Lecture Notes in Computer Science

Lecture Notes in Artificial Intelligence 16583

Founding Editor

Jörg Siekmann

Series Editors

Randy Goebel, *University of Alberta, Edmonton, Canada*
Wolfgang Wahlster, *DFKI, Berlin, Germany*
Zhi-Hua Zhou, *Nanjing University, Nanjing, China*

The series Lecture Notes in Artificial Intelligence (LNAI) was established in 1988 as a topical subseries of LNCS devoted to artificial intelligence.

The series publishes state-of-the-art research results at a high level. As with the LNCS mother series, the mission of the series is to serve the international R & D community by providing an invaluable service, mainly focused on the publication of conference and workshop proceedings and postproceedings.

Emmanuel G. Blanchard · Guanliang Chen ·
Min Chi · Seiji Isotani

Editors

Artificial Intelligence in Education

27th International Conference, AIED 2026
Seoul, South Korea, June 27–July 3, 2026
Proceedings, Part III

 Springer

Editors
Emmanuel G. Blanchard
Le Mans University
Le Mans, France

Min Chi
North Carolina State University
Raleigh, NC, USA

Guanliang Chen
Monash University
Clayton, VIC, Australia

Seiji Isotani
University of Pennsylvania
Philadelphia, PA, USA

ISSN 0302-9743   ISSN 1611-3349 (electronic)
Lecture Notes in Artificial Intelligence
ISBN 978-3-032-29759-4   ISBN 978-3-032-29760-0 (eBook)
https://doi.org/10.1007/978-3-032-29760-0

LNCS Sublibrary: SL7 – Artificial Intelligence

Preface

Welcome to the 27th International Conference on Artificial Intelligence in Education, taking place from June 27–July 3rd, 2026 in Seoul, South Korea. AIED is ranked A in CORE[1] (top 13.09% of 825 ranked venues). AIED is clearly growing and attracting more submissions, this year with 1,241 initial submissions. For more than three decades, the AIED community has advanced a rich body of research at the intersection of computer science, learning sciences, cognitive science, and artificial intelligence. From early intelligent tutoring systems to contemporary data-driven and adaptive platforms, the field has consistently pushed the boundaries of how technology can support teaching and learning. These contributions have not only deepened our theoretical understanding of learning but have also shaped educational practice across diverse contexts worldwide. Today, we stand at a pivotal moment. The rapid emergence of Generative AI and increasingly capable learning technologies challenges long-standing assumptions about the role of AI in education. Systems are no longer confined to delivering content, scaffolding problem solving, or modeling student knowledge; they are now capable of engaging in dialogue, generating explanations, co-creating artifacts, and participating in complex, context-aware interactions. This transformation compels us to reconsider a fundamental question: what does it mean for AI to meaningfully participate in the learning process?

The theme of **AIED 2026, "From Tools to Teammates: Human–AI Synergy for Augmented Learning"**, reflected this shift. Over decades of innovation, the AIED community has developed powerful tools and insights that have transformed learning worldwide. As these foundations continue to shape the field, emerging technologies, especially Generative AI, demand that we rethink how AI engages with learners and educators. Our field is entering a new era in which AI must evolve from simply supporting human learning to enabling richer human–AI collaboration. As AI becomes deeply embedded in everyday educational practice, AIED 2026 called for systems that foster genuine human–AI partnerships. This year's theme highlighted research on human and AI agency, collaborative intelligence, and the co-evolution of humans and AI. We invited work that reimagines AIED systems not merely as instruments, but as adaptive teammates that complement teachers and learners, align with human goals, and dynamically participate in shared educational processes. Such systems raise new opportunities and challenges: how to design for trust, transparency, and alignment; how to balance autonomy and control; how to support equity and inclusion; and how to rigorously evaluate learning in settings where humans and AI jointly construct knowledge.

AIED 2026 brought together a diverse and interdisciplinary community of researchers, practitioners, and policymakers to explore these questions. The contributions in these proceedings reflect a wide spectrum of perspectives—ranging from theoretical frameworks and empirical studies to system design, deployment, and real-world

---

[1] https://portal.core.edu.au/conf-ranks.

impact. Collectively, they illustrate a field that is both grounded in its intellectual heritage and boldly looking ahead.

The main conference program comprised three tracks:

- **Track 1 – Technical Aspects of AIED** focused on the computer science and engineering foundations that drive innovation in the field, emphasizing contributions where the primary novelty is technical. This track brought together work on novel AIED architectures, system engineering, and computational approaches to cognition and reasoning, including advances in knowledge representation, domain modeling, and agentic as well as multi-agent systems. Submissions span cutting-edge methods in machine learning, deep learning, generative models, natural language processing, and multimodal and video-based systems, alongside data mining, feature engineering, and predictive modeling techniques. The track also highlighted the design and implementation of intelligent tutoring systems, including those tailored for special education and resource-constrained (frugal) settings. Contributions were expected to demonstrate rigor through computational evaluation metrics such as accuracy, validity, and reliability, advancing the technical backbone of AIED while enabling more robust, scalable, and adaptive learning technologies.
- **Track 2 – Human Aspects of AIED** centered on the learning sciences, pedagogical foundations, and human-centered perspectives that underpin meaningful educational innovation. The primary insights emerge from theories of learning, empirical studies of human behavior, and humanities-informed analyses of educational practice. Topics include investigations of human agency, co-regulation, and human–AI collaboration, as well as rigorous evaluations of AIED systems using quantitative, qualitative, or mixed methods. Submissions draw on cognitive, motivational, metacognitive, and affective theories to better understand how learners and educators engage with AI-enabled environments, alongside work on instructional design, collaborative and social learning, and informal or game-based contexts. By foregrounding learners, teachers, and educational phenomena, this track advanced a deeper understanding of learning processes and aimed to ensure that AIED technologies are grounded in robust pedagogical and human-centered principles.
- **Track 3 – Societal Aspects of AIED** addressed the ethical, equitable, and policy-oriented dimensions of AIED, emphasizing contributions that critically examine the broader societal impact of AIED technologies. This track invited work on algorithmic fairness, bias, transparency, and accountability, as well as issues of privacy, surveillance, and data governance in educational contexts. It highlighted the importance of cultural awareness and sensitivity, alongside research focused on low-resource settings, unplugged AIED, and efforts to bridge the AIED divide across socio-economic, gender, and racial lines. Contributions also explored ethical frameworks for the design and deployment of AIED systems, policy implications of AI integration in education, and approaches to fostering AI literacy and critical understanding among learners and educators. By foregrounding responsibility, inclusion, and societal impact, this track sought to ensure that advances in AIED contribute to equitable and trustworthy educational futures.

AIED 2026 attracted an exceptionally broad range of submissions. We received 1,241 submissions across all tracks, of which 922 met the eligibility criteria and were accepted for review. From the full paper submissions, 143 were accepted as full papers, and an additional 168 were accepted as short papers. The acceptance rates for both full and short papers were 16.5% and 15.3% respectively. More specifically, 69 full and 71 short were accepted for Track 1; 54 full and 74 short were accepted for Track 2, and 20 full and 20 short were accepted for Track 3.

Every paper and presentation at AIED 2026 underwent a rigorous, double-blind peer-review process designed to ensure the highest scholarly standards and fair evaluation. We ensured that each paper was reviewed by three reviewers, including at least one senior reviewer. This rigorous collaborative effort—fueled by leading scholars and seasoned experts—resulted in a premier program spanning the complete spectrum of AIED innovation.

Beyond the scholarly sessions and paper presentations compiled in these conference proceedings, AIED 2026 offered a rich program of keynote addresses, panel discussions, interactive demonstrations, and specialized sessions which are compiled in the supplementary CCIS volumes of the conference. Specifically, this year was part of the Festival of Learning, co-organized with sister conferences Educational Data Mining (EDM 2026) and ACM Learning @ Scale (L@S 2026), which were co-located in Seoul, South Korea. Attendees had the opportunity to participate in the Doctoral Consortium, Workshops and Tutorials, Late-Breaking Results sessions, and dedicated tracks for Practitioners, Industry and Policy (PIP). The BlueSky track also invited visionary reflections on past progress and future trajectories in AIED, while the WideAIED track amplified perspectives from underrepresented regions and communities. Additionally, the conference offered presentations on the latest publications in the International Journal of Artificial Intelligence in Education (IJAIED)[2]. As a member of the International Alliance to Advance Learning in the Digital Era (IAALDE)[3], AIED 2026 also hosted presentations of the best papers from other IAALDE conferences.

This conference would not have been possible without the unwavering commitment of the International Artificial Intelligence in Education Society, the Organizing Committee, the Program and Senior Program Committees, the sponsors and partners who support our mission, and the Festival of Learning organizers. Their passion and dedication to advancing intelligent educational systems are the foundation of AIED's continued success and innovation.

We invite you to share your insights, spark new debates, and connect with peers to help drive the future of education. Together, we are exploring AI's potential as a powerful catalyst for inclusive, personalized, and ethical education globally. Welcome to AIED

---

[2] https://www.sciencedirect.com/journal/international-journal-of-artificial-intelligence-in-education.

[3] https://alliancelss.com/.

2026: where we aren't just predicting the future; we are actively reimagining it through every new innovation.

June 2026

Emmanuel G. Blanchard
Guanliang Chen
Min Chi
Seiji Isotani

Organization

Conference General Co-chair

Seiji Isotani   University of Pennsylvania, USA

Program Co-chairs

Emmanuel G. Blanchard   Le Mans Université, France
Guanliang Chen   Monash University, Australia
Min Chi   North Carolina State University, USA

Workshop and Tutorials Co-chairs

Engin Bumbacher   University of Teacher Education Vaud,
                                                          Switzerland
Shiyan Jiang   University of Pennsylvania, USA

Doctoral Consortium Co-chairs

Irene-Angelica Chounta   University of Duisburg-Essen, Germany
Yu Lu   Beijing Normal University, China
Ido Roll   Technion - Israel Institute of Technology, Israel

Late Breaking Results (Posters) Co-chairs

Davide Taibi   Consiglio Nazionale delle Ricerche, Italy
Renzhe Yu   Columbia University, USA
Zheng Yuan   University of Sheffield, UK

Blue Sky Co-chairs

Ivon Arroyo	University of Massachusetts Amherst, USA
Xiangen Hu	Hong Kong Polytechnic University, China
H. Chad Lane	University of Illinois Urbana-Champaign, USA

WideAIED Co-chairs

Alexandra I. Cristea	Durham University, UK
Rafael Ferreira Mello	Federal Rural University of Pernambuco, Brazil

Practitioners, Industry and Policy (PIP) Co-chairs

Christian M. Stracke	University of Bonn, Germany
Lixiang Yan	Tsinghua University, China
Diego Zapata-Rivera	Educational Testing Service, USA

Interactive Events (Demos) Co-chairs

Yuheng Li	Hong Kong Polytechnic University, China
Miguel Portaz	Universidad Nacional de Educación a Distancia, Spain
Sreecharan Sankaranarayanan	Extuitive Inc., USA

DEIA Fellowship Chairs

Ig Ibert Bittencourt	Federal University of Alagoas, Brazil
Valery Psyché	Université TÉLUQ, Canada

Lifetime Award Chair

Bruce M. McLaren	Carnegie Mellon University, USA

Awards Co-chairs

Gautam Biswas	Vanderbilt University, USA
Riichiro Mizoguchi	Japan Advanced Institute of Science and Technology, Japan
Olga C. Santos	Universidad Nacional de Educación a Distancia, Spain

Virtual Experiences Co-chairs

Patricia A. Jaques	Federal University of Paraná, Brazil
Huiyong Li	Kyushu University, Japan

Publicity Co-chairs

Cristian Cechinel	Universidade Federal de Santa Catarina, Brazil
Xinyuan Hao	University College London, UK

Proceedings Co-chairs

Matthieu Branthôme	University of Rennes, France
Diego Dermeval	Federal University of Alagoas, Brazil
Jionghao Lin	University of Hong Kong, China
Namrata Srivastava	Vanderbilt University, USA

Website Chair

Yuheng Li	Hong Kong Polytechnic University, China

Main Track

Senior Program Committee Members

Mohammed Abdel Razek	Al-Azhar University, Egypt
Bita Akram	North Carolina State University, USA
Laia Albó	Universitat de Vic, Spain

Vincent Aleven	Carnegie Mellon University, USA
Giora Alexandron	Weizmann Institute of Science, Israel
Laura Allen	University of Minnesota, USA
Ivon Arroyo	University of Massachusetts Amherst, USA
Roger Azevedo	University of Central Florida, USA
Ryan Baker	University of Pennsylvania, USA
Ayan Banerjee	Arizona State University, USA
Tiffany Barnes	North Carolina State University, USA
Abhinava Barthakur	University of South Australia, Australia
Brian Belland	Pennsylvania State University, USA
Yoav Bergner	New York University, USA
Gautam Biswas	Vanderbilt University, USA
Ig Ibert Bittencourt	Federal University of Alagoas, Brazil
Geoffray Bonnin	Université de Lorraine - LORIA, France
Conrad Borchers	Carnegie Mellon University, USA
Anthony F. Botelho	University of Florida, USA
François Bouchet	Sorbonne Université - LIP6, France
Kristy Elizabeth Boyer	University of Florida, USA
Bert Bredeweg	University of Amsterdam, Netherlands
Julien Broisin	Université de Toulouse, France
Christopher Brooks	University of Michigan, USA
Armelle Brun	LORIA - Université de Lorraine, France
Peter Brusilovsky	University of Pittsburgh, USA
Ilona Buchem	Berlin University of Applied Sciences, Germany
Simon Buckingham Shum	University of Technology Sydney, Australia
Okan Bulut	University of Alberta, Canada
Engin Bumbacher	University of Teacher Education Vaud, Switzerland
Dan Carpenter	North Carolina State University, USA
Paulo Carvalho	Carnegie Mellon University, USA
Cristian Cechinel	Universidade Federal de Santa Catarina, Brazil
Penghe Chen	Beijing Normal University, China
Irene-Angelica Chounta	University of Duisburg-Essen, Germany
Jaroslaw A. Chudziak	Warsaw University of Technology, Poland
Ruth Cobos	Universidad Autónoma de Madrid, Spain
Cesar Collazos	Universidad del Cauca, Colombia
Alexandra I. Cristea	Durham University, UK
Jennifer Cromley	University of Illinois Urbana-Champaign, USA
Mutlu Cukurova	University College London, UK
Maria Cutumisu	McGill University, Canada
Carrie Demmans Epp	University of Alberta, Canada
Vanessa Dennen	Florida State University, USA

Diego Dermeval	Federal University of Alagoas, Brazil
Michel Desmarais	Polytechnique Montréal, Canada
Daniele Di Mitri	DIPF | Leibniz Institute for Research and Information in Education, Germany
Vania Dimitrova	University of Leeds, UK
Blazenka Divjak	University of Zagreb, Croatia
Mohsen Dorodchi	University of North Carolina at Charlotte, USA
Shayan Doroudi	University of California, Irvine, USA
Vanessa Echeverria	RMIT University, Australia
Ralph Ewerth	University of Marburg and hessian.AI – Hessian Center for Artificial Intelligence, Germany
Yizhou Fan	Peking University, UK
Mingyu Feng	WestEd, USA
Shihui Feng	University of Hong Kong, China
Márcia Fernandes	Federal University of Uberlândia, Brazil
Rafael Ferreira Mello	Federal Rural University of Pernambuco/CESAR School, Brazil
Brendan Flanagan	Kyoto University, Japan
Reva Freedman	Northern Illinois University, USA
Francisco José García-Peñalvo	University of Salamanca, Spain
Dragan Gasevic	Monash University, Australia
Isabela Gasparini	Santa Catarina State University, Brazil
Sébastien George	LIUM, Le Mans Université, France
Michael Glass	Valparaiso University, USA
Janice Gobert	Rutgers University, USA
Sabine Graf	Athabasca University, Canada
Monique Grandbastien	LORIA, Université de Lorraine, France
Floriana Grasso	University of Liverpool, UK
Beate Grawemeyer	Coventry University, UK
Jason Harley	McGill University, Canada
Peter Hastings	DePaul University, USA
Yugo Hayashi	Ritsumeikan University, Japan
Neil Heffernan	Worcester Polytechnic Institute, USA
Tsukasa Hirashima	Hiroshima University, Japan
Sharon I-Han Hsiao	Santa Clara University, USA
Xiao Hu	University of Arizona, USA
Stephen Hutt	University of Denver, USA
Gwo-Jen Hwang	National Taiwan University of Science and Technology, Taiwan
Tomoo Inoue	University of Tsukuba, Japan
Shoya Ishimaru	Osaka Metropolitan University, Japan
Mirjana Ivanovic	University of Novi Sad, Serbia

Patricia Jaques	Universidade Federal do Paraná/Universidade Federal de Pelotas, Brazil
Johan Jeuring	Utrecht University, Netherlands
Yang Jiang	Columbia University, USA
Srecko Joksimovic	University of South Australia, Australia
Jelena Jovanovic	University of Belgrade, Serbia
David Joyner	Georgia Institute of Technology, USA
Akihiro Kashihara	University of Electro-Communications, Japan
Judy Kay	University of Sydney, Australia
Mohammad Khalil	University of Bergen, Norway
Hassan Khosravi	University of Queensland, Australia
Yeo Jin Kim	North Carolina State University, USA
Kirsty Kitto	University of Bergen, Norway
Rene Kizilcec	Cornell University, USA
Simon Knight	University of Technology Sydney, Australia
Irena Koprinska	University of Sydney, Australia
Vitomir Kovanovic	University of South Australia, Australia
Amruth Kumar	Ramapo College of New Jersey, USA
Tanja Käser	EPFL, Switzerland
Sébastien Lallé	Sorbonne University, France
Andrew Lan	University of Massachusetts Amherst, USA
Yunshi Lan	East China Normal University, China
H. Chad Lane	University of Illinois Urbana-Champaign, USA
Mikel Larrañaga	University of the Basque Country UPV/EHU, Spain
Hady Lauw	Singapore Management University, Singapore
Nguyen-Thinh Le	Humboldt Universität zu Berlin, Germany
James Lester	North Carolina State University, USA
Carla Limongelli	Università Roma Tre, Italy
Fuhua Lin	Athabasca University, Canada
Jionghao Lin	University of Hong Kong, China
Zitao Liu	Guangdong Institute of Smart Education, Jinan University, China
Chee-Kit Looi	Education University of Hong Kong, China
Yu Lu	Beijing Normal University, China
Vanda Luengo	Sorbonne Université - LIP6, France
Collin Lynch	North Carolina State University, USA
Sonsoles López-Pernas	University of Eastern Finland, Finland
Mirko Marras	University of Cagliari, Italy
Roberto Martinez-Maldonado	Monash University, Australia
Jeffrey Matayoshi	McGraw Hill ALEKS, USA
Noboru Matsuda	North Carolina State University, USA

Manolis Mavrikis	University of Edinburgh, UK
Agathe Merceron	Berliner Hochschule für Technik - Berlin State University of Applied Sciences, Germany
Wookhee Min	North Carolina State University, USA
Tanja Mitrovic	University of Canterbury, New Zealand
Riichiro Mizoguchi	Japan Advanced Institute of Science and Technology, Japan
Phaedra Mohammed	University of the West Indies, Trinidad and Tobago
Inge Molenaar	Radboud University, Netherlands
Steven Moore	Carnegie Mellon University, USA
Bradford Mott	North Carolina State University, USA
Chrystalla Mouza	University of Illinois Urbana-Champaign, USA
Kasia Muldner	Carleton University, Canada
Tomohiro Nagashima	Saarland University, Germany
Nia Nixon	University of California, Irvine, USA
Roger Nkambou	Université du Québec à Montréal, Canada
Benjamin Nye	University of Southern California, USA
Jaclyn Ocumpaugh	University of Houston, USA
Eduardo Oliveira	University of Melbourne, Australia
Luc Paquette	University of Illinois Urbana-Champaign, USA
Abelardo Pardo	University of Adelaide, Australia
Radek Pelánek	Masaryk University, Czechia
Niels Pinkwart	Humboldt-Universität zu Berlin, Germany
Vitaliy Popov	University of Michigan, USA
Sasha Poquet	University of South Australia, Australia
Kaska Porayska-Pomsta	University College London, UK
Valéry Psyché	Université TÉLUQ, Canada
Anna Rafferty	Carleton College, USA
Mladen Rakovic	Monash University, Australia
Steve Ritter	Carnegie Learning, Inc., USA
Maria Mercedes T. Rodrigo	Ateneo de Manila University, Philippines
Ido Roll	Technion - Israel Institute of Technology, Israel
Vasile Rus	University of Memphis, USA
Demetrios Sampson	Curtin University, Australia
Sreecharan Sankaranarayanan	Amazon.com, Inc., USA
Olga C. Santos	Universidad Nacional de Educación a Distancia, Spain
Mohammed Saqr	University of Eastern Finland, Finland
Filippo Sciarrone	Universitas Mercatorum, Italy
Lei Shi	Newcastle University, UK
Yang Shi	Utah State University, USA

Sean Siqueira	Federal University of the State of Rio de Janeiro, Brazil
Sergey Sosnovsky	Utrecht University, Netherlands
Namrata Srivastava	Vanderbilt University, USA
John Stamper	Carnegie Mellon University, USA
Angela Stewart	University of Pittsburgh, USA
Christian M. Stracke	University of Bonn, Germany
Daner Sun	Education University of Hong Kong, China
Bill Swartout	University of Southern California, USA
Davide Taibi	Italian National Research Council, Italy
Tamara Tate	University of California, Irvine, USA
Michelle Taub	University of Central Florida, USA
Marco Temperini	Sapienza - Università di Roma, Italy
Craig Thompson	University of British Columbia, Canada
Stefan Trausan-Matu	University Politehnica of Bucharest, Romania
Yi-Shan Tsai	Monash University, Australia
Maomi Ueno	University of Electro-Communications, Japan
Julita Vassileva	University of Saskatchewan, Canada
Olga Viberg	KTH Royal Institute of Technology, Sweden
Rosa Vicari	Universidade Federal do Rio Grande do Sul, Brazil
Xu Wang	University of Michigan, USA
Alistair Willis	Open University, UK
Beverly Woolf	University of Massachusetts Amherst, USA
Marcelo Worsley	Northwestern University, USA
Lixiang Yan	Tsinghua University, China
Lan Yang	Education University of Hong Kong, China
Amel Yessad	LIP6, Sorbonne Université, France
Zheng Yuan	King's College London, UK
Diego Zapata-Rivera	Educational Testing Service, USA
Xiaoming Zhai	University of Georgia, USA
Guojing Zhou	South China Normal University, USA
Xiaofei Zhou	University of Rochester, USA
Gaoxia Zhu	Nanyang Technological University, Singapore
Craig Zilles	University of Illinois Urbana-Champaign, USA
Gustavo Zurita	Universidad de Chile, Chile
Benedict du Boulay	University of Sussex, UK

Program Committee Members

Noorhan Abbas	University of Leeds, UK
Sophie Abel	University of Wollongong, Australia
Abdelghafour Aboukacem	Mohammed VI Polytechnic University, Morocco
Hasan Abu-Rasheed	Goethe University Frankfurt, Germany
Tomoki Aburatani	Osaka Metropolitan University, Japan
Ifeoma Adaji	University of British Columbia, Canada
Seth Adjei	Northern Kentucky University, USA
Imran S. A. Khan	Laboratoire d'Informatique de l'Université du Mans (LIUM), France
Dishank Aggarwal	IIT Bombay, India
Mahir Akgun	Pennsylvania State University, USA
Nazia Alam	North Carolina State University, USA
Veljko Aleksić	University of Kragujevac, Serbia
Azza Abdullah S. Alghamdi	King Abdulaziz University, Saudi Arabia
Samah Alkhuzaey	Umm Al-Qura University, Saudi Arabia
Isaac Alpizar-Chacon	Utrecht University, Netherlands
Ainhoa Alvarez	University of the Basque Country, UPV/EHU, Spain
Ioannis Anastasopoulos	University of California, Berkeley, USA
Moriah Ariely	Weizmann Institute of Science, Israel
Pablo Arnau-González	Universidad de Valencia, Spain
Burcu Arslan	Educational Testing Service, USA
Yuya Asano	University of Pittsburgh, USA
Gabriel Astudillo	Pontificia Universidad Católica de Chile, Chile
Berk Atil	Boğaziçi University, Turkey
Shen Ba	Education University of Hong Kong, China
Costin Badica	University of Craiova, Romania
Michelle P. Banawan	Asian Institute of Management, Philippines
Amanda Barany	University of Pennsylvania, USA
Alvaro Becerra	Universidad Autónoma de Madrid, Spain
Beata Beigman Klebanov	Educational Testing Service, USA
Francisco Bellas	Universidade da Coruna, Spain
Avia Ben-Ari	Technion - Israel Institute of Technology, Israel
Luca Benedetto	University of Cambridge, UK
El Houcine Bergou	Mohamed VI Polytechnic University, Morocco
Ismail Berrada	Mohamed VI Polytechnic University, Morocco
Susan Beudt	German Research Center for Artificial Intelligence (DFKI), Germany
Gabriele Biagini	Università degli Studi di Firenze, Italy

Wolfgang Bitter	TIB – Leibniz Information Centre for Science and Technology, Germany
Maria Bolsinova	Tilburg University, Netherlands
Anis Boubaker	École de Technologie Supérieure, Canada
Mariah Bradford	Colorado State University, USA
Matthieu Branthôme	University of Rennes, IRISA, CNRS, France
Rex Bringula	University of the East, Philippines
George Buchanan	University of Melbourne, Australia
Jill Burstein	Duolingo, USA
Marina Buzzi	IIT-CNR, Italy
Minghao Cai	University of Alberta, Canada
Jie Cao	University of Oklahoma, USA
Jie Cao	University of Pittsburgh, USA
May Kristine Jonson Carlon	RIKEN Center for Brain Science, Japan
Alberto Casas-Ortiz	Universidad Nacional de Educación a Distancia, Spain
Héctor Ceballos	Tecnológico de Monterrey, Mexico
Jeevan Chapagain	University of Memphis, USA
Ziyan Che	Central China Normal University, China
Eason Chen	Carnegie Mellon University, USA
Fu Chen	University of Macau, China
Shigeng Chen	King's College London, UK
Shijun Cindy Chen	University of Hong Kong, China
Wei-Peng Chen	Fujitsu Labs of America, USA
Xinyue Chen	University of Michigan, USA
Youjie Chen	University of Hong Kong, China
Yixin Cheng	Monash University, Australia
Thomas K. F. Chiu	Chinese University of Hong Kong, China
Chih-Yueh Chou	Yuan Ze University, Taiwan
Elizabeth Cloude	Michigan State University, USA
Keith Cochran	DePaul University, USA
Jade Mai Cock	EPFL, Switzerland
Maria de Los Angeles Constantino González	Tecnológico de Monterrey Campus Laguna, Mexico
Evandro Costa	Federal University of Alagoas, Brazil
Steven Coyne	Tohoku University; RIKEN, Japan
Jeffrey Cross	Tokyo Institute of Technology, Japan
Stefano D'Urso	Universitas Mercatorum, Italy
Rafael D. Araújo	Universidade Federal de Uberlândia, Brazil
Wei Dai	University of Hong Kong, China
Yiling Dai	Hiroshima University, Japan
Syaamantak Das	Indian Institute of Technology Bombay, India

Mihai Dascalu	University Politehnica of Bucharest, Romania
Rahul Dass	Georgia Tech, USA
Eduardo Davalos Anaya	Trinity University, USA
Erwan David	Le Mans University, France
Richard Lee Davis	Stanford University, USA
Jeanine DeFalco	University of New Haven, USA
Oscar Deho	Charles Sturt University, Australia
M. Ali Akber Dewan	Athabasca University, Canada
Nicholas Diana	Colgate University, USA
Yannis Dimitriadis	University of Valladolid, Spain
Heejin Do	ETH Zurich, Switzerland
Konomu Dobashi	Aichi University, Japan
Fabiano Dorça	Universidade Federal de Uberlândia, Brazil
Zhangqi Duan	University of Massachusetts Amherst, USA
Cristina Dumdumaya	University of Southeastern Philippines, Philippines
Nicholas Duran	Arizona State University, USA
Martin Ebner	Graz University of Technology, Austria
Yo Ehara	Tokyo Gakugei University, Japan
Bobbie Eicher	Georgia Institute of Technology, USA
Nour El Mawas	Université de Lille, France
Lara Ceren Ergenç	King's College London, UK
Kelechi Ezema	University of Colorado Boulder, USA
Xiuyi Fan	Nanyang Technological University, UK
Zhilin Fan	Beijing Normal University, China
Paolo Fantozzi	LUMSA University, Italy
Abdolali Faraji	Leibniz Information Centre for Science and Technology (TIB), Germany
Alexandra Farazouli	Stockholm University, Sweden
Effat Farhana	Auburn University, USA
Cassia Fernandez	University of São Paulo, Brazil
Gloria Milena Fernandez-Nieto	University of Technology, Sydney, Australia
Alessio Ferrato	Roma Tre University, Italy
Carol Forsyth	Educational Testing Service, USA
Kazuma Fuchimoto	University of Electro-Communications, Japan
Mari Fukuda	Kyoto University, Japan
Nikki G. Lobczowski	McGill University, Canada
Kobi Gal	Ben-Gurion University of the Negev, Israel
Cristiano Galafassi	Universidade Federal do Rio Grande do Sul, Brazil
Selen Galiç	Hacettepe University, Turkey
Jie Gao	McGill University, Canada

Zhen Gao	McMaster University, Canada
Zhikai Gao	Western Carolina University, USA
Sai Gattupalli	University of Massachusetts Amherst, USA
Gabrielle Gaudeau	University of Cambridge, UK
Jadon Geathers	Cornell University, USA
Thierry Geoffre	University of Luxembourg, Luxembourg
Alireza Gharahighehi	imec - KU Leuven, Belgium
Ashok Goel	Georgia Institute of Technology, USA
Sebastian Gombert	DIPF	Leibniz Institute for Research and Information in Education, Germany
Guher Gorgun	University of Alberta, Canada
Alex Goslen	North Carolina State University, USA
Vikram Goyal	IIIT-Delhi, India
Quanlong Guan	Jinan University, China
Jiong Guo	Northwest Normal University, China
Zhihan Guo	University of Hong Kong, China
Shivang Gupta	Carnegie Mellon University, USA
Ashish Gurung	Carnegie Mellon University, USA
Ella Haig	University of Portsmouth, UK
Songhee Han	University of Texas at Austin, USA
Jiangang Hao	Educational Testing Service, USA
Soroush Hashemifar	Iran University of Science and Technology, Iran
Carl Haynes-Magyar	University of Pittsburgh, USA
Liqun He	University College London, UK
Xinyu He	Central China Normal University, China
Owen Henkel	University of Oxford, UK
Davinia Hernandez-Leo	Universitat Pompeu Fabra, Spain
Ben Hicks	University of Technology Sydney, Australia
Camila Hidalgo	Technical University of Munich, Germany
Langdon Holmes	Vanderbilt University, USA
Joanna Holt	Amsterdam University of Applied Sciences, Netherlands
Anett Hoppe	Philipps-Universität Marburg & Hessian Center for AI; TIB Leibniz Information Centre for Science and Technology, Germany
Chenyu Hou	Nanyang Technological University, Singapore
Xinying Hou	University of Michigan, USA
Zhifei Hu	Durham University, UK
Kevin Huang	WestEd, USA
Lingyun Huang	Education University of Hong Kong, China
Xiaoshan Huang	McGill University, Canada
Samuel Hum	University of Illinois Urbana-Champaign, USA

Hui-Chun Hung	National Central University, Taiwan
Haerim Hwang	Chinese University of Hong Kong, China
Kevin Hwang	Glenelg High School, USA
Soo Hyoung Joo	Columbia University, USA
Eleni Ilkou	TIB Leibniz Information Centre for Science and Technology, Germany
Paul Inventado	California State University Fullerton, USA
Sehrish Iqbal	Monash University, Australia
Tsunenori Ishioka	National Center for University Entrance Examinations, Japan
Md Mirajul Islam	North Carolina State University, USA
Daneih Ismail	DePaul University, USA
Percy Jardine	Monash University, Australia
Vimukthini Jayalath	University of South Australia, Australia
Hyangeun Ji	Temple University, USA
Qiao Jin	North Carolina State University, USA
Yueqiao Jin	Monash University, Australia
Julian Marvin Jörs	Otto-von-Guericke-Universität Magdeburg, Germany
Jiyoon Jung	Valdosta State University, USA
Vishav Jyoti	IIT Gandhinagar, India
Shiming Kai	Columbia University, USA
Hamid Karimi	Utah State University, USA
Enkelejda Kasneci	Technical University of Munich, Germany
Stamos Katsigiannis	Durham University, UK
Mizue Kayama	Shinshu University, Japan
Priyanka Khare	North Carolina State University, USA
Beaumie Kim	University of Calgary, Canada
Chanmin Kim	Pennsylvania State University, USA
Min Kyu Kim	Georgia State University, USA
Badmavasan Kirouchenassamy	LIP6 - Sorbonne Université, France
Aleksandra Klasnja-Milicevic	University of Novi Sad, Serbia
Ekaterina Kochmar	Mohamed Bin Zayed University of Artificial Intelligence, United Arab Emirates
Elizabeth Koh	National Institute of Education, Nanyang Technological University, Singapore
Kento Koike	Tokyo University of Science, Japan
Kazuaki Kojima	Teikyo University, Japan
Maria Konte	Georgia Institute of Technology, USA
Sotiris Kotsiantis	University of Patras, Greece
Nikhil Krishnaswamy	Colorado State University, USA
Zuzana Kubincová	Comenius University, Bratislava, Slovakia

Christine Kwon	Carnegie Mellon University, USA
Eleni Kyza	Cyprus University of Technology, Cyprus
Adnan Labib	King's College London, UK
Salima Lamsiyah	Université Sidi Mohamed Ben Abdellah Fès, Morocco
Tai Le Quy	University of Koblenz, Germany
Haejin Lee	University of Illinois Urbana-Champaign, USA
Jaewook Lee	University of Massachusetts Amherst, USA
Junyoung Lee	Nanyang Technological University, Singapore
Morgan Lee	Worcester Polytechnic Institute, USA
Seiyon Lee	University of Florida, USA
Unggi Lee	Korea University, South Korea
Marie Lefevre	LIRIS - Université Lyon 1, France
Juho Leinonen	Aalto University, Finland
Arun Balajiee Lekshmi Narayanan	University of Pittsburgh, USA
Barbara Leporini	University of Pisa, Italy
Pascal Leroux	Centre de Recherche en Education de Nantes, France
Haiying Li	University of Pennsylvania, USA
Jianwei Li	Beijing University of Posts and Telecommunications, China
Jiazheng Li	King's College London, UK
Liang-Yi Li	National Taiwan Normal University, Taiwan
Lin Li	Monash University, Australia
Shan Li	Lehigh University, USA
Tengju Li	Ocean University of China, China
Tongguang Li	Monash University, Australia
Xiu Li	Stockholm University, Sweden
Yuheng Li	Monash University, Australia
Zhaohui Li	Penn State University, USA
Zhi Li	University of California, Berkeley, USA
Qianru Liang	Jinan University, China
Zhiping Liang	Monash University, Australia
Chang-Yen Liao	National Central University, Taiwan
Paul Libbrecht	IU International University of Applied Sciences, Germany
Fun Siong Lim	Nanyang Technological University, Singapore
Lisa-Angelique Lim	University of Technology Sydney, Australia
Wen Chiang Lim	Worcester Polytechnic Institute, USA
Bibeg Limbu	University of Duisburg-Essen, Germany
Chang Liu	Colorado School of Mines, USA
Lei Liu	Educational Testing Service, USA

Naiming Liu	Rice University, USA
Qinyi Liu	University of Bergen, Norway
Shiqi Liu	Central China Normal University, China
Tianqiao Liu	TAL AI Lab, China
Zhichun Liu	University of Hong Kong, China
Ziyuan Liu	Singapore Management University, USA
Giosué Lo Bosco	Università di Palermo, Italy
Angelica Lo Duca	IIT-CNR, Italy
Xinyi Lu	University of Michigan, USA
Nicholas Lytle	Georgia Institute of Technology, USA
Bailing Lyu	University of Utah, USA
Boxuan Ma	Kyushu University, Japan
Qianou Ma	Carnegie Mellon University, USA
Konrad Maciborski	Polish-Japanese Academy of Information Technology, Poland
John Magee	Clark University, USA
George Magoulas	Birkbeck College, University of London, UK
Subhankar Maity	ECE Paris, France
Aditi Mallavarapu	North Carolina State University, USA
Ivana Marenzi	L3S Research Center, Germany
Leonardo Brandão Marques	Federal University of Alagoas, Brazil
Alejandra Martínez-Monés	Universidad de Valladolid, Spain
Wannisa Matcha	Prince of Songkla University, Thailand
Yuichiroh Matsubayashi	Tohoku University, Japan
Tatsunori Matsui	Waseda University, Japan
Lindsay Clare Matsumura	University of Pittsburgh, USA
Hunter McNichols	University of Massachusetts Amherst, USA
Guilherme Medeiros Machado	ECE Paris, France
Paola Mejia Domenzain	EPFL, Switzerland
Grzegorz Meller	KU Leuven, Belgium
Xianghui Meng	Columbia University, USA
Donatella Merlini	Università di Firenze, Italy
Marcus Messer	Imperial, UK
Jamie Mikeska	Educational Testing Service, USA
Marcelo Milrad	Linnaeus University, Sweden
Tsunenori Mine	Kyushu University, Japan
Sein Minn	Inria, France
Kamila Misiejuk	FernUniversität Hagen, Germany
Tsegaye Misikir Tashu	University of Groningen, Netherlands
Yoshimitsu Miyazawa	National Center for University Entrance Examinations, Japan
Mukesh Mohania	IIIT Delhi, India

Wesley Morris — Vanderbilt University, USA
Ana Mouta — University of Salamanca, Spain
Hanni Muukkonen — University of Oulu, Finland
Pedro J. Muñoz-Merino — Universidad Carlos III de Madrid, Spain
Shatha N. Alkhasawneh — Pompeu Fabra University, Spain
Takashi Nagai — Institute of Technologists, Japan
Nurun Nahar — University of Greater Manchester, UK
Nidhi Nasiar — University of Pennsylvania, USA
Tanya Nazaretsky — EPFL, Switzerland
Léo Nebel — Sorbonne Université, France
Seyed Parsa Neshaei — EPFL, Switzerland
Jeremy T. D. Ng — University of Hong Kong, China
Manh Hung Nguyen — Max Planck Institute for Software Systems, Germany

Yasuhiro Noguchi — Shizuoka University, Japan
Ange Adrienne Nyamen Tato — Université Laval, Canada
Xavier Ochoa — New York University, USA
Soon Young Oh — Michigan State University, USA
Santiago Ojeda-Ramirez — University of California, Irvine, USA
Jeroen Ooge — Utrecht University, Belgium
María Óskarsdóttir — Reykjavík University, Iceland
Erin Ottmar — Worcester Polytechnic Institute, USA
Abdelkader Ouared — LIUM: Laboratoire d'Informatique de l'Université du Mans, France

Ranilson Paiva — Universidade Federal de Alagoas, Brazil
Martha Palmer — University of Colorado Boulder, USA
Viktoria Pammer-Schindler — Graz University of Technology, Austria
Prajakt Pande — Southern Methodist University, USA, and Aarhus University, Denmark

Maciej Pankiewicz — University of Pennsylvania, USA
Zaki Pauzi — University College London, UK
Bernardo Pereira Nunes — Australian National University, Australia
Margaret Perkoff — University of Pennsylvania, USA
Tung Phung — Max Planck Institute for Software Systems, Germany

Yang Pian — Beijing Normal University, China
Benjamin Pierce — University of Pittsburgh, USA
Gerti Pishtari — University for Continuing Education Krems (Danube University), Austria

Eduard Pogorskiy — Open Files LTD, UK
Allison Poh — University of Massachusetts Amherst, USA
Miguel Portaz — Universidad Nacional de Educación a Distancia, Spain

Victor Prado	Federal University of Rio de Janeiro, Brazil
Vijay Prakash	Indian Institute of Technology Bombay, India
Ethan Prihar	EPFL, Switzerland
James Pustejovsky	Brandeis University, USA
Pipob Puthipiroj	Northwestern University, USA
Mar Pérez-Sanagustín	Université de Toulouse, France
Ronald Pérez-Álvarez	Universidad de Costa Rica, Costa Rica
Kun Qian	Columbia University, USA
Liu Qiang	Sichuan Chengdu Shude High School, China
Emanuel Queiroga	Federal University of Pelotas, Brazil
Napol Rachatasumrit	Carnegie Mellon University, USA
Anna Radtke	Center for Advanced Internet Studies, Germany
Yuvaraj Rajamanickam	Anna University, India
Yasitha Rajapaksha	North Carolina State University, USA
Ramkumar Rajendran	IIT Bombay, India
Ilana Ram	Technion Israel Institute of Technology, Israel
Sowmya Ramachandran	Stottler Henke Associates Inc, USA
Injila Rasul	University of Massachusetts Amherst, USA
Manikandan Ravikiran	Thoughtworks AI Research Labs/IIT Mandi, India
Traian Rebedea	University Politehnica of Bucharest, Romania
Marcelo Reis	Universidade Federal de Alagoas, Brazil
Valérie Renault	Le Mans University, France
Shannon Rios	University of Melbourne, Australia
Sina Rismanchian	University of California, Irvine, USA
Luiz Rodrigues	Federal University of Technology - Paraná, Brazil
Carlos Felipe Rodriguez-Hernandez	Tecnológico de Monterrey, Mexico
José Raúl Romero	University of Córdoba, Spain
Rinat B. Rosenberg-Kima	Technion - Israel Institute of Technology, Israel
Daniela Rotelli	Sorbonne Université, France
José A. Ruipérez Valiente	University of Murcia, Spain
Stefan Ruseti	University "Politehnica" of Bucharest, Romania
Sylvio Rüdian	Humboldt-Universität zu Berlin, Germany
John Sabatini	University of Memphis, USA
Isabella Saccardi	Utrecht University, Netherlands
Nicy Scaria	Indian Institute of Science, India
Daniele Schicchi	CNR ITD, Italy
Ratan Sebastian	TIB Leibniz Information Centre for Science and Technology, Germany
Martha Shaka	University of Dodoma, Tanzania
Kshitij Sharma	Norwegian University of Science and Technology, Norway

Paras Sharma	University of Pittsburgh, USA
Vyom Sharma	Hippocratic AI, USA
Ryan Shea	Columbia University, USA
Bruce Sherin	Northwestern University, USA
Wanruo Shi	Tsinghua University, China
Atsushi Shimada	Kyushu University, Japan
Kazutaka Shimada	Kyushu Institute of Technology, Japan
Machi Shimmei	Tohoku University, Japan
Jinnie Shin	University of Florida, USA
Hajime Shirouzu	National Institute for Educational Policy Research, Japan
Momin Siddiqui	Georgia Institute of Technology, USA
Abubakir Siedahmed	Worcester Polytechnic Institute, USA
Aditi Singh	Cleveland State University, USA
Daevesh Singh	Indian Institute of Technology Bombay, India
Jasbir Singh	University of Otago, New Zealand
Andy Smith	North Carolina State University, USA
David Smith	Virginia Tech, USA
Shashank Sonkar	Rice University, USA
Deniz Sonmez Unal	University of Pittsburgh, USA
Marcus Specht	Delft University of Technology, Netherlands
Frank Stinar	University of Illinois Urbana-Champaign, USA
Amy Stornaiuolo	University of Pennsylvania, USA
Abhijit Suresh	University of Colorado Boulder, USA
Juan Andrés Talamás Carvajal	Tecnológico de Monterrey, Mexico
May Marie P. Talandron-Felipe	University of Science and Technology of Southern Philippines, Philippines
Danielle R. Thomas	Carnegie Mellon University, USA
Xiaoyi Tian	North Carolina State University, USA
Sutapa Dey Tithi	North Carolina State University, USA
Paula Toledo Palomino	São Paulo State College of Technology (FATEC) - Matão | Center for Excellence in Social Technologies (NEES-UFAL), Brazil
Christos Troussas	University of West Attica, Greece
Anne Trumbore	University of Virginia, USA
Ashwin Tudur Sadashiva	Vanderbilt University, USA
Onuralp Ulusoy	Utrecht University, Netherlands
Sam Urmian	University of Bergen, Norway
Masaki Uto	University of Electro-Communications, Japan
Giacomo Valente	University of L'Aquila, Italy
Enrique Valero-Leal	Universidad Politécnica de Madrid, Spain
Gerben van der Hoek	SG Huizermaat, Netherlands

Jessica Vandenberg	North Carolina State University, USA
Caleb Vatral	Tennessee State University, USA
Esteban Vazquez-Cano	Universidad Nacional de Educación a Distancia, Spain
Rémi Venant	Le Mans Université - LIUM, France
Mikel Villamañe	University of the Basque Country (UPV/EHU), Spain
Maureen Villamor	University of Southeastern Philippines, Philippines
Alessandro Vivas	Universidade Federal dos Vales do Jequitinhonha e Mucuri, Brazil
Candace Walkington	Southern Methodist University, USA
Chengliang Wang	East China Normal University, China
Deliang Wang	Beijing Normal University, China
Haoming Wang	East China Normal University, China
Judy Wang	Hosei University, Japan
Ning Wang	University of Southern California, USA
Christabel Wayllace	New Mexico State University, USA
Zhanlan Wei	University of Pennsylvania, USA
Stephan Weibelzahl	Private University of Applied Sciences Göttingen, Germany
Daniel Weitekamp	Carnegie Mellon University, USA
Denise Whitelock	Open University, UK
Megan Wiedbusch	University of Central Florida, USA
Eryka Wilson	Keiser University, USA
Jacqueline Wong	Utrecht University, Netherlands
Kester Yew Chong Wong	Nanyang Technological University, National Institute of Education, Singapore
Eamon Worden	Worcester Polytechnic Institute, USA
Anna Wróblewska	Warsaw University of Technology, Poland
Jiahui Wu	Beijing University of Posts and Telecommunication, China
Zihan Wu	University of Michigan, USA
Zhen Xu	Teachers College, Columbia University, USA
Saumya Yadav	IIIT-Delhi, India
Sedat Yalcin	Hisar School, Turkey
Özge Nilay Yalçın	Simon Fraser University, Canada
Masanori Yamada	Kyushu University, Japan
Sho Yamamoto	Kindai University, Japan
R. Yamamoto Ravenor	Ochanomizu University, Japan
Koichi Yamashita	Tokoha University, Japan
Takayoshi Yamashita	Chubu University, Japan
Hongxin Yan	Athabasca University, Canada

Kaixun Yang	Monash University, Australia
Kexin Yang	University of Pennsylvania, USA
Pingjing Yang	University of Illinois Urbana-Champaign, USA
Weipeng Yang	Education University of Hong Kong, China
Yin Nicole Yang	Education University of Hong Kong, China
Zhiwei Yang	Jinan University, China
Chengyuan Yao	Teachers College, Columbia University, USA
Mingrui Ye	King's College London, UK
Seyma N. Yildirim-Erbasli	Concordia University of Edmonton, Canada
Hao Yu	Boston University, USA
Annie Yuan	University of Sydney, Australia
Guangji Yuan	National Institute of Education, Nanyang Technological Universit, Singapore
Andres Felipe Zambrano	University of Pennsylvania, USA
Andrew Zamecnik	University of South Australia, Australia
Franck Zenasni	Université Paris Cité, France
Chenwei Zhang	University of Hong Kong, China
Jianwei Zhang	University at Albany, USA
Jiayi Zhang	University of Pennsylvania, USA
Shan Zhang	University of Florida, USA
Shugang Zhang	Ocean University of China, China
Yi Zhang	Beijing Normal University, China
Yujing Zhang	University of Hong Kong, China
Chenyan Zhao	University of Illinois Urbana-Champaign, USA
Chloe Qianhui Zhao	Carnegie Mellon University, USA
Linxuan Zhao	Monash University, Australia
Yiling Zhao	Stanford University, USA
Jinxin Zhu	Education University of Hong Kong, China
Min Zhuang	North Carolina State University, USA
Stefano Zingaro	Università di Bologna, Italy

International Artificial Intelligence in Education (IAIED) Society

IAIED Management Board

President

Seiji Isotani	University of Pennsylvania, USA

Secretary

Olga C. Santos   Universidad Nacional de Educación a Distancia,
                                  Spain

Journal Editors

Vincent Aleven   Carnegie Mellon University, USA
Cristina Conati   University of British Columbia, Canada
Marcus Specht   Delft University of Technology, Netherlands

Finance Chair

Benedict du Boulay   University of Sussex, UK

Membership Chair

Benjamin D. Nye   University of Southern California, USA

Publicity Chair

Irene-Angelica Chounta   University of Duisburg-Essen, Germany

IAIED Officers

Xinyuan Hao   University College London, UK
Jionghao Lin   University of Hong Kong, China

IAIED Executive Committee

Ig Ibert Bittencourt   Universidade Federal de Alagoas, Brazil
Min Chi   North Carolina State University, USA
Irene-Angelica Chounta   University of Duisburg-Essen, Germany
Cristina Conati   University of British Columbia, Canada
Alexandra I. Cristea   Durham University, UK

Neil Heffernan	Worcester Polytechnic Institute, USA
Seiji Isotani	University of Pennsylvania, USA
Noboru Matsuda	North Carolina State University, USA
Bruce M. McLaren	Carnegie Mellon University, USA
Tanja Mitrovic	University of Canterbury, New Zealand
Andrew M. Olney	University of Memphis, USA
Erin Walker	University of Pittsburgh, USA
Beverly Park Woolf	University of Massachusetts Amherst, USA
Diego Zapata-Rivera	Educational Testing Service, USA

International Alliance to Advance Learning in the Digital Era (IAALDE)

The IAIED Society is a member of the International Alliance to Advance Learning in the Digital Era (IAALDE) and belongs to its board. IAIED is currently represented at IAALDE by Seiji Isotani (University of Pennsylvania, USA) as president of IAIED.

AIED 2026 Sponsors

Platinum

Silver

Bronze

I= Eedi

Best Paper Award Sponsorship

🐴 Springer

How Best to Harness AI's Great Potential to Improve Education? (AIED 2026 Keynote)

Vincent Aleven

Human-Computer Interaction Institute, Carnegie Mellon University, USA

Abstract. AI has tremendous potential to improve education. For example, a substantial amount of scientific evidence shows that AI-based tutoring systems can help students learn better than other forms of instruction. Also, some scientific evidence suggests that AI-based tutoring systems can help reduce inequalities in the educational system, even if not all available evidence points in this direction. Yet, in the USA, standardized test scores are stagnant, including in K-12 mathematics learning, where AI-based tutoring systems are often used. Nor is there evidence that existing inequalities within the educational system are shrinking. These results are beginning to lead to calls to outlaw the use of computers in classrooms, in the USA and elsewhere. How might we reconcile these seemingly opposing views from research and educational practice? More importantly, what might researchers do to help improve educational outcomes? We propose that it is important to focus on creating favorable circumstances for the use of AI-based tutoring systems. To this end, it is productive to view the smart classroom as a socio-technical ecosystem with many stakeholders: students, in the first place, and "facilitators" such as teachers, peers, human tutors, and parents/caregivers. By carefully designing human-AI interactions to support these stakeholders, we stand a good chance to harness AI's great potential to improve education and reduce educational inequalities. We illustrate this vision with several example projects and promising empirical results from our lab. In these projects, students use AI-based tutoring software and facilitators are helped by a variety of novel AI-based tools, including a mixed-reality analytics-based awareness tool for teachers, support for goal setting for students, and small-dosage AI-supported remote human tutoring.

Biography

Dr. Vincent Aleven is a Professor of Human-Computer Interaction at Carnegie Mellon University. As the head of the Creating Adaptive Tutoring Software (CATS) Lab, he investigates how AI can enhance education. His lab focuses on prototyping new designs for the smart classroom, with projects ranging from optimizing the design of AI-based tutoring systems, to a real-time mixed-reality teacher awareness tool, to easy-to-use authoring tools for creating AI-based tutoring systems. His work builds on cognitive theory and theories of self-regulated learning and helps extend the empirical science of how people learn with adaptive learning technologies. He has over 300 publications, is co-editor-in-chief of the International Journal of Artificial Intelligence in Education, received over 25 major research grants, and won 12 best paper awards at international conferences.

Contents

Track 2 - Human Aspects of AIED - Full Papers (1/2)

Agnoagentia: The Illusion of Agency in AI-Assisted Learning

Iris Delikoura[1]([⊠]) [iD], Pantelis M. Papadopoulos[2] [iD], and Pan Hui[3] [iD]

[1] Hong Kong University of Science and Technology, Clear Water Bay,
Hong Kong SAR
`idelikoura@connect.ust.hk`
[2] University of Twente, Enschede, Netherlands
`p.m.papadopoulos@utwente.nl`
[3] Hong Kong University of Science and Technology, Guangzhou, China
`panhui@ust.hk`

Abstract. This study examines learners' perceived and enacted agency when interacting with different AI systems during collaborative writing tasks. A total of 52 university students, randomly grouped into 26 dyads consecutively completed three collaborative writing tasks under three conditions: (a) "Baseline" collaboration via chat and collaborative text editor, (b) "Clair", same as the Baseline, but with a pedagogically structured collaborative conversational agent (Clair) supporting student discussions, and (c) "ChatGPT", same as Baseline, but students had additionally individual access to ChatGPT (using GPT-5). Perceived agency was assessed by self-reported measures based on the Sense of Agency Scale. Enacted agency was evaluated through coding dyad dialogues using Bandura's four core properties: *forethought, self-reactiveness, intentionality, self-reflectiveness*. Whereas Clair had some positive impact on self-reflectiveness, ChatGPT significantly reduced the communication volume, while increasing offloading behaviour, i.e., delegating the task to ChatGPT. Results revealed a paradox: ChatGPT-assisted students reported high perceived agency, while demonstrating low enacted agency. We term this phenomenon *agnoagentia*, the illusory perception of agency that emerges when learners interact with GenAI tools, unaware that their enacted agency has been displaced.

Keywords: Agnoagentia · Agency · Collaborative Learning · Collaborative Conversational Agents · AI · GenAI

1 Introduction

AI systems employed in learning environments vary significantly in their design intent, specifically whether they are pedagogically structured or general-purpose. Popular and readily available generative AI (GenAI) tools (e.g., ChatGPT) are not based on underlying pedagogy and can be used for multiple purposes. In contrast, AI-driven pedagogical agents, such as collaborative conversational

E. G. Blanchard et al. (Eds.): AIED 2026, LNAI 16583, pp. 1–9, 2027.
https://doi.org/10.1007/978-3-032-29760-0_1

agents (CCAs), are aimed at fostering learning by implementing theory-informed instructional approaches such as the Socratic method [1], the argumentative dialogue [2], and the productive talk [3].

Given that student agency is particularly valuable in collaborative learning, understanding how different AI designs support or hinder agency is essential. Yet, empirical research examining AI's role in collaborative learning still remains in development [4], which motivates our study. By comparing these two tools against a baseline of human-only collaboration, we aim to identify how specific AI designs shape students' *perceived* and *enacted* agency. *Perceived agency* refers to the subjective sense of control and autonomy of the students. *Enacted agency*, in contrast, captures the observable behaviour through which students exercise control. This comparison, to our knowledge, has not yet been undertaken.

2   Theoretical Background

2.1   Collaborative Learning in the Age of AI

With the rapid adoption of ChatGPT in educational contexts, understanding how students collaborate when using such tools is important for designing activities that optimize engagement and knowledge exchange [5]. Darmawansah et al. [6] found that integrating ChatGPT into collaborative argumentation activities led to improvements in English as a Foreign Language, critical thinking awareness, and willingness to collaborate. Conversely, Albadarin et al. [7] reported that students working on group projects tend to use ChatGPT individually, rather than engaging in collective brainstorming or peer collaboration. This pattern suggests that even within collaborative settings, learners may bypass peer interaction in favour of AI assistance, effectively offloading cognitive processes that would otherwise be distributed among group members [8]. Such offloading can diminish collaboration, and cognitive functions such as memory, engagement, attention, and critical thinking [9].

However, not all AI-mediated interactions carry the same risks. Conversational Agents (CAs) have long served as study partners, improving students' academic performance, psychological engagement and metacognitive development [10]. While typical CAs have a single-learner facing interface, CCAs analyse patterns in dialogue and deliver automatic interventions to foster group exchange and guide toward productive dialogue. Research has demonstrated that when CCAs function as group members, they can improve learning outcomes, increase participation, and promote transactive exchange [11].

2.2   Agency: Properties and Development

As students increasingly interact with AI systems, the capacity to maintain autonomous decision-making becomes essential. The ability to exercise agency underpins both personal development and collective progress, enabling responsible citizenship and meaningful participation in society [12]. Bandura [13] posits that agentic learners can act intentionally and take responsibility for their self-development, adaptation, and self-renewal. There are four core properties of human agency [14]:

- *Intentionality* refers to the formation of intentions, including the development of action plans and strategies for achieving them.
- *Forethought* builds on intentionality through goal setting and the anticipation of future outcomes, which guide and motivate effort in advance.
- *Self-reactiveness* moves from planning to action by involving self-management and self-motivation processes that allow learners to monitor and regulate their behaviour during task execution.
- *Self-reflectiveness* complements the other properties by describing the capacity to examine and evaluate one's own thoughts, actions, and their effectiveness.

2.3   Study Motivation and Research Question

The focus of our study is the relationship between perceived and enacted agency in the context of online collaborative writing tasks. Given the prevalence of AI tools in education, we aim to compare how two distinct types of tools, a general-purpose and a pedagogy driven one, affect student agency when compared with a baseline setting of no AI support. Therefore, the study aims to answer the following research question: *How do different types of AI tools affect students' perceived and enacted agency during collaborative writing?*

3   Methods

3.1   Participants

A total of 68 students, randomly grouped into dyads, were recruited from a university in Hong Kong. The study was integrated into the standard curriculum, and students received a 5% course credit upon completion. Data from 16 participants were excluded due to incomplete post-task surveys. The final sample consisted of 52 participants (26 dyads; 27 female, 24 male, 1 prefer not to say; $M_{\mathrm{age}} = 22.15$, SD $= 1.87$). The study protocol was approved by the institutional ethics committee, and informed consent was obtained prior to the study.

3.2   Materials and Instruments

Go-Lab, Clair and ChatGPT. Our study used the freely available Go-Lab environment [15]. Go-Lab offers a wide range of virtual labs and tools. This includes a chat tool, a collaborative text editor in which students can co-author in real time, a collaborative conversational agent (Clair), and a tool to interact individually with ChatGPT (using GPT-5). Clair is an agent within Go-Lab that monitors student dialogues in the chat and intervenes when necessary, using "talk moves" based on the academically productive talk framework [16], to nudge students into a more productive dialogue. Clair's talk moves include prompts to link current to prior parts of the dialogue ("How does this connect with what has been discussed so far?"), note agreement ("Do you agree or disagree with what your partner just said?"), deepen the reasoning ("Could you elaborate more on what you just said?") and other.

Agency Instrument. For this study, we developed our own instrument to measure perceived agency, based on the Sense of Agency Scale (SoAS) [17]. A shorter questionnaire was necessary to minimise participant fatigue and maintain engagement. Our adapted instrument consisted of four 7-point Likert scale statements asking students to denote their level of agreement regarding their sense of agency, (1 = Strongly Disagree, 7 = Strongly Agree):

1. During this task, I felt in control of how the text developed.
2. I could influence or redirect my partner's ideas when I wanted to.
3. Decision-making felt balanced between us.
4. I feel personally responsible and accountable for the final abstract.

3.3 Study Design and Procedure

The study applied a within-subject design, with all dyads completing three consecutive collaborative writing tasks. For each task, every dyad had to read preparation learning material and jointly draft a 400-word abstract, using the collaborative text box in Go-Lab. One member of the dyad was provided with information about the risks of a given topic, while the other received information about its benefits. This asymmetry required dyad members to collaborate, share their respective knowledge, and negotiate what each would contribute to the joint text. To mitigate the effects of prior domain knowledge, we selected neutral topics unlikely to favour either member: (i) the future of work and automation, (ii) NFTs and copyright ethics, and (iii) food technology. All students progressed at the same time through the three study conditions of the three writing tasks, presented below in order:

1. **Baseline:** The students discussed in the chat and wrote the abstract collaboratively with their partner without the presence of AI tools.
2. **Clair:** The same as the Baseline condition, but with Clair present in the chat using talk moves to make the dialogue more productive.
3. **ChatGPT:** The same as the Baseline condition, but students had, in addition, individual access to ChatGPT in a separate window.

Each writing task lasted 20 min, with an additional 5 min allocated for completing the agency instrument. The total study duration was approximately 80 min. Students' activity (chat logs, ChatGPT logs, and abstracts) in each condition and their answers in the respective self-reported agency instrument were the dependent variables of the study, while the role of AI tools in each condition was the independent variable.

3.4 Data Analysis

Enacted agency was measured through chat logs that were deductively coded. Two coders annotated independently 15% of the data, achieving substantial inter-rater agreement ($\kappa = 0.81$). Discrepancies were resolved through discussion, and the first author coded the remaining dataset. The coding scheme is presented in Table 1. In addition to the four core properties of Bandura's theory [13], we also included *offloading* and *neutral* messages. We conducted repeated measures analysis of variance (ANOVA) to compare the levels of perceived agency and the absolute and relative frequencies of messages in each condition. Analysis showed that no test assumption was violated, therefore we opted for parametric tests. Finally, we used $\alpha = 0.05$ for all statistical analyses.

Table 1. Codebook: Terminology, Definitions, and Examples

Term	Definition	Example
Forethought	Setting goals and anticipating consequences of actions	"What is our strategy?"
Self-reactiveness	Monitoring and adjusting the process	"Hurry, only five minutes left"
Intentionality	Expressing a specific goal or outlining concrete steps	"I will do this part"
Self-Reflectiveness	Reflecting on one's own functioning and adequacy of actions	"Wait maybe we should do...instead"
Offloading	Delegating tasks to other entities	"ChatGPT will write this part"
Neutral	Chatter about unrelated topics	"My name is..."

4 Results

4.1 Perceived Participant Agency

Reliability analysis for the individual self-reported agency instrument was acceptable across conditions (Baseline: $\alpha = 0.72$; Clair: $\alpha = .74$; ChatGPT: $\alpha = .73$). Repeated measures ANOVA results showed a significant difference ($F(2, 102) = 3.20, p = .04, \eta_p^2 = .05$) of perceived agency between the Baseline ($M = 4.75, \text{SD} = 0.92$), Clair ($M = 5.07, \text{SD} = 0.99$), and ChatGPT ($M = 5.14, \text{SD} = 0.94$) conditions, but no significant difference in pairwise comparisons ($p > .05$).

4.2 Agency State Frequencies

Table 2 shows the average number of messages per dialogue in the three conditions, along with the number of messages coded under each of the six categories of Table 1. Clair's 70 interventions ($M = 2.69, \mathrm{SD} = 1.93$) were not counted towards the total. Repeated measures ANOVA with a Greenhouse-Geisser correction showed a significant difference in the number of messages between dyad members in the three conditions of the study ($F(1.87, 46.64) = 23.83, p < .01, \eta_p^2 = .48$). Pairwise comparisons with Bonferroni correction revealed that during the Baseline condition, the dialogues were significantly longer than the ones in the second condition, during which Clair was present in the chat ($p < .01$, $d = 0.62$), and the third condition when individual access to ChatGPT became available ($p < .01$, $d = 1.47$). Similarly, the dialogues during the second condition were also significantly longer than the ones in the third condition ($p < .01$, $d = 0.86$).

Since the length of the dialogues differed significantly in the three conditions, it was expected that the average number of messages per agency category would also differ. Indeed, repeated measures ANOVA with a Greenhouse-Geisser correction revealed significant differences for forethought, self-reactiveness, intentionality, offloading, and neutral messages ($p < .01$), but not for self-reflectiveness ($p = .23$). Pairwise comparisons with Bonferroni correction showed that during the Baseline condition, dialogues had significantly more agency-coded messages than the Clair condition in forethought, intentionality, and neutral ($p < .05$), and higher than the ChatGPT condition in all categories except self-reflectiveness ($p < .01$). Similarly, the Clair condition dialogues had significantly more agency-coded messages than the ChatGPT condition in forethought, self-reactiveness, and intentionality ($p < .05$). Notably, the ChatGPT condition was the only one where offloading behaviour was observed ($M = 1.31$, SD $= 1.26$), compared to zero instances in the Baseline condition and minimal instances in the Clair condition ($M = 0.54$, SD $= 1.07$).

Table 2. Number of messages per core property in the three conditions.

	Baseline ($n = 26$)		Clair ($n = 26$)		ChatGPT ($n = 26$)	
	M	(SD)	M	(SD)	M	(SD)
# of total messages*	24.12	12.42	17.15	10.42	9.96	6.14
# of Forethought messages*	8.04	5.05	5.35	3.31	1.69	1.54
# of Self-Reactiveness messages*	2.38	2.52	2.62	2.84	0.73	1.00
# of Intentionality messages*	2.12	2.16	1.27	1.49	0.42	0.70
# of Self-Reflectiveness messages	2.15	2.62	1.58	2.18	1.08	2.08
# of Offloading messages*	0.00	0.00	0.54	1.07	1.31	1.26
# of Neutral messages*	9.42	5.11	5.81	3.48	4.73	4.14

* $p < .05$

5   Discussion

Participants in the ChatGPT condition reported the highest perceived agency, followed by Clair, then Baseline. Enacted agency, however, moved in the opposite direction: Baseline participants demonstrated the highest enacted agency, followed by Clair, then ChatGPT. As shown in Table 2, the length of dialogues and the number of messages of each type, with the exception of offloading, generally decreases when transitioning from conditions 1–3. In ChatGPT, offloading increased significantly at the expense of forethought. While cognitive offloading is not inherently negative, we focus on its unproductive form, which has been characterized as cognitive surrender [18]. In summary, the perceived and enacted measures moved in opposite directions: when students felt most agentic, they demonstrated the least enacted agency.

The uncontested delegation of control to ChatGPT produced a paradoxical perception of heightened agency. We term this *Agnoagentia*: from Greek a- (without), gnōsis (knowledge), and Latin agentia (agency). This phenomenon emerges when learners interact with GenAI tools, unaware that their enacted agency has been displaced by the system. Agnoagentia comprises two observable features: (a) a perception-enactment gap, where subjective reports of agency exceed behavioural indicators; and (b) diminished forethought, where planning is replaced by prompting. In the presence of ChatGPT, the combination of high offloading and short dialogues contrasts with participants' subjective reports of feeling in control. Agnoagentia represents a learning blind spot: learners believe they are exercising agency because they direct a tool, yet the cognitive processes that constitute enacted agency have been outsourced.

This blind spot is reminiscent of *metacognitive calibration* [19], which describes the alignment between perceived and actual cognitive performance, reflecting how accurately individuals perceive their internal processes [20]. Well-calibrated learners monitor their engagement and adjust accordingly; poorly calibrated learners overestimate their understanding or control [21]. The perception-enactment gap observed in agnoagentia reflects a similar phenomenon, but applied specifically to learner agency. Bandura's components of agency all require accurate awareness of one's current state. When learners believe they are already in control, engagement with these agentic processes disappears. In short, agnoagentia not only reflects poor calibration but perpetuates it: learners who do not recognise their diminished agency have no drive to reclaim it, as they are unaware it has been displaced.

5.1   Implications for AIED

First, collaboration is necessary for both the development of learner agency and the construction of knowledge. By bypassing human collaboration in favour of an AI tool, we risk both displacing learner agency and fostering over-reliance on AI. The Baseline condition, despite producing the lowest perceived agency, demonstrated significantly higher message exchange and forethought than both AI conditions. This aligns with Vygotsky's [22] insight that collaborative struggle drives cognitive development. The productive friction of peer collaboration may feel less agentic precisely because it demands accommodation. Yet, this very friction triggers the cognitive processes that education seeks to develop. Learner agency should be co-developed, not outsourced. Second, the pattern of offloading observed in our study resonates with concerns raised by Dwivedi et al. [23], who cautioned that over-reliance on GenAI may lead to atrophy of the cognitive competencies education should foster. These implications remain provisional and are bounded by the limitations of the present study. Nonetheless, they point to a broader set of questions about how AI tools reshape the nature of learner agency in educational contexts.

6   Conclusion

This study reveals a paradox in AI-based learning: the tools that feel most empowering may be the least educationally productive. ChatGPT-assisted participants reported the highest sense of agency, while demonstrating the lowest enacted agency; a dissociation we term agnoagentia. Meanwhile, the productive struggle in peer collaboration, though subjectively experienced as less agentic, sustained the processes through which agency develops. Despite potential limitations, our findings carry important implications for the design and integration of AI tools in collaborative learning environments.

References

1. Xi, L., Zhang, Y., Wang, Q.: Investigating the effects of an LLM-based Socratic conversational agent on students' academic performance and reflective thinking in higher education. Comput. Educ. **241**, 105494 (2026)
2. Aicher, A., Matsuda, Y., Yasumoto, K., Minker, W., André, E., Ultes, S.: Enhancing reflective and conversational user engagement in argumentative dialogues with virtual agents. Multimodal Technol. Interact. **8**(8) (2024)
3. Tegos, S., Demetriadis, S., Papadopoulos, P.M., Weinberger, A.: Conversational agents for academically productive talk: a comparison of directed and undirected agent interventions. Int. J. Comput.-Support. Collab. Learn. **11**(4), 417–440 (2016)
4. Gilson, A., et al.: How does chatGPT perform on the united states medical licensing examination? the implications of large language models for medical education and knowledge assessment. JMIR Med. Educ. **9**(1), e45312 (2023)
5. Perifanou, M., Economides, A.A.: Students collaboratively prompting ChatGPT. Computers **14**(5) (2025)
6. Darmawansah, D., Rachman, D., Febiyani, F., Hwang, G.-J.: ChatGPT-supported collaborative argumentation: integrating collaboration script and argument mapping to enhance efl students' argumentation skills. Educ. Inf. Technol. **30**(3), 3803–3827 (2025)
7. Albadarin, Y., Saqr, M., Pope, N., Tukiainen, M.: A systematic literature review of empirical research on chatGPT in education. Discov. Educ. **3**(1), 60 (2024)
8. Risko, E.F., Gilbert, S.J.: Cognitive offloading. Trends Cogn. Sci. **20**(9), 676–688 (2016)

9. Kosmyna, N., et al.: Your brain on chatGPT: accumulation of cognitive debt when using an AI assistant for essay writing task (2025)
10. Ganguly, A., Mehjabin, N., Malik, A., Johri, A.: Conversational AI agents in education: an umbrella review of current utilization, challenges, and future directions for ethical and responsible use. AI Ethics **6**(1), 72 (2026)
11. Adamson, D., Dyke, G., Jang, H., Rosé, C.P.: Towards an agile approach to adapting dynamic collaboration support to student needs. Int. J. Artif. Intell. Educ. **24**(1), 92–124 (2014)
12. Mouta, A., Pinto-Llorente, A.M., Torrecilla-Sánchez, E.M.: "Where is Agency Moving to?": exploring the Interplay between AI Technologies in Education and Human Agency. Digit. Soc. **4**(2), 49 (2025)
13. Bandura, A.: Social cognitive theory: an agentic perspective. Annu. Rev. Psychol. **52**(1), 1–26 (2001)
14. Bandura, A.: Toward a psychology of human agency. Perspect. Psychol. Sci. **1**(2), 164–180 (2006)
15. Jong, T.D., et al.: Understanding teacher design practices for digital inquiry-based science learning: the case of Go-Lab. Education Tech. Research Dev. **69**(2), 417–444 (2021)
16. de Araujo, A., Papadopoulos, P.M., McKenney, S., de Jong, T.: A learning analytics-based collaborative conversational agent to foster productive dialogue in inquiry learning. J. Comput. Assist. Learn. **40**(6), 2700–2714 (2024)
17. Tapal, A., Oren, E., Dar, R., Eitam, B.: The sense of agency scale: a measure of consciously perceived control over one's mind, body, and the immediate environment. Front. Psychol. **8** (2017)
18. Shaw, S.D., Nave, G.: Thinking—Fast, Slow, and Artificial: How AI is Reshaping Human Reasoning and the Rise of Cognitive Surrender (2026)
19. Pieschl, S.: Metacognitive calibration–an extended conceptualization and potential applications. Metacogn. Learn. **4**(1), 3–31 (2009)
20. Stone, N.J.: Exploring the relationship between calibration and self-regulated learning. Educ. Psychol. Rev. **12**(4), 437–475 (2000)
21. Thiede, K.W., Dunlosky, J.: Toward a general model of self-regulated study: an analysis of selection of items for study and self-paced study time. J. Exp. Psychol. Learn. Mem. Cogn. **25**(4), 1024–1037 (1999)
22. Vygotsky, L.S.: Development of Higher Psychological Processes. Harvard University Press, Cambridge (1978)
23. Dwivedi, Y.K., Kshetri, et al.: Opinion Paper: "So what if ChatGPT wrote it?" Multidisciplinary perspectives on opportunities, challenges and implications of generative conversational AI for research, practice and policy. Int. J. Inf. Manage. **71**, 102642 (2023)

Do Instructional Behaviors Generalize Across Disciplines? an Empirical Study with Fine-Tuned Multimodal LLMs

Cunling Bian, Saisai Ye, and Weigang Lu

Department of Education, Ocean University of China, Qingdao, China
{clbian, luweigang}@ouc.edu.cn, yesaisai@stu.ouc.edu.cn

Abstract. Instructional behavior description extracts instructional behavior labels and structured descriptions from multimodal classroom data to support teaching evaluation and student feedback. Although instructional behaviors are often assumed to generalize across domains, examining cross-domain differences is essential for understanding how pedagogical intent and classroom enactment vary in practice. Accordingly, this study adopts cross-disciplinary comparison as a concrete research object to empirically examine domain-context dependence in instructional behavior description. We construct a multimodal classroom dataset composed of nearly 1,000 classroom video segments from authentic secondary school lessons, organized into Humanities and Science contexts to provide empirical data support. To enhance Multimodal Large Language Models' (MLLMs) instructional behavior recognition and description under educational data and computational constraints, we apply LoRA, a parameter-efficient fine-tuning method, to adapt three representative open-source MLLMs. We conduct intra-disciplinary evaluations, cross-disciplinary train–test swap experiments, and discipline-specificity analyses to systematically examine how instructional behavior recognition and description vary within and across disciplines. Results show that LoRA consistently improves performance in both contexts, while cross-disciplinary transfer leads to substantial performance degradation and clear directional asymmetry. Discipline-specificity analysis further reveals systematic differences in instructional behavior distributions and description keywords between Humanities and Science. These results provide empirical evidence that instructional behavior description is discipline-context dependent rather than one-size-fits-all, highlighting the risk of deploying discipline-agnostic instructional analytics in real classrooms and underscoring the necessity of discipline-aware educational AI systems.

Keywords: Instructional Behavior Description · Cross Disciplinary Generalization · Multimodal Large Language Model · Parameter Efficient Fine Tuning

E. G. Blanchard et al. (Eds.): AIED 2026, LNAI 16583, pp. 10–18, 2027.
https://doi.org/10.1007/978-3-032-29760-0_2

1 Context and Problem Statement

Instructional behavior description refers to recognizing instructional behavior labels and generating structured descriptions from multimodal classroom data. It provides empirical evidence for instructional evaluation and serves as a critical means for analyzing teacher–student interactions and supporting student feedback analysis. However, instructional behaviors are not fully universal: the same behavior label may exhibit systematic variation across disciplinary contexts in pedagogical intent, classroom enactment, and learning outcomes. For example, demonstration and explanation in Humanities typically involve interpreting texts or concepts using slides or the blackboard, whereas in Science they more often consist of step-by-step demonstrations grounded in physical artifacts or experimental procedures. Despite these differences, prior studies have largely focused on generic instructional behavior recognition, with limited investigation of discipline-specific realizations and little controlled evaluation of cross-disciplinary generalization (e.g., [1, 2]).

From a methodological perspective, instructional behavior analysis has evolved alongside advances in multimodal learning. Early approaches relied on traditional machine learning, followed by deep learning models such as two-stream networks, 3D CNNs, and skeleton-based methods, which primarily target behavior recognition rather than structured language generation [3]. With the emergence of Transformers as a dominant paradigm in visual and video understanding [4], Multimodal Large Language Models (MLLMs) have recently opened new opportunities for instructional behavior description by jointly performing recognition and generating interpretable, structured textual outputs. These models are particularly appealing for educational settings with limited labeled data.

Nevertheless, MLLMs trained for general-purpose multimodal tasks may not align well with the specific requirements of instructional behavior description. Zero- or few-shot prompting often yields unstable performance in educational scenarios [5], while full-parameter fine-tuning is computationally expensive and risks catastrophic forgetting. Parameter-Efficient Fine-Tuning (PEFT) methods address this challenge by updating only a small subset of model parameters, enabling efficient task adaptation under practical constraints [6]. In this work, we adopt LoRA, a representative PEFT approach, to adapt three open-source MLLMs for instructional behavior description in both Humanities and Science contexts.

Building on these motivations, this study uses cross-disciplinary comparison as a concrete and theoretically grounded research setting to examine domain-context dependence in instructional behavior description. We conduct intra-disciplinary evaluations, cross-disciplinary train–test swap experiments, and discipline-specificity analyses to systematically assess within-discipline performance, cross-disciplinary transferability, and discipline-dependent behavioral patterns. Specifically, we address the following research questions:

RQ1: How can MLLMs' ability to perform instructional behavior description be improved under educational data and computational constraints?

RQ2: Is instructional behavior description discipline-context dependent across Humanities and Science classrooms?

RQ3: How does discipline-context dependence manifest in instructional behavior descriptions, in terms of behavior distributions and description keywords?

2 Method

2.1 Overview and Research Design

This study adopts a discipline-aware experimental design to investigate discipline-context dependence in instructional behavior description. As illustrated in Fig. 1, the method consists of three interconnected stages aligned with the research questions. First, we construct a multimodal classroom dataset organized into Humanities and Science contexts to provide empirical grounding for examining disciplinary effects. Second, we adapt representative MLLMs using LoRA-based PEFT to improve instructional behavior recognition and structured description under educational data and computational constraints. Third, we design a set of evaluation protocols, including intra-disciplinary evaluation, cross-disciplinary train–test swap experiments, and discipline-specificity analysis, to systematically examine performance improvement, cross-disciplinary generalization, and discipline-dependent behavioral patterns.

This design enables us to move beyond generic performance comparison and explicitly link model behavior to disciplinary context. In particular, intra-disciplinary evaluation assesses whether MLLMs can effectively model instructional behaviors within a given discipline, cross-disciplinary testing probes the extent and directionality of generalization across disciplinary contexts, and discipline-specificity analysis reveals how instructional behavior distributions and descriptive semantics differ between Humanities and Science classrooms.

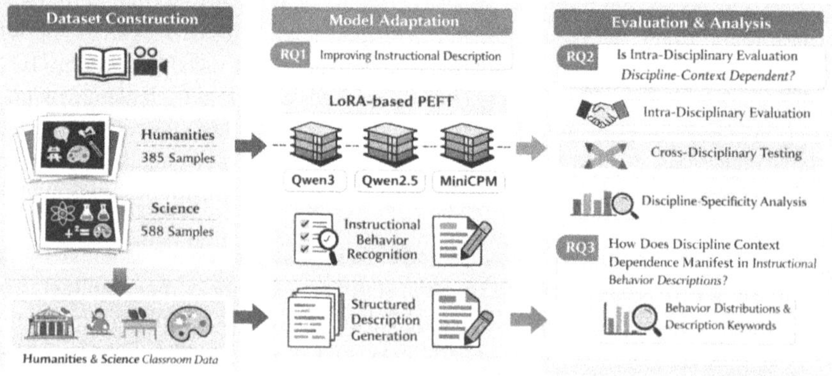

Fig. 1. Overview of the discipline-aware instructional behavior description framework.

2.2 Dataset Construction and Disciplinary Organization

We construct a multimodal classroom dataset composed of 973 classroom video segments extracted from authentic secondary school lessons across seven subjects: Chemistry, History, Fine Arts, Biology, Mathematics, Physics, and Chinese Language. To operationalize disciplinary context, the dataset is organized into two broad categories grounded in disciplinary teaching theory: Humanities (History, Fine Arts, Chinese) and Science (Physics, Chemistry, Biology, Mathematics). This grouping reflects fundamental differences in knowledge representation, instructional organization, and behavioral enactment across disciplines. Instructional behaviors in each video segment were manually annotated following the Flanders Interaction Analysis System (FIAS), and organized using the Initiation–Response–Feedback (IRF) interaction pattern. Each video segment is approximately one minute in length, and may contain multiple instructional behavior labels, which are further synthesized into structured textual descriptions reflecting the temporal flow of classroom interaction. After preprocessing, the final dataset includes 385 Humanities samples and 588 Science samples, with an 80/20 split for training and testing within each disciplinary context. While the dataset presents an uneven class distribution between Humanities and Science, this imbalance does not materially undermine the statistical validity and interpretability of the core findings.

2.3 Model Adaptation with PEFT

Multimodal LLMs. To support instructional behavior description from classroom videos, we select three representative open-source MLLMs: Qwen2.5-Omni-3B (Qwen2.5), Qwen3-VL-4B-Thinking (Qwen3), and MiniCPM-V-4.5 (MiniCPM). Qwen2.5 supports end-to-end multimodal inputs for video-based description, Qwen3 emphasizes multimodal reasoning for fine-grained inference, and MiniCPM focuses on efficient vision–language alignment with long-video understanding. These models were chosen because they are open-source, comparable in scale, and capable of lightweight deployment, enabling fair and controlled comparisons across adaptation settings.

PEFT. To enhance MLLMs' instructional behavior description under educational data scarcity and computational constraints, we adopt LoRA, a PEFT method. LoRA freezes the pretrained model parameters and introduces low-rank trainable adapters into intermediate layers, substantially reducing the number of trainable parameters while preserving general model capabilities. Instructional behavior description is formulated as a multi-task problem combining multi-label instructional behavior recognition and structured textual description generation. All three models are fine-tuned using LLaMA-Factory with identical hyperparameters, rank $= 16$, batch size $= 4$, learning rate 1.8×10^{-5}. This controlled setup allows performance differences to be attributed to parameter-efficient adaptation rather than architectural or data variations.

Baseline Models. To evaluate the effectiveness of LoRA-based adaptation, we use the native versions of Qwen2.5, Qwen3, and MiniCPM as baselines. Baseline models are executed under the same LLaMA-Factory framework with pretrained weights and no parameter updates. Their performance serves as a reference for quantifying gains achieved through parameter-efficient fine-tuning on instructional behavior description.

2.4 Experimental Design for Discipline-Context Dependence Analysis

Intra-Disciplinary Evaluation. Intra-disciplinary evaluation assesses model performance within the same disciplinary context. Models fine-tuned on Humanities data are evaluated on the Humanities test set, and models fine-tuned on Science data are evaluated on the Science test set. This setting measures the effectiveness of LoRA-based adaptation for instructional behavior description when training and testing contexts are aligned.

Cross-Disciplinary Train–Test Swap Evaluation. To assess cross-disciplinary generalization, we design a train–test swap protocol. Models fine-tuned on Humanities training data are evaluated on the Science test set, and vice versa. This setting explicitly examines the extent and directionality of generalization across disciplinary contexts and serves as the primary experimental basis for evaluating discipline-context dependence in instructional behavior description.

Discipline-Specificity Analysis. To further analyze discipline-context dependence beyond performance metrics, we conduct discipline-specificity analysis by comparing instructional behavior label distributions and keyword statistics in generated descriptions across Humanities and Science contexts. This analysis focuses on aggregated statistical patterns rather than individual cases, revealing systematic differences in behavioral prevalence and semantic emphasis between disciplines.

Evaluation Metrics. For instructional behavior recognition, we report F1-score, Precision, Recall, and exact-match Accuracy, where Accuracy denotes strict multi-label exact match. For structured description generation, we use ROUGE-1, ROUGE-2, ROUGE-L, and BLEU-4. Together, these metrics capture both recognition accuracy and descriptive quality.

3 Results

3.1 Intra-disciplinary Performance

Tables 1 and 2 summarize intra-disciplinary results for instructional behavior recognition and structured description generation in Humanities and Science. Across both disciplines, LoRA fine-tuning consistently improves performance for all three multimodal LLMs, including Qwen3, Qwen2.5, and MiniCPM, on both multi-label recognition and text generation metrics. Among the evaluated models, Qwen3 achieves the strongest overall performance across disciplines, followed by Qwen2.5 and MiniCPM, a ranking that remains stable before and after fine-tuning. These results indicate that LoRA effectively enhances both behavior identification accuracy and the quality of structured instructional descriptions, regardless of the underlying model architecture. Across all models, Science consistently outperforms Humanities in both native and fine-tuned settings. While part of this gap can be attributed to the larger amount of Science training data, it more fundamentally reflects disciplinary differences in instructional structure. Science instruction tends to follow more standardized and operational routines, which align well with multimodal representation learning, whereas Humanities instruction is more interpretive and context-dependent, making recognition and description more challenging.

Table 1. Performance comparison of native and fine-tuned multimodal LLMs in Humanities

Method	Model	F1	Accuracy	Precision	Recall	R-1	R-2	R-L	B-4
Native	Qwen3	**0.6572**	**0.1169**	**0.6485**	**0.6639**	**0.3559**	**0.1654**	**0.3315**	**0.0943**
	Qwen2.5	0.6291	0.1039	0.6205	0.6392	0.3345	0.1491	0.3104	0.0842
	MiniCPM	0.5827	0.0649	0.5732	0.5929	0.3012	0.1243	0.2795	0.0691
Fine-Tuned	Qwen3	**0.7758**	**0.2857**	**0.7702**	**0.7815**	**0.4524**	**0.2324**	**0.4215**	**0.1475**
	Qwen2.5	0.7475	0.2338	0.7458	0.7492	0.4294	0.2148	0.4101	0.1165
	MiniCPM	0.7241	0.2078	0.7265	0.7293	0.3892	0.1865	0.3702	0.1091

Table 2. Performance comparison of native and fine-tuned multimodal LLMs in Science

Method	Model	F1	Accuracy	Precision	Recall	R-1	R-2	R-L	B-4
Native	Qwen3	**0.6892**	**0.1525**	**0.6812**	**0.6927**	**0.3829**	**0.1851**	**0.3572**	**0.1059**
	Qwen2.5	0.6605	0.1271	0.6568	0.6715	0.3587	0.1692	0.3324	0.0945
	MiniCPM	0.6121	0.0847	0.6027	0.6219	0.3231	0.1459	0.3015	0.0762
Fine-Tuned	Qwen3	**0.8076**	**0.3475**	**0.7985**	**0.8142**	**0.4869**	**0.2637**	**0.4592**	**0.1607**
	Qwen2.5	0.7802	0.2881	0.7791	0.7825	0.4627	0.2412	0.4351	0.1462
	MiniCPM	0.7597	0.2542	0.7583	0.7612	0.4281	0.2092	0.4105	0.1294

3.2 Cross-Disciplinary Generalization

Table 3 reports cross-disciplinary generalization results under train–test swaps between Humanities and Science. All models experience clear performance degradation compared to intra-disciplinary evaluation, indicating limited cross-disciplinary transferability of instructional behavior understanding. Performance drops are not symmetric across transfer directions. Models trained on Humanities exhibit larger degradation when tested on Science than vice versa. This asymmetry suggests that instructional behaviors learned from Science data are more broadly transferable, whereas Humanities-trained models struggle to recognize discipline-specific behaviors prevalent in Science contexts. Overall, these findings highlight the strong dependence of instructional behavior representations on disciplinary context.

Table 3. Cross-disciplinary train–test swap performance of LoRA-fine-tuned multimodal LLMs

Method	Model	F1	Accuracy	Precision	Recall	R-1	R-2	R-L	B-4
Humanities train → Science test	Qwen3	**0.7042**	**0.1695**	**0.6978**	**0.7103**	**0.4032**	**0.1921**	**0.3746**	0.1102
	Qwen2.5	0.6729	0.1356	0.6465	0.6857	0.3815	0.1890	0.3543	**0.1118**

(continued)

Table 3. (*continued*)

Method	Model	F1	Accuracy	Precision	Recall	R-1	R-2	R-L	B-4
	MiniCPM	0.6305	0.1017	0.6238	0.6459	0.3507	0.1512	0.3252	0.0846
Science train → Humanities test	Qwen3	**0.7368**	**0.2208**	**0.7307**	**0.7458**	**0.4251**	**0.2139**	**0.3972**	**0.1220**
	Qwen2.5	0.7065	0.1942	0.6950	0.7159	0.4022	0.1930	0.3744	0.1121
	MiniCPM	0.6642	0.1299	0.6505	0.6728	0.3714	0.1663	0.3454	0.0945

3.3 Discipline-Specificity Findings

To explain the limited cross-disciplinary generalization, Table 4 presents the distribution of instructional behavior labels across Humanities and Science. The results reveal substantial and systematic disciplinary differences. Only a small subset of labels shows similar proportions across disciplines, while most instructional behaviors exhibit clear distribution shifts. Science classrooms are dominated by behaviors related to demonstration, procedural explanation, and probing questions, whereas Humanities classrooms more frequently emphasize reading, interpretation, and information seeking. Keyword-level analysis of the generated structured descriptions further confirms these differences: Science descriptions focus on procedures, observations, and reasoning, while Humanities descriptions emphasize textual materials, conceptual meaning, and interpretation. These stable discipline-specific patterns explain both the overall performance drop under cross-disciplinary transfer and the observed asymmetry. Behaviors prevalent in Science are underrepresented in Humanities data, leading Humanities-trained models to misrecognize them during Science evaluation.

Table 4. Disciplinary Differences in Instructional Behavior Distribution

Instructional behavior label	Humanities (%)	Science (%)	Difference (%)
Blackboard demonstration	1.04	15.31	+14.27
Probing and follow-up questioning	9.87	23.64	+13.77
Student reporting and sharing	4.16	15.48	+11.32
Independent thinking	7.79	19.22	+11.43
Student read-aloud	7.53	0.68	−6.85
Information seeking	2.60	0.51	− 2.09

3.4 Exemplary Case of Instructional Behavior Description

Figure 2 illustrates an example of instructional behavior description from a Humanities classroom clip. Given a video segment and a constrained prompt, the model first identifies instructional behavior labels based on the FIAS framework. It then organizes these labels using the IRF (Initiation–Response–Feedback) interaction structure to produce a coherent, temporally ordered description. By combining static behavior coding with dynamic interaction modeling, the model generates interpretable instructional behavior descriptions that capture both the occurrence and organization of classroom interactions.

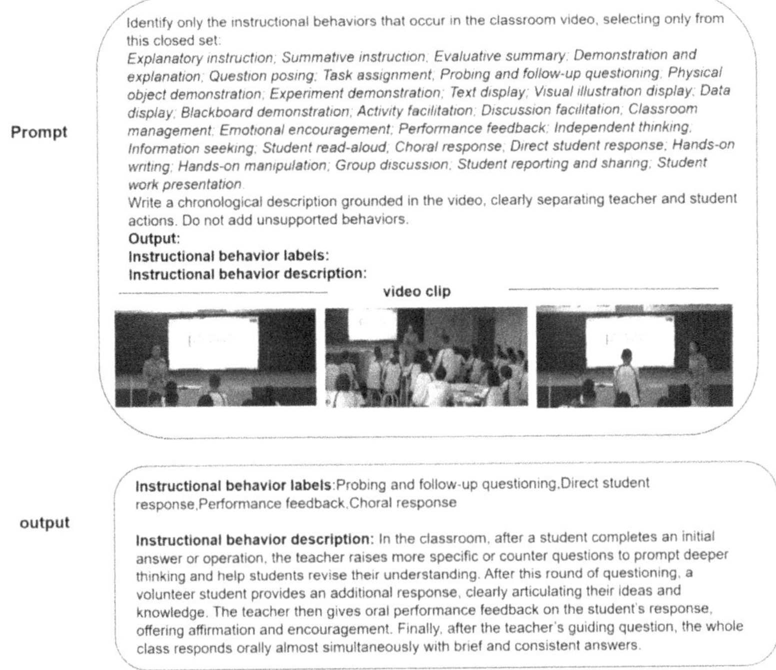

Fig. 2. Exemplary Case of instructional behavior description

4 Discussion and Conclusion

Our results provide coherent answers to the three research questions through complementary experimental analyses. Regarding RQ1, intra-disciplinary evaluations show that LoRA-based parameter-efficient fine-tuning consistently improves multimodal large language models' performance in instructional behavior recognition and structured description generation under educational data and computational constraints, demonstrating an effective and practical strategy for enhancing instructional behavior description. Addressing RQ2, results from both intra-disciplinary performance comparisons and cross-disciplinary train–test swap experiments indicate that instructional behavior description is discipline-context dependent across Humanities and Science classrooms. Models trained and evaluated within the same disciplinary context achieve substantially higher performance than those transferred across contexts, providing empirical evidence against a one-size-fits-all assumption. With respect to RQ3, discipline-specificity analyses reveal how this dependence manifests in practice: instructional behavior labels exhibit systematic distribution shifts between Humanities and Science, and the generated descriptions emphasize different keywords and semantic focuses even for the same behavior labels, reflecting distinct disciplinary instructional practices. Together, these findings demonstrate that instructional behavior description requires discipline-aware modeling rather than discipline-agnostic analytics. A limitation of this study is that it considers only two broad disciplinary contexts with imbalanced sample sizes; future work should extend to finer-grained disciplines and explore strategies to better accommodate discipline-context dependence.

References

1. Huang, C.L., Zhu, J., Ji, Y.L., et al.: A multi-modal dataset for teacher behavior analysis in offline classrooms. Sci. Data **12**(1) (2025)
2. Jacobs, J., Scornavacco, K., Harty, C., Suresh, A., Lai, V., Sumner, T.: Promoting rich discussions in mathematics classrooms: using personalized, automated feedback to support reflection and instructional change. Teach. Teach. Educ. **112**, 103631 (2022)
3. Heo, S., Moon, J., Jung, S.K.: Action recognition: a comprehensive survey of tasks, methods, and challenges. ICT Express (2025, in press). https://doi.org/10.1016/j.icte.2025.11.015
4. Arnab, A., Dehghani, M., Heigold, G., Sun, C., Lučić, M., Schmid, C.: ViViT: a video vision transformer. In: Proceedings of the IEEE/CVF International Conference on Computer Vision (2021)
5. Yue, X., et al.: MMMU: a massive multi-discipline multimodal understanding and reasoning benchmark for expert AGI. In: Proceedings of the IEEE/CVF Conference on Computer Vision and Pattern Recognition, pp. 9556–9567 (2024)
6. Hu, E.J., et al.: LoRA: low-rank adaptation of large language models. In: Proceedings of the International Conference on Learning Representations (2022)

From Black-Box Generation to Pedagogically Controllable Creation: A Text-to-Image Interactive System in Design Education

Jian Xu[1] and Wangda Zhu[2]

[1] Universiti Malaya, Kuala Lumpur, Malaysia
[2] The Hong Kong Polytechnic University, Kowloon, Hong Kong
wz334@cornell.edu

Abstract. Text-to-image (T2I) technology improves design students' work efficiency. However, this efficiency still functions in a black-box manner, with limited interactivity to align with design pedagogy and enhance design thinking. To address this gap, first, we propose an iterative framework of "attribute extraction, compositional control, regeneration," which maps the image generation process to an intentional design process. Second, using data from multiple design workshops containing 32,028 images, we construct a human-annotated attribute dictionary a process-oriented dataset as a stable intermediate representation to reduce semantic drift and improve interpretability and operational consistency. Third, we built a T2I interactive system for design educational settings. On the frontend, we adopt a node-based interactive composition interface that visually organizes and combines attributes such as color, mood, texture, and object; these attributes are then aggregated on an empty canvas and synthesized into structured prompts by a large language model (LLM). On the backend, we encode text and images within a unified semantic space and perform attribute localization and confidence estimation through attention alignment and metric matching. We conducted a user study with 10 participants, comparing our approach against a baseline T2I method and mainstream "LLM + T2I" approaches. The results demonstrate that our method produces superior design outcomes for both fixed and open-ended design problems. Participants also reported a better overall user experience and stronger perceived support for design thinking when using our system. These results indicate that extending T2I to an interpretable and controllable iterative process can effectively enhance design education.

Keywords: Interactive Text-to-image · Design Education · Multi-round Iterative Generation · Process-oriented Learning Dataset

1 Introduction

Text-to-image (T2I) techniques can rapidly concretize abstract knowledge points into observable and comparable visual examples, and are therefore well suited to the "demonstration, feedback, re-creation" loop in classroom instruction, after-class self-study, and

© The Author(s), under exclusive license to Springer Nature Switzerland AG 2027
E. G. Blanchard et al. (Eds.): AIED 2026, LNAI 16583, pp. 19–26, 2027.
https://doi.org/10.1007/978-3-032-29760-0_3

inquiry-based practice. T2I has been widely adopted in design education, however, such efficiency gains may also render the design process insufficiently explained and controlled, thereby harming design thinking. This issue is manifested in the fact that mainstream systems still rely primarily on one-shot black-box generation: learners often can only approach a target outcome through repeated prompt rewriting and trial-and-error. This not only increases cognitive load and ineffective operations, but also reduces the space for teachers to provide process-oriented guidance and for students to conduct self-regulated learning (planning-monitoring-reflection), ultimately making it difficult to stably achieve personalized learning goals. Therefore, there is a need to design a controllable text-to-image interaction model for the learning process, i.e., a controllable T2I interaction model, that transforms "prompt trial-and-error" into an iterative procedure of "visualized goals-step-by-step adjustment-immediate feedback," to reduce ineffective operations and cognitive switching, while supporting teachers' process-oriented scaffolding and students' self-regulated learning.

Existing research on text-to-image (T2I) generation has primarily focused on models and systems, including studies on prompt guidebooks [1] and design processes [2–4], as well as widely used models such as general diffusion frameworks [5], Stable Diffusion [6], DALL·E [7], and earlier generative adversarial network (GAN) [8]. Despite continuous advances in realism, semantic coverage, and generation efficiency, their deployment in educational and instructional settings still faces key gaps: (1) the process is invisible, uncontrollable, and untraceable. Most existing systems remain in a black-box "single prompt-single output" paradigm, where learners cannot visualize and revise intentions, and can only rely on repeated prompt rewriting and trial-and-error, leading to increased ineffective operations and cognitive switching, and making it difficult for personalized goals to converge stably; meanwhile, the lack of reusable and interpretable intermediate representations and process records makes it difficult for teachers to provide process-oriented scaffolding and for learning process modeling and instructional analytics to be conducted. (2) In classroom settings, it is difficult to simultaneously ensure timely responses and high-quality image generation. In classroom scenarios, systems often struggle to balance responsiveness and high-quality generation: on the one hand, high-quality generation typically requires more complex operations and higher computational costs, resulting in slower responses and increased latency; on the other hand, simplifying matching or reducing computation to lower latency can easily cause semantic deviations and unstable outputs, making iterative feedback unreliable and consequently limiting high-frequency iteration and immediate feedback in the classroom.

To address the above issues, we propose an education-oriented controllable interactive T2I framework consisting of a frontend and a backend. The frontend explicitly represents factors such as color/composition/atm through an attribute panel and supports reuse and weighted iteration, while the backend performs alignment and extraction based on a dataset-driven attribute dictionary and synthesizes controlled prompts, forming a traceable closed loop to support process-oriented feedback. Our main contributions are as follows: (1) From black-box to controllable interaction: we restructure "prompt-driven implicit trial-and-error" into a visual, attribute-level operational workflow, enabling learners to iteratively adjust explicit controllable variables, reducing ineffective operations and more stably meeting personalized needs. (2) From outcome to process: we construct a process-oriented dataset containing 32,028 images, recording inputs-outputs-iteration trajectories, and build an annotated attribute dictionary as a stable intermediate representation to reduce semantic discrepancies and improve interpretability and consistency; meanwhile, it provides evidence for teachers' process-oriented guidance and learning analytics, and offers learners an expressive scaffold. (3) From static alignment to efficient matching: in a unified semantic space, we replace cosine distance with Mahalanobis distance to improve matching robustness, and introduce deformable attention to reduce computational overhead and improve inference efficiency, supporting real-time interaction and multi-round iterative generation in the classroom.

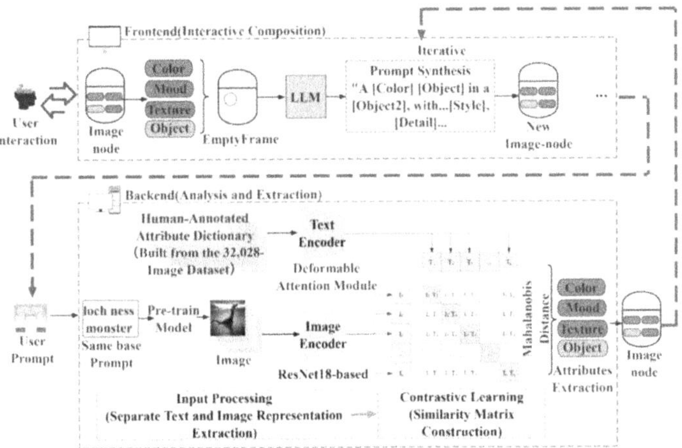

Fig. 1. Overall Architecture of the Proposed System Framework.

2   Method

As shown in Fig. 1, we propose an interactive text-to-image generation framework for intelligent augmented instruction. The system consists of a frontend and a backend. The frontend is responsible for explainable interaction and visual orchestration, while the backend handles attribute parsing, cross-modal alignment, conflict detection, and synthesis of generation instructions.

2.1   Frontend

The front end adopts a "control panel + dynamic canvas" workspace (Fig. 2). The control panel supports prompt input, generation triggering, model switching (DALL·E 2/3, Stable Diffusion, custom), and configuration of key parameters such as resolution and quality. On the canvas side, each generation is encapsulated as an image node that preserves the corresponding prompt, and an expandable/collapsible attribute panel is used to present, in a structured manner, elements such as color, style, objects, composition, and atmosphere. Users reuse attributes by drag-and-drop connections to an Empty Frame, and

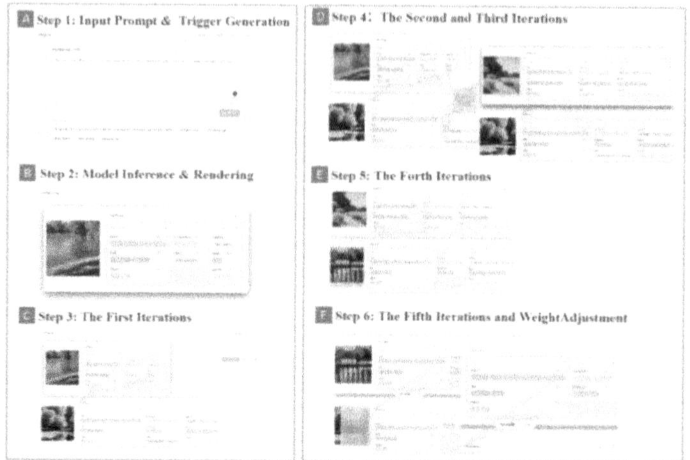

Fig. 2. Interactive T2I Iteration Process

assign weights to each connection. The system provides real-time visual encoding along the connection lines to reflect weight changes, enabling controllable fine-grained iteration that rapidly transforms abstract concepts into intuitive images, thereby improving the efficiency of knowledge delivery and learner engagement in teaching.

2.2 Backend

Process-Oriented Dataset Construction (32,028 Images). Existing datasets are limited in scale, which not only makes it difficult to provide students with sufficient reference examples, but also leads to inadequate model training. To address this gap, we construct a process-oriented dataset for generative learning scenarios, comprising 32,028 labled designed high-detail images that cover multiple everyday themes (e.g., leisure and entertainment, home renovation). To mitigate generation bias caused by class imbalance, we adopt a relatively balanced sampling strategy across themes (approximately 3,000 images per theme), and the entire data construction pipeline is completed by design students in educational settings (Fig. 3).

Construction of the Attribute Dictionary. To support interpretable interaction and reusable analysis in instructional settings, we build an attribute dictionary based on the above dataset, organizing visual factors that learners care about, such as appearance, composition, and atmosphere, into semantic units that are retrievable, composable, and comparable (Fig. 4). After each generation, we conduct manual annotation by jointly considering the image content and the creative intent, and map the annotation text into a unified representation space (word2Vector), thereby transforming visual outputs into computable attribute representations. The attributes span dimensions including color, texture, lighting, objects, and composition, and are hierarchically organized into a stable vocabulary and category system under Appearance/Composition/Atmosphere. To improve consistency and cross-sample comparability, we introduce text-image aligned representations to calibrate attribute semantics and reduce synonymy/ambiguity drift, thereby

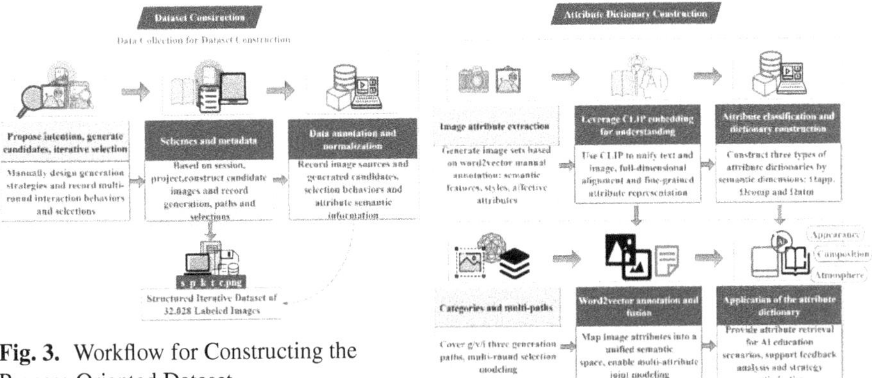

Fig. 3. Workflow for Constructing the Process Oriented Dataset.

Fig. 4. Workflow for Constructing the Attribute Dictionary Based on the Process-Oriented Dataset.

enabling stable retrieval, composition, and statistical analysis, and providing reusable support for creative assessment, style diagnosis, and personalized recommendation.

Input Representation (ResNet18 Image Encoding). We conduct comparative experiments between ResNet18 and ResNet50. The results show that ResNet50 achieves a slight advantage in detail fidelity, but it has a larger parameter size and higher computational overhead, demands stronger hardware resources, and increases inference latency. In contrast, ResNet18 offers superior inference speed and computational efficiency while achieving comparable generation quality. Balancing quality and efficiency, we ultimately adopt ResNet18 as the image encoder to meet the requirements of high-frequency iteration and immediate feedback in classroom scenarios.

Deformable-Attention Cross-Modal Alignment. To closely align the prompt-editing intent in the front-end interaction (e.g., "what is good/what is not good, and how it should be adjusted"), we encode the user input as a query vector Q, and construct the key/value K, V from the visual features of the current image node, thereby performing cross-modal alignment retrieval in a unified semantic space. Considering that full attention incurs high computational cost, we adopt deformable attention, which sparsely samples and aggregates only a small number of locations most relevant to the prompt, enabling low-latency alignment.

Mahalanobis-Distance Similarity Matrix and Attribute Extraction. Traditional Euclidean distance in Euclidean space is essentially more suitable for measuring linear feature differences. However, image-generation representations are affected by factors such as rotation, illumination intensity, brightness, and resolution, and thus often exhibit stronger nonlinear variations; therefore, Euclidean distance cannot sufficiently characterize such nonlinear feature discrepancies. To this end, we adopt Mahalanobis distance to measure feature differences.

2.3 Experiments and User Studies

We recruited 10 participants (aged 19–23; 5 males and 5 females; 6 undergraduates and 4 postgraduates) and conducted user studies in lab settings. The experiment adopted a within-subject design to compare three conditions (Baseline, LLM + GenAI, and Ours). All three shared the same T2I backend (DALL·E 2/3 and Stable Diffusion; identical versions and sampling hyperparameters), differing only in interaction mechanisms: Baseline used the native "Prompt → Generate → Select" workflow; LLM + GenAI additionally used GPT-5.2 Thinking for prompt rewriting. Ours further introduced structured attribute extraction and attribute-level compositional iteration. To cover both open-ended exploration and goal-oriented creation, the study consisted of two consecutive stages: (1) self-directed theme exploration and (2) task-card-constrained creation (e.g., "an evening urban street scene"). Each stage was allocated a fixed budget of five iterations, during which participants could adjust prompts and parameters and select a preferred output as the starting point for the next iteration. The presentation order of the three conditions was counterbalanced with randomization. Throughout the study, we logged generated images, prompt versions, parameter adjustments, and interaction traces. Outcome measures were summarized into two categories: UX (User Experience), an overall satisfaction rating for the three systems, and Design Thinking, a subjective choice of "the tool is helpful for improving design thinking, assessed on a 1–5 rating scale.

3 Results

In the open exploration task (Fig. 5), the Baseline exhibits trial-and-error prompt rewriting with limited quality gains, while LLM + GenAI increases descriptiveness but often leads to dispersed intentions and stylistic instability. Our method structures key attributes and supports reuse and weighted composition, enabling more focused iterations with improved consistency, stability, and controllability. In the instruction-constrained creation task (Fig. 6), our approach continuously enforces extracted constraints across iterations, resulting in higher stability, stronger semantic consistency, and more explainable convergence than both Baseline and LLM + GenAI.

Users rated higher user experience using our system compared with the others, while the design thinking support is similar (Fig. 7).

4 Discussion

4.1 Implications of the Framework and Insights from the User Study

Reconstructing "black-box single-round generation" into an interpretable, attribute-iterative loop. This study proposes a controllable interactive T2I framework for education and teaching, reconstructing the traditional black-box single-round paradigm of "Prompt → Generate → Select" into an attribute-driven multi-round iterative loop. On the client side, an attribute panel explicitly represents elements such as color, objects, composition, and atmosphere, supporting cross-node reuse, weighted combination, and conflict annotation, thereby shifting revisions from "language trial-and-error" to "traceable operations." On the server side, a process-oriented dataset and a manually curated

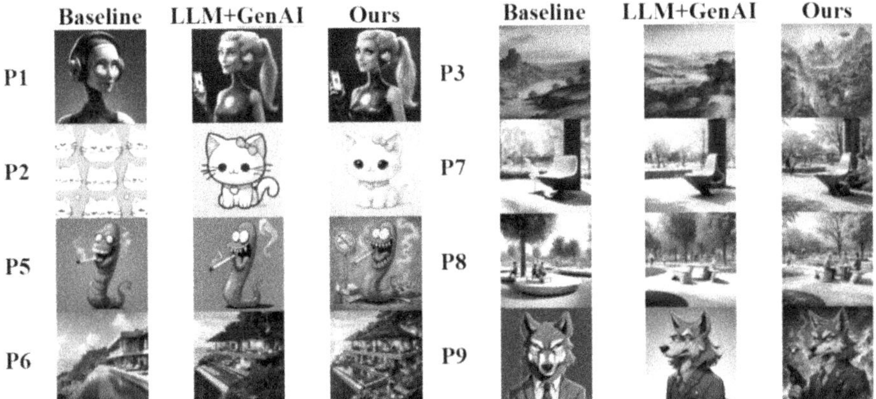

Fig. 5. Qualitative Comparison on the Open-Ended Exploration Task.

Fig. 6. Qualitative Comparison on the Instruction-Constrained Creative Task

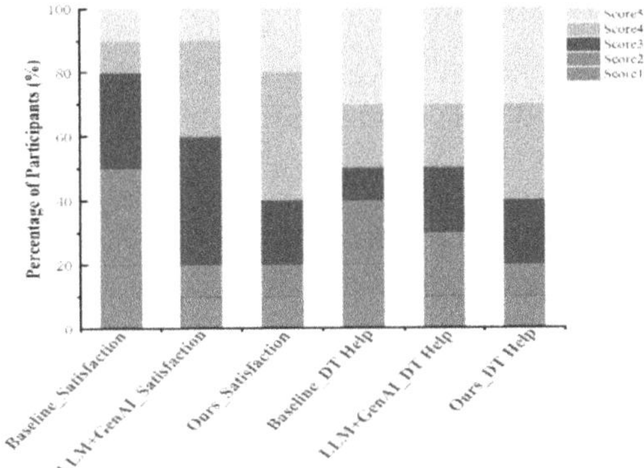

Fig. 7. User Experience (UX) Rating Distribution

attribute lexicon provide a stable intermediate representation, and efficient alignment and caching mechanisms are employed to reduce repeated encoding overhead, thereby supporting high-frequency iteration and real-time feedback in classroom settings.

Structured controllability yields more continuous and more stable iterative trajectories. Under the same backend, identical parameters, and a fixed budget of five iterations, a within-subject experiment compared Baseline, LLM + GenAI, and Ours, covering both open exploration and instruction-constrained tasks. Results show that Baseline mainly relies on natural-language trial-and-error, with scattered modification directions and unstable details. LLM + GenAI, while improving the richness of prompt expressions, lacks attribute-level constraints and reuse mechanisms and thus is prone to style/semantic drift; Ours grounds edits in controllable attributes, making iterations more continuous, styles more consistent, constraint satisfaction more stable, and the "edit-result" correspondence easier for learners to understand.

From a design-thinking perspective, the key is not only obtaining "better images," but whether one can achieve controllable divergence and faster convergence through iteration: the open exploration stage requires rapid divergence to form comparisons, while the instruction-constrained stage requires stabilizing alignment to core requirements. Baseline's pure text trial-and-error is closer to "blind search," with high divergence cost and an unclear convergence path; LLM + GenAI increases "description volume," but in the absence of structured constraints, it more easily accompanies intention drift, which in turn interferes with convergence. Ours decomposes creative factors into operable attributes and supports weighted reuse, making divergence focus on controllable variables and making convergence manifest as stepwise alignment to constraints, thereby better enabling creativity to be steadily externalized and accumulated across multiple iterations. Combined with the 1–5 creativity ratings and the subjective choice of "which tool better supports design thinking," this difference can be attributed to whether the system provides traceable iterative evidence, reduces ineffective trial-and-error and cognitive switching, and offers clear operational handles for creative decision-making.

4.2 Limitations and Future Work

The sample size is relatively small (10 participants), and Design Thinking is measured only by "creativity" on a 1–5 scale and a subjective choice; conclusions still need validation across more classrooms and task types. Future works including: (1) Expand real-classroom samples and introduce teacher evaluations to examine instructional transferability. (2) Add process metrics (e.g., number of iterative branches, number of rollbacks, span/frequency of attribute edits) to quantify "faster convergence" and learning-process gains.

References

1. Liu, V., Chilton, L.B.: Design guidelines for prompt engineering text-to-image generative models. In: Proceedings of the 2022 CHI Conference on Human Factors in Computing Systems, pp. 1–23 (2022)
2. Zhu, W., Guo, R., Zhu, G., Li, C., Li, H., Song, Y.: GAI4DE: harnessing the design process to integrate GAI into design studios. Int. J. Hum.-Comput. Interac., 1–24 (2025)
3. Zhu, W., et al.: Integrating image-generative AI into conceptual design in computer-aided design education. Educ. Technol. Soc. **28**(3), 166–183 (2025)
4. Zhu, W., L. Li, and S. Kim, A Generative AI Design Education Paradigm: from Scenario Space to Artifact Space. (2025)
5. Saharia, C., et al.: Photorealistic text-to-image diffusion models with deep language understanding. Adv. Neural Inf. Proces. Syst. **35**, 36479–36494 (2022)
6. Rombach, R., Blattmann, A., Lorenz, D., Esser, P., Ommer, B.: High-resolution image synthesis with latent diffusion models. In: Proceedings of the IEEE/CVF Conference on Computer Vision and Pattern Recognition, pp. 10684–10695 (2022)
7. Ramesh, A., et al.: Zero-shot text-to-image generation. In: International Conference on Machine Learning, pp. 8821–8831. PMLR (2021)
8. Zhang, H., et al.: Stackgan: text to photo-realistic image synthesis with stacked generative adversarial networks. In: Proceedings of the IEEE International Conference on Computer Vision, pp. 5907–5915 (2017)

Scaffolding-First Constraint Design for LLM Tutors in Data-Science Problem Solving

Stefania Zourlidou[✉] [ID], Shokooh Ebri, Tai Le Quy [ID],
and Frank Hopfgartner [ID]

Institute of Web Science and Technologies (WeST), University of Koblenz,
Koblenz, Germany
`{zourlidou,ebri,tailequy,hopfgartner}@uni-koblenz.de`
`https://www.uni-koblenz.de/de/informatik/west`

Abstract. Large language models (LLMs) can serve as on-demand tutors, but in computation-heavy STEM tasks they can also *over-help* by disclosing complete worked solutions too early. This undermines productive struggle and can shift effort from reasoning to copying. We study this risk in a data-science learning setting where an LLM tutor supports clustering exercises with solution keys and stepwise feedback. Using interaction logs (516 turns, 10 learners), we operationalize *premature solution disclosure* as tutor turns that reveal a complete solution *before any attempt is observed in the current question episode* or *immediately after direct answer-seeking*. We propose a *scaffolding-first constraint layer*: a lightweight, stateful policy that enforces a hint ladder, delays full solutions until attempts are observed, and reframes answer-seeking into diagnostically useful next steps. We further use counterfactual log replay to estimate how often such constraints would have delayed or reframed observed full-solution behavior. We discuss implications for designing LLM tutors whose *learning-safety* objectives complement content-safety guardrails.

Keywords: LLM tutoring · scaffolding · productive struggle · constraint design · data science education

1 Introduction

LLM-based tutors are now easy to deploy and often feel "helpful" because they can answer in fluent natural language, adapt the level of detail, and compute intermediate steps. Yet the same capability can become a pedagogical liability: when learners ask for "the answer" (or simply signal confusion), a model can comply by producing a complete worked solution. For tasks that are meant to be learned through reasoning—such as clustering by hand, interpreting distance functions, or identifying DBSCAN core/border/noise points—this *premature disclosure* short-circuits the learning opportunity. This concern is not only

E. G. Blanchard et al. (Eds.): AIED 2026, LNAI 16583, pp. 27–35, 2027.
`https://doi.org/10.1007/978-3-032-29760-0_4`

theoretical. Controlled evidence in programming education suggests that unrestricted solution-giving LLMs can reduce frustration and improve short-term performance while leaving learning gains unchanged, creating a "comfort trap" where user preferences misalign with pedagogical effectiveness [2]. Classical intelligent tutoring systems (ITS) research has long argued that effective guidance is neither absent nor maximal: learners benefit from prompts and feedback that keep them doing the cognitive work [1,9,10]. The challenge for LLM tutors is that natural language makes *solution giving* effortless, and the boundary between "help" and "answer" can blur quickly.

This paper focuses on a design mechanism that is available even when we do not (or cannot) retrain a tutor model: *constraints* that regulate *when* and *how* the system is allowed to reveal solutions. We treat anti-overhelping as a *learning-safety* goal: protecting the learner's opportunity to practice reasoning. Our contributions are: (i) an operationalization of premature solution disclosure in real tutoring logs for clustering problem solving, (ii) a scaffolding-first constraint policy that implements a hint ladder and disclosure gates, and (iii) a counterfactual simulation that estimates how often the policy would have delayed or reframed disclosure in our setting. Rather than introducing a new tutoring model, we frame *anti-overhelping* as a *learning-safety* objective and show that a thin, stateful constraint layer can regulate *when* and *how* solutions are revealed *without retraining* the underlying LLM. We focus on two practical questions:

- In our procedural clustering dialogs, how often does the tutor *give away the full solution* before the learner has made an attempt?
- If we apply a simple scaffolding-first constraint policy in counterfactual replay, how often would it *delay or reframe* those full-solution responses?

The rest of our paper is structured as follows. Section 2 gives an overview of the related work. The methodology is presented in Sect. 3. Then, we describe the results in Sect. 4 and discuss them in Sect. 5. Finally, the conclusion and outlook are summarized in Sect. 6.

2   Related Work

Recent LLM tutors often pair flexible natural-language responses with traditional ITS elements such as scaffolding, hints, and constraints. Chowdhury et al. [3] propose an LLM tutor with a hand-authored pedagogy and guardrails that mitigate answer leakage. Levonian et al. [5] analyze safety and relevance constraints in generative math chats, highlighting that strong problem-solving ability does not automatically yield good teaching. MathTutorBench [6] reports a trade-off between subject expertise and pedagogical quality and shows that longer dialogs are harder to tutor well. A complementary line of work aims to *steer* LLM tutoring behavior toward productive struggle. Puech et al. [7] study pedagogical steering that encourages learners to attempt solutions while maintaining correctness. Systematic evidence syntheses emphasize benefits and risks of LLMs in education, including over-reliance and assessment fairness concerns [8]. In programming and data-management education, students already use LLMs as help sources. Comparative studies characterize how LLM help-seeking differs from web search and how it affects interaction patterns [4].

Our work connects these strands by treating *over-helping* as a measurable failure mode and by evaluating a constraint layer via counterfactual log replay. In contrast to systems such as Chowdhury et al. [3], which combine handcrafted pedagogy with guardrails inside a predefined tutoring structure, our approach focuses on a lightweight post-hoc constraint layer that regulates disclosure without retraining the underlying model. It also differs from pedagogical steering approaches such as Puech et al. [7], whose aim is to guide tutor behavior more broadly across a multi-turn teaching strategy. Our focus is narrower and more operational, with particular emphasis on controlling *when* full solutions may be revealed in procedural problem solving. This makes the proposed mechanism lightweight, auditable, and readily adaptable to course-specific tutoring policies without requiring retraining of the underlying LLM.

3   Methodology

We analyze a classroom deployment where learners solved clustering exercises with an LLM tutor. The study involved 10 university students, each of whom completed an individual session with the tutor. The deployment took place in the context of a machine learning course and focused on six predefined clustering tasks drawn from the course materials and lecture examples. These tasks progressed from conceptual questions to more procedural sub-tasks, including k-means and DBSCAN computations. Each session followed the same structure: a pre-survey, a short introduction to the tutor and its use, the task sequence, and a post-survey. The activity was conducted as a non-graded study task. Pre-survey responses indicated that all participants had at least some prior familiarity with clustering concepts, and most reported previous experience using AI-based tools for learning. Participation was voluntary, responses were treated as confidential, and conversational logs were de-identified before analysis. We used GPT-4o as the underlying tutor model for this deployment because it provided stable performance across the clustering tasks considered in the study.

The exercise set combined conceptual prompts (applications, method selection, and feature scaling) with computation-heavy sub-tasks, including k-modes with Hamming distance, k-means assignment and centroid updates, and DBSCAN core/border/noise identification. The tutor had access to solution keys and was prompted to provide stepwise help rather than immediate full answers. The resulting dataset contains 516 turns (253 learner turns and 263 tutor turns), together with pre- and post-questionnaire data on background, confidence, and perceptions. The questionnaires were brief study-specific instruments used to collect background information, self-reported confidence, and perceptions of the tutor, and were used for descriptive exploratory analysis rather than as validated outcome measures. We logged timestamps and question identifiers to define episode boundaries. Here, Qi denotes the i-th assignment question and $Qi.j$ its sub-question. Disclosure analysis focuses on procedural sub-tasks: Q3.1 (k-modes with Hamming distance), Q4.1–Q5.2 (k-means assignment and centroid updates), and Q6 (DBSCAN labeling). A *turn* is one timestamped message (learner or tutor). An *episode* is the contiguous sequence of turns for one sub-question, from its prompt to the next prompt.

Our goal is not to "make the model refuse" in a generic sense, but to shape a tutoring dialogue that is both respectful and instructionally effective. We model constraint design as a thin, stateful layer between the learner and the LLM. It consumes observable signals (attempt cues, answer-seeking, number of tries, time-on-task) and decides what the LLM is *allowed* to do next. We use a four-level ladder inspired by scaffolding theory and ITS practice: (0) *Orientation*: restate the goal, ask for a first step, (1) *Hint*: point to the next operation, not the result, (2) *Targeted feedback*: verify a learner step; correct one local mistake, (3) *Partial worked step*: demonstrate one sub-step with new numbers but leave the remaining work to the learner. Level (4) *Full worked solution* is allowed only when disclosure conditions are met. This structure operationalizes a simple pedagogical intuition: it should be easier for the learner to act *next* than to merely read *more*.

We implement a per-episode controller that selects an allowed response *action* on a hint ladder. Let the episode state be

$$s = (\texttt{attempt\_seen}, \texttt{scaffold\_depth}, \texttt{failed\_tries}, \texttt{last\_request}).$$

On each learner turn we update s using rule-based detectors for *attempt* and *answer-seeking*. On each tutor turn we choose

$$a \in \{\text{ORIENT}, \text{HINT}, \text{FEEDBACK}, \text{PARTIAL}, \text{FULL}\}$$

Algorithm 1 summarizes one simple instantiation of the scaffolding-first controller. This policy can be implemented without retraining: the controller constrains the prompt to the chosen action type and updates s after each turn. The constraint layer also shapes tone. Short empathetic acknowledgments ("that step is genuinely tricky") plus a concrete next action ("compute the distances for point P3") keep the dialogue collaborative without surrendering the cognitive work. We operationalize premature disclosure using transparent, rule-based detectors applied to the dialog logs. The rule-based patterns were designed by the authors based on the structure of the clustering tasks and then applied consistently across the recorded dialogues. Label consistency was checked through discussion among the authors on a representative sample of turns. A formal inter-rater reliability study remains part of future validation. The goal is not to perfectly label pedagogy, but to quantify a high-impact failure mode, namely the delivery of complete solutions without sufficient learner work.

On each learner turn we detect: *Attempt* (computations, intermediate results, or substantive reasoning), *Answer-seeking* (explicit request for "answer/solution"), and *Skip* ("next question" or similar). On tutor turns we detect *Full solution* when the message discloses final assignments/centroids or

---

Algorithm 1. Scaffolding-first response controller (per episode)

Require: Episode state $s = (\texttt{attempt\_seen}, \texttt{scaffold\_depth}, \texttt{failed\_tries}, \texttt{last\_request})$
Require: Detectors on learner turn: ATTEMPT?, ANSWERSEEKING?
Ensure: Chosen action $a \in \{\text{ORIENT}, \text{HINT}, \text{FEEDBACK}, \text{PARTIAL}, \text{FULL}\}$

1: **Action semantics:**
    ORIENT: restate goal $+$ ask for the first concrete step
    HINT: point to the next operation (no final result)
    FEEDBACK: verify/correct one local step
    PARTIAL: work exactly one sub-step, then hand back

2: **Gating rule (learning-safety):**
    FULL is permitted only if $\texttt{attempt\_seen} = 1$ and $\texttt{scaffold\_depth} \geq 1$

3: **Selection heuristic:**
4: **if** ANSWERSEEKING and $\neg\texttt{attempt\_seen}$ **then**
5:    $a \leftarrow$ ORIENT   ▷ request intermediate artifact
6: **else if** $\neg\texttt{attempt\_seen}$ **then**
7:    $a \leftarrow$ HINT
8: **else if** $\texttt{scaffold\_depth} = 0$ **then**
9:    $a \leftarrow$ FEEDBACK
10: **else if** $\texttt{failed\_tries} \geq 2$ **then**
11:    $a \leftarrow$ PARTIAL
12: **else**
13:    $a \leftarrow$ HINT **or** FEEDBACK
14: **end if**
15: **return** a

---

enumerates DBSCAN clusters/core/noise. For each episode, we compute: (i) *Immediate disclosure*: whether the tutor's first reply after the learner begins the question is a full solution; and (ii) *Premature full-solution turns*: full-solution tutor turns that occur *before any attempt has been observed in the current episode* or *immediately after direct answer-seeking*. These metrics capture two different risks: "giving away" the episode from the start versus escalating to a complete solution before learners have engaged with the computation.

For example, if a learner requests *"the final cluster assignments"*, an unconstrained tutor may disclose the full table immediately. Our constrained tutor instead elicits an intermediate artifact: *"Share your assignments for P1–P3 (or compute distances for one point), and I'll check before we update centroids together."* To make labels auditable, we used transparent patterns. Learner *attempts* included distance arithmetic, partial assignments, centroid-update calculations, or DBSCAN neighborhood reasoning; *answer-seeking* included explicit requests for the final result (e.g., "give me the answer", "final assignments", "what are the centroids?"), and tutor *full solutions* disclosed the complete set of final assignments/centroids for the episode or enumerated DBSCAN outcomes (clusters plus core/border/noise labels) for all relevant points.

4   Results

Across procedural sub-tasks, the tutor produced full solutions in $23.5\%(42/179)$ of its messages. This is substantial for a tutor intended to provide stepwise help. In $22/55$ procedural episodes, the first tutor reply was already a full solution

(40%, Wilson 95% CI [28.1, 53.2]). Figure 1a breaks this down by question and Table 1 summarizes episode-level disclosure and turn-level premature rates by question. Two patterns stand out. First, Q6 (DBSCAN) is consistently high: every observed episode contained at least one full solution, and immediate disclosure occurred in the majority of episodes. Second, Q4.1 had lower episode-level disclosure rates, suggesting that the tutor sometimes succeeded at eliciting learner work before revealing results. This heterogeneity supports the case for *task-specific* constraint tuning rather than one-size-fits-all refusal behavior. Overall, learners produced 8 answer-seeking turns, and the tutor responded with a full solution next in 4 cases (50.0%). In our dataset, all detected answer-seeking occurred within procedural questions. All observed disclosure rates are computed on the *baseline (prompt-only)* tutoring logs; constraint effects are reported via counterfactual replay rather than a live A/B deployment.

Table 1. Per-question disclosure metrics (no constraint layer). "Immediate": the tutor's first reply in an episode was a full solution. "Any full": full solution within the episode. n_{fs} counts full-solution tutor turns. "Premature%": the fraction occurring before any observed attempt or immediately after answer-seeking.

Task	Immediate	Immediate%	Any full	Any%	n_{fs}	Premature%
Q3.1	1/10	10.0	8/10	80.0	13	23.1
Q4.1	5/10	50.0	7/10	70.0	7	57.1
Q4.2	1/8	12.5	1/8	12.5	1	100.0
Q5.1	4/10	40.0	5/10	50.0	5	40.0
Q5.2	4/7	57.1	4/7	57.1	4	50.0
Q6	7/10	70.0	10/10	100.0	12	58.3

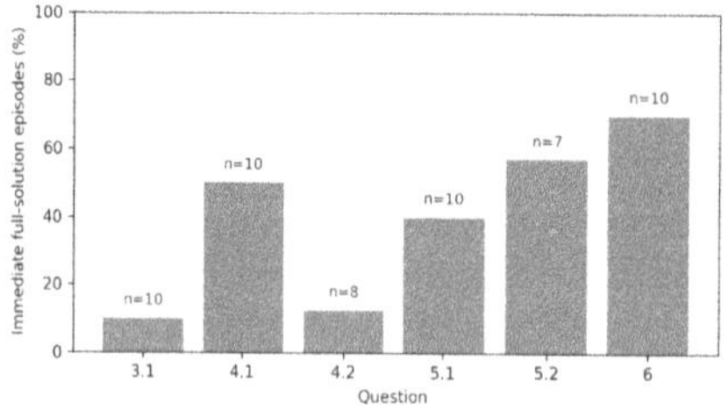

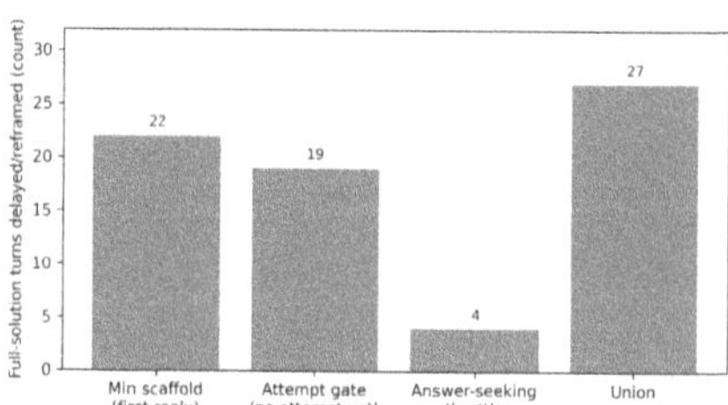

(a) Immediate full-solution replies by question (procedural tasks). Bars show the percentage of episodes in which the tutor's *first* reply disclosed a full solution.

(b) Counterfactual simulation: number of observed full-solution turns that would be delayed or reframed by each gate (and by their union) in procedural tasks.

Fig. 1. Results on procedural tasks.

These aggregate rates reflect a recurring episode-level pattern in the logs: a learner requests the final outcome for a procedural question (e.g., DBSCAN labeling) without providing intermediate work, and the tutor responds by listing complete clusters and point roles (core/border/noise), constituting a full-solution turn before any attempt is observed. Under the proposed scaffolding-first constraints, the same learner request would be reframed into a diagnostic next step (e.g., eliciting ε-neighbors for one point) and only later permit a complete solution after attempt evidence and at least one scaffold step.

The counterfactual replay estimates how often the constraint policy could intervene on the *timing and form* of tutor responses (delay/reframe), assuming the same episode structure and learner messages; it does not estimate causal effects on learning outcomes. We replay the observed dialogs under hypothetical constraints to estimate how often a scaffolding-first policy would have *delayed or reframed* full-solution disclosure. We evaluate three lightweight gates on tutor turns already classified as full solutions. All gates *delay or reframe* the response (e.g., switch to a hint or ask for the next step) rather than refusing help:

- *Minimum scaffolding step*: the first tutor reply in an episode cannot be a full solution.
- *Attempt gate*: full solutions are blocked until any attempt is observed in the current episode.
- *Answer-seeking throttle*: if the immediately preceding learner turn explicitly seeks the answer *and* the learner has not yet attempted the episode, a full solution is blocked.

Across the 42 observed full-solution tutor turns (procedural tasks), the proposed constraint layer would have delayed or reframed 22 turns under the minimum-step rule, 19 turns under the attempt gate, 4 turns under the answer-seeking throttle, and 27 turns under their union ($27/42 = 64.3\%$, Fig. 1). In other words, nearly two-thirds of observed full-solution disclosures occurred in contexts where a lightweight, stateful controller could have intervened to preserve learner agency by keeping the dialogue on a hint ladder. The remaining $15/42$ turns (35.7%) were not blocked by any gate because they occurred after attempt evidence and/or after at least one scaffold step, or were not triggered by immediate answer-seeking. Under our design, these represent cases where full disclosure is *permitted* rather than clearly premature. Importantly, this counterfactual does not claim learning gains. It estimates how often policy-level constraints could change the *timing and form* of assistance.

Learners rated the tutor positively on post-questionnaire items (1–5 Likert; means ranged from 3.9 to 4.7 across items). Confidence increased slightly from pre (mean $= 0.80$) to post (mean $= 0.82$), but the change was small (Wilcoxon signed-rank $p = 0.748$, paired t-test $p = 0.811$, $d_z = 0.08$; $n = 10$). Open-ended comments praised "detailed explanations" and the ability to get "precise help", while suggesting simpler explanations for novices and clearer step visualization in the interface.

5   Discussion and Implications

Content-safety guardrails prevent harmful or disallowed content, but they do not prevent pedagogical failure modes such as answer leakage. In our observed logs *without* the proposed constraint layer, the tutor sometimes produced full worked solutions despite a stepwise tutoring prompt: 35/55 procedural episodes (63.6%) contained at least one full solution, and 22/55 (40%) began with one. Designers should treat *learning-safety*—including anti-overhelping constraints— as an explicit objective alongside accuracy and user satisfaction. From a learner's perspective, premature disclosure is not always experienced as a "mistake": it can feel like smooth, reassuring help, especially under time pressure.

But the same interaction quietly removes a valuable moment—the few minutes where learners wrestle with distances, centroids, or neighbor definitions and build procedural fluency. Scaffolding constraints aim to keep the experience supportive while preserving that productive struggle: the system can still answer, but it answers *in steps*. Model training and preference optimization can reduce answer leakage [7], but many deployments rely on general models. A constraint layer provides a lightweight, auditable mechanism that can be tuned per task, per instructor, and per assessment policy. This is useful when instructors need predictable behavior (e.g., during graded homework) and when the same model is reused across many courses.

Based on the observed failure modes and the simulation, we recommend: (1) *Start with a scaffold step* in procedural questions, even when the learner asks for the answer, (2) *Require attempt evidence* before full solutions, (3) *Make escalation transparent*: explain what would unlock more help, and (4) *Separate explanation from computation*: encourage the learner to compute, while the system explains the method and checks intermediate results. Constraint layers that throttle solution disclosure should be communicated clearly to learners to avoid deception. Logs should be de-identified and used only with consent, and instructors should consider fairness: learners who already know the answer should not be penalized by a rigid policy. At the same time, our findings are bounded by the study design. We used rule-based detectors for attempts, answer-seeking, and full solutions, which may misclassify ambiguous turns. Our setting is task- and course-specific, and the counterfactual replay quantifies potential intervention frequency rather than learning gains. Although we evaluate the constraint layer in clustering tasks from a machine learning course, the mechanism itself is not specific to data science and may transfer to other procedural learning domains. Broader validation will require further controlled experiments.

6   Conclusions and Outlook

Premature solution disclosure is measurable in real LLM tutoring logs and can be frequent in procedural data-science tasks. In our setting, we proposed a scaffolding-first constraint layer that implements a hint ladder and disclosure gates, and counterfactual log replay estimated that it could delay or reframe

64.3% of observed full-solution turns. Future work should (i) validate disclosure detectors with human annotation, (ii) incorporate contextual signals (assessment stakes, time pressure), and (iii) explore personalization that adapts the hint ladder to learner proficiency without defaulting to solution giving. The broader message is that effective LLM tutoring requires not only correctness, but also principled control of when answers are revealed.

References

1. Aleven, V., Stahl, E., Schworm, S., Fischer, F., Wallace, R.: Help seeking and help design in interactive learning environments. Rev. Educ. Res. **73**(3), 277–320 (2003). https://doi.org/10.3102/00346543073003277
2. Bassner, P., Lenk-Ostendorf, B., Beinstingel, R., Wasner, T., Krusche, S.: Less stress, better scores, same learning: the dissociation of performance and learning in AI-supported programming education. Comput. Educ. Artif. Intell. **10**, 100537 (2026). https://doi.org/10.1016/j.caeai.2025.100537
3. Chowdhury, S.P., Zouhar, V., Sachan, M.: AutoTutor meets large language models: a language model tutor with rich pedagogy and guardrails. In: Proceedings of the Eleventh ACM Conference on Learning @ Scale (L@S 2024), Atlanta, GA, USA, 18–20 July 2024. ACM (2024). https://doi.org/10.1145/3657604.3662041
4. Kumar, H., Reza, M., Mitchell, J., Musabirov, I., Zhang, L., Liut, M.: Understanding help-seeking behavior of students using LLMs vs. web search for writing SQL queries. arXiv:2408.08401 (2024). https://doi.org/10.48550/arXiv.2408.08401
5. Levonian, Z., Henkel, O., Li, C., Postle, M.-E.: Designing safe and relevant generative chats for math learning in intelligent tutoring systems. J. Educ. Data Mining **17**(1), 66–97 (2025). https://doi.org/10.5281/zenodo.14751365
6. Macina, J., Daheim, N., Hakimi, I., Kapur, M., Gurevych, I., Sachan, M.: MathTutorBench: a benchmark for measuring open-ended pedagogical capabilities of LLM tutors. In: Proceedings of the 2025 Conference on Empirical Methods in Natural Language Processing, Suzhou, China, pp. 204–221. Association for Computational Linguistics (2025). https://doi.org/10.18653/v1/2025.emnlp-main.11
7. Puech, R., Macina, J., Chatain, J., Sachan, M., Kapur, M.: Towards the pedagogical steering of large language models for tutoring: a case study with modeling productive failure. In: Findings of the Association for Computational Linguistics: ACL 2025, Vienna, Austria, pp. 26291–26311. Association for Computational Linguistics (2025). https://doi.org/10.18653/v1/2025.findings-acl.1348
8. Shi, Y., Yu, K., Dong, Y., Chen, F.: Large language models in education: a systematic review of empirical applications, benefits, and challenges. Comput. Educ. Artif. Intell. **10**, 100529 (2026). https://doi.org/10.1016/j.caeai.2025.100529
9. VanLehn, K.: The behavior of tutoring systems. Int. J. Artif. Intell. Educ. **16**(3), 227–265 (2006). https://dl.acm.org/doi/10.5555/1435351.1435353
10. Wood, D., Bruner, J., Ross, G.: The role of tutoring in problem solving. J. Child Psychol. Psychiatry **17**(2), 89–100 (1976). https://doi.org/10.1111/j.1469-7610.1976.tb00381.x

Representation Learning to Study Temporal Dynamics in Tutorial Scaffolding

Conrad Borchers[1]([envelope]) [ORCID], Jiayi Zhang[2] [ORCID], and Ashish Gurung[1] [ORCID]

[1] Carnegie Mellon University, Pittsburgh, PA, USA
{cborcher,agurung}@cs.cmu.edu
[2] Worcester Polytechnic Institute, Worcester, MA, USA
jzhang31@wpi.edu

Abstract. Adaptive scaffolding enhances learning, yet the field lacks robust methods for measuring it within authentic tutoring dialogue. This gap has become more pressing with the rise of remote human tutoring and large language model-based systems. We introduce an embedding-based approach that analyzes scaffolding dynamics by aligning the semantics of dialogue turns, problem statements, and correct solutions. Specifically, we operationalize alignment by computing cosine similarity between tutor and student contributions and task-relevant content. We apply this framework to 1,576 real-world mathematics tutoring dialogues from the Eedi Question Anchored Tutoring Dialogues dataset. The analysis reveals systematic differences in task alignment and distinct temporal patterns in how participants ground their contributions in problem and solution content. Further, mixed-effects models show that role-specific semantic alignment predicts tutorial progression beyond baseline features such as message order and length. Tutor contributions exhibited stronger grounding in problem content early in interactions. In contrast, student solution alignment was modestly positively associated with progression. These findings support scaffolding as a continuous, role-sensitive process grounded in task semantics. By capturing role-specific alignment over time, this approach provides a principled method for analyzing instructional dialogue and evaluating conversational tutoring systems.

Keywords: Adaptive Learning · Scaffolding · Dialogue Moves · Tutoring

1 Introduction

Scaffolding refers to the dynamic adjustment of instructional support in response to learners' evolving needs. Understanding scaffolding dynamics is critical for explaining instructional effectiveness and informing the design of tutoring systems. Prior research emphasizes that this effectiveness arises from the bidirectional nature of tutoring dialogue, in which learner responses continuously shape subsequent feedback and scaffolding. This interactive structure enables

E. G. Blanchard et al. (Eds.): AIED 2026, LNAI 16583, pp. 36–45, 2027.
https://doi.org/10.1007/978-3-032-29760-0_5

well-designed tutoring systems to approximate the effectiveness of human tutors [20].

Scaffolding remains difficult to operationalize in naturalistic tutorial dialogue. Prior research in AIED has typically relied on rule-based representations of instructional support. For example, dialog-based systems such as AutoTutor provide scaffolding through predefined tutorial dialogue moves, including prompts, hints, and summaries, while using latent semantic analysis to assess student contributions against expert-authored expectation texts [9]. In contrast, step-based systems operationalize scaffolding through structured hint sequences and quantitative measures of hint usage level, such as assistance scores [14]. While these approaches have been influential, they impose categorical distinctions on inherently continuous instructional phenomena and are often tied to specific tasks or system architectures. As conversational tutoring increasingly occurs in open-ended, text-based settings (e.g., remote tutoring [11] or through large language models (LLMs) [18]), there is a growing need for task-grounded, scalable measures of scaffolding that generalize across task contexts.

We propose an embedding-based framework that models scaffolding as a continuous semantic property of tutorial dialogue. We characterize tutor and student turns by their alignment with two task anchors: the problem statement and the correct solution. Alignment with the problem reflects dialogue that remains close to the task formulation, whereas alignment with the solution captures the extent to which support becomes more directly oriented toward the target answer. Together, these dimensions define a continuum of scaffolding from problem-focused reasoning to directive, solution-oriented support, consistent with prior work on multi-level hinting that progresses from reflective prompts to explicit solution disclosure [2]. We apply this approach to real-world tutoring data to examine role differences in alignment and test whether these measures predict instructional progression beyond message order and length. Accordingly, we ask: **RQ1**: How do tutor and student roles differ in their semantic alignment to the problem statement and the correct solution during problem solving? **RQ2**: How does semantic alignment between tutorial dialogue and problem statement or solution *evolve* during problem solving? **RQ3**: Do role-specific patterns of semantic alignment predict problem progression beyond message order and length?

This work makes three contributions. First, we introduce a continuous operationalization of scaffolding based on semantic alignment to task content. Second, we show that embedding-based similarity captures role-specific and temporal patterns of instructional support in natural dialogue. Third, we demonstrate that these measures predict instructional progression beyond turn-based measures. Together, these contributions advance task-grounded methods for studying scaffolding in both human and conversational tutoring systems.

2 Related Work

2.1 Scaffolding in Natural Language Dialogue for Learning

Conversational tutoring systems support learning through natural language interaction that resembles human tutoring [9,18]. Dialogical systems prompt learners to articulate their reasoning and engage in mixed-initiative exchanges with the tutor. This shift from action-based input in step-based tutoring systems to language-based interaction enables richer modeling of student understanding and has been shown to support learning across domains and educational levels [15].

A prominent example is AutoTutor, which models tutoring as a sequence of predefined dialogue moves, including questions, prompts, hints, and summaries [8,9]. AutoTutor assesses learning by analyzing the semantic content of students' natural language responses. Using latent semantic analysis (LSA), the system compares student input to expert-authored expectation texts that represent ideal answer components. Conceptual coverage is quantified through cosine similarity between these representations, with predefined thresholds determining whether specific expectations have been satisfied. These similarity estimates are used to update a student model and guide subsequent instructional moves.

This architecture enables adaptive scaffolding within dialogue. When student responses are incomplete or vague, the system prompts elaboration and provides progressively specific hints to guide learners toward target concepts without directly revealing answers [9,10]. However, these approaches rely on expert-authored expectation texts, manually defined similarity thresholds, and task-specific representations of knowledge. Such dependencies limit scalability and constrain applicability in open-ended tutoring contexts, including remote human tutoring and emerging LLM-based systems [11,18].

2.2   Advances in Analyzing Tutorial Dialogue and Educational Text

LSA represents meaning through distributional word co-occurrence but remains static and limited in capturing context-dependent semantics. In contrast, LLM-based sentence embeddings provide representations with large context windows [16]. Unlike LSA's fixed semantic space derived from expert corpora, these embeddings leverage general-purpose models to produce richer and more adaptable representations of learning discourse [3]. This shift supports more generalizable approaches to modeling language in educational settings.

Accordingly, LLMs have been increasingly integrated into digital learning systems, including tools such as Khanmigo and MathTutor [19,21]. Recent work has applied LLMs to support problem solving, estimate student knowledge, and generate adaptive feedback aligned with established tutoring principles [17,18,21]. Beyond direct tutoring, sentence embeddings have also been used to analyze instructional dialogue, including identifying effective tutoring strategies and modeling students' conceptual understanding [3,13]. This body of work motivates the hypothesis that embedding-based semantic similarity can operationalize instructional scaffolding as a continuous property of tutor and learner behavior during problem solving, which we investigate in this study.

3   Methods

3.1   Data Set

We analyzed the Eedi-2K "Question-Anchored Tutoring Dialogues" dataset, an open-source corpus containing real-world, chat-based math tutoring interventions [22]. Eedi is an online platform that provides students with practice problems aligned with school mathematics curricula and facilitates one-to-one chat-based tutoring during problem solving. The dialogues in this dataset are anchored to individual mathematics problems, with each interaction centered on helping a student work through a specific problem. From this corpus, we analyzed 1,576 complete dialogues, totaling 55,322 conversational moves. The dataset included 25 unique human tutors across several students and no student IDs.

3.2   Data Preprocessing and Feature Engineering

We used sentence embeddings to transform dialogue into high-dimensional vector representations, enabling quantitative analysis of semantic relationships. Specifically, we used the `all-MiniLM-L6-v2` transformer model from the Sentence Transformers library [16] to generate 384-dimensional semantic embeddings for all textual content. We encoded three textual components: (1) individual tutor and student dialogue messages, (2) the diagnostic math problem text, and (3) the correct solution text. We then computed cosine similarity between sentence embedding vectors to measure the semantic alignment of dialogue moves with the problem statement and the correct solution.

We examined two temporal features as baselines: (1) absolute message sequence rank within a dialogue, and (2) relative normalized position within the dialogue. For each dialogue, we computed relative position as n/N, where n is the message's sequence index and N is the total number of messages. Relative position is operationalized as the progression of dialogue toward problem completion (0 = start, 1 = end). This normalization by dialogue length allows progression to be compared across interactions.

3.3   Investigating Temporal Scaffolding Dynamics (RQ1 & RQ2)

To answer **RQ1**, we compared (i) the distributions of alignment scores by role using density histograms and (ii) the role-specific temporal trajectories described above. Together, these distributional and temporal comparisons show how tutors and students align with problem and solution content during tutoring. To answer **RQ2**, we quantified how semantic alignment to the problem statement and the reference solution changes over time. We computed cosine similarity between each dialogue turn and (i) the problem text and (ii) the solution text, then summarized these scores as a function of dialogue progress. Specifically, we normalized each turn's position within its dialogue to n/N (0 = start, 1 = end), averaged alignment scores across all turns at each relative position, and applied Gaussian smoothing to estimate the overall temporal trajectories.

3.4   Predicting Progression from Semantic Alignment (RQ3)

To answer **RQ3**, we tested whether semantic alignment to the problem statement and reference solution predicts *relative dialogue progression* beyond non-semantic baselines. Our outcome variable was dialogue progress (see Sect. 3.3). We fit a series of linear mixed-effects regression models while logit-transforming progression scores to account for the bounded outcome. All continuous predictors were standardized (mean = 0, SD = 1) for interpretability. All models included tutor random intercepts to account for clustering of messages within tutors. We also checked model assumptions, finding no notable multicollinearity (all VIFs < 1.44), approximately normally distributed residuals (skewness = 0.03, kurtosis = 0.33), and no evidence of heteroscedasticity.

We established a baseline model (Model 0) using only absolute message sequence rank as a measure of dialogue progress. Model 1 added message length as a predictor. Model 2 introduced cosine similarity to the problem statement and to the reference solution, testing whether semantic alignment explains variation in progression beyond message order and length. Model 3 further allowed these semantic effects to vary by tutor and student. Model comparisons were based on the Bayesian Information Criterion (BIC) and likelihood ratio tests. Supplemental analysis code to reproduce our analyses is available online [1].

4   Results

Descriptively, tutors contributed 59.4% of messages across an average of 65.6 problems. Dialogue sessions averaged 35.1 messages (median = 31; range = 20–148). Messages were short (M = 29.3 characters; median = 21.0; SD = 29.1).

4.1   Temporal Alignment Trends (RQ1 & RQ2)

We begin by examining the distributions of semantic alignment in dialogues (RQ1). Figure 1 presents the density distributions of alignment scores for tutor and student moves. The distribution of tutor alignment to the problem statement is bimodal (Fig. 1A). This suggests that tutors alternate between two instructional modes: one more aligned with the problem content (peak around 0.4) and another, more conversational or exploratory (peak around 0.1). In contrast, the student moves cluster exclusively at lower alignment values, indicating limited convergence toward the problem language. For solution alignment (Fig. 1B), both distributions are left-skewed with minimal tutor-student differentiation.

The temporal analysis for RQ2 (Fig. 2) demonstrates that tutor alignment to the problem statement decreases (after initially rising) as the normalized position progresses from 0 to 1. In contrast, student alignment to the problem remains consistently low. Both roles show minimal alignment to the solution throughout dialogues. These temporal patterns suggest tutors and students maintain problem focus while gradually increasing solution-related content.

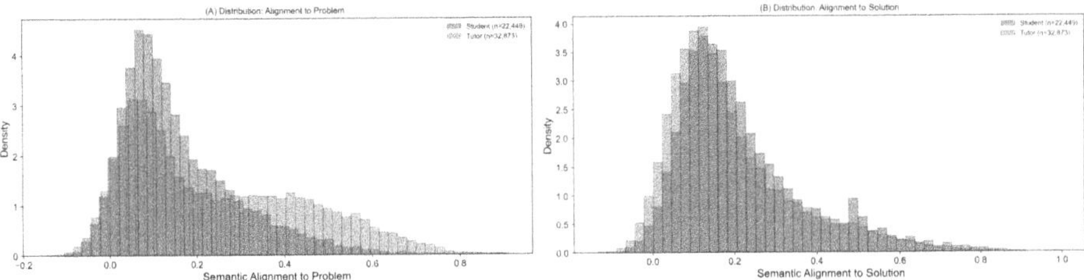

Fig. 1. Density distributions of semantic alignment scores for tutor and student moves. **(A)** Alignment to the problem statement. **(B)** Alignment to the correct solution.

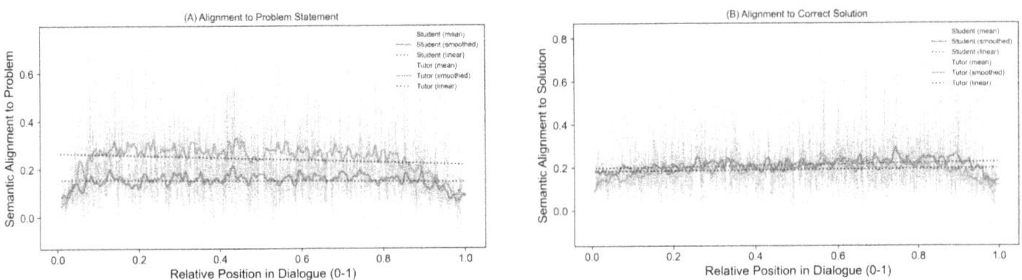

Fig. 2. Temporal evolution of semantic alignment. **(A)** Alignment to the problem statement. **(B)** Alignment to the correct solution.

4.2 Predicting Progression from Semantic Alignment (RQ3)

We examined whether semantic similarity measures predicted progression (the % of total dialogue completed at a given dialogue move; see Sect. 3.2) through tutoring dialogues using four nested linear mixed models with logit-transformed progression scores, with tutor random effects to account for across-tutor variance. All predictors were standardized. Adding message length significantly improved fit over sequence alone, $\chi^2(1) = 78.24$, $p < .001$, BIC $= 264500$. Adding cosine similarity to question and solution provided further improvement, $\chi^2(2) = 28.29$, $p < .001$, BIC $= 264494$. Allowing these effects to differ by role yielded additional improvement, $\chi^2(2) = 32.43$, $p < .001$, with the full model achieving BIC $= 264483$, indicating the best balance of fit and parsimony.

For the chosen model, tutor random effects were small (ICC $= .01$). Sequence position was the strongest positive predictor of dialogue progression ($\beta = 1.72$, $p < .001$), with a smaller positive effect of message length ($\beta = 0.14$, $p < .001$). Question similarity (tutor: $\beta = -0.04$, $p = .004$; student: $\beta = -0.09$, $p < .001$) and tutor solution similarity ($\beta = -0.07$, $p < .001$) were negatively associated with progression, whereas student solution similarity was positively associated ($\beta = 0.07$, $p < .001$). These results indicate that problem-focused alignment occurs earlier in dialogues, while solution-focused alignment emerges later, particularly in student contributions (controlling for all other predictors).

5   Discussion

This study examined an embedding-based approach to modeling instructional scaffolding in tutorial dialogue as a continuous, semantically grounded process. The results demonstrate the effectiveness of embedding-based methods for evaluating student–tutor interactions, extending their use in AIED beyond prior applications such as knowledge tracing [17].

5.1   Semantic Alignment with the Problem

The distribution of semantic alignment between dialogue turns and the problem statement sheds light on how tutors construct scaffolding during interaction (RQ1). Student turns cluster around low alignment, indicating minimal reuse of problem language. In contrast, tutor turns exhibit a bimodal pattern, with a dominant low-alignment mode and a smaller peak near 40%. The former may reflect dialogue focused on prompting and feedback, while the latter captures moments when tutors restate or paraphrase key problem elements to establish instructional grounding [7]. This pattern is consistent with prior accounts of scaffolding, in which tutors primarily guide learners through questioning while selectively restating task constraints to clarify goals and reduce cognitive load [6].

Temporal analyses (RQ2) show that tutors continue to occasionally reference problem content as solutions develop. This suggests that restatement is deployed opportunistically to diagnose understanding and consolidate progress, consistent with micro-adaptive models of tutoring [12]. Overall, these findings characterize scaffolding as a continuous, flexible process grounded in task semantics.

5.2   Across-Turn Semantic Alignment with the Solution

Solution alignment exhibits a distinct pattern from problem alignment. Both tutor and student turns follow overlapping, unimodal distributions, and alignment to the reference solution remains largely stable over time. This pattern is consistent with effective scaffolding that supports learners in constructing solutions while avoiding conditions associated with the "fluency heuristic" [6], whereby smooth interaction is mistaken for understanding. If tutors frequently revealed answers or students primarily sought confirmation, one would expect higher and increasing solution alignment, along with dialogue that promotes shallow learning and inflates perceived proficiency through misleading performance cues [5].

5.3   Predicting Progression Using Semantic Alignment

Using mixed-effects regression models (RQ3), we examined how the semantic similarity of tutor and student utterances to the problem statement and reference solution relates to dialogue progression, while adjusting for message order and length. Students and tutors exhibited distinct trends. Both referenced problem content more frequently early in the dialogue. In contrast, their solution similarity increased over time, suggesting greater use of solution-aligned language as they approach task completion, consistent with task progression.

Although statistically reliable, these effects are modest in magnitude. Nevertheless, the results support cosine similarity as a meaningful proxy for further study of scaffolding. Embedding-based measures enable fine-grained analysis of instructional dynamics beyond traditional metrics such as assistance scores [2], and provide a foundation for studying both human and LLM-based tutoring.

5.4 Limitations and Future Work

Scaffolding occurs both within problems, as studied here, and across problems through processes such as fading. The absence of student identifiers prevents analysis of longitudinal scaffolding and its optimality for learning. We leave validation against learning outcomes and systematic evaluation of potentially excessive LLM scaffolding to future work [4]. Additionally, incorporating alternative semantic anchors could capture forms of scaffolding beyond the problem-solution spectrum, including metacognitive support and multiple reasoning paths, perhaps in a direct comparison with LSA-based approaches [8,9].

Several extensions can broaden the scope of our framework. First, scaffold episodes could be identified by detecting bursts of high tutor problem alignment and testing whether these precede increases in student solution alignment, providing evidence for targeted restatement of task constraints [6,12]. Second, clustering tutors by alignment trajectories may reveal distinct scaffolding profiles and clarify whether observed bimodality reflects stable strategies or adaptive behavior, extending prior work on dialogue-based support [9,12].

6 Conclusion

Despite scaffolding's central role in tutoring, existing approaches provide limited means for analyzing how instructional support unfolds in natural dialogue. We introduce an embedding-based framework that models scaffolding as continuous semantic alignment between dialogue, problems, and solutions. This approach captures interpretable, role-specific dynamics in tutorial interaction. Tutors predominantly ground early exchanges through alignment with problem content, while students increasingly adopt solution-aligned language as they progress, controlling for move sequence. This transition reflects a gradual transfer of responsibility from tutor to learner. More broadly, these findings demonstrate the value of embedding-based representations for analyzing instructional dialog.

References

1. Open study repository. https://github.com/conradborchers/scaffolding-cosine/
2. Aleven, V., Roll, I., McLaren, B.M., Koedinger, K.R.: Help helps, but only so much: research on help seeking with intelligent tutoring systems. Int. J. Artif. Intell. Educ. **26**, 205–223 (2016)
3. Borchers, C., Patel, M., Lee, S.M., Botelho, A.F.: Disentangling learning from judgment: Representation learning for open response analytics. In: Proceedings of the LAK26: 16th International Learning Analytics and Knowledge Conference, pp. 744–750 (2026)
4. Borchers, C., Vie, J.J., Azevedo, R.: Large language models as students who think aloud: overly coherent, verbose, and confident. arXiv preprint arXiv:2602.01015 (2026)
5. Carpenter, S.K., Endres, T., Hui, L.: Students' use of retrieval in self-regulated learning: implications for monitoring and regulating effortful learning experiences. Educ. Psychol. Rev. **32**(4), 1029–1054 (2020)
6. Chi, M.T., Siler, S.A., Jeong, H., Yamauchi, T., Hausmann, R.G.: Learning from human tutoring. Cogn. Sci. **25**(4), 471–533 (2001)
7. Clark, H.H., Brennan, S.E.: Grounding in communication (1991)
8. Graesser, A.C., Chipman, P., Haynes, B.C., Olney, A.: Autotutor: an intelligent tutoring system with mixed-initiative dialogue. IEEE Trans. Educ. **48**(4), 612–618 (2005)
9. Graesser, A.C., Person, N., Harter, D., Group, T.R., et al.: Teaching tactics in autotutor. Modelling human teaching tactics and strategies. Int. J. Artif. Intell. Educ. **11**, 1020–1029 (2000)
10. Graesser, A.C., Person, N.K., Magliano, J.P.: Collaborative dialogue patterns in naturalistic one-to-one tutoring. Appl. Cogn. Psychol. **9**(6), 495–522 (1995)
11. Gurung, A., et al.: Human tutoring improves the impact of AI tutor use on learning outcomes. In: International Conference on Artificial Intelligence in Education, pp. 393–407. Springer (2025)
12. Katz, S., Albacete, P., Jordan, P.: Summarization during tutoring: Implications for developing micro-adaptive tutoring systems. Grantee Submission (2014)
13. Lin, J., et al.: Is it a good move? Mining effective tutoring strategies from human-human tutorial dialogues. Futur. Gener. Comput. Syst. **127**, 194–207 (2022)
14. Long, Y., Aleven, V.: Supporting students' self-regulated learning with an open learner model in a linear equation tutor. In: International Conference on Artificial Intelligence in Education, pp. 219–228. Springer (2013)
15. Paladines, J., Ramirez, J.: A systematic literature review of intelligent tutoring systems with dialogue in natural language. IEEE Access **8**, 164246–164267 (2020)
16. Reimers, N., Gurevych, I.: Sentence-BERT: sentence embeddings using Siamese BERT-networks. In: Proceedings of the 2019 Conference on Empirical Methods in Natural Language Processing. Association for Computational Linguistics (2019)
17. Scarlatos, A., Baker, R.S., Lan, A.: Exploring knowledge tracing in tutor-student dialogues using LLMs. In: Proceedings of the 15th International Learning Analytics and Knowledge Conference, pp. 249–259 (2025)
18. Schmucker, R., Xia, M., Azaria, A., Mitchell, T.: Ruffle&Riley: insights from designing and evaluating a large language model-based conversational tutoring system. In: International Conference on Artificial Intelligence in Education, pp. 75–90. Springer (2024)

19. Shetye, S.: An evaluation of Khanmigo, a generative AI tool, as a computer-assisted language learning app. Stud. Appl. Linguist. TESOL **24**(1) (2024)
20. VanLehn, K.: The relative effectiveness of human tutoring, intelligent tutoring systems, and other tutoring systems. Educ. Psychol. **46**(4), 197–221 (2011)
21. Venugopalan, D., Yan, Z., Borchers, C., Lin, J., Aleven, V.: Combining large language models with tutoring system intelligence: a case study in caregiver homework support. In: Proceedings of the 15th International Learning Analytics and Knowledge Conference, pp. 373–383 (2025)
22. Zent, M., Smith, D., Woodhead, S.: PIIvoT: a lightweight NLP anonymization framework for question-anchored tutoring dialogues. In: Proceedings of the 2025 Conference on Empirical Methods in Natural Language Processing, pp. 27467–27476 (2025)

Enabling Multi-agent Systems as Learning Designers: Applying Learning Sciences to AI Instructional Design

Jiayi Wang[1]([✉]) [iD], Ruiwei Xiao[2] [iD], Xinying Hou[3] [iD], and John Stamper[2] [iD]

[1] Northwestern University, Evanston, IL 60208, USA
`jiayiwang2025@u.northwestern.edu`
[2] Carnegie Mellon University, Pittsburgh, PA 15213, USA
`{ruiweix,jstamper}@cmu.edu`
[3] University of Michigan, Ann Arbor, MI 48109, USA
`xyhou@umich.edu`

Abstract. K–12 educators increasingly use large language models (LLMs) to draft lesson plans and learning activities, but outputs often lack the pedagogical structure needed for high-quality instruction. While sophisticated prompting can help, it requires substantial teacher time and expertise. We therefore shift pedagogical expertise from prompts into system architecture by embedding the Knowledge–Learning–Instruction (KLI) framework in two multi-agent systems (MAS), and compare them with a single-agent baseline that simulates typical teacher prompting. We evaluated the three systems on secondary math and science activity generation in a teacher study using an adapted Quality Matters K–12 rubric and open-ended feedback. Overall rubric score differences were not statistically significant across systems. However, MAS-CMD received the highest mean total score and received more favorable qualitative feedback, particularly around engagement, collaboration, and differentiation. More broadly, this study positions theory-guided AI instructional design as a promising direction for further investigation.

Keywords: Large language models · Generative AI · Multi-agent systems · Instructional design · Learning sciences · Knowledge–Learning–Instruction (KLI) framework · K–12 education · Teacher–AI interaction

1 Introduction

Generative AI is increasingly used in education for lesson drafting, activity generation, and adaptation for diverse learners [1,4,7,15]. However, prior work suggests LLMs still struggle with pedagogically grounded tasks requiring instructional judgment and learning-theoretic reasoning [11–14]. Strong learning activities require identifying what students must learn, selecting suitable learning processes, and designing supports aligned with evidence-based principles. Without this grounding, LLM outputs can be shallow, inconsistently structured, or

© The Author(s), under exclusive license to Springer Nature Switzerland AG 2027
E. G. Blanchard et al. (Eds.): AIED 2026, LNAI 16583, pp. 46–56, 2027.
https://doi.org/10.1007/978-3-032-29760-0_6

misaligned with learning goals, often requiring substantial teacher revision [11–14]. Approaches such as prompt engineering and retrieval-augmented generation (RAG) can improve outputs but place substantial demands on users [3]. Producing pedagogically strong results often requires prompts that encode instructional intent, yet many teachers may lack prompt-engineering experience, tool training, or time to do this consistently. This "prompting gap" limits what teachers can practically achieve with LLMs [3, 11].

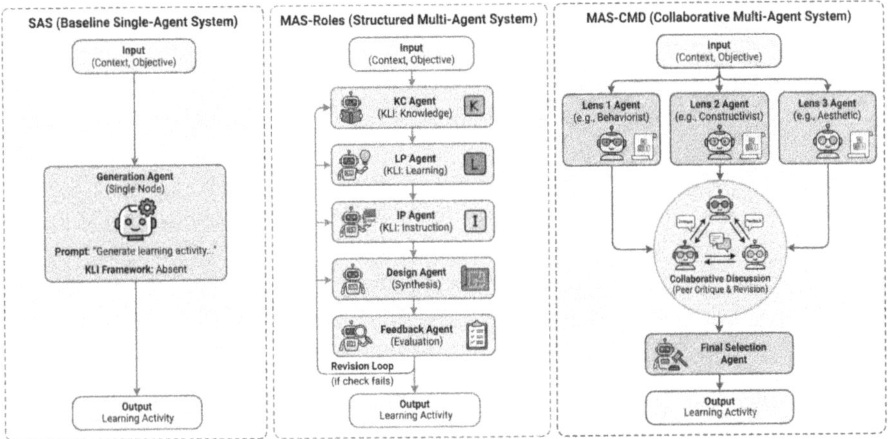

Fig. 1. System Architecture Comparison and KLI Theoretical Mapping.

We reimagine teacher–AI interaction by shifting pedagogical expertise from user prompts into system architecture. We adopt the Knowledge–Learning–Instruction (KLI) framework, which links knowledge components, learning processes, and instructional principles to support robust learning [8]. KLI captures learning-sciences expertise that is hard to encode in ad hoc prompts, such as identifying knowledge components and prerequisites, selecting learning processes, and choosing instructional principles [8]. We argue these steps should be handled by the system rather than reinvented through prompt iteration. To handle this multi-step reasoning, we use LLM-based multi-agent systems (MAS), which distribute decision-making across specialized agents and iterative critique [9]. MAS is well-suited to instructional design because agents can enact complementary pedagogical expertise and perform sub-tasks that are difficult for teachers to specify under time constraints.

We investigate: *Compared to a baseline of simple prompts teachers might use, do KLI-guided multi-agent systems produce higher-quality learning activities?* In a teacher evaluation using an adapted Quality Matters K–12 rubric and open-ended feedback, collaborative MAS received the highest mean total score and more favorable qualitative feedback.

2   Related Work

2.1   Generative AI and MAS in Instructional Design

Since late 2022, K–12 teachers have increasingly used LLMs for lesson planning, activity design, and differentiation. In fall 2023, 18% reported using AI for teaching and another 15% had tried it [4]. By spring 2025, a study of 2,232 public-school teachers found that 60% had used AI during the 2024–25 school year, with 32% using it at least weekly [1]. For instructional design, multi-agent systems (MAS) show promise by coordinating specialized agents to improve lessons, worksheets, and assessments. For example, EduPlanner uses evaluator, optimizer, and question-analysis agents to create math lessons tailored to student knowledge, and FACET uses simulated learner profiles to generate worksheets teachers judged as well structured and appropriate [6,19]. Generator–critic pipelines also produce classroom-usable AI literacy MCQs aligned with Bloom's taxonomy [17]. Overall, MAS can improve scalability and pedagogical quality over single-agent prompting, but most current designs are not explicitly guided by learning sciences principles.

Studies caution that novice prompting often produces shallow, misaligned, or inconsistent materials. In mathematics, analyses of ChatGPT-generated tasks found procedural bias, gaps in conceptual representation, and occasional inaccuracies even after prompt variation, suggesting unguided prompts can underdeliver on cognitive demand [13]. Other evaluations describe some AI-generated curriculum as "a mile high and an inch deep," with repetitive activities misaligned to specifications [14]. In foreign-language lesson planning, researchers found high run-to-run variability and historical-pedagogical bias without careful prompt design [5]. More broadly, without explicit scaffolds (e.g., role constraints, exemplars, rubrics), LLMs can produce hallucinations or surface-level plans requiring substantial teacher editing [12]. Although more schools and districts now offer AI training [4], simple and zero-shot prompting remains common [3], which may be insufficient for pedagogically robust materials.

2.2   The Knowledge–Learning–Instruction (KLI) Framework

Developed to bridge cognitive science research and real-world educational practice, the KLI framework provides a structured, theory-driven approach to instructional design [8]. It states that effective instruction requires careful alignment among three core elements: Knowledge Components (KCs), which are the goals of learning (e.g., concepts, skills, facts); Learning Processes, which describe how learning occurs (e.g., memory and fluency building, induction and refinement, understanding and sense-making); and Instructional Principles, which are the specific methods used to facilitate those learning processes (e.g., spacing and testing, worked examples, prompted self-explanation) [8]. By using the KLI framework to guide the reasoning of our multi-agent systems, we explicitly ground our systems' design in a well-established, evidence-based instructional theory that aims to produce robust student learning. This helps create a more pedagogically-informed instructional design process.

3   Methods

3.1   System Design and Implementation

This study designs, implements, and compares three systems (Fig. 1, Table 1) that generate K–12 learning activities: a baseline single-agent system (**SAS**); a role-based, sequential multi-agent system (**MAS-Roles**); and a collaborative multi-agent system with conquer-and-merge discussion (**MAS-CMD**) [18]. Prior case studies indicate that educators new to generative AI often use simple single-verb requests with "copy-paste" context [11,16], and teacher-written prompts in our survey followed the same general pattern; we therefore treat SAS as a standardized, conservative baseline. To induce complementary instructional priorities, MAS-CMD uses five lesson-planning approaches from McConnell et al. [10] as prompt-based teaching lenses: behaviorist, constructivist, aesthetic, ecological, and integrated social-emotional. These lenses diversify draft generation and critique rather than represent fixed teacher identities. All systems used the `gemini-2.5-flash` model and the `LangGraph` framework[1], with *temperature* $= 1.0$ and *top_p* $= 0.95$ (source code and prompts[2]).

3.2   Experimental Design and Procedure

A corpus of 10 secondary learning objectives (5 Math, 5 Science) was selected from the Oak Ridge Institute for Science and Education (ORISE) lesson plan library[3]. Each objective included subject domain, grade level, standard alignment, and learning objectives. Each of the three systems generated one learning activity per objective (30 total) for teacher evaluation.

Evaluation Rubric. To ensure a rigorous and standardized evaluation, we adapted the Quality Matters (QM) K–12 Rubric[4], focusing on four review standards from General Standard 5 (Learning Activities and Learner Interaction). Each criterion used an ordinal scale where higher values indicate stronger quality; 5.1C–5.3C were scored from 0–3, and 5.4C was scored from 0–2. Our survey presented multiple-choice, plain-language descriptors that correspond to the rubric's performance levels. Each item was aligned to the scale used in the QM rubric, and teachers selected the descriptor that best matched the activity.

Participants. We recruited 21 U.S.-based secondary math ($N = 12$) and science ($N = 9$) teachers via Prolific[5]. Eligibility required teaching grades 7–12 in the United States. One response was excluded for off-topic feedback and unusually rapid completion, leaving 20 participants (11 Math, 9 Science). Sessions took

---

[1] https://www.langchain.com/langgraph.
[2] https://osf.io/3gyqb/overview?view_only=48b332dc217c4c1fa07bde91eee00ad0.
[3] https://orise.orau.gov/k12/teachers/lesson-plans.html.
[4] https://qualitymatters.org/sites/default/files/PDFs/StandardsFromTheQMK-12RubricSixthEdition.pdf.
[5] https://www.prolific.com/.

Table 1. Comparative Analysis of System Architectures and KLI Theoretical Mapping

SAS	MAS-Roles	MAS-CMD
KLI Framework Integration Strategy		
Absent: The KLI framework is absent in the system, imitating a naive interaction paradigm with the LLM.	**Decomposed:** The KLI framework is broken into discrete steps across specialized nodes for KC analysis, Learning Processes, and Instructional Principles.	**Holistic:** The full KLI framework is provided as a complete reference string within the prompt for each agent involved in the generation process.
Workflow and Architectural Structure		
Single-Node: A linear architecture that generates output in one pass through a single node without internal feedback loops.	**Sequential Pipeline:** A 5-node state graph where each node represents one specialized functional step in the KLI design process.	**Multi-Stage Orchestration:** A graph involving nodes for parallel agent generation, peer-to-peer cross-critique, and final selection.
Guidance Mechanism		
Internal Weights: Relies on the base model's internal pre-training and default weights for instructional structure.	**Functional Decomposition:** Directs the model to focus on specific, isolated KLI framework components one node at a time.	**Perspectival Variation:** Directs the model to interpret the full KLI framework through specific teaching lenses.
Refinement and Evaluation Logic		
None: Generates output once without any internal critique or iterative revision nodes.	**Targeted Feedback:** A `Feedback_Agent` node checks alignment and can trigger a return to specific failed nodes to generate a revised activity.	**Peer Critique:** Agents with different teaching lenses review each other's content within a discussion node to generate revisions based on multi-perspective feedback.

approximately 15–30 min with $4–6 compensation. The study was approved by the authors' institutional IRB.

3.3 Data Collection and Analysis

We collected data via Qualtrics[6]. The survey used branching so math teachers saw math objectives and science teachers saw science objectives, and used survey randomization to distribute the 10 objectives evenly across participants. Each session then followed three stages: participants first wrote a baseline prompt

---

[6] https://www.qualtrics.com/.

from the provided context (subject domain, grade level, standard alignment, and learning objective), then evaluated three system-generated activities (SAS, MAS-Roles, MAS-CMD) in fully randomized order, and finally provided rubric-based scores and open-ended feedback on each version.

Data Analysis. We employed a mixed-methods approach to compare the three system architectures, combining quantitative statistical analysis of rubric scores with qualitative thematic analysis [2] of teacher feedback. **Quantitative Analysis** Quantitative analysis focused on comparing the three systems across total scores and individual QM rubric items (5.1, 5.2, 5.3, 5.4). Given the small sample size ($N = 20$) and non-normal distribution of scores (Shapiro-Wilk tests: $p < 0.05$ for all systems), we used non-parametric statistical tests. We conducted Kruskal-Wallis tests to compare three systems simultaneously, followed by Mann-Whitney U tests for pairwise comparisons when appropriate. We also examined whether evaluation patterns differed between math and science teachers using Mann-Whitney U tests. **Qualitative Analysis** We conducted thematic analysis [2] of open-ended teacher feedback using an iterative coding process. We developed descriptive codes capturing recurring pedagogical aspects in teacher feedback. To connect qualitative results to our theoretical framing, we organized these codes using the KLI framework. For each coded excerpt, we recorded sentiment (Positive or Negative). We then counted unique teachers mentioning each code by system and sentiment, and summarized results in Table 3.

Table 2. Mean Scores by Quality Matters Item and System

Item	SAS	MAS-Roles	MAS-CMD	p-value
5.1 (Alignment)	2.70 (0.47)	2.60 (0.50)	2.85 (0.49)	0.130
5.2 (Active Learning)	2.75 (0.44)	2.55 (0.60)	2.95 (0.22)	**0.031***
5.3 (Feedback)	2.35 (0.88)	2.20 (0.83)	2.45 (0.83)	0.491
5.4 (Interaction)	1.75 (0.44)	1.70 (0.47)	1.80 (0.41)	0.769

*Statistically significant at $p < 0.05$. Standard deviations in parentheses.

4 Results

4.1 Quantitative Results

Overall System Comparison. For total Quality Matters scores across the three systems ($N = 20$ per system), SAS had a mean of 9.55 ($SD = 1.43$, median = 9.5), MAS-Roles had a mean of 9.05 ($SD = 1.76$, median = 9.0), and MAS-CMD had a mean of 10.05 ($SD = 1.43$, median = 11.0). A Kruskal-Wallis test revealed no statistically significant difference between the three systems ($H = 4.14, p = 0.127$). We found no significant subject area differences except for MAS-CMD item 5.3, where math teachers scored higher than science teachers.

Item-Level Analysis. We examined differences across individual Quality Matters items (5.1–5.4). Table 2 shows mean scores for each item by system. A Kruskal-Wallis test revealed a statistically significant difference only for item 5.2 (Learning activities provide opportunities for interactions that support active learning) across systems ($H = 6.95$, $p = 0.031$). Post-hoc pairwise comparisons using Mann-Whitney U tests with Bonferroni correction showed that MAS-CMD ($M = 2.95$, $SD = 0.22$) scored significantly higher than MAS-Roles ($M = 2.55$, $SD = 0.60$) on this item ($U = 120.0$, $p = 0.008$). No other pairwise comparisons reached statistical significance.

4.2   Qualitative Results

In total, MAS-CMD received 57 positive mentions and 12 negative mentions (net +45), compared to SAS (43 positive, 23 negative, net +20) and MAS-Roles (37 positive, 20 negative, net +17) (Table 3). Overall, MAS-CMD showed the strongest profile across Knowledge, Learning, and Instruction, including zero negative mentions in Learning. MAS-Roles showed clear strengths in Instruction structure and Knowledge alignment but weaker learning-process signals. SAS was valued for hands-on activities but struggled with structure and organization.

Knowledge (K): MAS-CMD led with 13 positive mentions, especially in *Completeness & Resource Quality* and *Academic Language & Rigor*. MAS-Roles was strongest in *Alignment & Appropriateness*, with one teacher noting: *"The activities are well connected to the learning goals."* SAS showed its largest weakness in *Completeness & Resource Quality*.

Learning (L): MAS-CMD received the most positive mentions (24) and no negative mentions, followed by SAS and MAS-Roles. MAS-CMD led in *Collaboration/Group Work* and *Metacognition/Reflection*. As one teacher said of MAS-CMD: *"I really like this lesson plan as well. It still involves students generating ideas, sets the SEL expectations, and involves group work and collaboration."* SAS's clearest strength was *Hands-On Activities*. MAS-Roles showed a concerning pattern for *Collaboration/Group Work*, with one teacher noting: *"students are not expected to engage in discussion"*.

Instruction (I): MAS-CMD led overall, followed by MAS-Roles and SAS. For *Clear Structure/Organization*, SAS received 7 negative mentions, compared to 1 for MAS-Roles and 2 for MAS-CMD. One teacher commented on SAS: *"I am not quite sure 'how' to set up the stations, and I think this information needs to be clearer."* MAS-CMD showed strength in *Assessment/Feedback* and *Differentiation/Scaffolding*. MAS-Roles showed mixed results for *Teacher Guidance & Instructional Sequencing*, with explicit sequencing steps sometimes perceived as overly rigid.

Table 3. Number of Teachers Mentioning Each Code by System and Sentiment

Code	SAS		MAS-Roles		MAS-CMD	
	+	−	+	−	+	−
Knowledge (K)						
Academic Language & Rigor	1	0	2	0	3	0
Alignment & Appropriateness	1	0	4	0	3	1
Completeness & Resource Quality	3	4	2	3	6	2
Innovation/Creativity	1	1	0	1	1	1
Knowledge Total	**6**	**5**	**8**	**4**	**13**	**4**
Learning (L)						
Engagement Strategies	4	1	4	2	3	0
Real-World Application	2	1	2	1	3	0
Hands-On Activities	6	1	1	0	4	0
Collaboration/Group Work	5	0	0	2	6	0
Student-Centered Approach	2	0	2	0	3	0
Visual Aids/Materials	2	0	3	0	2	0
Metacognition/Reflection	1	0	1	0	3	0
Learning Total	**22**	**3**	**13**	**5**	**24**	**0**
Instruction (I)						
Clear Structure/Organization	4	7	5	1	3	2
Teacher Guidance & Instructional Sequencing	1	1	3	3	2	0
Differentiation/Scaffolding	2	0	1	3	4	0
Assessment/Feedback	4	3	5	1	6	2
Instruction Total	**11**	**11**	**14**	**8**	**15**	**4**
Implementation (non-KLI): feasibility and classroom constraints						
Time Management	2	1	1	2	2	4
Use Intent Statements	1	3	1	0	2	0
Suitable for New Teachers	1	0	0	1	1	0
Implementation Total	**4**	**4**	**2**	**3**	**5**	**4**

"+" = positive mentions; "−" = negative mentions.

Implementation Considerations: For *Time Management*, MAS-CMD received 4 negative mentions, with one teacher noting: *"It is long - definitely multiple class periods."* For *Use Intent Statements*, only SAS received 3 negative mentions where teachers explicitly stated they would not use the activities.

5 Discussion, Limitations, and Future Work

While LLMs can help draft instructional materials, producing pedagogically strong activities often still depends on user prompting skill, time, and instructional expertise. In response, we shifted pedagogical guidance from the user prompt into the system architecture by embedding the KLI framework into two multi-agent designs and comparing them with a simpler single-agent baseline.

Our findings suggest that how pedagogical guidance is embedded may shape the kinds of qualities teachers notice in AI-generated activities. Quantitatively, we did not find statistically significant differences in total QM scores across systems. At the same time, the results are not null in a practical sense. MAS-CMD received the highest mean total score and was described more favorably in teachers' open-ended feedback. These findings suggest that collaborative, discussion-based orchestration may be particularly useful for surfacing learning-process qualities that teachers value. The contrast across systems is also informative for design. MAS-Roles showed strengths in structure and alignment, suggesting that decomposing KLI into explicit stages can help the system attend to core instructional components. However, its weaker qualitative profile on collaboration and other learning-process features suggests that stepwise decomposition may also narrow the space of pedagogical possibilities if not carefully balanced. SAS, by contrast, was sometimes appreciated for hands-on activity ideas, but teachers more often noted weaknesses in clarity, structure, and completeness. This pattern suggests that theory-guided orchestration may be most useful not because it always raises every rubric score, but because it can redistribute model attention toward aspects of instructional quality that are often underdeveloped in simpler prompting workflows.

Several future work directions can help overcome the limitations of our current study. First, we should expand system testing across more subject areas, grade levels, teachers, learning contexts, and LLMs. Our sample size was relatively small ($N = 20$), included only math and science teachers, and relied on a single LLM model, which limits our ability to assess performance across diverse educational settings and models. Second, we should develop or identify evaluation rubrics that better capture pedagogical depth. The disconnect between quantitative scores and qualitative teacher feedback suggests that the current rubric does not fully capture the pedagogical sophistication experienced teachers recognize and value. Third, teachers should use these systems in actual teaching and classrooms with students to test validity. While our multi-agent systems generated learning activities teachers valued for pedagogical features, our current evaluation only asked teachers to evaluate learning objectives we selected, rather than testing effectiveness in authentic classroom contexts. Future work should investigate how teachers adapt and implement AI-generated activities in practice and the resulting student learning outcomes.

In conclusion, this paper does not show that KLI-guided multi-agent systems universally outperform simpler instructional generation approaches. It does, however, provide early evidence that theory-guided architectural choices can influence the pedagogical qualities teachers notice in AI-generated activities. We see this as an initial step toward AI instructional design systems that are more explicitly grounded in learning-sciences theory.

References

1. Ash, A.M.: Three in 10 teachers use AI weekly, saving six weeks a year (2025). https://news.gallup.com/poll/691967/three-teachers-weekly-saving-six-weeks-year.aspx
2. Braun, V., Clarke, V.: Using thematic analysis in psychology. Qual. Res. Psychol. **3**(2), 77–101 (2006)
3. Chen, E., Wang, D., Xu, L., Cao, C., Fang, X., Lin, J.: A systematic review on prompt engineering in large language models for k-12 stem education. arXiv preprint arXiv:2410.11123 (2024)
4. Diliberti, M.K., Schwartz, H.L., Doan, S., Shapiro, A., Rainey, L.R., Lake, R.J.: Using Artificial Intelligence tools in k–12 classrooms. Technical report. RR-A956-21, RAND Corporation (2024)
5. Dornburg, A., Davin, K.: To what extent is chatGPT useful for language teacher lesson plan creation? (2024)
6. Gonnermann-Müller, J., Haase, J., Fackeldey, K., Pokutta, S.: FACET: teacher-centred LLM-based multi-agent systems-towards personalized educational worksheets (2025)
7. Klopfer, E., Reich, J., Abelson, H., Breazeal, C.: Generative AI and K-12 Education: An MIT Perspective. An MIT Exploration of Generative AI (2024). https://mit-genai.pubpub.org/pub/4k9msp17
8. Koedinger, K.R., Corbett, A.T., Perfetti, C.: The knowledge-learning-instruction framework: bridging the science-practice chasm to enhance robust student learning. Cogn. Sci. **36**(5), 757–798 (2012)
9. Li, X., Wang, S., Zeng, S., Wu, Y., Yang, Y.: A survey on LLM-based multi-agent systems: workflow, infrastructure, and challenges. Vicinagearth **1**(1), 9 (2024)
10. McConnell, C., Conrad, B., Uhrmacher, P.B.: Lesson Planning with Purpose: Five Approaches to Curriculum Design. Teachers College Press (2020)
11. Octavio, M.M., Argüello, M.V.G., Pujolà, J.T.: ChatGPT as an AI L2 teaching support: a case study of an EFL teacher. Technol. Lang. Teach. Learn. **6**(1), 1142 (2024)
12. Powell, W., Courchesne, S.: Opportunities and risks involved in using chatGPT to create first grade science lesson plans. PLoS ONE **19**(6), e0305337 (2024)
13. Sapkota, B., Bondurant, L.: Assessing concepts, procedures, and cognitive demand of chatGPT-generated mathematical tasks. Int. J. Technol. Educ. **7**(2), 218–238 (2024)
14. Sawyer, A.G., Aga, Z.G.: A mile high and an inch deep: exploring chatGPT as a mathematics curriculum development tool. School Sci. Math. (2025)
15. Tan, X., Cheng, G., Ling, M.H.: Artificial intelligence in teaching and teacher professional development: a systematic review. Comput. Educ. Artif. Intell. **8**, 100355 (2025)
16. Tassoti, S.: Assessment of students use of generative artificial intelligence: prompting strategies and prompt engineering in chemistry education. J. Chem. Educ. **101**(6), 2475–2482 (2024)
17. Wang, J., Xiao, R., Tseng, Y.J.: Generating AI literacy MCQs: a multi-agent LLM approach. In: Proceedings of the 56th ACM Technical Symposium on Computer Science Education V. 2, pp. 1651–1652 (2025)

18. Wang, Q., Wang, Z., Su, Y., Tong, H., Song, Y.: Rethinking the bounds of LLM reasoning: are multi-agent discussions the key? arXiv preprint arXiv:2402.18272 (2024)
19. Zhang, X., Zhang, C., Sun, J., Xiao, J., Yang, Y., Luo, Y.: EduPlanner: LLM-based multi-agent systems for customized and intelligent instructional design (2025)

Multi-label Collaborative Dialogue Act Recognition for Adaptive Team Training Environments

Jay Pande[1]([✉]), Wookhee Min[1], Randall Spain[2], Vikram Kumaran[1], and James Lester[1]

[1] North Carolina State University, Raleigh, NC 27695, USA
{jpande,wmin,vkumara,lester}@ncsu.edu
[2] U.S. Army Combat Capabilities Development Command, Soldier Center, Orlando, FL 32826, USA
randall.d.spain.civ@army.mil

Abstract. Adaptive team training environments support team members as they learn to effectively coordinate their collaborative activities through cross-team communication. Team communication analytics, which informs automated team assessment and coaching in adaptive team training environments, requires accurate and efficient natural language dialogue act recognition (i.e., classifying team members' utterances to determine their communicative intent). Allowing multiple dialogue act recognition labels for each utterance can support analysis of complex utterances. However, the complexity and variability in team communication pose significant computational challenges for team dialogue act recognition. Large language models (LLMs) show promise for analyzing team communication but require context-specific fine-tuning to capture specialized terminology and each team member's role-based patterns. In this work, we investigate open-source LLMs for multi-label team dialogue act recognition for team communication analysis. We compare (1) fine-tuning all parameters of a 77-million-parameter Flan-T5-based model and (2) fine-tuning an 8-billion-parameter Llama-3.1-based model using model parameter quantization and low-rank adapters (QLoRA), with bidirectional LSTMs as a baseline. Empirical results show that, when performing dialogue act recognition on spoken dialogue from dialogue-rich medical team training scenarios, LLM-based dialogue act recognition models outperform the non-LLM baseline on all dialogue acts. This work paves the way toward robust team dialogue act recognition for team communication analytics to support adaptive team training environments.

Keywords: Collaborative Dialogue Analysis · Collaborative Learning · Team Training · Adaptive Training Environments · Team Communication Analytics

1 Introduction

During team training, team members must proficiently communicate with each other to exchange information about the status of the activity and collectively progress towards a desired end state [9]. In many team training contexts, developing effective communication and coordination skills as collaborative processes is a key training objective

E. G. Blanchard et al. (Eds.): AIED 2026, LNAI 16583, pp. 57–65, 2027.
https://doi.org/10.1007/978-3-032-29760-0_7

[5]. A substantial body of research on team training has demonstrated that the quality of team communication impacts a team's performance [14]. Because communication is instrumental to teamwork and team training, automated analysis of team communication has great potential to advance our understanding of team performance and the methods through which teams receive real-time or after-action feedback about their performance [10].

Dialogue act recognition (i.e., identifying communicative intent in dialogue) is particularly valuable because it enables AI-driven feedback that targets collaborative processes, such as how teams exchange information, coordinate actions, and maintain shared situational awareness [7]. (See Fig. 1 for an example of how such feedback can be used in team training.) It is especially important to automate multi-label dialogue act recognition, because, in real-world scenarios, an utterance may consist of multiple sentences with different intents (e.g., [1]).

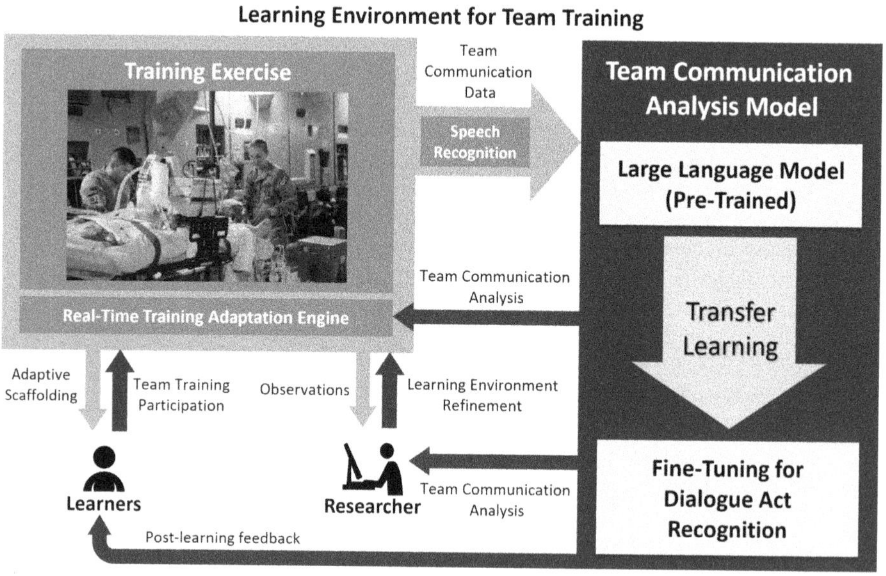

Fig. 1. LLM-based team communication analysis framework for facilitating adaptive team training.

Natural language processing (NLP) techniques, especially large language models (LLMs), have made it possible to automate dialogue act recognition with remarkable accuracy (e.g., [16]). LLMs typically require extensive fine-tuning to perform well on highly contextual tasks. For team training contexts, fine-tuning can help LLMs learn specialized terminology team members use to communicate key information, differentiate between dialogue act labels (which are often designed for a specific training context), and understand the roles each team member occupies during a training exercise.

In this paper, we investigate LLM-based, fine-tuned models for multi-label team dialogue act recognition on utterances spoken by team members during high-fidelity, scenario-based training exercises. We investigate two types of non-proprietary LLM-based approaches: firstly, we fine-tune an 8-billion-parameter Llama 3.1 model [13] using QLoRA [4], which mitigates the computational cost of fine-tuning LLMs by reducing the precision and number of tunable parameters, and secondly, we fine-tune a 77-million-parameter Flan-T5 model [3]. We compare these LLM approaches to baseline Bidirectional Long Short-Term Memory network (BiLSTM) models [11] using a Sentence-BERT embedding [17] to represent each utterance. We also explore methods that include previous utterances as context for the utterance that is the current target for dialogue act recognition. Our experiments show that team dialogue act recognition models based on both LLMs outperform the BiLSTM baselines. These results demonstrate the potential to create improved team dialogue act recognition models that can drive a team communication analysis framework, enabling adaptive learning and assessment in team training environments.

2 Related Work

LLMs are driving recent progress in learning analytics and AI-assisted learning, including when analyzing dialogue in educational settings. Khare et al. [12] found that zero-shot Llama 3.1 models outperform fine-tuned models and non-LLM baselines at predicting when the intervention of a facilitator is warranted in a group game-based learning activity. Vitale and colleagues [22], using transcripts of classroom interactions, found that a fine-tuned GPT-4o model was more accurate than a zero-shot approach at identifying when teachers posed questions aimed to increase student engagement.

Analyzing multi-party dialogue is particularly complex in NLP because, unlike a straightforward, back-and-forth discussion between two individuals, multi-party dialogue involves three or more participants who often engage in multiple concurrent conversation threads [21]. Team members intentionally exchange information to anticipate each other's needs [5], react appropriately to stressful situations [2, 20], and act in a unified manner [10, 19]. Analysis of multi-party dialogue must therefore consider the group dynamics that motivate each participant to contribute differently to the dialogue. Team communication analysis models must learn characteristics that distinguish each team member, while also capturing the team's shared goals and interactions [8].

Deep learning-based NLP approaches have been shown to be well-suited for labeling utterances from team training exercises to enable deeper analysis of multi-party dialogue [15]. Subsequent approaches based on fine-tuned T5 models have demonstrated enhanced performance on dialogue act recognition and information flow classification, leveraging the flexibility of text-based input to integrate the speaker's role and utterance [16]. This work aims to address three limitations of prior work. First, while prior work has used datasets with only a few hundred utterances [1] or a few thousand utterances [15, 16], the dataset used in the current work has nearly 50,000 utterances in total. This enables dialogue act recognition models to develop a more generalizable understanding of when each dialogue act applies to an utterance, making the models more robust to unseen data. Second, prior work largely explores single-label team dialogue act recognition, while this work focuses on multi-label team dialogue act recognition. Third, this work explores the use of LLMs with substantially more parameters than those used in prior research, enabling richer representations of contextual and domain-specific communication patterns in team dialogue.

Table 1. Example utterances and their dialogue act labels

Speaker	Utterance	Dialogue Acts
Nurse	Do you have any ketamine or anything?	Request update, Closing the loop
Doctor	<inaudible> right now his map is 66 at the moment	Provide update (unprompted), Closing the loop
Nurse	Yeah	Request update, Closing the loop
Respiratory Therapist	So based off his ph ratio he has <medical term> so his goal is CO2 should be 88 to 95 percent	Provide update (unprompted), Stating a goal

3 Team Training Dialogue Dataset

The dialogue dataset used for this study consists of labeled transcripts (47,580 total utterances) from 96 distinct training sessions involving medical air transport teams. The teams consisted of a nurse, doctor, and respiratory therapist (See Table 1 for example utterances). The data was compiled and labeled for a study approved by the Naval Medical Research Unit Dayton Institutional Review Board [18]. Team members participating in these exercises were expected to work together to provide care for critical illnesses or injuries to simulated patients controlled by course staff [18]. Building on the work of Robinson et al. [18], we extracted 11 dialogue acts and assigned a new "Other" label to any utterance not labeled with any of the 11 dialogue acts, resulting in 12 labels. The 11 dialogue acts [18] include Closing the Loop, Provide Update/Clarification (Prompted/Unprompted), Request Update/Clarification, Activity Coordination, Getting Attention, Communication Quality, and Stating a Goal. The most frequent label is Closing the Loop (13,499 utterances; 28.4%), while the least frequent is Stating a Goal (399 utterances; 0.8%). The "Other" label was assigned to 5,097 utterances (10.7%). Since an utterance can have more than one dialogue act label (see Table 1.), this dialogue act recognition task is cast as multi-label classification. Inter-rater reliability (Cohen's Kappa) across the 11 labels (excluding "Other") had a macro-average of 0.654 (Rater 1 vs. Rater 2) and 0.576 (Rater 1 vs. Rater 3), indicating moderate to substantial agreement in most categories [18].

4 Team Training Dialogue Act Recognition Models

We evaluate two approaches to dialogue act recognition in team-based medical training scenarios. The first is Llama 3.1 (8B parameters) [13] with QLoRA fine-tuning [4], an efficient approach for fine-tuning LLMs using limited memory resources. Llama 3.1

is known for its strong performance in general language understanding tasks, while QLoRA enables us to efficiently adapt the model to our dialogue act recognition task while minimizing computational overhead. This approach helps us assess the effectiveness of parameter-efficient fine-tuning techniques for team dialogue act recognition. For our second LLM-based approach, we fine-tune Flan-T5 (77M parameters) [3] on our dataset. Flan-T5 is a transformer model fine-tuned through instruction learning; it has demonstrated strong performance across various NLP tasks, particularly those requiring structured responses. Unlike the Llama-based approach, which freezes most weights during fine-tuning, we fine-tune all parameters of Flan-T5, as its smaller model size enables efficient fine-tuning on standard GPUs within a feasible timeframe. Comparing these approaches, we aim to examine (1) whether LLMs provide significant improvements over a BiLSTM baseline for dialogue act recognition, and (2) whether Llama's parameter-efficient fine-tuning (QLoRA) can achieve competitive results compared to Flan-T5's full fine-tuning.

For the BiLSTM baseline, each step of the input sequence consisted of 396 features: a 12-dimensional one-hot vector representing the speaker of the utterance concatenated with a 384-dimensional Sentence-BERT embedding of the utterance. Our BiLSTM model had one BiLSTM layer with 32 hidden units each for the forward and backward directions and one fully connected linear layer. We fine-tuned and evaluated the BiLSTM model using 5 and 10 previous utterances as context.

For all models used in this work, training was conducted using an AdamW optimizer with learning rate 3e-4, 8 epochs of training, and batch size 16. For the LLM experiments, after each epoch of fine-tuning, the model was evaluated on the validation set, and at the end of training, the tunable parameters were restored to the state that demonstrated the best performance on the validation set. The final model was then evaluated on the test set.

For our Llama-based team dialogue act recognition model with QLoRA, we use a Llama 3.1 model [13] as the base model and fine-tune it using QLoRA [4]. QLoRA quantizes model weights such that, for a given block of weights, the entire range of values is used in the quantization to maximize available precision. QLoRA also freezes the weights of the base model and adds matrices called low rank adapters to the architecture whose values are tuned to minimize training loss. For example, the adapter added to a weight matrix with dimensionality $h*o$ would consist of an $h*r$-dimensional matrix multiplied by an $r*o$-dimensional matrix, where r is the rank, a relatively small number. This decomposition substantially reduces the number of tunable parameters [4]. Our base model for this approach is unsloth/Meta-Llama-3.1-8B-bnb-4bit, a Llama 3.1 model with 8 billion parameters where model weights have been quantized to 4 bits [6]. We add low-rank adapters with rank $r = 16$, alpha of 16, and a dropout rate of 0.

Our second LLM model for team dialogue act recognition is based on Flan-T5 [3]. Flan-T5 models are transformer-based models that have been fine-tuned on various tasks via instruction prompts. The additional context in the instructions enhances the effect of fine-tuning, enabling Flan-T5 to exceed the performance of earlier models such as T5. We use the flan-t5-small model and fine-tune all 77 million parameters. The number of tunable parameters for this model is thus comparable to the number of parameters in the low-rank adapters of the Llama QLoRA approach. We retained 32-bit floating-point precision for Flan-T5's parameters, forgoing quantization.

5 Evaluation

We evaluate the performance of both LLM-based approaches in dialogue act recognition across various utterance history configurations. We evaluate both approaches with no previous utterances as context and with one or two previous utterances as context. We use a maximum of two previous utterances to minimize training and inference time. Results on the BiLSTM baseline are also included in the table. The 96 transcripts in the dataset were randomly partitioned into three subsets with 32 transcripts each. Each experiment was run three times, and on each run each subset was assigned to be either the training set, validation set, or test set. As our performance metric, we use the mean F1 score on the test set across all three runs.

Table 2. F1 score results (multi-label classification) across 12 dialogue act labels, with the highest score for each in bold. "current" means no previous utterances were used as context.

Dialogue Act Label	Llama 3.1 with QLoRA			Flan-T5			BiLSTM	
	current	1 prev.	2 prev.	current	1 prev.	2 prev.	5 prev.	10 prev.
Closing the loop	0.6369	0.6088	0.6170	0.6560	**0.6765**	0.6748	0.5228	0.4867
Provide update (unprompted)	0.7104	0.7009	0.6831	0.7681	**0.8057**	0.8046	0.5462	0.4999
Activity coordination	0.7867	0.7128	0.6797	0.8088	0.8039	**0.8122**	0.5032	0.6594
Request update	0.7259	0.6939	0.6942	0.7619	0.7725	**0.7770**	0.5435	0.4668
Provide update (prompted)	0.1875	0.5075	0.5401	0.1363	0.6258	**0.6352**	0.1760	0.0859
Getting attention	0.7449	0.7125	0.6491	0.8069	0.8074	**0.8091**	0.4131	0.1278
Request clarification	0.4677	0.4753	0.4729	0.5162	**0.5937**	0.5619	0.1308	0.1601
Provide clarification (prompted)	0.0859	0.1860	0.2228	0.0784	**0.4090**	0.4028	0.0578	0.0875
Provide clarification (unprompted)	0.1089	**0.1115**	0.0860	0.0226	0.0898	0.0898	0.0000	0.0244
Communication quality	**0.2979**	0.1841	0.1993	0.1511	0.2349	0.2639	0.0234	0.0135
Stating a goal	**0.5214**	0.4272	0.3861	0.4571	0.3888	0.4859	0.1483	0.0553
Other	0.5317	0.4893	0.5006	0.5880	0.6312	**0.6325**	0.3174	0.4405

Table 2 presents the F1 scores across the 12 dialogue act labels examined in our dialogue act recognition task for the medical team training dataset. Considering the average performance across all labels, the highest macro-F1 score for Llama 3.1 is 0.4841 (using 1 previous utterance) and for Flan-T5 is 0.5791 (using 2 previous utterances). The BiLSTM achieves its highest average macro-F1 score of 0.2819 with five previous utterances as context. For every dialogue act label, the best-performing model for each of the two LLM approaches consistently outperforms the baseline models.

6 Conclusion

Dialogue act recognition is key to enabling adaptive training environments by supporting automated coaching, team communication analysis, and performance assessment. We have introduced fine-tuned LLM-based team dialogue act recognition models and evaluated their multi-label classification performance on team dialogue from dialogue-rich medical training scenarios. Empirical results show that the LLM-based models outperform non-LLM baselines on all dialogue acts. Furthermore, the best-performing fine-tuned Flan-T5-based team dialogue act recognition model outperforms the best-performing QLoRA-fine-tuned Llama-3.1-based team dialogue act recognition model on almost all dialogue acts, suggesting that tuning all weights of an LLM is superior to using a larger LLM with frozen weights mediated by adapters.

Using two previous utterances as context tends to work best with Flan-T5, but with Llama 3.1, many dialogue acts achieve the best performance using only the current utterance. Llama 3.1 seems to rely more on its general language understanding abilities gained from pretraining rather than picking up on patterns in the context. Future work could explore unfreezing some parameters of the base Llama model instead of relying solely on the parameters in the adapters. Other promising directions for future work include using error analyses to identify any commonly misclassified labels and using LLMs to identify nuanced misclassifications and adjust label definitions to better handle them. Future work should also investigate transfer performance in medical and non-medical high stakes team training to quantify the models' generalizability and capacity.

Acknowledgments. The research described herein has been sponsored by the U.S. Army DEVCOM, Soldier Center under Cooperative Agreement W912CG-19-2-0001. The statements and opinions expressed in this article do not necessarily reflect the position or the policy of the United States Government, and no official endorsement should be inferred. This material is based upon work supported by the National Science Foundation Graduate Research Fellowship Program under Grant No. 2137100. Any opinions, findings, and conclusions or recommendations expressed in this material are those of the authors and do not necessarily reflect the views of the National Science Foundation. This work used Jetstream2 at Indiana University through allocation SEE250001 from the Advanced Cyberinfrastructure Coordination Ecosystem: Services & Support (ACCESS) program, which is supported by National Science Foundation grants #2138259, #2138286, #2138307, #2137603, and #2138296. The authors would like to thank Eric Robinson for providing the dataset used in this research.

Disclosure of Interests. The authors have no competing interests to declare that are relevant to the content of this article.

References

1. Baber, C., Mustafa, R., Leggett, A., Attfield, S., Gibson, W.H., Raywood-Burke, G., et al.: Automating the analysis of speech acts in teams to understand distributed sensemaking. Proc. Human Factors Ergonomics Soc. Annual Meeting **68**(1), 130–136 (2024)
2. Butchibabu, A., Sparano-Huiban, C., Sonenberg, L., Shah, J.: Implicit coordination strategies for effective team communication. Hum. Factors **58**(4), 595–610 (2016)

3. Chung, H.W., Hou, L., Longpre, S., Zoph, B., Tay, Y., Fedus, W., et al.: Scaling instruction-finetuned language models. J. Mach. Learn. Res. **25**, 1–53 (2024)

4. Dettmers T., Pagnoni, A. Holtzman, A., Zettlemoyer, L.: QLoRA: efficient finetuning of quantized LLMs. In: Oh, A., Naumann, T., Globerson, A., Saenko, Hardt, M., Levine, S. (eds.) NeurIPS 2023, pp. 10088–10115. Curran Associates Inc., Red Hook (2023)

5. Entin, E.E., Serfaty, D.: Adaptive team coordination. Hum. Factors **41**(2), 312–325 (1999)

6. Fine-tune Llama 3.1 Ultra-Efficiently with Unsloth. https://huggingface.co/blog/mlabonne/sft-llama3. Accessed 19 Feb 2025

7. Foltz, P.W., Martin, M.J.: Automated communication analysis of teams. In: Salas, E., Goodwin, G.F., Burke, C.S. (eds.) Team Effectiveness in Complex Organizations, 1st edn., pp. 445–466. Routledge, New York (2008)

8. Ganesh, A., Palmer, M., Kann, K.: A survey of challenges and methods in the computational modeling of multi-party dialog. In: Chen, Y.-N., Rastogi, A. (eds.) NLP4ConvAI 2023, pp. 140–154. Association for Computational Linguistics, Stroudsburg (2023)

9. Garosi, E., Kalantari, R., Zanjirani Farahani, A., Zuaktafi, M., Hosseinzadeh Roknabadi, E., Bakhshi, E.: Concerns about verbal communication in the operating room: a field study. Hum. Factors **62**(6), 940–953 (2020)

10. Gorman, J.C., Grimm, D.A., Stevens, R.H., Galloway, T., Willemsen-Dunlap, A.M., Halpin, D.J.: Measuring real-time team cognition during team training. Hum. Factors **62**(5), 825–860 (2020)

11. Graves, A., Schmidhuber, J.: Framewise phoneme classification with bidirectional LSTM and other neural network architectures. Neural Netw. **18**(5–6), 602–610 (2005)

12. Khare, P., Acosta, H., Carpenter, D., Bae, H., Feng, C., Mott, B., et al.: Predicting facilitator interventions in collaborative game-based learning with student dialogue analysis. In: Cristea, A.I., Walker, E., Lu, Y., Santos, O.C., Isotani, S. (eds.) AIED 2025, LNCS, vol. 15879, pp. 104–117. Springer, Cham (2025). https://doi.org/10.1007/978-3-031-98420-4_8

13. Llama Team, AI @ Meta: The Llama 3 herd of models. Technical report. Meta (2024)

14. Marlow, S.L., Lacerenza, C.N., Paoletti, J., Burke, C.S., Salas, E.: Does team communication represent a one-size-fits-all approach?: a meta-analysis of team communication and performance. Organ. Behav. Hum. Decis. Process. **144**, 145–170 (2018)

15. Min, W., Spain, R., Saville, J.D., Mott, B., Brawner, K., Johnston, J., et al.: Multidimensional team communication modeling for adaptive team training: A hybrid deep learning and graphical modeling framework. In: Roll, I., McNamara, D., Sosnovsky, S., Luckin, R., Dimitrova, V. (eds.) AIED 2021, LNCS, vol. 12748, pp. 293–305. Springer, Cham (2021). https://doi.org/10.1007/978-3-030-78292-4_24

16. Pande, J., Min, W., Spain, R.D., Saville, J.D., Lester, J.: Robust team communication analytics with transformer-based dialogue modeling. In: Wang, N., Rebolledo-Mendez, G., Matsuda, N., Santos, O.C., Dimitrova, V. (eds.) AIED 2023, LNCS, vol. 13916, pp. 639–650. Springer, Cham (2023). https://doi.org/10.1007/978-3-031-36272-9_52

17. Riemers, N., Gurevych, I.: Sentence-BERT: sentence embeddings using siamese BERT-networks. In: Inui, K., Jiang, J., Ng, V., Wan, X. (eds.) EMNLP 2019, pp. 3982–3992. Association for Computational Linguistics, Stroudsburg (2019)

18. Robinson, F.E., et al.: Team coordination style is an adaptive, emergent property of interactions between critical care air transport team personnel. Air Med. J. **42**(3), 174–183 (2023)

19. Stucky, C.H., De Jong, M.J., Kabo, F.W.: Military surgical team communication: implications for safety. Mil. Med. **185**(3–4), e448–e456 (2020)

20. Su, L., Kaplan, S., Burd, R., Winslow, C., Hargrove, A., Waller, M.: Trauma resuscitation: can team behaviors in the pre arrival period predict resuscitation performance? BMJ Simulat. Technol. Enhanced Learn. **3**(3), 106 (2017)

21. Tan, M., Wang, D., Gao, Y., Wang, H., Potdar, S., Guo, X., et al.: Context-aware conversation thread detection in multi-party chat. In: Inui, K., Jiang, J., Ng, V., Wan, X. (eds.) EMNLP 2019, pp. 6456–6461. Association for Computational Linguistics, Stroudsburg (2019)
22. Vitale, J., Kocabagli, K.B., Sanghi, S., Van Camp, A., Miller, S., Coker, B.: From noisy classroom transcripts to actionable feedback: fine-tuning GPT-4o to detect teachers' opportunities to respond. In: Cristea, A.I., Walker, E., Lu, Y., Santos, O.C., Isotani, S. (eds.) AIED 2025, LNCS, vol. 15878, pp. 149-162. Springer, Cham (2025). https://doi.org/10.1007/978-3-031-98417-4_11

Circuit Complexity of Hierarchical Knowledge Tracing

Naiming Liu[1]([✉]) [iD], Richard Baraniuk[1] [iD], and Shashank Sonkar[2] [iD]

[1] Rice University, Houston, USA
nl35@rice.edu
[2] University of Central Florida, Florida, USA
shashank.sonkar@ucf.edu

Abstract. Knowledge tracing models mastery over interconnected concepts, often organized by prerequisites. We analyze hierarchical prerequisite propagation through a circuit-complexity lens to clarify what is provable about transformer-style computation on deep concept hierarchies. Using recent results that log-precision transformers lie in logspace-uniform TC^0, we formalize prerequisite-tree tasks including recursive-majority mastery propagation. Unconditionally, recursive-majority propagation lies in NC^1 via $O(\log n)$-depth bounded-fanin circuits, while separating it from uniform TC^0 would require major progress on open lower bounds. Under a monotonicity restriction, natural for prerequisite aggregation where mastering additional prerequisites should not reduce readiness, we obtain an unconditional barrier: alternating ALL/ANY prerequisite trees yield a strict depth hierarchy for *monotone* threshold circuits. Via a simple reduction, this monotone barrier extends to recursive-majority prerequisite trees. These results delineate a complexity-theoretic landscape for prerequisite propagation and motivate structure-aware objectives and depth-adaptive mechanisms for knowledge tracing on deep hierarchies.

Keywords: Knowledge Tracing · Circuit Complexity · Transformer Models

1 Introduction

Knowledge tracing, modeling how learners master interconnected concepts over time, is fundamental to student modeling, intelligent tutoring systems, and adaptive learning [5,10,18]. A central challenge is capturing how mastery of prerequisite concepts propagates through a concept hierarchy to enable (or block) mastery of more advanced concepts. While a large body of work has explored neural architectures for knowledge tracing, the *computational* capabilities and limitations of these models remain poorly characterized [6,15,17,22,24].

This paper takes a circuit-complexity perspective on hierarchical prerequisite reasoning. Recent results show that *log-precision transformers*, transformers

E. G. Blanchard et al. (Eds.): AIED 2026, LNAI 16583, pp. 66–74, 2027.
https://doi.org/10.1007/978-3-032-29760-0_8

whose activations use $O(\log n)$ bits on inputs of length n, can be simulated by logspace-uniform constant-depth threshold circuits, i.e., they lie in logspace-uniform TC^0 [11,12]. This connection suggests a natural route to transformer limitations: exhibit knowledge-tracing functions that lie beyond (uniform) TC^0. However, proving such lower bounds for *general* TC^0 is notoriously difficult and is intertwined with major open questions in circuit complexity, for example separating TC^0 from NC^1 [21].

We formalize prerequisite propagation on deep concept hierarchies using balanced prerequisite trees and study what can be proved *unconditionally* versus what remains open for standard (non-monotone) transformers. We define a natural hierarchical mastery rule in which each internal concept is mastered if a majority of its prerequisites are mastered; computing the root mastery then corresponds to evaluating a depth-$\Theta(\log n)$ majority formula, placing the task in NC^1 [21]. Showing that this function is *not* in (uniform) TC^0 would yield an immediate limitation for log-precision transformers, but would also constitute a significant circuit lower bound beyond current techniques.

To provide unconditional evidence that layered prerequisite structure can resist shallow parallelization, we analyze an *alternating* prerequisite model (ALL/ANY requirements) under *monotone* threshold computation. From an educational modeling perspective, prerequisite aggregation is naturally monotone: mastering additional prerequisites should not reduce a learner's readiness for an advanced concept. In this principled restricted setting, classical results establish a strict depth hierarchy for monotone threshold circuits: increasing prerequisite depth provably increases the computational power required, and reducing depth forces exponential size [9,23]. Via a simple reduction we show that this monotone barrier extends to recursive-majority prerequisite trees. While these lower bounds do not directly apply to standard transformers (which are not monotone), they delineate a principled barrier and clarify which additional restrictions would be needed for unconditional transformer impossibility results.

Our contributions are as follows:

1. **Formalization and complexity accounting.** We formalize prerequisite propagation on balanced concept trees under natural mastery rules, including recursive majority, and connect these tasks to standard circuit-evaluation problems.
2. **What is provable today.** Unconditionally, for fixed arity k, recursive-majority prerequisite propagation is computable by logarithmic-depth bounded-fanin circuits, placing it in NC^1; in contrast, proving separation from (uniform) TC^0 would require major progress on circuit lower bounds.
3. **Unconditional monotone barrier.** For an alternating ALL/ANY prerequisite rule, classical results yield a strict depth hierarchy for *monotone* threshold circuits, showing that layered prerequisite structure can resist shallow parallelization under monotonicity constraints. We extend this barrier to majority-tree knowledge tracing via a reduction from alternating AND/OR gates to ternary majority.

Taken together, these results clarify both the promise and the limits of current theory for transformer-based knowledge tracing. Hierarchical prerequisite reasoning naturally induces logarithmic-depth computation, and unconditional lower bounds for general TC^0 remain out of reach; yet under the natural monotonicity restriction, deep prerequisite structure provably resists shallow parallelization.

2   Related Work

Our work connects two threads: (i) circuit-complexity characterizations of transformer like architectures, and (ii) modeling choices in knowledge tracing, especially prerequisite structure.

2.1   Theoretical Analysis of Transformer Computation

A growing line of work characterizes transformers via circuit complexity. Merrill and Sabharwal [11] show that *log-precision* transformers, those whose activations use $O(\log n)$ bits on length-n inputs, can be simulated by logspace-uniform constant-depth threshold circuits, placing them within logspace-uniform TC^0. Related analyses of restricted or saturated transformer variants connect attention-based computation to constant-depth threshold circuit families [12]. These results motivate a principled route to expressivity limitations: if a target function can be shown to lie beyond (uniform) TC^0, then it is unreachable by log-precision transformers in this single-pass setting.

Other work studies how specific architectural choices (e.g., attention constraints, normalization) affect expressivity on formal-language tasks [4,7]. Strobl et al. [19] provide a useful synthesis, which harmonizes expressivity results across transformer variants and situates them in the standard circuit hierarchy $\mathsf{AC}^0 \subset \mathsf{TC}^0 \subseteq \mathsf{NC}^1 \subseteq \mathsf{L}$. Importantly, while many natural recursive computations (e.g., Boolean formula evaluation) lie in NC^1, proving that such problems are *not* computable by general TC^0 circuits would imply major open lower bounds (e.g., separating TC^0 from NC^1). Our paper is explicitly motivated by this gap: we identify educationally meaningful hierarchical reasoning tasks that naturally land in NC^1, and we clarify what is currently provable versus what remains open for general TC^0-style transformer computation.

2.2   Knowledge Tracing Methods and Prerequisite Structure

Knowledge tracing (KT) began with Bayesian Knowledge Tracing (BKT) [5], which models binary mastery via hidden states. Deep learning shifted KT toward representation learning: Deep Knowledge Tracing (DKT) [15] applies RNNs to student-event sequences, while DKVMN [24] introduces key-value memory to separate concept representations from student mastery states. Transformers have since become prominent in KT [6,14], illustrating that architectural choices materially affect performance.

A parallel line explicitly models concept structure and prerequisites. Graph-based KT methods such as GKT [13] incorporate concept graphs via message passing. Other approaches directly encode prerequisite influence or constraints, including SKT [20] and prerequisite-driven extensions to sequence models [3].

Despite substantial empirical progress, most KT work evaluates architectures experimentally rather than characterizing which *structural* reasoning patterns (e.g., deep hierarchical prerequisite propagation) are compatible with their underlying computational model. Our work addresses this gap by formalizing prerequisite-tree propagation as a circuit-evaluation task and relating it to the transformer-TC^0 literature.

3 Background: Circuit Complexity and Transformers

Circuit complexity studies computation via families of Boolean circuits and characterizes problems by resources such as circuit size and depth [2,21]. Circuit *depth* is the length of the longest path from any input bit to the output.

The class TC^0 consists of Boolean functions computable by *uniform* families of constant-depth, polynomial-size circuits with unbounded fan-in threshold (majority) gates [8]. Logspace-uniformity ensures the circuit for each input length can be constructed by a logspace algorithm [16].

Recent work shows that log-precision transformers, meaning transformers whose activations use $O(\log n)$ bits on inputs of length n, *can be simulated by* logspace-uniform constant-depth threshold circuits. That is, they lie in logspace-uniform TC^0 [11,12]. Thus, any separation from logspace-uniform TC^0 would immediately yield a limitation for log-precision transformers.

4 Prerequisite-Tree Knowledge Tracing: Upper Bound, Monotone Barrier, and an Open Question

We formalize prerequisite propagation on deep concept hierarchies and clarify what is known unconditionally versus what remains open for *general* TC^0 (and hence standard log-precision transformers).

4.1 Definitions

Concept Tree and Inputs. We consider prerequisite *trees*. Let n denote the number of leaf concepts (input mastery bits), and let N denote the total number of concepts (nodes).

Fix an integer $k \geq 3$. Consider a perfectly balanced k-ary tree of depth d (root at depth 0), where each internal node has exactly k children. The number of leaves is $n = k^d$ (equivalently, $d = \log_k n$). The total number of nodes is

$$N = 1 + k + k^2 + \cdots + k^d - \frac{k^{d+1} - 1}{k - 1} = \frac{kn - 1}{k - 1} = O(n).$$

Majority Prerequisite Rule. Leaves are labeled by input mastery bits in $\{0,1\}$. Each internal node computes the (strict) majority of its k children:

$$\mathrm{MAJ}_k(x_1,\ldots,x_k) = 1 \quad \text{iff} \quad \sum_{i=1}^{k} x_i \geq \left\lfloor \frac{k}{2} \right\rfloor + 1.$$

(For odd k this is the usual majority; for even k this fixes a tie-breaking convention.) Let $\mathrm{KT}_{\mathrm{MAJ}}$ denote the problem of computing the root value.

4.2   Unconditional Upper Bound: $\mathbf{KT_{MAJ} \in NC^1}$

Theorem 1 (Upper Bound).   *For every fixed $k \geq 3$, $\mathrm{KT}_{\mathrm{MAJ}}$ on balanced k-ary trees with n leaves is computable in NC^1.*

Proof. The root value is the evaluation of a depth-$d = \Theta(\log n)$ formula whose internal gates are constant-fanin majorities MAJ_k. Because k is a fixed constant, each MAJ_k can be implemented by a constant-size bounded-fanin Boolean subcircuit; substituting these yields a bounded-fanin Boolean circuit of depth $O(d) = O(\log n)$ and polynomial size. Hence the problem lies in NC^1 [21].

Important Caveat. Theorem 1 does *not* imply $\mathrm{KT}_{\mathrm{MAJ}} \notin \mathsf{TC}^0$. Proving $\mathrm{KT}_{\mathrm{MAJ}} \notin$ (general) TC^0 would be a major circuit lower bound and would separate TC^0 from NC^1 [21].

4.3   A Monotone Barrier (unconditional): Alternating Prerequisite Trees Resist Shallow *monotone* threshold circuits

We next record an unconditional limitation for a *restricted* model, namely *monotone* threshold circuits (no negated inputs and nonnegative weights in threshold gates).

Why Monotonicity is a Meaningful Restriction. When mastery is represented as binary prerequisite indicators, a natural desideratum is *monotonicity*: mastering additional prerequisites should not decrease predicted readiness for a target concept. This aligns with the semantics of prerequisite structure and supports interpretability for prerequisite-aware interventions. Standard transformers are not monotone in general due to negative weights and non-monotone feature interactions.

We use this restriction as a normative baseline for prerequisite aggregation, rather than as a direct model of transformer computation. Even in this restricted setting, layered prerequisite structure can resist shallow parallelization.

Alternating ALL/ANY Prerequisite Trees. Define $\mathrm{KT}_{\wedge/\vee}$ as prerequisite propagation on a tree whose internal nodes alternate between: (i) ALL prerequisites required (AND), and (ii) ANY prerequisite sufficient (OR). This is exactly evaluation of an alternating $\wedge/\vee$ tree on the leaf bits. This task is monotone in the leaf mastery bits, so it aligns with the monotonicity desideratum above.

Theorem 2 (Monotone threshold depth hierarchy via alternating prerequisite formulas). *For every integer $t \geq 2$, there exists an explicit monotone Boolean function f_t that is computed by a depth-t alternating $\wedge/\vee$ read-once formula of linear size (allowing unbounded fan-in gates), but for which every depth-$(t-1)$ monotone threshold circuit requires size $\exp\!\left(n^{\Omega(1/t)}\right)$.*

Proof (Justification and references). Yao introduced monotone threshold circuits and proved a strict depth hierarchy by exhibiting explicit monotone functions computable at larger depth that require exponential size when the depth is reduced [23]. Håstad and Goldmann strengthened and streamlined these results using an explicit family f_t defined by a depth-t alternating $\wedge/\vee$ read-once formula of linear size (with unbounded fan-in), and proving lower bounds of the form $\exp(n^{\Omega(1/t)})$ for depth-$(t-1)$ monotone threshold circuits [9].

How to Read Theorem 2. This theorem states that *no fixed constant depth* of monotone threshold circuits can, in general, compress away the layered prerequisite structure captured by alternating ALL/ANY trees. (It does *not* claim that the specific balanced k-ary tree from our $\mathrm{KT}_{\mathrm{MAJ}}$ definition is hard in this model.)

Reduction from $\wedge/\vee$ Trees to Majority Trees (Restriction). We now connect this monotone barrier to majority-tree prerequisite propagation.

Lemma 1 (AND/OR as restricted ternary majority). *For Boolean inputs $a, b \in \{0, 1\}$,*

$$\mathrm{MAJ}_3(a, b, 0) = a \wedge b, \qquad \mathrm{MAJ}_3(a, b, 1) = a \vee b.$$

Corollary 1 (Monotone lower bound transfers to majority-tree KT). *Fix any $t \geq 2$ and let f_t be as in Theorem 2. Replacing each $\wedge/\vee$ gate in the defining alternating tree for f_t using Lemma 1 (and adding constant leaves) yields a ternary-majority tree function g_t such that any depth-$(t-1)$ polynomial-size monotone threshold circuit for g_t would imply one for f_t. In particular, g_t also requires superpolynomial size at depth $(t-1)$ in the monotone threshold model.*

Proof. Replacing each $\wedge/\vee$ internal node by $\mathrm{MAJ}_3(\cdot, \cdot, 0/1)$ yields a ternary-majority tree whose function restricts (by fixing the added constant leaves) to the original $\wedge/\vee$ tree function. Monotone threshold circuits are closed under restrictions, so any depth-$(t-1)$ monotone threshold circuit for g_t would give one for f_t, contradicting Theorem 2.

On the Monotone vs. General TC^0 *Gap.* Theorems 2–1 are unconditional but apply only to *monotone* threshold circuits. In contrast, these (and related) tree-evaluation families can be far easier for *general* threshold circuits, and obtaining comparable lower bounds for general TC^0 remains open. For example, Håstad–Goldmann note that their monotone-hard functions admit much shallower *general* threshold circuits via known simulations [1,9].

4.4   Implications for Log-Precision Transformers (Conditional)

Corollary 2 (Conditional transformer implication). *If* $\mathrm{KT}_{\mathrm{MAJ}}$ *(recursive majority on balanced trees) is not computable by logspace-uniform (general)* TC^0 *circuits, then log-precision transformers cannot compute* $\mathrm{KT}_{\mathrm{MAJ}}$.

Proof. Log-precision transformers lie in logspace-uniform TC^0 [11,12]. The claim follows immediately.

Takeaway. Unconditionally, $\mathrm{KT}_{\mathrm{MAJ}} \in \mathsf{NC}^1$, and alternating prerequisite-tree propagation exhibits strong limitations for *monotone* threshold circuits in the form of a strict depth hierarchy. Any unconditional limitation for standard (log-precision) transformers would require progress on open lower bounds for *general* TC^0.

5   Discussion and Conclusion

Prerequisite-based knowledge tracing fundamentally requires an *aggregation* operation: given mastery signals over prerequisite concepts, infer readiness for a target concept. Real curricula rarely match the extremes of requiring *all* prerequisites (too strict) or *any* prerequisite (too lenient); instead they behave like a threshold rule, where students need *enough* prerequisite mastery to progress. Modeling this as recursive threshold aggregation over a concept hierarchy yields a principled abstraction of prerequisite propagation.

Our complexity analysis clarifies that this propagation is inherently layered: for fixed arity, evaluating recursive-majority prerequisite trees is a logarithmic-depth computation (in NC^1), and collapsing deep prerequisite structure into a constant-depth computation would require resolving major open circuit lower bounds. Under the natural monotonicity restriction, where mastering additional prerequisites should not reduce readiness, we obtain an unconditional barrier: alternating ALL/ANY prerequisite trees yield a strict depth hierarchy for monotone threshold circuits, and this barrier extends to majority-tree prerequisite propagation. Thus, rather than claiming an impossibility for transformers, we use complexity as a lens to explain why deep prerequisite propagation is a non-trivial capability that constant-depth architectures may struggle to implement.

For AIED, the practical takeaway is that prerequisite structure should be treated as a first-class object in KT evaluation and model design. Our analysis motivates two actionable design principles: (i) incorporate mechanisms that explicitly represent and update intermediate prerequisite mastery, such as multi-task supervision on intermediate concept nodes or structured propagation modules, and (ii) support depth-adaptive computation for curricula with long prerequisite chains, for example through iterative inference, recurrent computation, or hybrid KT models that delegate propagation to a structured component.

Several open questions remain. Foremost, resolving whether recursive-majority tree evaluation lies outside (uniform) TC^0 would yield a direct limitation for log-precision transformers, but this would constitute major progress on the long-standing TC^0 versus NC^1 separation. Empirically validating the theoretical predictions, for example by testing whether transformer-based KT models learn hierarchical prerequisite propagation or converge to shallow shortcuts, is an important direction for future work. Finally, extending the analysis beyond balanced trees to more realistic curriculum structures (e.g., DAGs with variable branching and shared prerequisites) would strengthen the connection between circuit-complexity theory and practical knowledge tracing.

Acknowledgments. This work was supported by NSF SafeInsights and cooperative agreement 2153481.

References

1. Allender, E.: A note on the power of threshold circuits. In: 30th Annual Symposium on Foundations of Computer Science, pp. 580–584. IEEE Computer Society (1989)
2. Arora, S., Barak, B.: Computational complexity: a modern approach. Cambridge University Press (2009)
3. Chen, P., Lu, Y., Zheng, V.W., Pian, Y.: Prerequisite-driven deep knowledge tracing. In: 2018 IEEE International Conference on Data Mining (ICDM), pp. 39–48. IEEE (2018)
4. Chiang, D., Cholak, P.: Overcoming a theoretical limitation of self-attention, arXiv preprint. arXiv:2202.12172 (2022)
5. Corbett, A.T., Anderson, J.R.: Knowledge tracing: modeling the acquisition of procedural knowledge. User Model. User-Adap. Inter. **4**(4), 253–278 (1994)
6. Ghosh, A., Heffernan, N., Lan, A.S.: Context-aware attentive knowledge tracing. In: Proceedings of the 26th ACM SIGKDD International Conference on Knowledge Discovery & Data Mining, pp. 2330–2339 (2020)
7. Hahn, M.: Theoretical limitations of self-attention in neural sequence models. Trans. Associat. Comput. Linguist. **8**, 156–171 (2020)
8. Hajnal, A., Maass, W., Pudlák, P., Szegedy, M., Turán, G.: Threshold circuits of bounded depth. J. Comput. Syst. Sci. **46**(2), 129–154 (1993)
9. Håstad, J., Goldmann, M.: On the power of small-depth threshold circuits. Comput. Complexity **1**(2), 113–129 (1991)
10. Liu, N., Wang, Z., Baraniuk, R., Lan, A.: Open-ended knowledge tracing for computer science education. In: Proceedings of the 2022 Conference on Empirical Methods in Natural Language Processing, pp. 3849–3862 (2022)
11. Merrill, W., Sabharwal, A.: The parallelism tradeoff: limitations of log-precision transformers. Trans. Associat. Comput. Linguist. **11**, 531–545 (2023)

12. Merrill, W., Sabharwal, A., Smith, N.A.: Saturated transformers are constant-depth threshold circuits. Trans. Associat. Comput. Linguist. **10**, 843–856 (2022)
13. Nakagawa, H., Iwasawa, Y., Matsuo, Y.: Graph-based knowledge tracing: modeling student proficiency using graph neural network. In: IEEE/WIC/ACM International Conference on Web Intelligence, pp. 156–163. (2019)
14. Pandey, S., Karypis, G.: A self-attentive model for knowledge tracing, arXiv preprint, arXiv:1907.06837 (2019)
15. Piech, C., et al.: Deep knowledge tracing. In: Advances in Neural Information Processing Systems, p. 28 (2015)
16. Ruzzo, W.L.: On uniform circuit complexity. J. Comput. Syst. Sci. **22**(3), 365–383 (1981)
17. Sonkar, S., Baraniuk, R.G.: Deduction under perturbed evidence: probing student simulation (knowledge tracing) capabilities of large language models. In: LLM@ AIED, pp. 26–33 (2023)
18. Sonkar, S., Waters, A.E., Lan, A.S., Grimaldi, P.J., Baraniuk, R.G.: qdkt: question-centric deep knowledge tracing, arXiv preprint arXiv:2005.12442 (2020)
19. Strobl, L., Merrill, W., Weiss, G., Chiang, D., Angluin, D.: What formal languages can transformers express? a survey. Trans. Associat. Comput. Linguist. **12**, 543–561 (2024)
20. Tong, S., et al.: Structure-based knowledge tracing: an influence propagation view. In: 2020 IEEE international Conference on Data Mining (ICDM), pp. 541–550. IEEE (2020)
21. Vollmer, H.: Introduction to circuit complexity: a uniform approach. Springer Science & Business Media (1999)
22. Worden, E., Heffernan, C., Heffernan, N., Sonkar, S.: Foundationalassist: an educational dataset for foundational knowledge tracing and pedagogical grounding of llms. arXiv preprint arXiv:2602.00070 (2026)
23. Yao, A.C.: Circuits and local computation. In: Proceedings of the Twenty-First Annual ACM Symposium on Theory of Computing, pp. 186–196. (1989)
24. Zhang, J., Shi, X., King, I., Yeung, D.Y.: Dynamic key-value memory networks for knowledge tracing. In: Proceedings of the 26th International Conference on World Wide Web, pp. 765–774 (2017)

Beyond the Gold Standard: Reliability Estimation of Human and GenAI Scoring

Ji Yoon Jung[(✉)] [iD], Ummugul Bezirhan [iD], and Matthias von Davier [iD]

TIMSS and PIRLS International Study Center at Boston College,
Chestnut Hill, MA 02467, USA
{jungjg,bezirhan,vondavim}@bc.edu

Abstract. Generative AI (GenAI) has advanced rapidly, yet current evaluations of GenAI-based automated scoring continue to rely on traditional metrics that assume human scores represent the gold standard. However, human scoring is inherently prone to subjectivity and rater variability. To address these limitations, this study applied the Linguistic-integrated Reliability Audit (LiRA) framework, which automatically generates data-driven benchmark scores. We estimated and compared the reliability of human and GenAI scoring for six constructed response items from PIRLS across all participating countries. Results demonstrated that GenAI scoring achieved consistently higher reliability (97.21%) than human scoring (95.23%) across items and countries. These findings challenge the conventional reliance on human scores as the gold standard and support a paradigm shift toward automated, reproducible reliability estimation.

Keywords: Generative AI · Automated Scoring · Scoring Reliability

1 Introduction

Generative AI (GenAI) has revolutionized automated scoring (AS). Powered by large language models (LLMs) such as GPT and Gemini, GenAI-based AS (GenAI-AS) has demonstrated impressive performance across diverse assessment contexts [1–3]. A key advantage of GenAI-AS is its task-agnostic nature; unlike supervised approaches that require extensive, task-specific training data, it is highly adaptable to new items, domains, and languages. This flexibility makes it particularly valuable for international large-scale assessments (ILSAs), which process vast volumes of multilingual responses. Moreover, GenAI-AS can incorporate contextual information (e.g., item stems, scoring guides, and exemplar responses), and can be prompted to function as an informed exam grader. This contrasts with supervised AS, which typically relies on surface-level features like grammar, response length, or lexical variety.

Despite its promise, GenAI-AS evaluation typically relies on agreement with human scores [4]. Although widely used, this dependence raises a fundamental validity concern: are human scores an absolute "gold standard"? Prior research

E. G. Blanchard et al. (Eds.): AIED 2026, LNAI 16583, pp. 75–83, 2027.
https://doi.org/10.1007/978-3-032-29760-0_9

has consistently shown that human scoring (HS) is prone to construct-irrelevant variance, including rater effects and inconsistency [5,6]. Even with rigorous training, rater performance can still be compromised by scoring complexity, task type, individual background, and training experience [7]. These limitations underscore the need for complementary evaluation metrics that move beyond scoring agreement and function independently of human subjectivity.

To address this challenge, this paper leverages the Linguistic-integrated Reliability Audit (LiRA) framework [8] as a scoring-agnostic, reliability-centered evaluation approach. LiRA can be applied to both HS and AS, enabling reliability to be assessed against common, data-driven benchmarks rather than treating HS as a fixed reference. By directly comparing the reliability of HS and GenAI-AS, this study offers a new standard for reliability assessment that transcends traditional, human-dependent estimation.

2   Related Work

Evaluating AS systems conventionally relies on human-machine score agreement, assuming that human scores are the gold standard. However, prior studies have consistently demonstrated the intrinsic subjectivity of HS [9,10]. Bejar [9] noted that human raters develop internal scoring rubrics shaped by individual interpretation and idiosyncratic biases. This can lead to divergent scores, particularly for hard-to-score or borderline responses. Even with extensive training, achieving high levels of scoring reliability remains challenging in ILSAs, since ensuring consistency across raters, countries, and languages is inherently complex. Furthermore, the resource-intensive nature of HS often makes it infeasible to obtain human scores for every response across all items to estimate reliability.

Previous studies have proposed more practical alternatives for evaluating scoring reliability. Some studies [11,12] introduced partial double scoring, which estimates reliability using a random subset of responses. While this reduces costs and time, it raises validity concerns; for instance, if sampled responses overrepresent hard-to-score cases, it can lead to an underestimation of reliability [13]. Powers et al. [14] proposed a refined human-machine agreement model that differentiates raters by experience and expertise. Their findings indicated that AS aligns more closely with highly trained raters than with novices, suggesting that the gold standard itself requires refinement. This highlights the limitations of assuming rater equivalence and the practical difficulty of maintaining uniform expertise. However, this approach remains operationally demanding at scale, as it necessitates rigorous quality control to validate rater expertise.

3   Method

3.1   Dataset

The Progress in International Reading Literacy Study (PIRLS) has assessed the reading comprehension of fourth-grade students globally in five-year cycles since

2001. For this study, six one-point constructed response items were selected: three from the digital PIRLS 2021 and three from the PIRLS 2026 field test. Detailed item information is provided in Table 1.

Table 1. Item information used in this study.

Item	Cycle	Passage	Purpose	Process	N
1	2021	A	Informational	Focus on & retrieve	14,087
2	2021	B	Literary	Straightforward inferences	13,138
3	2021	C	Informational	Straightforward inferences	14,718
4	2026	D	Literary	Focus on & retrieve	14,622
5	2026	E	Literary	Straightforward inferences	13,335
6	2026	F	Informational	Straightforward inferences	14,104

3.2   GenAI-Based Automated Scoring

Student responses were scored via the GPT-4.1 API, using a scoring prompt integrated with the Chain-of-Thought (CoT) technique [15]. The model was instructed to evaluate multilingual responses by referencing contextual information, including task instructions, reading passages, item stems, and scoring guides. Following Jung et al. [16], we utilized condensed versions of the reading passages and scoring guides instead of the original lengthy texts. This approach optimized token efficiency while preserving the key information required for accurate scoring. Each response was assigned a score of 0 or 1, with a corresponding English translation generated for quality control purposes.

3.3   Benchmark Generation and Reliability Analysis

Response Flagging. Following the LiRA framework [8], we identified and flagged two types of responses: "untranslated" and "meaningless". The "untranslated" flag was applied when the English translation was deemed insufficient for validation despite a generated machine score. Specifically, a response was marked if (1) GPT explicitly labeled it as "untranslatable", or (2) English vocabulary comprised less than 75% of the translation. These responses were excluded from subsequent reliability analysis. Next, we flagged "meaningless" responses, representing low-effort attempts characterized by extreme brevity or semantic irrelevance to the item (e.g., off-topic responses). In such cases, the LiRA framework automatically assigned a score of 0.

Similarity-Weighted Benchmark Scoring. To generate the LiRA benchmark score (s^*), we produced response embeddings using the all-MiniLM-L6-v2 model and retrieved the top three nearest neighbors based on cosine similarity.

$$N_i = TopK_{j \neq i,\, k=3} \operatorname{sim}(e_i, e_j) \tag{1}$$

The benchmark score is determined by maximizing the cumulative similarity within each score category $s \in \{0,1\}$. The algorithm sums the similarities between the target embedding e_i and the neighbor embeddings e_j within the set $S_{i,s}$, which denotes the top three neighbors for response i that share score s:

$$S_{i,s} = \{j \in N_i | s_j = s\} \tag{2}$$

$$s_i^* = \mathrm{argmax}_{s \in \{0,1\}} \sum_{j \in S_{i,s}} \mathrm{sim}(e_i, e_j) \tag{3}$$

Finally, s^* is assigned only if the weighted similarity proportion exceeds a threshold of 0.60; otherwise, the response was flagged as "inconsistent" because its nearest neighbors are too semantically diverse to establish a benchmark score.

For instance, Fig. 1 illustrates the process using the response, "Plants need sunlight to grow well". The algorithm retrieves its three nearest neighbors: two with a score of 1 (each with a cosine similarity of 0.98) and one with a score of 0 (similarity 0.93). The candidate score is identified as 1, as the summed similarity for score 1 (0.98+0.98=1.96) outweighs that for score 0 (0.93). The weighted score proportion is calculated as: (0.98+0.98)/(0.98+0.98+0.93) ≈ 0.68. Since this value exceeds the 0.60 threshold (established via grid search), the response is assigned a final benchmark score of 1.

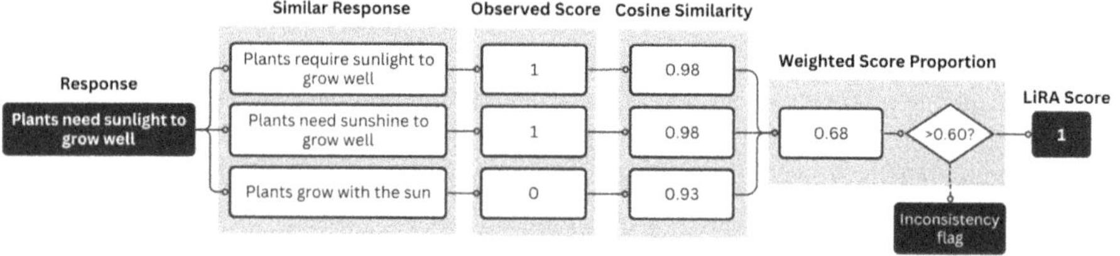

Fig. 1. Illustrative example of benchmark score generation.

Reliability Estimation. Once benchmark scores were generated, we estimated scoring reliability using Weighted Exact Agreement (WEA). Unlike standard agreement metrics, WEA weights each response by its local semantic similarity. This ensures that responses with higher semantic proximity to their neighbors, reflecting a more robust benchmark assignment, contribute more significantly to the final reliability score. The metric is defined as:

$$\mathrm{WEA} = \frac{\sum_{i=1}^{N} w_i \cdot \mathbf{1}(s_i = s_i^*)}{\sum_{i=1}^{N} w_i} \times 100 \tag{4}$$

where s_i and s_i^* represent the observed and benchmark scores, respectively. The agreement is adjusted by the weighting factor w_i, defined as the average cosine similarity among the response's semantic neighbors. The resulting WEA value represents a scoring reliability percentage ranging from 0 to 100.

4   Results

4.1   Item-Level Scoring Reliability

Table 2 presents the scoring reliability estimates for both HS (WEA_{HS}) and GenAI-AS (WEA_{AS}). While both scoring methods achieved high reliability, averaging above 95% across all six items, the GenAI-AS consistently outperformed HS. Specifically, WEA_{AS} exceeded WEA_{HS} for every item, with an average reliability gain of 1.98% points.

Table 2. Item-level scoring reliability.

Item	WEA_{HS}	WEA_{AS}	ΔWEA
1	93.83	94.90	+1.07
2	93.72	97.02	+3.30
3	96.38	97.75	+1.37
4	97.69	98.75	+1.06
5	94.92	97.60	+2.68
6	94.83	97.24	+2.41
Avg.	95.23	97.21	+1.98

4.2   Country-Level Scoring Reliability

Figure 2 illustrates the distribution of scoring reliability at the country level. Each point represents a country's reliability for GenAI-AS (x-axis, WEA_{AS}) and HS (y-axis, WEA_{HS}). Most data points fall below the 45-degree line, indicating that GenAI-AS achieved higher consistency than HS across most countries. Notably, substantial discrepancies were observed where GenAI-AS significantly outperformed HS. For example, in Item 4, one country showed a reliability gap of 17.5% points ($WEA_{HS} = 74.64\%$, $WEA_{AS} = 92.14\%$). Similarly, for Item 5, another country's GenAI-AS reliability reached 97.37%, markedly higher than its HS reliability of 88.16%. These cases are further examined in the Discussion section.

4.3   Benchmark Score Distributions and Flag Evaluation

Table 3 presents the distribution of benchmark scores (0 and 1) alongside the flags ("inconsistent" and "untranslated"). The LiRA framework successfully generated valid benchmark scores for the vast majority ($> 99\%$) of responses across all items and scoring methods, resulting in a negligible number of flagged cases. Specifically, the rates of "inconsistent" flags were minimal, ranging from 0.00%

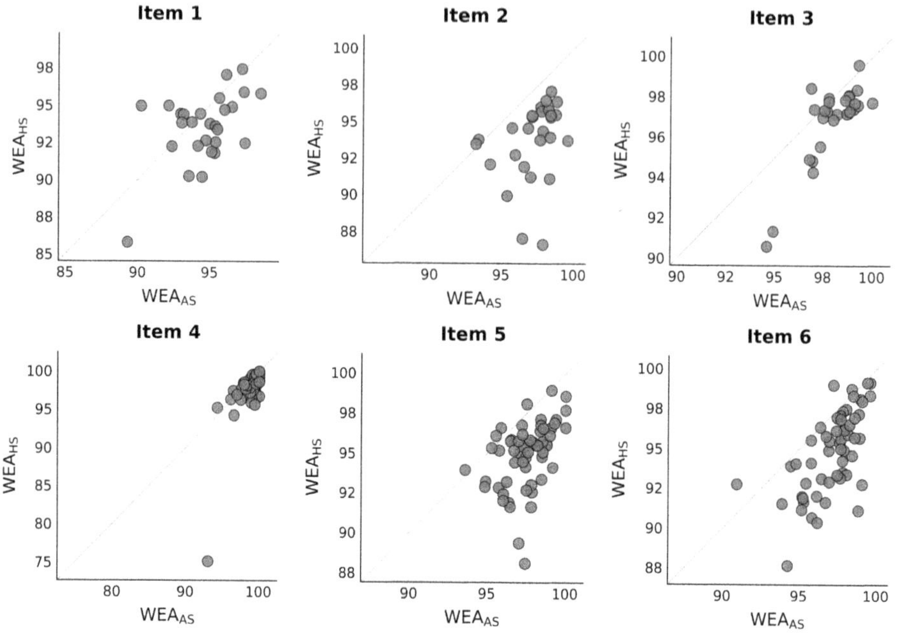

Fig. 2. Country-level scoring reliability by item.

to 0.05% for HS and 0.01% to 0.05% for GenAI-AS. Similarly, the proportion of "untranslated" responses was consistently low, ranging from 0.15% to 1.03% across items. These results demonstrate that LiRA provides a robust and comprehensive basis for reliability with very low levels of data loss.

Table 3. Distribution of benchmark scores by item and scoring method (%).

Item	Method	Score 0	Score 1	Inconsistent	Untranslated
1	HS	43.20	56.51	0.00	0.28
	AS	42.97	56.71	0.04	0.28
2	HS	16.00	83.83	0.02	0.15
	AS	12.90	86.94	0.02	0.15
3	HS	20.73	79.00	0.04	0.23
	AS	19.01	80.75	0.01	0.23
4	HS	9.01	90.27	0.02	0.70
	AS	8.85	90.43	0.02	0.70
5	HS	46.31	52.91	0.03	0.75
	AS	45.23	53.99	0.03	0.75
6	HS	29.64	69.28	0.05	1.03
	AS	28.79	70.13	0.05	1.03

Additionally, we examined the distributions of scores for responses flagged as "meaningless" and "untranslated" (Fig. 3). Under the LiRA framework, "meaningless" responses are automatically assigned a benchmark score of 0. This mechanism proved highly effective, as nearly all such responses received a score of 0 from both HS and GenAI-AS. A similar pattern was observed for "untranslated" flags, with the vast majority being scored as 0. A qualitative review revealed that these instances were predominantly off-topic, nonsensical, or rife with severe spelling errors. This suggests that the "untranslated" flag was primarily triggered by a limited response legibility, which precluded accurate translation and meaningful assessment.

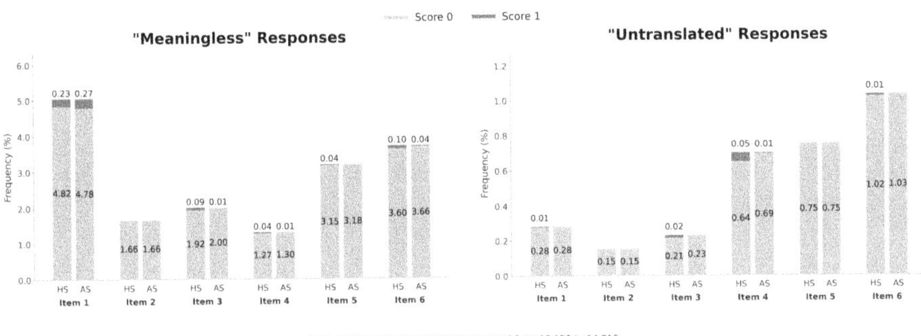

Fig. 3. Score distribution of "meaningless" and "untranslated" responses.

5   Discussion and Future Work

This study evaluated the reliability of HS and GenAI-AS by leveraging the LiRA framework, which operates independently of additional human scores. Unlike traditional evaluation practices that rely on agreement with human scores, LiRA generates robust, data-driven benchmark scores and utilizes WEA to assess scoring reliability. By assigning greater weight to responses with high semantic consensus and down-weighting ambiguous, low-similarity cases, LiRA provides a more stable and valid assessment of scoring consistency. Furthermore, LiRA's flagging algorithm effectively identifies responses that are inherently challenging to score (labeled as "inconsistent"), thereby signaling the need for targeted human-in-the-loop review. Beyond reliability estimation, LiRA offers valuable diagnostic insights by detecting "untranslated" or "meaningless" entries.

Crucially, LiRA enabled direct reliability comparisons between HS and GenAI-AS across various items, countries, and languages. The results demonstrated that GenAI-AS consistently achieved higher reliability than HS. Notably, LiRA identified specific countries where the reliability of GenAI-AS substantially exceeded that of IIS, particularly for Items 4 and 5. Expert review indicated that human raters in these countries tended to be inconsistent or overly lenient when scoring borderline responses requiring highly nuanced distinctions, leading to increased scoring variability. Further investigation is needed to examine whether these discrepancies stem from rater training practices, cultural nuances, or administrative challenges.

While LiRA offers a robust alternative to conventional evaluation, several limitations remain. First, future research should investigate the framework's generalizability beyond the PIRLS (reading) dataset to other assessment domains, such as science and mathematics. Expanding to these subjects may require recalibrating semantic similarity thresholds and the number of semantic neighbors. Second, although LiRA generated benchmark scores for the vast majority of responses, a small subset remained flagged as "inconsistent". Future strategies to resolve these cases could include iterative re-scoring, utilizing alternative LLMs (e.g., Gemini, Claude), or incorporating systematic human-in-the-loop review. Such hybrid approaches will further enhance the precision and scalability of the LiRA framework.

Disclosure of Interests. The authors have no competing interests to declare that are relevant to the content of this article.

References

1. Shermis, M.D.: Using ChatGPT to score essays and short-form constructed responses. Assess. Writ. **66**, 100988 (2025)
2. Latif, E., Zhai, X.: Fine-tuning ChatGPT for automatic scoring. Comput. Educ. Artifi. Intell. **6**, 100210 (2024)
3. Jung, J.Y., Tyack, L., von Davier, M.: Towards the implementation of automated scoring in international large-scale assessments: scalability and quality control. Comput. Educ. Artifi. Intell. **8**, 100375 (2025)
4. Williamson, D.M., Xi, X., Breyer, F.J.: A framework for evaluation and use of automated scoring. Educ. Meas. Issues Pract. **31**(1), 2–13 (2012)
5. Brown, A.: The effect of rater variables in the development of an occupation-specific language performance test. Lang. Test. **12**(1), 1–15 (1995)
6. Ling, G., Mollaun, P., Xi, X.: A study on the impact of fatigue on human raters when scoring speaking responses. Lang. Test. **31**(4), 479–499 (2014)
7. Myford, C.M., Wolfe, E.W.: Detecting and measuring rater effects using many-facet Rasch measurement: Part I. J. Appl. Meas. **4**(4), 386–422 (2003)
8. Jung, J.Y., Bezirhan, U., von Davier, M.: Reconceptualizing scoring reliability through linguistic similarity. Educ. Psychol. Measurem. (2025). https://doi.org/10.1177/00131644251397428
9. Bejar, I.I.: Rater cognition: implications for validity. Educ. Meas. Issues Pract. **31**(3), 2–9 (2012)
10. McClellan, C.A.: Constructed-response scoring–doing it right. R&D Connections **13**, 1–7 (2010)
11. Miao, J., Cao, Y.: Development and evaluation of a partial double scoring procedure for preservice teacher portfolio assessment. AERA Online Paper Repository (2019)

12. Xu, Y., Wind, S.A.: Examining the psychometric impact of targeted and random double-scoring in mixed-format assessments. Educ. Meas. Issues Pract. **44**(1), 18–30 (2025)
13. Song, Y.A., Lee, W.C.: Effects of using double ratings as item scores on IRT proficiency estimation. Appl. Measur. Educ. **35**(2), 95–115 (2022)
14. Powers, D.E., Escoffery, D.S., Duchnowski, M.P.: Validating automated essay scoring: a (modest) refinement of the "gold standard." Appl. Measur. Educ. **28**(2), 130–142 (2015)
15. Kojima, T., Gu, S.S., Reid, M., Matsuo, Y., Iwasawa, Y.: Large language models are zero-shot reasoners. In: Proceedings of the 35th International Conference on Neural Information Processing Systems (NeurIPS), pp. 22199–22213 (2022)
16. Jung, J.Y., Bezirhan, U., von Davier, M.: Optimizing reliability scoring for ILSAs. In: Proceedings of the AI in Measurement and Evaluation Conference (AIME-Con): Full Papers, pp. 43–49 (2025)

CODE-GEN: A RAG-Based Agentic AI System for Multiple-choice Question Generation

Xiaojing Duan[✉][iD], Frederick Nwanganga[iD], and Chaoli Wang[iD]

University of Notre Dame, Notre Dame, IN 46556, USA
{xduan,fnwangan,chaoli.wang}@nd.edu

Abstract. We present CODE-GEN, a retrieval-augmented generation (RAG)-based agentic AI system for generating context-aligned multiple-choice questions to develop learners' code comprehension. CODE-GEN employs a dual-agent architecture in which a Generator agent produces questions aligned with course-specific learning objectives and a Validator agent independently assesses quality across seven pedagogical dimensions, both augmented with specialized tools for computational accuracy and code verification. To evaluate CODE-GEN, six subject-matter experts (SMEs) judged 288 AI-generated questions, producing 2,016 human-AI rating pairs and 131 instances of qualitative feedback. Results show strong system performance, with human-validated success rates ranging from 79.9% to 98.6%. CODE-GEN achieves high reliability on dimensions suited to computational verification and explicit criteria matching, including question clarity, code validity, concept alignment, and correct answer validity. In contrast, human expertise remains essential for dimensions requiring deeper instructional judgment, such as distractor design and feedback quality. These findings provide evidence-based design guidelines for the strategic allocation of human and AI effort in AI-assisted educational content generation.

Keywords: LLMs · Retrieval-augmented generation · Agentic AI · Multi-agent architecture · Human evaluation · Pedagogical alignment

1 Introduction

Recent advances in large language models (LLMs) have generated substantial interest in their potential to support teaching and learning in educational contexts [4,15]. While prior studies demonstrate that LLMs can generate a wide range of educational artifacts [1,7], their adoption in authentic classroom settings remains limited [10,12]. This limitation stems from two persistent challenges. First, content produced by general-purpose LLMs is often overly generic and insufficiently aligned with course-specific learning objectives [8,14], undermining instructional validity and reducing instructor trust in AI-assisted content generation. Second, although recent work in agentic AI has introduced multi-agent systems with specialized roles for generation, critique, and revision to

E. G. Blanchard et al. (Eds.): AIED 2026, LNAI 16583, pp. 84–92, 2027.
https://doi.org/10.1007/978-3-032-29760-0_10

improve content quality [9,18], these systems frequently assume that automated critique agents provide reliable evaluations. In practice, such assumptions are problematic, as LLM-based evaluators are known to exhibit hallucinations, bias, and inconsistent judgment [11,16]. Without systematic validation against human expert judgment, errors introduced at the evaluation stage risk being amplified rather than corrected.

To address these challenges, we present CODE-GEN (Context-aligned, Output-validated, Dual-agent, Expert-guided GENeration), an agentic AI system for generating contextually grounded multiple-choice coding comprehension questions. CODE-GEN integrates retrieval-augmented generation (RAG) with a dual-agent architecture in which a Generator agent produces multiple-choice coding questions aligned with course-specific learning objectives, and a Validator agent independently assesses question quality across seven pedagogical dimensions derived from established multiple-choice item-writing guidelines. Both agents are augmented with specialized tools to support computational accuracy and reliable code execution verification. To evaluate the effectiveness of this agentic approach, we conducted a comprehensive human evaluation study in which six subject-matter experts (SMEs) judged 288 AI-generated questions, yielding 2,016 human-AI judgment pairs and 131 instances of qualitative feedback. Analysis of these SME judgments provides empirical evidence of where agentic AI systems can reliably support educational content generation and where human expertise remains essential, thereby characterizing both the strengths and limitations of LLM-based approaches to AI-assisted educational content generation.

The main contributions of the study include: (1) We introduce CODE-GEN, an agentic AI system that generates context-aligned multiple-choice questions validated against explicit pedagogical criteria. (2) Unlike prior multi-agent systems that assume automated critique agents are reliable, we treat automated assessment as an empirical object of study, systematically comparing Validator assessments against SME judgments across seven pedagogical dimensions to identify where automated assessment succeeds and where it falls short. (3) We derive evidence-based design guidelines demonstrating that AI can provide scalable, first-line quality control for dimensions involving computational verification and explicit criteria matching, while human experts remain essential for pedagogical judgment, including plausible distractor design and instructionally rich feedback.

2   Method

2.1   CODE-GEN

CODE-GEN is a RAG-based agentic AI system for generating and validating multiple-choice coding comprehension questions that are closely aligned with course-specific learning objectives.

Figure 1 illustrates the end-to-end workflow for CODE-GEN. The workflow begins with instructors uploading instructional materials, including learning

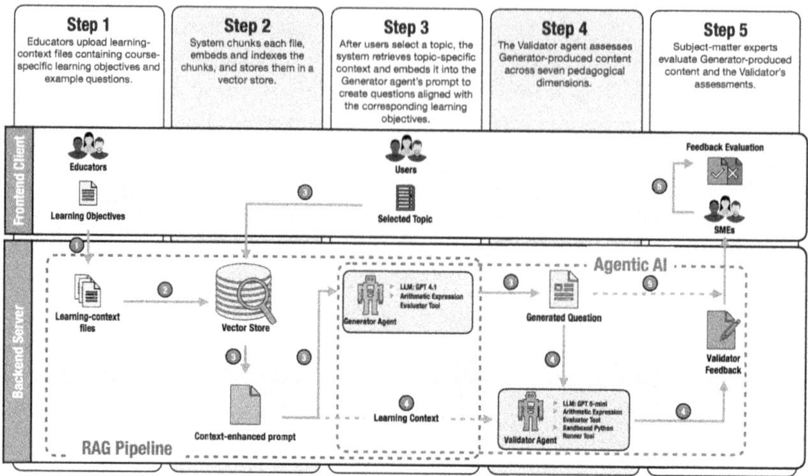

Fig. 1. CODE-GEN end-to-end system workflow.

objectives and example questions. These materials define the authoritative pedagogical context and are indexed through a RAG pipeline. When a user selects a topic, relevant instructional examples are retrieved and provided to a Generator agent, which produces multiple-choice questions grounded in the provided context. The Validator agent then independently aesses each question item across seven pedagogical dimensions as described in Table 1. The dimensions are: question stem clarity [6], code validity [3], concept alignment [2], correct answer validity [17], distractor quality [5], correct answer feedback quality [6], and distractor feedback quality [5].

RAG Pipeline. To ensure the generated questions are contextually aligned with course-specific learning objectives, CODE-GEN employs a RAG pipeline tailored for coding comprehension multiple-choice questions. Uploaded instructional materials are segmented using a domain-specific chunking strategy that preserves semantic coherence. Each semantically coherent chunk is embedded using the OpenAI text-embedding-3-small model and indexed in a Facebook AI Similarity Search (FAISS) vector store. When a user initiates question generation for a given topic, the system identifies the most relevant instructional examples through nearest-neighbor retrieval. These retrieved examples are embedded into the Generator agent's prompt, constraining generation to the intended instructional context.

Model Selection. To select models for the Generator and Validator agents, we conducted comparative experiments across state-of-the-art commercial LLMs at the time of the study (Claude Sonnet 4.5, Gemini 2.5 Pro, GPT-5-mini, and GPT-4.1), prioritizing API-accessible options to ensure reproducibility and practical deployability. Generator selection criteria emphasized novelty relative to retrieved context, answer correctness, and response latency; GPT-4.1 was

Table 1. Evaluation dimensions and Validator assessment outputs.

Evaluation Dimension	Description	Classification Output	Rationale Output
Question Stem Clarity	Clarity of the question stem	Yes/No	Why the question stem is or is not clear
Code Validity	Validity of the generated code	Yes/No	Why the code is or is not valid
Concept Alignment	Alignment of the generated question with the provided context	Yes/No	Why the question does or does not align with the provided context
Correct Answer Validity	Validity of the marked correct answer	Yes/No	Why the marked correct answer is or is not valid
Distractor Quality	Plausibility and pedagogical value of incorrect options	Good/Poor	Why the distractor quality is good or poor
Correct Answer Feedback Quality	Quality of feedback in explaining why the answer is correct and reinforcing the underlying concept	Good/Poor	Why is the correct answer feedback quality good or poor
Distractor Feedback Quality	Quality of feedback in explaining why the distractors are incorrect	Good/Poor	Why the distractor feedback quality is good or poor

selected for its balance across all three dimensions. Validator selection focused on detecting common quality issues such as incorrect answer keys and answer-feedback inconsistencies; GPT-5-mini was selected for its reliable error detection and concise validation output.

Tool Augmentation. Augmenting AI agents with external tools is an established strategy for extending capabilities beyond pure language generation [13]. In CODE-GEN, we adopt this approach to address two well-documented LLM limitations. First, because LLMs frequently miscalculate multi-step arithmetic expressions involving operator precedence, we developed an Arithmetic Expression Evaluator to support the Generator and Validator with deterministic arithmetic computation and verification. Second, to support automated validation of code execution results, we developed a Sandboxed Python Runner for the Validator to execute code in a restricted environment, capture outputs, and inspect variable states. Together, these tools improve quality assurance while maintaining operational security.

Prompt Engineering. The Generator and Validator agents use structured prompts designed to ensure pedagogical alignment, reliable tool usage, and strict output formatting for consistent parsing and scalable downstream analysis. The complete prompts are available on GitHub.[1]

---

[1] https://github.com/XiaojingDuan/CODE-GEN/.

2.2   Human Subject-Matter Expert Evaluation

CODE-GEN leverages human expertise to verify the Validator's assessments and mitigate the risk of propagating incorrect or misleading feedback during iterative refinement cycles. We recruited six SMEs (three men and three women), all with extensive experience teaching introductory programming. Following an orientation session to establish a shared understanding of evaluation criteria, SMEs evaluated 288 questions and the associated validations using CODE-GEN. Figure 2 illustrates an example of the evaluation interface using a while-loop-related question created by the Generator. Adjacent to the question, the user interface displays the Validator's analysis across seven evaluation dimensions.

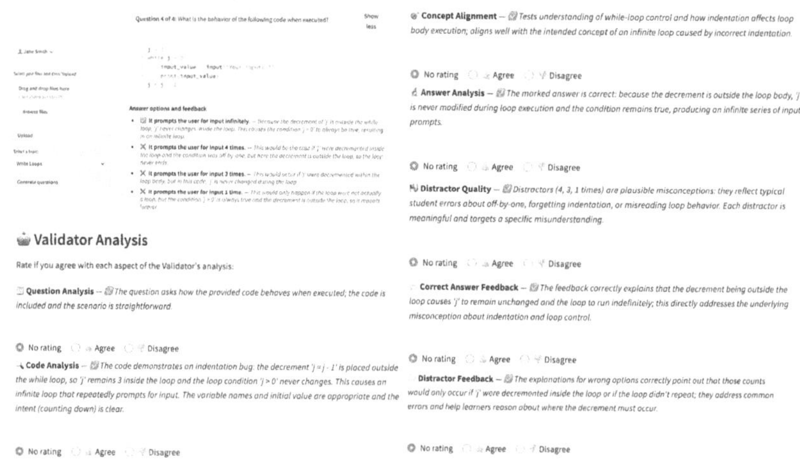

Fig. 2. CODE-GEN web user interface.

For each question, SMEs judged the generated items alongside the Validator's assessments, indicated agreement or disagreement for each dimension using the explicit Agree or Disagree button, and provided textual rationales when they disagreed. Across all experts and dimensions, this process yielded 2,016 SME-Validator rating pairs and 131 instances of qualitative feedback. Because CODE-GEN generates unique questions for each user, SMEs evaluated distinct question sets. As such, traditional inter-rater reliability measures such as Cohen's κ are not applicable, as they require multiple raters judging the same items. To assess evaluator consistency, we examined the SME-Validator agreement rates across all SMEs. Results show consistent agreement rates across all dimensions (82.5%–98.4%), with five of seven exhibiting standard deviations of 3.8% or below, indicating that SMEs applied comparable evaluation standards despite reviewing different question sets.

3   Results and Discussion

3.1   System-Level Quality Analysis Results

To evaluate CODE-GEN's performance, we treated human SMEs' judgments as ground truth and the Validator's assessments as predictions in a binary classification framework. Each SME-Validator rating pair was assigned to one of four outcome categories: **Success (TP)**, representing high-quality content correctly accepted; **Failure (FP)**, representing low-quality content incorrectly accepted; **Safeguarding (TN)**, representing low-quality content correctly rejected; and **Inefficiency (FN)**, representing high-quality content incorrectly rejected. Figure 3 shows system performance by outcome category across all seven evaluation dimensions.

Overall, CODE-GEN performed strongly. Five of the seven dimensions achieved human-validated success rates of 92% or higher. Concept alignment exhibited the highest success rate (98.6%), with only 0.3% failure. This exceptional performance validates that the RAG-based agentic design enables CODE-GEN to produce highly targeted questions.

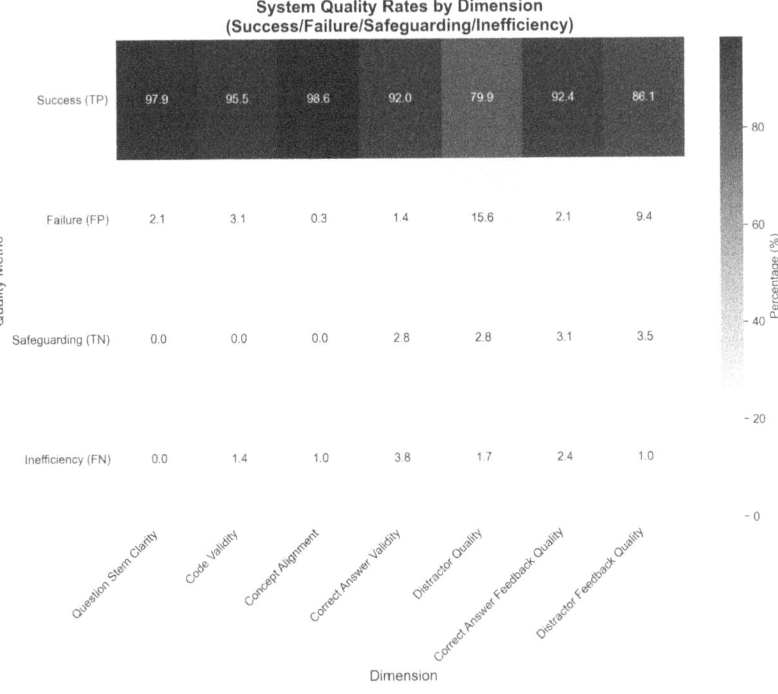

Fig. 3. System quality by evaluation dimension.

The other dimensions grounded in explicit criteria and tool-augmented verification, including question stem clarity, code validity, correct answer validity, and correct answer feedback quality, consistently achieved high success rates. In contrast, dimensions that require nuanced pedagogical judgment achieved comparatively lower success rates. Distractor quality yielded the lowest success rate (79.9%) and the highest failure rate (15.6%), while distractor feedback quality showed a success rate of 86.1% with a comparatively elevated failure rate (9.4%). These findings reinforce the continued need for human oversight in evaluating whether distractors effectively target common misconceptions and whether feedback adequately elaborates on underlying concepts.

3.2 System-Level Limitation Analysis Results

To better understand the limitations of CODE-GEN, we analyzed qualitative feedback from SMEs in the FP and FN cases. FP cases predominantly reflected limitations in pedagogical judgment rather than technical correctness. In the distractor quality dimension, the Generator often produced distractors that were syntactically valid and superficially plausible but failed to target common misconceptions. SMEs consistently noted that higher-quality distractors would better reflect known novice confusions. For example, when the Validator approved low-quality distractors, one SME critiqued: *"These distractors are obviously wrong. Better examples include pop('Leprechaun'), remove(4), and remove(3). They reflect students' common confusion with whether to use index position or values in .pop() vs. .remove() and miscount the index position by 1."* Similarly, FP cases in feedback-related dimensions showed that the Validator approved explanations that correctly described surface-level mechanics but lacked deeper pedagogical elaboration. For example, when the Validator approved low-quality feedback, an SME noted: *"The feedback didn't explain the given while loop reiterates after printing 'stop' because it reaches the end of the current iteration."*

FN cases exposed structural weaknesses in the Validator's reasoning process. A common pattern involved misinterpretation of answer schemas, where the Validator correctly analyzed the code output but confused the answer value with the option position. For example, when the correct answer was 2, the Validator correctly derived 2 but identified the 2nd option as marked correct even though the 1st option was the designated correct answer. An SME noted *"The marked answer is the value 2 (option 1), not option 2 (value 3)."* Another recurring issue was internal inconsistency, in which the Validator's detailed textual analysis affirmed alignment or correctness while its final binary classification indicated the opposite. For example, the Validator's analysis explicitly affirmed concept alignment yet generated negative classifications. An SME commented, *"The question aligns with the concept as stated above, but the final evaluation shows disagreement, which doesn't make any sense."*

3.3 Discussion

The empirical results show that CODE-GEN achieves strong human-validated success on dimensions grounded in explicit criteria and computational verification, with success rates ranging from 79.9% to 98.6%. In particular, the RAG pipeline played a central role in ensuring alignment between generated questions and course-specific learning objectives, as reflected in the exceptionally high concept alignment success rate. The agentic separation between generation and validation enabled systematic, dimension-level quality control, while tool augmentation substantially improved reliability on technically grounded dimensions, such as code validity, correct-answer validity, and correct-answer feedback quality. However, the analysis of human-AI disagreement cases shows automated validation was prone to approving technically correct but instructionally shallow items, underscoring the need for human oversight on pedagogically sensitive dimensions such as distractor design and feedback quality. Taken together, these findings offer evidence-based design guidelines for AI-assisted educational content generation: AI can provide scalable first-line quality control while human experts remain essential for ensuring pedagogical depth and overall instructional quality.

4   Limitations and Future Work

While this study focused on introductory Python, the underlying architecture, including the dual-agent workflow, RAG-based retrieval, and a dimension-level evaluation framework, is domain-agnostic. Future work can extend CODE-GEN to other domains by adapting domain-specific components such as the chunking strategy and tool augmentation. Another important future direction is iterative refinement. CODE-GEN currently uses single-pass generation by design, as iterative refinement requires confidence in the Validator's reliability, which this study was designed to establish. The findings now provide an empirical basis for future selective iterative refinement.

Acknowledgments. We gratefully acknowledge the six subject matter experts whose rigorous evaluations provided the empirical foundation for this research.

Disclosure of Interests. The authors have no competing interests to declare that are relevant to the content of this article.

References

1. Barros, J., Moraes, L.O., Oliveira, F., Delgado, C.A.D.M.: Large language models generating feedback for students of introductory programming courses. In: Cristea, A.I., Walker, E., Lu, Y., Santos, O.C., Isotani, S. (eds.) Artificial Intelligence in Education, vol. 15878, pp. 421–433. Springer Nature Switzerland, Cham (2025). https://doi.org/10.1007/978-3-031-98417-4_30
2. Butler, A.C.: Multiple-choice testing in education: are the best practices for assessment also good for learning? J. Appl. Res. Mem. Cogn. **7**(3), 323–331 (2018). https://doi.org/10.1016/j.jarmac.2018.07.002
3. Doughty, J., et al.: A Comparative Study of AI-Generated (GPT-4) and Human-crafted MCQs in Programming Education. In: Proceedings of the 26th Australasian Computing Education Conference. pp. 114–123. ACM, Sydney NSW Australia (Jan 2024). https://doi.org/10.1145/3636243.3636256

4. Dutulescu, A., Ruseti, S., Iorga, D., Dascalu, M., McNamara, D.S.: YMCQ: reasoning-enhanced MCQ generation. In: Cristea, A.I., Walker, E., Lu, Y., Santos, O.C., Isotani, S. (eds.) Artificial Intelligence in Education, vol. 15882, pp. 308–315. Springer Nature Switzerland, Cham (2025). https://doi.org/10.1007/978-3-031-98465-5_39

5. Gierl, M.J., Bulut, O., Guo, Q., Zhang, X.: Developing, analyzing, and using distractors for multiple-choice tests in education: a comprehensive review. Rev. Educ. Res. **87**(6), 1082–1116 (2017). https://doi.org/10.3102/0034654317726529

6. Haladyna, T.M., Downing, S.M., Rodriguez, M.C.: A review of multiple-choice item-writing guidelines for classroom assessment. Appl. Measur. Educ. **15**(3), 309–333 (Jul 2002)

7. Hoq, M., et al.: Facilitating Instructors-LLM Collaboration for Problem Design in Introductory Programming Classrooms (May 2025). https://doi.org/10.48550/arXiv.2504.01259

8. Kasneci, E., et al.: ChatGPT for good? On opportunities and challenges of large language models for education. Learn. Individ. Differ. **103**, 102274 (Apr 2023). https://doi.org/10.1016/j.lindif.2023.102274

9. Kostopoulos, G., Gkamas, V., Rigou, M., Kotsiantis, S.: Agentic AI in education: state of the art and future directions. IEEE Access **13**, 177467–177491 (2025). https://doi.org/10.1109/ACCESS.2025.3620473

10. Kurdi, G., Leo, J., Parsia, B., Sattler, U., Al-Emari, S.: A systematic review of automatic question generation for educational purposes. Int. J. Artif. Intell. Educ. **30**(1), 121–204 (2019). https://doi.org/10.1007/s40593-019-00186-y

11. Lin, X., et al.: LLM-based Agents Suffer from Hallucinations: A Survey of Taxonomy, Methods, and Directions (2025). https://doi.org/10.48550/ARXIV.2509.18970

12. Lyu, W., Wang, Y., Chung, T.R., Sun, Y., Zhang, Y.: Evaluating the effectiveness of LLMs in introductory computer science education: a semester-long field study. In: Proceedings of the Eleventh ACM Conference on Learning @ Scale, pp. 63–74. ACM, Atlanta (Jul 2024). https://doi.org/10.1145/3657604.3662036

13. Masterman, T., Besen, S., Sawtell, M., Chao, A.: The Landscape of Emerging AI Agent Architectures for Reasoning, Planning, and Tool Calling: A Survey (2024). https://doi.org/10.48550/ARXIV.2404.11584

14. Memarian, B., Doleck, T.: ChatGPT in education: methods, potentials, and limitations. Comput. Hum. Behav. Artifi. Hum. **1**(2), 100022 (2023). https://doi.org/10.1016/j.chbah.2023.100022

15. Scaria, N., Chenna, S.D., Subramani, D.: Automated Educational Question Generation at Different Bloom's Skill Levels using Large Language Models: Strategies and Evaluation (2024). https://doi.org/10.48550/ARXIV.2408.04394

16. Stureborg, R., Alikaniotis, D., Suhara, Y.: Large Language Models are Inconsistent and Biased Evaluators (2024). https://doi.org/10.48550/ARXIV.2405.01724

17. Towns, M.H.: Guide To developing high-quality, reliable, and valid multiple-choice assessments. J. Chem. Educ. **91**(9), 1426–1431 (2014). https://doi.org/10.1021/ed500076x

18. Yuksel, K.A., Sawaf, H.: A Multi-AI Agent System for Autonomous Optimization of Agentic AI Solutions via Iterative Refinement and LLM-Driven Feedback Loops (Dec 2024). https://doi.org/10.48550/arXiv.2412.17149

Content-Grounded Learning Behavior Analysis for Contextualized Feedback

Atsushi Shimada$^{(\boxtimes)}$, Yuma Miyazaki, and Saiki Hirotaka

Kyushu University, Fukuoka, Japan
`atsushi@ait.kyushu-u.ac.jp`

Abstract. Fine-grained learning behavior analysis based on interaction logs enables detailed investigation of students' study strategies, but the resulting representations are often difficult for educators to interpret. This study proposes a content-grounded learning behavior analysis framework that generates contextualized feedback by grounding behavior differences in instructional content. Learning behaviors are analyzed independently, while instructional pages are grouped into semantically coherent content clusters that serve as explanatory contexts, and a large language model (LLM) is used solely as an explanation layer to transform fixed analysis results into human-readable feedback. The framework is evaluated using learning logs and lecture materials from real-world university courses through a within-subject user study. Results show that feedback integrating analytical evidence with explanatory descriptions is perceived as more understandable and useful than feedback presenting either component alone.

Keywords: Learning Analytics · Learning Behavior Analysis · Explanation · Instructional Content · Large Language Models

1 Introduction

Digital learning materials generate detailed interaction logs that capture students' learning behaviors and have been widely used in learning analytics (LA) for tasks such as performance prediction, behavioral clustering, and recommendation [1,8,14]. Recent studies have adopted fine-grained representations of learning behavior that capture action sequences and temporal patterns, enabling more expressive analysis of learners' study strategies [6]. However, while these representations improve analytical fidelity, they are often difficult for educators to interpret directly.

The key challenge is therefore not the detection of learning behavior differences, but the explanation of such differences in a form that is meaningful and actionable for educators. In particular, when behavior analysis relies on distributed representations, additional contextual grounding is required to clarify where and in relation to which instructional content these differences emerge.

E. G. Blanchard et al. (Eds.): AIED 2026, LNAI 16583, pp. 93–102, 2027.
https://doi.org/10.1007/978-3-032-29760-0_11

To address this challenge, this study proposes a content-grounded learning behavior analysis framework that uses instructional content as an explicit explanatory context. Learning behaviors are analyzed independently, and a large language model (LLM) is employed solely as an explanation layer to transform fixed analytical results into human-readable feedback.

The contributions of this study are threefold. First, we present a framework that grounds fine-grained learning behavior analysis in instructional content, enabling behavior differences to be examined in context. Second, we demonstrate how group-level differences in learning behavior patterns can be summarized within instructional contexts. Third, we show that constraining an LLM as an explanation layer improves the interpretability and perceived usefulness of learning analytics feedback.

2   Related Work

Digital learning logs have been widely used for analyzing student behaviors, predicting academic performance, and clustering learners [1,7,8]. Traditional approaches rely on aggregated features such as interaction frequency and total study time [1,8,14], which are easy to interpret but fail to capture fine-grained temporal and sequential patterns. Recent work has therefore explored representation learning methods, including embedding-based approaches [4] and entropy-based weighting schemes [10]. E2Vec further encodes action sequences and temporal relationships into distributed representations, enabling more detailed behavior analysis [6]. However, these representations are often difficult for educators to interpret directly.

Instructional content has been incorporated into learning analytics primarily to improve prediction and recommendation performance. Embedding-based and hybrid approaches integrating content features with learner interactions have been shown to improve accuracy in educational settings [2,5]. While effective for modeling performance, these approaches do not explicitly use content as an explanatory context. This limitation becomes critical when behavioral differences are represented in high-dimensional latent spaces and require contextual grounding for interpretation.

Large language models (LLMs) have recently been applied to generate explanations and feedback in educational settings. Prior studies have shown that LLM-generated feedback can support teachers' understanding of student performance and engagement patterns [3,9,11,12], while also raising concerns about transparency and reliability [13]. When applied directly to raw data or complex analytical outputs, LLMs may function as opaque black boxes. This motivates approaches that constrain LLMs to act as explanation layers, separating analytical computation from natural language generation to improve interpretability.

3   Proposed Method

This study proposes a content-grounded learning behavior analysis framework for generating interpretable and contextualized feedback from student

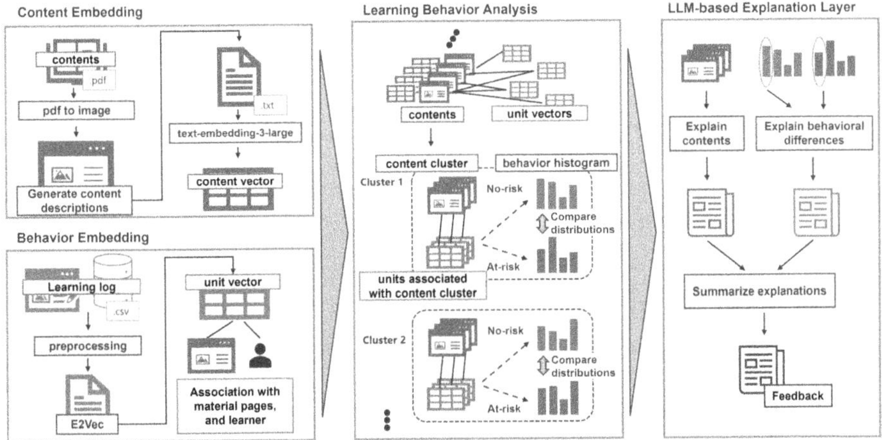

Fig. 1. Overview of the proposed framework.

interaction logs. The key idea is to use instructional content as an explicit explanatory context for organizing and interpreting learning behavior differences.

Figure 1 illustrates the overall framework. Learning behaviors are analyzed independently using distributed representations, while instructional content is represented at the page level and grouped into semantically coherent content clusters. These two representations are linked via page indices recorded in the logs, enabling learning behavior differences to be grounded in instructional context and translated into contextualized feedback.

3.1 Problem Definition and Design Rationale

Fine-grained learning behavior analysis based on interaction logs enables detailed investigation of learners' study strategies, but the resulting representations are often difficult for educators to interpret directly. In particular, distributed representations capture complex temporal and sequential patterns, making analytical outcomes less transparent without additional context.

The key challenge addressed in this study is therefore not the detection of learning behavior differences, but the explanation of such differences in a form that is meaningful and actionable for educators. Specifically, it is necessary to clarify where and in relation to which instructional content these differences emerge. To address this challenge, the proposed framework treats instructional content as an explicit explanatory context. Learning behavior analysis is conducted independently in the behavior representation space, and the resulting differences are subsequently grounded in instructional context by associating interaction units with the pages they reference.

Importantly, learning behavior representations and content representations are not merged into a shared vector space. Their association is established solely via page indices recorded in the interaction logs, preserving a clear analytical structure while supporting interpretability.

3.2 Representing Instructional Content as Context

In the proposed framework, instructional content is represented as an explicit context for organizing and explaining learning behavior differences. Each lecture slide is converted into a semantic representation by first generating a textual description using a large language model (LLM), and then embedding the description into a fixed-dimensional vector space. This process captures both textual and visual information contained in the instructional materials.

The resulting page-level representations are used to measure semantic similarity among instructional pages. Hierarchical clustering is then applied to group pages into semantically coherent content clusters. In this study, these clusters correspond to instructional themes, defined as local topical or conceptual units within the lecture materials derived from content embeddings rather than predefined pedagogical categories.

Importantly, content representations are used solely for organizing instructional context and are not incorporated into learning behavior representations. This separation enables behavior analysis to remain independent while allowing results to be interpreted within meaningful instructional contexts.

3.3 Learning Behavior Analysis with E2Vec

Learning behavior analysis in the proposed framework is conducted independently of instructional content, using distributed representations learned from student interaction logs. Interaction logs are represented as short sequences of learner actions that capture both temporal and sequential patterns. These sequences are segmented into units, each corresponding to a fine-grained learning behavior pattern. Each unit is mapped to a distributed representation using E2Vec, which encodes similarities in action sequences into a continuous vector space. As a result, behavior patterns with similar temporal and structural characteristics are located close to each other in the embedding space.

To compare learning behaviors between No-risk and At-risk students, unit-level embeddings are aggregated into histogram-based representations using a codebook of representative behavior patterns. This Bag-of-Words-style representation summarizes the distribution of fine-grained learning behaviors within each group. While this representation enables detailed comparison of behavior patterns, the resulting distributions are not directly interpretable for educators, motivating the need for contextualized explanation.

3.4 Grounding Behavior Analysis in Content Context

The proposed framework grounds learning behavior analysis results in instructional content by associating behavior units with the related pages. Each behavior unit retains the indices of the instructional pages involved in the corresponding learner actions. Using these page indices, units are linked to instructional pages, which have been grouped into semantically coherent content clusters.

Each content cluster represents an instructional context, such as a specific topic or conceptual unit, and serves as the basis for interpreting learning behavior differences. For each cluster, associated behavior units are collected and aggregated into histogram-based representations for No-risk and At-risk student groups. These histograms capture the distribution of learning behavior patterns within each instructional context.

To quantify differences between the two groups, the Chi-square distance is computed between their histograms for each content cluster. This allows behavioral differences to be analyzed in relation to where they occur within the instructional materials, rather than only in the abstract behavior space.

3.5 Generating Contextualized Feedback with LLMs

A large language model (LLM) is used solely as an explanation layer that transforms fixed analysis results into human-readable text. In this study, GPT-4o is employed for generating feedback, while all analytical results remain unchanged.

The LLM takes as input (1) a summary of the instructional content for each content cluster, (2) a description of learning behavior differences between No-risk and At-risk student groups derived from histogram-based representations, and (3) a specification of the intended audience (educators). Based on these inputs, the LLM generates feedback that contextualizes behavioral differences in relation to the corresponding instructional content.

4 Experiments

4.1 Experimental Setting

Learning logs and lecture materials from two university courses (A-2022 and D-2022) were used for evaluation. Course A is an exercise-oriented programming course (52 students, 197,389 logs), while Course D is a lecture-oriented course (93 students, 282,478 logs). Students were categorized into No-risk and At-risk groups based on final grades (A-2022: 23 vs. 29; D-2022: 60 vs. 33). Historical logs from 2020 (129 students, 396,351 logs) were used only to train E2Vec and were excluded from evaluation.

Based on identical underlying analysis results, three feedback presentation methods were prepared: (1) Baseline A (analytical results only), (2) Baseline B (explanatory descriptions only), and (3) the proposed method (integration of analytical results and explanations). Across all methods, the analytical results were identical, and only the presentation format differed. All feedback was generated at the level of content clusters obtained by grouping pages based on semantic similarity.

A within-subject user study was conducted with 47 participants, each evaluating all three methods across four evaluation sets. The participants were volunteer students with prior experience using information tools and web-based systems. The sets were selected from the two courses, including content clusters with the largest behavioral differences between No-risk and At-risk students (A-max and D-max in Table 2). For each set, five criteria were rated on a five-point Likert scale: understandability, convincingness, information amount, reliability, and usefulness for instructors.

Table 1. Quantitative evaluation results (mean ± SD) for the three feedback presentation methods.

Criterion	Baseline A	Baseline B	Proposed
Understandability	2.09 ± 0.93	4.49 ± 0.75	3.43 ± 1.21
Convincingness	2.51 ± 1.06	3.34 ± 1.29	3.79 ± 1.06
Information amount	3.11 ± 1.17	2.23 ± 0.81	3.91 ± 0.83
Reliability	3.36 ± 0.74	2.91 ± 1.19	3.64 ± 0.87
Usefulness for instructors	3.09 ± 1.10	3.36 ± 1.15	3.64 ± 0.94

Table 2. Friedman test results for each evaluation set (five criteria). A-max and D-max denote the content clusters with the largest behavioral distances in Course A and Course D, respectively.

Set	Criterion	χ^2	df	p-value	Kendall's W
A-max	Understandability	60.40	2	$< .001$	0.64
	Convincingness	25.32	2	$< .001$	0.27
	Information amount	52.33	2	$< .001$	0.56
	Reliability	13.58	2	.001	0.14
	Usefulness for instructors	6.25	2	.044	0.07
D-max	Understandability	59.27	2	$< .001$	0.63
	Convincingness	23.53	2	$< .001$	0.25
	Information amount	55.94	2	$< .001$	0.60
	Reliability	31.39	2	$< .001$	0.33
	Usefulness for instructors	15.46	2	$< .001$	0.16

4.2   Quantitative Results

Table 1 reports the mean scores and standard deviations for each feedback presentation method across the five evaluation criteria.

Friedman tests revealed significant differences among the three methods across all criteria and evaluation sets ($p < .05$; Table 2), with large effect sizes for understandability and information amount and smaller effects for reliability and usefulness.

Post-hoc Wilcoxon tests with Holm correction showed that the proposed method significantly outperformed Baseline A across all criteria, and also outperformed Baseline B for understandability, information amount, and reliability, while differences in usefulness were not consistent.

For the information amount criterion, the proposed method produced scores closer to the midpoint, indicating a more balanced perception.

Table 3. Example of feedback generated by the proposed method.

Content context

This feedback corresponds to a content cluster related to *program design methods*, focusing on recursive data processing and conditional function definitions. The materials emphasize systematic program construction through purpose statements, examples, definitions, and testing.

Observed behavioral differences

No-risk students frequently revisited pages and intermittently opened and closed materials (e.g., repeated O/C and P operations), often with short to medium time intervals. Their action sequences were relatively shorter and interspersed, indicating careful confirmation of content. In contrast, At-risk students exhibited longer action sequences dominated by consecutive next-page operations (N), reflecting rapid skimming with limited revisiting behavior.

Interpretation

The observed behaviors suggest that No-risk students tended to review program structure and logic incrementally, which aligns with the conceptual demands of program design involving recursion and conditional branching. At-risk students appeared to prioritize speed and coverage over depth, potentially leading to superficial engagement with complex design concepts.

4.3   Qualitative Results

This subsection reports qualitative findings derived from open-ended questionnaire responses, focusing on how users perceived differences among the three feedback presentation methods.

Baseline A, which presented analytical results without explanatory descriptions, was commonly perceived as information-rich but difficult to interpret. Participants noted that although behavioral differences between No-risk and At-risk students were observable, understanding their educational implications required substantial effort and prior knowledge.

Baseline B, which provided explanatory descriptions without underlying analytical evidence, was generally regarded as easy to read. However, participants frequently raised concerns regarding transparency and credibility, noting that explanations could be perceived as subjective or insufficiently grounded in data.

In contrast, the proposed method was often described as both understandable and convincing. As illustrated in Table 3, participants appreciated that explanations were explicitly linked to concrete behavioral patterns and instructional content, which reduced cognitive effort and supported more confident interpretation of learning analytics results.

Overall, the qualitative results indicate that while the baseline methods exhibited trade-offs between interpretability and credibility, the proposed method was perceived as achieving a better balance by integrating analytical evidence with explanatory descriptions.

4.4   Discussion

The results indicate that the perceived usefulness of learning analytics feedback is strongly influenced by its presentation format. In particular, feedback that integrates analytical evidence with explanatory descriptions was perceived as more understandable and useful than feedback presenting either component alone.

A key implication is that interpretability and credibility should not be treated as competing objectives. Rather than prioritizing either raw analytical transparency or narrative simplicity, explicitly linking explanations to observable behavioral patterns enables users to interpret results with both clarity and confidence. This evidenceexplanation integration appears to reduce cognitive burden while preserving access to the analytical basis of the feedback.

The findings also highlight potential limitations of explanation-only feedback. When explanatory statements are presented without visible analytical evidence, some participants interpreted them as implying causal relationships between learning behaviors and performance. By contrast, the proposed method mitigates this risk by grounding explanations in observable behavioral patterns and instructional context, supporting interpretation without asserting causality.

Another implication concerns the unit of feedback. Organizing feedback at the level of content clusters, rather than individual pages or global summaries, allowed users to relate behavioral differences to coherent instructional topics. This content-level framing supports interpretation without requiring detailed knowledge of underlying representations.

Several limitations should be noted. The evaluation focused on participants' perceptions rather than actual instructional impact, and was conducted on a limited set of courses and content clusters. In addition, qualitative responses suggest that the amount and structure of explanatory text may influence usability.

Future work should investigate the effects of such feedback on instructional decision-making and learning outcomes, as well as explore adaptive presentation strategies that balance detail, readability, and transparency.

5 Conclusion

This study proposed a content-grounded learning behavior analysis framework for generating contextualized feedback from student interaction logs. By grounding behavior differences in instructional content and using LLMs as explanation layers, the approach improves the interpretability of learning analytics results.

Experimental results showed that feedback integrating analytical evidence with explanatory descriptions was perceived as more understandable and useful than feedback presenting either component alone.

Acknowledgments. This work was supported by JST CREST Grant Number JPMJCR22D1 and JSPS KAKENHI Grant Number JP22H00551, Japan.

References

1. Chen, C.H., Yang, S.J., Weng, J.X., Ogata, H., Su, C.Y.: Predicting at-risk university students based on their e-book reading behaviours by using machine learning classifiers. Australas. J. Educ. Technol. **37**(4), 130–144 (2021)
2. Haque, M.A., Rahman, M.M., Islam, M.R.: Contextual course clustering: Bert-enhanced text analytics for personalized education. Inter. J. Intell. Syst. Appli. Eng. **12**(4) (2024)
3. Jia, Q., et al.: Llm-generated feedback in real classes and beyond: perspectives from students and instructors. In: Proceedings of the 17th International Conference on Educational Data Mining, pp. 862–867 (2024)
4. Kogishi, S., Minematsu, T., Shimada, A., Kawashima, H.: Predicting student scores using browsing data and content information of learning materials. In: The 24th International Conference on Artificial Intelligence in Education (AIED2023), vol. 2, pp. 555–560 (2023)
5. Li, X., Henriksson, A., Duneld, M., Nouri, J., Wu, Y.: Evaluating embeddings from pre-trained language models and knowledge graphs for educational content recommendation. Future Internet **16**(1) (2024)
6. Miyazaki, Y., Švábenský, V., Taniguchi, Y., Okubo, F., Minematsu, T., Shimada, A.: E2vec: feature embedding with temporal information for analyzing student actions in e-book systems. In: Proceedings of the 17th International Conference on Educational Data Mining, pp. 434–442 (2024)
7. Murata, R., Okubo, F., Minematsu, T., Taniguchi, Y., Shimada, A.: Recurrent neural network-fitnets: improving early prediction of student performance by time-series knowledge distillation. J. Educ. Comput. Res. **61**(3), 639–670 (2023)
8. Okubo, F., Yamashita, T., Shimada, A., Konomi, S.: Students' performance prediction using data of multiple courses by recurrent neural network. In: Proceedings of the 25th International Conference on Computers in Education, ICCE 2017, pp. 439–444. Asia-Pacific Society for Computers in Education (2017)

9. Pinargote, A., Calderón, E., Cevallos, K., Carrillo, G., Chiluiza, K., Echeverria, V.: Automating data narratives in learning analytics dashboards using genai. In: 2024 Joint of International Conference on Learning Analytics and Knowledge Workshops, pp. 150–161 (2024)
10. Qiu, F., et al.: E-learning performance prediction: mining the feature space of effective learning behavior. Entropy **24**(5) (2022)
11. Ruwe, T., Mayweg-Paus, E.: Embracing llm feedback: the role of feedback providers and provider information for feedback effectiveness. Frontiers in Education **9** (2024)
12. Tang, X., Wong, S., Huynh, M., He, Z., Yang, Y., Chen, Y.: Sphere: scaling personalized feedback in programming classrooms with structured review of llm outputs (2024)
13. Xu, H., Gan, W., Qi, Z., Wu, J., Yu, P.S.: Large language models for education: a survey (2024)
14. Yin, C., et al.: Exploring the relationships between reading behavior patterns and learning outcomes based on log data from e-books: A human factor approach. Inter. J. Hum.-Comput. Interact. **35**(4–5), 313–322 (2019)

Evaluating a Data-Driven Redesign Process for Intelligent Tutoring Systems

Qianru Lyu[1], Conrad Borchers[1]([✉]), Meng Xia[2], Karen Xiao[3], Paulo F. Carvalho[1], Kenneth R. Koedinger[1], and Vincent Aleven[1]

[1] Carnegie Mellon University, Pittsburgh, PA, USA
{qlyu,cborcher,pcarvalh,krk,aleven}@cs.cmu.edu
[2] Texas A&M University, College Station, TX, USA
mengxia@tamu.edu
[3] Wellesley College, Wellesley, MA, USA
kx100@wellesley.edu

Abstract. Past research has defined a general process for the data-driven redesign of educational technologies and has shown that in carefully-selected instances, this process can help make systems more effective. In the current work, we test the generality of the approach by applying it to four units of a middle-school mathematics intelligent tutoring system that were selected not based on suitability for redesign, as in previous work, but on topic. We tested whether the redesigned system was more effective than the original in a classroom study with 123 students. Although the learning gains did not differ between the conditions, students who used the Redesigned Tutor had more productive time-on-task, a larger number of skills practiced, and greater total knowledge mastery. The findings highlight the promise of data-driven redesign even when applied to instructional units *not* selected as likely to yield improvement, as evidence of the generality and wide applicability of the method.

Keywords: Data-driven redesign · Intelligent tutoring systems · K-12

1 Introduction and Related Work

Iterative, data-driven redesign promises to improve AIED systems but is not widespread [10,11]. Even carefully designed instructional systems are rarely optimal at first deployment [11]. Data-driven redesign uses data from prior use to inform targeted revisions, which has been shown to lead to improvement of educational technologies [3,15]. Intelligent tutoring systems (ITS) are particularly well-suited to this approach because they generate rich log data.

Although many data mining methods improve the prediction of student performance, few drive interventions with measurable effects on learners [6]. Prior

Q. Lyu and C. Borchers—Equal contribution.

E. G. Blanchard et al. (Eds.): AIED 2026, LNAI 16583, pp. 103–112, 2027.
https://doi.org/10.1007/978-3-032-29760-0_12

research has created a redesign strategy, focused on the refinement of knowledge component (KC) models, that has repeatedly yielded benefits in past studies [10,11,13]. A KC model decomposes a domain into fine-grained skills. KC models can guide instructional design in many ways, including the design of problem sets (i.e., practice items), the design of scaffolding within problems, tracking knowledge growth for mastery learning [16]. Many core functions of an ITS depend on an accurate KC model. Structuring instruction around a well-specified KC model can substantially improve learning by aligning practice with the cognitive operations required for problem solving [17]. However, KC models often contain deficiencies that undermine their effectiveness when used in instruction. Prior work has shown that student performance data can be used to diagnose deficiencies in KC models and guide systematic redesign [2,13]. These works provided "close-the-loop" evidence linking data-driven KC refinement to pedagogical effectiveness, a connection we extend in the present study. Additional close-the-loop studies reporting learning improvements from data-driven redesign include [12,15], as well as related syntheses and applied redesign efforts [11,17].

Building on this work, Huang et al. [10] introduced the General Multi-method Approach to Data-Driven Redesign, which integrates KC model refinement, instructional redesign, and optimization of individualized learning. The approach addresses misallocated practice across KCs, insufficient scaffolding for hard KCs identified by persistently high learning curves, and recurring errors. It combines newly proposed methods, such as Difficulty Factors Effect Analysis (to identify difficulty factors), with established techniques from educational data mining, many supported by DataShop [18]. A central strategy in Huang et al. [10] was focused practice, which directs additional practice to difficult KCs while avoiding redundant practice on easier or untargeted skills. In a one-month high school classroom study, the Redesigned Tutor produced significantly higher learning outcomes than the original while reducing both over- and underpractice [10].

Despite these promising results, evidence for the generality of these approaches is limited. The redesign process proposed by Huang et al. [10] has been evaluated on a narrow range of middle-school mathematics content, leaving open whether it reliably improves learning when applied to new instructional units. Assessing generality requires applying the process across additional content areas and instructional contexts. Moreover, prior evaluations have focused largely on aggregate learning gains, providing limited insight into how redesign affects students' learning processes during practice. To address these gaps, the present study applies the data-driven redesign process to multiple new instructional units and evaluates both learning outcomes and practice efficiency at the process level. Three questions are explored in this study:

RQ1: How does Huang et al. [10]'s redesign process, applied to an ITS for middle-school mathematics, reveal tutor limitations and help generate redesign ideas? **RQ2:** How does the Redesigned Tutor affect students' learning *outcome*, compared to the Original Tutor? **RQ3:** How does the Redesigned Tutor affect students' learning *process*, compared to the Original Tutor?

We examined a redesign of MathTutor, an ITS shown to effectively support middle-school mathematics learning [4]. MathTutor implements the core ITS features described above. We redesigned four of its 65 problem sets: graph interpretation, plotting, and two equation-solving units. These units have also undergone multiple rounds of refinement based on classroom use and teacher feedback, though not through data-driven redesign. Hence, they constitute a strong test case for evaluating the potential impact of a systematic redesign process.

2   Data-Driven Redesign Process (RQ1)

We used existing log data from four MathTutor units (including 103 students, 22,529 transactions; 50.19 practice hours) for the data-driven redesign of these units. We followed a three-step data-driven redesign process [10]. Table 1 summarizes how the three redesign goals were instantiated across units. First, we examined learning curves in DataShop [18] to identify ill-specified KCs or KCs ineffectively supported and redefined the KC model. Candidate KC models were evaluated by whether they exhibited gradual learning, reflected in smooth learning curves and good AFM fit [15]. Applying this step yielded different results in each unit; see Table 1. In Unit 7.05 (Graph Interpretation), some problems required students to infer coordinates between labeled grid points, yet the tutor treated these as simple lookup tasks; learning-curve analysis, therefore, revealed an unmodeled interpolation skill, motivating KC splitting for inferring coordinates with and without interpolation and adding two skills. In Unit 7.06, model comparison did not support refinement. For equation solving, operations involving negative terms (e.g., subtracting -3 or interpreting "-x" as "-1x") are more difficult for students, but were previously modeled as equivalent to positive cases; separating these sign-handling skills [16] improved fit and parsimony (AIC).

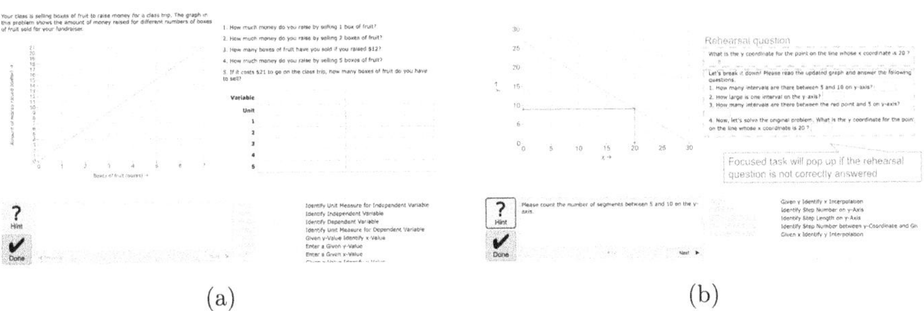

(a)   (b)

Fig. 1. Original (left) and redesigned (right) Unit 7.05 Graph Interpretation tutor. The redesigned version begins with an interpolation rehearsal and conditionally reveals focused tasks when the rehearsal is answered incorrectly.

Second, we redesigned the tutor units to better scaffold and practice challenging or newly identified KCs with changes to the problem types, scaffolding, and problem selection algorithm (Table 1). We designed new tasks for targeted practice of difficult KCs ("focused part tasks" [10]) that isolate a KC for efficient practice and dynamically replace whole tasks when mastery is lacking, reducing overpractice. For example, in Unit 7.05, we created new tasks that scaffold the reasoning steps needed for interpolating when reading a point off of a graph (see Fig. 1). All redesigns were implemented in CTAT [1].

Third, we implemented an adaptive problem selection algorithm [10], which prioritizes unmastered KCs, reduces redundant practice on mastered skills, and allocates practice more efficiently. Offline simulation was conducted to check under-practice and over-practice of specific KCs. As a result, we added problems to the equation-solving unit to ensure sufficient practice for newly split KCs, including negative subtraction, negative division, and division with "-x." We also enabled *Mastered Step Skipping* [19], which automatically completes remaining steps once all relevant KCs are estimated as mastered at a 95% threshold. With this mechanism, the student would only need to reduce more advanced equations (e.g., those involving variables on both sides or composite terms in parentheses) to a form that was already familiar (e.g., two-step equations), without having to solve that familiar form, thus avoiding over-practice.

Table 1. Unit-specific realization of redesign goals.

Goal	Unit 7.05	Unit 7.06	Equation Solving I, II
Goal 1: Discoveries made in data	Identified a hidden interpolation skill; split graph-reading KCs based on AFM evidence.	The *draw-a-line* KC remained highly difficult; no KC refinement supported.	Separated sign-handling cases (positive, negative, and $-x$), building on Long et al. [16].
Goal 2: Tutor redesign	Added focused interpolation tasks; revised wording; improved graph clarity and scaffolding.	Relaxed step-order constraints; refined hints; added focused graphing tasks with pre-filled tables.	Updated hints and scaffolds to align with refined KCs; added adaptive step support.
Goal 3: Adaptive support	Adaptive problem selection following Huang et al. [9].	Adaptive problem selection following Huang et al. [9].	Adaptive problem selection [9], mastered step skipping [19].

3   Classroom Evaluation (RQ2 & RQ3)

3.1   Participants and Procedure

A total of 123 students from 5 middle schools in the U.S. participated in the study. The sample spanned 8 classes from grades 7 and 8, taught by six different teachers. The study was conducted during students' regularly scheduled mathematics periods and followed an approved IRB protocol. All data from the study are available in DataShop (datasets #5868 and #6283) [18]. The study design and primary analyses were preregistered prior to data analysis (https://osf.io/xh584/).

The study followed a randomized within-subjects crossover design with two tutor conditions and pre-, mid-, and post-tests to measure learning gains (Fig. 2). Students completed a pre-test on Day 1, practiced with a tutor on Days 2–4, took a mid-test on Day 5, practiced again on Days 6–8, and completed a post-test on Day 9. During the first practice phase, students were randomly assigned to either the Original or Redesigned Tutor; after the mid-test, the groups switched conditions. Each practice session lasted approximately 20–25 min. Two isomorphic test forms (A and B) and test order were counterbalanced across conditions, with about 20 min allotted per test. All tutoring features, including hints, feedback, and skill bars, were disabled during testing.

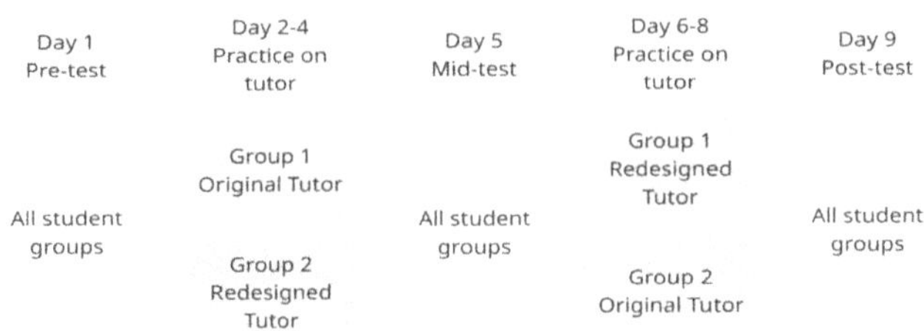

Fig. 2. Experimental design. The crossover happened between Days 4 and 6.

3.2   Data Analysis

Learning Gains (RQ2). To examine whether the Redesigned Tutor affected learning gains (post minus pre) relative to the Original Tutor (RQ2), we analyzed pre–post test performance using a linear mixed-effects model. The model included fixed effects of *condition* (Original vs. Redesigned), *test time* (Pre vs. Post), and their interaction (the differential gain by condition). Random intercepts for student, school, and content unit accounted for the hierarchical structure of the data. Students missing either pre- or post-test scores were excluded (final $N = 95$). Model diagnostics indicated model assumptions were tenable. All mixed-model tests were conducted with the `lmerTest` package in R [14].

Learning Processes and Within-Tutor Learning (RQ3). To address RQ3, we analyzed log data to compare student practice behavior across the two tutor versions. Time-on-task was computed by subtracting idle periods, defined as more than two minutes of inactivity following [8], from total logged-in time, yielding a measure of active engagement. To estimate within-tutor learning, we derived end-of-practice knowledge using two complementary approaches. First, we fit an Additive Factors Model (AFM) that predicts step correctness based on prior practice opportunities on each KC [5]. Using the fitted model, we estimated each student's knowledge at their final opportunity per KC and aggregated these estimates into total and average mastery measures. This approach was replicated using the tutor's Bayesian Knowledge Tracing (BKT) estimates. To avoid confounding, this analysis was conducted with the refined KC model applied to both conditions. All process analyses are reported as exploratory, as the preregistered analysis focused on test-score learning gains. Exploratory linear mixed-models adjusted for repeated measures across students, though we also confirmed the robustness of results after additionally adjusting for class periods.

3.3   Results: Effect on Students' Learning Gains (RQ2)

The main effect of test time was significant, indicating substantial pre-to-post learning gains across conditions ($t(279) = 6.14$, $p < .001$). Both conditions exhibited comparable improvements: students using the Original Tutor increased from $M = 0.41$ ($SD = 0.34$) to $M = 0.63$ ($SD = 0.34$), corresponding to a mean gain of 0.21 ($SD = 0.38$, $d = 0.57$), while students using the Redesigned Tutor improved from $M = 0.39$ ($SD = 0.33$) to $M = 0.59$ ($SD = 0.36$), yielding a mean gain of 0.20 ($SD = 0.31$, $d = 0.64$). Learning gains did not differ significantly by condition ($t(279) = -0.30$, $p = .760$), nor by unit or their interaction ($ps > .20$).

3.4   Results: Effect on Students' Learning Processes (RQ3)

Manipulation Checks. Our theory of change predicts that the Redesigned Tutor reallocates practice toward previously hidden, split KCs. It further predicts greater overall difficulty due to prioritizing harder KCs [9]. To test these predictions, we extended the AFM with a condition effect. Practice was significantly more difficult in the Redesigned condition ($\beta = -0.10$, $p = .020$). A linear mixed-effects model of practice opportunities showed that students in the Redesigned condition received more opportunities overall ($\beta = 0.30$, $p < .001$). Although new KCs received fewer opportunities than established KCs ($\beta = -0.74$, $p < .001$), the Redesigned condition allocated relatively more practice to them ($\beta = 0.23$, $p = .041$). There was no reliable evidence that the redesign reduced overpractice beyond 80% mastery, as neither the main effect ($\beta = 0.16$, $p = .080$) nor the interaction with KC type ($\beta = 0.28$, $p = .083$) reached significance.

Time-on-Task. Students in the Redesigned Tutor, despite equivalent session durations, spent more time logged into the ITS ($M = 47.7$, $SD = 25.7$) than those in the Original Tutor ($M = 39.3$, $SD = 27.0$), $t(235) = 2.44$, $p = .015$. They also engaged in more active, non-idle time ($M = 38.9$, $SD = 21.8$) compared to the Original Tutor ($M = 31.6$, $SD = 20.4$), $t(234) = 4.62$, $p < .001$. Idle time was comparable across conditions (Redesigned: $M = 8.80$, $SD = 17.5$; Original: $M = 7.70$, $SD = 15.8$), with no significant difference, $t(234) = 0.46$,

$p = .650$, indicating that increased logged-in time reflects greater productive engagement.

Productivity and Unit-Level Differences. Next, we compared productivity between conditions, measured as the number of completed problem steps. In a mixed-effects model predicting the number of completed steps, the main effect of condition was not significant ($\beta = -2.73$, $p = .699$). However, exploratory analyses revealed a significant condition-by-unit interaction such that in Unit 7.06 (Graphs and Equations), where students in the Redesigned Tutor completed more steps than those in the Original Tutor ($\beta = 37.76$, $p = .001$) (but not in other units). In this unit, differences were most pronounced in logged-in time: relative to the Original Tutor, the Redesigned Tutor showed a 28% increase in Unit 7.06, compared to a 16% increase in Unit 7.05, a 4% decrease in Unit 1 Equations, and an 18% increase in Unit 2 Equations.

Knowledge Mastered. Based on iAFM estimates, students mastered more knowledge in the Redesigned condition (M = 7.61, SD = 2.88) than in the Original condition (M = 6.03, SD = 2.26), $t(115) = 4.33$, $p < .001$, $d_p = 0.40$. A similar pattern was observed using BKT-based estimates (Redesigned: M = 8.96, SD = 3.44; Original: M = 7.30, SD = 2.53), $t(115) = 3.67$, $p < .001$, $d_p = 0.34$. Importantly, this increase reflected broader coverage of skills (since the Redesigned condition included five more skills than the Original condition; see Sect. 2). Average KC mastery did not differ significantly between conditions using either AFM (0.683 vs. 0.658, $t(115) = 1.11$, $p = .270$) or BKT estimates (0.687 vs. 0.672, $t(115) = 0.48$, $p = .630$).

4   Discussion

Data from instructional technology often inspires how to improve it. We tested the generality of the data-driven instructional redesign process by Huang et al. [10]. Our study examined whether the application of the framework could yield interesting discoveries and redesigns, and ultimately improve student learning in four problem sets of an ITS for middle-school mathematics.

The Redesigned Tutor changed students' learning processes by increasing time-on-task and total knowledge mastered. Although the average mastery level per skill was comparable between conditions, students in the redesigned condition practiced five additional skills within the same class time. This increase can be attributed to greater amounts of completed steps. This was especially evident in Unit 7.06, where reduced complexity likely decreased idle time. The adaptive problem selection algorithm distributed practice across KCs, especially new KCs [10,19]. Students also were logged in longer in the redesigned condition, consistent with prior evidence of variability in classroom time use [7]. These differences may reflect motivational factors, a question for future work.

These results are consistent with the idea that making difficult or implicit KCs explicit and supporting them with targeted practice improves learning efficiency [10,13,15]. Compared to past work on "focused practice" approaches, our redesign contributes positive evidence for novel scalable mechanisms such as fast-forwarding over mastered steps [19] and the use of partially completed problems and part tasks, as in Unit 7.06. However, limited classroom time and variable student engagement likely constrained downstream learning gains.

This study provides further evidence that data-driven redesign, following Huang et al. [10] and centered on KC model refinement, can improve learning outcomes. We applied this approach flexibly across units, adapting to data-driven issues: algebra units emphasized skill splitting and KC refinement, whereas Unit 7.06 focused on task design and interface scaffolding to improve efficiency. This flexibility aligns with prior work highlighting the importance of domain-specific redesign, including KC modeling [13] and curricular structure [17].

Unlike prior work [10, 13, 15], we observed no significant differences in learning gains between the Original and Redesigned tutor, despite differences in estimated mastery. One explanation is limited post-test coverage of newly introduced skills, including the absence of interpolation items for Unit 7.05, which constrains our ability to detect gains. A second, likely factor is limited practice time. Students completed only six 20-minute sessions across four units, substantially less exposure than in prior studies [10]. Accordingly, students in both conditions failed to reach mastery on average: AFM estimates remained below 70%. These results suggest that the benefits of the redesign were limited by insufficient practice.

4.1   Limitations, Future Work, and Outlook

Although the redesign process was highly iterative, students had limited opportunities to reach mastery. Longer practice periods and improved methods for estimating time to mastery are therefore needed, potentially by incorporating indicators of disengagement and struggle into simulations. Although this study extends data-driven redesign to a broader set of content, it remains close to prior mathematics and STEM domains [10, 13, 15, 17], prompting domain extensions.

In closing, data-driven redesign aims to optimize educational technologies, yet its implementation and evaluation remain challenging. We examined a data-driven redesign of a middle-school mathematics ITS grounded in KC model refinement and focused practice. Results show that such refinements can improve productive engagement and expand opportunities for skill practice and mastery, while revealing challenges in ensuring sufficient practice allocation to satisfy mastery criteria. These findings illustrate the promise of data-driven redesign and the need for continued refinement to support instructional technologies.

Acknowledgments. This research was funded by the Institute of Education Sciences (IES) of the U.S. Department of Education (Award #R305A220386).

References

1. Aleven, V., et al.: An integrated platform for studying learning with intelligent tutoring systems: CTAT+TutorShop. arXiv preprint arXiv:2502.10395 (2025)
2. Aleven, V., McLaughlin, E.A., Glenn, R.A., Koedinger, K.R.: Instruction based on adaptive learning technologies. Handbook Res. Learn. Instruct. **3**, 477–518 (2025)
3. Bakharia, A., et al.: A conceptual framework linking learning design with learning analytics. In: Proceedings of the Sixth International Conference on Learning Analytics & Knowledge, pp. 329–338. ACM (2016)
4. Borchers, C., Carvalho, P.F., Xia, M., Liu, P., Koedinger, K.R., Aleven, V.: What makes problem-solving practice effective? comparing paper and ai tutoring. In: European Conference on Technology Enhanced Learning, pp. 44–59. Springer (2023). https://doi.org/10.1007/978-3-031-42682-7_4
5. Cen, H., Koedinger, K., Junker, B.: Learning factors analysis – a general method for cognitive model evaluation and improvement. In: Ikeda, M., Ashley, K.D., Chan, T.-W. (eds.) ITS 2006. LNCS, vol. 4053, pp. 164–175. Springer, Heidelberg (2006). https://doi.org/10.1007/11774303_17
6. Clow, D.: The learning analytics cycle. In: Proceedings of the 2nd International Conference on Learning Analytics and Knowledge, pp. 134–138. ACM (2012)
7. Gurung, A., et al.: Starting seatwork earlier as a valid measure of student engagement. In: 18th International Conference on Educational Data Mining, pp. 303–316 (2025)
8. Holstein, K., McLaren, B.M., Aleven, V.: Student learning benefits of a mixed-reality teacher awareness tool in ai-enhanced classrooms. In: Penstein Rosé, C., et al. (eds.) AIED 2018. LNCS (LNAI), vol. 10947, pp. 154–168. Springer, Cham (2018). https://doi.org/10.1007/978-3-319-93843-1_12
9. Huang, Y., Brusilovsky, P., Guerra, J., Koedinger, K., Schunn, C.: Supporting skill integration in an intelligent tutoring system for code tracing. J. Comput. Assist. Learn. **39**(2), 477–500 (2023)
10. Huang, Y., et al.: A general multi-method approach to data-driven redesign of tutoring systems. In: LAK21: 11th International Learning Analytics and Knowledge Conference, pp. 161–172 (2021)
11. Koedinger, K.R., Brunskill, E., Baker, R.S.J.d., McLaughlin, E.A., Stamper, J.: New potentials for data-driven intelligent tutoring system development and optimization. AI Mag. **34**(3), 27–41 (2013)
12. Koedinger, K.R., McLaughlin, E.A.: Closing the loop with quantitative cognitive task analysis. Inter. Educ. Data Mining Soc. (2016)
13. Koedinger, K.R., Stamper, J.C., McLaughlin, E.A., Nixon, T.: Using data-driven discovery of better student models to improve student learning. In: Lane, H.C., Yacef, K., Mostow, J., Pavlik, P. (eds.) AIED 2013. LNCS (LNAI), vol. 7926, pp. 421–430. Springer, Heidelberg (2013). https://doi.org/10.1007/978-3-642-39112-5_43
14. Kuznetsova, A., Brockhoff, P.B., Christensen, R.H.: lmertest package: tests in linear mixed effects models. J. Stat. Softw. **82**, 1–26 (2017)
15. Liu, R., Koedinger, K.R.: Going beyond better data prediction to create explanatory models of educational data. In: Handbook of Learning Analytics, pp. 69–76. SoLAR (2017)
16. Long, Y., Holstein, K., Aleven, V.: What exactly do students learn when they practice equation solving? refining knowledge components with the additive factors model. In: Proceedings of the 8th International Conference on Learning Analytics and Knowledge, pp. 399–408 (2018)

17. Lovett, M., Meyer, O., Thille, C.: The open learning initiative: measuring the effectiveness of the oli statistics course in accelerating student learning. J. Interact. Media Educ. **2008**(1), 13 (2008)
18. Stamper, J.C., Koedinger, K.R.: Human-machine student model discovery and improvement using datashop. In: Biswas, G., Bull, S., Kay, J., Mitrovic, A. (eds.) AIED 2011. LNCS (LNAI), vol. 6738, pp. 353–360. Springer, Heidelberg (2011). https://doi.org/10.1007/978-3-642-21869-9_46
19. Xia, M., Schmucker, R., Borchers, C., Aleven, V.: Optimizing mastery learning by fast-forwarding over-practice steps. In: European Conference on Technology Enhanced Learning, pp. 549–563. Springer (2025). https://doi.org/10.1007/978-3-032-03870-8_3

Time-Window ONA: Model the Impact of Utterances in Ordered Network Analysis

Wangda Zhu[1]([✉]) [iD], Guang Chen[1] [iD], and Yin Yang[2] [iD]

[1] School of Design, The Hong Kong Polytechnic University, Hong Kong SAR, China
wangda.zhu@polyu.edu.hk
[2] Department of Mathematics and Information Technology, The Education University of Hong Kong, Hong Kong SAR, China

Abstract. In collaborative learning dialogues, Ordered Network Analysis (ONA) effectively models the epistemic patterns of learners but relies on fixed windows or a single shared decay function, implicitly assuming that all prior utterances lose influence at the same rate. In this paper, we propose a time-window ONA to model the heterogeneity of utterances influence regarding different learners. In this approach, the influence of each utterance is represented using a binary window function with learner-specific parameters, estimated through grid search within a one-vs-rest classification framework based on low-dimensional network projections. To validate the proposed method, we analyzed dialogue data from 26 university students, each interacting with five AI pedagogical roles, i.e., Tutor, Teaching Assistant, Peer, Excellent Student, and Struggling Student, in a human-AI collaborative learning setting. Dialogue utterances were coded using the 5E Instructional Model (Engage, Explore, Explain, Elaborate, Evaluate), and the time-window ONA was applied to examine how utterance impacts varied across AI roles. Results revealed distinct cross-role patterns: the Excellent Student condition was most distinctive, exhibiting a large AI window size and an explain-centered structure; Teaching Assistant and Peer roles showed asymmetric learner-AI window patterns, whereas Tutor and Struggling Student conditions were weakly separable. Overall, time-window ONA provides a method for capturing learner-specific variations in utterance influence and offers an empirical foundation for the design of AI pedagogical roles in collaborative learning environments.

Keywords: Ordered Network Analysis · Learner Roles · Time Window · Utterance Impact Modelling

1 Introduction

In collaborative learning settings, learners may differ in how quickly the influence of prior utterances fades over time within their subsequent discourse. Understanding such learner-specific influential patterns is important because they reflect how individuals sustain, integrate, or shift attention and ideas over time. Capturing these temporal dynamics provides deeper insight into the mechanisms of knowledge construction and coordination in collaborative learning environments, enabling more precise modeling of epistemic

© The Author(s), under exclusive license to Springer Nature Switzerland AG 2027
E. G. Blanchard et al. (Eds.): AIED 2026, LNAI 16583, pp. 113–121, 2027.
https://doi.org/10.1007/978-3-032-29760-0_13

patterns and more informed design of learning environments. However, existing state-dependent learning models (e.g., Epistemic Network Analysis (ENA) [11], Ordered Network Analysis (ONA) [13] and lag sequential analysis (LSA) [1]) typically rely on fixed windows or a single, shared decay function. These models implicitly assume that all previous utterances lose their influence at the same rate over time, making it difficult to account for learner-specific differences in time effects.

Transmodal Analysis (TMA) offers a more flexible framework by replacing fixed windows with a Time Influence (TI) function. However, in current implementations, TI is still determined by expert specification. As a result, it remains unclear whether TI varies by conversational role, and whether learner-specific TI can be learned in a data-driven way.

To address this gap, we propose a time-window ONA (TW-ONA) approach that estimates learner-specific TI functions for each learner role in collaborative learning dialogues. We employ a binary window function and use grid search for parameter estimation and model selection. This method helps us to answer research questions such as:

RQ1: How do time influence patterns (window parameters) differ across learners in collaborative learning environments?

RQ2: How do epistemic network structures differ under time-window ONA?

We applied the TW-ONA to a dataset of mathematical modeling collaborative learning environments with five AI roles. We found cross-role differences in TI functions, accompanied by clear differences in network connectivity patterns. We discuss the implications of this method that offers a computable, empirical basis for designing AI pedagogical roles.

2   Background

State-dependent models of learning, including LSA [1], ENA [11], and ONA [13], have been widely used to model dependencies among events during learning. A common design choice in these models is a fixed window (e.g., the last seven utterances) to define event weighting [1, 11, 13]. This choice implicitly assumes that the influence of all prior utterances functions in the same way [12]. In multi-learner contexts, this assumption is particularly questionable. Instructions from a tutor, explanations from a peer, and demonstrations from an excellent student can all be treated as utterances in dialogue, but they differ in influence and scaffolding functions [4, 14]. These differences plausibly lead to distinct time influence profiles on students' subsequent modeling behaviors: some utterances may persist longer in their influence, while others may be quickly overwritten by subsequent utterances.

Moving beyond fixed windows, Shaffer et al. [12] recently introduced Transmodal Analysis (TMA), which replaces the fixed window assumption with a set of influence functions, including TI, Learner Influence (LI), and Horizon (H). The central claim of TMA is that different event types, learner populations, and environmental structures should be associated with different influence functions, better reflecting the heterogeneity and dynamics of real learning processes.

In existing TMA applications, however, TI is still often derived from empirical influence-derivation procedures or specified a priori, and parameters are typically shared globally (e.g., using the same θ for all instances of an event type). While LI is conceptually available to capture group differences, there has been limited work treating conversational role identity as a key moderator of TI, and little empirical work identifying learner-specific window parameters automatically via optimization.

Our study advances that direction by proposing time-window ONA, which integrates TMA's time influence framework into ONA using single-modality dialogue coding data (the 5E Instructional framework [2]). We parameterize TI in a role-aware manner and estimate learner-specific window parameters via grid search. This enables direct comparison and interpretation of time persistence across roles, which is consistent with TMA's theoretical motivation but has not yet been fully realized in prior empirical work. To investigate optimal AI scaffolding in education, we designed five distinct AI roles to model distinct forms of instructional, peer, and cognitive support commonly observed in mathematics classrooms and collaborative learning contexts [9, 15, 17]. Drawing on research in scaffolding, social regulation of learning [7], each role embodies a different pedagogical stance and level of epistemic agency.

3 Methods

3.1 Dataset

We collected chat logs from 26 university students (Mean age $= 22.3$) who participated in a within-subjects randomized controlled trial. Each participant collaborated with five AI pedagogical roles (Tutor, Teaching Assistant (TA), Peer, Excellent Student, and Struggling Student) across five mathematical modeling tasks. All interactions were recorded and coded by two researchers using the 5E Instructional Model [2]. Each utterance was binary-coded (1/0) for the presence of each dimension, with discrepancies resolved through consensus. The resulting coded sequences formed the input for our TW-ONA (as shown in Table 1).

Each participant completed five 4-min mathematical modeling tasks, collaborating with a different AI role in each round (total interaction time ≈ 20 min per participant). After excluding corrupted data, 126 experimental dialogue sessions were analyzed. In total, these sessions yielded 1302 utterances. The mean number of utterances per session was 10.33 (SD $= 5.47$). The short interaction duration (4 min per task) captures initial interaction patterns under controlled conditions; longer-term dynamics remain for future work.

3.2 Time-Window ONA

We implemented TW-ONA using the *tma* package and *ona* packages in R. To capture heterogeneous time persistence across speakers, we parameterized the TMA time window as a speaker-conditional function. Let Δt denote the distance in utterance intervals between a focal utterance and a candidate historical utterance within the accumulation window defined by TMA contexts. In this study, TI refers to how the impact of prior utterances decays over time, and the TW is its binary instantiation, where utterances

Table 1. Sample data table: learner interaction with an AI pedagogical role (Tutor)

Dialogue ID	Utterance	Speaker	Engage	Explore	Explain	Elaborate	Evaluate
1	**How to view this issue?**	**Learner**	**1**	**1**	**0**	**0**	**0**
1	**Shall we start from the perspective of friction?**	**AI**	**1**	**1**	**0**	**0**	**0**
1	**I think friction is related to mass**	**Learner**	**0**	**1**	**1**	**0**	**0**
1	**You're absolutely right. Sliding friction is actually related to the coefficient of friction. What do you think now?**	**AI**	**1**	**1**	**0**	**1**	**1**
1	$f = \mu mg$	**Learner**	**1**	**1**	**0**	**0**	**0**
1	**Great, you've grasped the core of this issue**	**AI**	**0**	**0**	**0**	**0**	**1**

within a window are assigned full influence. Each historical utterance received a weight:

$$w(\Delta t | W) = \begin{cases} 1 \ \textit{if } \Delta t \leq W \\ 0 \ \textit{otherwise} \end{cases}$$

Utterances produced by the learner were weighted with $W_{learner}$, while utterances produced by the AI pedagogical role were weighted with W_{AI}. Larger W values correspond to longer TI.

Optimization Objective: The goal of parameter optimization is to find window parameters $(W_{learner}, W_{AI})$ such that the resulting network representation maximally differentiates a target pedagogical role from others. We operationalized this goal through a two-level optimization framework.

Inner Level: Logistic Regression for Role Discrimination. For a fixed role r ∈ roles, we defined a binary classification task with label:

$$y = \mathbb{I}(\textit{AI Role} = r),$$

and trained a logistic regression classifier using the two low-dimensional network projections as predictors:

$$Pr(y = 1) = \text{logit}^{-1}(\beta_0 + \beta_1 \text{SVD1} + \beta_2 \text{SVD2}).$$

The parameters $\beta = (\beta_0, \beta_1, \beta_2)$ were estimated by maximum likelihood, minimizing the negative log-likelihood:

$$\mathcal{L}(\beta) = -\sum_{i=1}^{N}\left[y_i \log \hat{p}_i + (1 - y_i) \log(1 - \hat{p}_i)\right]$$

where $\hat{p}_i$ is the predicted probability for observation i.

Outer Level: Grid Search for Time Windows. While the inner-level logistic regression finds the best linear classifier for a given network representation, the quality of that representation depends on the window parameters used in accumulation. To quantify representation quality, we used McFadden-style pseudo-R^2 [10] as the objective function:

$$R^2 = 1 - \frac{\log L_{full}}{\log L_{null}},$$

where L_{full} is the likelihood of the logistic model with SVD1 and SVD2, and L_{null} is the likelihood of an intercept-only model. Higher R^2 indicates that the network projections explain more variance in role membership, meaning the window parameters produce a representation that better separates the target role from others.

For each role r, we used Grid search [8] to solve:

$$\left(W_{learner}^{(r)}, W_{AI}^{(r)}\right) = \underset{W_{learner}, W_{AI} \in [1,10]}{\arg \max} \; R^2(W_{learner}, W_{AI}; r).$$

The search space consisted of all integer combinations within the range, yielding 100 candidate parameter pairs per role. Using the best parameters, we rebuilt the final TW-ONA model for that role and computed the final pseudo-R^2 and AIC. Given the small sample size, the grid search may introduce overfitting. We mitigate this by constraining the parameter space and using low-dimensional projections. Importantly, our goal is comparative structural analysis rather than predictive generalization.

3.3 TW-ONA Visualization Design

To ensure interpretability and consistency, our visualizations follow core ONA [13] conventions with targeted extensions to highlight TI effects. Node size indicates how often a code appears as a "response." The colored dot at the node center indicates the strength of self-connections. Directed edges are rendered as triangles: the base points to the "response," and the apex originates from the "ground." Edge thickness and saturation represent connection strength. We additionally report contrast (difference) networks. In these plots, edge color indicates the direction of the difference in edge weights: red indicates edges with higher weights in the target role, while blue indicates edges with higher weights in the remaining roles.

4 Results

After running a one-vs-rest test for each role condition (Table 2 and Fig. 1), roles exhibited varying degrees of separability based on interaction structures. Excellent Student was the most distinct from the other roles ($R^2 = 0.594$, AIC $= 58.13$). Its best settings were $W_{learner} = 1$ and $W_{AI} = 10$, suggesting that the AI maintains a long-range TI, while the learner responds based on the most recent context. TA was the second most separable ($R^2 = 0.366$, AIC $= 81.93$) and showed asymmetric learner–AI window patterns ($W_{learner} = 1$, $W_{AI} = 6$): the AI side retained longer-term structure, while the learner side was more driven by the most recent utterances. Peer was moderately separable ($R^2 = 0.172$, AIC $= 112.18$) but showed the opposite asymmetric pattern ($W_{learner} = 10$, $W_{AI} = 1$), meaning the longer-range structure came more from the learner, while the AI responses were more short-term. Struggling Student was only weakly separable ($R^2 = 0.115$, AIC $= 117.09$; $W_{learner} = 1$, $W_{AI} = 6$). Tutor was the hardest to separate ($R^2 = 0.028$, AIC $= 130.74$; $W_{learner} = 2$, $W_{AI} = 1$), suggesting that with our current codes, Tutor was weakly separable and look structurally similar to the other roles. Overall, Excellent Student and TA showed the clearest structural patterns, while Tutor largely overlapped with the rest.

Table 2. Learner-Specific window parameters and classification performance

Role Condition	$W_{learner}$	W_{AI}	R^2	AIC
Tutor	2	1	0.0276	130.74
TA	1	6	0.3659	81.93
Peer	10	1	0.1724	112.18
Struggling Student	1	6	0.1151	117.09
Excellent Student	1	10	0.5936	58.13

In the contrast networks (Fig. 2), red edges indicate stronger code co-occurrence in the target role, whereas blue edges indicate stronger co-occurrence in the remaining roles. Excellent Student showed the clearest signature ($R^2 = 0.594$), with an Explain-centered structure featuring stronger links to Elaborate/Evaluate, shifting away from an Engage-Explore pattern dominant in other roles. TA was also distinguishable ($R^2 = 0.366$), with relatively stronger Engage-Explore coupling compared to others. Peer showed a weaker but consistent tendency toward Engage-Explore ($R^2 = 0.172$). In contrast, Struggling Student ($R^2 = 0.115$) and Tutor ($R^2 = 0.028$) exhibited largely overlapping structures with the remaining roles.

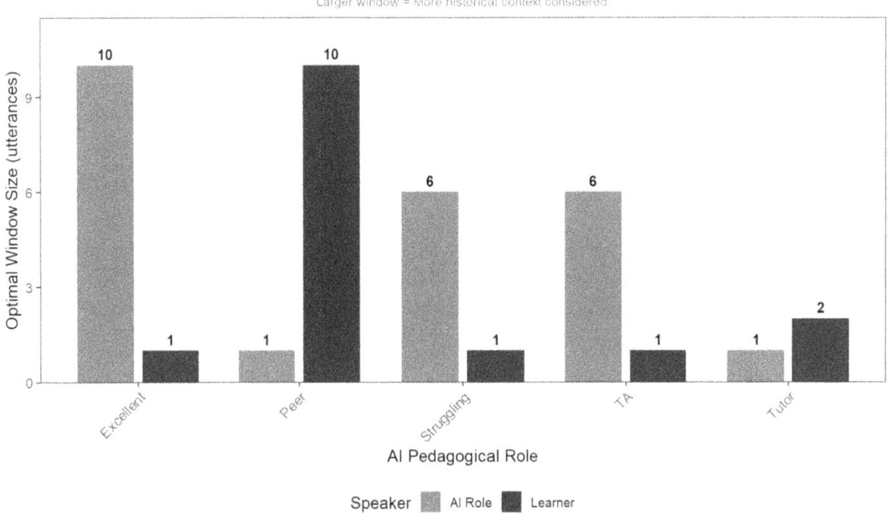

Fig. 1. Five role conditions' time window parameters.

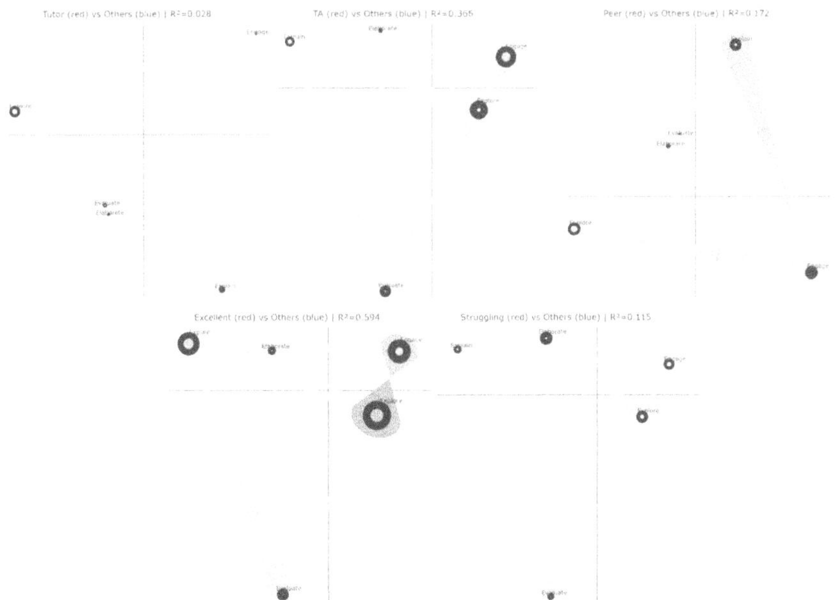

Fig. 2. Contrast Networks and Learner-Specific Structural Signatures

5 Discussion

This study examined whether learner-AI conversations with different role prompts exhibit distinct interaction structures, using TW-ONA networks over five discourse codes (Engage, Explore, Explain, Elaborate, Evaluate) and learner-specific window parameters. Overall, the results suggest that Excellent Student and TA roles produce clear and distinctive structural signatures, while Tutor and Struggling Student overlap substantially with the rest.

We interpret the window parameter W as a proxy for the time-scale preference that different AI pedagogical roles and students have for organizing dialogue: larger W reflects "continuously binding earlier concepts with the current utterance," thereby supporting conceptual integration and consistency modeling across turns; smaller W reflects "progressing closely aligned with the most recent turn," being more sensitive to local responsiveness, immediate error correction, or contextual reaction.

Within this framework, the smaller W for the learner and the larger W for the AI ($W_{learner}$, W_{AI}) in the Excellent Student condition corroborates its network structure where Explain is central and more strongly connected to Elaborate and Evaluate. This suggests that the role may provide stronger explanatory chains and reasoning continuity over a longer span. This aligns with arguments in the learning sciences emphasizing that explanation facilitates deep processing and knowledge integration [3, 16, 18].

The TA and Peer conditions show a different kind of role effect: an asymmetric time window pattern between learner and AI. TA is relatively separable and is best fit by $W_{learner}$ low and W_{AI} high, implying that the structural signal is driven more by the AI maintaining longer-range organization, while learner utterances contribute more locally. A plausible interaction-level reading is that, under a TA framing, the AI may take responsibility for keeping the thread of reasoning coherent across utterances, while learners respond to the most recent prompt or question. In contrast, Peer shows the opposite pattern ($W_{learner}$ high and W_{AI} low) and a stronger Engage-Explore tendency, suggesting that learners may carry more of the longer-range coherence in peer-like conversations, while the AI responds more immediately and collaboratively in the moment. The asymmetric time window patterns in the TA and Peer conditions resonate with work on peer tutoring and collaborative dialogue, where tutors or more knowledgeable partners often take primary responsibility for structuring explanations and maintaining coherence, while tutees contribute more local, reactive turns [5, 6].

Finally, Struggling Student and especially Tutor are weakly separable. This likely means that, with our current 5E Instructional Model, these conditions do not produce a stable interaction structure that consistently differs from the rest. One possibility is that the relevant differences are expressed less through broad discourse functions and more through finer-grained behaviors (e.g., types of feedback, scaffolding moves, repair, affective support) [5], which would not be visible in the present network.

Overall, TW-ONA provides a method for capturing learner-specific variations in temporal influence of utterances and offers an empirical foundation for the design of AI pedagogical roles in collaborative learning environments. Finally, the identified optimal time windows are data-driven and maximize statistical separability, but do not necessarily reflect theoretically optimal or pedagogically meaningful temporal scales.

References

1. Bakeman, R., Quera, V.: Sequential Analysis and Observational Methods for the Behavioral Sciences. Cambridge University Press (2011)
2. Bybee, R.W., et al.: The BSCS 5E instructional model: origins and effectiveness. Colorado Springs, Co BSCS **5**, 88–98 (2006)
3. Chi, M.T., De Leeuw, N., Chiu, M.H., LaVancher, C.: Eliciting self-explanations improves understanding. Cogn. Sci. **18**(3), 439–477 (1994)
4. Dillenbourg, P.: What do you mean by collaborative learning?. In: Collaborative-Learning: Cognitive and Computational Approaches, pp. 1–19 (1999)
5. Duran, D.: Cooperative interactions in peer tutoring: patterns and sequences in paired writing. Middle Grades Res. J. **5**(1), 47–60 (2010)
6. Flores, M., Ribosa, J., Duran, D.: How does peer tutoring contribute to the development of reading comprehension? Evidence from ten years of practice. Revista de Psicodidáctica (English ed.) **29**(2), 176–184 (2024)
7. Järvelä, S., Hadwin, A.F.: New frontiers: regulating learning in CSCL. Educ. Psychologist **48**(1), 25–39 (2013)
8. Liashchynskyi, P.: Grid Search, Random Search, Genetic Algorithm: A Big Comparison for NAS. arXiv preprint arXiv:1912.06059 (2019)
9. Malik, R., Abdi, D., Wang, R., Demszky, D.: Scaffolding middle school mathematics curricula with large language models. Br. J. Edu. Technol. **56**(3), 999–1027 (2025)
10. McFadden, D.: The measurement of urban travel demand. J. Public Econ. **3**(4), 303–328 (1974)
11. Shaffer, D.W., Collier, W., Ruis, A.R.: A tutorial on epistemic network analysis: analyzing the structure of connections in cognitive, social, and interaction data. J. Learn. Anal. **3**(3), 9–45 (2016)
12. Shaffer, D.W., Wang, Y., Ruis, A.: Transmodal analysis. J. Learn. Anal. **12**(1), 271–292 (2025)
13. Tan, Y., Ruis, A.R., Marquart, C., Cai, Z., Knowles, M.A., Shaffer, D.W.: Ordered network analysis. In: International Conference on Quantitative Ethnography, pp. 101–116. Springer Nature, Cham, Switzerland (2022)
14. Wood, D., Bruner, J.S., Ross, G.: The role of tutoring in problem solving. J. Child Psychol. Psychiatry **17**(2), 89–100 (1976)
15. Yavuz, S., Tekin, A.: Investigation of the use of AI as a scaffolding tool during mathematical discussion in geometry problem-solving. In: Proceedings of the Fourteenth Congress of the European Society for Research in Mathematics Education (CERME14), no. 19 (2025)
16. Yi, S., Sintawati, W., Zhang, Y.: Facilitating depth of explanation: utilising reflective feedback in collaborative learning environments. J. Comput. Assist. Learn. **41**(2), e70010 (2025)
17. Zhang, F., Gou, J., Shen, K.N., Camarinha-Matos, L.M., Wang, Z.: Effects of AI teammates on learning behavior in human-AI collaboration environments: a perspective on self-regulated learning. Educ. Inf. Technol., 1–25 (2025)
18. Zhu, W., Wang, F., Mayer, R.E., Liu, T.: Effects of explaining a science lesson to others or to oneself: a cognitive neuroscience approach. Learn. Instr. **91**, 101897 (2024)

On Generating and Validating Erroneous Examples in CS1 Using LLMs

Yuxuan Chen[(✉)], Chenyan Zhao, Jacob Levine, Kangyu Feng,
Max Fowler, and Mariana Silva

University of Illinois Urbana-Champaign, Urbana, USA
{yuxuan19,chenyan4,jlevine4,kangyuf2,mfowler5,mfsilva}@illinois.edu

Abstract. Erroneous examples are structured problem examples that intentionally contain mistakes, encouraging learners to identify and correct them as a means of strengthening their conceptual understanding. Constructing effective erroneous examples is challenging as it requires careful planning and a detailed knowledge of common student misconceptions, posing a time burden on educators. In this paper, we present a framework that leverages Large Language Models (LLMs) to automatically generate and validate erroneous examples and explanations tailored for introductory computer science instruction. Additionally, we design a rubric that formalizes key dimensions of erroneous example quality. Using this rubric, we evaluate six state-of-the-art LLMs on the generation task. We then assess the feasibility of automated validation via an LLM-as-a-judge approach using GPT-5, with human ratings serving as the gold standard. Our results indicate that current LLMs are generally capable of producing realistic erroneous examples with coherent explanations, with GPT-5 consistently achieving the strongest performance in terms of error validity and explanation clarity. We find that LLM-based judging can reliably evaluate erroneous examples and their explanations at scale, substantially reducing the need for manual evaluation effort.

Keywords: Erroneous Examples · Large Language Models · Rubrics

1 Introduction

In computer science (CS) education, instructors commonly use worked examples, which are correct solutions presented step by step, to demonstrate problem-solving processes to students [12,18]. Extending this approach, erroneous examples are structured problem examples that intentionally contain mistakes, encouraging learners to identify and correct them as a means of strengthening their conceptual understanding [19]. Previous work has begun exploring the use of Large Language Models (LLMs) to generate buggy programming examples for introductory computer science (CS1) practice [13]. Our work advances this direction by providing, to our knowledge, the first systematic evaluation of

© The Author(s), under exclusive license to Springer Nature Switzerland AG 2027
E. G. Blanchard et al. (Eds.): AIED 2026, LNAI 16583, pp. 122–131, 2027.
https://doi.org/10.1007/978-3-032-29760-0_14

several state-of-the-art LLMs for generating erroneous examples for CS1 instruction. We present in this paper: (i) an LLM-based algorithmic framework for the generation and validation of erroneous examples in CS1, and (ii) a rigorously developed rubric for evaluating the quality of the generated erroneous examples.

2   Related Works

Worked Examples and Erroneous Examples. A worked example presents a step-by-step solution to a problem, allowing learners to focus on understanding the problem-solving process [12,18]. This can reduce cognitive load and can help students more effectively learn and apply common problem-solving strategies within the subject area [9,18,22]. Studies have shown that worked examples can enhance learning outcomes, especially for novice learners [9,18,20].

An erroneous example is a structured problem example that intentionally includes misconceptions for students to identify and correct [19]. Erroneous examples have shown effective across a range of educational domains, such as mathematics [2,5,11] and statistics [7]. Prior research has demonstrated that erroneous examples can foster students' conceptual understanding [2], improve procedural knowledge while reducing misconception [5], and lead to better learning outcomes [11]. Erroneous examples may be beneficial as a reinforcement strategy after core concepts have been established through worked examples [7,15].

Within CS1 education, erroneous examples have been used as a pedagogical strategy to correct common novice misconceptions [1,6]. Ginat et al. [6] showed that engagement with erroneous examples can help reduce students' misconceptions about object-oriented programming. Designing pedagogically useful erroneous examples in CS1 remains challenging, as they must align with specific novice misconceptions instead of arbitrary bugs. CS1 consists of a wide range of misconceptions that vary by programming language and topic, making it difficult to identify and curate appropriate erroneous examples [4,14].

LLMs in CS Education. With the growing capabilities of LLMs, a large body of prior work has explored their use in CS education, including chatbot feedback [8], programming exercise generation [16], and worked example generation [10]. Concurrently, LLMs are being used as automatic evaluators of task outputs, commonly referred to as LLM-as-a-judge [21,23]. This framework allows for scalable and consistent evaluation of large volumes of model outputs, approximating human evaluation when manual judgments are costly.

There is limited research on the use of LLMs specifically for generating pedagogically meaningful erroneous examples. Pădurean et al. [13] proposed BugSpotter, an LLM-based system for generating debugging exercises for students by producing buggy code from problem sets. Given a specific programming problem, BugSpotter prompts an LLM to generate a buggy solution and a corresponding fixed solution, and then performs validation through code execution.

Our work differs in input condition and validation. BugSpotter is problem-conditioned and centers on debugging practice for a specific task, whereas we generate erroneous examples conditioned on high-level CS1 topics. Our framework additionally incorporates an LLM-as-a-judge validator that applies a rigorously refined rubric to assess generated erroneous examples, allowing for scalable quality control. We explore whether LLMs can generate sufficient quality erroneous examples across a broad range of CS1 topics for instructional use.

3   Algorithmic Framework

We propose a two-stage framework: generation of candidate erroneous examples for CS1, and validation of the generated erroneous examples.

Generation. In the generation stage, the instructor provides three primary inputs. First, the instructor specifies a CS1 topic (e.g., for/while loops, functions, exception handling), which constrains the generation process to a particular conceptual area. Second, the instructor specifies the number of erroneous examples to generate for the selected topic. Third, the instructor selects an LLM from a provided set of state-of-the-art models. The selected model then generates syntactically valid Python code snippets that contain intentional conceptual errors aligned with the specified topic. The model is also prompted to produce a natural-language explanation that describes the underlying misconception responsible for the error. Together, the generated code and explanation form an erroneous example–explanation pair. Table 1 shows a representative example pair. Figure 1 presents key components of the full prompt used in this stage.

Table 1. Example output from the framework, consisting of an erroneous Python code snippet and a corresponding explanation describing the misconception.

Code snippet	```python
	#Create a class representing a student and an instance of it
	class Student:
	    def __init__(self, name, age):
	        name = name
	        age = age
	
	student1 = Student("Alice", 20)
	print(student1.name)
	``

Explanation	The constructor does not use 'self' to assign attributes, so 'name' and 'age' are local variables rather than instance attributes. Accessing 'student1.name' will result in an AttributeError.

Validation. In the validation stage, generated erroneous example–explanation pairs are filtered to ensure that they are syntactically valid, exhibit a clear CS1-level conceptual error, and include explanations that accurately describe the underlying misconception. We adopt an LLM-as-a-judge approach, using GPT-5 to evaluate each candidate according to a rubric specifically designed for this task. We describe the rubric and scoring scheme in detail in Sect. 4. Pairs that fail the rubric are discarded and regenerated, enabling more scalable deployment of the system by reducing the need for instructors to manually verify all outputs.

```
system_prompt = f"""You are a helpful CS1 teaching assistant. Always
write Python code suitable for first-semester programming students.
Use simple syntax, clear variable names, and avoid advanced or
abstract features or built-in Python functions. The code should
resemble structured pseudocode in Python format."""

input_prompt = f"""You are given a task to generate
**erroneous Python code** to help students understand common
CS1-level programming mistakes.

You will be provided with:
- [input_topic]: a general topic like loops, functions, classes, etc.

Based on the user's input below, generate {num_examples} different
erroneous Python code snippet(s) that reflect CS1 misconceptions.
......"""
```

Fig. 1. Prompt Template for LLM Generation.

4   Methods

We aim to assess both the generator and the validator in our framework. We conduct a human evaluation of raw generator outputs to establish ground-truth quality labels and characterize generator performance. We then evaluate the validator by measuring its agreement with these human judgments. Our evaluation focuses on two aspects of quality in a CS1 context: (i) **error validity**, the extent to which the LLM-generated examples contain genuine errors, and (ii) **explanation clarity**, how understandable the explanations accompanying the generated erroneous examples are. To ensure consistency in the evaluation process, we designed a rubric (Table 2) to assess the quality of each erroneous example–explanation pair. The rubric was adapted from an evaluation framework proposed by Scaria et al. [17] and modified to reflect the characteristics of erroneous programming examples and their explanations.

The rubric is structured hierarchically, with certain items serving as prerequisites for the evaluation of subsequent items. The "Python Syntax" item (R1) is evaluated on a binary {Yes, No} scale. All subsequent items are evaluated on a ternary {Yes, No, Null} scale. If R1 is rated No, then all subsequent items are assigned Null. Similarly, if R2 is rated No, all items under R3 are assigned Null. All items in R3 are evaluated at the same hierarchical level. A No judgment on any R3 item does not preclude evaluation of the remaining R3 items.

Table 2. Rubric for evaluating LLM-generated erroneous example–explanation pairs. R1 is evaluated on a binary {Yes, No} scale, while subsequent items use a ternary {Yes, No, Null} scale to reflect hierarchical dependencies.

Rubric item	Description
(R1) Python Syntax	Output erroneous example is Python code
(R2) Erroneous	Output erroneous example contains an error based on common CS1-level misconceptions
(R3.1) Topic matching	Output erroneous example contains an error relevant to the provided CS1 programming topic
(R3.2) Explanation understandable	Output explanation text is grammatically correct and logically coherent
(R3.3) Explanation matching erroneous example	Output explanation text accurately describes and aligns with the output erroneous example

We identified seven representative programming topics based on the curriculum of a recently redesigned CS1 course [3]. The topics are variables and data types, lists and dictionaries, for loops and while loops, function definition and return, file input and output, exception handling, and classes. These topics cover foundational concepts commonly taught in CS1.

Across these seven selected topics, six LLMs each generated five erroneous example–explanation pairs, yielding 210 pairs. The evaluated models are GPT-4o, GPT-5, GPT-o4-mini, DeepSeek-V3.1, DeepSeek-R1-0528 (DeepSeek-R1), and Llama-4-Maverick-17B-128E-Instruct-FP8 (Llama-4-Maverick). Five examples per topic were selected as a trade-off between capturing within-model variability and maintaining a feasible human evaluation workload. Each output was generated via the API and independently evaluated by two graduate students with extensive CS1 background, both of whom are authors of this work. In the initial round of independent ratings, the raters agreed on 175 of 210 examples (83.3%), while 35 examples exhibited at least one mismatch across the five rubric items. The raters then met to resolve discrepancies and reach consensus on all rubric judgments. This process produced a consensus-labeled dataset, which we treat as a human-validated gold standard for subsequent analysis.

5   Results

5.1   Evaluation Results

Table 3 summarizes performance across the six evaluated LLMs using the rubric from Table 2. We define model performance of each rubric item as the proportion of outputs rated as Yes for that item. Under our hierarchical rubric, downstream items are labeled Null exactly when a parent item is labeled No. As a result, matching the parent No decisions implies matching the downstream Null labels, making a separate Null-only comparison less informative. Therefore, scores for Erroneous (R2) and the subsequent explanation-related items (R3.1–R3.3) are computed only over valid (non-Null) cases.

Table 3. Performance of erroneous example–explanation pairs on the rubric items across LLMs. Parentheses give the number of evaluated pairs (n). R1 is evaluated on all pairs ($n = 35$), while R2 and R3.1–R3.3 are evaluated only on valid (non-Null) pairs, yielding smaller n when the hierarchy renders an item not applicable.

LLM model	R1	R2	R3.1	R3.2	R3.3
GPT-4o	100% (35)	91.43% (35)	93.75% (32)	100% (32)	81.25% (32)
GPT-5	100% (35)	100% (35)	97.14% (35)	100% (35)	100% (35)
GPT-o4-mini	100% (35)	97.14% (35)	100% (34)	100% (34)	94.12% (34)
DeepSeek-V3.1	100% (35)	68.57% (35)	95.83% (24)	100% (24)	95.83% (24)
DeepSeek-R1	100% (35)	88.57% (35)	100% (31)	100% (31)	96.78% (31)
Llama-4-Maverick	100% (35)	88.57% (35)	87.10% (31)	100% (31)	83.87% (31)

All models consistently produced syntactically valid Python code. They also showed a strong ability to introduce specific errors into otherwise valid code, with five of the six models exceeding 88% on this criterion. For all six models, the generated examples aligned with the intended CS1 programming topics at least 87% of the time. Together, these results provide evidence of **error validity**, suggesting that within the scope of CS1 topics, current LLMs can generate erroneous examples that are syntactically valid and contain genuine errors, even without in-context examples.

All models consistently generated grammatically clear and logically coherent explanations. Most explanations accurately described the corresponding error, with four of the six models ranging above 94%. These results provide evidence of **explanation clarity**, showing that within the scope of CS1 topics, current LLMs generally are capable of producing explanations that are both understandable and well-aligned with the erroneous code they are meant to explain. Among the evaluated models, GPT-5 demonstrated the highest and most consistent performance across items, followed by GPT-o4-mini.

5.2 LLM-Based Validation

To test whether an LLM can serve as a reliable validator, we implemented an LLM judge using GPT-5. The judging prompt encodes the full rubric in Table 2, including hierarchical dependencies (subsequent items are Null when prerequisites fail). We applied this evaluator to all 210 generated example–explanation pairs and compared its outputs against the human gold-standard labels obtained from the consensus evaluation in Sect. 4.

Table 4. Agreement between the LLM judge and human labelers. R1 is evaluated on all pairs ($n = 210$), while R2 and R3.1–R3.3 are evaluated only on valid (non-Null) pairs, yielding smaller n when the hierarchy renders an item not applicable.

Metrics	R1	R2	R3.1	R3.2	R3.3
#TP	210	186	178	186	168
#FP	0	11	5	0	6
#FN	0	1	0	0	4
#TN	0	12	3	0	8
Accuracy	100%	94.29%	97.31%	100%	94.62%
Recall	100%	99.47%	100%	100%	97.67%
Precision	100%	94.42%	97.27%	100%	94.62%

Table 4 reports agreement between GPT-5 judgments and human evaluations for each rubric item. Similarly to Table 3, we report on non-Null cases to measure scoring quality for applicable items. GPT-5 matches human ratings perfectly on "Python Syntax" (R1) and "Explanation understandable" (R3.2). For "Erroneous" (R2) and "Topic Matching" (R3.1), recall is near-perfect (99.47%, 100%) while precision remains high (94.42%, 97.27%). This suggests GPT-5 has occasional over-acceptance of borderline cases. GPT-5 achieves high performance for "Explanation Matching" (R3.3). These results suggest that GPT-5 can function as an effective automated validator under our rubric, enabling the filtering of low-quality candidates and triggering regeneration without human intervention.

6   Discussion and Conclusion

We present, to our knowledge, the first systematic evaluation of state-of-the-art LLMs for generating erroneous examples for CS1 instruction. We also introduce a replicable generation-and-validation framework using a rubric-guided LLM-as-a-judge validator. Across seven representative CS1 topics and six LLMs, our human evaluation shows that current models such as GPT-5 and GPT-o4-mini can consistently produce CS1-topic erroneous examples with error validity and explanation clarity. The LLM judge results suggest that GPT-5 can act as an effective automated validator under our rubric. Near-perfect recall across rubric items suggests it rarely rejects examples that humans deem acceptable. Slightly lower precision on error presence and explanation matching indicates occasional acceptance of borderline cases, which could be addressed through a brief instructor skim of the curated outputs.

In practice, we believe our framework lowers the barrier for instructors to incorporate erroneous examples into CS1 instruction by shifting effort from manual authoring to lightweight selection and adaptation. Instructors can apply erroneous examples in several instructional formats. For in-class or homework activities, instructors can use erroneous code snippets as open-ended response questions, asking students to describe the error and propose a correction with explanations. In discussion-oriented settings (e.g., peer instruction or think–pair–share), instructors can present multiple variants of a topic-level error and ask students to compare diagnoses. Erroneous examples can be adapted as multiple-choice questions where students choose the most accurate reasoning. The generated explanations may help streamline grading and feedback, and can be integrated into both manual and AI-assisted workflows.

Our evaluation rubric captures several core properties of the generated erroneous examples, but it does not yet measure whether an erroneous example is instructionally effective for a particular student population. One missing aspect is error subtlety: an error that is too obvious may yield limited learning value by making diagnosis trivial, whereas an overly subtle error may frustrate novices or increase cognitive load beyond the intended learning objective. A second limitation is that our study focuses on Python programming language, which may limit generalizability to CS1 courses taught in other languages. Finally, our evaluation does not include classroom deployment: we do not yet know how instructors would incorporate these artifacts into their workflows, nor how students would respond to them in authentic learning activities. Future work should (i) extend generation and validation to additional languages, (ii) expand the rubric with explicit pedagogical criteria, and (iii) conduct instructor- and student-centered studies to evaluate usability and learning impact in authentic CS1 settings.

Disclosure of Interests. The authors have no competing interests to declare that are relevant to the content of this article.

References

1. Beege, M., Schneider, S., Nebel, S., Zimm, J., Windisch, S., Rey, G.D.: Learning programming from erroneous worked-examples. Which type of error is beneficial for learning? Learn. Instruct. **75**, 101497 (2021). https://doi.org/10.1016/j.learninstruc.2021.101497
2. Booth, J.L., Lange, K.E., Koedinger, K.R., Newton, K.J.: Using example problems to improve student learning in algebra: differentiating between correct and incorrect examples. Learn. Instr. **25**, 24–34 (2013). https://doi.org/10.1016/j.learninstruc.2012.11.002
3. Chen, Y., Zhao, C., Feng, K., Beckman, M.A., Silva, M.: A complete redesign of CS1 for engineering students. In: 2025 ASEE Annual Conference & Exposition (2025). https://doi.org/10.18260/1-2-55349
4. Chiodini, L., Moreno Santos, I., Gallidabino, A., Tafliovich, A., Santos, A.L., Hauswirth, M.: A curated inventory of programming language misconceptions. In: Proceedings of the 26th ACM Conference on Innovation and Technology in Computer Science Education, ITiCSE 2021, vol. 1, pp. 380–386. ACM, New York, NY, USA (2021). https://doi.org/10.1145/3430665.3456343
5. Durkin, K., Rittle-Johnson, B.: The effectiveness of using incorrect examples to support learning about decimal magnitude. Learn. Instr. **22**(3), 206–214 (2012). https://doi.org/10.1016/j.learninstruc.2011.11.001

6. Ginat, D., Shmalo, R.: Constructive use of errors in teaching CS1. In: Proceeding of the 44th ACM Technical Symposium on Computer Science Education, SIGCSE 2013, pp. 353–358. ACM, New York, NY, USA (2013). https://doi.org/10.1145/2445196.2445300

7. Große, C.S., Renkl, A.: Finding and fixing errors in worked examples: can this foster learning outcomes? Learn. Instr. **17**(6), 612–634 (2007). https://doi.org/10.1016/j.learninstruc.2007.09.008

8. Hassan, M., Chen, Y., Denny, P., Zilles, C.: On teaching novices computational thinking by utilizing large language models within assessments. In: Proceedings of the 56th ACM Technical Symposium on Computer Science Education, SIGCSETS 2025, vol. 1, pp. 471–477. ACM, New York, NY, USA (2025). https://doi.org/10.1145/3641554.3701906

9. Jalani, N.H., Sern, L.C.: The example-problem-based learning model: applying cognitive load theory. Procedia. Soc. Behav. Sci. **195**, 872–880 (2015). https://doi.org/10.1016/j.sbspro.2015.06.366

10. Jury, B., Lorusso, A., Leinonen, J., Denny, P., Luxton-Reilly, A.: Evaluating LLM-generated worked examples in an introductory programming course. In: Proceedings of the 26th Australasian Computing Education Conference, ACE 2024, pp. 77–86. ACM, New York, NY, USA (2024). https://doi.org/10.1145/3636243.3636252

11. McLaren, B.M., Adams, D.M., Mayer, R.E.: Delayed learning effects with erroneous examples: a study of learning decimals with a web-based tutor. Int. J. Artif. Intell. Educ. **25**(4), 520–542 (2015). https://doi.org/10.1007/s40593-015-0064-x

12. Muldner, K., Jennings, J., Chiarelli, V.: A review of worked examples in programming activities. ACM Trans. Comput. Educ. **23**(1) (2022). https://doi.org/10.1145/3560266

13. Pădurean, V.A., Denny, P., Singla, A.: BugSpotter: automated generation of code debugging exercises. In: Proceedings of the 56th ACM Technical Symposium on Computer Science Education, SIGCSETS 2025, vol. 1. pp. 896–902. ACM, New York, NY, USA (2025). https://doi.org/10.1145/3641554.3701974

14. Qian, Y., Lehman, J.: Students' misconceptions and other difficulties in introductory programming: a literature review. ACM Trans. Comput. Educ. **18**(1) (2017). https://doi.org/10.1145/3077618

15. Richey, J.E., et al.: More confusion and frustration, better learning: the impact of erroneous examples. Comput. Educ. **139**, 173–190 (2019). https://doi.org/10.1016/j.compedu.2019.05.012

16. Sarsa, S., Denny, P., Hellas, A., Leinonen, J.: Automatic generation of programming exercises and code explanations using large language models. In: Proceedings of the 2022 ACM Conference on International Computing Education Research - Volume 1, ICER 2022, pp. 27–43. ACM, New York, NY, USA (2022). https://doi.org/10.1145/3501385.3543957

17. Scaria, N., Dharani Chenna, S., Subramani, D.: Automated educational question generation at different bloom's skill levels using large language models: strategies and evaluation. In: Artificial Intelligence in Education, pp. 165–179. Springer Nature Switzerland, Cham (2024)

18. Sweller, J., Cooper, G.A.: The use of worked examples as a substitute for problem solving in learning algebra. Cogn. Instr. **2**(1), 59–89 (1985)

19. Tsovaltzi, D., Melis, E., McLaren, B.M., Meyer, A.-K., Dietrich, M., Goguadze, G.: Learning from erroneous examples: when and how do students benefit from them? In: Wolpers, M., Kirschner, P.A., Scheffel, M., Lindstaedt, S., Dimitrova, V. (eds.) EC-TEL 2010. LNCS, vol. 6383, pp. 357–373. Springer, Heidelberg (2010). https://doi.org/10.1007/978-3-642-16020-2_24

20. Vieira, C., Yan, J., Magana, A.J.: Exploring design characteristics of worked examples to support programming and algorithm design. J. Comput. Sci. Educ. **6**, 2–15 (2015). https://doi.org/10.22369/issn.2153-4136/6/1/1
21. Zheng, L., et al.: Judging LLM-as-a-Judge with MT-bench and chatbot arena (2023). https://arxiv.org/abs/2306.05685
22. Zhi, R., Price, T.W., Marwan, S., Milliken, A., Barnes, T., Chi, M.: Exploring the impact of worked examples in a novice programming environment. In: Proceedings of the 50th ACM Technical Symposium on Computer Science Education, SIGCSE 2019, pp. 98–104. ACM, New York, NY, USA (2019). https://doi.org/10.1145/3287324.3287385
23. Zhu, L., Wang, X., Wang, X.: JudgeLM: fine-tuned large language models are scalable judges (2025). https://arxiv.org/abs/2310.17631

Contrastive Network-Based Similarity for Zero-Shot Automatic Scoring of Very Short Handwritten Answers

Nam Tuan Ly[1,2]($\boxtimes$) , Hung Tuan Nguyen[1] , Thanh-Nghia Truong[1] ,
Masamitsu Ito[3], and Masaki Nakagawa[1]

[1] Tokyo University of Agriculture and Technology, Tokyo, Japan
`nakagawa@cc.tuat.ac.jp`
[2] Tokyo Metropolitan University, Tokyo, Japan
`namly@tmu.ac.jp`
[3] Wacom Co., Ltd., Saitama, Japan
`masamitsu.ito@wacom.com`

Abstract. Automatic scoring for handwritten answers based on handwriting recognition rely on predefined dictionaries and can result in false positives when handling out-of-vocabulary characters or wrong characters that resemble dictionary entries. This is serious for beginners to learn languages. To address this limitation, this paper proposes a contrastive learning network-based automatic scoring method to improve the scoring of single- or few-character answers that are often scored strictly by human teachers. The proposed method consists of two main components: a contrastive learning network-based pattern similarity and a similarity-based automatic scoring algorithm for classifying an answer as correct, incorrect, or rejected based on its similarity to the expected answer. The proposed contrastive learning network is trained end-to-end by a novel data-sampling method using a dataset of handwritten answers. Experiments on a collection of handwritten answers from elementary school students demonstrate the superiority of the proposed method over the previous recognizer-based methods and its effectiveness for zero-shot automatic scoring, making it useful in low-resource settings. We also compare different backbones on the proposed scorer.

Keywords: Handwritten Answer Scoring · Contrastive Learning · Pattern Similarity · Zero-shot Automatic Scoring · Very Short Answers

1 Introduction

Exams and tests are essential for verifying learners' knowledge acquisition and problem-solving abilities. However, scoring constructed-response questions is typically done by humans, which requires significant time and effort, and it often takes time to provide feedback to learners on the scored results. Human scoring may also be subject to error, variability, and bias, thereby reducing the effectiveness of the examinations [1]. Thus, automatic scoring has become a promising technique in computer-aided education and has attracted the attention of numerous researchers [2, 3].

E. G. Blanchard et al. (Eds.): AIED 2026, LNAI 16583, pp. 132–140, 2027.
https://doi.org/10.1007/978-3-032-29760-0_15

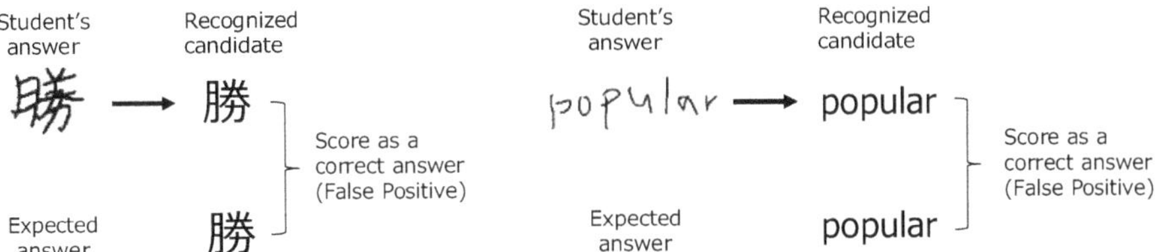

Fig. 1. Some examples of False Positive in the recognizer-based methods.

Recently, with the growing popularity and development of pen- and touch-based tablets, automatic scoring methods for answers written on tablets or electronic paper are being studied [4–6]. These methods enable students to answer questions by hand, and the automatic scoring system evaluates their answers immediately after the exams. Both the assessment time and the teacher's workflow can be reduced. For scoring students' answers, handwriting recognizers are used to recognize the answers and compare them with the expected ones. The recognizer-based methods perform well on short- to medium-length text answers in mathematics, English, and Japanese, and achieve a low false-positive rate (incorrect answers are scored as correct) [5, 6]. However, these methods exhibited a high false-positive rate when scoring single- or few-character answers (named very short answers). The main reason is that handwriting recognition methods often rely on predefined dictionaries, which can lead to false positives when encountering out-of-vocabulary characters or non-character symbols resembling dictionary entries. This is particularly evident in lower grade levels, where neat handwriting is strongly emphasized by teachers. For example, if a student's answer resembles the expected answer but differs in a few strokes and does not form a valid character, the recognizer may still classify it as the expected answer, which appears in the pre-defined dictionary. This results in a false positive. Figure 1 shows some examples of false positive in Japanese and English.

Real-world automatic scoring systems must generalize to score student answers to unseen questions that were not available during training, without collecting labeled answers or performing any fine-tuning. This setting aligns with zero-shot automatic scoring, where the model is expected to transfer what it learned from previously seen questions to new questions "as is," which is especially important because students' answer collection and annotation are expensive and limit scalability in practice. However, recognizer-based methods often perform poorly in zero-shot settings. Because they rely on a fixed vocabulary, out-of-vocabulary or rare characters are typically replaced with the closest known symbols. This issue becomes more severe for unseen questions.

In this paper, inspired by Siamese networks, we propose a contrastive learning network-based automatic scoring method to overcome the limitations of handwriting-recognition-based approaches for scoring very short answers. We further propose a training data sampling strategy for contrastive learning networks and evaluate our approach on zero-shot automatic scoring. To our knowledge, this is the first study on a contrastive learning network for zero-shot automatic scoring.

The remainder of this paper is structured as follows. Section 2 overviews the related works. Section 3 introduces the proposed methods. Section 4 presents experimental results. Finally, Sect. 5 concludes the paper.

2   Related Work

Research on automatic short-answer scoring (SAS) began following the success of automatic essay scoring [7–9]. Most studies have focused on SAS using keyboard input responses, except [10]. Burrows et al. reviewed studies from 1996 to 2013, categorizing them into five key eras: concept mapping, information extraction, corpus-based methods, machine learning, and evaluation initiatives [3]. Over the past decade, Deep Neural Networks and Deep Learning have had a significant impact on SAS [2, 11, 12].

Short answers that are to be filled in at certain positions in the text are called fill-the-gap answers. Typed answers are considered solved [3]. Handwritten answers, however, pose a challenging problem. Teachers require single or few-character answers to be written precisely and neatly. Context should not be used to recognize them, and even the state-of-the-art handwriting recognizers can produce false positives.

Recent studies have examined the implementation of a pen-based tablet system with an automatic scoring technique in everyday learning contexts [4–6]. For automatic scoring of the students' answers, handwritten text recognizers are used to recognize the handwritten answers and score them into three groups: correct answers, incorrect answers, and rejection by the two proposed algorithms of RCR (recognition confidence-based rejection) and CAS (content-awareness similarity) [6]. Their systems perform well on the answers with short or medium-length text of expected answers, but struggle with very short text of expected answers.

3   Methods

To address the limitations of the recognizer-based methods, we propose a contrastive learning network-based automatic scoring method for automatically scoring very short text answers. The proposed method consists of two main components: a contrastive learning network and a similarity-based automatic scoring algorithm. The contrastive learning network takes a handwritten answer pattern and an expected answer pattern as input and computes their similarity. Then, the similarity-based automatic scoring algorithm scores the handwritten answer as correct, incorrect, or rejected based on its similarity with the expected answer. We describe them in detail in the following sections.

3.1   Contrastive Learning Network

The proposed network comprises a vision encoder for extracting vision features and a merger module for computing visual feature similarity, as shown in Fig. 2. Given two answers, the vision encoder processes each answer independently and extracts a visual feature grid, yielding two feature grids. The two feature grids are fed into the merger module to compute the similarity between the two answers ranging from 0 to 1.

Vision Encoder.

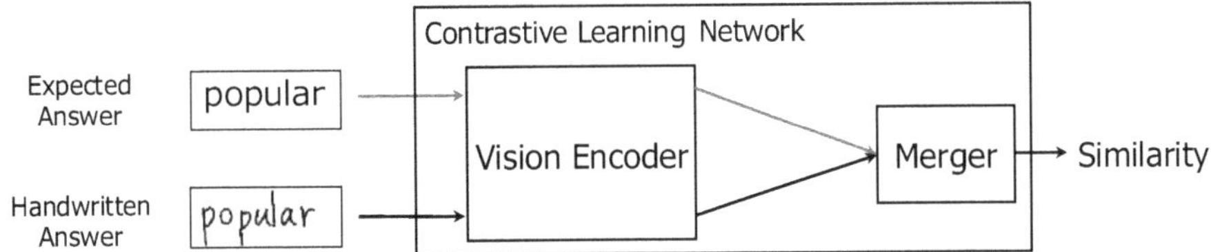

Fig. 2. The architecture of the proposed network for pattern similarity.

At the bottom of the proposed model, the vision encoder extracts a visual feature grid from an answer image. Given an answer image of the size $\{h, w, c\}$, the vision encoder extracts a feature grid F of size $\{h', w', c'\}$, where c', h', and w' depend on the h and w of the input image and the network architecture of the backbone. A CNN backbone is often used, such as ResNet, or a Transformer backbone, such as ViT. Each of these backbones have their advantages and disadvantages. In this work, to build a robust vision encoder, we evaluate three popular backbones (ResNet-18 [13], ViT [14], and Swin [15]) and select the best-performing one.

Merger Module. At the top of the vision encoder, the merger module takes the two feature grids produced by the vision encoder as input and predicts the similarity between the two input answers. In this work, we employ two fully connected layers and one Sigmoid layer to construct the merger module.

Training and Data Sampling. The proposed contrastive learning network can be trained end-to-end using stochastic gradient descent and a binary cross-entropy loss function on pairs of answers and their similarity annotations. The binary cross-entropy loss for a minibatch $B = \{x_i, y_i, s_i\}_{i=1}^{n}$ is defined as follows:

$$\mathcal{L}(B) = -\frac{1}{n} \sum_{i=1}^{n} \left[s_i \times logS_i + (1 - s_i) \times log(1 - S_i) \right] \tag{1}$$

here x_i, y_i and s_i are the two answers and the annotation of their similarity of the i-th sample in the minibatch B. S_i is the predicted similarity between x_i and y_i.

Training the proposed contrastive learning network requires samples comprising a handwritten answer, the expected answer, and their corresponding similarity. Let (X, E, S) be one of the training samples. Here, X, E, and S are the handwritten answer, the expected answer, and their similarity, respectively. The similarity S equals 1 if the handwritten answer is correct for the question. We refer to them as a positive-pair sample. Otherwise, the similarity S is 0. We refer to them as negative-pair samples. To prepare training samples from a handwritten-answer dataset, we propose a data sampling algorithm that generates (X, E, S) samples by randomly selecting an equal number of correct and incorrect answers for each question in order to maintain the balance between the positive and negative-pair samples.

3.2 Similarity-Based Automatic Scoring Algorithm

Based on the similarity between the handwritten answer and the rendered image of the expected answer, the similarity-based automatic scoring algorithm scores the handwritten answer as correct, incorrect, or rejected using the two thresholds of False threshold (α) and True threshold (β). Specifically, an answer is classified as correct if the similarity exceeds β, and as incorrect if it falls below α. Otherwise, it is labeled as reject. The two thresholds α and β are determined empirically. Answers classified as reject are forwarded to human graders for manual evaluation.

3.3 Zero-Shot Automatic Scoring

A key advantage of the proposed method is that it naturally supports zero-shot automatic scoring for unseen questions. For a new question, the system only requires the rendered image of the expected answer and does not require additional training samples or retraining of the network. The similarity between the handwritten answer and the expected answer is directly calculated, and the final decision is made according to the predicted similarity and the thresholds α and β. This is useful in low-resource settings.

4 Experiments

This section presents experiments to evaluate the model for very short answers.

4.1 Datasets

In this paper, we conduct experiments on a collection of handwritten answers [4] from Japanese elementary school students. This dataset was collected using an electronic paper device equipped with an electronic pen and eraser, which provides a paper-like experience. The collection and use of student responses were conducted with approval from the institutional ethics review board for research involving human subjects at the institution (Approval No. 240104-0411). The questions are extracted from a series of educational workbooks in Japanese, English, and Math across all grade levels of Japanese elementary school and have been digitized with the publisher's authorization [4]. In each grade level, 50 students are asked to answer all questions from their grade level. Note that the English subject in Japan starts from the 5th grade. This paper focuses on the Japanese and English subsets of the dataset, which contain 98,547 and 15,900 answers, respectively.

4.2 Implement Details and Evaluation Metrics

In the proposed contrastive learning network, we employ the two fully connected layers having 1024 and 128 nodes, respectively, to construct the merger module. The proposed network is implemented in PyTorch and trained on one NVIDIA RTX A6000 48 GB with a batch size of 16. The learning rate is initialized at 0.0001. All input images are resized to a height of 224 pixels before being fed into the vision encoder.

For the evaluation metrics, we employ correct scoring rate, rejection rate, claim rate (rejection rate + false negative rate likely disputed by students and subsequently re-evaluated by teachers), and risky scoring rate (false positive rate unlikely reported by students in the same way as [6].

Table 1. Performance (%) in different backbones.

Backbone	Correct Scoring Rate	Rejection Rate	Claim Rate	Risky Scoring Rate
ResNet	94.61	N/A	2.22	3.17
ViT	94.01	N/A	2.99	2.99
Swin	95.13	N/A	1.71	3.16

4.3 Backbone Network Selection

To identify the optimal backbone for the vision encoder, we conduct an experiment to investigate the impact of the backbone. We compare three representative architectures: ResNet-18, which benefits from convolutional inductive biases such as locality and translation equivariance; Vision Transformer (ViT), which relies on global self-attention to model long-range interactions; and Swin Transformer, which employs shifted window-based self-attention to efficiently capture local structure while enabling cross-window contextual modeling. To ensure a fair comparison across all settings, we keep all training and evaluation conditions identical and use the same true and false thresholds (0.5) across all experiments. Table 1 shows that the Swin Transformer backbone achieves the best performance. This result suggests that modeling fine-grained both local and global context is beneficial for the proposed method.

4.4 Single Character Answers

This section evaluates the method for Japanese single-character answers.

Thresholds Selection

This experiment evaluates the performance of the proposed method in threshold selection. Table 2 shows the correct scoring rate, rejection rate, claim rate, and risky scoring rate in different thresholds. We observe that if we decrease the False threshold (α) while keeping the True threshold (β), the claim rate is decreased; however, the rejection rate is increased, and the correct scoring rate is decreased. If we increase the True threshold (β) while keeping the False threshold (α), the risky scoring rate is decreased; however, the rejection rate is increased, and the correct scoring rate is decreased. In summary, when selecting the thresholds, we need to consider the balance between the evaluation metrics of the automatic scoring systems.

Zero-Shot Automatic Scoring

To evaluate the performance of the proposed method for zero-shot automatic scoring, we create test and training samples based on the questions (i.e., the expected answers) rather than on the students. This ensures that the questions in the test set are not in the training set. Specifically, the training set comprises 780 expected answers, and the test set comprises 195. The proposed method achieved a correct scoring rate of 73.19%, a rejection rate of 21.11%, a risky scoring rate of 2.58%, and a claim rate of 3.12%. These results demonstrate the performance of the proposed method for zero-shot automatic scoring.

Comparison with Previous Works

This experiment evaluates the performance of the proposed method in comparison with the previous works [6] of the two recognizer-based methods RCR and CAS. Table 3 shows that the proposed method achieved significantly lower claim and risky scoring rates than RCR and CAS. Most of doubtful answers are rejected and re-scored by the teachers. These results demonstrate the superiority of the proposed method over recognizer-based methods for the automatic scoring of single-character answers.

Table 2. Performance (%) in different thresholds for single-character answers.

Thresholds (α, β)	Correct Scoring Rate	Rejection Rate	Claim Rate	Risky Scoring Rate
$\alpha = 0.4, \beta = 0.6$	93.53	1.36	2.20	2.91
$\alpha = 0.4, \beta = 0.8$	90.79	4.61	2.20	2.40
$\alpha = 0.3, \beta = 0.8$	90.85	5.25	1.77	2.40
$\alpha = 0.25, \beta = 0.9$	86.71	9.85	1.55	1.89
$\alpha = 0.25, \beta = 0.95$	80.95	16.06	1.55	1.44

Table 3. Comparison with previous works on Japanese answers.

Scorer	Correct Scoring Rate	Rejection Rate	Claim Rate	Risky Scoring Rate
Our	88.61	9.85	1.55	1.89
RCR	87.14	0.31	7.25	5.03
CAS	88.11	0.19	6.21	5.22

4.5 Short Text Answers

This experiment evaluates the performance of the proposed method for short text answers in Japanese. As shown in Table 4, we observe that when the number of characters is increased, the risky scoring rate is decreased. However, the claim and rejection rates increase, while the correct scoring rate declines sharply. These results indicate that as the number of characters increases, the proposed model's performance decreases. If the number of characters exceeds 6, the rejection rate exceeds 38%, negatively impacting automatic scoring performance. These experimental results suggest that the proposed method performs well on very short answers (fewer than six characters), but performance declines as the number of characters increases.

We also evaluate the performance of the proposed method on short text answers in English. Note that the number of English answers is much less than that of Japanese answers. The proposed method achieves a low risky scoring rate of 1.51%; however, claim rates are higher (around 10%) than the Japanese short text answers. One reason for the high claim rate is that most teachers score students' answers regardless of letter cases, whereas the proposed method is case-sensitive. Another reason is the lack of training data compared to Japanese answers. Note that the primary objective of automatic scoring is to minimize the risky scoring rate, while keeping the claim rate below 15%. This is satisfied by the proposed method.

Table 4. Performance (%) on Japanese short text answers in different numbers of characters.

Number Char	Correct Scoring Rate	Rejection Rate	Claim Rate	Risky Scoring Rate
1	79.95	17.21	0.83	2.02
2–3	77.47	19.64	0.96	1.94
4–5	70.22	26.64	1.81	1.33
≥6	45.06	38.94	15.22	0.77

5 Conclusions

In this paper, we presented a contrastive learning network-based automatic scoring method to address the limitations of the recognizer-based methods for automatic scoring of very short text answers. Extensive experiments on the handwritten answer dataset demonstrate that the proposed method performs well for very short answers. Moreover, it is expected to be even more effective when combined with recognizer-based automatic scoring methods for short text answers (longer than six characters) and NLP-based methods for long text answers (longer than 30 characters). The experimental results also demonstrate the performance of our method for zero-shot automatic scoring, which is useful in low-resource settings.

In future work, we plan to integrate our approach with complementary techniques, including recognizer- and NLP-based methods.

Acknowledgments. This work is partially supported by the joint research budget from WACOM Co., Ltd. and by KAKENHI (JP24H00738, JP24K20789).

References

1. Heffernan, N.T., Heffernan, C.L.: The ASSISTments ecosystem: building a platform that brings scientists and teachers together for minimally invasive research on human learning and teaching. Int. J. Artif. Intell. Educ. **24**, 470–497 (2014). https://doi.org/10.1007/S40593-014-0024-X/FIGURES/7

2. Riordan, B., Horbach, A., Cahill, A., Zesch, T., Lee, C.M.: Investigating neural architectures for short answer scoring. In: Tetreault, J., Burstein, J., Leacock, C., Yannakoudakis, H. (eds.) Proceedings of the 12th Workshop on Innovative Use of NLP for Building Educational Applications, pp. 159–168. Copenhagen, Denmark (2017). https://doi.org/10.18653/v1/W17-5017

3. Burrows, S., Gurevych, I., Stein, B.: The eras and trends of automatic short answer grading. Int. J. Artif. Intell. Educ. **25**, 60–117 (2015). https://doi.org/10.1007/S40593-014-0026-8/TABLES/11

4. Asakura, T.: Digitalizing educational workbooks and collecting handwritten answers for automatic scoring. In: iTextbooks@AIED 2023, pp. 78–87 (2023)

5. Nakagawa, M., et al.: Two experiments for automatic scoring of handwritten descriptive answers. In: Document Analysis Systems. DAS 2024, pp. 3–19 (2024). https://doi.org/10.1007/978-3-031-70442-0_1

6. Truong, N.T., Nguyen, H.T., Ly, N.T., Horie, T., Nakagawa, M.: Content-based similarity for automatic scoring of handwritten descriptive answers. In: Proceedings of 18th International Conference on Document Analysis and Recognition (ICDAR2024). LNCS, vol. 14805, pp. 268–281 (2024). https://doi.org/10.1007/978-3-031-70536-6_16

7. Burstein, J., et al.: Automated scoring using a hybrid feature identification technique. In: Proceedings of the Annual Meeting of the Association for Computational Linguistics, vol. 1, pp. 206–210 (1998). https://doi.org/10.3115/980845.980879

8. Wild, F., Stahl, C., Stermsek, G., Neumann, G.: Parameters driving effectiveness of automated essay scoring with LSA. In: In: 9th Conference on Computer Assisted Assessment, pp. 485–494 (2005)

9. Ishioka, T., Kameda, M.: Automated Japanese essay scoring system: Jess. In: International Conference on Database and Expert Systems Applications – DEXA, vol. 15, pp. 4–8 (2004). https://doi.org/10.1109/DEXA.2004.1333440

10. Srihari, S., Srihari, R., Babu, P., Srinivasan, H.: On the automatic scoring of handwritten essays. In: International Joint Conference on Artificial Intelligence, pp. 2880–2884 (2007)

11. Sung, C., Dhamecha, T.I., Mukhi, N.: Improving short answer grading using transformer-based pre-training. In: Isotani, S., Millán, E., Ogan, A., Hastings, P., McLaren, B., Luckin, R. (eds.) Artificial Intelligence in Education. LNCS (LNAI), vol. 11625, pp. 469–481. Springer, Cham (2019). https://doi.org/10.1007/978-3-030-23204-7_39

12. Li, Z., Tomar, Y., Passonneau, R.J.: A semantic feature-wise transformation relation network for automatic short answer grading. In: Moens, M.-F., Huang, X., Specia, L., Yih, S.W. (eds.) Proceedings of the 2021 Conference on Empirical Methods in Natural Language Processing, pp. 6030–6040 (2021). https://doi.org/10.18653/v1/2021.emnlp-main.487

13. He, K., Zhang, X., Ren, S., Sun, J.: Deep residual learning for image recognition. In: 2016 IEEE Conference on Computer Vision and Pattern Recognition (CVPR), pp. 770–778. IEEE (2016). https://doi.org/10.1109/CVPR.2016.90

14. Dosovitskiy, A., et al.: An image is worth 16x16 words: transformers for image recognition at scale. In: International Conference on Learning Representations (2020)

15. Liu, Z., et al.: Swin transformer: hierarchical vision transformer using shifted windows. In: IEEE International Conference on Computer Vision, pp. 9992–10002 (2021). https://doi.org/10.1109/ICCV48922.2021.00986

MAML-KT: Addressing Cold Start Problem in Knowledge Tracing for New Students via Few-Shot Model-Agnostic Meta Learning

Indronil Bhattacharjee$^{(\boxtimes)}$ and Christabel Wayllace

New Mexico State University, Las Cruces, NM, USA
{indronil,cwayllac}@nmsu.edu

Abstract. Knowledge tracing (KT) models are commonly evaluated by training on early interactions from all students and testing on later responses. While effective for measuring average predictive performance, this evaluation design obscures a cold start scenario that arises in deployment, where models must infer the knowledge state of previously unseen students from only a few initial interactions. Prior studies have shown that under this setting, standard empirically risk-minimized KT models such as DKT, DKVMN and SAKT exhibit substantially lower early accuracy than previously reported. We frame new-student performance prediction as a few-shot learning problem and introduce MAML-KT, a model-agnostic meta learning approach that learns an initialization optimized for rapid adaptation to new students using one or two gradient updates. We evaluate MAML-KT on ASSISTment data using a controlled cold start protocol that trains on a subset of students and tests on held-out learners across early interaction windows, scaling cohort sizes from 10 to 50 students. Across datasets, MAML-KT achieves higher early accuracy than prior KT models in nearly all cold start conditions. Overall, optimizing KT models for rapid adaptation reduces early prediction error and sharpens the interpretation of early accuracy fluctuations.

Keywords: Predictive Models · Educational Data Mining · Classifiers

1 Introduction

Personalized tutoring systems rely on accurate early estimates of a learner's mastery to decide what to present next and how to adapt difficulty. Knowledge Tracing (KT) models this as sequential prediction over student responses to tutoring items. Modern deep KT approaches, including recurrent models [14] and memory-based architectures [1,17], are typically trained via empirical risk minimization (ERM).

While these models capture temporal structure and concept dynamics, they can struggle in cold start settings [3,18]. When a new student has only a few

E. G. Blanchard et al. (Eds.): AIED 2026, LNAI 16583, pp. 141–149, 2027.
https://doi.org/10.1007/978-3-032-29760-0_16

interactions, parameters optimized for average performance may not personalize quickly, and early errors can influence subsequent instructional decisions. Prior work has formally characterized the new-student cold start problem under disjoint train–test splits, documenting unstable early-phase performance but leaving open the question of how to explicitly mitigate it [3]. To address this limitation, we frame new-student KT as a few-shot adaptation problem and apply Model-Agnostic Meta Learning (MAML) [6]. Rather than optimizing a single global solution, MAML learns an initialization that can be rapidly adapted to a new student from a small support prefix.

Our contributions are threefold: (1) we formulate new-student knowledge tracing as a few-shot adaptation problem under a strictly causal support–query split; (2) we introduce MAML-KT, a model-agnostic meta-learning approach tailored to sequential student data for rapid personalization; and (3) we provide a systematic evaluation of cold-start performance across multiple datasets and cohort sizes (10–50 students), showing that meta-learned initialization improves early-phase prediction and scales to larger, more realistic deployment settings.

2   Background and Related Works

Knowledge Tracing [4] estimates a learner's latent mastery from interaction sequences to predict future performance. DKT uses RNNs to model interaction histories [14], while DKVMN externalizes concept representations via memory and attention-based models weight relevant past interactions [7,12,17]. Despite strong average performance, these globally trained models require multiple observations before predictions stabilize for a new student, exposing the new-student cold start problem [3].

Cold start arises when a model must personalize to a new student with only a few interactions or when new skills are introduced. Unlike standard evaluation, the focus is performance over early interactions. Architectural approaches improve early predictions through inductive bias [2], and some methods incorporate auxiliary information to reduce uncertainty [8,9], but most KT models remain optimized for global prediction rather than rapid per-student adaptation.

Meta learning trains models to adapt quickly across tasks. In MAML [6], parameters are optimized so that a few gradient steps on a support set yield strong query performance. This paradigm has been effective in cold-start recommendation settings, where each user defines a task with sparse interactions [5,10,16].

3   Problem Statement and Research Approach

3.1   Problem Statement: New-Student Cold Start in KT

We consider knowledge tracing (KT) in the new-student cold start setting [3], where an unseen student has no prior history and the model must predict correctness on upcoming items using only the first K interactions. Our goal is to learn parameters that can be quickly personalized via a few gradient steps on these initial interactions.

Let a student's sequence be $S_s = (q_t, a_t)_{t=1}^{T_s}$, where q_t denotes the question (with one or more associated skills) and $a_t \in 0, 1$ its correctness label. For each unseen student s, we define a causal split: $S_s^{support} = (q_t, a_t)_{t=1}^{K}$ and $S_s^{query} = (q_t, a_t)_{t=K+1}^{T_s}$.

We evaluate next-step correctness on the query segment, emphasizing early-phase performance for small K.

3.2 Key Research Questions

Our study aims to address the following research questions:

1. Does meta learning improve early-phase new student performance over ERM baselines (DKT, DKVMN, SAKT) at small K?
2. Does the proposed MAML-KT approach scale with cohort size, i.e., do its cold start accuracy change when moving from the prior settings (10 students) to larger cohorts (20 and 50 students)?
3. Under which sequence and content conditions does MAML-KT trail other ERM baselines?

3.3 Few-Shot Task Construction

For each student trajectory $\{(q_t, a_t)\}_{t=1}^{T}$, we construct a few-shot task under next-step prediction. At timestep t, the model receives the history token $x_t = (q_t, a_t)$ and predicts the subsequent outcome a_{t+1} conditioned on the target item q_{t+1}.

Thus, per-timestep training examples are (x_t, q_{t+1}, a_{t+1}) for $t = 1, \ldots, T-1$. Given a support size K, we split each sequence into a causal support prefix and query suffix. The support set consists of the first K timesteps, and the query set consists of the remaining timesteps. To ensure a non-empty query, we require $1 \leq K \leq T - 1$ and discard sequences with $T < 2$. Padding is applied during preprocessing and does not affect interaction order.

3.4 Meta Learning Objective

Following the MAML paradigm [6], the meta-parameter θ_T is optimized such that after inner-loop adaptation on the support set of a student task T, the adapted parameters θ_T' minimize the query loss with inner learning rate α:

$$\min_{\theta} \mathbb{E}_{T \sim p(T)}[\mathcal{L}_T^{query}(\theta_T')] \quad \text{s.t.} \quad \theta_T' = \theta - \alpha \nabla_\theta \mathcal{L}_T^{support}(\theta)$$

Here, θ denotes the shared initialization parameters, θ_T' the task-adapted parameters for student T, and $\mathcal{L}$ is the binary cross-entropy loss over next-step prediction.

3.5   Training Procedure

During meta-training, we iterate over meta-batches of student tasks. For each student s in the batch:

Support Adaptation. For each student, we update the shared parameters using gradient descent on the support loss $\mathcal{L}^{(s)}_{support}$. The update is differentiable, enabling the outer meta-optimization to account for how the model adapts to new students.

Meta-loss on Query. Using the adapted parameters θ'_s, we compute the query loss $\mathcal{L}^{(s)}_{query}$ on the remaining timesteps. These per-task query losses are averaged across the meta-batch to form the meta-objective.

Outer Update. We backpropagate through the inner updates and update the shared initialization, $\theta \leftarrow \theta - \beta \nabla_\theta \left(\frac{1}{B} \sum_{s=1}^{B} \mathcal{L}^{(s)}_{\text{query}} \right)$ using Adam with meta learning rate β.

3.6   Evaluation Protocol

Let N denote the total number of query predictions aggregated across all test students. We calculate Overall accuracy and Windowed early-phase accuracy.

$$\text{ACC} = \frac{1}{N} \sum_{t=1}^{N} (\mathbf{1}[\hat{p}_t \geq 0.5] = y_t) \tag{1}$$

For a window $[Q_{min}, Q_{max}]$ and coldstart zone $\in \{\text{Critical}, \text{Moderate}\}$, the average windowed accuracy is

$$\overline{ACC}_{\text{coldstart zone}} = \frac{1}{N_Q} \sum_{Q=Q_{min}}^{Q_{max}} ACC(Q) \tag{2}$$

3.7   Algorithm

We retain the standard MAML objective [6], optimizing query loss after inner adaptation, and adapt it to sequential student–response data (Algorithm 1). Each student trajectory defines a task.

The backbone is a GRU-based Deep KT model with a projected target-item embedding fused before the readout layer. Inner adaptation performs R steps of task-local SGD on the support loss. We train second-order MAML by backpropagating through the inner updates and applying the meta-update to the averaged query loss across tasks.

The algorithm has the same meta-objective and inner/outer optimization as standard MAML. The differences are limited to task construction and model design: a causal support–query split with auto-shrink, sequence-aware preprocessing, and a KT-specific GRU with target fusion. The objective and meta-optimization remain unchanged. The code is available at **github.com/Indronil-Prince/MAML-KT**.

Algorithm 1: MAML-KT (GRU backbone, second-order)

Input: Training set $\mathcal{D}_{train}$, support size K, inner steps R, LR α, meta LR β
        meta-batch B

1 **Preprocess**: For each student trajectory $\{(q_t, a_t)\}_{t=1}^{T}$, form next-step pairs
    (x_t, q_{t+1}, a_{t+1}) with $x_t = (q_t, a_t)$; discard $T < 2$ and enforce $1 \leq K \leq T - 1$.

2 **Model**: GRU over interaction tokens with projected target-item embedding.

3 **for** $epoch = 1, 2, \ldots$ **do**

4   Sample meta-batch $\{(X_i, y_i, T_i)\}_{i=1}^{B}$ from $\mathcal{D}_{train}$;

5       $L_{\mathrm{meta}} \leftarrow 0$, $V \leftarrow 0$;

6   **for** $i = 1$ **to** B **do**

7   **if** $T_i \leq K$ **continue**

8   support $(X^s, y^s) = (X_i[1{:}K], y_i[1{:}K])$;

9   query $(X^q, y^q) = (X_i[K{+}1{:}T_i - 1], y_i[K{+}1{:}T_i - 1])$; // `Causal split`

10          $\phi \leftarrow \theta$;   // `fast parameters`

11   **for** $r = 1$ **to** R **do**

12              $\ell_r \leftarrow \mathrm{BCE}\big(f(X^s; \phi), y^s\big)$;

13              $\phi \leftarrow \phi - \alpha \nabla_\phi \ell_r$;

14   **end**

15          $\ell_q \leftarrow \mathrm{BCE}\big(f(X^q; \phi), y^q\big)$;

16          $L_{\mathrm{meta}} \leftarrow L_{\mathrm{meta}} + \ell_q$; $V \leftarrow V + 1$;

17   **end**

18   **if** $V > 0$, **then** $\theta \leftarrow \theta - \beta \nabla_\theta (L_{\mathrm{meta}}/V)$;

19 **end**

---

4 Experiment Setup and Methodology

4.1 Datasets

We use three ASSISTments benchmarks: ASSIST2009 Skill-Builder [11], ASSIST2015 [15], and ASSIST2017 Challenge [13]. These datasets contain student-problem interactions from mathematics curricula, including question IDs, binary correctness labels and question–skill mappings.

4.2 Data Segregation and Problem Setup

We follow Bhattacharjee et al. (2025) [3], applying a minimum-length filter before sampling: students must have ≥ 20 interactions in ASSIST2009 and ASSIST2015, and ≥ 30 in ASSIST2017. From each filtered dataset, we adopt the same new-student protocol used in [3] for cohort size 10. We additionally construct cohorts of 20 and 50 students via uniform random sampling of student IDs. We define the critical (Q = 3–10) and moderate (Q = 11–15) cold-start windows following prior work, corresponding to phases where limited interaction history constrains personalization and where early instructional decisions are most impactful [3].

For each dataset and cohort size, we generate five independent splits. We frame meta-training as per-student tasks. Each training student's sequence is split chronologically into a support prefix and query suffix, one fast gradient update on the support adapts the KT backbone and the adapted model is evaluated on the query segment to refine the shared initialization. No cross-student leakage is allowed.

At test time, each held-out student's earliest interactions are used once for adaptation; subsequent interactions are predicted with the adapted weights and no further learning occurs.

Hyperparameters, including learning rates (α, β), number of inner-loop steps, and hidden dimensions, were selected via validation on training students to maximize early-phase accuracy.

5 Results and Discussion

We analyze results along three dimensions: (1) early-phase accuracy (lift-off), (2) stability under limited history, and (3) sensitivity to skill transitions. To isolate the effect of meta-learning, we compare MAML-KT against its ERM counterpart (DKT), which shares the same GRU backbone but is trained without task-level adaptation, as well as standard KT baselines (DKVMN and SAKT).

Table 1. Critical (Q = 3–10) and Moderate cold start (Q = 11–15): best (first row) and second-best (second row) accuracies per dataset × set × cohort size.

Critical Cold Start						Moderate Cold Start				
Dataset	Set 1	Set 2	Set 3	Set 4	Set 5	Set 1	Set 2	Set 3	Set 4	Set 5
10 New Students										
ASSIST	**75.3**^{M}	**75.9**^{M}	**72.3**^{M}	**67.2**^{M}	**66.8**^{M}	**79.4**^{M}	**78.1**^{M}	**76.6**^{M}	**71.9**^{M}	**70.5**^{M}
2009	72.0^D	68.1^S	68.8^S	63.9^S	61.6^S	76.6^D	73.3^S	72.6^S	70.4^S	64.7^D
ASSIST	**84.5**^{M}	**78.1**^{M}	**70.0**^{M}	**72.1**^{M}	**66.0**^{M}	**88.3**^{M}	**78.7**^{M}	**76.8**^{M}	**77.9**^{M}	**75.6**^{M}
2015	76.1^N	69.8^D	61.2^S	65.7^S	59.9^D	81.0^N	78.5^N	71.2^S	74.9^N	69.7^N
ASSIST	**67.4**^{M}	**71.9**^{M}	**72.9**^{M}	**70.6**^{M}	**71.7**^{M}	**69.1**^{M}	**72.8**^{M}	**69.4**^{M}	**72.7**^{M}	**73.0**^{M}
2017	62.7^S	69.9^S	66.5^S	68.2^S	66.3^S	68.9^S	71.4^S	69.0^S	70.2^S	69.7^S
20 New Students										
ASSIST	**81.1**^{M}	**76.8**^{M}	**81.0**^{M}	**75.5**^{M}	**81.9**^{M}	**82.6**^{M}	**80.9**^{M}	**82.7**^{M}	**82.0**^{M}	**84.6**^{M}
2009	70.8^S	76.2^S	76.9^S	74.0^S	80.3^S	77.9^S	80.5^S	78.0^S	79.1^S	81.8^S
ASSIST	**73.6**^{M}	**77.3**^{M}	79.5^S	**77.3**^{M}	**76.0**^{M}	**76.8**^{M}	**80.7**^{M}	**78.0**^{M}	**81.7**^{M}	**80.1**^{M}
2015	73.4^S	76.8^S	**75.9**^{M}	75.9^S	74.7^S	75.3^D	79.1^D	76.1^S	74.3^D	73.2^S
ASSIST	**75.7**^{M}	75.8^S	76.3^S	**65.1**^{M}	**67.6**^{M}	**72.5**^{M}	69.9^S	71.7^S	**78.4**^{M}	**73.8**^{M}
2017	71.3^S	**72.1**^{M}	**71.9**^{M}	74.7^D	74.2^S	68.3^S	**68.8**^{M}	**70.3**^{M}	73.9^D	72.0^D
50 New Students										
ASSIST	**80.1**^{M}	**77.8**^{M}	**74.4**^{M}	**77.1**^{M}	**77.5**^{M}	**85.0**^{M}	**78.4**^{M}	**72.0**^{M}	**79.6**^{M}	**77.2**^{M}
2009	77.9^S	76.7^S	71.7^S	73.9^S	76.7^S	81.3^S	77.9^S	70.9^S	79.3^S	75.5^S
ASSIST	**78.2**^{M}	**79.9**^{M}	**79.3**^{M}	**77.2**^{M}	**81.5**^{M}	**79.7**^{M}	81.8^S	**82.6**^{M}	**80.1**^{M}	**80.2**^{M}
2015	76.5^S	78.9^D	78.6^S	76.3^S	78.3^D	79.4^S	**81.4**^{M}	81.0^S	77.8^S	76.8^S
ASSIST	**71.9**^{M}	**67.6**^{M}	**74.0**^{M}	**65.1**^{M}	**67.6**^{M}	**71.4**^{M}	**69.7**^{M}	**73.0**^{M}	**65.6**^{M}	**68.1**^{M}
2017	71.2^N	66.6^D	71.5^N	64.9^N	66.1^N	69.6^N	67.1^D	69.6^D	64.9^N	65.0^D

** M: MAML, D: DKT, N:DKVMN, S: SAKT*

5.1 Results on 20 and 50 New Student Cohorts

We evaluate cold-start performance on larger held-out cohorts of 20 and 50 students to assess whether meta-learned adaptation scales beyond prior small-cohort settings.

Across datasets (Table 1), two consistent patterns emerge. 1) MAML-KT maintains higher early-phase accuracy than ERM baselines in both the critical (Q = 3–10) (Fig. 1a) and moderate (Q = 11–15) windows (Fig. 1b). 2) This advantage remains stable as cohort size increases, indicating that the learned initialization generalizes across larger and more diverse student populations rather than overfitting to small evaluation sets.

Compared to prior work limited to cohorts of 10 students [3], these results show that meta-learned adaptation produces consistent gains under more realistic deployment conditions, where models must generalize to many unseen learners simultaneously.

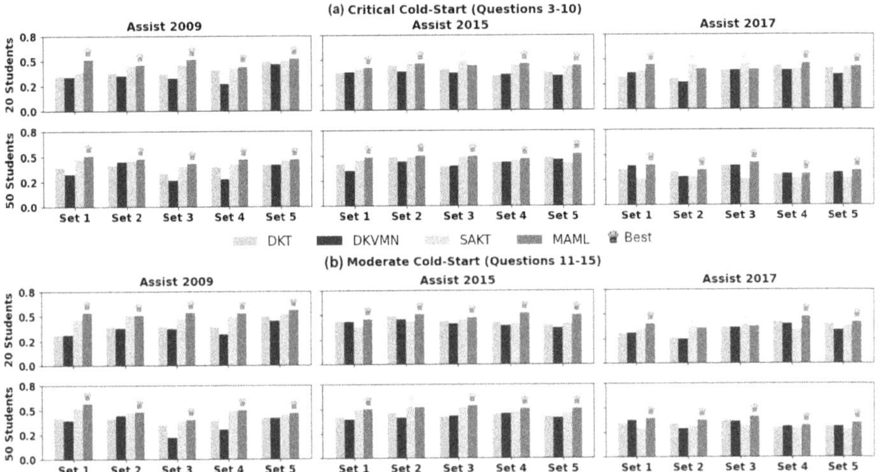

Fig. 1. (a) Critical (Questions 3–10) and (b) Moderate Cold Start (Questions 11–15): Average Accuracy across 5 Datasets × 4 Models × 2 Cohort Sizes (20 and 50)

5.2   Cold Start Performance

Beyond cohort scaling, we examine how models behave across interaction sequences. Two consistent patterns emerge: (1) faster lift-off, where MAML-KT reaches stable accuracy earlier, and (2) improved stability under limited history, with smoother trajectories across student sets.

On ASSIST2015, these gains are more pronounced despite weaker KC signals, suggesting that task-level adaptation compensates for limited item structure. On ASSIST2017, MAML-KT maintains strong early performance despite greater skill heterogeneity.

These results suggest that training models for rapid adaptation, rather than a single global optimum, better matches the early-stage personalization requirements of tutoring systems.

5.3 When Does MAML-KT Trail?

On ASSIST2017, we observe a localized dip around $Q = 8$ where MAML-KT briefly trails SAKT before recovering by $Q = 13$. Per-student panels (Fig. 2(b)) show that many learners encounter new skills around $Q = 6$–8.

Because MAML-KT adapts on the K-step support, it specializes to seen skills; when the query introduces unseen skills, performance temporarily drops. In contrast, SAKT does not adapt per student and is less sensitive to this mismatch.

This effect is strongest on ASSIST2017 due to frequent early skill introductions, highlighting a boundary of meta-learning in KT: adaptation relies on short-term skill continuity. When new skills appear, the model effectively faces a form of skill-level cold start. This suggests that early prediction performance is shaped not only by model adaptation capacity, but also by the structure of students' learning trajectories, particularly the timing and diversity of skill exposure.

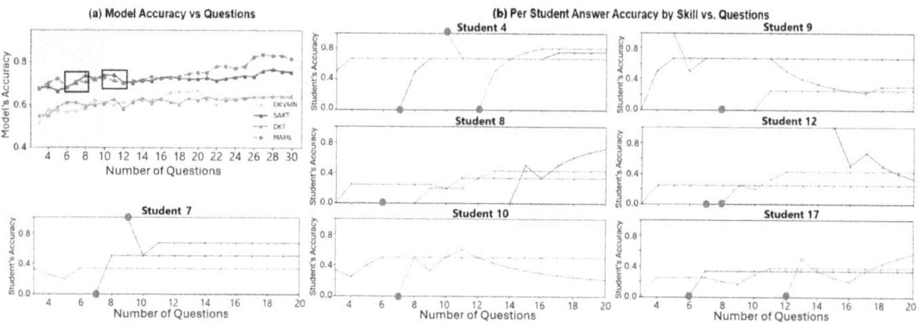

Fig. 2. Assist2017 - 20 New Students - Set 2, Questions 6–8 and 10–12. (a) Model Accuracy vs Questions (b) Per Student Answer Accuracy by Skill vs Questions (The lines represent a skill and start of new skills are marked with red circles)

6 Conclusion and Future Work

We studied MAML for cold-start knowledge tracing by framing each new student as a few-shot adaptation task. Across datasets and cold-start regimes, MAML-KT improved early-phase prediction over ERM baselines, demonstrating that a shared initialization can enable rapid personalization from limited interactions.

Our analysis also reveals an important limitation: gains depend on short-term skill continuity and diminish when new skills appear in the query, highlighting an interaction between student-level and skill-level cold start.

While we instantiate MAML-KT using a GRU-based backbone for comparability with prior KT work, the formulation is model-agnostic and can be extended to other KT architectures.

Future work will investigate adaptation strategies that are more robust to skill shifts, including skill-level task construction and uncertainty-aware updates, toward more reliable and scalable personalization in real instructional settings.

References

1. Abdelrahman, G., Wang, Q.: Knowledge tracing with sequential key-value memory networks. In: Proceedings of the 42nd ACM SIGIR, pp. 175–184 (2019)
2. Bai, Y., Li, X., Liu, Z., Huang, Y.: csKT: addressing cold-start problem in knowledge tracing via kernel bias and cone attention. Expert Syst. Appl. **266** (2025)
3. Bhattacharjee, I., Wayllace, C.: Cold start problem: an experimental study of knowledge tracing models with new students. In: AIED-2025, pp. 425–432 (2025)
4. Corbett, A.T., Anderson, J.R.: Knowledge tracing: modeling the acquisition of procedural knowledge. User Model. User-adapt Interact. **4**(4), 253–278 (1995)
5. Du, Y., Zhu, X., Chen, L., Fang, Z., Gao, Y.: MetaKG: meta-learning on knowledge graph for cold-start recommendation. IEEE Trans. KDE **35** (2022)
6. Finn, C., Abbeel, P., Levine, S.: Model-agnostic meta-learning for fast adaptation of deep networks. In: Proceedings of the 34th ICML, vol. 70, pp. 1126–1135 (2017)
7. Ghosh, A., Heffernan, N., Lan, A.S.: Context-aware attentive knowledge tracing. In: Proceedings of the 26th ACM SIGKDD, pp. 2330–2339 (2020)
8. Guo, Y., et al.: Mitigating cold-start problems in knowledge tracing with large language models: an attribute-aware approach. In: Proceedings of the 33rd ACM CIKM, pp. 727–736 (2024)
9. Jung, H., Yoo, J., Yoon, Y., Jang, Y.: CLST: cold-start mitigation in knowledge tracing by aligning a generative language model as a students' knowledge tracer. J. Educ. Data Mining **17**(2), 86–117 (2025)
10. Lu, Y., Fang, Y., Shi, C.: Meta-learning on heterogeneous information networks for cold-start recommendation. In: Proceedings of the 26th ACM SIGKDD (2020)
11. Mao, S.: Assistment2009 (2024). https://doi.org/10.21227/k80b-0n66
12. Pandey, S., Karypis, G.: A self-attentive model for knowledge tracing (2019). arXiv preprint arXiv:1907.06837
13. Patikorn, T., Heffernan, N.T., Baker, R.S.: ASSISTments longitudinal data mining competition 2017: a preface. In: Proceedings of the EDM Workshops (2018)
14. Piech, C., et al.: Deep knowledge tracing. In: NeurIPS, vol. 28 (2015)
15. Selent, D., Patikorn, T., Heffernan, N.: ASSISTments dataset from multiple randomized controlled experiments. In: 3rd ACM Learning@Scale, pp. 181–184 (2016)
16. Wang, C., Zhu, Y., Liu, H., Zang, T., Wang, K., Yu, J.: Multifaceted relation-aware meta-learning with dual customization for user cold-start recommendation. ACM Trans. Knowl. Discovery Data **17**(9) (2023)
17. Zhang, J., Shi, X., King, I., Yeung, D.Y.: Dynamic key-value memory networks for knowledge tracing. In: 26th World Wide Web Conference, pp. 765–774 (2017)
18. Zhang, J., Das, R., Baker, R., Scruggs, R.: Knowledge tracing models' predictive performance when a student starts a skill. In: EDM 2021, pp. 625–629 (2021)

Peer and Tutor in One: A Productive Failure-Based Architecture for Multi-role Conversational Agents in Physics Learning

Junbo Koh[1], Minsun Cho[1], and Sunyoung Keum[2]([⊠])

[1] Seoul National University, Seoul, South Korea
{gtkobo92,moon05}@snu.ac.kr
[2] Korea Institute for Curriculum and Evaluation, Jincheon-gun, Chungcheongbuk-do, South Korea
keum0815@kice.re.kr

Abstract. Large language model-based conversational agents are increasingly adopted in education. However, most existing systems are constrained by single-role configurations, with research primarily focused on technical implementation rather than pedagogically grounded design. This study aims to design and validate a multi-role conversational agent that assumes two contrasting roles—tutor and peer—grounded in the productive failure learning theory to facilitate learners' conceptual change in physics. A dialogue management system architecture was employed to categorize learner difficulties as intents, define role-specific dialogue acts, and establish dialogue policies that map each intent to appropriate acts. The system design was refined through two rounds of expert validation involving five specialists in AI, science education, and educational technology. Subsequently, a usability test was conducted with 46 high school students. Quantitative analysis of dialogue logs between the system and students, along with qualitative analysis of their feedback, confirmed the system's technical validity and educational usefulness. This study contributes to both theory and practice by proposing a learning-theory-based multi-role conversational agent architecture and demonstrating the potential to develop pedagogically aligned AI systems.

Keywords: Multi-Role Conversational Agents · Dialogue Management System · Productive Failure · Physics Education

1 Introduction

As Large Language Models (LLMs) advance, research on conversational agents that interact with learners through natural language dialogue is also growing rapidly. However, a significant portion of prior research focuses on technical feasibility, limiting the theoretical grounding for designing learning environments [12]. Furthermore, evaluations of these systems often merely report learner perceptions [4]. When utilizing conversational agents in education, it is crucial to

E. G. Blanchard et al. (Eds.): AIED 2026, LNAI 16583, pp. 150–158, 2027.
https://doi.org/10.1007/978-3-032-29760-0_17

support learners in thinking deeply to derive solutions, rather than providing immediate answers to their questions. This goes beyond relying on the efficient text generation capabilities of LLMs and requires pedagogically effective design of how the agent responds to learner needs.

Such pedagogical design is particularly required during learner-centered productive failure (PF) processes. PF is divided into an exploration stage where learners reveal their prior concepts and experience failure, and a subsequent consolidation stage where concepts are structured through elaborate explanation, comparison, and organization [6]. To implement this at the system level, rather than having a single role interact throughout all stages, it is necessary to manage peer role agents that facilitate exploration and tutor role agents that perform elaboration according to the learner's state.

To achieve this objective, the study developed peer and tutor multi-role conversational agents based on PF and implemented them within a Dialogue Management System (DMS) architecture. Specifically, (1) we classified the types of difficulties learners encounter into an intent taxonomy based on prior research, and (2) defined role-specific dialogue act inventories for peers and tutors based on PF theory. (3) Furthermore, a dialogue policy was designed to ensure each role acts appropriately according to the intent. This integrated the system into a white-box DMS, revealing educational intent rather than using the LLM as a black box. The system developed in this study underwent two rounds of expert validation. Subsequently, quantitative analysis based on learner dialogue logs and usability evaluations was conducted to confirm its technical validity and educational usefulness.

2   Related Works

Pedagogical conversational agents interact with learners through natural language and provide personalized support such as tutoring and motivation. Recent studies have increasingly focused on multi-role conversational agents that assume diverse roles such as tutor, peer, and coach. Prior research has explored various approaches, such as designing management structures that coordinate multiple agents or comparing the educational effects of different agent roles [2,13]. However, few studies have developed an act inventory grounded in learning theory and designed an act policy that enables educationally meaningful interactions based on learners' intents, while also presenting a corresponding system architecture.

Recently, there has been a growing effort to integrate LLMs into DMS frameworks to enable adaptive conversations that respond flexibly to learners' inputs [1,9]. In educational contexts, it is essential to carefully design when and how feedback should be delivered. Puech et al. [10] implemented 'Pedagogical Steering' in an LLM-based mathematics tutor to optimize prompts at each turn, promoting cognitive engagement through hints rather than immediate answers. Such work suggests that DMS in education is evolving toward a system grounded in pedagogical theory that provides appropriate instructional interventions throughout the learning process.

PF is an instructional approach that promotes learning through learners' initial experiences of failure, positing that cognitive conflict from early unsuccessful attempts leads to deeper conceptual understanding [6]. It consists of two phases: an unsupported exploration phase and a consolidation phase in which instruction helps learners compare their ideas with canonical solutions [5]. Therefore, to implement PF within conversational agents, it is necessary to develop distinct policies for a peer agent that promotes exploration and a tutor agent that supports consolidation.

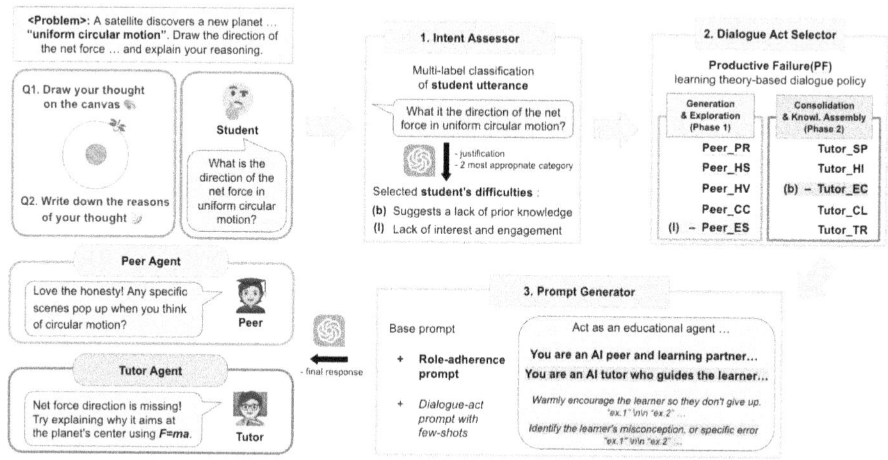

Fig. 1. System architecture of the PF-based multi-role dialogue management system.

3   Pedagogical Design and System Architecture

The proposed system was developed based on the DMS architecture to implement PF learning theory through multi-role conversational agents (Fig. 1). A DMS typically consists of four modules: Natural Language Understanding (NLU) for identifying user intent, Dialog State Tracker (DST) for managing conversation state, Dialog Policy Manager (DP) for selecting appropriate dialogue scenarios, and Natural Language Generation (NLG) for producing final responses. The proposed system aligns with these core modules and consists of three components: an Intent Assessor, a Dialogue Act Selector, and a Prompt Generator.

First, the Intent Assessor corresponds to the NLU module and identifies the learner's intent, classifying it into predefined learning state indicators. These indicators represent categories of difficulties that students encounter in physics learning and were derived from prior literature. By synthesizing the conversation history, system prompts, and the user's query, it selects the two most relevant indicators representing the learner's current state.

Second, the Dialogue Act Selector corresponds to the DST and DP modules and selects the appropriate dialogue act that the agents should perform based on the identified learning state indicators. The dialogue acts were designed based on PF's two-phase instructional framework. In Phase 1 (Generation & Exploration), five dialogue acts were developed as scaffolding strategies to promote students' thinking. In Phase 2 (Consolidation & Knowledge Assembly), five additional dialogue acts were designed as feedback strategies to address misconceptions and provide direct instruction.

The mapping between learning state indicators and dialogue acts is automatically determined based on predefined rules. Each indicator is mapped to a single dialogue act (one-to-one mapping), and the final act selection is determined by the highest-ranked indicator (Table 1). A distinctive feature is that even when the same indicator is identified, it may be linked to different dialogue acts depending on the learner's current phase and the agent's role.

Third, the Prompt Generator corresponds to the NLG module and constructs the final system prompt based on the selected dialogue act. A role-adherence prompt is incorporated to assign distinct personas depending on the instructional phase, and few-shot prompts tailored to each dialogue act are included to facilitate effective response generation and enhance role consistency.

4   Development and Evaluation

The DMS developed in this study was integrated into the physics learning platform previously introduced by Koh et al. [7]. The platform is a simulation-based AI system prototype designed to support the physics inquiry process and consists of five instructional stages. Students respond to the inquiry problem by drawing a diagram and explaining their reasoning in text. The conversational agent analyzes both inputs through multimodal processing to assess the student's answer and its underlying rationale. The newly integrated platform was developed to induce cognitive conflict, facilitate conceptual clarification, and promote transfer in alignment with each stage of learning. At each stage, the conversational agent assumes either the role of a peer or a tutor, evaluating students' responses and providing feedback throughout the learning process.

4.1   Expert Evaluation

Two rounds of expert validation were conducted with a panel of five specialists—two in educational technology, two in science education, and one in computer science—to examine the validity of the dialogue acts implemented in the AI chatbot. The first round evaluated the appropriateness of the dialogue acts in the context of science learning and the adequacy of the chatbot's interactions. Based on the results, the dialogue acts and example prompts were revised, and a second round assessed both the refined dialogue acts and their alignment with categorized types of student difficulties in scientific inquiry.

Validity was assessed using a four-point Likert scale, and the content validity index (CVI) and inter-rater agreement (IRA) were calculated to quantify item validity and assess the consistency of expert judgments across items. In the first validation, mean scores for dialogue act items were 3.2 or higher (CVI = 0.6–1.0; IRA = 0.69). Most chatbot-related items scored 3.4 or higher; however, the "activation of prior knowledge" item showed a low mean (2.4) and CVI (0.2), due to an overly strict response evaluation threshold that caused repetitive dialogue loops.

Table 1. Examples of intent-to-act mapping across learning stages.

Learning Stage	Agent Role	Student Intent (description)	dialogue act	
			label	description
Stage 2: Thinking	Peer	Eliciting misconceptions (inaccurate understanding of scientific concepts)	Induce cognitive conflict (Peer_CC)	Questions that surface discrepancies between the learner's prior conceptions and observed/expected phenomena trigger cognitive conflict
Stage 3: Experimenting	Peer	Fragmented knowledge (difficulty connecting related concepts coherently)	Hypothesis validation (Peer_HV)	Questions that help the learner logically link their hypothesis to simulation/experiment results
Stage 4: Reflecting	Tutor	Eliciting misconceptions (inaccurate understanding of scientific concepts)	Error correction (Tutor_EC)	Feedback that identifies the learner's misconception, points out what is incorrect, and guides them toward the correct understanding
		Fragmented knowledge (difficulty connecting related concepts coherently)	Concept clarification (Tutor_CL)	Concrete explanations that clarify the learned concepts and connect them coherently

In the second validation, mean scores for dialogue act items increased to 3.4 or higher (CVI = 1.0 for all but one item; IRA = 0.92). The alignment between student difficulty types and dialogue acts also demonstrated acceptable validity ($M \geq 3.0$; CVI = 0.6–1.0; IRA = 0.81). Based on expert feedback, the system was further refined to clarify stage-specific difficulty types and explicitly link student utterance analysis to dialogue act selection within the prompts.

4.2   Technical Evaluation

The system was implemented with 46 eleventh-grade students in South Korea, who interacted with the system for approximately 25 min. The collected dialogue logs were analyzed quantitatively.

To measure role-adherence performance, we employed BERT-Score, which calculates semantic similarity using contextual embeddings [14]. As a semantic similarity metric, BERT-Score is used to validate design fidelity, specifically whether the system produces role-distinct outputs as intended, rather than pedagogical impact. Using 100 randomly sampled dialogue pairs, the analysis showed high within-role similarity for both Peer ($M = 0.71$) and Tutor ($M = 0.77$) roles, while between-role similarity was comparatively low (see Fig. 2), indicating that the agents exhibit semantically distinct interaction patterns.

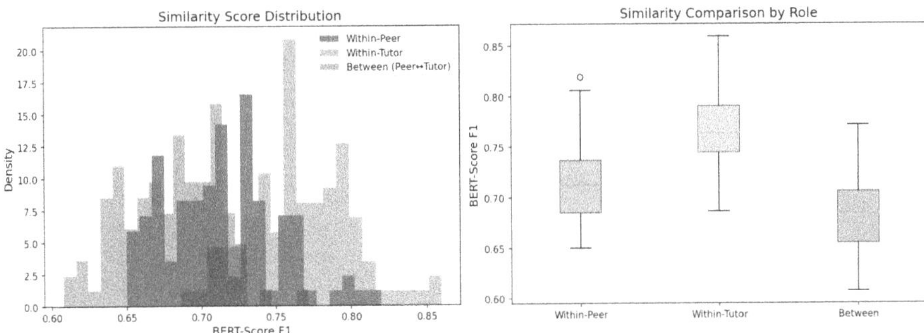

Fig. 2. Distribution and comparison of BERT-Score F1 for within-role (Peer, Tutor) and between-role (Peer $\leftrightarrow$ Tutor) response pairs.

Additionally, a rubric-based evaluation was conducted to assess the educational effectiveness of generated utterances during Phases 2–4. The rubric was developed based on Scarlatos et al. [11] and adapted to the context of this study. For the Peer agent, four criteria were used: Guide Hypotheses (GH), Deepen Reasoning (DR), Cognitive Conflict (CC), and Encouraging (Enc). For the Tutor agent, four criteria were applied: Accuracy (Acc), Progress (Pro), Error Identification (EI), and Strategic Hinting (SH). Each criterion was evaluated using a binary label, and an overall score (Ove) was assigned on a 5-point scale.

To ensure reliability, an in-service teacher and a physics education major manually rated approximately 20% of total responses to establish a human evaluation standard. IRA values were 0.82 in Phase 2, 1.0 in Phase 3, and 0.93 in Phase 4. An automated evaluation prompt was then iteratively refined to align with human judgment. Since the system was built on OpenAI's GPT-4.1, we used Claude-Sonnet-4.5 as the evaluation model to mitigate self-preference bias [8]. The finalized prompt was used to evaluate the entire dataset, which consisted of 335 dialogue pairs in Phase 2, 165 in Phase 3, and 46 in Phase 4. Results are presented in Table 2.

Table 2. Rubric-based evaluation results across learning phases.

	GH	DR	CC	Enc	Acc	Pro	EI	SH	Ove
Phase 2	0.797	0.891	0.516	0.969	–	–	–	–	4.03
Phase 3	0.873	0.441	0.126	0.983	–	–	–	–	3.32
Phase 4	–	–	–	–	0.935	0.543	0.935	0.783	3.94

4.3   User Evaluation

Based on one-on-one usability interviews conducted with 16 students, the following findings emerged. First, when compared to a general-purpose LLM such as ChatGPT, participants reported that the educational AI system developed in this study was more trustworthy. Because the system was specifically designed for educational purposes, students noted that it reduced concerns about hallucinations and did not provide excessive information beyond the intended scope of learning. However, one area for improvement was that, compared to technically advanced general-purpose AI systems, the conversation did not feel "as fast and smooth" (Student E).

Second, in terms of the user interface (UI), students indicated that long blocks of text were difficult to grasp at a glance and that it was challenging to review responses from previous stages. Future improvements should therefore consider enhancing user convenience by adjusting the size and placement of the chatbot dialogue window and enabling easier access to conversation history from earlier stages.

Third, there was a demand for functional improvements and broader implementation of the system. Functionally, some students suggested that the agent's persona could be more customizable to fit individual learner preferences. For example, when interacting with the peer agent, students expressed a desire to choose different interaction styles depending on whether they wanted to "focus seriously on studying from the beginning" or "engage in a lighter, more exploratory conversation" (Student G).

5   Discussion and Conclusion

The system developed in this study is not a black-box model that merely relies on an LLM, but rather a DMS designed as a white-box model with explicit pedagogical intentions. As the development of LLM-based AI agents rapidly expands, concerns have been raised about the limitations of constructing prompts without sufficient theoretical grounding and without fully considering the educational impact of the developed systems [12]. In this context, the present study aimed to develop a model that ensures both technical and pedagogical validity through iterative expert validation. To this end, two rounds of expert validation were conducted, involving specialists in AI, educational technology, and science education.

For technical validation, within-role and between-role similarities were analyzed using BERT-Score. The results confirmed that the peer and tutor agents generated semantically distinct utterances within a shared architecture. Notably, the tutor agent showed higher within-role similarity than the peer agent. This is interpreted as reflecting the tutor agent's design, which emphasizes structured explanations of scientific concepts, leading to more stable and convergent responses. In contrast, the peer agent was designed to generate exploratory utterances that induce cognitive conflict, resulting in greater expressive variability and consequently lower within-role similarity. These findings also provide a basis for interpreting learners' requests for more "natural conversations," as identified in the usability evaluation.

Unlike general-purpose LLM, the developed system operates through an educationally intentional DMS architecture. As a result, its utterances—designed to support productive failure within a predefined scope of educational content— may at times appear somewhat mechanical. While this characteristic may enhance learners' trust in the AI agent as an educational tool, it may simultaneously reduce the perceived naturalness of conversation. To foster a stronger sense of presence and engagement in educational interactions with AI agents, further improvements are needed to enable more natural conversational flows.

Regarding architecture scalability, the DMS developed in this study is designed to be domain-transferable. By modifying the intent taxonomy and act inventory according to the target domain, it is possible to develop multi-role conversational agents aligned with educational intentions through a dialogue policy framework. For instance, in economics education, misconceptions about supply and demand could be defined as specific intents, with corresponding peer agent acts designed to induce cognitive conflict and tutor agent acts providing explicit explanations. In this way, multi-role conversational agents supporting productive failure–based learning could also be implemented in economics.

This study has several limitations. First, the field implementation involved only 46 high school students, resulting in a limited sample size. As this study focused on chatbot development, further validation of its educational effectiveness with larger samples is required. Second, the evaluation was based on approximately 25 min of short-term use; longer-term exposure and more rigorous evaluation designs, such as controlled studies, are needed to assess changes in students' conceptual understanding. Third, the current system employs a rule-based dialogue policy that deterministically maps each intent to a predefined dialogue act. While this may oversimplify complex learner states, it is an intentional trade-off to ensure interpretable and faithful implementation of PF-aligned pedagogy. More adaptive policies may better capture learner complexity.

Future work could draw on multi-agent orchestration approaches [3], in which agent roles and interaction structures are dynamically configured based on evolving task states rather than being fixed a priori. For example, an orchestration layer could monitor learner states in real time and selectively invoke tutor-like acts during the exploration phase when persistent misconceptions are detected, enabling role composition and dialogue policies to co-adapt to the learner's trajectory while preserving the overall PF instructional sequence. Additionally, future research could compare multi-role conversational agents with single-role agents and general-purpose LLM to enable more rigorous evaluation of their effectiveness.

References

1. Algherairy, A., Ahmed, M.: A review of dialogue systems: current trends and future directions. Neural Comput. Appl. **36**(12), 6325–6351 (2024). https://doi.org/10.1007/s00521-023-09322-1
2. Cao, C.C., Ding, Z., Lin, J., Hopfgartner, F.: AI chatbots as multi-role pedagogical agents: transforming engagement in CS education (2023). arXiv preprint arXiv:2308.03992
3. Dang, Y., et al.: Multi-agent collaboration via evolving orchestration (2025). arXiv preprint arXiv:2505.19591
4. Debets, T., Banihashem, S.K., Joosten-Ten Brinke, D., Vos, T.E., de Buy Wenniger, G.M., Camp, G.: Chatbots in education: A systematic review of objectives, underlying technology and theory, evaluation criteria, and impacts. Comput. Educ. **234**, 105323 (2025)
5. Hmelo-Silver, C.E., Kapur, M., Hamstra, M.: Learning through problem solving. In: International Handbook of the Learning Sciences, pp. 210–220. Routledge (2018). https://doi.org/10.4324/9781315617572-21
6. Kapur, M.: Productive failure. Cogn. Instr. **26**(3), 379–424 (2008). https://doi.org/10.1080/07370000802212669
7. Koh, J., Park, J., Kim, C., Kim, Y., Keum, S.: Development of a prototype simulation-based AI system to support physics inquiry learning. J. Educ. Inf. Media **31**(2), 493–517 (2025). https://doi.org/10.15833/KAFEIAM.31.2.493
8. Li, D., et al.: From generation to judgment: opportunities and challenges of LLM-as-a-judge. In: Proceedings of the 2025 Conference on Empirical Methods in Natural Language Processing, pp. 2757–2791 (2025). https://doi.org/10.18653/v1/2025.emnlp-main.138
9. Pian, Y., Lu, Y.: Leveraging large language models to enhance the inner loops of intelligent tutoring systems. In: International Conference on Artificial Intelligence in Education, pp. 218–230. Springer Nature Switzerland, Cham (2025). https://doi.org/10.1007/978-3-031-98420-4_16
10. Puech, R., Macina, J., Chatain, J., Sachan, M., Kapur, M.: Towards the pedagogical steering of large language models for tutoring: a case study with modeling productive failure. In: Findings of the Association for Computational Linguistics: ACL 2025, pp. 26291–26311 (2025). https://doi.org/10.18653/v1/2025.findings-acl.1348
11. Scarlatos, A., Liu, N., Lee, J., Baraniuk, R., Lan, A.: Training LLM-based tutors to improve student learning outcomes in dialogues. In: International Conference on Artificial Intelligence in Education, pp. 251–266. Springer Nature Switzerland, Cham (2025). https://doi.org/10.1007/978-3-031-98414-3_18
12. Stamper, J., Xiao, R., Hou, X.: Enhancing LLM-based feedback: insights from intelligent tutoring systems and the learning sciences. In: International Conference on Artificial Intelligence in Education, pp. 32–43. Springer Nature Switzerland, Cham (2024). https://doi.org/10.1007/978-3-031-64315-6_3
13. Xu, Z., Zhang, J., Tang, A., Lee, Y.C.: Who you explain to matters: Learning by explaining to conversational agents with different pedagogical roles (2026). arXiv preprint arXiv:2601.16583
14. Zhang, T., Kishore, V., Wu, F., Weinberger, K.Q., Artzi, Y.: Bertscore: Evaluating text generation with bert (2019). arXiv preprint arXiv:1904.09675

EduArt-Bench: A Benchmark and Lightweight Scoring Calibration for K-12 Art Education

Zekun Huang, Shuyan Chen, Yiwen Chen, Xun Zhou, and Wei Xu[✉]

School of Electronic Information and Communication, Huazhong University of
Science and Technology, Wuhan, China
{huangzekun,chen_shuyan,chenyiwen,zhouxun,xuwei}@hust.edu.cn

Abstract. In conventional K-12 art education, teachers often struggle to provide timely and fine-grained feedback for each student's high-frequency practice, which leads to delayed assessments and inconsistent criteria. Developing a K-12 art automatic assessment system can effectively reduce teachers' assessment burden, improve evaluation efficiency, and promote educational equity as well as personalized learning. In this paper, we introduce EduArt-Bench, a task-driven benchmark for K-12 art automatic assessment. It contains 334 authentic student works spanning 12 instructional tasks and covers both drawings and handicrafts. Two art experts exhaustively annotate all samples across seven dimensions and overall quality. Building on this benchmark, we conduct a systematic comparison of three progressively constrained prompting strategies and find that the integration of explicit scoring rubrics and prototypical examples significantly enhances the scoring agreement between multimodal large language models (MLLMs) and expert ratings. Furthermore, inspired by multi-dimensional calibration-based automatic assessment, we propose Aesthetic Feature Extraction–Deep Calibration (Aesthetic-FEDC), which mounts an ultra-lightweight MLP calibrator onto a small-to-medium MLLM backend and achieves strong alignment with expert scoring standards with limited training data.

Keywords: Benchmark · Image aesthetics assessment · MLP calibrator · Multimodal large language models · Rubric-based prompting

1 Introduction

With the rapid development of artificial intelligence, assessment in K-12 art education is gaining an opportunity to shift from experience-based judgment toward intelligent and fine-grained evaluation. Due to the inherent subjectivity of art, assessment has often relied on individual teachers' aesthetic experience and professional judgment. As a result, it is difficult to provide timely and detailed feedback for every student's high-frequency practice, leading to delayed evaluation and inconsistent standards. Therefore, building an automated assessment

E. G. Blanchard et al. (Eds.): AIED 2026, LNAI 16583, pp. 159–167, 2027.
https://doi.org/10.1007/978-3-032-29760-0_18

system for K-12 art can not only reduce teachers' workload but also improve evaluation efficiency.

The research area most closely related to K-12 art automatic assessment is Image Aesthetic Assessment (IAA), which aims to predict the overall aesthetic quality of a given image. Recent IAA advancements have evolved from score-only predictions [11] to interpretable aesthetic analyses. However, applying these general-purpose models to K-12 art introduces significant challenges. For example, models such as AesCLIP [10] and ArtiMuse [2] can learn aesthetic preferences from professional works and output an overall score together with aesthetic analyses. However, directly transferring such general-purpose aesthetic models to K-12 art automatic assessment introduces notable issues. Their evaluation criteria are often calibrated to standards far above children's artistic proficiency, which can cause students' works to cluster in low-score ranges and thus fail to form a discriminative competence spectrum. Moreover, models like ArtiMuse lack support for user-defined prompts, failing to meet task-driven instructional requirements where assessment must align with specific learning objectives rather than just surface-level aesthetics.

From the dataset perspective, existing datasets and benchmarks for image aesthetic assessment have not been sufficiently adapted to the instructional needs of K-12 art education. Mainstream aesthetic datasets, such as AVA [9], AADB [8], PCCD [3], and APDDv2 [7], primarily focus on professional artworks and photographic images, rather than defining evaluation targets and test instances around concrete K-12 instructional tasks. In recent years, datasets targeting children's works have begun to emerge. While recent datasets like AACP [6] and KidsArtBench [13] focus on children's art, they emphasize general aesthetic attributes rather than customizable, dimension-specific instructional criteria. Similarly, ArtMentor [14] explores interactive critique but ignores assignment-specific requirements. Consequently, it is difficult for such data and settings to directly support standardized assessment aligned with instructional objectives and calibrated scoring scales.

To address these limitations, we are among the first to propose a K-12 art automatic assessment framework that enables teachers to explicitly specify instructional goals and task requirements. First, we construct EduArt-Bench, a K-12 art automatic assessment benchmark comprising 334 student works that cover 12 core instructional tasks. Professional education experts provide systematic annotations for all samples, including scores on seven fine-grained dimensions and an overall quality score. Second, based on EduArt-Bench, we conduct experiments with multiple mainstream MLLMs and systematically compare the effectiveness of three prompting strategies, namely *Direct*, *+Rubric*, and *+Rubric+Examples*. We find that *+Rubric+Examples* yields the best assessment performance. Finally, we propose a lightweight alignment framework, Aesthetic Feature Extraction–Deep Calibration(Aesthetic-FEDC), which attaches an ultra-lightweight MLP calibrator to a small-to-medium-scale MLLM backend. With only limited training data, Aesthetic-FEDC achieves strong alignment between model outputs and expert scoring standards, providing an effective solu-

Table 1. Unified evaluation dimensions (covering both 2D artworks and 3D handicrafts).

ID	Dimension	Brief description
D1	Task Fulfillment	Degree of alignment with assignment requirements and key task features
D2	Theme Clarity	How clearly the theme is conveyed and how easily it can be recognized and understood
D3	Composition	Quality of layout and spatial organization or coherence and balance of the 3D structure
D4	Color & Value	Appropriateness of color/value usage or effectiveness of color and decoration for recognition and aesthetics
D5	Line & Form	Clarity and stability of lines and forms or reliability of craftsmanship and construction details
D6	Creativity	Novelty and personalization of ideas, including imaginative content or inventive material use
D7	Completeness	Overall completion and refinement with adequate details and finishing quality
Overall	Overall Performance	Overall quality as an assignment product and level of instructional attainment

tion for K-12 art automatic assessment. We provide the complete repository for reproducibility at https://github.com/hopeSerendipity/EduArt-Bench.

2   Method

2.1   EduArt-Bench

We constructed a dataset of 334 authentic art works created by elementary school students, collected from a central region of China. The dataset covers 12 instructional tasks and includes both drawings and handicraft pieces.

Following the *Compulsory Education Art Curriculum Standards (2022 Edition)* issued in China, we decomposed art-education objectives into seven actionable assessment dimensions (see Table 1 for the dimension definitions). Each work was independently scored by two professionally trained art-education raters on a 1–5 scale. The final discrete label for each dimension is the mean of the two scores rounded to the nearest integer. To ensure scoring consistency, we introduced a calibration stage prior to formal annotation: for each dimension, the two raters selected anchor samples representing different proficiency levels and conducted rubric alignment and discussions of prototypical cases, ensuring that the evaluation framework remained consistent and professionally appropriate in complex artistic contexts. The expert panel achieved an average quadratic weighted kappa (QWK) [4] of 0.7814 across dimensions, indicating high inter-rater agreement for subjective art assessment.

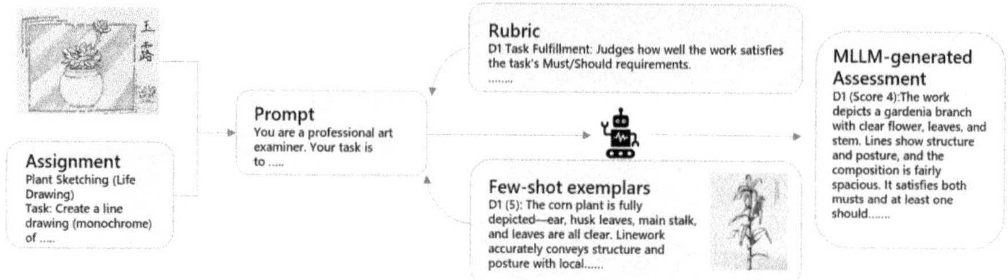

Fig. 1. *Direct,+Rubric*, and *+Rubric+Examples*: Three constraint settings for a multi-dimensional art assignment grading prompting pipeline.

2.2   Prompting Strategies for MLLM-Based Grading

To identify an effective paradigm for automated assessment of children's art assignments, we benchmark a diverse set of general-purpose MLLMs under progressively stronger prompting constraints, covering both proprietary and open-source models with different parameter scales. Specifically, we evaluate GPT-5.1, GPT-4o, Gemini 3 Pro, Qwen3-VL-235B-A22B-Instruct [1], GLM-4.6V-Flash [12], and Qwen3-VL-8B-Instruct. We consider three prompting modes with increasing supervision namely *Direct*, *+Rubric*, and *+Rubric+Examples*.

In the *Direct* mode, we provide only the names of the eight dimensions, aiming to assess the MLLM's zero-shot performance under minimal instructions. The *+Rubric* mode further incorporates tiered criteria for each dimension, enabling us to examine the regularizing effect of structured scoring rules. The *+Rubric+Examples* mode additionally supplies, for each assignment, three prototypical cases that span distinct quality levels, together with their scores and feedback comments. This few-shot setup offers explicit anchors for the scoring scale. This progressive design mirrors the evolution of assessment practices from coarse judgments to fine-grained diagnosis, allowing us to analyze the performance limits of different MLLMs as knowledge constraints are strengthened (Fig. 1).

2.3   Aesthetic Feature Extraction–Deep Calibration

Inspired by the multi-dimensional and calibratable evaluation paradigm proposed in LLM-rubric [5], we extend calibration-based assessment from natural language tasks to the visual evaluation of K-12 art automatic assessment. In the data-scarce setting of art assignment scoring, aligning model outputs with expert raters' scoring rubrics remains particularly challenging. To address this, we propose Aesthetic-FEDC.

Specifically, for each scoring item $d \in \{1, \ldots, 8\}$, we perform dimension-wise prompted inference so that the MLLM produces a scoring signal only for the target dimension. Instead of reading the full vocabulary distribution or directly using the generated text, we extract logits only for the candidate score tokens

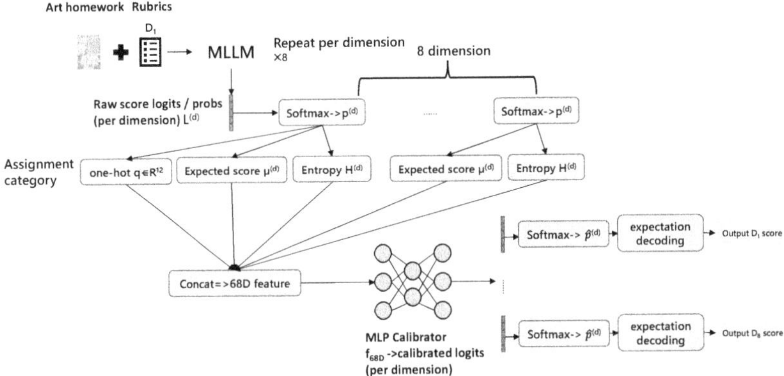

Fig. 2. End-to-End Pipeline of MLLM-based Art Assessment with Aesthetic-FEDC

$\{1, 2, 3, 4, 5\}$, denoted as $\mathbf{L}^{(d)} \in \mathbb{R}^5$, and normalize them into a probability distribution $\mathbf{p}^{(d)} = \mathrm{softmax}(\mathbf{L}^{(d)})$. This feature captures the MLLM's relative preference and confidence structure over the ordinal scale $\{1, \ldots, 5\}$. Concatenating $\mathbf{p}^{(d)}$ across the eight dimensions yields an 8×5-dimensional input feature, denoted as 40D.

Since art assessment often involves controversial or ambiguous samples, we further compute the expected score and information entropy from $\mathbf{p}^{(d)}$ to explicitly encode both tendency and uncertainty. The final feature vector augments the 40D concatenation with $\mu^{(d)}$ and $H^{(d)}$ for all eight dimensions and a one-hot encoding of the assignment category index over 12 task types, $\mathbf{q} \in \mathbb{R}^{12}$, resulting in a 68-dimensional vector, denoted as 68D. We call the calibrator ultra-lightweight because it trains only a small MLP on top of frozen MLLM outputs, using this 68-dimensional feature vector rather than end-to-end visual fine-tuning, which substantially reduces trainable parameters and computational cost. Compared with the underlying MLLM, the MLP introduces only a tiny fraction of additional parameters, making it highly efficient and practical for small-scale art assessment.

During training, we supervise the calibrator with the consensus discrete label $y^{(d)} \in \{1, \ldots, 5\}$ and minimize an equally weighted cross-entropy loss across dimensions. The model outputs a 5-way logit vector for each dimension, and we apply a per-dimension softmax to obtain $\hat{p}^{(d)}$. At inference time, we decode $\hat{p}^{(d)}$ by its expectation to produce a continuous score (Fig. 2).

3 Experiments

3.1 Evaluation Metrics

To evaluate each model's consistency with expert raters' annotations under different strategies and to quantify the improvements brought by the calibration module, we use Mean Absolute Error (MAE) to measure the average magnitude

Table 2. Performance of MLLMs on K-12 art automatic assessment under three prompting strategies. Macro (D1–D7) denotes the mean of per-dimension results computed separately for each dimension. Overall is an independently annotated holistic score.

Model	Direct Macro(D1–D7)			Direct Overall			+Rubric Macro(D1–D7)			+Rubric Overall			+Rubric+Examples Macro(D1–D7)			+Rubric+Examples Overall		
	QWK↑	MAE↓	ACC↑	QWK↑	MAE↓	ACC↑	QWK↑	MAE↓	ACC↑	QWK↑	MAE↓	ACC↑	QWK↑	MAE↓	ACC↑	QWK↑	MAE↓	ACC↑
GPT-5.1	**0.272**	**0.8135**	**0.382**	**0.270**	**0.814**	**0.377**	**0.335**	**0.741**	**0.436**	**0.256**	1.06	0.293	**0.480**	**0.620**	**0.491**	0.465	0.811	0.377
GPT-4o	0.238	0.900	0.328	0.236	0.912	0.355	0.267	0.852	0.352	0.254	0.915	0.332	0.420	0.712	0.428	0.458	**0.739**	**0.401**
Gemini 3 Pro	0.142	1.103	0.282	0.187	0.890	0.341	0.159	0.996	0.323	0.207	**0.882**	0.323	0.342	0.818	0.389	0.361	0.831	0.353
Qwen3-VL-235B-A22B-Instruct	0.097	1.255	0.228	0.108	1.214	0.235	0.091	1.011	0.307	0.086	0.961	**0.337**	0.388	0.781	0.422	0.417	0.868	0.349
GLM-4.6V-Flash	0.083	0.973	0.178	0.106	1.102	0.127	0.097	1.294	0.208	0.071	1.671	0.108	0.156	1.215	0.217	0.135	1.485	0.147
Qwen3-VL-8B-Instruct	0.132	1.205	0.201	0.142	1.368	0.108	0.126	1.096	0.231	0.068	1.569	0.105	0.101	1.318	0.213	0.048	1.659	0.123
ArtiMuse (Overall-only)	–			0.009	1.075	0.216	–			–			–			–		

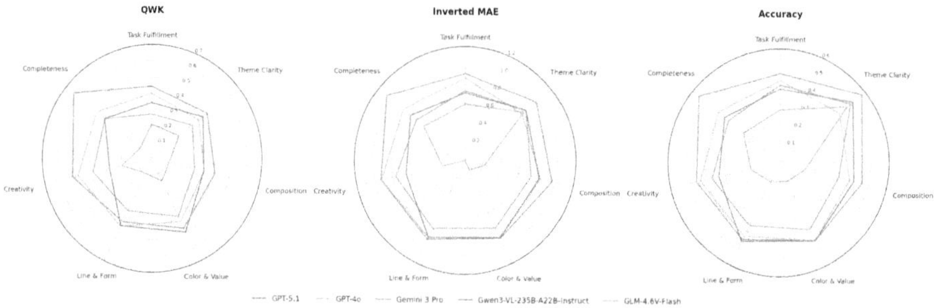

Fig. 3. Performance Distribution of MLLMs Across Evaluation Dimensions Under the *+Rubric+Examples* Prompting Setting. *Note:* MAE values are inverted as $\text{MAE}_{max} -$ MAE, where MAE_{max} denotes the maximum MAE across all models.

of deviation between predicted and annotated scores (treating the 15 ratings as an interval scale). We also report QWK to assess agreement on ordered categories, and use Accuracy (ACC) as a strict exact-match metric.

3.2   Effects of Prompt Constraints on Model Scoring

We reserve 36 of the 334 works in EduArt-Bench as exemplars for *+Rubric +Examples* and evaluate all three prompting strategies on the remaining 298 works. Table 2 presents the grading performance of GPT-5.1, GPT-4o, Qwen3-VL-235B, and Gemini 3 Pro under the three prompting constraints described in Sect. 2.2. Overall, the *+Rubric* setting outperforms *Direct* on most metrics, indicating that structured, dimension-level criteria help constrain the basis for model judgments. The *+Rubric+Examples* setting achieves the best performance, suggesting that introducing scored exemplars and corresponding feedback further calibrates the model's scoring scale (Fig. 3).

In contrast, for small-parameter models such as GLM-4.6V-Flash and Qwen3-VL-8B-Instruct, the gains from *+Rubric* and *+Rubric+Examples* are unstable, and some metrics even degrade. This implies that model scale plays an important role in supporting the comprehension of rubric constraints and the effective use

Table 3. Performance impact of the Aesthetic-FEDC calibrator across varying model scales.

Size	Model	Macro (D1–D7)			Overall		
		QWK↑	MAE↓	ACC↑	QWK↑	MAE↓	ACC↑
8B	Base-MLLM	0.151	1.468	0.149	0.162	1.774	0.056
	MLLM + Aesthetic-FEDC	**0.314**	**0.669**	**0.222**	**0.311**	**0.639**	**0.278**
30B	Base-MLLM	0.179	1.209	0.151	0.200	1.422	0.069
	MLLM + Aesthetic-FEDC	**0.448**	**0.637**	**0.224**	**0.534**	**0.604**	**0.241**

Table 4. Input feature ablation for the Aesthetic-FEDC module (68D vs. 40D).

Size	Input	Macro (D1–D7)			Overall		
		QWK↑	MAE↓	ACC↑	QWK↑	MAE↓	ACC↑
8B	40D	0.240	0.698	0.212	0.155	0.709	0.222
	68D	0.314	0.669	0.222	0.311	0.639	**0.278**
30B	40D	0.401	0.681	0.177	0.454	0.696	0.138
	68D	**0.448**	**0.637**	**0.224**	**0.534**	**0.604**	0.241

of exemplar references. Moreover, as an aesthetics-assessment model, ArtiMuse does not allow custom prompts or reference images, and thus cannot produce results under *+Rubric* or *+Rubric+Examples*. Even under *Direct*, its performance is not satisfactory. Although KidsArtBench supports custom prompting, its training-time scoring dimensions are fixed and differ from those used in this work, making a direct score-level comparison infeasible.

3.3 Performance and Ablation Studies of Aesthetic-FEDC

To develop the Aesthetic-FEDC, the EduArt-Bench dataset was partitioned into training, validation, and test sets following an 8:1:1 distribution. We compare the performance of Aesthetic-FEDC across different parameter scales. As shown in Table 3, Aesthetic-FEDC consistently and substantially outperforms the corresponding baseline models on both Qwen3-VL-8B-Instruct and Qwen3-VL-30B-A3B-Instruct, confirming the importance of calibration for improving scoring agreement. In addition, relative to the 8B setting, Aesthetic-FEDC achieves markedly better QWK and MAE in the 30B setting, reflecting stronger modeling capacity at larger scale. The slight fluctuation in ACC may be attributed to the small test set size and the relatively strict matching criterion.

We further compare Aesthetic-FEDC under different input feature settings described in Sect. 2.3. As shown in Table 4, the 68D feature configuration consistently outperforms the 40D configuration for both the 8B and 30B backends, with particularly pronounced gains on the *Overall* dimension. For example, with the 30B backend, the *Overall* QWK increases from 0.454 to 0.534, and ACC improves from 0.138 to 0.241. These results indicate that calibration based solely on the score-token probability distribution is limited. Incorporating uncertainty cues captured by entropy, directional information conveyed by the expected score, and complementary signals from the task-type one-hot encoding enables a more stable fit to expert scoring criteria.

4   Conclusion

In this paper, we build EduArt-Bench, a task-driven benchmark for K-12 art automatic assessment. We systematically compare three progressively constrained prompting strategies on general-purpose MLLMs and find that introducing explicit scoring rubrics and prototypical examples substantially improves the agreement between MLLM-based scoring and expert ratings. Moreover, we introduce a multi-dimensional calibration mechanism for open-source MLLMs and propose Aesthetic-FEDC, which attaches an ultra-lightweight MLP calibrator to a small-to-medium-scale MLLM backend. With limited training data, Aesthetic-FEDC achieves strong alignment with expert scoring standards. In future work, we plan to construct a larger-scale dataset and further explore fine-tuning and post-training strategies for MLLMs. We expect that richer data and stronger adaptation pipelines will further improve grading accuracy, robustness, and generalization.

Acknowledgments. This work is supported by the National Key Research and Development Program of China under Grant 2021YFC3340803.

Disclosure of Interests. The authors have no competing interests to declare that are relevant to the content of this article.

References

1. Bai, S., et al.: Qwen3-VL technical report (2025). https://arxiv.org/abs/2511.21631
2. Cao, S., et al.: ArtiMuse: fine-grained image aesthetics assessment with joint scoring and expert-level understanding. arXiv preprint arXiv:2507.14533 (2025)
3. Chang, K.Y., Lu, K.H., Chen, C.S.: Aesthetic critiques generation for photos. In: Proceedings of the IEEE International Conference on Computer Vision, pp. 3514–3523 (2017)
4. Cohen, J.: Weighted kappa: nominal scale agreement provision for scaled disagreement or partial credit. Psychol. Bull. **70**(4), 213 (1968)
5. Hashemi, H., Eisner, J., Rosset, C., Van Durme, B., Kedzie, C.: LLM-Rubric: a multidimensional, calibrated approach to automated evaluation of natural language texts. In: Proceedings of the 62nd Annual Meeting of the Association for Computational Linguistics (Volume 1: Long Papers), pp. 13806–13834 (2024)
6. Jiang, S., Li, N., Shi, C., Guo, L., Wang, C., Li, C.: AACP: aesthetics assessment of children's paintings based on self-supervised learning. In: Proceedings of the AAAI Conference on Artificial Intelligence, vol. 38, pp. 2534–2542 (2024)

7. Jin, X., et al.: APDDv2: aesthetics of paintings and drawings dataset with artist labeled scores and comments, **8**(9) (2024). arXiv preprint arXiv:2411.08545
8. Kong, S., Shen, X., Lin, Z., Mech, R., Fowlkes, C.: Photo aesthetics ranking network with attributes and content adaptation. In: Leibe, B., Matas, J., Sebe, N., Welling, M. (eds.) ECCV 2016. LNCS, vol. 9905, pp. 662–679. Springer, Cham (2016). https://doi.org/10.1007/978-3-319-46448-0_40
9. Murray, N., Marchesotti, L., Perronnin, F.: AVA: a large-scale database for aesthetic visual analysis. In: 2012 IEEE Conference on Computer Vision and Pattern Recognition, pp. 2408–2415. IEEE (2012)
10. Sheng, X., et al.: AesCLIP: multi-attribute contrastive learning for image aesthetics assessment. In: Proceedings of the 31st ACM International Conference on Multimedia, pp. 1117–1126 (2023)
11. Talebi, H., Milanfar, P.: NIMA: neural image assessment. IEEE Trans. Image Process. **27**(8), 3998–4011 (2018)
12. Hong, W., et al.: GLM-4.5V and GLM-4.1V-thinking: towards versatile multimodal reasoning with scalable reinforcement learning (2025). https://arxiv.org/abs/2507.01006
13. Ye, M., et al.: KidsArtBench: multi-dimensional children's art evaluation with attribute-aware MLLMs. In: Proceedings of the 19th Conference of the European Chapter of the Association for Computational Linguistics (Volume 1: Long Papers), pp. 5702–5722 (2026)
14. Zheng, C., et al.: ArtMentor: AI-assisted evaluation of artworks to explore multimodal large language models capabilities. In: Proceedings of the 2025 CHI Conference on Human Factors in Computing Systems, pp. 1–18 (2025)

Conceptualization of Thinking Activities-Specific Metacognitive Knowledge Ontology

Tomoki Aburatani[✉] [iD], Yuki Hayashi [iD], and Kazuhisa Seta [iD]

Osaka Metropolitan University, 1-1 Gakuen-cho, Naka-ku, Sakai, Osaka, Japan
{aburatani.tomoki,hayapy,seta}@omu.ac.jp

Abstract. Thinking tasks such as research and active learning activities, which aim to solve problems in the mental world rather than the physical world, require the conscious exercise of metacognition to control the co-evolutionary problem-solving process where both problem and solution spaces evolve simultaneously. Although the learning and application of metacognitive knowledge is essential for such tasks, there is no systematic framework for representing task-specific metacognitive knowledge in a context-sensitive manner. This study proposes an ontology (TACTO: Thinking ACTivities-specific metacognitive knowledge Ontology) for representing metacognitive knowledge in thinking tasks. Drawing on task ontology and functional ontology, we define three core concepts: "cognitive act" representing events that transform artifacts from an unthought state to a thought state, "cognitive act achievement way" representing sequences of cognitive acts effective for accomplishing a specific cognitive act, and "goal-way rationale" explaining why such achievement ways are effective.

Keywords: Metacognitive knowledge · Thinking tasks · Formal ontology · Conceptualization

1 Introduction

Research activities and autonomous learning activities involve ill-defined problems, in which the final goal state, constraints, and solutions cannot be predetermined [22]. In the problem-solving process for such problems, a co-evolutionary process is known to occur, whereby both the approach to solving the problem (solution space) and the problem itself (problem space) change simultaneously and interactively [3,13]. In this study, we refer to activities that dynamically reconstruct the problem space and solution space as mental representations while working toward a solution to such ill-defined problems as '*thinking tasks.*' Such thinking tasks require exercising metacognition over the co-evolutionary process and steering it toward purposeful problem solving [26]. By acquiring and exercising metacognitive knowledge—the knowledge referenced during the execution of metacognitive activities—one can effectively perform thinking tasks in which

E. G. Blanchard et al. (Eds.): AIED 2026, LNAI 16583, pp. 168–177, 2027.
https://doi.org/10.1007/978-3-032-29760-0_19

goals are not clearly defined [5,8]. However, no mechanism has been proposed to support the explicit and systematic learning of metacognitive knowledge.

For example, in research tasks in educational systems and information science, researchers must consciously consider what they should think about—such as *'what difficulties do learners face?'*—and for each such consideration, multiple solution processes can be envisioned as options. Selecting an appropriate process requires metacognitive knowledge, which is currently left to the heuristics of individual faculty members. Similarly, in autonomous learning about technology aimed at specific problem solving (technology domain learning tasks), learners need to go beyond memorizing what is explicitly written in texts and deepen their understanding by reading what is not written, such as *'what problems does the technology solve'* [2,10]. Here too, multiple solution processes exist, and learners must select appropriate ones guided by metacognitive knowledge. Although educational programs that encourage learners to construct metacognitive knowledge have been proposed [1], the metacognitive knowledge to be constructed must be specified ad hoc for each learning domain.

Thus, although the acquisition and exercise of metacognitive knowledge is important for performing thinking tasks, no comprehensive mechanism to support this has been established. The underlying issue is that frameworks for expressing metacognitive knowledge that address the content and context of thinking tasks have not been sufficiently discussed, making it difficult to discuss support methods for exercising and learning metacognitive knowledge under a common framework. If a conceptual foundation could be constructed that enables people, (computer) systems, or both to share a common understanding of the metacognitive knowledge referenced to observe and control the solution process, this could lead to more purposeful execution of thinking tasks and adaptive support for learning them.

Therefore, in this study, we pose the research question *'What is the conceptual definition for expressing metacognitive knowledge in thinking tasks?'* and examine an ontology for expressing metacognitive knowledge specific to thinking tasks, focusing on research tasks and learning tasks as the primary subjects. More specifically, we propose a thinking activities-specific metacognitive knowledge ontology with *'cognitive-acts,'* their *'cognitive-act achievement ways,'* and *'the rationale for why those ways are considered effective'* as the constituents of metacognitive knowledge.

2   Requirements Definition

2.1   Necessity of Formal Representation of Metacognitive Knowledge

Figure 1 illustrates the process of constructing, referencing, and sharing metacognitive knowledge (MK) in thinking tasks. Metacognitive activities (MCA) are positioned as a sequence of meta-level cognitive-acts (Cog-act)—higher-order problem-solving activities involving monitoring, planning, and control—relative to a sequence of object-level cognitive-acts, i.e., problem-solving activities (PSA) that transition through state spaces in the mind [9]. Metacognitive knowledge is referenced during the execution of these meta-level cognitive-acts and used to control the sequence of object-level cognitive-acts [18]. Through trial and error and reflection on these meta-level cognitive-acts, MK construction acts—meta-learning activities (MLA) that learn metacognitive knowledge deemed effective—are executed and retained in the memory of the thinking task performer [1]. Ideally, metacognitive knowledge constructed by individuals should be shared and refined within organizations (communities of practice) that share a common orientation, such as laboratory members, academic societies, or companies [12,24].

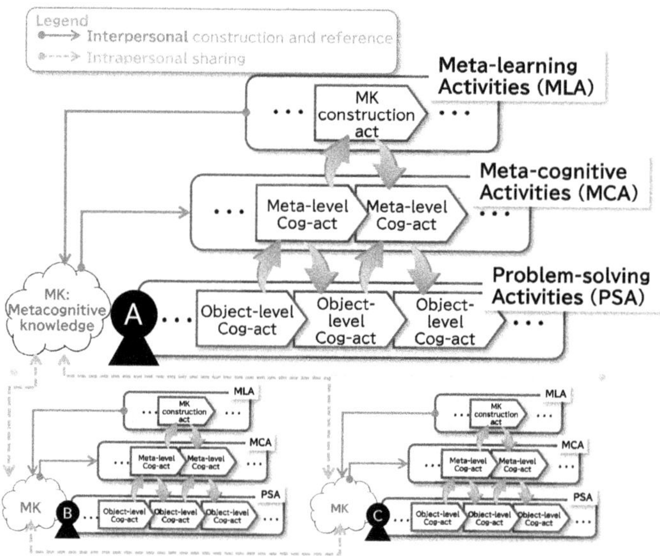

Fig. 1. Process of construction, reference, and sharing of metacognitive knowledge

However, metacognitive activities are often executed implicitly [23], and metacognitive knowledge accumulates as tacit knowledge that remains unformalized within individuals. For example, in research-based education, faculty members often implicitly convey metacognitive knowledge through dialogue rather than explicitly verbalizing it; similarly, in learning tasks, teachers find it difficult to explicitly convey knowledge about how to learn. The need to make such knowledge explicit is further amplified in environments where generative AI is used, as thinking task performers must develop the ability to critically evaluate AI responses [4,25].

Making metacognitive knowledge explicit in a form interpretable by computer systems would lay a foundation for its construction, reference, and sharing within communities of practice, and contribute to adaptive diagnosis and intervention by systems supporting problem solving and learning. Therefore, in this study, we aim to formally represent metacognitive knowledge in thinking tasks using an ontology—an explicit specification of conceptualization for knowledge representation that is processable by both humans and computers [6].

2.2 Requirements for Metacognitive Knowledge Ontology

We discuss the requirements that an ontology should satisfy in order to express metacognitive knowledge in thinking tasks as knowledge processable by both humans and computers.

Requirement 1. Expressibility of Cognitive-Acts that Enter into the Context of Specific Thinking Tasks

Hayashi et al. have defined general metacognition-related concepts—such as *'metacognition of learning process'* and *'metacognition of problems that learners themselves have'*—as part of an ontology (OMNIBUS) targeting learning support [7]. While this provides guidelines for classifying metacognitive-acts in learning activities, it does not serve as a framework for defining how metacognition is executed within the context of specific thinking tasks. To exercise metacognitive knowledge in actual execution contexts, it is necessary to define cognitive-acts with executable specificity.

Requirement 2. Expressibility of Diverse Solution Processes

As noted in Sect. 1, in thinking tasks that tackle ill-defined problems, there can be situations where multiple solution processes (sequences of actions) are available as options. That is, diversity can be expected in the sequences of cognitive-acts that can be selected in light of the current purpose. In such cases, exercising metacognition to consider *'which solution process is promising to adopt in what situation'* is important.

To enable metacognition that brings the purposefulness of each solution process up for consideration, it is necessary to explicitly distinguish the differences between solution processes and express them as distinct metacognitive knowledge.

Requirement 3. Expressibility of *'Knowledge'* that can be Used in the Future

Nolte et al. have proposed an ontology (MOI) that captures metacognitive experiences in robot agents as state transitions and causal chains of mental activities [19]. Their approach expresses *'what kind of mental activity, in what order, brought about what kind of result,'* but is designed to represent phenomena as they occurred, rather than the rationale for *'why a sequence of actions led to good results.'* To transform metacognitive experiences into *'strategic knowledge'* usable in future thinking tasks, it is necessary to explicitly specify *'what is metacognitive knowledge referenced for goal achievement?'* based on sequences of cognitive-acts together with their significance and conditioning [21].

3   Design Policy of the Ontology

3.1   Cognitive-Act Definition Based on Task Ontology (Corresponding to Requirement 1)

To systematically define cognitive-act concepts specific to the execution context of particular tasks—such as research tasks in educational systems and information science, and learning tasks in technology domains—we regard thinking tasks as *'problem-solving tasks whose purpose is to change cognitive states'* and examine a framework for defining cognitive-acts based on the philosophy of task ontology, which defines the conceptual structure of tasks.

In the problem-solving task ontology by Mizoguchi et al., an 'action' is defined as an event that changes a pre-state (input) to a post-state (output), and a 'task' is a sequence of such actions aimed at goal achievement [16]. Building on this, we define cognitive-acts in thinking tasks as events that receive conceptual or material artifacts [20] as inputs and transform them into different artifacts as outputs. For example, the cognitive-act of *'thinking about learners' difficulties'* in educational systems and information science research can be defined as a cognitive-act that takes the artifact *'(not yet considered) learner difficulties'* as input and produces the artifact *'(considered) learner difficulties'* as output. Similarly, in learning tasks, the cognitive-act of *'understanding the difficulties that the technology solves'* in technology domain learning tasks can be defined as a cognitive-act that takes *'(not yet understood) difficulties that the technology solves'* as input and produces *'(understood) difficulties that the technology solves'* as output.

In this way, even when the types of thinking tasks differ (e.g., research and learning), task-specific cognitive-acts can be made concrete by defining artifacts specific to each thinking task.

3.2   Cognitive-Act Achievement Ways Definition Based on Functional Concept Ontology (Corresponding to Requirement 2)

To systematically accommodate the diversity of possible solution processes for the same purpose, we introduce the *'achievement way (Way) concept for systematizing interpretation processes of functional knowledge'* proposed by Kitamura et al. [11].

An achievement way is a sequence of sub-purposes (functions) for achieving a given purpose (function), and serves as a conceptual device for distinguishing and expressing different procedures and methods. For example, for the purpose of *'to generate electricity,'* the *'steam power generation method'* is characterized by the sub-purpose sequence *'to raise liquid temperature'* → *'to turn the turbine'* → *'to generate electricity,'* while the *'hydroelectric power generation method'* replaces the first sub-purpose with *'to run the water.'*

We apply this achievement way concept—originally proposed for the functions of physical devices—to cognitive-acts, thereby defining *'cognitive-act achievement ways'* that express the diversity of solution processes. For example, when the cognitive-act *'to think learner difficulties'* is the goal, multiple achievement ways can be defined: the *'persona-driven method (Way1),'* beginning with *'to assume a concrete learner profile,'* or the *'approach-driven method (Way2),'* beginning with *'to remember designed support approach.'*

3.3 Metacognitive Knowledge Definition Referencing Cognitive-Act Achievement Ways Concepts (Corresponding to Requirement 3)

As shown by Schraw & Dennison [21], metacognitive knowledge can be regarded as a concept containing three elements: *'when,' 'what,'* and *'why'* to think effectively. The expression of the conditioning *'why it is effective'* is an important cue for researchers to utilize metacognitive knowledge.

In this study, we map the *'purpose'* in the cognitive-act achievement way introduced in Sect. 3.2 to concepts constituting *'when'* to think in metacognitive knowledge, and the sub-action sequence to *'what'* to think. We then adopt a framework in which information about *'why'* these cognitive-act achievement ways are effective, retained during the execution of metacognitive-acts, constitutes *'metacognitive knowledge specific to thinking tasks.'* For example, in educational systems and information science research,

- (When) When *'thinking about learners' difficulties'*
- (What) Executing the *'persona-driven method'* is
- (Why) Effective *'because concretely conceptualizing learner personas may enable defining difficulties in an experientially grounded manner'*

Such metacognitive knowledge can be expressed. This enables the expression of metacognitive knowledge that includes conditional knowledge specific to thinking tasks.

4 TACTO: Thinking Activities-Specific Metacognitive Knowledge Ontology

Based on the design policy discussed in Sect. 3, we developed the Thinking Activities-Specific Metacognitive Knowledge Ontology (TACTO: Thinking ACTivities-specific metacognitive knowledge Ontology). Figure 2 shows the core concept definitions.

This ontology was constructed on the basis of YAMATO [14]—an upper ontology with expressive power to precisely define action and function concepts—using the Hozo ontology editor [15], which supports export to OWL and RDFs.

The core concepts of TACTO consist of four elements: *'artifacts'* (Fig. 2(a)), *'cognitive-acts'* (Fig. 2(b)) that produce them, *'cognitive-act achievement ways'* (Fig. 2(c)), and *'metacognitive knowledge'* (Fig. 2(d)) that is established with these concepts as constituents. More specific concept definitions are described below.

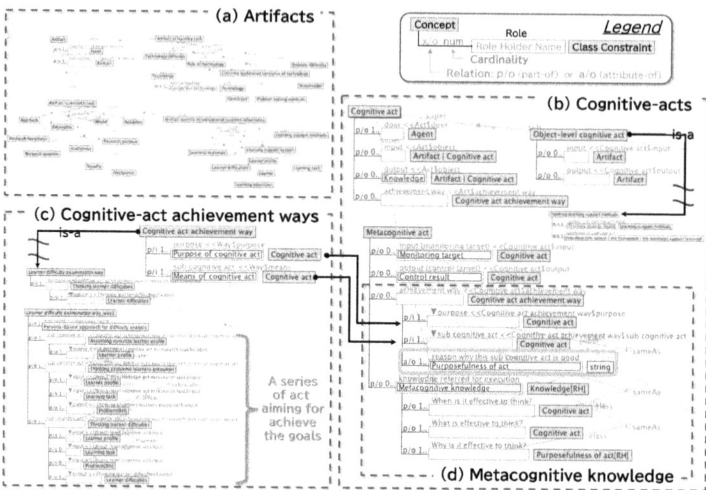

Fig. 2. Core concepts of thinking activities-specific metacognitive knowledge ontology

We conceptually define '*artifacts*' as deliverables produced as a result of cognitive-acts (Fig. 2(a)). This concept is defined as a subconcept of '*quasi-abstract objects*' in YAMATO. For research tasks, we define conceptual artifacts such as research purpose, novelty, and rationality; for learning tasks, we define conceptual artifacts such as learner difficulties, learning objectives, learning support methods, and learning support systems. These concept definitions are expected to increase as the definition of cognitive-acts is refined.

We conceptually define '*cognitive-acts*' as actions that take these conceptual artifacts as input and output (Fig. 2(b)). Input and output are defined as being able to reference other '*cognitive-acts*' in addition to '*artifacts.*' This is to allow expressing that while the deliverables (outputs) of object-level cognitive-acts (problem-solving activities) are '*artifacts,*' meta-level cognitive-acts (metacognitive activities) are actions that transform inappropriate cognitive-acts (e.g., a state of executing '*thinking about learners' difficulties*' in an ad hoc manner) into more appropriate cognitive-acts (e.g., a state of executing '*thinking about learners' difficulties*' in a planned manner). Through this, metacognitive-acts can also be conceptually defined within the framework of task ontology consisting of input and output, just as cognitive-acts are.

We conceptually define '*cognitive-act achievement way*' as a set and sequence of '*cognitive-acts*' designated as a '*goal*' to be achieved, together with a sequence of sub-cognitive-acts effective for its achievement (Fig. 2(c)).

'*Metacognitive knowledge*' is defined as what is regarded as knowledge, in the context of '*metacognitive-acts*', about the '*cognitive-act achievement way*' and '*its purposefulness*' (Fig. 2(d)). More specifically, it is mapped as follows:

- (When) when achieving the *'cognitive-act'* that plays the role of *'goal'* in the achievement way, it is effective to think about
- (What) executing the sequence of *'cognitive-acts'* that play the role of *'sub-cognitive-acts'* in the achievement way, which is
- (Why) desirable from the perspective of *'purposefulness'*

Through these explicit concept definitions, when specifying metacognitive knowledge in thinking tasks, a common understanding can be formed among multiple people and systems that metacognitive knowledge consists of three elements—*'cognitive-acts,'* their *'achievement ways,'* and their *'purposefulness'*—and that agreement on these elements is required.

5   Conclusion

In this study, we proposed an ontology (TACTO) for establishing a common understanding of metacognitive knowledge in thinking tasks—among people, between people and systems, and among systems.

More specifically, we developed a method for defining cognitive-act achievement way concepts by defining cognitive-acts based on task ontology and by applying achievement way concepts from functional ontology. We then formulated that *'metacognitive knowledge'* is what is referenced in the context of metacognitive-acts as a triplet of the *'cognitive-act'* playing the role of *'goal'* in the cognitive-act achievement way, the sequence of *'cognitive-acts'* playing the role of *'sub-cognitive-acts,'* and their *'purposefulness.'*

In future work, we plan to redefine the ontology referenced by a thought organization support system [17] using TACTO to empirically validate its utility for adaptive support regarding metacognitive knowledge. We also plan to examine whether TACTO facilitates systematic metacognitive knowledge template construction when expanding meta-learning programs to different technology domains, and how semi-automatic diagnostic functions for learners' metacognitive knowledge can be realized.

Disclosure of Interests. The authors have no competing interests to declare that are relevant to the content of this article.

References

1. Aburatani, T., Seta, K., Hayashi, Y.: Meta-learning program based on abstraction of learning experiences. In: EdMedia+ Innovate Learning, pp. 567–576 (2024)
2. Chi, M.T.H., De Leeuw, N., Chiu, M.H., Lavancher, C.: Eliciting self-explanations improves understanding. Cogn. Sci. **18**(3), 439–477 (1994)
3. Dorst, K., Cross, N.: Creativity in the design process: co-evolution of problem-solution. Des. Stud. **22**(5), 425–437 (2001)
4. Fan, Y., et al.: Beware of metacognitive laziness: effects of generative artificial intelligence on learning motivation, processes, and performance. Br. J. Edu. Technol. **56**(2), 489–530 (2025)

5. Flavell, J.H.: Metacognition and cognitive monitoring: a new area of cognitive-developmental inquiry. Am. Psychol. **34**(10), 906–911 (1979)
6. Gruber, T.R.: A translation approach to portable ontology specifications. Knowl. Acquis. **5**(2), 199–220 (1993)
7. Hayashi, Y., Bourdeau, J., Mizoguchi, R.: Using ontological engineering to organize learning/instructional theories and build a theory-aware authoring system. Int. J. Artif. Intell. Educ. **19**(2), 211–252 (2009)
8. Jonassen, D.H.: Instructional design models for well-structured and ill-structured problem-solving learning outcomes. Educ. Tech. Res. Dev. **45**, 65–94 (1997)
9. Kayashima, M., Inaba, A., Mizoguchi, R.: What do you mean by to help learning of metacognition? In: Proceedings of the 2005 Conference on Artificial Intelligence in Education, pp. 346–353 (2005)
10. Kieras, D.E., Bovair, S.: The role of a mental model in learning to operate a device. Cogn. Sci. **8**(3), 255–273 (1984)
11. Kitamura, Y., Mizoguchi, R.: Ontology-based description of functional design knowledge and its use in a functional way server. Expert Syst. Appl. **24**(2), 153–166 (2003)
12. Lave, J., Wenger, E.: Situated Learning: Legitimate Peripheral Participation. Cambridge University Press (1991)
13. Maher, M., Tang, H.: Co-evolution as a computational and cognitive model of design. Res. Eng. Design **14**(1), 47–64 (2003)
14. Mizoguchi, R., Borgo, S.: Yamato: yet-another more advanced top-level ontology. Appl. Ontol. **17**(1), 211–232 (2022)
15. Mizoguchi, R., Sunagawa, E., Kozaki, K., Kitamura, Y.: The model of roles within an ontology development tool: HOZO. Appl. Ontol. **2**(2), 159–179 (2007)
16. Mizoguchi, R., Vanwelkenhuysen, J., Ikeda, M.: Task ontology for reuse of problem solving knowledge. In: Towards Very Large Knowledge Bases: Knowledge Building & Knowledge Sharing, vol. 46, pp. 46–59 (1995)
17. Mori, N., Hayashi, Y., Seta, K.: Ontology-based thought organization support system to prompt readiness of intention sharing and its long-term practice. J. Inf. Syst. Educ. **18**(1), 27–39 (2019)
18. Nelson, T.O.: Metamemory: a theoretical framework and new findings. In: Bower, G.H. (ed.) Psychology of Learning and Motivation, vol. 26, pp. 125–173. Academic Press (1990)
19. Nolte, R., Pomarlan, M., Beßler, D., Porzel, R., Malaka, R., Bateman, J.A.: Towards an ontology for robot introspection and metacognition. In: Proceedings of the 13th International Conference Formal Ontology in Information Systems (FOIS 2023), vol. 377, pp. 318–333 (2023)
20. Orlikowski, W.J., Iacono, C.S.: Research commentary: desperately seeking the "IT" in IT research – a call to theorizing the IT artifact. Inf. Syst. Res. **12**(2), 121–134 (2001)
21. Schraw, G., Dennison, R.S.: Assessing metacognitive awareness. Contemp. Educ. Psychol. **19**(4), 460–475 (1994)
22. Shin, N., Jonassen, D.H., McGee, S.: Predictors of well-structured and ill-structured problem solving in an astronomy simulation. J. Res. Sci. Teach. **40**(1), 6–33 (2003)
23. Son, L.K., Schwartz, B.L., Kornell, N.: Implicit metacognition, explicit uncertainty, and the monitoring/control distinction in animal metacognition. Behav. Brain Sci. **26**(3), 355–356 (2003)
24. Wenger, E., McDermott, R., Snyder, W.M.: Cultivating Communities of Practice. Harvard Business School Press, Boston, MA (2002)

25. Xu, X., Qiao, L., Cheng, N., Liu, H., Zhao, W.: Enhancing self-regulated learning and learning experience in generative ai environments: the critical role of metacognitive support. Br. J. Edu. Technol. **56**(5), 1842–1863 (2025)
26. Zhang, Q., Lockee, B.B.: Designing a framework to facilitate metacognitive strategy development in computer-mediated problem-solving instruction. J. Format. Des. Learn. **6**(2), 127–143 (2022)

Mix and Match: Context Pairing
for Scalable Topic-Controlled Educational Summarisation

Nathikan Yodthap[1], Thanapong Intharah[1], and Sahan Bulathwela[2(✉)]

[1] Visual Intelligence Laboratory, Department of Statistics, Faculty of Science,
Khon Kaen University, Khon Kaen 40002, Thailand
nathikan@kkumail.com, thanin@kku.ac.th
[2] Centre for Artificial Intelligence, Department of Computer Science, University
College London, London WC1E 6BT, UK
m.bulathwela@ucl.ac.uk

Abstract. Topic-controlled summarisation enables users to generate summaries focused on specific aspects of source documents. This paper investigates a data augmentation strategy for training small language models (sLMs) to perform topic-controlled summarisation. We propose a pairwise data augmentation method that combines contexts from different documents to create contrastive training examples, enabling models to learn the relationship between topics and summaries more effectively. Using the SciTLDR dataset enriched with Wikipedia-derived topics, we systematically evaluate how augmentation scale affects model performance. Results show consistent improvements in win rate and semantic alignment as the augmentation scale increases, while the amount of real training data remains fixed. Consequently, a T5-base model trained with our augmentation approach achieves competitive performance relative to larger models, despite using significantly fewer parameters and substantially fewer real training examples.

Keywords: Topic-controlled summarisation · TCS · T5 model · Data augmentation · SciTLDR · Transformer · Natural language processing (NLP)

1 Introduction

The growing volume of academic literature creates significant challenges for learners, particularly in science education, where students must efficiently access information aligned with specific learning objectives. For instance, a student studying neural networks may only need to understand how backpropagation works from a paper, rather than reading the entire work. Generic summaries often fail to meet these needs, as they provide broad overviews rather than being

E. G. Blanchard et al. (Eds.): AIED 2026, LNAI 16583, pp. 178–187, 2027.
https://doi.org/10.1007/978-3-032-29760-0_20

focused on targeted topics. Topic-controlled summarisation addresses this limitation by enabling summaries to be generated with explicit topical constraints, reducing cognitive load and supporting more effective learning.

Although large language models (LLMs) have demonstrated strong performance in summarisation tasks, their high computational and data requirements limit their applicability in many educational settings. Smaller language models (sLMs) provide a more practical alternative; however, their performance is particularly sensitive to the quality and availability of labelled training data. In educational domains, high-quality labelled data is often scarce. As a result, improving data efficiency by maximising the utility of limited high-quality data becomes essential for enabling effective topic-controlled summarisation with sLMs.

In this work, we propose a pairwise data augmentation strategy that improves data efficiency for topic-controlled summarisation by constructing contrastive training examples while keeping the amount of real training data fixed. We conduct a controlled study on the augmentation scale, demonstrating consistent improvements in semantic alignment and relative topical alignment as augmentation increases, with stable performance at higher scales. Under limited real-data conditions, we further show that a T5-base model trained with our approach achieves performance comparable to larger topic-controllable summarisation models, despite using substantially fewer parameters and training examples, highlighting its suitability for resource-constrained educational applications.

Research Questions. The research questions are formulated as follows:
RQ1: Can pairwise data augmentation improve topic-controlled summarisation under limited data conditions?
RQ2: How does augmentation scale affect topic alignment as measured by win rate?
RQ3: Can a small language model trained with this strategy achieve performance comparable to larger models?

2   Related Work

Recent advances in transformer-based architectures [19] have substantially improved abstractive text summarisation. Building on this foundation, pretrained models such as T5 [17], BART [12], and PEGASUS [21] achieve strong performance on standard benchmarks by generating fluent, human-like summaries. These models have further enabled controllable summarisation, where generation is guided toward specific topics or attributes. For example, controllable summarisation methods guide generation toward specific topics using explicit control mechanisms. Early approaches explore entity-planning strategies [14], followed by control-code-based methods such as CTRLsum [10], and more recent work on query-based control [6]. These methods are effective but are commonly implemented on large pretrained models and require substantial labelled data, which can limit their practicality in resource-constrained educational settings.

In educational contexts, topic-controlled generation is particularly valuable for aligning generated content with learners' objectives. Li et al. propose topic-controlled educational question generation using scalable topic annotation via Wikification, demonstrating the potential of topic guidance for personalised learning. While this line of work targets question generation rather than summarisation, it highlights the importance of topic control in educational applications. In parallel, data augmentation techniques have been explored to address data scarcity in summarisation. For instance, [15] propose ExtraPhrase, which constructs pseudo training pairs via extractive summarisation followed by paraphrasing, demonstrates effectiveness in low-resource settings. However, such approaches focus on improving surface-level diversity rather than reinforcing specific topic–summary associations. In the aspect-based summarisation setting, [20] addresses data scarcity by constructing a large-scale dataset from Wikipedia to enable aspect-focused generation. While effective, this approach relies on large-scale data collection rather than augmenting limited labelled data. In contrast, our work introduces a pairwise augmentation strategy adapted from [13] that explicitly targets topic–summary alignment by exposing the model to contrastive contexts, enabling effective training of small language models without requiring additional labelled data or large-scale corpora.

3   Methodology

3.1   Models

We use T5-base as the foundation model due to its compact size and strong empirical performance in summarisation. T5 is a transformer-based encoderdecoder model with approximately 220 million parameters, making it suitable for conditional generation under resource constraints. Input sequences are truncated to 512 tokens, and generated summaries are limited to 128 tokens. For RQ 3 experiments, we use CTRLSum [10], a strong topic-controlled summarisation model that is twice as large as T5-base (406M params).

3.2   Dataset Construction

Source Dataset. We base our experiments on the SciTLDR-A corpus, which contains scientific paper abstracts paired with expert- or author-written TLDR-style summaries [5]. The dataset is split into training (1,992 abstracts), validation (618), and test (619) sets. While the validation and test splits may include multiple reference summaries per abstract, each training instance contains a single abstractsummary pair. Importantly, SciTLDR-A does not provide explicit topic annotations, which are required for topic-controlled summarisation.

Topic Annotation. To enable topic-controlled training, we augment the training split with topic labels using Wikification [1], following prior work on topic-guided generation [13]. Wikification maps text to relevant Wikipedia concepts and assigns confidence scores based on graph-based ranking. For each abstract–summary pair (A_i, s_i), where A_i denotes the abstract and s_i the corresponding summary, we select a salient topic t_i, resulting in topic-annotated training instances of the form (A_i, t_i, s_i). During evaluation, t_i' denotes an alternative topic drawn from the same document, used as a contrastive reference in win rate computation.

New Datasets with Novel Augmentation: For the experiments, we create three versions of datasets from the source SciTLDR training data using the exact method used in [13], but instead of questions as labels, we have summaries in this work. From training data that has the following composition

$$D \in \{\ldots, (A_i, s_i), (A_j, s_j), \ldots\}$$

We create three new training datasets using topic annotation with Wikification [1]. The dataset families are shown in Table 1.

Table 1. The resultant structure of training examples in different training datasets D. under different augmentation settings. $+$ indicates the concatenation of two abstracts.

Dataset Name	Dataset Composition
Baseline	$D_{\text{Baseline}} \in \{\ldots, (A_i, t_i, s_i), (A_j, t_j, s_j), \ldots\}$
TCS · X	$D_{\text{TCS1X}} \in \{\ldots, (A_i + A_j, t_i, s_i), (A_i + A_j, t_j, s_j), \ldots\}$
TCS · XX	$D_{\text{TCS1XX}} \in \{\ldots, (A_i + A_j, t_i, s_i), (A_i + A_j, t_j, s_j), (A_j + A_i, t_i, s_i), (A_j + A_i, t_j, s_j), \ldots\}$

3.3 Evaluation Metrics

We evaluate models using two automatic metrics for summary quality and topic alignment, respectively:

BERTScore, an indicator of summary quality, measures semantic similarity between the generated and reference summaries using contextualised embeddings, allowing for a flexible comparison beyond surface-level token overlap.

Win Rate evaluates topic alignment between the topic t_i and summary s_i using cosine similarity computed over sentence embeddings. Specifically, we encode the generated summary and topic representations using a pretrained sentence embedding model, and compare the cosine similarity between the generated summary and its intended reference salient topic $\cos(\text{emb}(s_i), \text{emb}(t_i))$ against similarity with the next alternative topic in the same summary $\cos(\text{emb}(s_i), \text{emb}(t_i'))$. A win is recorded when the similarity to the intended topic t_i is higher than that to the alternating topic t_i'. The win rate is defined as the proportion of such wins across all evaluated instances. The alternative topic t_i' is derived from the structure of the SciTLDR test set, where each record contains multiple expert-written summaries with corresponding topics. We expand each record into multiple instances, each using one summary-topic pair (s_i, t_i) as the target, while the remaining topics serve as alternative topics t'_i. This design reflects realistic evaluation conditions, as the alternative topics are semantically close to the intended topic, making the distinction more challenging and better aligned with real-world data distribution. Although cosine similarity is used as the underlying measure, win rate provides a relative comparison that focuses on topic control rather than direct similarity to a single gold label summary.

3.4　Experimental Setup

Table 2 summarises the experimental configuration used across all models. To ensure fair comparison under resource-constrained settings, all experiments share the same training and optimisation setup.

The test data split of the SciTLDR dataset contains multiple summaries created by several experts (author, domain expert, etc.) for each unique example. Due to this, we do not carry out abstract pairing in the test set and use different summaries that have different salient topics as topic-controlled examples. This allows us to do a truly realistic evaluation that aligns with the real-world data distribution.

Table 2. Experimental setup and training configuration for T5 Models

Component	Setting
Model	T5-base encoder–decoder
Input format	$Summarize:\ topic = t_i,\ context = A_i + A_j$
Max input length	512 tokens
Max output length	128 tokens
Optimiser	AdamW (weight decay 0.05)
Learning rate	5×10^{-6} with linear warm-up (10%)
Batch size	8
Training epochs	Up to 10
Loss function	Sequence-to-sequence cross-entropy
Regularisation	Dropout (0.3 hidden, 0.1 attention)
Gradient clipping	1.0
Early stopping	Validation loss (patience 1, $\delta = 10^{-4}$)

4　Results

4.1　Impact of Data Augmentation on Model Performance (RQ1)

Table 3 reports the performance of the baseline model and its augmented variants under small-scale topic-controlled sampling (TCS). Using $1\times$ augmentation (TCS1X) does not lead to clear improvements over the baseline in either

BERTScore or win rate. Although TCS1XX introduces reversed-context samples to increase diversity, the resulting gains remain marginal, with win rate matching the baseline and only slight stabilisation in BERTScore.

When the augmentation scale is increased to 2× (TCS2X), a modest but consistent improvement in win rate is observed, while BERTScore remains comparable across all settings. This indicates that limited augmentation alone is insufficient to substantially improve topic alignment, whereas moderate increases in augmented data begin to yield measurable benefits without degrading summary quality.

Table 3. Results of summarisation models under different training data settings. The best and second-best results are indicated in **bold** and *italic* respectively.

Model	BERTScore	Win rate (%)
Baseline	**0.8795**	36.56
TCS1X	0.8779 ± 0.0004	35.69 ± 1.0988
TCS1XX	0.8783 ± 0.0007	36.56 ± 1.0825
TCS2X	0.8780 ± 0.0003	**36.80 ± 0.5098**

4.2 Effects of Augmentation Scale on Pairwise Topic-Controlled Summarisation (RQ2)

Table 4 presents model performance across a wider range of TCS augmentation scales. BERTScore remains relatively stable across all configurations, suggesting

Table 4. Performance increase when models are trained with new datasets created by the proposed data augmentation method in different multipliers of the original training dataset size, ultimately leading to beating CTRLSum with no additional examples.

Model	Params	Unique Training Examples	BERTScore	Win rate (%)
Baseline	220M	1,992	0.8795	36.56
TCS1X	220M	1,992	0.8779 ± 0.0004	35.69 ± 1.0988
TCS2X	220M	1,992	0.8780 ± 0.0003	36.80 ± 0.5098
TCS3X	220M	1,992	0.8783 ± 0.0002	38.22 ± 0.1651
TCS4X	220M	1,992	0.8783 ± 0.0001	37.51 ± 0.2423
TCS5X	220M	1,992	0.8781 ± 0.0002	37.43 ± 1.0041
TCS10X	220M	1,992	0.8789 ± 0.0003	38.38 ± 0.2859
TCS15X	220M	1,992	0.8789 ± 0.0003	38.86 ± 0.1651
TCS25X	220M	1,992	0.8714 ± 0.0146	39.81 ± 0.2747
TCS30X	220M	1,992	**0.8799 ± 0.0001**	39.97 ± 0.5200
CTRLsum	406M	50,000	0.8545	**39.97**

that increasing the amount of augmented data does not negatively affect overall summary quality. In contrast, the win rate shows a clearer upward trend as the augmentation scale increases, indicating progressively better topic alignment.

Improvements in win rate are already observable at small augmentation scales (2x to 3x) and continue to increase at larger scales, peaking at 15x30x. Notably, TCS1X performs below the baseline, and win rate improvements only become more apparent from TCS3X onward, suggesting that a certain level of contrastive exposure may be needed for the augmentation to take effect. The decreasing standard deviation at larger scales may also suggest improved training stability.

Despite relying on a substantially smaller model and significantly fewer real training instances, TCS30X achieves a win rate comparable to CTRLsum, which uses a larger backbone and a much larger labelled dataset. This comparison suggests that pairwise topic-controlled augmentation can effectively improve topic alignment under limited data and model capacity constraints.

5   Discussion

Our results indicate that pairwise augmentation improves topic-controlled summarisation primarily by increasing contextual diversity rather than merely enlarging the training set. As shown in Table 3, the basic paired setting (TCS1X) does not outperform the baseline, suggesting that naive pairing alone is insufficient. Introducing reversed-context samples (TCS1XX) stabilises performance, while moderate scaling (TCS2X) leads to measurable improvements in win rate, indicating better topic alignment. This further suggests that exposing the model to diverse paired contexts helps it learn more robust topicsummary associations.

The observed pattern across augmentation scales offers further insight into how pairwise augmentation affects model learning. At low scales (1x-2x), the paired contexts may introduce additional noise without providing sufficient contrastive signal, which could explain why the model does not consistently outperform the baseline. As the scale increases (3x-10x), a greater variety in topic–context pairings may help the model develop more robust topic–summary associations. At larger scales (15x-30x), the accumulated contrastive signal appears to stabilise training, as reflected in both higher win rates and reduced variance across runs, though the underlying mechanism warrants further investigation.

Compared to CTRLsum, which uses a larger model and labelled data, our T5-base models achieve similar win rates with far fewer parameters and only 1,992 documents. While CTRLsum benefits from greater capacity and supervision, these results suggest that pairwise topic-controlled augmentation can help small models approach the performance of larger models under data constraints. From an educational perspective, higher win rates indicate that the model's summaries align more closely with the intended topic, supporting learners' objectives and potentially reducing instructor workload and learner cognitive overload in Intelligent Tutoring Systems.

Unlike prior work, such as ExtraPhrase [15] and OASum [20], which emphasise data diversity, our gains occur without changes in BERTScore, suggesting that pairwise augmentation primarily improves topic alignment rather than surface-level diversity. Explicit modelling of contrastive topiccontext relationships may thus aid topic-controlled summarisation in low-resource settings.

6   Conclusion

This study demonstrates that pairwise data augmentation can effectively train a T5-base model for topic-controlled summarisation under limited real-data conditions. Our results show that augmentation improves performance primarily by increasing contextual diversity rather than merely enlarging the dataset. As the augmentation scale increases, win rate consistently improves, indicating stronger topic alignment, while BERTScore remains stable across settings, suggesting preserved semantic quality.

At larger augmentation scales, gains in win rate continue without sacrificing overall summary quality, highlighting the robustness of the proposed pairwise training strategy. Compared with CTRLsum, our approach achieves comparable topic alignment using a substantially smaller model and only 1,992 real training examples. These findings underscore the data efficiency of pairwise topic-controlled augmentation and suggest its potential as a practical alternative for controllable summarisation in resource-constrained settings. Future work will explore alternative augmentation strategies and evaluate generalisation across different domains and datasets.

7   Limitation and Future Work

Several limitations should be noted. Evaluation relies solely on automatic metrics, and human evaluation has not been conducted. Formal statistical significance testing was not performed, and results should be interpreted with caution. Comparisons are limited to CTRLsum; benchmarking against general-purpose LLMs, broader topic annotation methods, and cross-domain generalisation remains as future work.

Acknowledgments. This work is co-funded by the European Commission's projects "Teacher-AI Complementarity (TaiCo)" (Project ID: 101177268), "Humane AI" (Grant No. 820437) and "X5GON" (Grant No. 761758).

References

1. Brank, J., Leban, G., Grobelnik, M.: Annotating documents with relevant Wikipedia concepts. In: Proceedings of the Slovenian Conference on Data Mining and Data Warehouses (SiKDD 2017), Ljubljana, Slovenia (2017)
2. Brown, T.B., et al.: Language models are few-shot learners. In: Advances in Neural Information Processing Systems, vol. 33, pp. 1877–1901 (2020)
3. Bulathwela, S., Perez-Ortiz, M., Yilmaz, E., Shawe-Taylor, J.: Truelearn: a family of Bayesian algorithms to match lifelong learners to open educational resources. In: Proceedings of the AAAI Conference on Artificial Intelligence, pp. 565–573 (2020)

4. Bulathwela, S., Muse, H., Yilmaz, E.: Scalable educational question generation with pre-trained language models. In: Proceedings of the International Conference on Artificial Intelligence in Education, pp. 327–339 (2023)
5. Cachola, I., Lo, K., Cohan, A., Smith, N.A.: TLDR: extreme summarisation of scientific documents. In: Proceedings of the 2020 Conference on Empirical Methods in Natural Language Processing (EMNLP), pp. 4766–4777 (2020)
6. Chen, N.F., Zhang, Y., Liu, S.: Instructive dialogue summarisation with query aggregations. In: Proceedings of the 2023 Conference on Empirical Methods in Natural Language Processing (EMNLP), pp. 8542–8557 (2023)
7. Etemad, M., Ramezanian, S., Ghassemian, M.: Fine-tuning T5 for abstractive text summarisation. In: Proceedings of the 2021 International Conference on Advances in Computer Science and Engineering, pp. 1–6 (2021)
8. Fawzi, F., Balan, S., Cukurova, M., Yilmaz, E., Bulathwela, S.: Towards human-like educational question generation with small language models. In: Proceedings of the International Conference on Artificial Intelligence in Education, pp. 295–303 (2024)
9. Goodwin, K., Poria, S., Cambria, E.: A comparative study of T5, BART, and PEGASUS for multi-document summarisation in few-shot settings. arXiv preprint arXiv:2010.05779 (2020)
10. He, J., et al.: CTRLsum: towards generic controllable text summarisation. In: Proceedings of the 2022 Conference on Empirical Methods in Natural Language Processing (EMNLP), pp. 5776–5793 (2022)
11. Hidey, C., Musi, E., Muresan, S., Passonneau, R., McKeown, K.: Leveraging topic relatedness for argument persuasion. In: Proceedings of the 15th Conference of the European Chapter of the Association for Computational Linguistics, pp. 492–502 (2017)
12. Lewis, M., Liu, Y., Goyal, N., Ghazvininejad, M., Mohamed, A., Levy, O.: BART: denoising sequence-to-sequence pre-training for natural language generation, translation, and comprehension. In: Proceedings of the 58th Annual Meeting of the Association for Computational Linguistics (2020)
13. Li, Z., Cukurova, M., Bulathwela, S.: A novel approach to scalable and automatic topic-controlled question generation in education. In: Proceedings of the 15th Learning Analytics and Knowledge Conference (LAK 2025). ACM (2025)
14. Liu, Z., Wang, C., Huang, M., Zhu, X.: Controllable neural dialogue summarisation with personal named entity planning. In: Proceedings of the 2021 Conference on Empirical Methods in Natural Language Processing (EMNLP), pp. 92–103 (2021)
15. Loem, M., Takase, S., Kaneko, M., Okazaki, N.: ExtraPhrase: efficient data augmentation for abstractive summarisation. In: Proceedings of the 2022 Conference of the North American Chapter of the Association for Computational Linguistics: Human Language Technologies: Student Research Workshop, pp. 16–24, Seattle, Washington (2022)
16. Narayan, S., Maynez, J., Liu, Y., Bansal, M.: Planning with topic control for abstractive summarisation. In: Proceedings of the 2021 Conference on Empirical Methods in Natural Language Processing (EMNLP), pp. 4838–4850 (2021)
17. Raffel, C., et al.: Exploring the limits of transfer learning with a unified text-to-text transformer. J. Mach. Learn. Res. 21(140), 1–67 (2020)
18. Szymański, P., Mandzy, T.: Wikify! A keyword extraction and linking system for general text. In: Proceedings of the 2019 International Conference on Artificial Intelligence and Soft Computing, pp. 1–8 (2019)
19. Vaswani, A., et al.: Attention is all you need. In: Advances in Neural Information Processing Systems, vol. 30 (2017)

20. Yang, X., et al.: OASum: large-scale open domain aspect-based summarisation. In: Findings of the Association for Computational Linguistics: ACL 2023, Toronto, Canada, pp. 4381–4401 (2023)
21. Zhang, J., Zhao, Y., Saleh, M., Liu, P.J.: PEGASUS: pre-training with extracted gap-sentences for abstractive summarisation. In: Proceedings of the 37th International Conference on Machine Learning (ICML), pp. 11328–11339 (2020)

Study Program Curriculum Development with AI

Blaženka Divjak[(✉)] [iD], Petra Vondra [iD], Darko Grabar [iD], Barbi Svetec [iD], and Josipa Bađari [iD]

Faculty of Organization and Informatics, University of Zagreb, Varaždin, Croatia
{bdivjak,petra.vondra,dgrabar,basvetec,jobadjari}@foi.hr

Abstract. This paper presents the latest research and development regarding the Balanced Design Planning (BDP) learning design (LD) tool, focusing on supporting curriculum mapping at the study program (SP) level through curriculum analytics and AI assistance. SP-level curriculum analytics enables the examination of coherence, balance, progression, and alignment across multiple courses. Support for horizontal alignment between learning outcomes, teaching and learning activities and assessment has previously been enabled through course design analytics. This latest development supports vertical alignment of courses and SPs through advanced curriculum analytics, focusing on analyzing mapped representations of the intended curriculum, and extends AI support for LD from the course level to the SP level. While studies have shown that AI-supported LD tools can scaffold educators' design decisions and support reflective practice while preserving human agency, limitations have been identified at higher, more abstract levels of LD. Therefore, as part of the BDP tool's design cycle, we present the technical upgrade and architecture of an AI assistant for curriculum design.

Keywords: Curriculum Design · Curriculum Mapping · Curriculum Analytics · Learning Analytics · Learning Design · AI Assistance · Study Program

1 Introduction

Today, (re)designing higher education (HE) curricula is challenging, requiring balance between theory and practice, alignment across course and study program (SP) intended outcomes, adaptation to external expectations and internal quality assurance (QA) [12].

Learning design (LD) at the SP level, i.e. curriculum design, presents a valuable tool in achieving these goals. *Curriculum design* is the intentional organization of learning outcomes (LOs), content, pedagogical approaches, learning activities, and assessment across courses to support student progression and achievement of program goals [2]. A more practical aspect is *curriculum mapping*, providing a systematic and visual representation of curriculum structures and relationships [18]. Using structured tools to develop curriculum design is a basis for systematic analysis beyond individual courses - *curriculum analytics.* Curriculum design and analytics are the focus of recent developments related to the Balanced Design Planning (BDP) tool for LD, so far used by almost 3000 users worldwide and iteratively validated by users in international contexts.

E. G. Blanchard et al. (Eds.): AIED 2026, LNAI 16583, pp. 188–197, 2027.
https://doi.org/10.1007/978-3-032-29760-0_21

This paper presents the latest upgrades of the BDP tool, supporting educators in designing not only courses but entire SPs (curricula). One aspect is curriculum analytics based on analyzing patterns of balance, alignment, and progression across courses. Another aspect is the upgrade of the AI assistant for LD (LeDA) [7].

2 Background

2.1 Learning Design, BDP and LeDA

While literature offers several definitions, in its essence, LD refers to the sequence of TLAs, related resources and student support [14], which should be done by educators and students to enable acquisition of the intended LOs [13]. LD supports educators in making informed decisions aligned with intended pedagogical approaches [4], and interest has been rising in the synergy between LD and learning analytics [14, 17].

This synergy is reflected in the innovative BDP concept and tool. The tool has been developed since 2021, following the design science methodology, with each design cycle leading to new innovative features [5–7], with the development thus far being focused on course LD supported by real-time design analytics. The BDP concept is strongly based on LOs and the principle of constructive alignment between LOs, TLAs, assessment, and student workload, paying great attention to student-centeredness. Accordingly, in the tool, LD starts with LOs and their prioritization [8], followed by detailed planning of topics, units and TLAs linked to the LOs. At the TLA level, planning includes student workload, delivery modes, collaboration and group work, assessment, learning types, etc. The BDP learning types include acquisition, discussion, investigation, practice, production, assessment, and are particularly valuable in designing learning in line with innovative pedagogies. Course-related design analytics is presented in a dashboard, providing insights to support sound pedagogical planning. [5–7] A recent innovative feature is the AI assistant in LD (LeDA) using API calls to an LLM (GPT) to support educators in developing sound LD, while preserving human agency and decision-making. The beta-version [7] provided assistance in course-level LD.

With the latest upgrades, the BDP approach has been extended to include more features related to SP LD, i.e. curriculum design. This includes two essential components: curriculum mapping and analytics, and a curriculum-level AI assistant.

2.2 Curriculum Design

The term 'curriculum' is often used interchangeably with terms like program, course, and educational experience. The nature of curricula is dynamic, including both structured and unstructured learning experiences [2, 12].

Curriculum mapping refers to a systematic process of documenting and visualizing relationships between curriculum elements, such as LOs, course content, TLAs, assessment methods, and progression; making explicit how individual courses contribute to SP goals and qualification frameworks. It is described as "a procedure that creates a visual representation of curriculum based on real time information" [18].

Curriculum analytics applies analytical and computational methods to create insights and interpretations, extending curriculum mapping which focuses on representation.

Using data from mapped curricula, it enables quantitative and qualitative analysis of curriculum characteristics, such as distribution of LOs, balance of learning types, assessment load, progression of cognitive demand, and alignment with qualification standards [14]. Curriculum analytics is commonly applied at SP level, as its main purpose is to examine coherence, progression, and alignment across courses [2, 5, 14, 18].

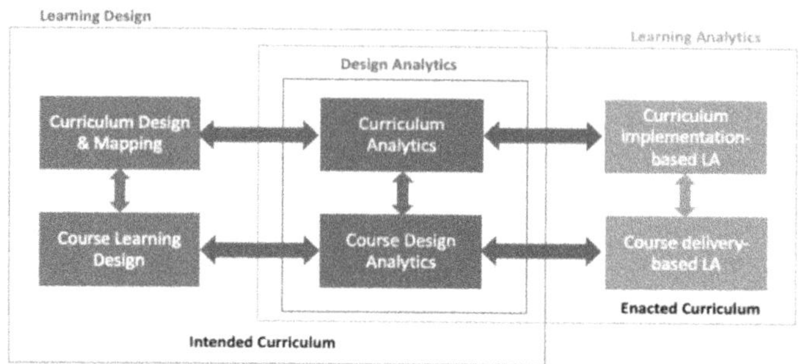

Fig. 1. Relationships between the key practices related to curriculum design

Curriculum analytics is also conceptualized as a form of design analytics, with curriculum structures captured in LD serving as a data source for evaluation and enhancement [5]. Combined with learning analytics derived from LMSs (focused on enacted learning), curriculum analytics supports comparison between intended and enacted curricula (Fig. 1), informing curriculum enhancement, QA, and strategic decision-making. Capturing LD through structured tools such as the BDP fosters this.

2.3 Generative AI, Learning Design and Curriculum Development

In course design, human–AI partnerships can yield outcomes that surpass the creativity and efficiency of individual efforts. Educational developers and learning designers increasingly combine human expertise with GenAI tools to create interactive learning content aligned with pedagogical intent [15]. Applications of GenAI extend across multiple aspects of teaching and learning, including curriculum and course design [3, 19]. Still, domain expertise and instructional design competence are essential to ensure the quality, coherence, and reliability of AI-generated outputs [3]. GenAI is a design partner that can augment educators' capacity to create context-sensitive learning experiences, with an emphasis on ethics, transparency, and human oversight. [11].

Recent work explores how these principles can be operationalized through AI-supported LD tools. Divjak et al. [7] demonstrate how an AI assistant embedded within an LD tool can assist an educator to scaffold design decisions, support reflective practice, and facilitate constructive alignment at the course level. However, besides positive pilot feedback, this work also highlights a limitation: the reduced effectiveness of AI support at more abstract levels of LD. Building on this, this study extends AI assistance beyond individual courses by enabling LeDA's support in LD at the SP level, i.e. curriculum design, thereby contributing to broader curricular coherence and QA goals.

3   Methodology

The BDP concept and tool have been developed in line with the design science methodology, using an agile approach and responding to the current user needs and QA requirements. In this sense, all the major phases of the BDP development have included three main tasks of the design cycle: problem investigation, treatment design and treatment validation [5]. This applies also to curriculum design, as follows.

With respect to **problem investigation**, feedback from previous phases of the BDP tool development has been considered, especially user feedback related to the pilot study on AI assistance in course LD [7]. Specifically, this study follows up on the recommendation to support the SP perspective and enable links between courses and SPs. Furthermore, the requirements of the QA processes in HE were considered [9]. To widen the understanding of the requirements of curriculum design, a literature review has been conducted, presented in the Background section.

Regarding **treatment design**, a technical upgrade was introduced to the BDP tool, and a beta-version of curriculum design enabled. This includes course LD informed by SP requirements, curriculum mapping, advanced curriculum analytics focusing on analyzing mapped representations of the intended curriculum, and extending AI support for LD from the course level to the SP level. The details of the curriculum design functionalities and the AI assistant architecture are presented in the Results section.

As part of **treatment validation**, the beta-version of the curriculum design support is currently piloted in the revision of a postgraduate-level SP, as a platform for experimentation. The entire curriculum (15 courses) is being revised in line with QA principles [9], using the BDP tool, course-level design analytics, and insights provided at three levels: SP board, course teachers, student feedback.

4   Results and Discussion

The beta-version of curriculum design support includes curriculum mapping and advanced curriculum analytics, and extending AI support for LD to the SP level. The upgrade responds to the quality requirements applied in HE, reflected in accreditation and QA processes [9], as well as contemporary research related to curriculum design [17].

4.1   Curriculum Mapping

While SP LD, i.e. curriculum design, had been envisaged in the BDP concept since its inception, with the latest upgrade, additional aspects of curriculum mapping have been introduced, and more elaborate curriculum-related information is to be provided by the educator. This includes SP details (description, workload, target groups, delivery mode), SP LOs, and distribution of six BDP learning types. It also includes identification of the SP type (more theoretical, practical, or mixed), links between course and SP LOs, with degrees of contribution (low, medium, high), and marking obligatory/elective student workload. This approach enables structured comparison across courses.

Regarding the SP type, curriculum literature often distinguishes between theoretical knowledge and practical application, recognizing the need for their integration in curriculum design [2]. The classification of courses into theoretical, practical, and mixed types is employed in this study to support systematic LD and curriculum analysis. Rather than representing fixed or mutually exclusive categories, these types capture dominant orientations reflected in learning types, LOs, TLAs, and assessment. The approach relying on prevalence and emphasis helps avoid deterministic mappings between cognitive levels, learning activities, and program orientation.

The SP integration into the overall design process enables systematic mapping of course-level LOs to program-level LOs, thereby ensuring vertical alignment between program and course design [5]. Course LOs contribute to the achievement of program LOs to varying degrees, commonly operationalised through three developmental stages (e.g. introduced–reinforced–mastered; slightly, moderately, or substantively) [1, 10, 16] or graded levels of contribution (e.g. low, medium, high).

4.2 Curriculum Analytics

Curriculum analytics (design analytics at the SP level) enables an overview of TLAs at the SP level (all courses). It also enables comparisons among courses based on characteristics of TLAs (collaboration, group work, delivery mode, feedback), workload (per learning type: course – SP, planned - designed workload), assessment (type, provider) and LOs. In this sense, it aggregates course design analytics available so far.

The upgrade enables some new, curriculum-specific insights. The BDP concept and tool rely strongly on two principles: horizontal and vertical constructive alignment [5]. The first principle refers to the alignment between LOs, TLAs and assessment, and has been enabled by course-level design analytics as a fundamental part of BDP. The second principle refers to the alignment among courses and SPs. This upgrade enables educators to identify those links and provides respective curriculum analytics, with insights into contribution of course LOs to SP LOs, mapping of course-level assessment to SP LOs, and alignment of assessment at course and SP level. It also enables comparison between intended and designed distribution of learning types, as well as between the average distribution of learning types at the SP level and within a particular course (Fig. 2). Together with vertical constructive alignment, this feature is valuable in QA, especially when it comes to fostering the use of innovative pedagogies.

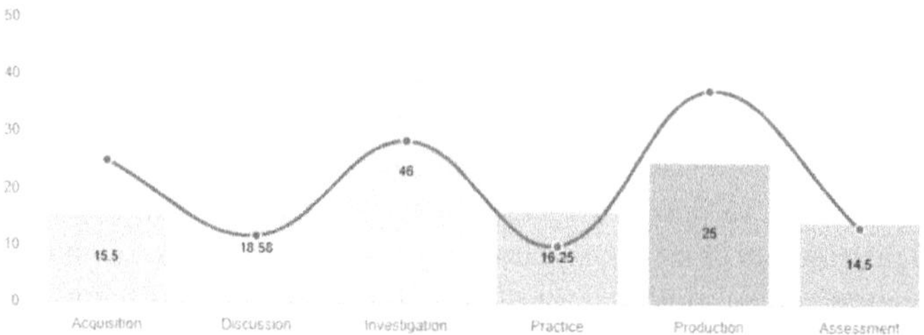

Fig. 2. Comparison of SP average (curve) and course-level learning types (bars)

4.3 Upgraded AI Assistant

The upgraded AI assistant (LeDA) architecture extends the original AI-assisted LD tool [7] by integrating curriculum design support and enhancing contextualization and data retrieval mechanisms. The key novelties of the upgraded architecture are (1) the integration of SP design support into the LD process, (2) introduced AI support for curriculum design and enhanced AI support at course level, with a feedback loop from SP to course level, (3) Contextual Data Retrieval System, and (4) Knowledge Base.

At the curriculum-level, LeDA now supports educators in formulating and revising LOs, using information from the Knowledge Base (e.g. levels of Bloom's taxonomy, qualification frameworks), and taking into account the SP description (e.g., type of the SP, educational level, mode of delivery, target groups, etc.). It also helps identify the most appropriate distribution of learning types based on the SP descriptors, interpret curriculum analytics, and develop course LD which takes into account curriculum-level inputs (e.g. LOs, SP type, other courses of the SP). Finally, it includes a general conversational AI assistant (agent) providing feedback to the curriculum mapping.

The LeDA architecture is structured around three main layers (Fig. 3): BDP LD environment, AI-powered LeDA subsystem, and external LLM services.

When users request AI assistance, the request is forwarded to the LeDA subsystem, consisting of four core components. **GenAI Application Module** prepares structured prompts, communicates with the LLM and returns structured responses to users. **Contextual Data Retrieval System** selects and aggregates relevant program- and course-level data and Knowledge Base for each AI query. **Knowledge Base** stores curated LD resources, examples, and domain knowledge (e.g., Bloom's taxonomy, program/course type, course structure, definition of weight, horizontal and vertical constructive alignment) and structured data collected through the Data Importer. **Data Importer** collects data from external data sources (e.g. institutional regulations, LO frameworks, pedagogical and didactic frameworks, accreditation requirements).

The GenAI Application Module integrates user queries with contextual data retrieved from the BDP environment and the Knowledge Base. These enriched prompts are then sent to the LLM (GPT 4o) via API calls. Returned responses are post-processed and adapted to the BDP data model before being presented to users. This ensures semantic coherence, and compatibility with program and course data structures. Users retain full decision-making authority and may accept, modify, or reject AI-generated suggestions. Selected AI-generated suggestions can be directly implemented at course and program levels, enabling seamless integration of AI-supported design elements.

At the SP level, LeDA supports users through predefined prompts structured across several design dimensions. These include prompts for generating LOs, generating LOs based on selected levels of Bloom's taxonomy, and revising LOs. Dedicated prompts also enable targeted revision and refinement of individual LOs. Additional prompts support analysis and alignment of intended learning types with program LOs, and interpretation of curriculum analytics related to program overview, workload distribution, assessment–LO alignment, constructive alignment, and AI use.

In addition to predefined prompts, users have access to a general conversational AI assistant at the program level, enabling open ended dialogue, reflective inquiry, and holistic discussion of curriculum design and mapping.

Integration of curriculum design support also enhances AI-supported design at the course level. By incorporating program-level details, LOs and intended learning types into contextual retrieval, LeDA generates more relevant, consistent, and pedagogically grounded recommendations for individual courses. This multi-level contextualization strengthens alignment between course-level LD and program design. Furthermore, the introduction of a Contextual Data Retrieval System and Knowledge Base strengthens the grounding of LLM outputs, reduces generic recommendations, and facilitates the application of retrieval-augmented generation principles. This architecture supports responsible human-AI collaboration, where AI acts as an intelligent assistant [11].

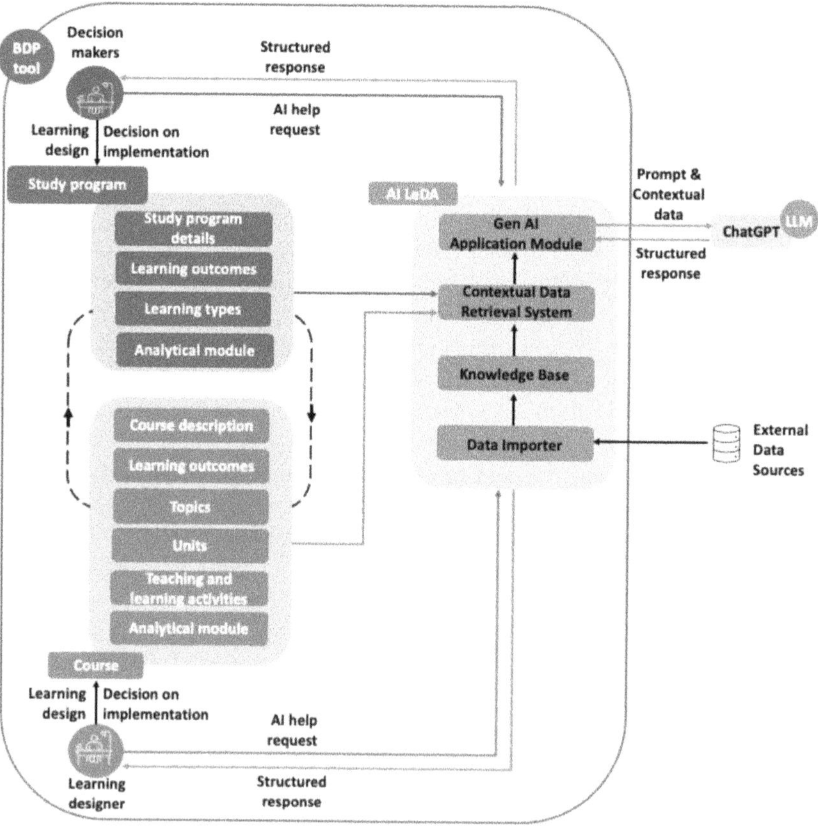

Fig. 3. The upgraded LeDA architecture

4.4 Examples of AI Assistance

AI Assistant Analysis. LeDA generates a structured response to a prompt related to the comparison between targeted and designed ECTS distribution across all courses within the SP. The response is organized into sections, including analytical summary, pedagogical interpretation, and actionable recommendations for improvement. Educators can translate numerical indicators into pedagogically grounded insights.

Feedback Loop From Curriculum to Course LOs. LeDA supports revision of course-level LOs by incorporating SP LOs when generating suggestions. A user can request the revision of an existing LO with an instruction to LeDA to maintain alignment with program LOs. LeDA generates a revised LO that is more concise, pedagogically sound, and aligned with program LO. This way the integration of SP data supports vertical alignment and enhances the quality of course design.

Prompts. LeDA currently includes 25 actions done by GPT which use pre-designed prompts (example below), and which take into account the SP descriptions and data, course details and contextually relevant entries from the Knowledge Base.

Learning Types Alignment:
Context: "You are a Learning Design assistant. You are given the details of a study program in JSON format, including its learning outcomes, currently planned learning types (and their percentages), and a list of all available learning types with their descriptions and examples. Your task is to analyze if the planned learning types are aligned with the learning outcomes. If 'plannedLearningTypes' is missing or empty, suggest an appropriate distribution of learning types from 'availableLearningTypes' that would best support the achievement of the learning outcomes. Provide a brief explanation of your analysis and then suggest optimized percentages for the learning types. IMPORTANT: You MUST ONLY use the names of the learning types provided in 'availableLearningTypes'. Ensure the total percentage of suggested learning types is exactly 100. Format your response as a JSON object with two keys: 'explanation' (string) and 'suggestions' (array of objects with 'name' and 'percentage')."
 message: "Analyze the alignment for the study program data provided below in JSON format.\n\n### STUDY PROGRAM JSON DATA ###\n{spJson}\n### END OF JSON DATA ###".

4.5 Further Research and Development

The essential track, already in progress, is the validation of curriculum design support. In an ongoing pilot study, the BDP tool is used to revise a postgraduate level SP. We plan to extend the validation of curriculum design support in the revision of additional SP, followed by collection of user feedback, which will provide us with deeper insights into the practical usefulness of the functionalities and possibly inspire further development. Further development will include building the Knowledge Base further to enable more targeted, pedagogically sound and research-informed suggestions, helping educators in both course-level and curriculum-level LD. Further upgrades will also enable transparency, flexibility and adaptability of the Knowledge Base and prompts.

5 Conclusions

We present further development of the BDP concept and tool, which enables curriculum design support enhanced by an AI assistant using API calls to GPT 4o and a carefully designed Knowledge Base. New functionalities cover curriculum mapping, curriculum analytics and the AI assistant with the supporting architecture. We provide examples of concrete curriculum analytics and discuss links with curriculum design. Curriculum and design analytics supported by an AI assistant provide visual representations and structured data, and curriculum mapping enables educators to identify gaps, redundancies and misalignments within and across courses.

Acknowledgments. The study is part of the Erasmus+ SAILeR project (2025-1-HR01-KA220-HED-000355135) financed by the European Union and the TRUELA project (IP-2022-10-2854) financed by the Croatian Science Foundation.

Disclosure of Interests. The authors declare that they have no competing interests.

References

1. Allen, M.J.: Assessing Academic Programs in Higher Education. Anker Publishing (2004)
2. Barnett, R., Coate, K.: Engaging the Curriculum in Higher Education. SRHE/Open University Press, Maidenhead (2005)
3. Choi, G.W., et al.: Utilizing generative ai for instructional design: exploring strengths, weaknesses, opportunities, and threats. TechTrends **68**(4), 832–844 (2024). https://doi.org/10.1007/s11528-024-00967-w
4. Conole, G.: Designing for Learning in an Open World. Springer New York, New York (2013). https://doi.org/10.1007/978-1-4419-8517-0
5. Divjak, B., et al.: Balanced learning design planning: concept and tool. J. Inf. Organ. Sci. **46**(2) (2022). https://doi.org/10.31341/jios.46.2.6
6. Divjak, B., et al.: Enhancing learning design through user experience research: insights from a survey in four European countries. In: Proceedings of the Central European Conference on Information and Intelligent Systems, pp. 213–221 (2023)
7. Divjak, B., et al.: Learning design with an AI assistant. In: Cristea, A.I. et al. (eds.) Artificial Intelligence in Education, pp. 207–220 Springer Nature Switzerland, Cham (2025). https://doi.org/10.1007/978-3-031-98414-3_15
8. Divjak, B., et al.: The use of decision-making methods to ensure assessment validity. In: 2021 IEEE Technology & Engineering Management Conference - Europe (TEMSCON-EUR), pp. 1–6 IEEE (2021). https://doi.org/10.1109/TEMSCON-EUR52034.2021.9488580
9. EHEA: Standards and guidelines for quality assurance in the European higher education area (2015). https://ehea.info/page-standards-and-guidelines-for-quality-assurance
10. Felder, R.M., Brent, R.: Designing and teaching courses to satisfy the ABET engineering criteria. J. Eng. Educ. **92**(1), 7–25 (2003). https://doi.org/10.1002/j.2168-9830.2003.tb00734.x
11. Giannakos, M., et al.: The promise and challenges of generative AI in education. Behav. Inf. Technol. **44**(11), 2518–2544 (2025). https://doi.org/10.1080/0144929X.2024.2394886
12. Hicks, O.: Curriculum in higher education: confusion, complexity and currency (2018)
13. Koper, R., Olivier, B.: Representing the learning design of units of learning. Educ. Technol. Soc. **7**(3), 97–111 (2004)
14. Lockyer, L., et al.: Informing pedagogical action: aligning learning analytics with learning design. Am. Behav. Sci. **57**(10), 1439–1459 (2013). https://doi.org/10.1177/0002764213479367
15. McInnes, R., et al.: Unleashing the power of gen-AI for digital education development. ASCILITE Publications (2023). https://doi.org/10.14742/apubs.2023.520

16. Plaza, C.M., et al.: Curriculum mapping in program assessment and evaluation. Am. J. Pharmaceut. Educ. **71**(2), 20 (2007). https://doi.org/10.5688/aj710220
17. Rienties, B., et al.: Applying and translating learning design and analytics approaches across borders. In: Viberg, O. and Grönlund, Å. (eds.) Practicable Learning Analytics, pp. 35–53. Springer, Cham (2023). https://doi.org/10.1007/978-3-031-27646-0_3
18. Uchiyama, K.P., Radin, J.L.: Curriculum mapping in higher education: a vehicle for collaboration. Innov. High. Educ. **33**(4), 271–280 (2009). https://doi.org/10.1007/s10755-008-9078-8
19. Ullmann, T.D., et al.: Towards generative AI for course content production: expert reflections. Eur. J. Open, Distance E-Learn. **26**(S1), 20–34 (2024). https://doi.org/10.2478/eurodl-2024-0013

Cross-Dataset Bloom Question Classification: Supervised Models and Prompted LLMs

Abdolali Faraji[1], Mohammadreza Molavi[1]([✉]), Zohreh Rasoulkhani[2], Mohammadreza Tavakoli[1], and Gábor Kismihók[1]

[1] Leibniz Information Centre for Science and Technology (TIB), Hanover, Germany
{abdolali.faraji,mohammadreza.molavi,reza.tavakoli,gabor.kismihok}@tib.eu
[2] University of Genoa, Genoa, Italy

Abstract. Automatic Bloom's taxonomy classification of assessment questions can substantially reduce instructor workload, but labeling is subjective and teacher-dependent. Prior machine learning (ML) and deep learning (DL) approaches reported strong within-dataset results, yet were rarely evaluated in cross-dataset settings, leaving real-world generalizability unclear; meanwhile, LLM effectiveness for Bloom question classification has not been systematically studied. We evaluated the cross-dataset generalization of existing ML/DL methods and assessed LLMs with multiple prompting strategies on five datasets; the best prompting strategy combined in-context examples with course-specific action verbs. Supervised ML/DL models degraded substantially on unseen datasets, whereas LLMs were more stable, suggesting a robust alternative across diverse educational contexts. Based on the best prompting strategy, we also presented a lightweight UI that supports instructors in automatically classifying large question banks; a usability study indicated low workload and high usability.

Keywords: Bloom's Taxonomy · Question Classification · Cross-Dataset Generalization · Prompting Strategies · Large Language Models

1 Introduction

Bloom's taxonomy [5] and its revised formulation [3] have long served as foundational frameworks for organizing learning objectives and assessment items according to levels of cognitive complexity. By structuring cognitive processes from lower-order to higher-order skills, Bloom's taxonomy supports the systematic design, analysis, and alignment of instructional activities and assessments.

Despite its importance, manually classifying assessment questions based on Bloom's taxonomy is time-consuming, especially for large item banks or repeated

A. Faraji and M. Molavi—These authors contributed equally to this work.

course offerings [14]. This has motivated interest in automating Bloom-level classification to reduce instructor workload and improve efficiency. A key challenge, however, is that Bloom labeling is inherently context- and teacher-specific: the same question may be interpreted differently depending on instructional goals, course content, or instructor perspective [11]. Developing automated tools that perform reliably across teachers and contexts thus remains a non-trivial problem.

Most existing efforts to automate Bloom-level question classification rely on ML and DL methods [7,9]. While these approaches often achieve high performance, evaluations are generally conducted using train-test splits from the same dataset. Consequently–given the context- and instructor-specific nature of Bloom labeling discussed above–the generalizability of these models to other datasets or instructors remains unclear, limiting their practical utility.

More recently, large language models (LLMs) have emerged as an alternative to traditional ML and DL approaches, demonstrating strong performance across a wide range of text classification tasks [2]. However, despite their growing use in educational applications, their potential for Bloombased classification of assessment questions has not yet been examined in a focused manner.

Motivated by these gaps, this study investigated automatic Bloom classification of assessment questions. First, we examined the cross-dataset generalization of existing ML and DL approaches, assessing how well models trained in one context transferred to unseen datasets. Second, we evaluated the performance of LLMs for Bloom-based question classification across datasets and prompting strategies. Finally, to support teachers in automating the classification of large question banks, we designed and evaluated the usability of a user interface (UI) based on the best-performing method. Accordingly, we addressed the following research questions, which are also depicted in Fig. 1:

RQ1: How well do developed ML and DL models for Bloom-based question classification generalize across unseen datasets?

RQ2: How do LLMs perform on Bloom classification of assessment questions?

RQ3: How can Bloom-based question classification be supported through a practical UI?

2   Related Work

This section positions our work by summarizing prior research. We group prior work into two methodological categories: ML/DL methods and more recent studies that leverage LLMs for cognitive classification.

2.1   ML and DL Approaches for Bloom Classification

Early Bloom question-classification work used traditional ML. Yahya et al. [14] framed the task as supervised learning with SVMs and analyzed the impact of frequency features and stopword removal. Mohammed and Omar [9] proposed POS-aware TF IDF that emphasizes verbs, combined it with word embeddings, and evaluated several classifiers (SVM, logistic regression, KNN), improving

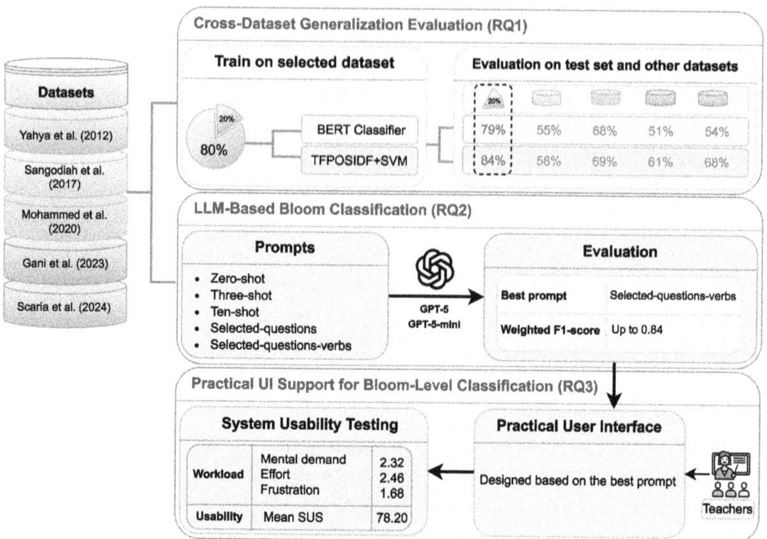

Fig. 1. Paper overview. The section corresponding to RQ1 illustrates cross-dataset evaluation using one dataset as the training source, highlighting performance drops when testing on other datasets. The RQ2 section presents the evaluation of LLMs across datasets under different prompting strategies and the selection of the best-performing prompt. The RQ3 section shows the usability study of the UI built on this prompt.

over standard TF–IDF baselines. Other work explored alternative approaches: Das et al. [6] applied LLDA for *multi-class* Bloom classification, while Wang et al. [13] proposed a *weakly supervised* method to reduce labeling needs.

More recent work has increasingly adopted DL models. Shaikh et al. [12] applied LSTM networks with pretrained word embeddings to classify both assessment questions and course learning outcomes. Gani et al. [7] investigated convolutional neural networks combined with various pretrained embeddings, including both non-contextual (Word2Vec, GloVe, FastText) and contextual representations (BERT, RoBERTa, ELECTRA), reporting their strongest results when using CNNs with RoBERTa embeddings. Das et al. [6] further evaluated transformer-based models by fine-tuning BERT for multi-class Bloom classification, demonstrating substantial gains over traditional methods.

Despite strong reported performance, evaluations typically used random within-dataset train–test splits. As a result, models trained on one dataset were rarely tested on different datasets, leaving generalization across instructors and educational contexts largely unexplored and limiting applicability to unseen data.

2.2   Large Language Models for Cognitive Classification

Recent work has explored LLMs for cognitive classification in educational settings. Scaria et al. [11] focused on Bloom-level question generation and used Bloom classification only for evaluating generated questions, offering an initial (but not dedicated) look at the classification task.

Almatrafi et al. [2] studied GPT-4 for Bloom-based categorization of course learning outcomes, comparing multiple prompting strategies (zero-shot, few-shot, and chain-of-thought). Faraby et al. [1] analyzed ChatGPT for educational question classification using the Graesser taxonomy, which characterizes question types by underlying cognitive processes rather than Bloom's levels.

Overall, prior LLM work focuses on learning outcomes, uses other taxonomies, or uses Bloom classification only to evaluate generated questions. Systematic multi-dataset evaluations of LLMs for Bloom question classification remain limited, suggesting the area is still in its infancy.

3   Method

This section provides an overview of our methodology, including datasets, models, evaluation procedures, and results. The code, prompts, and datasets are available in our repository[1].

3.1   Datasets

This study uses five Bloom's taxonomyannotated question datasets, totaling 4,179 questions. Four datasets consist of human-authored assessment questions that have been frequently adopted in Bloom classification research: Yahya et al. (2012) [14], Sangodiah et al. (2017) [10], Mohammed and Omar (2020) [9], and Gani et al. (2023) [7], containing 600, 415, 126, and 1,200 questions, respectively. In addition to human-generated questions, we incorporate an LLM-generated question dataset from Scaria et al. (2024) [11] (1,838 questions). This dataset is included to reflect the growing prevalence of AI-generated educational content in contemporary learning environments.

While all datasets provide Bloom-based labels, some follow the original Bloom taxonomy, whereas others use the revised Bloom taxonomy. To ensure consistency and comparability across datasets, we map all labels to the revised Bloom cognitive levels; the resulting class distribution is shown in Table 1.

3.2   Cross-Dataset Generalization Evaluation (RQ1)

Classification Models. To examine the generalizability of Bloom's taxonomy question classification models, we evaluate two representative approaches from prior work, covering both traditional ML and DL paradigms.

---

[1] https://gitlab.com/zrasoulkhani/bloom-classification-aied2026.

Table 1. Distribution of questions across revised Bloom levels in the five datasets.

Dataset	Remember	Understand	Apply	Analyze	Evaluate	Create	Total
Yahya et al. (2012)	100	100	100	100	100	100	600
Sangodiah et al. (2017)	50	135	72	56	45	57	415
Mohammed and Omar (2020)	22	20	15	19	29	21	126
Gani et al. (2023)	669	107	100	149	99	76	1 200
Scaria et al. (2024) (LLM-generated)	218	412	338	220	344	306	1 838
Total	1 059	774	625	544	617	560	4 179

TFPOSIDF+SVM. This model is an SVM-based classifier that represents questions using TF–IDF features weighted by part-of-speech (POS) information. In this approach, words are assigned different weights according to their POS tags, with higher importance given to verbs, as they provide strong indicators of Bloom's cognitive levels [9].

Fine-tuned BERT. As a deep learning reference model, we employ a BERT-based text classification model fine-tuned on Bloom-labeled data in our experiments. We adopt the model architecture and hyperparameter configuration reported in prior work that applied BERT to Bloom-based classification [2].

Evaluation Protocol. For each dataset, we perform a cross-dataset generalization evaluation. Specifically, one dataset is selected as the source dataset and randomly split into 80% training and 20% test sets. Models are trained on the training portion, and performance is first measured on the test set using weighted F1-score, reflecting the evaluation protocol commonly reported in prior studies. The trained models are then evaluated on the remaining four datasets, which are treated as unseen test sets. This procedure is repeated for each dataset, such that every dataset serves once as the training source and multiple times as an unseen test set.

Results and Discussion. Table 2 reports the weighted F1-scores for TFPOSIDF+SVM and fine-tuned BERT across the five datasets. Diagonal values correspond to performance on the test split of the training dataset, while the other values represent cross-dataset test results. For TFPOSIDF+SVM, test scores range from 0.68 to 0.82 depending on the training dataset, but performance decreases on unseen datasets by an average of 0.25, ranging between 0.40 and 0.70. Similarly, fine-tuned BERT achieves test scores between 0.76 and 0.91, which drop on average by 0.28 when evaluated on other datasets, ranging from 0.31 to 0.76.

These results highlight the inherent subjective and context-dependent nature of Bloom's classification of questions: models trained on questions from one instructor or context do not generalize reliably to unseen datasets from different contexts. The only exception observed in our results occurs when

TFPOSIDF+SVM is trained on the Sangodiah dataset and tested on the Gani dataset, showing a small increase of 0.02 in weighted F1-score. For BERT, no increase is observed, but the performance drop is only 0.04, which is considerably smaller than the average cross-dataset decrease of 0.28. This asymmetry suggests that the diversity and context present in the Gani questions are already represented in the Sangodiah dataset, allowing better transfer in this direction.

Table 2. Cross-dataset generalization results (weighted F1-score).

Model	Train dataset	Test datasets				
		Yahya	Sangodiah	Mohammed	Gani	Scaria
TFPOSIDF+SVM	Yahya	**0.79**	0.55	0.68	0.51	0.54
	Sangodiah	0.43	**0.68**	0.54	0.70	0.52
	Mohammed	0.46	0.44	**0.73**	0.55	0.53
	Gani	0.40	0.59	0.49	**0.82**	0.41
	Scaria	0.41	0.46	0.51	0.54	**0.78**
Fine-tuned BERT	Yahya	**0.84**	0.58	0.69	0.61	0.68
	Sangodiah	0.47	**0.80**	0.48	0.76	0.53
	Mohammed	0.46	0.37	**0.76**	0.31	0.36
	Gani	0.56	0.68	0.59	**0.91**	0.52
	Scaria	0.55	0.53	0.58	0.60	**0.84**

3.3 LLM-Based Bloom Classification (RQ2)

Large Language Models. To examine the potential of LLMs for Bloom's taxonomy question classification, we evaluate two models: GPT-5 and GPT-5-mini. Both models are used in a prompt-based inference setting via the Batch API with default configurations and do not undergo task-specific fine-tuning. Instead, they rely on in-context instructions and examples to assign Bloom's cognitive levels to input questions. GPT-5 represents a higher-capacity model, while GPT-5-mini serves as a smaller and more economical alternative, allowing us to examine performance across both state-of-the-art and cost-efficient LLM settings.

Prompting Strategies. To classify questions with LLMs, we evaluated five different prompting strategies. All prompts were designed to produce outputs in JSON format, enabling automatic evaluation across datasets.

- **Zero-shot:** The model is provided only the question and asked to assign a Bloom cognitive level.
- **Three-shot:** Three randomly selected examples per cognitive level, drawn from the same dataset, are provided to give minimal contextual guidance.
- **Ten-shot:** Ten randomly selected examples per cognitive level, again drawn from the same dataset, are included to provide richer contextual information.

- **Selected-questions:** Up to ten examples per level are manually selected to better represent the diversity of question types. Selection was performed jointly by two experts with at least five years of teaching and assessment experience for each dataset.
- **Selected-questions-verbs:** Building on the *selected-questions* prompt, we added the curated sets of key action verbs selected by the experts for each Bloom cognitive level within each dataset to the prompt.

Evaluation Protocol. For each dataset, LLMs classify all questions using each prompting strategy, and predicted Bloom levels are evaluated against gold labels with weighted F1-score.

Results and Discussion. Table 3 reports the weighted F1-scores of GPT-5 and GPT-5-mini across all datasets and prompting strategies. The results show that prompting strategies based on carefully selected examples are particularly effective. Specifically, the *selected-questions-verbs* prompt achieves the strongest performance, reaching weighted F1-scores of up to 0.84 on the Yahya dataset. This indicates that selecting representative examples, together with incorporating level-specific action verbs, provides valuable guidance for Bloom classification.

More generally, the use of in-context examples consistently improves model performance. Both three-shot and ten-shot prompting outperform zero-shot prompting across datasets, suggesting that additional contextual information helps to align model predictions with Bloom's cognitive levels. Nevertheless, zero-shot prompting still yields reasonable performance, with GPT-5 achieving weighted F1-scores around 0.75 on most datasets, indicating that LLMs retain useful classification capability even in the absence of examples. At the model level, across all prompting strategies and datasets, GPT-5 consistently performs better than GPT-5-mini; however, the performance gap remains modest, making GPT-5-mini a viable alternative when computational efficiency or cost is a concern, with an average weighted F1-score only 0.03 lower.

Compared to the supervised models evaluated in RQ1, LLM performance shows substantially less sensitivity to dataset shifts, indicating stronger cross-dataset robustness. Although LLMs do not surpass the within-dataset test performance of fine-tuned models, their comparatively stable performance across diverse datasets highlights their potential as a practical alternative for Bloom classification in heterogeneous educational settings. This robustness is particularly valuable given the subjective and context-dependent nature of Bloom's taxonomy, where labeled data from a single instructional context may not generalize reliably to unseen sources.

3.4   User Interface to Support Bloom Classification (RQ3)

Bloom-level question classification is difficult to do manually at scale, as instructors often need to label large numbers of questions [14]. To support this process,

Table 3. Weighted F1-score results of GPT-5 and GPT-5-mini on various datasets.

LLM	Prompt	Test datasets				
		Yahya	Sangodiah	Mohammed	Gani	Scaria
gpt-5	selected-questions-verbs	**0.84**	**0.76**	**0.81**	**0.83**	**0.82**
	selected-questions	0.79	0.75	0.80	0.80	**0.82**
	10-shot	0.79	0.74	0.79	0.75	**0.82**
	3-shot	0.76	0.74	0.76	0.75	0.80
	0-shot	0.75	0.71	0.76	0.75	0.75
gpt-5-mini	selected-questions-verbs	0.80	0.71	0.77	0.80	0.81
	selected-questions	0.79	0.71	0.77	0.77	0.80
	10-shot	0.75	0.69	0.76	0.73	0.79
	3-shot	0.74	0.67	0.73	0.72	0.79
	0-shot	0.74	0.65	0.72	0.71	0.73

we developed a lightweight tool based on our best-performing prompting strategy (*selected-questions-verbs*). Instructors can provide a small set of example questions per Bloom level for their specific context (e.g., course, topic, or learning objectives); the tool extracts key action verbs from these examples and uses them—together with the examples themselves—to construct the prompt for classifying new questions. Users can then upload question sets (CSV/Excel) and receive Bloom-level predictions in a structured output.

To assess usability, we conducted a user study with $N = 50$ participants recruited via Prolific[2]. Participants (1) interacted with the UI for 10 min for one of their real courses and added Bloom-level examples, (2) answered three NASA-TLX items (mental demand, effort, frustration; 1–5 scale) [8], and (3) completed the System Usability Scale (SUS) [4]. Participants reported low perceived workload (means: mental demand 2.32, effort 2.46, frustration 1.68), and the tool achieved very good usability (mean SUS $= 78.2$, SD $= 14.07$)[3].

4   Conclusion

In this work, we examined the generalizability of prior Bloom-level question classification methods and the potential of LLMs for this task. Our cross-dataset experiments on five datasets show that models trained on a single dataset suffer substantial performance drops when applied to unseen datasets, highlighting limitations in their real-world applicability. In contrast, LLMs demonstrate more stable performance across datasets, with GPT-5 achieving weighted F1-scores up to 0.84 under the best prompt, indicating their potential as a more robust

---

[2] https://www.prolific.com.
[3] The detailed study data are available online: https://bit.ly/4asf6ZA.

solution for Bloom-based question classification. To support practical use, we implemented a UI based on the *selected-questions-verbs* workflow; a user study ($N = 50$) reported low workload (NASA-TLX means: mental demand 2.32, effort 2.46, frustration 1.68) and very good usability (mean SUS = 78.2).

There are a few aspects that warrant further investigation. For cross-dataset evaluation, we only tested a subset of ML and DL models, and additional models could be explored. Regarding LLMs, more models, particularly open-source alternatives, could be evaluated to assess robustness and cost-effectiveness. Finally, while our UI design was tested with pilot users, feedback from real instructors would provide more precise insights for practical deployment

References

1. Al Faraby, S., Romadhony, A., et al.: Analysis of LLMs for educational question classification and generation. Comput. Educ. Artif. Intell. **7**, 100298 (2024)
2. Almatrafi, O., Johri, A.: Leveraging generative AI for course learning outcome categorization using bloom's taxonomy. Comput. Educ. Artif. Intell. **8**, 100404 (2025)
3. Anderson, L.W., Krathwohl, D.R.: A taxonomy for learning, teaching, and assessing: a revision of Bloom's taxonomy of educational objectives, complete edition. Addison Wesley Longman, Inc. (2001)
4. Brooke, J.: Sus: a "quick and dirty" usability scale. In: Jordan, P.W., Thomas, B., McClelland, I.L., Weerdmeester, B. (eds.) Usability Evaluation in Industry, pp. 189–194. Taylor & Francis (1996)
5. BS, B.: Taxonomy of educational objectives: the classification of educational goals. Handbook; Cognitive domain **1** (1956)
6. Das, S., Mandal, S.K.D., Basu, A.: Identification of cognitive learning complexity of assessment questions using multi-class text classification. Contemp. Educ. Technol. **12**(2), ep275 (2020)
7. Gani, M.O., Ayyasamy, R.K., Sangodiah, A., Fui, Y.T.: Bloom's taxonomy-based exam question classification: The outcome of CNN and optimal pre-trained word embedding technique. Educ. Inf. Technol. **28**(12), 15893–15914 (2023)
8. Hart, S.G., Staveland, L.E.: Development of NASA-TLX (task load index): results of empirical and theoretical research. In: Advances in Psychology, vol. 52, pp. 139–183. North-Holland (1988)
9. Mohammed, M., Omar, N.: Question classification based on bloom's taxonomy cognitive domain using modified TF-IDF and word2vec. PLoS ONE **15**(3), e0230442 (2020)
10. Sangodiah, A., Ahmad, R., Wan Ahmad, W.F.: Taxonomy based features in question classification using support vector machine. J. Theoret. Appl. Inf. Technol. **95**(12) (2017)
11. Scaria, N., Dharani Chenna, S., Subramani, D.: Automated educational question generation at different bloom's skill levels using large language models: strategies and evaluation. In: Olney, A.M., Chounta, IA., Liu, Z., Santos, O.C., Bittencourt, I.I. (eds.) AIED 2024. LNCS, vol. 14830, pp. 165–179. Springer, Cham (2024). https://doi.org/10.1007/978-3-031-64299-9_12
12. Shaikh, S., Daudpotta, S.M., Imran, A.S.: Bloom's learning outcomes' automatic classification using LSTM and pretrained word embeddings. Ieee Access **9**, 117887–117909 (2021)

13. Wang, Z., Manning, K., Mallick, D.B., Baraniuk, R.G.: Towards blooms taxonomy classification without labels. In: Roll, I., McNamara, D., Sosnovsky, S., Luckin, R., Dimitrova, V. (eds.) AIED 2021. LNCS (LNAI), vol. 12748, pp. 433–445. Springer, Cham (2021). https://doi.org/10.1007/978-3-030-78292-4_35
14. Yahya, A.A., Toukal, Z., Osman, A.: Bloom's taxonomy–based classification for item bank questions using support vector machines. In: Ding, W., Jiang, H., Ali, M., Li, M. (eds.) Modern advances in intelligent systems and tools, pp. 135–140. Springer, Heidelberg (2012). https://doi.org/10.1007/978-3-642-30732-4_17

Decoding Latent Reasoning: Mechanistic Interpretability of Chain of Continuous Thought with Sparse Autoencoders

Shlok Sand[(⊠)], Chaitanya Shah, and Vasudeva Varma

International Institute of Information Technology, Hyderabad, India
shlok.sand@research.iiit.ac.in, chaitanya.shah@students.iiit.ac.in,
vv@iiit.ac.in

Abstract. Large language models are going silent. As mathematical reasoning evolves from explicit Chain-of-Thought to efficient "latent reasoning," models using methods like Chain of Continuous Thought (CoConut) no longer show their work, they "think" through continuous, inscrutable hidden states. For education, this creates a critical transparency crisis: how can we trust an AI tutor that solves problems without revealing its reasoning process? When should it intervene if we cannot detect its uncertainty or errors? We break open this black box by applying Sparse Autoencoders (SAEs) to interpret CoConut's internal reasoning states during step-by-step problem solving on GSM8k. Through systematic analysis of 7,914 reasoning steps and manual annotation of problems across 9 mathematical skills, we discover something remarkable: buried within these inscrutable activations are interpretable features that reliably detect specific reasoning patterns ($F1=0.542$, 135% better than random). When we surgically ablate these features, performance collapses. Removing the top feature causes a 44.6% drop, with some skills degrading by 67%, proving these aren't spurious correlations but causally important mechanisms. Most strikingly, we reveal that features detecting uncertainty and logical contradictions are nearly perfectly correlated ($r=0.988$, $p<0.0001$): the model maintains a unified internal "reasoning quality monitor." These findings reveal that latent reasoning, despite its opacity, contains structured representations that enable skill detection and error monitoring, providing a foundation for more transparent mathematical reasoning systems.

Keywords: Sparse Autoencoders · Latent Reasoning · Mechanistic Interpretability · AI Tutoring · Error Detection

1 Introduction

When a student struggles with a math problem, a good tutor does more than provide answers i.e. they reveal their reasoning, explain their thought process, and make their uncertainty visible [6]. But as AI tutors evolve toward "latent reasoning", models using Chain of Continuous Thought (CoConut) [1] are doing the

E. G. Blanchard et al. (Eds.): AIED 2026, LNAI 16583, pp. 208–216, 2027.
https://doi.org/10.1007/978-3-032-29760-0_23

opposite: solving problems through continuous hidden states without generating observable reasoning steps. This efficiency comes at a cost as we can no longer see *how* these models think, *when* they become uncertain, or *why* they make errors.This opacity poses fundamental challenges for educational AI [7]. How can we trust an AI tutor that refuses to show its work? When should the system intervene to scaffold a struggling student [8] if we cannot detect the model's own confusion? Without answers to these questions, even highly accurate AI tutors remain black boxes which are powerful but untrustworthy [9].Recent advances in mechanistic interpretability like Sparse Autoencoders (SAEs) [2,4] have emerged as a powerful technique for discovering interpretable features in neural networks by learning overcomplete dictionaries that decompose activations into sparse, semantically meaningful components.While SAEs have successfully revealed features for sentiment and linguistic patterns in language models, their application to mathematical reasoning, particularly latent reasoning remains unexplored.

We address this gap by training SAEs on the internal representations of GPT-2 Medium, obtained by applying CoConut during step-by-step problem solving on the GSM8k dataset [3]. We use GPT-2 Medium to maintain direct comparability with the original CoConut work, which demonstrated latent reasoning capabilities on this architecture.Through systematic analysis combining manual skill annotation, feature discovery, and causal validation via ablation studies [10], we transform inscrutable hidden states into interpretable, actionable signals for educational AI. We make 4 primary contributions:

(1) Skill Detection via Interpretable Features. We manually annotate 200 GSM8k problems across 9 mathematical skills and discover feature ensembles that reliably detect each skill (average F1=0.542), significantly outperforming random baselines (+135%).

(2) Causal Validation through Ablation. We prove that discovered features are causally important by systematically removing them and measuring performance degradation. Removing the top feature causes an average 44.6% F1 drop, with some skills experiencing catastrophic 67% degradation.

(3) Discovery of Unified Error Detection. We identify features that detect uncertainty and logical contradictions during reasoning. Strikingly, these features are nearly perfectly correlated (r=0.988, p<0.0001), revealing that CoConut maintains a single internal "reasoning quality monitor" rather than separate error-checking mechanisms.

(4) Practical Educational Applications. Our interpretable features enable real-time capabilities for AI tutoring systems. For example, when a student attempts a problem, active features reveal required skills i.e. if Features 787 (Group-Based Partitioning) and 1599 (Unit Rate Conversion) activate, the system can provide targeted scaffolding: "This problem involves dividing quantities into groups and calculating rates." When Feature 296 (error detector) spikes mid-solution, the system can intervene proactively: "You seem stuck, would you like a hint?" This transforms opaque model activations into actionable pedagogical decisions.

2   Related Work

Sparse Autoencoders for Interpretability. Sparse coding has long been used to discover interpretable representations [11], but recent work has scaled SAEs to large language models [2,4]. Unlike methods that analyze individual neurons [12], SAEs learn overcomplete dictionaries where features better align with human-interpretable concepts. Our work extends SAEs to mathematical reasoning.

Mathematical Reasoning in LLMs. Mathematical problem-solving has become a critical benchmark [13]. Datasets like GSM8k [3] test arithmetic and word problems. Chain-of-thought prompting [5] improves performance by encouraging step-by-step reasoning. CoConut [1] introduces latent reasoning where models think in continuous hidden states rather than language, but understanding *how* these models solve problems remains challenging [14].

Mechanistic Interpretability. This aims to reverse-engineer neural networks by discovering circuits [15,16]. Techniques include attention visualization [17], probing classifiers [12], and causal interventions [10]. SAEs complement these by discovering monosemantic features.

AI in Education. Intelligent tutoring systems have a rich history [18,19] but face transparency challenges [20]. Recent systems leverage LLMs for explanations [21] but treat models as black boxes [22]. Our interpretable features enable transparent skill assessment and proactive error detection.

3   Methodology

3.1   Dataset and Model

We use the GSM8k dataset [3], which contains 8,792 grade school math word problems requiring multi-step arithmetic reasoning. We leverage the latent reasoning annotations provided by the CoConut authors [1], which include reasoning step boundaries for 7,914 training examples. These annotations mark the transitions between consecutive reasoning steps in the model's latent space indicating when the model completes one reasoning operation and begins the next. Each annotation specifies the token position where a reasoning step concludes, enabling us to extract the corresponding hidden state activations at these critical reasoning boundaries. We analyze a GPT-2 Medium model trained using the Chain of Continuous Thought (CoConut) paradigm [1]. Unlike traditional chain-of-thought models [5], CoConut performs reasoning in a continuous latent space by feeding hidden states back iteratively. Rather than decoding intermediate reasoning steps into language tokens, CoConut uses the last hidden state from each reasoning step as the input embedding for the next step, enabling efficient reasoning without language constraints.

3.2 Sparse Autoencoder Training

We train a SAE to discover interpretable features in CoConut's reasoning process. SAEs learn an overcomplete dictionary that decomposes activations into sparse linear combinations [2]:

$$\mathbf{x} \approx \sum_{i=1}^{d} f_i(\mathbf{x})\mathbf{d}_i \tag{1}$$

where $\mathbf{x}$ is the input activation, $\mathbf{d}_i$ are learned dictionary vectors, and $f_i(\mathbf{x})$ are sparse activation coefficients.

We use a GPT2-Medium architecture (355M parameters) trained on CoConut's residual stream activations. Our training corpus consists of 7,914 reasoning steps. The SAE learns 4,096 features with L1 sparsity penalty to encourage interpretable representations.

3.3 Manual Skill Annotation

We randomly sample 200 problems from GSM8k test set for manual annotation. Two independent annotators identified 9 distinct mathematical skills: (1) Multi-Step Proportional Scaling (48 problems), (2) Group-Based Partitioning (65 problems), (3) Fractional and Percentage Partitions (48 problems), (4) Large Magnitude Arithmetic (13 problems), (5) Unit Rate and Time Conversion (42 problems), (6) Periodic Change and Net Balance (32 problems), (7) Relational Domino Chains (21 problems), (8) Threshold Capacity Analysis (11 problems), (9) Geometric Progression and Iterative Scaling (7 problems). Problems can involve multiple skills simultaneously (e.g., a problem may require both proportional scaling and unit conversion), so the per-skill counts sum to more than 200. Each problem was labeled with all applicable skills, and skill detection was evaluated independently per skill. Two independent annotators achieved Cohen's $\kappa = 0.82$ inter-rater agreement, indicating substantial agreement. Disagreements were resolved through discussion until consensus.

3.4 Feature Ensemble Discovery and Ablation

For each skill k, we identify features whose activations correlate with skill presence using point-biserial correlation [23], which measures the relationship between a binary variable (skill present/absent) and a continuous variable (feature activation). We compute problem-level activations by max-pooling across all reasoning steps for each problem. For each feature i and skill k:

$$r_{pb}(i, k) = \frac{\mu_1 - \mu_0}{\sigma} \sqrt{\frac{n_1 n_0}{n(n-1)}} \tag{2}$$

where r_{pb} is the point-biserial correlation coefficient, μ_1 and μ_0 are mean activations for problems with and without skill k, σ is pooled standard deviation, and

n_1, n_0 are sample sizes. We select the top 10 features per skill (ranked by $|r_{pb}|$) as an ensemble [24]. A skill is detected if any ensemble feature exceeds threshold $\tau = 1.0$:

$$\text{Detected}_k = \mathbb{1}\left[\max_{i \in \text{Ensemble}_k} f_i > \tau\right] \tag{3}$$

We evaluate using precision, recall, and F1 score. To validate causal importance [10], we conduct systematic ablation studies, removing the top $k \in \{1, 3, 5\}$ features and re-evaluating performance. Large performance drops indicate features play a mechanistic role. We compare against a random baseline: 10 randomly selected features from the full 4,096 feature set.

3.5 Error Detection Analysis

We investigate whether SAE features can detect reasoning errors and uncertainty using two approaches: **Uncertainty Detection**: Features with high variance across reasoning steps within a problem, indicating inconsistent activation patterns that suggest the model is exploring multiple solution paths and **Contradiction Detection**: Features with sudden activation spikes between consecutive steps, potentially capturing moments when the model revises its reasoning or encounters logical inconsistencies.

4 Results

4.1 Skill Detection Performance

Table 1. Feature ensemble performance for detecting 9 mathematical skills. High recall demonstrates reliable detection.

Skill	Precision	Recall	F1
Multi-Step Proportional Scaling	0.440	1.000	0.611
Group-Based Partitioning	0.616	0.877	0.724
Fractional & Percentage Partitions	0.461	1.000	0.631
Large Magnitude Arithmetic	0.277	1.000	0.434
Unit Rate & Time Conversion	0.429	0.929	0.587
Periodic Change & Net Balance	0.375	1.000	0.545
Relational Domino Chains	0.321	0.952	0.480
Threshold Capacity Analysis	0.280	0.909	0.428
Geometric Progression & Iterative Scaling	0.297	0.857	0.441
Average	**0.388**	**0.947**	**0.542**

Table 1 presents feature ensemble performance for detecting 9 mathematical skills across 200 problems. Average F1 score is 0.542, demonstrating that SAE features reliably capture mathematical reasoning patterns.

4.2 Ablation Study: Features are Causally Important

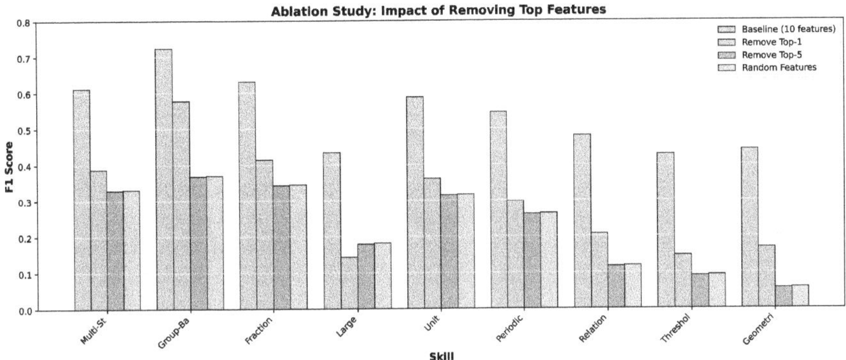

Fig. 1. Ablation showing performance collapse when removing top features. Green=baseline, orange/red=ablated, gray=random. (Color figure online)

Figure 1 visualizes ablation results. Removing the top-1 feature drops average F1 from 0.542 to 0.300 i.e. a 44.6% degradation. Some skills experience catastrophic drops: Large Magnitude Arithmetic (67.1%), Threshold Capacity Analysis (65.7%), and Geometric Progression (61.6%), indicating highly specialized feature learning. Crucially, even the degraded SAE ensembles (F1=0.300 after removing top-1, F1=0.229 after removing top-5) remain comparable to random 10-feature baselines (F1=0.231), demonstrating that the top features carry most of the discriminative signal. This validates that correlation-based feature selection identifies causally important patterns rather than noise.

4.3 Discovery of Unified Error Detection

Features detecting uncertainty and contradiction are nearly perfectly correlated (r=0.988, p<0.0001). We identified top 5 uncertainty features (high within-problem variance) and top 5 contradiction features (high step-to-step spikes). 4 of 5 top features appear in *both* lists: Features 296, 1040, 1880, and 976, suggesting a unified "reasoning quality monitor."

Feature 296 emerges as the master error detector, ranking first in both uncertainty (variance=7.69) and contradiction (max spike=4.15). Figure 2 shows Feature 296's patterns across 5 problems. In simple problems (Problem 0), it remains stable (range 5–12). In complex problems (Problems 150, 199), it exhibits dramatic fluctuations (range 0–12), spiking when encountering difficult sub-problems. Other features (F2471, F1102, F1040, F976) show similar but weaker patterns, confirming Feature 296 as the dominant error signal. This unified mechanism enables single-feature intervention signaling for AI tutoring.

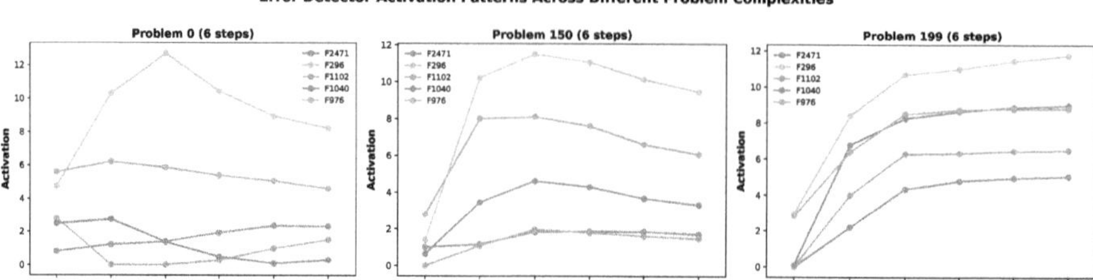

Fig. 2. Error detector activation patterns across 3 problems of increasing complexity. Feature 296 (orange) shows strongest signal which is stable in simple problems (left), fluctuating in medium complexity (center), highly variable in complex ones (right). All 5 features track complexity, but Feature 296 provides clearest signal. (Color figure online)

5   Discussion

Implications for Educational AI. Our findings enable practical applications: (1) **Real-Time Skill Assessment** as feature ensembles identify which mathematical skills a problem requires, enabling adaptive curriculum sequencing. (2) **Intelligent Intervention Timing** as Feature 296's unified error detection provides a single signal for when to intervene. (3) **Transparent Feedback Generation** as interpretable features enable explanations like "This problem requires unit conversion (Feature 1599) and multi-step reasoning (Feature 787)." The high recall (0.947) with moderate precision (0.388) represents a deliberate trade-off: the system may over-predict required skills, potentially leading to unnecessary scaffolding, but ensures that struggling students receive support rather than being overlooked. In educational settings, false positives (offering unneeded help) are often preferable to false negatives (missing students who need intervention).

Insights for Mechanistic Interpretability. Our work demonstrates that latent reasoning models, despite their opacity, contain structured, interpretable representations. Three key insights emerge: (1) Sparse features generalize across reasoning paradigms. (2) Mathematical skills have dedicated features as the strong ablation results (44.6% average drop, up to 67% for some skills) indicate that reasoning is implemented through specialized circuits. (3) Error Detection Shows Strong Unification as the near-perfect correlation (r=0.988) between uncertainty and contradiction features indicates substantial overlap in error monitoring mechanisms, suggesting shared representations for tracking reasoning quality rather than separate systems.

Limitations. Our analysis covers 200 manually annotated GSM8k problems. Our 9 skills may not capture all mathematical reasoning dimensions. We analyze only CoConut; testing similar features in other latent reasoning models would strengthen claims about universal mechanisms.

6   Conclusion

As mathematical reasoning models transition from explicit chain-of-thought to efficient latent reasoning, they risk becoming inscrutable black boxes unsuitable for educational applications. We demonstrate that Sparse Autoencoders can break open this opacity, revealing interpretable features for skill detection and error monitoring. Through systematic ablation, we prove these features are causally important as removing the top feature causes 44.6% average performance degradation, with some skills collapsing by 67%. Most strikingly, we discover that uncertainty and contradiction detection are not separate mechanisms but a unified "reasoning quality monitor." These findings reveal that latent reasoning, despite its opacity, contains structured representations that enable skill detection and error monitoring, providing a foundation for more transparent mathematical reasoning systems. Future work extending these techniques to larger models and diverse reasoning domains could enable fully interpretable AI tutoring systems that explain their reasoning as clearly as human teachers.

References

1. Hao, S., et al.: Training Large Language Models to Reason in a Continuous Latent Space. arXiv:2412.06769 (2024)
2. Cunningham, H., Ewart, A., Riggs, L., Huben, R., Sharkey, L.: Sparse Autoencoders Find Highly Interpretable Features in Language Models. arXiv:2309.08600 (2023)
3. Cobbe, K., et al.: Training Verifiers to Solve Math Word Problems. arXiv:2110.14168 (2021)
4. Templeton, A., et al.: Scaling Monosemanticity: Extracting Interpretable Features from Claude 3 Sonnet. Anthropic (2024)
5. Wei, J., et al.: Chain-of-Thought Prompting Elicits Reasoning in Large Language Models. NeurIPS (2022)
6. Chi, M.T., et al.: Learning from human tutoring. Cogn. Sci. **25**(4), 471–533 (2001)
7. Roll, I., Wylie, R.: Evolution and revolution in artificial intelligence in education. Int. J. Artif. Intell. Educ. **26**(2), 582–599 (2016). https://doi.org/10.1007/s40593-016-0110-3
8. Koedinger, K.R., Corbett, A.T., Perfetti, C.: The knowledge-learning-instruction framework. Cogn. Sci. **36**(5), 757–798 (2012)
9. Ribeiro, M.T., Singh, S., Guestrin, C.: Why Should I Trust You?: Explaining the Predictions of Any Classifier. KDD (2016)
10. Geiger, A., Lu, H., Icard, T., Potts, C.: Causal Abstractions of Neural Networks. NeurIPS (2021)
11. Olshausen, B.A., Field, D.J.: Emergence of simple-cell receptive field properties. Nature **381**, 607–609 (1996)
12. Belinkov, Y.: Probing classifiers: promises, shortcomings, and advances. Comp. Ling. **48**(1), 207–219 (2022)
13. Hendrycks, D., et al.: Measuring Mathematical Problem Solving with the MATH Dataset. NeurIPS (2021)
14. Stolfo, A., Belinkov, Y., Sachan, M.: A Mechanistic Interpretation of Arithmetic Reasoning. EMNLP (2023)

15. Elhage, N., et al.: A Mathematical Framework for Transformer Circuits. Transformer Circuits Thread (2021)
16. Wang, K., et al.: Interpretability in the Wild. ICLR (2023)
17. Clark, K., et al.: What Does BERT Look at? ACL Workshop BlackboxNLP (2019)
18. Anderson, J.R., Corbett, A.T., Koedinger, K.R., Pelletier, R.: Cognitive tutors: lessons learned. J. Learn. Sci. **4**(2), 167–207 (1995)
19. VanLehn, K.: The relative effectiveness of human tutoring, intelligent tutoring systems, and other tutoring systems. Ed. Psychol. **46**(4), 197–221 (2011)
20. Holmes, W., Bialik, M., Fadel, C.: Artificial Intelligence in Education. Center for Curriculum Redesign (2019)
21. Kasneci, E., et al.: ChatGPT for Good? On opportunities and challenges of large language models for education. Learn. Individ. Differ. **103**, 102274 (2023)
22. Conati, C., Porayska-Pomsta, K., Mavrikis, M.: AI in Education Needs Interpretable Machine Learning. arXiv:1807.00154 (2018)
23. Tate, R.F.: Correlation Between a Discrete and a Continuous Variable. PointBiserial Correlation. Ann. Math. Stat. **25**(3), 603–607 (1954)
24. Dietterich, T.G.: Ensemble Methods in Machine Learning. In: Multiple Classifier Systems, pp. 1–15 (2000)

Personalizing Mathematical Game-Based Learning for Children: A Preliminary Study

Jie Gao and Adam K. Dubé[✉]

McGill University, Montreal, Quebec, Canada
`jie.gao3@mail.mcgill.ca, adam.dube@mcgill.ca`

Abstract. Game-based learning (GBL) is widely adopted in mathematics education. It enhances learners'engagement and critical thinking throughout the mathematics learning process. However, enabling players to learn intrinsically through mathematical games still presents challenges. In particular, effective GBL systems require dozens of high-quality game levels and mechanisms to deliver them to appropriate players in a way that matches their learning abilities. To address this challenge, we propose a framework, guided by adaptive learning theory, that uses artificial intelligence (AI) techniques to build a classifier for player-generated levels. We collect 206 distinct game levels created by both experts and advanced players in Creative Mode, a new tool in a math game-based learning app, and develop a classifier to extract game features and predict valid game levels. The preliminary results show that the Random Forest model is the optimal classifier among the four machine learning classification models (k-nearest neighbors, decision trees, support vector machines, and random forests). This study provides insights into the development of GBL systems, highlighting the potential of integrating AI into the game-level design process to provide more personalized game levels for players.

Keywords: Personalize · Game-based Learning · Machine Learning · Mathematics

1 Introduction

Game-based learning (GBL) has been widely examined for its effectiveness and affordance in enhancing students' critical thinking, problem-solving, and conceptual understanding [1,7,11,14]. The recent meta-analysis research shows that GBL has a significant positive overall effect on students' critical thinking [15]. These findings align with previous research and also highlight the critical role of specific game mechanics [10]. A good math game goes beyond gamification and turns the core math skill into game mechanics (i.e., what the player does) to make learning the game [20]. Ke [11] called these intrinsically integrated educational games and showed they are far more effective than games where learning is extrinsic to gameplay (i.e., play the game then solve math problems).

E. G. Blanchard et al. (Eds.): AIED 2026, LNAI 16583, pp. 217–225, 2027.
https://doi.org/10.1007/978-3-032-29760-0_24

Making intrinsic games requires dedicated designers and hours of labor for each level, while mastering math skills requires cumulative practice over dozens of levels [16]. However, most GBL systems face this challenge [8]. Konca [12] evaluated 30 popular STEM applications and showed that most math applications paid more attention to content quality, design, functionality, and technical features. Some researchers also indicated that both intrinsic motivation for math and the quality of the playing experience impact students' learning success [18].

To make the game levels more intrinsically mathematical and to improve students' learning of mathematical knowledge, a math game-based learning app developed a tool, Creative Mode, that helps players enhance their creative thinking skills. Through this tool, players can design new game levels and expert-selected user levels can be delivered to other players. Yet, manually identifying which player-levels are suitable for sharing with other players is untenable, thousands of levels have to be reviewed by the experts. Additionally, it is challenging to provide adaptive game levels that match individuals' learning abilities. Previous research focuses on using machine learning (ML) methods to predict learner performance. However, there is limited research on filtering player-generated game levels using ML models [4,13]. To address this concern, we aimed to design a framework that (1) uses a machine learning classifier to identify and classify valid player-generated levels and (2) provide personalized game levels to appropriate players, all guided by adaptive learning theory.

2   Related Work

2.1   GBL in Mathematics

GBL is defined as a learning method that integrates digital games into the learning environment [3]. Some researchers suggested that well-designed math games can provide multi-level behavioural, cognitive, and affective interactions that increase children's interest and performance in math [10,17]. Previous studies have indicated that GBL can address pedagogical concerns by providing low-stakes, student-centered contexts where abstract laws and concepts are concretized during gameplay [20], improve students' meaning-making abilities when interacting with multiple external representations framed by the GBL mechanics [19], and provide adaptive challenges matching students' learning abilities [5,20].

An increasing body of evidence has indicated that GBL improves not only students' learning outcomes but also their critical thinking skills [6,15]. By simulating real-world problems in a learning environment, students can try different strategies over time and adjust their solutions based on the feedback; thereby improving their critical thinking [15]. Furthermore, moving beyond the role of a player, the transition to a game level creator encourages students to engage in higher-order thinking. In this role, they are tasked with the complex challenge of constructing innovative levels that effectively balance entertainment value with pedagogical efficacy [9].

2.2   Math Game Adaptivity

Previous research [20] suggests that games can be designed to adapt to students' actions and level of learning, achieving game adaptivity. However, Cayton-Hodges and her colleagues [2] reviewed 64 math apps on four dimensions, including mathematical content, feedback, scaffolding, interactions, and adaptability. They found that not all apps focused on adaptability. Some researchers indicated that most educational games today implement a low-resolution adaptivity form at the level of individual players [21]. They argue that a micro-adaptive, dynamic, fine-grained, and player-centered approach to game design is critical.

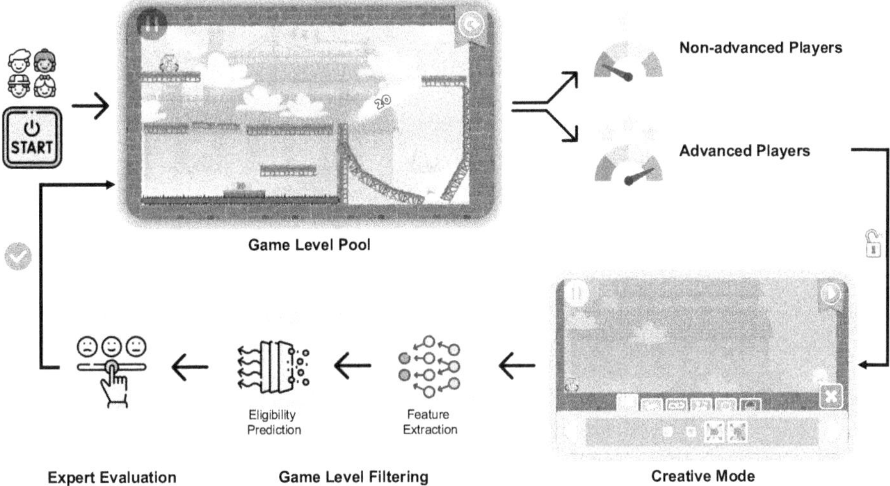

Fig. 1. Overview of the player-generated levels selection pipeline.

2.3   Current Study

The present study focuses on exploring an effective approach to identifying valid play-generated game levels and providing personalized levels to individual players, better fulfilling their learning needs. The purpose of this work is to provide insights into how artificial intelligence (AI) techniques can be integrated into GBL for math learning. It also addresses a critical question, which is whether intrinsic educational games can be designed to provide sufficient practice for students to achieve mastery.

3   Methodology

3.1   Dataset

In this study, we employ a game level dataset from a math game-based learning app, gathered between 2024 and 2025. This app builds conceptual understanding

Table 1. Four variable groups: player character, goal, physics objects, and obstacles.

Groups	Variable Examples	Level Examples
Player Character	Player Character, Player Character Value	
Goal	Goal	
Physics Objects	Ice Block x1, Ice Block x 10, Lava Block x1, Lava Block x10, Bubble, One-way Platform, Slimy Platform, Sticky Platform	
Obstacles	Cloud, Could Value, Door, Door Value, Spiky Platform, Breakable Wall, Breakable Wall Value	

through game-based learning, supporting children ages 5-10 around the world. Creative Mode is a tool within the game, allowing advanced players to design and create new game levels based on their own ideas. This mode helps advanced players improve their creative thinking with math and provides the cumulative practice that other players need through player-generated levels.

The dataset includes 206 distinct game levels from Creative Mode: 86 expert-designed levels and 120 player-generated levels. Each level is associated with a JSON file that encodes all game features. Among player-generated levels, 44 of them were validated and selected by experts at the game company for other peers to play, while the remaining levels were excluded from the active pool. We extract key variables for this study, including the counts of features (N=25) and their associated values (N=12). Note that some features appear more than once within a level. The dataset is fully anonymous.

3.2   Design Pipeline

As illustrated in Figure 1, advanced players gain access to the Creative Mode and can drag elements (e.g., ice blocks, lava blocks, bubbles, and platforms) into the board to design a game level. After creating the game levels, we extract the key variables from each level and apply a machine learning approach to filter the levels. Selected levels identified by the model are sent to experts for a final review. Only validated levels are approved and deployed into the public game pool for other players to play.

3.3   Data Processing and Analysis

The data processing mainly consists of the following steps. First, we extracted key variable values from each level and stored the data in a structured dataset. Second, we classified the 61 extracted variables into four groups: player character, goal, physics objects, and obstacles (see Table 1). The player character group includes variables related to the game character. The goal group represents the completion goal of the game. Each game level includes a single goal. The physics objects group comprises diverse game objects, including ice blocks, lava blocks, and platforms. Some of these objects have individual values. When the character approaches such an object, the character's value merges (e.g., addition, subtraction) with the object's value. The obstacles group includes game objects that may prevent the character from moving, such as clouds, doors, and breakable walls. Third, missing values were recoded as missing. Fourth, we used Lasso, a regression analysis method, to further select features and reduce the dimensionality of the data, enhancing prediction accuracy and result interpretability.

This study applied four ML models to identify the optimal predictive model: k-nearest neighbors (KNN), decision trees (DT), support vector machines (SVM), and random forests (RF). We selected these algorithms because they represent a diverse range of classification mechanisms. Moreover, model performance is assessed using nested cross-validation, which can minimize evaluation bias.

4   Preliminary Results

This section presents the results of the model performance metrics of four selected ML models. The metrics include accuracy, precision, recall, F1-score, ROC-AUC score, and the confusion matrix. The results are preliminary, mainly focusing on the phase of selecting the most effective model as the game level classifier.

Performance Comparison. Table 2 reports the performance of four classifiers evaluated using nested cross-validation to identify an effective model for screening player-generated game levels. Performance was stable across inner and outer loops, indicating limited overfitting and reasonable generalization to unseen levels. Among the models tested, RF demonstrated the strongest overall performance, achieving the highest recall and F1-score while maintaining high overall

Table 2. Results of the classification performance evaluation (Inner vs. Outer loop).

Model	Accuracy	Precision	Recall	F1-Score	ROC-AUC
Inner loop					
KNN	$81.42 \pm 1.53\%$	$73.85 \pm 3.92\%$	$65.32 \pm 3.13\%$	$66.41 \pm 3.53\%$	$84.77 \pm 4.71\%$
DT	$83.89 \pm 1.54\%$	$78.06 \pm 3.57\%$	$73.40 \pm 4.72\%$	$73.63 \pm 3.96\%$	$81.58 \pm 3.66\%$
SVM	$82.42 \pm 1.19\%$	$75.90 \pm 3.14\%$	$66.67 \pm 3.23\%$	$68.11 \pm 3.64\%$	$\mathbf{86.84 \pm 2.20\%}$
RF	$82.07 \pm 1.37\%$	$74.43 \pm 2.64\%$	$70.46 \pm 2.18\%$	$71.12 \pm 2.27\%$	$85.86 \pm 1.85\%$
Outer loop					
KNN	$79.90 \pm 4.01\%$	$68.60 \pm 10.79\%$	$62.97 \pm 8.19\%$	$63.66 \pm 9.10\%$	$84.12 \pm 8.45\%$
DT	$82.23 \pm 3.88\%$	$75.45 \pm 7.54\%$	$71.72 \pm 7.39\%$	$71.86 \pm 6.60\%$	$81.69 \pm 7.62\%$
SVM	$81.93 \pm 2.53\%$	$74.90 \pm 6.93\%$	$65.52 \pm 4.98\%$	$67.50 \pm 5.19\%$	$86.22 \pm 4.87\%$
RF	$82.42 \pm 5.71\%$	$74.53 \pm 8.91\%$	$72.69 \pm 9.75\%$	$72.70 \pm 9.22\%$	$\mathbf{86.57 \pm 6.32\%}$

discrimination. Confusion matrix results (Figure 2a) further show that RF was least likely to discard expert-validated levels, a critical requirement for preserving high-quality user-generated content in the proposed screening pipeline. Although SVM also achieved a strong ROC-AUC performance, it was more conservative in identifying selectable levels. Taken together, these results indicate that RF provides the most suitable balance of robustness and sensitivity for identifying high-quality player-generated game levels. Figure 2b further compares the performance of the four classifiers. RF and SVM consistently consistently outperformed the other classifiers. SVM (86.22%) demonstrated strong classification performance, whereas RF (86.57%) achieves the best overall performance across four models.

Feature Importance. To improve interpretability and reduce the dimensionality of the dataset, Lasso regression was used to identify the most informative features for predicting whether a player-generated level would be selected by experts. The analysis indicates that selection decisions are primarily associated with a small set of core structural features, including the number of player characters and goals, as well as the presence of one-way platforms, platform bubbles, and poppable bubbles. These features are central to gameplay mechanics, suggesting that expert judgments of level quality are closely tied to how mathematical actions and objectives are structured within a level rather than to peripheral or decorative elements.

5   Discussion

The present study identified the top actionable predictors of game features using the best-performing machine learning model, RF, out of all the classifiers compared and contrasted in this study. Of these predictors, player characters and goals emerged as the most critical elements. While these features represent fundamental game-based mechanics rather than explicit mathematical symbols, they

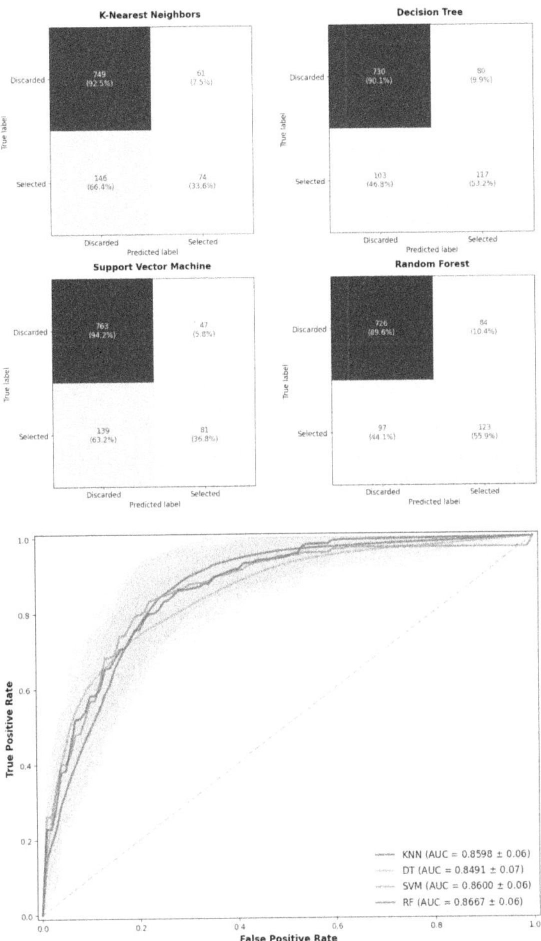

Fig. 2. Top (a): Confusion matrix. Bottom (b): ROC-AUC of four models.

serve as the essential interactive vessel for the learning content. The player character acts as the mathematical problem solver, whereas the goal defines the successful resolution of the game level. The findings demonstrate that the structural integrity of the game is a prerequisite for effective math learning during gameplay. Also, features from physics objects groups play more important roles than features from obstacles, suggesting that the model prioritizes features that allow more constructive manipulation (related to calculation and logical reasoning) over passive barriers. Our study uses machine learning methods to identify game features and predict selectable game levels, provide guidance for GBL systems in developing more intrinsic game levels. This automates the game level selection process and replaces labor-intensive manual curation. The proposed framework shows the possibility of using AI techniques to handle large volumes of player-generated game levels on the GBL systems and provide high-quality, intrinsically integrated learning experiences to players.

This study has several limitations. First, the size of the dataset constrains the model comparison. Future work includes collecting additional game levels to improve the robustness and generalizability of the results. Second, the Creative Mode includes other game modules with different features. More predictors could be manually selected and explored for further study. Third, as these are preliminary findings, further exploration is needed and could focus on adaptive and personalized mathematical GBL informed by the proposed framework.

6   Conclusion

This paper proposes a novel screening framework for mathematical GBL systems, applying machine learning methods to identify key game features and predict effective player-generated levels. Our findings rigorously demonstrate that RF is the optimal model for screening game levels in this case. By bridging a critical gap in the existing literature, our approach provides new insights for the development of mathematical GBL systems and enhances the creation of sufficiently intrinsic games. Furthermore, the ML classifier can maintain consistency and standardization in the screening process, ensuring the quality and reliability of game levels. Ultimately, this study provides a theoretical and practical foundation for the development of math learning games, also improving students' motivation, engagement, and critical thinking skills through gameplay.

References

1. Alam, S.S., Gao, J., Dubé, A.K.: A systematic review and meta-analysis of digital mathematics interventions for k-12 students with mathematical learning disabilities. Int. J. Sci. Math. Educ. 1–28 (2025)
2. Cayton-Hodges, G.A., Feng, G., Pan, X.: Tablet-based math assessment: what can we learn from math apps? J. Educ. Technol. Soc. **18**(2), 3–20 (2015)
3. Chang, C.Y., Kao, C.H., Hwang, G.J., Lin, F.H.: From experiencing to critical thinking: a contextual game-based learning approach to improving nursing students' performance in electrocardiogram training. Education Tech. Research Dev. **68**(3), 1225–1245 (2020)
4. Chi, M., Schwartz, D., Blair, K.P., Chin, D.B.: Choice-based assessment: can choices made in digital games predict 6th-grade students' math test scores? In: Educational Data Mining 2014 (2014)
5. Chiotaki, D., Poulopoulos, V., Karpouzis, K.: Adaptive game-based learning in education: a systematic review. Front. Comput. Sci. **5**, 1062350 (2023)
6. Cicchino, M.I.: Using game-based learning to foster critical thinking in student discourse. Interdisc. J. Problem-Based Learn. **9**(2) (2015)
7. Dai, C.P., Ke, F., Pan, Y.: Narrative-supported math problem solving in digital game-based learning. Education Tech. Research Dev. **70**(4), 1261–1281 (2022)
8. Dubé, A.K., Keenan, A.: Are games a viable home numeracy practice? In: Early childhood mathematics skill development in the home environment, pp. 165–184. Springer (2016)

9. Hsiao, H.S., Chang, C.S., Lin, C.Y., Hu, P.M.: Development of children's creativity and manual skills within digital game-based learning environment. J. Comput. Assist. Learn. **30**(4), 377–395 (2014)

10. Kacmaz, G., Dubé, A.K.: Examining pedagogical approaches and types of mathematics knowledge in educational games: a meta-analysis and critical review. Educ. Res. Rev. **35**, 100428 (2022)

11. Ke, F.: Designing and integrating purposeful learning in game play: a systematic review. Education Tech. Research Dev. **64**(2), 219–244 (2016)

12. Konca, A.S.: Digital technology usage of young children: screen time and families. Early Childhood Educ. J. **50**(7), 1097–1108 (2022)

13. Lee, J.E., Jindal, A., Patki, S.N., Gurung, A., Norum, R., Ottmar, E.: A comparison of machine learning algorithms for predicting student performance in an online mathematics game. Interact. Learn. Environ. **32**(9), 5302–5316 (2024)

14. Liljedahl, P., Santos-Trigo, M., Malaspina, U., Bruder, R.: Problem solving in mathematics education. Springer Nature (2016)

15. Mao, W., Cui, Y., Chiu, M.M., Lei, H.: Effects of game-based learning on students' critical thinking: a meta-analysis. J. Educ. Comput. Res. **59**(8), 1682–1708 (2022)

16. Mayfield, K.H., Chase, P.N.: The effects of cumulative practice on mathematics problem solving. J. Appl. Behav. Anal. **35**(2), 105–123 (2002)

17. McEwen, R.N., Dube, A.: Engaging or distracting: children's tablet computer use in education. Int. Forum Educ. Technol. Soc. (2015)

18. Ninaus, M., Moeller, K., McMullen, J., Kiili, K.: Acceptance of game-based learning and intrinsic motivation as predictors for learning success and flow experience. Int. J. Serious Games **4**(3), 15–30 (2017)

19. Pan, Y., Ke, F., Dai, C.P.: Patterns of using multimodal external representations in digital game-based learning. J. Educ. Comput. Res. **60**(8), 1918–1941 (2023)

20. Sharma, R., Lajoie, S.P., Dubé, A.K.: Game design for mathematics education. Math. Educ. Res. Innov. 25–37 (2022)

21. Vandewaetere, M., Cornillie, F., Clarebout, G., Desmet, P.: Adaptivity in educational games: including player and gameplay characteristics. Int. J. Higher Educ. **2**(2), 106–114 (2013)

A Hybrid Human-AI Content Generation Framework for Safe and Personalized Dialogic Learning with Children

Elena Malnatsky[1], Shenghui Wang[2]([✉]), Kuhu Sinha[1],
Koen V. Hindriks[1], and Mike E. U. Ligthart[1]

[1] Vrije Universiteit Amsterdam, De Boelelaan 1105, 1081HV Amsterdam,
The Netherlands
{e.malnatsky,kuhu.sinha,k.v.hindriks,m.e.u.ligthart}@vu.nl
[2] University of Twente, Drienerlolaan 5, 7522NB Enschede, The Netherlands
shenghui.wang@utwente.nl

Abstract. Educational conversational systems for children must balance personalization, safety, and pedagogical alignment to support engaging and meaningful learning interactions. While large language models (LLMs) can support personalised dialogue, direct runtime generation risks factual errors, pedagogical drift, and developmentally inappropriate content. We present a Hybrid Human-AI Content Generation Framework that combines rule-based pedagogical scaffolding, constrained offline LLM authoring, and a two-stage validation pipeline with automated evaluation and expert moderation. We evaluated the framework in an in-school study with 51 children (ages 8 – 11) engaged in book-related dialogues with a social robot across four sessions over two months. Results show strong pedagogical alignment (94% of utterances), robust safety (zero unsafe utterances), meaningful personalization (54% achieving both book and personal relevance), and 93.5% human – AI validator agreement with only 10.7% of utterances requiring manual intervention, though humor generation remained the most challenging category for automated evaluation. Together, these findings suggest that hybrid offline authoring with human-AI validation can support safe, pedagogically grounded, and personalized child-facing dialogue in bounded school deployments.

Keywords: Educational Dialogue Systems · Child-Robot Interaction · Hybrid Intelligence · Dialogic Learning · Personalization · Large Language Models · Safety Assurance · Human-in-the-loop

1 Introduction

Personalized educational dialogue systems offer strong potential to support children's engagement, reflection, and learning, but they must also remain pedagogically grounded, developmentally appropriate, and safe [7,8]. This creates

E. G. Blanchard et al. (Eds.): AIED 2026, LNAI 16583, pp. 226–235, 2027.
https://doi.org/10.1007/978-3-032-29760-0_25

a central challenge for trustworthy AI in Education: how to support meaningful adaptation without sacrificing educational control and reliability. Recent Large language models (LLMs) offer new opportunities for generating adaptive and personalized dialogue, yet their direct runtime use in child-facing systems remains problematic [4,11]. In open-ended interaction, generated content may be factually incorrect, pedagogically misaligned, or inappropriate for the developmental level of the learner. In child – robot interaction, these risks are especially salient because dialogue should feel responsive and engaging while remaining carefully constrained in content.

Prior work in child – robot interaction and educational robotics has shown the value of personalization, for example by adapting conversational content or educational support to user characteristics, preferences, or prior interaction history [5,7]. However, many such systems rely on scripted or rule-based pathways, which support control but can limit scalability across learners, topics, and longer-term interactions [1,10]. At the same time, LLMs have begun to expand what is possible in educational applications, including question generation [6], personalized feedback [9,13], and discussion support [2]. Yet child-facing educational settings impose stronger assurance requirements than most prior deployments: runtime generation complicates auditability, and consistent pedagogical quality cannot be assumed without explicit validation.

Hybrid approaches that combine automated checks with human oversight offer a promising middle ground [12]. Yet existing work has not integrated pedagogically structured dialogue scaffolding, constrained offline LLM authoring, and auditable validation with automated screening and human judgment into a reusable design pattern for child-facing educational dialogue [3]. This gap matters especially in settings where safeguarding, developmental appropriateness, and pedagogical accountability are non-negotiable.

To address this gap, we present a Hybrid Human-AI Content Generation Framework for safe and personalized dialogic learning with children. The framework treats LLMs as collaborative offline content authors rather than runtime autonomous generators, combining a rule-based pedagogical scaffold, constrained offline generation, and a two-stage validation pipeline that integrates automated evaluation with expert moderation before any utterance reaches the child. We instantiate and evaluate it in a robot-mediated reading intervention with 51 children (ages 8 – 11) across four sessions over two months in primary schools. Results indicate strong pedagogical alignment, robust safety, meaningful personalization, and generally effective automated triage, while highlighting the limits of rubric-based evaluation for affective content such as humor.

Our contributions are: (1) a general hybrid human – AI content generation framework for child-facing educational dialogue that separates content generation from delivery while preserving pedagogical structure and auditability; (2) an instantiation in a real-school deployment for personalized book discussions with children; and (3) empirical insights into the strengths and limits of automated validation for child-facing educational dialogue, especially for affective content such as humor.

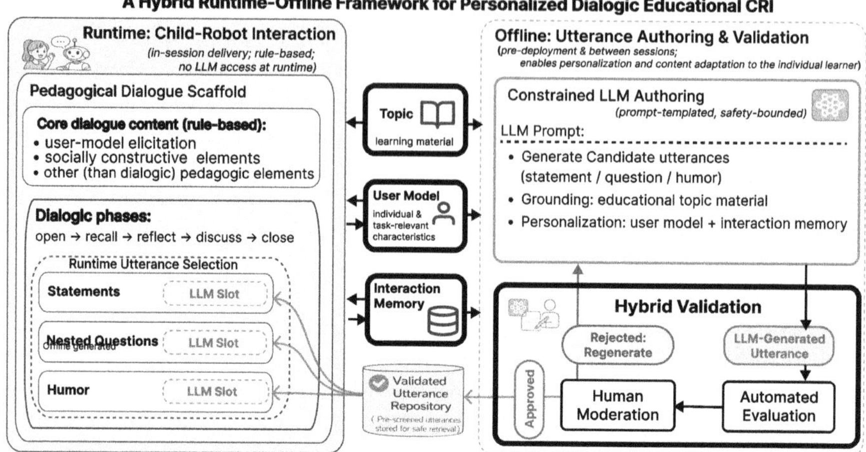

Fig. 1. Hybrid runtime-offline framework. A rule-based scaffold governs runtime interaction using only pre-validated utterances; offline, constrained LLM authoring and hybrid validation populate the dialogue repository.

2   Hybrid Human-AI Content Generation Framework

We present a Hybrid Human-AI Content Generation Framework for safe, personalized child-facing dialogic learning. The framework is designed for settings where auditability and developmental appropriateness are essential, and is guided by five requirements: (1) pedagogically grounded structure, (2) accurate educational content, (3) scalable personalization, (4) sustained cognitive and affective engagement, and (5) assurance of safety and developmental appropriateness.

The framework operationalizes these requirements through three interlinked components (Fig. 1): (1) a rule-based pedagogical scaffolding maintaining dialogue structure while defining insertion points for adaptive content, (2) constrained offline LLM generation producing personalized utterances grounded in educational knowledge and user models, and (3) a two-stage validation pipeline combining automated evaluation with expert moderation.

Rule-Based Pedagogical Scaffold. The pedagogical scaffold provides a fixed dialogue structure organized into phases (opening, recall, reflection, discussion, closing) with predefined insertion slots for LLM-generated content (Fig. 1, left). Dialogue is realized through three units - statements, questions, and humor - allowing adaptive content to be inserted while preserving pedagogical coherence and developmental appropriateness.

Constrained LLM Generation. LLM generation is constrained by three inputs (Fig. 1, top right): (1) educational topic material (for books: title, author, genre, age, plot summary), (2) a user model capturing demographics, interests, and learning preferences (reading motivation, favorite genres), and (3) interaction memory preserving prior exchanges for longitudinal personalization.

Utterances are pre-generated offline through modular prompts specifying the robot's educational role, grounded topic content, and personalization cues from the user model and interaction memory. Prompts balance explicit constraints, such as age-appropriateness and factual accuracy, with enough flexibility to produce personalized statements, questions, or humor.

Two-Stage Hybrid Validation Pipeline. All LLM-generated utterances undergo two-stage validation before deployment (Fig. 1, bottom right). During child-facing interaction, the system retrieves only pre-validated utterances from the repository; no LLM is accessed at runtime.

Candidate utterances are evaluated against a rubric derived from dialogic learning requirements. Core criteria assess appropriateness and linguistic suitability; standard criteria assess educational alignment, personalization, dialogic quality, accuracy, and engagement; humor is additionally assessed for cultural relevance and amusement.

Stage 1: Automated Evaluation. Each candidate is scored by an independent LLM-based evaluator (1–10) on all criteria, with brief justifications. Utterances scoring ≥ 7 on all criteria pass the automated gate and are eligible for deployment, subject to spot-check audits of above-threshold items for obvious false accepts; any utterance scoring below 7 on any criterion is routed to expert moderation. The cutoff of 7 was used as a pragmatic triage threshold rather than a formally calibrated optimum, based on an initial inspection suggesting that overall quality was generally good and that the automated scores were directionally sensible while still leaving substantial content for human review. This stage concentrates expert effort on potentially problematic content. The validation layer is modular by design and can accommodate different evaluators depending on domain risk and operational constraints.

Stage 2: Expert Moderation. Below-threshold utterances are reviewed by expert moderators, who assess usability, verify rubric alignment, and decide whether each item should be approved, revised, or regenerated. Spot-checks of above-threshold utterances provide lightweight audits for obvious false accepts. Only moderator-approved utterances enter the validated repository, and all scores and moderation decisions are logged for traceability.

3   Case Study: Robot-Mediated Reading Intervention

3.1   Study Setup

Fifty-one children (ages 8–11; 27 boys, 24 girls) were recruited via collaborating primary schools. The study was approved by the institutional ethics committee (ref. 2023-015). Children completed pre-study questionnaires on interests and reading preferences, then participated in four one-on-one sessions over approximately two months with an autonomous NAO robot in a quiet school setting. Sessions lasted 8–15 min and were supervised by a research assistant.

Session 1 elicited information for the user model through a "getting to know each other" interaction. Afterward, each child was assigned a unique book matched to their interests. In Session 2, the robot introduced the book and explained why it suited the child's preferences. In Sessions 3 and 4, the robot engaged the child in reflective discussion using pre-validated statements, questions, and occasional humor; full details of the interaction design and session structure are reported in [8]. Children read the assigned book independently between sessions, and each child's dialogue content was tailored to both the book and the child profile.

The interaction scripts were executed by a GOAL-based dialogue agent, which managed turn-taking, triggered pre-validated utterances from the dialogue repository, and logged interaction data for subsequent analysis.

3.2   Content Generation and Validation in Practice

In this instantiation, the pedagogical scaffold structured Sessions 2–4 into opening, recall, reflection, discussion, and closing phases, with adaptive content inserted only at predefined slots.

The study setting creates two practical challenges for personalized content generation: grounding was limited to short book summaries and metadata, while each child had a different book and profile, creating high demand for scalable individualized content. We used GPT-4o to generate candidate utterances offline via eight modular prompt templates: *Connections, Questions, Humor (Joke Script), Opinions, Interests (Interest Script), Hooks, Favourites,* and *Active Reading Connections,* producing 15 utterance types grouped at runtime into three higher-level units: statements, questions, and humor. All templates were conditioned on book material, child profile, and interaction memory, while enforcing format and style constraints for developmental appropriateness.[1]

All candidate utterances were processed through the two-stage validation pipeline; only validated items entered the runtime repository. Five trained moderators reviewed subsets of utterances by child and session, assessing deployment suitability and whether backup or regeneration was required; disagreements were resolved via consultation with the lead researcher. Above-threshold utterances were spot-checked against the child profile without full rubric re-scoring, flagging only obvious false accepts. Review took approximately 30 s for clearly acceptable utterances, around 1 min when a backup was selected, and 3 – 5 min when regeneration was required.

---

[1] Prompt templates and evaluation rubrics are available at: https://github.com/Social-AI-VU/robot-bookworm.

Table 1. Validation Pipeline Outcomes by Utterance Type.

Category	Flagged for Review (<7)	Evaluator-Moderator Disagreement	Rejected by Moderator	Total Utter.
Statement	90 (16.04%)	17 (3.03%)	22 (3.92%)	561
Question	20 (13.07%)	4 (2.61%)	8 (5.23%)	153
Humor	14 (13.73%)	32 (31.37%)	57 (55.88%)	102
Total	124 (15.20%)	53 (6.50%)	87 (10.66%)	816

3.3 Evaluation Metrics

We evaluated feasibility and content quality along three dimensions: personalization and book alignment, dialogic quality and engagement, and safety and appropriateness. Evaluation combined (1) pre-deployment hybrid validation metrics based on automated rubric scores and moderator decisions, (2) a post-hoc corpus audit using a separate GPT-4o prompt to assess book alignment, personalization, personalized alignment, and hallucination, and (3) child self-reports after Session 4 on personalization/alignment, dialogic quality, appropriateness, linguistic suitability, accuracy, and humor. Multi-item scales showed acceptable reliability (Cronbach's $\alpha > .70$).

4 Results

4.1 Hybrid Validation Pipeline Performance

We analyzed the outcomes of the hybrid validation pipeline applied to 816 utterances (561 statements, 153 questions, 102 humorous utterances).

Automated Evaluation Scores Automated scores were high overall: appropriateness ($M = 9.94$, $SD = 0.33$), comprehensibility ($M = 9.78$, $SD = 0.53$), accuracy ($M = 9.51$, $SD = 0.94$), and book alignment ($M = 9.51$, $SD = 1.00$) all scored strongly, while humor-related criteria were comparatively lower (cultural relevance: $M = 8.26$, $SD = 0.92$; amusement: $M = 8.08$, $SD = 0.85$). This suggests that the generator reliably produced age-appropriate and educationally aligned content, with humor as the least stable category.

Human Moderation Outcomes. Table 1 summarizes review flags, evaluator – moderator disagreement, and final rejection rates. Overall agreement between the automated evaluator and moderators was 93.5%, with disagreement concentrated in humor (31.37%). Across 816 utterances, 124 (15.2%) were flagged for review and 87 (10.66%) were rejected or regenerated. Rejections were mainly due to mismatch with scripted material, humor quality, excessive complexity, or hallucinated assumptions about the child. No utterance was judged unsafe.

4.2 Content Quality Analysis (Post-Hoc)

Table 2 reports post-hoc alignment and personalization by utterance type. Overall, 94.24% of utterances aligned with book content, 57.40% were personalized to the child model, and 54.19% achieved both. Hallucinations were rare (1.96% overall) and absent in questions, indicating that the framework generally produced content that was both grounded and individually relevant.

Table 2. Post-hoc Analysis of Book Alignment, Personalization, and Hallucinations

	Statement	Question	Humor	All
Book Alignment	98.93%	98.69%	61.76%	94.24%
Personalization	67.65%	59.48%	23.53%	57.40%
Personalized Alignment	65.36%	55.56%	18.63%	54.19%
Hallucinations	2.50%	0%	–	1.96%

4.3 Child Self-reported Experience

Child self-reports were analyzed descriptively using medians and interquartile ranges. Children reported high perceived personalization and book fit (Mdn = 4.00 [3.00, 4.50]; *Personalized Book Fit*: 4.00 [4.00, 5.00]), high appropriateness (*Unpleasant statements*: 5.00 [4.50, 5.00]; *Odd statements*: 4.00 [3.50, 4.50], reverse coded), and strong dialogic quality (4.12 [3.78, 4.75]). Linguistic suitability was also rated positively (4.00 [3.75, 4.62]), consistent with high automated ratings for appropriateness ($M = 9.94$, $SD = 0.33$) and comprehensibility ($M = 9.80$, $SD = 0.53$). Humor was the clearest exception: children moderately appreciated individual jokes (3.50 [3.00, 4.50]) despite high humor desirability (5.00 [4.00, 5.00]), mirroring the elevated moderator rejection rate for humor and underscoring the limits of rubric-based evaluation for affective content.

5 Discussion

Affective Content as the Hard Case: Humor. Humor revealed the clearest mismatch between rubric-based automated evaluation and children's affective experience. Although the evaluator scored humor relatively highly (cultural relevance $M = 8.26$; amusement $M = 8.08$), evaluator–moderator disagreement was highest in this category (31%), and many jokes were rejected as "not funny" or "too complex." Children's reports reinforced this pattern: appreciation of individual jokes was moderate (Mdn= 3.5/5), while humor desirability was high overall (Mdn= 5/5), suggesting that playfulness can support rapport even when specific jokes fall flat. More broadly, affective content appears less amenable to static rubric-based validation than safety, clarity, or topical relevance, and may require complementary mechanisms such as curated templates, multimodal feedback, or selective human authorship.

Deployment Trade-offs. The framework achieves personalization at the content-authoring stage rather than at runtime; real-time adaptivity is deliberately sacrificed for pre-deployment assurance, which is the appropriate trade-off for this deployment context, where safeguarding and structured dialogue are non-negotiable. In practice, we envision content review being performed by curriculum specialists or reading coordinators on a per-book cycle basis. In lower-stakes or adult-facing contexts, simpler templates or runtime guardrails may be more appropriate.

Limitations. Several limitations remain. The evaluation focused on book-related dialogue with children aged 8 – 11; transfer to other domains, age groups, or more dynamic interaction styles remains an open empirical question. No systematic human review of the deployed session dialogues was conducted, limiting assessment of in-situ interaction quality. Personalization was constrained by lightweight book metadata and a basic user model, limiting responsiveness to unexpected child input. The sample reflected participating schools without detailed demographic data, so cultural transferability—especially for humor—requires further study. Finally, the validation pipeline was operational rather than fully calibrated: the threshold was chosen pragmatically, and moderation cost was estimated from the deployment workflow rather than compared experimentally against fully human authoring; both content generation and evaluation used GPT-4o, which has since been superseded; future deployments should assess whether more capable models reduce rejection rates, particularly for humor. Future work should examine richer user modeling, constrained runtime adaptation, broader cross-domain and cross-cultural validation, and more systematic threshold calibration.

6   Conclusion

This paper presented a hybrid human–AI framework for safe and personalized dialogic learning with children where offline content generation and validation are separated from runtime delivery. In a robot-mediated reading intervention with 51 children, the framework supported pedagogically grounded, developmentally appropriate, and meaningfully personalized dialogue while focusing expert review on a relatively small set of uncertain cases. Humor remained the most challenging category, highlighting that affective and subjective qualities are harder to evaluate automatically than formal and topical aspects of content. Overall, for child-facing educational systems, generative AI may therefore be most promising not as an unconstrained runtime interlocutor, but as a bounded partner in an auditable human–AI workflow oriented toward shared educational goals.

AI tool use disclosure: We used ChatGPT (OpenAI) for language editing and clarity improvements in portions of this manuscript. The authors reviewed and revised all suggested changes and take full responsibility for the final content.

Acknowledgments. We sincerely thank the participating schools for their invaluable contributions. This work was supported by the Gravitation Programme Hybrid Intelligence, funded by the Nederlandse Organisatie voor Wetenschappelijk Onderzoek (NWO). Grant No. 024.004.022.

References

1. Van den Berghe, R., Verhagen, J., Oudgenoeg-Paz, O., Van Der Ven, S., Leseman, P.: Social robots for language learning: a review. Rev. Educ. Res. **89**(2), 259–295 (2019). https://doi.org/10.3102/0034654318821286
2. Dietz Smith, G., Prasad, S., Davidson, M.J., Findlater, L., Shapiro, R.B.: ContextQ: Generated Questions to Support Meaningful Parent-Child Dialogue While Co-Reading. In: Proceedings of the 23rd Annual ACM Interaction Design and Children Conference, pp. 408–423. IDC '24, Association for Computing Machinery, New York, NY, USA (2024). https://doi.org/10.1145/3628516.3655809
3. Gao, M., Hu, X., Ruan, J., Pu, X., Wan, X.: LLM-based NLG Evaluation: Current Status and Challenges (2024). https://doi.org/10.48550/arXiv.2402.01383, arXiv:2402.01383
4. Hadi, M.U., et al.: Large Language Models: A Comprehensive Survey of its Applications, Challenges, Limitations, and Future Prospects (2023). https://doi.org/10.36227/techrxiv.23589741
5. Irfan, B., Ramachandran, A., Spaulding, S., Glas, D., Leite, I., Koay, K.: Personalization in Long-Term Human-Robot Interaction, pp. 685–686 (2019). https://doi.org/10.1109/HRI.2019.8673076
6. Lee, U., et al.: Few-shot is enough: exploring ChatGPT prompt engineering method for automatic question generation in English education. Educ. Inf. Technol. 1–33 (2023)
7. Ligthart, M.E.U., Neerincx, M.A., Hindriks, K.V.: Memory-Based Personalization for Fostering a Long-Term Child-Robot Relationship. In: Proceedings of the 2022 ACM/IEEE International Conference on Human-Robot Interaction, pp. 80–89. HRI '2022, IEEE Press, Sapporo, Hokkaido, Japan (2022)
8. Malnatsky, E., et al.: The Robot Bookworm: Fostering Children's Reading Motivation through Personalized Book Discussions. In: Proceedings of the 21st ACM/IEEE International Conference on Human-Robot Interaction, pp. 1010–1019. HRI '2026, Association for Computing Machinery, New York, NY, USA (2026). https://doi.org/10.1145/3757279.3785618
9. Meyer, J., et al.: Using LLMs to bring evidence-based feedback into the classroom: AI-generated feedback increases secondary students' text revision, motivation, and positive emotions. Comput. Educ. Artif. Intell. **6**, 100199 (2024)
10. Michaelis, J.E., Mutlu, B.: Reading socially: Transforming the in-home reading experience with a learning-companion robot. Sci. Robo. **3**(21), eaat5999 (2018). https://doi.org/10.1126/scirobotics.aat5999. Publisher: American Association for the Advancement of Science

11. Pozdniakov, S., et al.: Large language models meet user interfaces: the case of provisioning feedback. Comput. Educ. Artif. Intell. **7**, 100289 (2024). https://doi.org/10.1016/j.caeai.2024.100289
12. Schroeder, H., Roy, D., Kabbara, J.: Just put a human in the loop? Investigating LLM-assisted annotation for subjective tasks. In: Che, W., Nabende, J., Shutova, E., Pilehvar, M.T. (eds.) Findings of the Association for Computational Linguistics: ACL 2025, pp. 25771–25795. Association for Computational Linguistics, Vienna, Austria (2025). https://doi.org/10.18653/v1/2025.findings-acl.1323
13. Stahl, M., Biermann, L., Nehring, A., Wachsmuth, H.: Exploring LLM Prompting Strategies for Joint Essay Scoring and Feedback Generation. arXiv preprint arXiv:2404.15845 (2024)

Likelihood-Based Diagnosis with Generative Models: Confidence-Aware Measurement from Student Writing

S. Thomas Christie[1,2(✉)], Matthew Zent[3,4], Markus Hauru[1], Anna N. Rafferty[2], and Simon Woodhead[4]

[1] Renaissance Philanthropy, Washington D.C., USA
`{thomas.christie,markus.hauru}@renphil.org`
[2] Carleton College, Northfield, MN, USA
`arafferty@carleton.edu`
[3] University of Minnesota, Minneapolis, MN, USA
`zentx005@umn.edu`
[4] Eedi, Inc., London, UK
`simon.woodhead@eedi.com`

Abstract. Generative modeling is rapidly reshaping student educational experiences, yet assessment still heavily relies on selected-response items like multiple-choice questions. A strong benefit of selected-response-based inference is its grounding in probabilities: beliefs about student skills are derived via likelihood functions relating student abilities to observed behavior. Inspired by this approach, we propose a method that leverages the likelihood computations of Large Language Models (LLMs) to produce analogous probabilistic judgments for student-written text. Specifically, we use an open-weight LLM to evaluate the likelihood of student-written text conditioned on contextual skill and misconception descriptions. Rather than generate new text or produce a rubric-based score, the LLM assigns conditional probabilities to observed student outputs. Inferences are made using posterior probabilities over conditioning statements, similar to latent class modeling. We illustrate the approach using student explanations to mathematics problems by comparing classifications to human labels. Early results show that accuracy on high-confidence predictions is competitive with zero-shot label generation from state-of-the-art models with orders of magnitude more parameters. In addition to providing classifications, our method produces a confidence signal computed from model likelihoods that is strongly correlated with classification accuracy, providing a principled route to educational measurement using free-response text.

Keywords: Large Language Models · Educational Assessment · Measurement · Generative AI · Automated Scoring

E. G. Blanchard et al. (Eds.): AIED 2026, LNAI 16583, pp. 236–244, 2027.
https://doi.org/10.1007/978-3-032-29760-0_26

1   Introduction

For thousands of years, learning progress has been evaluated through expert observation of rich, high-dimensional student behavior. From a journeyman blacksmith crafting a blade to a doctoral student defending their dissertation, assessment has long involved observation and judgment of student behavior on domain-specific tasks. Unfortunately, expert attention does not scale, and the past century has witnessed the emergence of an assessment industry focused on increasing assessment scalability and reliability through the use of selected-response items (SRIs). SRIs offer many operational benefits, including the affordance of a probabilistic approach to assessment (see Sect. 2). Use of a probabilistic framework transforms the process of assessment from a series of human judgments into a mechanistic process of evidence accumulation designed to produce a trustworthy and useful score. However, filtering student behavior through SRIs also has drawbacks. While a categorical response selection is recorded, the behavior process leading to the selection is typically neither recorded nor factored into the student evaluation. Moreover, SRIs must be carefully constructed to induce students to perform a specific, well-defined behavioral or mental operation— reasoning or knowledge recall, for example—to make a correct selection. Even then, a correct response could be a guess or the result of using an unanticipated strategy, invalidating the intended skill inference.

We wish to broaden the set of behaviors that can be used for assessment while retaining the mechanistic, probabilistic evidence-gathering framework described above. As such, our work follows in the tradition of automated scoring of open-ended student responses [16]. Automated scoring approaches are rich and varied, and include quantifying student writing with hand-crafted metrics [2], training classifiers to predict expert ratings [15], and measuring similarity to expert responses [11]. More recent techniques leverage the power of Large Language Models (LLMs), typically by providing models with both student writing and an expert-authored rubric and prompting the model to generate a score [6]. These methods typically produce point-estimate scores but lack principled estimates of score uncertainty. However, uncertainty quantification is a critical component of educational measurement, driving decisions about assessment length, reliability (*Do I have enough evidence?*), and adaptivity (*Is this the best question to ask?*).

To address this gap, we propose a method that leverages LLM likelihood computations to produce confidence-aware probabilistic judgments of skills and misconceptions from student writing. Unlike standard LLM-powered scoring approaches, our approach does not use LLMs to predict labels or generate text. Instead, we leverage LLMs to compute the conditional probability of observed student text to create a probabilistic measurement equation for student behavior. An analogous approach has been applied to text classification tasks, there referred to as a 'noisy channel language model' [10]. While this paper's application to automated scoring is a proof-of-concept, if successful, the proposed method could allow scalable and evidence-oriented likelihood-based assessment of learning using a much wider range of ecologically valid behaviors such as writing, speech, or even movement. Our contributions are as follows:

1. We introduce likelihood-based diagnosis with generative models, an approach to performing educational measurement using student writing.
2. We outline theoretical parallels between likelihood-based diagnosis and other latent variable approaches like Item Response Theory: parameters are replaced by interpretable skill statements, and the LLM likelihood function is analogous to the probabilistic measurement equation.
3. We apply our method to an expert-labeled dataset of student explanations to multiple choice questions. Using a 3B model, likelihood-based diagnosis achieves state-of-the-art accuracy for high-confidence predictions while simultaneously demonstrating a smooth relationship between accuracy and confidence, a property required for principled measurement but missing from LLM-as-a-Judge approaches like those in [6].

2   Likelihood-Based Latent Class Diagnosis from Text

Psychometrics treats educational assessment as a problem of measurement. A student has certain abilities or skills that exist as unobserved potential; the assessor's task is to elicit observable behaviors to gather evidence about the student's skills. The student's skill (θ) is latent and related to behavior (x) only probabilistically. We model this as $\mathcal{L}(\theta\,;x) = \Pr(X = x \mid \Theta = \theta) = p(x \mid \theta)$ for a set of student attributes Θ. Observed behavior x is treated as a realization of a random variable X. Multiple behavior 'events' are treated as independent, a fact that can be used to compute the posterior:

$$p(\theta \mid x) \propto p(x_1, x_2, ..., x_n \mid \theta)p(\theta) = p(\theta) \prod_{i=1}^{n} p(x_i \mid \theta) \tag{1}$$

The likelihood function $p(x \mid \theta)$ is a parameterized logistic model in Item Response Theory with continuous-valued θ [3]. In Cognitive Diagnostic Models, it is a probability contingency table with discrete-valued latent attributes [1]. In both cases, the likelihood functions evaluate the conditional likelihood of discrete categorical events, which are then combined to compute a posterior and produce a score, with reliability demands dictating the number of items needed.

2.1   Computing Conditional Likelihoods Using LLMs

We propose using the likelihood computations inherent in generative models in an analogous manner to serve as the likelihood function for inference. In particular, the core operation of a pretrained Large Language Model is to compute the conditional likelihood of tokens given previous tokens. While the conditional likelihood distribution is typically used to generate new tokens via sampling, it can also be used to compute the likelihood of observed tokens given a prompt.

Let S_k be a text statement describing a latent ability $k \in K$ and let C represent the text of a particular assessment context such as a math problem or essay prompt. Let $T = (t_1, t_2, ..., t_n)$ represent written text that can be decomposed into a sequence of tokens t_i. Given an LLM L, we compute the likelihood of each token in T conditional on the previous tokens:

$$p_L(T \mid C, S_k) = p_L(t_1 \mid C, S_k) \cdot p_L(t_2 \mid C, S_k, t_1) \cdot p_L(t_3 \mid C, S_k, t_1, t_2) \ldots \quad (2)$$

$$= \prod_{i=1}^{n} p_L(t_i \mid C, S_k, t_{j<i}) \quad (3)$$

The logarithmic form of Eq. 3 can be computed by invoking, e.g., an AutoModel from Hugging Face's `transformers` library.

Given a set of mutually exclusive skill statements $k \in K$, we wish to evaluate the relative likelihood of each given the student's response and use that to determine which conditioning statement S_k best accounts for the response. That is, we wish to compute the posterior probability of a discrete multinomial distribution as shown in Algorithm 2.1, Eq. 5. Assuming that statements in K are mutually exclusive is a modeling assumption shared by more common methods like Naive Bayes.

Algorithm 2.1: Likelihood-based latent class diagnosis

Inputs: context C, student text $T = (t_1, \ldots, t_n)$, statements $\{S_k\}_{k=1}^{K}$, priors $p(S_k)$, entropy threshold τ, model L.

Step 1: Compute token-likelihood score

$$\ell_k = \sum_{i=1}^{n} \log p_L(t_i \mid C, S_k, t_{<i}) \quad \text{(sum over tokens in } T \text{ only).} \quad (4)$$

Step 2: Compute posterior

$$p(S_k \mid C, T) = \mathrm{softmax}_k(\ell_k + \log p(S_k)) \quad (5)$$

Prediction: $\hat{k} = \arg\max_k p(S_k \mid C, T)$.
Confidence: $p(S_{\hat{k}} \mid C, T)$.
Posterior entropy: $H = -\sum_k p(S_k \mid C, T) \log p(S_k \mid C, T)$.
Decision: output $\hat{k}$ iff $H \leq \tau$; else abstain.

Equation 5 represents a posterior belief over mutually exclusive values for a latent attribute (i.e., which skill statement best accounts for a student's response T to the problem context C) and corresponds to Eq. 1 in traditional measurement. Prior probabilities over skill or misconception categories are provided by the user. Rather than prompting to generate labels, we use an open-weight LLM to compute the conditional likelihood of student-provided text. Inference occurs via comparing the likelihoods of the *same text* under conditioning hypotheses S_k, making length normalization unnecessary for within-response comparisons. In our experiments, we use pretrained (non-instruction-tuned) models, since preference-tuning distorts likelihoods relative to observed text.

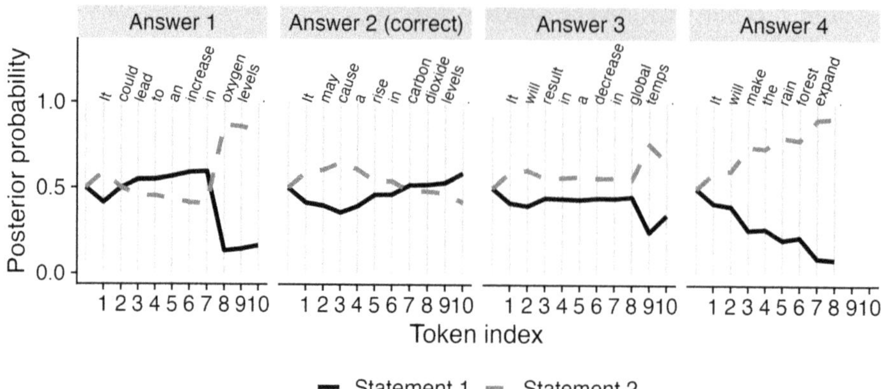

Fig. 1. Plots show four possible responses to the passage/question in Sect. 2.2. Lines show the posterior probability of the response token sequence up-to-and-including the token at each index. Solid and dashed lines show probabilities conditioned on Statement 1 and Statement 2, respectively. In practice, probabilities are used to compute an aggregate confidence metric, which is compared to a pre-specified threshold. The model used is `meta-llama/Llama-3.2-3B`.

2.2   A Dichotomous Worked Example

Suppose a student is given an assessment to measure their ability to make correct inferences from a written passage. Consider the following, shortened for brevity:

Passage: The Amazon Rainforest, often called the "lungs of the Earth," produces approximately 20% of the world's oxygen. [*truncated*] Scientists warn that continued destruction could lead to severe consequences, including loss of biodiversity and increased carbon dioxide levels in the atmosphere.

Question: What is one major concern scientists have about deforestation in the Amazon Rainforest?

This passage is our assessment context C. We can specify two mutually exclusive statements S_1 and S_2 describing the student's abilities:

S_1: "The student responding to the following question comprehends the written passage and makes a correct inference."

S_2: "The student responding to the following question has difficulty comprehending the written passage or makes an incorrect inference."

Figure 1 shows posterior probabilities for skill statements S_1 and S_2 for four possible student responses to the prompt, calculated using Eqs. 3 and 5. The method supports token-wise evidence accumulation, though in practice, the entire student statement would be used to make inferences. In this example, the method requires fewer tokens to infer that students do not have a skill (Statement 2 receives a higher posterior probability in Answers 1, 3, and 4) than the converse. While beyond the scope of this paper, multiple student statements, responses to questions, or dialogue turns can be combined to build evidence of a student's latent skills or knowledge.

3   Misconception Diagnosis from Text

To investigate the performance characteristics of likelihood-based diagnosis on multi-class inference, we use our method to infer misconceptions about mathematical operations revealed by short reasoning statements written by students. The full dataset consists of 36,696 multiple-choice questions and responses collected by the Eedi platform and used with permission. Each response is accompanied by a one-sentence student explanation justifying their answer (e.g., the following explanation for an incorrect response in the dataset labeled *Additive*):

Question: $\frac{A}{10} = \frac{9}{15}$. What is the value of A?
MC Response: 4
Explanation: If you do $5 + 10 = 15$ then you need to do $A + 5 = 9$, which
             means thee answer must be four.

We filtered the dataset to responses that were both incorrect and contained expert-supplied misconception labels, resulting in 9,457 responses. We then randomly split the data in half by question, using 50% to develop misconception labels and 50% for evaluation. For this exploration, misconception descriptions were created by prompting GPT-5.2 to provide mutually exclusive misconception descriptions that account for student text responses in the dataset, where each misconception description begins with the sentence "While explaining the answer to the following math problem, the student..." For example, the "Additive" misconception proceeded with "... tries to create equivalent fractions by adding or subtracting the same amount to the numerator as was added or subtracted to the denominator (additive scaling), rather than scaling numerator and denominator by the same multiplicative factor." This process resulted in 35 misconception labels with associated descriptions. We sampled up to 20 responses from each misconception category for the analysis, resulting in 583 responses.

4   Results

Inference results from applying our method to predicting one of 35 possible misconceptions in the Eedi dataset are shown in Fig. 2. We compare to two baselines: 1) LLM-as-a-Judge with tool-calling for categorical predictions (horizontal lines) and 2) LLM self-evaluation adapted from [8] (black lines) where label decisions are converted into a sequence of binary predictions and resulting token likelihoods are normalized across misconceptions. Misconceptions were randomized

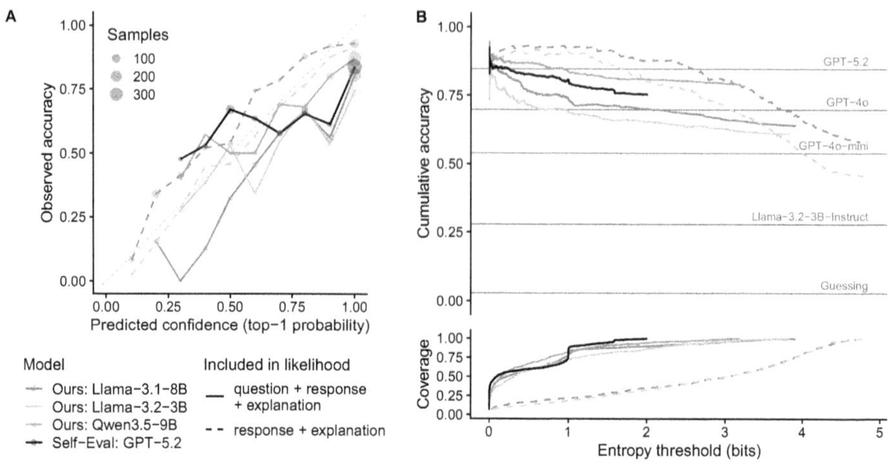

Fig. 2. Misconception inference results comparing prompt-based LLM-as-a-Judge generative predictions (horizontal lines), the self-evaluation method from [8] with GPT-5.2 (black), and our method with various open-weight LLMs (colors). Dashed line results include only the per-token likelihood of the student's answer and explanation. Solid lines also include the problem text in likelihood computations to align with the self-evaluation baseline. **A** shows each model's confidence in its prediction vs accuracy. The $x = y$ diagonal represents the ideal case. Dot size marks the number of samples at each confidence threshold. **B** shows the cumulative accuracy (top), and cumulative coverage (bottom) of predictions with entropy below a threshold (x-axis).

to mitigate position bias for both baseline methods. Figure 2A illustrates that posterior uncertainty provides a critical signal about inference trustworthiness in the absence of an unobservable ground-truth. Figure 2B demonstrates the accuracy achieved with smaller LLMs and the strong correlation between accuracy and entropy.

Characteristic of a calibrated measurement model and in contrast to the baseline approaches, our method using only student responses and explanations exhibits a smooth relationship between posterior uncertainty and classification accuracy, with posterior uncertainty quantified as either confidence or entropy. This signal of trustworthiness indicates when predictions should be trusted and when more data is needed. For data points where our method is highly confident, classification accuracy is competitive with state-of-the-art models utilizing many orders of magnitude more parameters. Where the method reveals a lack of confidence, more behavioral evidence can be collected from students.

5   Discussion and Conclusion

The purpose of educational measurement is to gather evidence in support of a claim about an unobservable property of a student. Framed this way, measurement is an inference problem that critically relies on a *degree of belief* to determine when sufficient evidence has been collected to be confident in a particular claim. Principled confidence estimates are an information-bearing signal for adaptive item selection and test length requirements. Recent work (e.g. [7,12]) illustrates the utility of LLMs for high-accuracy scoring of open-assessment items, mirrored by our comparison results here to GPT-5.2. However, methods using LLMs-as-judges [6] lack a principled quantification of degree-of-belief that allows practitioners to know when to be confident in an inferential claim and when more evidence is needed (though again, see [8] as a notable exception).

Here, we introduce a method that uses an LLM to compute the likelihood of observed student writing given several 'latent' interpretable skill or misconception statements. Our approach addresses two fundamental limitations of LLM use to date by providing: (1) interpretable skill/misconception statements and token-level evidence, and (2) a method of quantifying the degree of evidence for, or against, particular claims. The paradigm is a step towards leveraging powerful generative modeling for principled inference-based educational measurement.

Limitations and Future Work. The method presented here represents a methodological proof-of-concept. Subsequent investigations will include evaluations of larger open-weight LLMs, quantifying the utility of fine-tuning, and modifying the wording used to describe latent skills and misconceptions in conditioning statements. In particular, tweaking human-interpretable skill statements is amenable to optimization using targeted context adjustments [4] or neuro-symbolic approaches similar to DeepMind's FunSearch [14].

The current analysis only evaluated model performance on a single dataset; prior to any use of the method in a real-world assessment context, more thorough validation across a range of datasets is needed. Such validation should explore calibration across subject areas, response lengths, and numbers of skills or misconceptions. The existing dataset we used classified each student as exhibiting one of 35 different misconceptions, meaning that the dataset treated these misconceptions as mutually exclusive. As noted above, care must be taken in creating the ontology of skills or misconceptions that maximizes mutual exclusivity. Future work could explore classifying responses as exhibiting multiple misconceptions, for example by creating two contexts for each misconception: one indicating the presence of the misconception, and one indicating its absence.

More broadly, the field of psychometrics has an established set of validation and reliability methodologies that can be readily applied to the approach described in this paper (e.g. [5,9]). Moreover, our method has the potential to address some biases in LLM-based scoring, such as overrating highly likely responses [13], by focusing on relative likelihoods. Re-orienting the use of generative modeling from *generation* to *likelihood estimation* creates an exciting possibility to dramatically broaden the range of student behavior that can be validly and reliably assessed.

Acknowledgments. The authors thank the Learning Engineering Virtual Institute for supporting the development of this work.

Disclosure of Interests. The authors have no competing interests to declare that are relevant to the content of this article.

References

1. Almond, R.G., Mislevy, R.J., Steinberg, L.S., Yan, D., Williamson, D.M.: Bayesian networks in educational assessment. Springer (2015)
2. Attali, Y., Burstein, J.: Automated essay scoring with e-rater® v. 2. J. Technol. Learn. Assess. **4**(3) (2006)
3. Cai, L., Choi, K., Hansen, M., Harrell, L.: Item response theory. Ann. Rev. Stat. Appl. **3**(1), 297–321 (2016)
4. Chu, Y., et al.: Confusion-aware rubric optimization for LLM-based automated grading. arXiv preprint arXiv:2603.00451 (2026)
5. Eignor, D.R.: The standards for educational and psychological testing (2013)
6. Gu, J., et al.: A survey on LLM-as-a-judge. Innov. **7**(6), 101253 (2026)
7. Impey, C., Wenger, M., Garuda, N., Golchin, S., Stamer, S.: Using large language models for automated grading of student writing about science. IJAIED. 1–35 (2025)
8. Kadavath, S., et al.: Language models (mostly) know what they know. arXiv preprint arXiv:2207.05221 (2022)
9. Kane, M.: The argument-based approach to validation. Sch. Psychol. Rev. **42**(4), 448–457 (2013)
10. Min, S., Lewis, M., Hajishirzi, H., Zettlemoyer, L.: Noisy channel language model prompting for few-shot text classification. In: Muresan, S., Nakov, P., Villavicencio, A. (eds.) Proceedings of the 60th Annual Meeting of the Association for Computational Linguistics (Volume 1: Long Papers), pp. 5316–5330. Association for Computational Linguistics, Dublin, Ireland (2022). https://doi.org/10.18653/v1/2022.acl-long.365
11. Mohler, M., Mihalcea, R.: Text-to-text semantic similarity for automatic short answer grading. In: Proceedings of the 12th Conference of the European Chapter of the ACL (EACL 2009), pp. 567–575 (2009)
12. Morris, W., Holmes, L., Choi, J.S., Crossley, S.: Automated scoring of constructed response items in math assessment using large language models. IJAIED **35**(2), 559–586 (2025)
13. Ohi, M., Kaneko, M., Koike, R., Loem, M., Okazaki, N.: Likelihood-based mitigation of evaluation bias in large language models. In: Ku, L.W., Martins, A., Srikumar, V. (eds.) ACL 2024, pp. 3237–3245. Association for Computational Linguistics, Bangkok, Thailand (2024)
14. Romera-Paredes, B., et al.: Mathematical discoveries from program search with large language models. Nature **625**(7995), 468–475 (2024)
15. Sung, C., Dhamecha, T.I., Mukhi, N.: Improving short answer grading using transformer-based pre-training. In: International Conference on Artificial Intelligence in Education, pp. 469–481. Springer (2019)
16. Williamson, D.M., Xi, X., Breyer, F.J.: A framework for evaluation and use of automated scoring. Educ. Meas. Issues Pract. **31**(1), 2–13 (2012)

Delegating Educational Tasks to LLMs: A Content Analysis of Evaluation Approaches

Badmavasan Kirouchenassamy[1], Chloé Conrad[2]([✉]), Maëva Somny[2],
and Léo Nebel[1,3]

[1] CNRS, LIP6, Sorbonne Université, 75005 Paris, France
{badmavasan.kirouchenassamy,leo.nebel}@lip6.fr
[2] LIRIS, UMR5205, Université Claude Bernard Lyon 1, CNRS, École Centrale de
Lyon, INSA Lyon, Université Lumière Lyon 2, 69622 Villeurbanne, France
{chloe.conrad,maeva.somny}@univ-lyon1.fr
[3] EvidenceB, Paris, France

Abstract. LLMs have gone from theoretical computer science research to widespread use by the general public, with the emergence of increasingly powerful and popular LLMs models. These effective models have been incorporated into AIED research, but they raise several questions, since in this field, every prediction and every decision can have a significant impact on the learner. In this paper, we propose a study of LLMs' use in education, focusing on the evolution of the presence of these systems, their evaluation, and the tasks assigned to them. To this end, we conducted a meta-analysis, leading to the construction of a codebook based on the articles published from 2023 to 2025 editions of the *AIED* conference, ensuring agreement between annotators on a sample.

Keywords: Large Scale Language Models · Education · Content Analysis

1 Introduction

The landscape of educational technology is undergoing a "generative turn". Large Language Models (LLMs), with their transformer architectures and emergent reasoning capabilities, have moved beyond sophisticated auto-complete to serve as multifaceted instruments within the pedagogical ecosystem, facilitating functions such as learning, supporting content creation, dialogue-based learner assistance, assessment, and feedback [5]. However, this rapid integration has outpaced our theoretical understanding of its impact. Initially confined to low-stakes support functions—such as text summarization or grammar correction—LLMs are increasingly being delegated "High-Level Cognitive Tasks" (HLCTs). In education, these include instructional design, learner misconception modeling, and even acting as pseudo-tutors in collaborative learning environments [7]. This

E. G. Blanchard et al. (Eds.): AIED 2026, LNAI 16583, pp. 245–253, 2027.
https://doi.org/10.1007/978-3-032-29760-0_27

shift makes rigorous socio-technical evaluation all the more important: LLM outputs are probabilistic, sensitive to prompt and context variations, and prone to generating fluent but nonfactual content–commonly known as "hallucinations" – which poses real risks to educational validity and trust. This article presents early findings from a broader, ongoing review of generative AI in education. This broader review addresses educational uses of LLMs, approaches for evaluating such uses, ethical and governance considerations, and prompting strategies for different educational uses.

We restrict the present synthesis to papers published in the *AIED* (Artificial Intelligence in Education) Conference over the most recent three-year window. This scope is motivated (*i*) temporally because widely accessible LLM systems entered public use at the end of 2022 and the first sustained wave of educational research followed in 2023 and (*ii*) venue-wise because *AIED* is a long-standing, field-defining conference at the intersection of AI and the learning sciences, and its proceedings provide a concentrated view of methodological norms and emergent application patterns in AI-in-education research. This scope might be expanded in future works. Given the identified need for rigorous evaluation methods for LLM systems in education, we narrow the focus to a foundational **research question** that structures the first phase of synthesis: ***How are different tasks assigned to LLMs in educational settings evaluated?***

2   Related Works

Recent syntheses have studied LLM's appearance in education. Position and survey-style papers outline opportunities and risks across student-facing support (explanations, dialogue tutoring, practice generation, writing support) and teacher-facing work (lesson/assessment authoring, feedback drafting), emphasizing the socio-technical implications of deploying probabilistic text generators in instructional settings [4,5]. Scoping and systematic reviews further catalogue applications and recurring challenges (e.g., transparency/replicability, privacy, bias), often grouping findings by use-case families such as feedback, grading, content generation, and teaching support [3,9,11]. These syntheses also focus on specific application domains evaluation, especially assessment and tutoring. Reviews and empirical studies report mixed evidence on reliability/validity when LLMs grade or score open-ended work, and highlight sensitivity to prompts, rubrics, and rater disagreement [2,6,8]. In tutoring, recent work proposes pedagogy-grounded evaluation taxonomies and benchmarks, reflecting the lack of shared standards for assessing "instructional quality" beyond surface plausibility. Human-centered evaluation frameworks in adjacent fields stress multidisciplinary protocols and validity threats in human judgment of generative systems [1,10].

But a key gap still remains: most reviews organize studies by application area rather than by what is actually delegated to the LLM. This is important because different delegated tasks require distinct evaluation designs and outcome measures. When studies with fundamentally different delegation choices are grouped, results are harder to compare and may not reflect genuine learning effects. A task-level lens makes the unit of analysis explicit, aligns evaluation methods with the delegated function, and supports more educationally valid interpretations. Addressing this gap, our content analysis (restricted to the last three years of *AIED*) builds a task-level delegation taxonomy and synthesizes, by task, the evaluation approaches used

3   Methodology

3.1   Annotation Process

Because the application of LLM to education is both recent and rapidly diversifying, existing reviews organize the space from multiple angles (applications, risks, stakeholders, technical approaches) but do not yet provide a shared, ready-to-use taxonomy that directly operationalizes the constructs needed for our research question on the evaluation of the different tasks provided to LLMs. We have therefore developed a purpose-built coding scheme using a hybrid content-analysis strategy: categories were inductively derived and iteratively refined from the corpus, while individual labels and decision rules were anchored in established frameworks, such as canonical prompting and adaptation methods (see 3.2).

To this end, the authors formed a team of **four annotators** and followed an iterative codebook-development procedure common in systematic content analysis. First, we jointly read a small subset of papers to determine which variables were necessary to address the research questions and draft an initial codebook specifying constructs, admissible values, and explicit decision rules. We then conducted a broader pilot annotation on additional papers, during which we applied the draft codebook and logged ambiguities, missing categories, and recurrent edge cases. These observations informed successive refinements (merging/splitting categories, tightening definitions, and adding decision rules) until the coding scheme stabilized—i.e., newly sampled papers rarely prompted new categories and the rules could be applied consistently. To quantify reliability, we ran a two-round agreement assessment: in Round 1, we coded 24 of 86 papers in the 2025 subset, and we computed Cohen's κ for single-choice variables and Krippendorff's α for multi-label variables (alongside percent agreement, following reporting recommendations). We then held a structured calibration meeting to resolve disagreements, clarify definitions, and revise decision rules, to read all papers again with these adjusted guidelines, and repeated the procedure with the same codebook on a second sample of 24 papers to verify improved consistency. Second-round κ and α scores (and percent agreement) are reported for each variable in the next subsection. After this calibration-and-verification cycle, we applied the finalized codebook to annotate the full set of included papers (all papers from 2024 and 2023).

3.2   Coding Scheme

This section documents the operational definitions used in our annotation protocol. We grouped our annotations in three main categories: (A) Technical Architecture and Implementation, (B) Task, and (C) Evaluation (specifically to answer RQ). Table 1 sum up all the categories, variables, and labels. In line with our research question, we confined our meta-analysis to variables that were both pertinent and supported by strong annotator agreement. Variables deemed non-essential for the questions at hand were omitted, as were those with unresolved annotator disagreement—an issue we interpret as reflecting insufficient definitional clarity. Some variables that were kept still yielded low κ or α scores while

Table 1. Annotation Scheme Summary: Features and Reliability

Category/Variable	Definition & Rules	Labels (Values)	Reliability (κ/α & %)
Category A: Technical Architecture & Implementation			
Model Used	Name of the model used.	*Free text*	
Adaptation Level	Level of adaptation to the task.	**Zero-Shot, Few-Shot, Fine-Tuning...**	$\alpha = 0.84$ - 83.3%
Deployment Mode	How is the model accessed and executed?	**Local, API, Unspecified**	$\kappa = 0.75$ - 91.7%
Reproducibility	Was the prompt given or the method detailed?	**Prompt, Method, Unspecified**	$\kappa = 0.58$ - 74.8%
Category B: Task			
Task Category	What is the category of the educational task that was delegated to LLM according to our taxonomy	**Evaluation, Generation, Chatbot, Other**	$\alpha = 0.72$ - 84.7%
Task Type	What educational task was delegated to LLM ?	**Scoring, Feedback...**	$\alpha = 0.64$ - 72.2%
Category C: Evaluation			
Evaluation Focus	What was the LLM evaluated on?	**Performance, Usefulness, Usability**	$\alpha = 0.84$ - 91.7%
Human evaluation	Were there any human evaluation? And if so, were they experts?	**Yes/No**	$\kappa = 0.75$ - 91.7% $\kappa = 0.81$ - 91.7%
LLM evaluation	Were there any LLM-as-judge? And if so, were they validated by experts?	**Yes/No**	$\kappa = 0.59$ - 87.5% $\kappa = 0.00$ - 91.7%
A/B Testing	Were there any A/B Testing protocol?	**Yes/No**	$\kappa = 1.0$ - 100%
Statistical tests	Were there any statistical tests ?	**Yes/No**	$\kappa = 0.83$ - 91.7%
Surveys	Were there any standardized survey used and if so, which one?	**Yes/No** + *Free text*	$\kappa = 0.57$ - 83.3%
Datasets	Were there any external dataset used and if so, which one?	**Yes/No** + *Free text*	$\kappa = 0.80$ - 91.7%
Metrics	What metrics were used?	*Free text*	

having an acceptable percentage of agreement. They represent potentially imbalanced categories that should be clarified. Moreover, our results for these few might be mitigated by this limitation (Category A: reproducibility, Category C: LLM Evaluation, surveys).

Category A: Technical Architecture & Implementation captures implementation-level descriptors that can be coded directly from the methods: **(A1)** the model family used (verbatim model IDs and parameter scales were first recorded, then collapsed to families such as GPT/Llama/Mistral for analysis), **(A2)** the adaptation level describing how an off the shelf LLM was personalized for the use case (from prompt-based in-context learning and structured prompting to parameter-efficient and full fine-tuning) and, **(A3)** the deployment mode at inference time (API/hosted, local/self-hosted, or unspecified)

Category B: Task identifies the educational task(s) assigned to the LLM (coded as multi-label when applicable) in order to situate each study's evaluation within its functional intent. We also define a task-level delegation taxonomy: **Generation** (educational content generation, feedback...), **Evaluation** (assessment, educational content difficulty...), **Chatbots**, and **Other**. This category could also be coded as multi-label when necessary.

Category C: Evaluation records how studies evaluate LLM-based systems and is the primary basis for our **research question**: we coded an **Evaluation Focus** as **Performance** (output quality against a reference/criterion), **Usefulness** (perceived or measured educational value/outcomes), or **Usability** (interaction quality in terms of effectiveness/efficiency/satisfaction), and additionally captured structured metadata about the evaluation design (e.g., instruments, raters, agreement metrics, statistical tests).

Overall, the methodology combines data-driven codebook construction with iterative annotator calibration and inter-annotator agreement checks, yielding a coding scheme that is both grounded in the corpus and sufficiently operationalized for reproducible application.

4 Results

4.1 Tendencies and Global Observations

A global examination of the results confirms a steady rise in the use of LLMs either as standalone systems or as components within systems over the last three years in our research domain, increasing from 7 articles in 2023 (8.98% of articles) to 21 in 2024 (27.63%) and 86 in 2025 (34.40%). These figures exclude papers that discuss LLMs without actually deploying them, which also grow over time: from 1 (1.28%) in 2023 to 13 (17.11%) in 2024 and 53 (21.2%) in 2025. These results show that LLMs are a subject that is growing enormously in importance, accounting for half of all articles published in 2025. Regarding the specific models employed, Fig. 1 presents their evolution across years. A total of 128 different models were used. While only 1 article used more than one model in 2023, this number rose to 9 in 2024 (42.9% of LLM-operating papers) and 29 in 2025 (33.7% of LLM-operating papers), enabling broader comparative

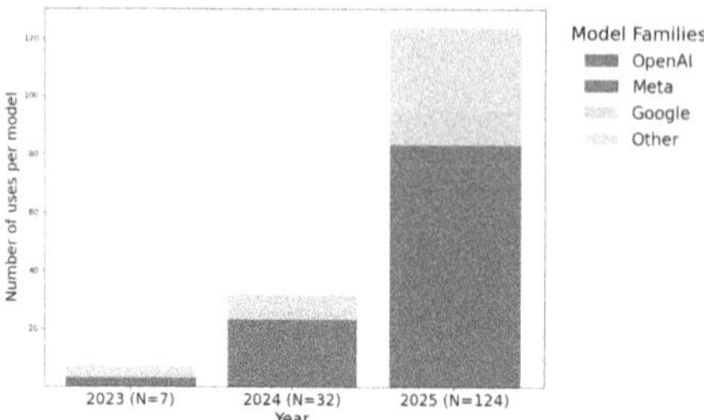

Fig. 1. Model supplier evolution across years.

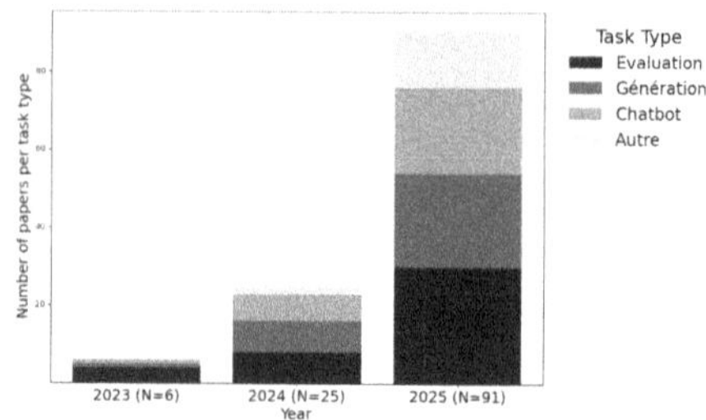

Fig. 2. Task type distribution evolution across years.

evaluations across systems. We observe the strong predominance of OpenAI models (specifically coming from GPT-4o in the 2025 graph) in the last two years, along with the emergence of an increasingly diverse range of alternatives, captured in the expanding "Other" category. Regarding models' openness, $70, 3\%$ of the 78 models used in our scope were proprietary, $21, 9\%$ the models were open weights, and 7.8% were open source. 72.6% were online models only usable through APIs or interfaces, and 27.4% were downloadable models. Figure 2 shows how the tasks delegated to LLM evolved throughout the year according to our taxonomy. Although there are slightly more papers with an evaluation task, the proportions of the 3 task types remain balanced throughout the year.

4.2 Evaluation Methods

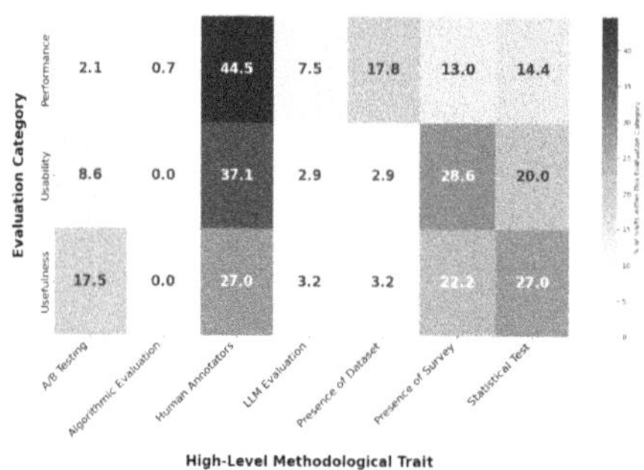

Fig. 3. Methodologies of evaluation used depending on evaluation category.

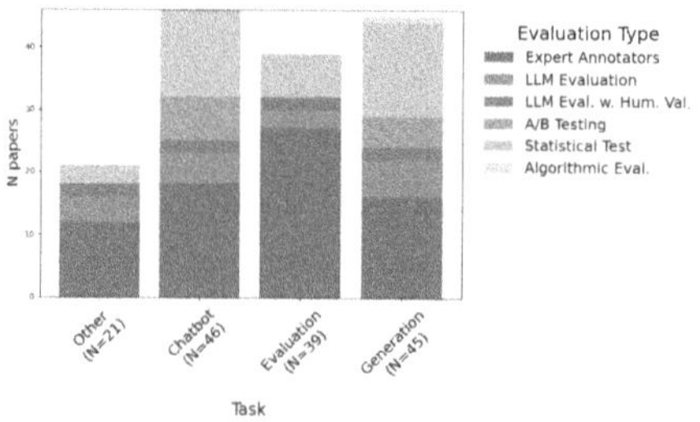

Fig. 4. Methodologies of evaluation per task delegating to the LLM system.

Of the 115 papers that used LLM as or within a system, 19 evaluated it on multiple dimensions. Most assessed performance ($N = 86$, 74.8%), while fewer examined usefulness ($N = 26$, 22.6%) or usability ($N = 17$, 14.8%). Only three papers did not evaluate either the LLM or its host system.

When diving into details, 67.8% of articles evaluate their models through human annotation, among which 84.6% are experts' annotations (the others might be from the learners or users of the system). 31.3% of articles performed statistical tests, 30% used surveys, 22.6% used existing datasets. LLM was used as a judge in 14 (12.2%) articles, and these evaluations were validated by humans in 6 cases. A/B testing protocol was used in 10.4% of studies. Figure 3 illustrates the prevailing methods used to evaluate the system, broken down by the performed evaluation types. However, this visualization has a limitation: several papers include multiple evaluation types, sometimes applying a method to only one aspect. For example, a study might assess both performance and usefulness, while A/B testing is used only for usefulness, yet it still appears on the performance line. Nearly half of the studies (44.5%) used human annotation to evaluate performance. When it was not the case, they often relied on existing datasets (17.8%). Usability shows an important survey uses (28.6%), usefulness of statistical tests (27.0%), and A/B Testing (17.5%).

Figure 4 shows how different tasks are evaluated. We can see that systems for Chatbot or Generation tasks are generally similarly assessed. For Evaluation tasks, there is a clear prevalence of expert labeling and an absence of A/B testing. This tends to indicate that, for this type of system (mostly classification systems), authors aim to develop systems focusing on performance metrics but do not consider the possible pedagogical impact these systems could have.

We can note that 28 studies (24.5%) did not evaluate model performance, focusing instead on the usefulness and/or usability aspects. This shift is particularly evident in studies utilizing proprietary models (89.3% of the 28 studies), where the research objective moves from benchmarking technical capabilities to assessing educational impact. These studies employed human-centric methodologies such as surveys and A/B testing, representing a "qualitative turn" in LLM-assisted education. In a sensitive area like education, the accuracy of systems and their performance in a given task seems to be a first and necessary assessment step. The fact that only 67% of the total corpus utilized either Expert Annotators or existing datasets **suggests a potential "validation gap" where the pedagogical safety of a system is assumed rather than tested**, especially when automated performance metrics are bypassed. A weakness of the LLMs lies in their exploratory nature, especially for proprietary models where results are harder to replicate. To try to answer this issue, we underline that 45.6% of articles detailed their prompting methods while 28.9% even gave an example of their prompt. Lastly, 30 papers (26.3%) did not propose any method or prompt to illustrate their approach, limiting reproducibility of the work.

An interesting methodological shift identified in the recent AIED proceedings is the emergence of the "LLM-as-judge" paradigm, which reflects a growing tension between scalability and pedagogical validity. Our analysis shows that 14 articles (12.3%) entrust the assessment of learner outputs or system performance to an LLM, yet this automation is not always subjected to rigorous oversight. Specifically, only 6 of these 14 integrate expert validation to verify alignment with educational standards. This trend reveals a growing validation gap, where system reliability is assumed rather than empirically proven. Without a robust "human-in-the-loop" framework to audit these automated judges, **we risk embedding algorithmic biases that remain invisible to both learners and educators.**

5   Conclusion

This work on the evaluation of LLM-based systems raises important questions about the trust placed in such technologies, especially in education, where sensitive data is handled. Although LLMs are powerful and effective tools, it is crucial to remember that every decision or output they produce can significantly affect learners, as sustaining their motivation, confidence, and engagement is inherently challenging. Our work also shows how some studies try to keep "Expert-in-the-loop" and persist in rigorous evaluation protocols, evaluating performance, usability, and utilisability. The growing use of LLMs on HLCTs in education should still make us keep these conclusions in mind to ensure pedagogical safety.

In this paper, we present a preliminary overview of our work. Although we are focusing on a subset of our annotations, there is already much to be seen in the AIED publications of the last three years. We still explore other aspects of the corpus to evaluate more precisely the techniques used or how the use of LLM was compared to existing works. This global study aims to engage a discussion within our research community over our practices and the use of these technologies.

Acknowledgments. This work was partly supported by Génération 5 (Cifre PhD scholarship).

References

1. Elangovan, A., Liu, L., Xu, L., Bodapati, S.B., Roth, D.: Considers-the-human evaluation framework: rethinking human evaluation for generative large language models. In: Proceedings of ACL'2024 (Volume 1), pp. 1137–1160 (2024)
2. Emirtekin, E.: Large language model-powered automated assessment: a systematic review. Appl. Sci. **15**(10), 5683 (2025)
3. Guizani, S., Mazhar, T., Shahzad, T., Ahmad, W., Bibi, A., Hamam, H.: A systematic literature review to implement large language model in higher education: issues and solutions. Discover Educ. **4**(1), 1–25 (2025)
4. Holmes, W., Miao, F., et al.: Guidance for generative AI in education and research. UNESCO Publishing (2023)
5. Kasneci, E., et al.: Chatgpt for good? on opportunities and challenges of large language models for education. Learn. Individ. Differ. **103**, 102274 (2023)
6. Pack, A., Barrett, A., Escalante, J.: Large language models and automated essay scoring of English language learner writing: insights into validity and reliability. Comput. Educ. Artifi. Intell. **6**, 100234 (2024)
7. Pal Chowdhury, S., Zouhar, V., Sachan, M.: Autotutor meets large language models: a language model tutor with rich pedagogy and guardrails. In: Proceedings of the Eleventh ACM Conference on Learning@ Scale, pp. 5–15 (2024)

8. Seo, H., et al.: Large language models as evaluators in education: verification of feedback consistency and accuracy. Appl. Sci. **15**(2), 2076–3417 (2025)
9. Shi, Y., Yu, K., Dong, Y., Chen, F.: Large language models in education: a systematic review of empirical applications, benefits, and challenges. Comput. Educ. Artifi. Intell. 100529 (2025)
10. Tam, T.Y.C., et al.: A framework for human evaluation of large language models in healthcare derived from literature review. NPJ Digit. Med. **7**(1) (2024)
11. Yan, L., et al.: Practical and ethical challenges of large language models in education: a systematic scoping review. BJET **55**(1), 90–112 (2024)

An ORID-Structured GenAI Reading Companion Integrating Structured Book Chat and Virtual Labs for Science Reading

Chen Hu[1]([✉]), Hui-Chun Hung[1] [iD], Chih-Hao Hsu[2], Shu-I Fang[2],
Chen-Chung Liu[3] [iD], Chia-Hui Chang[3] [iD], and Ying-Tien Wu[1] [iD]

[1] Graduate Institute of Network Learning Technology, National Central University,
Taoyuan City, Taiwan
gigihu0309@gmail.com, hch@cl.ncu.edu.tw
[2] Taoyuan Municipal Nan-Shi Elementary School, Taoyuan City, Taiwan
[3] Department of Computer Science and Information Engineering, National Central University,
Taoyuan City, Taiwan

Abstract. This study proposes an ORID-structured generative AI reading companion to regulate AI-learner interaction during science reading. The system orchestrates structured AI-supported book chat and, in one condition, integrates a virtual laboratory to connect textual claims with observable phenomena. A nine-week classroom study with 62 sixth-grade students employed an AB/BA counterbalanced design. Students completed pretest, midtest, and posttest measures of science knowledge and reading motivation, and provided open-ended reflections. Linear mixed models with baseline as a covariate and midtest/posttest as repeated measures indicated that science knowledge showed descriptive improvement from baseline to midtest in both sequence groups, but the added effect of the virtual laboratory condition on science knowledge was not statistically reliable after controlling for baseline and within-student dependence. In contrast, over-all reading motivation was significantly higher when the GenAI companion was combined with virtual laboratory support. Qualitative feedback suggested a trade-off: many learners found simulations engaging and helpful for making ideas concrete, while some reported distraction that reduced focus on reading. Overall, the findings provide classroom-based evidence and practical design guidance for orchestrating ORID-structured GenAI book talk with virtual laboratories to support elementary science reading, with motivational benefits emerging more clearly than knowledge gains.

Keywords: Science Reading Companion · ORID discussion method · virtual laboratory

1 Introduction

In K–12 science education, science reading requires learners not only to decode text but also to connect textual information with explanatory ideas. When science and literacy are integrated, students can improve science understanding [1]. However, science reading becomes difficult when texts are conceptually demanding, disciplinary language is

E. G. Blanchard et al. (Eds.): AIED 2026, LNAI 16583, pp. 254–261, 2027.
https://doi.org/10.1007/978-3-032-29760-0_28

dense, and classroom time is limited. Greater science-text difficulty can hinder learning outcomes, suggesting that learning science through text alone may require additional support [2].

Structured classroom talk can support comprehension and reasoning [3], and dialogic reading can support literacy-related learning [4]. Recent advances in generative AI have made AI learning companions more capable of providing adaptive conversational support. Reviews suggest that educational chatbots can support self-regulated learning when prompts and guidance are well structured [5], and meta-analytic evidence indicates that ChatGPT-supported instruction can improve learning outcomes, although effects vary across contexts [6]. At the same time, educational uses of large language models require clear pedagogical framing to avoid superficial or weakly grounded interaction [7].

Accordingly, a promising direction is to use GenAI not as a free-form chatbot but as a structured dialogue partner. In this study, that structure is provided by ORID, which guides learners from identifying information to expressing responses, constructing interpretations, and making judgments [8]. Prior work has shown the potential of chatbot-based companions for science learning [9], while reviews also note that many educational chatbots still lack strong theoretical grounding [10]. In reading-related contexts, AI chatbot interaction has been associated with reading interest [11], and chatbot-supported dialogic reading has been found to support comprehension and word learning [12]. ORID is relevant here because it offers a concise and teachable framework for organizing dialogue, and it has also been associated with deeper reflection [13].

However, structured dialogue alone may not be sufficient for deeper science understanding, because learners also need opportunities to connect textual claims with observable phenomena. Virtual laboratories can complement reading when hands-on experiments are constrained, and prior work suggests that they can support content learning when well-integrated into instruction [14, 15]. Reading motivation is also important because it is related to reading behavior and competence [16], and can be fostered through instructional designs that support engagement and strategic reading [17]. In science education, structured virtual-lab designs have also been associated with improved motivation and inquiry-related outcomes [18]. Yet previous studies have more often examined GenAI-supported dialogue and virtual-laboratory learning separately than as part of the same classroom routine. To address this gap, the present study investigates two conditions of an ORID-structured GenAI reading companion in a nine-week AB/BA counterbalanced classroom study: Condition A provided ORID AI-supported book talk only, whereas Condition B additionally provided virtual-laboratory support. The study focused on science knowledge and overall reading motivation. Accordingly, the following research questions are proposed:

(RQ1) Does integrating a virtual laboratory into ORID-structured GenAI reading companion lead to significantly different outcomes in students' science knowledge compared to using ORID-structured GenAI reading companion alone?

(RQ2) Does integrating a virtual laboratory into ORID-structured GenAI reading companion lead to significantly different outcomes in students' overall reading motivation compared to using ORID-structured GenAI reading companion alone?

2 Method

2.1 Participants

Participants were 62 sixth-grade students from two intact classes at an elementary school in northern Taiwan (31 students per class; 33 boys and 29 girls). The study adopted an AB/BA counterbalanced design in which the two classes experienced the two learning conditions in opposite orders across two phases (Sequence Groups 1 and 2). Students participated with their original classroom enrollment, used school-provided tablets during regular class time, and all data were anonymized for academic analysis.

2.2 ORID-GenAI Reading Companion

The system used gpt-5-chat-latest in a stage-aware RAG pipeline, where each turn prompt combined a companion persona, paragraph-level retrieved passages from the assigned reading, ORID interaction rules, virtual-lab instructions when applicable, and the current session history. Paragraph-level retrieval was adopted to preserve explanatory completeness in concept-dense popular science texts.

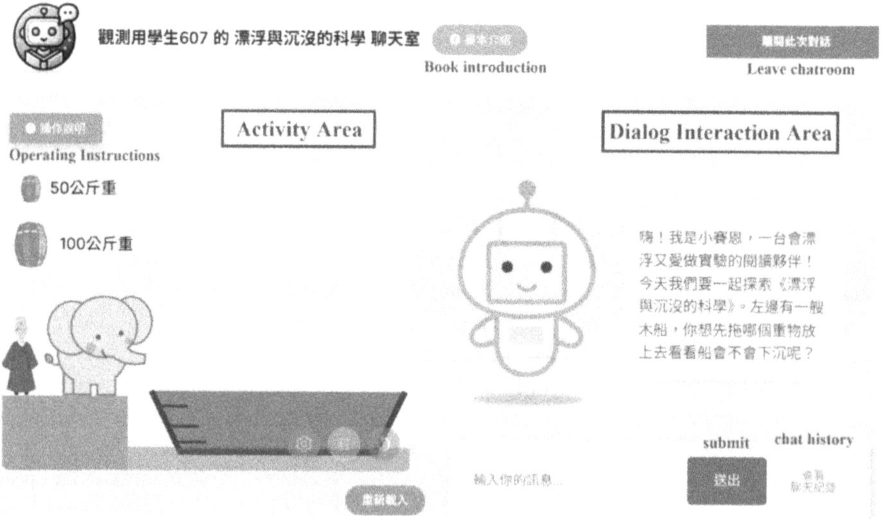

Fig. 1. System interface

ORID functioned as both a pedagogical scaffold and a framework for turn-by-turn dialogue guidance, sequencing Objective, Reflective, Interpretive, and Decisional prompts and, in Condition B, linking students' reported observations from the virtual lab to the assigned text.

The learning activity was organized as a structured book talk routine. Before each weekly session, students completed the assigned popular science reading. During class, they used tablets to interact with the system in a 40-min dialogue session. The system guided students through ORID-based discussion while keeping each turn grounded in retrieved text and the ongoing session context.

Figure 1 illustrates the interface used in the present study. Both conditions shared the same dialogue workspace and ORID-based prompting mechanism, whereas the only instructional difference was whether the activity area provided CoSci-linked simulation support or a brief topic introduction. In the dialogue area, prompts were generated from retrieved text, session history, and student responses. In the experimental condition, the system additionally incorporated observation-oriented lab instructions so that students could connect reported observations with ideas in the assigned reading. Rather than relying on automatic simulation-log analysis, the system grounded this integration in students' reported observations and interpretations during dialogue.

2.3 Design and Procedure

The study followed a nine-week AB/BA counterbalanced design with three measurement points and two three-week intervention phases. Week 1 served as the pretest and orientation session, Week 5 as the midtest, and Week 9 as the posttest.

Reading motivation was measured using a shortened version of the Motivation for Reading Questionnaire [19] on a 5-point Likert scale. Items were translated and adapted to match the reading materials and Grade 6 classroom context, with high internal consistency at pretest (Cronbach's $\alpha = .922$). Science knowledge was measured with a 20-item multiple-choice test aligned with the focal concepts of the weekly readings and reviewed by domain experts for content alignment.

The intervention was implemented from Weeks 2 to 8 and divided into Phase 1 (Weeks 2–4) and Phase 2 (Weeks 6–8). During intervention weeks, students completed one popular science topic per week, read three short texts on the same theme, and then engaged in a 40-min ORID-guided book talk session with the system. Two learning conditions were used: Condition A provided AI-supported book talk only, whereas Condition B additionally provided access to a virtual laboratory for exploring phenomena related to the weekly topic. The two classes experienced both conditions in opposite orders, with Sequence Group 1 following A → B and Sequence Group 2 following B → A across the two phases. Aside from the presence or absence of the virtual laboratory, the interface layout, dialogue mechanism, and classroom schedule were held constant across conditions. Week 9 also included open-ended responses, which were thematically coded to complement the quantitative findings.

3 Results

3.1 Science Knowledge Outcomes and Learner Reflections

Descriptively, science knowledge increased from baseline to midtest in both se-quence groups. Sequence Group 1 (A → B) rose from baseline (M = 59.60, SD = 16.95) to midtest (M = 68.85, SD = 19.86) and posttest (M = 75.60, SD = 21.42), whereas Sequence Group 2 (B → A) increased from baseline (M = 53.17, SD = 20.06) to midtest (M = 61.67, SD = 23.21) and remained similar at posttest (M = 61.33, SD =

27.13). In the LMM, the Period × Treatment interaction showed a trend-level pattern, $F(1, 52.168) = 3.205, p = .079$. Baseline science knowledge significantly predicted subsequent performance, $F(1, 52.311) = 30.167, p < .001$, whereas the main effects of Period, $F(1, 52.402) = 1.652, p = .204$, Treatment, $F(1, 52.402) = 1.984, p = .165$, and Sequence, $F(1, 52.168) = 3.205, p = .079$, were not significant. Adjusted EMMs showed that in Period 1, Condition A was higher than Condition B (67.895 vs. 63.431), whereas in Period 2, Condition B was higher than Condition A (75.178 vs. 63.098), consistent with the trend-level interaction (see Table 1).

Qualitative responses provided a richer view of this pattern. Many students reported that combining dialogue with experimentation made ideas more concrete and engaging, for example, that it helped them "directly know what this unit is talking about" (S14), that "participation and fun both increase" (S40), and that it "makes learning feel interesting" (S41). Some also noted that the activity helped clarify what the questions were asking and how to approach them (S48). At the same time, some students preferred the AI-only condition because the added activity could distract attention from reading, noting that "with a game, it is easy to get distracted" (S04) or that "the game may distract me" (S37). Students also highlighted the value of structured questioning across both conditions: prompts for locating key points were often seen as helpful (e.g., S23), whereas explanation- and judgment-oriented prompts were described as more difficult, though sometimes also "the most helpful" (S30). Overall, the qualitative findings suggest a trade-off: the virtual laboratory could make ideas more concrete and engaging, but it could also introduce competing attentional demands, while the ORID-guided questioning appeared to support comprehension monitoring and explanation building across conditions.

Table 1. Fixed effects from LMMs for science knowledge and reading motivation.

Outcome	Fixed effect	df (num)	df (den)	F	p
Science knowledge	Period	1	52.402	1.652	.204
	Sequence	1	52.168	3.205	.079
	Treatment (A vs B)	1	52.402	1.984	.165
	Baseline (covariate)	1	52.311	30.167	< .001***
	Period × Treatment	1	52.168	3.205	.079
Reading motivation	Period	1	54.001	0.454	.503
	Sequence	1	53.014	1.131	.292
	Treatment (A vs B)	1	54.001	5.028	.029*
	Baseline (covariate)	1	53.001	126.926	< .001***

(continued)

Table 1. (*continued*)

Outcome	Fixed effect	df (num)	df (den)	F	p
	Period × Treatment	1	53.014	1.131	.292

3.2   Reading Motivation Outcomes and Learner Reflections

For overall reading motivation, the Period × Treatment interaction was not significant, $F(1, 53.014) = 1.131$, $p = .292$, indicating that the treatment difference was comparable across midtest and posttest. Baseline motivation significantly predicted subsequent scores, $F(1, 53.001) = 126.926$, $p < .001$. After adjustment for baseline, the main effect of Treatment was significant, $F(1, 54.001) = 5.028$, $p = .029$, with higher adjusted motivation under Condition B than under Condition A. The estimated marginal means were 3.541 (SE $= 0.062$) for Condition B and 3.397 (SE $= 0.061$) for Condition A, yielding an adjusted mean difference of 0.143 (B - A), 95% CI [0.015, 0.271], $p = .029$. The main effects of Period and Sequence were not significant ($p > .05$), suggesting relatively stable adjusted motivation across occasions (see Table 1).

Qualitative responses aligned with this result and suggested that the virtual laboratory generally increased students' willingness to engage in reading activities by making the learning experience more novel, interesting, and participatory. Students reported that it "made me a bit more willing to read, and it felt novel" (S02), that "it is more interesting, so I feel more engaged and I have more patience to read" (S55), and that it "improved my sense of participation" (S04) and helped them "focus very well" (S11). At the same time, some students still preferred AI-only book talk for understanding and focus because the additional activity could distract them, noting that "with a game, it is easy to get distracted" (S04) or that "the game may distract me" (S37). One student also reported that continued questioning from the AI felt "novel rather than annoying" (S14), suggesting that structured dialogue itself may also help sustain engagement. Overall, the qualitative findings indicate that integrating the virtual laboratory tended to increase reading motivation, although individual differences in attentional demands may have influenced how consistently students benefited from the combined workflow.

4   Discussion and Conclusion

This study examined an ORID-structured GenAI reading companion for popular science reading, with and without an integrated virtual laboratory, using an AB/BA counterbalanced classroom design. Science knowledge showed descriptive improvement over time in both sequence groups, but mixed-model results indicated that the added effect of the virtual laboratory condition was not statistically reliable after controlling for baseline and repeated measures. This pattern is consistent with prior work suggesting that science-text difficulty can constrain learning and that additional supports may be needed when students learn science through text [2].

By contrast, overall reading motivation was higher under the virtual-laboratory-supported condition than under the AI-only condition. This aligns with research linking motivation to reading engagement and persistence and suggesting that instructional designs can enhance motivation when activities provide meaningful involvement and feedback [16, 17]. Students' reflections converged with this interpretation: many described the CoSci-supported activities as more engaging and helpful for making ideas concrete, while also reporting increased willingness to read and participate. This is consistent with the view that the educational value of virtual labs depends on purposeful integration rather than add-on exploration [15].

Qualitative feedback also highlighted an implementation trade-off. Some learners reported distraction from the added activity, suggesting that virtual laboratories require careful orchestration to guide attention and connect observations to explanatory ideas [20, 21]. Across both conditions, students emphasized the value of structured questioning for identifying key points and organizing explanations, supporting the use of ORID as a pragmatic script for keeping GenAI dialogue coherent and goal-directed [3, 4, 7, 8]. Overall, the findings suggest that integrating virtual laboratories into ORID-structured GenAI book talk can yield motivational benefits in elementary science reading, although stronger scaffolds may be needed to translate experiential evidence into more robust science knowledge gains.

Several limitations warrant caution. Because the study involved only two intact classes (N = 62), sequence effects were confounded with class context and teacher factors, and statistical power for detecting small treatment effects—particularly for science knowledge after controlling for baseline and repeated measures—was limited. In addition, the nine-week implementation may have been too brief for knowledge advantages to emerge reliably. The science knowledge test primarily targeted concept understanding and was reviewed for content alignment, but formal reliability evidence was not established; moreover, cognitive load was not measured quantitatively, so the study could not directly test whether students' reported distraction reflected split attention or cognitive overload. Future studies should involve more classes and strengthen scaffolds that explicitly link text-based claims to simulation-based evidence.

Acknowledgments. This study was funded by the National Science and Technology Council of Taiwan (NSTC113-2628-H-008-001-MY3; NSTC114-2423-H-008-002-) and by Research Center for Science and Technology for Learning, National Central University, Taiwan.

References

1. Cervetti, G.N., Barber, J., Dorph, R., Pearson, P.D., Goldschmidt, P.G.: The impact of an integrated approach to science and literacy in elementary school classrooms. J. Res. Sci. Teach. **49**, 631–658 (2012)
2. Jian, Y.-C.: Influence of science text reading difficulty and hands-on manipulation on science learning: an eye-tracking study. J. Res. Sci. Teach. **59**, 358–382 (2022)

3. Murphy, P.K., Wilkinson, I.A.G., Soter, A.O., Hennessey, M.N., Alexander, J.F.: Examining the effects of classroom discussion on students' comprehension of text: a meta-analysis. J. Educ. Psychol. **101**, 740–764 (2009)
4. Pillinger, C., Vardy, E.J.: The story so far: a systematic review of the dialogic reading literature. J. Res. Reading **45**, 533–548 (2022)
5. Guan, R., Raković, M., Chen, G., Gašević, D.: How educational Chatbots support self-regulated learning? A systematic review of the literature. Educ. Inf. Technol. **30**, 4493–4518 (2025)
6. Deng, R., Jiang, M., Yu, X., Lu, Y., Liu, S.: Does ChatGPT enhance student learning? A systematic review and meta-analysis of experimental studies. Comput. Educ. **227**, 105224 (2025)
7. Kasneci, E., et al.: ChatGPT for good? On opportunities and challenges of large language models for education. Learn. Individ. Differ. **103**, 102274 (2023)
8. Stanfield, R.: The Art of Focused Conversations: 100 Ways to Access Group Wisdom in the Workplace. The Institute for Cultural Affairs, Chicago (2000)
9. Ng, D.T.K., Tan, C.W., Leung, J.K.L.: Empowering student self-regulated learning and science education through ChatGPT: a pioneering pilot study. Br. J. Edu. Technol. **55**, 1328–1353 (2024)
10. Debets, T., Banihashem, S.K., Joosten-Ten Brinke, D., Vos, T.E.J., Maillette de Buy Wenniger, G., Camp, G.: Chatbots in education: a systematic review of objectives, underlying technology and theory, evaluation criteria, and impacts. Comput. Educ. **234**, 105323 (2025)
11. Liu, C.-C., Liao, M.-G., Chang, C.-H., Lin, H.-M.: An analysis of children' interaction with an AI Chatbot and its impact on their interest in reading. Comput. Educ. **189**, 104576 (2022)
12. Cheng, X., et al.: Chatbot dialogic reading boosts comprehension for Chinese kindergarteners with higher language skills. J. Exp. Child Psychol. **240**, 105842 (2024)
13. Kayan Fadlelmula, F., Qadhi, S.M.: Beyond the classroom: integrating the ORID model for in-depth reflection and assessment in service-learning. Educ. Sci. **14**, 987 (2024)
14. Brinson, J.R.: Learning outcome achievement in non-traditional (virtual and remote) versus traditional (hands-on) laboratories: a review of the empirical research. Comput. Educ. **87**, 218–237 (2015)
15. de Jong, T., Linn, M.C., Zacharia, Z.C.: Physical and virtual laboratories in science and engineering education. Science **340**, 305–308 (2013)
16. Schiefele, U., Schaffner, E., Möller, J., Wigfield, A.: Dimensions of reading motivation and their relation to reading behavior and competence. Read. Res. Q. **47**, 427–463 (2012)
17. Guthrie, J.T., McRae, A., Klauda, S.L.: Contributions of concept-oriented reading instruction to knowledge about interventions for motivations in reading. Educ. Psychol. **42**, 237–250 (2007)
18. Chen, C., Rabu, S.N.A., Jamiat, N.: Enhancing physics learning achievement, motivation and inquiry skills in a flipped classroom: a structured inquiry-based virtual lab approach. J. Balt. Sci. Educ. **24**, 37–52 (2025)
19. Wigfield, A.: A questionnaire measure of children's motivations for reading. National reading research center (1996)
20. Liu, C.-C., et al.: Augmenting the effect of virtual labs with "teacher demonstration" and "student critique" instructional designs to scaffold the development of scientific literacy. Instr. Sci. **50**, 303–333 (2022)
21. van der Graaf, J., Segers, E., de Jong, T.: Fostering integration of informational texts and virtual labs during inquiry-based learning. Contemp. Educ. Psychol. **62**, 101890 (2020)

Large Language Models for Automated Bloom's Taxonomy Classification in Computer Science Assessment

Alessio Ferrato[1]([envelope]) [iD], Carla Limongelli[1] [iD], Daniele Schicchi[2] [iD], and Davide Taibi[3] [iD]

[1] Department of Engineering, Roma Tre University, Via della Vasca Navale 79, Rome 00146, Italy
{alessio.ferrato,carla.limongelli}@uniroma3.it
[2] Independent Researcher, Palermo, Italy
[3] Institute for Educational Technology, National Research Council of Italy, Via Ugo La Malfa 153, Palermo 90146, Italy
davide.taibi@cnr.it

Abstract. Bloom's Taxonomy plays a central role in assessment design by helping instructors align evaluation tasks with learning objectives. However, applying Bloom's framework in practice, especially in programming education, requires substantial effort and often leads to divergent interpretations among educators. This study explores the extent to which Large Language Models (LLMs) can support the automated classification of programming assessment items across Bloom's cognitive levels. We evaluate Bloom-based classification on a dataset of items from an introductory undergraduate Computer Science course, covering four cognitive levels (Remember, Understand, Apply, and Analyze), comparing proprietary LLMs with open-source alternatives. Our methodology considers two strategies: zero-shot prompting and a council-based ensemble approach. Results show that proprietary models achieve accuracies of up to 78%, while locally deployable models reach 59–73%, within the range of human inter-annotator variability. By lowering the technical and economic barriers to adoption, our approach can assist educators in designing balanced assessments. Dataset and framework are available at: https://doi.org/10.5281/zenodo.19332485.

Keywords: Assessment · Bloom taxonomy · LLMs · Council

1 Introduction

Aligning instructional objectives with assessment strategies is a critical challenge for teachers. The Revised Bloom's Taxonomy (RBT) [3] serves as the *de facto* standard for categorizing educational outcomes across six cognitive levels, from *Remembering* to *Creating*, and plays a central role in Constructive Alignment [5]. This is particularly evident in Computer Science (CS) Education, where

E. G. Blanchard et al. (Eds.): AIED 2026, LNAI 16583, pp. 262–270, 2027.
https://doi.org/10.1007/978-3-032-29760-0_29

programming in low-level languages like C imposes significant cognitive load [11], and educators must design assessments that are pedagogically balanced across cognitive levels.

However, the manual classification of items according to RBT is labor-intensive and prone to subjectivity, with inter-rater agreement often falling below acceptable thresholds [8,13]. LLMs offer new possibilities for automating this process [4,14]. While early approaches relied on keyword matching [18], modern architectures capture semantic variations in educational texts more effectively [12,25], though they still struggle with adjacent cognitive levels [17].

We investigate whether LLMs can automate Bloom-based classification of CS assessment items, and whether multi-agent collaboration can compensate for individual model limitations. Our research questions are:

RQ1: To what extent can LLMs replicate expert Bloom classification, and how does their performance compare to human inter-rater variability?

RQ2: What is the impact of council-based ensembles compared to individual proprietary models?

RQ3: Which cognitive levels are most frequently confused, and how severe are the errors?

Our contributions are: (i) a comparative evaluation of proprietary and open-weight LLMs against a multi-annotator human baseline; (ii) a council-based ensemble of small, locally deployable models that narrows the gap with the best proprietary system to ~5 percentage points while enabling privacy-preserving deployment; (iii) an error analysis showing that misclassifications concentrate between adjacent levels with complementary error profiles across model families; and (iv) a publicly released annotated dataset and evaluation framework.

2   Related Work

Despite its broad applicability across educational disciplines, the use of Bloom's Taxonomy becomes more complex in CS. Programming and algorithmic problem solving impose high cognitive demands, requiring the integration of abstract reasoning, procedural knowledge, and domain-specific skills. Several studies propose refinements to Bloom's categories for computing-specific outcomes [23,24], while others focus on quantifying cognitive difficulty of assessments [9]. Classifying items by cognitive level allows instructors to design balanced assessments, a capability particularly important in Intelligent Tutoring Systems where accurate metadata about question complexity is essential for scaffolding and personalization.

A substantial body of literature has addressed automated Bloom classification, especially for multiple-choice questions. Early approaches relied on traditional machine learning and handcrafted features [1], while ensemble-based methods subsequently improved robustness [19]. More recently, [20] investigates LLMs for generating and classifying questions at different Bloom levels, demonstrating that LLMs capture semantic information beyond surface-level keyword matching. [12] examines how LLM performance aligns with Bloom's cognitive hierarchy, highlighting limitations in distinguishing adjacent categories. Research on inclusive education further underscores the importance of Bloom-aligned frameworks in AI-driven systems [2]. Multi-agent LLM architectures have also gained traction for improving reasoning [26]. Notably, [26] find that a single agent with a strong prompt can sometimes match multi-agent discussion, challenging the assumption that collaboration inherently improves outputs. However, prior work has not yet applied multi-agent architectures to Bloom classification in CS education.

3   Methodology

Dataset. The dataset consists of items from six years of exams of an introductory undergraduate CS course, covering computer architecture, operating systems, binary arithmetic, boolean operations, algorithms, data structures and programming. To eliminate redundancy, the 231 original questions were grouped by question root and one representative was selected per cluster, yielding 75 unique items in three formats: multiple-choice, numerical open-response, and true/false. Table 1 shows the distribution.

Table 1. Dataset overview by question type and Bloom's Taxonomy level.

Question type	Remember	Understand	Apply	Analyze	Total
Multiple-choice	22	12	18	4	56
Numerical	0	0	0	1	1
True/False	10	7	0	1	18
Total	32	19	18	6	75

Human Annotation and Ground Truth. Four CS educators (a senior professor, an adjunct professor, a secondary school teacher, and a PhD candidate) independently labeled the 75 items without prior calibration, to capture natural variation in expert interpretation. Annotators received the same Bloom category descriptions used in the LLM prompts. Importantly, no ground truth existed prior to this campaign: final labels were established through consensus discussion among all annotators, informed by their independent classifications. Fleiss' Kappa yielded $\kappa = 0.4758$ (moderate agreement), consistent with prior findings on Bloom classification subjectivity [8,13]. The ground truth spans four levels (*Remember, Understand, Apply, Analyze*); *Evaluate* and *Create* are absent due to structural constraints of closed-form formats [3].

Zero-Shot Evaluation. Individual LLMs were evaluated using a standardized system prompt defining all six cognitive levels. The models span proprietary architectures (OpenAI, Anthropic, Google, X-AI, Z-AI, DeepSeek) and open-weight families (Qwen, Phi, DeepSeek) for resource-constrained settings. Outputs were constrained to a predicted Bloom level with a brief rationale. Prompt templates are provided in the supplementary materials [10].

LLM Council Architecture. To mitigate single-model reliance, we employ a *Multi-Agent Council* of heterogeneous LLMs [6,7], implementing a three-stage pipeline: (1) *Divergence*: each model independently classifies the item and produces a rationale; (2) *Dialectical Review*: anonymized blind peer-review where agents critique alternative classifications and rank responses; (3) *Convergence*: a designated *Chairman* meta-reasoner synthesizes critiques into a final classification. The adversarial validation in Stage 2, where agents cross-examine each other's rationales, acts as a filter for reasoning errors, ensuring the output results from distributed deliberation rather than simple ensemble averaging.

Evaluation Protocol. Each configuration was executed over five independent runs; we report mean accuracy and standard deviation. We adopt accuracy as the primary metric (proportion of items matching the ground truth). While ordinal agreement measures could complement this analysis given Bloom's hierarchical nature, accuracy provides a transparent baseline facilitating comparison with human annotators. Inference temperature was set to each model's default, as zero-temperature induced reasoning loops in some local models; the low observed variance (Table 2) confirms this did not introduce instability. Proprietary models were accessed via OpenRouter[1]; open-weight models were deployed locally using Ollama[2] on an NVIDIA RTX 3090 GPU with 64 GB RAM. For the Council, four open-weight models (Phi4-14b, DeepSeek-R1-8b, GPT-OSS-20b, Qwen3-8b) served as members, with the Chairman role rotating. Invalid outputs were treated as incorrect predictions. The full framework is publicly available [10].

4 Results

Table 2 presents classification accuracy for human annotators, proprietary LLMs, and Council configurations. Confusion matrices (Fig. 1) are aggregated across all five runs.

Human judgment varies substantially: Human 1 achieved 90.7% while Human 2 (69.3%) and Human 4 (68.0%) fell behind many automated models. Among LLMs, Claude-Opus-4.5 achieved the highest accuracy (78.1%). The best Council (qwen3-8b chairman) reached 73.6%, outperforming both lower-performing annotators, with a gap of only ~5% to the best proprietary model despite substantially lower computational requirements. The Council also stabilized the volatile accuracy in models. For, example *phi4-14b* improved from 58.9% to 73.3%, with SD dropping from ±4.0 to ±1.6.

The per-category breakdown reveals that *Apply* yields consistently high accuracy (several models at 100.0%), while Council architectures achieve strong

---

Table 2. Accuracy (overall and per Bloom level) for human evaluators (👤), councils (🖧), and individual LLMs (🤖). The chairman is in parentheses. Locally deployable systems in blue, API-based in red, humans in green.

Category	Overall (%)	Remember (%)	Understand (%)	Apply (%)	Analyze (%)
👤 Human 1	$90.7 \pm 0.0\%$	$100.0 \pm 0.0\%$	$84.2 \pm 0.0\%$	$94.4 \pm 0.0\%$	$50.0 \pm 0.0\%$
👤 Human 3	$82.7 \pm 0.0\%$	$96.9 \pm 0.0\%$	$68.4 \pm 0.0\%$	$100.0 \pm 0.0\%$	$0.0 \pm 0.0\%$
🤖 Claude-Opus-4.5	$78.1 \pm 0.7\%$	$96.2 \pm 1.4\%$	$35.8 \pm 2.4\%$	$96.7 \pm 3.0\%$	$60.0 \pm 9.1\%$
🤖 Grok-4.1-Fast	$77.9 \pm 2.6\%$	$91.2 \pm 4.1\%$	$35.8 \pm 5.8\%$	$100.0 \pm 0.0\%$	$73.3 \pm 9.1\%$
🤖 Gpt-5.2	$76.8 \pm 2.2\%$	$88.8 \pm 3.6\%$	$47.4 \pm 5.3\%$	$95.6 \pm 4.6\%$	$50.0 \pm 11.8\%$
🤖 Gemini-2.5-Flash	$76.5 \pm 2.6\%$	$78.8 \pm 4.6\%$	$55.8 \pm 4.7\%$	$94.4 \pm 0.0\%$	$76.7 \pm 9.1\%$
🤖 Grok-Code-Fast-1	$74.9 \pm 1.1\%$	$88.1 \pm 1.4\%$	$33.7 \pm 8.0\%$	$100.0 \pm 0.0\%$	$60.0 \pm 19.0\%$
🤖 Claude-Haiku-4.5	$74.4 \pm 1.7\%$	$83.1 \pm 1.7\%$	$49.5 \pm 4.7\%$	$91.1 \pm 5.0\%$	$56.7 \pm 9.1\%$
🤖 Glm-4.7	$73.9 \pm 0.7\%$	$85.0 \pm 1.4\%$	$43.2 \pm 2.4\%$	$97.8 \pm 3.0\%$	$40.0 \pm 14.9\%$
🖧 Council (qwen3-8b)	$73.6 \pm 2.6\%$	$93.1 \pm 2.6\%$	$16.8 \pm 9.4\%$	$98.9 \pm 2.5\%$	$73.3 \pm 9.1\%$
🖧 Council (phi4-14b)	$73.3 \pm 1.6\%$	$90.6 \pm 3.8\%$	$22.1 \pm 7.8\%$	$96.7 \pm 3.0\%$	$73.3 \pm 25.3\%$
🖧 Council (gpt-oss-20b)	$73.1 \pm 2.0\%$	$93.1 \pm 2.6\%$	$17.9 \pm 4.7\%$	$97.8 \pm 3.0\%$	$66.7 \pm 0.0\%$
🤖 qwen3-8b	$72.8 \pm 1.5\%$	$91.9 \pm 1.7\%$	$12.6 \pm 4.7\%$	$98.9 \pm 2.5\%$	$83.3 \pm 20.4\%$
🖧 Council (deepseek-r1-8b)	$72.8 \pm 1.2\%$	$92.5 \pm 1.7\%$	$15.8 \pm 3.7\%$	$97.8 \pm 3.0\%$	$73.3 \pm 9.1\%$
🤖 Gpt-Oss-120B	$72.3 \pm 2.6\%$	$92.5 \pm 3.6\%$	$21.1 \pm 3.7\%$	$98.9 \pm 2.5\%$	$46.7 \pm 13.9\%$
🤖 Gemini-2.5-Pro	$71.7 \pm 3.8\%$	$88.1 \pm 4.1\%$	$17.9 \pm 6.0\%$	$97.8 \pm 5.0\%$	$76.7 \pm 14.9\%$
🤖 Gpt-5-Mini	$71.5 \pm 1.2\%$	$94.4 \pm 2.6\%$	$16.8 \pm 4.4\%$	$100.0 \pm 0.0\%$	$36.7 \pm 7.5\%$
🤖 Claude-Sonnet-4.5	$70.9 \pm 0.6\%$	$86.9 \pm 1.4\%$	$29.5 \pm 2.9\%$	$85.6 \pm 3.0\%$	$73.3 \pm 14.9\%$
👤 Human 2	$69.3 \pm 0.0\%$	$78.1 \pm 0.0\%$	$52.6 \pm 0.0\%$	$77.8 \pm 0.0\%$	$50.0 \pm 0.0\%$
🤖 Deepseek-V3.2	$69.1 \pm 3.5\%$	$89.4 \pm 2.8\%$	$20.0 \pm 6.9\%$	$88.9 \pm 6.8\%$	$56.7 \pm 19.0\%$
👤 Human 4	$68.0 \pm 0.0\%$	$90.6 \pm 0.0\%$	$47.4 \pm 0.0\%$	$72.2 \pm 0.0\%$	$0.0 \pm 0.0\%$
🤖 Gpt-5-Nano	$66.4 \pm 1.1\%$	$89.4 \pm 1.7\%$	$14.7 \pm 2.4\%$	$78.9 \pm 4.6\%$	$70.0 \pm 7.5\%$
🤖 gpt-oss-20b	$66.1 \pm 3.6\%$	$91.2 \pm 2.6\%$	$24.2 \pm 9.6\%$	$75.6 \pm 8.4\%$	$36.7 \pm 13.9\%$
🤖 deepseek-r1-8b	$65.9 \pm 2.6\%$	$89.4 \pm 5.2\%$	$9.5 \pm 4.4\%$	$85.6 \pm 6.3\%$	$60.0 \pm 19.0\%$
🤖 phi4-14b	$58.9 \pm 4.0\%$	$63.1 \pm 6.8\%$	$30.5 \pm 7.8\%$	$94.4 \pm 5.6\%$	$20.0 \pm 7.5\%$

Remember results (93.1%), outperforming proprietary models like Gemini-2.5-Flash (78.8%). The largest human–LLM gap is in *Understand*: Human 1 scored 84.2% versus 55.8% for the best model and 16.8% for Council (qwen3-8b). In *Analyze*, results were variable but several models surpassed human annotators.

The confusion matrices (Fig. 1) confirm errors concentrate between adjacent levels, but with differing patterns. Claude-Opus-4.5 (Fig. 1a) distributes *Understand* errors across *Remember* (31), *Apply* (10), and *Analyze* (20), suggesting overinterpretation. In contrast, qwen3-8b (Fig. 1b) skews toward *Remember* (38) and *Analyze* (32), defaulting to frequent categories. The Council (Fig. 1c) partially mitigates this (149/160 correct on *Remember*), though *Understand* remains challenging. The best human (Fig. 1d) achieves 160/160 on *Remember* and 80/95 on *Understand*.

5 Discussion

LLMs can support Bloom-based classification at a level within human inter-rater variability [22,24]. The moderate proprietary–open-source gap suggests that Bloom classification is inherently ambiguous and approximate consistency may matter more than strict correctness [27]. Errors between adjacent levels, especially *Apply/Analyze*, reflect long-standing debates about cognitive demands

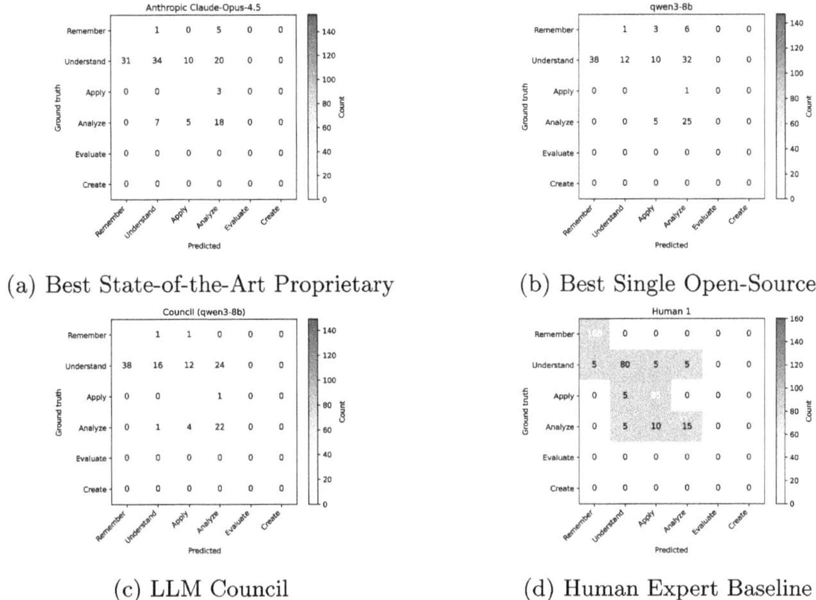

(a) Best State-of-the-Art Proprietary   (b) Best Single Open-Source

(c) LLM Council   (d) Human Expert Baseline

Fig. 1. Confusion matrices comparing classification performance. Diagonal = correct predictions. In (d), human counts are multiplied by 5 for comparability with the 5 model runs.

of programming tasks [15] and the fact that programming questions often engage multiple cognitive processes simultaneously [27].

The *Understand* category reveals qualitatively different error profiles across model families. Smaller models misclassify *Understand* as *Remember* (surface-level matching), while proprietary models distribute errors more evenly (over-interpreting complexity). We attribute this to: (i) the thin semantic boundary between recall and comprehension in CS, where "Understand" items involve terminology models may interpret as retrieval cues; (ii) class imbalance; and (iii) insufficient signal in zero-shot prompts to distinguish comprehension from recall without examples. These complementary biases partially explain why the Council, aggregating diverse perspectives, achieves competitive performance despite smaller components. The Council's parity with large proprietary systems, consistent with ensemble learning [16], has practical implications: locally deployable, privacy-preserving solutions reduce dependence on commercial APIs, important for institutions with strict data governance or limited resources [21]. However, systematic biases could distort assessment balance if unchecked, reinforcing the need for human oversight.

Limitations. The dataset comprises 75 items with imbalanced classes (six *Analyze*; no *Evaluate/Create*), reflecting introductory CS exams but limiting generalizability. Only zero-shot prompting was evaluated; few-shot learning may improve classification, particularly for *Understand*. We do not compare with prior non-LLM methods (e.g., [18,19]), as dataset differences make direct comparison non-trivial. Given the dataset size, we interpret minor accuracy differences as indicative of comparable capability rather than superiority.

6 Conclusion and Future Works

This study presented a systematic evaluation of LLMs for the automated classification of CS assessment items according to Bloom's Revised Taxonomy, comparing proprietary systems, open-source alternatives, and a novel council-based ensemble architecture against expert human annotators.

With respect to RQ1, our results demonstrate that LLMs can classify programming assessment items at accuracy levels that fall within the range of human inter-annotator variability. The best proprietary model, Anthropic Claude-Opus-4.5, achieved 78.1% overall accuracy, while the best council configuration reached 73.6%, both outperforming two of the four expert human annotators. For RQ2, the council-based ensemble of small, locally deployable models narrowed the gap with large proprietary systems to approximately five percentage points, validating a cost-effective and privacy-preserving alternative. Regarding RQ3, the analysis of confusion matrices revealed that misclassifications are predominantly concentrated between adjacent levels, most notably involving the *Understand* category. Smaller open-source models tend to conflate *Understand* with *Remember* while larger proprietary models exhibit the opposite tendency. These complementary error profiles suggest that combining models with diverse biases, as the council architecture does, can partially compensate for individual weaknesses, and that the residual errors largely reflect genuine ambiguity inherent in Bloom's framework rather than model failure.

Future work will address these limitations along several directions. First, we plan to expand the dataset to include assessment items from multiple CS courses and levels, with broader coverage of higher-order Bloom categories through open-ended assessment formats. Second, we intend to investigate few-shot and retrieval-augmented prompting strategies, as well as fine-tuning lightweight models on Bloom-annotated corpora, to improve classification of the most challenging categories. Third, we aim to integrate the council architecture into a practical tool for educators to provide real-time Bloom-level feedback during assessment authoring. Finally, a longitudinal study examining how automated Bloom classification influences instructors' assessment design practices would provide valuable evidence on the pedagogical impact of such tools in authentic educational settings.

References

1. Abduljabbar, D.A., Omar, N.: Exam questions classification based on bloom's taxonomy cognitive level using classifiers combination. J. Theor. Appl. Inf. Technol. **78**(3), 447 (2015)
2. Ahmed, S., Rahman, M.S., Kaiser, M.S., Hosen, A.S.: Advancing personalized and inclusive education for students with disability through artificial intelligence: perspectives, challenges, and opportunities. Digital **5**(2), 11 (2025)

3. Anderson, L.W., Krathwohl, D.R.: A taxonomy for learning, teaching, and assessing: a revision of bloom's taxonomy of educational objectives: complete edition (2001)
4. Banujan, K., Kumara, S., Prasanth, S., Ravikumar, N.: Revolutionising educational assessment: automated question classification using bloom's taxonomy and deep learning techniques-a case study on undergraduate examination questions. Int. J. Educ. Dev. Inf. Commun. Technol. **19**(3), 259–278 (2023)
5. Biggs, J., Tang, C., Kennedy, G.: Teaching for Quality Learning at University 5e. McGraw-Hill Education, London (UK) (2022)
6. Chen, J., Saha, S., Bansal, M.: Reconcile: round-table conference improves reasoning via consensus among diverse LLMs. In: Proceedings of the 62nd Annual Meeting of the Association for Computational Linguistics (ACL) (2024)
7. Cohen, R.: LM-as-a-judge: the definitive guide to using LLMs for evaluation. Towards Data Sci. (2024). focus on consensus mechanisms in evaluation
8. Coleman, V.: On the reliability of applying educational taxonomies (2017)
9. Dorodchi, M., Dehbozorgi, N., Frevert, T.K.: "i wish i could rank my exam's challenge level!": an algorithm of bloom's taxonomy in teaching cs1. In: 2017 IEEE Frontiers in Education Conference (FIE), pp. 1–5. IEEE (2017)
10. Ferrato, A., Limongelli, C., Schicchi, D., Taibi, D.: "large language models for automated bloom's taxonomy classification in computer science assessment" (supplementary materials: Dataset and reproducibility code) (2026)
11. Harrington, B., Cheng, N.: Tracing vs. writing code: beyond the learning hierarchy. In: Proceedings of the 49th ACM Technical Symposium on Computer Science Education, pp. 423–428. SIGCSE '18, Association for Computing Machinery, New York, NY, USA (2018)
12. Huber, T., Niklaus, C.: LLMs meet bloom's taxonomy: a cognitive view on large language model evaluations. In: Proceedings of the 31st International Conference on Computational Linguistics, pp. 5211–5246 (2025)
13. Karpen, S.C., Welch, A.C.: Assessing the inter-rater reliability and accuracy of pharmacy faculty's bloom's taxonomy classifications. Curr. Pharm. Teach. Learn. **8**(6), 885–888 (2016)
14. Kim, T., Joo, K.: Automated bloom's taxonomy classification of teacher questions using whisper and GPT-4. Architect. Image Stud. **7**(1), 119–127 (2026)
15. Krathwohl, D.R.: A revision of bloom's taxonomy: an overview. Theory Into Pract. **41**(4), 212–218 (2002)
16. Li, J., Zhang, Q., Yu, Y., Fu, Q., Ye, D.: More agents is all you need arXiv preprint arXiv:2402.05120 (2024)
17. Ming, N., Sharma, S., Noh, J.: Youleqd: decoding the cognitive complexity of questions and engagement in online educational videos from learners' perspectives. arXiv preprint arXiv:2501.11712 (2025)
18. Mohammed, M., Omar, N.: Question classification based on bloom's taxonomy cognitive domain using modified TF-IDF and word2vec. PLoS ONE **15**(3) (2020)
19. Osadi, K., Fernando, M., Welgama, W., et al.: Ensemble classifier based approach for classification of examination questions into bloom's taxonomy cognitive levels. Int. J. Comput. Appl. **162**(4), 1–6 (2017)
20. Scaria, N., Dharani Chenna, S., Subramani, D.: Automated educational question generation at different bloom's skill levels using large language models: strategies and evaluation. In: International Conference on Artificial Intelligence in Education, pp. 165–179. Springer (2024)
21. Sharples, M.: Towards social generative ai for education: theory, practices and ethics. Learn. Res. Practice **9**(2), 159–167 (2023)

22. Stanny, C.J.: Reevaluating bloom's taxonomy: what measurable verbs can and cannot say about student learning. Educ. Sci. **6**(4) (2016). https://www.mdpi.com/2227-7102/6/4/37
23. Starr, C.W., Manaris, B., Stalvey, R.H.: Bloom's taxonomy revisited: specifying assessable learning objectives in computer science. ACM SIGCSE Bull. **40**(1), 261–265 (2008)
24. Thompson, E., Luxton-Reilly, A., Whalley, J.L., Hu, M., Robbins, P.: Bloom's taxonomy for cs assessment. In: Proceedings of the Tenth Conference on Australasian Computing Education. vol. 78, pp. 155–161 (2008)
25. Waheed, A., Goyal, M., Mittal, N., Gupta, D., Khanna, A., Sharma, M.: BloomNet: a robust transformer based model for bloom's learning outcome classification. In: Abbas, M., Freihat, A.A. (eds.) Proceedings of the 4th International Conference on Natural Language and Speech Processing (ICNLSP 2021), pp. 209–218. Association for Computational Linguistics, Trento, Italy (2021)
26. Wang, Q., Wang, Z., Su, Y., Tong, H., Song, Y.: Rethinking the bounds of LLM reasoning: are multi-agent discussions the key? In: Ku, L.W., Martins, A., Srikumar, V. (eds.) Proceedings of the 62nd Annual Meeting of the Association for Computational Linguistics (Volume 1: Long Papers), pp. 6106–6131. Association for Computational Linguistics, Bangkok, Thailand (2024)
27. Zhang, J., Wong, C., Giacaman, N., Luxton-Reilly, A.: Automated classification of computing education questions using bloom's taxonomy. In: Proceedings of the 23rd Australasian Computing Education Conference, pp. 58–65. ACE '21, Association for Computing Machinery, New York, NY, USA (2021)

A Framework for Human-AI Q-Matrix Refinement: A NeuralCDM Evaluation

Ying Zhang, Ningxi Cheng, Yizhu Gao, Hongmei Li, Lehong Shi, Nicholas Young, Geng Yuan, and Xiaoming Zhai[✉]

AI4STEM Education Center, University of Georgia, Athens, GA, USA
{zhying,EdwardCheng,yizhu.gao,hongmei.li1,ls77437,nicholas.young, geng.yuan,Xiaoming.Zhai}@uga.edu

Abstract. Q-matrices are a cornerstone of theory-driven assessment and learning analytics, making item demands—and students' underlying knowledge components and misconceptions—explicit and actionable. However, Q-matrices are typically crafted by experts, making them time-consuming to build, prone to subjectivity, and difficult to validate empirically. We propose a framework for *human-AI Q-matrix refinement* in which large language models (LLMs) generate candidate Q-matrices using structured, misconception-aware prompting, and NeuralCDM provides an empirical evaluation layer to compare candidates based on how well they explain student response data. We apply the framework to a thermodynamics assessment dataset and benchmark locally deployed LLMs against cloud-served models. Results show that iteratively refined LLM-generated Q-matrices can exceed expert-baseline model fit (AUC 0.780 vs. 0.717), and that locally deployed models achieve comparable performance to cloud APIs, supporting privacy-preserving deployment.

Keywords: Q-Matrix · Cognitive Diagnosis · NeuralCDM · Large Language Models · Misconceptions · Thermodynamics

1 Introduction

The Q-Matrix is a binary mapping that specifies which latent Knowledge Components (KCs) or misconceptions are required by each assessment item [3,11]. By defining the cognitive requirements of each item, Q-matrices enable Cognitive Diagnosis Models (CDMs) to produce multidimensional student profiles. The accuracy of proficiency estimation depends critically on Q-Matrix quality [9].

Despite its importance, Q-Matrix construction remains challenging [2]. Expert-driven approaches are subjective, exhibit low inter-rater reliability, and fail to scale to expanding item banks [4]. Data-driven refinement methods—including statistical techniques such as the General Discrimination Index (GDI) [12] and neural approaches like NeuralCDM [14], offer objectivity but often lack semantic interpretability.

Large Language Models (LLMs) offer a promising avenue for Q-Matrix construction through their semantic reasoning capabilities [7,8]. However, LLM outputs can be unreliable, raising the question of how to leverage their reasoning

E. G. Blanchard et al. (Eds.): AIED 2026, LNAI 16583, pp. 271–278, 2027.
https://doi.org/10.1007/978-3-032-29760-0_30

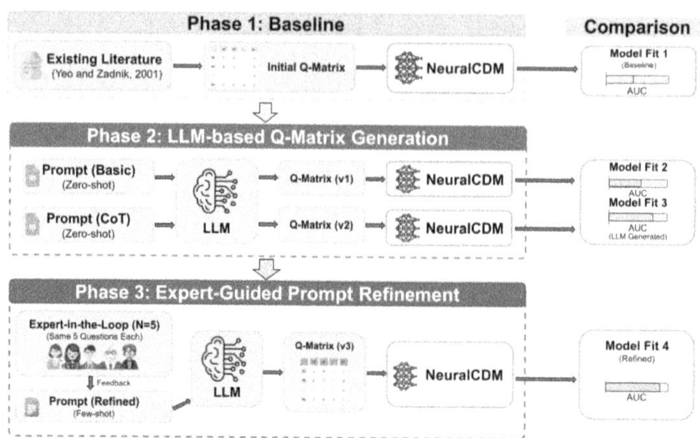

Fig. 1. LLM-Augmented Q-Matrix Validation Pipeline.

while maintaining empirical validity. We propose a *Generate-and-Validate* framework combining LLM-based generation with NeuralCDM validation (Fig. 1), guided by:

- **RQ1**: To what extent can LLMs generate Q-matrices aligned with expert-defined mappings?
- **RQ2**: How do prompting strategies affect alignment quality, and does expert feedback further improve LLM-generated Q-matrices?
- **RQ3**: Do refined Q-matrices achieve better CDM fit than the expert baseline?

We evaluate cloud-hosted models (GPT-4o, GPT-5, GPT-5.1) and locally deployable open-weight models (Qwen3 [16], Llama3 [5]) as privacy-preserving alternatives.

2   Related Work

Q-Matrix Construction and Validation. The Q-Matrix ($\mathbf{Q} \in \{0,1\}^{I \times K}$) bridges I items with K latent attributes [3,11]. Traditional expert-driven construction is limited by subjective bias and scalability constraints [4]. Statistical refinement methods address these limitations: Chiu [2] proposed residual-sum-of-squares minimization, Sun et al. [10] introduced matrix factorization, and de la Torre and Chiu [12] developed the GDI for empirical Q-matrix validation. While GDI and related non-parametric methods provide theoretically grounded validation within psychometric frameworks, they assume specific CDM structures (e.g., DINA) and may not capture the non-linear interactions present in complex STEM domains. NeuralCDM [14] offers an alternative by modeling flexible student-item interactions through neural networks, enabling direct comparison of candidate Q-matrices via predictive fit metrics.

LLMs for Cognitive Modeling. Recent work has explored LLMs for KC extraction [13] and cognitive diagnosis enrichment [1], though with limited empirical validation against student data. Chain-of-Thought prompting [15] enhances interpretability but existing validations rely primarily on agreement with human experts rather than psychometric frameworks. Our work addresses this gap by using NeuralCDM as an empirical validator.

Human-AI Collaboration. Traditional generate-then-edit workflows scale linearly with expert effort [8]. We implement a *Lightweight Expert-in-the-Loop* protocol that shifts expert intervention upstream to prompt calibration, reducing annotation burden while maintaining pedagogical validity.

3   Methodology

3.1   Dataset

We use thermodynamics assessment data ($N = 614$ students) based on the Thermal Concept Evaluation (TCE) [17], a 26-item instrument with distractors mapped to documented misconceptions. The TCE's item-to-misconception mapping serves as our expert-defined Q-Matrix baseline.

3.2   Prompt Engineering

We developed an iterative prompting strategy through four phases (Table 1): **Phase 0 (Baseline)**: Zero-shot prompting produced severe hallucinations. **Phase 1 (V1)**: Introduced a structured Misconception Library and confidence calibration (High/Medium/Low tiers), reducing hallucinations but causing keyword-driven over-tagging. **Phase 2 (V2)**: Added Critical Evaluation Principles requiring item-content alignment, error attribution, and distractor mapping validation before labeling. **Phase 3 (V3)**: Five physics education researchers, each holding a doctoral degree, independently annotated the same subset of five items (25 response options). Their annotations were synthesized through discussion into few-shot examples demonstrating exclusionary reasoning.

Table 1. Evolution of Prompt Engineering Strategy

Features	V0 (Baseline)	V1 (Structured)	V2 (Rule-Based)	V3 (Expert-FewShot)
Misconception Library	✗	✓	✓	✓
Confidence Calibration	✗	✓	✓	✓
Evaluation Principles	✗	✗	✓	✓
Few-Shot Examples	✗	✗	✗	✓
Reasoning Depth	Shallow	Structured	Logical	Expert-Sim.

3.3   NeuralCDM Evaluation

We use NeuralCDM [14] as an empirical comparator, evaluating candidate Q-matrices via AUC and RMSE on student response prediction. We trained Neural-CDM with an 80/20 train-test split, repeated over 5 random seeds (reported as mean ± std). We do not treat better model fit as definitive evidence of cognitive validity, but as empirical support indicating greater consistency with student performance data.

3.4   Experimental Setup

Local inference used 4× NVIDIA L40S GPUs with vLLM [6]. We evaluated Qwen3-30B, Qwen3-8B, and Llama 3.1 8B locally, and GPT-4o, GPT-5, and GPT-5.1 via OpenAI API, all at temperature 0.0.

4   Results

4.1   Expert–LLM Alignment (RQ1)

Table 2 presents confusion-matrix metrics treating the expert Q-Matrix as the reference. Cloud models consistently achieved higher alignment: GPT-5 (High-Only) achieved the highest Recall (0.54) and Micro-F1 (0.49), outperforming Llama 3.1 8B (Recall = 0.18, Micro-F1 = 0.21). Regarding RQ1, LLMs show moderate reproductive consistency with expert mappings, with cloud models substantially outperforming local alternatives. Additionally, expanding from High-Only to High+Medium confidence thresholds improved recall at the cost of precision across all models: GPT-5's recall increased from 0.54 to 0.74, while precision dropped from 0.44 to 0.31.

It is critical to interpret these metrics with nuance. A "False Positive" denotes a misconception flagged by the LLM that was absent in the original expert list; this does not necessarily constitute a hallucination but may represent a valid misconception that experts overlooked. We frame these metrics as a measure of reproductive consistency rather than absolute diagnostic quality.

4.2   Role of Prompt Engineering (RQ2)

Prompt engineering proved critical for transforming raw LLM capabilities into psychometrically valid outputs. Each phase addressed specific failure modes: V1's structured misconception library eliminated hallucinated codes but introduced keyword-driven over-tagging; V2's evaluation principles reduced false positives by enforcing distractor-level evidence; V3's expert few-shot examples further sharpened exclusionary reasoning. As shown in Table 3, this progression yielded consistent AUC improvements across all models and confidence tiers. Notably, the gains were not limited to frontier models: Qwen3-8B's AUC rose from 0.692 (V1) to 0.752 (V3), demonstrating that prompt design can compensate substantially for model scale. Regarding RQ2, iterative, expert-informed prompt calibration is the primary driver of Q-matrix quality, with each phase contributing complementary constraints.

Table 2. Q-Matrix Comparison Stats. **Colored cells** indicate the best value in that column for Local and Cloud groups, respectively. Lighter shades denote Local models; Darker shades denote Cloud models.

Model	Config	TP	FP	FN	TN	TPR	TNR	Precision	Recall	Micro F1	Macro F1
Llama 3.1 8B	High-only	14	43	62	765	0.1842	0.9468	0.2456	0.1842	0.2105	0.5801
Qwen3-30B	High-only	27	70	49	738	0.3553	0.9134	0.2784	0.3553	0.3121	0.6213
Qwen3-8B	High-only	24	58	52	750	0.3158	0.9282	0.2927	0.3158	0.3038	0.6203
gpt-4o	High-only	23	31	53	777	0.3026	0.9616	0.4259	0.3026	0.3538	0.6582
gpt-5	High-only	41	52	35	756	0.5395	0.9356	0.4409	0.5395	0.4852	0.746
gpt-5.1	High-only	36	41	40	767	0.4737	0.9493	0.4675	0.4737	0.4706	0.7198
Llama 3.1 8B	High+Med	18	85	58	723	0.2368	0.8948	0.1748	0.2368	0.2011	0.5659
Qwen3-30B	High+Med	37	151	39	657	0.4868	0.8131	0.1968	0.4868	0.2803	0.5797
Qwen3-8B	High+Med	32	124	44	684	0.4211	0.8465	0.2051	0.4211	0.2759	0.5861
gpt-4o	High+Med	31	69	45	739	0.4079	0.9146	0.31	0.4079	0.3523	0.6528
gpt-5	High+Med	56	126	20	682	0.7368	0.8441	0.3077	0.7368	0.4341	0.7023
gpt-5.1	High+Med	50	96	26	712	0.6579	0.8812	0.3425	0.6579	0.4505	0.6984
Llama 3.1 8B	All Tiers	23	130	53	678	0.3026	0.8391	0.1503	0.3026	0.2009	0.5587
Qwen3-30B	All Tiers	41	235	35	573	0.5395	0.7092	0.1486	0.5395	0.233	0.5264
Qwen3-8B	All Tiers	32	184	44	624	0.4211	0.7723	0.1481	0.4211	0.2192	0.5449
gpt-4o	All Tiers	38	109	38	699	0.5	0.8651	0.2585	0.5	0.3408	0.6355
gpt-5	All Tiers	61	188	15	620	0.8026	0.7673	0.245	0.8026	0.3754	0.6459
gpt-5.1	All Tiers	56	145	20	663	0.7368	0.8205	0.2786	0.7368	0.4043	0.6604

4.3   NeuralCDM Model Fit (RQ3)

Table 3 compares NeuralCDM fit across all configurations against the expert-defined Q-matrix baseline (AUC = 0.717, RMSE = 0.400). The best configuration (GPT-5, V3, High-Only) achieved AUC of **0.780** and RMSE of **0.386**, substantially exceeding the expert baseline. This result suggests that when state-of-the-art models express high certainty, their semantic reasoning aligns closely with empirical patterns of student misconceptions.

Remarkably, locally deployed open-weight models proved highly competitive despite being orders of magnitude smaller. Qwen3-8B (V3, High-Only) achieved an AUC of 0.752, surpassing the expert baseline while operating with a fraction of the computational footprint. This finding challenges the assumption that high-quality LLM-based Q-matrix generation requires frontier model scale, demonstrating that smaller, privacy-preserving models, when guided by optimized prompting and confidence filtering, can capture the core semantic structures of the domain effectively.

Table 3. NeuralCDM performance metrics. **Colored cells** indicate the best value in that column for Local and Cloud groups respectively. Lighter shades denote Local models; Darker shades denote Cloud models.

| Model | Prompt | High Confidence | | Medium/High | | All Choices | |
		AUC	RMSE	AUC	RMSE	AUC	RMSE
Expert Baseline		0.717 ±.011	0.400 ±.002	–	–	–	–
GPT-5 (v0)		0.642 ±.026	0.614 ±.025	–	–	–	–
Open-Weights (Local)							
Qwen3-8B	v1	0.692 ±.014	0.576 ±.015	0.707 ±.020	0.533 ±.015	0.707 ±.032	0.515 ±.009
	v2	0.722 ±.005	0.404 ±.002	0.723 ±.011	0.406 ±.004	0.726 ±.009	0.406 ±.003
	v3	0.752 ±.005	0.396 ±.003	0.753 ±.011	0.403 ±.005	0.754 ±.009	0.406 ±.004
Llama3.1 8B	v1	0.667 ±.013	0.587 ±.010	0.683 ±.025	0.560 ±.021	0.699 ±.017	0.544 ±.026
	v2	0.724 ±.003	0.394 ±.002	0.729 ±.005	0.400 ±.002	0.734 ±.008	0.402 ±.003
	v3	0.741 ±.008	0.396 ±.003	0.744 ±.009	0.400 ±.004	0.758 ±.005	0.399 ±.001
Qwen3-30B	v1	0.705 ±.013	0.544 ±.013	0.685 ±.018	0.534 ±.013	0.682 ±.013	0.521 ±.010
	v2	0.733 ±.011	0.397 ±.004	0.743 ±.011	0.402 ±.004	0.750 ±.010	0.400 ±.006
	v3	0.737 ±.009	0.398 ±.002	0.748 ±.007	0.405 ±.005	0.762 ±.006	0.399 ±.004
Cloud APIs							
GPT-4o	v1	0.668 ±.022	0.664 ±.027	0.703 ±.043	0.556 ±.029	0.720 ±.027	0.543 ±.024
	v2	0.704 ±.010	0.394 ±.006	0.716 ±.008	0.406 ±.003	0.734 ±.010	0.413 ±.004
	v3	0.740 ±.006	0.395 ±.001	0.742 ±.011	0.397 ±.003	0.738 ±.011	0.406 ±.003
GPT-5	v1	0.715 ±.022	0.549 ±.027	0.702 ±.013	0.538 ±.012	0.701 ±.020	0.525 ±.013
	v2	0.727 ±.009	0.398 ±.002	0.743 ±.006	0.402 ±.003	0.749 ±.007	0.406 ±.004
	v3	0.780 ±.008	0.386 ±.002	0.776 ±.006	0.397 ±.005	0.775 ±.007	0.405 ±.005
GPT-5.1	v1	0.673 ±.014	0.584 ±.025	0.707 ±.025	0.542 ±.016	0.708 ±.024	0.525 ±.019
	v2	0.718 ±.006	0.400 ±.003	0.728 ±.005	0.410 ±.004	0.743 ±.009	0.411 ±.004
	v3	0.749 ±.005	0.393 ±.002	0.755 ±.010	0.404 ±.003	0.778 ±.007	0.402 ±.003

5 Discussion

Our framework connects three elements: LLMs as semantic hypothesis generators, NeuralCDM as an empirical evaluation layer, and lightweight expert input for prompt calibration. This shifts Q-matrix development from exhaustive manual labeling to an iterative, evidence-informed workflow.

The framework operationalizes human–AI collaboration through a clear division of labor: LLMs contribute breadth by generating candidate mappings, NeuralCDM provides a data-grounded filter, and experts contribute depth through targeted feedback on high-leverage cases. Expert effort concentrates on prompt calibration rather than scaling linearly with item count, making the approach viable for large item banks.

Limitations. First, the evaluation uses a single thermodynamics instrument; the framework is designed to be domain-agnostic, but generalization requires validation across subjects and item formats. Second, our expert baseline may itself contain omissions. Third, NeuralCDM model fit depends on modeling assumptions and dataset representativeness; fit differences may change under alternative CDMs. Fourth, we did not compare against psychometric Q-matrix validation methods such as GDI [12] or non-parametric approaches, which offer complementary validation within specific CDM frameworks; integrating such comparisons is a direction for future work. Fifth, we evaluate model fit rather than downstream learning outcomes; improved Q-matrix accuracy does not automatically translate to better diagnostic feedback or instruction.

6 Conclusion

We presented a framework for human–AI Q-matrix refinement combining LLM-based generation, NeuralCDM evaluation, and targeted expert feedback. Iterative prompt refinement improved both expert alignment and model fit, with the best configuration exceeding the expert-baseline AUC (0.780 vs. 0.717). Locally deployed models achieved competitive results, supporting privacy-preserving deployment. Future work should examine generalization across domains, integrate psychometric validation methods, and assess downstream effects on diagnostic feedback and learning outcomes.

Acknowledgments. This work was supported by the Institute of Education Sciences (GENIUS, #R305C240010) and the National Science Foundation (TALENT, #2507128). The opinions expressed are those of the authors and do not represent views of the funding agencies.

Disclosure of Interests. The authors have no competing interests to declare that are relevant to the content of this article.

References

1. Chen, X., Zhang, J., Zhou, T., Zhang, F.: LLM-CDM: a large language model enhanced cognitive diagnosis for intelligent education. IEEE Access (2025)
2. Chiu, C.Y.: Statistical refinement of the q-matrix in cognitive diagnosis. Appl. Psychol. Meas. **37**(8), 598–618 (2013)
3. De La Torre, J.: The generalized dina model framework. Psychometrika **76**(2), 179–199 (2011)
4. Desmarais, M.C., Naceur, R.: A matrix factorization method for mapping items to skills and for enhancing expert-based Q-matrices. In: Lane, H.C., Yacef, K., Mostow, J., Pavlik, P. (eds.) AIED 2013. LNCS (LNAI), vol. 7926, pp. 441–450. Springer, Heidelberg (2013). https://doi.org/10.1007/978-3-642-39112-5_45

5. Grattafiori, A., et al.: The llama 3 herd of models. arXiv preprint arXiv:2407.21783 (2024)
6. Kwon, W., et al.: Efficient memory management for large language model serving with pagedattention. In: Proceedings of the ACM SIGOPS 29th Symposium on Operating Systems Principles (2023)
7. Latif, E., Fang, L., Ma, P., Zhai, X.: Knowledge distillation of LLMs for automatic scoring of science assessments. In: Olney, A.M., Chounta, I.A., Liu, Z., Santos, O.C., Bittencourt, I.I. (eds.) Artificial Intelligence in Education. Posters and Late Breaking Results, Workshops and Tutorials, Industry and Innovation Tracks, Practitioners, Doctoral Consortium and Blue Sky. CCIS, vol. 2151, pp. 166–174. Springer, Cham (2024)
8. Lee, G.G., Latif, E., Wu, X., Liu, N., Zhai, X.: Applying large language models and chain-of-thought for automatic scoring. Comput. Educ. Artifi. Intell. **6**, 100213 (2024)
9. Rupp, A.A., Templin, J.: The effects of q-matrix misspecification on parameter estimates and classification accuracy in the Dina model. Educ. Psychol. Measur. **68**(1), 78–96 (2008)
10. Sun, Y., Ye, S., Inoue, S., Sun, Y.: Alternating recursive method for q-matrix learning. In: Educational Data Mining 2014 (2014)
11. Tatsuoka, K.K.: Rule space: an approach for dealing with misconceptions based on item response theory. J. Educ. Meas. **20**(4), 345–354 (1983)
12. de la Torre, J., Chiu, C.Y.: A general method of empirical q-matrix validation. Psychometrika **81**(2), 253–273 (2016)
13. Wang, C., Lin, J., Koedinger, K.R.: Leveraging large language models for identifying knowledge components. arXiv preprint arXiv:2511.09935 (2025)
14. Wang, F., et al.: Neural cognitive diagnosis for intelligent education systems. In: Proceedings of the AAAI Conference on Artificial Intelligence. vol. 34, pp. 6153–6161 (2020)
15. Wei, J., et al.: Chain-of-thought prompting elicits reasoning in large language models. Adv. Neural. Inf. Process. Syst. **35**, 24824–24837 (2022)
16. Yang, A., et al.: Qwen3 technical report. arXiv preprint arXiv:2505.09388 (2025)
17. Yeo, S., Zadnik, M.: Introductory thermal concept evaluation: assessing students' understanding. Phys. Teach. **39**(8), 496–504 (2001)

MCQ Difficulty Prediction via Modeling Learner Heterogeneity Using Data-Driven Cognitive Profiling

Dhriti Krishnan[✉] and Jaromir Savelka

Carnegie Mellon University, Pittsburgh, PA, USA
{dhritik,jsavelka}@andrew.cmu.edu

Abstract. Predicting the difficulty of multiple-choice questions (MCQs) is important for effective assessment, yet current methods typically assume a unimodal student ability distribution, overlooking the heterogeneous nature of student misconceptions. We propose a persona-driven framework that replaces theoretical ability sampling with data-driven cognitive profiling. Using student interactions from the EEDI dataset, we identify behavioral personas via latent class analysis (LCA), then condition a large language model (LLM) to simulate response distributions for each persona. These signals are aggregated with topic context and fed into a Ridge Regression model to predict the item response theory (IRT) difficulty parameter. With five-fold cross-validation, our method improves over a recent baseline (MSE: $0.367 \rightarrow 0.274$; R^2: $0.525 \rightarrow 0.686$). The discovered personas are interpretable and offer insights into why items are difficult, with potential applications to diagnostic assessment design.

Keywords: Item difficulty prediction · Large language models · Cognitive profiling · Learner heterogeneity · Item response theory · Student simulation

1 Introduction

Accurate estimates of item difficulty are fundamental to effective testing, item calibration, and curriculum design [23]. Traditional approaches based on item response theory (IRT) [6,19] require substantial pretesting data, meaning newly authored items, particularly multiple-choice questions (MCQs) [5], cannot be deployed until sufficient student responses have been collected. Recent work has explored predicting difficulty without pretesting, by inferring it from the question text [9,13], learned semantic representations [4,8], or LLM-simulated student responses [10,18]. However, these approaches typically assume a unimodal student population, overlooking heterogeneity in learner behavior.

Our central hypothesis is that student errors are not random but reflect systematic patterns tied to distinct cognitive profiles. Learners with comparable

E. G. Blanchard et al. (Eds.): AIED 2026, LNAI 16583, pp. 279–288, 2027.
https://doi.org/10.1007/978-3-032-29760-0_31

overall performance may differ in the types of mistakes they make and the concepts they fail to apply [16], and student knowledge is better characterized by multiple knowledge components than a single ability parameter [15]. If this heterogeneity is ignored, simulated response distributions, and the difficulty estimates derived from them, may poorly reflect how diverse learner populations interact with assessment items.

Our contributions presented in this work are as follows:

1. We propose a novel persona-driven framework that (i) uses Latent Class Analysis (LCA) on student response data to discover interpretable behavioral personas that capture how different types of learners systematically differ in their knowledge and misconceptions; (ii) conditions an LLM on these personas to simulate response distributions, replacing the standard assumption of a unimodal ability distribution.
2. We demonstrate improved prediction of IRT difficulty parameters over a recent state-of-the-art baseline [8] on the EEDI dataset using five-fold cross-validation (MSE: $0.471 \rightarrow 0.274$; R^2: $0.525 \rightarrow 0.686$), while producing interpretable personas with potential applications to diagnostic assessment design.

2   Related Work

LLMs as Simulated Students. He-Yueya et al. [10] introduced psychometric alignment as a metric for quantifying how well LLMs reflect human knowledge distributions. Park et al. [18] demonstrated that LLMs can exhibit graded proficiency levels in a zero-shot setting without fine-tuning, suggesting their potential as proxies for learners at different ability levels. Building on this, Hu and Collier [12] showed that conditioning LLMs on persona variables systematically alters response patterns, while Yuan et al. [24] argued that valid student simulation requires explicitly specifying the epistemic scope of a simulated learner's knowledge. In our work, we extend this line of research by deriving behavioral personas directly from observed student response patterns to ensure that the simulated students reflect the actual capabilities and misconceptions found in real-world classrooms.

Modeling Learner Ability. LLM-based difficulty prediction has gained attention through the BEA 2024 Shared Task [22], where participating systems showed competitive zero-shot performance but generally struggled to model distractor plausibility. Subsequent work has focused on how to represent variation in student ability within simulation pipelines. Feng et al. [8] sampled scalar knowledge levels from a standard normal distribution, while Scarlatos et al. [20] used direct preference optimization to align simulated students with IRT ability parameters. These approaches implicitly assume that student errors vary in frequency rather than in kind. Our framework relaxes this assumption by conditioning on discrete cognitive profiles that capture qualitative differences in error patterns across learner subpopulations.

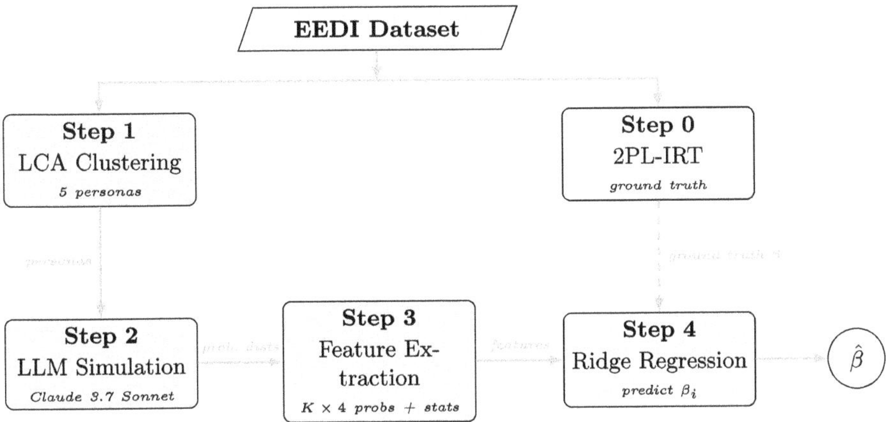

Fig. 1. The Proposed Pipeline. LCA discovers 5 learner personas from student response data (Step 1). An LLM simulates per-persona response distributions (Step 2), which are aggregated into features (Step 3) and used to predict IRT difficulty via Ridge Regression (Step 4). Ground truth is estimated independently via 2PL-IRT (Step 0).

The Homogeneity Gap. A recurring finding across literature is that LLMs tend to produce expert-biased responses, generating unrealistically accurate answers rather than reflecting the error patterns of typical learners [10]. Feng et al. [7] observed a similar pattern in distractor generation: LLMs produce mathematically valid distractors but failed to target the misconceptions that real students actually held. Taken together, these results point to a fundamental mismatch between how LLMs reason and how students err. Our work tackles this by grounding simulation in cognitive personas discovered from actual student response data (Fig. 1).

3   Methodology

We propose a four-stage framework for estimating MCQ difficulty that combines psychometric profiling with LLM-based student simulation: (1) data pre-processing and ground truth estimation, (2) psychometric profiling, (3) profile-conditioned response simulation, (4) predictive modeling of difficulty.

3.1   Data Pre-processing and Ground Truth Estimation

We use tasks 3 & 4 of the EEDI Dataset [21], which contains 948 mathematics MCQs answered by 4,918 students. Each of the 1,382,728 interaction records contains a student ID, question ID, selected answer option, and binary correctness indicator. Questions are provided as images; we extract their textual content using Tesseract OCR applied to grayscale-converted images. Questions where OCR indicated image-only content were excluded.

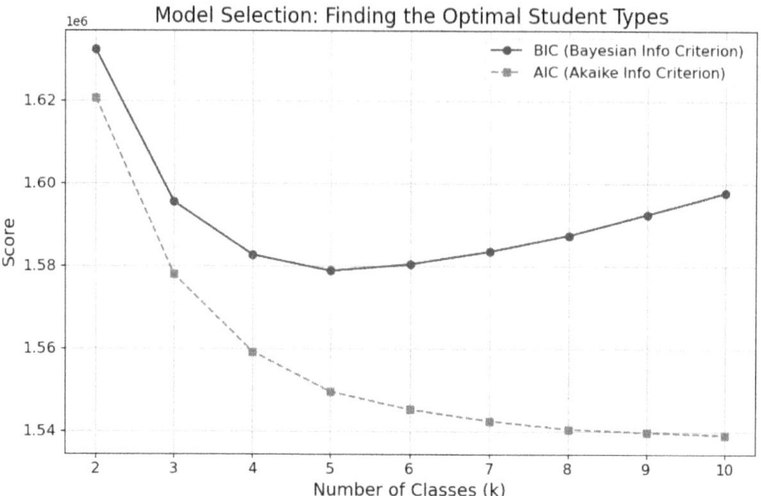

Fig. 2. Model selection for psychometric profiling. Bayesian Information Criterion (BIC) and Akaike Information Criterion (AIC) for Latent Class models with varying numbers of latent classes. BIC reaches a global minimum at $k = 5$, indicating the optimal number of learner profiles.

We partition the dataset into two disjoint subsets: a **profiling set** for discovering student personas, and an **estimation set** for ground truth estimation and difficulty prediction. For the profiling set, we apply dense core filtering, retaining questions with ≥ 50 responses and students with ≥ 10 attempts. For the estimation set, we retain questions with ≥ 20 responses, yielding 900 items. We fit a 2PL-IRT model on this subset using py-irt [17], estimating item difficulty (β) and discrimination (α) parameters that serve as ground truth targets (Fig. 2).

3.2   Psychometric Profiling

We partition students into latent performance classes using LCA with a binary measurement model (StepMix). Each student is assigned to a latent class $c_u \in \{1, \ldots, k\}$ based on maximum posterior probability, and classes are ordered by mean accuracy.

To interpret each cluster, we compute a deviation score for each question i and cluster c:

$$\delta_i^{(c)} = a_i^{(c)} - \frac{1}{K} \sum_{k=1}^{K} a_i^{(k)}, \tag{1}$$

where $a_i^{(c)}$ is the accuracy of cluster c on question i. We select the 5 questions with the largest $\delta_i^{(c)}$ (strengths) and the 5 with the most negative $\delta_i^{(c)}$ (weaknesses) per cluster. These questions, with their topic labels and accuracy figures, are provided to Claude Opus 4.5 [2], which produces a persona name and description capturing the cognitive gap between each cluster's strengths and weaknesses (Table 1). For instance, "The Conceptual Reasoner" can explain why dividing by a fraction increases a number but cannot execute $2/9 \div 3/4$.

3.3   Profile-Conditioned Response Simulation

Table 1. Summary of Discovered Personas. Five profiles with distinct procedural and conceptual capabilities.

Persona	Core Strength	Core Weakness
The Rule Memorizer	Applies formulas (e.g., multiplication) accurately.	Lacks number sense; misconceptions on magnitude.
The Procedural Calculator	Strong on single-step arithmetic.	Fails inverse reasoning and multi-step logic.
The Abstract Reasoner	High logical/proportional reasoning.	Weak automaticity with basic arithmetic.
The Conceptual Reasoner	Strong mathematical intuition ("Why").	Breakdown in procedural fluency ("How").
The Fraction Calculator	Solves standard fraction equations well.	Fails proportional reasoning in real contexts.

Given an assessment item Q_i and a persona description π_c, we need to estimate how each type of learner would respond. A direct regression from item text to difficulty would bypass the learner entirely; instead, we use an LLM as a simulation engine because it can process both the question content (provided as an image) and the persona description jointly, producing response distributions that reflect persona-specific reasoning patterns rather than optimal problem-solving.

Each question image is sent to Claude 3.7 Sonnet [1] along with a system prompt containing the persona name and description. The model is instructed to estimate, as that student type, the probability of selecting each answer option rather than solve the item optimally. We denote the profile-conditioned option selection distribution as:

$$\mathbf{p}_i^{(c)} = \left[p_{iA}^{(c)}, p_{iB}^{(c)}, p_{iC}^{(c)}, p_{iD}^{(c)} \right], \qquad \sum_{o \in \{A,B,C,D\}} p_{io}^{(c)} = 1. \qquad (2)$$

This produces a $K \times 4$ matrix of option probabilities per item, where $K{=}5$ personas each contribute a four-option distribution.

3.4   Predictive Modeling of Item Difficulty

For each item i, we construct a feature vector from the simulated probabilities in Eq. 2. For each persona c, we extract the probability assigned to the correct option, $p_{i,\text{correct}}^{(c)}$, and compute aggregate statistics across personas: mean, variance, and range of $p_{i,\text{correct}}^{(c)}$. Each item's mathematical topic (Number, Algebra, or Geometry and Measure) is one-hot encoded. All numeric features are standardised before modeling.

We predict the IRT difficulty parameter β_i using Ridge Regression [11] with cross-validated regularisation strength ($\alpha \in \{0.1, 1, 10, 100, 500\}$).

4   Experiments

4.1   Baseline Methods

We compare against four baselines from Feng et al. [8], evaluated on the same EEDI dataset:

- **LR:** Linear regression on nine handcrafted syntactic and mathematical features.
- **FT:** Longformer-base-4096 [3] finetuned to predict difficulty from tokenised question text.
- **FTWR:** FT augmented with GPT-4o-generated [14] reasoning steps for the correct answer and feedback messages for each distractor.
- **Two-Stage Likelihood:** The primary method in [8]. It samples student knowledge levels from a standard normal distribution, predicts per-option selection likelihoods, and regresses difficulty from these likelihoods.

4.2   Results

We use five-fold cross-validation, reporting mean and standard deviation across folds. We evaluate with MSE and R^2. Table 2 summarises difficulty prediction performance. Our method reduces MSE by 25% relative to the strongest baseline and improves R^2 from 0.525 to 0.686, explaining substantially more variance in IRT-estimated difficulty.

5   Discussion

The improvement from $R^2 = .525$ to $.686$ is consistent with our central hypothesis: student errors on mathematical items are structured, not random. Different learner profiles make different kinds of mistakes, and modelling this explicitly produces simulated response distributions that better match empirically estimated difficulties.

Our results also suggest that item difficulty is not an intrinsic property of question text alone but emerges from the interaction between an item and the

Table 2. Item difficulty prediction performance. Baseline results are reported from [8]

Method	MSE	R^2
Our method	**0.274 $\pm$ 0.022**	**0.686 $\pm$ 0.012**
Two-Stage Likelihood [8]	0.367 $\pm$ 0.082	0.525 $\pm$ 0.101
FTWR [8]	0.471 $\pm$ 0.149	0.390 $\pm$ 0.181
FT [8]	0.522 $\pm$ 0.079	0.329 $\pm$ 0.048
LR [8]	0.688 $\pm$ 0.028	0.084 $\pm$ 0.059

learner population. An item requiring multi-step symbolic manipulation may be straightforward for *Rule Memorizers* but challenging for *Conceptual Reasoners*, even when both groups have similar overall ability under a unidimensional IRT model [19]. The persona-conditioned simulation makes these differences visible and feeds them into difficulty prediction.

To illustrate the depth of the discovered profiles, Fig. 3 shows the full LLM-generated analysis for "The Conceptual Reasoner" (Cluster 3). This student understands mathematical logic but fails at symbolic execution—they can reason about why dividing by a fraction increases a number, but cannot carry out the procedure. Conditioning the LLM on this behavioural signature allows it to simulate realistic "right logic, wrong answer" errors.

Persona Spotlight: Cluster 3 – "The Conceptual Reasoner"

LLM Analysis: The Conceptual Reasoner has developed strong mathematical intuition and can think logically about number relationships, proportional reasoning, and abstract concepts. They excel when problems require understanding 'why' mathematics works — reasoning about factors, analyzing how operations affect quantities, or thinking through sharing scenarios. However, they have critical gaps in procedural skills, particularly fraction operations: finding equivalent fractions, converting between representations, and applying the reciprocal method for division. The cognitive gap is striking — they can reason abstractly about what happens when you divide by a fraction, but cannot execute $(2/9 \div 3/4)$.

Fig. 3. LLM-Generated Description for "The Conceptual Reasoner". The pipeline uses these descriptions to prompt the simulation LLM.

5.1   Implications for Teaching Practice

Cold-Start Problem. Our framework enables approximate difficulty estimation at the time of item authoring, without requiring pretesting data. This supports earlier integration of new items into adaptive systems, particularly in domains where content must be frequently refreshed.

Diagnostic Item Design. Rather than a single difficulty score, our approach yields profile-specific response patterns showing which learner types are likely to struggle. This helps instructors assess whether an item measures its intended concept or instead reflects a specific procedural or representational challenge.

Targeted Instruction. Linking personas to error patterns helps interpret *why* students struggle. If *Rule Memorizers* frequently fail an item, the item likely depends on conceptual understanding rather than procedural recall—suggesting that conceptual explanations would be more useful than additional drill.

5.2   Limitations

The EEDI dataset is specific to UK mathematics education, so the discovered personas (e.g., "The Fraction Calculator") would not transfer directly to other domains or curricula without re-running the profiling stage. Our model also treats persona assignments as static, whereas real students shift between profiles as they learn. Finally, baseline results are taken directly from [8], whose setup differs from ours: they use 327 MCQs (excluding diagram items) with a 65/15/20 train/validation/test split, versus our 900 MCQs with five-fold cross-validation, and IRT ground truth was estimated independently in both studies. These differences should be kept in mind when interpreting the comparison.

6   Conclusions and Future Work

We presented a persona-driven framework for MCQ difficulty prediction that derives learner profiles via LCA and conditions LLM simulation on these profiles. On the EEDI dataset, this improves IRT difficulty estimation over existing methods [8], suggesting that accounting for learner heterogeneity matters more than increasing model complexity alone.

Future work includes applying the framework to subjects beyond mathematics to test whether the discovered profiles are domain-specific, incorporating temporal models such as knowledge tracing to capture how students shift between profiles, and using persona-conditioned simulations to design distractors that target specific misconceptions.

Acknowledgments. This research is funded in part by the Carnegie Mellon-Accenture Center of Excellence in AI-Enabled Workforce Training (ACE-AI). The content of the information does not necessarily reflect the position or the policy of the funder and no official endorsement should be inferred. Generative AI was used in writing this article to improve surface language features.

References

1. Anthropic: Claude 3.7 sonnet (2025)
2. Anthropic: Introducing claude opus 4.5 (2025
3. Beltagy, I., Peters, M.E., Cohan, A.: Longformer: the long-document transformer. arXiv preprint arXiv:2004.05150 (2020)
4. Binz, M., Schulz, E.: Turning large language models into cognitive models. In: The Twelfth International Conference on Learning Representations (2024)
5. Butler, A.C.: Multiple-choice testing in education: are the best practices for assessment also good for learning? J. Appl. Res. Mem. Cogn. **7**(3), 323–331 (2018)
6. De Ayala, R.J.: The Theory and Practice of Item Response Theory, Guilford Publications (2013)
7. Feng, W., et al.: Exploring automated distractor generation for math multiple-choice questions via large language models. In: Findings of NAACL 2024, pp. 3067–3082 (2024)
8. Feng, W., Tran, P., Sireci, S., Lan, A.S.: Reasoning and sampling-augmented MCQ difficulty prediction via LLMs. In: Artificial Intelligence in Education (AIED 2025). LNCS, pp. 31–45. Springer (2025)
9. Ha, L.A., Yaneva, V., Baldwin, P., Mee, J.: Predicting the difficulty of multiple choice questions in a high-stakes medical exam. In: Proceedings of BEA Workshop 2019, pp. 11–20 (2019)
10. He-Yueya, J., Ma, W.A., Gandhi, K., Domingue, B.W., Brunskill, E., Goodman, N.D.: Psychometric alignment: capturing human knowledge distributions via language models. arXiv preprint arXiv:2407.15645 (2024)
11. Hoerl, A.E., Kennard, R.W.: Ridge regression: Biased estimation for nonorthogonal problems. Technometrics **12**(1), 55–67 (1970)
12. Hu, T., Collier, N.: Quantifying the persona effect in LLM simulations. In: Proceedings of ACL 2024, pp. 10289–10307 (2024)
13. Huang, Z., Qi, Y., Shen, C., Ding, G.: Question difficulty prediction for multiple choice problems in medical exams. In: Proceedings of CIKM (2019)
14. Hurst, A., Lerer, A., Goucher, A.P.: Gpt-4o system card. arXiv preprint arXiv:2410.21276 (2024)
15. Koedinger, K.R., Corbett, A.T., Perfetti, C.: The knowledge-learning-instruction framework: bridging the science-practice chasm. Cogn. Sci. **36**(5), 757–798 (2012)
16. Koedinger, K.R., Nathan, M.J.: The real story behind story problems: effects of representations on quantitative reasoning. J. Learn. Sci. **13**(2), 129–164 (2004)
17. Lalor, J.P., Wu, H., Yu, H.: Learning latent parameters without human response patterns: item response theory with artificial crowds. In: Proceedings of EMNLP 2019 (2019)
18. Park, J.W., Park, S.J., Won, H.S., Kim, K.M.: Large language models are students at various levels: zero-shot question difficulty estimation. In: Findings of EMNLP 2024, pp. 8157–8177 (2024)
19. Rasch, G.: Probabilistic Models for Some Intelligence and Attainment Tests. University of Chicago Press (1960)
20. Scarlatos, A., Fernandez, N., Ormerod, C., Lottridge, S., Lan, A.: Smart: simulated students aligned with item response theory for question difficulty prediction. In: Proceedings of EMNLP 2025 (2025)
21. Wang, Z., et al.: Diagnostic questions: the neurips 2020 education challenge arXiv preprint arXiv:2007.12061 (2020)

22. Yaneva, V., et al.: Findings from the first shared task on automated prediction of difficulty and response time for multiple-choice questions. In: Proceedings of BEA Workshop at NAACL 2024, pp. 470–482 (2024)
23. Yang, F.M., Kao, S.T.: Item response theory for measurement validity. Shanghai Arch. Psychiatry **26**(3), 171 (2014)
24. Yuan, Z., et al.: Towards valid student simulation with large language models (2026). arXiv:2601.05473

Can Large Language Models Learn to Grade Like Teachers? A Few-Shot Study on Open-Ended Assessment

Valentina Scorza[(✉)] [iD], Giacomo Cassano [iD], and Nicoletta Di Blas [iD]

Politecnico di Milano, Piazza Leonardo da Vinci 32, 20133 Milano, Italy
{valentina.scorza,giacomo.cassano,nicoletta.diblas}@polimi.it
https://www.polimi.it

Abstract. Open-ended questions are effective for assessing students' conceptual understanding and higher-order reasoning, but in large-scale educational contexts, such as university courses, their grading is time-consuming, which limits their practical use. Although recent work shows that large language models (LLMs) can automate grading under pre-defined or explicit criteria, failing to account for instructors' implicit and individual grading standards risks overlooking a core component of authentic evaluation. This work addresses this gap by examining whether LLMs can infer and align with such latent criteria from a small number of graded examples. A few-shot grading setting is considered in which a teacher provides a set of scored student responses, and the model assigns scores consistent with the teacher's evaluation scale. Several GPT-based models (GPT-4o, GPT-4.1, GPT-5, and their mini variants) are evaluated under few-shot conditions ($k \in \{1, 3, 5, 7\}$) using student answers graded by a human instructor. Alignment with teacher grading is assessed using strict accuracy, relaxed accuracy with tolerance, mean absolute error, and quadratic weighted kappa, complemented by grading error analysis. Results show that all models benefit from few-shot examples, with gains emerging at low k and diminishing returns beyond approximately five examples. Higher-capacity models achieve stronger alignment, while smaller variants consistently exhibit lower performance. Remaining discrepancies are predominantly local, reflecting confusion between adjacent score levels rather than severe misgradings. These findings suggest that few-shot LLM-based grading can approximate a teacher's evaluation criteria with limited instructor effort, providing scalable decision support for open-ended question evaluation.

Keywords: Automatic Short Answer Grading (ASAG) · Large Language Models · Few-Shot Learning · Teacher-Aligned Grading

1 Introduction

Open-ended questions play a central role in the assessment of student learning, as they allow learners to articulate reasoning, demonstrate conceptual understanding, and integrate knowledge in ways that closed-form questions often fail

E. G. Blanchard et al. (Eds.): AIED 2026, LNAI 16583, pp. 289–297, 2027.
https://doi.org/10.1007/978-3-032-29760-0_32

to capture [4,12,16]. Despite their pedagogical value, evaluating such responses is inherently time-consuming and cognitively demanding [15,18], particularly in educational contexts characterized by large student populations, such as university-level courses. As student numbers increase, the manual grading of open-ended answers becomes a substantial and often unsustainable workload for instructors, limiting the scalability of this assessment practice.

Recent advances in AI, and in particular in large language models (LLMs), have enabled a wide range of educational applications [3,7,17], raising the question of whether these systems can also support the evaluation of open-ended responses while maintaining alignment with human judgment. However, beyond raw model performance, the feasibility of AI-assisted grading critically depends on the effort required from instructors. While prior work shows that LLMs can grade open-ended responses under predefined criteria, these approaches rely on detailed rubrics or structured prompts that are difficult to design and fail to capture implicit, individualized criteria that often guide real-world grading practices. This mismatch between prevailing research assumptions and instructional reality highlights the need for lightweight approaches that minimize teacher effort while preserving alignment with authentic evaluation.

This study investigates whether LLMs can infer a teacher's implicit grading criteria from a small set of scored examples. Specifically, we consider a few-shot setting in which the model learns from a limited number of graded responses and is tasked with assigning scores consistent with the teacher's evaluation scale, without requiring explicit rubrics or additional configuration.

Using this constrained and realistic setup, multiple generations of GPT-based models are compared to assess their ability to align with teacher-assigned evaluations of open-ended responses, providing insight into progress toward AI-based grading systems that approximate human assessment under minimal supervision.

This study is guided by the following research questions:

- **RQ1.** How does the grading performance of LLMs vary as a function of the number of few-shot examples (k)?
- **RQ2.** How accurately do different LLMs evaluate open-ended student responses compared to teacher-assigned scores under a few-shot setting?
- **RQ3.** What grading discrepancies arise under few-shot LLM-based evaluation of open-ended responses, and what is their pedagogical relevance?

2 Background and Related Works

Accurate grading is central to education, providing feedback, supporting learning, and ensuring fair evaluation. However, assessing open-ended responses is challenging due to their variability and the diversity of valid reasoning strategies. Automatic Short Answer Grading (ASAG) aims to evaluate short, open-ended responses using computational methods, reducing instructor workload while preserving the assessment of semantic understanding and reasoning. Compared to closed-form formats, open-ended responses allow for multiple valid expressions, making automated evaluation inherently more complex.

Early ASAG systems [1,9] relied on surface-level similarity, such as string matching and shallow syntactic or semantic analysis. While these approaches enabled partial automation, they were sensitive to wording and struggled with paraphrase. Later approaches [8] introduced statistical and embedding-based methods to better capture semantic similarity, improving robustness to lexical variation but remaining limited in modeling reasoning. More recent neural methods [13,14] improved contextual modeling, yet typically require task-specific training data, limiting practical adoption.

LLMs introduce a shift by enabling prompt-based evaluation via in-context learning. Studies show they can achieve moderate to high agreement with human graders across domains when supported by rubrics or carefully designed prompts [2,5,10,11]. However, these approaches generally rely on predefined grading criteria and do not address alignment with instructors' implicit practices in subjective assessments. Recent work explores whether LLMs can approximate instructor judgment from limited signals. Impey et al. [6] show that GPT-4 can generate rubrics from minimal context, achieving performance comparable to instructor-defined criteria, suggesting that LLMs can recover core evaluative principles.

Building on this, we investigate whether LLMs can infer grading criteria directly from a small set of scored examples, and whether such criteria can be consistently applied to new responses. We further examine how alignment improves with additional examples, aiming to identify an effective and pedagogically feasible few-shot setup.

3 Experimental Setup

3.1 Implementation

A single prompt template is used for all questions. The prompt instructs the model to assign a score on a 0–5 ordinal scale, reflecting the instructor's grading scheme, and to provide a brief explanation, without question-specific prompt engineering or an explicit grading rubric. The template is dynamically populated with: (1) the question, (2) the student response, (3) an instructor-identified ideal answer, (4) a set of graded examples (depending on the few-shot condition), and (5) output-format instructions. The full prompt template and additional materials are available at https://github.com/valentinascorza/llm-fewshot-grading-materials.

Few-shot conditions vary the number of examples k. For $k = 1$, only the ideal answer is provided. For higher values, additional graded examples are selected to ensure coverage of the grading scale and avoid bias toward specific score ranges. In the $k = 3$ condition, examples with the minimum and maximum instructor scores are included. For $k = 5$ and $k = 7$, further examples are added to approximate a balanced distribution across intermediate scores; when exact balance is not possible, the closest available scores are selected. Examples are selected prior to inference, and the model is not informed of the selection strategy. They are provided as plain-text blocks, including the student response, the instructor-assigned score, and feedback for all non-maximum scores. Model outputs have a predefined structure consisting of a numerical score and a brief explanation. Experiments are conducted on multiple GPT-based models (GPT-4o, GPT-4.1, GPT-5, and mini variants) under identical settings. All evaluations use deterministic decoding, with each prompt evaluated once. To reduce stochasticity, the temperature is set to 0, except for GPT-5 models where explicit control is unavailable. The evaluation uses two datasets from examinations of a *Communication Skills* course at a large technical university, comprising 222 responses from 37 students and 258 responses from 43 students, respectively, across six reasoning- and argumentation-focused open-ended questions per exam. Responses are short, typically ranging from a few sentences to short paragraphs, falling within the scope of Automatic Short Answer Grading (ASAG).

3.2   Evaluation Metrics

Model performance is evaluated by comparing model-assigned scores with teacher-assigned scores using metrics aligned with the three RQs.

For **RQ1**, we compute the *Mean Absolute Error* (MAE), which measures the average absolute difference between model and teacher scores. To explicitly capture performance changes relative to the ideal-answer-only baseline, we also report:

$$\Delta\mathrm{MAE}(k) = \mathrm{MAE}(k) - \mathrm{MAE}(k = 1),$$

capturing performance variation as the number of few-shot examples increases.

For **RQ2**, we evaluate grading accuracy using *strict accuracy* (exact score match) and *relaxed accuracy* (within ± 1 point), reflecting the inherent subjectivity of open-ended grading. We also report *Quadratic Weighted Kappa* (QWK) to measure ordinal agreement while penalizing larger discrepancies.

For **RQ3**, we analyze confusion matrices between model and teacher scores to examine the distribution of errors, distinguishing between adjacent-score disagreements and more severe misgradings.

Together, these metrics provide a comprehensive evaluation of grading performance, capturing error magnitude, agreement, ordinal consistency, and the nature of discrepancies under varying few-shot conditions.

4   Results

4.1   Effect of Few-Shot Examples (RQ1)

Figure 1 reports the effect of the number of few-shot examples k on grading performance. It shows that the MAE between AI-generated and teacher-assigned scores decreases monotonically as k increases across all models. The reduction in MAE is limited when moving from $k = 1$ to $k = 3$, becomes more pronounced between $k = 3$ and $k = 5$, and then diminishes beyond $k = 5$, with only small differences observed between $k = 5$ and $k = 7$, indicating a stabilization of performance.

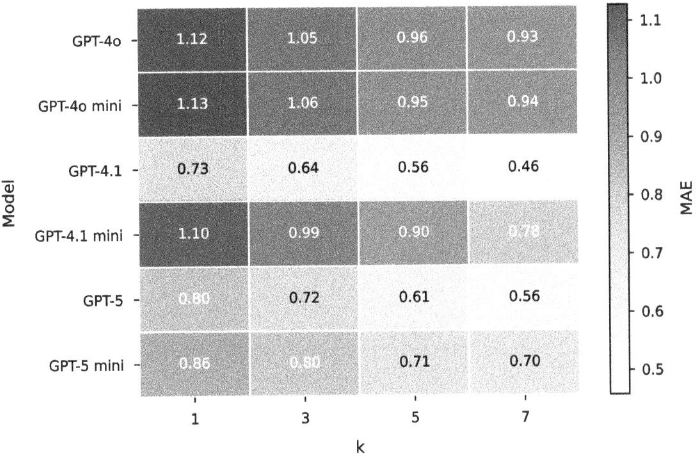

Fig. 1. MAE between AI-generated and teacher-assigned scores, averaged over all questions and both datasets, for each model and k. Darker colors indicate higher error.

4.2 Overall Grading Accuracy (RQ2)

Table 1 reports overall agreement with teacher-assigned scores at $k=5$, aggregated across all questions from datasets A and B and evaluated using accuracy, relaxed accuracy (± 1), and Quadratic Weighted Kappa (QWK). We focus on $k=5$ because, as shown in Fig. 1, MAE decreases consistently as k increases but shows limited additional variation beyond this point, making $k=5$ a stable configuration for model-level comparison.

GPT-5 achieves the highest accuracy, while GPT-4.1 attains the highest relaxed accuracy and QWK, indicating stronger ordinal alignment. Although the first is a more recent model, GPT-4.1 exhibits comparable and, in some metrics, stronger alignment with human grading, highlighting differences in grading behavior across model families. Full-sized models consistently outperform their mini variants. For both GPT-4.1 and GPT-5, the full versions show higher accuracy, higher QWK, and stronger relaxed agreement, while the mini variants exhibit reduced exact and ordinal alignment despite maintaining relatively high relaxed accuracy. In contrast, GPT-4o and GPT-4o mini display very similar performance across metrics, with both lagging behind GPT-4.1 and GPT-5, suggesting a lower overall grading agreement for this model family.

Taken together, the results indicate that grading accuracy varies substantially across model families. While newer models do not uniformly outperform earlier ones, higher-capacity models consistently achieve stronger agreement with teacher-assigned scores across exact, relaxed, and ordinal evaluation measures.

4.3 Analysis of Grading Discrepancies (RQ3)

Figure 2 shows row-normalized confusion matrices comparing teacher- and model-assigned scores at $k=5$ for GPT-4o, GPT-4.1, and GPT-5. Error pat-

Table 1. Agreement with teacher-assigned scores under a few-shot setting (k=5), aggregated across all questions from both datasets.

Model	Accuracy	Relaxed Acc. ±1	QWK
GPT-4o	0.354	0.744	0.666
GPT-4o mini	0.356	0.750	0.669
GPT-4.1	0.619	**0.877**	**0.798**
GPT-4.1 mini	0.365	0.798	0.679
GPT-5	**0.644**	0.838	0.776
GPT-5 mini	0.594	0.785	0.690

terns vary with the teacher score. Mid-range scores show the highest dispersion, reflecting greater ambiguity, whereas higher scores are predicted more consistently. GPT-4o tends to favor mid-range scores even for extreme teacher scores, unlike GPT-4.1 and GPT-5, which align more closely with high scores. Grading errors, therefore, depend on the score level, with mid-range teacher scores exhibiting the highest variability across models.

Overall, discrepancies are structured rather than random, with GPT-4.1 and GPT-5 showing tighter alignment and more consistent error patterns.

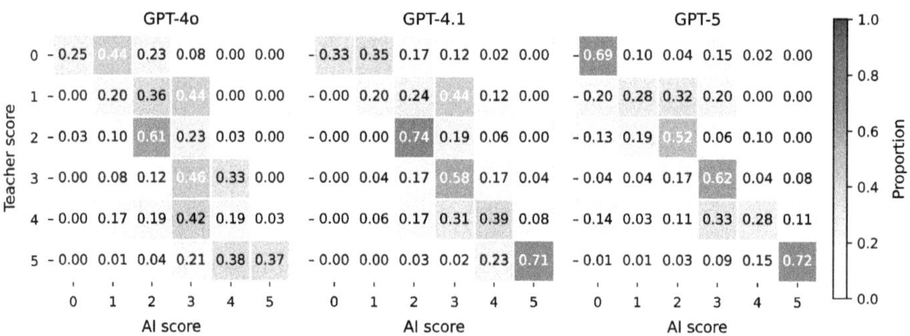

Fig. 2. Row-normalized confusion matrices comparing teacher- and model-assigned scores at $k = 5$, aggregated across all questions from both datasets.

5   Discussion

This study examined the feasibility of few-shot LLM-based grading of open-ended responses in a realistic setting with limited teacher input. The results show that LLMs can achieve meaningful alignment with human grading without explicit rubrics or fine-tuning. For **RQ1**, performance improves as the number of examples increases, but with clear diminishing returns, stabilizing around k=5.

This suggests that a small set of teacher-scored responses is sufficient for models to infer core aspects of the grading criteria. However, results may be influenced by the 0–5 ordinal scale, incomplete score coverage, and the limited number of responses per question, which reflect realistic constraints but may affect generalizability. **RQ2** highlights differences across model families and capacities. Larger models consistently achieve stronger agreement with teacher-assigned scores than their mini counterparts, confirming the role of model capacity in grading reliability. However, newer models do not uniformly outperform earlier ones across metrics: GPT-5 achieves higher exact agreement, while GPT-4.1 shows stronger relaxed accuracy and ordinal consistency, reflecting differences in how models internalize grading criteria. This indicates that grading performance cannot be reduced to a single metric and that model choice should be guided by the type of agreement that is most pedagogically meaningful. **RQ3** examines the structure of grading discrepancies. Rather than exhibiting random errors, all models show structured patterns of disagreement, with most errors confined to adjacent score categories. This behavior mirrors known challenges in human grading of open-ended responses, particularly for mid-range answers that admit multiple plausible interpretations. Higher-capacity models show sharper alignment with teacher scores, while lower-capacity models exhibit more diffuse predictions. These results suggest that LLM-based graders can capture meaningful aspects of the grading process even without exact agreement. Finally, performance varies considerably across questions, suggesting that grading outcomes depend not only on model characteristics and prompting, but also on the conceptual complexity and ambiguity of the assessed questions.

6 Limitations and Ethical Considerations

This study has several limitations that should be taken into consideration. First, the evaluation is based on a limited set of open-ended questions and responses, reflecting realistic classroom conditions but potentially limiting generalizability across larger cohorts, subjects, or more diverse answer distributions. As a result, alignment between model and teacher scores may depend on the size and composition of the response pool. Second, grading relies on a 0–5 ordinal scale with few-shot examples that do not always cover all score levels. While this reflects authentic scenarios (where complete and balanced coverage of all score levels is uncommon), incomplete coverage may reduce the model's ability to distinguish between adjacent scores. Third, the use of few-shot prompting without explicit rubrics or fine-tuning, while minimizing teacher effort, limits control over grading criteria and makes results sensitive to exemplar selection. Teacher-assigned scores are treated as the reference standard, and inter-rater reliability is not assessed, limiting conclusions about absolute validity beyond a single evaluator, but remaining consistent with the study's objective of modeling alignment with a specific instructor's grading practices.

From an ethical perspective, LLM-based grading raises concerns related to fairness, transparency, and accountability, as assessment impacts students' motivation and outcomes. At the same time, results suggest potential benefits for scalable formative assessment, reduced teacher workload, and timely feedback, given that discrepancies are often limited to adjacent score levels. When used as decision-support tools rather than autonomous evaluators, LLMs can support teaching while preserving human judgment. However, variability across questions and models highlights the need for human oversight, particularly in high-stakes contexts, and for clear guidelines on responsible use.

7   Conclusions

This paper examines the feasibility of using LLMs for grading open-ended responses through few-shot prompting under realistic constraints on teacher effort. Rather than relying on explicit rubrics or fine-tuning, the study investigates whether models can align with an instructor's grading criteria from a small set of scored examples. Results show that few-shot prompting improves agreement with teacher-assigned scores, with performance stabilizing after a limited number of examples ($k=5$). Even when the few-shot examples do not fully cover the grading scale, models are able to infer core aspects of the instructor's evaluation strategy, suggesting that meaningful alignment can be achieved with low instructional overhead. Across models, higher-capacity LLMs achieve stronger agreement than smaller variants, although newer models do not uniformly outperform earlier ones across all evaluation metrics. Error analysis shows that discrepancies are structured and mostly limited to adjacent score categories. Higher variability in mid-range scores reflects the inherent ambiguity of borderline cases rather than systematic failure, mirroring patterns of human grading disagreement. This suggests that LLM-based graders capture relevant aspects of human judgment while remaining sensitive to ambiguous cases.

Overall, few-shot LLM-based grading appears to be a viable support tool for assessment, particularly in formative or teacher-in-the-loop scenarios where minor grading differences can be reviewed by instructors. At the same time, variability across questions and models highlights the need for careful validation and human oversight in high-stakes assessment contexts. Future work will explore how question characteristics, score distribution, and prompt composition influence grading behavior, as well as hybrid human–AI approaches aimed at balancing efficiency with pedagogical validity.

Disclosure of Interests. The authors have no competing interests to declare that are relevant to the content of this article.

References

1. Burrows, S., Gurevych, I., Stein, B.: The eras and trends of automatic short answer grading. Int. J. Artif. Intell. Educ. **25**(1), 60–117 (2014). https://doi.org/10.1007/s40593-014-0026-8
2. Chang, L.H., Ginter, F.: Automatic short answer grading for finnish with Chat-GPT. In: Proceedings of AAAI, pp. 23173–23181 (2024). https://doi.org/10.1609/aaai.v38i21.30363

3. García-Méndez, S., de Arriba-Pérez, F., Somoza-López, M.: A review on the use of large language models as virtual tutors. Sci. Educ. **34**, 877–892 (2024). https://doi.org/10.1007/s11191-024-00530-2

4. Hauer, K., Boscardin, C., Brenner, J., van Schaik, S., Papp, K.: Twelve tips for assessing medical knowledge with open-ended questions. Med. Teach. **42**, 880–885 (2020). https://doi.org/10.1080/0142159x.2019.1629404

5. Henkel, O., Hills, L., Roberts, B., et al.: Can LLMs grade open response reading comprehension questions? Int. J. Artif. Intell. Educ. **35**, 651–676 (2025). https://doi.org/10.1007/s40593-024-00431-z

6. Impey, C., Wenger, M., Garuda, N., Golchin, S., Stamer, S.: Using large language models for automated grading of student writing. Int. J. Artif. Intell. Educ. (2025). https://doi.org/10.1007/s40593-024-00453-7

7. Kasneci, E., Sessler, K., Küchemann, S., Bannert, M., Dementieva, D., Fischer, F., et al.: ChatGPT for good? on opportunities and challenges of large language models for education. Learn. Individ. Differ. **103**, 102274 (2023). https://doi.org/10.1016/j.lindif.2023.102274

8. Landauer, T., Foltz, P., Laham, D.: An introduction to latent semantic analysis. Discourse Process. **25**, 259–284 (1998). https://doi.org/10.1080/01638539809545028

9. Leacock, C., Chodorow, M.: C-rater: automated scoring of short-answer questions. Lang. Resour. Eval. **37**, 389–405 (2003). https://doi.org/10.1023/A:1025779619903

10. Lee, G.G., Latif, E., Wu, X., Liu, N., Zhai, X.: Applying large language models and chain-of-thought for automatic scoring. Comput. Educ.: Artif. Intell. **6**, 100213 (2024). https://doi.org/10.1016/j.caeai.2024.100213

11. Lee, U., et al.: Can we use GPT-4 as a mathematics evaluator in education? Int. J. Artif. Intell. Educ. **35**(3), 1560–1596 (2025). https://doi.org/10.1007/s40593-024-00448-4

12. Mee, J., et al.: An experimental comparison of multiple-choice and short-answer questions on a high-stakes test for medical students. Adv. Health Sci. Educ. **29**(3), 783–801 (2024). https://doi.org/10.1007/s10459-023-10266-3

13. Ndukwe, I.G., Amadi, C.E., Nkomo, L.M., Daniel, B.K.: Automatic grading system using sentence-BERT network. In: Bittencourt, I.I., Cukurova, M., Muldner, K., Luckin, R., Millán, E. (eds.) AIED 2020. LNCS (LNAI), vol. 12164, pp. 224–227. Springer, Cham (2020). https://doi.org/10.1007/978-3-030-52240-7_41

14. Ormerod, C., et al.: Automated short answer scoring using neural networks and LSA. Int. J. Artif. Intell. Educ. **33**(3), 467–496 (2023). https://doi.org/10.1007/s40593-022-00294-2

15. Sychev, O., Anikin, A., Prokudin, A.: Automatic grading and hinting in open-ended text questions. Cogn. Syst. Res. **59**, 264–272 (2020). https://doi.org/10.1016/j.cogsys.2019.09.025

16. Tan, S., Thibault, G., Chew, A., Rajalingam, P.: Enabling open-ended questions in team-based learning using automated marking. J. Comput. Assist. Learn. **38**, 1347–1359 (2022). https://doi.org/10.1111/jcal.12680

17. Yan, L., et al.: Practical and ethical challenges of large language models in education. Br. J. Educ. Technol. **55**, 90–112 (2023). https://doi.org/10.1111/bjet.13370

18. Zhai, X., Nehm, R.: AI and formative assessment: the train has left the station. J. Res. Sci. Teach. (2023). https://doi.org/10.1002/tea.21885

ArguAgent: AI-Supported Real-Time Grouping for Productive Argumentation in STEM Classrooms

Jennifer Kleiman[ID], Yizhu Gao[ID], Xin Xia[ID], Zhaoji Wang[ID], Zipei Zhu[ID], Jongchan Park[ID], and Xiaoming Zhai[(✉)][ID]

AI4STEM Education Center, University of Georgia, Athens, GA, USA
{jennifer.kleiman,yizhu.gao,xin.xia,zhaoji.wang,zipei.zhu,jongchan.park,
xiaoming.zhai}@uga.edu

Abstract. Argumentation is a core practice in STEM education, but its productivity depends on who participates and how they interact. Higher-achieving students often dominate the talk and decision-making, while lower-achieving peers may disengage, defer, or comply without contributing substantive reasoning. As a result, forming groups strategically–based on students' stances and argumentation skills–is critical for sustaining inclusive, productive, and evidence-based discourse. In practice, however, teachers seldom implement such grouping because it requires real-time insight into students' positions and the quality of their argumentation—information that is difficult to assess reliably and at scale during instruction. We present a generative AI-powered system, ArguAgent, that creates groups optimizing for stance heterogeneity while constraining argumentation quality differences to ± 1 level on a validated learning progression. ArguAgent uses a two-component assessment pipeline: first scoring student arguments on a 0–4 rubric, then clustering positions via semantic analysis. We validated the scoring component against human expert consensus (Krippendorff's $\alpha = 0.817$) using 200 expert-generated scores. Testing three OpenAI models (GPT-4o-mini, GPT-5.1, GPT-5.2) with identical calibrated prompts, we found that systematic prompt engineering informed by human disagreement analysis contributed 89% of scoring improvement (QWK: $0.531 \rightarrow 0.686$), while model upgrades contributed an additional 11% (QWK: $0.686 \rightarrow 0.708$). Simulation testing across 100 classes demonstrated that the grouping algorithm achieves 95.4% of groups that meet both design criteria, a $3.2\times$ improvement over random assignment. These results suggest ArguAgent can enable real-time, theoretically grounded grouping that promotes productive STEM argumentation in classrooms.

Keywords: Scientific argumentation · Automated assessment · LLM scoring · Collaborative learning · Productive disagreement

1 Introduction

Argumentation is widely recognized as a core practice in STEM education because it supports learners in constructing, evaluating, and revising evidence-

E. G. Blanchard et al. (Eds.): AIED 2026, LNAI 16583, pp. 298–305, 2027.
https://doi.org/10.1007/978-3-032-29760-0_33

based explanations and models [2,19,21]. However, productive argumentation is difficult to realize in typical classrooms [2,19]. Particularly in small-group discussions, participation often becomes uneven: higher-achieving or more confident students may dominate talk and decision making, while lower-achieving peers may disengage, defer, or comply without contributing substantive reasoning [4,15,23].

Research suggests that group composition is a consequential design variable for argumentation outcomes [4,23]. Groups benefit from genuine differences in positions because disagreement can elicit deliberative argumentation–engagement with alternative claims and evidence rather than superficial consensus [1,9]. At the same time, large skill gaps can suppress equitable participation; narrower ability ranges can better support mutual regulation and sustained reasoning [23,27]. These findings motivate strategic grouping that simultaneously (a) promotes position heterogeneity to enable productive disagreement and (b) constrains within-group skill differences so that all members can participate meaningfully. Despite its promise, strategic grouping is rarely implemented because it requires timely, class-wide insight into what students think and how well they argue [7,22].

To address this gap, we present *ArguAgent*, a generative AI–powered system that addresses this challenge by linking automated argument assessment to group formation. After students produce an individual written argument, ArguAgent scores its quality using a validated 0–4 learning progression [18] and clusters student positions via semantic analysis. These outcomes feed a grouping algorithm that maximizes position heterogeneity while constraining within-group quality gaps to ± 1 level.

We address three research questions:

1. How accurately does ArguAgent score argumentation quality compared to trained human coders?
2. What contributes more to scoring accuracy: prompt calibration or model selection?
3. Does the grouping algorithm produce groups that satisfy the design criteria (position heterogeneity and bounded quality differences)?

2 Literature Review

Argumentation competencies improve through sustained dialogic practice [6,10, 11,13,14]. Critically, not all peer interaction produces equivalent gains. Iordanou and Kuhn [9] found that students arguing with opposing-view peers showed significantly greater gains than those arguing with same-side peers, and Zillmer and Kuhn [27] found that partners of similar ability regulate one another's thinking more effectively. These findings yield two design principles: groups should contain members with different positions, and skill levels should be similar enough that all members can participate meaningfully.

To operationalize "similar skill level" in argumentation, we rely on Osborne et al.'s learning progression work [18]. Their research shows how argumentation development can be related to a hierarchical series of states: students first make claims, then learn to ground them in evidence, then to connect evidence to claims through reasoning, and finally to engage with opposing positions. Each transition represents a qualitatively different kind of argument, not a better version of the same one. Our ± 1 constraint is grounded in this developmental structure, as adjacent LP levels identify students whose argument sophistication differs enough to create productive tension but not so much that the gap prevents mutual engagement.

Machine learning approaches have achieved reliable scoring of scientific arguments [24–26], and LLMs with prompt engineering strategies such as few-shot learning and chain-of-thought reasoning have shown strong performance on argument evaluation tasks [17]. However, these systems have been developed primarily for summative assessment. No prior work has combined automated stance detection with argumentation quality assessment to form instructionally optimal groups. Recent work has developed computer-supported collaborative argumentation environments [20], but the grouping problem remains unaddressed.

3   Methods

3.1   ArguAgent System Overview

ArguAgent forms discussion groups of 2–4 students by analyzing individual written arguments in two stages: (1) each student's argument is scored on a 0–4 quality scale using an adapted version of the Osborne et al. [18] learning progression, and (2) student positions are clustered into 2–4 stance categories via LLM-based semantic analysis. A grouping algorithm then forms discussion groups optimizing for stance heterogeneity while constraining quality differences to ± 1 level.

3.2   Dataset and Human Coding

Five researchers collaboratively authored 200 simulated student responses to a science argumentation task about object deformation during collisions. The prompt asked students to respond to the claim that "all objects change shape when they collide." Responses spanned the full range of argumentation quality (Levels 0–4) with realistic variation in language and complexity (Table 1).

Four coders independently scored a calibration set ($n = 21$), then convened for consensus, yielding five critical scoring principles incorporated into both the human codebook and AI prompt: (1) elaboration is not reasoning, (2) evaluate only explicit content, (3) logical chains are not evidence, (4) reasoning is not restating, and (5) mechanistic explanations count as reasoning. Inter-rater reliability on a subsequent set ($n=27$) reached Krippendorff's $\alpha = 0.817$ (ordinal), exceeding the 0.80 threshold for reliable data [8,12]. The remaining 152 responses were scored by coder pairs, with consensus computed as the rounded average.

Table 1. ArguAgent Argumentation Quality Rubric

Level	Label	Criteria
0	No Response	No claim, evidence, or reasoning. Includes "I don't know," blank responses, or irrelevant content.
1	Claim Only	A relevant claim without supporting evidence. Elaboration without citing evidence remains Level 1.
2	Claim + Evidence	A claim backed by observations, data, or examples. Evidence must be explicitly cited, not merely implied.
3	Argument	Claim + evidence + reasoning that explains why the evidence supports the claim. All three components must be present and connected.
4	Complete Argument	A Level 3 argument that additionally addresses counterarguments or considers alternate positions.

3.3 AI Scoring and Calibration

The AI prompt includes rubric definitions, evidence evaluation criteria, the five scoring principles, and a decision tree for systematic rubric application.[1] We compared three models (GPT-4o-mini, GPT-5.1, GPT-5.2) with identical calibrated prompts on the test set ($n = 179$), reporting Quadratic Weighted Kappa (QWK) [5], exact match, mean absolute error, and Pearson correlation.

The baseline (GPT-4o-mini, uncalibrated prompt) showed systematic over-scoring: Bias = +0.85 levels; QWK = 0.531. Root cause analysis revealed three error patterns: AI crediting elaborations as reasoning, accepting reasoning without grounded evidence, and inferring components students did not state. The calibrated prompt addressed each pattern directly.

3.4 Stance Detection and Grouping

One coder classified all 200 responses into three stance categories (ALL, SOME/NO, Unsure). AI-extracted claims were programmatically classified into the same categories. The grouping algorithm uses LLM-based position clustering (because stance categories emerge from student responses and are not predetermined), followed by a scoring-based optimization that forms discussion groups of 3 students. Groups are scored by a composite function rewarding stance heterogeneity (+40 for mixed positions) while enforcing the ± 1 level constraint (-100 for violations). We evaluated the algorithm via Monte Carlo simulation: 100 classes of 24 students each, with level distributions matching our coded data, producing 800 groups.

---

[1] Scoring prompts, simulation code, and data are available at https://github.com/jenniferbk/arguagent-aied-2026.

4   Results

4.1   Argumentation Quality Scoring

Table 2 presents scoring performance. All models with the calibrated prompt exceeded target thresholds. GPT-5.2 achieved QWK = 0.708, indicating substantial agreement [16].

Table 2. Model Comparison with Calibrated Prompt

Metric	GPT-4o-mini	GPT-5.1	GPT-5.2	Target
Exact Match	50.3%	67.6%	**68.7%**	>55%
Within ±1 Level	**91.1%**	89.9%	89.9%	>80%
Mean Absolute Error	0.60	0.45	**0.44**	<0.6
Bias (AI − Human)	−0.11	−0.06	**−0.03**	$< \pm 0.2$
QWK	0.686	0.687	**0.708**	>0.65

Table 3. Decomposing Improvement Sources

Comparison	QWK Change	% of Total
Prompt engineering (uncalibrated → calibrated)	+0.155	**89%**
Model upgrade (4o-mini → 5.2, calibrated)	+0.022	**11%**
Total improvement	**+0.177**	**100%**

Table 3 shows that prompt engineering contributed 89% of total improvement, while model upgrades contributed 11%. Schools with budget constraints can achieve near-optimal accuracy using GPT-4o-mini with the calibrated prompt.

Of 179 test responses, 56 (31.3%) showed AI-human disagreement: 39 off by 1 level (primarily borderline cases at the evidence/reasoning and reasoning/rebuttal boundaries) and 17 off by 2+ levels (concentrated at Level 0). Level 4 detection proved most challenging: GPT-5.2 achieved 64% recall with 8 false positives. This boundary is inherently difficult—human coders also disagreed on 63% of Level 4 assignments.

4.2   Stance Detection and Grouping

Stance detection achieved 85% overall agreement ($\kappa = 0.690$), with 94% accuracy on SOME/NO stances but only 74% on ALL stances due to hedging language. This validation is preliminary, relying on a single coder.

The grouping algorithm achieved 95.4% of groups meeting both design criteria, a 3.2× improvement over random assignment (Table 4).

Table 4. Grouping Algorithm Simulation Results

Algorithm	±1 Level	Mixed Positions	Both Criteria	vs. Random
Random assignment	~35%	~75%	30.3%	1.0×
ArguAgent grouping	**96.8%**	**98.6%**	**95.4%**	**3.2×**

5 Discussion

Our most striking finding is that prompt engineering contributed 89% of scoring improvement, with model upgrades contributing only 11%. The five scoring principles encode tacit knowledge that distinguishes expert from naive rubric application; the same calibrated prompt works across three model generations with minimal performance variation (QWK range: 0.686–0.708). Schools can achieve reliable scoring without expensive frontier models.

If validated in classroom settings, ArguAgent could enable teachers to employ principled grouping without the manual assessment burden that currently limits adoption [3]. The system handles assessment and grouping for a class of 30 students in under two minutes, and is designed to support teacher agency: all scores include explanations, and teachers can review and override both scores and groupings.

Despite the promising findings, this study has limitations. All 200 responses addressed a single topic and were researcher-generated. We validated scoring reliability, not whether ArguAgent-formed groups improve learning outcomes. Stance detection validation is preliminary (single coder, $\kappa = 0.690$). The system depends on commercial LLM APIs with cost and data privacy considerations. The rubric captures argument construction but not critique [18], and bias across diverse student populations remains an ongoing concern [24]. ArguAgent is intended for formative use; we caution against summative applications without stronger validation and human oversight.

6 Conclusion

We presented ArguAgent, a system combining automated quality assessment with position clustering to form groups optimized for productive argumentation. LLM-based scoring achieves substantial agreement with human consensus (QWK = 0.708), with prompt engineering contributing 89% of improvement. The grouping algorithm achieves 95.4% of groups meeting both design criteria, a 3.2× improvement over random assignment. The next step is classroom validation with authentic student data across multiple STEM topics.

Acknowledgments. This work was supported by the Institute of Education Sciences, U.S. Department of Education, through Grant No. R305C240010 (GENIUS). Any opinions, findings, conclusions, or recommendations expressed in this material are those of the authors and do not necessarily reflect the views of the Institute of Education Sciences.

Disclosure of Interests. The authors have no competing interests to declare that are relevant to the content of this article.

References

1. Asterhan, C.S.C., Schwarz, B.B.: Argumentation for learning: well-trodden paths and unexplored territories. Educ. Psychol. **51**, 164–187 (2016)
2. Berland, L.K., Reiser, B.J.: Classroom communities' adaptations of the practice of scientific argumentation. Sci. Educ. **95**(2), 191–216 (2011)
3. Buchs, C., Filippou, D., Pulfrey, C., Volpé, Y.: Challenges for cooperative learning implementation: reports from elementary school teachers. J. Educ. Teach. **43**(3), 296–306 (2017). https://doi.org/10.1080/02607476.2017.1321673
4. Cohen, E.G.: Restructuring the classroom: conditions for productive small groups. Rev. Educ. Res. **64**(1), 1–35 (1994)
5. Cohen, J.: Weighted kappa: nominal scale agreement provision for scaled disagreement or partial credit. Psychol. Bull. **70**(4), 213–220 (1968). https://doi.org/10.1037/h0026256
6. Crowell, A., Kuhn, D.: Developing dialogic argumentation skills: a 3-year intervention study. J. Cogn. Dev. **15**, 363–381 (2014)
7. Dillenbourg, P. (ed.): Collaborative Learning: Cognitive and Computational Approaches. Elsevier Science (1999)
8. Hayes, A.F., Krippendorff, K.: Answering the call for a standard reliability measure for coding data. Commun. Methods Meas. **1**, 77–89 (2007)
9. Iordanou, K., Kuhn, D.: Contemplating the opposition: does a personal touch matter? Discourse Process. **57**, 343–359 (2020)
10. Iordanou, K., Kuhn, D., Matos, F., Shi, Y., Hemberger, L.: Learning by arguing. Learn. Instr. **63**, 101207 (2019)
11. Iordanou, K., Rapanta, C.: "argue with me": a method for developing argument skills. Front. Psychol. **12**, 631203 (2021)
12. Krippendorff, K.: Content Analysis: An Introduction to Its Methodology, 2nd edn. Sage Publications, Thousand Oaks (2004)
13. Kuhn, D., Bruun, S., Geithner, C.: Enriching thinking through discourse. Cogn. Sci. **48**, 1–17 (2024)
14. Kuhn, D., Udell, W.: The development of argument skills. Child Dev. **74**, 1245–1260 (2003)
15. Kumpulainen, K., Mutanen, M.: The situated dynamics of peer group interaction: an introduction to an analytic framework. Learn. Instr. **9**, 449–473 (1999)
16. Landis, J.R., Koch, G.G.: The measurement of observer agreement for categorical data. Biometrics **33**(1), 159–174 (1977)
17. Lee, G.G., Latif, E., Wu, X., Liu, N., Zhai, X.: Applying large language models and chain-of-thought for automatic scoring. Comput. Educ. Artif. Intell. **6**, 100213 (2024)
18. Osborne, J.F., Henderson, J.B., MacPherson, A., Szu, E., Wild, A., Yao, S.Y.: The development and validation of a learning progression for argumentation in science. J. Res. Sci. Teach. **53**, 821–846 (2016)
19. Osborne, J.F.: An argument for arguments in science classes. Phi Delta Kappan **91**(4), 62–65 (2010)
20. Song, Y., Ferretti, R.P., Sabatini, J., Cui, W.: Insights into critical discussion: designing a computer-supported collaborative space for middle schoolers. ETS Res. Rep. Ser. **2024**, 1–20 (2024)

21. States, N.L.: Next generation science standards: for states, by states. National Academies Press (2013)
22. Van Leeuwen, A., Janssen, J., Erkens, G., Brekelmans, M.: Teacher interventions in a synchronous, co-located CSCL setting: Analyzing focus, means, and temporality. Comput. Hum. Behav. **29**(3), 1377–1386 (2013)
23. Webb, N.: Task-related verbal interaction and mathematics learning in small groups. J. Res. Math. Educ. **22**, 366–389 (1991)
24. Wilson, C.D., et al.: Using automated analysis to assess middle school students' competence with scientific argumentation. J. Res. Sci. Teach. **61**, 38–69 (2024)
25. Zhai, X., Haudek, K.C., Ma, W.: Assessing argumentation using machine learning and cognitive diagnostic modeling. Res. Sci. Educ. **53**, 405–424 (2023)
26. Zhai, X., Yin, Y., Pellegrino, J.W., Haudek, K.C., Shi, L.: Applying machine learning in science assessment: a systematic review. Stud. Sci. Educ. **56**, 111–151 (2020)
27. Zillmer, N., Kuhn, D.: Do similar-ability peers regulate one another in a collaborative discourse activity? Cogn. Dev. **45**, 68–76 (2018)

Minimizing Data Exposure in Higher Education LLM Applications: Evaluating the Model Context Protocol (MCP) for Preserving Privacy in Academic Advising

Bill Dong[1]([✉]) [iD] and Jessica Liebowitz[1,2] [iD]

[1] Brandeis University, Waltham, MA 02453, USA
{yingxuandong,jkl}@brandeis.edu
[2] Northeastern University, Boston, MA 02115, USA

Abstract. Large language models (LLMs) are increasingly used in academic advising and student dashboards. However, traditional full-record integrations send complete student profiles to third-party model providers. This paper checks if the Model Context Protocol (MCP) can lower exposure by making the model retrieve only necessary fields through logged tools. Using fully synthetic U.S. undergraduate records, we compare a traditional full-record tool design that includes seven profile fields in every request with an MCP per-field tool design across two advising tasks. We measure privacy risk with a tiered leakage score and evaluate response quality using an LLM-as-a-judge approach. Across three runs, the traditional approach gives the highest average leakage score of 30, while MCP reduces leakage to about 10 mainly by avoiding access to identifiers. However, this comes with a drop in quality that depends on the task (overall from about 5.0 to 3.1). These findings show that MCP can significantly reduce the exposure of confidential student information while still providing high-quality advising for tasks that require less data. Lastly, the tiered leakage metric and MCP tool-call logs together make privacy exposure transparent and measurable. The results motivate future work to understand and control field-level retrieval in MCP-based advising, explaining when and why models over- or under-retrieve specific student fields to support safer and more useful deployments.

Keywords: Model Context Protocol (MCP) · Data Minimization · Data Leakage Measurement · Educational AI Governance

1 Introduction

Universities are increasingly including large language models (LLMs) in academic advising systems, learning dashboards, and other tools. While personalizing guidance can improve outcomes, it often relies on sensitive education record data. In a typical advising situation, important context may include identifiers like student ID and name, academic details like major and GPA. When these details are shared with third-party model providers, institutions face increased privacy, governance, and compliance risks.

E. G. Blanchard et al. (Eds.): AIED 2026, LNAI 16583, pp. 306–314, 2027.
https://doi.org/10.1007/978-3-032-29760-0_34

Regulatory guidelines stress the need to limit what is shared. In the United States, the Family Educational Rights and Privacy Act (FERPA) restricts the disclosure of personally identifiable information from education records without consent. It also requires vendors to use student data only for approved purposes [1]. The European Union's General Data Protection Regulation (GDPR) similarly focuses on limiting purpose and minimizing data. It requires that personal data be adequate, relevant, and restricted to what is necessary for a specific task [2]. These rules raise concerns about common LLM integration methods that send more student data than is needed for a question.

Discussions about privacy risk in these integrations often remain at a general level. They rarely measure which fields were exposed and how sensitive those fields are. This paper innovatively offers a clear evaluation metric that takes sensitivity into account. It features a tiered leakage score that quantifies exposure by weighting record fields based on their sensitivity (for example, direct identifiers, academic progress, and general attributes). This metric allows for a clear and measurable view of privacy exposure.

Most LLM deployments use a full-record method. The application gathers a complete student profile and includes it in each API request, regardless of the prompt. This method is easy to use but tends to overshare and provides little insight into which fields were actually required. We explore an alternative design based on the Model Context Protocol (MCP), where the model starts with just the student's question and retrieves specific fields through clear, per-field tools operating within the institution's environment, with each access logged for auditing. Despite growing interest in tool-based LLM architectures, we find no published evaluation to our knowledge of MCP applications in student advising use case.

This paper addresses a specific research question: when an advising LLM has separate per-field MCP tools for accessing student data, does it reveal less sensitive information to the model provider compared to the traditional full-record method? Additionally, how does the quality of responses compare between an LLM using MCP and one that does not? We generated fully synthetic undergraduate records that closely resemble the characteristics of real undergraduate data to simulate an academic advisor LLM that answers two common questions, "Am I on track to graduate in four years?" and "Should I consider changing my major?", under both approaches. We measure exposure using the tiered leakage score that weighs each field based on its significance. We also evaluate response quality using an LLM-as-a-judge approach.

2 Related Work

2.1 LLM-Driven Educational Chatbots and Agents

Recent work views LLM-based educational systems as tools that combine memory, tool use, and planning. They support tasks like tutoring, feedback, and student assistance, while also facing ongoing challenges in deployment, such as privacy, hallucination, and integration with current platforms [3]. For example, MoodleBot includes an LLM chatbot within an LMS and employs retrieval-augmented generation (RAG) alongside user feedback, reporting strong alignment with course content in the classroom [4]. These systems mainly focus on improving helpfulness, grounding, and user experience, but there is less emphasis on considering data exposure to third-party model providers as an important design factor.

Previous work on secure GenAI adoption highlights risks from using public cloud LLMs, including unclear retention and training policies, governance issues, and compliance worries. This drives the need for stronger institutional controls or private, on-premise deployments [5]. These concerns are particularly important for student advising systems, where a full-record approach greatly increases the risk of oversharing sensitive student data.

2.2 Tool-Based and Retrieval-Augmented Architectures

Technically, our work is closest to retrieval and tool augmented LLM systems. RAG combines parametric generation with non-parametric retrieval to improve factuality and allow for updatable, inspectable evidence [7]. Toolformer demonstrates that language models can learn through self-supervision when to call external APIs and how to incorporate results [6]. This improves performance while maintaining generality. Building on these ideas, our contribution reframes tools not just as a capability mechanism but also as a privacy boundary. We propose an MCP per-field API design that minimizes the student data exposed to the model provider while allowing for auditable access and evaluation of privacy and utility.

2.3 Novelty and Contribution

To our knowledge, MCP has not previously been evaluated in an academic advising setting in the research literature. Prior work emphasizes chatbots, RAG, and application layer safety, but it does not examine MCP as a privacy protection technique for advising systems. This paper's innovation is to bring MCP into the advising context and empirically compare it to the full-record design. By running this first analysis, we can therefore specify which research questions must be answered to responsibly leverage MCP for LLM-integrated student affairs advising.

3 Methods

3.1 Synthetic Dataset Construction

To avoid using real student records while still showing realistic characteristics, we generated completely synthetic undergraduate profiles that represent typical U.S. four-year students. Each experimental run produced a new group of 50 students, and we repeated this process for three separate runs, resulting in 150 unique synthetic students in total. We conducted analyses for each run individually to maintain their independence.

Each student record was saved as a JSON object with seven fields: (1) student_id, a pseudo-identifier that starts with "S" followed by six digits; (2) full_name, which is a synthetic name; (3) email, which is generated from the name using an institutional domain; (4) major; (5) year, indicating class level; (6) gpa; and (7) credits_earned. We created names using a Node.js package called @faker-js/faker, and we generated emails from normalized names, handling collisions by adding numeric suffixes.

We generated synthetic student data by replicating the distributional characteristics of real undergraduate populations across four dimensions: major, class year, GPA, and credits earned. We sampled majors to match NCES field-of-study distributions while excluding the "Other and not classified" category [8]. The class year was sampled based on NCES undergraduate class-level proportions [11]. GPA values were taken from a left-skewed distribution centered between 3.0 and 4.0 to reflect realistic grade distributions [9], and credits earned were sampled within typical ranges according to class standing (Freshman: 0–29; Sophomore: 30–59; Junior: 60–89; Senior: 90 +).

3.2 Experimental Setup

We simulated an AI academic advisor accessible through a user interface. This assumes the backend can recognize the logged-in student and retrieve the full synthetic record. We used the advisor model Claude-sonnet-4–20250514. For every student, we instructed the model to respond to two fixed prompts, "Am I on track to graduate in four years?" and "Should I consider changing my major?". These questions were selected because they reflect common advising issues. Prompt 1 relies on detailed academic progress, while Prompt 2 can often be answered with more general information. We evaluated two architectural conditions:

- Condition 1: Traditional full-record integration. For every student and prompt, the application sent the full student record to the LLM provider as part of the request context. This included student_id, full_name, email, major, year, gpa, and credits_earned, regardless of which fields were necessary for the answer.
- Condition 2: MCP per-field API integration. In this MCP setup, the LLM did not receive the complete record. Instead, it accessed individual fields by calling specific MCP tools available through an MCP server (one tool for each field): get_student_id, get_name, etc. The model decided which tools to use and the order they were called; the server only returned the requested field values and logged each tool use. Since the backend already knows which student is logged in, the system assumes identifier tools are not needed for the prompts, and ideally, the model should not call for them. For analysis, the effective exposure in MCP was defined as the fields actually retrieved through tool calls in that interaction.

In each run, we generated 50 students and collected responses for both prompts under both conditions. This resulted in 4 responses per student per run, totaling 200 responses per run, along with MCP tool-call logs indicating which fields were accessed.

3.3 Data Leakage Measurement

To measure privacy risk, we grouped student record fields into three sensitivity levels:

- Tier 1 (most sensitive - direct identifiers): full_name, email, student_id
- Tier 2 (academic performance and progress): gpa, credits_earned
- Tier 3 (least sensitive - general attributes): major, year

For each response, we computed a Leakage Score (LS) based on how many fields from each tier were exposed to the LLM provider during that interaction:

$$LS = 3 \times (\# \textit{Tier 1 fields}) + 2 \times (\# \textit{Tier 2 fields}) + 1 \times (\# \textit{Tier 3 fields}) \tag{1}$$

Exposing all seven fields gives the highest LS of 15. In the traditional condition, LS is always 15 because the complete record is always included. Under MCP, LS changes based on the interaction and the tools used.

We reported leakage at two aggregate levels for each run and condition: the Total Leakage Score (TLS), which is the total of LS across all student-prompt interactions in that condition and run; and the Average Leakage Score (ALS), which is the average leakage per student across both prompts. This is calculated by adding each student's two prompt LS values and then averaging over the 50 students.

3.4 Response Quality Evaluation (LLM-as-a-Judge)

To determine if MCP's reduced exposure affected the quality of advising, we used an LLM-as-a-judge approach [10]. Claude generated responses for both conditions and also served as the judge. This avoided self-enhancement bias. For every student and prompt, the judge reviewed the student profile as the ground truth, the question, and the two responses (Traditional and MCP). Then, the judge assigned each response a score from 1 (very poor) to 5 (excellent). Scores needed to be in a strict JSON format to enable automated analysis. We defined quality in two ways:

1. Accuracy: This means correctly using the student's major and year, and when relevant, GPA and credits. Any fabricated or contradictory details received low scores.
2. Relevance: This refers to how well the response answers the specific prompt, avoiding generic or off-topic replies.

To avoid position bias, we evaluated each pair of responses twice, changing the order (Traditional first and MCP first). We then averaged the two scores assigned to each response to create a single score. Finally, we calculated the average quality by prompt and condition within each run (Prompt 1 vs. Prompt 2, and Overall).

4 Results

4.1 Data Leakage

In all three runs, the traditional approach always showed the complete student profile for each interaction. This fixed the leakage at LS = 15 per prompt and ALS = 30 per student (for two prompts). In contrast, the MCP approach varied the leakage based on which tools the model selected. This resulted in much lower exposure in every run (Run 1: ALS 10, TLS 500; Run 2: ALS 9.98, TLS 499; Run 3: ALS 10, TLS 500).

On average, the traditional ALS was 30, while the MCP ALS was ~ 9.99. This shows about a 66–67% reduction in per-student leakage with MCP. Total leakage showed a similar trend: over the 3 runs, the traditional totaled 4500 compared to 1499 for MCP.

Table 1. Average Leakage Scores and Total Leakage Scores by Run and Integration

Runs	Traditional		MCP	
	ALS	TLS	ALS	TLS
Run 1	30	1500	10	500
Run 2	30	1500	9.98	499
Run 3	30	1500	10	500

Table 2. Mean Response Quality Scores by Run, Prompt, and Integration

Runs	Traditional			MCP		
	P1	P2	Overall	P1	P2	Overall
Run 1	5	5	5	2.302	4.170	3.236
Run 2	4.917	5	4.959	2.021	4.133	3.077
Run 3	4.990	5	4.995	2.083	4.260	3.172
a						

4.2 Response Quality

Quality scores show a task-dependent trade-off. For Prompt 1 ("Am I on track to graduate in four years?"), the traditional responses were generally close to the maximum, with run means between 4.917 and 5. In contrast, MCP responses were much lower, with run means ranging from 2.021 to 2.302. Overall, the paper reports a mean quality for Prompt 1 of about 4.97 for traditional responses compared to around 2.14 for MCP.

For Prompt 2 ("Should I consider changing my major?"), the difference was smaller. Traditional responses scored an average of 5, while MCP responses averaged about 4.19, which still indicated relatively high quality.

When combining both prompts and all runs, traditional responses averaged ~ 4.98, while MCP averaged ~ 3.16. Most of the drop came from the data-intensive first prompt.

5 Discussion

5.1 Data Leakage vs. Response Quality

This experiment highlights a clear trade-off between the traditional and MCP approaches in terms of privacy and utility. In the traditional model, each interaction reveals the entire student profile, resulting in the highest ALS. In contrast, the MCP greatly limits exposure since the model only retrieves selected fields. Our logs show that the model never accessed identifier fields like student ID, name, or email, which accounts for most of the reduction in data exposure. The remaining difference came from occasionally skipping other academic or contextual fields. However, this decrease in data exposure has a downside: the overall quality of responses declines under MCP. This indicates that simply reducing access does not ensure same advising performance.

5.2 Task Dependence

The effect of MCP on quality depends a lot on the advising task. For the first question, "Am I on track to graduate in four years?" the traditional method performs much better. This is because accurate guidance needs precise information about academic progress, especially credits earned and GPA, along with more structured reasoning about requirements. Under MCP, responses are not as strong since the model sometimes fails to retrieve all important fields before answering. This leaves it with an incomplete understanding, which reduces accuracy and relevance. In contrast, for Prompt 2, "Should I consider changing my major?" MCP is close to the traditional method. Basic reasoning and general academic advice are usually enough in this situation. The model can provide good suggestions with just the student's current major and class year, along with some broad principles. This makes Prompt 2 need less context. These results indicate that the MCP works best for tasks that don't depend heavily on detailed academic data.

5.3 Transparency and Governance Benefits

Beyond reducing exposure, MCP offers a governance benefit through visibility. Unlike the traditional approach, where the full record is included into the prompt with little insight into its use, MCP clearly logs each data access. This allows institutions to track what was accessed, when it was accessed, and how often tools are used. This clear record helps with accountability and better supports data minimization, which is highly valued in higher education, given the sensitive nature of student data.

5.4 Limitations and Future Work

The study has several limitations. The dataset is entirely synthetic and does not reflect the variability and complexity of real student records. For instance, real-world student records contain far more than seven fields, including completed courses, ongoing courses, and sensitive information such as student gender and ethnicity. In addition, the study only evaluates two advising prompts, so the findings may not generalize to other advising workflows such as course planning or prerequisite checking. Future work will test MCP across a broader range of advising tasks.

Results may also vary across models, as both the responses and evaluations came from a single LLM. Future work will use separate judge models to evaluate response quality, including cross-model comparisons with systems such as ChatGPT or Gemini. This will enable examination of whether the observed quality differences vary depending on the choice of evaluator. Future work will also broaden examination of the quality criteria, beyond accuracy and relevance to include important advising qualities like tone and empathy.

Furthermore, the MCP tools were simple and only allowed per-field retrieval. A key question for our future research is why the quality drop for Prompt 1 was so severe under MCP. Future research will begin by investigating whether the failure to call necessary tools is the primary cause of the decline in the quality of model responses. Alternative tool designs could better balance privacy and utility: for example, returning GPA ranges (3.0–3.5) or narrative summaries ("on track for graduation") rather than exact values. Finally, the model should be tested with real advisors in actual institutional settings to determine if it genuinely reduces their workload while protecting student privacy.

6   Conclusion

This paper demonstrates that MCP-based field-level access controls can substantially reduce student data exposure to third-party LLM providers without sacrificing advising quality across all tasks. Our comparison shows that selective field access reduced average leakage scores from 30 to about 10, primarily by avoiding direct identifiers. This privacy gain came with minimal quality trade-offs for lower-data tasks like major changes, though performance declined predictably for data-intensive graduation audits.

Beyond these empirical findings, this work establishes a methodological foundation for evaluating privacy-utility trade-offs in educational AI systems. The tiered leakage metric and logged tool calls make data exposure transparent and auditable, which is critical for institutional governance. To our knowledge, this is the first empirical evaluation of MCP as a privacy protection mechanism in academic advising, where prior work has focused primarily on chatbot interfaces and application-layer safety.

Future research should investigate which student fields are genuinely necessary for different advising tasks, why models sometimes over- or under-retrieve information, and how to optimize MCP implementations for both safety and performance. As institutions integrate LLMs into student-facing systems, understanding these field-level access patterns will be essential for responsible deployment.

Acknowledgments. We are especially grateful to Professor Timothy Hickey and Professor Nianwen Xue, both of the Department of Computer Science at Brandeis University, for their engagement with this project and insightful feedback throughout this work.

Disclosure of Interests.   **Disclosure of Interests.** The authors have no competing interests to declare.

References

1. U.S. Department of Education: FERPA | Protecting Student Privacy. Accessed 01 Feb 2026
2. European Union: Regulation (EU) 2016/679 (General Data Protection Regulation), Art. 5. EUR-Lex. Accessed 01 Feb 2026
3. Chu, Z., et al.: LLM Agents for Education: Advances and Applications. arXiv preprint arXiv: 2503.11733 (2025)
4. Neumann, A.T., et al.: An LLM-driven chatbot in higher education for databases and information systems. IEEE Trans. Educ. **68**(1), 103–116 (2025). https://doi.org/10.1109/TE.2024.3467912

5. Jayaram, Y.: Private LLMs for higher education: secure GenAI for academic & administrative content. Am. Inter. J. Comput. Sci. Technol. **6**(4), 28–38 (2024). https://doi.org/10.63282/3117-5481/AIJCST-V6I4P103

6. Schick, T., et al.: Toolformer: Language Models Can Teach Themselves to Use Tools. arXiv preprint arXiv:2302.04761 (2023)

7. Lewis, P., et al.: Retrieval-Augmented Generation for Knowledge-Intensive NLP Tasks. arXiv preprint arXiv:2005.11401 (2021)

8. National Center for Education Statistics: Table 322.10. Bachelor's degrees conferred by postsecondary institutions, by field of study: Selected academic years, 1970–71 through 2021–22. Digest of Education Statistics 2023. U.S. Department of Education. (Table prepared September 2023.) https://nces.ed.gov/programs/digest/d23/tables/dt23_322.10.asp, last accessed 2026/01/31

9. Weiss, G.M., et al.: An Analysis of Grading Patterns in Undergraduate University Courses. In: 2023 IEEE 47th Annual Computers, Software, and Applications Conference (COMPSAC), Torino, Italy, pp. 310–315 (2023). https://doi.org/10.1109/COMPSAC57700.2023.00048

10. Gu, J., et al.: A Survey on LLM-as-a-Judge. arXiv preprint arXiv:2411.15594v6 [cs.CL] (2025)

11. Campbell, T., Wescott, J.: Profile of Undergraduate Students: Attendance, Distance and Remedial Education, Degree Program and Field of Study, Demographics, Financial Aid, Financial Literacy, Employment, and Military Status: 2015–16. Web Tables, U.S. Department of Education / National Center for Education Statistics, NCES 2019–467 (Jan 2019)

Re-imagine Knowledge Tracing
with Student Agency in a Generative AI
Language Tutor

Jiachen Gong[✉][iD], Anshula Bali[iD], Ishrat Ahmed[iD], Michelle Banawan[iD],
Tracy Arner[iD], and Danielle S. McNamara[iD]

Learning Engineering Institute, Arizona State University, Tempe, AZ 85281, USA
{jgong42,abali4,iahmed27,mbanawan,tarner,dsmcnama}@asu.edu

Abstract. Knowledge Tracing (KT) is widely used for personalization
in Intelligent Tutoring Systems (ITSs). However, it is typically implemented as a hidden component that autonomously makes learning decisions, leaving students with little control over their own learning. Generative AI (GenAI) creates an opportunity to rethink the relationship
between KT and student agency through natural language interaction,
enabling learners to contest KT-driven recommendations and take an
active role in learning decisions. Yet, few have examined how a GenAI-
based KT could be configured and evaluated to support ITSs' adaptivity
and student agency. In this paper, we first present a multi-agent ITS for
AI-assisted French learning (AIFL), where a KT agent drives adaptivity, and learners can contest topic recommendations, ask follow-up questions, and track progress via a learning analytics dashboard (LAD). We
then compared the KT agent's performance against Bayesian Knowledge
Tracing (BKT) with simulated students under experimental conditions.
Our results showed that with appropriate multi-agent design and prompt
engineering, a GenAI-based KT could achieve adaptivity comparable to
an established framework, and maintain adaptivity when learners exercise agency in topic selection.

Keywords: GenAI-based ITS · Knowledge Tracing · Student Agency

1 Introduction

Intelligent Tutoring Systems (ITSs) have demonstrated potential to improve student learning through personalization across diverse domains, from mathematics
to language learning [2,10,11]. Recent advances in generative AI (GenAI) have
introduced new opportunities for language learning ITSs by enabling flexible natural language interaction [4,8,13]. However, prior research has predominantly
focused on English language learning [12,13], and few studies systematically
examined how GenAI could support instructional adaptivity within ITSs [3,4].

A prevalent approach for personalization in ITSs is Knowledge Tracing (KT)
[10,18], which supports adaptive instruction by tailoring activities to learners'

© The Author(s), under exclusive license to Springer Nature Switzerland AG 2027
E. G. Blanchard et al. (Eds.): AIED 2026, LNAI 16583, pp. 315–324, 2027.
https://doi.org/10.1007/978-3-032-29760-0_35

inferred knowledge states [1]. KT models are commonly deployed as closed, invisible components that autonomously select learning activities, limiting learners' ability to make decisions or contest system inferences, thereby constraining student agency. Student agency, defined as learners' active role in knowledge construction and decision-making [24], is critical for deeper learning, self-regulation, and long-term outcomes [20]. By minimizing learner involvement, closed KT risks optimizing short-term adaptivity at the expense of these broader gains.

GenAI presents an opportunity to rethink this relationship: by interpreting natural language and supporting conversational interaction, a prompt-engineered GenAI agent can function as a KT [17] that not only provides adaptive recommendations but also invites learners to participate in instructional decision-making. However, recent benchmarking work has shown that GenAI exhibited limited adaptivity compared to traditional KT [5], and few studies have examined how a GenAI-based KT can be configured within a multi-agent system to enable reliable adaptivity. We argue that the key question is not whether GenAI can replicate ITS adaptivity, but how it is configured and integrated to do so.

To address these challenges, we introduce **AI-assisted French Learning (AIFL)**, a GenAI-based French language learning ITS grounded in insights from a user survey [9]. It provides after-class conversational grammar and vocabulary practice. This paper is guided by two research questions:

RQ1. How can a multi-agent GenAI-based ITS be designed to support both adaptive personalization and meaningful student agency in language learning?

RQ2. To what extent can LLMs function as reliable KT, and how closely do their mastery estimates align with established knowledge-tracing frameworks?

Our contributions are: (1) the design of AIFL, a multi-agent GenAI-based ITS for French learning with a GenAI-based KT agent and six collaborating agents supporting adaptive personalization and student agency; and (2) a quantitative evaluation of the KT agent using simulated students, comparing with a well-established KT framework, Bayesian Knowledge Tracing (BKT).

2   Related Work

Language Learning ITSs. Language education has a decades-long history assisted by computers [12]. Early language learning ITSs used natural language processing (NLP) to detect grammatical mistakes and deliver rule-based feedback, but were complex to develop and limited by technical constraints [11]. Recent advances in GenAI enabled more comprehensive language tutors, predominantly focusing on grammar and vocabulary feedback for writing [8,13]; through conversational interfaces, GenAI also enhances learners' motivation and provides immediate feedback [3,4]. However, several gaps remain. First, existing work has predominantly focused on English language learning [12,13], with little attention to other languages such as French. Second, although personalization was frequently cited as a key benefit of GenAI for language learning, relatively little research has systematically examined how GenAI modeled student knowledge states and adjusted instruction accordingly [3,4]. Third, most studies relied on off-the-shelf tools such as ChatGPT [8] rather than proposing a multi-agent system for language learning ITS.

Knowledge Tracing and Student Agency. Knowledge Tracing (KT) is a class of techniques that models and tracks students' evolving knowledge states over time to support personalization in ITSs [1]. Among KT models, Bayesian Knowledge Tracing (BKT) [7] is a well-established statistical model implemented in multiple ITSs [2,10]. LLM-based KT approaches have also emerged recently [17]. However, KT is commonly embedded as a closed model in which learners cannot view, question, or influence the model's representation of their knowledge, nor participate in decisions about what to practice next (e.g., [10,18]). Moreover, the obscure nature of most KT algorithms makes student-model negotiation difficult. Statistical and machine learning-based KT models makes it difficult to explain to learners how knowledge state estimates are derived or why specific instructional decisions are made [15]. Together, a lack of opportunities for student-algorithm negotiation and inadequate algorithmic transparency constrain student agency.

Student Agency with GenAI. Prior work has highlighted the importance of balancing student agency and system adaptivity for high learning gain and productivity, with most studies operationalizing agency as students' freedom to choose the order of tasks [19]. [22] proposed a multidimensional framework of student agency in AI-assisted learning, encompassing Content Agency, Feedback & Help Agency, Co-Orchestration Agency, and Data Agency. Moreover, GenAI can support a negotiable, open learner model [6] by making system inferences transparent and open to dialogue: through natural language interaction, students can question and contest the system's interpretations of their knowledge states. This enables the learner model to be co-constructed by both the system and the students, shifting from adaptation *for* learners to adaptation *with* learners.

3   AI-Assisted French Learning (AIFL) System

Learner-Centered Design. The design of AIFL is informed by a user survey (n = 22) examining students' learning challenges, practices, and expectations for GenAI-assisted language learning [9]. The participants were enrolled in lower-division French courses at a large public university in the United States. They expressed strong demand for supplemental grammar and vocabulary practice that adapts to their learning progress, while emphasizing that GenAI should supplement rather than replace human instruction. Guided by these findings, we designed AIFL to provide after-class conversational grammar and vocabulary practices personalized to students' individual needs. AIFL has two main components: the front-end web application and the multi-agent system backend.

Web Application The AIFL web application provides two interfaces (Fig. 1): a conversational UI (CUI) where students practice fill-in-the-blank questions and interact with the GenAI agents, and a student-facing Learning Analytics Dashboard (LAD) that tracks learning progress. The LAD aggregates practice statistics at both daily and chapter levels, reporting learning time, question counts, and accuracy rates per topic.

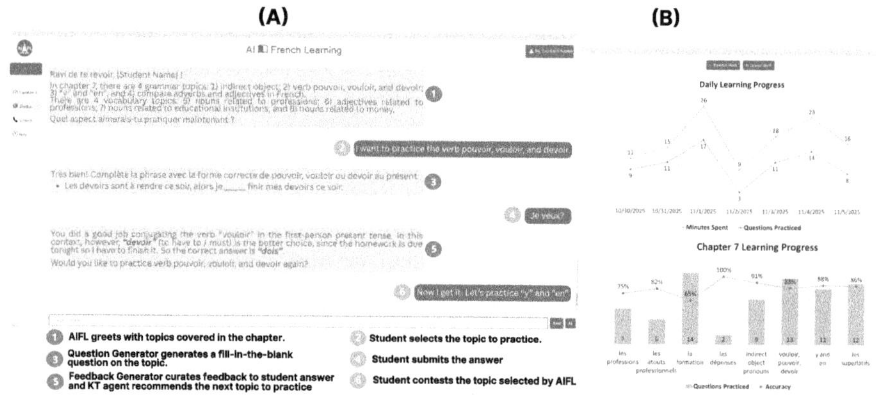

Fig. 1. (A) CUI a demo of the student-system interaction. (B) Student-facing LAD

Multi-agent System. AIFL is implemented as a multi-agent system where seven agents collaborate to generate practice questions in French, give immediate feedback, and answer follow-up questions. Most agents are prompt-engineered, and some are further customized by supervised fine-tuning or retrieval augmentation. Figure 2 describes the AIFL's agentic workflow. The *Manager Agent* serves as the central orchestrator, classifying learner intent and routing the student prompt to appropriate agents. The *KT Agent* serves as the KT model, estimating students' latent knowledge state and recommending the next best topic to practice. The *Question Generator* produces fill-in-the-blank French practices. The *Feedback Generator* evaluates student responses, identifies errors, and provides explanatory feedback. The *QA Chatbot* supports conversational follow-up by responding to learner-initiated clarification or explanation requests. The *Re-engagement Agent* sustains practice momentum by negotiating subsequent learning activities with the learner. Finally, the *Safeguard Agent* monitors safety-related signals and directs students to appropriate university support resources when needed. A typical interaction is illustrated in Fig. 1(A).

Student Agency Operationalization. We adopt the proposed framework from [22] to describe student agency in AIFL. First, AIFL preserves the content agency: students are able to decide the next topic to practice, and contest AIFL's topic selection. Second, it preserves the feedback/help agency: students receive

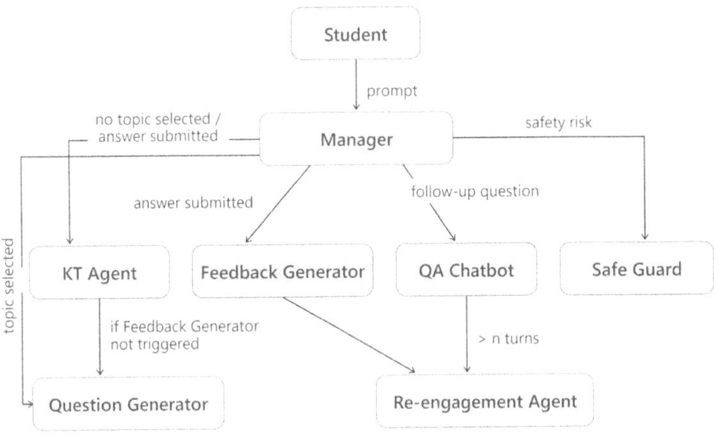

Fig. 2. AIFL Multi-Agent Design Framework

immediate feedback and ask follow-up questions. Third, it promotes data agency: AIFL provides an LAD that enables learners to track their learning progress.

4   KT Agent Evaluation Method

Before deploying AIFL with real learners, it is essential to verify that the KT agent reliably estimates knowledge states and maintains adaptivity when students exercise agency in topic selection. We therefore evaluated the KT agent using simulated students, a well-established approach in ITS research that enables controlled, ground-truth comparison prior to real-user deployment [21].

Experiment Design. We conducted two experiments with simulated students: Experiment 1 tested three prompt variants with incremental detailed information of the underlying student cognitive model, without student agency. Experiment 2 used the most information-rich prompt with student agency enabled, allowing simulated students to contest the system's topic selection. The simulation was grounded in instructional materials from one chapter of an intermediate-level French course with eight learning topics (e.g., use indirect object pronouns, describe professional attributes). Following the straightforward yet effective approach implemented by [21], we simulated five students based on BKT, which represented a real cognitive model where students could give an answer correctly by guessing, incorrectly by slipping, and be probable to learn when practicing. BKT agents were implemented as baselines for adaptivity comparison without (Control A) and with agency (Control B).[1]

---

[1] Simulation details see https://osf.io/dgehc/files/osfstorage/69cabf84d8e5444d0f 639a9c.

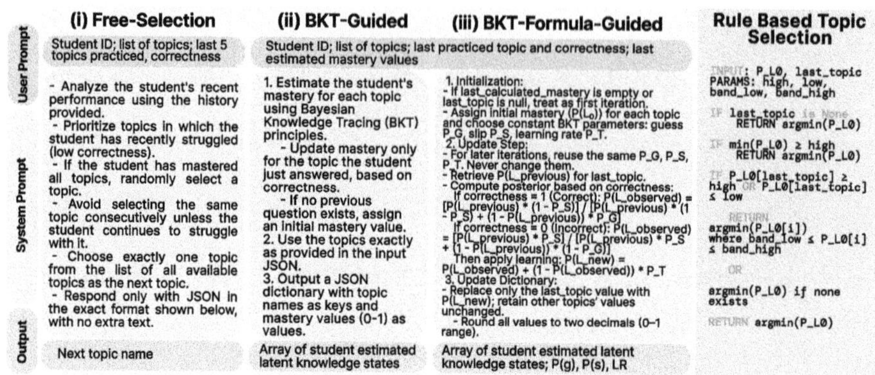

Fig. 3. User and system prompts, agent outputs, and the rule-based topic selection.

Experiment 1 (Prompt Design): Aiming to achieve higher adaptivity by incorporating more information suggested by previous research [16], we implemented three prompts with incremental information about the underlying student cognitive model. (i) *Free-Selection*: the KT agent was prompted to recommend the next topic based solely on recent performance history. (ii) *BKT-Guided*: the agent was asked to estimate latent knowledge states using BKT principles, returning a mastery array used by a rule-based topic selection function. (iii) *BKT-Formula-Guided*: the agent was additionally provided with explicit BKT formulas to estimate knowledge states and infer guess, slip, and learning rate parameters. The rule-based topic selection function kept practices at an appropriate difficulty level, paired with prompt (ii), (iii), and the baseline BKT agents. Full prompts and the topic selection function are detailed in Fig. 3.

Experiment 2 (Student Agency): With the KT agent configured with prompt (iii), simulated students were allowed to contest and override the system's recommended topic selection to simulate student agency. The likelihood of contesting increased with longer practice streaks, and was modeled as $Prob(Contest) = \frac{n-1}{m^2}x^2 + \frac{2(1-n)}{m}x + n$, where x is the streak length, with contest probability of n with 0 streak, and the student would definitely contest when the streak length reached m. In our experiments, n was set to 0.1 and m was set to 10.

Adaptivity Evaluation Metrics. We calculated Point-Biserial correlations between topic selection frequencies and simulated students' initial mastery values, and Pearson correlations between topic selection frequencies and their average accuracies, to assess adaptivity. Stronger negative correlations indicated more adaptive behavior, as an effective KT should allocate more practice to lower-mastery topics. We also calculated mean squared errors (MSEs) between the agent's estimated and the simulated students' true knowledge states to assess estimation accuracy. A lower MSE represented higher accuracy in the estimation.

5 KT Agent Evaluation Results

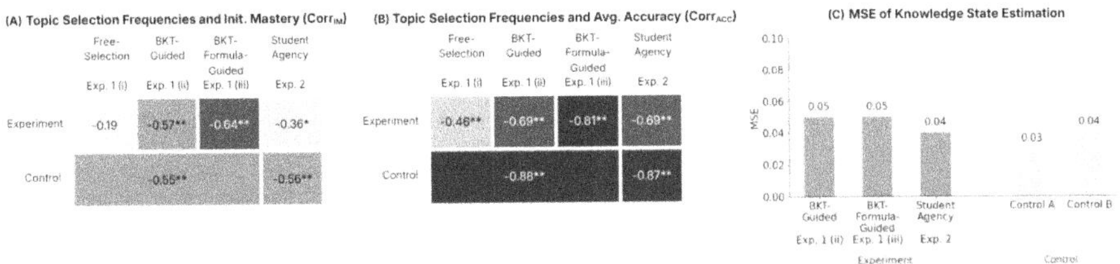

Fig. 4. Correlation between topic selection frequencies and (A) initial mastery values and (B) average accuracies. Asterisks denote statistical significance (* $0.01 \leq p < 0.05$; ** $p < 0.01$). (C) MSE of knowledge state estimations per condition.

Adaptivity to Student Knowledge States. Figure 4(A) showed that the correlation between topic selection frequency and initial mastery ($Corr_{IM}$) strengthened from -0.19 with prompt (i), to -0.57^{**} with prompt (ii), and further to -0.64^{**} with prompt (iii). Figure 4(B) showed that correlations with average accuracies ($Corr_{ACC}$) followed the same trend, strengthening from -0.46^{**}, to -0.69^{**}, then to -0.81^{**}, as the prompt incorporated increasingly explicit BKT guidance. The KT agent with prompt (iii) achieved comparable correlations ($Corr_{IM} = -0.64^{**}$; $Corr_{ACC} = -0.81^{**}$) to the baseline BKT agent (Control A: $Corr_{IM} = -0.55^{**}$; $Corr_{ACC} = -0.88^{**}$). When student agency was enabled in Experiment 2, the GenAI-based KT agent displayed weaker but still significant correlations ($Corr_{IM} = -0.36^{*}$; $Corr_{ACC} = -0.69^{**}$) compared to the BKT agent (Control B: $Corr_{IM} = -0.56^{**}$; $Corr_{ACC} = -0.87^{**}$).

Knowledge State Estimation Accuracy. Figure 4(C) reports the MSEs between the agent's estimated and the simulated students' true knowledge states. In Experiment 1, the KT agent with BKT-Guided and BKT-Formula-Guided prompts achieved low MSEs ($MSE_{Exp.1(ii)} = MSE_{Exp.1(iii)} = 0.05$), slightly higher than the baseline BKT ($MSE_{ControlA} = 0.03$). When student agency was introduced in Experiment 2, the KT agent achieved a lower MSE ($MSE_{Exp.2} = 0.04$), comparable to the baseline BKT ($MSE_{ControlB} = 0.04$).

6 Discussion, Limitations, and Future Work

This study introduced a multi-agent GenAI-based ITS for French language learning that balanced system adaptivity and student agency, and evaluated the KT agent's adaptivity using simulated students. Regarding **RQ1**, AIFL demonstrated three out of four dimensions of student agency in [22]'s framework: content agency through contestable topic selection, feedback/help agency through immediate feedback and follow-up questions, and data agency through the LAD. Regarding **RQ2**, our results showed that a prompt-engineered GenAI-based agent was able to function as a KT and showed significant adaptivity to simulated students' knowledge states. Adding detailed information of the underlying student cognitive model in the prompt increased the KT agent's adaptivity and could approximate the adaptivity of BKT. The KT agent also showed accurate knowledge state estimation comparable to the BKT baseline, and allowing students to contest topic selection did not reduce this accuracy.

Two major limitations in the current work point to important directions for future research. First, while AIFL grants learners full control over practice selection, system support is still needed to facilitate effective agency [23]. Future work should design a negotiation mechanism in which the KT agent explains its topic-selection rationale and engages learners in reflective dialogue, potentially incorporating students' self-evaluations of their own knowledge states into KT estimations to transform practice selection into a co-decision process. Second, the adaptivity evaluation relied on one type of student model (BKT) and was conducted in an isolated testing environment. Although this enabled controlled experimentation and fair comparison, future research should incorporate simulations with different cognitive models, and possibly GenAI-based simulated students [14]. Ultimately, real-world deployment will be necessary to better understand how a GenAI-based KT operates in authentic learning contexts.

Acknowledgments. The research reported here was supported by the Institute of Education Sciences, U.S. Department of Education, through Grant R305T240035 to Arizona State University. The opinions expressed are those of the authors and do not represent views of the Institute or the U.S. Department of Education.

References

1. Abyaa, A., Khalidi Idrissi, M., Bennani, S.: Learner modelling: systematic review of the literature from the last 5 years. Educ. Tech. Res. Dev. **67**, 1105–1143 (2019). https://doi.org/10.1007/s11423-018-09644-1
2. Aleven, V., McLaren, B.M., Sewall, J., Koedinger, K.R.: The cognitive tutor authoring tools (CTAT): preliminary evaluation of efficiency gains. In: Intelligent Tutoring Systems, pp. 61–70 (2006). https://doi.org/10.1007/11774303_7
3. AlGhamdi, E.M., Li, Y., Gašević, D., Chen, G.: Leveraging prompt-based LLMS for automated scoring and feedback generation in higher education. Comput. Educ. **243**, 105511 (2026). https://doi.org/10.1016/j.compedu.2025.105511
4. Barrot, J.S.: ChatGPT as a language learning tool: an emerging technology report. Technol. Knowl. Learn. **29**, 1151–1156 (2023). https://doi.org/10.1007/s10758-023-09711-4
5. Borchers, C., Shou, T.: Can large language models match tutoring system adaptivity? A benchmarking study (2025). https://arxiv.org/abs/2504.05570
6. Bull, S., Kay, J.: Open learner models, studies in computational intelligence, vol. 308, pp. 301–322. Springer-Verlag, Berlin Heidelberg (2010). https://doi.org/10.1007/978-3-642-14363-2_15

7. Corbett, A.T., Anderson, J.R.: Knowledge tracing: modeling the acquisition of procedural knowledge. User Modell. User-Adapted Interact. **4**(4), 253–278 (1994). https://doi.org/10.1007/bf01099821
8. Escalante, J., Pack, A., Barrett, A.: AI-generated feedback on writing: insights into efficacy and ENL student preference. Int. J. Educ. Technol. High. Educ. **20**(1), 1–20 (2023). https://doi.org/10.1186/s41239-023-00425-2
9. Gong, J., Ahmed, I., Yu, F., Arner, T., McNamara, D.S.: L2-French learners and generative AI (GenAI): challenges, needs, and design guidelines. In: Proceedings of the Learning Engineering Research Network Convening (LERN 2026) (2026). https://doi.org/10.59668/2551.25403
10. Gordon, G., Breazeal, C.: Bayesian active learning-based robot tutor for children's word-reading skills. In: Proceedings of the AAAI Conference on Artificial Intelligence, vol. 29, no. 1 (2015). https://doi.org/10.1609/aaai.v29i1.9376
11. Heift, T.: Developing an intelligent language tutor. CALICO J. **27**(3), 443–459 (2010). https://www.jstor.org/stable/calicojournal.27.3.443
12. Heift, T., Schulze, M.: Errors and intelligence in computer-assisted language learning: parsers and pedagogues. ReCALL **21** (2009). https://doi.org/10.1017/s0958344009000044
13. Law, L.: Application of generative artificial intelligence (GENAI) in language teaching and learning: a scoping literature review. Comput. Educ. Open **6**, 100174 (2024). https://doi.org/10.1016/j.caeo.2024.100174
14. Lu, X., Wang, X.: Generative students: Using LLM-simulated student profiles to support question item evaluation. In: Proceedings of the ACM Conference on Learning@Scale, pp. 16–27. Cornell University (2024).https://doi.org/10.1145/3657604.3662031
15. Lu, Y., Wang, D., Chen, P., Zhang, Z.: Design and evaluation of trustworthy knowledge tracing model for intelligent tutoring system. IEEE Trans. Learn. Technol. **17**, 1661–1676 (2024). https://doi.org/10.1109/tlt.2024.3403135
16. Neshaei, S.P., Davis, R.L., Hazimeh, A., Lazarevski, B., Dillenbourg, P., Käser, T.: Towards modeling learner performance with large language models. In: Proceedings of the 17th International Conference on Educational Data Mining. International Educational Data Mining Society (2024). https://doi.org/10.5281/zenodo.12729942
17. Park, S., Kim, H.: A comprehensive survey and taxonomy on large language model-based knowledge tracing. In: Generative Systems and Intelligent Tutoring Systems, pp. 246–258. Springer Nature Switzerland, Cham (2025). https://doi.org/10.1007/978-3-031-98281-1_20
18. Schodde, T., Bergmann, K., Kopp, S.: Adaptive robot language tutoring based on Bayesian knowledge tracing and predictive decision-making. In: Proceedings of the 2017 ACM/IEEE International Conference on Human-Robot Interaction (2017). https://doi.org/10.1145/2909824.3020222
19. Taub, M., Sawyer, R., Smith, A., Rowe, J., Azevedo, R., Lester, J.: The agency effect: the impact of student agency on learning, emotions, and problem-solving behaviors in a game-based learning environment. Comput. Educ. **147**, 103781 (2020). https://doi.org/10.1016/j.compedu.2019.103781
20. Thomas, J.W.: Agency and achievement: self-management and self-regard. Rev. Educ. Res. **50**(2), 213–240 (1980)

21. VanLehn, K., Niu, Z., Siler, S., Gertner, A.S.: Student modeling from conventional test data: a Bayesian approach without priors. In: Goettl, B.P., Halff, H.M., Redfield, C.L., Shute, V.J. (eds.) Intelligent Tutoring Systems, pp. 434–443. Springer, Berlin Heidelberg, Berlin, Heidelberg (1998). https://doi.org/10.1007/3-540-68716-5_49
22. Vincoli, M., Scholz, N., Nagashima, T.: Multidimensional student agency in learning with AI: a conceptual framework and design implications. In: Cristea, A.I., et al. (eds.) Artificial Intelligence in Education. LNAI, vol. 15880, pp. 218–232. Springer Nature Switzerland AG, Cham (2025). https://doi.org/10.1007/978-3-031-98459-4_16
23. Xu, X., Qiao, L., Cheng, N., Liu, H., Zhao, W.: Enhancing self-regulated learning and learning experience in generative AI environments: The critical role of metacognitive support. Br. J. Educ. Technol. **56**(5) (2025). https://doi.org/10.1111/bjet.13599
24. Zimmerman, B.J., Pons, M.M.: Development of a structured interview for assessing student use of self-regulated learning strategies. Am. Educ. Res. J. **23**(4), 614–628 (1986). https://doi.org/10.3102/00028312023004614

From Predictive Models to Actionable Recommendations: A Survey of Counterfactual Approaches in Student Dropout

Raylan Santos[1]([✉])(iD), Cristian Cechinel[1,2](iD), Ig Ibert Bittencourt[1](iD), Emanuel Queiroga[1,3](iD), and Thales Vieira[1](iD)

[1] Center of Excellence for Social Technologies (NEES), Federal University of Alagoas, Maceió, Brazil
{raylan.santos,cristian.cechinel,ig.ibert,emanuel.queiroga,
thales.vieira}@nees.ufal.br
[2] Federal University of Santa Catarina, Araranguá, Brazil
[3] Federal Technological University of Paraná, Dois Vizinhos, Brazil

Abstract. Student dropout remains a critical challenge in global education, representing a significant loss of human capital. Although data-driven approaches like predictive modeling have achieved high accuracy in identifying at-risk students, a "trust gap" persists among educators. Prediction alone is insufficient; stakeholders require interpretable insights to guide effective intervention. This survey explores the paradigm shift from passive "black-box" detection to "actionable prescription" through the lens of Counterfactual Explanations (CFE). We analyze 23 primary studies published between 2021 and 2026, categorizing them using a novel *Intervention Pipeline* taxonomy that bridges four levels: Identification (predictive models), Interpretation (XAI), Visual Analytics (interactive visualization and human-in-the-loop analysis), and Actionable Recommendations (counterfactuals). Adopting an analytical framework, we systematically interrogate the literature regarding variable risk definitions, data source diversity, prediction horizons, and feature actionability. Our analysis reveals a critical disconnect: while many models prioritize accuracy using immutable features, few focus on the actionable variables necessary for generating feasible pedagogical recommendations. We conclude that while CFE offers a promising path for personalized support, future research must address challenges regarding causal validity, explanation stability, and scalability (individual vs. institutional) to successfully bridge the gap between algorithmic output and practical pedagogical action.

Keywords: Student dropout · Predictive Models · Explainable AI · Counterfactual explanations · Learning analytics

1   Introduction

Educational discontinuity and attrition remain persistent challenges worldwide, with substantial social and economic consequences. UNESCO's latest education data estimate that the global out-of-school population increased since 2021 and now totals 250 million children and youth; the global out-of-school rate across primary to upper secondary is 16.1%, and Latin America and the Caribbean report a total rate of 7.6% [23].

This challenge is amplified in the Global South, where structural constraints limit the capacity to prevent dropout through timely and individualized support: in low-income countries, the share of out-of-school children and youth is 33%, compared to 3% in high-income countries, and large disparities in spending per learner reinforce a substantial financing gap for feasible interventions [23,24].

In Brazil, the problem is particularly salient in higher education, where dropout rates have been reported as nearing 60%, creating sustained pressure on institutional management and public policy; although many Brazilian federal universities have institutional policies and access to student profile data, most institutions still do not use these data proactively to support decision-making and prevention [14].

Against this backdrop, Learning Analytics (LA) has increasingly relied on predictive models to identify at-risk students, yet prediction alone often fails to translate into concrete pedagogical action [14]. In educational practice, risk scores are rarely sufficient: instructors and support teams need interpretable and actionable levers to decide when and how to intervene. Crucially, actionable prescription requires *feasible recourse*: recommendations must target variables that are changeable by an identified agent (student, instructor, or institution) within the available intervention window.

This survey examines the emerging shift from "black-box" identification toward actionable recommendation by synthesizing recent advances in explainable AI, visual analytics, and counterfactual explanations for student dropout prevention. Accordingly, we structure our analysis around four research questions: (RQ1) how dropout is defined across studies and which prediction and intervention horizons characterize the 20212026 literature; (RQ2) what data sources and feature modalities are used, and how they influence feature actionability and intervention feasibility; (RQ3) which modeling paradigms and evaluation strategies (including class imbalance handling) prevail and how they align with data modalities; and (RQ4) to what extent the literature progresses along the proposed Intervention Pipeline, and what barriers remain to achieving actionable prescription through counterfactual explanations.

2   Methodology and Conceptual Framework

This survey adopts a PRISMA-inspired screening protocol to examine how the student dropout literature progresses from predictive identification to actionable recommendations [15].

2.1   Search Protocol and Corpus Selection

We searched IEEE Xplore, ACM Digital Library, and Google Scholar from November 2025 to January 26, 2026, using the Boolean query ("student dropout" OR "attrition" OR "retention") AND ("counterfactual" OR "explainable AI" OR "actionable" OR "prescriptive"). We included studies published between 2021 and 2026 that explicitly addressed student dropout or retention and contributed to at least one stage of the intervention workflow, from risk identification to intervention-oriented analysis. We excluded studies focused only on academic performance prediction without a dropout- or retention-related intervention setting or early-warning use case, as well as purely conceptual papers without empirical evaluation.

The search returned 142 records. After removing 18 duplicates and excluding 79 out-of-scope records in title/abstract screening, we assessed 45 full-text articles and retained 23 primary studies (Fig. 1).

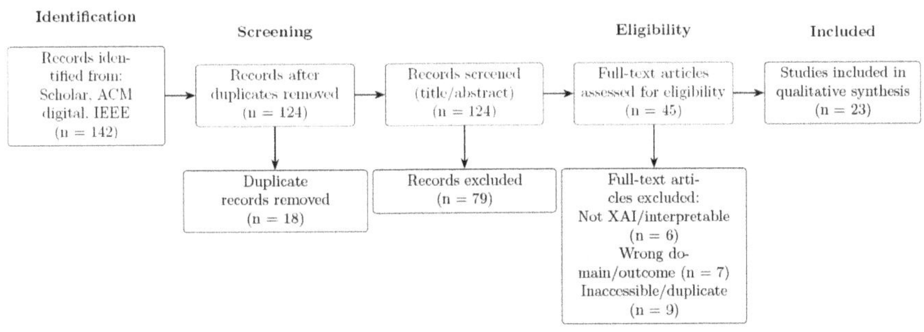

Fig. 1. PRISMA-inspired study selection flow for the 2021–2026 corpus.

For transparency and replication, we maintained a master coding table recording each study's educational context, dataset access, sample size, scope, operational dropout definition, prediction horizon, intervention level, and feature modalities. All studies were coded using the operational criteria and tie-breaking rules described in Sect. 2.2. After a short washout period, we conducted a second full-pass verification of key categorical fields, including Intervention Pipeline level and prediction horizon, correcting and logging inconsistencies.

2.2   Intervention Pipeline Taxonomy and Coding Rules

To organize the literature toward intervention-oriented evidence, we propose an *Intervention Pipeline* with four levels: (1) Identification (predictive modeling), (2) Interpretation (XAI), (3) Visual Analytics (interactive visualization and human-in-the-loop analysis), and (4) Actionable Recommendations (counterfactual explanations). This taxonomy captures the progression from risk detection to intervention-oriented outputs and makes heterogeneous contributions comparable under a common lens.

To operationalize the taxonomy, we use a single-label coding strategy in which each study is assigned to the *highest* level of intervention capability it demonstrated, avoiding double counting and supporting corpus-level coverage analysis. Level 1 includes studies that optimize predictive performance (e.g., AUC/F1) without user-facing explanations; Level 2 includes studies that provide feature-based explanations (e.g., SHAP/LIME); Level 3 includes studies that provide interactive visual interfaces such as dashboards; and Level 4 was assigned when a study explicitly generated counterfactual recommendations of the form $x \to x'$ intended to change the predicted outcome while addressing feasibility through actionability or immutability constraints. Thus, Level 4 requires actionable *recourse*, not only interpretive evidence about why risk is high.

When a study combined multiple components, we coded it at the highest level supported by implemented functionality. Interactive *what-if* exploration without explicit $x \to x'$ recommendations was coded as Level 3, whereas benchmark or evaluation papers analyzing explainers or counterfactual methods without deployable recommendations were coded up to Level 2. In ambiguous cases, we prioritized the artifact exposed to stakeholders over methodological discussion. In addition, we coded prediction horizon as *Early* when prediction was operationalized before the end of the instructional period, and as *End* otherwise, since this distinction directly affects the feasibility of prescriptive recommendations.

3   Systematic Analysis of the Literature

We analyze the 23 selected studies through four dimensions aligned with our research questions: risk definitions and prediction horizons, data sources and feature actionability, modeling choices, and the shift from identification to actionable prescription.

3.1   Definitions and Prediction Horizons

In this survey, we treat *dropout* as a study-specific attrition event rather than assuming a universal definition across modalities and institutions. As an illustrative example from Brazilian distance education, Queiroga et al. [16] operationalize dropout using institutional or administrative criteria (e.g., removal after prolonged inactivity or missing re-enrollment) and also employ an inactivity threshold over VLE logs to localize when dropout occurs. To make heterogeneous studies comparable, we coded each primary study by *scope* (course/module, program/degree, or school level) and by *operationalization* (e.g., inactivity thresholds, non re-enrollment or administrative withdrawal, and school abandonment). When a paper did not report an explicit operational definition, we recorded it as NR; when multiple definitions coexisted, we prioritized the definition used to label the experimental target outcome. At a coarse level, abandonment or withdrawal definitions dominate the corpus (13/23), followed by mixed outcome labels (8/23) and inactivity-threshold definitions (2/23).

Prediction timing is also uneven: 12 of the 23 studies (52.2%) rely on end-of-term evaluation, whereas 11 (47.8%) support early-warning or dynamic prediction settings. The corpus is dominated by Higher Education (18/23), with fewer MOOC studies (4/23) and a single K–12 study (1/23). In MOOCs, dropout is typically operationalized through inactivity or non-completion at the course or module level [10,17,28], whereas Higher Education studies more often rely on administrative signals or mixed institutional outcomes at the program level [18,26]; the K–12 study focuses on school abandonment [9]. This heterogeneity affects both what can be acted upon and when.

3.2 Data, Modeling, and Actionability

The effectiveness of intervention is constrained by the data used to train the model, since different feature modalities provide different levers for pedagogical action. We treat features as *actionable* when they can plausibly be changed by an identified agent within the intervention window, whereas demographic or background attributes are treated as *immutable*. Across the corpus, 17 of the 23 studies (73.9%) include demographic or immutable variables, while 15 (65.2%) include LMS/log features (i.e., behavioral interaction data from learning management systems), which are typically more actionable but often co-occur with immutable predictors. This actionability gap limits the feasibility of prescriptive recommendations.

A critical timing tension also emerges. Vaarma et al. [25] show that actionable features may gain predictive weight only later in the semester, and in our corpus LMS/log features appear less often in Early-warning studies than in End-of-term studies (6/11, 54.5%, vs. 9/12, 75.0%). As a result, early-warning systems may depend more heavily on early-available but less actionable information, which complicates the generation of feasible behavioral recommendations.

Modeling choices interact with these constraints. Tree-based ensembles are common in structured educational data [4,18], while deep learning is more common in sequential settings such as MOOCs [10,17]. From a recourse perspective, tabular pipelines rely on static and mixed-type attributes, whereas sequential models introduce additional challenges related to opacity and temporal realism in learner trajectories. Class imbalance complicates this picture: techniques such as SMOTE or weighting can distort local decision geometry, potentially affecting the validity and feasibility of counterfactual recommendations [3,8] (Table 1).

3.3 From Prediction to Actionable Prescription

Applying our coding rules, 10 studies (43.5%) remain at Level 1, 9 (39.1%) are located at Levels 2–3, and only 4 (17.4%) reach Level 4. This distribution suggests that the main bottleneck is not only predictive accuracy, but the translation of model outputs into feasible actions within realistic intervention windows.

Table 1. Feature modalities and Intervention Pipeline levels across the coded corpus.

Ref	Ctx	D	A	L	Lvl
[1]	HE/OULAD	●	●	●	4
[2]	HE/OULAD	●	●	●	2
[3]	HE/OULAD	○	○	●	2
[4]	HE/Korea	●	●	●	1
[5]	HE/Germany	●	●	○	4
[6]	HE/Peru	●	●	○	3
[7]	HE/Peru	●	●	○	3
[8]	HE/Korea	●	●	○	1
[9]	K12/Brazil	●	●	○	3
[10]	MOOC/KDD15	○	○	●	1
[11]	HE/USA	●	●	○	4
[12]	HE/Vietnam	●	●	●	1
[13]	HE/NR	●	●	●	1
[17]	MOOC/XuetangX	○	○	●	1
[18]	HE/Spain	●	●	○	1
[19]	HE/Portugal	●	●	○	1
[20]	HE/Australasia	●	●	●	4
[21]	HE/New Z.	●	●	●	3
[22]	MOOC/EPFL	○	○	●	2
[25]	HE/Finland	●	●	●	1
[26]	HE/NR	●	●	●	1
[27]	HE/Moodle	○	○	●	2
[28]	MOOC/XuetangX	○	○	●	3

Coverage: D = 73.9%, A = 73.9%, L = 65.2%

Abbreviations: D = demographics/immutable; A = academic/grades; L = LMS logs/actionable; Lvl = Intervention Pipeline level.

Post-hoc explainers such as SHAP are useful for diagnosing risk factors [9,11], but they typically explain why risk is high rather than how an actor can change the learner state under institutional and temporal constraints; Swamy et al. also report instability across explainers for the same learner [22]. Visual analytics systems reduce the cognitive gap between model output and educator interpretation [6,28], yet most dashboards remain descriptive or diagnostic and do not generate explicit recommendations of the form $x \rightarrow x'$ under feasibility constraints. Counterfactual approaches come closest to actionable prescription, including work on recourse quality [2,3], feasibility constraints [5], natural-language mediation [20], and group-level interventions [1], but they also expose unresolved challenges in aligning mathematical recourse with institutional practice.

Even among studies that attempt to provide actionable recommendations, structural limitations still hinder real-world deployment. Across the corpus, three barriers persist: causal validity, stability, and scalability. Without causal and temporal grounding, recommendations may be infeasible [5]; without robustness, they may fluctuate across perturbations or explainers [22]; and without scalable delivery, individualized recourse remains costly to validate and deploy, motivating alternatives such as group-level counterfactuals [1]. Accordingly, future work should report the prediction horizon, intended agent, actionable versus immutable variables, enforced feasibility constraints, robustness criteria, and operational cost.

4   Final Remarks

This survey analyzed 23 primary studies (2021–2026) to map the shift from dropout prediction to actionable prescription through counterfactual explanations. A central empirical finding is the *actionability gap*: in our coded corpus, 17 out of 23 studies (73.9%) include demographic/immutable variables (D), while 15 studies (65.2%) include LMS/log variables (L) that are typically more actionable, yet often co-occur with immutable predictors (Sect. 3.2). As discussed in Sects. 3.2 and 3.3, this gap constrains feasibility, stability, and scalability of actionable recommendations.

Despite a PRISMA-inspired protocol, this survey has some limitations. The corpus may omit relevant studies outside the queried sources and keywords or published after the search date. In addition, feasibility constraints, actionability schemas, and deployment costs are often under-specified in the primary studies, which limits what can be coded reliably. Our single-label Intervention Pipeline coding also prioritizes the highest demonstrated capability of each study and may therefore under-represent partial contributions across levels.

These findings also point to a clear research agenda. Future work should prioritize actionable signals by distinguishing mutable from immutable variables and by making agency and timing assumptions explicit. Counterfactual generation should incorporate causal assumptions and feasibility constraints to avoid unrealistic recommendations, while evaluation protocols should treat stability as a core criterion through robustness checks. At the same time, research should move beyond fully individualized recourse toward cohort- or group-level prescriptions, report operational costs, and translate recommendations into clear guidance with explicit actors and constraints. When demographic or other immutable variables are used for prediction, their role should be justified carefully and they should not be turned into prescriptive targets.

Acknowledgments. This work was supported by the Brazilian Ministry of Education (MEC) under Grants TED13914 and TED11476; by the Brazilian National Council for Scientific and Technological Development (CNPq) under Grant No. 445016/2024-8; by the project Ia.Edu National Institute of Artificial Intelligence in Unplugged Education (Process No. 4084883/2024-5); and by the Research Support Foundation of the State of Alagoas (FAPEAL) under Process No. FAPEAL 60030.0000001481/2025.

Disclosure of Interests. The authors have no competing interests.

References

1. Buñay-Guisñan, P., Cano, A., Anguera, A., Lara, J.A., Romero, C.: Group counterfactual explanations: a use case to support students at risk of dropping out in online education. Electronics **15**(51) (2026)
2. Cavus, M., Kuzilek, J.: The actionable explanations for student success prediction models: a benchmark study on the quality of counterfactual methods. In: HEXED 2024 (2024)
3. Cavus, M., Kuzilek, J.: An effect analysis of the balancing techniques on the counterfactual explanations of student success prediction models. J. Meas. Eval. Educ. Psychol. **15**, 302–317 (2024). Special issue
4. Cho, C.H., Yu, Y.W., Kim, H.G.: A study on dropout prediction for university students using machine learning. Appl. Sci. **13**(21), 12004 (2023)
5. Cohausz, L.: Towards real interpretability of student success prediction combining methods of XAI and social science. In: EDM 2022, pp. 361–367 (2022)
6. Garcia-Zanabria, G., Gutierrez-Pachas, D.A., Camara-Chavez, G., Poco, J., Gomez-Nieto, E.: SDA-VIS: a visualization system for student dropout analysis based on counterfactual exploration. Appl. Sci. **12**(12), 5785 (2022)
7. Garcia-Zanabria, G., Gutierrez-Pachas, D.A., Poco, J., Gomez-Nieto, E.: CSDA-vis: a what-if-and-when visual system for early dropout detection using counterfactual and survival analysis interactions. Comput. Graph. (2025). in press
8. Kim, S., Choi, E., Jun, Y.K., Lee, S.: Student dropout prediction for university with high precision and recall. Appl. Sci. **13**(10), 6275 (2023)
9. Krüger, J.G.C., Britto Jr., A.d.S., Barddal, J.P.: An explainable machine learning approach for student dropout prediction. Expert Syst. Appl. **233**, 120937 (2023)
10. Kumar, G., Singh, A., Sharma, A.: Ensemble deep learning network model for dropout prediction in MOOCS. Int. J. Electr. Comput. Eng. Syst. **14**(2), 187–195 (2023)
11. Mgonja, T.: Using interpretable machine learning approaches to predict and provide explanations for student completion of remedial mathematics. Educ. Inf. Technol. **29**, 1–32 (2024)
12. Nguyen Thi Cam, H., Sarlan, A., Arshad, N.I.: A hybrid model integrating recurrent neural networks and the semi-supervised support vector machine for identification of early student dropout risk. PeerJ Comput. Sci. **10**, e2572 (2024)
13. Niyogisubizo, J., Liao, L., Nziyumva, E., Murwanashyaka, E., Nshimyumukiza, P.C.: Predicting student dropout in university classes using two-layer ensemble machine learning approach: a novel stacked generalization. Comput. Educ. Artif. Intell. **3**, 100066 (2022)
14. Pacheco, A.S.V., Tete, M.F., Monsueto, S.E.: Actions to combat student dropout in higher education. Avaliação: Revista da Avaliação da Educação Superior **29**, e024026 (2024)
15. Page, M.J., et al.: The PRISMA 2020 statement: an updated guideline for reporting systematic reviews. BMJ **372**, n71 (2021)
16. Queiroga, E.M., et al.: A learning analytics approach to identify students at risk of dropout: a case study with a technical distance education course. Appl. Sci. **10**(11), 3998 (2020)

17. Roh, D., Han, D., Kim, D., Han, K., Yi, M.Y.: SIG-Net: GNN-based dropout prediction in MOOCS using student interaction graph. In: SAC 2024, pp. 29–37 (2024)
18. Segura, M., Mello, J., Hernández, A.: Machine learning prediction of university student dropout: does preference play a key role? Mathematics **10**(18), 3359 (2022)
19. Singh, A.K., Karthikeyan, S.: A federated learning neural network for student dropout prediction. In: ICCE 2025 (2025)
20. Susnjak, T.: Beyond predictive learning analytics modelling and onto explainable artificial intelligence with prescriptive analytics and ChatGPT. Int. J. Artif. Intell. Educ. **34**, 452–482 (2024)
21. Susnjak, T., Ramaswami, G.S., Mathrani, A.: Learning analytics dashboard: a tool for providing actionable insights to learners. Int. J. Educ. Technol. High. Educ. **19**(12) (2022)
22. Swamy, V., Radmehr, B., Krco, N., Marras, M., Käser, T.: Evaluating the explainers: black-box explainable machine learning for student success prediction in MOOCS. In: EDM 2022, pp. 98–109 (2022)
23. UNESCO: 250 million children out-of-school: what you need to know about UNESCO'S latest education data (2023). https://www.unesco.org/en/articles/250-million-children-out-school-what-you-need-know-about-unescos-latest-education-data. Accessed 2 Jan 2026
24. United Nations Office at Geneva: 251 million children still out of school worldwide, UNESCO reports (2024). https://www.ungeneva.org/en/news-media/news/2024/10/99797/251-million-children-still-out-school-worldwide-unesco-reports. Accessed 2 Jan 2026
25. Vaarma, M., Li, H.: Predicting student dropouts with machine learning: an empirical study in Finnish higher education. Technol. Soc. **76**, 102474 (2024)
26. Villar, A., Robledo Velini de Andrade, C.: Supervised machine learning algorithms for predicting student dropout and academic success: a comparative study. Discov. Artif. Intell. **4**(2) (2024)
27. Wijekoon, A., Wiratunga, N., Nkisi-Orji, I., Martin, K., Palihawadana, C., Corsar, D.: Counterfactual explanations for student outcome prediction with Moodle footprints. In: SICSA XAI Workshop 2021, pp. 1–8 (2021)
28. Zhang, H., Dong, J., Lv, C., Lin, Y., Bai, J.: Visual analytics of potential dropout behavior patterns in online learning based on counterfactual explanation. J. Visual. **26**, 359–374 (2023)

Simulating Validity: Modal Decoupling in MLLM Generated Feedback on Science Drawings

Arne Bewersdorff[1] , Nejla Yuruk[2] , and Xiaoming Zhai[1]

[1] University of Georgia, AI4STEM Education Center, Athens, GA 30602, USA
{arne.bewersdorff,xiaoming.zhai}@uga.edu
[2] Department of Mathematics and Science Education, Gazi University, Ankara 06560, Turkey
nejlayuruk@gazi.edu.tr

Abstract. Multimodal large language models (MLLMs) are increasingly used to generate feedback on students' hand-drawn scientific models. However, modal decoupling, where outputs remain pedagogically plausible while contradicting the drawing or treating depicted elements as missing, threatens feedback validity. Using $N = 150$ middle school drawings spanning five modeling tasks and three competence levels, we generated $N = 300$ feedback instances with GPT-5.1 and coded four grounding error types. Grounding failures were common: 41.3% of feedback contained at least one error. In the direct workflow, 49.3% of instances were flawed; the inventory-list-first workflow reduced this to 33.3%. False absence was the dominant failure mode and increased with drawing complexity. An inventory-list-first workflow reduced error rates but did not eliminate them: one in three outputs remained flawed. Linguistic surface cues like word count or physical-term density provided no diagnostic value for detecting invalid feedback. These findings indicate that valid feedback requires binding and verification mechanisms beyond prompting.

Keywords: MLLM · Generative AI · Feedback · Multimodal · Representational Competence · Modal Decoupling · Visual Grounding

1 Introduction

In science education, students frequently construct hand-drawn visual models of scientific phenomena. For MLLM-generated feedback on such drawings to be valid, model claims must be grounded in the specific visual evidence, that is, the depicted entities, their attributes, and their relations. However, modal decoupling can cause feedback that appears pedagogically sound yet is not anchored in the student's drawing: the model may contradict depicted content or treat present elements as missing. For instance, if a model correctly identifies a drawing as depicting particles but fails to register the student's added motion arrows, feedback claiming those arrows are missing is not grounded in the visual evidence. Prior work links this to architectural and optimization constraints in MLLMs, including geometric separation between modalities, unimodal optimization

E. G. Blanchard et al. (Eds.): AIED 2026, LNAI 16583, pp. 334–341, 2027.
https://doi.org/10.1007/978-3-032-29760-0_37

bias toward text, and weakening visual grounding during generation (Liang et al., 2022; Bai et al., 2024).

This paper demonstrates that modal decoupling leads to invalid feedback when using off-the-shelf pre-trained MLLMs and cannot be reliably mitigated by an inventory-list-first prompting workflow. Analyzing $N = 150$ student drawings, we show that directly generated feedback frequently exhibits grounding errors, and that generating an inventory list first (Yan et al., 2024) reduces but does not suppress these errors. Our contribution is an empirical characterization and comparison of grounding failures under two deployment-realistic prompting workflows; mechanistic accounts are discussed as plausible contributors rather than causally identified drivers.

2 Theoretical Background

2.1 Multimodal Representational Competence and Feedback

Scientific phenomena often involve abstract processes that are challenging to convey through text alone. Science education therefore relies on multimodal construction, where students demonstrate understanding by integrating visual models with explanatory meaning through entities, attributes, and relations (Ainsworth, 2006). Formative feedback on drawings is crucial for supporting students' scientific understanding (Black & Harrison, 2004; Chin & Teou, 2010). However, for feedback to be effective, its claims must be grounded in the student's drawing. Grounding invalidity can occur as (a) contradiction, where feedback asserts content the drawing does not support, or (b) false absence, where feedback treats a depicted element as missing.

2.2 Technical Constraints Underlying Modal Decoupling

Modal decoupling in MLLMs has been linked to three technical constraints. First, geometric separation: embeddings from different modalities concentrate in narrow, separated regions of the representation space, limiting fine-grained cross-modal alignment (Liang et al., 2022; Yi et al., 2025). Second, unimodal optimization bias: during training, the model relies more on the structured textual modality, causing the vision encoder to remain under-optimized and generating outputs based on textual priors rather than visual evidence (Zheng et al., 2025; Bai et al., 2024). Third, visual grounding decay: as generation proceeds, attention to visual features weakens and the model increasingly maintains linguistic consistency rather than re-examining the image (Chung et al., 2025; Favero et al., 2024). Together, these constraints can yield feedback that appears correct but is not grounded in the specific visual evidence.

However, in science education, where practitioners often rely on fixed, pre-trained MLLMs (Bewersdorff et al., 2025; Yin et al., 2024), model-centric mitigation strategies are often infeasible, making inference-time approaches more applicable. Among these, the inventory-list-first workflow prompts the model to verbalize visual elements before generating feedback, a strategy structurally analogous to Chain-of-Thought prompting (Yan et al., 2024). By serializing observation before evaluation, this approach aims to bridge the modality gap and keep visual evidence accessible. However, these mechanisms motivate why inventory lists might reduce observable modal decoupling; they do not imply elimination. Our study evaluates this empirically.

2.3 Construct Validity and the Risk of Fabricated Utility

When feedback is driven by model priors rather than the student's drawing, it introduces construct-irrelevant variance. If modal decoupling produces formally plausible but ungrounded feedback, a follow-up question arises: can validity be detected from surface text properties? Automated filters might assume that feedback with more concrete visual references or spatial language is better grounded, an assumption we test empirically.

3 Research Questions

RQ1. To what extent does off-the-shelf MLLM-generated feedback on student scientific drawings exhibit grounding failures?

RQ2. Which forms of grounding failures are most prevalent, and how do they vary across modeling tasks and competence levels?

RQ3. To what extent do grounding failures persist under an inventory-list-first workflow?

RQ4. Do automated linguistic indicators of visual grounding predict fewer grounding failures, or does decoupling persist despite grounding-oriented linguistic profiles?

4 Method

4.1 Sample

The dataset consists of $N = 150$ student-generated scientific drawings from a middle school curriculum unit on Kinetic Molecular Theory. Students drew visual models of particle-level mechanisms to explain macroscopic phenomena. Drawings cover five modeling tasks (Table 1): (R1) red dye diffusion, (R2) balloon expansion/contraction, (R3) heating a solid, (R4) water condensation, and (R5) boiling water. Each drawing was pre-classified into one of three competence levels reflecting visual complexity and representational sophistication.

Table 1. Distribution of student drawings over competency levels and tasks.

Level	R1	R2	R3	R4	R5	Total
Level 1	7	10	10	6	18	51
Level 2	8	6	9	9	10	42
Level 3	9	9	10	9	20	57
Total	24	25	29	24	48	150

4.2 Experimental Design

We evaluated two workflows for generating feedback using the OpenAI Chat Completions API (GPT-5.1; temperature $= 0$; single-image input via base64). In C1 (direct feedback), the model generates feedback immediately. In C2 (inventory-list-first), the model first produces a structured inventory of objects, attributes, and relationships present in the drawing, which then serves as the observational basis for feedback.

4.3 Analysis

All feedback (C1 and C2) was coded for grounding failures operationalized as four error types distinguishing false evidence (E1-E3) from false absence (E4):

- E1 (Object mismatch): Feedback references an entity not present in the drawing.
- E2 (Attribute mismatch): Feedback assigns an attribute contradicting the drawing.
- E3 (Relation mismatch): Feedback asserts a spatial or relational structure contradicting the drawing.
- E4 (False absence): Feedback states that a depicted element is missing.

Each error was coded binary; multiple types could co-occur. Interrater reliability on a 10% subset was high (Cohen's $\kappa = .83$; 94% agreement).

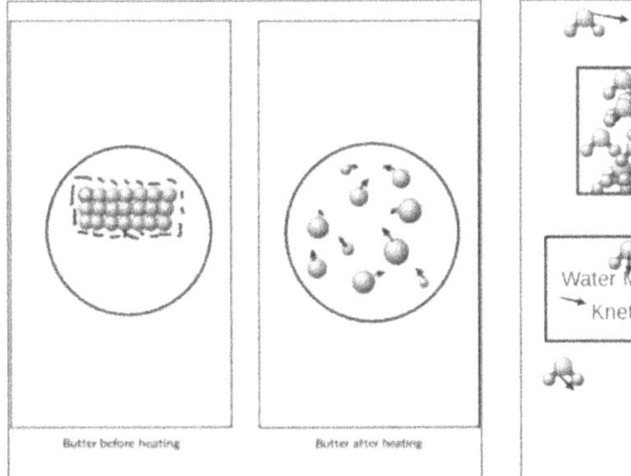

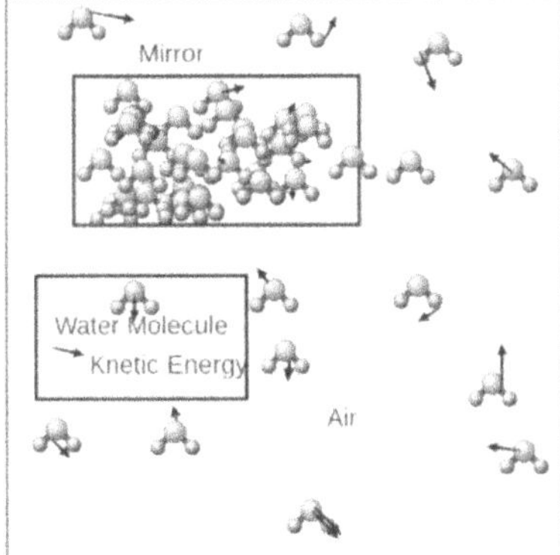

Fig. 1. False absence errors (E4) persisting across both workflows. Panel A (R3, Level 3); Panel B (R4, Level 3).

To illustrate these error types, Fig. 1 presents two examples. In Panel A (R3: heating a solid), a student drew butter particles before and, with motion arrows, after heating. Yet the feedback requests "vibration arrows", a false absence error (E4), as motion arrows are already depicted. In Panel B (R4: water condensation), the student drew water molecules with differentiated kinetic energy arrows on both the mirror and in the air, yet the feedback claims this indication is "missing" (E4). In both cases, the error persists under C2.

For RQ1, prevalence was estimated with 95% Wilson score confidence intervals. For RQ2, error rates (errors per instance) were examined by task and competence level. For RQ3, paired McNemar's tests compared error prevalence between C1 and C2 (N = 150 paired instances), with effects quantified as risk differences (Δ Risk, pp). For RQ4, cluster-robust logistic regression models predicted grounding failures from linguistic features (word count, physical-term density, spatial-term density, hedging density), controlling for task, level, and workflow. Discrimination was assessed via AUC comparison.

5 Results

Across N = 300 feedback instances, grounding failures were common. The inventory-list-first workflow reduced several error categories, but grounding invalidity remained substantial, with false absence as the dominant failure mode.

5.1 Prevalence of Modal Decoupling (RQ1)

In C1, 49.3% of instances were flawed (74/150; 95% CI [41.4%, 57.3%]). In C2, 33.3% were flawed (50/150; 95% CI [26.3%, 41.2%]). Pooled across workflows, 41.3% of feedback contained at least one grounding failure (124/300; 95% CI [35.9%, 47.0%]).

5.2 Profiles and Boundary Conditions (RQ2)

False absence (E4) was the dominant failure mode. The pooled E4 rate was 0.327 errors/feedback, exceeding the contradiction-type rate (E1-E3: 0.207). E4 increased with competence level (Level 1: 0.127; Level 2: 0.33; Level 3: 0.50), whereas contradiction-type errors remained comparatively stable (0.17–0.24). This suggests that information-dense drawings offer more opportunities for the model to overlook depicted elements. Task-level analyses revealed complementary boundary conditions: R4 and R3 showed the highest E4 rates, while R2 and R1 showed the highest contradiction-type rates. R5 showed the lowest rates for both.

5.3 Persistence Under Inventory-List-First (RQ3)

Despite the enforced inventory step, 33.3% of C2 feedback remained flawed (Table 2). Mean errors decreased from 0.654 (C1) to 0.414 (C2) per instance, with reductions in both contradiction-type (0.267 to 0.147) and false absence errors (0.387 to 0.267).

Table 2. Frequency of modal decoupling types by workflow.

Error type	C1: n (%)	C2: n (%)	Δ Risk (pp)	p-Value (McNemar)
E1 (object mismatch)	7 (4.7)	8 (5.3)	0.7	1.00
E2 (attribute mismatch)	11 (7.3)	4 (2.7)	−4.7	.039 *
E3 (relation mismatch)	22 (14.7)	10 (6.7)	−8.0	.017 *
E4 (false absence)	58 (38.7)	40 (26.7)	−12.0	.003 *
Any flaw (E1-E4)	74 (49.3)	50 (33.3)	−16.0	.001 *

*Note. Values indicate the number of feedback in which the error type was present (binary coding: absent = 0, present = 1). A single feedback may contain multiple error types. p-values were computed using McNemar's test on paired per-instance indicators (C1 vs C2; N = 150 drawings). * p < .05*

C2 reduced E2 (11 → 4, $p = .039$), E3 (22 → 10, $p = .017$), and E4 (58 → 40, $p = .003$), while E1 did not change significantly (7 → 8, $p = 1.000$). False absence remained the dominant residual failure under C2 (40 instances vs. 22 for E1-E3 combined). The inventory-list-first workflow shifted error composition but did not eliminate modal decoupling.

5.4 Linguistic Indicators and Modal Decoupling (RQ4)

Flawed and non-flawed feedback were similar on all measured text features. Cluster-robust logistic regression showed no reliable associations between grounding failures and physical-term density, spatial-term density, or hedging (all $p > .34$). The only text-related signal was that higher word count predicted more E4 errors ($OR = 1.046$, $p = .017$). Adding linguistic features improved AUC only negligibly (0.746 to 0.755; ΔAUC = 0.009). Surface linguistic cues provide no practically useful signal for identifying flawed feedback.

6 Discussion

This study provides an empirical grounding validity analysis for an applied setting: under two deployment-realistic workflows, off-the-shelf MLLM feedback on student scientific drawings is frequently not grounded in the visual evidence. The dominant failure mode is false absence, i.e., feedback treating depicted elements as missing, rather than explicit contradiction. This pattern is consistent with the technical constraints underlying modal decoupling: geometric separation, optimization bias, and grounding decay (Sect. 2.2). The increase of E4 with drawing complexity suggests that the main bottleneck is maintaining evidence coverage when drawings become information-dense, consistent with models falling back to high-probability pedagogical patterns when visual signal is difficult to sustain throughout generation. Task-level variation further supports that decoupling is shaped by representational demands: some tasks preferentially elicited contradiction-type errors, while others showed elevated false absence.

The inventory-list-first workflow reduced several error categories, especially E2, E3, and E4, compatible with its intended function of frontloading observation. However, roughly one in three outputs remained flawed, with E4 still dominant and E1 unchanged. This suggests a ceiling: inventory prompting can improve downstream specificity once entities are identified, but cannot correct early failures in establishing a correct object set. In short, inventory-list-first behaves as a risk-reduction heuristic, not a grounding validity mechanism.

That linguistic surface cues failed to distinguish grounded from ungrounded feedback (RQ4) challenges a common implicit safety assumption: that more concrete references, more spatial language, or more hedging indicates better alignment with the drawing. Feedback can read as specific and well-formed while containing grounding failures, implying that fabricated utility is difficult to detect from the feedback text alone. For practice, this means that automated quality filters based on text properties cannot serve as a substitute for explicit grounding verification.

When feedback is driven by model priors rather than the student's drawing, it introduces construct-irrelevant variance into assessments of students' representational competence. The increase of E4 with competence level raises a specific concern: the system may fail most where student work is richest and most diagnostic, potentially disadvantaging more advanced drawings by ignoring relevant structure and requesting redundant additions. When the model fails to recognize what is already depicted, it risks undermining students' confidence in their own representational choices, leading them to revise correct work unnecessarily.

Given these findings, prompting should be framed as risk reduction, not validation. This points away from "generate then justify" approaches (Ji et al., 2023) and toward "generate only what can be grounded," with explicit support for verification and abstention when grounding is uncertain. Valid feedback systems will likely require structured intermediate representations of depicted entities, attributes, and relations (e.g., semantic graph representations; Latif et al., 2025), along with explicit checks that each feedback claim maps back to supporting evidence. Neither inventory-list-first strategies nor linguistic signals offer a dependable correctness screen. Consequently, such systems should operate under human oversight rather than as direct, autonomous feedback agents for students.

7   Conclusion

Off-the-shelf MLLMs frequently generate feedback that seems pedagogically plausible yet visually unanchored, confirming the validity risk of modal decoupling where linguistic priors override specific visual evidence. Inventory-list-first improves some grounding but cannot resolve modal decoupling. The path to valid feedback therefore lies not primarily in more elaborate prompting, but in workflows and system designs that treat visual evidence as a binding constraint on what feedback may claim. Consequently, prompt-level scaffolds with off-the-shelf MLLMs are insufficient for valid autonomous feedback; such systems should operate under human oversight.

Acknowledgements. This study was funded by the Institute of Education Sciences, U.S. Department of Education (Grant R305C240010, PI Zhai). The opinions expressed are those of the authors and do not represent views of the Institute or the U.S. Department of Education.

References

Bewersdorff, A., Hartmann, C., Hornberger, M., Seßler, K., Bannert, M., Kasneci, E., et al.: Taking the next step with generative artificial intelligence: THe transformative role of multimodal large language models in science education. Learn. Individ. Differ. **118**, 102601 (2025)

Ainsworth, S.: DeFT: a conceptual framework for considering learning with multiple representations. Learn. Instr. **16**(3), 183–198 (2006)

Bai, Z., et al.: Hallucination of multimodal large language models: a survey. arXiv:2404.18930 (2024)

Black, P., Harrison, C.: Science Inside the Black Box. nferNelson, London (2004)

Chin, C., Teou, L.: Formative assessment: using concept cartoon, pupils' drawings, and group discussions to tackle children's ideas about biological inheritance. J. Biol. Educ. **44**(3), 108–115 (2010)

Chung, J., Kim, J., Kim, S., Lee, J., Kim, M.S., Yu, Y.: Learning to point visual tokens for multimodal grounded reasoning. arXiv:2505.18842 (2025)

Favero, A., Zancato, L., Trager, M., Choudhary, S., Perera, P., Achille, A., et al.: Multi-modal hallucination control by visual information grounding. In: Proceedings IEEE/CVF Conference Computer Vision and Pattern Recognition (CVPR), pp. 1–12. arXiv:2403.14003 (2024)

Ji, Z., Lee, N., Frieske, R., Yu, T., Su, D., Xu, Y., et al.: Survey of hallucination in natural language generation. ACM Comput. Surv. **55**(12), 1–38 (2023)

Latif, E., Khan, Z., Zhai, X.: SketchMind: a multi-agent cognitive framework for assessing student-drawn scientific sketches. arXiv:2507.22904 (2025)

Liang, W., Zhang, Y., Kwon, Y., Yeung, S., Zou, J.: Mind the gap: understanding the modality gap in multi-modal contrastive representation learning. arXiv:2203.02053 (2022)

Yan, A., Yang, Z., Wu, J., Zhu, W., Yang, J., Li, L., et al.: List items one by one: a new data source and learning paradigm for multimodal LLMs. arXiv:2404.16375 (2024)

Yi, L., Douady, R., Chen, C.: Decipher the modality gap in multimodal contrastive learning: from convergent representations to pairwise alignment. arXiv:2510.03268 (2025)

Yin, S., et al.: A survey on multimodal large language models. Nat. Sci. Rev. **11**(12), nwae403 (2024). https://doi.org/10.1093/nsr/nwae403

Zheng, X., Liao, C., Fu, Y., Lei, K., Lyu, Y., Jiang, L., et al.: MLLMs are deeply affected by modality bias. arXiv:2505.18657 (2025)

Confidence-Aware Automated Assessment of Student-Drawn Scientific Models

Luyang Fang[1,2], Yingchuan Zhang[2], Jongchan Park[1], Zhaoji Wang[1], Ping Ma[2], and Xiaoming Zhai[1]

[1] AI4STEM Education Center, Athens, GA, USA
{Luyang.Fang,Jongchan.Park,zhaojiwang,xiaoming.zhai}@uga.edu
[2] Department of Statistics, University of Georgia, Athens, GA, USA
{Yingchuan.Zhang,pingma}@uga.edu

Abstract. Student-generated drawings are widely used in science education to assess learners' conceptual understanding in modeling-based tasks aligned with the Next Generation Science Standards (NGSS). However, scoring such drawings requires expert human judgment to interpret complex visual representations, making large-scale assessment costly to implement and sustain in classroom settings. In this work, we study automated scoring of student-generated scientific drawings using a vision-based model. We evaluate a Vision Transformer (ViT) with parameter-efficient adaptation and propose a confidence-aware scoring framework that derives response-level confidence from test-time predictive distributions. This confidence signal enables selective automation by scoring high-confidence responses automatically while deferring uncertain cases for human review. Experiments on six NGSS-aligned middle school assessment items show that the proposed approach improves scoring reliability while supporting a practical trade-off between automated coverage and scoring risk, highlighting the value of confidence-aware methods for trustworthy educational assessment.

Keywords: Student-Generated Drawings · Automated Scoring · Confidence-Aware Scoring · Vision Transformers · Science Education

1 Introduction

In science education, assessing scientific modeling practice involves eliciting and interpreting evidence of students' understanding through a combination of drawings and written explanations [12]. Since drawings can externalize structures, relationships, and mechanisms that may remain implicit in text-only responses, modeling assessments often rely on rubric-based evaluation of student-generated drawings alongside written explanations [16]. However, consistent rubric-based scoring of drawings requires careful human judgment and sustained attention to scoring quality; in everyday classroom contexts, the time, expertise, and attention required for consistent and reliable scoring are often limited [12]. At scale, reliance on human scoring becomes a major hurdle because scoring students'

© The Author(s), under exclusive license to Springer Nature Switzerland AG 2027
E. G. Blanchard et al. (Eds.): AIED 2026, LNAI 16583, pp. 342–350, 2027.
https://doi.org/10.1007/978-3-032-29760-0_38

drawings is labor-intensive and costly [13]. These constraints have motivated automated scoring approaches that aim to support rubric-aligned interpretation of student drawings more efficiently [11].

Prior research has demonstrated the feasibility of computational analysis of student-generated visual artifacts. Early work focused on extracting quantifiable visual features from drawings and linking them to rubric-aligned scoring criteria to support automated assessment [13,15]. More recently, advances in artificial intelligence have enabled modern models, including Vision Transformer (ViT) architectures [6], to directly learn scoring-relevant representations from student responses [3,10,11,14].

Despite these advances, existing automated scoring approaches typically produce only a single score or proficiency label, offering limited support for how such outputs should be used in instructional decision-making. In formative assessment contexts, teachers must judge not only the predicted score but also its reliability, particularly for visually complex and ambiguous student drawings. The absence of explicit confidence information makes it difficult to determine when automated scores can be trusted and when manual review is warranted, limiting the practical usability of automated assessment systems [2,5].

To address these gaps, we propose a confidence-aware *vision-based* approach for automated scoring of student-generated scientific drawings. Building on the confidence-guided inference research [1,4,17], the approach derives a response-level confidence score from the stability of a ViT-based model's predictions under semantic-preserving test-time perturbations. We further incorporate *test-time selection with selective trust* to emphasize reliable perturbed predictions when forming the final scoring decision. The resulting confidence score enables selective automated scoring: the system can auto-score responses with strong predictive support while deferring low-confidence cases for human review, helping teachers triage responses and calibrate reliance on automated scores in practice.

Our study evaluates the proposed framework on student-generated drawings from six NGSS-aligned middle school science modeling assessment items with rubric-based proficiency levels. Empirically, the approach improves agreement with expert scoring and provides an intuitive confidence score indicating when automated predictions are reliable, supporting informed decisions about when human review is needed in classroom assessment.

2   Methodology

Problem Setup. We consider an automated scoring task with training data $\mathcal{D} = \{(x_i, y_i)\}_{i=1}^{n}$, where $x_i \in \mathcal{X}$ is a student-generated drawing represented as an image and $y_i \in \{1, \ldots, K\}$ is the corresponding rubric-based proficiency level. We train a scoring model $f_\theta : \mathcal{X} \rightarrow [0, 1]^K$, where $f_\theta(x) = (p_1(x), \ldots, p_K(x))$ is a probability distribution over the K score levels.

In educational assessment settings, automated scoring systems must decide not only what score to assign, but also whether that score can be trusted. We therefore adopt a confidence-aware scoring paradigm in which the model outputs both a predicted score and a confidence value that determines whether a response is automatically scored or deferred to human review. This confidence is derived from the model's test-time predictive distribution and is therefore directly aligned with the final scoring decision.

Parameter-Efficient Task Adaptation via LoRA. To implement this confidence aware scoring framework in a practical classroom assessment setting, we adapt a pretrained transformer-based vision backbone using a parameter-efficient fine-tuning strategy. Specifically, we employ Low-Rank Adaptation (LoRA) [9], which enables efficient task-specific adaptation while updating only a small subset of parameters [7].

Concretely, rather than updating all parameters in the transformer, LoRA introduces low-rank updates into the linear projection layers. For a weight matrix $W \in \mathbb{R}^{d \times p}$, the adapted layer is parameterized as

$$W' = W + \Delta W, \quad \Delta W = BA,$$

where $A \in \mathbb{R}^{r \times p}$ and $B \in \mathbb{R}^{d \times r}$ are trainable low-rank matrices with $r \ll \min\{d, p\}$. During training, only the LoRA parameters $\{A, B\}$ are optimized, while the pretrained weights W remain fixed. This yields an adapted scoring function $f_{\theta + \Delta \theta}(x)$ that captures task-specific scoring patterns with only a small number of additional trainable parameters.

Confidence via Test-Time Predictive Distribution. Once the scoring model is adapted to the task, we estimate prediction confidence by examining the stability of scoring decisions under plausible test-time variations of the input, following the direction of [1,4].

Given a response x, we generate M semantic-preserving perturbations, such as crops or rotations, $\tilde{x}_j = T_j(x), j = 1, \ldots, M$. For each perturbed input, the model produces a predictive distribution $p^{(j)} = f_\theta(\tilde{x}_j)$. We then define the test-time predictive distribution as the average over these perturbations: $\bar{p}(x) = \frac{1}{M} \sum_{j=1}^{M} p^{(j)}$. The automated score is then given by $\hat{y}(x) = \arg\max_k \bar{p}_k(x)$.

We define the *response-level confidence score* as the probability mass assigned to the predicted score:

$$\kappa(x) = \max_k \bar{p}_k(x) = \bar{p}_{\hat{y}(x)}(x) = \frac{1}{M} \sum_{j=1}^{M} p_{\hat{y}(x)}^{(j)}.$$

Here, $\kappa(x) \in [0, 1]$ measures how strongly the final predictive distribution supports the chosen score. Intuitively, a high confidence value indicates that plausible test-time variations of the response largely agree on the same score, whereas a low value suggests disagreement among these variations.

Selective Automated Scoring. Using the response-level confidence score defined above, we implement a selective automated scoring strategy that defers low-confidence cases to human graders. Given a confidence threshold τ, define $g_\tau(x) = \mathbf{1}\{\kappa(x) \geq \tau\}$. The selective scoring rule is:

$$h_\tau(x) = \begin{cases} \hat{y}(x), & g_\tau(x) = 1, \\ \text{defer to human review}, & g_\tau(x) = 0. \end{cases}$$

This formulation allows the system to automatically score responses with sufficient confidence while deferring uncertain cases for manual evaluation. By varying τ, we control the trade-off between automated coverage and scoring risk.

Test-Time Selection with Selective Trust. While the test-time predictive distribution already provides a response-level confidence score, we further improve robustness by selectively trusting individual test-time predictions. Importantly, this step operates at the *view level* and uses an internal *selection score*, which is distinct from the response-level confidence $\kappa(x)$ defined above.

For each augmented prediction $p^{(j)}$, let $\hat{y}^{(j)} = \arg\max_k p_k^{(j)}$ denote the predicted class under that perturbation. We then compute a selection score:

$$c^{(j)} = -\frac{1}{K-1} \sum_{k \neq \hat{y}^{(j)}} \log\left(p_k^{(j)}\right), \tag{1}$$

which measures how strongly that perturbed prediction suppresses probability mass on competing classes. Larger values of $c^{(j)}$ indicate more decisive predictions for that test-time view and are used solely for ranking and selecting reliable perturbations.

We adopt a Top-η filtering strategy at test time. Given M perturbed views of an input x, we retain only the top $\lceil \eta M \rceil$ perturbations with the largest selection scores $c^{(j)}$, where $\eta \in (0,1]$. Let $\mathcal{J}(x) \subseteq \{1,\ldots,M\}$ denote the indices of these selected views. The filtered predictive distribution is then defined as

$$\bar{p}_\eta(x) = \frac{1}{|\mathcal{J}(x)|} \sum_{j \in \mathcal{J}(x)} p^{(j)}.$$

The refined prediction and response-level confidence are given by

$$\hat{y}_\eta(x) = \arg\max_k \bar{p}_{\eta,k}(x), \quad \kappa_\eta(x) = \max_k \bar{p}_{\eta,k}(x).$$

3 Dataset Details

We use a dataset of student-generated scientific drawings collected from middle school science modeling assessments in the northeastern United States [8]. The assessment items are aligned with the Next Generation Science Standards (NGSS) and require students to construct visual models to explain observed scientific phenomena. Our experiments focus on the visual components of student responses from six assessment items, each targeting a distinct scientific concept. All responses are provided as images and independently scored by domain experts using rubric-based criteria. Following the original annotation protocol, each drawing is assigned to one of three ordered proficiency levels: *Beginning*, *Developing*, or *Proficient*.

Figure 1 shows an example item illustrating the open-ended and visually complex nature of the student drawings. Example student drawings are available in the GitHub repository[1]. Dataset statistics for each item, including the number of responses and label distributions, are summarized in Table 1.

---

[1] https://github.com/LuyangFang/CA-Drawing.

Table 1. Summary of the student drawing dataset used in this study.

Item	Item Description	Total	Beginning	Developing	Proficient
Item 1	Red dye diffusion	477	195	205	77
Item 2	Jane's inflated ball	538	177	288	73
Item 3	Melting butter	520	155	266	99
Item 4	Hot shower effect	772	494	107	171
Item 5	Heated cup of water	453	61	262	130
Item 6	Jennifer's teapot	816	390	271	155

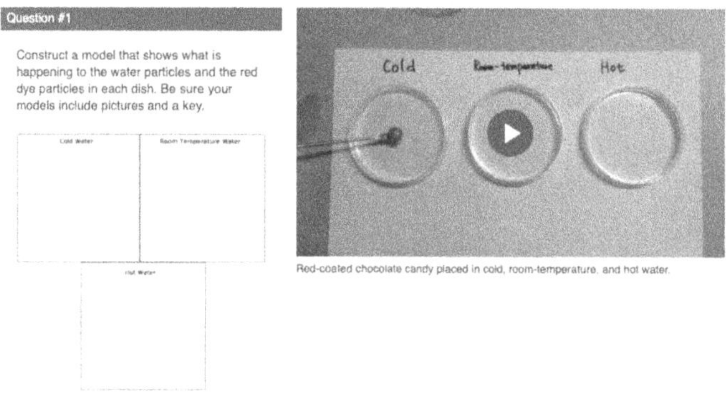

Fig. 1. Example science modeling assessment item. Students observe red dye diffusion in cold, room-temperature, and hot water and are asked to construct a visual model representing the behavior of water and dye particles. (Color figure online)

4 Experimentation and Results

We evaluate the proposed confidence-aware automated scoring framework on the student drawing assessment dataset described in Sect. 3. For each assessment item, the task is formulated as a supervised multi-class classification problem, where the scoring model predicts one of $K = 3$ rubric-aligned proficiency levels: Beginning, Developing, or Proficient.

Baselines. We compare four approaches: (1) **ViT (Frozen)**, a pretrained vision transformer without task-specific fine-tuning; (2) **ViT+LoRA**, where the backbone is adapted using low-rank adaptation; (3) **CA-Uniform**, a confidence-aware scoring method that uniformly trusts all test-time predictions; and (4) **CA-Selective**, our proposed confidence-aware selective scoring method based on test-time selection with selective trust.

Evaluation Metrics. We report performance using (1) standard classification metrics, including accuracy, Cohen's κ, precision, recall, and F1 score, computed separately for each item and averaged across items; and (2) evaluation of the confidence score introduced by the proposed CA-Selective method.

Training Details. Models are trained using a stratified train/validation/test split to preserve proficiency distributions. We adopt a pretrained ViT model (`vit_base_patch16_224`) backbone. Standard image preprocessing and data augmentation are applied. Models are optimized using cross-entropy loss for three-class classification, and the best checkpoint for each item is selected based on validation Cohen's κ. We use $M = 20$ and $\eta = 0.75$. All models are trained independently for each assessment item.

Table 2. Comparison of four methods across six items. Best performance for each item is shown in bold.

Metric	Method	Item 1	Item 2	Item 3	Item 4	Item 5	Item 6	Avg
Accuracy	ViT (Frozen)	0.438	0.482	0.212	0.244	0.174	0.183	0.289
	ViT + LoRA	**0.792**	0.833	0.769	**0.821**	0.761	0.622	0.766
	CA-Uniform	**0.792**	**0.852**	0.808	**0.821**	**0.783**	**0.659**	0.786
	CA-Selective	**0.792**	**0.852**	**0.827**	**0.821**	**0.783**	**0.659**	**0.789**
Kappa	ViT (Frozen)	-0.048	0.134	-0.110	0.040	-0.112	0.000	-0.016
	ViT + LoRA	**0.796**	0.759	0.708	0.788	0.589	0.608	0.708
	CA-Uniform	**0.796**	**0.789**	0.747	**0.813**	0.610	**0.643**	0.733
	CA-Selective	**0.796**	**0.789**	**0.826**	**0.813**	**0.694**	**0.643**	**0.760**
Precision	ViT (Frozen)	0.314	0.304	0.246	0.411	0.258	0.061	0.266
	ViT + LoRA	**0.774**	0.905	0.728	**0.721**	0.813	0.585	0.754
	CA-Uniform	**0.774**	**0.914**	0.774	0.708	0.829	**0.638**	0.773
	CA-Selective	**0.774**	**0.914**	**0.805**	0.708	**0.836**	**0.638**	**0.779**
Recall	ViT (Frozen)	0.350	0.327	0.259	0.347	0.255	0.333	0.312
	ViT + LoRA	**0.758**	0.695	0.736	**0.702**	0.695	0.596	0.697
	CA-Uniform	**0.758**	**0.713**	0.782	0.679	**0.707**	**0.639**	0.713
	CA-Selective	**0.758**	**0.713**	**0.815**	0.679	**0.707**	**0.639**	**0.719**
F1 Score	ViT (Frozen)	0.257	0.299	0.196	0.152	0.173	0.103	0.196
	ViT + LoRA	**0.765**	0.729	0.731	**0.708**	0.724	0.571	0.705
	CA-Uniform	**0.765**	**0.745**	0.778	0.687	0.739	**0.612**	0.721
	CA-Selective	**0.765**	**0.745**	**0.809**	0.687	**0.743**	**0.612**	**0.727**

4.1 Automated Scoring Performance

Table 2 reports automated scoring performance across six NGSS-aligned modeling items. Overall, the confidence-aware methods improve average performance relative to standard fine-tuning, with the clearest gains observed in Cohen's kappa and, in most cases, F1 score. Higher kappa values indicate improved agreement with human rubric-based scoring beyond chance, suggesting that confidence-aware modeling can support more reliable scoring decisions across diverse student drawings.

Comparing the two confidence-aware variants, CA-Selective achieves the best overall performance on average across items, suggesting that selective aggregation can improve scoring quality by reducing the influence of less informative test-time predictions. From an assessment perspective, this leads to rubric-aligned predictions that are less sensitive to superficial variability in students' representational styles. Such robustness is especially important in open-ended drawing tasks, where similar ideas may be expressed visually in different ways.

Table 3 summarizes model complexity across scoring methods. All approaches share the same ViT backbone (86.4M parameters), so performance differences are not attributable to model capacity. LoRA introduces only 0.6M additional trainable parameters while keeping the backbone fixed, and the confidence-aware variants add no further trainable parameters. Confidence-aware scoring incurs a higher inference cost because it aggregates multiple test-time augmented views to obtain response-level confidence, but all methods remain substantially lighter than LLM-based scoring approaches.

Table 3. Model complexity and computational cost of different scoring methods.

Method	Backbone Params	Trainable Params	Inference Latency (ms)
ViT (Frozen)	86.4M	0	1.0341
ViT + LoRA	86.4M	0.6M	1.0355
CA-Uniform	86.4M	0.6M	20.532
CA-Selective	86.4M	0.6M	20.572

To provide comparison with modern open-source multimodal foundation models, we additionally evaluated a vision-language model (Qwen3-VL-8B-Instruct) in a zero-shot setting using the same test split and rubric-aligned prompts. In this configuration, the model achieved lower agreement with expert scoring and substantially higher inference latency than the task-adapted ViT-based approaches. Details are provided in the GitHub repository. This does not indicate a limitation of the multimodal model itself, as effective use of VLMs for rubric-aligned assessment typically benefits from careful prompt design, few-shot exemplars, or task-specific adaptation. Instead, the comparison provides a practical reference showing that lightweight task-adapted vision backbones remain competitive and efficient in this setting.

4.2 Confidence Scores

To validate the intuitive rationality of our confidence metric $\kappa(x)$, we analyze the correlation between mean confidence and predictive accuracy across all proficiency labels. We find that there is a significant positive correlation ($r = 0.649, p < 0.01$) between the two. The linear fit demonstrates that higher confidence scores consistently align with higher scoring accuracy, particularly for the 'Beginning' level. This alignment ensures that $\kappa(x)$ serves as a reliable proxy for scoring quality, providing a solid foundation for the subsequent selective automated scoring strategy. Additional visualization results are available in the GitHub repository. We are also conducting expert review to verify the qualitative validity of these results.

In assessment contexts, the key question is not only whether a model can generate a score, but whether that score should be acted upon without further review. In this regard, the confidence score may provide a practical basis for deciding when an automated score may be used and when teacher review is still needed. This is especially relevant for student drawings, where visually ambiguous or unconventional drawings may be difficult for automated systems to interpret reliably and therefore may require teacher review.

5   Conclusion

In this work, we studied confidence-aware automated scoring of student-generated scientific drawings using a vision-based approach. By deriving response-level confidence from test-time predictive distributions and selectively aggregating reliable predictions, the proposed framework enables automated scoring that balances efficiency and reliability. Experiments on six NGSS-aligned science modeling tasks demonstrate that confidence-aware methods improve agreement with human scoring while providing an intuitive signal for deciding when automated scores can be trusted. Beyond performance gains, this work highlights the importance of integrating confidence estimation into automated assessment systems to support responsible deployment in classroom settings. At the same time, findings in this study should be interpreted in light of the dataset context. The data were collected from middle school science classrooms in one region of the United States, and students' representational practices may reflect local curricular and classroom contexts. In addition, because expert-provided scores were used as the reference, any systematic tendencies in human scoring may also be reflected in model performance. With these caveats, future work will examine the proposed approach across more diverse student populations and assessment contexts, as well as explore extensions to multimodal student responses and more fine-grained feedback aligned with instructional use.

Acknowledgments. This work was partially supported by the U.S. National Science Foundation (NSF) [2101104, DMS-2124493, DMS-2311297, DMS-2319279, DMS-2318809]. Any opinions, findings, conclusions, or recommendations expressed in this material are those of the authors and do not necessarily reflect the views of NSF.

Disclosure of Interests. The authors have no competing interests to declare.

References

1. Bahat, Y., Shakhnarovich, G.: Classification confidence estimation with test-time data-augmentation arXiv preprint. arXiv:2006.16705 (2020)
2. Black, P., Wiliam, D.: Assessment and classroom learning assessment in education. Principles, Policy & Practice, **5**(1), 7–74 (1998)
3. Fang, L., Wang, T., Ma, P., Zhai, X.: Generalizable and efficient automated scoring with a knowledge-distilled multi-task mixture-of-experts. In: Proceedings of the AAAI Conference on Artificial Intelligence, vol. 40, pp. 40831–40839 (2026)
4. Fu, Y., Wang, X., Tian, Y., Zhao, J.: Deep think with confidence arXiv preprint (2025). arXiv:2508.15260
5. Gürtl, S., Schimetta, G., Kerschbaumer, D., Liut, M., Steinmaurer, A.: Automated feedback on student-generated UML and er diagrams using large language models arXiv preprint. arXiv:2507.23470 (2025)
6. Han, K., et al.: A survey on vision transformer. IEEE Trans. Pattern Anal. Mach. Intell. **45**(1), 87–110 (2022)
7. Han, Z., Gao, C., Liu, J., Zhang, J., Zhang, S.: Parameter-efficient fine-tuning for large models: a comprehensive survey. arXiv preprint arXiv:2403.14608 (2024)
8. Harris, C.J., Krajcik, J.S., Pellegrino, J.W.: Creating and Using Instructionally Supportive Assessments in NGSS Classrooms. NSTA Press, National Science Teaching Association (2024)
9. Hu, E.J., Shen, Y., Wallis, P., Allen-Zhu, Z., Li, Y., Wang, S., Wang, L., Chen, W.: LoRA: Low-Rank Adaptation of large language models. In: International Conference on Learning Representations (ICLR) (2022)
10. Latif, E., Fang, L., Ma, P., Zhai, X.: Knowledge distillation of LLMS for automatic scoring of science assessments. In: International Conference on Artificial Intelligence in Education, pp. 166–174. Springer (2024). https://doi.org/10.1007/978-3-031-64312-5_20
11. Lee, G., Zhai, X.: NERIF: GPT-4V for automatic scoring of drawn models. J. Sci. Educ. Technol., 1–18 (2025)
12. Lee, J., Lee, G.G., Hong, H.G.: Automated assessment of student hand drawings in free-response items on the particulate nature of matter. J. Sci. Educ. Technol. **32**(4), 549–566 (2023)
13. Leong, C.W., Liu, L., Ubale, R., Chen, L.: Toward large-scale automated scoring of scientific visual models. In: Proceedings of the Fifth Annual ACM Conference on Learning at Scale, pp. 1–4 (2018)
14. Li, T., Haudek, K., Krajcik, J.: Utilizing deep learning ai to analyze scientific models: overcoming challenges. J. Sci. Educ. Technol., 1–22 (2025)
15. Pei, B., Xing, W., Lee, H.S.: Using automatic image processing to analyze visual artifacts created by students in scientific argumentation. Br. J. Edu. Technol. **50**(6), 3391–3404 (2019)
16. Rahaman, M.A., Rahman, T., Hossain, M.M.: Automated grading and classification of hand-drawn sketches using deep learning. In: 2024 International Conference on Innovations in Science, Engineering and Technology (ICISET), pp. 1–6. IEEE (2024)
17. Wang, G., Li, W., Aertsen, M., Deprest, J., Ourselin, S., Vercauteren, T.: Aleatoric uncertainty estimation with test-time augmentation for medical image segmentation with convolutional neural networks. Neurocomputing **338**, 34–45 (2019)

Exploring Question Isomorphism Through Different Numerical Representations

Matheus Valentim[✉][iD] and Max Fowler[iD]

University of Illinois Urbana-Champaign, Champaign, USA
`mfowler5@illinois.edu`

Abstract. Despite their useful applications, isomorphic questions — questions that assess the same underlying concept with comparable difficulty while differing in surface features—- have received less attention than related problems such as question difficulty estimation. To offer a foundation for future research, we investigate whether different questions' numerical representations (question solutions' code embeddings, question stem embeddings, labeling of programming plans required in the solutions and solution code ASTs) can approximate isomorphism. We (1) compare the representations' similarity to items that were designed to be isomorphic (members of their "isomorphic family") against their similarity to items from other families and (2) test if they can recreate the original isomorphic families in an open pool of questions. While three out of four representations hold higher similarity within their own isomorphic families, all representations we investigated perform somewhat poorly in the open pool setting. We discuss what these findings mean for capturing pedagogically meaningful notions of question isomorphism.

Keywords: Question isomorphism · Embeddings · Clustering

1 Introduction and Prior Work

Among multiple interpretations, a question is said to be "isomorphic" if it changes certain aspects of a prior question while otherwise assessing the same "core" ideas [14,17,23]. These changes are variably referred to as a "narrative" change [13]; as "any change that keeps an aspect of the original" [17]; as "superficial" changes that require similar solving approaches [7]; and as changes to aspects of the question that do not affect its difficulty – i.e., "incidentals" [14]. In Computer Science, examples include questions with differing numerical constants, data structures, and function names [7,8,17].

The phenomenon of question isomorphism is fundamental for a range of educational applications [6,9,10,15,18–20,23]. Isomorphic questions can be used as a learning strategy, allowing students to see an underlying concept in different themes and contexts [10,15,18]; as a way to assess student learning on those underlying concepts [6,19,23]; and as a foundation for building large question pools for secure large-scale examinations and high-enrollment courses [9,20].

E. G. Blanchard et al. (Eds.): AIED 2026, LNAI 16583, pp. 351–360, 2027.
https://doi.org/10.1007/978-3-032-29760-0_39

Despite its relevance, there is still a significant gap in the isomorphism literature, particularly regarding a more quantitative identification, especially given the availability of modern tools. In the following sections we briefly review such tools, the initial steps that have been taken towards a more quantitative characterization of the phenomenon and explain our plan to extend it.

1.1   Other Quantitative Approaches Using Question Data

Questions' stems, solution code, and solutions' abstract syntax trees (ASTs), have been widely used to characterize questions, though mostly for question difficulty estimation (QDE). Examples of question stem usage include using stems with IRT-calculated difficulties [2]; experimenting with number of words, average word size and text embeddings [11]; relying on whether the questions were phrased as "true or false", and on the visual aid contained in their stem [5]; and using the position of the correct answer among the multiple choice items and the topic covered in the stem [3]. Examples of questions' solutions and solutions' ASTs include using a combination of historical student data and SQL prompts' ASTs [22]; embeddings for both questions' stems and questions' code solutions [21]; and code similarity - via code embeddings - to analyze assessment bias [12].

In addition to the usage precedent, prior work also suggests these approaches effectively capture question characteristics. Transformer-based architectures perform strongly in text-based difficulty estimation [1]; code embeddings are among the best to indicate similarity in assignment submissions [12]; text embeddings outperform other question-stem proxies [11]; and both text and AST-based representations contribute meaningfully to QDE [22]. In short, embeddings and AST-based representations are often effectively used for characterizing questions.

1.2   Prior Quantitative Work in Isomorphism

Despite the potentially portable efforts mentioned from QDE, most work that has looked at isomorphism through quantitative lenses, did it looking its effect on student performance. Lievens and Sackett [14] explored the correlation between exam grades and how strictly isomorphic questions are defined, finding that looser definitions (e.g. questions about the same topic are isomorphs) had much less correlated exams scores. More recently, both Fowler et al. [7,8] and Parker et al. [17] find that altering what could be considered "non-essential" parts of the question mostly result in similar difficulty statistics, an initial step towards the understanding of the extent to which questions can be considered isomorphic.

Even these efforts, however, have (1) largely remained tied to historical student performance data, (2) have not yet brought new computational tools to the field, and ultimately (3) have not yet laid enough foundations for a more systematic understanding of the phenomenon of isomorphism itself. In this work, we take a first step toward addressing these limitations by systematically exploring numerical and computational representations for question isomorphism. We collected items from an introductory Computer Science course, and used four different representations to assess how well they align with literature-informed notion of isomorphism. We explored questions' solution code embeddings, programming-plan based embeddings, question stem text embeddings and question solution code ASTs to answer the following research question. **RQ:** To what extent do these numerical and computational representations capture or encode the concept of question isomorphism?

We found that while CodeEmb and CodeAST seem to encode isomorphism better than other representations, all representations struggled to accurately recreate original isomorphic families in an open pool of questions.

2   Methods

2.1   Collecting Questions

We collected 461 questions from an introductory Python course aimed at non-CS majors in STEM. It covers a typical suite of concepts, ranging from syntax and basic control flow to a brief introduction to classes and objects, from a large public university in the United States. Questions were labeled as members of an already known "isomorphic family": a collection of isomorphic questions designed to differ only on "superficial features" as defined by Fowler et al. [7,8]. Table 1 contains examples of two different isomorphic families, and question variants belonging to each.

In total we had 461 questions, with 190 isomorphic families. 352 questions were in the 81 isomorphic families that had from two to nine members and 109 questions were in families with one member only. This leads to an average of 2.43 and a standard deviation of 1.98 questions per family. From each of the questions, we extracted the question's stem, question's isomorphic family and an instructor crafted solution (that should capture the *intended* solution for that question given the course) which we used in our numerical representations.

2.2   Generating Numerical Representations

Each question was encoded with four different representations:

1. Solution-code embeddings (CodeEmb, hereinafter), obtained by inputting question solution code in the ada-text-002 embedding generator. Added as it aligns with prior literature [12] and due to the expectation of encoding a "sweetspot" in being sufficiently similar to other isomorphic questions in their family, and different enough from other questions. A text embedding generator was chosen (for this and other representations) for higher comparability between code-based representations and stem-based representations.

2. Question stem embeddings (StemEmb, hereinafter), obtained by inputting question solution code in the ada-text-002 embedding generator. Added as we expected them to encode more information from the "student-facing" side of the question, which would be unique among our representations, as others encode information from the "solution" side;

Table 1. Two example isomorphic question families. Each family contains variants where only **superficial aspects** (highlighted in bold when in the prompt) are modified. Some repeated text is replaced with —...—.

Function	Prompt	Variation
def sum_even_nums(input_list):	The function below takes an argument: a list, input_list add all **even** numbers from the **input_list** and return that sum.	Base question
def sum_odd_nums(input_list):	[...] add all **odd numbers** from the **input_list** and return that sum.	**even → odd**
def mult_even_nums(input_list):	[...] multiply all **even numbers** from the **input_list** and return that result (return 1 if none).	**sum → product**
Family 2: Counting numbers from a list (polarity, variable name variants)		
def count_over_100(number_list):	The function below takes one parameter: a list of numbers (**number_list**). Complete the function to count how many of the numbers in the list are **greater than 100**.	Base question
def count_over_100(number_list):	[...] count how many of the numbers in the list are **greater than or equal to 100**.	**greater than → greater than or equal to**
def count_over_100(info_list):	[...] count how many of the numbers in the list are **greater than 100**.	**number_list → info_list**

Table title "Family 1: Aggregate values from list (even/odd, sum/multiply variants)" spans the first grouping.

3. Programming-plan embeddings (PPEmb, hereinafter), obtained by prompting ChatGPT 4.1 with the question solution and asking it to identify programming plans in it with *"You are a programming teacher. Identify which programming plans are present in the solution, e.g. pps_list Respond only with the name of the plans. There may be more than one plan.".* Where pps_list is a compilation of 10 programming plans based on prior literature:"Looping adding values", "Looping looking for best", "Looping indefenetely", "Looping processing items", "Selection With Two Alternatives", "Selection With Multiple Alternatives", "Selection with multiple possible non-alternating results", "Eveness Check", "Recursion", "Finding a minimum or a maximum", and "Triangular Swap". This follows a succesful method by Demirtas et al. [4] that finds ChatGPT4.o highly capable (around 86% to 95%) of finding plans,

all while using a cheaper and widely considered more capable model. For each unique combination of identified programming plans (even the ones with "none", 9% of total), we averaged all CodeEmb (our first representation) for that combination.

4. Question solution's Abstract Syntax Tree (CodeAST, hereinafter), obtained by applying Python's ast package on the solution code. Added also due to the expectation of "sweetspot" encoding.

2.3   Evaluating Similarity Intra and Inter Isomorphic Families

For our first experiment, we tested each of our four question representations to check if they had a higher similarity with representations of items of the same isomorphic family than with items' representations from other isomorphic families. As a metric for similarity between the items, we used cosine similarity for the 3 embedding-based representations. For CodeAST we used the AST simple distance function from the *ast* Python package. To calculate the intra-family similarity, we chose a question representation, calculated the similarity from one item to all other items in one family, using that representation, and then averaged those similarities. Similarly, for the inter-famility similarity, one representation a time, we calculate the similarity of each item with all items that do not belong to its family, then we average all these similarities.

To calculate these metrics, we had to cut out the 109 questions which were in families with a single question, retaining 76% of our questions for this step. Having done that, we had four intra-family similarities and four inter-family similarity for each of the remaining 352 questions, one similarity for each of the numerical representations. To determine whether the similarity was significantly higher among members of the same family than with members of other families, we conducted, for each representation a pair-wise t-test using the 352 long vectors.

2.4   Clustering in an Open Question Pool

For our second experiment, we used each of our four representations, independently, to cluster both all 461 questions and then just the 352 questions that belonged to a family with more than one question. We then evaluate how well they could recreate the original boundaries of the isomorphic families. We used HDBSCAN [16] as our clustering algorithm mainly because we didn't want to directly chose a number of clusters (as we'd have to in k-means). HDBSCAN also accommodates the variability of cluster size (varying size isomorphic families) better. We transformed our embedding-based representations (which were too high dimensional) using standard PCA, reaching 40, 60, 70 and 80 dimensions for CodeEmb and StemEmb and 4,6 and 7 dimensions for our PPEmb (those dimensions maintained 60% to 80% of their variance, following common practice). We also changed our CodeAST (originally not in a numerical-vectorial format) by using an anchor-based distance encoding. We created a vectorial representation for each question by calculating 40 AST distances (using *ast* Python package's "simple distance") from that question's AST representation and to a set of fixed, randomly chosen, "anchor" questions.

3   Findings

Across two experiments, we found that, in response to our **RQ**, (1) some representations seem to encode isomorphism better than others, but (2) no representation is capable of accurately recreating the original isomorphic families (Table 2).

3.1   Some Representations Yield Greater Intra-/inter-Family Separation Than Others

Table 2. Intra- and Inter-Family Statistics for Question Representations (Cosine similarity for embeddings and AST distance for ASTs, p-value shown for mean difference)

Rep	Intra-Family				Inter-Family				
	Mean	Std	25%	75%	Mean	Std	25%	75%	p-value
CodeEmb	0.778	0.117	0.718	0.855	0.210	0.039	0.188	0.236	0***
PPEmb	0.952	0.096	0.965	1.000	0.857	0.089	0.860	0.905	0***
StemEmb	0.252	0.080	0.200	0.297	0.239	0.039	0.217	0.265	0.98
CodeAST	17.478	23.239	0.000	31.000	129.196	35.991	105.454	136.628	0***

When testing whether representations yield higher intra- than inter-family similarity, distinct patterns emerge. CodeEmb and CodeAST show the largest, statistically significant separations in intra- and inter-family similarity. In CodeEmb, for example, 75% of intra-family similarities are at or above 0.718, while 75% of inter-family similarities were at 0.236 or lower. This means that the these methods achieved the goal of high similarity within question families and lower similarity across other items. This may indicate that code-based representations have less noise than other representations. It may also be that, given isomorphic questions are designed to have similar solutions, solution-based embeddings will capture this similarity.

PPEmb also achieved statistically significant differences between intra- and inter-family similarities, but their values were much closer. It may be that PPEmb is a much coarser representation due to the small number of programming plans, which means even non-isomorphic questions share plans. StemEmb suffered from the opposite problem. Embedding question stems seems to have made the questions representations too specific, resulting in the lowest similarity values and no statistical significance.

3.2   No Representation Adequately Recreated the Original Families from the Full Open Question Set

When clustering in an open pool of questions, our results were consistent across both the full dataset and the 352-question subset of questions from multi-member families. Our representations exhibited two distinct patterns: CodeEmb and StemEmb produced 40 clusters, whereas PPEmb and CodeAST produced only two. These reduced number of clusters compared to our initial set of families shows how our representations were seemingly not granular enough to capture our specific isomorphs. To capture our original isomorphic families, at least 81 (the number of multi-member families in our dataset) clusters should have been found.

The ARI metrics for our clustering provide further insight into this failure to reproduce the original isomorphic families. CodeEmb, the best ARI, was *only* 0.21, while the others scored near the performance of random clustering. The pairwise metric indicates that very few pairs of questions that were together in the original families remained together in our prediction. Despite the low ARI, CodeEmb and StemEmb retained information about the families' original structure, as reflected in their higher NMI scores (Table 3). Together, these metrics confirm that the representations capture structure but lack granularity.

3.3   Our Representations Encode Some but Not All Traits of Isomorphism

Even though some of our representations were successful in our first analysis, their struggle in accurately recreating the original families during clustering indicates that they only encode isomorphism to *some* extent. It may be that these representations can be useful for removing unfitting items from an isomorphic family but they are not yet appropriate for producing full isomorphic families. Educational applications that require them to fully define the proximity of questions are, therefore, still likely out of reach.

In addition to their general performance, the representations also displayed patterns that allowed us to speculate whether certain traits correlate with an improvement in representing isomorphism. First, being solution-focused seemed to positively impact the representations. CodeEmb, CodeAST and PPEmb all managed to differentiate between members of their own family and other families at some level of statistical significance, and CodeEmb had the best results in clustering. We believe they could encode isomorphism better because a defining trait of isomorphic questions is having similar approaches to their solutions, which these representations capture. Second, granularity also seemed to positively impact isomorphism encoding. Our coarser representation, PPEmb, led to comparatively higher similarity with items from other isomorphic families than more fine-grained representations. More granular representations also yielded better results in clustering. Finally, natural language based embeddings may be at a disadvantage in this context as our code-based representations yielded overall better results: CodeEmb, for example, was consistently more effective than StemEmb. It may be that shared words between stems introduce added difficulty in delineating between isomorphs.

Table 3. Clustering Performance Metrics for Different Representations. AST does not use PCA, so the "PCA dims" should be read "dimensions" (*) for AST.

Representation	PCA dims	ARI (range)	NMI (range)
StemEmb	40–80	0.002–0.005	0.553–0.581
CodeEmb	40–80	0.132–0.210	0.769–0.804
PPEmb	4–7	0.002	0.112–0.120
AST	40*	0.010	0.208

4 Limitations, Future Work and Conclusion

Our analysis holds some limitations, as our investigation methods are exploratory. First, the chosen ways we used to create PPEmb and to adapt CodeAST, especially in our clustering leaves uncertainty about whether some results reflected true deficiencies in the representations or limitations of our choices. Especially for PPEmb, different sets of programming plans, at different granularities, could have potentially yielded different results. We particularly hope future work extends the foundation we attempted to build and explores new methods for determining useful representations of isomorphism.

Disclosure of Interests. The authors have no competing interests to declare that are relevant to the content of this article.

References

1. Benedetto, L., Wang, N., Rebolledo-Mendez, G., Dimitrova, V., Matsuda, N.: Artificial intelligence in education. Posters and late breaking results, workshops and tutorials, industry and innovation tracks, practitioners, doctoral consortium and blue sky. In: A Quantitative Study of NLP Approaches to Question Difficulty Estimation (2023). https://doi.org/10.1007/978-3-031-36336-8_67
2. Benedetto, L., Aradelli, G., Cremonesi, P., Cappelli, A., Giussani, A., Turrin, R.: On the application of transformers for estimating the difficulty of multiple-choice questions from text. In: Proceedings of the 16th Workshop on Innovative Use of NLP for Building Educational Applications (2021)
3. Boldt, R.F., Freedle, R.: Using a neural net to predict item difficulty. ETS Res. Rep. Ser (2) (1996). https://doi.org/10.1002/j.2333-8504.1996.tb01709.x
4. Demirtaş, M.A., Zheng, C., Cunningham, K.: Detecting programming plans in open-ended code submissions. In: Proceedings of the 56th ACM Technical Symposium on Computer Science Education V. 2, pp. 1435–1436. Association for Computing Machinery, New York, NY, USA (2025). https://doi.org/10.1145/3641555.3705166 SIGCSETS 2025
5. El Masri, Y.H., Ferrara, S., Foltz, P.W., Baird, J.A.: Predicting item difficulty of science national curriculum tests: the case of key stage 2 assessments. Curricul. J. **28**(1), 59–82 (2017). https://doi.org/10.1080/09585176.2016.1232201

6. Fleisher, D.S., Schwenker, J.: Isomorphic patient management problems: a method of creating equivalent problem-solving tests. Med. Educ. **21**(3), 207–212 (1987). https://doi.org/10.1111/j.1365-2923.1987.tb00692.x
7. Fowler, M., Smith, D.H., Zilles, C.: Quickly producing "'isomorphic" exercises: quantifying the impact of programming question permutations. In: Proceedings of the 2024 on Innovation and Technology in Computer Science Education V. 1, pp. 178–184. ACM, Milan Italy (2024). https://doi.org/10.1145/3649217.3653617
8. Fowler, M., Zilles, C.: Superficial code-guise: investigating the impact of surface feature changes on students' programming question scores. In: Proceedings of the 52nd ACM Technical Symposium on Computer Science Education, pp. 3–9. ACM, Virtual Event USA (2021). https://doi.org/10.1145/3408877.3432413
9. Goolsby-Cole, C., Bass, S.M., Stanwyck, L., Leupen, S., Carpenter, T.S., Hodges, L.C.: Issues of question equivalence in online exam pools. J. Coll. Sci. Teach. **52**(4), 24–30 (2023). https://doi.org/10.1080/0047231X.2023.12290629
10. Greer, B., Harel, G.: The role of isomorphisms in mathematical cognition. J. Math. Behav. **17**(1), 5–24 (1998). https://doi.org/10.1016/S0732-3123(99)80058-3
11. Ha, L.A., Yaneva, V., Baldwin, P., Mee, J.: Predicting the difficulty of multiple choice questions in a high-stakes medical exam. In: Proceedings of the Fourteenth Workshop on Innovative Use of NLP for Building Educational Applications, pp. 11–20. Association for Computational Linguistics (2019). https://doi.org/10.18653/v1/W19-4402
12. Johnson-Yu, S., Bowman, N., Sahami, M., Piech, C.: SimGrade: using code similarity measures for more accurate human grading (2024). https://doi.org/10.48550/arXiv.2403.14637, arXiv:2403.14637
13. Kotovsky, K., Hayes, J., Simon, H.: Why are some problems hard? Evidence from Tower of Hanoi. Cogn. Psychol. **17**(2), 248–294 (1985). https://doi.org/10.1016/0010-0285(85)90009-X
14. Lievens, F., Sackett, P.R.: Situational judgment tests in high-stakes settings: issues and strategies with generating alternate forms. J. Appl. Psychol. **92**(4), 1043–1055 (2007). https://doi.org/10.1037/0021-9010.92.4.1043
15. Lin, S.Y., Singh, C.: Using isomorphic problems to learn introductory physics. Phys. Rev. Spec. Top. Phys. Educ. Res. **7**(2), 020104 (2011). https://doi.org/10.1103/PhysRevSTPER.7.020104
16. Malzer, C., Baum, M.: A hybrid approach to hierarchical density-based cluster selection. In: 2020 IEEE International Conference on Multisensor Fusion and Integration for Intelligent Systems (MFI), pp. 223–228. IEEE (2020). https://doi.org/10.1109/mfi49285.2020.9235263
17. Parker, M.C., Garcia, L., Kao, Y.S., Franklin, D., Krause, S., Warschauer, M.: A pair of ACES: an analysis of isomorphic questions on an elementary computing assessment. In: Proceedings of the 2022 ACM Conference on International Computing Education Research - Volume 1, pp. 2–14. ACM, Lugano and Virtual Event Switzerland (2022). https://doi.org/10.1145/3501385.3543979
18. Pastoriko, F.M., Retnowati, E.: How to create isomorphic example-problem pairs for facilitating analogical thinking. J. Phys: Conf. Ser. **1397**(1), 012083 (2019). https://doi.org/10.1088/1742-6596/1397/1/012083
19. Singh, C.: Assessing student expertise in introductory physics with isomorphic problems. II. Effect of some potential factors on problem solving and transfer. Phys. Rev. Special Top. Phys. Educ. Res. **4**(1), 010105 (2008). https://doi.org/10.1103/PhysRevSTPER.4.010105

20. Sinharay, S., Johnson, M.: Analysis of data from an admissions test with item models. ETS Res. Rep. Ser. **2005**(1), 32 (2005). https://doi.org/10.1002/j.2333-8504.2005.tb01983.x
21. Wang, Z., Zhang, W., Wang, J.: Estimating difficulty levels of programming problems with pre-trained model. ArXiv abs/2406.08828 (2024). https://api.semanticscholar.org/CorpusID:270440564
22. Xu, J., Tingting Wei, Lv, P.: SQL-DP: A novel difficulty prediction framework for SQL programming problems. In: Proceedings of the 15th International Conference on Educational Data Mining (2022). https://doi.org/10.5281/ZENODO.6852986, publisher: Zenodo
23. Zingaro, D., Porter, L.: Tracking student learning from class to exam using isomorphic questions. In: Proceedings of the 46th ACM Technical Symposium on Computer Science Education, pp. 356–361. ACM, Kansas City Missouri USA (2015). https://doi.org/10.1145/2676723.2677239

A Generator-Aligner Pipeline for LLM-Based Situational Judgment Test Generation

Xinyi He[1,2] , Cixiao Wang[1] , and Feng Ji[2(✉)]

[1] Beijing Normal University, No. 19, Xinjiekouwai Street, Haidian,
Beijing 100875, China
`wangcixiao@bnu.edu.cn`
[2] University of Toronto, Toronto, ON M5S 1A1, Canada
`f.ji@utoronto.ca`

Abstract. Situational Judgment Tests (SJTs) are widely used to assess practice-oriented competencies, yet their development remains labour-intensive and difficult to scale across contexts. Recent advances in large language models (LLMs) offer new opportunities for automating SJT generation, yet concerns remain about the validity of AI-generated items. This study proposes a generatoraligner workflow that separates generation from validation and examines the distinct and combined roles of these components through a four-condition comparative design. Specifically, the workflow incorporates a retrieval-augmented Generator to enhance situational authenticity and contextual richness, and an Aligner to strengthen construct relevance and alignment during validation. A total of 54 LLM-generated SJT scenarios were independently evaluated by four human reviewers in terms of construct relevance and situational authenticity. The results show that retrieval augmentation improves contextual richness but does not consistently strengthen construct alignment when used without supervisory validation. In contrast, pipelines incorporating alignment mechanisms achieve higher and more stable authenticity and relevance. Moreover, the combined pipeline improves convergence efficiency by reducing the number of iterative revisions required to reach alignment acceptance.

Keywords: Multi-agent · Situational judgment tests · AI pedagogy · Retrieval-augmented generation · Construct alignment

1 Introduction

Situational Judgment Tests (SJTs) assess competencies by placing individuals in realistic scenarios and examining their judgments or actions [3]. In education, they are increasingly used to measure non-cognitive, practice-oriented competencies such as professional judgment, self-regulation, and socialemotional dispositions [4,5], for example in teacher professional development and the assessment of instructional practice. However, designing high-quality SJTs is highly

E. G. Blanchard et al. (Eds.): AIED 2026, LNAI 16583, pp. 361–369, 2027.
https://doi.org/10.1007/978-3-032-29760-0_40

resource-intensive: it requires substantial expert input, multiple review rounds, and extensive validation, limiting their scalability and adaptability in educational contexts.

Recent advances in large language models (LLMs) have opened new avenues for automatic item generation. With their ability to produce coherent, linguistically diverse text, LLMs are increasingly used for item development [13]. Empirical validation studies have begun to examine the psychometric quality of LLM-generated items. Attali and Powers [1] evaluated ChatGPT-generated questions and found that they could approximate human-authored items in difficulty and discrimination, though expert oversight remained essential for quality assurance. A large-scale validation by Muszyński [8] using TIMSS Grade 4 items further showed that while many LLM-generated items met basic quality thresholds, they exhibited misaligned difficulty levels and low discrimination without systematic human review. These findings suggest that, while LLMs can support assessment development, more rigorous, process-oriented methods are needed to ensure quality and methodological soundness. Key challenges include ensuring construct–item alignment and producing defensible validity evidence [7,9]. These concerns are amplified in SJTs, where scenarios must be both construct-faithful and ecologically plausible [12]; without safeguards, LLM-generated scenarios may trade off realism against construct specificity, undermining interpretive usefulness.

A growing line of work explores multi-agent LLM architectures to address quality limitations inherent in single-pass generation. In automated scoring, Wang et al. [11] proposed AutoSCORE, a two-agent framework in which one agent extracts rubric-relevant components from student responses and another assigns scores, achieving consistent improvements over single-agent baselines on complex rubrics. For item generation, Guo et al. [2] introduced ReQUESTA, a hybrid multi-agent system that decomposes multiple-choice question authoring into parallel cognitive-level subtasks, producing items that are more discriminative and better aligned with reading comprehension performance than single-pass baselines. These studies demonstrate the promise of distributing generation and evaluation across specialized agents, yet no prior work has applied such architectures to SJT scenario development, where scenarios must simultaneously satisfy construct fidelity and contextual authenticity.

To address these challenges, this study proposes a dual-agent GeneratorAligner architecture for LLM-based SJT scenario generation. The Generator produces candidate scenarios grounded in explicit construct definitions and, optionally, authentic teaching cases retrieved via RAG; the Aligner evaluates construct correspondence and provides iterative revision feedback. The present study implements this architecture under four pipeline configurations that vary the use of retrieval augmentation and supervisory validation, enabling descriptive comparisons of their independent and combined effects on scenario quality and stability. Accordingly, we address the following research question.

RQ: How do different combinations of generation support and alignment filtering affect the quality and efficiency of SJT item generation?

Table 1. Operational definitions of AI Pedagogy constructs

Construct	Operational Definition
AI-Supported Instructional Planning	Purposeful integration of AI into lesson design, including task formulation, learning objective alignment, activity structuring, and anticipation of AIstudent interaction while maintaining pedagogical coherence.
AI-Mediated Classroom Enactment	Real-time orchestration of AI-enhanced classroom interactions, including management of student AI use, facilitation of inquiry and dialogue, regulation of over-reliance on AI outputs, and maintenance of human-centered authority.
AI-Informed Assessment and Feedback	Interpretation, validation, and strategic use of AI-generated analytics and feedback, with attention to system limitations, bias, reliability, and ethical justification of assessment decisions.

2 Method

2.1 Construct Framework

The development of SJT scenarios was grounded in a construct framework of *AI Pedagogy*, developed by the authors for the purposes of this study. Drawing on the UNESCO AI Competency Framework for Teachers [10], which delineates foundational, intermediate, and advanced competencies for teaching with AI, we adapted and extended its competency dimensions to the specific instructional contexts targeted by our SJT scenarios. AI Pedagogy conceptualizes teachers' competencies in integrating AI into instructional practice while maintaining pedagogical coherence and human-centered decision-making. To reflect the temporal structure of instructional practice, the construct was organized into three phase-level components: planning (pre-class), enactment (in-class), and assessment (post-class). The operational definitions of the constructs are summarized in Table 1.

2.2 Dual-Agent Architecture

The dual-agent architecture separates scenario creation from construct verification. The two agents operate in an iterative generationvalidation loop: the Generator produces candidate scenarios, and the Aligner evaluates their construct consistency. When misalignment is detected, the Aligner's feedback is incorporated into the Generator's current-item memory to guide revision.

Generator: Scenario Generation Agent. The Generator creates SJT scenarios from structured task instructions. It takes as input (a) the focal construct and its definition, (b) information about the instructional stage and sub-process, (c) optional few-shot examples, and (d) authentic cases retrieved via RAG. The authentic cases come from submissions to the 2025 AI Teaching Innovation Case Competition (https://mp.weixin.qq.com/s/gIKnTK_kK30PIypaogDfpg) and reflect AI-supported instructional practices implemented in real educational settings. Together, these inputs constrain the structure, contextual boundaries, and central decision dilemma of the scenario, thereby ensuring that the resulting scenarios are grounded in instructional practice.

Aligner: Supervisory Validation Agent. The Aligner applies a set of structured criteria that parallel human judgments of construct relevance (see Table 2). For each scenario, it produces a binary validation decision along with a brief rationale. To ensure comparability across conditions, each scenario is allowed up to **10** revision attempts. If this limit is reached, the version with the highest alignment score is retained for subsequent human review.

Language Models and Inference Settings. Both the Generator and the Aligner were powered by GPT-4o-mini (OpenAI). The Generator used a temperature of 0.4 with a maximum output length of 500 tokens to balance creativity and coherence in scenario generation. The Aligner used a lower temperature of 0.1 with a maximum output length of 1,200 tokens to promote deterministic and consistent validation judgments. For retrieval-augmented conditions, case embeddings were computed using `text2vec-base-chinese` and indexed in a vector store; the top-k ($k = 3$) most similar cases were retrieved and injected into the Generator prompt.

2.3   Human Review Rubric

Four independent reviewers evaluated each generated SJT scenario on a 5-point Likert scale (1 = very low, 5 = very high). Two doctoral students in educational technology independently rated construct relevance, and two in-service teachers (each with at least five years of classroom experience) independently rated situational authenticity. Relevance refers to the degree of alignment with the intended AI Pedagogy construct, while authenticity pertains to the plausibility of the situation in a real classroom. The evaluation criteria are summarized in Table 2. To assess inter-rater reliability, intraclass correlation coefficients (ICC[2,1], two-way random, single measures, absolute agreement) were computed for each dimension. The ICC for construct relevance was 0.72 (95% CI [0.59, 0.84]), indicating moderate-to-good agreement, and the ICC for situational authenticity was 0.56 (95% CI [0.35, 0.72]), indicating moderate agreement [6].

2.4   Experimental Design and Conditions

The dual-agent architecture was implemented under four pipeline configurations that vary the use of RAG and supervisory validation. As shown in Fig. 1, four conditions are constructed:

Table 2. Human evaluation rubric for SJT scenarios

Dimension	Description
Construct Relevance	Assesses whether the scenario specifically targets the intended AI Pedagogy construct rather than general teaching knowledge. Reviewers evaluated whether the construct is necessary to differentiate meaningful responses. Higher scores indicate clear reliance on AI-integration competencies.
Situational Authenticity	Assesses whether the scenario reflects situations plausibly occurring in AI-supported classrooms. Reviewers evaluated whether teachers could realistically encounter or imagine the situation. Higher scores indicate strong contextual grounding.

- **Baseline**: Few-shot prompting without RAG or supervisory validation.
- **Group 1 (RAG-only)**: Few-shot prompting augmented with RAG, without supervisory validation.
- **Group 2 (Aligner-only)**: Zoro-shot generation with supervisory validation via the Aligner to minimize exemplar effects.
- **Group 3 (RAG + Aligner)**: Few-shot generation augmented with RAG and followed by supervisory validation.

A total of 54 SJT scenarios were generated across conditions (Baseline: $n = 14$; Group 1: $n = 13$; Group 2: $n = 13$; Group 3: $n = 14$). Each scenario was independently evaluated by four reviewers: two doctoral students in educational technology assessed construct relevance, and two in-service teachers assessed situational authenticity. All ratings used 5-point Likert scales.

3   Results

Table 3 presents human-rated construct relevance and authenticity across conditions. With respect to authenticity, the Baseline condition showed relatively low authenticity ratings ($M = 3.07$, $SD = 0.83$). Introducing RAG without alignment (Group 1) was associated with a modest increase in authenticity ($M = 3.23$, $SD = 0.83$), accompanied by substantial variability. In contrast, both Aligner-mediated conditions demonstrated higher authenticity ratings, with Group 2 reaching a mean of $M = 4.31$ ($SD = 0.75$) and Group 3 achieving the highest authenticity score ($M = 4.36$, $SD = 0.50$). With respect to construct relevance, both non-aligned conditions exhibited comparatively low relevance ratings (Baseline: $M = 3.14$, $SD = 1.29$; Group 1: $M = 3.62$, $SD = 1.56$). In contrast, the two Aligner-mediated pipelines achieved higher relevance scores, with Group 2 obtaining the highest mean relevance ($M = 4.60$, $SD = 0.84$), followed closely by Group 3 ($M = 4.57$, $SD = 0.51$).

Figure 2 presents the distributions of human-rated authenticity and relevance across pipelines. With respect to authenticity, the Baseline condition shows the widest dispersion, with a low-end tail extending to 1, whereas Groups 1, 2, and 3 are largely concentrated in the 4–5 range. With respect to construct relevance,

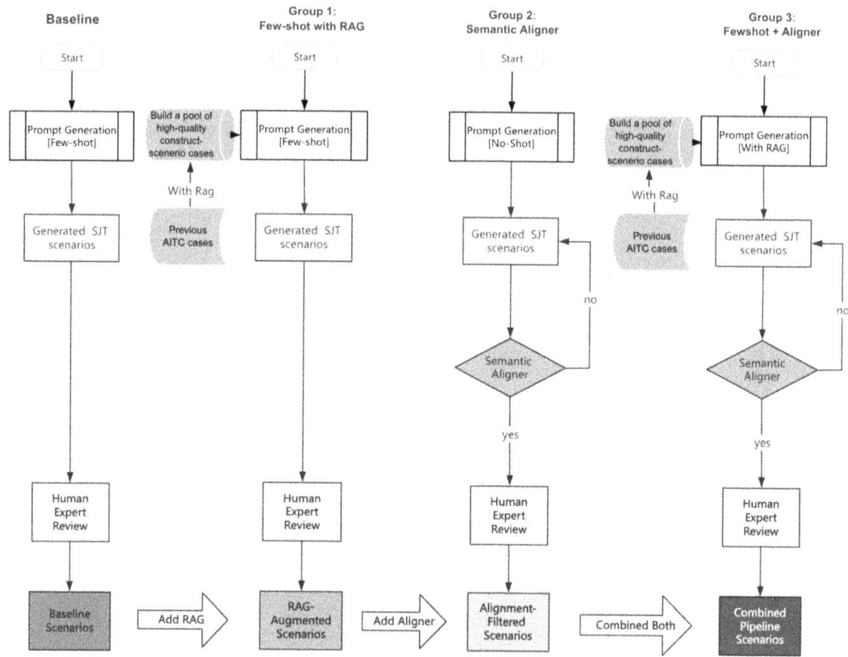

Fig. 1. Dual-agent experimental pipelines for SJT generation across varying generation and supervisory validation conditions

Table 3. Human evaluation metrics across experimental conditions

Group	n	Authenticity M (SD)	Relevance M (SD)
Baseline	14	3.07 (0.83)	3.14 (1.29)
Group 1	13	3.23 (0.83)	3.62 (1.56)
Group 2	13	4.31 (0.75)	4.60 (0.84)
Group 3	14	4.36 (0.50)	4.57 (0.51)

Note. Relevance = mean human rating of construct alignment; Authenticity = mean human rating of contextual realism.

the Baseline condition exhibits a collapsed distribution around the midpoint (approximately 3) with several outliers; Group 1 shifts upward to a 3–4 range, while Groups 2 and 3 cluster in the 45 range with medians close to 5.

Table 4 further illustrates the validation trade-offs introduced by LLM-mediated alignment. Among the aligned pipelines, Group 3 achieved the highest LLM acceptance rate (51.9%) and required the fewest revision attempts (M = 6.26), suggesting more efficient convergence during automated validation. In contrast, Group 2 required more revision cycles on average (M = 7.44), indicating higher iterative cost to reach acceptance.

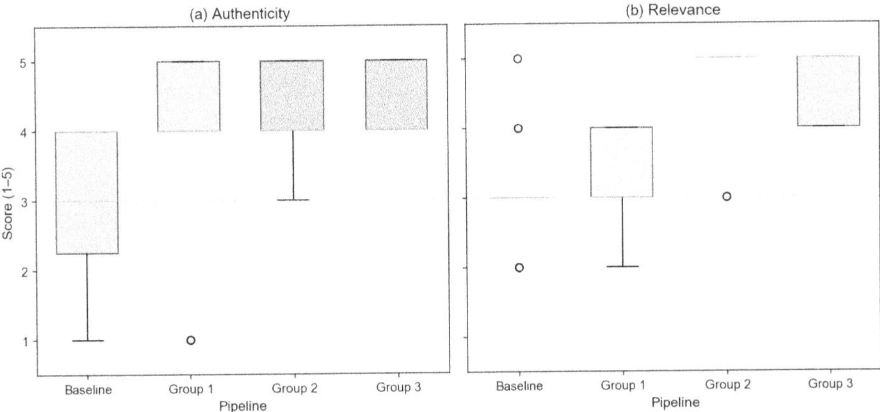

Fig. 2. Distribution of human-rated authenticity and relevance across pipelines.

Table 4. Validation trade-offs introduced by LLM-mediated alignment.

Group	Alignment	LLM pass (%)	Mean attempts
Aligner-only (G2)	Yes	40.7	7.44
RAG + Aligner (G3)	Yes	51.9	6.26

Note. LLM pass was calculated at the validation-attempt level. Mean attempts refers to the average number of revision attempts required for accepted scenarios.

Table 5 reports human ratings for items the Aligner accepted versus those it rejected. In Group 2, accepted items received slightly higher average authenticity scores (4.67 vs. 4.00), while their relevance ratings were similar to those of rejected items (4.67 vs. 4.50). In Group 3, by contrast, items accepted by the Aligner had lower mean relevance (4.44 vs. 4.80) and authenticity (4.22 vs. 4.80) than items that were rejected.

Table 5. Human ratings by Aligner pass status

Group	Aligner status	n	Relevance M	Authenticity M
Group 2	Passed	6	4.67	4.67
Group 2	Not passed	7	4.50	4.00
Group 3	Passed	9	4.44	4.22
Group 3	Not passed	5	4.80	4.80

4   Discussion, Implication and Limitations

This study moves beyond prompt-only LLM item generation by separating item creation from construct verification in a dual-agent pipeline. Relative to generation-only baselines [13], adding an Alignment Agent improved human-rated construct relevance and authenticity, whereas retrieval augmentation mainly enhanced contextual plausibility without consistently strengthening construct alignment. Notably, Aligner scores did not always mirror human judgments: in Group 3, items rejected for containing embedded resolution cues were often rated as more relevant and authentic than Aligner-accepted items (Table 5). This divergence points to a trade-off between structural compliance and contextual richness, suggesting automated alignment should serve as a first-pass filter that complements, rather than replaces expert review in assessment development.

These results should be interpreted in light of several scope conditions. The item pool and sample sizes were chosen to enable controlled comparison of pipeline components rather than to maximize generalizability; larger-scale replications would therefore help estimate effect sizes more precisely and extend findings across content domains. A further methodological boundary concerns the Aligner: while it provides a rigid, rule-based operationalization of constraint, it may not capture the full range of expert nuances, suggesting that hybrid approaches combining rules with learned signals are a promising next step. More broadly, following Song et al. [9], future work should scale to larger item pools and incorporate additional sources of validity evidence to move from proof-of-concept toward operational deployment.

References

1. Attali, Y., Powers, D.: Evaluating the psychometric properties of ChatGPT-generated questions. Comput. Educ. Artif. Intell. **7**, 100267 (2024). https://doi.org/10.1016/j.caeai.2024.100284
2. Guo, Q., McNamara, D.S., Lan, A.: Cognitively diverse multiple-choice question generation: a hybrid multi-agent framework with large language models. arXiv preprint arXiv:2602.03704 (2026)
3. Kepes, S., Keener, S.K., Lievens, F., McDaniel, M.A.: An integrative, systematic review of the situational judgment test literature. J. Manag. **51**(6), 2278–2319 (2025). https://doi.org/10.1177/01492063241288545
4. Kiessling, C., et al.: Development and validation of a computer-based situational judgement test to assess medical students' communication skills in the field of shared decision making. Patient Educ. Couns. **99**(11), 1858–1864 (2016). https://doi.org/10.1016/j.pec.2016.06.006
5. Klassen, R., et al.: Developing a proof-of-concept selection test for entry into primary teacher education programs. Int. J. Assess. Tools Educ. **4**(2), 96–114 (2016). https://doi.org/10.21449/ijate.275772, http://dergipark.gov.tr/doi/10.21449/ijate.275772, source: DOI.org (Crossref)
6. Koo, T.K., Li, M.Y.: A guideline of selecting and reporting intraclass correlation coefficients for reliability research. J. Chiropr. Med. **15**(2), 155–163 (2016). https://doi.org/10.1016/j.jcm.2016.02.012

7. Liu, O.L., Mao, L., Frankel, L., Xu, J.: Assessing critical thinking in higher education: the HEIghten^{TM} approach and preliminary validity evidence. Assess. Eval. High. Educ. **41**(5), 677–694 (2016). https://doi.org/10.1080/02602938.2016.1168358
8. Muszyński, M.: Using large language models for automatic item generation: development and validation for TIMSS fourth grade. Tech. rep., International Association for the Evaluation of Educational Achievement (IEA) (2025). https://www.iea.nl/publications/rd-outcomes/using-LLM-automatic-item-generation
9. Song, Y., Du, J., Zheng, Q.: Automatic item generation for educational assessments: a systematic literature review. Interact. Learn. Environ. **33**(9), 5386–5405 (2025). https://doi.org/10.1080/10494820.2025.2482588
10. UNESCO: AI Competency Framework for Students. UNESCO, Paris (2024). https://doi.org/10.54675/JKJB9835
11. Wang, Y., Ding, Z., Wu, X., Sun, S., Liu, N., Zhai, X.: AutoSCORE: enhancing automated scoring with multi-agent large language models via structured component recognition. In: Proceedings of the AAAI Conference on Artificial Intelligence (2026)
12. Whetzel, D., Sullivan, T., McCloy, R.: Situational judgment tests: an overview of development practices and psychometric characteristics. Personnel Assess. Decis. **6**(1) (2020). https://doi.org/10.25035/pad.2020.01.001, https://scholarworks.bgsu.edu/pad/vol6/iss1/1/
13. Zhang, Z., Tu, Z., Chen, Y., Xiao, X., Feng, Y., Zhang, W.: Automated item generation for personality assessment: development and validation of large-language-model-derived HEXACO situational judgment tests. J. Res. Pers. **120**, 104680 (Feb2026). 10.1016/j.jrp.2025.104680, https://www.sciencedirect.com/science/article/pii/S0092656625001126

When Can We Trust AI Coding of Student-Generated Text? A Committee-Based Approach to Diagnosing Agreement and Uncertainty at Scale

Fanjie Li[(✉)] , Madison Lee Mason , Daniel T. Levin ,
and Alyssa Friend Wise

Vanderbilt University, Nashville, TN, USA
{fanjie.li,madison.j.lee,daniel.t.levin,alyssa.wise}@vanderbilt.edu

Abstract. This paper operationalizes a committee-based performance diagnostic framework that combines inter-model agreement, consensus entropy, and borderline rate to support interpretable monitoring of AI coding of student text on unlabeled data. In a pilot application to nursing simulation reflections, these complementary metrics revealed distinct ensemble patterns, including stable consensus and divergence between agreement and decisiveness. The results illustrate how committee diagnostics can support ongoing oversight of AI coding as systems encounter new learners, contexts, and language use at scale.

Keywords: Automated Coding · LLMs · Uncertainty Quantification

1 Introduction

AIED systems increasingly rely on automated interpretation of student-generated text such as written explanations, short responses, and dialogue to deliver adaptive support [2,11]. Recent advances in large language models have lowered the barriers to large-scale automated text analysis; but the value of such systems depends on maintaining coherent behavior beyond training and testing as models encounter new learners, contexts and forms of expression. In practice, however, such AI coding pipelines rarely include systematic mechanisms for ongoing post-deployment validation or monitoring. Even when methods such as confidence monitoring or drift detection [4] are employed, these techniques typically focus on changes in individual predictions or input distributions, offering limited visibility into whether models continue to produce consistent, aligned interpretations of target constructs once deployed. In educational settings, this can result in misleading feedback, inappropriate agent responses, or misaligned system actions. As the use of LLM-based coding rapidly expands, ensuring that AIED systems continue to respond appropriately to the constructs they are intended to detect across learners, contexts, and time requires new approaches to monitoring automated AI analysis of student-generated text throughout the system lifecycle. To address this gap, this paper introduces a committee-based diagnostic framework that integrates measures of inter-model agreement, decisiveness, and certainty to support interpretable monitoring of automated coding on unlabeled data. The contribution lies not in the individual metrics themselves, which build on established approaches, but in how they are used together to characterize ensemble behavior for each construct and support actionable interpretation over time. We first introduce the *Reflect* system as a motivating context in nursing education, then describe the proposed approach and diagnostics, and finally demonstrate feasibility through an initial proof-of-concept using pilot data.

2   Background: Nursing Simulations and *Reflect* System

Simulation-based education is central to nursing preparation, giving students realistic clinical practice while cultivating the cognitive and metacognitive work required for clinical judgment [7,15]. Currently, much of the structured opportunity for guided reflection happens in post-simulation debriefings, but they are often constrained by time, instructor variability, and group dynamics [3]. Structured individual written reflection, especially when anchored in student-identified meaningful events, can extend debriefing by prompting deeper sense-making about actions and reasoning. In practice, however, these reflections are rarely reviewed beyond learner themselves. This represents a missed opportunity to support reflective skills, a core component of professional learning that rarely develops without structured support; and to provide instructional teams insight into students' clinical judgment development across contexts and time.

Reflect is a post-simulation reflection system designed to support nursing students' analysis of their simulation experiences [9]. It was developed as part of a larger project that leverages AI-powered tools to support experiential learning in nursing simulation. *Reflect* promotes sustained re-engagement with the simulation experience by having students segment first-person video into meaningful events and identify associated actions, goals, and cognitive states. The broader project's long-term goals include developing reflection analytics to support adaptive feedback, instructional insight, and indicators of competency development.

While standard test set evaluation of automated reflection coding helps establish baseline performance, it cannot guarantee stability as the system encounters new cohorts and simulation contexts. Without mechanisms for ongoing monitoring, automated coding may drift or produce misleading signals in consequential ways. To address this challenge, we developed a committee-based diagnostic framework that can characterize model behavior on unlabeled data over time.

3   AI Coding Approach and Monitoring Diagnostics

The elements described below augment a standard LLM-based coding pipeline [2,10] using a committee based approach, with mechanisms to surface uncertainty at three levels: within individual judgments of code presence (via guided chain-of-thought [1] with explicit uncertainty flagging), across each AI coder's repeated inference attempts (via decision stability quantification [10,14]), and among multiple LLMs, each acting as an "AI coder" (via committee agreement [17]). Building on components of our prior active learning framework (Sects. 3.1–3.2), this study extends the approach with diagnostic metrics that support ongoing oversight on unlabeled data (Sect. 3.3; see Fig. 1). Below, we describe the approach in its simplest form: binary detection of a single construct on unlabeled data using AI coders calibrated through active learning on labeled training and test sets [8]. Although we present the full suite of techniques here, the approach is modular, allowing adoption of components as appropriate.

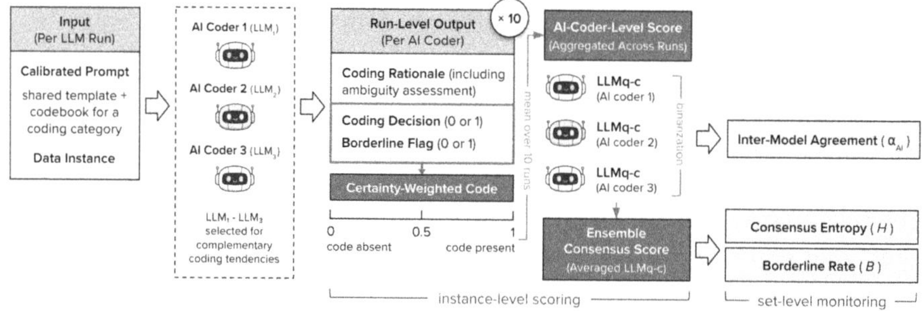

Fig. 1. Committee-based diagnostic framework for performance monitoring.

3.1   AI Coding System Elements

Guided Reasoning with Uncertainty Flags. When LLMs are used for automated coding, they are typically prompted to produce label predictions with little visibility into decision confidence. Prior work has shown that chain-of-thought prompting, where models articulate step-by-step reasoning before reaching conclusions, can improve both performance and interpretability [2]. We extend this approach by embedding explicit uncertainty signaling within the reasoning process. Specifically, the AI coder is prompted to: (1) reason through application of codebook to a data instance, (2) note moments of decision difficulty (e.g., competing interpretations) and (3) flag cases where code presence or absence cannot be determined with confidence. The output includes both a binary judgment (code present/absent) and an explicit uncertainty flag (raised or not), which together can be used to derive an uncertainty-adjusted score (Sect. 3.2).

Repeated Inference for Decision Stability. Beyond single-shot inference, each AI coder processes every data item through multiple independent runs (e.g., N=10) with a non-zero temperature (e.g., temperature = 1), following prior work using repeated inference to examine LLM decision stability [10,14]. This approach draws on the self-consistency hypothesis [16], which posits that, when a construct is well operationalized, multiple valid reasoning paths should converge on the same coding decision. In contrast, variability across repeated inferences signals intra-coder decision instability, often reflecting latent ambiguity or competing interpretations that warrant closer human inspection.

Committee-Based Coding with Multiple LLMs. As a single AI coder's uncertainty estimate may reflect model-specific biases or overconfidence, the system employs a committee of AI coders, each using a different LLM. This ensemble approach follows Query by Committee methods from active learning [12], which use disagreement among diverse models to identify ambiguous cases near the decision boundary. When multiple models independently flag uncertainty or reach different coding decisions, the ensemble provides more robust signals of collective uncertainty not subject to a particular model's training biases.

3.2 Instance-Level Scoring

For each data instance, run-level outputs are aggregated within each AI coder to produce an AI-coder-level score ($LLMq{-}c \in [0,1]$ described below) summarizing decision stability and uncertainty across stochastic runs. The resulting set of AI-coder-level scores is then used to derive committee-level decisions, and compute diagnostic measures of agreement and decisiveness across the dataset.

Certainty-Weighted LLMq ($LLMq\text{-}c$). At the individual coder level, we build on Tai et al. [14]'s Large Language Model quotient (LLMq). LLMq measures model confidence in code presence by averaging binary codes across repeated LLM queries and has recently been used in learning analytics to characterize model behavior across multiple coding runs [10]. Our certainty-weighted variant extends LLMq by down-weighting uncertainty-flagged outputs to the neutral midpoint (0.5), then averaging these uncertainty-adjusted scores across runs (e.g. if 5 LLM runs yield outputs $\{1,1,1,1,1_{flag}\}$, then $LLMq{=}1$, $LLMq\text{-}c{=}0.9$). This weighting scheme treats uncertainty-flagged codes as providing no directional information, preventing hesitant decisions from artificially inflating or deflating the resulting $LLMq\text{-}c$ score.

Ensemble Consensus Score ($\hat{p}$). Given prior work demonstrating improved robustness through ensemble aggregation [4,17], we compute the committee's collective judgment as mean of three AI coders' $LLMq\text{-}c$ scores; applying a 0.5 threshold produces the final binary decision for downstream analysis.

3.3 Performance Monitoring Metrics

On unlabeled data, traditional validation metrics (e.g., F1) are unavailable. However, the committee-based, uncertainty-aware framework allows system health to be diagnosed through three complementary metrics that require no ground truth labels.

Inter-Model Agreement (α_{AI}). Krippendorff's α [6], a robust and widely used measure of inter-rater reliability, is used to assess inter-model agreement.

Based on the three models' thresholded decisions derived from binarized $LLMq\text{-}c$, this metric indexes how often the model committee converges on the same coding decision ($\alpha > 0.67$ indicates moderate agreement; $\alpha > 0.80$ strong agreement [6]). Sustained high agreement indicates consistent codebook application across models, while declining α_{AI} signals potential drift, suggesting models beginning to diverge in how they interpret the codebook when applied to new data.

Consensus Entropy (H). This metric is computed as the Shannon entropy $H \in [0, 1]$ over the instance-level, cross-model consensus score ($\hat{p}$) [15], where: $H = -[\hat{p} \times \log_2(\hat{p}) + (1 - \hat{p}) \times \log_2(1 - \hat{p})]$. Following [17], average consensus entropy across items serves as a summary indicator of ensemble decisiveness on unlabeled data. Lower H indicates more decisive ensemble judgments ($\hat{p}$ near 0 or 1); higher H indicates greater indecisiveness ($\hat{p}$ near 0.5) which can occur when models confidently disagree or are uncertain or unstable across runs.

Borderline Rate (B). While consensus entropy summarizes overall decisiveness, it does not distinguish between pervasive uncertainty and uncertainty concentrated on a few items. Building on prior work [5], we distinguish between broad-based uncertainty and uncertainty localized to a subset of ambiguous instances using borderline rate (B), the percentage of items for which $L \leq \hat{p} \leq U$, where L and U are probability bounds defining a region of decisional ambiguity.

Summary of Contribution. While existing studies have explored guided reasoning [1], coding stability scoring [10,14], and ensemble methods [17] independently, our contribution lies in their novel integration to enable performance monitoring on unlabeled data. Building on our prior work on calibrating AI coders via active learning [8], the present study repurposes consensus entropy (H) and extends the set of diagnostics with borderline rate (B) and inter-model agreement (α_{AI}), using all three metrics for deployment-time monitoring of potential degradation in coding quality. Rather than treating these metrics as traditional measures of reliability or validity, we interpret them as complementary diagnostics of agreement, decisiveness, and certainty, relative to patterns established during calibration and testing. These diagnostics can be continuously monitored in settings where ground truth labels are unavailable or themselves subject to uncertainty [13]. Interpreted together, they provide actionable insight into which codes are likely to be applied robustly across models and repeated inferences and for which further investigation is warranted.

4   Proof-of-Concept Pilot

4.1   Context, Data and Coding Scheme

This pilot uses an event-level Reflect corpus from a nursing school at a U.S. research university (Summer 2024) of 213 reflections from 16 students reflecting on key moments from a range of adult and pediatric simulations. The project's first coding scheme was a simulation-general activity framework aligned with models of clinical judgement [15] and self-regulation [7]. By surfacing behavioral and cognitive elements not fully visible in simulation video, reflections provide a useful basis for interpreting student engagement with key dimensions of practice. The nine-activity coding scheme (Table 1) was iteratively developed through inductive analysis and deductive refinement grounded in nursing education and reflective learning theory [7,15], informed by consultation with nursing education experts. The resulting codebook includes code definitions, indicators, and decision heuristics; full details are reported elsewhere [8].

Table 1. Simulation-general nursing activity codes for student reflections.

Code	Code Name	Definition
GATHER	Gathering information	Collecting or receiving clinical data related to the patient needed for safe and effective nursing care.
IMPLMT	Implementation of nursing care	Hands-on execution of direct care procedures to address patient needs or problems.
T-COMM	Communication with healthcare team	Communicating or collaborating with healthcare team members to share info or coordinate care.
P-COMM	Communication with patient (family)	Communicating with patients or families to build rapport, share info and address questions.
INTRPT-SIT	Interpret info to understand patient situation	Connecting clinical info to form understanding, hypotheses, or clinical judgments about a patient.
INTRPT-VLDT	Interpret info to validate care plan	Ensuring correctness, safety, and readiness of a planned nursing intervention for implementation.
INTRPT-EVAL	Interpret info to evaluate outcome	Assessing a patient's response to nursing care to determine therapeutic or adverse effects.
GOALS	Establish goals and generate solutions	Planning nursing care by identifying therapeutic goals and appropriate interventions.
TIME	Prioritization and time management	Managing time, tasks, and/or priorities during care delivery.

The codebook was used by three researchers to double code 60 reflections (IRR: $0.63 < \alpha < 0.91$). Following reconciliation, data was split into training (N=36) and test sets (N=24). A relatively large test set was used to ensure sufficient positive instances for a rare category (INTRP-EVAL). Three AI coders (o3, Claude-Sonnet-4, DeepSeek-r1) were calibrated through iterative active learning using a shared system prompt with dynamically inserted relevant codebook sections. These models were selected based on observed differences in coding tendencies during calibration (e.g., more conservative vs. more inclusive labeling), providing complementary perspectives for committee-based assessment. Data instances with high uncertainty triggered targeted human review and prompt refinement until human-AI agreement stabilized, after which performance was evaluated on held-out data. Full prompt engineering and training workflow details are reported in [8]. Here we characterize model behavior on both the test set and unlabeled data using the three diagnostic metrics introduced above: inter-model agreement (α_{AI}), consensus entropy (H), and a borderline rate (B) of $0.35 \leq \hat{p} \leq 0.65$. Bounds were chosen based on patterns in uncertainty observed during calibration. The goal is to provide a proof-of-concept demonstrating how complementary diagnostic signals can be jointly interpreted to characterize ensemble behavior in the absence of ground truth (see Fig. 2).

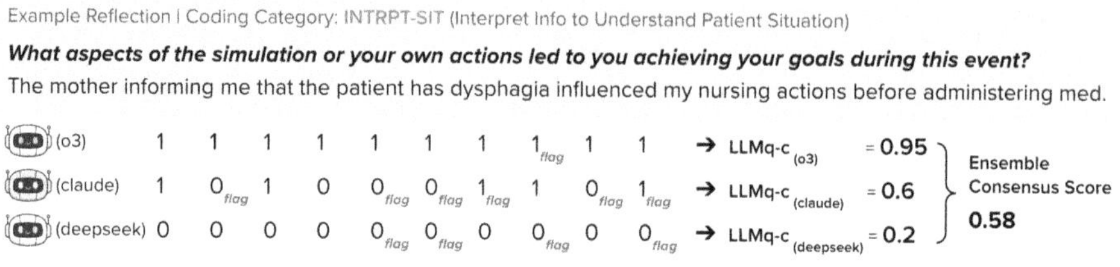

Example Reflection | Coding Category: INTRPT-SIT (Interpret Info to Understand Patient Situation)

What aspects of the simulation or your own actions led to you achieving your goals during this event?
The mother informing me that the patient has dysphagia influenced my nursing actions before administering med.

(o3)   1   1   1   1   1   1   1 1_{flag} 1   1   → $LLMq\text{-}c_{(o3)}$ = 0.95 ⎫
(claude)   1 0_{flag} 1   0 0_{flag} 0_{flag} 1_{flag} 1 0_{flag} 1_{flag} → $LLMq\text{-}c_{(claude)}$ = 0.6   ⎬ Ensemble Consensus Score
(deepseek) 0   0   0   0 0_{flag} 0_{flag} 0 0_{flag} 0 0_{flag} → $LLMq\text{-}c_{(deepseek)}$ = 0.2   ⎭ **0.58**

Fig. 2. Example of committee disagreement due to differing expectations for explicit versus implicit evidence of interpretation work (recognizing implications of dysphagia).

4.2   Results

Table 2 summarizes diagnostic indicators and test-set performance metrics by activity code, comparing agreement and uncertainty patterns across constructs for both held-out test and unlabeled data. For the first four behaviorally explicit codes (GATHER, IMPLMT, T-COMM, P-COMM) with very high test-set performance (F1 > .9), the ensemble showed stable high inter-model agreement across test and unlabeled data (all α_{AI} > .8). Consensus entropy remained relatively stable and borderline rates stayed below 10% with minimal changes. This stable-consensus profile is consistent with expectations for behaviorally explicit constructs and suggests diagnostically stable generalization beyond held-out evaluation. While very high test-set F1 scores raise overfitting concerns, diagnostics on unlabeled corpus provide complementary evidence that ensemble behavior remained stable rather than brittle on additional data.

The latter five codes require more inference about cognitive activity, yielding a broader range of diagnostically informative patterns. INTRP-SIT showed lower test-set performance (F1=0.77) than behaviorally explicit codes, consistent with its more interpretive nature (Fig. 2). However, inter-model agreement, entropy, and borderline rates remained stable across test and unlabeled data $(\alpha_{AI}=0.683/0.756, H=0.344/0.276, B=8.33\%/9.40\%)$, suggesting that the lower accuracy did not translate into unstable ensemble behavior when applied to additional unlabeled data. In contrast, INTRP-VLDT showed perfect test set agreement $(\alpha_{AI}=1.0)$ paired with modest ensemble entropy $(H=0.321)$ but no borderline cases, indicating unanimous but weakly decisive judgments. On unlabeled data, a rise in borderline cases without a corresponding increase in entropy, together with an expected decline in inter-model agreement, suggests uncertainty

Table 2. Performance metrics for test data and unlabeled data.

Activity Code	Test Data				Unlabeled Data		
	F1	α_{AI}	H	B	α_{AI}	H	B
GATHER	0.966	0.942	0.295	4.17%	0.885	0.275	7.69%
IMPLMT	0.941	1.000	0.322	0.00%	0.951	0.218	5.13%
T-COMM	0.923	0.877	0.295	8.33%	0.946	0.230	2.56%
P-COMM	0.923	0.944	0.214	8.33%	0.917	0.131	3.42%
INTRPT-SIT	0.770	0.683	0.344	8.33%	0.756	0.276	9.40%
INTRPT-VLDT	0.947	1.000	0.321	0.00%	0.837	0.343	9.40%
INTRPT-EVAL	1.000	0.844	0.195	0.00%	0.532	0.163	1.71%
GOALS	0.824	0.698	0.506	25.00%	0.719	0.456	12.82%
TIME	1.000	0.735	0.379	4.17%	0.644	0.309	11.11%

concentrated in a subset of cases. As validating a nursing care plan requires attention to safety-critical practices varying by clinical contexts, this pattern is consistent with context-sensitive variation in how validation reasoning is expressed and points to a need for targeted human review of emerging edge cases.

INTRP-EVAL was a rare code in the dataset, making its perfect test-set accuracy (F1=1.0) potentially misleading. On unlabeled data, α_{AI} dropped substantially (0.884 → 0.532), while entropy and borderline rates remained low ($H < 0.2$, $B < 2\%$). This pattern reflects confident consensus on code absence for most items, paired with disagreement on the small number of candidate positive cases. In large unlabeled datasets, this pattern can be used to flag a small subset of instances where an AI coder indicates potential code presence, enabling targeted human review.

GOALS showed good performance on the test set ($F1 = 0.824$) with moderate agreement (α_{AI}=0.698/0.719) but midrange entropy (H=0.506/0.456) and elevated borderline rates (B=25%/13%) indicating pervasive uncertainty across test and unlabeled data. This pattern suggests potential ambiguity in how the GOALS construct is operationalized. Consistent with challenges in human coding, this reflects a tension between a theoretically grounded GOALS construct and the partial or emergent ways novice learners express goal setting and solution generation. This points to a need to refine code definitions or prompt guidance, rather than concerns about model stability when applied to new data.

Finally, TIME also showed perfect test-set accuracy (F1=1.0), with only moderate inter-model agreement (α_{AI}=0.735). On unlabeled data, agreement declined further (α_{AI}=0.644) while borderline rate rose (4%→11%) without a corresponding rise in entropy, indicating increased uncertainty in a subset of cases. This pattern of declining agreement and increased localized uncertainty suggests difficulty distinguishing *prioritization and time management* (TIME) from adjacent clinical reasoning, consistent with the construct's cognitive complexity and indicating a need for further construct clarification or training data.

5 Limitations and Conclusion

Using a committee-based framework, this paper operationalizes complementary metrics for continuous monitoring of AI coding performance on unlabeled data. In a pilot application, these diagnostics revealed recurring ensemble patterns, including stable consensus and divergence between agreement and decisiveness, illustrating how the metrics can be jointly interpreted to monitor AI coding in the absence of ground truth. Limitations include the small pilot scale and its focus on reflection data from a single nursing program using one coding framework. Further validation is needed to assess whether the metrics function as useful diagnostics across other forms of student-generated text, coding schemes, and instructional contexts. The computational cost of committee-based inference is also non-trivial; future work will explore sparse and adaptive monitoring strategies to balance efficiency with ongoing oversight. Overall, this work addresses an important challenge in AIED: maintaining the robustness of AI coding of complex, open-ended student work as systems encounter new populations, contexts, and patterns of expression at scale.

Acknowledgments. This work was supported by the National Science Foundation under Grant No. DRL-2418602. The opinions, findings, and conclusions or recommendations expressed in this material are those of the authors and do not necessarily reflect the views of the National Science Foundation.

References

1. Anthropic: Let Claude think (CoT). https://platform.claude.com/docs/en/build-with-claude/prompt-engineering/chain-of-thought
2. Cohn, C., Hutchins, N., Le, T., Biswas, G.: A chain-of-thought prompting approach with LLMs for evaluating students' formative assessment responses in science. In: Proceedings of AAAI Conference on Artificial Intelligence, pp. 23182–23190 (2024)
3. Decker, S., et al.: Standards of best practice: simulation standard VI: The debriefing process. Clin. Simul. Nurs. **9**(6), 26–29 (2013)
4. Herrera-Poyatos, D., et al.: An overview of model uncertainty and variability in LLM-based sentiment analysis: challenges, mitigation strategies, and the role of explainability. Front. Artif. Intell. **8**, 1–24 (2025)
5. Jamison, E., Gurevych, I.: Noise or additional information? Leveraging crowd-source annotation item agreement for natural language tasks. In: Proceedings of 2015 Conference on Empirical Methods in Natural Language Processing, pp. 291–297 (2015)
6. Krippendorff, K.: Content Analysis: An Introduction to its Methodology (2019)
7. Lajoie, S.P., Gube, M.: Adaptive expertise in medical education: accelerating learning trajectories by fostering self-regulated learning. Med. Teach. **40**(8) (2018)
8. Li, F., Mason, M.L., Levin, D., Wise, A.: Using RE-LLM coding uncertainty to resolve codebook ambiguities: an example of the CLARIFY toolset and workflow in action. In: Joint Proceedings of LAK 2026 Workshops, pp. 1–10 (2026)
9. Mason, M.L., Jessee, M.A., Levin, D.T.: Transforming experiences into expertise: leveraging event cognition to support self-regulation in a practical learning system (2026), in review

10. Ramanathan, S., Lim, L.A., Mottaghi, N.R., Buckingham Shum, S.: When the prompt becomes the codebook: grounded prompt engineering (GROPROE) and its application to belonging analytics. In: LAK'25 Proceedings, pp. 713–725. ACM (2025)
11. Scarlatos, A., Baker, R.S., Lan, A.: Exploring knowledge tracing in tutor-student dialogues using LLMs. In: LAK'25 Proceedings, pp. 249–259. ACM (2025)
12. Settles, B.: Active learning literature survey, University of Wisconsin-Madison Department of Computer Sciences (2009). TR1648 Tech. Rep
13. Song, H., et al.: In validations we trust? the impact of imperfect human annotations as a gold standard on the quality of validation of automated content analysis. Polit. Commun. **37**(4), 550–572 (2020)
14. Tai, R.H., et al.: An examination of the use of large language models to aid analysis of textual data. Int J Qual Methods **23**, 1–14 (2024)
15. Tanner, C.A.: Thinking like a nurse: a research-based model of clinical judgment in nursing. J. Nurs. Educ. **45**(6), 204–211 (2006)
16. Wang, X.: Self-consistency improves chain of thought reasoning in language models (2023). arXiv:2203.11171 cs.CL
17. Zhang, Y.: Consensus entropy: Harnessing multi-VLM agreement for self-verifying and self-improving OCR (2025). arXiv:2504.11101 cs.CV

From Rule-Based to LLM-Based Agents: A Calibrated Simulation Framework for Classroom Social Networks

Kyosuke Takami[1,2](✉) and Masahiko Haruno[2]

[1] Osaka Kyoiku University, Osaka, Japan
`takami-k75@cc.osaka-kyoiku.ac.jp`
[2] Center for Information and Neural Networks, Osaka, Japan

Abstract. Peer interactions are fundamental to social and emotional learning (SEL) yet modeling how classroom social networks emerge over time remains challenging, particularly when interaction rules are hand-crafted and difficult to validate empirically. This paper proposes a simulation framework for classroom social networks that enables controlled comparisons between interpretable rule-based agents and large language model (LLM)–based agents under identical conditions. In the framework, students are modeled as autonomous agents who repeatedly select a fixed number of interaction partners based on individual attributes, such as Big Five personality traits, and classroom climate indicators derived from questionnaire data. Repeated interactions reinforce social ties, allowing weighted network structures to emerge endogenously. As a reference, we calibrate a rule-based interaction model using random search to reproduce multiple observed network properties, including density, modularity, community structure, reciprocity, and personality–degree correlations. Using this calibrated model as a baseline, we replace the hand-crafted scoring function with an LLM-based decision module that operates under the same simulation context but without calibration to observed networks. Across multiple classrooms, results suggest that LLM-based agents can approximate coarse-grained interaction patterns, while exhibiting systematic deviations in socially meaningful network properties. Rather than validating LLMs as social simulators, this work contributes a flexible framework for evaluating how different agent decision mechanisms shape emergent classroom social networks.

Keywords: Classroom Social Networks · Agent-Based Simulation · Large Language Models · Big Five Personality · Classroom Climate

1 Introduction

Peer interactions play a central role in learning and development in classroom settings. Through everyday interactions, students form friendships, experience conflict, and develop a sense of belonging, all of which are foundational to social and emotional learning (SEL) [1, 2]. Understanding how such classroom social networks emerge and evolve over time is therefore a longstanding concern in learning sciences, educational

© The Author(s), under exclusive license to Springer Nature Switzerland AG 2027
E. G. Blanchard et al. (Eds.): AIED 2026, LNAI 16583, pp. 380–388, 2027.
https://doi.org/10.1007/978-3-032-29760-0_42

psychology, and learning analytics, and aligns with broader goals in computational social science [3]. Beyond descriptive analysis, simulation-based approaches offer a powerful means to explore how individual-level characteristics and decision-making processes give rise to collective social structures [4, 5]. Agent-based models (ABMs) have been widely used to simulate social network formation in educational and developmental contexts. In these models, students are represented as agents who repeatedly select interaction partners based on predefined rules, such as homophily, personality traits, or classroom climate. While rule-based ABMs provide interpretability and explicit control over mechanisms, their validity critically depends on hand-crafted interaction rules and parameter choices. Designing rules that are both psychologically plausible and capable of reproducing observed classroom network structures remains challenging, and poorly calibrated models can easily generate unrealistic social dynamics [5]. In parallel, statistical network evolution models (e.g., stochastic actor-oriented models) provide principled frameworks for studying micro–macro links in network dynamics, highlighting the importance of carefully specifying and validating behavioral mechanisms [6].

Recent advances in large language models (LLMs) have introduced a new paradigm for agent-based simulation. LLMs can generate context-sensitive decisions by leveraging broad patterns learned from large-scale text corpora, raising the possibility of using them as flexible social decision-making agents. In educational research, LLM-based agents have been explored for tutoring, dialogue, and role-play simulations, while also raising concerns about reliability and bias [7]. In the simulation literature, LLM-driven "generative agents" have demonstrated the ability to produce coherent individual behaviors and emergent interaction patterns in sandbox environments [8]. Related work has also explored LLMs as proxies for human decision-makers in multi-agent settings, suggesting both promise and methodological caveats [9]. However, their potential for simulating social network formation—particularly in classroom settings—remains underexplored. A key open question is whether LLM-based agents, when provided with the same contextual information as traditional agents, can produce realistic emergent social structures without explicit rule engineering or parameter tuning.

In this paper, we propose a simulation framework for classroom social networks that enables a controlled comparison between rule-based and LLM-based agents under identical conditions.

2 Methods

Our proposed simulation framework for classroom social network consists of three phases. **Phase A** (Calibration) obtains questionnaire-based data—students' Big Five personality traits (openness, conscientiousness, extraversion, agreeableness, neuroticism) and classroom climate perceptions (friction, satisfaction, closeness)—together with an observed classroom social network to calibrate the parameters of a rule-based interaction model via parameter search. The target network is used only in this calibration phase. **Phase B** (Simulation) generates classroom social networks over discrete time steps (t = 1 to T) starting from an empty network (nodes only). At each step, agents select top-k interaction partners based on either a calibrated rule-based scoring function or an LLM-based scoring function, followed by deterministic edge-weight reinforcement. During this phase, agents have no access to the target network. **Phase C** (Evaluation & Comparison) compares the simulated networks produced by the rule-based and LLM-based agents against the observed target network using multiple structural and relational metrics, enabling a controlled assessment of how different decision mechanisms influence emergent classroom social structures.

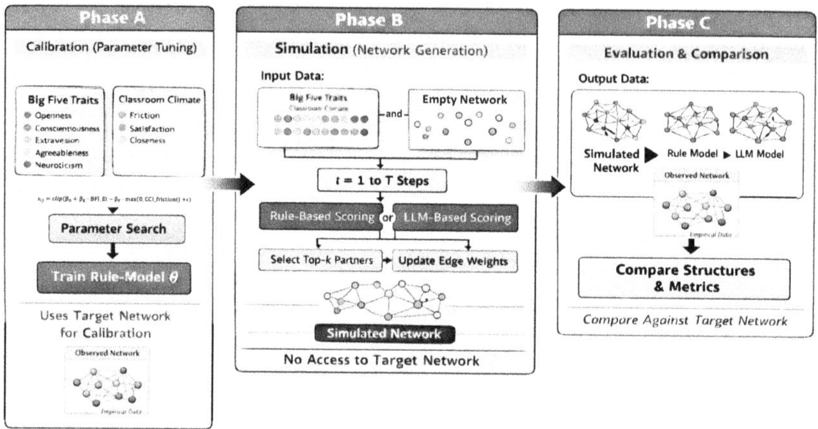

Fig. 1. Overview of the simulation framework[1] for classroom social network formation and evaluation. Phase A (Calibration), Phase B (Simulation), Phase C (Evaluation & Comparison).

2.1 Phase a: Data Representation and Model Calibration.

Classroom Network Representation: Classroom peer interactions are represented as undirected, weighted social networks, where nodes correspond to students and edge weights reflect the cumulative strength of interactions. Each classroom network consists of 40 students. Empirical target networks are constructed from questionnaire-based peer interaction data and are used only for calibration and evaluation, not during simulation. Each observed classroom network is denoted as.

$G^{\mathrm{obs}} = (V, E^{\mathrm{obs}})$, where V is the set of students and E^{obs} is the set of weighted edges.

In this study, we obtained friendship nomination data from 160 high school students across four classrooms (A, B, C and D as shown in Results section). This study was conducted with informed consent obtained from all participating students and was approved by the school principal and the student guidance committee. We used this empirical data for Observed Network and Target Network.

Student Attributes from Questionnaires: Each student node is associated with attributes derived from self-report questionnaires, including:

---

[1] Our proposed framework is available at GitHub: https://github.com/KyosukeTakami/llm-sna-sim.

- **Personality traits**: Big Five dimensions [10] (Openness, Conscientiousness, Extraversion, Agreeableness, Neuroticism), z-standardized.
- **Classroom climate perception**: Classroom Climate Inventory [11] (Friction, satisfaction, and closeness), also z-standardized.

These attributes serve as inputs to both rule-based and LLM-based agents when computing interaction propensities.

Rule-Based Interaction Model: As a baseline, we implemented a parametric rule-based agent that computes interaction propensity as:

$$s_{ij} = clip(\beta_0 + \beta_E \cdot \text{BFI\_Ei} - \beta_F \cdot \max(0, \text{CCI\_frictioni}) + \epsilon),$$

where β_0 is a base interaction rate, β_E captures the effect of extraversion, β_F penalizes perceived classroom friction. BFI_Ei denotes the z-standardized extraversion score of student i, and CCI_friction_i represents perceived classroom friction. $\epsilon \sim \mathcal{U}(0, 0.02)$ introduces stochasticity. The *clip* function denotes a truncation function defined as $clip(x) = \min(1, \max(0, x))$, , ensuring that interaction scores lie within the [0, 1] interval. This formulation reflects interpretable behavioral assumptions, where socially outgoing students are more likely to initiate interactions, while negative classroom climate suppresses interaction tendencies.

Parameter Calibration Using Target Networks: Model parameters are calibrated exclusively in Phase A using the observed target networks. The calibration procedure is formulated as a simulation-based random search. Specifically, model parameters governing interaction behavior (e.g., baseline interaction rate, personality effects, interaction constraints, and edge reinforcement mechanisms) are sampled from predefined ranges. For each parameter set, multiple simulation runs are conducted to account for stochasticity in the interaction process. The resulting simulated networks are compared to the observed network using a weighted multi-metric distance function. This distance captures discrepancies in key structural properties, including network density, modularity, number of communities, isolation rate, degree distribution, and the correlation between extraversion and degree. Modularity is computed using greedy modularity maximization (Clauset–Newman–Moore) with the Newman formulation; single-community cases are assigned zero modularity. For each parameter set, we compute the mean distance across repeated simulations, and the parameter configuration that minimizes this value is selected as the calibrated model. Calibration is performed separately for each classroom. The selected parameter set is then fixed and used as the rule-based baseline in subsequent simulations. Importantly, the observed target network is used only during this calibration phase and is not accessible during the simulation phase, ensuring a clear separation between model fitting and evaluation. This procedure improves robustness by averaging over multiple stochastic realizations of the network formation process.

2.2 Phase B: Simulation of Classroom Social Networks

Simulation Procedure and Temporal Dynamics: Simulations start from an empty graph G^0, containing nodes only and no edges. The simulation proceeds for T = 20 discrete time steps. At each step, students are visited in random order. For a focal student i, an agent assigns interaction scores $s_{ij} \in [0,1]$ to all other students $j \neq i$. Based on these scores, the top-k candidates are selected as interaction partners. For each selected candidate, the edge weight is updated according to a predefined reinforcement rule, which depends on the candidate's rank, score, or their combination. If an edge does not already exist, it may be created with probability p_{new}. The resulting simulated network after T steps is denoted G^{sim}. No information from the observed target network is used during this phase. During simulation, the rule-based agent uses the calibrated parameters obtained in Phase A but does not access any observed network statistics. Interaction decisions depend solely on individual attributes and stochasticity. This process introduces path dependence, where early interactions influence subsequent network evolution through cumulative reinforcement of social ties.

LLM-Based Agent: To model more flexible and context-sensitive decision-making, we replaced the rule-based scoring function with an LLM-based agent. For each focal student, the LLM receives a structured JSON input containing:

- the student's personality and classroom climate attributes,
- global simulation parameters (e.g., base rate, friction penalty),

as shown below Prompt:

```
You are a decision-making agent in a classroom social network
simulation.
Given the input JSON, score each candidate in [0,1] where higher
means more likely to interact next.
Return ONLY valid JSON. Do not include any extra text.
Required output JSON schema:{"scores": [{"id": "CANDIDATE_ID",
"score": 0.0}]}
Constraints:Use only candidate ids provided in input
JSON.Provide up to top_k items, sorted by descending score.score
must be a number between 0 and 1.
Input JSON:{"self_id": "D020", "BFI_E_z": 0.0696733014291618,
"BFI_A_z": -0.8657035928395885, "BFI_C_z": -0.1488799238561821,
"BFI_N_z": 0.5085028986045035, "BFI_O_z": 0.5780485010628444,
"CCI_friction_z": 1.491254742020745, "CCI_satisfaction_z": -
0.8425741333011361, "CCI_closeness_z": -1.3145633350599792,
"use_persona": true, "use_climate": true, "candidates": ["D016",
"D023",…], "top_k": 3}.
```

The LLM is instructed to output interaction scores in $[0,1]$ for the provided candidates, returning at most the top-k items sorted by score. To ensure reproducibility, the temperature is fixed to 0.0, candidate pools are capped, and random seeds are controlled. The LLM-based agent uses the same selection threshold and update rules as the rule-based agent; differences arise solely from the scoring mechanism.

Edge Weight Update and Reinforcement Mechanism: Edges are updated deterministically following each interaction. Let $w_{ij}^{(t)}$ denote the edge weight between students i and j at step t. When student i selects student j at rank $r_{ij}^{(t)}$ with score $s_{ij}^{(t)}$, the edge weight is updated as:

$$w_{ij}^{(t)} = w_{ij}^{(t)} + \alpha \cdot \frac{1}{r_{ij}^{(t)}} \cdot s_{ij}^{(t)},$$

with $\alpha = 1.0$. New edges are created automatically upon first interaction. This reinforcement mechanism introduces path dependence, allowing social ties to strengthen through repeated interactions. The same update rule is applied to both agent types.

Evaluation Metrics: After simulation, the generated network G^{sim} is compared with the observed network G^{obs}. Evaluation metrics include network density, modularity, number of communities, isolation rate, degree distribution, and the correlation between extraversion and degree.

3 Results

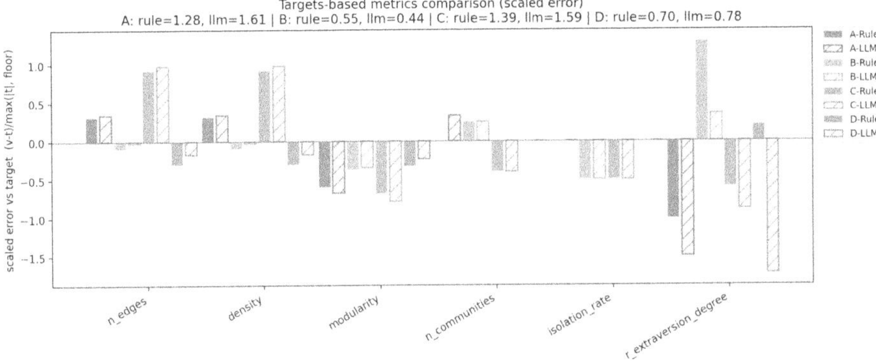

Fig. 2. Targets-based comparison of global network metrics between calibrated rule-based and LLM-based (GPT-4o) simulations across classrooms A–D.

This section reports the results of simulation experiments comparing a calibrated rule-based interaction model and a large language model (LLM)–based agent under identical simulation settings. As a LLM based agent, we used **GPT-4o**-2024–08-06 (OpenAI API). The comparison focuses on how well each approach reproduces observed classroom social network properties across four classrooms (A–D) empirically obtained from high school students. Importantly, while the rule-based model was calibrated to empirical data using random search (REP = 20, TRIALS = 60, T = 20), and the best-performing parameter set for each classroom was retained and fixed for all subsequent simulations, the LLM-based agent operated without access to any calibrated parameters and relied solely on the same contextual inputs (student attributes and classroom climate indicators).

3.1 Reproduction of Classroom Network Structure

Figure 2 compares global network properties of simulated networks generated by the calibrated rule-based model and the LLM-based agent across four classrooms (A–D). Scaled errors are reported relative to the observed target networks, with smaller values indicating better reproduction. Overall, the calibrated rule-based model consistently reproduced the observed classroom networks across all metrics and classrooms, including edge counts, density, modularity, community structure, isolation rate, and the correlation between extraversion and degree. This indicates that the calibration procedure successfully aligned local interaction rules with empirically grounded classroom structures. In contrast, the LLM-based agent reproduced coarse-grained properties such as total edge count and network density in some classrooms but showed substantially larger deviations on meso-level and relational metrics. In particular, modularity, the number of detected communities, and personality–degree correlations were inconsistently reproduced across classrooms. These results suggest that, although LLM-based agents generate socially plausible interaction patterns, they do not reliably recover empirically observed classroom social structures when operating without calibration.

3.2 Temporal Interaction Dynamics

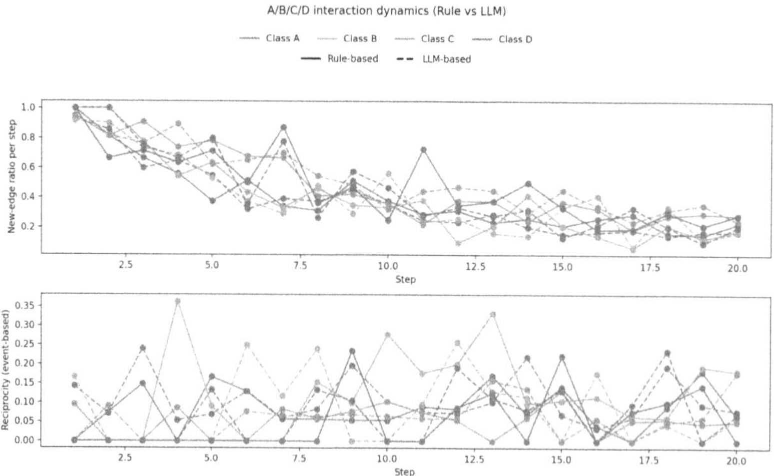

Fig. 3. Temporal interaction dynamics in four classrooms (A–D), comparing rule-based and LLM-based agents under identical simulation settings. The top panel shows the proportion of newly formed edges at each simulation step, illustrating how interaction opportunities gradually shift from exploratory to reinforcing existing ties. The bottom panel reports event-based reciprocity, defined as the fraction of interactions that are immediately reciprocated within the same step. Both agent types exhibit a declining rate of new edge formation over time. However, LLM-based agents consistently display higher and more variable reciprocity, indicating a stronger tendency toward immediate mutual interactions.

Figure 3 summarizes temporal interaction dynamics derived from simulation logs. For both agent types, the proportion of newly formed edges declined over simulation steps, indicating a common transition from exploratory interactions to reinforcement of existing ties. However, LLM-based agents tended to exhibit higher and more variable reciprocity than the rule-based model across classrooms. This indicates a stronger tendency toward immediate mutual interactions in LLM-driven decision-making. In contrast, the calibrated rule-based model produced stable reciprocity trajectories that closely matched observed classroom patterns. These temporal results suggest that deviations in LLM-based network structure arise from systematic biases in interaction decisions rather than from differences in initial conditions or network growth dynamics.

4 Conclusion

This paper proposed a simulation framework for classroom social networks that enables controlled comparisons between calibrated rule-based agents and large language model (LLM)–based agents under identical conditions. A key methodological distinction is that the rule-based model is calibrated using empirical target networks, whereas the LLM-based agent operates without parameter tuning; thus, the calibrated model serves as an empirical reference rather than a strictly comparable baseline. Rather than making strong claims about the validity of LLM-based social simulation, the framework provides a systematic approach to examine how different decision-making mechanisms influence emergent network structures. Illustrative results suggest that LLM-based agents can generate locally plausible interaction patterns, while also exhibiting systematic deviations from empirically grounded baselines. Overall, this work contributes an extensible methodological framework for evaluating LLM-based agents in educational social systems and clarifying their potential and limitations in future research. These findings highlight the need for careful interpretation when using LLM-based agents in classroom social network simulations.

Acknowledgments. This work was supported by JST CREST Grant Number JPMJCR15E4 including AIP challenge program, Japan and partly supported by JSPS Grant-in-Aid for Scientific Research (Early Career) JP23K17012, (B) JP20H01722.

Disclosure of Interests.. The authors have no competing interests to declare that are relevant to the content of this article.

References

1. Durlak, J.A., Weissberg, R.P., Dymnicki, A.B., Taylor, R.D., Schellinger, K.B.: The impact of enhancing students' social and emotional learning: a meta-analysis of school-based universal interventions. Child Dev. **82**(1), 405–432 (2011). https://doi.org/10.1111/j.1467-8624.2010.01564.x
2. Erstad, O., Černochová, M., Knezek, G., Furuta, T., Takami, K., Liang, C.: Social and emotional modes of learning within digital ecosystems: Emerging research agendas. Technol. Knowl. Learn. **29**(4), 1751–1766 (2024). https://doi.org/10.1007/s10758-024-09775-w

3. Lazer, D., et al.: Computational social science. Science **323**(5915), 721–723 (2009). https://doi.org/10.1126/science.1167742
4. Epstein, J.M.: Generative Social Science: Studies in Agent-Based Computational Modeling. Princeton University Press, Princeton (2012)
5. Railsback, S.F., Grimm, V.: Agent-Based and Individual-Based Modeling: A Practical Introduction. Princeton University Press, Princeton (2019)
6. Snijders, T.A.B., van de Bunt, G.G., Steglich, C.E.G.: Introduction to stochastic actor-based models for network dynamics. Soc. Netw. **32**(1), 44–60 (2010). https://doi.org/10.1016/j.socnet.2009.02.004
7. Kasneci, E., Sessler, K., Küchemann, S., Bannert, M., Dementieva, D., Fischer, F., et al.: ChatGPT for good? On opportunities and challenges of large language models for education. Learn. Individ. Differ. **103**, 102274 (2023). https://doi.org/10.1016/j.lindif.2023.102274
8. Park, J.S., O'Brien, J., Cai, C.J., Morris, M.R., Liang, P., Bernstein, M.S.: Generative agents: interactive simulacra of human behavior. arXiv preprint arXiv:2304.03442 (2023)
9. Aher, G.V., Arriaga, R.I., Kalai, A.T.: Using large language models to simulate multiple humans. arXiv preprint arXiv:2208.10264 (2022)
10. John, O.P., Donahue, E.M., Kentle, R. L.: Big Five Inventory. University of California, Berkeley, Institute of Personality and Social Research, Berkeley (1991)
11. Ayako, I., Hitoshi, M.: Construction Of The Classroom Climate Inventory. Japanese J. Educat. Psychol. **49**(4), 449–457. https://doi.org/10.5926/jjep1953.49.4_449

Making Advanced Temporal Visualizations Accessible to Educators Using Generative AI

Debarshi Nath[1,2]($\boxtimes$) , Yash Desai[3] , Ramkumar Rajendran[2] ,
and Dragan Gašević[1]

[1] Department of Data Science and AI, Monash University, Melbourne, Australia
{debarshi.nath,dragan.gasevic}@monash.edu
[2] Centre for Educational Technology, Indian Institute of Technology Bombay,
Mumbai, India
ramkumar.rajendran@iitb.ac.in
[3] Department of Computer Engineering, Sardar Patel Institute of Technology,
Mumbai, India

Abstract. Advanced temporal learning analytics can model how learning unfolds over time. However, the results of these analyses are often expressed through complex visual representations that are difficult for educators to interpret and are rarely combined into coherent explanations that can inform instructional decisions. This study examines whether a large language model can serve as an interpretation layer that translates multiple temporal representations into educator-oriented natural language explanations. We focus on three complementary perspectives on temporality: *passage of time, order in time,* and *cotemporality.* These perspectives were operationalized using raincloud plots, transition network analysis, and epistemic network analysis. We evaluated zero-shot model interpretations of these representations using trace data from 31 middle school students completing a 45-minute reading-to-write task. Consolidated interpretations across representations produced coherent and well-grounded temporal descriptions of the learning activity over consecutive time windows. Although the model made some overreaching claims in its current setup, it successfully identified key behavioral patterns that distinguish high and low scorers, including premature transitions to essay writing and reduced engagement with task instructions, conforming to prior findings in education literature. Our findings suggest that generative AI can improve the intelligibility of complex temporal learning analytics for educators, offering a pathway towards augmenting educators' capabilities in supporting students.

Keywords: Temporal learning analytics · Temporal visualizations · Generative AI · Learning strategies · Human-AI collaboration

1   Introduction

Understanding how learning unfolds over time is central to supporting self-regulation. Learners plan, monitor, and adapt their strategies dynamically, and recognizing when students shift between reading, planning, writing, or revising can provide critical insight for teachers [10,13]. While contemporary learning analytics can model these temporal dynamics in detail, the resulting analyses are rarely accessible to educators in practice.

A key barrier lies in the complexity of temporal representations, which require substantial methodological expertise to interpret. Temporality can be examined from multiple perspectives: *passage of time* (when actions occur), *order in time* (how actions transition), and *cotemporality* (which actions occur in close proximity) [9]. Prior research shows that combining these perspectives leads to richer interpretations of learning processes [11], yet they are frequently presented separately and are not comprehensible for common educators.

Democratizing AI in education requires that complex analytic outputs be understandable to educators and classroom practitioners. LLMs offer a promising interpretation layer, translating research-grade temporal visualizations into natural language explanations teachers can act upon. In this paper, we examine whether an LLM can interpret, integrate, and generate textual explanations from three complementary temporal visualizations: raincloud plots, transition network analysis (TNA), and epistemic network analysis (ENA), using data from a reading-to-write task, and whether such interpretations can meaningfully articulate differences between learner groups.

2   Background

2.1   Temporality and its Multiple Perspectives

Despite the recognition that learning unfolds over time, its temporal nature remains underexplored [9,15]. Two fundamental perspectives anchor temporality in learning: (i) *passage of time*, indicating when events occur on an absolute timeline, and (ii) *order in time*, indicating the relative sequencing of events. A third perspective (iii) *Cotemporality* emphasizes events in close temporal proximity [20], particularly valuable where temporally clustered actions reveal meaningful relationships [9]. Consolidating these perspectives proves very effective for understanding learning processes and supporting decision-making [11,13].

Each perspective requires distinct methods. For example, raincloud plots can capture *passage of time* by combining exact event timing with distributional measures [11]. TNA [17] merges relational and transitional metrics to express *order in time*. ENA [18] uses a sliding window to foreground *co-temporal* relationships. While powerful, their complexity creates an accessibility barrier limiting practical utility beyond the research community [15].

2.2   The Accessibility Challenge and LLMs as Interpreters

Temporal insights from methods like TNA and ENA remain largely inaccessible to teachers, compounded by limited visualization literacy and cognitive overload when presented with multiple visualizations [14]. Recent dashboards have begun incorporating temporal perspectives (e.g., MORF-ENA [22], CADA [6]), yet substantial analytical expertise is still required to interpret these dashboards.

LLMs offer a promising solution. Rather than requiring stakeholders to interpret visualizations directly, temporal analytics can be represented in structured text formats that LLMs process to generate accessible narratives [24]. Emerging work suggests LLMs can generate contextual insights from structured learning data [3,5]. However, it remains unclear whether LLMs can interpret specialized temporal analytics like TNA and ENA across multiple temporality perspectives, consolidate insights into coherent narratives, and produce actionable descriptions for educators. This study addresses these gaps.

3   Current Context

To facilitate the temporal investigations for this study, we created TemporLA, a Streamlit-based dashboard integrating raincloud plots (*passage of time*), TNA (*order in time*), and ENA (*co-temporality*). A demo is available in the supplementary material. While consolidating multiple temporal methods isn't exactly novel [16], recent work demonstrated that combining complementary perspectives like *passage of time* and *order in time* yields richer findings than single-perspective approaches [11,19]. TemporLA extends this by integrating the perspective of *co-temporality*. The dashboard enables researchers to upload temporal learning data, configure analytical parameters, and generate comparative visualizations for up to two groups, with an interactive *time slider* for temporal slicing and dynamic updates. As its current design primarily serves researchers, we investigate whether LLMs can transform its structured outputs into interpretable narratives for educators, positioning TemporLA as a platform for translating temporal insights into actionable pedagogical knowledge.

Research questions driving the current work are – **RQ1**: To what extent can a large language model generate grounded interpretations of the temporal evolution of learning behaviours using visualizations capturing multiple perspectives of temporality? **RQ2**: To what extent can a large language model articulate temporal differences between learner groups, based on visualizations capturing multiple perspectives of temporality?

4   Methodology

4.1   Learning Task and Data

We evaluate our approach using data from a 45-minute essay writing task where 31 middle school students (ages 12–15; M=15, F=16) read materials on artificial intelligence and medicine, then composed a 200–300 word essay on AI's future impact in medicine. Ethics approval and parental consent were obtained. The task was conducted in FLoRA [7], an open-source learning environment featuring a reading interface, navigation panel, and self-regulatory tools (highlighter, note-taker, planner, timer, writing window). Trace data captured fine-grained learner interactions including navigational logs, keystrokes, and mouse events.

4.2 Temporal Analysis Setup and Experimental Procedure

Following prior work [4], we analyzed behavior across six time windows (0–7, 7–14, 14–21, 21–28, 28–35, 35–45 min) chosen to capture meaningful behavioral shifts. For each window, we generated three temporal representations: raincloud plots (passage of time), TNA (order in time), and ENA (co-temporality), and converted these to structured markdown text for LLM processing. Inputs were: minute-level action frequency tables (for raincloud); normalized cumulative adjacency matrix resulting from singular value decomposition (for ENA) [18]; and transition probability matrix (for TNA) [17]. Our pilot investigation using image inputs (see supplementary material) found image quality confounded LLM interpretations, reinforcing prior findings [2] and motivating text representations used in the current study. The experimental procedure is depicted in Fig. 1.

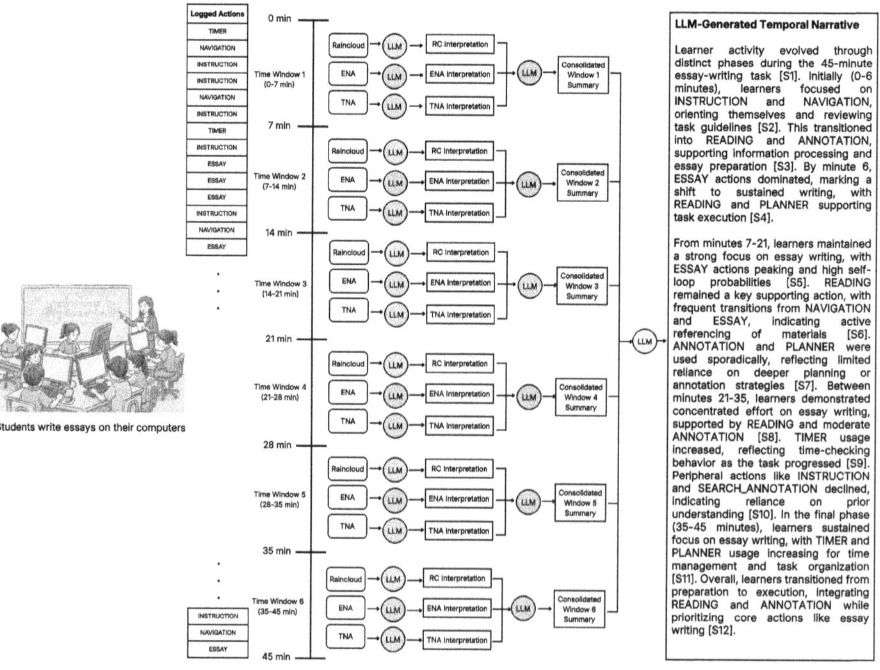

Fig. 1. The setup for the temporal analysis of learner behaviours over 45 min essay writing activity, and the LLM-generated temporal narrative for RQ1

For RQ1, the LLM received all three visualization representations for the full group of learners per time window, interpreted each independently, consolidated into window-level summaries, and finally synthesized into a temporal narrative. For RQ2, students were divided into high and low scorers via tertile split of their essay scores; the LLM received two raincloud plots, two TNA plots, and one ENA difference network per window, then generated a consolidated narrative of behavioral divergence. Group performance labels were withheld to avoid bias.

We adopted structured zero-shot prompting using ChatGPT-4o (free-tier API, GitHub Marketplace) with four prompt components: (i) *role definition*; (ii) *context definition*; (iii) *action library*; and (iv) *task requirements*. Temperature was set to 0.2 to ground outputs in data, with instructions to anchor claims to specific graph elements [23]. Full details are in the supplementary material.

4.3   Analysing LLM Responses

LLM outputs were segmented into minimal verifiable claims and independently coded by two human raters for ~40% of output as: *Correct* (fully supported), *Partially Correct* (right direction but overstated), *Unsupported* (no evidence), or *Incorrect* (contradicts data). Inter-rater reliability was computed using Gwet's AC1 (to account for imbalance of codes), and was found to be 0.67 (substantial agreement) [25]. Only *Correct* labels were treated as valid; all others as incorrect, penalizing even partial over-interpretations. Accuracy was computed across single graph interpretations, window-level summaries, and final temporal narratives, with additional qualitative review by the first author.

5   Results

5.1   RQ1: Single Group Analysis

Individual graph interpretations achieved 87% accuracy (Fig. 2). Consolidation into window-level summaries improved accuracy to 91%, suggesting effective synthesis of complementary temporal perspectives. The final temporal narrative across all 31 learners achieved 89% accuracy (Fig. 1). Qualitatively, the LLM correctly identified an initial orientation phase involving task guidelines review (S2, Fig. 1), followed by strategic reading to support essay writing (S3, S4). It captured nuanced patterns like referencing reading materials while composing (S8), increased time-checking towards task deadline (S11), and the broader shift from preparation to execution (S12). A notable over-interpretation was conflating decreased annotation search and instruction reviewing with reliance on prior understanding (S10), an interpretive leap not directly supported by trace data.

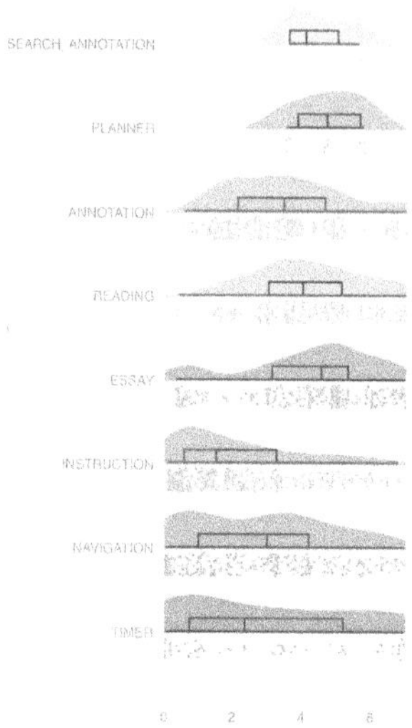

LLM-generated interpretation
· Early focus on instructions and navigation (Minute 0-1): At the start of the task, learners heavily engaged with INSTRUC-TION (95 actions at minute 0, 68 at minute 1) and NAVIGA-TION (63 actions at minute 0, 39 at minute 1). This suggests learners were orienting themselves within the platform and re-viewing task guidelines before actively engaging in essay writing.
· Shift to annotation and reading (Minute 2-4): ANNOTATION and READING actions increased significantly between minutes 2-4 (e.g., ANNOTATION peaked at 57 actions at minute 3, while READING peaked at 54 actions). This indicates learners were actively analyzing and processing information, likely to support essay development.
· Essay writing gains momentum (Minute 3-6): ESSAY actions steadily increased, peaking at 59 actions at minute 4 and remain-ing high (50+ actions) through minute 6. This suggests learners transitioned from preparation to sustained writing activity.
· Decline in instruction and navigation (Minute 3-6): Actions related to INSTRUCTION and NAVIGATION dropped signif-icantly after minute 3 (e.g., INSTRUCTION fell from 27 actions at minute 3 to 9 at minute 6). This reflects learners shifting focus away from platform exploration toward task execution.

Fig. 2. Raincloud plot and its LLM-generated interpretation for 0–7 min (RQ1)

5.2 RQ2: Group Difference Analysis

The group comparison analysis achieved 76% accuracy for single-graph inter-pretations, 65% for window summaries, and 74% for the final temporal narrative. Without being informed of group performance labels, the LLM identified tem-porally distinct behavioral patterns aligning with differences documented in the self-regulated learning literature [10,11,26]. It detected that g2 transitioned more rapidly into essay writing within the first 7 min (S3, Fig. 3), while g1 devoted substantially more time to reviewing task instructions (S2) – consistent with research on premature task execution and lower performance [11,21,26]. Fur-ther valid observations included g2's alternating engagement between reading and essay composition (S5, S10) and heavier time-checking in the final phase (S11). These subtle differences emerged clearly only when insights were con-solidated across multiple temporal perspectives. However, the LLM exhibited interpretive overreach, framing g2's quick transition as "exploratory behavior" (S2) and attributing favorable descriptors like "diverse", "reflective", "iterative" to g2's approach (S11, S13), contradicting actual performance data and likely reflecting the LLM's tendency toward balanced framings rather than critical analysis.

6 Discussion

6.1 LLM Capabilities in Temporal Analytics Interpretation

Our findings provide evidence that LLMs can interpret complex temporal learn-ing analytics and generate accessible narratives for educators, addressing a

Over the 45-minute essay-writing task, g1 and g2 exhibited evolving differences in their approaches, reflecting distinct strategies and priorities [S1]. Early on (w1), g1 demonstrated a structured, goal-oriented approach, focusing heavily on INSTRUCTION and ANNOTATION with strong connections to ESSAY, suggesting deliberate preparation [S2]. In contrast, g2 transitioned quickly to ESSAY writing, emphasizing exploratory behaviors with weaker planning connections [S3]. By w2, g2's focus on ESSAY intensified, integrating ANNOTATION and NAVIGATION strategically, while g1 maintained a preparatory focus with more evenly distributed READING and ANNOTATION actions [S4].

In w3, g2 sustained higher ESSAY engagement, alternating iteratively with READING, while g1 exhibited more frequent NAVIGATION and PLANNER use, reflecting a less linear workflow [S5]. G2's iterative writing process contrasted with g1's later integration of ANNOTATION and READING [S6]. By w4, g2's ESSAY writing remained dominant, with exploratory use of tools like SEARCH_ANNOTATION and PLANNER, though connections between ANNOTATION and other actions weakened [S7]. G1, meanwhile, showed stronger NAVIGATION -> READING transitions, indicating effective resource use but a more linear approach [S8].

In w5, g1 sustained consistent ESSAY engagement, with stronger NAVIGATION -> ESSAY transitions, reflecting structured task re-engagement [S9]. G2 balanced ESSAY writing with increased READING and ANNOTATION, suggesting a focus on refining ideas but with weaker integration of resources [S10]. Finally, in w6, g2 adopted a diverse, strategic approach, engaging heavily with ANNOTATION, TIMER, and PLANNER, while g1 focused narrowly on ESSAY writing, peaking later in the window [S11]. G2's stronger integration of READING and ANNOTATION into writing contrasted with g1's exploratory NAVIGATION behaviors [S12].

Overall, g1 displayed a structured, resource-focused approach with consistent ESSAY engagement, while g2 evolved toward a more strategic, reflective, and iterative workflow, emphasizing integration and time management [S13]. These differences highlight distinct learning strategies and priorities over time [S14].

Fig. 3. LLM-generated temporal narrative for RQ2

critical gap in translating researcher-grade insights into actionable pedagogical knowledge. Despite operating under constraints (free-tier API limits, restricted context windows, zero-shot prompting), ChatGPT-4o generated coherent, data-grounded temporal narratives across both research questions. Notably, claims regarding graph edges, nodes, and action labels were remarkably free from hallucinations when visualizations were provided as text, whereas prior investigations using image inputs revealed susceptibility to misidentifications from resolution issues, overlapping labels, and spatial ambiguities [2], suggesting text-based representations may prove more reliable for LLM interpretation at the current state of the technology. Qualitative analysis further revealed theoretically-informed interpretations aligned with established findings in self-regulated learning [11,26].

6.2 Implications for Educational Practice and Research

Our results demonstrate that LLMs can generate valid interpretations of temporal analytics in accessible language for educators who lack expertise in complex visualizations like ENA and TNA. A real-time system converting classroom insights into actionable narratives could prove transformative, enabling data-driven pedagogical adjustments without requiring specialized analytical skills. Incorporating knowledge bases with expert graph interpretations and educator perspectives could further improve grounding. Pairing LLM-generated narratives with simpler visualisations like raincloud plots (as in Fig. 2) can enhance teacher autonomy while supporting human-AI synergy. Beyond educators, LLM-assisted interpretation could expedite temporal exploration in time-sensitive scenarios and improve decision-making, given that even expert analysts are prone to misinterpretation and bias [1]. Systematic testing is needed to examine how context-specific inputs like action labels, temporal granularities, and graph representations shape LLM interpretations, and whether resulting narratives yield insights that generalize beyond the context in which they were generated [10].

6.3   Limitations and Future Directions

Free-tier API constraints impose context window limits, and zero-shot prompting, although chosen to evaluate whether interpretations could be generated through prompting only for a particular context, likely understates the technology's potential, given that fine-tuning and few-shot examples can substantially improve graph interpretation performance [5,8]. This evaluation used a single learning context; establishing generalizability requires systematic testing across diverse activities, temporal durations, and learner populations, alongside investigation of different LLM architectures and hybrid human-AI workflows. Incorporating multimodal channels like eye-tracking as LLM inputs may further enable deeper automated temporal insights into learning processes [12].

References

1. Glazer, N.: Challenges with graph interpretation: a review of the literature. Stud. Sci. Educ. **47**(2), 183–210 (2011)
2. Gutierrez, S., et al.: Seeing the forest and the trees: solving visual graph and tree based data structure problems using large multimodal models. In: Proceedings of the 27th Australasian Computing Education Conference (2025)
3. Iyengar, A.I.K.N., Mukhopadhyay, S., Qidwai, A., Singh, S., Roth, D., Gupta, V.: InterChart: benchmarking visual reasoning across decomposed and distributed chart information (2025). arXiv:2508.07630 arXiv preprint
4. Jin, F.J.Y., et al.: Analytics of self-regulated learning in learning analytics feedback processes: associations with feedback literacy in secondary education. J. Comput. Assisted Learn. **41**(4) (2025)
5. Jin, Y., et al.: Chatting with a learning analytics dashboard: the role of generative AI literacy on learner interaction with conventional and scaffolding chatbots. In: Proceedings of the 15th International Learning Analytics and Knowledge Conference, pp. 579–590 (2025)
6. Kaliisa, R., Dolonen, J.A.: CADA: a teacher-facing learning analytics dashboard to foster teachers' awareness of students' participation and discourse patterns in online discussions. Technol. Knowl. Learn. **28**(3), 937–958 (2023)
7. Li, X., et al.: The FLoRA Engine: using analytics to measure and facilitate learners' own regulation activities. J. Learn. Anal **12**(1), 391–413 (2025)
8. Li, Y., Hu, B., Shi, H., Wang, W., Wang, L., Zhang, M.: VisionGraph: leveraging large multimodal models for graph theory problems in visual context. In: Proceedings of the 41st International Conference on Machine Learning (2024)
9. Molenaar, I., Wise, A.F.: Temporal aspects of learning analytics: grounding analyses in concepts of time. In: The Handbook of Learning Analytics, pp 66–76 (2022)
10. Nath, D., Fan, Y., Gašević, D., Rajendran, R.: Balancing contextualization and generalization in trace-based measurement of self-regulated learning: a systematic review of theoretically grounded studies. Review Educat. Res., 00346543251382238 (2025)

11. Nath, D., Gasevic, D., Fan, Y., Rajendran, R.: CTAM4SRL: a consolidated temporal analytic method for analysis of self-regulated learning. In: Proceedings of the 14th Learning Analytics and Knowledge Conference, pp. 645–655 (2024)
12. Nath, D., Gašević, D., Fan, Y., Rajendran, R.: How do learners read the content in a multi-source reading-to-write task?-A multimodal study. In: International Conference on Artificial Intelligence in Education, pp. 293–300 (2025)
13. Nazeri, S., Hatala, M., Salehian Kia, F.: When to intervene? Utilizing two facets of temporality in students' SRL processes in a programming course. In: LAK23: 13th International Learning Analytics and Knowledge Conference, pp. 293–302 (2023)
14. Pozdniakov, S., Martinez-Maldonado, R., Tsai, Y.S., Srivastava, N., Liu, Y., Gasevic, D.: Single or multi-page learning analytics dashboards? Relationships between teachers' cognitive load and visualisation literacy. In: European Conference on Technology Enhanced Learning, pp. 339–355 (2023)
15. Saint, J., Fan, Y., Gašević, D., Pardo, A.: Temporally-focused analytics of self-regulated learning: a systematic review of literature. Comput. Educ. Artif. Intell. **3**, 100060 (2022)
16. Saint, J., Gašević, D., Matcha, W., Uzir, N.A., Pardo, A.: Combining analytic methods to unlock sequential and temporal patterns of self-regulated learning. In: Proceedings of the Tenth International Conference on Learning Analytics & Knowledge, pp. 402–411 (2020)
17. Saqr, M., López-Pernas, S., Törmänen, T., Kaliisa, R., Misiejuk, K., Tikka, S.: Transition network analysis: A novel framework for modeling, visualizing, and identifying the temporal patterns of learners and learning processes. In: Proceedings of the 15th International Learning Analytics and Knowledge Conference, (2025)
18. Shaffer, D., Ruis, A.: Epistemic network analysis: a worked example of theory-based learning analytics. In: Handbook of Learning Analytics (2017)
19. Shah, M., Tan, Y., Eagan, B., Chabalowski, B., Chen, Y.: A dual-method examination of nursing students' teamwork in simulation-based learning: combining CORDTRA and ordered network analysis to reveal patterns and dynamics. In: Proceedings of the 15th International Learning Analytics and Knowledge Conference, pp. 858–864 (2025)
20. Swiecki, Z., Lian, Z., Ruis, A., Shaffer, D.W.: Does order matter? Investigating sequential and cotemporal models of collaboration. In: Proceedings of the International Conference on Computer Supported Collaborative Learning (2019)
21. Thiede, K.W., de Bruin, A.B.: Self-regulated learning in reading. In: Handbook of self-Regulation of Learning and Performance, pp. 124–137. Routledge (2017)
22. Wei, Z., et al.: MORF ENA–a tool for making MOOC discussion forum data more accessible for epistemic network analysis. In: Proceedings of the 19th International Conference of the Learning Sciences-ICLS 2025, pp. 1569-1573. International Society of the Learning Sciences (2025)
23. Yan, L., et al.: VizChat: enhancing learning analytics dashboards with contextualised explanations using multimodal generative AI chatbots. In: International Conference on Artificial Intelligence in Education, pp. 180–193 (2024)
24. Ye, Y., et al.: Generative AI for visualization: State of the art and future directions. Vis. Info. **8**(2), (2024)
25. Zec, S., Soriani, N., Comoretto, R., Baldi, I.: High agreement and high prevalence: the paradox of Cohen's kappa. Open Nurs. J. **11**, 211 (2017)
26. Zhao, L., Raković, M., Cloude, B., Li, E., Gašević, X., Bardach, D., L.: The effect of sequential transition of self-regulated learning processes on performance: insights from ordered network analysis. In: Proceedings of the 15th International Learning Analytics and Knowledge Conference, pp. 516–526. (2025)

FairDetect: Training-Time Fairness for AI-Generated Text Detection via Perplexity-Adaptive Focal Loss

Salima Lamsiyah[✉][iD]

Department of Computer Science, Faculty of Science, Technology and Medicine,
University of Luxembourg, Luxembourg, Luxembourg
salima.lamsiyah@uni.lu

Abstract. Automated detectors of AI-generated student writing are increasingly used in educational settings, yet growing evidence shows that they disproportionately misclassify writing by non-native English speakers (NNES) as AI-generated. We argue that this disparity reflects a representational limitation rather than a thresholding artifact, as modern transformer-based detectors often rely on a spurious shortcut that associates syntactic simplicity and low language-model perplexity with AI authorship. To mitigate this issue, we propose *FairDetect*, a training-time approach based on *Perplexity-Adaptive Focal Loss* (PAFL), which down-weights low-perplexity AI samples during optimization and discourages reliance on fluency-based cues while preserving hard-example learning. We evaluate PAFL on a multi-source benchmark comprising native English essays, NNES learner writing, and AI-generated text. Results show that FairDetect consistently reduces NNES false positive rates and narrows native-NNES disparities while maintaining competitive overall detection performance. These findings suggest that suppressing perplexity-based shortcuts during training can support fairer and more reliable AI-generated text detection for educational assessment. To support reproducibility, the source code is publicly available at https://github.com/lamsiyah/FairDetect.

Keywords: AI-Generated Text Detection · Fairness in Educational Assessment · NNES Bias · Academic Integrity

1 Introduction

AI-generated text detectors are increasingly used in educational settings to support academic integrity. However, recent surveys and reviews raise serious concerns about their reliability, transparency, and fairness, reporting high false positive rates and negative impacts on trust, assessment practices, and student well-being [1,6,9,11,16]. These concerns are especially critical in high-stakes academic contexts, where erroneous accusations can carry lasting academic and psychological consequences.

E. G. Blanchard et al. (Eds.): AIED 2026, LNAI 16583, pp. 398–406, 2027.
https://doi.org/10.1007/978-3-032-29760-0_44

A growing body of empirical work shows that current AI detectors disproportionately misclassify non-native English speakers as AI-generated [3,5,13,17].
Similar misclassification patterns have also been reported for other marginalized
writing styles, including autistic authors [4]. Prior analyses attribute these disparities to detectors' reliance on surface-level statistical signals such as fluency,
syntactic simplicity, and low perplexity, which overlap with legitimate linguistic variation rather than authorship intent [7,8,19]. As a result, low linguistic
complexity becomes a spurious proxy for AI authorship during model training.

Several mitigation strategies have been proposed, including group-aware
thresholding [15], post hoc calibration, behavioral signals such as keystroke
dynamics [14], and benchmark-based bias auditing [2]. While these approaches
can reduce observed disparities, most operate at inference time or focus on evaluation, leaving the underlying shortcut learning mechanism unaddressed.

In this work, we propose *FairDetect*, a training-time approach to fair AI-
generated text detection. *FairDetect* introduces a *Perplexity-Adaptive Focal Loss*
that explicitly down-weights low-perplexity AI samples during optimization, discouraging reliance on predictability-based shortcuts while preserving detection
utility. Experiments on educationally motivated benchmarks demonstrate substantial reductions in NNES false positive rates and group disparities with minimal impact on overall performance. PAFL is complementary to post-hoc thresholding and representation-level invariance methods: unlike threshold adjustment,
it modifies the training signal itself, and unlike group-aware approaches, it does
not require sensitive attributes at inference time. By targeting fairness during
training through loss shaping rather than post hoc correction, this work contributes a practical perspective for research on fairness-aware AI-generated text
detection.

2   *FairDetect* Method

We present *FairDetect*, a training-time approach for AI-generated text detection
that reduces NNES false positives by limiting reliance on perplexity-based cues
during learning, with the full optimization procedure outlined in Algorithm 1.

2.1   Problem Setup

We study binary AI-generated text detection in educational settings, where false
accusations against NNES are particularly harmful. Each text sample is an essay
x with an authorship label $y \in \{\text{HUMAN}, \text{AI}\}$. For analysis and evaluation only,
we additionally consider a group label $g \in \{\text{NATIVE}, \text{NNES}\}$ indicating the
writer's language background.

Our primary fairness objective is to reduce both the false positive rate (FPR)
on NNES writing and the disparity in false positive rates across groups:

$$\Delta_{\text{FPR}} = |\text{FPR}_{\text{Native}} - \text{FPR}_{\text{NNES}}|, \tag{1}$$

Algorithm 1: Training FairDetect with Perplexity-Adaptive Focal Loss (PAFL)

Input: Training set $\mathcal{D} = \{(x_i, y_i)\}_{i=1}^{N}$,
Pretrained encoder f_θ,
Fixed external language model $\mathcal{M}_{\mathrm{ppl}}$,
Focal loss parameters α_y, γ,
Perplexity modulation strength η
Output: Trained detector parameters θ
Preprocessing:
foreach $x_i \in \mathcal{D}$ **do**
> Compute perplexity $\mathrm{ppl}(x_i)$ using $\mathcal{M}_{\mathrm{ppl}}$
> Compute normalized score $z_i = (\log \mathrm{ppl}(x_i) - \mu)/\sigma$
> Compute $\tilde{p}_i = \mathrm{clip}(\sigma(z_i), 0, 1)$

Training:
foreach *mini-batch* $\mathcal{B} \subset \mathcal{D}$ **do**
> **foreach** $(x_i, y_i) \in \mathcal{B}$ **do**
>> Compute prediction $\hat{p}_i = \mathrm{Pr}_\theta(y = \mathrm{AI} \mid x_i)$
>> Compute focal loss $\mathcal{L}_{\mathrm{FL}}(p_{t,i})$
>> **if** $y_i = \mathrm{AI}$ **then**
>>> Set $w_i = \tilde{p}_i^\eta$
>>
>> **else**
>>> Set $w_i = 1$
>>
>> Compute $\mathcal{L}_{\mathrm{PAFL}}(x_i, y_i) = w_i \cdot \mathcal{L}_{\mathrm{FL}}(p_{t,i})$
>
> Update θ by minimizing the average $\mathcal{L}_{\mathrm{PAFL}}$ over $\mathcal{B}$

return θ

---

where $\mathrm{FPR}_g = \mathrm{Pr}(\hat{y} = \mathrm{AI} \mid y = \mathrm{HUMAN}, g)$ denotes the probability that a human-authored essay from group g is incorrectly classified as AI-generated. Minimizing Δ_{FPR} therefore seeks to reduce unequal exposure to false accusations between native and non-native English speakers. By defining fairness in terms of parity of false positive errors on human-authored text, the objective reflects educational risk more directly than aggregate performance metrics, which can mask group-level harms.

2.2   Backbone Detector

We formulate AI-generated text detection as a binary classification task with labels $y \in \{\mathrm{HUMAN}, \mathrm{AI}\}$. Given an input essay x, a transformer-based encoder with parameters θ produces a contextual representation $h = f_\theta(x)$ using standard pooling (e.g., [CLS]). A classification head then estimates the probability $\hat{p} = \mathrm{Pr}_\theta(y = \mathrm{AI} \mid x)$.

We instantiate f_θ with DeBERTa-v3 [12], which provides strong performance on text classification. This backbone serves as a standard detector architecture, while fairness considerations are addressed through the training objective described in the following section.

2.3 Perplexity-Adaptive Focal Loss (PAFL)

Motivation. A recurring failure mode of AI-text detectors is to over-rely on a spurious shortcut: *"low perplexity $\Rightarrow$ AI"*. This shortcut is harmful in educational contexts because NNES writing can exhibit syntactic simplicity and repetitive constructions that also yield low perplexity under common language models. We therefore propose a training objective that (i) emphasizes hard-to-classify samples and (ii) explicitly discourages learning from low-perplexity artifacts in the AI class.

Base Focal Loss. Let p_t denote the probability assigned by the detector to the ground-truth class. We start from focal loss [18]:

$$\mathcal{L}_{\mathrm{FL}}(p_t) = -\alpha_y(1 - p_t)^\gamma \log(p_t), \tag{2}$$

where α_y is a class-balancing factor and $\gamma > 0$ focuses learning on hard examples.

Perplexity Modulation. Let $\mathrm{ppl}(x)$ be the perplexity of x computed by a fixed external language model (e.g., GPT-2), used only to derive a training-time weight. We normalize log-perplexity using training-set statistics:

$$z(x) = \frac{\log \mathrm{ppl}(x) - \mu}{\sigma}, \tag{3}$$

then map it to $[0, 1]$ via a bounded squashing function:

$$\tilde{p}(x) = \mathrm{clip}\big(\sigma(z(x)), 0, 1\big), \tag{4}$$

where $\sigma(\cdot)$ denotes the logistic sigmoid and clip prevents extreme values.

We define a perplexity-adaptive weight $w(x, y)$ that down-weights *low-perplexity AI* samples:

$$w(x, y) = \begin{cases} \tilde{p}(x)^\eta, & \text{if } y = \text{AI}, \\ 1, & \text{if } y = \text{Human}, \end{cases} \tag{5}$$

where $\eta > 0$ controls the strength of the modulation. Intuitively, if an AI sample has very low perplexity, its contribution to the gradient is reduced, limiting the incentive to learn a trivial perplexity-based decision boundary.

Final Objective. The proposed Perplexity-Adaptive Focal Loss is:

$$\mathcal{L}_{\mathrm{PAFL}}(x, y) = w(x, y) \cdot \mathcal{L}_{\mathrm{FL}}(p_t). \tag{6}$$

PAFL combines the benefits of focal loss (hard-example emphasis) with explicit suppression of perplexity-driven shortcuts on the AI class. This encourages the detector to rely more on semantic and discourse cues rather than fluency or predictability proxies.

2.4   Training Procedure

We fine-tune the detector using mini-batch optimization with early stopping on a validation set. Perplexity scores are computed once per sample using a fixed external language model (GPT-2) and cached prior to training. Hyperparameters γ and η are tuned on the validation set while monitoring both overall utility (Macro F1) and fairness metrics such as FPR_{NNES} and Δ_{FPR}. Group labels (Native vs. NNES) are used only for evaluation and are not required at inference time. Likewise, GPT-2 serves only as a fixed and inexpensive source of relative perplexity scores for training-time weighting, not as a detector itself. This setup avoids additional deployment-time requirements. We instantiate FairDetect with DeBERTa-v3 as a standard and well-established detector backbone so that the contribution of the proposed loss shaping can be assessed without architectural confounds.

Computational Overhead. PAFL introduces minimal computational overhead relative to standard fine-tuning. The only additional preprocessing step is a one-time computation of essay perplexities with a fixed external language model, after which the scores are cached. During optimization, PAFL adds only a scalar sample weight to the focal loss, and inference-time cost remains unchanged because neither perplexity nor group information is required at deployment.

3   Experimental Results

In this section, we evaluate the efficacy of *FairDetect* in mitigating bias against NNES while maintaining good overall detection performance. We aim to address the following research questions: **RQ1 (Fairness):** Does *FairDetect* reduce the disparity in False Positive Rates (FPR) between native and non-native writers? **RQ2 (Utility):** Does penalizing perplexity-based shortcuts degrade general detection performance? **RQ3 (Mechanism):** Does the proposed objective decouple the detector's predictions from spurious perplexity cues?

3.1   Datasets

We construct a composite evaluation benchmark from open-access corpora to reflect realistic educational deployment with linguistically diverse writing.

NNES Human Essays (Hard Negatives). We use the *ELLIPSE* corpus[1], which contains approximately 6,500 essays written by non-native English speakers and annotated with proficiency information. Due to their syntactic simplicity and limited lexical diversity, these essays frequently trigger false positives in standard detectors and therefore serve as hard negatives for fairness evaluation.

Native Human Essays. Native-speaker writing is sampled from the human-authored portion of the *HC3* corpus [10], which provides high-quality English prose and serves as the reference group for measuring disparity.

---

[1] https://www.kaggle.com/datasets/mpware/ellipse-corpus?resource=download.

AI-Generated Text. AI-generated samples are drawn from the ChatGPT portion of *HC3* [10]. Human and AI texts are drawn from matched topical settings within HC3, which helps reduce confounding effects due to content differences.

Splits and Usage. We create document-level stratified train, validation, and test splits using a 60/20/20 ratio, ensuring no prompt or near-duplicate overlap across splits. Group labels (Native vs. NNES) are used exclusively for evaluation. All detectors are trained on the same pooled training distribution, so observed disparities reflect model behavior rather than corpus-specific supervision.

3.2 Baselines

We compare *FairDetect* against three representative baselines: **DeBERTa-v3 (Standard):** A DeBERTa-v3-base classifier fine-tuned using cross-entropy loss, representing a strong supervised baseline without fairness constraints. **Detect-GPT (Zero-Shot):** A curvature-based zero-shot detector [20] that explicitly relies on likelihood and perplexity signals, serving as a proxy for *pure* perplexity-based detection. **Reweighting (Class-Balancing):** A standard fairness baseline in which training samples are weighted inversely to their class frequency to mitigate majority-class bias.

3.3 Main Results

Table 1 reports the detection and fairness performance of all models. We report the FPR for NNES essays (ELLIPSE), the FPR for native essays (HC3-Human), and the overall Macro F1 score on the balanced test set.

Table 1. Detection performance and fairness metrics. **FPR-NNES** denotes the false positive rate on ELLIPSE (hard negatives), and **FPR-Native** denotes the false positive rate on HC3 human essays. Lower values indicate better fairness.

Method	Macro F1 ↑	FPR-Native ↓	FPR-NNES ↓	Δ_{FPR} ↓
DetectGPT (Zero-Shot)	0.76	0.02	0.61	0.59
DeBERTa-v3 (Standard)	**0.97**	**0.01**	0.16	0.15
Reweighting (Class-Bal.)	0.95	0.02	0.11	0.09
FairDetect (Ours)	0.96	**0.01**	**0.03**	**0.02**

Vulnerability of Standard Detectors. Consistent with prior findings on linguistic bias, the zero-shot *DetectGPT* method falsely flags 61% of NNES essays as AI-generated. Although the supervised DeBERTa-v3 classifier achieves high aggregate performance, it inherits this bias, yielding an FPR_{NNES} of 16% compared to just 1% for native essays. This indicates that standard fine-tuning implicitly exploits a *simplicity shortcut* correlated with non-native writing.

Efficacy of FairDetect. *FairDetect* successfully suppresses this shortcut. The NNES false positive rate is reduced from 16% to 3%, corresponding to an improvement of over 80%. The disparity gap Δ_{FPR} is reduced to 0.02, indicating near parity between native and non-native writers. This fairness gain comes with minimal cost to utility: the Macro F1 score decreases by only 0.01 relative to the standard baseline.

Mechanism Analysis. To analyze the mechanism underlying these improvements, we compute the correlation between text perplexity and the predicted probability of AI authorship, $\hat{p}_{\mathrm{AI}}$. For the standard DeBERTa model, we observe a strong negative Pearson correlation on the NNES subset ($r = -0.74$), indicating that lower perplexity strongly increases AI confidence. In contrast, *FairDetect* substantially weakens this relationship ($r = -0.28$), suggesting reduced reliance on perplexity-related cues and greater use of alternative signals beyond surface-level predictability. This confirms that the Perplexity-Adaptive Focal Loss effectively suppresses reliance on spurious statistical shortcuts.

Discussion. These results point to an important limitation of current AI-generated text detectors: the overlap between statistical properties commonly associated with AI text, such as low perplexity, and legitimate linguistic characteristics of non-native English writing. By explicitly discouraging reliance on this signal during training, *FairDetect* encourages the model to draw on a broader set of cues beyond surface-level predictability. While no detector can fully eliminate errors, the proposed approach consistently reduces false positives for NNES writers with minimal impact on overall performance, representing a step toward fairer use of AI-generated text detection in educational contexts.

Implications for Educational Deployment. FairDetect is intended as a decision-support component rather than an automated accusation system. In practice, we envision it being used with conservative operating points that prioritize low false positive rates, especially for human-authored student writing, and with all detector outputs treated as signals for instructor review rather than final judgments. Because PAFL does not require group labels or additional behavioral signals at inference time, it can be integrated into existing detection pipelines while remaining compatible with human-in-the-loop workflows, confidence-based flagging, and institutional review policies.

Limitations and Future Work

This study has several limitations. First, our experiments focus on a single detector backbone, DeBERTa-v3, and one training-time mitigation strategy, PAFL. Although this design isolates the effect of the proposed loss shaping, additional experiments with other architectures and fine-tuning setups are needed to assess generality more fully. Second, fairness is evaluated using a binary grouping of Native versus NNES writers and measured through false positive rate parity on human-authored essays. While this captures a central educational risk, it does not account for finer-grained variation such as proficiency levels, first-language backgrounds, dialectal differences, or intersectional factors.

Third, the evaluation benchmark combines corpora from multiple sources, which may introduce residual domain differences despite pooled training and consistent evaluation protocols. Fourth, PAFL relies on perplexity scores produced by a fixed external language model, and its behavior may therefore vary across domains, time periods, or alternative perplexity estimators. A related trade-off is that reducing reliance on low-perplexity AI samples may weaken sensitivity to highly fluent machine-generated text in some settings, or shift the detector toward other superficial cues. In our experiments, this risk appears limited, since fairness improves substantially while Macro F1 decreases only marginally, but a broader analysis of alternative shortcut features remains necessary.

Finally, we do not evaluate robustness under adversarial transformations such as paraphrasing, translation, or human post-editing, nor do we study mixed-authorship settings or downstream classroom decision workflows. Future work will extend PAFL to a broader range of detector architectures, external language models, and training configurations, and will examine fairness across more fine-grained learner populations. We also plan to investigate robustness under realistic text transformations, calibrated confidence reporting, and human-in-the-loop deployment settings in which detector outputs are used as decision-support signals rather than automated judgments.

References

1. Ardito, C.G.: Generative AI detection in higher education assessments. New Dir. Teach. Learn. **2025**(182), 11–28 (2025)
2. Basu, P., Zhang, Y., Raheja, V.: BAID: a benchmark for bias assessment of AI detectors, (2025). arXiv:2512.11505 arXiv preprint
3. Chaka, C.: Accuracy pecking order-how 30 AI detectors stack up in detecting generative artificial intelligence content in university English 11 and English 12 student essays. J. Appl. Learn. Teach. **7**(1), 127–139 (2024)
4. Chambers, S., Kelley, M.C.: The misclassification of autistic writing as AI-generated. In: International Conference on Artificial Intelligence in Education, pp. 89–103. Springer (2025)
5. Chan, A.L., Chua, R.C., Del Rio, D., Lee, B.C., Ong, R.E., Tiam-Lee, T.J.: The reliability of AI text detectors on Filipino student essays. In: International Conference in Methodologies and Intelligent Systems for Techhnology Enhanced Learning, pp. 47–58. Springer (2025)
6. Deep, P.D., Edgington, W.D., Ghosh, N., Rahaman, M.S.: Evaluating the effectiveness and ethical implications of ai detection tools in higher education. Information **16**(10), 905 (2025)
7. Gegg-Harrison, W., Quarterman, C.: AI detection's high false positive rates and the psychological and material impacts on students. In: Academic Integrity in the Age of Artificial Intelligence, pp. 199–219. IGI Global Scientific Publishing (2024)
8. Giray, L.: The problem with false positives: AI detection unfairly accuses scholars of ai plagiarism. Ser. Libr. **85**(5–6), 181–189 (2024)

9. Giray, L., Sevnarayan, K., Ranjbaran Madiseh, F.: Beyond policing: AI writing detection tools, trust, academic integrity, and their implications for college writing. Int. Ref. Serv. Q. **29**(1), 83–116 (2025)
10. Guo, B., et al.: How close is ChatGPT to human experts? Comparison corpus, evaluation, and detection (2023). arXiv:2301.07597 arXiv preprint
11. Han, J., Yang, Y., Liu, G.: Are teachers assessing work written by students or by AI? A rapid literature review of research on detecting content generated by generative AI. Eur. J. Educ. **60**(4), e70240 (2025)
12. He, P., Gao, J., Chen, W.: DeBERTaV3: improving DeBERTA using electra-style pre-training with gradient-disentangled embedding sharing (2021). arXiv:2111.09543 arXiv preprint
13. Jiang, Y., Hao, J., Fauss, M., Li, C.: Detecting ChatGPT-generated essays in a large-scale writing assessment: is there a bias against non-native English speakers? Comput. Educ. **217**, 105070 (2024)
14. Jiang, Y., Zhang, M., Hao, J., Deane, P., Li, C.: Using keystroke behavior patterns to detect nonauthentic texts in writing assessments: Evaluating the fairness of predictive models. J. Educ. Meas. **61**(4), 571–594 (2024)
15. Jung, M., Panizo, C.F., Dugan, L., Chen, P.Y., Liang, P.P.: Group-adaptive threshold optimization for robust AI-generated text detection (2025). arXiv:2502.04528 arXiv preprint
16. Kangwa, D., Msafiri, M.M., Fute, A.: Exploring the factors that promote a balance between academic integrity and the effective use of GenAI tools in higher education: A systematic review. J. Comput. Assist. Learn. **41**(5), e70109 (2025)
17. Liang, W., Yuksekgonul, M., Mao, Y., Wu, E., Zou, J.: GPT detectors are biased against non-native English writers. Patterns **4**(7) (2023)
18. Lin, T.Y., Goyal, P., Girshick, R., He, K., Dollár, P.: Focal loss for dense object detection. In: Proceedings of the IEEE International Conference on Computer Vision, pp. 2980–2988 (2017)
19. Markl, N.: Language variation and algorithmic bias: understanding algorithmic bias in British English automatic speech recognition. In: Proceedings of the 2022 ACM Conference on Fairness, Accountability, and Transparency, pp. 521–534 (2022)
20. Mitchell, E., Lee, Y., Khazatsky, A., Manning, C.D., Finn, C.: DetectGPT: zero-shot machine-generated text detection using probability curvature. In: International Conference on Machine Learning, pp. 24950–24962 (2023) PMLR

Reliability as a Teammate: Budgeted Verifier-in-the-Loop (BVIL) Policies for Reliable LLM Tutoring Actions

Partha Sarathi Purkayastha[✉][iD]

ETH Zürich, Zürich, Switzerland
`ppurkayastha@ethz.ch`

Abstract. Large language models (LLMs) are increasingly deployed as tutors, yet "tutor-like" behavior in interactive intelligent tutoring system (ITS) interfaces remains brittle. TutorGym operationalizes this gap by evaluating whether a tutor agent can (i) grade candidate actions as correct/incorrect and (ii) produce a correct next-step demonstration action (selection–action–input) for a given tutor state. We study a compute-frugal setting: no new datasets, no finetuning, and only TutorGym's established metrics and baselines. We introduce a *budgeted verifier-in-the-loop* (BVIL) policy: a tutor proposes candidate actions and may query a check-only verifier up to a fixed budget B per state; optionally, minimal verifier feedback is injected to diversify subsequent attempts. Using a local open model (Qwen3-8B in non-thinking mode), BVIL yields large improvements in next-action accuracy under small budgets. With $B=5$, $K=3$ candidates per round, and feedback enabled, next-action accuracy increases from $25.88\% \rightarrow 32.58\%$ (CTAT), $45.22\% \rightarrow 62.70\%$ (Apprentice), and $36.35\% \rightarrow 55.82\%$ (OATutor). Ablations show that increasing candidate count alone produces modest gains, while verifier-guided feedback accounts for most improvements. These results support an AIED "tools-to-teammates" framing: bounded verification can act as a practical guardrail that makes LLM tutoring actions more reliable under realistic resource constraints.

Keywords: LLM tutoring · Intelligent Tutoring Systems · Tool use · Verification · TutorGym

1 Introduction

LLMs can generate explanations, hints, and worked solutions on demand, which has accelerated interest in "LLM tutors" across formal and informal learning contexts. This interest is fueled by rapid advances in general-purpose language modeling and instruction following [4,19]. However, much of the optimism is still grounded in benchmarks that score final answers or free-form explanations, rather than the grounded, step-level behaviors that ITSs have historically relied on to detect mistakes early and scaffold learning effectively. Decades of ITS

E. G. Blanchard et al. (Eds.): AIED 2026, LNAI 16583, pp. 407–416, 2027.
https://doi.org/10.1007/978-3-032-29760-0_45

research argues that the granularity of interaction matters: step-based tutoring can approach the effectiveness of human tutoring while providing adaptive feedback and practice selection at fine skill resolutions [3,6,27]. Modern tutoring prototypes also inherit the broader trajectory of instruction-tuned LLMs: large pretrained models (e.g., In-context learners) can follow natural-language tutoring prompts surprisingly well [4], and reinforcement learning from human feedback has further improved instruction-following and helpfulness [19]. Yet instruction following alone is not sufficient for step-level tutoring, where a tutor must act in a constrained interface and where each action can be mechanically verified.

TutorGym makes this mismatch concrete by embedding AI agents inside real tutor interfaces (CTAT, Apprentice Tutors, OATutor) and evaluating step-level tutoring behaviors directly [1,15,20,30]. In TutorGym's tutoring evaluation, several strong commercial LLMs failed to exceed chance at labeling incorrect actions, while next-step demonstration accuracy remained only about 52–70% [30]. Those results highlight both (i) the fragility of step-level tutoring with LLMs and (ii) the value of grounded interface-based correctness signals.

This provides us with a practical opportunity to integrate LLMs with executable correctness checks (domain models, behavior graphs, rule engines), producing better reliable tutoring systems without requiring any re-training or new data. In our work, we explore this direction and contribute (1) a simple, reproducible *budgeted verifier-in-the-loop* (BVIL) policy for TutorGym next-action generation, (2) a configuration sweep over budget B, candidate count K, and feedback toggle F using a single local open model, and (3) an analysis of the accuracy–budget trade-off and the role of verifier-guided feedback.

2 Related Work

Step-based ITSs utilize domain models to recognize partial progress, diagnose errors, and provide tailored hints (e.g., model tracing, example tracing) [1–3,9]. Their success motivates evaluating tutoring behaviors at the interface-action level rather than just final outcomes [27]. TutorGym extends this tradition, providing a standardized API and completeness profiles to evaluate tutoring behaviors across domains [30]. Recent reviews highlight the rapid expansion of LLM-based tutoring and automated feedback, while noting persistent concerns regarding reliability, bias, privacy, and over-reliance [10,25]. While existing work often focuses on rubric-based grading or pedagogical response quality (e.g., mistake identification and guidance) [21,22], we focus on grounding tutoring behaviors within executable tutor interfaces. Inference-time accuracy can be improved by generating multiple candidates and selecting via verifiers or self-consistency [5,28,29]. Tool-augmented agents and iterative self-refinement methods further interleave reasoning with actions and external feedback to revise outputs [17,24]. Verification-oriented prompting and hallucination reduction methods also use explicit checking steps for improved performance [7,11,18]. BVIL adapts these verification-oriented prompting and search strategies to the step-level tutoring context using a strict query budget and a check-only verifier.

3 TutorGym Evaluation

TutorGym evaluates tutor agents with *completeness profiles*, which pair each tutor state with: (i) all valid demonstration actions for that state, and (ii) when available, both correct and incorrect student actions. A fully reliable tutor should therefore do three things in each state: (a) mark correct actions as correct, (b) reject incorrect actions, and (c) produce at least one valid next action as a demonstration, or bottom-out hint. Accordingly, TutorGym reports three metrics: *Correct Accuracy* for recognizing valid actions, *Incorrect Accuracy* for rejecting invalid ones, and *Demo (Next-Action) Accuracy* for generating a correct next step. It covers three major tutor paradigms: (1) CTAT example-tracing tutors, which involve complex interface widgets and branching control flow [1,2]; (2) Apprentice Tutors, which are rule-based and can use symbolic tools for flexible answer matching [15,16]; and (3) OATutor, which combines adaptive content sequencing with Bayesian knowledge tracing [6,20]. These platforms differ in action spaces, input constraints, and how strongly the tutor model restricts "correct" next steps.

4 Budgeted Verifier-in-the-Loop (BVIL)

In TutorGym, next-step tutoring is not free-form text generation but structured action selection: each tutor move is a selection–action–input (SAI) triple, so even a plausible explanation fails if the selected element, action type, or input is wrong. Crucially, TutorGym can execute a proposed action and check it against the tutor's domain model. BVIL uses this check as a budgeted tool, turning the ITS into an interactive teammate rather than a passive content source, yielding an explicit reliability-cost trade-off. This is not trivial brute force as BVIL limits checks to a budget B, studies performance across budgets, and uses a check-only verifier that never supplies the answer, so the tutor must still solve the step itself, within that budget B. We study three policy families on the same states and metrics: sampling-only, verifier-filtering, and verifier plus feedback-guided resampling, with the last producing the largest gains.

4.1 Policy Definition

BVIL wraps an LLM action proposer with a check-only verifier:

- The **proposer** outputs one or more candidate actions in TutorGym's SAI format.
- The **verifier** executes a candidate action in the environment and returns a binary signal CORRECT/INCORRECT. (We treat the verifier as non-generative as it does not propose actions or explain solutions.)

  We parametrize BVIL by:

- B: maximum number of verifier checks per state ("budget").

- K: number of candidate actions proposed per round.
- $F \in \{0, 1\}$: whether minimal verifier feedback is injected into the next prompt (e.g., "Avoid selecting X"), enabling controlled diversification.

4.2 Algorithm

Algorithm 1 shows the core next-action procedure. Intuitively, BVIL turns next-step tutoring into a small bounded search problem: propose candidates, verify, and stop early if a correct action is found.

Algorithm 1. BVIL for next-action generation in a TutorGym state

---

Require: Tutor state s; LLM proposer π; verifier V; budget B; candidates per round K; feedback toggle F.

```
 1: C ← ∅                                          ▷ context / optional feedback
 2: for t = 1 to B do
 3:     {a₁, ..., a_K} ← π(s, C)                   ▷ propose structured SAI actions
 4:     for i = 1 to K do
 5:         y ← V(s, aᵢ)                           ▷ y ∈ {CORRECT, INCORRECT}
 6:         if y = CORRECT then
 7:             return aᵢ
 8:         else
 9:             if F = 1 then
10:                 C ← C ∪ {minimal feedback about (s, aᵢ, y)}
11:             end if
12:         end if
13:     end for
14: end for
15: return a₁                        ▷ fallback: first proposal (or highest-likelihood)
```

---

5 Experimental Setup

Benchmark and Metrics. We use TutorGym tutoring evaluation completeness profiles (CTAT, Apprentice, and OATutor) and report three accuracies: correct-action grading accuracy, incorrect-action grading accuracy, and next-action (demo) accuracy, matching the platform splits as reported in TutorGym [30]. Since BVIL is designed specifically as a policy for grounded next-step action generation under bounded verification, our configuration sweep focuses primarily on next-action accuracy across all three platforms.

Model and Baseline. We use **Qwen3-8B** as a local open model, in "non-thinking" mode, without finetuning [23] with deterministic decoding (temperature 0, top-p 1) to isolate the impact of BVIL's bounded verification and feedback mechanism. As BVIL can solicit multiple candidates ($K > 1$) and can incorporate feedback ($F = 1$), the method still explores a small action neighborhood even under deterministic decoding. We then compare the results to TutorGym's reported LLM baselines (Sonnet-3.5, Haiku-3.5, GPT-4o, and DeepSeek-v2.5).

6   Results

Baseline Comparison. Table 1 compares our local Qwen3-8B baseline (bold) with TutorGym's published baseline accuracies. On next-action accuracy, our baseline is below the strongest commercial models but comparable to the weaker baselines across CTAT, Apprentice, and OATutor. Notably, our baseline incorrect-action grading accuracy is substantially higher than TutorGym's reported baselines for CTAT and OATutor, despite using a smaller, local model. This makes it a meaningful, compute-frugal starting point for BVIL, where the main question is not raw frontier performance but how much bounded verification can improve a practical local tutor.

Table 1. Comparison of TutorGym tutoring evaluation baselines with our local Qwen3-8B baseline (bold). *Correct* and *Incorrect* denote grading accuracy on correct and incorrect student actions, respectively; *Demo* denotes next-action generation accuracy.

Tutor platform	Model	Correct	Incorrect	Demo
CTAT (10)	Sonnet-3.5	61.92	36.21	56.50
	Haiku-3.5	81.06	25.05	36.49
	GPT-4o	28.11	42.63	38.89
	DeepSeek-v2.5	59.96	30.84	39.33
	Qwen3-8B (ours, B0_K1_F0)	**56.78**	**54.63**	**25.88**
Apprentice (30)	Sonnet-3.5	86.54	46.56	64.20
	Haiku-3.5	88.36	22.34	49.73
	GPT-4o	74.61	49.80	70.75
	DeepSeek-v2.5	82.00	48.92	58.35
	Qwen3-8B (ours, B0_K1_F0)	**72.01**	**47.13**	**45.22**
OATutor (183)	Sonnet-3.5	79.59	38.85	52.10
	Haiku-3.5	92.36	10.82	36.63
	GPT-4o	71.20	38.69	51.07
	DeepSeek-v2.5	90.87	17.21	43.89
	Qwen3-8B (ours, B0_K1_F0)	**79.40**	**47.70**	**36.35**

Table 2. BVIL configuration sweep on Next-action accuracy over verifier budget B, candidate count K, and feedback setting F across CTAT, Apprentice, and OATutor. Cells report next-action accuracy for each setting, with gains relative to the baseline $B0\_K1\_F0$ indicated in parentheses. Best per platform is bold, second-best underlined.

Configuration (B, K, F)	CTAT	Apprentice	OATutor
B0_K1_F0	25.88 (+0.00)	45.22 (+0.00)	36.35 (+0.00)
B3_K1_F0	27.46 (+1.58)	48.06 (+2.84)	37.47 (+1.12)
B5_K1_F0	27.46 (+1.58)	48.06 (+2.84)	37.47 (+1.12)
B0_K3_F1	24.68 (−1.20)	46.06 (+0.84)	36.35 (+0.00)
B1_K3_F1	24.62 (−1.26)	45.65 (+0.43)	35.23 (−1.12)
B3_K3_F0	26.26 (+0.38)	49.98 (+4.76)	39.14 (+2.79)
<u>B3_K3_F1</u>	<u>31.88 (+6.00)</u>	<u>61.13 (+15.91)</u>	<u>52.75 (+16.40)</u>
B5_K3_F0	25.88 (+0.00)	48.86 (+3.64)	37.47 (+1.12)
B5_K3_F1	**32.58 (+6.70)**	**62.70 (+17.48)**	**55.82 (+19.47)**
B0_K15_F0	25.69 (−0.19)	46.36 (+1.14)	36.35 (+0.00)
B0_K15_F1	25.69 (−0.19)	46.36 (+1.14)	36.35 (+0.00)

Performance Across BVIL Design Space. Table 2 summarizes next-action accuracy for a sweep over BVIL configurations, reporting absolute values and gains (Δ) relative to the $B0\_K1\_F0$ baseline.

We observe three consistent trends across platforms - (i) Increasing the verification budget alone provides only modest improvements; moving from $B0$ to $B5$ with a single candidate ($K = 1, F = 0$) yields +1–3 points before saturating, suggesting that "just checking" a single deterministic proposal offers limited leverage (ii) Increasing the candidate count without verifier feedback has negligible impact, with $B5\_K3\_F0$ showing minimal gains over the baseline across platforms, and (iii) Integrating multiple candidates with verifier-guided feedback ($K = 3, F = 1$) produces the most significant performance jumps; under the $B5\_K3\_F1$ regime, accuracy rises to 32.58% (+6.70) on CTAT, 62.70% (+17.48) on Apprentice, and 55.82% (+19.47) on OATutor. Notably, the OATutor result also surpasses the best reported TutorGym demo baseline of 52.10% [30].

This stepwise decomposition confirms that while raw budget or candidate counts independently offer marginal benefits, iterative feedback is the primary driver of pedagogical reliability. However, despite these gains, performance remains far from perfect (particularly on CTAT), highlighting the need for further validation across diverse platforms and tasks.

7   Analysis and Future Work

The large gap between $B5\_K3\_F0$ and $B5\_K3\_F1$ shows that gains do not come from making more attempts alone, but from combining repeated attempts with grounded verification. When $F = 1$, the model conditions on a compact external error signal that acts as a structured constraint, helping eliminate repeated failure modes such as repeatedly selecting the wrong interface element. In this sense, BVIL resembles a test-time analogue of reflection and critique methods [8,17,26], but crucially relies on an externally grounded verifier rather than self-critique. By contrast, increasing K without feedback yields only marginal benefit, consistent with evidence that LLMs do not reliably self-correct without trustworthy external signals [11].

BVIL also makes the reliability-latency trade-off explicit: in Algorithm 1, each round checks at most K candidates, so the worst-case number of verifier calls per state is $B \times K$, while one proposer call returns K structured SAIs, making the worst-case number of proposer calls B and total generated candidates $B \times K$. For $B{=}5, K{=}3$, this gives at most 15 checks and 3–15 LLM generations. We also ran direct 15-candidate settings (worst case total generated candidates), and results stayed near baseline even with feedback: CTAT 25.69% versus 25.88%, Apprentice 46.36% versus 45.22%, and OATutor 36.35% versus 36.35%. Thus, extra compute alone does not buy meaningful gains, they come from spending limited verification budget strategically. For future work, such trade-offs should be evaluated not only in terms of action quality, but also with respect to deployment criteria such as latency, cost, and privacy, which recent works argue are central to real-world educational feedback systems, especially when using smaller local models [12,13,31].

Additionally, CTAT remains harder because its tutors often involve complex control flow, specialized widgets, and more structurally invalid but superficially plausible actions [1,30]. More broadly, bounded verification is a guardrail for action correctness, not a full tutoring policy, though it aligns with tool-augmented reliability mechanisms [14,24]. Since TutorGym measures action correctness rather than learning outcomes, future work should connect verification budgets to pedagogical strategy, learner state, and downstream outcomes such as learning gains, help-seeking, and over-reliance.

8 Limitations

Our verifier uses the tutor environment's own correctness check, which also defines benchmark correctness, so access to it can appear privileged. We view this as educationally realistic, since deployed ITSs already rely on executable domain models for step-level feedback. Moreover, this is not trivial as the verifier is still check-only, so the tutor must still solve the step itself, that too checked to a budget B. Accordingly, BVIL should be understood as a method for allocating limited verification, not replacing the tutor. It applies most naturally in grounded tutor interfaces with executable checkers, as in TutorGym [2,3,30], while freer chat-based tutoring would require learned or heuristic verifiers [5,7,8,14]. We also evaluate many runs only on next-action accuracy and do not measure downstream learning gains, so connecting bounded verification to pedagogical outcomes remains open [25].

9   Conclusion

We presented a compute-frugal study of tool-augmented LLM tutoring in Tutor-Gym. A simple budgeted verifier-in-the-loop policy substantially improves next-action demonstration accuracy for a local open model, with especially large gains on Apprentice and OATutor completeness profiles. However, absolute accuracies remain quite low and BVIL should be understood as a guardrail for action correctness rather than a complete tutoring policy. Our results suggest that bounded verification is a practical mechanism for making LLM tutor actions more reliable without new data or training, and an important next step is to connect budgeted verification to pedagogical strategy, evaluated on downstream learner outcomes.

References

1. Aleven, V., McLaren, B.M., Sewall, J., Koedinger, K.R.: The cognitive tutor authoring tools (CTAT): preliminary evaluation of efficiency gains. In: Intelligent Tutoring Systems. LNCS, vol. 4053, pp. 61–70. Springer (2006). https://doi.org/10.1007/11774303_7
2. Aleven, V., McLaren, B.M., Sewall, J., et al.: Example-tracing tutors: intelligent tutor development for non-programmers. Int. J. Artif. Intell. Educ. **26**(1), 224–269 (2016). https://doi.org/10.1007/s40593-015-0088-2
3. Anderson, J.R., Boyle, C.F., Corbett, A.T., Lewis, M.W.: Cognitive modeling and intelligent tutoring. Artif. Intell. **42**(1), 7–49 (1990)
4. Brown, T.B..: Language models are few-shot learners (2020). arXiv:2005.14165 arXiv preprint
5. Cobbe, K., et al.: Training verifiers to solve math word problems (2021). arXiv:2110.14168 arXiv preprint
6. Corbett, A.T., Anderson, J.R.: Knowledge tracing: modeling the acquisition of procedural knowledge. User Model. User-Adap. Inter. **4**(4), 253–278 (1994)
7. Dhuliawala, S., Komeili, M., Xu, J.: Chain-of-verification reduces hallucination in large language models. In: Findings of the Association for Computational Linguistics: ACL 2024, pp. 1895–1914. Association for Computational Linguistics (2024). https://doi.org/10.18653/v1/2024.findings-acl.111
8. Gou, Z., Shao, Z., Gong, Y.: CRITIC: Large language models can self-correct with tool-interactive critiquing (2023). arXiv:2305.11738 arXiv preprint
9. Graesser, A.C., Lu, S., Jackson, G.T., et al.: AutoTutor: a tutor with dialogue in natural language. Behav. Res. Meth. Instr. Comput **36**(2), 180–192 (2004). https://doi.org/10.3758/BF03195563
10. Guizani, S., Mazhar, T., Shahzad, T., Ahmad, W., Bibi, A., Hamam, H., et al.: A systematic literature review to implement large language model in higher education: issues and solutions. Discover Educ. **4**, 35 (2025). https://doi.org/10.1007/s44217-025-00424-7
11. Huang, J.: Large language models cannot self-correct reasoning yet. In: The Twelfth International Conference on Learning Representations (2024)
12. Kotalwar, N., Gotovos, A., Singla, A.: Hints-in-browser: benchmarking language models for programming feedback generation. In: Advances in Neural Information Processing Systems, vol. 37, pp. 29864–29877. Curran Associates, Inc (2024)

13. Koutcheme, C., Woodrow, J., Piech, C.: Aligning small language models for programming feedback: towards scalable coding support in a massive global course. In: Proceedings of the 57th ACM Technical Symposium on Computer Science Education V. 1, pp. 610–616. Association for Computing Machinery (2026). 10.1145/3770762.3772539

14. Lewis, P., Perez, E., Piktus, A.: Retrieval-augmented generation for knowledge-intensive NLP tasks (2020). arXiv:2005.11401 arXiv preprint

15. MacLellan, C.J.: Closing the loop between learning theory and educational data: a computational theory of learning with the Apprentice Learner architecture. Ph.D. Thesis, University of Pittsburgh (2016)

16. MacLellan, C.J., Koedinger, K.R.: Domain-general tutor authoring with apprentice learner models. Int. J. Artif. Intell. Educ. **32**(1), 76–117 (2022). https://doi.org/10.1007/s40593-020-00214-2

17. Madaan, A., et al.: Self-refine: iterative refinement with self-feedback (2023). arXiv:2303.17651 arXiv preprint

18. Manakul, P., Liusie, A., Gales, M.J.F.: SelfCheckGPT: zero-resource black-box hallucination detection for generative large language models. In: Proceedings of the 2023 Conference on Empirical Methods in Natural Language Processing, pp. 9004–9031. Association for Computational Linguistics (2023). https://doi.org/10.18653/v1/2023.emnlp-main.557

19. Ouyang, L., et al.: Training language models to follow instructions with human feedback (2022). arXiv:2203.02155 arXiv preprint

20. Pardos, Z.A., Tang, M., Anastasopoulos, I., et al.: OATutor: an open-source adaptive tutoring system and curated content library for learning sciences research. In: Proceedings of the 2023 CHI Conference on Human Factors in Computing Systems, pp. 1–17. Association for Computing Machinery (2023). 10.1145/3544548.3581574

21. Park, G., Song, J., Choi, G.: K-NLPers at BEA 2025 shared task: evaluating the quality of AI tutor responses with GPT-4.1. In: Proceedings of the 20th Workshop on Innovative Use of NLP for Building Educational Applications, pp. 1145–1163. Association for Computational Linguistics (2025). https://doi.org/10.18653/v1/2025.bea-1.90

22. Pathak, A., Gandhi, R., Uttam, V.: Rubric is all you need: improving LLM-based code evaluation with question-specific rubrics. In: Proceedings of the 2025 ACM Conference on International Computing Education Research, pp. 181–195. Association for Computing Machinery (2025)

23. Qwen Team: Qwen3 technical report (2025). arXiv:2505.09388 arXiv preprint

24. Schick, T., Dwivedi-Yu, J., Dessi, R.: ToolFormer: language models can teach themselves to use tools (2023). arXiv:2302.04761 arXiv preprint

25. Shi, Y., Yu, K., Dong, Y., Chen, F.: Large language models in education: a systematic review of empirical applications, benefits, and challenges. Comput. Educ. Artif. Intell **10**, 100529 (2026). https://doi.org/10.1016/j.caeai.2025.100529

26. Shinn, N., Cassano, F., Berman, E.: Reflexion: language agents with verbal reinforcement learning (2023). arXiv:2303.11366 arXiv preprint

27. VanLehn, K.: The relative effectiveness of human tutoring, intelligent tutoring systems, and other tutoring systems. Educat. Psychol. **46**(4), 197–221 (2011). https://doi.org/10.1080/00461520.2011.611369

28. Wang, X., Wei, J., Schuurmans, D.: Self-consistency improves chain of thought reasoning in language models (2022). arXiv:2203.11171 arXiv preprint

29. Wei, J., Wang, X., Schuurmans, D.: Chain-of-thought prompting elicits reasoning in large language models (2022). arXiv:2201.11903 arXiv preprint

30. Weitekamp, D., Siddiqui, M.N., MacLellan, C.J.: TutorGYM: a testbed for evaluating AI agents as tutors and students. arXiv preprint arXiv:2505.01563 (2025)
31. Zeng, Z., Wang, J., Yang, J., et al.: PrivacyRestore: privacy-preserving inference in large language models via privacy removal and restoration. In: Proceedings of the 63rd Annual Meeting of the Association for Computational Linguistics, (vol. 1: Long Papers), pp. 10821–10855. Association for Computational Linguistics, Vienna, Austria (2025). 10.18653/v1/2025.acl-long.532

Estimating Learners' Skill Acquisition Without Temporal Information

Ryosuke Nagai[1(✉)] , Kyohei Atarashi[1] , Koh Takeuchi[1] , Jill-Jênn Vie[2] ,
and Hisashi Kashima[1]

[1] Kyoto University, Kyoto, Japan
`nagai.ryosuke@ml.kyoto-u.ac.jp`,
`{atarashi,takeuchi,kashima}@i.kyoto-u.ac.jp`
[2] Inria, Paris, France
`jill-jenn.vie@inria.fr`

Abstract. Recent research in educational data mining, especially knowledge tracing, has focused on predicting learners' future knowledge states to support adaptive instruction. However, in many real-world educational settings, learning data are often available only as single-time-point assessments without temporal information, making existing time-series-based approaches difficult to apply. In this paper, we propose a novel framework for predicting future skill acquisition using only snapshot data. Specifically, we address the problem of predicting the next skill to be acquired from skill mastery patterns estimated by cognitive diagnostic models (CDMs). In the absence of temporal information, we exploit inclusion relations among learners' skill sets to induce a pseudo-temporal ordering, interpreting expanding skill sets as a proxy for learning progression. To efficiently approximate unobserved acquisition paths, we introduce a neural model that captures latent skill acquisition dynamics through expected skill increments. Experiments on both synthetic and real-world datasets demonstrate that the proposed method consistently outperforms baseline approaches, with particularly strong advantages as the skill space becomes larger. These results indicate that meaningful skill acquisition patterns can be inferred from snapshot data alone, providing a practical framework for adaptive learning support in data-constrained educational environments.

Keywords: Educational Data Mining · Next Skill Prediction · Snapshot Data · Cognitive Diagnostic Models · Pseudo-temporal Ordering

1 Introduction

Understanding and predicting how learners develop knowledge over time is a central problem in educational data mining and learning analytics. Accurate prediction of learners' future knowledge can support a wide range of educational interventions, including personalized learning pathways, instructional planning,

E. G. Blanchard et al. (Eds.): AIED 2026, LNAI 16583, pp. 417–426, 2027.
https://doi.org/10.1007/978-3-032-29760-0_46

and early detection of learning difficulties. To address this problem, a substantial body of research, most notably knowledge tracing, has focused on modeling the evolution of latent knowledge states from time-stamped learner interaction logs [2, 8, 10]. However, unlike classical knowledge tracing, many practical educational settings do not provide learner-wise temporal sequences, making it difficult to apply such models directly.

This limitation is particularly evident in large-scale and periodic assessment settings, where learner data are often collected as snapshots rather than as rich temporal traces. For example, international and national assessment programs such as PISA and NAEP evaluate learners at a particular stage of schooling through periodic assessments, and PISA explicitly characterizes each cycle as a cross-sectional study that provides a snapshot of students' developmental status [6, 7]. In addition, many large-scale assessments are administered in school-based, group-oriented formats that support population-level monitoring but do not directly provide learner-wise temporal logs [3].

Cognitive Diagnostic Models (CDMs) offer a widely used approach for representing learners' knowledge states from snapshot response data [4, 11, 14]. Based on a predefined mapping between items and skills, CDMs estimate learners' mastery of individual skills as binary skill mastery patterns. CDMs have also been applied to large-scale assessments; for example, prior work has used cognitive diagnostic assessment to infer learners' subskill profiles from PIRLS data [12]. While CDMs are effective for static diagnosis, comparatively little attention has been paid to predicting future skill acquisition without temporal learning logs.

In this paper, we address this limitation by proposing a framework that predicts the next skill to be acquired using only snapshot-based skill mastery patterns. Our research question is: **Can learners' next skill acquisition be predicted solely from snapshot skill mastery patterns?**

This capability has practical implications for settings in which only snapshot assessments are available. Estimating the next likely skill can help identify plausible next learning targets and support assessment-driven instructional decisions even in the absence of longitudinal logs. Our contributions are twofold: (i) we formulate the problem of next-skill prediction based exclusively on CDM-derived snapshot representations, and (ii) we propose a pseudo-temporal transition model that learns skill-acquisition dynamics from snapshot inclusion patterns and predicts the next skill.

2   Problem Setting

We consider the problem of predicting the next skill to be acquired by a learner based solely on their current skill mastery pattern. Let K denote the total number of skills and N the number of observed learners.

Observations. For each learner i, the current skill mastery pattern is represented as a binary vector $\boldsymbol{s}_i \in \{0, 1\}^K$, where $\boldsymbol{s}_i[k] = 1$ indicates that skill k has been mastered. The observed dataset is given by $\mathcal{D} = \{\boldsymbol{s}_i\}_{i=1}^{N}$.

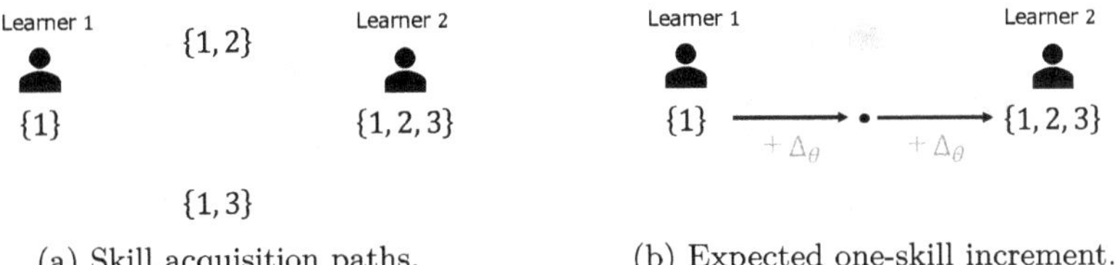

(a) Skill acquisition paths.   (b) Expected one-skill increment.

Fig. 1. Illustration of path approximation via pseudo-temporal ordering.

Goal. Given a learner's current mastery pattern s_i, our goal is to estimate the conditional distribution of the next acquired skill, denoted by $P^*(y_i \mid s_i)$. Here, $y_i = e_{t_i} \in \{0,1\}^K$ is a one-hot vector corresponding to skill $t_i \in \{1, 2, \ldots, K\}$, indicating the newly acquired skill.

Assumption (Non-forgetting). We assume a non-forgetting learning process, in which once a skill is mastered, it remains mastered. Formally, if $s_i[k] = 1$ for skill k, the learner is assumed to retain that skill in all future states.

3 Proposed Method

3.1 Basic Idea: Pseudo-Temporal Ordering

The main challenge in our study is that no explicit temporal information is observed for each learner. To address this, we focus on the diversity of skill mastery patterns in the observed data and construct a pseudo-temporal axis from these patterns. This is particularly reasonable when plausible acquisition tendencies are broadly shared across learners, whether due to common skill dependencies or aggregate differences in skill difficulty.

We consider set-inclusion relations among mastered-skill sets across learners, where each learner's mastered-skill set consists of the skills that the learner has mastered. For example, in Fig. 1a, learner 2's mastered-skill set is a superset of learner 1's. Under the non-forgetting assumption (Sect. 2), once a skill is mastered, it is never forgotten, and a learner's mastered-skill set expands monotonically over time. Therefore, a learner whose mastered-skill set is a superset of another learner's set can be viewed as one plausible later state. Such inclusion relations provide a useful structural signal for estimating latent skill acquisition dynamics from snapshot data.

In our pseudo-temporal view, acquiring one new skill constitutes the atomic step. In practice, however, explicit skill acquisition paths are rarely observable from the data. Moreover, as the number of skills increases, the number of possible acquisition paths grows exponentially, making direct path enumeration infeasible. Therefore, instead of modeling complete acquisition paths, we introduce the expected increment of a single skill, denoted by Δ_θ, as the basic modeling unit (Fig. 1b). Since our target is the next acquired skill, this formulation provides a compact and task-aligned approximation of latent learning dynamics. Repeatedly accumulating these expected increments allows us to approximate intermediate states as continuous-valued representations.

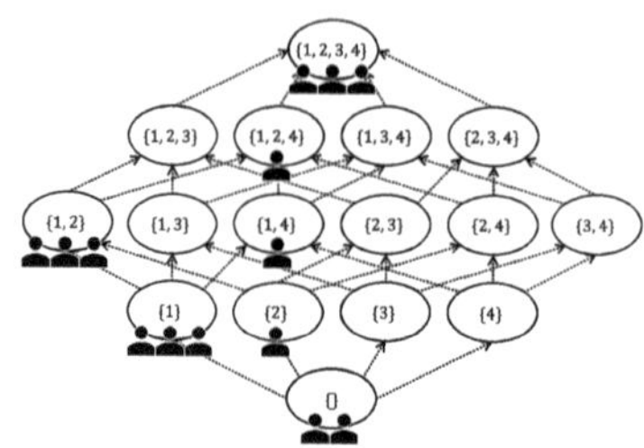

Fig. 2. Skill mastery lattice for $K = 4$, represented as a Hasse diagram. Each node denotes a mastery pattern, and each edge corresponds to the acquisition of one additional skill.

3.2 State Update Formulation via Expected Increments

Each observed binary mastery pattern can be viewed as a node in a skill lattice, illustrated as a Hasse diagram in Fig. 2. In this representation, moving along an edge corresponds to acquiring exactly one new skill. Therefore, an observed state $s \in \{0,1\}^K$ can be interpreted as the result of $\|s\|_1$ successive one-skill acquisitions starting from the empty set.

Directly modeling all possible discrete acquisition paths is infeasible because their number grows rapidly with the number of skills. To obtain a tractable approximation, we introduce continuous intermediate states $\tilde{s}^{(h)} \in [0,1]^K$ for $h \in \{0, \ldots, K\}$, representing a relaxed mastery state after h successive skill acquisitions. We then model learning as the accumulation of *expected one-skill increments*. Formally, given an expected skill increment function Δ_θ (defined in the next subsection), we define the state update as

$$\tilde{s}^{(h+1)} := \tilde{s}^{(h)} + \Delta_\theta(\tilde{s}^{(h)}), \qquad \tilde{s}^{(0)} = \mathbf{0}. \tag{1}$$

Starting from the empty state, we repeatedly add the expected next-skill increment to obtain a sequence of intermediate states. For learner i, we reconstruct the observed pattern s_i by applying this update $\|s_i\|_1$ times, and define $\hat{s}_i = \tilde{s}_i^{(\|s_i\|_1)}$ as the predicted state corresponding to s_i.

3.3 Expected Skill Increment Model Δ_θ

The expected skill increment function Δ_θ maps a continuous mastery state to a distribution over the next skill to be acquired. By Eq. (1), Δ_θ should satisfy the following requirements: **(1) relaxed input**: it is defined on *continuous* intermediate representations, and **(2) output constraint**: it assigns probability mass only to currently unmastered skills, i.e., $\Delta_\theta(\tilde{s}) \in \Delta^K \cap [0, \mathbf{1} - \tilde{s}]$, where Δ^K is the K-dimensional probability simplex.

To satisfy these conditions, we employ a feed-forward neural network with the Upper Bounded Softmax (UBSoftmax) function [1,5], which is an extension of Softmax with upper-bound constraints. Formally, we define Δ_θ as

$$\Delta_\theta(\tilde{\boldsymbol{s}}) = \text{UBSoftmax}(z(\tilde{\boldsymbol{s}}), \mathbf{1} - \tilde{\boldsymbol{s}}) := \underset{p \in \Delta^K \cap [\mathbf{0}, \mathbf{1} - \tilde{\boldsymbol{s}}]}{\operatorname{argmax}} \boldsymbol{p}^\top z(\tilde{\boldsymbol{s}}) - \sum_{k=1}^{K} p_k \log p_k, \quad (2)$$

$$z(\tilde{\boldsymbol{s}}) = \boldsymbol{W}\tilde{\boldsymbol{s}} + \boldsymbol{b}, \quad (3)$$

where $\boldsymbol{W} \in \mathbb{R}^{K \times K}$ and $\boldsymbol{b} \in \mathbb{R}^K$ are parameters to be trained. By construction, $\Delta_\theta(\tilde{\boldsymbol{s}})$ lies in $\Delta^K \cap [\mathbf{0}, \mathbf{1} - \tilde{\boldsymbol{s}}]$.

The model parameters $\theta = \{\boldsymbol{W}, \boldsymbol{b}\}$ are learned by minimizing

$$\mathcal{L}(\theta) = \frac{1}{N} \sum_{i=1}^{N} \left\| \boldsymbol{s}_i - \tilde{\boldsymbol{s}}_i^{(\|\boldsymbol{s}_i\|_1)} \right\|_2^2 + \lambda \|\theta\|_1,$$

where $\lambda \geq 0$ is the hyperparameter of regularization-strength. The squared error term encourages accurate reconstruction of observed mastery patterns, while the ℓ_1 regularization promotes sparse and interpretable dependencies among skills.

Through this training procedure, the model captures aggregate tendencies of skill set expansion along the induced pseudo-temporal axis.

4 Experiments on Next-Skill Prediction

4.1 Experimental Setup

Evaluation Metrics. We evaluate the model's performance on the test set by predicting the subsequently acquired skills $\Delta \boldsymbol{s}_i$ from the current mastery pattern $\boldsymbol{s}_i$. Let $r = \|\Delta \boldsymbol{s}_i\|_1$ denote the number of newly acquired skills and p_k be the predicted probability for skill k.

- **New-Skill Accuracy (Acc.):** Recall@r over unmastered skills.
- **Acquisition Cross-Entropy (ACE):** $-\frac{1}{r} \sum_{k \in \Delta \boldsymbol{s}_i} \log p_k$, evaluating confidence on actually acquired skills.
- **Skill-State MSE (MSE):** Mean squared error between predicted and true additional skill vectors.

For synthetic data, we additionally evaluate the reconstruction of next-skill probability distributions using **KL divergence (KL)** and **Jensen–Shannon divergence (JSD)**, weighted by the frequency of each mastery pattern.

Baselines. We compare our approach with baselines applicable to prediction from single-time-point observations without learner-wise temporal logs: structure-based modeling (Bayesian Network), frequency-based prediction (Popularity), local transition estimation (Simple Markov), and an uninformed reference (Random).

Table 1. Results on synthetic data (mean ± std).

Method	Acc. ↑	ACE ↓	MSE ↓	KL ↓	JSD ↓
Bayesian Network	0.780 ± 0.103	0.500 ± 0.278	0.0774 ± 0.0426	<u>3.15 ± 3.04</u>	<u>0.700 ± 0.592</u>
Popularity	**0.822 ± 0.089**	<u>0.420 ± 0.248</u>	<u>0.0580 ± 0.0278</u>	3.66 ± 4.14	0.861 ± 0.795
Simple Markov	0.756 ± 0.124	1.466 ± 0.983	0.0778 ± 0.0395	34.6 ± 23.7	1.348 ± 0.977
Random	0.695 ± 0.136	0.492 ± 0.261	0.0750 ± 0.0354	5.70 ± 4.84	1.326 ± 1.110
Proposed	<u>0.820 ± 0.091</u>	**0.397 ± 0.209**	**0.0571 ± 0.0288**	**2.68 ± 2.43**	**0.687 ± 0.639**
Oracle Upper Bound	0.832 ± 0.085	0.385 ± 0.203	0.0540 ± 0.0265	2.61 ± 2.47	0.673 ± 0.644

Best and second-best results are shown in **bold** and <u>underlined</u>, respectively.

- **Bayesian Network** [9,13]: learns skill structures as a DAG using hill-climbing with BIC.
- **Popularity**: ranks skills by empirical acquisition frequency.
- **Simple Markov**: estimates next-skill probabilities from the observed frequency of next acquisition patterns given the current skill pattern.
- **Random**: assigns uniform probabilities to unmastered skills.
- **Oracle Upper Bound**: uses the same architecture as our model but is trained with true future skill labels, serving only as a reference upper bound.

All methods output a probability distribution over the next acquired skill. When multiple skills are observed as newly acquired, predictions are proportionally scaled to match the number of additions.

4.2 Synthetic Data

To evaluate performance under controlled learning dynamics, we generate synthetic datasets based on predefined skill prerequisite graphs. Learners acquire skills sequentially following these dependencies, with injected noise allowing occasional prerequisite violations. We evaluate 675 configurations (10 runs each), varying the number of learners, skills, noise levels, and acquisition tendencies.

Mean and Standard Deviation. As shown in Table 1, across all settings, the proposed method consistently outperforms baseline approaches on all metrics except Acc. and closely approaches the oracle upper bound performance, indicating that meaningful signals of latent learning dynamics can be inferred from snapshot data.

Effect of Skill Size and Noise. Figures 3 and 4 illustrate the win rates of the proposed method against each baseline across varying skill sizes and noise rates. The win rate represents the proportion of trials in which the proposed method outperformed the baseline. As shown in these figures, the proposed method exhibits robust performance; in particular, its win rate consistently increases or remains high as the number of skills grows, indicating strong robustness to state-space expansion. While the performance of several baselines degrades under higher noise rates, the proposed method maintains high win rates across all evaluation metrics, suggesting stable behavior even under noisy conditions.

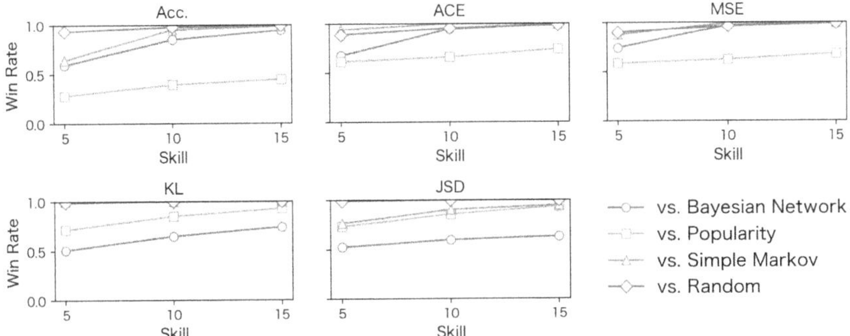

Fig. 3. Win rate of the proposed method vs. number of skills (Synthetic Data).

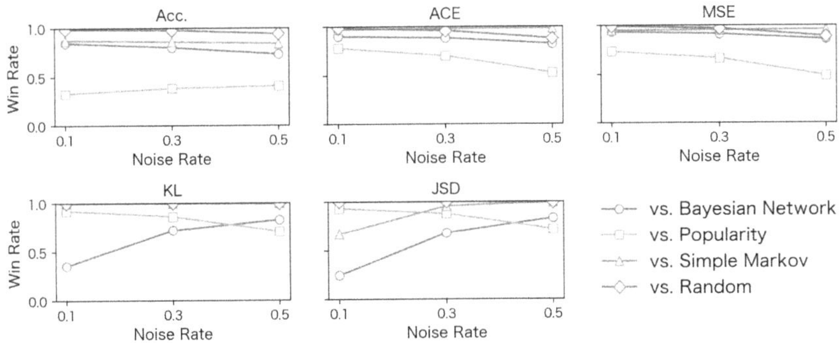

Fig. 4. Win rate of the proposed method vs. noise rate (Synthetic Data).

4.3   Real-World Data

We further evaluate our method on the ASSISTments 2009–2010 dataset. To simulate a snapshot setting, we split each learner's interaction log into an early segment and the full log, and estimate current mastery from the early segment and future mastery from the full log using a DINA model [4]. We selected 95 learners who attempted all 15 skills so that both current and future mastery patterns could be estimated consistently over a common skill space. This filtering yields a cleaner testbed for evaluation, but limits sample representativeness and should be relaxed in future work. We performed 100 random train/test splits (70:30).

Mean and Standard Deviation. As shown in Table 2, the proposed method achieves the best performance across all metrics on the real-world dataset, outperforming all baseline methods. These results suggest that the proposed approach can effectively predict future skill acquisition in this real-world benchmark setting.

Table 2. Results on real-world data (15 skills, mean ± std.).

Method	Acc. ↑	ACE ↓	MSE ↓
Bayesian Network	$0.648 \pm 0.061^{\dagger}$	$0.853 \pm 0.122^{\dagger}$	$0.0786 \pm 0.0118^{\dagger}$
Popularity	$\underline{0.760 \pm 0.046}^{\dagger}$	$0.645 \pm 0.072^{\dagger}$	$0.0599 \pm 0.0060^{\dagger}$
Simple Markov	$0.581 \pm 0.066^{\dagger}$	$1.811 \pm 0.720^{\dagger}$	$0.0738 \pm 0.0083^{\dagger}$
Random	$0.525 \pm 0.065^{\dagger}$	$0.780 \pm 0.090^{\dagger}$	$0.0696 \pm 0.0056^{\dagger}$
Proposed	$\mathbf{0.769 \pm 0.052}$	$\mathbf{0.626 \pm 0.081}$	$\mathbf{0.0571 \pm 0.0063}$
Oracle Upper Bound	0.807 ± 0.056	0.562 ± 0.075	0.0458 ± 0.0053

† indicates that the proposed method significantly outperforms the corresponding baseline (Wilcoxon signed-rank test, $p < 0.05$).

Effect of Skill Size. Consistent with the synthetic experiments, Fig. 5 shows that the proposed method maintains high win rates against baselines as the number of skills increases. In particular, it consistently performs strongly on ACE and MSE, indicating better calibration and lower prediction error under higher-dimensional skill settings.

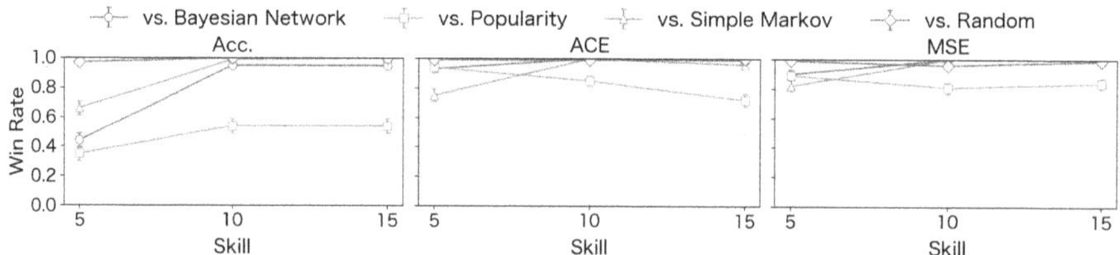

Fig. 5. Win Rate of the proposed method vs. number of skills (Real-World Data).

5   Conclusion

In this paper, we addressed the challenge of predicting learners' future skill acquisition in educational settings where temporal data is unavailable. We proposed a novel framework that infers latent learning dynamics solely from snapshot skill mastery patterns. By interpreting the inclusion relations among learners' skill sets as a pseudo-temporal ordering, we modeled skill expansion as a proxy for learning progression. Experiments on synthetic and real-world datasets demonstrate that our method consistently outperforms baselines. The results highlight the model's robustness to noise and skill space expansion, suggesting that meaningful acquisition patterns can be effectively inferred from snapshot data to support forward-looking instructional decisions.

Several limitations remain. Our current formulation relies on a non-forgetting assumption and is evaluated on a restricted real-world subset, so future work should examine more heterogeneous learning settings. An important next step is to incorporate forgetting mechanisms and further validate the framework on larger and more complex skill structures.

Acknowledgments. This work was supported by JST CREST Grant Number JPMJCR21D1.

References

1. Atarashi, K., Oyama, S., Arai, H., Kashima, H.: Probability bounding: post-HOC calibration via box-constrained softmax (2025). arXiv:2506.10572 arXiv preprint
2. Corbett, A.T., Anderson, J.R.: Knowledge tracing: modeling the acquisition of procedural knowledge. User Model. User-Adap. Inter. **4**(4), 253–278 (1994)
3. Cresswell, J., Schwantner, U., Waters, C.: A review of international large-scale assessments in education: assessing component skills and collecting contextual data. OECD Pub. World Bank (2015). https://doi.org/10.1787/9789264248373-en
4. Junker, B.W., Sijtsma, K.: Cognitive assessment models with few assumptions, and connections with nonparametric item response theory. Appl. Psychol. Meas. **25**(3), 258–272 (2001)
5. Martins, A.F.T., Kreutzer, J.: Learning what's easy: fully differentiable neural easy-first taggers. In: Proceedings of the Conference on Empirical Methods in Natural Language Processing, pp. 349–362 (2017)
6. National Center for Education Statistics: About NAEP. National Assessment of Educational Progress (NAEP) website (2025). Accessed 29 Mar 2026
7. OECD: PISA 2022 Assessment and Analytical Framework. OECD Publishing, Paris (2023). https://doi.org/10.1787/dfe0bf9c-en
8. Piech, C., et al.: Deep knowledge tracing. In: Advances in Neural Information Processing Systems, vol. 28 (2015)
9. Plajner, M., Vomlel, J.: Student skill models in adaptive testing. In: Proceedings of the Conference on Probabilistic Graphical Models, pp. 403–414 (2016)
10. Shen, S., et al.: A survey of knowledge tracing: models, variants, and applications. IEEE Trans. Learn. Technol. **17**, 1858–1879 (2024)

11. Templin, J., Henson, R.A.: Diagnostic Measurement: Theory, Methods, and Applications, Guilford Press (2010)
12. Toprak-Yildiz, T.E.: An international comparison using cognitive diagnostic assessment: fourth graders' diagnostic profile of reading skills on pirls 2016. Stud. Educ. Eval. **70**, 101057 (2021)
13. Vomlel, J.: Bayesian networks in educational testing. Internat. J. Uncertain. Fuzziness Knowl. Based Syst **12**(1), 83–100 (2004)
14. Wang, F., et al.: A survey of models for cognitive diagnosis: new developments and future directions. arXiv preprint arXiv:2407.05458 (2024)

Multimodal Analytics of Cybersecurity Crisis Preparation Exercises: What Predicts Success?

Conrad Borchers[1]([✉])[iD], Valdemar Švábenský[2][iD], Sandesh K. Kafle[2][iD],
Kevin K. Tang[1][iD], and Jan Vykopal[2][iD]

[1] Carnegie Mellon University, Pittsburgh, PA, USA
`cborcher@cs.cmu.edu, kktang@andrew.cmu.edu`
[2] Faculty of Informatics, Masaryk University, Brno, Czechia
`valdemar@mail.muni.cz, {xkafle,vykopal}@fi.muni.cz`

Abstract. Instructional alignment, the match between intended cognition and enacted activity, is central to effective instruction but hard to operationalize at scale. We examine alignment in cybersecurity simulations using multimodal traces from 23 teams (76 students) across five exercise sessions. Study 1 codes objectives and team emails with Bloom's taxonomy and models the completion of key exercise tasks with generalized linear mixed models. Alignment, defined as the discrepancy between required and enacted Bloom levels, predicts success, whereas the Bloom category alone does not predict success once discrepancy is considered. Study 2 compares predictive feature families using grouped cross-validation and ℓ_1-regularized logistic regression. Text embeddings and log features outperform Bloom-only models (AUC $\approx$ 0.74 and 0.71 vs. 0.55), and their combination performs best (Test AUC $\approx$ 0.80), with Bloom frequencies adding little. Overall, the work offers a measure of alignment for simulations and shows that multimodal traces best forecast performance, while alignment provides interpretable diagnostic insight.

Keywords: Bloom · simulation-based learning · tabletop exercises · prediction

1 Introduction

Instructional alignment, the coherence among learning objectives, activities, and assessment, is foundational to effective learning design [8,30]. Bloom's taxonomy and later revisions [2,9] provide a shared language for articulating cognitive demands, ranging from remembering and understanding to analyzing, evaluating, and creating. Despite their ubiquity in instructional design, such frameworks are rarely used to *measure* alignment in practice, particularly at scale, where learners' enacted activities may diverge from intended objectives [35]. The present study contributes empirical evidence that alignment between collaborative learner actions and instructional objectives, inferred from multimodal learning analytics, predicts problem-solving performance. For the AIED community, this demonstrates how theory-driven cognitive frameworks can be operationalized to support performance prediction and complex collaborative learning environments.

This challenge is especially pronounced in simulation-based learning (SBL), where open-ended, team-based tasks generate rich but noisy multimodal traces that are difficult to relate to targeted cognitive processes [15,48]. Cybersecurity tabletop exercises (TTXs; see Sect. 2.3) exemplify this problem: teams must coordinate under time pressure, interpret evolving information, and communicate with diverse stakeholders, producing behaviors that are pedagogically valuable yet methodologically hard to code and assess [39,43]. Although past work has modeled such traces to support instructional intervention [45], it remains unclear whether Bloom-aligned discrepancies between objectives and enacted behavior predict performance, or which trace types are most informative.

We address these questions using cybersecurity TTXs conducted on the open-source INJECT Exercise Platform [39], analyzing platform logs and in-exercise email communications from 23 teams (76 students) across five sessions. RQ1 examines whether *alignment*, operationalized as the Bloom-level discrepancy between milestone objectives (i.e., the successful completion of key tasks in the exercise) and the highest Bloom level evidenced in team communications, predicts team performance, while RQ2 compares the predictive utility of Bloom-coded categories, linguistic features from emails and logs, and engineered behavioral log features, individually and in combination. Study 1 codes objectives and communications using Bloom's taxonomy and applies generalized linear mixed models [7] to test the contribution of discrepancy beyond raw Bloom levels, and Study 2 evaluates predictive models using Bloom-only features, text embeddings, behavioral aggregates, and their combinations with grouped cross-validation and ℓ_1-regularized logistic regression.

We contribute a data-driven measure of instructional alignment in SBL and show that Bloom-level discrepancy between objectives and team communication predicts performance in cybersecurity tabletop exercises. Linguistic and behavioral traces were more predictive than Bloom-frequency features, while discrepancy remains valuable for instructional diagnosis.

2   Background

2.1   Bloom's Taxonomy for the Prediction of Learning Performance

Bloom's Taxonomy is an established framework for characterizing learning objectives across cognitive levels, including in computing education [2,9]. AIED research has operationalized this framework by inferring cognitive levels from observable learner behaviors, such as clickstream activity, assignment artifacts, and rubric-based assessments, to predict performance and cognitive progression [6,26,27]. Despite their success, these approaches rely primarily on unimodal digital traces, which limits their ability to capture learning processes distributed across multiple forms of interaction.

Recent AI-oriented reinterpretations, including the proposed "AIEd Bloom's taxonomy," replace cognitive levels with process-focused stages such as Collect and Adapt [20]. While motivated by modernization, this shift weakens Bloom's theoretical grounding by obscuring distinctions between lower- and higher-order thinking and offering limited support for differentiating surface engagement from critical reasoning. Both traditional and AI-driven adaptations largely overlook the application of Bloom's framework to multimodal learning contexts, including collaborative communication artifacts, which require explicit coding schemes and ground-truth labeling [26]. We address these gaps by combining multimodal evidence from team communication transcripts and interaction logs with predictive modeling to operationalize Bloom's Taxonomy in a rich learning setting. To address validity concerns in mapping trace data to cognition, we interpret email and log features as indicators of collaborative processes such as coordination and shared problem framing, which have been shown to provide observable evidence of learning in collaborative learning settings [32].

2.2 Cybersecurity Education in the AIED Context

Cybersecurity is a key component of contemporary computing education, integrating technical systems with human, informational, and organizational concepts to protect operations against adversarial threats [21,36]. Alongside rapidly expanding areas such as artificial intelligence, cybersecurity has gained increasing prominence, and mastery of cybersecurity competencies is now widely viewed as core preparation for graduates in computer science and related fields [31,36].

Despite its importance, cybersecurity remains marginal in AIED and learning analytics research. A systematic review found only 35 relevant studies among more than 3,000 publications, most using primarily shallow descriptive measures [41]. Furthermore, most past papers on the topic focused on privacy or infrastructure rather than cybersecurity learning itself [4,17].

Existing research on cybersecurity education within AIED and learning analytics focused on privacy awareness, informal learning environments, program-level analyses, and online courses [5,14,18,24,38]. None of these studies examined students in dedicated higher-education cybersecurity degree programs. Although cybersecurity education has gained visibility in computing education research [40], it remains rare within AIED. This study addresses that gap by presenting learning analytics evidence from a higher education program centered on cybersecurity.

2.3 Tabletop Exercises (TTXs)

Tabletop exercises (TTXs) are a form of experiential learning in which small groups collaboratively work through complex, time-constrained scenarios in a shared instructional setting [3,43]. Instructors issue common prompts, while teams develop responses independently and submit outcomes orally or through digital systems of varying sophistication. This structure supports coordinated engagement without requiring fully synchronized group activity.

TTXs help learners practice responses to realistic, high-stakes situations that are difficult to reproduce in classrooms, including disaster response, public health emergencies, healthcare crises, and cybersecurity, which is the focus of the present study [23]. More broadly, TTXs belong to the tradition of simulation-based pedagogy, which is well established in AIED and learning analytics research [48]. Compared to technical exercises in cyber ranges – another popular approach for realistic cybersecurity simulations [42] – TTXs are much more lightweight and relevant also for less technically-oriented roles (e.g., IT management).

3   The INJECT Exercise Platform

Tabletop exercises were traditionally conducted offline using printed materials, which imposed substantial preparation demands on instructors and required labor-intensive manual assessment. In response, digital tools have emerged to support TTX-based instruction, as documented in a recent survey [43]. Our study uses the open-source INJECT Exercise Platform (IXP) [39], a browser-based system supporting the full exercise lifecycle while reducing instructor workload. IXP provides scenario-critical information, is freely available and actively maintained, and has been refined over time through sustained feedback from instructors.

3.1   Educational Goals and Learning Objectives

While TTXs apply across many instructional domains (Sect. 2.3), we focus on cybersecurity. Here, TTXs enable learners to practice responses to cyber crises that disrupt IT operations, such as data breaches. Teams collaboratively address technical incidents alongside communication and coordination challenges, developing competencies in conditions that mirror professional practice and support workforce readiness in a rapidly evolving field [31,36].

The exercises model the work of a Computer Security Incident Response Team (CSIRT) in medium- to large-scale organizations. Participants engage in open-ended scenarios that require prioritizing and resolving multiple, simultaneous incidents under time constraints of roughly 90 min, reflecting the pace and uncertainty of real incident response. Learning outcomes align with the Incident Response role in the NICE Cybersecurity Workforce Framework [28]. In addition to technical skills, the activities emphasize professional dispositions [31,36], including teamwork, decision-making under pressure, and effective communication within the CSIRT and with external stakeholders. Specific tasks that the teams address include investigating connections from suspicious IP addresses to an organization's infrastructure, advising non-expert users affected by cyber attacks, and writing up a report documenting the findings.

3.2   How Students Learn Using the INJECT Exercise Platform

Tabletop exercises unfold through *injects*, predefined messages released during the activity to introduce new information and advance the scenario [39]. An inject may, for example, inform students of a breach in their simulated organization. In traditional TTXs, instructors typically deliver such messages verbally or on paper. The INJECT Exercise Platform instead automates inject delivery, presenting them directly within each team's web interface, as shown in Fig. 1.

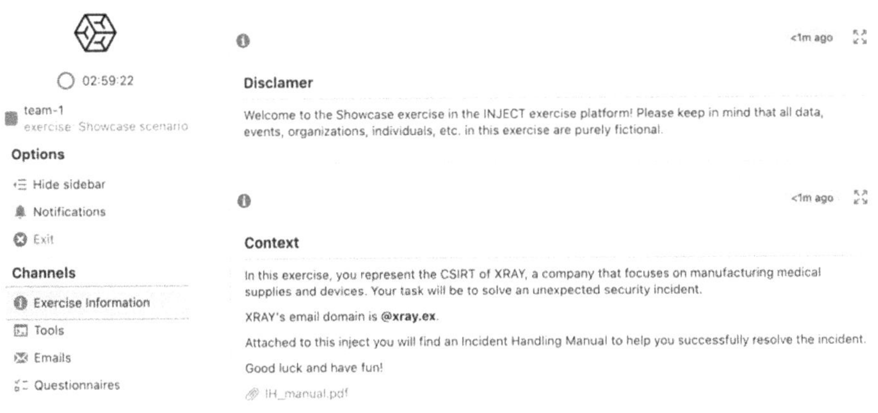

Fig. 1. IXP from the student perspective, displaying recent injects.

Upon receiving an inject, teams decide how to respond and enact their decisions through the platform (Fig. 1). These tools abstract real-world applications, allowing teams to carry out actions that resemble professional practice and receive immediate feedback. Professional communication is also central to TTXs, and in IXP, this is modeled through emails from simulated stakeholders that pose questions or requests requiring deliberation. Teams must compose appropriate replies under time pressure as the incident unfolds. Responses to these emails require both lower- and higher-order cognitive processes, such as confirming information or applying procedures (Table 1). Email is the only tool for communicating with simulated in-exercise actors. Spoken communication between team members is also relevant but outside the scope of our analysis.

Every team action, including tool use and email communication, is logged with full metadata and microsecond-resolution timestamps in JSONL format. These logs support the identification of milestones that mark key events in the TTX and allow instructors to monitor progress and, if desired, assign grades.

4   Methods

4.1   Participant Sample

By including participants from multiple nations and contexts, we aim to improve the external validity of our findings [19]. In the Czech Republic, four sequential tabletop exercises (TTX0–3) were run as a capstone in a semester-long cyber-security incident response course at a public university, involving 36 computing majors per exercise, organized into 13 skill-balanced teams (10 teams of three and three teams of two). The exercises were spaced out across several weeks. In Estonia, a fifth exercise (TTX4) included 11 teams at a cross-border cybersecu-rity event: five university teams, five vocational-school teams, and one educator team.

In late 2024, 24 teams with 81 learners participated. One team declined research consent, leaving 23 teams and 76 learners for analysis. The sample is comparable to or larger than prior studies of collaborative cybersecurity work [46]. All teams in our sample completed up to 18 milestones in a fixed order (though multiple milestones can be worked on simultaneously), limiting task difficulty confounds. Finally, 68 (20%) milestone completions included no email. Such milestones mostly included simple tasks such as blocking an IP address, which did not require communication with the simulated exercise stakeholders.

4.2   Coding of Emails

Annotating emails is substantially more complex than annotating exercise objec-tives, which are few and brief, and therefore requires dedicated qualitative cod-ing. We developed a codebook to classify security and incident-response emails by the highest cognitive demand imposed on the recipient. We ensured that the scheme was sufficiently grounded in Bloom's taxonomy by initially starting codebook development based on ACM CCECC's Bloom's taxonomy for comput-ing [2]. The codebook defines six categories spanning simple acknowledgments to higher-order demands involving analysis, evaluation, or creation; Table 1 presents the categories, definitions, and representative examples.

Three independent coders applied the codebook to individual emails from the INJECT Exercise Platform using a three-stage process of independent cod-ing, discussion-based reconciliation, and final consolidation. When text reflected multiple Bloom levels, coders assigned the highest level; when no emails were present, no code was assigned. Inter-rater reliability was moderate to substantial. Pairwise Cohen's κ ranged from 0.555 to 0.678 across coder pairs, and Fleiss' kappa for three raters on complete cases was 0.636. Reliability varied by cate-gory, with higher agreement for Applying and Creating, moderate agreement for Analyzing, Remembering, and Evaluating, and the lowest agreement for Under-standing. Given the inherent ambiguity of cognitive constructs, κ values around 0.6 are commonly considered acceptable in related research [22, 25]. We provide anonymized analysis and preprocessing code via a public Git repository.[1] The study data are also open source [1].

---

[1] https://github.com/conradborchers/bloom-ttx/.

Table 1. Overview of the Codebook categories.

Category	Definition	Example
Remembering	Pure acknowledgement or status updates with no action required.	"Thanks for the info."
Understanding	Provide trivial self-facts or confirm information already known.	"What is your email?"
Applying	Execute known steps or fetch specified resources.	"Send 48h access logs for `nice-project.uni.ex`."
Analyzing	Investigate without prescribed steps; decide what data or methods to use.	"What is going on? Please provide more information."
Evaluating	Make judgments under uncertainty (policy, impact, authenticity).	"Should we inform NCISA about this incident?"
Creating	Produce new artifacts such as summaries, advisories, or drafts.	"Please draft the public statement about the breach."

5   Study 1: Explaining Performance via Bloom (RQ1)

Study 1 tested whether (a) Bloom-coded cognitive demand in team emails predicted milestone success and whether (b) misalignment between required and observed Bloom levels predicted outcomes.

5.1   Method

For each team and milestone, we coded the highest Bloom level evident in the related email exchange. Milestone completion was a binary outcome (1 for completion, 0 for non-completion). We computed a discrepancy score as the distance between the Bloom level required and that observed, coded as 0 for exact matches, 1 for adjacent levels, and 2 otherwise. Missing data were coded as 2, since no response is conceptually similar to an inadequate response.

We fit a sequence of generalized linear mixed models predicting the log-odds of milestone achievement. All models included a random intercept for each team to account for repeated observations. The baseline model included the observed Bloom level as a fixed effect. The second model added the discrepancy score to capture misalignment between required and enacted cognitive levels. The final model further included the interaction between Bloom level and discrepancy to test whether the effect of misalignment depended on the absolute cognitive level at which teams were communicating.

Models were compared sequentially using likelihood-ratio tests, retaining the best-fitting specification. Fixed effects are reported as odds ratios with 95% confidence intervals, which quantify multiplicative changes in the odds of success in logistic models. An odds ratio above one indicates increased odds, while values below one indicate reduced odds, for a one-unit increase or category presence. Odds ratios describe relative changes rather than absolute probabilities.

5.2   Results

Adding discrepancy significantly improved fit over a Bloom-only baseline, $\chi^2(1) = 7.18$, $p = .007$, whereas the Bloom-discrepancy interaction did not, $\chi^2(2) = 0.45$, $p = .800$. In the selected additive model, greater discrepancy reduced the odds of success (OR $= 0.65$, 95% CI $[0.48, 0.90]$, $p = .008$), and Bloom category was no longer significant (p's $> .077$). Between-team variability was substantial (ICC $= .20$), but fixed effects explained little variance (marginal $R^2 = .04$; conditional $R^2 = .23$), indicating limited explanatory power of Bloom alignment.

A complementary χ^2 test across discrepancy levels (0–2) showed a significant but weak association with milestone achievement, $\chi^2(2, N = 340) = 6.41$, $p = .041$, Cramr's $V = .14$, suggesting that smaller discrepancies were associated with higher success rates but with modest practical impact.

6   Study 2: What Predicts Performance? (RQ2)

The second study examined which feature families best predict milestone achievement. Moving beyond Study 1's theoretical focus, we compared models using Bloom-coded email categories, linguistic features from team communication, and log-based behavioral indicators, alone and in combination, to assess whether Bloom coding adds predictive value beyond automated text and log traces.

6.1   Method

In the second study, we fused system logs and email with Bloom-coded indicators into text sequences and numeric features. All timestamps were converted to UTC and aligned by `teamID`. For each milestone, we aggregated logs and emails since the previous milestone or session start. Emails were concatenated with a delimiter token (`<|CHAIN|>`). We also computed counts of logs and emails, action-type frequencies, average log and email lengths, elapsed time since the prior milestone, email response times, number of unique senders, and Bloom code frequencies. Together, these features constituted the milestone-level indicators. We grouped the resulting predictors into three groups:

- **Text features:** embeddings of `chained_logs` and `chained_emails` generated using the `all-MiniLM-L6-v2` model from `SentenceTransformers`.
- **Log features:** numeric aggregates derived from system interactions, excluding Bloom-coded variables.
- **Bloom features:** counts of Bloom taxonomy codes (e.g., *remembering, applying*) extracted from coded emails within objectives.

Evaluation Design. To assess predictive value, we trained ℓ_1-regularized logistic regression models using different feature combinations, with milestone achievement as the binary outcome. Data were split into 80% training and 20% test sets, stratified by outcome and grouped by `teamID`, with 5-fold `GroupKFold` cross-validation on the training set. Inputs were standardized. ℓ_1 regularization mitigates overfitting and enforces feature selection (by shrinking irrelevant coefficients to 0 and effectively dropping them out of the model). Performance was evaluated using AUC with 95% confidence intervals, computed across folds and via stratified bootstrap on the test set.

Interpretability. Interpretation relied on coefficients from the ℓ_1-regularized logistic regression. With standardized features, the coefficient sign and magnitude directly reflect the direction of the association with milestone achievement. Accordingly, post-hoc explainers designed for complex, non-linear architectures (e.g., SHAP/LIME) were unnecessary, reducing overfitting risk and avoiding known inconsistencies in these interpretability methods [34]. We report the ten largest absolute weights, spanning text embeddings and engineered indicators.

6.2   Results

Table 2 reports predictive performance across feature sets. Bloom-coded features alone performed at near-chance levels, whereas text and log features were substantially more predictive. Combining text and log features yielded the strongest results (test AUC = 0.80), indicating a complementary signal, with Bloom features adding little incremental value beyond embeddings.

Table 2. Cross-validated and test set performance for different feature sets.

Model	CV AUC	CV 95% CI	Test AUC	Test 95% CI
Bloom only	0.551	[0.468, 0.634]	0.541	[0.469, 0.615]
Text only	0.740	[0.720, 0.760]	0.727	[0.666, 0.786]
Log only	0.714	[0.667, 0.761]	0.727	[0.669, 0.783]
Text + Bloom	0.740	[0.720, 0.760]	0.727	[0.666, 0.786]
Log + Bloom	0.714	[0.667, 0.761]	0.727	[0.669, 0.783]
Text + Log	0.790	[0.760, 0.821]	0.804	[0.747, 0.856]
All (Text + Log + Bloom)	0.790	[0.760, 0.821]	0.804	[0.747, 0.856]

Figure 2 displays the ten strongest predictors from the full model. Most derive from `chained_emails` embeddings, reinforcing the predictive value of email communication, with additional contributions from temporal and structural features. The coefficient sign indicates the direction of association with milestone achievement.

7   General Discussion

Instructional alignment has long been treated as a central principle of learning design [8,30], yet it is rarely operationalized in authentic, data-rich contexts such as SBL. Most prior work examines alignment through curriculum artifacts or rubric-based analyses [6], or reviews scaffolding in simulations without measuring alignment as it occurs during activity [16].

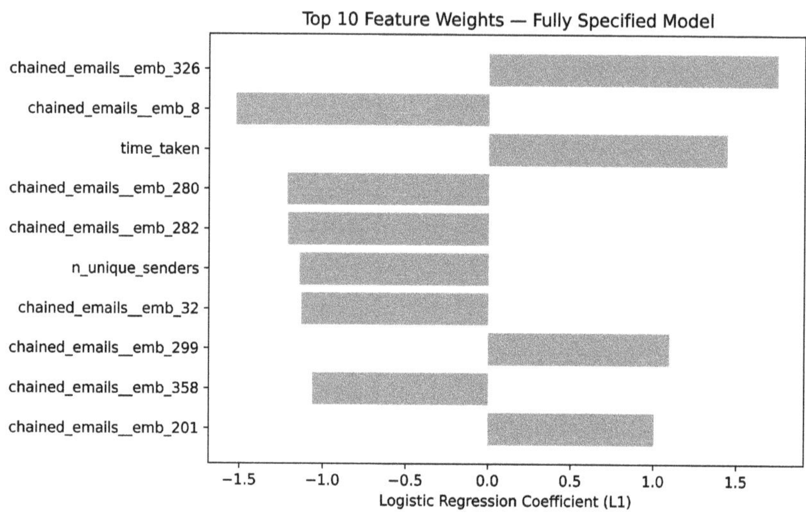

Fig. 2. Top ten features in the fully specified model (Text+Log+Bloom). Positive weights indicate higher predicted probability of milestone achievement. Subscripts for embedding-based features represent the n-th dimension of the vector.

This article addresses this gap by integrating theory-driven coding with predictive modeling of multimodal team data. Study 1 frames alignment as a discrepancy between instructional objectives and enacted communication, while Study 2 compares the predictive value of Bloom-coded features with text and log data. Together, the studies connect interpretable, theory-based measures of alignment with scalable analytics that support accurate prediction.

7.1   Study 1: Alignment and Milestone Success

From a constructive alignment perspective, Study 1 results explain why discrepancy, rather than nominal Bloom levels, predicts success. Biggs' account of alignment emphasizes that learning improves when activities and assessment elicit the same cognitive work as the intended objectives [8]. Our finding that misaligned teams underperform extends this principle to simulation-based contexts using trace data. Prior meta-analyses of scenario-based learning similarly show that scaffolds improve outcomes by aligning what learners actually do with the targeted cognitive demands, not by merely increasing task difficulty [15,16]. In tabletop exercises, where reasoning is enacted primarily through time-pressured communication [39,43], a Bloom gap likely reflects coordination without the intended analytic, evaluative, or generative thinking, consistent with work distinguishing surface participation from deeper cognition [44].

For TTX design, these results suggest prioritizing scaffolds that help teams maintain reasoning at the intended cognitive level rather than adding more complex injects. Because TTXs generate rich communication traces, they enable real-time alignment diagnosis by combining transcription, automated classification, and predictive modeling. Comparable methods have captured self-regulated learning processes as they unfold [13]. Applied to TTXs, such approaches could enable timely prompts or feedback when misalignment emerges, turning Bloom discrepancy from a post-hoc indicator into a mechanism for just-in-time support in high-pressure learning environments.

7.2 Study 2: Predictive Value of Feature Families

Study 2 frames Bloom codes as interpretable diagnostics while showing that linguistic and interaction traces are more predictive of performance. This mirrors prior discourse-analytic and learning analytics work demonstrating that models grounded in communication structure, language use, and temporal participation outperform coarse categorical labels, and that combining multiple trace types yields complementary value [11,33,47]. Our results hence support combining fine-grained behavioral and linguistic signals for forecasting performance.

The limited contribution of Bloom frequencies beyond embeddings could indicate limited value for our prediction task. Alternatively, it could indicate that their information is already captured in the semantic structure of communication traces. This aligns with evidence that large language models achieve strong classification performance while reducing interpretability [37]. Practically, this suggests a division of labor: Bloom coding supports explanation and design, whereas embeddings and engineered features support real-time risk detection. Similar complementarities between rich interaction logs and textual analysis have been reported in large-scale cyber and simulation-based exercises [29,33].

Across both studies, Bloom discrepancy helps explain why teams succeed or struggle, while multimodal features indicate who is likely to do so and when. For AIED, this suggests a pipeline in which predictive models flag at-risk moments using text and log traces, and alignment analytics provide cognitively meaningful rationales for feedback and redesign. Analytics related to this feedback could be directly shown to students to enhance learning or to instructors to improve instruction accompanying the simulation-based training or curricular redesign. This synthesis responds to calls for analytics that are simultaneously accurate and pedagogically actionable [45], and it links platform-level telemetry with discourse-level evidence of thinking in TTXs and related simulations. Future work should extend these diagnostics beyond Bloom categories toward network-based representations, such as epistemic network analytics, to support more nuanced and instructionally useful insights [12].

7.3 Limitations and Future Work

Despite diverse data spanning two countries, our findings are bounded by the specific cybersecurity platform and TTXs, each lasting approximately 1.5 h. Broader validity will require replication across domains and longer SBL formats, ideally incorporating milestone-level difficulty controls and alternative operationalizations that model reasoning trajectories rather than peak Bloom levels. Our results are also correlational in nature, calling for quasi-experimental studies potentially matching groups with different Bloom discrepancies by prior knowledge, ability, or similarly adjusting for milestone difficulty.

We prioritized interpretable linear models, but more complex architectures could improve predictive performance, and so could more complex measures of Bloom discrepancy in larger samples, such as penalizing larger discrepancies more strongly instead of treating all Bloom taxonomy gaps as equally-spaced. Future work should also examine hybrid approaches that pair high-performing multimodal models with explanations instructors can readily use. We also acknowledge that more qualitative analysis will be needed to make embedding-based features consumable for students and teachers (e.g., by sampling prototypical examples corresponding to changes in salient embedding dimensions [10]). Finally, correlating milestone performance with assessments of learning (e.g., via external pre-post tests) as well as studying fine-grained process measures of remote collaboration (e.g., email revisions) are subject to future work.

8 Conclusion

We operationalize constructive alignment as a trace-based measure for simulation learning and show how it complements multimodal prediction by integrating linguistic communication (email/text embeddings) and behavioral interaction logs. In cybersecurity tabletop exercises, alignment, measured as Bloom-level discrepancy between intended objectives and enacted communication, predicted milestone success, whereas nominal Bloom level did not. At the same time, linguistic and interaction traces outperformed Bloom frequencies in prediction, separating explanation from detection: alignment explains why teams succeed or fail, while multimodal features indicate who is at risk and when.

This supports an actionable AI-based pipeline: text and log models flag impending milestone failures, and alignment diagnostics guide targeted, cognitively grounded support such as prompts to analyze or justify. Although evaluated in cybersecurity TTXs with human-coded labels, the approach generalizes to other domains, semi-automated coding, and embedded interventions triggered by misalignment. By combining predictive accuracy with explanatory clarity, this work advances AIED toward timely, pedagogically meaningful guidance.

Acknowledgments. This research was supported by the Open Calls for Security Research 2023–2029 (OPSEC) program granted by the Ministry of the Interior of the Czech Republic under No. VK01030007 – Intelligent Tools for Planning, Conducting, and Evaluating Tabletop Exercises.

References

1. Study dataset. https://doi.org/10.5281/zenodo.19249686
2. ACM Committee (CCECC): Bloom's for computing: Enhancing bloom's revised taxonomy with verbs for computing disciplines (2023). https://ccecc.acm.org/assessment/blooms-for-computing
3. Angafor, G., Yevseyeva, I., Maglaras, L.: Malaware: a tabletop exercise for malware security awareness education and incident response training. Internet Things Cyber-Phys. Syst. **4**, 280–292 (2024)
4. Asatryan, H., et al.: Exploring student expectations and confidence in learning analytics. In: Proceedings of the 14th Learning Analytics and Knowledge Conference, LAK 2024, pp. 892–898. ACM, New York (2024)
5. Asif, R., Merceron, A., Pathan, M.K.: Investigating performance of students: a longitudinal study. In: Proceedings of the Fifth International Conference on Learning Analytics And Knowledge, LAK 2015, pp. 108–112. Association for Computing Machinery, New York (2015). https://doi.org/10.1145/2723576.2723579
6. Ayyanathan, N.: Learning analytics model and bloom's taxonomy based evaluation framework for the post graduate students' project assessment – a blended project based learning management system with rubric referenced predictors. Shanlax Int. J. Educ. **10**(3), 48–60 (2022)
7. Bates, D., Mächler, M., Bolker, B., Walker, S.: Fitting linear mixed-effects models using lme4. J. Stat. Softw. **67**, 1–48 (2015)
8. Biggs, J.: Enhancing teaching through constructive alignment. High. Educ. **32**(3), 347–364 (1996)
9. Bloom, B.S., Engelhart, M.D., Furst, E.J., Hill, W.H., Krathwohl, D.R.: Taxonomy of educational objectives: the classification of educational goals. In: Handbook 1: Cognitive Domain. Longman (1956)
10. Borchers, C., Patel, M., Lee, S.M., Botelho, A.F.: Disentangling learning from judgment: representation learning for open response analytics. In: Proceedings of the LAK26: 16th International Learning Analytics and Knowledge Conference, pp. 744–750 (2026, April)
11. Borchers, C., Tian, X., Boyer, K.E., Israel, M.: Combining log data and collaborative dialogue features to predict project quality in middle school AI education, arXiv preprint arXiv:2506.11326 (2025)
12. Borchers, C., Wang, Y., Karumbaiah, S., Ashiq, M., Shaffer, D.W., Aleven, V.: Revealing networks: understanding effective teacher practices in AI-supported classrooms using transmodal ordered network analysis. In: Proceedings of the 14th Learning Analytics and Knowledge Conference, pp. 371–381 (2024)
13. Borchers, C., et al.: Large language models generalize SRL prediction to new languages within but not between domains. J. Educ. Data Mining **17**(2), 24–54 (2025)
14. Brennan, R., Perouli, D.: Generating and evaluating collective concept maps. In: LAK22: 12th International Learning Analytics and Knowledge Conference, LAK 2022, pp. 570–576. Association for Computing Machinery, New York (2022). https://doi.org/10.1145/3506860.3506918
15. Chernikova, O., Heitzmann, N., Stadler, M., Holzberger, D., Seidel, T., Fischer, F.: Simulation-based learning in higher education: a meta-analysis. Rev. Educ. Res. **90**(4), 499–541 (2020)
16. Chernikova, O., et al.: Personalization through adaptivity or adaptability? A meta-analysis on simulation-based learning in higher education. Educ. Res. Rev. **46**, 100662 (2025)

17. Drachsler, H., Greller, W.: Privacy and analytics: it's a delicate issue a checklist for trusted learning analytics. In: Proceedings of the Sixth International Conference on Learning Analytics & Knowledge, LAK 2016, pp. 89–98. Association for Computing Machinery, New York (2016). https://doi.org/10.1145/2883851.2883893

18. Franco, A., Holzer, A.: Fostering privacy literacy among high school students by leveraging social media interaction and learning traces in the classroom. In: LAK23: 13th International Learning Analytics and Knowledge Conference, LAK 2023, pp. 538–544. Association for Computing Machinery, New York (2023)

19. Guzdial, M., du Boulay, B.: The history of computing education research. In: The Cambridge Handbook of Computing Education Research, chap. 1, pp. 11–39. Cambridge University Press, UK (2019)

20. Hmoud, M., Ali, S.: Aied bloom's taxonomy: a proposed model for enhancing educational efficiency and effectiveness in the artificial intelligence era. Int. J. Technol. Learn. **31**, 111–128 (2024)

21. Joint Task Force on Cybersecurity Education: Cybersecurity curricular guideline (2017). http://cybered.acm.org

22. Karpen, S.C., Welch, A.C.: Assessing the inter-rater reliability and accuracy of pharmacy faculty's bloom's taxonomy classifications. Curr. Pharm. Teach. Learn. **8**(6), 885–888 (2016)

23. Kävrestad, J., Johansson, S., Bergström, E.: Using tabletop exercises to raise cybersecurity awareness of decision-makers. In: Oliva, G., Panzieri, S., Hämmerli, B., Pascucci, F., Faramondi, L. (eds.) Critical Information Infrastructures Security, pp. 231–248. Springer, Cham (2025)

24. Kitto, K., Sarathy, N., Gromov, A., Liu, M., Musial, K., Buckingham Shum, S.: Towards skills-based curriculum analytics: can we automate the recognition of prior learning? In: Proceedings of the Tenth International Conference on Learning Analytics & Knowledge, LAK 2020, pp. 171–180. Association for Computing Machinery, New York (2020). https://doi.org/10.1145/3375462.3375526

25. Levin, N., Baker, R., Nasiar, N., Hutt, S.: Evaluating gaming detector model robustness over time. In: Proceedings of the 15th International Conference on Educational Data Mining. International Educational Data Mining Society (2022)

26. Li, Y., Rakovic, M., Poh, B.X., Gasevic, D., Chen, G.: Automatic classification of learning objectives based on bloom's taxonomy. In: Proceedings of the 15th International Conference on Educational Data Mining, p. 530 (2022)

27. Muhamad Sori, Z., Wan Mustapha, W.H.: Bloom's taxonomy for effective teaching and learning. SSRN Electron. J. **25** (2025)

28. Nat. Initiative for Cybersecurity Careers and Studies (NICCS): Incident response (2020). https://niccs.cisa.gov/tools/nice-framework/work-role/incident-response

29. Pfaller, T., Skopik, F., Reuter, L., Leitner, M.: Data collection in cyber exercises through monitoring points: observing, steering, and scoring (2025)

30. Porter, A.C.: Measuring the content of instruction: uses in research and practice. Educ. Res. **31**(7), 3–14 (2002)

31. Raj, R., et al.: Professional competencies in computing education: pedagogies and assessment. In: Working Group Reports on Innovation and Technology in Computer Science Education. ITiCSE-WGR, pp. 133–161. ACM, New York (2022)

32. Roschelle, J., Teasley, S.D.: The construction of shared knowledge in collaborative problem solving. In: Computer Supported Collaborative Learning, pp. 69–97. Springer (1995)

33. Suraworachet, W., Seon, J., Cukurova, M.: Predicting challenge moments from students' discourse: a comparison of GPT-4 to two traditional natural language

processing approaches. In: Proceedings of the 14th Learning Analytics and Knowledge conference, pp. 473–485 (2024)
34. Swamy, V., Radmehr, B., Krco, N., Marras, M., Käser, T.: Evaluating the explainers: Black-box explainable machine learning for student success prediction in MOOCs. In: Proceedings of the 15th International Conference on Educational Data Mining, p. 98 (2022)
35. Tello, A.B., Wu, Y.-T., Perry, T., Yu-Pei, X.: A novel yardstick of learning time spent in a programming language by unpacking Bloom's taxonomy. In: Arai, K., Kapoor, S., Bhatia, R. (eds.) SAI 2020. AISC, vol. 1228, pp. 785–794. Springer, Cham (2020). https://doi.org/10.1007/978-3-030-52249-0_53
36. The Joint Task Force on Computer Science Curricula: Computing Curricula 2023. ACM, New York (2024). https://doi.org/10.1145/3664191
37. Vajjala, S., Shimangaud, S.: Text classification in the LLM era-where do we stand?, arXiv preprint arXiv:2502.11830 (2025)
38. Vogelsang, T., Ruppertz, L.: On the validity of peer grading and a cloud teaching assistant system. In: Proceedings of the Fifth International Conference on Learning Analytics And Knowledge, LAK 2015, pp. 41–50. Association for Computing Machinery, New York (2015). https://doi.org/10.1145/2723576.2723633
39. Švábenský, V., Vykopal, J., Horák, M., Hofbauer, M., Čeleda, P.: From paper to platform: evolution of a novel learning environment for tabletop exercises. In: Innovation and Technology in Computer Science Education, pp. 213–219. ACM, New York (2024). https://doi.org/10.1145/3649217.3653639
40. Švábenský, V., Vykopal, J., Čeleda, P.: What are cybersecurity education papers about? A systematic literature review of SIGCSE and ITiCSE conferences. In: Proceedings of the 51st ACM Technical Symposium on Computer Science Education, SIGCSE 2020, pp. 2–8. Association for Computing Machinery, New York (2020). https://doi.org/10.1145/3328778.3366816
41. Švábenský, V., Vykopal, J., Čeleda, P., Kraus, L.: Applications of educational data mining and learning analytics on data from cybersecurity training. Educ. Inf. Technol. **27**, 12179–12212 (2022)
42. Vykopal, J., Čeleda, P., Seda, P., Švábenský, V., Tovarňák, D.: Scalable learning environments for teaching cybersecurity hands-on. In: Proceedings of the 51st IEEE Frontiers in Education Conference, FIE 2021, pp. 1–9. IEEE, New York (2021). https://doi.org/10.1109/FIE49875.2021.9637180
43. Vykopal, J., Čeleda, P., Švábenský, V., Hofbauer, M., Horák, M.: Research and practice of delivering tabletop exercises. In: 29th Conference on Innovation and Technology in Computer Science Education, ITiCSE 2024, pp. 220–226. ACM, New York (2024). https://doi.org/10.1145/3649217.3653642
44. Wine, M., Hoffman, A.M.: Reinforcing Webb's depth of knowledge: laterally extending DoK by acknowledging proficiency's impact on cognitive demand. In: 2023 Aera Annual Meeting: Interrogating Consequential Education Research in Pursuit of Truth, pp. 13–16 (2023)
45. Wise, A.F.: Designing pedagogical interventions to support student use of learning analytics. In: Proceedings of the Fourth International Conference on Learning Analytics and Knowledge, pp. 203–211 (2014)
46. Won, M., Carrington, L.R., Espinoza, D.M., Ali, M.H., Dasgupta, D.: A cybersecurity summer camp for high school students using autonomous R/C cars. In: Tech. Symposium on Comp. Sci. Educ., SIGCSE, pp. 1435–1441. ACM, New York (2024). https://doi.org/10.1145/3626252.3630758

47. Wong, K., Wu, B., Bulathwela, S., Cukurova, M.: Rethinking the potential of multimodality in collaborative problem solving diagnosis with large language models. In: International Conference on Artificial Intelligence in Education, pp. 18–32. Springer (2025)
48. Yan, L., et al.: The role of indoor positioning analytics in assessment of simulation-based learning. Br. J. Edu. Technol. **54**(1), 267–292 (2023). https://doi.org/10.1111/bjet.13262

From Exploration to Creation: How Teachers Orchestrate AI-Supported Learning in History Classrooms

Hyungwoo Song, Kieun Park, and Bongwon Suh

Department of Intelligence and Information, Seoul National University,
Seoul, South Korea
{rotto95,kieun.park,bongwon}@snu.ac.kr

Abstract. As Artificial Intelligence (AI) becomes increasingly integrated into classrooms, how teachers organize AI-supported learning in practice remains underexplored. This study examines teacher orchestration in AI-supported history instruction by analyzing how teachers designed and enacted lessons using *HistoriaCraft*, an LLM-based platform for authoring and exploring historical simulations, in Grade 6 and Grade 8 classrooms. Following a formative study with 15 teachers, we co-designed three-session lesson sequences with four teachers and observed their implementation with 118 students across six classes. The lessons were structured as a sequence of exploration and creation activities, which we conceptualize as two instructional modes: Exploration Mode, in which students engaged with teacher-authored simulations, and Creation Mode, in which students authored their own. Drawing on classroom observations and teacher interviews, we characterize how teachers organized instruction differently across these modes, adopting distinct roles in structuring sense-making and fostering student ownership and inquiry. We further analyze differences in student engagement across modes using interaction logs, observational data, and surveys, identifying systematic shifts in student discourse, participation structures, and perceived agency. These findings illustrate how teachers actively orchestrate AI-supported learning through deliberate instructional design, offering a classroom-based account of teacher agency in AI-integrated instruction and implications for supporting teachers as designers of AI-mediated learning.

Keywords: AI in Education · Teacher Orchestration · Instructional Design · Instructional Sequencing · Classroom Study

---

H. Song and K. Park—These authors contributed equally to this work.

E. G. Blanchard et al. (Eds.): AIED 2026, LNAI 16583, pp. 443–458, 2027.
https://doi.org/10.1007/978-3-032-29760-0_48

1 Introduction

As Artificial Intelligence (AI) becomes increasingly integrated into classrooms, it is reshaping how teaching and learning are organized [19,21]. Across educational settings, AI systems are commonly framed as providing personalized feedback, adaptive content, and analytics, with growing attention to their potential to reconfigure instructional practices [24,28]. As these systems become embedded within everyday classroom activity rather than treated as peripheral tools, they increasingly function as part of the instructional infrastructure through which learning unfolds [7,10]. This shift highlights the need to examine how classroom learning is practically organized and sequenced around AI-supported interactions and responsibilities.

How teachers organize and sequence AI-supported learning in situated classroom practice remains comparatively underexplored in prior AI-in-education research [8,22]. Existing work has predominantly focused on system development, learning outcomes, or learner-facing perceptions [13,19]. Although some studies have examined teachers' engagement with AI, they have tended to emphasize attitudes, professional development, or broad role adoption rather than teachers' instructional decision-making in everyday classroom activity [4, 18,20]. Related syntheses similarly suggest that educators' instructional work is underrepresented relative to technology-centered perspectives in the literature [27].

In this work, we focus on teacher orchestration in AI-supported classrooms. Rather than examining AI tools in isolation, we analyze how teachers design, sequence, and enact AI-supported learning as a coherent instructional process. We report findings from a field study conducted in Grade 6 and Grade 8 history classrooms using *HistoriaCraft*, an LLM-based platform for authoring and exploring historical simulations, drawing on classroom observations, teacher interviews, student interaction logs, and surveys.

Through a formative study with 15 teachers, we iteratively developed *HistoriaCraft* and identified key pedagogical needs for classroom use. Building on these insights, we worked with four teachers across six classrooms (118 students) to co-design three-session lesson sequences organized as a progression from exploration to creation on the same platform, consistent with prior work suggesting that structured sense-making supports subsequent open-ended inquiry [1,17].

We conceptualize this sequence as two instructional modes: Exploration Mode, in which students engage with teacher-authored simulations, and Creation Mode, in which students author their own. Drawing on classroom observations, teacher interviews, interaction logs, and surveys, we characterize how teachers adopted distinct instructional roles across modes and document associated shifts in student discourse, participation, and perceived agency.

This paper contributes a classroom-based empirical account of how teachers orchestrate AI-supported learning across two instructional modes, characterizes their distinct roles and associated differences in student discourse and agency, and derives design implications for AI learning environments that support teachers as designers of AI-mediated learning.

2 Related Work

While AI systems in education are increasingly capable, understanding how teachers organize AI-supported learning in real classrooms remains limited. We review research on AI-supported learning in classroom contexts and teacher orchestration practices, highlighting gaps our study addresses.

2.1 AI-Supported Learning in Classroom Contexts

Prior research in Artificial Intelligence in Education (AIED) has primarily examined how AI systems support learning through automated feedback, personalization, and adaptive guidance [21,27]. Intelligent tutoring systems, learning analytics dashboards, and more recently generative AI tools have been reported to improve efficiency, engagement, or short-term learning outcomes under specific conditions [24,26]. Within this line of work, learning processes are often explained through system affordances, algorithmic adaptation, or optimization-oriented features designed to enhance individual performance.

However, research in the learning sciences has long emphasized that identical technologies can support qualitatively different learning processes depending on how they are pedagogically organized [14,25], with teachers playing a central role in shaping how tools are introduced, sequenced, and integrated into classroom activity [5,16]. Despite these insights, AIED research has paid comparatively limited attention to how teachers organize AI-supported learning in authentic classroom settings, particularly how they orchestrate transitions between different instructional modes of AI-supported activity [8,27].

2.2 Teacher Orchestration and Instructional Sequencing

A growing body of research has examined teachers' roles in AI-integrated educational contexts. Prior studies have emphasized teachers' evolving roles as learning designers and facilitators, as well as their needs for AI literacy and professional development [11,15,28]. Frameworks such as TPACK and its AI-oriented extensions have articulated the knowledge domains required for effective integration of emerging technologies into instruction [16].

However, much of this work remains at a conceptual or survey-based level, focusing on teachers' perceptions, attitudes, or preparedness rather than their instructional practices in real classrooms [4,18,20]. Empirical studies that closely examine how teachers enact these roles during classroom instruction remain relatively limited, particularly in AI-mediated settings [21,22]. Within the learning sciences, research on orchestration has highlighted how teachers manage classroom complexity, coordinate multiple activities, and sequence tasks to support learning progression [6]. Related work on inquiry-based learning further emphasizes the importance of moving from guided sense-making toward more open-ended inquiry and student-led knowledge construction [12].

Within this broader literature, prior work has provided theoretical grounds for sequencing structured sense-making activities before open-ended construction tasks. Barron et al. (1998) [1] demonstrated that structured problem-solving activities can establish the conceptual foundation necessary for productive engagement in subsequent project-based learning, suggesting that guided experience with domain content supports more meaningful student-driven inquiry. Relatedly, Miyake and Norman (1979) [17] argued that the capacity to formulate meaningful questions presupposes relevant prior understanding, implying that learners benefit from processing domain knowledge before generating their own representations. These perspectives suggest that sequencing guided exploration before creative construction may support learners in building the cognitive prerequisites for productive authorship. However, how such sequencing operates in AI-supported classroom environments—where AI agents mediate both exploration and creation—remains an open empirical question.

Despite these contributions, limited research has examined how teachers orchestrate instructional sequencing in AI-supported classrooms, particularly how they organize transitions between different instructional modes and the roles they adopt in each mode. As a result, the relationship between teacher orchestration, instructional design decisions, and classroom learning processes in AI-integrated environments remains insufficiently understood.

Our study addresses these gaps by documenting how teachers designed and enacted AI-supported learning across two instructional modes—Exploration Mode and Creation Mode—in real classroom settings, examining both their orchestration practices and the associated patterns in student learning processes.

3   HistoriaCraft

We developed *HistoriaCraft*, an LLM-based historical simulation platform, through an iterative design process with teachers. This section describes the platform's core functionality and the formative study that shaped its dual-mode design.

3.1   Platform Overview

HistoriaCraft enables users to author and explore historical simulations. Users author historical maps by defining background narratives, characters representing different historical perspectives, and quests—structured inquiry tasks guiding investigation. Once authored, simulations can be explored by navigating the map, engaging in AI-driven dialogue with characters, and completing quests. In this context, a simulation refers to a structured historical scenario consisting of a background narrative, interactive characters, and inquiry-based quests, all situated within a navigable map environment.

As shown in Fig. 1, the platform supports two instructional modes. In **Exploration Mode** (left panel), students explore teacher-authored simulations, interacting with AI-driven characters and completing quests to investigate historical scenarios from multiple perspectives. In **Creation Mode** (right panel), students author their own historical simulations, designing maps, characters, and quests with AI assistance. LLM-based agents support both modes: maintaining character dialogue consistency in Exploration Mode and providing authoring suggestions in Creation Mode, all grounded in teacher-authored background narratives to ensure historical accuracy and curricular alignment.

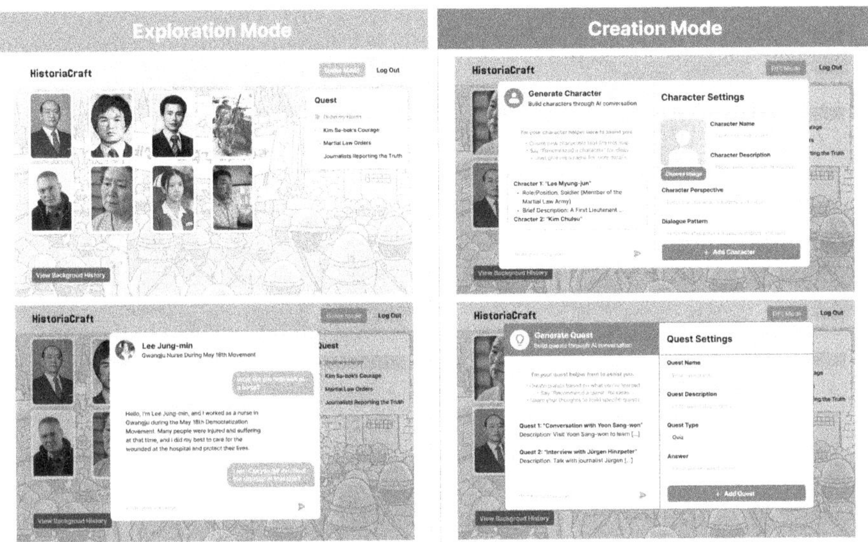

Fig. 1. Exploration Mode and Creation Mode interfaces for *HistoriaCraft*. In Exploration Mode (left), students explore teacher-authored simulations, interact with AI-driven characters, and complete quests. In Creation Mode (right), teachers or students author simulations by defining background stories, characters, and quests.

3.2 Formative Study and Design Iterations

To inform the design of HistoriaCraft, we evaluated an early prototype through a formative study with 15 elementary and middle school history teachers. This process surfaced key design considerations for classroom use, which guided subsequent system refinement. Each teacher explored a pre-configured scenario as a student, then used the authoring interface to design instructional content, providing feedback through think-aloud protocols and interviews.

The formative study revealed three key design considerations: **adaptive extensibility** across topics and grade levels, **student authorship** as a pedagogically desirable mode of engagement, and **robust classroom behavior handling** to reorient off-task interactions toward instructional goals. These considerations informed the development of a dual-mode platform balancing guided exploration with student-driven creation.

3.3   AI Agent Framework

In practice, students in Exploration Mode navigate maps, converse with characters, and answer quests, while in Creation Mode they define background narratives, design characters, and author quests with AI assistance. HistoriaCraft employs four specialized AI agents, each designed for specific educational functions. The *Character Dialogue Agent* manages conversations between students and historical figures, maintaining character consistency and historical accuracy through continuous reference to user-defined background narratives. The *Character Generation Assistant* and *Quest Generation Assistant* support student authoring by suggesting historically appropriate character traits and educationally meaningful quest structures, while requiring student validation of all suggestions. The *Quest Verification Agent* evaluates student responses through semantic understanding rather than keyword matching, providing contextual feedback that guides further exploration.

To minimize hallucination and preserve historical accuracy, all AI prompts incorporate the background story as a grounding reference. Safeguard guidelines embedded in every prompt ensure age-appropriate tone and accessible language, and can be configured by teachers through an administrative mode. The platform supports classroom-scale deployment with concurrent multi-user access.

4   Classroom Study

Following the formative study, we collaborated with teachers to implement *HistoriaCraft* in real classroom settings. This section describes how teachers designed and structured their lessons, and our data collection and analysis methods.

4.1   Classroom Implementation

We worked with four teachers across six classrooms with 118 students total. Participants included three sixth-grade elementary teachers (each teaching one class, 46 students total) and one eighth-grade middle school history teacher (teaching three classes, 72 students total).

Prior to classroom deployment, each teacher participated in an approximately one-hour orientation session where we introduced *HistoriaCraft*'s functionality and discussed classroom integration strategies. Teachers then independently designed three 40-min lesson sequences aligned with their curricular goals.

Teachers consistently structured lessons around two sequential instructional modes. Session 1 (Exploration Mode) engaged students with teacher-authored historical simulations, where they interacted with AI-driven characters and completed quests. Sessions 2–3 (Creation Mode) involved student authoring of historical simulations—designing maps, characters, and quests—followed by peer-sharing activities where students explored and critiqued each other's work. A key implementation difference emerged by grade level: elementary teachers organized Creation as individual work, while the middle school teacher used group-based activities (4 students per group).

4.2 Data Collection and Analysis

We collected multiple forms of data across all classroom sessions. Classroom observations documented lesson flow, teacher moves, and participation patterns through timestamped field notes. Post-implementation teacher interviews (60 min each) captured instructional decisions and reflections on organizing learning across modes. Student surveys were administered after Session 3 using 5-point Likert scales (1 = strongly disagree, 5 = strongly agree) adapted from the in-game Game Experience Questionnaire (GEQ), measuring perceived control and ownership separately for each mode. System logs automatically recorded all student interactions and created content.

Teacher interviews were transcribed and analyzed following reflexive thematic analysis [2,23]. Three researchers engaged in iterative and interpretive coding, independently examining subsets of the data to surface diverse perspectives and collaboratively refining candidate themes through discussion. This process yielded primary themes related to instructional sequencing rationales and teacher roles across modes.

Student discourse was analyzed separately using a structured coding approach applied to interaction logs containing 11,164 utterances (5,582 student messages and 5,582 AI responses) across all six classes. We developed a coding scheme adapted from the DAMSL dialogue act framework, distinguishing curricular-aligned exchanges (historical reasoning, perspective-taking, causal explanation), off-topic interactions, and others (e.g., procedural utterances). Within curricular exchanges, we further coded for historical significance discussions, and AI responses were additionally coded for redirection, defined as instances where the agent steered off-topic inputs back toward curricular themes. Two researchers coded the dataset using a negotiated, discussion-based approach informed by prior work on collaborative qualitative coding [3]. An initial subset was independently coded to refine category boundaries and resolve definitional ambiguities, followed by full dataset coding with disagreements addressed through structured discussion until mutual agreement was reached. This process was designed to ensure analytic consistency through iterative refinement of shared interpretations, rather than to establish statistical intercoder agreement [2].

Survey data were analyzed descriptively, comparing mean scores across modes. Observation notes were systematically reviewed to document orchestration practices and participation structures. System logs provided supplementary context for interpreting engagement patterns across modes.

5 Findings

This section describes how teachers structured and enacted AI-supported learning using *HistoriaCraft* in real classrooms, focusing on how their instructional roles differed between Exploration and Creation modes.

5.1 Instructional Framing: Sequencing Exploration and Creation

Teachers consistently framed the system as a sequenced instructional process, deliberately ordering activities as *Exploration → Creation* based on their expectations of students' cognitive readiness.

Several teachers expressed concern that initiating lessons directly with creative tasks could lead to disorientation or historically shallow outputs. As T2 explained, *"If students start by making something right away, they often don't know what to make or why. They need to understand the situation first."* Similarly, T4 noted, *"When context is missing, students focus on making it fun, not historically meaningful."* T4 described this observation as arising from a prior lesson in which students, given a creation task without preceding exploration, produced characters that reflected popular media stereotypes rather than historically grounded perspectives.

In response, teachers positioned Exploration Mode as a phase for establishing shared historical context through teacher-designed maps, characters, and quests. T1 described this phase as setting a baseline for inquiry: *"Exploration is where students figure out who is involved, what the conflict is, and why it matters."* Teachers also emphasized exposure to multiple perspectives, with T3 noting, *"By meeting different characters first, students start asking why people thought differently, instead of assuming there's just one story."*

Only after this phase did teachers transition students into Creation Mode, where students designed their own historical representations based on prior exploration. Teachers viewed creation as a way to externalize historical understanding rather than free-form expression. As T1 explained, *"What students make shows how they understood the history."* Peer-sharing was often used to surface differences in interpretation, as T4 observed: *"Students start asking whether each other's ideas really make sense historically."*

5.2 Teacher Role in Exploration Mode: Guided Sense-Making

In Exploration Mode, teachers described their role not as delivering historical explanations but as structuring how students navigated the inquiry space.

First, teachers acted as starting-point providers by designing initial storylines, guiding questions, and quest flows to prevent students from becoming directionless. As T1 explained, *"If we don't set a starting point, students just wander around without knowing what to look for."*

Second, teachers intentionally orchestrated perspectives by placing characters with contrasting social positions and viewpoints within the same historical scenario. This design choice encouraged students to interpret events relationally rather than as a single narrative. As T3 noted, *"When students hear different characters talk, they naturally start comparing who says what and why."*

Finally, teachers positioned themselves as cognitive boundary regulators when students interacted with AI-generated content. Rather than treating AI responses as authoritative, teachers prompted students to question accuracy, sources, and plausibility. As T4 emphasized, *"We always tell students that AI can be wrong, so they need to check and think about whether it makes sense."*

Together, these practices show that in Exploration Mode, teachers did not transfer knowledge directly but orchestrated the conditions under which students' historical understanding could emerge.

5.3 Teacher Role Transformation in Creation Mode: From Sense-Making to Ownership and Inquiry

In Creation Mode, teachers described their role not as structuring students' sense-making but as engineering ownership and inquiry.

First, teachers acted as ownership designers by requiring students to define their own historical characters, quests, and contextual settings. Teachers consistently emphasized in interviews that meaningful engagement depended on students' sense of authorship. As T2 explained, *"Creating directly has much greater educational effect than conversation."* Classroom observations confirmed this intention: rather than supplying content, teachers guided students to make substantive design decisions about narrative direction and historical framing. Consistent with these practices, post-session surveys indicated high levels of perceived control (sixth grade: M = 4.46, SD = 0.61; eighth grade: M = 4.11, SD = 1.06) and ownership (sixth grade: M = 4.03, SD = 0.95; eighth grade: M = 4.06, SD = 1.09) on a 5-point scale.

Second, teachers positioned themselves as inquiry quality controllers to prevent student work from collapsing into superficial fact listing. During quest creation, teachers regularly examined whether students' questions reflected historical significance and causal reasoning, intervening when tasks became merely descriptive or fragmented. As T4 observed, *"In Creation Mode, I heard students asking questions I'd never heard from them before—not just 'Is this right?' but 'How would this person really think?' and 'What would motivate them to act this way?'"* Although the AI system provided suggestions for content and structure, final judgments about the direction and rigor of inquiry were negotiated between teachers and students.

Finally, teachers orchestrated peer-learning by embedding structured sharing and critique into the classroom workflow. Teachers deliberately designed peer-sharing activities in which students exchanged maps and quests, identified errors, and compared alternative historical interpretations. Observation data revealed that these sessions generated new patterns of collaboration and redistributed participation across groups. As one student reflected, *"Looking at my friend's work helped me notice mistakes and understand the history better."*

Together, these practices show that in Creation Mode, teachers did not simply facilitate student activity but actively reconfigured the learning environment to promote ownership, inquiry, and collaborative historical reasoning.

5.4   Student Discourse and Engagement Across Instructional Modes

Analysis of student interactions across Exploration and Creation Modes revealed systematic differences in discourse patterns and engagement. These differences, observed consistently across all six classrooms, aligned with the distinct instructional roles teachers adopted in each mode.

Table 1. Student Discourse Patterns Across Modes by Grade Level

Grade	Discourse Type	Exploration	Creation
Sixth	Curricular	30.0%	44.9%
	Off-topic	46.9%	26.4%
	Others	23.1%	28.7%
	HS (in curricular)	9.9%	19.6%
	Redirection (in AI responses)	27.4%	20.5%
Eighth	Curricular	42.9%	41.0%
	Off-topic	41.4%	29.8%
	Others	15.7%	29.2%
	HS (in curricular)	13.8%	59.0%
	Redirection (in AI responses)	23.6%	24.9%

Note: N = 11,164 utterances (5,582 student, 5,582 AI responses) HS = Historical Significance discussions within curricular exchanges Representative examples – Curricular: "Why did workers decide to strike instead of negotiating?"; Off-topic: "Do you like pizza?"; HS: "Was the revolution really necessary, or could reform have worked?"; Redirection: [AI] "That's an interesting thought – how might it connect to what the factory workers experienced?"

Discourse Patterns. Coding of 11,164 student utterances showed substantial shifts in how students engaged with historical content (Table 1).

In Exploration Mode, student discourse was characterized by lower rates of curricular-aligned exchanges (sixth grade: 30.0%, eighth grade: 42.9%) and higher rates of off-topic interaction (sixth grade: 46.9%, eighth grade: 41.4%). Within curricular exchanges, discussions of historical significance—questions about why events mattered, how they should be remembered, or whether interpretations were justified—comprised a small fraction (sixth grade: 9.9%, eighth grade: 13.8%). Students more often requested factual information or sought clarification about quest requirements.

In Creation Mode, particularly during peer-sharing activities, discourse patterns shifted markedly. Curricular-aligned exchanges increased (sixth grade: 44.9%, eighth grade: 41.0%), while off-topic interactions decreased substantially (sixth grade: 26.4%, eighth grade: 29.8%). More notably, discussions centered on historical significance rose dramatically (sixth grade: 19.6%, eighth grade: 59.0%). As students examined and critiqued peer-created simulations, they engaged less in fact-focused questions and more in interpretive reasoning about historical meaning and perspective. For example, whereas Exploration Mode exchanges were often factual in nature (e.g., *"What were the orders for the Gwangju suppression operation?"*), Creation Mode exchanges reflected more interpretive engagement, such as a student asking a peer-authored character, *"If Chun Doo-hwan in 1980 had learned about the Nazis, what would he have thought?"*, a counterfactual question that connects historical contexts across time and probes a figure's moral reasoning rather than retrieving information. These shifts suggest that the authoring and peer-review process prompted students to move beyond information retrieval toward evaluating and constructing historical interpretations. This pattern is consistent with teachers' observations that Creation Mode elicited qualitatively different forms of historical questioning (see Sect. 5.3).

In addition, AI responses frequently redirected off-topic student inputs toward curriculum-relevant themes (Table 1). Rather than terminating interaction, these responses often guided conversations back into curricular dialogue.

Relationship to Teacher Orchestration. These systematic differences across modes corresponded with teachers' distinct instructional approaches. Teachers deliberately sequenced Exploration before Creation based on their judgment that structured sense-making should precede open-ended construction, and their distinct instructional roles in each mode aligned with the observed shifts in student discourse and engagement. While task affordances differed between modes, the consistency of patterns across all six classrooms suggests that teachers' orchestration practices shaped how students engaged with the same AI platform.

6 Discussion

Our findings illustrate how teachers organized AI-supported learning through deliberate instructional design decisions. We discuss three implications: how teacher orchestration shapes learning processes beyond AI affordances, the tension between student autonomy and teacher control in AI-mediated classrooms, and the evolving role of teachers as designers of AI-supported learning.

6.1 Teacher-Orchestrated Learning Shifts Beyond AI Affordances

Although the same AI system was used across both modes, classrooms exhibited systematic changes in student discourse, participation, and perceived agency. Exploration was characterized by fact-oriented sense-making and guided navigation, whereas Creation involved interpretive reasoning, ownership, and more equitable participation. These patterns were consistent across grades and classrooms.

While prior AIED research often explains learning outcomes through system capabilities or adaptive features [19,21], our results indicate that the same technology supported different learning processes depending on how it was pedagogically organized by teachers. This observation is consistent with learning sciences work emphasizing instructional framing and task design over tool characteristics [5,25], and further illustrates how teachers can reorganize learning trajectories within AI-supported environments.

We note that the Exploration-to-Creation sequence itself draws on well-established pedagogical principles, including scaffolded inquiry and constructionist learning [1,17]. The contribution of this study lies not in proposing a novel instructional model, but in providing empirical evidence of how teachers enacted and adapted such sequencing within an AI-supported classroom environment. In particular, our findings illustrate how the same AI platform supported qualitatively different instructional modes depending on teachers' orchestration decisions, a dynamic that existing theoretical accounts of instructional sequencing have not examined in AI-mediated settings.

These findings point to the importance of attending not only to what AI systems are capable of, but also to how teachers organize learning activities around them. From this perspective, AI systems may benefit from supporting pedagogical flexibility, rather than assuming fixed learning outcomes based solely on system functionality.

6.2 Balancing Student Autonomy and Teacher Control in AI-Mediated Classrooms

Across both the formative study and classroom deployment, teachers consistently expressed concerns that open-ended AI-mediated dialogue could drift into off-topic interactions, a pattern confirmed by our analysis of student chat logs. To address this without restricting student interaction, the system incorporated a redirection-based mechanism in which AI agents acknowledged off-topic inputs while steering conversations back toward curricular themes. As reported in Sect.5.4, such redirection occurred at a substantial rate and often guided students back into content-relevant trajectories.

Together, these findings surface a core tension in AI-supported classrooms between fostering student autonomy through immersive interaction and maintaining instructional control [9]. Teachers emphasized that effective orchestration involved continuously calibrating this balance, and several expressed interest in additional control-oriented affordances, such as real-time alerts or visibility into studentagent exchanges. Designing AI systems that support flexible redirection and teacher-in-the-loop oversight may therefore be critical for sustaining both immersive learning and classroom manageability.

6.3 Reframing Teacher Roles in AI-Supported Classrooms

Teachers' roles differed across modes. In Exploration, they structured sensemaking by controlling entry points, perspectives, and cognitive boundaries. In Creation, they engineered ownership, regulated inquiry quality, and orchestrated peer learning. These instructional moves preceded observable changes in student interaction and collaboration.

These findings are consistent with views of teaching as orchestration rather than content delivery [6,16]. Importantly, orchestration in this context involved designing the conditions under which learning unfolded, rather than directing student behavior moment by moment.

Taken together, these findings suggest a view of teachers as key designers of AI-mediated learning. For AIED research and practice, this underscores the value of tools, curricula, and professional development that attend to teachers' design and orchestration work, alongside advances in AI functionality.

7   Conclusion

This study examined how teachers organized AI-supported learning in Grade 6 and Grade 8 history classrooms using *HistoriaCraft*, an LLM-based platform enabling users to author and explore historical simulations. Through formative development with 15 teachers and classroom implementation with 4 teachers across 6 classrooms (118 students), we documented how teachers designed and enacted instruction across two sequential modes: Exploration Mode, where students explored teacher-authored simulations, and Creation Mode, where students authored their own simulations. Our findings contribute an empirical account of how teachers orchestrated AI-supported learning across distinct instructional modes, characterize associated differences in student discourse and agency, and articulate design implications for AI learning environments that support teachers as designers of AI-mediated learning.

Limitations. First, this paper deliberately focuses on teachers' orchestration practices; while student-level data were extensively collected, our sample of four teachers and 118 students provides rich qualitative insight but limits statistical generalization, and student-centered analyses will be examined in future work. Second, the study was conducted in a specific domain (history education), with a limited age range (Grades 6 and 8), a single instructional sequence, and a design that does not support causal claims, which together constrain the generalizability of findings to other subjects, sequencing strategies, or outcome measures. Third, our three-session implementation captures initial use but does not reveal how orchestration practices might evolve with sustained use over time.

Future Directions. Future research should address these limitations through several directions. Future work could examine teacher orchestration across different domains, grade levels, and alternative instructional sequences, and employ longitudinal or experimental designs to establish how orchestration expertise develops and how instructional decisions shape learning outcomes. Additionally, future studies could examine student and teacher agency across modes through dedicated measurement instruments, and employ multilevel analyses to account for nested classroom structures in larger-scale implementations. Finally, design research exploring how AI learning environments can better support teacher orchestration—including tools for planning, monitoring, and reflecting on instructional sequences—represents an important next step for the field.

By foregrounding teacher orchestration in AI-supported learning, this study contributes to understanding how educators shape the educational potential of AI technologies through deliberate instructional design decisions. As AI becomes increasingly integrated into classrooms, attending to teachers' orchestration practices alongside technological capabilities will be essential for realizing AI's promise in education.

Acknowledgments. Supported by IITP [RS-2021-II211343] and NRF [RS-2025-25421701, RS-2025-25429940] (MSIT, MOE, Korea). We thank Hana Oh, Hoyeol Yang, Yeonjoon Kim, Jung Lee, Dongseok Heo, Jaehoon Choi, Minchae Kim, and Jueon Lee from Seoul National University for their assistance with the experiments, result analysis, and figure preparation.

References

1. Barron, B.J.S., et al.: Doing with understanding: lessons from research on problem- and project-based learning. J. Learn. Sci. **7**(3–4), 271–311 (1998). https://doi.org/10.1207/s15327809jls0703&4_2
2. Braun, V., Clarke, V.: Reflecting on reflexive thematic analysis. Qual. Res. Sport Exerc. Health. **11**(4), 589–597 (2019). https://doi.org/10.1080/2159676X.2019.1628806
3. Campbell, J.L., Quincy, C., Osserman, J., Pedersen, O.K.: Coding in-depth semistructured interviews: problems of unitization and intercoder reliability and agreement. Sociol. Methods Res. **42**(3), 294–320 (2013). https://doi.org/10.1177/0049124113500475
4. Chounta, I.A., Bardone, E., Raudsep, A., Pedaste, M.: Exploring teachers' perceptions of artificial intelligence as a tool to support their practice in Estonian K-12 education. Int. J. Artif. Intell. Educ. **32**(3), 725–755 (2022)
5. Cope, C., Ward, P.: Integrating learning technology into classrooms: the importance of teachers' perceptions. J. Educ. Technol. Soc. **5**(1), 67–74 (2002)
6. Dillenbourg, P.: Design for classroom orchestration. Comput. Educ. **69**, 485–492 (2013). https://doi.org/10.1016/j.compedu.2013.04.013
7. Giannakos, M., et al.: The promise and challenges of generative AI in education. Behav. Inf. Technol. **44**(11), 2518–2544 (2025)
8. Harvey, E., Koenecke, A., Kizilcec, R.F.: "Don't Forget the Teachers": towards an educator-centered understanding of harms from large language models in education. In: Proceedings of the CHI Conference on Human Factors in Computing Systems (CHI 2025). ACM (2025). https://doi.org/10.1145/3706598.3713210
9. Holstein, K., McLaren, B.M., Aleven, V.: Co-designing a real-time classroom orchestration tool to support teacher–AI complementarity. J. Learn. Anal. **6**(2), 27–52 (2019). https://doi.org/10.18608/jla.2019.62.3. https://learning-analytics.info/index.php/JLA/article/view/6336
10. Huber, S.E., Kiili, K., Nebel, S., Ryan, R.M., Sailer, M., Ninaus, M.: Leveraging the potential of large language models in education through playful and game-based learning. Educ. Psychol. Rev. **36**(1), 25 (2024)

11. Kaspersen, M.H., et al.: From primary education to premium workforce: drawing on K-12 approaches for developing AI literacy. In: Proceedings of the 2024 CHI Conference on Human Factors in Computing Systems, pp. 1–16 (2024)
12. Kirschner, P., Sweller, J., Clark, R.E.: Why unguided learning does not work: an analysis of the failure of discovery learning, problem-based learning, experiential learning and inquiry-based learning. Educ. Psychol. **41**(2), 75–86 (2006)
13. Kotamjani, S.S., Shirinova, S., Muratova, K., Sharma, M.: Exploring students' perspectives on generative AI for academic purposes in Uzbekistan's higher education. In: Proceedings of the 8th International Conference on Future Networks & Distributed Systems, pp. 986–994 (2024)
14. Lave, J., Wenger, E.: Situated Learning: Legitimate Peripheral Participation. Cambridge University Press, Cambridge (1991)
15. Long, D., Magerko, B.: What is AI literacy? Competencies and design considerations. In: Proceedings of the 2020 CHI Conference on Human Factors in Computing Systems, pp. 1–16. ACM (2020). https://doi.org/10.1145/3313831.3376727
16. Mishra, P., Koehler, M.J.: Technological pedagogical content knowledge: a framework for teacher knowledge. Teach. Coll. Rec. **108**(6), 1017–1054 (2006). https://doi.org/10.1111/j.1467-9620.2006.00684.x
17. Miyake, N., Norman, D.A.: To ask a question, one must know enough to know what is not known. J. Verbal Learn. Verbal Behav. **18**(3), 357–364 (1979). https://doi.org/10.1016/S0022-5371(79)90200-7
18. Moura, A., Carvalho, A.A.A.: Teachers' perceptions of the use of artificial intelligence in the classroom. In: International Conference on Lifelong Education and Leadership for All (ICLEL 2023), pp. 140–150. Atlantis Press (2024)
19. Mustafa, M.Y., et al.: A systematic review of literature reviews on artificial intelligence in education (AIED): a roadmap to a future research agenda. Smart Learn. Environ. **11**(1), 59 (2024). https://doi.org/10.1186/s40561-024-00350-5
20. Nazaretsky, T., Ariely, M., Cukurova, M., Alexandron, G.: Teachers' trust in AI-powered educational technology and a professional development program to improve it. Br. J. Edu. Technol. **53**(4), 914–931 (2022)
21. Roll, I., Wylie, R.: Evolution and revolution in artificial intelligence in education. Int. J. Artif. Intell. Educ. **26**(2), 582–599 (2016). https://doi.org/10.1007/s40593-016-0110-3
22. Tan, M., Subramonyam, H.: More than model documentation: Uncovering teachers' bespoke information needs for informed classroom integration of ChatGPT. In: Proceedings of the CHI Conference on Human Factors in Computing Systems (CHI 2024). ACM (2024). https://doi.org/10.1145/3613904.3642592
23. Terry, G., Hayfield, N., Clarke, V., Braun, V.: Thematic analysis. In: Willig, C., Stainton Rogers, W. (eds.) The SAGE Handbook of Qualitative Research in Psychology, 2 edn., pp. 17–37. SAGE Publications Ltd, London (2017). https://uwe-repository.worktribe.com/output/888518/thematic-analysis
24. Thomas, D.R., et al.: Improving student learning with hybrid human-AI tutoring: a three-study quasi-experimental investigation. In: Proceedings of the 14th Learning Analytics and Knowledge Conference (LAK 2024), pp. 404–415. ACM (2024). https://doi.org/10.1145/3636555.3636896
25. Vygotsky, L.S., Cole, M.: Mind in Society: Development of Higher Psychological Processes. Harvard University Press (1978)
26. Wang, S., Wang, F., Zhu, Z., Wang, J., Tran, T., Du, Z.: Artificial intelligence in education: a systematic literature review. Expert Syst. Appl. **252**, 124167 (2024). https://doi.org/10.1016/j.eswa.2024.124167. https://www.sciencedirect.com/science/article/pii/S0957417424010339

27. Zawacki-Richter, O., Marín, V.I., Bond, M., Gouverneur, F.: Systematic review of research on artificial intelligence applications in higher education - where are the educators? Int. J. Educ. Technol. High. Educ. **16**(1), 39 (2019). https://doi.org/10.1186/s41239-019-0171-0
28. Zhai, X.: Transforming teachers' roles and agencies in the era of generative AI: perceptions, acceptance, knowledge, and practices. J. Sci. Educ. Technol. **34**(6), 1323–1333 (2025). https://doi.org/10.1007/s10956-024-10174-0

Explaining, Solving, or Generating? Functional Differences in Students' AI Use in a University Database Course

Piret Luik[(✉)] [ID]

University of Tartu Institute of Computer Science, Tartu 51009, Estonia
`piret.luik@ut.ee`

Abstract. The increasing use of artificial intelligence (AI) in computer science education has highlighted the need to better understand how students use AI in learning, rather than treating AI use as single, uniform behavior. This study examines dimensions of students' AI use and their associations with motivational as well as individual and contextual characteristics. Survey data were collected from 236 students enrolled in an undergraduate database course. Using confirmatory factor analysis, three distinct dimensions of AI use were identified: AI use for explanations, AI use for task solving, and generative AI use. Multiple regression analyses showed that AI use is functionally differentiated. Perceived trust in AI emerged as a cross-cutting predictor across all three usage dimensions, whereas more differentiated patterns were observed for other factors, and several background characteristics, including gender, showed no meaningful associations. These findings underscore the importance of distinguishing between different forms of AI use when studying learner–AI interaction and designing pedagogically informed approaches to AI integration in computer science education.

Keywords: dimensions of AI usage · associations · computer science education

1 Introduction

In recent years, artificial intelligence (AI) has rapidly spread across many areas of human activity, bringing significant scientific, educational, and ethical challenges. The integration of AI tools into higher education has transformed how students engage with academic tasks and have led to a growing body of research examining students' AI use in learning contexts. Learners employ AI for a wide range of purposes, including searching for learning materials [1], idea generation [1, 2], explaining new concepts [1–3], obtaining feedback [4, 5], and programming support [6, 7]. Prior studies have documented this diversity of AI-supported learning activities, often focusing on usage frequencies or general purposes of AI use.

Beyond describing AI usage, research in educational psychology and human–technology interaction has identified several factors that may shape learners' engagement with AI-based tools. Motivational variables such as achievement goal orientations [8–10], academic help-seeking tendencies and resources [11–13], and trust in technological

© The Author(s), under exclusive license to Springer Nature Switzerland AG 2027
E. G. Blanchard et al. (Eds.): AIED 2026, LNAI 16583, pp. 459–474, 2027.
https://doi.org/10.1007/978-3-032-29760-0_49

systems [14, 15] have been linked to students' use of learning technologies, including AI. However, findings across these studies are often inconsistent, and certain aspects, such as help-avoidance behaviors, remain underexplored [16].

Moreover, individual and contextual characteristics are typically examined in isolation, which may partly explain the mixed results reported in the literature. For example, some studies report higher AI use among male students in computer science courses [17], whereas others find no meaningful gender differences in usage frequency [18]. Contextual and learning-behavior factors, such as time investment in learning and the timing of help-seeking, have received comparatively limited attention. Existing research rarely examines motivational factors, individual and contextual characteristics simultaneously within a comprehensive analytical framework.

Given the rapid proliferation of AI tools in education and the diversity of ways in which students use them, there is a growing need for studies that capture AI use as a multidimensional and context-dependent phenomenon. In particular, understanding how different forms of AI use relate to motivational, individual, and contextual factors is essential for developing pedagogically informed approaches to AI integration. Addressing this need, the present study combines factor analysis and regression analysis to identify key dimensions of AI usage and to examine their associations with motivational factors as well as individual and contextual characteristics in an introductory database course. Accordingly, the study addresses the following research questions:

RQ1. What are the dimensions of AI usage among learners, as revealed through factor analysis of self-reported purposes and frequency of use?

RQ2. How are motivational factors (goal orientation, academic help-seeking behavior including timing of help-seeking), perceived trust in AI tools, individual (gender, prior knowledge), and contextual characteristics (study mode, course requirement status, time investment) related to these AI usage dimensions?

2 Related Work

2.1 AI Use in Computer Science

The integration of AI into classroom practice has accelerated rapidly in recent years, particularly following the emergence of generative AI tools such as ChatGPT [19, 20]. In higher education, AI-based tools are increasingly used to support adaptive learning experiences and to provide real-time, personalized feedback to learners [4, 5, 20]. However, it has long been emphasized that the effectiveness of AI-supported learning depends not only on the capabilities of the system but also on how learners engage with it [21]. Within this broader landscape, Computer Science (CS) students have emerged as particularly intensive users of AI tools, reflecting the close alignment between AI capabilities and programming-related tasks. Prior research shows that CS students primarily use AI for coding-related activities, including writing code, debugging, and generating explanations of code functionality [1, 22]. In addition to direct coding support, CS students use AI for getting a shorter overview of the lengthy learning materials [1], explaining new concepts [1–3], and creating new content [1, 3].

Recent studies further differentiate between the roles of various AI tools in CS learning. For example, Echeverry and Narayanan [22] report that CS students tend to use AI coding assistants for writing code from scratch, while conversational AI systems such as ChatGPT are more often employed for debugging, problem decomposition, and conceptual clarification. Similarly, Amoozadeh et al. [14] found that students primarily rely on AI for seeking programming help and understanding existing code rather than for generating entirely new code. Although trust AI has been identified as a critical factor regulating students' adoption of these technologies [23], its role in shaping concrete AI usage patterns in CS education remains largely unexplored.

2.2 Achievement Goal Orientation and its Relationship with AI Use

Achievement goal orientation is a central framework in educational psychology that describes the motivational standards individuals use to interpret, approach, and evaluate achievement-related tasks [24]. One of the most widely used distinctions differentiates between mastery (learning) goals and performance goals, a framework rooted in Elliot and Dweck foundational work [25]. Mastery goals emphasize developing competence and understanding, whereas performance goals focus on demonstrating competence relative to others.

A growing body of research suggests that achievement goal orientations are associated with students' engagement with digital technologies [24] and use of AI tools [8, 9]. In studies focusing on CS students, mastery-oriented learners tend to engage more frequently in learning-supportive uses of technology, such as taking notes, reviewing materials, and using digital tools to facilitate deeper information processing [24].

Recent studies examining AI use specifically suggest that mastery goal orientation is often negatively associated with AI use for academic tasks [8, 9]. Mastery-oriented students may avoid AI tools out of concern that such tools could compromise conceptual understanding or lead to unoriginal work and when they do use AI, it is more likely to serve as a support for skill development, idea structuring, or self-checking rather than as a substitute for effort [8]. Consistent with this view, mastery-oriented students report greater confidence in their ability to program without AI assistance and are more likely to critically inspect and test AI-generated code [10].

In contrast, findings regarding performance goal orientation and AI use are more mixed. Some studies suggest that performance-oriented students may benefit from AI use, particularly when AI tools are perceived as enhancing efficiency or competitive performance [9]. Other research, however, indicates that strong performance goals may be associated with lower AI usage, as students perceive AI as potentially undermining the authenticity of demonstrated competence [10].

2.3 Academic Help-Seeking and its Relationship with AI Use

Help-seeking has been extensively studied in AIED as part of learner interaction with AI-driven systems [26, 27]. Academic help-seeking (AHS) is a self-regulated learning strategy that involves recognizing the need for assistance, deciding to seek help, and selecting appropriate resources to achieve academic goals [16, 28]. Prior research distinguishes between different forms of AHS. Instrumental (or adaptive) help-seeking refers to seeking guidance or hints that enable learners to complete tasks independently, whereas expedient (or executive) help-seeking involves requesting solutions with little intention to engage in the underlying problem-solving process [29]. In addition to these strategies, learners may engage in help-seeking avoidance when help is needed but not requested, often due to social or affective barriers, and may experience help-seeking threats, which reflects fear of negative evaluation or appearing incompetent [16, 29].

In CS education, AHS plays a particularly critical role due to the high cognitive demands associated with learning programming concepts, syntax, and debugging [30]. Even prior to the widespread adoption of AI tools, CS students tended to seek help first from online resources or peers before turning to instructors or teaching assistants [11, 23], but nowadays the introduction of AI-based tools has further transformed help-seeking practices in CS education [12, 13, 23]. AI systems provide immediate, on-demand, and personalized assistance that can resemble human interaction [14] and may support guided self-discovery during learning [30]. Recent study using a mixed-methods approach indicates that while peers remain an important source of support, AI tools are increasingly prioritized, particularly by students who are more introverted or who experience fear related to asking for help from others [23].

Despite this growing interest, significant gaps remain in understanding academic help-seeking in AI-mediated contexts, especially regarding help-seeking avoidance and maladaptive patterns of AI use [28]. Emerging evidence suggests that AI tools can also facilitate unproductive help-seeking behaviors. For example, case studies report that a substantial proportion of students attempt to complete programming tasks by submitting entire problem descriptions to AI systems without engaging in independent effort [14].

2.4 Individual and Contextual Factors and their Relationship with AI Use

Individual and contextual factors have long been examined in research on technology use in education, yet their role in shaping students' AI use remains comparatively under-explored. Among individual characteristics, gender differences have received the most attention. Several studies report that male students in higher education use AI tools more frequently and across a wider range of learning activities than female students, even when no differences in prior AI training are observed [31, 32]. Other research suggests that gender differences in AI use are more pronounced in STEM disciplines, whereas in non-STEM fields such differences are less evident [33].

Findings are particularly mixed in CS education. Some studies indicate that male students use AI tools more frequently in CS courses, while female students rely more on instructor-provided troubleshooting resources [17]. In contrast, other work reports no substantial gender differences in overall AI usage frequency, although men may be more likely to use AI specifically for problem solving [18]. Taking together, these results suggest that gender effects are context-dependent and may vary by discipline, task type, and available instructional support.

Beyond individual characteristics, contextual factors related to learning environments remain largely underexamined in the context of AI use. While prior research has demonstrated that AI technologies can support learning in online settings such as MOOCs [34], there is limited empirical evidence on how the mode of study (online versus on-campus) influences students' AI usage patterns. Moreover, other contextual characteristics - including time investment in learning and whether a course is compulsory or elective - have received little systematic attention in existing AI-in-education research.

3 Methodology

3.1 Sample

The study was conducted during the spring semester of 2025 in the course "Databases", which enrolled a total of 345 students. Data for the present analysis were collected from 236 students who voluntarily completed an online questionnaire administered as part of the course. Prior to participation, all respondents were informed about the purpose of the study and provided informed consent. The study protocol was reviewed and approved by the institutional ethics committee, and all procedures were conducted in accordance with established ethical guidelines for research involving human participants.

The sample consisted of 155 male students (65.7%) and 70 female students (33.5%), with two participants choosing not to disclose their gender. Participants represented a wide range of academic backgrounds. Most respondents ($n = 193$) were enrolled in computer science, mathematics, and statistics curricula, while the remaining students came from other disciplines (for example Economics and Business Administration, Biology, Medicine, English Language and Literature, Semiotics etc.).

3.2 Instrument

Data were collected in 2025 using a structured questionnaire consisting of three sections, each targeting a different set of constructs relevant to the study. The first section of the questionnaire addressed students' use of AI in learning within the context of the course. Students were presented with a list of thirteen course-specific AI usage activities. The items were not derived from an existing validated instrument but were intended to capture course-specific patterns of AI use. These items were constructed by the author based on qualitative responses to an open-ended question included in a course feedback survey administered in 2024. In that survey, students were asked to describe, in their own words, how they had used AI tools in the same course. The responses were reviewed and grouped to identify recurring types of AI use. Based on this process, items were formulated and aligned with the actual learning activities of the course. The final set of thirteen items reflects the most common and contextually relevant AI usage activities (e.g., gaining an overview of theoretical topics, solving SQL-related tasks, supporting group work). For each activity, students reported how often they had used AI during the course on the five-point frequency scale (1 = never, 2 = rarely, 3 = sometimes, 4 = often, 5 = always).

In addition, perceived trust in AI tools was measured using a single-item indicator. Students rated their agreement on a five-point Likert-type scale (1 = strongly disagree to 5 = strongly agree) with the statement: "I trust the responses of AI tools used in the course." The item was intended to capture students' overall, general trust in the AI tools used in the course rather than task-specific trust.

The second section assessed students' motivational factors. Scale of the achievement goal orientations based on the model proposed by Elliot and Dweck [25]. The scale was translated and adapted into Estonian and has previously been used in a similar higher education context with CS students. Items of this scale were rated on a five-point Likert-type scale ranging from 1 (strongly disagree) to 5 (strongly agree). Three items measured Mastery Approach (Cronbach's alpha (α) was 0.84 and McDonald's omega (ω) was 0.85) and three items measured Performance Approach ($\alpha = 0.72$ and $\omega = 0.78$). The second motivational scale focused on AHS behavior, measured using Karabenick's [29] four-category framework of help-seeking behaviors. This scale was also translated and adapted into Estonian and has been used in a comparable higher education context. Items in this section were rated similarly to previous ones on a five-point Likert-type scale ranging from 1 (strongly disagree) to 5 (strongly agree). The factor structure and reliability of the scale were examined in the present dataset: Instrumental Help-seeking ($\alpha = 0.66$ and $\omega = 0.68$), Expedient Help-seeking ($\alpha = 0.67$ and $\omega = 0.68$), Help-seeking Threat ($\alpha = 0.83$ and $\omega = 0.84$) and Help-seeking Avoidance ($\alpha = 0.88$ and $\omega = 0.89$).

In addition, describing students' AHS their typical timing of help-seeking when encountering difficulties was measured on 5-point scale ranging from immediate help-seeking upon reading the task to seeking help only after prolonged independent effort.

The final section of the questionnaire collected individual and contextual information. Individual-level variables included gender and prior knowledge of SQL. Contextual characteristics comprise study mode (participation in an online or on-campus group), the course's status within the student's curriculum (compulsory, optional, or elective) and students' average weekly time investment in the course (with response options ranging from less than two hours to more than ten hours).

The questionnaire was administered at the end of the course, prior to the final exam, when students had completed the main learning activities. Participation was voluntary and anonymous. Students were informed that their responses would not be accessible to the course instructor in identifiable form and would not affect their course grades.

3.3 Data Analysis

All statistical analyses were conducted using IBM SPSS Statistics and AMOS (version 30.0). The analytical procedure proceeded in several stages. To examine the underlying structure of students' AI usage activities, an exploratory factor analysis (EFA) was first performed in SPSS. Maximum Likelihood (ML) extraction with an oblique rotation method (Oblimin) was applied.

Following the exploratory phase, confirmatory factor analyses (CFA) were conducted using AMOS to test the factor structure identified in the EFA. The models were estimated using the Maximum Likelihood method, and multiple goodness-of-fit indices were employed to evaluate model adequacy. Model fit was judged according to commonly accepted criteria: values of CFI, GFI, and TLI equal to or greater than.90 indicating appropriate fit [35], RMSEA values below .08 [36], and SRMR values below .08 indicating good fit [35]. Given the sensitivity of the χ^2 statistic to sample size, the ratio of χ^2 to degrees of freedom (χ^2/df) was also considered, with values between 1 and 3 indicating acceptable fit [37]. The internal consistency of the resulting AI usage dimensions was assessed using reliability analyses. Both Cronbach's alpha and McDonald's omega were calculated to evaluate scale reliability.

Based on the confirmed factor structure, composite scores for each AI usage dimension were computed by averaging the items loading on the corresponding factor. A repeated-measures analysis of variance with Bonferroni correction as post-hoc pairwise comparisons were used to identify differences between the factors. To examine associations between AI usage dimensions and individual, contextual, and motivational variables, multiple regression analyses using the Enter method were conducted to assess the unique contribution of each predictor. Regression analysis was chosen to provide a more nuanced understanding of these relationships, as bivariate correlations alone do not account for shared variance or indirect effects among predictors [38].

Assumptions underlying the regression analyses were evaluated prior to interpretation. Multicollinearity was assessed using Variance Inflation Factor (VIF) and tolerance statistics, with VIF values below 10 and tolerance values above 0.10 considered acceptable [39]. The normality of standardized residuals was examined using the Kolmogorov–Smirnov test.

4 Results

4.1 Dimensions of AI Use

The Kaiser–Meyer–Olkin (KMO) measure of sampling adequacy was .866, exceeding the recommended threshold of .60, and Bartlett's test of sphericity was significant, $\chi^2(78) = 1138.584, p < .001$, indicating that the data were suitable for factor analysis. The EFA revealed a three-factor structure, which described 53.7% of the variance and all factor loadings were over 0.35. To verify the factor structure identified through the EFA, the CFA was then performed.

This model showed an unsatisfactory fit to the data: $\chi^2(59) = 161.633, p < .001$; CFI $= 0.901$; GFI $= 0.876$; TLI $= 0.869$; RMSEA $= 0.109$; SRMR $= 0.0583$ As standardized factor loading of the item 'To explain quiz answers' was below 0.40, it was removed from further factor analysis as it was considered insufficiently representative of their latent construct. The Goodness of Fit statistics of the modified model were: $\chi^2 = 113.037$, df $= 45$, χ^2/df $= 2.51$, CFI $= 0.940$, GFI $= 0.902$, TLI $= 0.912$, RMSEA $= 0.081$, SRMR $= 0.0472$. Although the RMSEA value was slightly above the conventional cut-off of .08, the CFI and TLI values exceeded .90 and the SRMR was well below .05, indicating an overall acceptable model fit. Following recommendations to evaluate model adequacy based on multiple indices rather than a single criterion [35], the model was considered to provide a reasonable representation of the data. The standardized factor loadings and items' reliabilities are shown in Table 1.

As the first factor consisted of items to explain tasks or code or topic, to get extra material, to get overview, the factor was named Explaining. Three items related to SQL tasks formed the second factor, which was named Task solving. The last factor included three items from four which described purpose of using AI for generating something and this factor was named Generating.

All correlation between the emerged factors were positive: between Factor 1 and Factor 2 r $= 0.673$, between Factor 1 and Factor 3 r $= 0.531$ and between Factor 2 and

Table 1. Three factors of using AI with indicators according to CFA.

Factor	Items	Reliability	Standardized factor loadings	Item reliability
F1 – Explaining	Getting an overview of a topic	$\alpha = 0.84$	0.852	0.725
	Explaining a topic	$\omega = 0.85^{a}$	0.851	0.724
	Obtaining additional learning materials		0.694	0.482
	Explaining code		0.809	0.655
	Explaining a task		0.762	0.580
F2 - Task Solving	Solving a task	$\alpha = 0.88$	0.692	0.478
	Identifying errors in code	$\omega = 0.88$	0.842	0.709
	Generating alternative solutions		0.734	0.539
F3 – Generating	Assisting with group work generation	$\alpha = 0.92$	0.605	0.366
	Editing text	$\omega = 0.95$	0.800	0.640
	Generating coding tasks for practice		0.633	0.401
	Generating theoretical questions for practice		0.586	0.343

a α – Cronbach's alpha, ω - McDonald's Omega

Factor 3 r $= 0.477$. The observed correlation does not indicate redundancy between the two factors. In factor-analytic research, correlations below .85 are generally considered acceptable and do not threaten discriminant validity, particularly when constructs are conceptually distinct [37]. Therefore, despite their association, the factors represent distinct patterns of AI engagement, as evidenced by their different item compositions. Therefore, the factor structure was retained for subsequent analyses.

The mean values of the three AI usage dimensions were 2.26, 2.26, and 1.54. A repeated-measures analysis of variance revealed a significant difference between the factors, $F(2, 234) = 151.11$, $p < 0.01$. Post-hoc pairwise comparisons with Bonferroni correction indicated that AI use for explanations and AI use for task solving both had significantly higher mean values than generative AI use ($p < 0.01$), whereas no significant difference was observed between the first two factors ($p > 0.05$).

4.2 Relationships Between Individual, Contextual, and Motivational Factors and AI Use Dimensions

The multiple regression models to find relationships with the three factors were statistically significant ($p < 0.01$). The model describing the use of AI for explaining (Table 2) accounted for approximately 33.6% of the variance, suggesting a medium effect. Variables *Study mode of the practicals*, *Time investment for the course*, *Instrumental Goal*, *Help-seeking Threat*, and *Perceived trust in AI tools* had significant positive and *Mastery Approach* significant negative relationships with the AI first dimension - using AI for explaining. The distribution of the standardized residuals was not statistically significantly different from the normal distribution (with Kolmogorov-Smirnov test $D = 0.043$, $p > 0.05$).

Table 2. Multiple regression analysis on using AI for explaining.

R	F	Model	β	T	Tolerance	VIF
0.336	4.445**	**Mastery Approach**	−0.220	−2.361*	0.668	1.496
		Performance Approach	0.041	0.444	0.685	1.459
		Instrumental Help-seeking	0.191	2.098*	0.701	1.426
		Expedient Help-seeking	0.089	0.955	0.676	1.480
		Help-seeking Threat	0.251	2.514*	0.582	1.718
		Help-seeking Avoidance	−0.121	−1.187	0.564	1.772
		Timing of help-seeking	−0.071	−0.843	0.827	1.209
		Perceived trust in AI tools	0.200	2.466*	0.884	1.131
		Gender	0.038	0.428	0.759	1.317
		Prior Knowledge	0.000	−0.002	0.830	1.205
		Study mode of the practicals	0.170	2.078*	0.868	1.152
		Course requirement status	0.046	0.569	0.874	1.144
		Time investment for the course	0.354	4.395**	0.900	1.112

* $p < 0.5$, ** $p < 0.01$

Multiple regression model to find relationships with the factor describing using AI for task solving (Table 3) described approximately 29.0% of the variance. According to standardized regression coefficients *Time investment for the course* and *Perceived trust in AI tools* had significant positive and *Mastery Approach* significant negative relationships with the AI second dimension - using AI for task solving. The distribution of the standardized residuals was not statistically significantly different from the normal distribution (with Kolmogorov-Smirnov test $D = 0.056$, $p > 0.05$).

The model describing the use of AI for generating (Table 4) described approximately 22.3% of the variance, indicating a small effect. According to standardized regression coefficients, only two variables were significantly associated with the AI third dimension - using AI for generating. Both variables - *Help-seeking Threat* and *Perceived trust in AI tools* - demonstrated positive relationships. The distribution of the standardized residuals was not statistically significantly different from the normal distribution (with Kolmogorov-Smirnov test $D = 0.77$, $p > 0.05$). VIF values in all models were well below 10, and Tolerance values were all above 0.,1 indicating no multicollinearity in the data [40].

Table 3. Multiple regression analysis on using AI for task solving.

R	F	Model	β	T	Tolerance	VIF
0.290	3.575[**]	**Mastery Approach**	-0.270	-2.797[**]	0.668	1.496
		Performance Approach	0.050	0.523	0.685	1.459
		Instrumental Help-seeking	0.114	1.206	0.701	1.426
		Expedient Help-seeking	0.085	0.889	0.676	1.480
		Help-seeking Threat	0.156	1.505	0.582	1.718
		Help-seeking Avoidance	-0.109	-1.034	0.564	1.772
		Timing of help-seeking	-0.087	-1.006	0.827	1.209
		Perceived trust in AI tools	0.302	3.598[**]	0.884	1.131
		Gender	-0.059	-0.655	0.759	1.317
		Prior Knowledge	0.079	0.911	0.830	1.205
		Study mode of the practicals	0.103	1.217	0.868	1.152
		Course requirement status	-0.100	-1.179	0.874	1.144
		Time investment for the course	0.227	2.724[**]	0.900	1.112

$* p < 0.5$, $** p < 0.01$

Table 4. Multiple regression analysis on using AI for generating.

R	F	Model	β	T	Tolerance	VIF
0.223	2.523[**]	Mastery Approach	-0.007	-0.067	0.668	1.496
		Performance Approach	0.109	1.094	0.685	1.459
		Instrumental Help-seeking	0.006	0.062	0.701	1.426
		Expedient Help-seeking	-0.061	-0.611	0.676	1.480
		Help-seeking Threat	0.245	2.263[*]	0.582	1.718
		Help-seeking Avoidance	0.112	1.023	0.564	1.772
		Timing of help-seeking	-0.097	-1.068	0.827	1.209
		Perceived trust in AI tools	0.188	2.141[*]	0.884	1.131
		Gender	0.006	0.065	0.759	1.317
		Prior Knowledge	0.144	1.592	0.830	1.205
		Study mode of the practicals	0.117	1.324	0.868	1.152
		Course requirement status	0.012	0.131	0.874	1.144
		Time investment for the course	0.125	1.439	0.900	1.112

[*] $p < 0.5$, [**] $p < 0.01$

5 Discussion

First, this study identified distinct dimensions of AI usage among students in an introductory database course. A three-factor model - comprising AI use for explanations, AI use for task solving, and generative AI use - provided an adequate representation of students' AI-related activities, with satisfactory fit indices in the confirmatory factor analysis. Although the correlation between the explanation and task-solving factors was relatively high ($r > 0.68$), such overlap is expected in learning contexts where different forms of support-seeking often co-occur rather than operate independently.

The factor structure suggests that students' AI engagement can be meaningfully described using three distinct yet related dimensions. AI use for explanations reflects reliance on AI for clarifying theoretical concepts and course material, consistent with prior work describing AI as an on-demand explanatory resource for explaining new concepts [1–3] and programming code [6, 22]. AI use for task solving captures AI use for completing course-related tasks, such as solving SQL assignments, identifying errors in code, or generating alternative solutions. This dimension emphasizes task execution rather than conceptual explanation, as explaining code loaded on the first factor. While prior studies suggest that CS students primarily use AI for understanding code rather than producing solutions [14], the present study found no significant difference in mean usage between explanatory and task-solving AI use, indicating that students may integrate both functions to a similar extent in a database course.

The third factor, generative AI use, encompassed a heterogeneous set of activities, including generating course-related artifacts as well as potentially learning-oriented practices such as generating coding tasks or theoretical questions for practice. This heterogeneity indicates that generative AI use cannot be treated as a uniform category. While prior research has raised concerns about generative AI reducing active engagement [4, 7] and has largely focused on content creation [2, 3], the relatively low mean value of this factor suggests that such uses were less prevalent in the present context and warrant further investigation.

Beyond these functional distinctions, patterns of AI use may also be shaped by contextual factors related to how AI tools perform in the given learning environment. Preliminary findings from the authors' related work suggest that variations in domain-specific terminology and naming conventions may influence the quality of AI-generated solutions, which in turn may influence how students use AI for different purposes.

Second, we examined how motivational, individual, and contextual factors were associated with these AI usage dimensions. *Perceived trust in AI tools* emerged as a consistent positive predictor across all three dimensions, aligning with prior research identifying trust as a key determinant of AI adoption [23] and reliance on automated systems more generally [40]. While this finding aligns with prior assumptions that trust is a prerequisite for engaging with AI tools, the cross-sectional design of the study does not allow for causal interpretations. It is also possible that the relationship is bidirectional, such that continued use of AI tools may further strengthen students' trust in them.

Beyond this shared pattern, more differentiated associations emerged. AI use for explanations and AI use for task solving were both positively associated with *time invested in the course* and negatively associated with *Mastery Approach*, consistent with earlier findings that mastery-oriented students may be reluctant to use AI due to concerns about reduced depth of understanding [8, 9]. Notably, Mastery Approach was also negatively related to explanatory AI use, suggesting that mastery-oriented students may avoid AI even for explanatory purposes if such use is perceived as misaligned with course expectations as previously found [8]. From an instructional perspective, this highlights the importance of clearly communicating which forms of AI use are considered permissible and compatible with deep learning goals.

The positive association between time investment and the first two dimensions warrants a nuanced interpretation. On the one hand, students who experience greater difficulty with course material may invest more time and seek explanations from AI and use AI for solving tasks when they can't find a solution themselves. On the other hand, frequent use of AI for explanations may expose students to additional examples and clarifications, which can extend study time as students engage more deeply with the content.

Help-seeking Threat was positively associated with AI use for explanations and generative AI use, but not with task-solving AI use. This pattern suggests that AI may reduce social and affective barriers related to asking questions, consistent with prior findings that students reluctant to seek interpersonal help rely more on AI-based resources [23]. The absence of a relationship with task-solving AI use may reflect the pragmatic and private nature of task-focused activities, where interpersonal concerns play a less central role [29]. Finally, *Instrumental Help-seeking* and *participation in online practicals* were uniquely associated with explanatory AI use, highlighting AI's role as a low-threshold explanatory resource in contexts where opportunities for spontaneous instructor interaction are limited. This finding is consistent with earlier claims that AI tools can support learning in online environments [34]. Importantly, online participation predicted only AI use for explanations, not task-solving or generative uses, underscoring the function-specific nature of AI engagement.

6 Conclusion

This study identified three distinct dimensions of students' AI use in an introductory database course: AI use for explanations, AI use for task solving, and generative AI use. Across these dimensions, Perceived trust in AI tools emerged as a consistent positive predictor, indicating that students' willingness to engage with AI depends broadly on their trust in the reliability and appropriateness of these tools. More differentiated patterns were observed for other factors. However, individual characteristics such as gender and prior knowledge showed no consistent effects. Taken together, these patterns imply that instructional interventions should prioritize affective and behavioral drivers (trust and help-seeking), while attending to motivation (mastery) and course design (time and online formats), rather than targeting demographic groups.

Clear guidance on permissible and learning-oriented AI use may help support mastery-oriented students, while AI tools can serve as low-threshold support resources in online learning contexts. AI technology should be taken as an opportunity for broadening learning, as an opportunity to ask for help from a tool that mimics human interaction, but is not a human, so that those who are afraid to ask for help can also benefit from AI tools.

Several limitations should be noted. First, the study was conducted in a single undergraduate computer science course (an introductory database course), which may limit the generalizability of the findings to other disciplines and educational contexts. In addition, the cross-sectional design does not allow for causal interpretations. Second, the study relied on self-reported measures, which may be subject to bias. This includes both the reporting of AI usage and contextual characteristics such as time investment. Third, some constructs were measured in a simplified manner. Perceived trust in AI was assessed using a single-item indicator capturing general trust, which does not account for potential task-specific variations. Furthermore, the AI usage items were developed specifically for this course context and were not derived from an established validated instrument.

While prior research, including qualitative and mixed-methods studies, has provided valuable insights into how students use AI tools, there is a growing need for approaches that capture these patterns in an integrated, multivariate framework. Future research should examine these AI usage dimensions longitudinally and in relation to learning outcomes, extend the analysis to other disciplinary and instructional contexts.

Acknowledgments. This work was sponsored by the Estonian Research Council grant "Developing human-centric digital solutions" (TEM-TA120).

Disclosure of Interests. The author has no competing interests to declare that are relevant to the content of this article.

References

1. Smith, C.E., Shiekh, K., Cooreman, H., Rahman, S., Zhu, Y., et al.: Early adoption of generative artificial intelligence in computing education: emergent student use cases and perspectives in 2023. In: Proceedings of ITiCSE 2024, pp. 1–7. ACM, New York, NY, USA (2024)
2. Budhiraja, R., Joshi, I., Akolekar, H., Challa, J.S., Kumar, D.: "It's not like Jarvis, but it's pretty close": examining ChatGPT's usage among undergraduate students in computer science. In: Proceedings of ACE 2024, pp. 1–10. ACM, New York, NY, USA (2024)
3. Xiao, R., Hou, X., Kumar, H., Moore, S., Stamper, J., Liut, M.: A preliminary analysis of students' help requests with an LLM-powered chatbot when completing CS1 assignments. In: Proceedings of CSEDM 2024. ACM, New York, NY, USA (2024)
4. Nazaretsky, R., Mejia-Domenzain, P., Swamy, S., Frej, J., Käser, T.: The critical role of trust in adopting AI-powered educational technology for learning: an instrument for measuring student perceptions. Comput. Educ.: Artif. Intell. **8**, 100368 (2025)
5. Seco, D., Groesser, S.N., Pedrosa, A.M.: Use of generative artificial intelligence tools in university environments. Multidiscip. J. Educ. Soc. Technol. Sci. **12**(1), 156–175 (2025)
6. Becker, B.A., Denny, P., Finnie-Ansley, J., Luxton-Reilly, A., Prather, J., Santos, E.A.: Programming is hard—or at least it used to be: educational opportunities and challenges of AI code generation. In: Proceedings of SIGCSE 2023, vol. 1, pp. 500–506. ACM, New York, NY, USA (2023)
7. Zawacki-Richter, O., Marín, V.O., Bond, M., Gouverneur, F.: Systematic review of research on artificial intelligence applications in higher education – where are the educators? Int. J. Educ. Technol. High. Educ. **16**, 39 (2019)
8. Daha, E.S., Altelwany, A.A.: Exploring the impact of using ChatGPT in light of goal orientations and academic self-efficacy. Int. J. Instr. **18**(2), 167–184 (2025)
9. Kwan, L.Y.Y., Hung, Y.S.: Does AI usage diminish human creativity? How goal orientation theory moderates the negative effects between AI usage and creative output. Soc. Sci. Comput. Rev. **0**(0), 1–21 (2025)
10. Vadaparty, A., Geng, F., Smith IV, D.H., Benario, J.G., Zingaro, D., Porter, L.: Achievement goals in CS1-LLM. In: Proceedings of ACE 2025, pp. 144–153. ACM, New York, NY, USA (2025)
11. Doebling, A., Kazerouni, A.M.: Patterns of academic help-seeking in undergraduate computing students. In: Proceedings of Koli Calling '21, pp. 1–13. ACM, New York, NY, USA (2021)
12. Hou, I., Nguyen, H.V., Man, O., MacNeil, S.: The evolving usage of GenAI by computing students. In: Proceedings of SIGCSE Technical Symposium 2025, vol. 2, pp. 1481–1482. ACM, New York, NY, USA (2025)

13. Kumar, H., Reza, M., Thomas-Mitchell, J., Musabirov, I., Zhang, L., Liut, M.: Understanding help-seeking behavior of students using LLMs vs. web search for writing SQL queries. In: Proceedings of the 4th International Workshop on Data Systems Education: Bridging Education Practice with Education Research (DataEd@SIGMOD 2025), pp. 23–28. ACM, New York, NY, USA (2025)

14. Amoozadeh, M., Nam, D., Prol, D., Alfageeh, A., Prather, J., Hilton, M., et al.: Student–AI interaction: a case study of CS1 students. In: Proceedings of Koli Calling '24, pp. 1–13. ACM, New York, NY, USA (2024)

15. Martín-Moncunill, D., Alonso Martínez, D.: Students' trust in AI and their verification strategies: a case study at Camilo José Cela University. Educ. Sci. 15(10), 1307 (2025)

16. Gillies, C., Turner, J.: Looking for answers: a scoping review of academic help-seeking in digital higher education research. Educ. Sci. 15(9), 1095 (2025)

17. Luik, P.: Learning in a database course: the same regardless of gender? In: Proceedings of the 8th International Conference on Gender Research, pp. 240–248. Academic Conferences International Ltd (2025)

18. Bikanga, A.M.: It helps with crap lecturers and their low effort: investigating computer science students' perceptions of using ChatGPT for learning. Educ. Sci. 14(10), 1106 (2024)

19. Bond, M., Khosravi, H., De Laat, M., Bergdahl, N., Negrea, V., Oxley, E., et al.: A meta-systematic review of artificial intelligence in higher education: a call for increased ethics, collaboration, and rigour. Int. J. Educ. Technol. High. Educ. 21(4), 4 (2024)

20. Deng, R., Jiang, M., Yu, X., Lu, Y., Liu, S.: Does ChatGPT enhance student learning? A systematic review and meta-analysis of experimental studies. Comput. Educ. 227, 105224 (2025)

21. Baker, R.S.: Stupid tutoring systems, intelligent humans. Int. J. Artif. Intell. Educ. 26(2), 600–614 (2016)

22. Echeverry, N., Narayanan, A.L.: How are CS students using resources and AI tools for coding tasks? In: MIT AI & Education Summit. Cambridge, MA, USA (2025)

23. Hou, I., Mettille, S., Li, Z., Man, O., Zastudil, C., MacNeil, S.: The effects of generative AI on computing students' help-seeking preferences. In: Proceedings of ACE 2024, pp. 39–48. ACM, New York, NY, USA (2024)

24. McGloin, R., McGillicuddy, K.T., Christensen, J.L.: The impact of goal achievement orientation on student technology usage in the classroom. J. Comput. High. Educ. 29(4), 695–714 (2017)

25. Elliot, E.S., Dweck, C.S.: Goals: an approach to motivation and achievement. J. Pers. Soc. Psychol. 54(1), 5–12 (1988)

26. Aleven, V., Roll, I., McLaren, B.M., Koedinger, K.R.: Help helps, but only so much: research on help seeking with intelligent tutoring systems. Int. J. Artif. Intell. Educ. 26(1), 205–223 (2016)

27. Roll, I., Aleven, V., McLaren, B.M., Koedinger, K.R.: Can help-seeking be tutored? Searching for the secret sauce of metacognitive tutoring. In: Luckin, R., Koedinger, K.R., Greer, J. (eds.) AIED 2007 LNCS (LNAI), vol. 4733, pp. 203–210. Springer, Heidelberg (2007)

28. Karabenick, S.A., Berger, J.-L.: Help seeking as a self-regulated learning strategy. In: Zimmerman, B.J., Bembenutty, H., Cleary, T.J., Kitsantas, A. (eds.) Applications of Self-Regulated Learning across Diverse Disciplines: a Tribute to Barry Zimmerman, pp. 237–261. IAP, Charlotte, NC, USA (2013)

29. Karabenick, S.A.: Seeking help in large college classes: a person-centered approach. Contemp. Educ. Psychol. 28, 37–58 (2003)

30. Amiri, S.M.H., Islam, M.M.: Enhancing python programming education with an AI-powered code helper: design, implementation, and impact. Software Eng. 11(1), 1–17 (2025)

31. Møgelvang, A., Bjelland, C., Grassini, S., Ludvigsen, K.: Gender differences in the use of generative artificial intelligence chatbots in higher education: characteristics and consequences. Educ. Sci. **14**, 1363 (2024)
32. Stöhr, C., Ou, A.W., Malmström, H.: Perceptions and usage of AI chatbots among students in higher education across genders, academic levels and fields of study. Comput. Educ.: Artif. Intell. **7**, 100259 (2024)
33. Wen, S.: A study on gender differences in the use of generative artificial intelligence for assisted learning among university students: a review and outlook. J. Soc. Sci. Humanit. **7**(7), 14–19 (2024)
34. Yang, C., Huan, S., Yang, Y.: A practical teaching mode for colleges supported by artificial intelligence. Int. J. Emerg. Technol. Learn. **15**(17), 195–206 (2020)
35. Hu, L.T., Bentler, P.M.: Cutoff criteria for fit indexes in covariance structure analysis: conventional criteria versus new alternatives. Struct. Equ. Model. **6**(1), 1–55 (1999)
36. Browne, M.W., Cudeck, R.: Alternative ways of assessing model fit. In: Bollen, K.A., Long, J.S. (eds.) Testing Structural Equation Models, pp. 136–162. Sage, Newbury Park, CA (1993)
37. Kline, R.B.: Principles and Practice of Structural Equation Modeling, 4th edn. Guilford Press, New York, NY (2016)
38. Cohen, J., Cohen, P., West, S.G., Aiken, L.S.: Applied Multiple Regression/Correlation Analysis for the Behavioral Sciences, 3rd edn. Routledge, New York, NY (2003)
39. Field, A.P.: Discovering Statistics Using SPSS, 3rd edn. Sage, London (2009)
40. Lee, J.D., See, K.A.: Trust in automation: designing for appropriate reliance. Hum. Factors. **46**(1), 50–80 (2004)

Leveraging Human-AI Collaboration for a Passage-Based Question Authoring Tool

Mehmet Arif Demirtaş[1,2(✉)] , Sungjin Nam[2] , and Gabrielle Griffin[2]

[1] University of Illinois Urbana-Champaign, Urbana, IL 61801, USA
mad16@illinois.edu
[2] ACT Education Corp, Iowa City, IA 52243, USA
{sungjin.nam,gabrielle.griffin}@act.org

Abstract. Passage-based reading comprehension questions are common in standardized tests, yet they are often manually authored by content specialists with minimal computational assistance despite a growing body of work on LLM-based question generation. To understand this gap, we interviewed content specialists working for a national standardized test, identified the challenges they face, and examined how their work can be complemented by human-AI collaboration. Based on these observations, we designed a human-in-the-loop system that uses large language models to model connections between parts of the passage and items. Our results from a mixed-methods evaluation with 11 content specialists show that human-in-the-loop features can lead to lower cognitive demands and higher productivity. We discuss design insights into where content specialists want support from LLMs and how they can leverage this support efficiently for authoring passage-based questions.

Keywords: large language models · multiple-choice question generation · human-AI collaboration

1 Introduction

Passage-based multiple-choice questions that measure students' reading comprehension are commonly used to estimate academic outcomes on standardized tests (e.g., SAT/ACT in the U.S.) [21]. However, creating high-quality reading comprehension questions is difficult and time-consuming [20]. At the item level, each question should go beyond asking students to locate details in the passage and should encourage engagement with the text [9]. At the test level, a high-quality reading comprehension test should include multiple items that cover each important concept in the passage, but these items should not overlap or provide hints for one another, so that each question yields a strong and unbiased statistical signal about students' competencies. Although computational approaches exist for automated question generation [16], such approaches are not widely adopted

M. A. Demirtaş—Work done during an internship at ACT Education Corp.

E. G. Blanchard et al. (Eds.): AIED 2026, LNAI 16583, pp. 475–489, 2027.
https://doi.org/10.1007/978-3-032-29760-0_50

by content specialists who create questions for high-stakes standardized tests. For content specialists, these automated systems do not provide opportunities for incorporating their pedagogical content knowledge into generated questions.

Human-in-the-loop systems informed by existing practices of content specialists can bridge this gap by augmenting existing processes without completely automating them. Human-AI collaboration approaches have achieved promising results in question authoring in various contexts [14,20], but prior studies have not focused on content specialists who author questions for high-stakes standardized tests and who have extensive experience designing high-quality items.

In this work, we conducted a human-centered design project with content specialists in an organization that administers a centralized assessment program at scale. Specifically, we address the following research questions:

- **RQ1**: What are the challenges in question authoring that should be supported by human-AI collaboration systems?
- **RQ2-5**: How does a question authoring tool with human-AI collaboration:
  - affect the cognitive demands experienced by content specialists?
  - affect the productivity of content specialists?
  - affect measures of item quality?
  - affect the user experience for content specialists?

We conducted formative focus group interviews to understand content specialists' workflows and the challenges they experience. We identified opportunities to support intermediate processes, such as identifying *testable constructs*— parts of interest in the passage that can be tested in an item— and modeling connections among test items. Informed by these opportunities, we designed a system to support question authoring by making intermediate processes salient through AI-supported knowledge representations. We explored design considerations from a mixed-methods user study with 11 content specialists. We show that human-in-the-loop systems that combine LLMs with human expertise can lead to productivity gains and reduced cognitive demands. We also analyzed qualitative data from think-aloud sessions that shed light on how domain experts want to interact with systems and incorporate LLMs into their creative processes. Our results reveal key dimensions for domain expert systems that can facilitate human-AI collaboration.[1]

2   Related Work

2.1   Automatic Question Generation

Automatic question generation has been a core problem for the natural language processing community [3,5,16]. Along with end-to-end question generation, authoring incorrect, but plausible distractors from a source passage is a challenging task [1,25,27]. Generating distractors with language models

---

[1] System prompts and study materials are available as supplementary material at: https://github.com/marifdemirtas/aied2026-136-supp.

has shown promising results, but their black-box architectures can limit interpretability, which may hinder the agency of domain experts over the output. Another challenging task is evaluating generated items. Recent works have used large language models to develop evaluation methods that incorporate pedagogical concerns and existing item writing rubrics [22]. These studies show that LLMs can model question quality in terms of alignment with human preferences. This approach shows promise for improving the question authoring experience. Our work focuses on *human-centered* approaches for question generation, which combine the power of language models with the domain expertise of content specialists to support high-quality, interpretable question generation.

2.2   Human-Centered Question Generation

Several researchers have proposed NLP interfaces that support domain experts in question authoring. For instance, ReadingQuizMaker [20] presents an interface where question authors can browse the source material, get suggestions for question types and distractors, and check coverage of the passage at a high level. TreeQuestion [6] supports instructors who write questions to test conceptual understanding (rather than passage-based reading comprehension) by creating an intermediate knowledge graph from a set of concepts and using LLMs to generate questions on this map. TutorCraftEase [14] is another question authoring tool that combines NLP support with human expertise by leveraging large language models, enabling efficient creation of pedagogically appropriate questions. We move beyond suggesting questions and focus on supporting the intermediate processes for high-quality question authoring, such as identifying parts of the passage for question authoring, developing distractors, or representing the relationship within the question set and to the passage. Moreover, our work focuses on supporting question authoring for high-stakes assessments, as opposed to the focus on engagement and formative assessments in prior work.

2.3   Instructor-in-the-Loop Systems

Human-AI collaboration systems have been shown to be beneficial for other educational tasks. These systems combine the expertise of domain experts with machine learning models to automate repetitive or tedious parts of instructional design tasks. The interest in this design paradigm has increased with the advent of large language models and their capability for generating plausible-looking text, but they fail to notice when the task requires domain knowledge [26]. This paradigm has been used to support grading and feedback [2,11], generating instructional content [7,19] and automating intermediate instructor workflows [12,13,23]. These studies have revealed some key design guidelines for LLM-based expert support systems. First, they support rapid ideation and iteration by providing initial draft materials and bypassing time-consuming tasks, such as formatting content. Second, they use interpretable representations, such as knowledge graphs [6] to record intermediate states. These explicit representations allow instructors to better understand the LLM output. Third, they give instructors control over the final output, such as providing multiple drafts to edit or choose from, or allowing customization of the LLM output [14].

3 Focus Group Interviews

3.1 Methods

To answer RQ1, we conducted two hour-long focus group interviews (FGIs) to understand how content specialists design passage-based reading comprehension questions for a standardized test. In the first FGI, three content specialists (F1, F2, and F3; Table 1) discussed their processes and common challenges across subject areas. In the second FGI, two content specialists (F3 and F4; Table 1) expanded on their processes for STEM questions, further highlighting common pain points in question authoring.

3.2 RQ1: What Are the Challenges in Question Authoring?

What do content specialists aim for? All content specialists at our institution develop passage-based question units, which include one reading passage and 10–20 multiple-choice questions (MCQs), depending on the unit type. Each unit is written for one of two main domains aligned with high school education in the United States: STEM and English Language Arts (ELA). The institution specifies which competencies are tested in each unit.

Our participants indicated that their pedagogical values shape their goals for a unit in addition to formally defined rubrics and specifications. They emphasized 1) achieving high *passage coverage* by distributing items evenly across the passage to ensure that students read and interpret the whole passage and 2) avoiding *thematic overlap*, such as multiple questions that test tightly connected information, to prevent test takers from missing multiple items due to a single misunderstanding or having one item provide hints for others.

How do content specialists start their units? Our participants explained that they start their workflows by finding a topic that fits the unit's focus. For instance, in STEM units, F3 said that they try to find a dataset or an experiment that is straightforward and "easily described in a paragraph", while also being "representative of scientific accuracy" even if details are omitted for simplicity. For ELA units, F1 described that they might write their own passages to measure students' ability to understand and select appropriate phrases and grammar while maintaining rhetorical consistency, or look for published excerpts from fiction or nonfiction sources to measure reading comprehension holistically.

How do participants approach a passage? The next step after selecting/writing a passage was "passage mapping". Content specialists defined this task as the process of keeping track of the testable constructs in the passage– parts of the passage that can be tested as an item, and stated that identifying testable constructs is a key challenge for a high-quality reading comprehension test. Participants explained that these constructs could include anything from key experimental details to interesting vocabulary. F1, who had classroom teaching experience, said they break down the passage "as if you were to teach it to a class". F4 said that they draft items iteratively while reading, editing the passage as necessary to create opportunities for items and align with the unit requirements. This dynamic can introduce thematic overlap between newly edited passages and items. F3 said that they sometimes even start by writing questions first to decide what should be tested in a passage, and then find/write an appropriate passage for those questions. This iteration highlights another challenge, which is to dynamically track how each question relates to particular parts and constructs from the passage.

What tools do participants use for passage mapping? Despite describing passage mapping as a key part of their processes, content specialists did not use any standardized tools or representations for passage mapping. F1 explained that they find it tedious to manually manage many aspects of the question authoring process (including the passage content, metadata on unit requirements, and reviewer comments) in a single development interface, and prefer to work on a printed copy of the passage and underline parts of the passage they plan to test in their items. F2 said that "most people do it in their heads" for STEM units. F3 said they used to do it on a word processor by manually annotating unique information in the passage to identify non-overlapping pieces to test with their items. These quotes underline another challenge, which is to manage specifications and metadata about questions in ways that do not require additional effort from content specialists. Specialists may prefer tools that match the main affordances of existing tools, such as text editors, rather than using intrusive systems, and standalone LLM interfaces might introduce unnecessary friction.

Table 1. Left: List of participants for the focus group interviews 1 and 2 (F1–F4). **Right**: Participants in the user study (P1–P11).

ID	Subject	Experience	Participation
F1	ELA	4-6	FGI 1
F2	STEM	4-6 years	FGI 1
F3	STEM	13-15	FGI 1 & 2
F4	STEM	13-15	FGI 2

ID	Subject	Experience	ID	Subj.	Exp.
P1	STEM	13-15 years	P7	CR	13-15
P2	ELA	4-6	P8	ELA	4-6
P3	ELA	10-12	P9	STEM	7-9
P4	STEM	13-15	P10	STEM	4-6
P5	ELA	13-15	P11	STEM	13-15
P6	ELA	10-12			

4 System Design

Based on the challenges and needs identified in the focus groups, we propose a system that supports content specialists during intermediate stages of question authoring and passage mapping through three key features.

Feature 1: Suggested Highlights. Content specialists can ask the system for suggestions about what parts of the passage can be tested in questions. The system addresses the challenge of identifying *testable constructs* by highlighting these spans that may point to a key detail or a main idea in the passage [left pane in Fig. 1] and adds them as nodes in the graph visualization [right pane in Fig. 1]. These LLM-generated highlights can support specialists as they identify key parts of the passage.

Feature 2: Links. After adding initial question items, content specialists can visualize the links between the items and the passage [right pane in Fig. 1] to address the challenge of dynamically keeping track of how questions and parts of the passage relate to each other. This feature connects each item to the most relevant testable constructs in the passage and provides confidence levels based on the semantic similarity between questions and passage constructs. This feature is designed to reveal potential thematic overlaps between question items and to facilitate an iterative item-editing workflow. Users can regenerate these links as they edit the questions.

Feature 3: Item Specifications. Finally, content specialists can enter the list of requirements for a unit and classify the items they have written so far under these requirements to see their progress for the unit. The classification is made by another LLM agent that is provided with the items and the descriptions of the unit requirements. By integrating this feature into users' ideation environment, we aim to address the challenge of managing many aspects of the unit development at the same time.

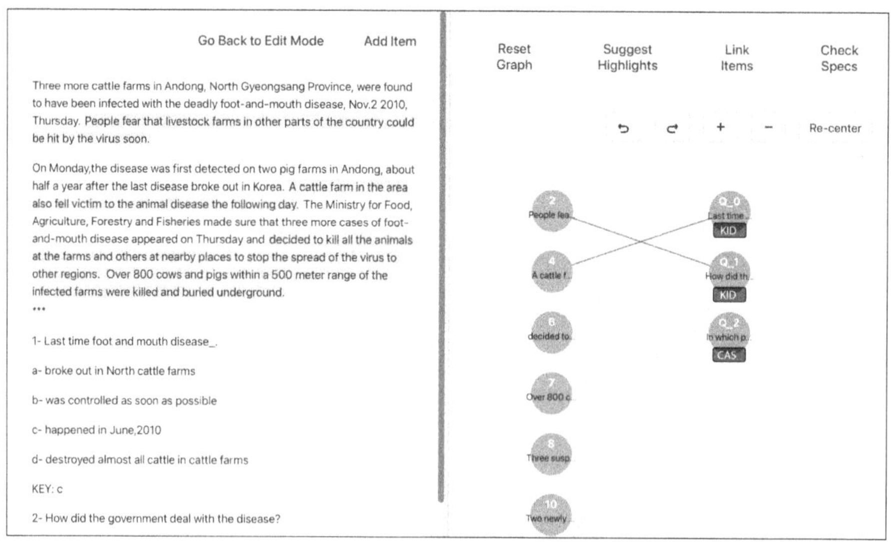

Fig. 1. A typical view of the system: Content specialists can ask for the LLM-suggested highlights on the passage (left), visualize links between questions and the passage (right), and show item specifications (e.g., KID, CAS labels on the right).

Implementation. Our system is implemented in an agentic structure in which we combine prompt calls to the LLM with tool calls (such as Python functions for validating the output). For feature 1, highlights are suggested by an agent that prompts the GPT-4o model with the contents of the editor to highlight parts of the passage that correspond to a "question type supported by text evidence" without "merging multiple concepts". For feature 2, the links are calculated by computing text embeddings using OpenAI's `text-embedding-3-small` model for each item and the correct answer, as well as all highlighted constructs from the passage, and computing cosine similarity to link the most similar nodes. For feature 3, item specifications are obtained by prompting GPT-4o to classify each item by sending them along with the descriptions of different item types.

5   Mixed Methods Evaluation

5.1   Methods

Demographics. We recruited 11 content specialists who develop tests across a diverse set of subjects, including ELA, STEM, and career readiness (CR). All of our participants have extensive experience developing standardized test items (see Table 1). Participants P3, P4, and P10 have also participated in our formative study (referred to as F1, F4, and F3, respectively).

Protocol. The lead author conducted an hour-long think-aloud session with each participant remotely, where participants completed a question authoring task under three conditions. The task was to develop up to 5 multiple-choice questions given a reading passage and one example question. These passages are taken from the RACE dataset [17], which consists of passage-based multiple-choice questions for measuring reading comprehension levels at a high school level. To account for order effects, participants worked on selected passages in randomized orders. Participants completed surveys and a short interview after the tasks. The three conditions were presented in a within-subjects design:

- Condition 1 (Baseline): We disabled all proposed features and asked participants to use our prototype as a text editor.
- Condition 2 (Suggestion Only): We presented highlights created using our tool as suggestions without the ability to regenerate [left pane from Fig. 1].
- Condition 3 (Suggestion + Visualization): We provided full access to features for highlighted suggestions, visualizing passage coverage, and automatically verifying against item specifications [full view from Fig. 1].

5.2   Results

RQ2: Cognitive Demands. Participants indicated the cognitive demands of the tasks on the NASA Task Load Index (NASA TLX) [10] after each task. We used the Friedman test to compare the ratings across conditions, as the ratings were ordinal and collected in a repeated-measures design [24]. We did not observe any significant differences in overall NASA TLX scores between the three conditions (p=.89). Differences in 4 out of 6 subscales (Physical Demand: p=.60, Temporal Demand: p=.07, Effort: p=.28, Frustration: p=.61) were not statistically significant according to the Friedman test. We observed significant differences in the Mental Demand and Performance scales (p<.05). Post-hoc Wilcoxon tests with Bonferroni corrections showed marginal significance between the second condition (highlight suggestions only) and the third condition (both suggestions and visualization) (Mental Demand: p=.06, Performance: p=.05).

These results imply that providing LLM-generated suggestions may significantly decrease perceived cognitive demands and improve performance. Moreover, content specialists reported better or comparable results in performance and cognitive demands compared to the baseline while using the full prototype (Fig. 2a), supporting their work *without additional cognitive effort*.

RQ3: Productivity Modeling. To understand how the additional affordances affect the productivity of content specialists, we fit a linear mixed-effects model to estimate the time to author a question. This time was measured from the moment a participant finished their previous question (or their initial reading of the passage), including the time spent re-reading the passage, coming up with an idea, and developing distractors. The fixed effects were the experimental conditions (baseline, suggestions only, suggestions and visualization), a passage identifier (one of three randomly assigned passages), and task progress (i.e., how many questions they had written so far for the passage). Participants were modeled as random effects to account for individual differences in expertise and experience. We had 11 participants with 98 observations in total. We checked for assumptions of linearity, normality, and homogeneity of variance on Q-Q and residuals vs. fitted plots and observed no violations.

The average time to author a question was 163 s. Participants who worked with suggestions (Condition 2) wrote questions significantly faster (42 s faster than baseline (Condition 1), p=.012) (Fig. 2b). Participants who worked with suggestions and visualizations (Condition 3) were only marginally faster than the baseline (by 8 s, p=.641). We did not observe significant differences between passages or progress in the task.

Similar to the results for cognitive demands, the productivity modeling results indicated that LLM-generated suggestions may improve productivity. Moreover, visualization and modeling features can provide additional information to content specialists without damaging their productivity.

RQ4: Item Quality. To evaluate the quality of the items generated under each condition, content specialists rated a random subset of items on a rubric adapted from prior literature with four items focusing on the correctness and difficulty of authored questions [8] and one item testing the reasoning level (word matching, paraphrasing, single-sentence reasoning, and multi-sentence reasoning) expected

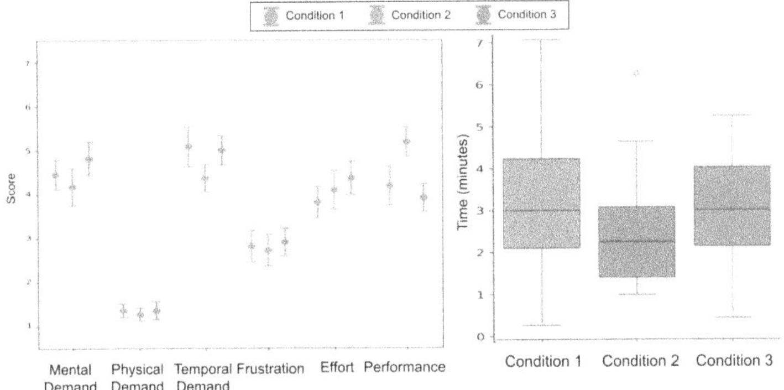

Fig. 2. a) (left) Average scores with standard errors on each subscale of the NASA-TLX survey, b) (right) Comparison of the question times between the three conditions.

from the student [17]. Five additional content specialists from the same organization rated 96 items collected from all three conditions, and each item was evaluated by at least two raters. We used the Kruskal-Wallis H-tests under the assumption of independence between items as items were randomly sampled. We did not observe statistically significant differences in any of the rubric items between conditions in Kruskal-Wallis H-tests, indicating that the introduction of LLM-supported interactions for question authoring does not reduce the perceived item quality for content specialists. However, we noticed that, in Condition 3, more questions required "Multi-sentence reasoning" (45.0%) compared to Conditions 1 (38.5%) and 2 (26.8%), and fewer questions were at the reasoning level of "Word matching" (17.5%) compared to Conditions 1 (21.2%) and 2 (31.0%). These results suggest that the visualization features may be helpful for questions that combine information from different parts of the passage.

We achieved Krippendorff's alpha [15] of 0.604 for inter-rater reliability, indicating relatively low agreement. This might be caused by the inherent difficulty of item evaluation. The evaluated questions were also the product of a time-limited, think-aloud session, and some items included typos or were incomplete, making the evaluation task more difficult. In cases of disagreement, the lower score for that rubric item was assigned as a conservative estimate.

RQ5: User Experience. Participants responded to four usability questions drawn from the PSSUQ [18] and rated the usefulness of four features (getting suggested highlights, visualizing highlights in a graph, connecting items to passage highlights, and classifying items based on item specs) on a 7-point Likert scale. The results show that content specialists found our system easy to use and helpful for completing tasks quickly. However, they also noted that it may take time to find features and use the system effectively. When asked to evaluate the usability of features, they rated suggestions and linking the highest (Fig. 3).

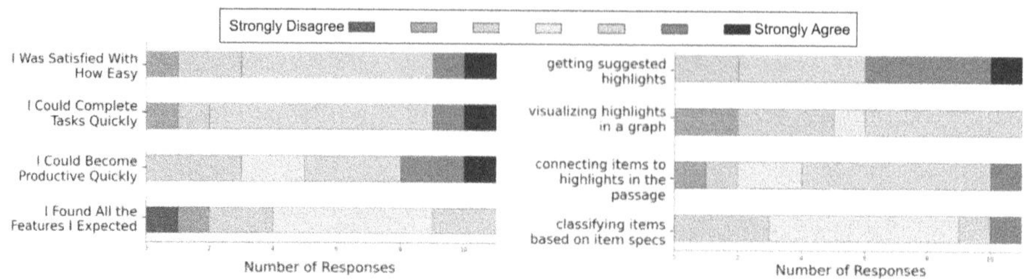

Fig. 3. Left: Distribution of scores for usability statements about the system. **Right**: Distribution of scores for system features.

We also collected transcripts from the think-aloud sessions and the post-task interviews to understand how content specialists worked with the prototype and experienced it. We present excerpts from these transcripts under four key themes.

Theme 1 - Repurposing Features in different contexts. Content specialists used the system's key features for various purposes to better fit their tried-and-tested workflows. Several specialists used the LLM suggestions **to initiate** their question authoring, for example, to "get me started if nothing else" (P6) and to get "ideas in a text-heavy passage" (P9). Some specialists (P1, P5, P7) appreciated having suggestions up front **as guidance** to direct their attention as they skimmed the passage, even if they did not necessarily write items based on suggestions alone. Some specialists preferred the third condition, which generated suggestions after they read the passage rather than showing suggestions up front. They wanted to form an unbiased first draft and then used the suggestions **as validation** to ensure that their items covered the whole passage. For instance, P2 said "it makes me drawn to those sections of the passage without reading through the whole thing without any bias first." They clarified that this was not about the suggestions' quality: "a couple of these are really good details [...] The highlights, it got a lot of the stuff that I would." (P2) Another use case for the suggestions was to create **distractors**. For instance, P6 wrote the question stem and the correct answer first and then returned to the suggestions to identify plausible distractors. Participants also switched between these use cases as the session progressed.

Theme 2 - Modifying workflows around key features. Content specialists also identified points where they would modify their workflows in response to the new features. For instance, P6 said: "When I see like the highlighted sentences, like details [that] would lend themselves well to detail items, I might just immediately start writing. That would be something a little different from my normal process, 'cause normally I would try to think of the big picture items first (...) rather than focusing on such small detail items." Other specialists (P3, P4) also agreed that having this system would motivate them to adapt and modify their workflows.

Theme 3 - Desire to intervene in automated processes. Content specialists emphasized the importance of being able to intervene and modify the suggestions generated by the system, for example, by adjusting the granularity and number of suggestions (P2, P5, P8, P11). For instance, P8 said, "There was a lot of highlighted [points], and so, in some ways, that becomes like nothing is highlighted". P11 said that when there were too many suggestions in a passage, it wasn't "that much different [than the baseline] where I was just starting from scratch and looking through the passage". They also wanted to see *why* a suggestion was presented (P3, P8) and ask for suggestions that could be used to write a particular item type (P2, P3, P5, P8). These requests showed that content specialists preferred to step in when necessary to ensure ownership over the output, rather than automating large chunks of their work.

Theme 4 - Appreciating automation that aligns with existing practices. Specialists welcomed automation that mirrored their existing practices. Many appreciated the linking feature because it automated a process they were already doing (P1, P2, P3, P4, P7). P3 said this feature was "the coolest one [...] take items that we have and link them to spots in the passage. That's kind of something that I do anyway when I write reading items". P2 said that they were "doing the same thing that [the tool] is doing almost in my head". This feature addressed questions like "have I have I mined the passage efficiently from top to bottom? Like do I have a good coverage of things and where might I have overlap" (P4), which was "something that [they] wrestle with a lot" (P4). These types of features may not enable participants to achieve completely new outcomes, but they improve existing workflows and the overall user experience.

6 Discussion and Conclusion

In this work, we conducted formative focus group interviews with content specialists with extensive experience in authoring passage-based questions for a standardized test in order to understand challenges and design opportunities for supporting question authoring. Informed by these findings, we designed an LLM-based human-AI collaboration system to facilitate early-stage question authoring and passage mapping by explicitly visualizing knowledge representations developed by content specialists. Our mixed-methods results showed that the system can reduce cognitive demands and increase productivity. However, we also found that content specialists valued salient representations of their expert knowledge, even when they did not experience clear gains in cognitive demand or productivity. In this section, we discuss key considerations for designing LLM-based systems to support content specialists in early-stage authoring of high-stakes assessment items, illuminated by our findings. Insights from question authoring can also inform designers interested in how other instructors with extensive domain knowledge might benefit from introducing AI support into their workflows.

We observed that content specialists follow iterative and flexible processes. To write sets of high-quality passage-based questions, they need to maintain a mental representation of how items relate to each other *and* to the passage. However, this "passage mapping" process is not explicitly represented or supported by existing support systems. While content specialists iterate and refine, most automated question generation approaches directly generate questions without considering the intermediate artifacts generated by content specialists (e.g., passage maps). As a result of this mismatch between what content specialists do and what automated systems do, specialists cannot incorporate systems into their existing workflows. Our findings heavily suggest that content specialists are willing to adopt AI support when their domain-specific knowledge is valued and supported with appropriate knowledge representations in the system.

We further note that content specialists repurposed features provided in the system in different contexts, using the same features to get inspiration for items, validate the quality of items, and create distractors (**theme 1**). However, this interaction was not unilateral. As participants became more familiar with the system, they speculated about how *their* workflows might change in response to the new affordances offered by the system (**theme 2**). As implied by these two themes, participants did not want the system to have prescriptive features with a single "correct" way of using them. Instead, they experimented with *when* to invoke a feature and *how* to incorporate the output into their work, maximizing the benefit they received from each feature. This aligns with the concept of *variable affordances*, which are affordances that change based on the context of the task and the user's values [4]. In educational content authoring tasks, providing variable affordances may be even more important, as users are domain experts with years of experience and pedagogical content knowledge, and may already have established ways of completing tasks that they wish to preserve.

Content specialists were interested in the potential benefits of the system, but they also wanted to keep control over the process. To empower content specialists in question authoring, a system should balance allowing experts to step in and use their domain knowledge to complement their workflow (**theme 3**) with reducing an expert's workload (**theme 4**). For instance, content specialists appreciated features such as linking items, which helped them get a head start on a task. However, rather than an "ideal" model that highlights *all* testable constructs, they wanted a tool that highlights the specific constructs they care about. They preferred not to fully delegate their workflow to the system, as their pedagogical expertise and content knowledge were central to doing their job. This aligns with prior findings that instructors prefer to delegate rote and tedious tasks, rather than fully automate their workflows when using automated systems [12]. Systems for authoring educational content should empower instructors to focus on the more sensitive parts of their workflow by carefully considering which parts can be automated and which require human expertise.

One important observation from our mixed-methods design is that there can be a trade-off between reducing cognitive demands (or increasing productivity) and improving the user experience. We consider this trade-off to be a powerful lens for designers working with domain experts. Compared to the second condition (in-line suggestions only), our third condition (visualizations) lost some productivity and cognitive gains, but it presented more information to the user and improved user satisfaction. Providing more informative output—at the cost of higher cognitive demands—may also enable content specialists to hold their work to a high standard. Our item quality analysis showed that this condition may have contributed to producing questions at higher reasoning levels. The contrast between quantitative metrics of productivity, task load, and cognitive demands and qualitative reports of improved user experience also highlights the importance of mixed-methods study designs for evaluating tools that support multifaceted instructional design. While a tool might not show immediate benefits in a short study session, domain experts can articulate how the tool can support them in authentic tasks and provide design directions for future work.

Our contributions in this work include a rich understanding of question authoring processes for high-stakes assessments from our focus groups, the design and implementation of a human-AI collaboration system for question authoring, and design guidelines for supporting question authoring and other educational content creation tasks from a mixed-method evaluation of the system.

6.1 Limitations and Future Work

Participants used the system for a limited time. Because they had to learn the system and complete the task simultaneously, this time constraint may have affected their ability to discover how the presented features would best fit into their workflows and may have influenced perceived cognitive demands in the final user study condition. For the quantitative measures, our sample size may not be enough to draw robust statistical conclusions. However, we observed significant decreases in cognitive demands and increases in productivity even with this small sample. We view these results as complementary to our qualitative observations.

This study focused on supporting content specialists with experience in passage-based question authoring. Future work can explore how similar systems would perform in different educational domains. Another opportunity is to explore how the capabilities of the underlying LLM, such as different models and prompt structures, could affect the user experience.

The research questions for the study focus on the perceptions of authoring tool by content specialists rather than the technical performance of the system, such as the accuracy of links and item specifications. We limited our scope to the perception of content specialists as we did not have the data to compare the system's generations against as this is a relatively novel problem space. Future work can propose metrics for technical evaluation of similar human-AI collaboration systems.s

References

1. Alhazmi, E., Sheng, Q.Z., Zhang, W.E., Zaib, M., Alhazmi, A.: Distractor Generation in Multiple-Choice Tasks: A Survey of Methods, Datasets, and Evaluation (Oct 2024)
2. Armfield, D., et al.: Avalon: a Human-in-the-Loop LLM Grading System with Instructor Calibration and Student Self-assessment. In: Cristea, A.I., Walker, E., Lu, Y., Santos, O.C., Isotani, S. (eds.) Artificial Intelligence in Education, pp. 111–118. Springer Nature Switzerland, Cham (2025)

3. Bhowmick, A.K., et al.: Automating question generation from educational text. In: Bramer, M., Stahl, F. (eds.) Artificial Intelligence XL, pp. 437–450. Springer Nature Switzerland, Cham (2023). https://doi.org/10.1007/978-3-031-47994-6_38

4. Borghi, A.M., Riggio, L.: Stable and variable affordances are both automatic and flexible. Front. Hum. Neurosci. **9** (2015)

5. Bulathwela, S., Muse, H., Yilmaz, E.: Scalable Educational question generation with pre-trained language models. In: Wang, N., Rebolledo-Mendez, G., Matsuda, N., Santos, O.C., Dimitrova, V. (eds.) Artificial Intelligence in Education, pp. 327–339. Springer Nature Switzerland, Cham (2023). https://doi.org/10.1007/978-3-031-36272-9_27

6. Cheng, Z., Xu, J., Jin, H.: TreeQuestion: assessing conceptual learning outcomes with LLM-generated multiple-choice questions. Proc. ACM Hum.-Comput. Interact. **8**(CSCW2), 431:1–431:29 (2024)

7. Choi, S., Lee, H., Lee, Y., Kim, J.: VIVID: human-AI collaborative authoring of vicarious dialogues from lecture videos. In: Proc. of the 2024 CHI Conf. on Human Factors in Computing Systems, CHI 2024, pp. 1–26. ACM, New York (May 2024)

8. Doughty, J., et al.: A comparative study of ai-generated (gpt-4) and human-crafted mcqs in programming education. In: Proc. of the 26th Australasian Computing Education Conf, pp. 114–123. ACM, Sydney NSW Australia (Jan 2024)

9. Fordham, N.W.: Crafting questions that address comprehension strategies in content reading. J. Adolescent & Adult Literacy **49**(5), 390–396 (2006)

10. Hart, S.G., Staveland, L.E.: Development of NASA-TLX (Task Load Index): results of empirical and theoretical research. In: Human Mental Workload, pp. 139–183. Advances in Psychology, vol. 52. North-Holland, Oxford, England (1988)

11. Hoq, M., et al.: Explainable AI in the Loop: An Instructor-Transformer Collaboration for Improving Explainability and Reliability of Feedback in Intr. Programming Classrooms

12. Jain, Y., Demirtas, M.A., Cunningham, K.I.: PLAID: supporting Computing Instructors to Identify Domain-Specific Programming Plans at Scale. In: Proc. of the 2025 CHI Conference on Human Factors in Computing Systems, CHI 2025, pp. 1–21. ACM, New York (2025)

13. Jin, H., Yoo, M., Park, J., Lee, Y., Wang, X., Kim, J.: TeachTune: reviewing pedagogical agents against diverse student profiles with simulated students. In: Proc. of the 2025 CHI Conf. on Human Factors in Computing Systems, CHI 2025, pp. 1–28. ACM, New York (Apr 2025)

14. Kang, W., .: TutorCraftEase: enhancing pedagogical question creation with large language models. In: Proc. of the 2025 CHI Conference on Human Factors in Computing Systems, CHI 2025, pp. 1–22. ACM, New York (Apr 2025)

15. Krippendorff, K.: Content Analysis: An Introduction to Its Methodology, 3 edn. SAGE Publications (2018)

16. Kurdi, G., Leo, J., Parsia, B., Sattler, U., Al-Emari, S.: A systematic review of automatic question generation for educational purposes. Int. J. Artif. Intell. Educ. **30**(1), 121–204 (2020)

17. Lai, G., Xie, Q., Liu, H., Yang, Y., Hovy, E.: RACE: large-scale reading comprehension dataset from examinations. In: Palmer, M., Hwa, R., Riedel, S. (eds.) Proc. of the 2017 Conf. on Empirical Methods in Natural Language Processing, pp. 785–794. ACL, Copenhagen, Denmark (Sep 2017)

18. Lewis, J.R.: Psychometric evaluation of the post-study system usability questionnaire: the PSSUQ. In: Proc. of the Human Factors Society Annual Meeting **36**(16), 1259–1260 (1992)

19. Lim, H., et al.: Co-creating question-and-answer style articles with large language models for research promotion. In: Proc. of the 2024 ACM Designing Interactive Systems Conf., DIS 2024, pp. 975–994. ACM, New York (Jul 2024)
20. Lu, X., Fan, S., Houghton, J., Wang, L., Wang, X.: ReadingQuizMaker: a human-NLP collaborative system that supports instructors to design high-quality reading quiz questions. In: Proc. of the 2023 CHI Conference on Human Factors in Computing Systems, CHI 2023, pp. 1–18. ACM, New York (Apr 2023)
21. Miller, A.C., et al.: Novel approaches to examine passage, student, and question effects on reading comprehension. Learn. Disabilities Res. & Prac. **29**(1), 25–35 (2014)
22. Moore, S., Costello, E., Nguyen, H.A., Stamper, J.: An Automatic Question Usability Evaluation Toolkit. In: Olney, A.M., Chounta, I.A., Liu, Z., Santos, O.C., Bittencourt, I.I. (eds.) Artificial Intelligence in Education, pp. 31–46. Springer Nature Switzerland, Cham (2024). https://doi.org/10.1007/978-3-031-64299-9_3
23. Reza, M., Anastasopoulos, I., Bhandari, S., Pardos, Z.A.: PromptHive: bringing subject matter experts back to the forefront with collaborative prompt engineering for educational content creation. In: Proc. of the 2025 CHI Conf. on Human Factors in Computing Systems, pp. 1–22. ACM, Japan (2025)
24. Sheldon, M.R., Fillyaw, M.J., Thompson, W.D.: The use and interpretation of the friedman test in the analysis of ordinal-scale data in repeated measures designs. Physiother. Res. Int. **1**(4), 221–228 (1996)
25. Susanti, Y., Tokunaga, T., Nishikawa, H., Obari, H.: Automatic distractor generation for multiple-choice English vocabulary questions. Res. Pract. Technol. Enhanc. Learn. **13**(1), 15 (2018)
26. Vats, V., et al.: A Survey on Human-AI Collaboration with Large Foundation Models (Sep 2025)
27. Xie, J., Peng, N., Cai, Y., Wang, T., Huang, Q.: Diverse distractor generation for constructing high-quality multiple choice questions. IEEE/ACM Trans. Audio Speech Lang. Process. **30**, 280–291 (2022)

Automating Supportive Psychological Processes: How Source Attribution Shapes Perceived Empathy, Working Alliance, and Acceptability of a Supportive Conversational Agent

Eryka Probierz[1]([✉]) [iD], Anita Gałuszka[2] [iD], Tomasz Grzejszczak[3] [iD], and Adam Gałuszka[3] [iD]

[1] Helena Chodkowska University of Technology and Economics in Warsaw, Jagiellońska 82F, 03-301 Warsaw, Poland
eryka.probierz@uth.edu.pl

[2] Katowice Business University, Harcerzy Września 1939 3, 40-659 Katowice, Poland
anita.galuszka@akademiagornoslaska.pl

[3] Silesian University of Technology, Akademicka 16, 44-100 Gliwice, Poland
{tomasz.grzejszczak,adam.galuszka}@polsl.pl

Abstract. As generative AI systems increasingly appear in supportive and self-regulatory contexts, understanding how users perceive affective qualities of human–AI interaction is critical for designing trustworthy AI-enabled learning environments. This study examined how source attribution (AI vs. human expert) shapes perceived empathy, working alliance, and acceptance of a supportive message attributed to a conversational agent. A randomized between-subjects design (N = 1,002) exposed participants to an identical standardized message labelled as AI- or human-authored. Outcomes included perceived empathy, working alliance, acceptability, trust, and intention to use, assessed with validated instruments. AI-labelled messages were rated as less empathic and relationally engaging than human-labelled messages. Acceptance-related outcomes were also lower, though AI support remained moderately acceptable for low-risk functions (e.g., reflection, psychoeducation). Positive attitudes toward AI increased acceptance, while privacy and responsibility concerns reduced it, especially for substitutive roles. Importantly, acceptance persisted for complementary, human-supervised uses. Findings indicate that attribution shapes relational and acceptance evaluations under minimal, non-interactive exposure. Although based on a single-message design, the results are relevant to AI-enabled learning environments where brief, text-based support is common. The study contributes to the design of human-centered AI systems that balance affective support with transparency, role clarity, and human oversight.

Keywords: Human–AI Interaction · Conversational Agents · Perceived Empathy · Trust in AI · Affective Processes · AI Acceptance

E. G. Blanchard et al. (Eds.): AIED 2026, LNAI 16583, pp. 490–504, 2027.
https://doi.org/10.1007/978-3-032-29760-0_51

1   Introduction

Conversational agents are increasingly used in health, wellbeing, and educational contexts to deliver psychoeducation, reflective prompts, and scalable support. Evidence on mental health chatbots is generally described as promising but heterogeneous, with short-term evaluations and variable reporting standards [1–3]. At the same time, ethical concerns remain central, including crisis handling, harmful recommendations, accountability, privacy, anthropomorphism, and risks of over-reliance or emotional dependency—particularly when AI is framed as a substitute rather than a supervised support tool [4–6]. In learning sciences and HCI, affective support is also a key design element; affective agents are associated with small-to-moderate improvements in learner affect and motivation, moderated by context and design [7, 8]. This highlights the need to examine how AI-delivered support is interpreted and how disclosure of AI involvement shapes perceived relational quality and trust [7, 8]. These perceptions are important because empathy and working alliance are core process variables linked to engagement and outcomes. The working alliance involves agreement on goals, tasks, and relational quality [9], and meta-analyses confirm its association with outcomes, including in digital contexts [10]. Empathy similarly predicts positive outcomes [11], although alliance formation in mediated settings depends on modality and requires empirical validation [12, 13]. A key question is whether source attribution alone (AI vs. human), with identical content, alters perceived empathy and relational quality and whether this affects acceptance and intention to use. Prior work shows that people form relationship-like evaluations of AI and apply legitimacy and accountability heuristics that may reduce trust under disclosure [14–20]. This is particularly relevant for AI-enabled learning environments, where brief, text-based interactions (e.g., prompts, feedback) may shape engagement through perceived empathy and trust.

2   Hypotheses and Related Work

2.1   Hypotheses

Source attribution is operationalised as an experimentally manipulated disclosure cue indicating that an identical supportive message is authored either by an AI assistant or by an experienced human expert. The primary outcomes are perceived empathy (the extent to which the message is experienced as understanding, validating, and responsive), working alliance (perceived collaboration and relational bond in terms of goals, tasks, and bond under minimal exposure), and acceptance of the supportive conversational agent, including acceptability, trust, and intention for future use. Conceptualisations of working alliance emphasise agreement on goals and tasks as well as an affective bond [11], while therapeutic empathy is widely treated as a relational process variable linked to outcomes in psychosocial interventions [9].

The first set of hypotheses concerns perceived empathy and working alliance.

H1 Perceived empathy will be lower under AI attribution than human attribution. Prior evidence indicates that empathy judgements are sensitive to author framing and disclosure even in text-based communication [5–7].

H2 Working alliance will be lower under AI attribution, particularly for the bond component [11–13].

The second set addresses trust, acceptability, and intention to use, including role-dependent differences.

H3 Trust, acceptability, and intention to use will be lower under AI attribution. Previous research suggests that AI disclosure can reduce trust via legitimacy and authenticity inferences, independent of message content quality [28, 29].

H4 Acceptance will be higher for low-risk than high-risk roles, with a larger difference under AI attribution. This low–high risk disparity is expected to be larger under AI attribution, reflecting heightened sensitivity to accountability and safety concerns when AI is framed as the source [30, 32–34].

The final set examines mediation and moderation processes underlying attribution effects.

H5 The effect of attribution on acceptance will be mediated by perceived empathy and working alliance. Specifically, AI attribution is expected to reduce empathy and alliance, which in turn is expected to reduce trust, acceptability, and intention to use, consistent with process-based models of psychosocial interventions [9, 12].

H6 Attribution effects will be moderated by individual differences (e.g., AI attitudes, privacy concerns). More favourable attitudes toward AI are expected to attenuate the negative impact of AI attribution on trust and acceptability, whereas stronger privacy and responsibility concerns are expected to amplify it, particularly for higher-risk and substitutive roles. Prior research indicates that trust and adoption of AI depend on user-, task-, and system-level factors, supporting moderation-based hypotheses [20, 31]. Together, these hypotheses test whether attribution influences acceptance outcomes through relational perceptions and individual differences.

2.2 Empathy and Working Alliance in Human–AI Mediated Support

Empathy and working alliance are central constructs in supportive communication, but are inconsistently operationalised in human–AI interaction research. In psychotherapy, empathy refers to understanding, validation, and responsiveness rather than polite language, and is strongly linked to outcomes [9]. Instruments such as the Consultation and Relational Empathy (CARE) measure capture perceived relational processes rather than linguistic features [10]. This distinction is important in AI contexts, where empathic-sounding language may not be perceived as genuine without clear cues of agency and intent [8]. Empirical findings are mixed: chatbot responses have sometimes been rated as more empathic than physicians' replies, but such comparisons often confound attribution with content differences [4, 9]. Experimental studies suggest a trade-off between warmth and perceived authenticity, and show that empathy judgments vary depending on attribution and disclosure [5–7, 10]. Reviews highlight substantial heterogeneity in definitions and measurement, supporting attribution-only designs that isolate disclosure effects under controlled conditions [8, 11, 12]. Working alliance is typically defined by agreement on goals, tasks, and relational quality [11], and is associated with outcomes across psychotherapy and digital interventions [12]. However, alliance formation depends on expectations and provider cues rather than being modality-invariant [13].

Reviews stress the need to distinguish alliance from related constructs such as satisfaction [13, 14]. Brief measures such as the Working Alliance Inventory—Short Revised (WAI-SR) allow testing whether attribution affects alliance perceptions when content is held constant [15, 16]. While alliance-like evaluations can emerge in AI-mediated support [17–19], attribution-only studies remain limited, constraining causal conclusions about AI labelling effects [16].

2.3 Trust, Acceptance, and Algorithm-Related Boundary Conditions in Supportive AI

Trust and acceptance are central to the adoption of AI-enabled support in learning and self-regulation contexts. Trust in automation guides reliance under uncertainty and should reflect alignment between perceived and actual system capabilities [20]. This is particularly important for supportive conversational agents, where fluent, empathic outputs may obscure limitations in higher-risk contexts, requiring calibrated trust [17]. Trust has been operationalised as a measurable construct linked to reliance behaviour [21], and meta-analytic evidence shows it is context-sensitive, shaped by performance cues, interface features, and user characteristics [22]. Integrative reviews further highlight the role of social framing and AI representation in shaping trust [31]. These findings justify examining trust in attribution research, as disclosure of AI authorship can influence perceived legitimacy even when content is constant [18]. Acceptance can be understood through multiple frameworks. Technology acceptance models emphasise perceived usefulness and ease of use [23], while broader models incorporate performance expectations and social influence [24]. In implementation science, acceptability is treated as a distinct outcome, measured with validated tools such as the Acceptability of Intervention Measure (AIM) [25]. These perspectives suggest that acceptance may follow attribution-driven changes in perceived empathy and alliance [19]. Research on algorithm aversion and appreciation further defines boundary conditions: people may reject algorithmic advice after errors, especially in socially sensitive tasks [21, 26], but may prefer it in other contexts [27]. In supportive domains, resistance is stronger when AI is framed as a substitute rather than an assistive tool [30]. This supports distinguishing low-risk from high-risk roles and expecting risk-contingent acceptance to interact with AI attribution [22, 23].

2.4 Ethical Considerations in AI-Enabled Learning and Self-Regulation Environments

Ethical challenges of conversational AI in mental health and related supportive contexts are well documented and include concerns regarding privacy and data governance, risk of harm, accountability, bias, anthropomorphism, and over-reliance [32–34]. Rather than reiterating these issues, it is important to consider how they intersect with empirical findings on user perception and acceptance. A scoping review emphasises that ethical evaluation must extend beyond efficacy to questions of governance, safety, and acceptable role boundaries [32]. However, prior ethical analyses are predominantly conceptual and are rarely linked to controlled empirical tests of how users interpret AI-mediated support. For example, although transparency is widely endorsed, socio-legal work shows that disclosure functions as a contextual communication act and may not ensure genuine understanding or accountability [35], while behavioural evidence indicates that disclosure can reduce trust through legitimacy-related mechanisms [29]. In learning and self-regulation contexts, affective support is often used to enhance motivation, yet meta-analytic evidence shows heterogeneous effects dependent on design and context [36], and systematic reviews highlight limited theoretical consistency and evaluation rigor in empathic conversational agents [37]. These literatures reveal a lack of integration between ethical concerns and measurable user responses. Similarly, alliance-like evaluations have been observed in digital contexts but vary substantially depending on interaction format and framing. Acceptance is consistently context-dependent, with greater acceptance for low-risk supportive roles and lower acceptance for substitutive or high-risk functions. At the same time, many studies confound attribution with content, interaction design, or system capability, limiting causal inference. Consequently, it remains unclear whether attribution alone can systematically shape perceived empathy, relational evaluation, and acceptance under controlled conditions. The present study addresses this gap by isolating source attribution while holding message content constant and examining relational, acceptance, and role-specific outcomes within a single experimental framework.

3 Research Design and Methodology

A randomised between-subjects experimental design with two conditions was employed. Participants were exposed to an identical supportive message differing only in source attribution (AI assistant vs. human expert). Random allocation (1:1) was used to minimise confounding and ensure balanced groups. The sample comprised adults (18+) recruited online, with eligibility requiring proficiency in Polish. As the study involved Polish-speaking participants, generalisability may be limited, as cultural norms related to emotional expression, trust in technology, and expectations toward professional support may influence perceptions of empathy and relational quality in AI-mediated messages. Participants indicating acute psychological crisis at screening were excluded and provided with appropriate support resources. The stimulus was a single, standardised supportive message (approx. 250–300 words), designed to be psychologically safe, non-clinical, and oriented toward reflection and self-regulation. It was developed by the authors using principles of supportive, non-directive communication, ensuring neutral wording and suitability for general adult populations, and was internally reviewed for clarity and consistency. A brief pilot check confirmed comprehensibility and perceived supportiveness, with preliminary indicators suggesting acceptable psychometric properties (e.g., $\alpha = .84$, high item coherence). The message was delivered via an online survey in a browser-based interface as a static text block labelled as AI- or human-authored. The display resembled a survey-style presentation rather than a conversational interface; no interactive exchange or adaptive dialogue was implemented. Accordingly, the design captures first-impression responses under minimal exposure rather than sustained interaction or relational development, with message content held constant across conditions and only attribution varying.

The following message was used as the experimental stimulus. The original message was developed in Polish and presented to participants in Polish. The version below provides an English translation for transparency.

"It sounds like you may be going through something that requires effort and emotional energy. Situations like this can feel difficult, especially when there is uncertainty or when things do not unfold as expected. It is understandable to experience a range of reactions, including tension, doubt, or fatigue. Sometimes it can be helpful to pause and notice what feels most important in the moment. You might consider what thoughts or concerns are most present for you right now, and how they are influencing how you feel. There is no need to resolve everything at once—small steps and gradual reflection can be enough. It may also be useful to recognise what has helped you cope with challenging situations in the past. Even if the current situation is different, some of those strategies or perspectives may still offer support. Paying attention to what is within your control, even in a limited way, can sometimes create a sense of stability. At the same time, it is okay if things feel unclear or unresolved. Many situations take time to process, and it is natural not to have immediate answers. Allowing yourself space to reflect, without pressure to reach conclusions too quickly, can be a helpful starting point. If you feel comfortable, you might also consider whether there are people, resources, or activities that usually support you in moments like this. Even small forms of support can make a difference. Whatever you are experiencing, it is valid to take it seriously and to approach it with patience and care."

Primary outcomes include perceived empathy, working alliance, and acceptance-related constructs. Representative items were adapted from established instruments to reflect evaluation of a single, text-based supportive message rather than an ongoing interaction. Example items include: perceived empathy (Consultation and Relational Empathy [CARE]–aligned; e.g., "This message made me feel understood"), working alliance (Working Alliance Inventory—Short Revised [WAI-SR]; e.g., "I felt that this support aligned with my needs"), acceptability (Acceptability of Intervention Measure [AIM]; e.g., "This type of support seems acceptable to me"), trust (based on trust in automation scales; e.g., "I would trust this source of support"), and intention to use (behavioural intention measures; e.g., "I would consider using this support again"). All items were phrased to capture first-impression evaluations under minimal exposure. Perceived empathy is assessed using a multi-item self-report measure operationalising relational empathy as perceived understanding, validation, and responsiveness. Item content is aligned with relational empathy traditions exemplified by the Consultation and Relational Empathy (CARE) measure, adapted for text-based supportive messaging contexts. Working alliance is assessed using the Working Alliance Inventory—Short Revised (WAI-SR), which measures alliance in terms of goals, tasks, and bond. In the present design, the WAI-SR is used to capture initial, minimal-exposure alliance impressions rather than a fully developed relational bond. This application is consistent with prior research indicating that alliance-like evaluations can emerge in early or brief interactions and can be meaningfully assessed under constrained exposure conditions. Accordingly, scores should be interpreted as reflecting perceived alliance potential or first-impression relational judgments, rather than sustained collaboration. Psychometric support for the WAI-SR has been documented across clinical samples.

Acceptance is operationalised through complementary constructs: perceived acceptability, trust, and intention to use the agent in the future. Perceived acceptability is assessed using the Acceptability of Intervention Measure (AIM), a brief psychometrically evaluated instrument developed within implementation science. Trust is assessed using established trust-in-automation measurement traditions, including psychometric approaches designed to capture trust in automated systems as a measurable construct, consistent with broader human factors perspectives on trust and appropriate reliance in automation contexts. Intention to use is assessed using a brief multi-item behavioural intention measure reflecting willingness to use the agent again under comparable circumstances. Additional measures capture hypothesised moderators. Attitudes toward AI and privacy/responsibility concerns are assessed using structured self-report items reflecting dispositional acceptance and governance-oriented concerns. Prior experience with human support services is assessed via self-report (e.g., prior engagement with counselling/psychotherapy or related support). Current emotional state is assessed using the Patient Health Questionnaire-4 (PHQ-4), an ultra-brief screening measure for anxiety and depression symptom burden. Data are collected using an online survey platform with embedded attention checks and monitoring of completion time to support data quality. After screening and consent, participants are randomised to one attribution condition, read the attributed supportive message, and complete the battery of outcome and moderator measures.

3.1 Statistical Analysis

Primary analyses test between-condition differences in perceived empathy, working alliance, and acceptance-related outcomes using independent-samples t-tests and analysis of variance, as appropriate. Moderation is examined using regression models including interaction terms between attribution condition and individual difference variables (attitudes toward AI, privacy/responsibility concerns, prior experience with human support services, and PHQ-4). Mediation analyses evaluate whether perceived empathy and working alliance account for (i.e., statistically mediate) the association between attribution condition and acceptance-related outcomes. Indirect effects are evaluated using contemporary mediation approaches that emphasise the indirect effect and resampling-based inference, such as bootstrapped confidence intervals, consistent with established conceptual analyses of moderator versus mediator relations. Role-specific acceptability is examined by comparing participant ratings for low-risk supportive functions (e.g., reflection, psychoeducation, between-session self-regulation support) versus high-risk or substitutive functions (e.g., crisis support, diagnostic judgement, replacement of human support), and by testing whether risk level interacts with source attribution. Assumptions for parametric analyses were examined prior to hypothesis testing. Normality was assessed via visual inspection and skewness/kurtosis indices, indicating no substantial deviations. Homogeneity of variance was tested using Levene's test; where violations occurred, Welch-adjusted statistics were used, with no change in inference. Given the large sample size, parametric tests were considered robust to minor departures from normality. Regression results are reported using standardised coefficients (β) to facilitate comparison across predictors.

4   Results

A total of N = 1,002 participants was analysed, with n = 501 in each condition (AI-labelled vs. human-expert-labelled). Randomisation yielded comparable groups across background variables, with no significant between-condition differences (all ps ≥ .09; Table 1). Internal consistency was satisfactory for all measures (α = .83–.93).

Table 1. Participant characteristics by attribution condition

Characteristic	Human-expert-labelled (n = 501)	AI-labelled (n = 501)
Age, years	31.39 (9.23)	31.08 (8.98)
Gender: female	265 (52.9%)	302 (60.3%)
Gender: male	218 (43.5%)	183 (36.5%)
Gender: non-binary/other	12 (2.4%)	10 (2.0%)
Gender: prefer not to say	6 (1.2%)	6 (1.2%)
Student status	183 (36.5%)	202 (40.3%)
Prior AI chatbot use	362 (72.3%)	359 (71.7%)
Prior human support experience	214 (42.7%)	200 (39.9%)
PHQ-4 score	3.24 (1.73)	3.18 (1.75)
Attitudes toward AI (1–7)	4.68 (1.22)	4.65 (1.22)
Privacy/responsibility concerns (1–7)	4.10 (1.24)	4.24 (1.26)

Note. Values are M (SD) for continuous variables and n (%) for categorical variables

4.1   Relational Outcomes (H1-H2)

Consistent with H1–H2, AI attribution reduced perceived empathy and working alliance (Table 2). Perceived empathy was lower in the AI-labelled condition (M = 4.71, SD = 0.79) than in the human-expert condition (M = 5.11, SD = 0.69), t ≈ 8.55, p < .001, d = −0.54. Working alliance was also lower under AI attribution (M = 3.50, SD = 0.57) compared with human attribution (M = 3.74, SD = 0.51), t ≈ 7.14, p < .001, d = −0.45.

Table 2. Primary outcomes by attribution condition

Outcome (scale range)	Human-expert-labelled M (SD)	AI-labelled M (SD)	Δ (AI − Human)	Cohen's d	p
Perceived empathy	5.11 (0.69)	4.71 (0.79)	−0.40	−0.54	p < .001
Working alliance	3.74 (0.51)	3.50 (0.57)	−0.24	−0.45	p < .001

(continued)

Table 2. (*continued*)

Outcome (scale range)	Human-expert-labelled M (SD)	AI-labelled M (SD)	Δ (AI − Human)	Cohen's d	p
Acceptability	3.64 (0.78)	3.31 (0.90)	−0.33	−0.39	p < .001
Trust	4.84 (1.00)	4.42 (1.19)	−0.41	−0.38	p < .001
Intention to use	4.66 (1.06)	4.19 (1.35)	−0.47	−0.39	p < .001

Note. Values are M (SD) for continuous variables and n (%) for categorical variables

4.2 Acceptance Outcomes (H3-H4)

In line with H3, acceptance-related outcomes were lower under AI attribution, with small-to-moderate effects on acceptability, trust, and intention to use (Table 2). Supporting H4, acceptance differed by role risk. Low-risk functions (reflection, psychoeducation, between-session support) were rated substantially more acceptable than high-risk or substitutive functions (overall $\Delta M = 1.76$, p < .001). This difference was larger in the AI-labelled condition (M = 1.86) than in the human-expert condition (M = 1.66), p < .001, indicating stronger differentiation of acceptable roles under AI attribution (Table 3).

Table 3. Role-specific acceptability by attribution condition

Role acceptability	Human-expert-labelled M (SD)	AI-labelled M (SD)	Δ (AI−Human)	Cohen's d	p
Low-risk composite	3.78 (0.67)	3.63 (0.78)	−0.15	−0.20	0.0013
Reflection	3.78 (0.82)	3.57 (0.91)	−0.21	−0.24	0.0001
Psychoeducation	3.78 (0.80)	3.66 (0.88)	−0.12	−0.15	0.0202
Between-session support	3.77 (0.79)	3.66 (0.85)	−0.11	−0.13	0.0381
High-risk/substitutive composite	2.11 (0.71)	1.77 (0.64)	−0.34	−0.51	p < .001
Crisis support	2.12 (0.82)	1.78 (0.74)	−0.33	−0.43	p < .001
Diagnostic judgement	2.11 (0.82)	1.76 (0.73)	−0.35	−0.45	p < .001
AI as substitute for human support	2.12 (0.82)	1.77 (0.78)	−0.35	−0.44	p < .001
Human-supervised	3.92 (0.85)	3.70 (0.92)	−0.21	−0.24	p < .001

Note. Negative d indicates lower acceptability in the AI-labelled condition

4.3   Moderation

Consistent with H6, the effect of attribution on acceptance-related outcomes was moderated by individual differences (Table 4). More positive attitudes toward AI were associated with higher acceptance, trust, and intention to use, and attenuated the negative effect of AI attribution. In contrast, privacy/responsibility concerns showed strong negative associations with acceptance and amplified attribution effects, particularly for higher-risk roles. Prior experience with human support was associated with lower acceptance of AI in high-risk and substitutive roles ($ps < .05$), consistent with role-boundary expectations.

Table 4. Role-specific acceptability by attribution condition

Outcome	Cond (AI = 1) β (SE)	AI attitude β (SE)	Privacy β (SE)	Cond × AI attitude β (SE)	Cond × Privacy β (SE)	R^2
Acceptability (AIM)	−0.286 (0.040)	0.388 (0.028)	−0.285 (0.028)	0.107 (0.040)	−0.062 (0.040)	0.463
Trust	−0.356 (0.051)	0.472 (0.036)	−0.321 (0.037)	0.189 (0.051)	−0.211 (0.051)	0.477
Intention to use	−0.412 (0.052)	0.597 (0.037)	−0.369 (0.037)	0.250 (0.052)	−0.151 (0.052)	0.556
Low-risk acceptability	−0.118 (0.039)	0.263 (0.028)	−0.157 (0.028)	0.100 (0.039)	−0.079 (0.039)	0.292
High-risk acceptability	−0.310 (0.036)	0.166 (0.026)	−0.333 (0.026)	−0.063 (0.036)	0.019 (0.036)	0.332

Note. Standardised regression coefficients (β) are reported; continuous predictors were standardised prior to analysis; models control for prior human support experience and PHQ-4. Positive Cond × AI attitude interaction terms indicate attenuation of the AI-labelling penalty as AI attitudes become more favourable

4.4   Mediation

Mediation analyses (H5) indicated statistically significant indirect associations consistent with mediation pathways linking attribution to acceptance outcomes through perceived empathy and working alliance (Table 5). AI attribution predicted lower empathy and alliance, which in turn were positively associated with acceptability, trust, and intention to use. Bootstrapped indirect effects supported statistically reliable mediation pathways across all outcomes. These mediation results reflect statistical associations observed in a single-exposure experimental context and should not be interpreted as evidence of fully developed or longitudinal relational processes.

Table 5. Mediation of attribution effects via perceived empathy and working alliance

Outcome	Indirect via empathy (95% CI)	Indirect via alliance (95% CI)	Total indirect (95% CI)	Direct effect (c′)
Acceptability	−0.097 [−0.129, −0.069]	−0.071 [−0.098, −0.048]	−0.168 [−0.209, −0.131]	−0.117
Trust	−0.139 [−0.181, −0.100]	−0.106 [−0.143, −0.074]	−0.245 [−0.304, −0.192]	−0.111
Intention to use	−0.156 [−0.199, −0.116]	−0.081 [−0.114, −0.053]	−0.237 [−0.290, −0.187]	−0.174

Note. Indirect effects are estimated from linear models with covariates and bootstrapped percentile confidence intervals. Negative indirect effects indicate that AI attribution reduced outcomes via reduced perceived empathy and/or alliance. Values represent unstandardised indirect effects

The results are consistent with a relationally mediated pattern of associations under minimal exposure, in which AI attribution is linked to lower perceived empathy and working alliance, which are in turn associated with lower acceptance-related outcomes.

5 Discussion

The present study examined how source attribution (AI vs. human expert), applied to an identical supportive message, shapes perceived empathy, working alliance, and acceptance-related outcomes. Overall, the findings indicate that attribution cues systematically influence both relational evaluations and acceptance. Consistent with H1–H2, AI attribution reduced perceived empathy and working alliance, suggesting that initial relational evaluations are shaped not only by message content but also by assumptions about agency and accountability. Under minimal exposure, AI-labelled support appears to constrain initial affective evaluation, particularly the bond component of alliance, while leaving task- and goal-related perceptions less affected. In line with H3, acceptability, trust, and intention to use were lower under AI attribution. However, these effects were smaller than those observed for relational outcomes, indicating that reduced perceived empathy does not preclude pragmatic acceptance. Supporting H4, acceptance varied by role risk: low-risk functions such as reflection and psychoeducation were rated more acceptable than high-risk or substitutive roles. This distinction was more pronounced under AI attribution, suggesting heightened sensitivity to responsibility and safety when support is framed as AI-generated. As predicted in H5, perceived empathy and working alliance were statistically consistent with partial mediation of the attribution–acceptance association, indicating that relational perceptions constitute an important pathway through which attribution shapes trust and intention to use. At the same time, the persistence of direct effects suggests that acceptance also reflects broader evaluative and normative considerations. Consistent with H6, attribution effects were moderated by individual differences: more positive attitudes toward AI attenuated the negative impact of AI attribution, whereas stronger privacy and responsibility concerns amplified it, particularly for higher-risk roles. Prior experience with human support was associated with lower acceptance of AI in substitutive roles, but not in complementary or supervised use. The findings support a differentiated, context-sensitive account of AI acceptance. Rather than supporting a replacement model, the results favour a complementarity perspective in which AI functions as a bounded and human-supervised support tool. Although AI attribution constrains relational evaluation, it does not eliminate acceptance when the role remains clearly defined and non-substitutive. These interpretations should be understood as reflecting first-impression judgments rather than sustained interaction or fully developed relational processes. These findings have direct implications for AI-enabled learning environments, where similar forms of brief, text-based support are used to scaffold self-regulation, reflection, and motivation. In such contexts, even minimal interactions may shape learners' engagement through perceived empathy and trust, influencing whether support is accepted or ignored.

Several limitations should be noted. The study is based on a single, static message and therefore reflects first-impression judgments under minimal exposure rather than sustained interaction or developed relational processes. Outcomes rely on self-report measures rather than behavioural or longitudinal indicators, and real-world systems vary in interaction style, adaptivity, and transparency, which may interact with attribution effects. Additionally, the use of a Polish-speaking sample limits cross-cultural generalisability, as perceptions of empathy, trust, and AI roles may differ across cultural contexts. These findings also raise ethical concerns. Anthropomorphic language without clear attribution may create ambiguity about whether users are interacting with a human or AI, increasing risks of miscalibrated trust, over-reliance, and misattributed responsibility. Transparency is therefore necessary but must be meaningful and aligned with system capabilities. Additionally, supportive AI may evoke emotional engagement that, in repeated use, could contribute to dependency if not clearly framed as non-relational support.

Future research should extend these findings to longitudinal and fully interactive conversational settings, where working alliance and perceived empathy may evolve over repeated exchanges. Experimental designs incorporating real-time, adaptive dialogue are needed to examine how attribution effects interact with responsiveness, personalisation, and conversational dynamics. Behavioural outcomes (e.g., actual engagement, continued use, dropout) should complement self-report measures to assess real-world impact. Further work should also compare different delivery formats and platforms (e.g., chat interfaces, mobile learning systems, embedded educational tools), as interface characteristics may shape attribution effects. Cross-cultural studies are required to examine variability in trust, empathy perception, and acceptance across linguistic and socio-cultural contexts. Finally, future research should explicitly contrast human-supervised versus substitutive AI roles in ecologically valid settings, testing how transparency, oversight, and role framing influence appropriate reliance and boundary-setting.

6 Conclusion

This study demonstrates that source attribution alone—AI assistant versus human expert—systematically shapes perceived empathy, working alliance, and acceptance of a supportive message attributed to an AI or human source, even when message content is identical. AI attribution is associated with lower relational and affective evaluations, which partially mediate reduced trust and intention to use. At the same time, AI-attributed supportive message is evaluated as moderately acceptable for clearly bounded, low-risk functions and in complementary, human-supervised roles. The findings differences in affective and relational evaluations under minimal exposure in supportive and self-regulatory contexts and provide empirical support for design approaches that emphasise transparency, role clarity, and hybrid human–AI collaboration. These conclusions should be interpreted within the constraints of a minimal-exposure, non-interactive design, capturing initial evaluations rather than sustained use or developed interaction. Rather than aiming to simulate human empathy or replace professional support, trustworthy AI-enabled learning and support systems should be designed to augment human practice in clearly bounded roles, with future systems requiring validation in longitudinal, interactive, and behaviourally grounded contexts.

Acknowledgements. This work was supported by the grant from SUT - subsidy for maintaining and developing the research potential in 2026, by Katowice Business University for scientific research in 2026 and by the Helena Chodkowska University of Technology and Economics in Warsaw through the subsidy for maintaining and developing the research potential grant in 2025/2026.

Disclosure of Interests.   The authors have no competing interests to declare that are relevant to the content of this article.

References

1. Vaidyam, A.N., Wisniewski, H., Halamka, J.D., Kashavan, M.S., Torous, J.B.: Chatbots and conversational agents in mental health: a review of the psychiatric landscape. Can. J. Psychiatry **64**(7), 456–464 (2019). https://doi.org/10.1177/0706743719828977
2. Hua, Y., et al.: Charting the evolution of artificial intelligence mental health chatbots from rule-based systems to large language models: a systematic review. World Psychiatry **24**(3), 383–394 (2025). https://doi.org/10.1002/wps.21352
3. Boucher, E.M., et al.: Artificially intelligent chatbots in digital mental health interventions: a review. Expert Rev. Med. Devices **18**(sup1), 37–49 (2021). https://doi.org/10.1080/17434440.2021.2013200
4. Ayers, J.W., et al.: Comparing physician and artificial intelligence chatbot responses to patient questions posted to a public social media forum. JAMA Intern. Med. **183**(6), 589–596 (2023). https://doi.org/10.1001/jamainternmed.2023.1838
5. Shen, J., DiPaola, D., Ali, S., Sap, M., Park, H.W., Breazeal, C.: Empathy toward artificial intelligence versus human experiences and the role of transparency in mental health and social support chatbot design: comparative study. JMIR Ment Health **11**, e62679 (2024). https://doi.org/10.2196/62679

6. Ovsyannikova, D., Oldemburgo de Mello, V., Inzlicht, M.: Third-party evaluators perceive AI as more compassionate than expert humans. Commun. Psychol. **3**, 4 (2025). https://doi.org/10.1038/s44271-024-00182-6

7. Seitz, L.: Artificial empathy in healthcare chatbots: does it feel authentic? Comput. Hum. Behav. Artif. Hum. **2**(1), 100067 (2024). https://doi.org/10.1016/j.chbah.2024.100067

8. Sanjeewa, R., Iyer, R., Apputhurai, P., Wickramasinghe, N., Meyer, D.: Empathic conversational agent platform designs and their evaluation in the context of mental health: systematic review. JMIR Ment Health **11**, e58974 (2024). https://doi.org/10.2196/58974

9. Elliott, R., Bohart, A.C., Watson, J.C., Murphy, D.: Therapist empathy and client outcome: an updated meta-analysis. Psychotherapy **55**(4), 399–410 (2018). https://doi.org/10.1037/pst0000175

10. Mercer, S.W., Maxwell, M., Heaney, D., Watt, G.C.M.: The consultation and relational empathy (CARE) measure: development and preliminary validation and reliability of an empathy-based consultation process measure. Fam. Pract. **21**(6), 699–705 (2004). https://doi.org/10.1093/fampra/cmh621

11. Bordin, E.S.: The generalizability of the psychoanalytic concept of the working alliance. Psychotherapy **16**(3), 252–260 (1979). https://doi.org/10.1037/h0085885

12. Flückiger, C., Del Re, A.C., Wampold, B.E., Horvath, A.O.: The alliance in adult psychotherapy: a meta-analytic synthesis. Psychotherapy **55**(4), 316–340 (2018). https://doi.org/10.1037/pst0000172

13. Berger, T.: The therapeutic alliance in internet interventions: a narrative review and suggestions for future research. Psychother. Res. **27**(5), 511–524 (2017). https://doi.org/10.1080/10503307.2015.1119908

14. Kaiser, J., Hanschmidt, F., Kersting, A.: The association between therapeutic alliance and outcome in internet-based psychological interventions: a meta-analysis. Comput Human Behav **114**, 106512 (2021). https://doi.org/10.1016/j.chb.2020.106512

15. Hatcher, R.L., Gillaspy, J.A.: Development and validation of a revised short version of the working alliance inventory. Psychother. Res. **16**(1), 12–25 (2006). https://doi.org/10.1080/10503300500352500

16. Munder, T., Wilmers, F., Leonhart, R., Linster, H.W., Barth, J.: Working Alliance Inventory-Short Revised (WAI-SR): psychometric properties in outpatients and inpatients. Clin. Psychol. Psychother. **17**(3), 231–239 (2010). https://doi.org/10.1002/cpp.658

17. Beatty, C., Malik, T., Meheli, S., Sinha, C.: Evaluating the therapeutic alliance with a free-text CBT conversational agent (Wysa): a mixed-methods study. Front Digit Health **4**, 847991 (2022). https://doi.org/10.3389/fdgth.2022.847991

18. He, L., Basar, E., Wiers, R.W., Antheunis, M.L., Krahmer, E.: Can chatbots help to motivate smoking cessation? A study on the effectiveness of motivational interviewing on engagement and therapeutic alliance. BMC Public Health **22**, 726 (2022). https://doi.org/10.1186/s12889-022-13115-x

19. Bickmore, T., Gruber, A., Picard, R.: Establishing the computer–patient working alliance in automated health behavior change interventions. Patient Educ. Couns. **59**(1), 21–30 (2005). https://doi.org/10.1016/j.pec.2004.09.008

20. Lee, J.D., See, K.A.: Trust in automation: designing for appropriate reliance. Hum. Factors **46**(1), 50–80 (2004). https://doi.org/10.1518/hfes.46.1.50_30392

21. Jian, J.Y., Bisantz, A.M., Drury, C.G.: Foundations for an empirically determined scale of trust in automated systems. Int. J. Cogn. Ergon. **4**(1), 53–71 (2000). https://doi.org/10.1207/S15327566IJCE0401_04

22. Schaefer, K.E., Chen, J.Y.C., Szalma, J.L., Hancock, P.A.: A meta-analysis of factors influencing the development of trust in automation: implications for understanding autonomy in future systems. Hum. Factors **58**(3), 377–400 (2016). https://doi.org/10.1177/0018720816634228

23. Davis, F.D.: Perceived usefulness, perceived ease of use, and user acceptance of information technology. MIS Q. **13**(3), 319–340 (1989). https://doi.org/10.2307/249008
24. Venkatesh, V., Morris, M.G., Davis, G.B., Davis, F.D.: User acceptance of information technology: toward a unified view. MIS Q. **27**(3), 425–478 (2003). https://doi.org/10.2307/30036540
25. Weiner, B.J., et al.: Psychometric assessment of three newly developed implementation outcome measures. Implement. Sci. **12**, 108 (2017). https://doi.org/10.1186/s13012-017-0635-3
26. Dietvorst, B.J., Simmons, J.P., Massey, C.: Algorithm aversion: people erroneously avoid algorithms after seeing them err. J. Exp. Psychol. Gen. **144**(1), 114–126 (2015). https://doi.org/10.1037/xge0000033
27. Logg, J.M., Minson, J.A., Moore, D.A.: Algorithm appreciation: people prefer algorithmic to human judgment. Organ. Behav. Hum. Decis. Process. **151**, 90–103 (2019). https://doi.org/10.1016/j.obhdp.2018.12.005
28. Jakesch M, French M, Ma X, Hancock JT, Naaman M (2019) AI-mediated communication: how the perception that profile text was written by AI affects trustworthiness. In: Proceedings of the 2019 CHI Conference on Human Factors in Computing Systems. https://doi.org/10.1145/3290605.3300469
29. Schilke, O., Reimann, M.: The transparency dilemma: how AI disclosure erodes trust. Organ. Behav. Hum. Decis. Process. **188**, 104405 (2025). https://doi.org/10.1016/j.obhdp.2025.104405
30. Longoni, C., Bonezzi, A., Morewedge, C.K.: Resistance to medical artificial intelligence. J. Consum. Res. **46**(4), 629–650 (2019). https://doi.org/10.1093/jcr/ucz013
31. Glikson, E., Woolley, A.W.: Human trust in artificial intelligence: review of empirical research. Acad. Manag. Ann. **14**(2), 627–660 (2020). https://doi.org/10.5465/annals.2018.0057
32. Rahsepar Meadi, M., Sillekens, T., Metselaar, S., van Balkom, A., Bernstein, J., Batelaan, N.: Exploring the ethical challenges of conversational AI in mental health care: scoping review. JMIR Ment. Health **12**, e60432 (2025). https://doi.org/10.2196/60432
33. Vilaza, G.N., McCashin, D.: Is the automation of digital mental health ethical? Applying an ethical framework to chatbots for cognitive behaviour therapy. Front. Digit. Health **3**, 689736 (2021). https://doi.org/10.3389/fdgth.2021.689736
34. Blease, C., Rodman, A.: Generative artificial intelligence in mental healthcare: an ethical evaluation. Curr Treat Opt. Psychiatry (2024). https://doi.org/10.1007/s40501-024-00340-x
35. Felzmann, H., Fosch Villaronga, E., Lutz, C., Tamò-Larrieux, A.: Transparency you can trust: transparency requirements for artificial intelligence between legal norms and contextual concerns. Big Data Soc. **6**(1), 1–14 (2019). https://doi.org/10.1177/2053951719860542
36. Wang, Y., Gong, S., Cao, Y., Lang, Y., Xu, X.: The effects of affective pedagogical agent in multimedia learning environments: a meta-analysis. Educ. Res. Rev. **38**, 100506 (2023). https://doi.org/10.1016/j.edurev.2022.100506
37. Ortega-Ochoa, E., Arguedas, M., Daradoumis, T.: Empathic pedagogical conversational agents: a systematic literature review. Br. J. Educ. Technol. **55**(3), 886–909 (2024). https://doi.org/10.1111/bjet.13413

Tailoring AI-Driven Reading Scaffolds to the Distinct Needs of Neurodiverse Learners

Soufiane Jhilal[1,2,3]([✉]) [iD], Eleonora Pasqua[4,5] [iD], Caterina Marchesi[4], Riccardo Corradi[6], and Martina Galletti[1,5] [iD]

[1] Sony Computer Sciences Laboratories, Paris, France
soufiane.jhilal@pasteur.fr, martina.galletti@sony.com
[2] Institut de l'Audition - Institut Pasteur, Paris, France
[3] Université Paris Cité, Paris, France
[4] Centro Ricerca e Cura di Roma, Rome, Italy
{e.pasqua,c.marchesi}@crc-balbuzie.it
[5] Sapienza Università di Roma, Rome, Italy
[6] I-Lab, Rome, Italy
r.corradi@Ilabroma.com

Abstract. Neurodiverse learners often require reading supports, yet increasing scaffold richness can sometimes overload attention and working memory rather than improve comprehension. Grounded in the Construction-Integration model and a contingent scaffolding perspective, we examine how structural versus semantic scaffolds shape comprehension and reading experience in a supervised inclusive context. Using an adapted reading interface, we compared four modalities: unmodified text, sentence-segmented text, segmented text with pictograms, and segmented text with pictograms plus keyword labels. In a within-subject pilot with 14 primary-school learners with special educational needs and disabilities, we measured reading comprehension using standardized questions and collected brief child- and therapist-reported experience measures alongside open-ended feedback. Results highlight heterogeneous responses as some learners showed patterns consistent with benefits from segmentation and pictograms, while others showed patterns consistent with increased coordination costs when visual scaffolds were introduced. Experience ratings showed limited differences between modalities, with some apparent effects linked to clinical complexity, particularly for perceived ease of understanding. Open-ended feedback of the learners frequently requested simpler wording and additional visual supports. These findings suggest that no single scaffold is universally optimal, reinforcing the need for calibrated, adjustable scaffolding and provide design implications for human–AI co-regulation in supervised inclusive reading contexts.

Keywords: AI for Special Education · Neurodiversity · Multimodal Scaffolding · Reading Comprehension · Inclusive Learning Technologies

E. G. Blanchard et al. (Eds.): AIED 2026, LNAI 16583, pp. 505–520, 2027.
https://doi.org/10.1007/978-3-032-29760-0_52

1 Introduction

Reading comprehension is a complex cognitive process that involves integrating information from the text, existing knowledge, and contextual cues to construct meaning [1]. This skill develops gradually, requiring learners to decode words, expand vocabulary, and synthesize textual ideas [2, 3]. For neurodiverse children with Special Educational Needs and Disabilities (SEND), such as learning disabilities, developmental disorders, and communication impairments, mastering reading comprehension poses additional challenges. These difficulties often originate from deficits in auditory and visual processing, language skills, attention, and working memory [4]. As a result, many learners experience persistent barriers to independent reading and to classroom participation when text is the dominant medium for instruction and assessment.

A long-standing response to these barriers is individualized intervention delivered by specialized professionals (e.g., speech-language therapy, targeted reading rehabilitation). While effective, this approach is resource-intensive and difficult to scale, especially where specialist availability is limited [5, 6]. This has motivated growing interest in technology-enhanced reading scaffolds that aim to make texts more accessible and provide additional cues for comprehension [7]. However, adding support is not inherently beneficial. In neurodiverse populations in particular, a scaffold that helps one learner may overload another by increasing sensory input, splitting attention, or introducing redundant information that competes with the primary reading task. The central challenge is therefore not simply to provide more supports, but to calibrate the type and intensity of support to the learner and the moment [8].

In this paper, we investigate how different scaffolds shape comprehension and reading experience for neurodiverse learners in a supervised reading context. We use an adapted version of the ARTIS reading interface [9–11] to present different forms of reading support, ranging from structural simplification through sentence segmentation to semantic scaffolds such as pictograms and pictogram-label pairs. In a within-subject pilot study with 14 primary school children with SEND, we combine comprehension outcomes with learner- and therapist-reported experience measures and feedback to characterize when particular scaffolds appear supportive versus distracting, and to derive design implications for calibrated, adjustable AI-enabled reading support in inclusive settings. The following sections review related work and the theoretical grounding that motivates these comparisons.

2 Related Work

AI has expanded what is possible in both educational [12] and clinical contexts [13, 14]. Yet comparatively less work has focused on AI-enabled supports that directly target language and reading comprehension for neurodiverse learners with SEND in supervised educational or rehabilitative practice.

Digital platforms increasingly use AI to support reading through features like summarization, question-answering, simplification, and semantic annotation. Earlier systems such as 3D Readers [15] and CACSR [16] illustrate valuable techniques (e.g., main-idea identification, self-questioning, inference generation) but were developed primarily for mainstream educational settings rather than heterogeneous rehabilitation-oriented contexts. RIDInet [17] platform represents a specialized effort in Italian telerehabilitation, providing inferential comprehension exercises but lacking multimodal augmentation. Overall, these approaches fail to address the multimodal needs of SEND learners, and to provide a framework suitable for clinical or scalable intervention.

A second strand of related work concerns semantic scaffolds that make key content easier to locate and interpret during reading. One common approach is to highlight keywords to direct attention to core concepts. Keyword cues have a long history in educational psychology [18, 19] and can now be automated with deep learning approaches [20]. However, for many SEND learners, linguistic cues alone may not fully address comprehension barriers. Research shows that students with dyslexia and language disorders often rely on non-verbal and visual-spatial abilities to compensate for linguistic difficulties [21–23], underscoring the value of multimodal interventions that provide visual support alongside textual information. Pictograms, which are simplified visual representations, are known to improve information processing, particularly in learners with language disorders, due to their concrete and universally interpretable nature [24]. On the technical side, text-to-pictogram translation has progressed from rule-based pipelines [25] to systems that incorporate data-driven neural approaches [26]. Despite this progress, relatively few studies examine keyword cues and pictogram scaffolds together as part of the reading experience for neurodiverse learners, or test whether increasing scaffold richness can backfire.

3 Theoretical Framework

Our study is grounded in the idea that scaffolds can reduce some demands while increasing others, so effects need not be monotonic. We adopt the Kintsch and van Dijk's Construction-Integration account of comprehension [27, 28], which theorizes that discourse comprehension proceeds in two main phases: (1) the construction phase, in which readers activate a network of propositions derived from textual input and prior knowledge, and (2) the integration phase, in which this network is refined into a coherent mental representation by resolving inconsistencies and strengthening relevant connections. This maps onto our scaffold mechanisms as sentence segmentation supports early processing by lowering linguistic density and enabling incremental construction, while pictograms and pictogram-label pairs target integration by grounding key concepts and making symbol-word mappings more explicit.

We also draw on a scaffolding perspective in which support is beneficial when it is contingent and aligned with the learner's current capabilities. In Vygotskian terms, assistance is most productive when it operates within the learner's zone of proximal development and supports gradual autonomy [29]. In supervised inclusive settings, such alignment is often actively managed by teachers and clinicians, who adjust task demands and supports in response to attention, fatigue, and comprehension difficulties.

Finally, we conceptualize multimodal scaffolds as a trade-off between grounding benefits and coordination costs. Visual symbols can reduce reliance on fragile decoding or lexical access, but they can also increase attentional switching and working-memory demands when learners must coordinate multiple representations or process redundant cues. This trade-off is particularly salient for neurodiverse learners for whom attentional and executive resources may be limited and fluctuate across time and tasks [4]. Accordingly, we interpret outcomes in terms of this balance and emphasize within-learner comparisons, rather than assuming average gains from adding features.

4 Methods

4.1 User Interface and Multimodal Presentation

ARTIS is an AI-powered reading support platform designed for supervised educational and rehabilitation sessions with neurodiverse learners, where a therapist or teacher can adjust scaffolding levels to the learner and session goals [9–11]. The text-to-pictogram pipeline used in this study is an adapted version of the original ARTIS workflow. The updated pipeline [30] is multilingual and context-aware. It first detects the input language and segments the text into sentences, then extracts the top candidate keywords per sentence using YAKE [31], prioritizing semantic salience. Each keyword is queried against ARASAAC [32], retrieving pictogram candidates accompanied by a semantic definition. A disambiguation module then selects the most contextually appropriate pictogram by matching sentence-context embeddings to pictogram definitions via cosine similarity using multilingual sentence transformers [33], reducing polysemy errors without manual intervention. Selected pictograms are then ordered to follow the original sentence structure and integrated into the interface so that pictograms align with the corresponding textual content. Prior to the study, clinicians performed a targeted review of representative outputs to ensure developmental and therapeutic appropriateness.

To examine progressively richer scaffolds, text was presented through four distinct modalities:

- **Modality A** serves as a baseline and shows the unmodified full text;
- **Modality B** segments the text into sentences for improved readability and reduced cognitive load;
- **Modality C** adds pictograms aligned to each segmented sentence, providing visual cues that aid semantic interpretation; and
- **Modality D** adds keyword labels beneath the pictograms, allowing for explicit associations between visual symbols and their corresponding textual terms.

These modalities are based on the Construction-Integration Model in which readers construct candidate propositions from text and integrate them into a coherent situation model by strengthening relevant links and resolving inconsistencies. Each modality was crafted to support these phases by reducing cognitive load and enhancing the formation of coherent propositional structures. By progressively augmenting the text from Modality A to Modality D with segmentation, imagery, and explicit labeling, the interface aligns with the Construction-Integration Model's emphasis on the interaction between surface structures, text base representations, and situation models, thereby scaffolding both micro-level sentence processing and macro-level discourse comprehension. Figure 1 illustrates the four modalities as presented in the interface.

Fig. 1. Interface screenshots showing the four reading modalities: plain text (A), sentence segmentation (B), segmentation with pictograms (C), and segmentation with pictograms and keyword labels (D).

4.2 Experimental Design

This exploratory pilot study examined how different scaffold types and levels of richness shape both reading comprehension and the reading experience for neurodiverse learners with SEND in a supervised context. We compared four interface modalities that progressively vary the form and intensity of support (Modality A–D), from unmodified text to sentence segmentation and symbol-based semantic cues (pictograms, with or without keyword labels). While this study focuses on the effects of these scaffolds on neurodiverse learners, a separate technical evaluation of the pipeline's multilingual performance, pictogram coverage, and semantic accuracy has also been conducted [30].

We used a within-subject design in which each participant experienced all four modalities. Passages were drawn from the standardized MT reading comprehension test bank [34], selected to match the participant's school grade. These materials were chosen for their well-established use in both didactic and clinical settings, and because they are standardized for primary education in Italy. Eight passages from the MT test bank were used in total, four per grade level (4th and 5th grade), each comprising 10–14 multiple-choice comprehension questions. Each participant completed one passage per modality, such that every modality was paired with a different text. To mitigate order and text effects, the assignment of passages to modalities was varied across participants, ensuring that no single text was consistently paired with the same modality. After each passage, participants answered the comprehension questions, with performance operationalized as the percentage of correct responses per modality.

To capture the lived experience of reading beyond accuracy alone, we collected brief post-condition questionnaires from both learners and supervising therapists. Learners reported perceived ease of reading and understanding, engagement, and concentration, and provided open-ended feedback on what would make the experience easier or more enjoyable. Therapists reported observations of motivation, attention, frustration, fatigue, and perceived usefulness of the support, alongside open-ended comments about difficulties encountered and any support or adjustments provided during the session. To minimize burden and avoid confusion for young participants, we used a short, age-appropriate learner questionnaire with a 3-point Likert scale (1 = Disagree, 2 = Neutral, 3 = Agree), while therapists completed a parallel set of items on a 5-point Likert scale (1 = Strongly disagree to 5 = Strongly agree) to allow for finer-grained clinical judgment. The learner questionnaire included only a small number of items to reduce fatigue and maintain attention. During completion, the supervising therapist guided the child through each question (e.g., clarifying the meaning and checking understanding), discussed how the child felt about the just-completed modality, and then recorded the child's response together with them. Table 1 summarizes all questionnaire items administered to learners and therapists.

Table 1. Questionnaire items for children and therapists. Children answered four Likert items on a 3-point scale (1–3) plus one open-ended question; therapists answered seven Likert items on a 5-point scale (1–5) plus two conditional open-ended follow-ups.

Children questions	
Question 1 - Likert (1–3)	The text was easy to read
Question 2 - Likert (1–3)	The text was easy to understand
Question 3 - Likert (1–3)	I was engaged while reading
Question 4 - Likert (1–3)	I was focused while reading
Question 5 - Open-ended	What would you change to make reading even easier or more fun in this mode?
Therapist questions	
Question 1 - Likert (1–5)	The child seems comfortable while reading
Question 2 - Likert (1–5)	The reading interface worked effectively
Question 3 - Open-ended	If you selected strongly disagree or disagree, specify what went wrong
Question 4 - Likert (1–5)	The child is attentive while reading
Question 5 - Likert (1–5)	The child was motivated in reading
Question 6 - Likert (1–5)	The child requested support from the operator
Question 7 - Open-ended	If you selected agree or strongly agree, specify what type of support was requested
Question 8 - Likert (1–5)	The child showed signs of fatigue in performing the activity
Question 9 - Likert (1–5)	The child showed signs of frustration in reading

4.3 Derived Measures of Comprehension Gains

In addition to raw comprehension scores, we computed two derived metrics to assess relative improvement (per participant) in performance across the scaffolded interface modalities. These metrics do not rely on the actual order in which modalities were presented to participants but instead reflect the logical progression of support from Modality A to Modality D.

Absolute Modality Gain represents the relative improvement in comprehension score for each modality compared to the participant's baseline in Modality A.

$$AbsoluteGain = \frac{Score_{currentmodality} - Score_{modalityA}}{Score_{modalityA}}$$

Relative Modality Gain measures the incremental improvement relative to the preceding modality, reflecting how each added support feature (sentence segmentation, pictograms, keyword labels) impacted comprehension.

$$RelativeGain = \frac{Score_{currentmodality} - Score_{priormodality}}{Score_{priormodality}}$$

These gain metrics normalize performance relative to each participant's own baseline or to the previous scaffolded step. They offer a more individualized assessment of how each added support feature contributes to comprehension, which is particularly valuable in small-sample, within-subject designs with heterogeneous cognitive profiles. In our dataset, comprehension scores were non-zero across all participants and modalities, so the ratio-based gain metrics were well-defined for all observations.

4.4 Participants

Fourteen neurodiverse primary-school children participated in this exploratory study. Participants were recruited through CRC (Centro Ricerca e Cura), a developmental rehabilitation center in Rome, Italy, where the study was conducted as part of supervised reading sessions. Participation occurred with informed consent from guardians and assent from children, and data were handled in a de-identified manner. The sample size (N = 14) and heterogeneity of profiles reflect the study's goal of generating early design evidence about how different scaffold types may help or overload different learners, rather than estimating population-level effects.

At the time of testing, children were 9–11 years old (M = 10.6), with 10 males and 4 females, and were enrolled in either 4th or 5th grade. All participants had at least one clinically established neurodevelopmental and/or learning-related diagnosis assigned by qualified professionals according to local clinical practice. These included:

- **Developmental Coordination Disorder (DCD)** characterized by impaired motor coordination that interferes with academic or daily functioning;
- **Attention-Deficit/Hyperactivity Disorder (ADHD)** marked by persistent inattention, hyperactivity, and/or impulsivity;
- **Language Disorder (LD)** involving significant difficulties in understanding or producing spoken language;
- **Specific Learning Disorder (SLD)** encompassing difficulties in reading, writing, or arithmetic (e.g., dyslexia, dysorthographia);
- **Mixed Developmental Disorder (MMD)** referring to combined delays in multiple developmental domains; and

- **Emotional Disorder (ED)** involving challenges in emotional regulation, such as heightened anxiety or mood related symptoms. Table 2 summarizes participant characteristics and diagnostic profiles.

Table 2. Participant profiles including demographic information and diagnosed conditions. Grade refers to school grade (4 = 4th grade, 5 = 5th grade). *X indicates the presence of a diagnosis; – indicates absence.*

ID	Gender	Age	Grade	DCD	ADHD	LD	SLD	MMD	ED
user1	Male	10	4	–	X	X	–	–	–
user2	Male	10	4	–	X	–	X	–	–
user3	Male	11	5	–	X	–	X	–	–
user4	Male	10	5	–	–	X	X	–	X
user5	Female	10	4	–	–	–	X	–	–
user6	Male	10	4	X	X	X	–	–	–
user7	Male	10	5	–	X	–	X	–	–
user8	Male	11	4	–	–	–	–	–	X
user9	Female	9	4	–	–	–	–	X	–
user10	Male	11	5	X	–	X	X	–	–
user11	Male	11	5	–	X	–	X	–	–
user12	Female	10	5	–	–	–	X	–	–
user13	Female	11	4	X	X	X	–	–	–
user14	Male	10	4	–	–	–	X	–	X

Clinical Complexity and Comorbidity. To better understand how individual clinical profiles influenced reading comprehension performance, we computed a comorbidity index for each participant, representing the total number of diagnosed neurodevelopmental or learning related conditions. This allowed us to assess how the degree of clinical complexity related to comprehension outcomes and different types of scaffolded support.

5 Results

We used mixed-design ANOVAs with Modality (A–D) as a within-participant factor and diagnostic indicator tested separately (presence vs. absence of each diagnosis) or comorbidity level as between-participant factors, to identify potentially meaningful patterns in scaffold response. Given the pilot scale (N = 14), these analyses are intended to highlight indicative trends that can inform interpretation and future hypothesis testing rather than to provide definitive population-level estimates. Prior to analysis, standard assumption checks were conducted for residual normality and homogeneity of variance. Post-hoc comparisons were corrected for multiple testing using a Bonferroni adjustment.

5.1 Diagnostic Group Differences in Performance

Mixed-design ANOVAs examining the effects of Modality and diagnosis on comprehension scores suggested systematic performance differences linked to several diagnoses (Fig. 2). In this sample, children with Developmental Coordination Disorder (DCD) scored lower than peers without DCD ($F(1,48) = 6.15$, $p = .017$), as did those with Language Disorders (LD) ($F(1,48) = 6.49$, $p = .014$), while learners with Emotional Disorders (ED) showed higher overall scores ($F(1,48) = 8.38$, $p = .006$). Children with DCD and LD tended to underperform across modalities, with an apparent increase in scores in Modality C. Conversely, children with ED performed relatively well in Modalities A and B (plain and segmented text), but their scores were lower in Modality C.

5.2 Diagnostic Modulation of Multimodal Benefit

To examine whether the relative benefit of multimodal scaffolds varied across diagnostic profiles, we analyzed both absolute gain from Modality A (Fig. 3) and relative gain between successive scaffolding steps (Fig. 4).

Relative Modality Gain showed interaction effects between Modality and diagnosis for ED ($F(3,48) = 4.18$, $p = .010$) and Language Disorders (LD) ($F(3,48) = 7.97$, $p < .001$), consistent with the possibility that scaffold effects differed across learner profiles. For ED, relative gain was near zero from Modality A to B (segmented text) but decreased in Modality C, suggesting that pictograms may have introduced additional coordination demands for some learners in this group. In contrast, learners with LD showed larger relative gains in Modalities B and C, consistent with the hypothesis that both sentence segmentation and pictograms can provide useful support in this sample. However, gains for the LD group decreased in Modality D relative to Modality C, suggesting that adding keyword labels may not provide additional benefit for some learners. Absolute Modality Gain also suggested interaction effects for DCD ($F(3,48) = 2.80$, $p = .050$) and a trend for LD ($F(3,48) = 2.39$, $p = .080$).

Overall, these patterns point to heterogeneous scaffold responses across modalities and learner profiles within this pilot sample.

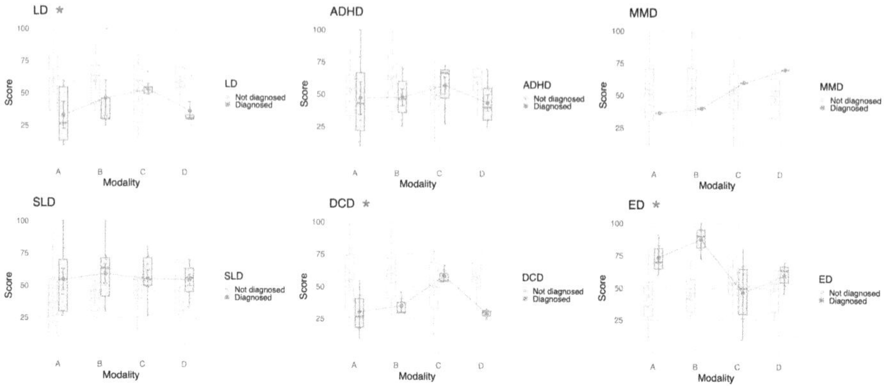

Fig. 2. Comprehension scores across modalities by diagnosis. *Red asterisk (*) = significant main effect of diagnosis.*

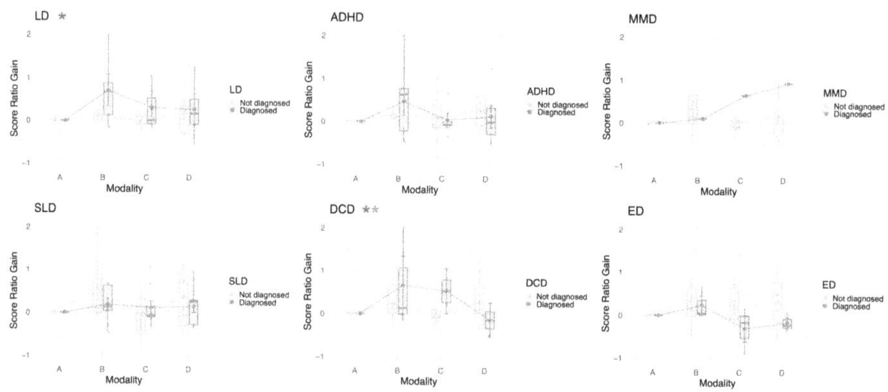

Fig. 3. Absolute Modality Gain by diagnosis. *Red asterisk (*) = significant main effect of diagnosis; Green asterisk (*) = significant interaction effect between Modality and diagnosis.*

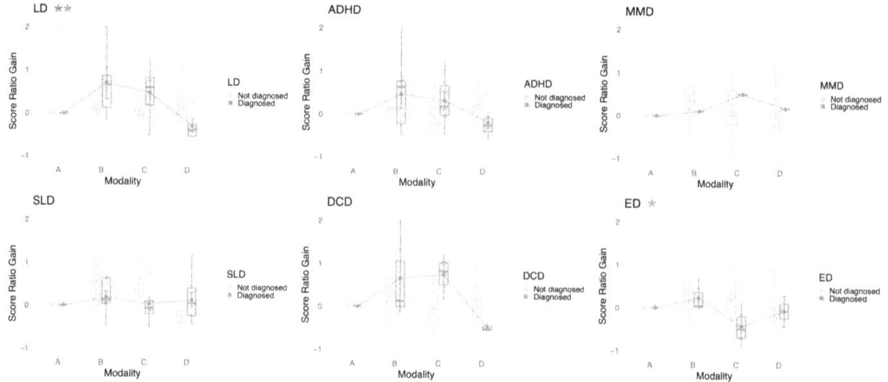

Fig. 4. Relative Modality Gain by diagnosis. *Red asterisk (*) = significant main effect of diagnosis; Green asterisk (*) = significant interaction effect between Modality and diagnosis.*

5.3 Impact of Comorbidity

We also examined whether clinical complexity, operationalized as the number of diagnosed conditions, was associated with comprehension or scaffold response. There was no main effect of comorbidity on comprehension scores ($F(2,44) = .81$, $p = .452$). However, an interaction between Modality and comorbidity was observed for Relative Modality Gain ($F(6,44) = 3.03$, $p = .014$), suggesting that learners with different levels of comorbidity showed different patterns of change across scaffold steps (Fig. 5).

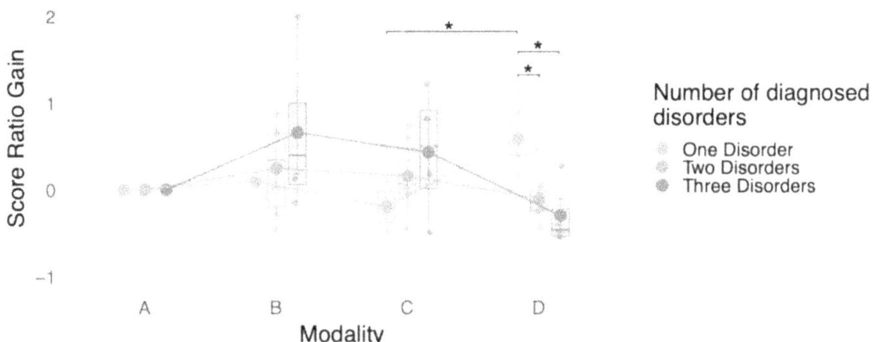

Fig. 5. Relative Modality Gain by number of diagnosed disorders across modalities. *Asterisk* (*) *indicates a significant post-hoc comparison.*

5.4 Qualitative Insights from Learner Feedback

Across the learner and therapist Likert-scale questionnaires, we observed limited variation in ratings between modalities for the group as a whole. However, a distinct pattern emerged regarding clinical complexity for the children's Question 1 ("*The text was easy to understand*", see Fig. 6). Ratings indicated that children with the highest comorbidity (3 diagnosed conditions) perceived the texts as harder to understand compared to peers with fewer diagnoses. This difficulty appeared most acute in the baseline condition (Modality A). Specifically, the 3-disorder subgroup rated the unmodified text notably lower than the scaffolded conditions (B, C, and D), suggesting that for clinically more complex learners, the baseline presentation was experienced as harder to follow relative to segmented and multimodally scaffolded variants.

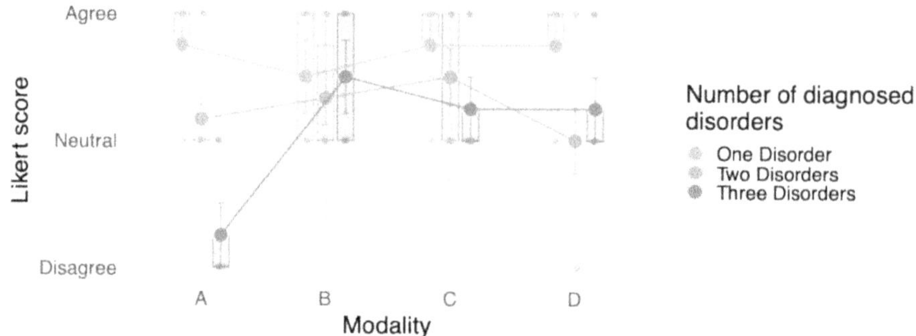

Fig. 6. Children's Likert scale ratings for Question 1 *"The text was easy to understand"* by number of diagnosed disorders across modalities.

Complementing these ratings, the open-ended responses provided additional context about perceived barriers and preferences. When asked what would make reading easier or more enjoyable, children most frequently requested simpler words, pointing to the overall difficulty of the texts. The second most common suggestion was to include more drawings or images, consistent with a perceived benefit or preference for visual support in the reading material.

6 Discussion

This exploratory pilot examined how progressively richer reading scaffolds (sentence segmentation, pictograms, and pictogram-keyword pairs) relate to comprehension and reading experience in a supervised SEND context. Rather than showing a uniform benefit of adding support, the results point to heterogeneous scaffold responses that vary across diagnostic profiles and clinical complexity, consistent with our framing of a trade-off between grounding benefits and coordination costs.

On comprehension outcomes, several diagnoses were associated with overall performance differences across modalities, indicating that baseline comprehension levels differed by profile in this sample. Beyond these main effects, analyses of gain metrics suggested that the pattern of change across scaffold steps may differ by learner group.

Children with Language Disorders (LD) appear to benefit the most from added scaffolds, especially when text was segmented (Modality B) and augmented with pictograms (Modality C). These results are in line with previous research suggesting that learners with decoding or attentional difficulties gain from structural simplification and visual cues [35, 36]. However, their benefit diminished in Modality D, where keyword labels were added beneath pictograms. This pattern suggests that additional textual information, despite being supportive in principle, may become redundant or even distracting when cognitive or linguistic resources are limited.

Conversely, learners with Emotional Disorders (ED) showed an opposite trend: they performed relatively well in Modality A (raw text) and Modality B (segmented text), but their performance declined in Modality C. The introduction of visual elements may have disrupted their cognitive processing, either due to increased sensory load or reduced ability to integrate multimodal content. This highlights the need to avoid over-scaffolding for some learners, as even well-intentioned supports can become counterproductive when not aligned with individual processing preferences.

Interestingly, learners with Developmental Coordination Disorder (DCD) and Language Disorders (LD), who initially showed lower performance, achieved comparable scores to peers in Modality C. One possible interpretation is that the addition of pictograms without text labels may have helped them bypass linguistic and decoding challenges by offering a more intuitive route to meaning-making. This could mean that visual support can enhance accessibility without overwhelming cognitive resources.

Comorbidity analyses similarly highlighted variability in scaffold response. Although comorbidity level was not associated with overall comprehension scores, it did modulate Relative Modality Gain, indicating that learners with different levels of clinical complexity showed different trajectories across scaffold steps. In the qualitative questionnaires, most Likert items did not show any clear modality differences. The exception was the children's *"text was easy to understand"* item (Fig. 6), which seems to show lower ratings in the 3-disorder subgroup, particularly for the baseline presentation (Modality A). Together, these results suggest that clinical complexity may relate not only to performance but also to perceived ease, and that baseline presentations can be harder to follow for some learners with more complex profiles.

Open-ended feedback provides additional context for these quantitative patterns. Children most frequently requested simpler words, reflecting the general difficulty of the standardized passages, and also commonly requested more drawings or images. While these comments do not establish efficacy, they indicate that visual supports are salient and often perceived as desirable, reinforcing the importance of offering scaffolds that can be adjusted to learner needs and tolerance for added information.

Overall, the findings argue against a one-size-fits-all approach to reading support in heterogeneous SEND populations and highlight several design implications for AI-driven reading interventions. First, scaffolds should dynamically adapt to individual learner profiles rather than relying solely on diagnostic categories, as substantial variability was observed even within groups. Second, systems should carefully balance informational support with cognitive load, as additional visual or semantic cues may either support comprehension or lead to overload depending on the learner. Finally, AI-driven interfaces should allow for adjustable scaffold intensity, enabling therapists or learners themselves to tailor the level and type of support to situational needs. However, these findings should be interpreted in light of the study's scope. As noted in the Participants section, this was an exploratory pilot with a small and clinically diverse sample, intended to explore patterns of differential response across scaffolds rather than produce population-level estimates. This approach enabled in-depth, diagnosis-specific observations that may be overlooked in larger but less targeted studies. Nonetheless, the limited sample size reduces statistical power, and diagnostic categories were not evenly represented. The absence of a neurotypical control group limits comparative interpretation. Therapist supervision, essential for accessibility and engagement, may have influenced task dynamics. Addressing these limitations in subsequent research, will be essential to establishing evidence-based guidelines for personalized reading support in educational technology.

7   Conclusion

This exploratory pilot study evaluated four progressively scaffolded reading interface modalities in a supervised SEND context, combining comprehension outcomes with learner- and therapist-reported experience measures. The results suggest that no single support modality is universally effective: optimal scaffolding depends on diagnosis and clinical complexity, with some learners benefiting from rich multimodal reinforcement and others from simpler structural interventions. This variability underscores the importance of dynamic learner modeling in future AI-education systems, enabling real-time adaptation of support strategies to maximize engagement and comprehension. Building on these preliminary insights, future research will scale to larger and more balanced cohorts, explore longitudinal effects, and integrate adaptive algorithms capable of adjusting scaffolding in real time based on continuous learner performance and feedback.

References

1. Hulme, C., Snowling, M.J.: Learning to read: what we know and what we need to understand better. Child Dev. Perspect. **7**, 1–5 (2013). https://doi.org/10.1111/cdep.12005
2. Scarborough, H., Fletcher-Campbell, F., Soler, J., Reid, G.: Connecting early language and literacy to later reading (dis)abilities: Evidence, theory, and practice. Approaching difficulties in literacy development: assessment, pedagogy, and programmes 23–39 (2009)
3. Castles, A., Rastle, K., Nation, K.: Ending the reading wars: reading acquisition from novice to expert. Psychol. Sci. Public Interest **19**, 5–51 (2018). https://doi.org/10.1177/152910061 8772271
4. Capin, P., Cho, E., Miciak, J., et al.: Examining the reading and cognitive profiles of students with significant reading comprehension difficulties. Learn. Disabil. Q. **44**, 183–196 (2021). https://doi.org/10.1177/0731948721989973
5. Billingsley, B.S.: Special education teacher retention and attrition: a critical analysis of the research literature. J. Spec. Educ. **38**, 39–55 (2004). https://doi.org/10.1177/002246690403 80010401
6. Squires, K.: Addressing the shortage of speech-language pathologists in school settings. J. Am. Acad. Spec. Educ. Prof. 131–137 (2013)
7. Yang, Y., Chen, L., He, W., et al.: Artificial intelligence for enhancing special education for K-12: a decade of trends, themes, and global insights (2013–2023). Int. J. Artif. Intell. Educ. **35**, 1129–1177 (2025). https://doi.org/10.1007/s40593-024-00422-0
8. Cesaroni, V., Pasqua, E., Bisconti, P., Galletti, M.: A participatory strategy for AI ethics in education and rehabilitation grounded in the capability approach. In: Cristea AI, Walker, E., Lu, Y., et al. (eds.): Artificial Intelligence in Education, pp 77–84. Springer, Cham (2025)
9. Galletti, M., Pasqua, E., Calanca, M., et al.: ARTIS: a digital interface to promote the rehabiliatation of text comprehension difficulties through Artificial Intelligence (2024)
10. Galletti, M., Pasqua, E., Bianchi, F., et al.: A reading comprehension interface for students with learning disorders. In: International Conference on Multimodal Interaction, Paris France, pp 282–287. ACM (2023)
11. Galletti, M.: A computational framework for AI-driven reading comprehension rehabilitation for neurodiverse learners. Università degli Studi di Roma "La Sapienza" (2026)
12. Wang, S., Wang, F., Zhu, Z., et al.: Artificial intelligence in education: a systematic literature review. Expert Syst. Appl. **252**, 124167 (2024). https://doi.org/10.1016/j.eswa.2024.124167

13. Zhang, Y., Weng, Y., Lund, J.: Applications of explainable artificial intelligence in diagnosis and surgery. Diagnostics **12**, 237 (2022). https://doi.org/10.3390/diagnostics12020237

14. Jhilal, S., Marchesotti, S., Thirion, B., et al.: Implantable Neural Speech Decoders: Recent Advances, Future Challenges. Neurorehabil Neural Repair (2025). https://doi.org/10.1177/15459683251369468

15. Johnson-Glenberg, M.C.: Web-based reading comprehension instruction: three studies of 3D-readers. In: Reading Comprehension Strategies: Theories, Interventions, and Technologies, Mahwah, NJ, US, pp 293–324. Lawrence Erlbaum Associates Publishers (2007)

16. Kim, A.-H., Vaughn, S., Klingner, J.K., et al.: Improving the reading comprehension of middle school students with disabilities through computer-assisted collaborative strategic reading. Remedial Spec. Educ. **27**, 235–249 (2006)

17. RIDInet. https://www.anastasis.it/ridinet/. Accessed 2 Feb 2026

18. McDaniel, M.A., Pressley, M.: Keyword and context instruction of new vocabulary meanings: effects on text comprehension and memory. J. Educ. Psychol. **81**, 204–213 (1989). https://doi.org/10.1037/0022-0663.81.2.204

19. Seki, Y., Akahori, K., Sakamoto, T.: Using key words to facilitate text comprehension. Educ. Technol. Res. **16**, 11–21 (1993)

20. Nadim, M., Akopian, D., Matamoros, A.: A comparative assessment of unsupervised keyword extraction tools. IEEE Access **11**, 144778–144798 (2023)

21. Danis, E., Nader, A.-M., Degré-Pelletier, J., Soulières, I.: Semantic and visuospatial fluid reasoning in school-aged autistic children. J. Autism Dev. Disord. **53**, 4719–4730 (2023). https://doi.org/10.1007/s10803-022-05746-1

22. Jhilal, S., Molinaro, N., Klimovich-Gray, A.: Non-verbal skills in auditory word processing: implications for typical and dyslexic readers. Lang. Cogn. Neurosci. **40**, 341–359 (2025). https://doi.org/10.1080/23273798.2024.2438012

23. Superbia-Guimarães, L., Bader, M., Camos, V.: Can children and adolescents with ADHD use attention to maintain verbal information in working memory? PLoS ONE **18**, e0282896 (2023). https://doi.org/10.1371/journal.pone.0282896

24. Vaschalde, C., Trial, P., Esperança-Rodier, E., et al.: Automatic pictogram generation from speech to help the implementation of a mediated communication. In: Conference on Barrier-free Communication. Geneva, Switzerland (2018)

25. Vandeghinste, V., Sevens, I.S.L., Eynde, F.V.: Translating text into pictographs. Nat. Lang. Eng. **23**, 217–244 (2015). https://doi.org/10.1017/S135132491500039X

26. Pereira, J.A., Macêdo, D., Zanchettin, C., et al.: PictoBERT: transformers for next pictogram prediction. Expert Syst. Appl. **202**, 117231 (2022)

27. Kintsch, W.: The role of knowledge in discourse comprehension: a construction-integration model. Psychol. Rev. **95**, 163–182 (1988). https://doi.org/10.1037/0033-295X.95.2.163

28. Kintsch, W., van Dijk, T.A.: Toward a model of text comprehension and production. Psychol. Rev. **85**, 363–394 (1978). https://doi.org/10.1037/0033-295X.85.5.363

29. Vygotsky, L.S.: Mind in Society: Development of Higher Psychological Processes. Harvard University Press (1978)

30. Jhilal, S., Galletti, M.: Robust Multilingual Text-to-Pictogram Mapping for Scalable Reading Rehabilitation (2026). https://doi.org/10.48550/arXiv.2603.24536

31. YAKE. https://github.com/INESCTEC/yake. Accessed 5 Feb 2026

32. ARASAAC. https://beta.arasaac.org/. Accessed 2 Feb 2026

33. SentenceTransformers. https://sbert.net/. Accessed 5 Feb 2026

34. Cornoldi, C., Colpo, G., Carretti, B.: Nuove prove di lettura MT per la scuola media inferiore. Giunti EDU, Firenze (1998)
35. Lorch, R.F., Jr., Lorch, E.P.: Effects of organizational signals on text-processing strategies. J. Educ. Psychol. **87**, 537–544 (1995). https://doi.org/10.1037/0022-0663.87.4.537
36. Chun, D.M., Plass, J.L.: Research on text comprehension in multimedia environments (1997). https://doi.org/10.64152/10125/25004

Should AI Ask First? Investigating the Effects of Proactive vs Reactive AI Mentoring in Self-directed Learning

Khaoula Otmani[1,2]($\boxtimes$)(iD), Anna Bodonhelyi[1,2](iD), Babette Bühler[1,2](iD), and Enkelejda Kasneci[1,2](iD)

[1] Human-Centered Technologies for Learning, Technical University of Munich, Munich, Germany
{khaoula.otmani,anna.bodonhelyi,babette.buehler,enkelejda.kasneci}@tum.de
[2] Munich Center for Machine Learning (MCML), Munich, Germany

Abstract. Motivated by decades of research on tutoring and help-seeking in intelligent learning environments, we ask an important but underexplored question: *Should an AI mentor wait for learners to ask for help, or ask first?* We compare proactive and reactive *initiative policies* in a between-subjects experiment ($N = 81$) using a 14-min instructional video about Bayes' theorem. The proactive mentor provided brief prompts on natural task boundaries using lightweight personalization and a cooldown mechanism to prevent overload. Proactive mentoring significantly increased interaction volume (10.5 vs. 2.9 messages on average, $p < .001$), reduced no-interaction rate (8.1% vs. 31.8%, $p = .013$), and reduced off-topic messaging (2.0% vs. 6.8% of messages, $p < .01$), shifting communication towards help-accepting behaviors and sustained conversations. Cluster analysis revealed a distinct help-accepting profile (observed only in the proactive condition). Knowledge gains showed a non-significant upward trend for the reactive group. The learners in the reactive group reported greater perceived choice and control, highlighting a design trade-off between interaction and agency. Together, these findings identify initiative-coupled scaffolding policy as a key determinant of help-seeking and learner-AI interaction patterns in self-directed learning settings.

Keywords: Self-directed learning · Help-seeking · Pedagogical conversational agent · LLM-based learning systems

1 Introduction

The effectiveness of one-to-one tutoring compared to conventional classroom instruction, as demonstrated by Bloom's "2-sigma" finding [4], has motivated decades of research into scalable forms of individualized support. While achieving tutoring-level learning outcomes at scale remains a long-term goal, prior work suggests that tutoring effectiveness depends not only on instructional quality, but

© The Author(s), under exclusive license to Springer Nature Switzerland AG 2027
E. G. Blanchard et al. (Eds.): AIED 2026, LNAI 16583, pp. 521–535, 2027.
https://doi.org/10.1007/978-3-032-29760-0_53

also on learners' consistent engagement, timely help-seeking, and willingness to accept support [3]. Recent advances in large language and multimodal models promise to change this landscape [22]. These models can act as conversational mentors, explaining, prompting, and scaffolding learners during self-directed study. Prior work further suggests that LLM-powered learning environments can influence learners' motivation and engagement [30]. However, early empirical work shows that many learners still underuse such AI tutors, mirroring the same help-seeking asymmetries observed in traditional intelligent tutoring systems (ITSs). In prior studies of Pedagogical Conversational Agents (PCAs), for example, a majority of learners engaged minimally or not at all with the available support [5,17,19,31]. These behavioral patterns suggest that simply providing an AI mentor does not guarantee its efficient use; learners must choose to and ideally know how to interact with it. To address this gap, research must move beyond system capability toward the dynamics of *initiative* in human–AI learning interactions: who speaks first, when, and why. The decision to let learners request support or have the AI proactively offer it has far-reaching implications for engagement, autonomy, and equity. In self-paced environments, overly reactive systems risk leaving less confident or less experienced learners unsupported, while overly proactive ones may disrupt flow or reduce perceived control and satisfaction [13]. Motivated by these challenges, we investigate an important but underexplored design question: how does the initiative policy of an AI mentor, reactive versus proactive, shape learners' engagement, communication behaviors, and short-term learning in self-directed settings? Rather than evaluating tutoring-level effectiveness, our goal is to isolate initiative-coupled scaffolding as an interaction control variable and examine how it influences learners' use of available support. To investigate this question, we introduce a model-agnostic experimental environment that allows systematic comparison of proactive and reactive mentoring policies in video-based learning. In our study, we instantiated a proactive policy that schedules brief, context-aware prompts at low cognitive load timing, and compared it against a purely reactive, on-demand baseline in a between-subjects experiment. Rather than proposing a new tutoring system per se, we make an empirical contribution by investigating how initiative shapes learner interaction and outcomes, and for whom proactive AI support is most beneficial or disruptive. We organize our investigation around four main research questions:

RQ1 Interaction and communication: *How does proactive AI mentoring affect learners' engagement and communication patterns compared to reactive mentoring?*

RQ2 Interaction profiles: *What distinct learner–AI interaction trajectories emerge under different initiative policies?*

RQ3 Learning outcomes: *How do different interaction trajectories relate to short-term learning signals in a single-session setting?*

RQ4 Learner experience: *How do initiative policies trade off engagement, autonomy, and perceived control?*

2   Related Work

Help Seeking and Metacognitive Support in Educational Technology.
A persistent challenge in self-directed and online learning is that some learners underuse available help, even when it demonstrably improves outcomes [9,26]. Research in Intelligent Tutoring Systems (ITS) shows that effective help-seeking is not only a matter of access but also of *metacognitive regulation*, knowing when and how to request assistance [2,27–29]. Learners often fail to recognize impasses, delay help requests, or ignore hints [2,17,19,28,31,32]. Adaptive scaffolding and self-regulation prompts can partly mitigate these tendencies [6,29], yet their effectiveness depends strongly on timing and user engagement [1,10,25]. These findings motivate systems that not only make help available but also anticipate when learners are most receptive to support.

Proactivity, Timing, and Interruption Etiquette in Learner Support.
Proactive systems initiate interactions without explicit user requests, lowering the activation threshold for engagement. In educational settings, proactive interventions can re-engage learners who would otherwise remain passive [33], but may also risk disrupting flow or reducing perceived autonomy [1,13,21,25]. HCI research on interruption management demonstrates that the *timing* of an intervention is often more important than its content: interruptions are less disruptive at natural task boundaries or periods of lower cognitive load [1,11,21,25]. Large observational studies of MOOC and lecture videos show systematic engagement patterns [16] and demonstrate that students use playback controls to self-pace and regulate cognitive load [24]; other work links transient confusion to productive learning when it is detected and resolved [15,23]. Recent multimodal work further shows that aware and unaware mind wandering during lecture viewing can be detected from behavioral and physiological signals, underscoring the importance of learner-state sensitivity in video-based support systems [7,8]. These findings support designs that leverage player events and engagement curves as real-time signals for adaptive interventions. While these bodies of research collectively advance our understanding of equitable, metacognitive, and timely AI-supported learning toward Bloom's ideal of scalable tutoring, they underexplore the direct empirical effects of initiative policies, specifically, proactive versus reactive mentoring, on engagement, communication dynamics, and outcomes in self-directed video-based contexts. Our work addresses this gap through a controlled between-subjects experiment to inform more effective, learner-centered AI designs.

3   Design of Proactive AI-Based Tutoring

Our proactive mentoring agent builds upon a previously developed context-aware reactive mentoring framework introduced by [5], extending its capabilities through the integration of a proactive policy mechanism. Importantly, the system is not intended as a novel tutoring solution but as an experimental instantiation that isolates initiative-coupled scaffolding as an interaction

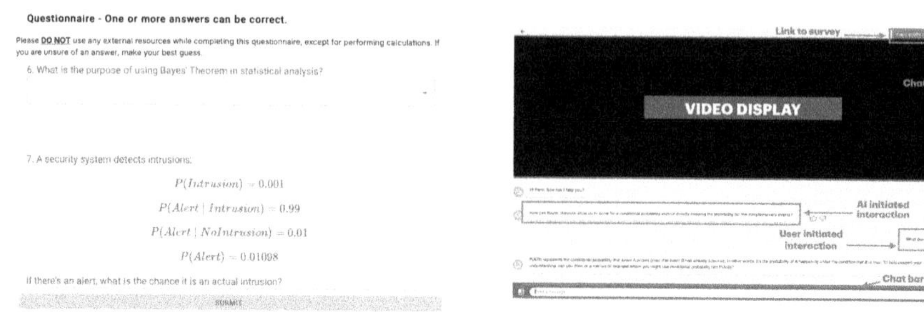

Fig. 1. Integrated 14-items knowledge questionnaire (left), Mentor interface with an example chat interaction (right).

control variable. In realistic self-directed learning settings, initiative and scaffolding content are tightly coupled: initiating an interaction necessarily entails delivering pedagogical material. Our design reflects this coupling rather than attempting to artificially decouple it. Throughout this paper, we use the term initiative-coupled scaffolding to refer to mentoring policies in which pedagogical actions are either system-initiated (proactive) or learner-initiated (reactive). Proactive initiative entails the system initiating instructional acts, while reactive initiative requires learners to explicitly request them. The proactive design is based on two fundamental principles derived from the literature: *temporal optimization* [1,21,23,25], and *personalization* [14,23]. Research has demonstrated that proactive interventions are most effective when delivered during moments of low cognitive load [1,11,25], while personalized interaction patterns significantly improve learning outcomes by adapting to individual needs and preferences [14,23]. The timing and content of the interactions are decided based on a multifactorial algorithm. For both conditions, our tutor uses GPT-4o with a custom prompt inspired by ChatGPT's study mode prompt.[1]

Content-Based Timing. The timing of proactive interactions in our system is governed by a multi-factor algorithm that balances content-based and user-specific signals. This approach ensures that interventions are both contextually relevant and minimally disruptive to the learning process. We strategically scheduled all proactive interventions to be at the very start of a new chapter in the video. In our current implementation, we utilize publicly available YouTube chapter segmentation points to separate the video into chapters. These transition periods to a new chapter represent ideal opportunities for knowledge consolidation through proactive questioning, as learners are not deeply involved in the new chapter yet [11].

User Adaptation. To avoid users being distracted by too many proactive interruptions, we use pre-test performance as an initialization parameter to person-

---

[1] https://simonwillison.net/2025/Jul/29/openai-introducing-study-mode/.

alize interaction frequency. Each pre-test question is mapped to specific video segments, enabling the system to create a personalized intervention schedule. Learners demonstrating strong prior knowledge for a specific section are less likely to receive a proactive question. User interactions with the mentor also trigger a cooldown mechanism (cooldown: **3** min) to avoid a proactive interruption immediately after a user-initiated conversation and to prevent overload. Lastly, the video player is continuously monitored to detect confusion or difficulty in real-time. This design is motivated by prior work showing that attentional states such as mind wandering during lecture viewing can be inferred from multimodal behavioral signals, making learner-state-aware support a promising direction for video-based learning systems [7]. Behaviors such as pausing or rewinding specific segments trigger the dynamic scheduling of a content-specific intervention at the end of the section (if not in a cooldown period). The content is based on the transcript right before and after the event (pause, rewind). The content and timing of the proactive interruptions are summarised in Fig. 2.

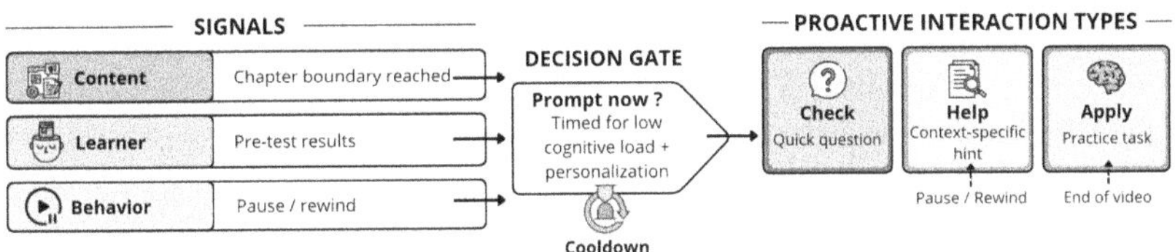

Fig. 2. Conceptual overview of the initiative-coupled proactive scaffolding.

4 Experimental Setup

4.1 Study Design

We conducted a between-subjects, pre/post experimental study to evaluate how the initiative policy of an AI mentor (Reactive vs. Proactive) influences interactions and learning during a short video lecture on Bayes' theorem. Participants were recruited via Prolific and randomly assigned to one of two conditions. The *Reactive* mentor provided assistance only upon learner request (on-demand help), whereas the *Proactive* mentor initiated brief pedagogical interventions during the video (Fig. 1). Thus, conditions differed in how support was surfaced (system-initiated vs. learner-initiated) while drawing from the same underlying mentor capabilities and prompt.

Learning outcomes were assessed with a 14-item knowledge test administered immediately before (pre-test) and after (post-test) the instructional video. The 14 knowledge-test items were designed to span multiple levels of cognitive processing. The instrument included items targeting conceptual knowledge and recall (e.g., identifying the correct formula for Bayes' theorem), as well as items assessing procedural application and transfer (e.g., applying Bayes' theorem to a novel scenario), as shown in Fig. 1. The participants received +1 point per item, yielding a possible range from 0 to max-score = 14. To quantify individual learning, we calculated each participant's normalized Hake gain [18] using the observed pre-test and post-test scores and the theoretical maximum of 14.

All participants completed an identical four-phase protocol, (1) Pre-test consisting of 14-item assessment of Bayesian concepts, (2) Video watching of an instructional video on Bayes' theorem and interacting with the mentor, (3) Post-test consisting of the same 14-item assessment as the pre-test, with question order permuted to reduce memory effects, (4) Final survey capturing perceived control, confusion, frustration, usability, workload, and other subjective experiences.

4.2   Participants

A total of 100 participants were recruited through Prolific (53 male, 44 female, 3 non-binary). Inclusion criteria were fluency in English, the ability to use a computer or laptop, and no prior participation in one of our system studies. Participants were randomly assigned to conditions (Reactive: 53; Proactive: 47). To ensure data validity, we excluded participants who did not pass the attention check and manually reviewed the chat for indications of malpractice (e.g., copying test items into the chat), excluding participants if applicable. After exclusions for the criteria above, the analysed dataset contained 81 participants (Reactive: $n = 44$, average age: 30.68, average pre-test score: 5.64, percentage of females: 47.7; Proactive: $n = 37$, average age: 31.92, average pre-test score: 6.08, percentage of females: 37.8).

5   Results

5.1   RQ1: Interaction and Communication

Interaction Volume and Breadth. To address RQ1, we analysed interaction logs to characterise how participants engaged with the AI mentors. We operationalized interaction using complementary behavioral proxies: the number of messages exchanged with the mentor, the proportion of participants with no interaction, and conversation depth. Total message counts differed markedly between conditions: participants in the Proactive condition exchanged substantially more messages with the mentor ($\overline{M} = 10.51$ messages per participant) than those in the Reactive condition ($\overline{M} = 2.89$), a statistically significant difference (Mann–Whitney U test, $p < .001$; Fig. 3). To better understand how proactive initiative shaped interaction dynamics, we manually decomposed message activity in the Proactive condition into two categories: (i) *proactive-elicited* messages, defined as messages produced within conversational threads initiated by a proactive mentor prompt, and (ii) *user-initiated* messages, defined as interactions independently initiated by the learner. Because proactive prompts create interaction opportunities by design, we report user-initiated messages separately as a proxy for voluntary help-seeking.

Although most interactions in the Proactive condition were elicited by mentor prompts ($\overline{M} = 8.73$ proactive-elicited messages), participants continued to initiate interactions independently ($\overline{M} = 1.78$ user-initiated messages). While the number of user-initiated messages was lower than in the Reactive condition ($\overline{M} = 2.89$), this difference did not reach statistical significance ($p = .084$), and the effect size was small ($d = 0.36$). Importantly, this reduction occurred alongside a substantial increase in total interaction volume, indicating a shift in conversational leadership rather than a suppression of learner initiative. Interaction differences were also reflected in participation breadth and time on task. The proportion of participants who never interacted with the mentor was significantly higher in the Reactive condition (14/44, 31.8%) than in the Proactive condition (3/37, 8.1%). The relative likelihood of interacting with the mentor was 3.92 times higher in the Proactive condition, a difference confirmed by Fisher's exact test ($p = .013$).

Finally, we examined conversation structure by segmenting learner–mentor interactions into topical sub-conversations occurring at distinct time points in the video. Learners in the Proactive condition engaged in significantly deeper conversations; we measure depth as the number of turns per topic ($\overline{M} = 2.24$ vs. 1.26, $p < .001$), and explored a greater number of distinct topics ($\overline{M} = 4.30$ vs. 1.64, $p < .001$). These findings suggest that proactive mentoring created opportunities to engage with a broader range of topics and sustain interaction within each topic for longer. In the absence of such guidance, reactive learners interacted minimally, rarely engaged in answer-based dialogue, and conducted short, isolated exchanges.

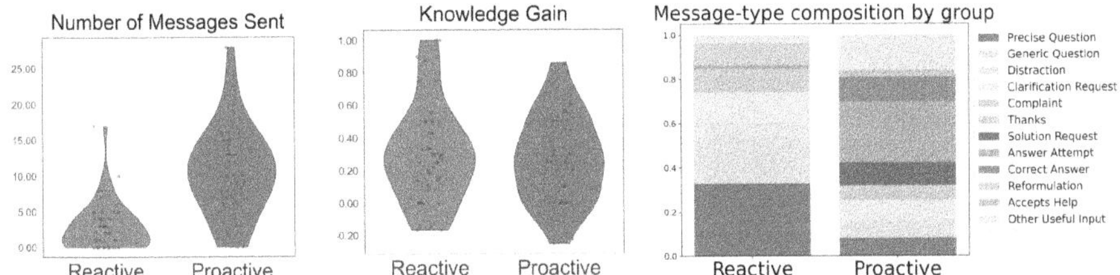

Fig. 3. Distribution of participant message counts by condition.

Fig. 4. Distribution of normalized learning gains by condition.

Fig. 5. Message-type composition by condition.

Communication Patterns. We developed a message coding scheme adapted from prior work [20] that captures both communicative function (e.g., questions, clarifications, acknowledgements) and cognitive orientation (e.g., precise versus generic questions). User messages were coded using a multilabel approach (Table 1), allowing a single message to receive multiple codes when appropriate. Two independent coders annotated the data, achieving substantial inter-rater reliability (IRR = 0.79, Cohen's k). Analysis of message types revealed qualitatively distinct communication patterns across conditions (Fig. 5).

A two-sample proportion test with FDR correction revealed significant differences in several message types between the Reactive and Proactive groups. The Reactive group used *Precise Question* (32.6%), *Generic Question* (20.5%), and *Reformulation* (9.8%) significantly more than the Proactive group (all $p < .01$). Conversely, the Proactive group used message types *Accepts Help* (11.7%) and *Other Useful Input* (14.5%) more frequently than the Reactive group (all FDR $p < .001$). Moreover, *Distraction* (6.8%) was significantly lower for the Proactive group ($p < .01$). Message types *Answer Attempt* (24.6%), *Solution Request* (9.4%), *Correct Answer* (10.2%), were by design also significantly more observed in the Proactive condition (all FDR $p < .001$). No significant differences were observed for *Clarification Request, Complaint,* or *Thanks* types. Differences in help acceptance were particularly pronounced. When normalized by the number of mentor help offers, the Reactive group showed a near-zero mean acceptance ratio ($M = 0.013$, $SD = 0.057$), whereas the Proactive group accepted help at substantially higher rates ($M = 0.232$, $SD = 0.245$), a statistically significant difference ($p < .001$). This indicates that proactive initiative not only increased opportunities for help but also elicited greater learner responsiveness to such support. These results suggest that the conversation in the proactive condition was guided by the proactive mentor, scaffolding the knowledge through proactive questioning and help offers.

Table 1. Message coding scheme for learner–AI interactions.

Message Type	Comment
Precise Question	Asks a precise or specific question to the AI mentor
Generic Question	Asks for a summary, simplification, or a basic question
Distraction	Distracting due to lecture-unrelated questions or comments
Clarification Request	Clarification question or utterance of confusion
Complaint	Complaints about task difficulty
Thanks	Thanks the AI mentor
Solution Request	Asks directly for the solution instead of trying
Answer Attempt	Attempts to answer a question
Correct Answer	Provides a correct answer
Reformulation	Reformulates previous statement, checks their own knowledge
Accepts Help	Accepts help from the AI mentor
Other Useful Input	Other useful input for the conversation

5.2   RQ2: Interaction Profiles

To assess the impact of initiative policy on individual learners, we conducted an exploratory clustering analysis based on frequencies of user message codes. This analysis is intended to generate hypotheses about emergent interaction profiles rather than to establish stable learner typologies. Given small cluster sizes, we treat cluster labels as descriptive summaries rather than stable learner types. To reduce the risk that clusters merely reflected structurally induced answer behavior in the Proactive condition, we excluded response-oriented codes (*Correct Answer*, *Attempt Answer*, and *Solution Request*) and normalized the *Accept Help* code prior to clustering. We applied K-means clustering to the remaining user message codes. The choice of K = 4 was guided by the Elbow and Calinski–Harabasz index diagnostics. The resulting clusters (Fig. 6, Table 2) correspond to four qualitatively distinct interaction patterns. The majority of participants were assigned to Cluster 1 (Low-Interaction), characterized by minimal interaction and predominantly composed of learners from the Reactive condition. Two smaller clusters, Cluster 0 (Passive–Distracted, N = 4) and Cluster 2 (Active Clarifiers, N = 6), exhibited more specialized behaviors but were limited in size, constraining the generalizability of their profiles. Notably, a help-accepting interaction pattern (Cluster 3) emerged exclusively under proactive mentoring, indicating an interaction profile associated with proactive initiative rather than spontaneously adopted, and accounted for approximately one-third of participants in the Proactive condition. Learners in this cluster exhibited higher conversational continuity and greater responsiveness to mentor support, consistent with the interaction and communication patterns observed in RQ1.

Table 2. Summary statistics by cluster with group size (N) and proactive proportions.

Cluster	N	Avg. Messages (#)	Proactive (%)	g
0—Passive–Distracted	4	9.00	50%	0.089
1—Low-Interaction	58	3.41	31%	0.26
2—Active Clarifiers	6	16.33	67%	0.24
3—Help-Accepting Learners	13	14.15	100%	0.45

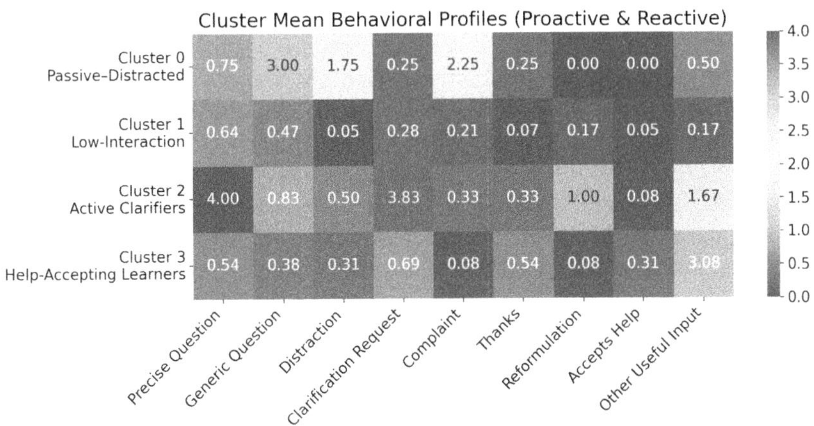

Fig. 6. Behavioral clusters of learner-AI interaction patterns

5.3 RQ3: Learning Outcomes

To assess whether initiative policy influenced learning outcomes, we compared participant-level normalized learning gains (g) between the two conditions. As shown in Fig. 4, the Reactive group exhibited a slightly higher mean normalized gain than the Proactive group; however, this difference did not reach statistical significance. To control for baseline and demographic differences, we conducted an ANCOVA on post-test scores with condition (Reactive vs. Proactive) as the between-subjects factor and pre-test score as the primary covariate. Age, education, work experience, gender, and test completion times (pre and post) were included as additional covariates. All ANCOVA assumptions were satisfied. Pre-test score ($p < .001$) and post-test completion time ($p = .026$) were significant predictors of post-test performance, while condition was not. No other covariates showed significant effects. We also examined learning gains across the exploratory interaction clusters identified in RQ2. Although the help-accepting interaction profile (Cluster 3) exhibited the highest mean normalized gain, a Kruskal–Wallis test revealed no statistically significant differences in gains across clusters ($p = .069$). Interpretation of these results is limited by small cluster sizes, inter-participant variability in gains, and the exploratory nature of the clustering procedure. Taken together, these findings indicate that initiative policy has a strong and reliable effect on learner–AI interaction structure, while short-term learning gains remain largely insensitive to initiative in a single-session, video-based setting. This dissociation underscores the importance of evaluating AI mentors not solely by immediate learning gains, but by the interaction patterns they elicit.

5.4 RQ4: Learner Experience

To complement behavioral and test-score analyses, we examined self-report data collected via the final questionnaire (including NASA-TLX, IMI subscales, and SUS). Two measures differed reliably between conditions after FDR correction. Participants in the Reactive condition reported substantially greater perceived choice regarding the interactions with our tutor (Proactive: $\overline{M} = 3.93$, $SD = 1.58$; Reactive: $\overline{M} = 5.45$, $SD = 1.30$). Similarly, perceived sense of control of the interactions was higher in the Reactive condition (Proactive: $\overline{M} = 3.81$, $SD = 1.52$; Reactive: $\overline{M} = 5.32$, $SD = 1.58$). Both effects indicate large, robust differences in favor of the Reactive condition (higher perceived choice and control). We ran an OLS regression with normalized gain as the dependent variable and questionnaire factors as predictors, controlling for condition. The regression revealed that two variables were significantly associated with knowledge gain, **IMI Perceived Competence** ($\beta = 0.0774$, $p = .015$) and **IMI Effort/Importance** ($\beta = 0.0941$, $p = .015$). Both predictors showed positive correlations with learning outcomes, suggesting that learners who felt more competent and valued the task put in more effort, and consequently gained more knowledge. This interpretation is in line with prior work on LLM-powered learning environments, suggesting that motivational dimensions are closely tied to how learners experience and benefit from AI-supported learning [30]. *Perceived Competence* and *Effort/Importance* scores did not significantly differ between both groups. In summary, participants in the Reactive condition reported a significantly greater sense of control and perceived choice in their interactions than those in the Proactive condition. This pattern is consistent with the literature and highlights an inherent design trade-off in proactive mentoring, between increasing interaction frequency and preserving learners' perceived choice and control.

6   Discussion

This study examined how an AI mentor's initiative policy shapes engagement, interaction patterns, and learning in a self-directed video-based learning task. The findings contribute empirical design knowledge for Pedagogical Conversational Agents by demonstrating that initiative policy is a consequential interaction control variable that substantially shapes engagement, non-interaction, and help-seeking behaviors. The primary contribution of this work lies in showing how initiative policy can reorganize learner–AI interaction trajectories. These trajectories, characterized by help acceptance and conversational continuation, constitute a central design outcome for pedagogical conversational agents, independent of immediate learning gains. The best predictors of learning gains remain *Perceived Competence* and *Effort/Importance*, which offer interesting insights for future design.

Interaction clustering revealed a distinct help-accepting profile associated with the highest normalized learning gains. This profile emerged exclusively through a proactive initiative, suggesting that proactive mentoring can scaffold learners into certain interaction patterns they may not initiate on their own. Rather than increasing interaction frequency alone, proactive initiative altered the qualitative structure of learner-agent dialogue, fostering help acceptance and conversational continuation. From a learning sciences perspective, these behaviors align with core components of self-regulated learning, particularly help-seeking and monitoring of understanding. We argue that interaction patterns themselves should be treated as primary design outcomes for pedagogical conversational agents. Initiative-coupled scaffolding policy directly shapes these outcomes, independent of short-term learning effects. This perspective aligns with prior work on self-regulated learning, help-seeking, and tutorial dialogue, where productive interaction is not merely a conduit to learning, but a central object of design.

Despite the behavioral benefits of proactive mentoring, learners in the reactive condition reported higher perceived autonomy and control. This finding highlights a well-established tension between providing adaptive support and preserving learner agency. Consistent with self-determination theory, these results suggest that while proactive interventions can engage otherwise passive learners, they may also risk undermining perceived autonomy if not carefully calibrated. From a mixed-initiative interaction perspective, initiative should be dynamically negotiated between the learner and the system rather than fixed (e.g., user-tunable proactivity or preference-adaptive prompting to preserve autonomy while maintaining engagement benefits). The AI mentor in this study implemented adaptive initiative by modulating proactivity based on behavioral indicators of disengagement or difficulty (e.g., pauses, rewinds, absence of response) and pretest-based personalization. This allowed the system to intervene selectively, approximating an early form of adaptive initiative control. Future PCAs could extend this approach by incorporating explicit models of learner preferences, confidence, or affective state to further refine when and how initiative is exercised. Importantly, these findings demonstrate that initiative-coupled scaffolding is an independent design lever that shapes learner experience, separate from the generative capabilities of the underlying AI model. This distinction underscores the need for research to examine interaction-control policies as first-class design variables in learning systems.

6.1   Limitations and Future Research Directions

This study examined a single short learning session within one domain, limiting generalizability to extended learning trajectories and diverse subject matter. The proactive initiative policy relied on predefined content boundaries and behavioral triggers, which, while adaptive, did not account for evolving learner preferences or longitudinal changes in self-regulation. Prior work suggests that sustained AI support may hinder the internalization of self-regulatory strategies when feedback is withdrawn [12], underscoring the importance of examining initiative policies over time. Future research should therefore investigate longitudinal and adaptive initiative strategies, including scaffold-to-fade approaches in which proactivity supports early onboarding and confidence-building before gradually diminishing as learners develop effective help-seeking behaviors. Additional limitations include potential test–retest and recall bias and reliance on pre-test indicators of prior knowledge. While appropriate for the present study, these measures capture only a limited temporal window. Future work could integrate repeated sessions and longitudinal performance data to support richer learner modeling and more robust estimation of knowledge and motivational states. Incorporating multimodal signals, such as gaze or posture estimation, may enable more precise and context-sensitive timing of proactive interventions. This direction is supported by recent multimodal evidence that learner states, such as aware and unaware mind wandering during lecture viewing, can be detected using eye tracking, facial video, and physiological data [7]. This work reframes a central design question from whether AI mentors should be proactive to when, how, and for whom proactivity is most effective. The findings suggest that initiative-coupled scaffolding policy is a powerful design dimension for PCAs when used to scaffold productive interaction patterns while preserving learner autonomy.

7   Conclusion

This study examined how initiative policy shapes interaction and learning in self-directed video-based learning. Using a model-agnostic experimental testbed, we isolated the effects of proactive versus reactive mentoring. A proactive initiative increased interaction, reduced non-interaction, and shifted communication toward more conversation continuity and help-accepting behaviors. These findings demonstrate that initiative-coupled scaffolding policy is a powerful mechanism for shaping learner-AI interaction trajectories. We contend that designing for such trajectories is a core challenge for AI-supported self-directed learning. At the same time, reactive mentoring was associated with higher perceived autonomy, highlighting a trade-off between engagement and agency. These findings support treating initiative as a first-class design dimension in intelligent learning environments, requiring careful calibration to elicit productive, tutoring-like interaction patterns while preserving learner autonomy.

Disclosure of Interests. No funds, grants, or other support were received. The authors have no relevant financial or non-financial interests to disclose.

Ethics Statement. This study was reviewed and approved by the ethics committee at TUM (approval no. 2025-151-NM-BA). All participants provided informed consent prior to participation and were compensated in accordance with the study protocol.

References

1. Adamczyk, P.D., Bailey, B.P.: If not now, when? The effects of interruption at different moments within task execution. In: Proceedings of the SIGCHI Conference on Human Factors in Computing Systems, CHI 2004, pp. 271–278. Association for Computing Machinery, New York, NY, USA (2004). https://doi.org/10.1145/985692.985727
2. Aleven, V., Roll, I., McLaren, B.M., Koedinger, K.R.: Help helps, but only so much: research on help seeking with intelligent tutoring systems. Int. J. Artif. Intell. Educ. **26**(1), 205–223 (2016). https://doi.org/10.1007/s40593-015-0089-1
3. Aleven, V., Stahl, E., Schworm, S., Fischer, F., Wallace, R.: Help seeking and help design in interactive learning environments. Rev. Educ. Res. **73**(3), 277–320 (2003). https://doi.org/10.3102/00346543073003277
4. Bloom, B.S.: The 2 sigma problem: the search for methods of group instruction as effective as one-to-one tutoring. Educ. Res. **13**(6), 4–16 (1984). https://doi.org/10.3102/0013189X013006004
5. Bodonhelyi, A., Thaqi, E., Özdel, S., Bozkir, E., Kasneci, E.: From passive watching to active learning: empowering proactive participation in digital classrooms with AI video assistant. In: Proceedings of the 2025 CHI Conference on Human Factors in Computing Systems, CHI 2025 (2025). https://doi.org/10.1145/3706598.3713513
6. Bouchet, F., Harley, J.M., Azevedo, R.: Impact of different pedagogical agents' adaptive self-regulated prompting strategies on learning with MetaTutor. In: Lane, H.C., Yacef, K., Mostow, J., Pavlik, P. (eds.) AIED 2013. LNCS (LNAI), vol. 7926, pp. 815–819. Springer, Heidelberg (2013). https://doi.org/10.1007/978-3-642-39112-5_120

7. Bühler, B., et al.: Detecting aware and unaware mind wandering during lecture viewing: a multimodal machine learning approach using eye tracking, facial videos and physiological data. In: Proceedings of the 26th International Conference on Multimodal Interaction, pp. 244–253 (2024)

8. Bühler, B., et al.: Temporal dynamics of meta-awareness of mind wandering during lecture viewing: implications for learning and automated assessment using machine learning. J. Educ. Psychol. (2024)

9. Bühler, B., Bueno, I., Kasneci, E.: Democratizing writing support with AI: insights from one year of real-world interactions with an open-access writing feedback tool. Proc. AAAI Conf. Artif. Intell. **40**(45), 38278–38286 (2026). https://doi.org/10.1609/aaai.v40i45.41167

10. Chen, V., Zhu, A., Zhao, S., Mozannar, H., Sontag, D., Talwalkar, A.: Need help? Designing proactive AI assistants for programming (2024). https://doi.org/10.48550/arXiv.2410.04596

11. Czerwinski, M., Cutrell, E., Horvitz, E.: Instant messaging: effects of relevance and timing. In: People and Computers XIV: Proceedings of HCI, vol. 2, pp. 71–76 (2000)

12. Darvishi, A., Khosravi, H., Sadiq, S., Gašević, D., Siemens, G.: Impact of AI assistance on student agency. Comput. Educ. **210**, 1–18 (2024). https://doi.org/10.1016/j.compedu.2023.104967

13. Diebel, C., Goutier, M., Adam, M., Benlian, A.: When AI-based agents are proactive: implications for competence and system satisfaction in human–AI collaboration. Bus. Inf. Syst. Eng. (2025). https://doi.org/10.1007/s12599-024-00918-y

14. D'mello, S., Graesser, A.: AutoTutor and affective AutoTutor: learning by talking with cognitively and emotionally intelligent computers that talk back. ACM Trans. Interact. Intell. Syst. **2**(4) (2013). https://doi.org/10.1145/2395123.2395128

15. D'Mello, S., Lehman, B., Pekrun, R., Graesser, A.: Confusion can be beneficial for learning. Learn. Instr. **29**, 153–170 (2014). https://doi.org/10.1016/j.learninstruc.2012.05.003

16. Guo, P.J., Kim, J., Rubin, R.: How video production affects student engagement: an empirical study of MOOC videos. In: Proceedings of the First ACM Conference on Learning @ Scale Conference, L@S 2014, pp. 41–50. Association for Computing Machinery (2014). https://doi.org/10.1145/2556325.2566239

17. Gupta, A., MacLellan, C.: Intelligent tutors beyond K-12: an observational study of adult learner engagement and academic impact (2025). https://arxiv.org/abs/2502.16613

18. Hake, R.R.: Interactive-engagement versus traditional methods: a six-thousand-student survey of mechanics test data for introductory physics courses. Am. J. Phys. **66**(1), 64–74 (1998). https://doi.org/10.1119/1.18809

19. Hanshaw, G., Sullivan, C.: Exploring barriers to AI course assistant adoption: a mixed-methods study on student non-utilization. Discover Artif. Intell. **5**(1), 178 (2025). https://doi.org/10.1007/s44163-025-00312-x

20. Hennessy, S., et al.: Developing a coding scheme for analysing classroom dialogue across educational contexts. Learn. Cult. Soc. Interact. **9**, 16–44 (2016). https://doi.org/10.1016/j.lcsi.2015.12.001

21. Iqbal, S.T., Bailey, B.P.: Leveraging characteristics of task structure to predict the cost of interruption. In: Proceedings of the SIGCHI Conference on Human Factors in Computing Systems, CHI 2006, pp. 741–750. Association for Computing Machinery, New York, NY, USA (2006). https://doi.org/10.1145/1124772.1124882

22. Kasneci, E., et al.: ChatGPT for good? On opportunities and challenges of large language models for education. Learn. Individ. Differ. **103**, 102274 (2023)

23. Kong, K., Isleem, H.F., Aluvalu, R., Tejani, G.G., Metwally, A.S.M.: Real-time cognitive and emotional state tracking in intelligent tutoring systems for enhanced learning outcomes. J. Big Data **12**(1), 266 (2025). https://doi.org/10.1186/s40537-025-01333-0
24. Merkt, M., Hoppe, A., Bruns, G., Ewerth, R., Huff, M.: Pushing the button: why do learners pause online videos? Comput. Educ. **176**, 104355 (2022). https://doi.org/10.1016/j.compedu.2021.104355
25. Pu, K., et al.: Assistance or disruption? Exploring and evaluating the design and trade-offs of proactive AI programming support. In: Proceedings of the 2025 CHI Conference on Human Factors in Computing Systems, CHI 2025, pp. 1–21. Association for Computing Machinery (2025). https://doi.org/10.1145/3706598.3713357
26. Qayyum, A.: Student help-seeking attitudes and behaviors in a digital era. Int. J. Educ. Technol. High. Educ. **15**(1), 17 (2018). https://doi.org/10.1186/s41239-018-0100-7
27. Roll, I., Aleven, V., McLaren, B.M., Koedinger, K.R.: Improving students' help-seeking skills using metacognitive feedback in an intelligent tutoring system. Learn. Instr. **21**(2), 267–280 (2011). https://doi.org/10.1016/j.learninstruc.2010.07.004
28. Roll, I., Aleven, V., McLaren, B.M., Ryu, E., Baker, R.S.J., Koedinger, K.R.: The help tutor: does metacognitive feedback improve students' help-seeking actions, skills and learning? In: Ikeda, M., Ashley, K.D., Chan, T.-W. (eds.) ITS 2006. LNCS, vol. 4053, pp. 360–369. Springer, Heidelberg (2006). https://doi.org/10.1007/11774303_36
29. Schwonke, R., Ertelt, A., Otieno, C., Renkl, A., Aleven, V., Salden, R.J.C.M.: Metacognitive support promotes an effective use of instructional resources in intelligent tutoring. Learn. Instr. **23**, 136–150 (2013). https://doi.org/10.1016/j.learninstruc.2012.08.003
30. Seßler, K., Kepir, O., Kasneci, E.: Enhancing student motivation through LLM-powered learning environments: a comparative study. In: European Conference on Technology Enhanced Learning, pp. 156–162. Springer (2024)
31. Thomas, D.R., et al.: Improving student learning with hybrid human-AI tutoring: a three-study quasi-experimental investigation. In: Proceedings of the 14th Learning Analytics and Knowledge Conference, LAK 2024, pp. 404–415. ACM (2024). https://doi.org/10.1145/3636555.3636896
32. Vanlehn, K.: The behavior of tutoring systems. Int. J. Artif. Intell. Ed. **16**(3), 227–265 (2006)
33. Xiao, X., Wang, J.: Context and cognitive state triggered interventions for mobile MOOC learning. In: Proceedings of the 18th ACM International Conference on Multimodal Interaction, ICMI 2016, pp. 378–385. Association for Computing Machinery, New York, NY, USA (2016). https://doi.org/10.1145/2993148.2993177

Uncertain AI – Better AI? Effects of Uncertainty Indicators in Collaborative Learning with a Human Peer or an Artificial Intelligence

Anna Radtke[1]([✉])[iD] and Lenka Schnaubert[2][iD]

[1] Center for Advanced Internet Studies (CAIS), Konrad-Zuse-Str. 2a, 44801 Bochum, Germany
anna.radtke@cais-research.de
[2] School of Education, University of Nottingham, Jubilee Campus, Wollaton Road, Nottingham NG8 1BB, UK
lenka.schnaubert@nottingham.ac.uk

Abstract. In learning, uncertainty is often associated with negative experiences and seen as something to be resolved immediately. However, research shows that uncertainty can increase learners' motivation, process regulation, and learning intention. In collaborative learning, learners not only confront their own uncertainty but also the uncertainty they perceive in their peers. Nevertheless, little empirical work has examined whether the effects of group uncertainty observed in human collaboration transfer to interactions between learners and AI peers. In this study, we analyzed the effects of group uncertainty in different collaborative settings (with a human peer vs. an AI agent) and investigated mechanisms of uncertainty expression through different uncertainty indicators (uncertainty markers and controversial arguments) as well as the role of perceived social presence. We conducted an online study ($N = 343$) in which participants learned about a controversial topic with a co-learner. Depending on the experimental condition, the co-learner was a human peer or an AI agent who provided participants with their research results that did or did not include uncertainty indicators. We found that uncertainty indicators increased learners' perceptions of their peer's uncertainty (indicating group uncertainty awareness), which affected their individual uncertainty and learning engagement. Individual uncertainty increased learning intention via confusion. The effects were largely independent of whether the partner was human or AI. Perceived social presence strengthened the influence of perceived partner uncertainty on individual uncertainty, though this effect was stronger for the human peer. Our findings advance understanding of uncertainty in collaborative learning and support design of effective AI peer agents.

Keywords: Artificial Intelligence as Learning Partner · Group Uncertainty Awareness · Uncertainty Indicators · Uncertainty Markers · Collaborative Learning · Metacognition

E. G. Blanchard et al. (Eds.): AIED 2026, LNAI 16583, pp. 536–551, 2027.
https://doi.org/10.1007/978-3-032-29760-0_54

1   Introduction

Imagine asking learners, 'How would you describe your ideal peer?' They would probably say 'smart', 'reliable', or 'creative'. But what about an *uncertain* peer? Most likely, uncertainty would not be among the first characteristics mentioned. When it comes to learning, uncertainty is often associated with negative experiences and is frequently seen as something that needs to be resolved right away [10, 34]. But might an artificial intelligence (AI) serve as such an ideal learning partner, and what if it demonstrated some uncertainty? AI-based chatbots, such as *ChatGPT*, show promising potential to function as digital peer agents, facilitating the application of collaborative learning practices similar to those in human-AI interactions [9, 33]. Indeed, students might be keen to use AI-powered peer agents because they are adaptive, interactive, and constantly available [31]. However, we also doubt that uncertainty would be considered one of the most desirable features of an ideal AI peer.

But does uncertainty live up to its negative reputation? And should it be avoided when designing learning processes? Metacognitive research provides substantial evidence to contradict it. Specifically, uncertainty is a metacognitive experience that provides valuable information for reliability of knowledge and understanding [25]. Previous research has also shown that experiencing uncertainty can increase learners' motivation [1, 36], draw their attention to knowledge gaps, and encourage deeper (meta)cognitive engagement in process regulation and with learning materials [40, 42]. Evidence from human-computer interaction research also suggests that collaborations with digital peer agents that involve uncertainty can encourage learners to confront their uncertainty and confusion, thereby promoting learning process regulation [30]. However, due to the recent adoption of AI peer agents, there is yet little empirical research on the effects of uncertainty in learning contexts involving digital peer agents. Exploring this aspect is crucial to fundamentally understanding the role of uncertainty in collaborative learning and also to developing effective designs for AI agents in practice.

In this study, we explored how the uncertainty of different learning partners (human peer vs. AI agent) impacts learners' metacognitive and affective states, as well as their learning intentions and behaviors. Moreover, to investigate the mechanisms of uncertainty expression, we tested the effects of two types of *uncertainty indicators*: (a) *uncertainty markers* (e.g., hedges, self-referential phrases; [15, 19]) and (b) *controversial arguments* [5, 26]. These indicators differ in how uncertainty in conveyed either in (a) metacognitive expressions or (b) the presence of conflicting cognitive information. These indicators have been shown not only to support learners' group awareness (i.e., their salient perception of relevant characteristics of the collaborating group; [39]) but also affect their individual metacognitions and learning behaviors [38]. However, it is unclear whether these mechanisms are transferable to collaboration with AI partners and whether AI uncertainty is perceived differently than human uncertainty. Additionally, we explored the impact of *perceived social presence* of different learning partners (human peer vs. AI agent) on perceived and individual uncertainty. We assumed that it would affect learners' (meta)cognitive processes and behaviors when confronted with their co-learner's uncertainty via social schemata activation [43].

2 Theoretical Background

2.1 Role of Uncertainty in Individual Learning Regulation

Metacognitive experiences, such as *uncertainty*, which may arise from the monitoring of limitations in one's knowledge or assumptions, play a key role in learning processes. Indeed, metacognitive experiences are strongly connected to learners' cognitive and emotional regulation and thus may impact their behaviors in several ways [12]. However, uncertainty is often associated with negative affectional states, such as *confusion*, which are frequently viewed as factors that must be reduced or resolved as quickly as possible [10]. Therefore, some teachers or learning environments provide students with support and explanations right away, thereby preventing metacognitive challenges from unfolding [34]. However, there is empirical evidence that contradicts the idea that uncertainty is an undesirable state in the learning process. When learners overcome challenges that trigger uncertainty, they can strategically adjust their learning behaviors to achieve better outcomes [10]. Additionally, experiencing uncertainty can motivate learners and stimulate their learning engagement [1, 36]. For instance, it may help learners identify knowledge gaps and encourage them to explore learning materials more deeply [40]. Moreover, uncertainty can positively influence learners' curiosity associated with the effort invested in learning as well as learning intentions [27]. In summary: while uncertainty indeed can lead to unpleasant mental states, these experiences can prompt control processes aimed at resolving these states, thereby enhancing learning and leading to knowledge gain.

2.2 Uncertainty Indicators in Collaborative Learning

For collaborative learning to be successful, learners need to gain accurate *group awareness* (GA), the salient perception of relevant characteristics of the collaborating group, which includes their peers'(meta)cognitive states [39]. Therefore, in addition to confronting their own uncertainty, learners often have to deal with the uncertainty they perceive in their peers (*group uncertainty awareness*, GUA). In written communication, uncertainty can be conveyed by using certain *uncertainty indicators*: (a) *uncertainty markers* and (b) *controversial arguments*.

(1) *Uncertainty markers* include, for instance, hedges (e.g., *somehow, perhaps*), self-referential phrases (e.g., *as far as I know*), certain frequency adverbs (e.g., *often, rarely*), and ellipses ('...'; [15, 19]). A peer's use of these markers represents metacognitive expressions that signal lacking internal certainty and can be related to knowledge gaps [20]. Consequently, if a peer displays uncertainty, their credibility as an information source and the persuasiveness of their assumptions can be undermined [4]. Previous empirical research has shown that adding uncertainty markers to text messages in a forum setting strengthens learners' self-indicated perception of the group's uncertainty and respective increases in GUA reinforce learners' individual uncertainty and learning intentions [38]. Thus, increased GUA can be a valuable trigger for further engagement with the subject matter and additional learning materials.

(2) Bringing up *controversial arguments* represents another indicator of uncertainty in collaborative learning, as these arguments may convey a lack of consensus or insecurity within the group [5, 26]. Providing learners with information about conflicting assumptions in a group has shown to trigger regulation processes to resolve these conflicts [41, 42]. When interacting with a single peer, that peer's contradictory arguments or conflicting sources cited can serve as controversial arguments [5, 10]. Empirical findings suggest that presenting controversial arguments highlights uncertainty about the validity of knowledge and assumptions and draws learners' attention to sources of controversial information [5]. As a result, learners engage more deeply with learning materials and particularly the sources, which may improve their comprehension.

2.3 Effects of Co-Learners' Uncertainty in Learning with a Human Peer or an AI

As a relevant dimension of group awareness, GUA has been shown to influence the regulation of individual and collaborative learning with the aim of resolving uncertainty within the group [41]. Indeed, learners' perception of their peers' uncertainty can impact the way they evaluate both their peers' expertise and the credibility of their contributions [42] as well as the task complexity [21]. Furthermore, empirical studies suggest that perceiving peers' uncertainty can 'rub off' on learners, increasing their individual uncertainty [10, 38] and confusion [10, 21]. Therefore, when learners perceive their peers' uncertainty, their own uncertainty increases, which can have a positive impact on their learning processes and outcomes, as explained in the Sect. 2.1.

In recent years, the adoption of AI-powered chatbots, particularly *ChatGPT*, by learners has increased rapidly. One promising benefit of this technology is the learner-AI interaction mode that allows students to engage in mutual, 'peer-to-peer' learning with AI [33, 35]. Through natural language processing, AI peer agents can engage learners in authentic discussions, thereby increasing their self-efficacy, enabling early detection of misunderstandings or knowledge gaps, and facilitating knowledge co-construction [11, 16]. As with collaborative learning with peers, learners need to develop a kind of *awareness of AI as a learning partner* when collaborating with it [9]. In practice, students may have different perceptions of and expectations for AI's role in the learning process, ranging from viewing AI as a mere search engine or virtual tutor to considering it a *digital peer* [23]. Indeed, learners' awareness of AI's features is important because it affects how they make sense of and interact with the tool and its outputs [31]. Notably, *awareness of AI as a learning partner*, or at least as a content generator, should extend beyond features prominent in 'conventional' human peers collaboration. For instance, learners should be aware of the data sources AI relies on, the algorithms it uses, and the limitations of the content it generates [9]. However, recent research has demonstrated that learners' awareness of AI in AI-assisted learning is limited when it comes to addressing AI's technical features [37]. Instead, learners attribute human-like characteristics (cognitive, mental, and emotional states) to AI and apply social interaction norms to human-AI interactions [7, 31]. This supports our assumption that learners are likely to attribute a *certain level of (un)certainty* to their AI digital peers as they would to human peers. Empirical studies on digital agents expressing uncertainty have shown that presenting controversial arguments in a dialogue between two AI agents significantly increases learners' confusion and uncertainty, yet positively impacts their learning performance [30]. Further study found that the use of hedges (~uncertainty markers) and incorrect statements (~controversial arguments) by a digital peer agent can prompt learners to take the initiative in learning regulation, which can be seen as increased learning intention [22].

Another key factor in collaborative learning and particularly building GUA, whether with human peers or AI agents, is learners' *perception of their co-learners' social presence*. Empirical findings suggest that a strong sense of social presence in digital learning environments increases learners' willingness to collaborate, facilitates knowledge exchange, and fosters a sense of belonging [2]. In human-computer interaction, social presence is defined as the sense of the presence of and interaction with other intelligent beings, even when they are non-human and merely simulate intelligence [28]. Empirical research revealed that increasing the perceived social presence of a digital agent can, for example, foster trust in that agent and satisfaction with the learning experience [18]. Therefore, we assume that perceiving more social cues would affect learners' (meta)cognitive processes and behaviors when confronted with their partner's *uncertainty* via social schemata activation [43]. In other words, learners would experience the impact of GUA on their individual learning more intensely if they perceive their peers' social presence as high.

2.4 Research Questions and Hypotheses

The aim of this study was to investigate the following research questions:

- **RQ1**: Do learners perceive the use of uncertainty indicators by their learning partner (human peer vs. AI agent), and is this perception similar for different indicators (uncertainty markers and controversial arguments)?
- **RQ2**: Does the co-learner's perceived uncertainty (human peer vs. AI agent) impact learners' individual metacognitive and affectional states? And how do the latter affect learning processes in turn?
- **RQ3**: Which role does the perceived social presence of the learning partner (human peer vs. AI agent) play in this learning setting?

Based on the evidence outlined above, we developed the following hypotheses.

- **H1**: Learners perceive their learning partner (human peer vs. AI agent) as less certain when that partner is using uncertainty indicators, such as uncertainty markers and/or controversial arguments.
- **H2**: Perceived uncertainty of the learning partner (human peer vs. AI agent) increases learners' individual uncertainty.
- **H3a–d**: Perceived uncertainty of the learning partner (human peer vs. AI agent) leads to (a) a greater intensity of engagement with the learning materials and (b) a stronger learning intention, mediated by learners' level of (c) individual uncertainty and (d) individual confusion.
- **H4a–b**: The impact of the co-learner's perceived uncertainty on learners' individual uncertainty is (a) moderated by perceived social presence and (b) particularly more pronounced for higher perceived social presence of the learning partner (human peer vs. AI agent).

We did not formulate any directed hypotheses regarding the differences between the two learning partners (human peer vs. AI agent) due to a lack of evidence regarding the possible contrasts. However, we accounted for possible differences between both co-learner types in each hypothesis.

3 Methods

We conducted an online experimental study in which participants learned about a controversially discussed topic (the existence of William Shakespeare as a real person) with a learning partner. Depending on randomly assigned experimental conditions, the learning partner was either a human peer or an AI agent. This learning partner provided participants with the textual research results, which did or did not include uncertainty indicators in the form of uncertainty markers and/or controversial arguments. The study (study ID: psychmeth_2022_UAH_04) was conducted online and approved by the local ethics committee (IRB ID: 2204PFRA6440).

3.1 Sample

The total sample consisted of $N = 343$ participants. In terms of gender, 71.1% identified as female, 28.0% as male, and 0.9% as non-binary. The average age was $M = 27.04$ years ($SD = 7.78$). Regarding highest educational attainment, the majority of participants indicated having a bachelor's degree (49.0%) or a high school diploma (32.4%). Most of the participants were high school or university students (72.3%). The average duration of the participation was $M = 13.90$ min ($SD = 5.69$).

3.2 Study Design and Procedure

In a $2 \times 2 \times 2$ experiment ($N = 343$), we varied (1) *the type of the learning partner* participants were co-learning with (*human peer* or *AI agent*) and *the presence or absence of uncertainty indicators* in the content provided by this learning partner: (2) *uncertainty markers* and (3) *controversial arguments*. This resulted in eight experimental conditions. The study was designed in a way that participants were not given content authentically generated by a human peer or an AI. Instead, all participants received the same pre-set materials, which were claimed to have been generated by a certain learning partner. This manipulation ensured that participants' perceptions and behaviors were primarily influenced by the experimental variations and not by other variations in the learning materials. As the experimental setting involved engagement with learning materials supposedly prepared by a certain learning partner rather than a real-time interaction with that partner, we showed participants a greeting video introducing their learning partner as either a *human peer* or an *AI agent*. This should reinforce the perception of a collaborative setting during the learning task (see Fig. 1).

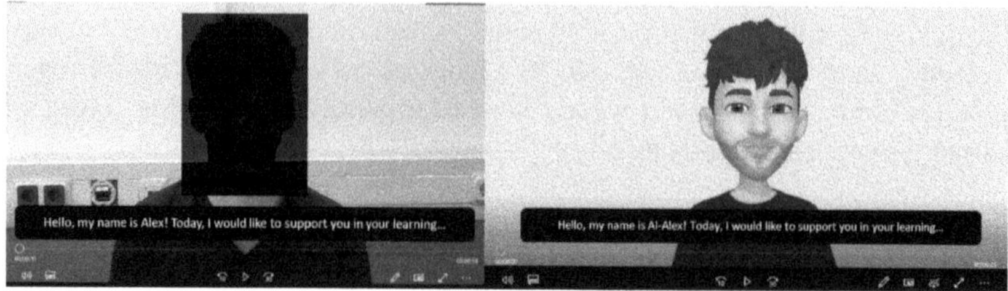

Fig. 1. Video presentation of the learning partner (human peer or AI agent). (The human peer's face is hidden in the figure for data protection reasons.)

In an online study (for the procedure see Fig. 2), all participants first read a text on the topic *'William Shakespeare: A real person or just a pseudonym?'* Then, they assessed ten text-related statements as either *true* or *false* and indicated their certainty in the correctness of each of those assumptions on a 6-point scale (see Fig. 3). After that, participants self-evaluated their current level of *confusion* and *learning intention.*

Next, participants were shown a greeting video in which their learning partner – either a human peer (*Alex*) or an AI avatar (*AI-Alex*) – introduced himself (see Fig. 1). After watching the video, participants were provided with the results of their learning partner's research on the topic *'William Shakespeare: A real person or just a pseudonym?'* These research results were presented in the form of ten text passages, each of those was followed by a 'source'-button (see Fig. 4). Participants could access the detailed description of the source by clicking on these buttons (used as a proximal measure of the *intensity of engagement with the learning material*). The buttons could be clicked several times in any order. Depending on experimental condition, the research results included (1) ten arguments for William Shakespeare being a pseudonym (no controversial arguments) or a combination of five arguments for William Shakespeare being a pseudonym and five arguments for William Shakespeare being a real person (controversial arguments; see Fig. 4, left column) and (2) no uncertainty markers or uncertainty markers (see Fig. 4, top row).

After engaging with the content provided by the learning partner, participants were asked to indicate how they rated their learning partner's uncertainty. To this end, we used a *Group Uncertainty Awareness Scale* developed in a preliminary study. Then, participants were asked to assess the same ten text-related statements again (including the individual certainty ratings; see Fig. 3). This was followed by the repeated assessment of the current level of *confusion* and *learning intention.* Finally, we measured participants' *perceived social presence of their learning partner* using the *Feeling of Social Presence Index* [29].

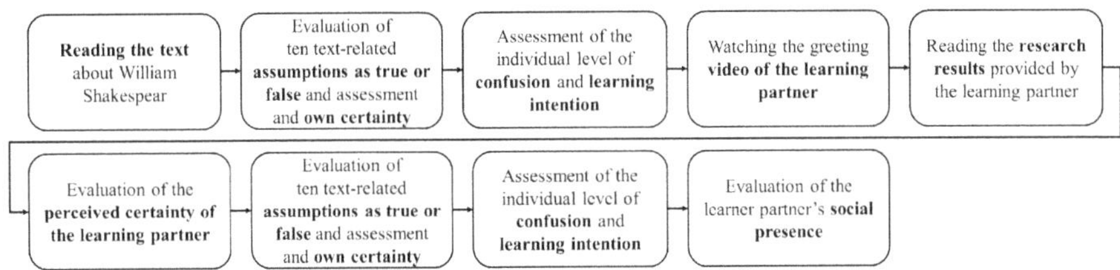

Fig. 2. Study procedure.

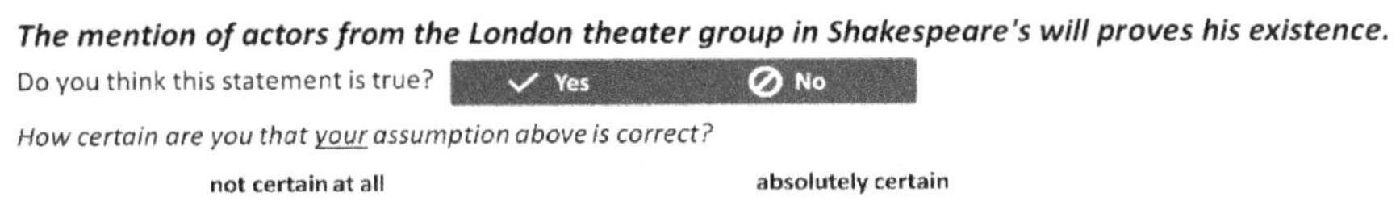

Fig. 3. Example for a text related statement to be assessed with the scale for indicating the certainty in the correctness of the assumption.

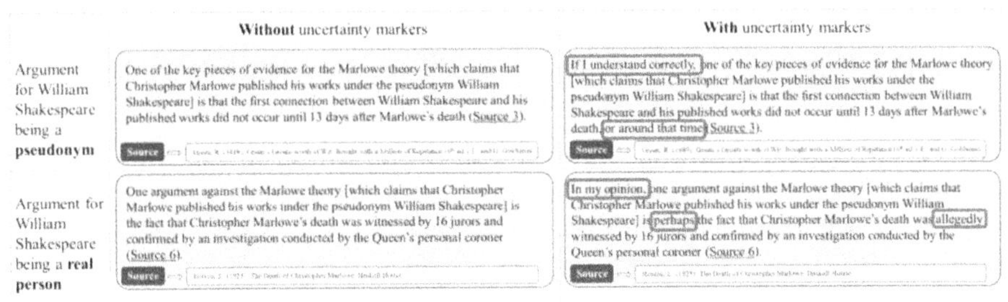

Fig. 4. Example for different arguments in the partner's research results, without and with uncertainty markers (marked red). (Color figure online)

3.3 Measures and Instruments

Perceived Uncertainty of the Learning Partner. Perceived uncertainty of the learning partner was measured with the *Group Uncertainty Awareness Scale* (Cronbach's α = .83), which was developed in a preliminary study ($N = 233$). The questionnaire contained three items and a 7-point Likert-type rating scale ranging from 1 (*strongly disagree*) to 7 (*strongly agree*). The items of the GUA scale were: (1) *My learning partner is certain that their assumptions are correct.* (2) *My learning partner believes that others should share their assumptions.* (3) *My learning partner is convinced that their assumptions are the only correct way to think about this topic.* For the subsequent analyses, the items were inverted to represent perceived learning partner *uncertainty*.

Changes in Individual Uncertainty. While assessing ten text-related statements as either *true* or *false*, learners were asked to indicate their certainty in the correctness of each of their assumptions: *'How certain are you that your assumption above is correct?'* The answers were collected on a 6-point Likert-type scale from 1 (*not certain at all*) to 6 (*absolutely certain*; see Fig. 2). To determine learners' current level of individual uncertainty, we calculated the mean of their responses to all ten 'certainty-questions'.

To determine learners' changes in individual uncertainty, we calculated the difference between learners' level of uncertainty after and prior to engaging with the research results of the learning partner. This measure ranged from –5 (*uncertainty decreased*) to 5 (*uncertainty increased*).

Changes in Individual Confusion. Learners' current level of confusion was measured with a single item: *'How confused do you feel right now?'* The 5-point Likert-type scale ranged from 1 (*not confused at all*) to 5 (*absolutely confused*). To determine learners' changes in individual confusion, we calculated the difference between learners' level of confusion after and prior to engaging with the research results of the learning partner (ranging from –4 (*confusion decreased*) to 4 (*confusion increased*)).

Intensity of Engagement with the Learning Materials. Learners' intensity of engagement with learning materials was determined by the number of times they clicked on 'source'-buttons while reading their partner's research results (see Fig. 4).

Changes in Learning Intention. Learners' learning intention was measured with a single item: *'How much time would you take to study additional learning materials on this topic?'* The 7-point Likert-type scale ranged from 1 (*very little*) to 7 (*very much*). To determine learners' changes in learning intention, we calculated the difference between learning intention after and prior to engaging with the research results of the learning partner (ranging from –6 (*intention decreased*) to 6 (*intention increased*)).

Social Presence of the Learning Partner. To measure learners' perception of the social presence of their partner, we used the *Feeling of Social Presence Index* [29] (Cronbach's $\alpha = .79$). The questionnaire contained seven items (e.g., *'How much did you feel as if you and your learning partner were communicating to each other?'*) and a 10-point Likert-type scale ranging from 1 (*not at all*) to 10 (*absolutely*).

4 Results

We analyzed the data in IBM SPSS Statistics (Version 31.0) by calculating multi-factor ANOVA, mediation, and moderation analyses using PROCESS v4.2. Initially, we assessed whether the dependent variables met the requirements for the chosen statistical analyses. Although the assumption of normality was not completely satisfied, this deviation was considered negligible given the outcomes presented in the Q-Q plots, the sample size, and the robustness of the chosen statistical methods [3]. To achieve more accurate results and reduce the impact of minor deviations from normality, we used the bias-corrected and accelerated bootstrap method for our mediation and moderation analyses. The modified Breusch–Pagan tests for the mediation and moderation analyses detected no heteroskedasticity in the data ($p \geq .268$).

4.1 Learners' Perception of Their Learning Partner's Uncertainty

We performed a $2 \times 2 \times 2$ ANOVA with *uncertainty markers* (no/yes), *controversial arguments* (no/yes), and *learning partner* (human peer/AI agent) as factors and *perceived uncertainty of learning partner* as dependent variable to test *H1* (see Table 1).

Table 1. Perceived uncertainty of the learning partner.

Uncertainty markers	Controversial arguments	Learning partner	M	SD	n
No	No	human peer	3.56	1.23	46
		AI agent	3.69	1.26	43
	Yes	human peer	4.05	1.28	42
		AI agent	3.43	1.34	43
Yes	No	human peer	4.59	1.28	42
		AI agent	4.47	1.44	45
	Yes	human peer	5.28	1.21	41
		AI agent	4.96	1.26	41

The results revealed that participants whose learning partner used *uncertainty markers* ($F(1, 335) = 66.871$, $p < .001$, $\eta_p^2 = .166$) or *controversial arguments* ($F(1, 335) = 6.496$, $p = .011$, $\eta_p^2 = .019$) perceived their *partner's uncertainty* as significantly higher than participants whose learning partner did not use any uncertainty indicators (see Fig. 5). Thus, *H1* was confirmed.

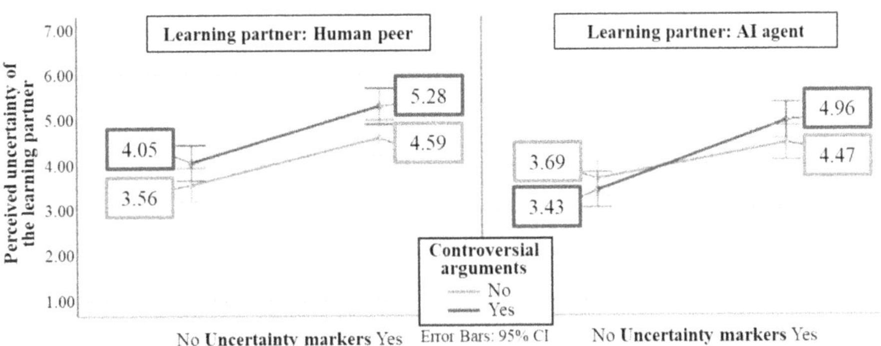

Fig. 5. Effects of uncertainty indicators on perceived uncertainty of the learning partner for human peer (left) and AI agent (right) as learning partner.

However, the type of the *learning partner* – human peer or AI agent – had no significant influence on the perceived uncertainty ($F(1,335) = 2.756$, $p = .098$, $\eta_p^2 = .008$). Moreover, we found no interaction effects, neither between both uncertainty indicators ($p = .088$, $\eta_p^2 = .009$) nor between the *learning partner* and uncertainty indicators ($p \geq .090$, $\eta_p^2 \leq .009$). Given that we did not find any differences between the learning partners, we performed the mediation analyses without distinguishing between the two types.

4.2 Effects of Perceived Uncertainty on Learners' Individual Uncertainty, Confusion, Engagement with Learning Materials, and Learning Intention

In the next step, we conducted mediation analyses for the effects of *perceived uncertainty of the learning partner* on the *intensity of engagement with the learning materials* (model A) and the *changes in learning intention* (model B), mediated by learners' *changes in individual uncertainty* and *changes in individual confusion*.

The results of the mediation analysis (model A; see Fig. 6, top) showed a significant positive total effect of the *perceived uncertainty of the learning partner* on the *intensity of engagement with the learning materials* (ß = .115, *p* = .033, [LLCI: .01, ULCI: .22]). The direct effect was also significant, although the confidence interval (CI) crossed zero, indicating rather weak statistical evidence (ß = .110, *p* = .045, [–.002, .22]). We found that learners' *individual uncertainty* increased as the *perceived learning partner's uncertainty* increased (*p* = .004). Thus, *H2* was confirmed. In addition, our findings indicated that *changes in individual uncertainty* had a reinforcing effect on *changes in individual confusion* (*p* < .001).

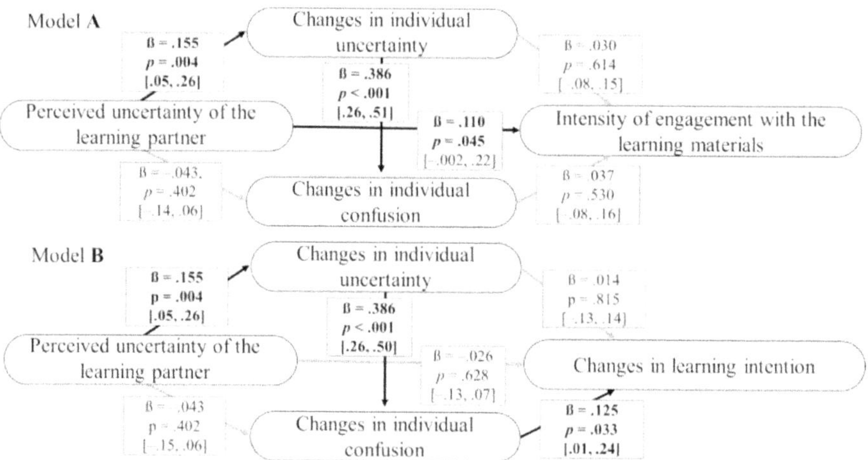

Note. ß are standardized coefficients. The values in square brackets are 95% confidence intervals. Significant values are bold.

Fig. 6. Mediation analysis for the effects of perceived on the intensity of engagement with the learning materials (model A, top) / on learning intention (model B, bottom).

The results of the second mediation analysis (model B; see Fig. 6, bottom) indicated a significant indirect positive effect of the *perceived uncertainty of the learning partner* on *changes in learning intention* (ß = .007, [.00, .02]): *Perceived uncertainty of the learning partner* caused *individual uncertainty* to increase (*p* = .004) which in turn raised *individual confusion* (*p* < .001) which fostered *learning intention* (*p* = .033). The total (ß = –.022, *p* = .682, [LLCI: –.13, ULCI: .08]) and direct effects (ß = –.026, *p* = .628, [–.13, .07]) were not significant. Thus, *H3a–d* were only partially confirmed.

4.3   Effects of Perceived Social Presence of the Learning Partner

Finally, we examined whether the *perceived social presence of the learning partner* affected the impact of the *perceived uncertainty* on learners' *individual uncertainty*, with the type of *learning partner* considered. As expected, participants who co-learned with a human peer ($M = 4.69$, $SD = 1.46$) perceived the social presence of their learning partner significantly higher than those who co-learned with an AI agent ($M = 4.10$, $SD = 1.59$; $t(341) = 3.575$, $p < .001$, Cohen's $d = 1.52$). However, both mean values were at the lower end of the 10-point scale which is likely due to the study's design. A moderated moderation analysis (see Fig. 7) revealed that strongly perceived *social presence of the learning partner* fostered the effect of the *perceived uncertainty of the learning partner* on learners' *changes in individual uncertainty* ($p = .005$), supporting *H4a–b*. Particularly, this moderating effect was pronounced when participants had a human peer as learning partner ($p = .022$, $[-.52, .02]$) as compared to the AI agent being a learning partner (see Fig. 8). The CI suggested rather weak statistical evidence.

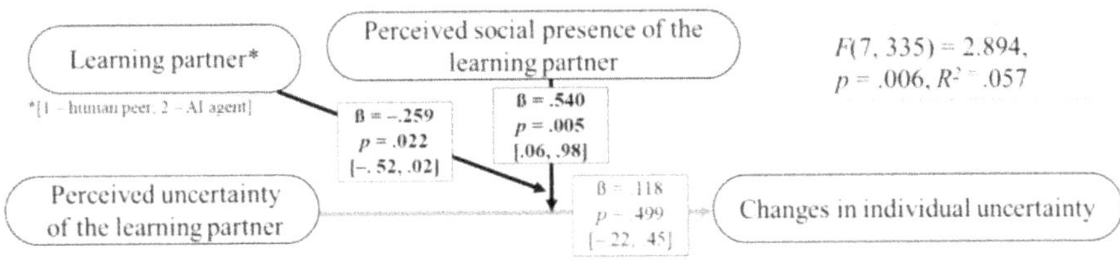

Fig. 7. Effect of perceived uncertainty on individual uncertainty moderated by the perceived social presence of the learning partner and learning partner's type.

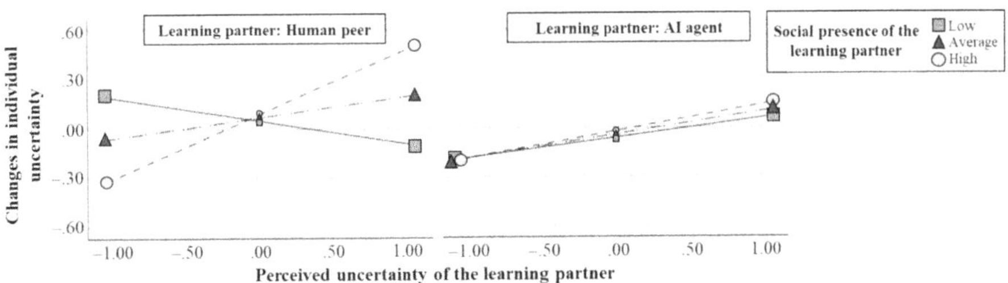

Fig. 8. Visualization of the moderation effect compared by the learning partner.

5   Discussion

In collaborative learning, perceiving and being influenced by peers' uncertainty is common and almost inevitable [10]. However, little empirical research has been conducted on whether uncertainty displayed by digital peer agents can promote learning as well. Such research would provide valuable insight into the fundamental effects of uncertainty in various collaborative learning settings and offer practical implications for designing effective AI-powered learning environments. The aim of this study was to investigate the impact of co-learners' perceived uncertainty (triggered by uncertainty indicators) on learners' metacognitive and affective states, behaviors, and learning intentions. Of particular interest was comparing the effects between learning scenarios involving a human peer or an AI agent as a co-learner. Additionally, we analyzed the mechanisms of uncertainty expression by testing the effects of two types of uncertainty indicators, *uncertainty markers* and *controversial arguments*, and explored the influence of *perceived social presence* on perceived and individual uncertainty.

The results of this study largely corroborate and extend previous empirical findings on the effects of uncertainty in collaborative learning with human peers [38, 40, 42]. First, we found that uncertainty indicators increased learners' perception of their partners' uncertainty, which in turn affected their individual uncertainty and engagement with learning materials. A particularly important new insight was that the effect size of *uncertainty markers* was considerably higher than that of *controversial arguments*. One possible explanation is that uncertainty markers trigger immediate metacognitive monitoring, whereas controversial arguments require deeper, content-based cognitive processing and can also be interpreted in multiple ways. Second, we found that individual uncertainty prompted learners' confusion, which increased their learning intention. These effects seem largely independent of whether the learning partner is a human peer or an AI agent. Thus, integrating uncertainty indicators into the dialogue strategies of AI peer agents seems to be a promising way to encourage learners' critical reflection and an effective metacognitive learning regulation [22, 30]. Furthermore, AI's use of uncertainty expressions could prevent learners from overreliance on its outputs [24], countering the development of technology dependence and poor self-regulation processes [13]. Indeed, this approach provides an intriguing alternative to current AI applications, which mostly appear knowledgeable without concern for veracity [17]. Similar to humans, AI tools such as *ChatGPT* are often 'overconfident' in the sense that they provide incorrect information with convincing confidence. However, unlike humans, these tools seem to lack the (metacognitive) regulatory mechanisms for adjusting confidence [6]. Thus, further work is needed to ensure that the level of confidence expressed by an AI in its responses, as indicated by (un)certainty cues, aligns with the estimated accuracy of those responses [32].

Further results suggest that not the type of co-learner per se – whether a human peer or an AI agent – affects the GUA's influences, but rather the *perceived social presence* of the partner. Higher perceived social presence comes with a stronger impact of perceived group uncertainty on individual uncertainty. Considering these findings, we suggest paying particular attention to social cues that promote social presence in learning environments assisted by AI agents [44]. Although the moderation analysis indicates a stronger effect of social presence for the human peer, this may be attributed to learners' preconceptions about human co-learners. Thus, it requires further investigation of perceptions that shape truly interactive human-AI collaborations [14]. Nonetheless, the impact of social presence might not be uniform, but different underlying mechanisms may influence the role of uncertainty in human-human and human-AI collaborations.

The experimental design that we implemented in this study enhanced the internal validity and precision of our exploratory investigation but also limits its generalizability. Next, investigating a more authentic real-time interaction between learners and their co-learners (human peers vs. AI agents) is necessary to better understand the mechanisms of uncertainty in collaborative learning settings. Additionally, this study primarily measured changes in learners' mental states and their effects using self-report data. Future research would benefit from supplementing this data with behavioral data, such as the amount of time learners actually spend with learning materials during subsequent study sessions. Moreover, to gain deeper insights into the investigated mechanisms, future studies could vary the roles of human peers and AI agents in the learning interactions, in a way that a learning partner is conceptualized as being more or less knowledgeable in the study topic (e.g., AI peer vs. AI tutor; [8, 10]). In addition, future studies could examine how varying the frequency and context of uncertainty indicators (e.g., across different tasks or types of learning partner's statements) might affect learners' perception of group uncertainty.

Acknowledgments. This work was supported by the PsychMeth: Technology, Learning, Collaboration Lab at the University of Duisburg-Essen (UDE), Germany, and the Center for Advanced Internet Studies (CAIS), Bochum, Germany. We thank Kevin Palzer from the PsychMeth: Technology, Learning, Collaboration Lab for assisting us in preparing the study materials.

References

1. Anselme, P.: The uncertainty processing theory of motivation. Behav. Brain Res. **208**(2), 291–310 (2010). https://doi.org/10.1016/j.bbr.2009.12.020
2. Bangert, A.: The influence of social presence and teaching presence on the quality of online critical inquiry. J. Comput. High. Educ. **20**(1), 34–61 (2008). https://doi.org/10.1007/BF03033431
3. Blanca Mena, M.J., Alarcón Postigo, R., Arnau Gras, J., Bono Cabré, R., Bendayan, R.: Non-normal data: is ANOVA still a valid option? Psicothema **29**(4), 552–557 (2017). https://doi.org/10.7334/psicothema2016.383
4. Blankenship, K.L., Holtgraves, T.: The role of different markers of linguistic powerlessness in persuasion. JLSP **24**(1), 3–24 (2005). https://doi.org/10.1177/0261927x04273034
5. Braasch, J.L., Rouet, J.F., Vibert, N., Britt, M.A.: Readers' use of source information in text comprehension. Mem. Cognit. **40**(3), 450–465 (2012). https://doi.org/10.3758/s13421-011-0160-6
6. Cash, T.N., Oppenheimer, D.M., Christie, S., Devgan, M.: Quantifying uncert-AI-nty: testing the accuracy of LLMs' confidence judgments. Mem. Cognit. **54**, 375–400 (2026). https://doi.org/10.3758/s13421-025-01755-4
7. Caspi, A., Blau, I.: Collaboration and psychological ownership: how does the tension between the two influence perceived learning? Soc. Psychol. Educ. **14**, 283–298 (2011). https://doi.org/10.1007/s11218-010-9141-z
8. Chou, C.Y., Chan, T.W., Lin, C.J.: Redefining the learning companion: the past, present, and future of educational agents. Comput. Educ. **40**(3), 255–269 (2003). https://doi.org/10.1016/S0360-1315(02)00130-6
9. Cress, U., Kimmerle, J.: Co-constructing knowledge with generative AI tools: reflections from a CSCL perspective. Int. J. Comput.-Support. Collab. Learn. **18**, 607–614 (2023). https://doi.org/10.1007/s11412-023-09409-w
10. D'Mello, S., Lehman, B., Pekrun, R., Graesser, A.: Confusion can be beneficial for learning. L&I **29**, 153–170 (2014). https://doi.org/10.1016/j.learninstruc.2012.05.003
11. de Araujo, A., Papadopoulos, P.M., McKenney, S., de Jong, T.: A learning analytics-based collaborative conversational agent to foster productive dialogue in inquiry learning. J. Comput. Assist. Learn. **40**(6), 2700–2714 (2024). https://doi.org/10.1111/jcal.13007

12. Efklides, A.: Metacognition: defining its facets and levels of functioning in relation to self-regulation and co-regulation. Eur. Psychol. **13**(4), 277–287 (2008). https://doi.org/10.1027/1016-9040.13.4.277

13. Fan, Y., et al.: Beware of metacognitive laziness: effects of generative artificial intelligence on learning motivation, processes, and performance. Br. J. Edu. Technol. **56**(2), 489–530 (2025). https://doi.org/10.1111/bjet.13544

14. Gomez, C., Cho, S.M., Ke, S., Huang, C.M., Unberath, M.: Human-AI collaboration is not very collaborative yet: a taxonomy of interaction patterns in AI-assisted decision making from a systematic review. Front. Comput. Sci. **6** (2025). Article 1521066. https://doi.org/10.48550/arXiv.2310.19778

15. Green, M.: Cognitive stage differences in types of speaker uncertainty markers. Lang. Speech **27**(4), 323–331 (1984). https://doi.org/10.1177/002383098402700403

16. Hao, Z., Cao, J., Li, R., Yu, J., Liu, Z., Zhang, Y.: Mapping student-AI interaction dynamics in multi-agent learning environments: supporting personalized learning and reducing performance gaps. Comput. Educ. **241** (2025). Article 105472. https://doi.org/10.1016/j.compedu.2025.105472

17. Hicks, M.T., Humphries, J., Slater, J.: ChatGPT is bullshit. Ethics Inf. Technol. **26** (2024). Article 38. https://doi.org/10.1007/s10676-024-09775-5

18. Janson, A.: How to leverage anthropomorphism for chatbot service interfaces: the interplay of communication style and personification. Comput. Hum. Behav. **149** (2023). Article 107954. https://doi.org/10.1016/j.chb.2023.107954

19. Jordan, M.E., McDaniel, R.R.: Managing uncertainty during collaborative problem solving in elementary school teams: the role of peer influence in robotics engineering activity. JLS **23**(4), 490–536 (2014). https://doi.org/10.1080/10508406.2014.896254

20. Juanchich, M., Gourdon-Kanhukamwe, A., Sirota, M.: "I am uncertain" vs "it is uncertain". How linguistic markers of the uncertainty source affect uncertainty communication. Judgm. Decis. Mak. **12**(5), 445–465 (2017). https://doi.org/10.1017/S1930297500006483

21. Karabenick, S.A.: Social influences on metacognition: effects of co-learner questioning on comprehension monitoring. J. Educ. Psychol. **88**(4), 689–703 (1996). https://doi.org/10.1037/0022-0663.88.4.689

22. Kersey, C., Di Eugenio, B., Jordan, P., Katz, S.: KSC-PaL: a peer learning agent that encourages students to take the initiative. In: Proceedings of the 4th Workshop on Innovative Use of NLP for Building Educational Applications, pp. 55–63. Association for Computational Linguistics, Boulder (2009). https://aclanthology.org/W09-2109.pdf

23. Kim, J., Yu, S., Detrick, R., Li, N.: Exploring students' perspectives on generative AI-assisted academic writing. Educ. Inf. Technol. **30**, 1265–1300 (2025). https://doi.org/10.1007/s10639-024-12878-7

24. Kim, S.S., Liao, Q.V., Vorvoreanu, M., Ballard, S., Vaughan, J.W.: "I'm not sure, but…": examining the impact of large language models' uncertainty expression on user reliance and trust. In: Proceedings of the 2024 ACM conference on fairness, accountability, and transparency, pp. 822–835. Association for Computing Machinery, New York, NY, United States (2024). https://doi.org/10.48550/arXiv.2405.00623

25. Koriat, A.: The self-consistency model of subjective confidence. Psychol. Rev. **119**(1), 80–113 (2012). https://doi.org/10.1037/a0025648

26. Koriat, A., Adiv, S., Schwarz, N.: Views that are shared with others are expressed with greater confidence and greater fluency independent of any social influence. Pers. Soc. Psychol. Rev. **20**(2), 176–193 (2015). https://doi.org/10.1177/1088868315585269

27. Lamnina, M., Chase, C. C.: Developing a thirst for knowledge: how uncertainty in the classroom influences curiosity, affect, learning, and transfer. Contemp. Educ. Psychol. **59** (2019). Article 101785. https://doi.org/10.1016/j.cedpsych.2019.101785

28. Lee, K.M., Nass, C.: Designing social presence of social actors in human computer interaction. In: Proceedings of the SIGCHI Conference on Human Factors in Computing Systems, pp. 289–296. ACM, New York (2003). https://doi.org/10.1145/642611.642662

29. Lee, K.M., Peng, W., Jin, S.A., Yan, C.: Can robots manifest personality? An empirical test of personality recognition, social responses, and social presence in human-robot interaction. JOC **56**(4), 754–772 (2006). https://doi.org/10.1111/j.1460-2466.2006.00318.x

30. Lehman, B., Graesser, A.: Impact of agent role on confusion induction and learning. In: Trausan-Matu, S., Boyer, K. E., Crosby, M., Panourgia, K. (eds.) ITS 2014, vol. 8474, pp. 45–54. Springer, Cham (2014). https://doi.org/10.1007/978-3-319-07221-0_6

31. Luther, T., Kimmerle, J., Cress, U.: Teaming up with an AI: exploring human–AI collaboration in a writing scenario with ChatGPT. AI **5**(3), 1357–1376 (2024). https://doi.org/10.3390/ai5030065

32. Mielke, S.J., Szlam, A., Dinan, E., Boureau, Y.L.: Reducing conversational agents' overconfidence through linguistic calibration. Trans. Assoc. Comput. Linguis. **10**, 857–872 (2022). https://doi.org/10.1162/tacl_a_00494

33. Nguyen, A., Hong, Y., Dang, B., Huang, X.: Human-AI collaboration patterns in AI-assisted academic writing **49**(5), 847–864 (2024). https://doi.org/10.1080/03075079.2024.2323593

34. O'Donnell, S.C., Yan, V.X., Bi, C., Oyserman, D.: Is difficulty mostly about impossibility? What difficulty implies may be culturally variant. Pers. Soc. Psychol. Bull. **49**(2), 309–328 (2021). https://doi.org/10.1177/01461672211065595

35. Oppenheimer, D.M., Cash, T.N., Connell Pensky, A.E.: You've got AI friend in me: LLMs as collaborative learning partners. Int. J. Artif. Intell. Educ. **35**, 3896–3921 (2025). https://doi.org/10.1007/s40593-025-00521-6

36. Ozcelik, E., Cagiltay, N.E., Ozcelik, N.S.: The effect of uncertainty on learning in game-like environments. C&E **67**, 12–20 (2013). https://doi.org/10.1016/j.compedu.2013.02.009

37. Radtke, A., Meyer, J., Rummel, N.: Learners' awareness of AI as originator of an academic text during revision: an exploratory study. In: Cristea, A.I., Walker, E., Lu, Y., Santos, O.C., Isotani, S. (eds.) AIED 2025. LNCS, vol. 15878, pp. 3–17, Springer, Cham (2025). https://doi.org/10.1007/978-3-031-98417-4_1

38. Radtke, A., Schnaubert, L.: Effects of uncertainty markers on metacognitive group awareness and regulation. In: Chinn, C., Tan, E., Chan, C., Kali, Y. (eds.) 16th ICLS Proceedings, pp. 274–281. ISLS, Hiroshima (2022). https://repository.isls.org//handle/1/9042

39. Schnaubert, L., Bodemer, D.: Group awareness and regulation in computer-supported collaborative learning. ijCSCL **17**, 11–38 (2022). https://doi.org/10.1007/s11412-022-09361-1

40. Schnaubert, L., Bodemer, D.: Prompting and visualising monitoring outcomes: guiding self-regulatory processes with confidence judgments. Learn. Instr. **49**, 251–262 (2017). https://doi.org/10.1016/j.learninstruc.2017.03.004

41. Schnaubert, L., Bodemer, D.: Providing different types of group awareness information to guide collaborative learning. Int. J. Comput.-Support. Collab. Learn. **14**(1), 7–51 (2019). https://doi.org/10.1007/s11412-018-9293-y

42. Schnaubert, L., Krukowski, S., Bodemer, D.: Assumptions and confidence of others: the impact of socio-cognitive information on metacognitive self-regulation. Metacogn. Learn. **16**(4), 855–887 (2021). https://doi.org/10.1007/s11409-021-09269-5

43. Schneider, S., Beege, M., Nebel, S., Schnaubert, L., Rey, G.D.: The cognitive-affective-social theory of learning in digital environments (CASTLE). Educ. Psychol. Rev. **34**, 1–38 (2022). https://doi.org/10.1007/s10648-021-09626-5

44. Xu, K., Chen, M., You, L.: The hitchhiker's guide to a credible and socially present robot: two meta-analyses of the power of social cues in human–robot interaction. Int. J. Soc. Rob. **15**(2), 269–295 (2023). https://doi.org/10.1007/s12369-022-00961-3

Using LLMs to Score Mathematics Lessons for Instructional Quality with the UTOP

Katie Bainbridge[1]([✉]) [ID], Jessica Vitale[2] [ID], and Candace Walkington[3] [ID]

[1] OpenStax, Rice University, Houston, TX, USA
Katie@OpenStax.org
[2] Vanderbilt University, Nashville, TN, USA
jessicavitale@teachfx.com
[3] Southern Methodist University, University Park, TX, USA
cwalkington@mail.smu.edu

Abstract. Validated classroom observation protocols are useful tools in educational research, but are expensive and invasive to implement. This study sought to investigate the use of AI to reliably score classroom recordings using a validated classroom observation protocol. The UTeach Observation Protocol (UTOP) was designed to assess active and inquiry-based teaching and learning in K-12 STEM classrooms, focusing on more complex and high-inference elements of instruction. We trained 4 experts in STEM education to rate lessons with the UTOP, drawing on a sample of mathematics lesson transcripts from classroom audio recordings. We then had the trained experts each rate 5 new lessons (grades 8-11 mathematics) using the UTOP, and compared their ratings to those generated by GPT-4.1-mini using two prompt-tuned approaches: a rubric-aligned rationale-generation approach and a quote-anchored evidence approach. We found that the reliability of two human raters surpassed the reliability of one human teamed with one AI. However, the AI ratings were substantially above chance in their agreement with human ratings and were moderately correlated to human ratings. The AI models did better on individual indicator ratings than synthesis ratings, and better at rating lesson structure and content than classroom environment or implementation. Using a g-theory approach, we found that having an AI rater to complement a human rater can increase consistency of ratings, particularly for assessing mathematics content. Implications for human-AI teaming to evaluate K-12 instructional quality are given.

Keywords: classroom observation · mathematics education · generative AI

1 Introduction

Classroom observation protocols are invaluable tools in education research; they provide indicators of implementation fidelity, and measures of teacher and student progress over the course of an intervention. However, classroom observations are expensive, difficult to scale, and potentially invasive, as they require a researcher or other trained observer to be physically present in the classroom [1, 2]. The experience of being observed can

E. G. Blanchard et al. (Eds.): AIED 2026, LNAI 16583, pp. 552–561, 2027.
https://doi.org/10.1007/978-3-032-29760-0_55

be disruptive to teachers and students, and it is financially and logistically impractical to observe every class over the course of an intervention. While LLMs have been primarily conceptualized in prior research as tools for student learning and instruction, there is a growing trend toward using generative AI for more evaluative and analytical uses [9, 11]. This study extends that trend by exploring whether LLMs could reliably score classroom recordings using a validated observation protocol. Specifically, we examined whether an AI-based approach could approximate human ratings on the UTeach Observation Protocol (UTOP) when applied to classroom audio recordings and transcripts.

If successful, this approach would enable more frequent and less intrusive measurement of instructional quality than traditional in-person observations, while substantially reducing cost and logistical burden. More broadly, establishing the feasibility of AI-assisted classroom observation could expand the use of validated observation protocols in large-scale and longitudinal research, increasing access to high-quality instructional data. Establishing the feasibility of AI-assisted classroom observation could expand the use of validated protocols in large-scale research. Such an approach aligns with emerging strategies for generative AI in the mobile learning era, while also addressing unresolved research issues surrounding the reliability and validity of AI-generated metrics in digital learning contexts [10].

This paper contributes to the existing literature by applying LLMs to a validated, high-inference observation protocol, systematically comparing two prompting strategies across protocol indicators, and providing evidence for human–AI teaming, rather than replacement, grounded in g-theory.

2 Method

To test the hypothesis that an AI tool could replicate a classroom observation protocol, we began by training 4 math teachers how to use the UTeach Observation protocol. They attended a 6-h training spread over two sessions to learn how to apply the UTOP to audio recordings of secondary math classes. After the training, they were given 5 new recordings and asked to score them using the UTOP. A large language model was prompt-engineered to use the UTOP with the same instructions as the human raters and given the same 5 recordings. We compared the scores generated by the human subject-matter experts and the model.

2.1 Materials

UTOP. The UTeach Observation Protocol (UTOP) is a comprehensive evaluation tool designed to assess the quality of STEM instruction by examining both general pedagogy and content-specific practices [3]. Developed to support the UTeach teacher preparation model [4], the instrument measures classroom performance across four domains: environment, lesson structure, implementation, and mathematics or science content. The instrument shows high internal consistency, with Cronbach's alpha ranging between 0.905 and 0.962 for each of the four sections. The UTOP shows a high disattenuated correlation ($r = 0.85$) with the Mathematical Quality of Instruction (MQI) rubric, demonstrating high convergent validity with measures of similar constructs. It has high predictive validity, showing a correlation of $r = 0.34$ when predicting student test score gains relative to the prior year. The UTOP was altered slightly to fit this particular application of the tool [5]. The version of the UTOP we used had 22 different indicators, with six in Classroom Environment, four in Lesson Structure, five in Implementation, and seven in Mathematics Content [6]. Each section concludes with a 1-5 synthesis rating which is not intended to be a numerical average but rather human weighted for the relative importance of different indicators.

Classroom Audio and Transcripts. The dataset consisted of five classroom transcripts from 8th-10th-grade math teachers derived from classroom audio recordings. Audio was captured via mobile devices and processed using "ABC's" (anonymized) automated speech recognition and diarization pipeline to produce time-aligned transcripts segmented by speaker (teacher vs. student talk). Additional details on the diarization and ASR pipeline are described in prior work [7]. The transcripts reflect the characteristics of real-world classroom audio, including overlapping speech, incomplete utterances, and occasional transcription errors. All transcripts were de-identified prior to human rating and automated analysis. The trained UTOP raters listened to the classroom audio recordings and consulted the corresponding transcripts to support their ratings and written rationales. In contrast, the AI models were provided only with the transcripts and did not have access to the audio.

Automated Rating Methods. Automated UTOP ratings were generated using GPT-4.1-mini with two structured prompting approaches designed to mirror different human rating strategies. Both approaches used the same underlying language model and differed only in the structure of the prompts and the form of evidence requested. For both approaches, the model was provided with the UTOP rubric and the training guide used to prepare the human raters, supplied as reference documents and explicitly cited in the prompts. When provided with the full classroom transcript, the model was instructed to apply the UTOP rubric as written and to base all ratings solely on evidence in the transcript.

In the rubric-aligned rationale-generation approach (Model 1), the model was prompted to assign a score to each UTOP indicator on a 1-5 scale (or NA where permitted), guided by the rubric language and training guidance. For each indicator, the model generated a brief written rationale summarizing the evidence supporting its score. Prompts emphasized conservative scoring, adherence to rubric anchors, and avoidance of inference beyond the transcript. In the quote-anchored evidence approach (Model 2), the model was prompted to assign scores for each indicator and to justify each score by extracting up to two short verbatim teacher utterances from the transcript when possible. When relevant behaviors were not directly reflected in teacher speech, the model was instructed to provide a concise descriptive summary instead. This approach was intended to more explicitly ground ratings in observable linguistic evidence and to parallel evidence-citation practices commonly used by human raters.

2.2 Participants

Our participants were 4 experienced Algebra teachers working in the United States. All four teachers were female and white. The participants underwent the standard training protocol to learn to use the UTOP, delivered by one of the original developers of the instrument via Zoom. During the two-day training, the raters learned about the different UTOP indicators, and then rated sample mathematics lessons from audio files. They discussed and compared their ratings with each other and with the UTOP trainer, clarifying their understanding of the rating procedures in the rating manually as necessary. The raters also read background literature about the UTOP and its rating practices. Each rater then rated 5 new mathematics lessons using the UTOP (due to a medical issue, Rater 4 only rated 4 of the 5 lessons). The means and standard deviations of the raters' UTOP scores are shown below.

Table 1. Indicators on the UTOP with their means and standard deviations

Indicator	Mean	SD
1-1 The classroom environment encouraged students to generate ideas, questions, conjectures, and/or propositions that reflected engagement or exploration with important mathematics concepts	3.05	1.39
1-2 Interactions reflected collegial working relationships among students. (e.g. students worked together productively and talked with each other about the lesson)	1.53	1.48
1-3 Based on conversations, interactions with the teacher, and/or work samples, students were intellectually engaged with important ideas relevant to the focus of the lesson	3.37	1.07
1-4 The majority of students (audible on feeds) were on task throughout the class	3.16	0.96
1-5 The teacher's classroom management strategies enhanced the classroom environment	3.58	1.12
1-6 The classroom environment established by the teacher reflected attention to issues of access, equity, and diversity for students	3.21	0.71
2-1 The lesson was well organized and structured (e.g. the objectives of the lesson were clear to students, and the sequence of the lesson was structured to build understanding and maintain a sense of purpose)	3.47	1.12
2-2 The structure of the lesson allowed students to engage with or explore important concepts in mathematics (instead of focusing on techniques that may only be useful on exams)	3.47	0.96
2-3 The structure of the lesson included opportunities for the instructor to gauge student understanding	3.26	1.28
2-4 The lesson included an investigative or problem-based approach to important concepts in mathematics	2.58	1.43
3-1 The teacher used questioning strategies to develop skills and facilitate interaction with students	3.63	1.12

(continued)

Table 1. (continued)

Indicator	Mean	SD
3-2 The teacher's questioning strategies developed student conceptual understanding of important mathematics content (e.g. emphasizing higher order questions, appropriately using "wait time," exploring incorrect answers)	2.74	1.33
3-3 The teacher used formative assessment effectively to be aware of the progress of all students	2.95	1.22
3-4 An appropriate amount of time was devoted to each part of the lesson	3.00	1.05
3-5 The instructional strategies and activities used in this lesson clearly connected to students' prior knowledge and experience	2.47	1.22
4-1 The mathematics content chosen was significant, worthwhile, and developmentally appropriate for this course (includes content standards covered, as well as examples and activities chosen by teacher)	3.74	0.73
4-2 Content communicated through direct and non-direct instruction by the teacher is consistent with deep knowledge and fluency with the mathematics concepts of the lesson (e.g. fluent use of examples, discussions and explanations of concepts, etc.)	3.42	1.35
4-3 Teacher verbal content information was accurate	4.21	0.92
4-4 Elements of mathematical abstraction (e.g., symbolic representations, theory building) were used appropriately	3.26	0.96
4-5 During the lesson, it was made explicit to students why the content is important to learn	1.53	0.84
4-6 Appropriate connections were made to other areas of mathematics and/or to other disciplines (including non-school contexts)	1.79	0.98
4-7 During the lesson, there was discussion about the content topic's role in history or current events	1.00	0.00

3 Results

3.1 Absolute Reliability of AI Compared to Human "Gold Standard"

We first calculated the absolute reliability of human versus AI ratings on the UTOP. This simulates a scenario where we are deciding if human raters could be replaced by AI raters. We calculated the mode of the human ratings for each indicator and lesson, and compared this mode to the rating of AI-Model 1 and AI-Model 2. For each AI model, we computed its bias (mean error), mean absolute error, and root mean squared error compared to the human rating, and also looked at Pearson and Spearman correlations between the AI ratings and gold standard ratings. The results are shown in Table 2.

Table 2. Reliability of AI-Models 1 and 2 compared to "gold standard" mode of 4 human ratings

UTOP Indicator	AI Model 1				AI Model 2			
	Bias	MAE	RMSE	Pearson	Bias	MAE	RMSE	Pearson
1-1	0.20	1.00	1.48	-0.27	0.80	1.20	1.55	−0.14
1-2	−1.00	1.00	1.29	0.87	−0.67	1.33	1.41	0.50
1-3	−0.20	1.00	1.18	0.27	0.40	1.20	1.26	0.14
1-4	0.00	0.80	0.89	0.35	0.40	0.40	0.63	0.91
1-5	−0.40	0.80	1.10	0.37	−0.80	1.20	1.41	−0.20
1-6	−0.40	0.40	0.63	0.25	-1.00	1.00	1.18	−0.25
3-1	−0.25	1.25	1.32	0.14	0.25	0.75	1.12	0.26
3-2	−0.40	1.20	1.55	0.08	0.60	1.40	1.73	−0.11
3-3	0.60	1.00	1.18	0.64	1.00	1.40	1.48	0.68
3-4	1.00	1.00	1.34	0.41	0.40	1.20	1.26	−0.41
3-5	0.40	1.20	1.26	0.26	0.80	1.20	1.41	0.27
2-1	0.00	0.40	0.63	−0.25	−0.20	0.60	0.78	−0.41
2-2	−0.40	0.40	0.63	0.79	−0.40	0.80	0.89	NA
2-3	0.00	0.80	1.10	0.46	0.40	0.80	1.10	0.58
2-4	−1.00	1.00	1.48	0.67	−0.40	1.20	1.55	0.00
4-1	0.40	0.40	0.63	0.65	0.60	0.60	1.00	−0.61
4-2	0.60	1.00	1.18	0.65	1.40	1.80	2.14	−0.65
4-3	0.60	0.60	1.00	NA	0.40	0.40	0.63	0.88
4-4	−0.67	0.67	0.82	0.87	−0.33	0.33	0.58	0.87
4-5	0.80	0.80	0.89	0.79	0.80	0.80	0.89	NA
4-6	0.00	0.80	1.10	0.29	0.00	0.80	1.10	NA
Average	**−0.01**	**0.83**	**1.08**	**0.41**	**0.21**	**0.97**	**1.20**	**0.13**

As can be seen from the table, overall the AI models do not rate substantially higher or lower than the humans, with the amount of bias varying greatly from indicator-to-indicator. On the UTOP's 5-point scale, the average error levels (MAE, RMSE) hover around 1, although some indicators have lower errors (AI-Model 1: 1-6, 3-1, 3-2, 4-1; AI-Model 2: 1-4, 3-1, 4-1, 4-4) and therefore may be more amenable to being rated by an AI. Other indicators have substantially higher errors (AI-Model 1: 2-1, 2-2, 2-5; AI-Model 2: 2-2, 2-3, 4-2), suggesting that AI struggles to rate aspects of Sect. 2, Lesson Structure, particularly.

The correlations also suggest areas of the AI Models' strengths and weaknesses. Both Models 1 and 2 show high correlation with human ratings for indicator 4.5. AI-Model 1 additionally has high correlations with human raters for indicators 1-2, 3-2, and 4-5, while AI-Model 2 shows strong correlations for 1-4 and 4-3. It may be that using some combination of AI-Models 1 and 2, depending on the indicator being rated, may allow for the best results. We also see negative correlations between the AI-Model ratings and the human ratings for some indicators - like 1-1, 1-5, 1-6, 2-2, 2-4, 3-1, 4-1, and 4-2, with this most often happening for Model 2. Overall, AI-Model 1 seems to be a better fit for the human ratings than AI-Model 2, based on the correlations.

3.2 Cohen's Kappa Reliability of Humans Versus AI Teams

We next looked at the inter-rater reliability of different combinations of raters, to see if human-AI teams would perform similarly to human-human teams. This simulates a scenario where we are deciding whether a second human rater could be replaced by an AI. For this analysis, we looked at overall reliability for all 22 indicators on the UTOP, and for all 4 synthesis ratings on the UTOP. We calculated weighted kappas with linear weights for each combination of raters (e.g., Rater 1 versus Rater 2 or Rater 1 versus AI Model-1). Then, kappas were averaged together based on whether they were from humans or AIs. The weighted kappas for each rater combination are given in Table 3.

Table 3. Weighted kappa values for different lesson rater combinations

Rater Combination	Kappa for Indicator Ratings	Kappa for Synthesis Ratings
Human + Human	0.45	0.35
Human + AI-Model 1	0.37	0.08
Human + AI-Model 2	0.29	0.07
AI-Model 1 + AI-Model 2	0.54	0.04

As can be seen from the table, two humans rating together have a kappa reliability of 0.45 on individual indicators of the UTOP, which corresponds to moderate agreement [8]. This is very similar to the inter-rater reliability figures quoted in prior articles on the UTOP, where a human-human indicator reliability of 0.41 was reported [3]. Having an AI rate a lesson instead of getting a second human reduces the reliability for the indicator ratings by a moderate amount, from 0.45 to 0.37 (AI-Model 1) or 0.29 (AI-Model 2), both corresponding to fair agreement [8]. Thus, AI raters do not appear to rate at the same reliability as humans, with AI-Model 1 showing stronger performance than AI-Model 2. AI-Model 1 and AI-Model 2 showed moderate agreement with each other, however.

For the synthesis ratings, we see substantially lower human-human inter-rater reliability than reported in previous UTOP documentation; indeed, Walkington and Marder [3] put inter-rater reliability of synthesis ratings at 0.63 (substantial agreement), while here that figure is only 0.35 (fair agreement). This may be because the raters in the present study were rating from audio only, rather than audio and video, and getting an overall sense of the teacher was more difficult in this context. As the remaining kappa values show, both of the AI models struggled with the "human weighted" importance approach for UTOP synthesis ratings, rating close to the chance level regardless of who they were rating with.

3.3 G-theory Analysis of Human-AI Teaming

We also used a *g*-theory approach to calculate the reliability of a human rating alone to a human teamed with an AI rater. This simulates a scenario in which only one human rater is available and we want to determine whether it is worthwhile to complement this rater with an AI. To calculate the reliability of a human rating with the UTOP alone, within one section of the UTOP, we fit a mixed effects linear regression model with lesson (lessons 1-5) and indicator (which UTOP indicator from Table 1) as random effects, and used this to calculate the intraclass correlation by looking at the proportion of the total variance that was at the Lesson level. To calculate the reliability of a human rating with the UTOP teamed with an AI (if the AI and human ratings were averaged), we fit a mixed effects linear regression model with lesson, indicator, rater (human or AI), and the interaction of lesson with indicator as random effects. We again calculated the ICC as the proportion of the total variance that was at the Lesson level. The intraclass correlation values are given in Table 4 below. The ICC of each rater's scores in each section of the UTOP when the rater rated alone was compared to the ICC when the rater rated with AI-Model 1 and with AI-Model 2. The ICCs were computed at the rater level, and then averaged together for all raters, depending on whether the rater was human or AI.

Table 4. Intraclass Correlation Values: The amount of variance attributed to underlying characteristics of the lesson

	Classroom Environment	Lesson Structure	Implementation	Math Content
Human Only	0.91975	0.79475	0.68975	0.758
Human + AI-Model1	0.91225	0.8675	0.871	0.84625
Human + AI-Model2	0.8155	0.71925	0.77925	0.69775

As shown in Table 4, adding a second AI rater did not improve upon human raters for the "Classroom Environment" section of the UTOP, with AI-Model 2 making the ratings less reliable. For the "Lesson Structure" section of the UTOP, AI-Model 1 (but not AI-Model 2) teaming with a human rater improved reliability in terms of the ICC, with AI-Model 2 making the ratings less reliable. For the "Implementation" section of the UTOP, both AI models improved the reliability of the human rating, but AI-Model 1 did so by more. And for the "Math Content" section of the UTOP, AI-Model 1 improved upon the human ratings while AI-Model 2 made them less reliable. We again see that AI-Model 1 seems to be a stronger rater than AI-Model 2, and that AI-Model 1 might be particularly useful at rating the Implementation and Math Content sections of the UTOP.

4 Discussion

This study examined whether large language models (LLMs) could approximate human ratings on a validated, high-inference classroom observation protocol (UTOP) using transcript-only classroom data. Overall, results suggest that while LLMs can produce non-random and moderately human-aligned scores for some UTOP indicators, further optimization is required before they can reliably replicate human observation ratings across the full protocol when applied to audio-derived transcripts alone.

Results from both absolute reliability and inter-rater agreement analyses suggest that LLMs, as used here, are not a drop-in replacement for trained human observers. However, g-theory analyses indicate that combining a human rater with an AI rater, particularly for lesson structure and mathematics content, can improve reliability relative to a single human rater alone. This pattern suggests a potential role for AI as a complementary rater that contributes consistency on indicators that are more text-amenable, rather than as a standalone observer. This aligns with work suggesting a role for AI as a complementary partner in educational research, contributing to a broader shift toward scalable, data-driven, and methodologically grounded evaluative uses of the technology [10, 11].

Several methodological factors likely constrained AI performance in this study. First, the UTOP was designed for in-person or video classroom observations, and some indicators rely on visual cues. Second, the dataset was small, consisting of five transcripts from different teachers. Prior work with the UTOP suggests that stable estimates of instructional quality require multiple observations of the same teacher [3]; this condition was not met here. Third, AI models were provided only with transcripts, whereas human raters had access to both audio and transcripts, which may have amplified modality-related differences. Finally, the model used was GPT 4.1, and newer models may prove more capable.

Future studies should consider the strengths and weaknesses of the technology and select a protocol that takes these into account. Our results suggest that LLMs may be better equipped to reliably detect specific, granular elements of a lesson rather than global, synthesis-level interpretations of the lesson as a whole. Additionally, researchers should consider altering or removing elements of the protocol that are easier to gauge with visual cues, and consider using a multimodal AI tool to capture these elements. Rather than using an existing protocol, it may be more fruitful to develop a scoring rubric from scratch with these strengths and limitations in mind, and conduct the reliability/validity testing process with both humans and AI throughout the development of this new protocol with the goal of having a trustworthy, AI-powered tool for classroom observation that can be used for research going forward.

Comparing multiple prompting strategies gave us useful insights into the strengths and weaknesses of using an LLM for this purpose. Given that the prompts used were more effective for some indicators than others, future research could explore making indicator-specific prompts or hybrid prompting designs to increase reliability for the global, holistic aspects of the observation protocol.

Acknowledgments. This work was supported, in whole or in part, by the Gates Foundation [INV-078985]. The conclusions and opinions expressed in this work are those of the author(s) alone and shall not be attributed to the Foundation.

Disclosure of Interests. None to disclose.

References

1. Loughland, T.: Classroom observation as method for research and improvement. In: Teacher Adaptive Practices, Springer Singapore, pp. 23–42 (2019). https://doi.org/10.1007/978-981-13-6858-5_3
2. O'Leary, M.: Classroom Observation: A Guide to the Effective Observation of Teaching and Learning, 2nd edn. Routledge (2020). https://doi.org/10.4324/9781315630243
3. Walkington, C., Marder, M.: Using the UTeach Observation Protocol (UTOP) to understand the quality of mathematics instruction. ZDM Math. Educ. **50**(3), 507–519 (2018). https://doi.org/10.1007/s11858-018-0923-7
4. McGuire, P., Urquhart, M., Enderson, M., Hughes, K., Marder, M., Goldberg, E.: UTeach a quarter of century in review: Impacts, challenges, and new directions in STEM teacher preparation. Am. J. STEM Educ. **16**, 59–76 (2025). https://doi.org/10.32674/fvsgr909
5. UTOP rating manual: UTOP-RAISE. https://sites.google.com/view/utop-raise/home. Accessed 2 Feb 2026
6. UTOP Scoring Sheet: UTOP-RAISE, adapted from Horizon Research, Inc. 2005-06 Core Evaluation Manual, Jun. 19, 2025. https://docs.google.com/document/d/1JLghF8Dnu8TE94eIzSj2GU-fBTxUHzIN/edit. Accessed 2 Feb 2026
7. Perez, M., Coker, B., Kocabagli, K.B., Vitale, J., Van Camp, A.: Multimodal Classroom Diarization with GPT Re-scoring: Teacher or Student?. In: Cristea, A.I., Walker, E., Lu, Y., Santos, O.C., Isotani, S. (Eds.) Artificial Intelligence in Education. AIED 2025, Lecture Notes in Computer Science, vol. 15881, Springer, Cham (2025). https://doi.org/10.1007/978-3-031-98462-4_29
8. Landis, J.R., Koch, G.G.: The measurement of observer agreement for categorical data. Biometrics **33**(1), 159–174 (1977). https://doi.org/10.2307/2529310
9. Chang, C.-Y., Chen, I.-H., Tang, K.-Y. (n.d.).: Roles and research trends of ChatGPT-based learning
10. Lai, C.L., Tu, Y.F.: Roles, strategies, and research issues of generative AI in the mobile learning era. Int. J. Mob. Learn. Organ. **18**(4), 516–537 (2024). https://doi.org/10.1504/IJMLO.2024.141836
11. Tu, Y.F., Lu, Y.C.: Trends of generative AI applications in educational settings. Int. J. Mob. Learn. Organ. **19**(4), 442–467 (2025). https://doi.org/10.1504/IJMLO.2025.149024

Making AI Planning Visible: Narrative-Centered Goal-Directed AI Reasoning to Foster AI Literacy

Bradford Mott[1]([✉]) [iD], Jessica Vandenberg[1] [iD], Srijita Chakraburty[2] [iD], Anne Ottenbreit-Leftwich[2] [iD], Emma Braaten[1] [iD], Cindy Hmelo-Silver[2] [iD], Amy Hutchison[3] [iD], Krista Glazewski[1] [iD], and James Lester[1] [iD]

[1] North Carolina State University, Raleigh, NC, USA
{bwmott,jvanden2,ekbraate,kdglazew,lester}@ncsu.edu
[2] Indiana University, Bloomington, IN, USA
{srichak,aleftwic,chmelosi}@iu.edu
[3] University of Alabama, Tuscaloosa, AL, USA
achutchison1@ua.edu

Abstract. As AI systems increasingly make autonomous, goal-directed decisions, enabling young learners to understand how these systems reason and act is a central challenge in AI education. However, many introductory AI learning experiences treat AI as a black box, limiting students' opportunities to reason about how AI systems represent goals, make decisions, and act in the world. This paper presents a narrative-centered game-based learning environment that makes AI planning visible as a form of goal-directed reasoning to support students' emerging AI literacy. Within the learning environment, students engage in a story-driven investigation, collaborating with an AI-driven agent to solve consequential problems. Students construct and revise representations of goals and actions using a block-based interface, observe how an AI planner generates and executes plans in the game world, and iteratively refine their representations through a Use–Modify–Create scaffolding progression. The narrative context provides concrete stakes for planning decisions, while the behavior of the AI-driven agent serves as interpretable feedback that supports students' sensemaking about goal-directed AI reasoning. We report findings from an implementation of the game with students ages 10–11, examining learning outcomes using pre- and post-assessments of AI knowledge. Results demonstrate statistically significant gains in students' understanding of AI planning concepts related to goal representation and decision-making. These findings illustrate how narrative-centered game design can make goal-directed AI reasoning visible and foster young learners' AI literacy.

Keywords: AI literacy · Elementary AI education · AI planning · Goal-directed reasoning · Game-based learning

1   Introduction

AI increasingly shapes everyday practices, from content recommendation and navigation to scientific analysis and automated problem solving [31]. As these AI-driven systems become more autonomous, supporting K–12 students in developing foundational AI literacy has emerged as an important educational goal [19,28,31]. A central challenge in this space is helping young learners understand that AI systems operate as goal-directed decision makers, relying on internal representations, available actions, and reasoning processes to determine how to act [26,28]. However, introductory AI learning experiences do not always provide students with opportunities to think about how and why AI systems behave as they do, despite the importance of such understanding for AI literacy [31]. When AI reasoning remains hidden, students may struggle to develop accurate mental models of AI behavior, limiting their ability to critically interpret, evaluate, and make sense of AI-driven systems. Addressing this challenge requires learning experiences that make AI reasoning visible and interpretable, enabling young learners to engage meaningfully with how AI systems pursue objectives and make decisions, including how goals, actions, and constraints interact in planning.

Narrative-centered game-based learning offers a promising approach for supporting AI literacy by embedding abstract ideas within meaningful contexts, objectives, and consequences [23,25,32]. Narratives naturally foreground goal-directed activity, as characters' actions are understood in relation to their goals, intentions, and the unfolding causal structure of events [24]. This makes narrative especially well suited for supporting learners' reasoning about how intelligent systems pursue objectives over time through sequences of decisions and actions. Within AI education, AI planning provides a concrete instantiation of goal-directed reasoning, emphasizing how systems represent goals, reason about possible actions, and generate plans to achieve desired outcomes. Unlike many data-driven AI techniques that rely on statistical inference over large datasets, planning systems rely on explicit symbolic representations of goals, actions, and constraints, making their decision processes more readily inspectable. This transparency makes planning particularly well suited for supporting young learners' understanding of how AI systems reason about intent, consequences, and trade-offs over time. When paired with interpretable representations and feedback, planning-based interactions can make AI reasoning processes visible rather than opaque. This perspective aligns with prior work on learning through structured problem solving, which emphasizes hypothesis generation, feedback, and reflection in relation to goals and outcomes [13].

PRIMARYAI is a narrative-centered game-based learning environment designed to support inquiry-based AI learning for upper elementary students ages 8 to 11. In the game, students investigate why penguin populations on a remote island are declining and solve challenges that require reasoning about goals, actions, and outcomes in collaboration with an AI-driven agent. As students interact with the agent, they observe how an AI planner generates and executes plans, use the agent's behavior as feedback, and iteratively refine their goal and action specifications for the agent. Learning is scaffolded through a Use–Modify–Create progression, in which students first use pre-built solutions, then modify them for specific tasks, and ultimately create their own solutions [17]. Through this design, PRIMARYAI aims to make goal-directed AI reasoning explicit, interpretable, and developmentally accessible for young learners in ways that support inquiry, reflection, and iterative problem solving.

To investigate how narrative-centered gameplay that makes AI planning visible supports the development of elementary students' AI literacy, we address the following research questions:

RQ1. To what extent does a narrative-centered game-based learning environment that makes AI planning visible support students' understanding of goal-directed AI reasoning?

RQ2. In what aspects of goal-directed AI reasoning do students show the strongest gains, and where do they continue to struggle?

We explore these questions using data collected during an implementation of the game with fifth-grade students, providing a preliminary investigation of learning outcomes through pre- and post-assessments of AI knowledge.

2 Related Work

2.1 AI Literacy in K–12 Education

Recent work in AI education has increasingly emphasized the development of core competencies that enable learners to engage meaningfully with AI systems, beyond simply interacting with AI-driven tools. Foundational frameworks proposed by Long and Magerko [19] and by Touretzky et al. [28] articulate AI literacy as encompassing an understanding of how AI systems perceive, represent, and learn from data; how training, evaluation, and feedback shape system behavior; and how AI capabilities and limitations influence real-world decision making. More recent consensus-driven efforts led by the Computer Science Teachers Association (CSTA) and the AI4K12 initiative further refine and prioritize these competencies for K–12 learners, emphasizing preparation for informed participation as consumers, creators, and citizens in an AI-enabled society [5]. Collectively, these frameworks highlight representation and reasoning as central dimensions of AI literacy that should be made accessible even to young learners.

A growing body of K–12 AI education research underscores the importance of contextualized and authentic learning experiences for supporting these AI competencies [8,16,31]. Prior work suggests that students develop stronger conceptual understanding when AI ideas are embedded in personally meaningful, real-world contexts rather than presented through abstract or decontextualized instruction alone [16,27]. Pedagogical approaches such as project-based learning [6,15], game-based learning [1,30], and disciplinary integration [2,29] have all been shown to support deeper conceptual engagement by helping learners connect AI concepts to observable phenomena and familiar practices. Recent work has also begun to explore scenario-based instructional interventions that support students' responsible and effective use of AI systems for learning through direct interaction and feedback [33]. Collectively, these approaches position students not only as consumers of AI technologies, but also as active participants who can experiment with data, models, and decision-making processes in ways that reflect authentic forms of AI use.

Despite this progress, students and teachers continue to face significant challenges in developing robust conceptual understandings of AI. Prior research documents persistent misconceptions about AI systems [7,21], including overgeneralized beliefs about autonomy, intelligence, and correctness. These challenges underscore the need for instructional supports and pedagogical designs that make otherwise invisible AI processes, such as internal representations, reasoning steps, and decision logic, more accessible and interpretable for learners [19,28,31]. Addressing these challenges is essential for supporting accurate mental models of AI behavior and for preparing learners to engage in ethical reasoning and informed decision-making about AI-driven systems.

2.2 Supporting AI Literacy Through Game-Based Learning

Game-based learning has emerged as a promising approach for supporting AI literacy by providing interactive environments in which learners engage with complex concepts through action, feedback, and iteration [12,18,22,30]. In contrast to static instructional materials, game-based learning environments enable students to test hypotheses, observe the consequences of decisions, and iteratively refine their understanding [10,25]. Furthermore, work on intelligent game-based learning highlights how adaptive feedback, learner modeling, and AI-supported decision making can foster learners' sensemaking [20].

Recent work has explored a wide range of game-based and interactive approaches to AI education, including simulations, competitive environments, and role-playing experiences that introduce concepts such as classification, reinforcement learning, and algorithmic decision making [1,12,16]. These approaches often emphasize learning through doing, enabling students to manipulate data, adjust model parameters, or compare system outputs in ways that make concepts more accessible [12,22]. Prior work also highlights important design challenges faced by AI learning environments [7,31]. Many approaches emphasize technical interaction with AI tools without sufficiently situating these activities within meaningful narrative, social, or decision-making contexts. As a result, learners may gain familiarity with AI mechanisms while continuing to struggle with questions of when, why, or for whom particular AI approaches are appropriate [34]. Moreover, AI systems may be perceived as black-box authorities [9,14] rather than as fallible, context-dependent systems that require human judgment [3]. For younger learners, such perceptions are particularly problematic, as they can reinforce over-trust, anthropomorphic interpretations of AI behavior, and the belief that AI systems are inherently objective or infallible. These findings underscore the need for game-based learning designs that support not only interaction with

AI systems, but also learners' reasoning about AI behavior, limitations, and decision processes [7,28].

3   PRIMARYAI Learning Environment

PRIMARYAI is a narrative-centered game-based learning environment designed to engage upper elementary students (ages 8–11) in AI-infused problem solving (Fig. 1). In the game, players investigate the decline of the penguin population on a remote island, engaging in challenges that require them to collect data, evaluate hypotheses, and reason about AI-supported decision making. The game is designed for use in classroom settings and is accompanied by a curriculum that includes "unplugged" AI learning activities. These unplugged activities introduce foundational AI concepts prior to gameplay, preparing students to engage with AI reasoning within the game. This section describes the design goals and design decisions for PRIMARYAI, focusing on how narrative-centered gameplay and AI planning are integrated to make goal-directed AI reasoning visible through interpretable representations, agent behavior, and iterative feedback.

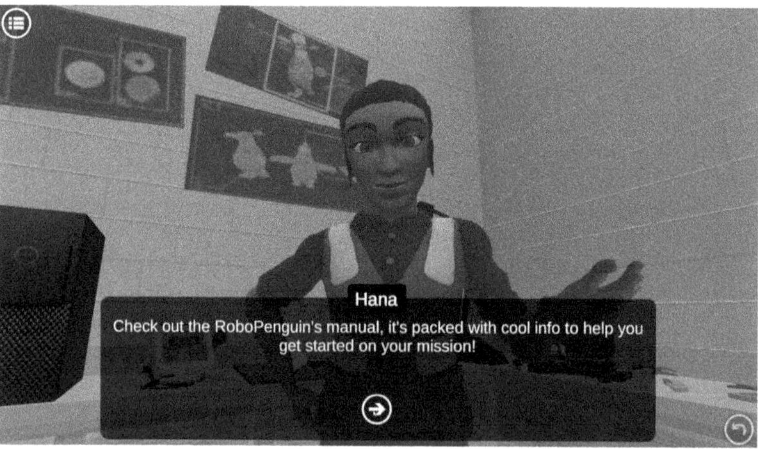

Fig. 1. In-game scene from PRIMARYAI, illustrating the game's interface and guidance from in-world characters.

3.1   Design Goals and Learning Aims

The design of PRIMARYAI is guided by the goal of supporting upper elementary students' emerging AI literacy by making goal-directed AI reasoning visible, interpretable, and developmentally accessible. Building on prior work that introduced the PRIMARYAI learning environment [11], this paper foregrounds the design rationale for helping students think about how AI systems represent goals, select actions, and generate plans. This focus aligns with AI literacy frameworks that emphasize representation and reasoning as core ideas students should understand, even at early grade levels [28]. A central design aim of the game is to position AI planning as an observable and manipulable form of goal-directed reasoning that students can engage with through interaction. To support this, PRIMARYAI prioritizes interpretable representations of goals and actions, immediate behavioral feedback from an AI-driven agent, and opportunities for iterative refinement (Fig. 2). AI reasoning is embedded within a meaningful narrative context that provides clear goals, constraints, and consequences, supporting inquiry-oriented learning while grounding abstract reasoning processes in concrete situations. Together, these design elements aim to help students develop accurate mental models of how AI systems reason and act, rather than treating AI behavior as opaque or magical.

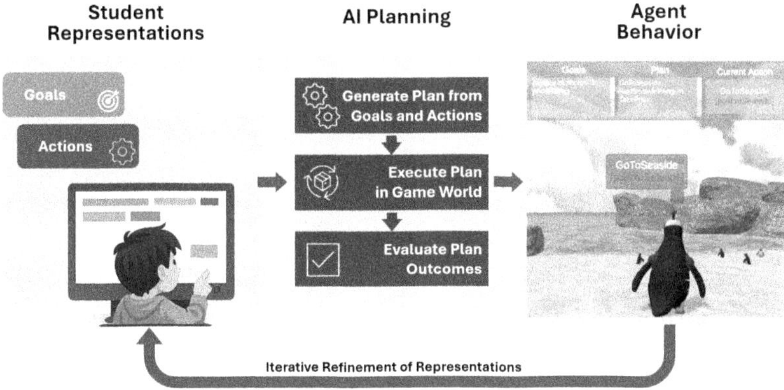

Fig. 2. Iterative gameplay model showing how student-defined goals and actions are used by an AI planner to generate, execute, and evaluate plans in the game world.

3.2 Narrative-Centered Gameplay and AI Planning Integration

PRIMARYAI engages students in a story-driven investigation focused on understanding environmental changes affecting the penguin population on a remote island. The narrative context provides a coherent structure in which goals are meaningful, actions have consequences, and decisions unfold over time, conditions that naturally support reasoning about goal-directed behavior. Within the game, students collaborate with an AI-driven agent, playfully known as *RoboPenguin*, a robot camouflaged as a penguin that assists in solving challenges related to the investigation. Rather than functioning as a passive tool, the robot operates as an autonomous entity that generates and executes plans to achieve specified goals. As students observe the robot's behavior in the game world, they connect abstract representations of goals and actions to concrete outcomes, experiencing AI planning as a visible form of reasoning embedded within narrative gameplay. Gameplay challenges are designed to prompt students to reason explicitly about what the robot is trying to accomplish, which actions are available, and how sequences of actions lead to success or failure. By situating AI planning within narrative-centered inquiry, the environment leverages storytelling to support students' understanding of decision-making over time, emphasizing how AI systems pursue goals under constraints rather than simply producing answers.

3.3 Making Goal-Directed AI Reasoning Visible

A core design feature of PRIMARYAI is making goal-directed AI reasoning visible through interpretable representations and behavior-based feedback. Students interact with a block-based interface in the game that allows them to construct and revise representations of goals and actions that guide the AI agent's behavior (Fig. 3). These representations are designed to be accessible to elementary learners while preserving the essential structure of goal-directed reasoning.

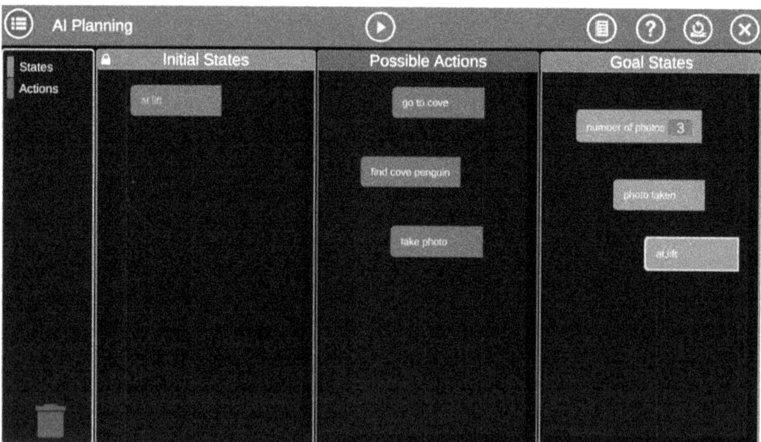

Fig. 3. In-game block-based interface for manipulating planning representations, including initial states, possible actions, and goal states.

The design makes reasoning visible through three tightly coupled mechanisms: (1) *Inspectable representations*, which allow students to add, modify, and delete planning goals and actions; (2) *Executable reasoning*, in which an AI planner generates plans directly from students' representations; and (3) *Behavior-as-feedback*, where the agent's execution of a plan reveals how those representations influence outcomes (Fig. 4). Successful plans advance the narrative, while unsuccessful plans prompt students to reconsider goal specifications or action choices. This coupling between representation, execution, and outcome supports iterative sensemaking by allowing students to observe how changes in representations affect AI behavior.

Fig. 4. AI-driven agent planning and executing a plan, with the current plan and action displayed in the game world.

Learning is further scaffolded through a Use–Modify–Create progression that structures students' engagement with goal-directed AI reasoning [17]. Students initially use pre-constructed representations to observe how the agent behaves, then modify these representations to address new challenges, and ultimately create their own goal and action specifications. This progression is intended to support a gradual shift from interpreting AI behavior to actively constructing and refining the representations that drive it. Through this combination of narrative context, interpretable representations, and iterative feedback, PRIMARYAI aims to make goal-directed AI reasoning explicit, understandable, and developmentally appropriate for elementary learners.

4   Method

To investigate our research questions, we use data collected during a multi-week implementation of PRIMARYAI with fifth-grade students.

4.1   Participants and Setting

The implementation involved a total of 60 students across three fifth-grade classrooms at a Midwestern elementary school in the United States as part of a multi-week AI-infused science curriculum. Informed parental consent and student assent were obtained prior to participation, in accordance with Institutional Review Board approval. Of the participating students, approximately 55% identified as female, 40% as male, and 5% did not specify a gender. Instruction took place during a structured field experience hosted on a university campus, where students attended weekly full-day sessions over six weeks.

4.2   Instructional Context and Procedure

PRIMARYAI was co-taught by an experienced elementary science teacher and a member of the research team, using the same curriculum and instructional materials employed in standard classroom implementations of the learning environment. Across the six-week period, the curriculum introduced foundational AI concepts, including computer vision, machine learning, and AI planning, through inquiry-based activities grounded in real-world science applications. At the start and end of each unit, students completed brief pre- and post-unit assessments aligned with the focal AI concepts. Prior to the AI planning unit, students engaged in unplugged activities, group discussions, and hands-on tasks designed to support understanding of how AI systems learn from data and make decisions. During the final phase of the curriculum, students engaged with the PRIMARYAI game across two instructional sessions. These gameplay sessions constitute the primary focus of the learning outcomes analyzed in this study, although they occurred within the broader instructional context of the multi-week curriculum.

4.3   Knowledge Assessment

To assess learning outcomes, students' conceptual knowledge was measured using assessments developed in our prior work and iteratively refined to capture understanding across instructional units [4]. For the AI planning unit, matched pre- and post-data were available for 24 out of the 60 participating students, due to absences and incomplete assessment responses across the implementation. This subset constituted the analytic sample used in all subsequent analyses.

The AI planning assessment consisted of 11 multiple-choice items designed to measure students' understanding of goal-directed AI reasoning across increasing levels of complexity. Items assessed students' understanding of core planning representations, including initial states, goal states, and actions, as well as their ability to apply these representations in configuring plans for an AI-driven agent. For example, one item asked students to identify the goal state of a robot tasked with collecting trash cans around a school, with the correct response indicating the robot's ending condition ("at the office, 3 trash cans collected"), requiring students to distinguish goal states from initial conditions or intermediate states. Additional items probed students' understanding of action constraints, including preconditions and postconditions, which are central to reasoning about why plans succeed or fail. For instance, students were asked to select the most appropriate precondition for an action (e.g., whether the robot must first locate a trash can before picking it up), targeting their understanding of dependencies between actions and world states. Internal consistency of the AI planning assessment at post-test was examined as a reliability check and demonstrated good internal reliability (Cronbach's α = .82); however, given the relatively small analytic sample, this result is reported as evidence of internal consistency rather than full-scale validation. For analyses related to RQ2, items were grouped by conceptual focus to examine patterns of learning gains and persistent difficulties.

5   Results

To address RQ1, we examined learning outcomes using paired-samples t-tests comparing students' pre- and post-assessment scores on the AI planning knowledge assessment, with possible scores ranging from 0 to 11. Assumption checks indicated no evidence of substantial deviation from normality in the pre–post difference scores (Shapiro–Wilk $W = .970$, $p = .670$), supporting the use of a paired-samples t-test. Effect sizes were calculated using Cohen's d to estimate the magnitude of observed learning gains. Results indicated a statistically significant increase in students' understanding of AI planning concepts from pre-test ($M = 6.00$, $SD = 2.52$) to post-test ($M = 7.04$, $SD = 2.88$), $t(23) = 2.44$, $p = .023$, corresponding to a small but meaningful effect size ($d = 0.39$). This reflects an average gain of 1.04 points, or approximately one additional item correct on the 11-item assessment.

To better understand where students made the greatest progress and where challenges persisted, we examined learning gains across specific components of goal-directed AI reasoning (RQ2). Assessment items were grouped into conceptual categories corresponding to key aspects of AI planning (i.e., *core concepts*, *planning setup*, *action constraints*, and *action prioritization*), and summed pre- and post-test scores were calculated within each category (Table 1). These categories reflect progressively more complex aspects of planning, from understanding core elements to configuring planning problems and reasoning about action constraints and preferences. Given the exploratory nature of these component-level analyses, we focused on descriptive pre–post patterns and Cohen's d effect sizes, computed using the average of the pre- and post-test standard deviations to characterize the magnitude of change within each component.

Table 1. Pre–Post performance across key aspects of AI planning. *Note. Values in parentheses indicate the number of assessment items in each category.*

AI Planning Aspect	Pre M	Pre SD	Post M	Post SD	d	Magnitude
Core concepts (4)	2.67	1.13	2.96	1.20	0.25	Small
Planning setup (3)	1.54	1.02	1.75	1.11	0.20	Small
Action constraints (3)	1.17	1.05	1.67	1.17	0.45	Small-to-moderate
Action prioritization (1)	0.63	0.49	0.67	0.48	0.09	Negligible

Results indicated that students demonstrated their strongest gains in reasoning about *action constraints*, which showed a small-to-moderate effect size (Cohen's $d = 0.45$). This suggests students became more adept at reasoning about how preconditions and postconditions govern action execution.

In contrast, gains for *core concepts* and *planning setup* were more limited, with small effect sizes (Cohen's $d = 0.25$ and $d = 0.20$, respectively). Performance on *core concepts* increased modestly, suggesting some growth in students' understanding of key planning elements. Although *planning setup* also improved slightly on average, students may have continued to experience difficulty coordinating initial states, goals, and actions into coherent plans.

Reasoning about *action prioritization* showed minimal change from pre-test to post-test, with a negligible effect size (Cohen's $d = 0.09$). This result should be interpreted with caution, as this aspect of planning was assessed using a single item, which likely constrained sensitivity to change.

6   Discussion

This study investigated how making AI planning visible within a narrative-centered game-based learning environment supports young learners' emerging AI literacy. Given the exploratory nature of this analysis, the findings should be interpreted as indicative rather than definitive. Overall, the results indicate that students demonstrated statistically significant learning gains in their understanding of goal-directed AI reasoning, with the strongest gains observed in reasoning about action constraints. These findings suggest that embedding AI planning within interpretable representations, agent behavior, and narrative context can help learners reason about how AI systems make decisions.

One of the most notable findings was that students showed their strongest learning gains in reasoning about *action constraints*, including preconditions and postconditions. Importantly, in the game, students do not directly author these constraints within the block-based planning interface. Instead, they are made visible through the AI-driven agent's execution of plans in the game world. As actions succeed or fail, students observe how satisfied or unmet conditions shape the agent's behavior, creating concrete opportunities for sensemaking. This design suggests that, even without direct authoring, exposure to interpretable agent behavior can support learners' understanding of otherwise invisible planning constraints. The tight coupling among representation, execution, and feedback appears to help students reason about why certain actions are possible in a given context, rather than treating AI behavior as arbitrary or opaque.

From a design perspective, these findings suggest that *action constraints* may serve as a particularly accessible entry point for helping elementary learners reason about goal-directed AI behavior. Unlike abstract planning structures, constraints are experienced through observable outcomes, making them well suited for developmentally appropriate learning environments. This reinforces the value of designing AI literacy experiences that emphasize interpretable feedback loops, where learners can connect internal reasoning processes to external behavior.

In contrast, modest gains in both *core concepts* and *planning setup* suggest that some aspects of AI planning remained challenging for learners. Although students showed some growth in understanding key planning elements, integrating initial states, goals, and actions into coherent planning tasks appeared to place greater cognitive demands on them. This pattern points to the difficulty of not only learning core planning ideas, but also coordinating multiple representations simultaneously, particularly for younger students. While the game provides opportunities for iterative refinement, additional scaffolding may be needed to support students in developing both a stronger grasp of foundational planning concepts and the ability to configure them into complete planning tasks.

Reasoning about *action prioritization* showed minimal change from pre-test to post-test. This may reflect both the relative complexity of prioritization as a planning concept and the fact that the current version of the game provides only minimal support for making prioritization visible to learners. Unlike preconditions and postconditions, which were directly reflected in action execution and feedback, prioritization was less explicitly represented in gameplay. The limited change observed in this area is therefore not entirely surprising. Supporting reasoning about prioritization may require richer instructional scaffolds, additional practice, or more explicit representation of action preferences and trade-offs within the learning environment.

Together, these findings underscore the importance of designing AI literacy experiences that move beyond surface-level interaction with AI tools to foreground how AI systems reason and act. The results suggest that making AI reasoning visible through interpretable representations and behavior-based feedback can support young learners' sensemaking, particularly for aspects of AI planning that are closely tied to observable outcomes.

For designers of AI literacy learning environments, these results highlight the value of narrative-centered game-based approaches that situate AI reasoning within meaningful contexts. Importantly, the findings also suggest that different components of AI reasoning may require different forms of scaffolding, with constraints and feedback serving as effective entry points and more abstract planning coordination requiring additional support.

7   Limitations and Future Work

While this study provides evidence for the potential of narrative-centered AI planning experiences, several limitations highlight important directions for future research. First, the analytic sample was limited to students with matched pre- and post-assessment data, resulting in a modest sample size and limited statistical power. Studies with larger samples will be valuable for assessing the robustness of these results across a broader range of learners and contexts. Second, participant demographic information (e.g., gender) was collected as part of the study; however, the size of the analytic sample did not permit meaningful subgroup or intersectional analyses. As a result, we report aggregate learning outcomes and interpret the findings as exploratory with respect to broader generalizability. Future work with larger and more diverse samples will be needed to examine potential differences in how students from different backgrounds engage with and learn about AI through narrative-centered game-based learning. Third, the assessment of *action prioritization* relied on one item, constraining sensitivity to change in this area. Developing richer measures of prioritization represents an important direction for future work. Finally, because gameplay was embedded within a broader instructional sequence that included unplugged activities, the study does not isolate the effects of the game alone.

More broadly, while this study focused on learning outcomes related to AI planning, future work could examine how students' reasoning processes evolve during gameplay using log data and related process analyses. Such analyses could provide deeper insight into how learners interact with representations and feedback over time. Finally, longitudinal studies are needed to explore how early experiences with goal-directed AI reasoning influence students' broader AI literacy and their ability to reason about AI systems in new contexts.

8   Conclusion

By embedding goal-directed AI reasoning within interpretable representations, agent behavior, and meaningful narrative context, PRIMARYAI provides learners with opportunities to think about how AI systems pursue goals and make decisions over time, rather than treating AI behavior as a black box. This perspective is increasingly relevant as learners encounter agentic AI systems that autonomously pursue goals, adapt to changing conditions, and act over time.

Results indicate that students demonstrated statistically significant gains in their understanding of AI planning, with the strongest improvements observed in *action constraints*. Notably, these gains occurred even though students did not directly author preconditions or postconditions, suggesting that observing AI behavior and feedback during plan execution can be an effective pathway for supporting learners' sensemaking about otherwise invisible reasoning processes. At the same time, more modest gains in *core concepts* and *planning setup* highlight ongoing challenges in supporting learners' coordination of multiple planning elements, pointing to opportunities for additional scaffolding and refinement.

These findings provide evidence that narrative-centered game-based learning can make goal-directed AI reasoning accessible and interpretable for elementary learners. More broadly, this work suggests that AI literacy experiences that foreground observable reasoning processes, rather than surface-level interaction with AI tools, can help young learners develop more accurate mental models of how AI systems reason and act.

Acknowledgments. This research was supported by the National Science Foundation (NSF) under grants DRL-2445720, DRL-2445721, DRL-2445722, DRL-1934153, and DRL-1934128. Any opinions, findings, and conclusions expressed in this material are those of the authors and do not necessarily reflect the views of the NSF.

Disclosure of Interests. The authors have no competing interests to declare.

References

1. Aguiar, C., Carpenter, D., Vandenberg, J., Min, W., Catete, V., Mott, B.: Fostering AI literacy through strategic play: a competitive pathfinding game for middle school. In: Proceedings of the IEEE Conference on Games, pp. 1–4. IEEE (2025)

2. Akram, B., Yoder, S., Tatar, C., Boorugu, S., Aderemi, I., Jiang, S.: Towards an AI-infused interdisciplinary curriculum for middle-grade classrooms. In: Proceedings of the AAAI Conference on Artificial Intelligence, vol. 36, pp. 12681–12688 (2022)
3. Amershi, S., et al.: Guidelines for human-AI interaction. In: Proceedings of the CHI Conference on Human Factors in Computing Systems, pp. 1–13 (2019)
4. Chakraburty, S., et al.: Measuring upper-elementary students' understanding of AI concepts-A RASCH model analysis. Inf. Learn. Sci. (2025)
5. CSTA & AI4K12: AI learning priorities for all K-12 students. Computer Science Teachers Association, New York, NY (2025). https://csteachers.org/ai-priorities
6. Druga, S., Otero, N., Ko, A.J.: The landscape of teaching resources for AI education. In: Proceedings of the ACM Conference on Innovation and Technology in Computer Science Education, vol. 1, pp. 96–102 (2022)
7. Druga, S., Williams, R., Breazeal, C., Resnick, M.: "Hey Google, is it ok if I eat you?" Initial explorations in child–agent interaction. In: Proceedings of the ACM Conference on Interaction Design and Children, pp. 595–600 (2017)
8. Eguchi, A., Okada, H., Muto, Y.: Contextualizing AI education for K-12 students to enhance their learning of AI literacy through culturally responsive approaches. KI-Künstliche Intelligenz $35(2)$, 153–161 (2021)
9. Felzmann, H., Fosch-Villaronga, E., Lutz, C., Tamò-Larrieux, A.: Towards transparency by design for artificial intelligence. Sci. Eng. Ethics $26(6)$, 3333–3361 (2020)
10. Gee, J.P.: What video games have to teach us about learning and literacy. Comput. Entertain. $1(1)$, 1–4 (2003)
11. Gupta, A., et al.: Supporting upper elementary students in learning AI concepts with story-driven game-based learning. In: Proceedings of the AAAI Conference on Artificial Intelligence, vol. 38, pp. 23092–23100 (2024)
12. Hinojosa, C., Kumar, P., Rajarajan, P.D., Martin, F.: TrainYourSnakeAI: a novel tool to teach reinforcement learning to middle school students. In: Proceedings of the ACM Technical Symposium on Computer Science Education, vol. 1, pp. 506–512 (2025)
13. Hmelo-Silver, C.E.: Problem-based learning: what and how do students learn? Educ. Psychol. Rev. $16(3)$, 235–266 (2004)
14. Kaur, H., Nori, H., Jenkins, S., Caruana, R., Wallach, H., Wortman Vaughan, J.: Interpreting interpretability: understanding data scientists' use of interpretability tools for machine learning. In: Proceedings of the CHI Conference on Human Factors in Computing Systems, pp. 1–14 (2020)
15. Kong, S.C., Cheung, M.Y.W., Tsang, O.: Developing an artificial intelligence literacy framework: evaluation of a literacy course for senior secondary students using a project-based learning approach. Comput. Educ. Artif. Intell. 6, 100214 (2024)
16. Lee, I., Ali, S., Zhang, H., DiPaola, D., Breazeal, C.: Developing middle school students' AI literacy. In: Proceedings of the ACM Technical Symposium on Computer Science Education, pp. 191–197 (2021)
17. Lee, I., et al.: Computational thinking for youth in practice. ACM Inroads $2(1)$, 32–37 (2011)
18. Lim, H., Min, W., Vandenberg, J., Cateté, V., Mott, B.: Unplugged K-12 AI learning: Exploring representation and reasoning with a facial recognition game. In: Proceedings of the AAAI Conference on Artificial Intelligence, vol. 38, pp. 23285–23293 (2024)
19. Long, D., Magerko, B.: What is AI literacy? Competencies and design considerations. In: Proceedings of the CHI Conference on Human Factors in Computing Systems, pp. 1–16 (2020)

20. McLaren, B.M., Nguyen, H.A.: Digital learning games in Artificial Intelligence in Education (AIED): a review. In: Handbook of Artificial Intelligence in Education, pp. 440–484 (2023)
21. Mertala, P., Fagerlund, J.: Finnish 5th and 6th graders' misconceptions about artificial intelligence. Int. J. Child-Comput. Interact. **39**, 100630 (2024)
22. Mott, B., et al.: Designing a narrative-centered game to promote AI literacy and health career exploration. In: Proceedings of the IEEE Conference on Games, pp. 1–4. IEEE (2025)
23. Naul, E., Liu, M.: Why story matters: a review of narrative in serious games. J. Educ. Comput. Res. **58**(3), 687–707 (2020)
24. Riedl, M.O., Young, R.M.: An intent-driven planner for multi-agent story generation. In: Proceedings of the Third International Joint Conference on Autonomous Agents and Multiagent Systems-Volume 1, pp. 186–193 (2004)
25. Rowe, J.P., Shores, L.R., Mott, B.W., Lester, J.C.: Integrating learning, problem solving, and engagement in narrative-centered learning environments. Int. J. Artif. Intell. Educ. **21**(1–2), 115–133 (2011)
26. Russell, S., Norvig, P.: Artificial Intelligence: A Modern Approach, 4th edn. Pearson (2020)
27. Sintov, N., et al.: Keeping it real: using real-world problems to teach AI to diverse audiences. AI Mag. **38**(2), 35–47 (2017)
28. Touretzky, D., Gardner-McCune, C., Martin, F., Seehorn, D.: Envisioning AI for K-12: what should every child know about AI? In: Proceedings of the AAAI Conference on Artificial Intelligence, vol. 33, pp. 9795–9799 (2019)
29. Walsh, B., Dalton, B., Forsyth, S., Yeh, T.: Literacy and STEM teachers adapt AI ethics curriculum. In: Proceedings of the AAAI Conference on Artificial Intelligence, vol. 37, pp. 16048–16055 (2023)
30. Wang, N., Greenwald, E., Montgomery, R., Leitner, M.: ARIN-561: an educational game for learning artificial intelligence for high-school students. In: Rodrigo, M.M., Matsuda, N., Cristea, A.I., Dimitrova, V. (eds.) AIED 2022. LNCS, vol. 13356, pp. 528–531. Springer, Cham (2022). https://doi.org/10.1007/978-3-031-11647-6_108
31. Wang, N., Lester, J.: K-12 education in the age of AI: a call to action for K-12 AI literacy. Int. J. Artif. Intell. Educ. **33**(2), 228–232 (2023)
32. Wang, T., Uttamchandani, S., Zou, X., Hmelo-Silver, C.E., Rowe, J., Lester, J.: Learning with stories: characteristics and learning outcomes in narrative-centered science learning environments. In: Proceedings of the International Society of the Learning Sciences (2023)
33. Xiao, R., et al.: Learning to use AI for learning: teaching responsible use of AI chatbot to K-12 students through an AI literacy module. In: Proceedings of the AAAI Conference on Artificial Intelligence, vol. 40, pp. 40721–40729 (2026)
34. Zhang, H., Lee, I., Ali, S., DiPaola, D., Cheng, Y., Breazeal, C.: Integrating ethics and career futures with technical learning to promote AI literacy for middle school students: an exploratory study. Int. J. Artif. Intell. Educ. **33**(2), 290–324 (2023)

A Comparative Study of Student Perspectives on Technical Writing Feedback Quality: Evaluating LLMs, SLMs, and Humans in Computer Science Topics

Suqing Liu[1], Runlong Ye[2(✉)], Christopher Eaton[3], Bogdan Simion[4],
and Michael Liut[4]

[1] McMaster University, Hamilton, ON, Canada
`liu2684@mcmaster.ca`
[2] Department of Computer Science, University of Toronto, Toronto, ON, Canada
`harryye@cs.toronto.edu`
[3] Research Institute for the Study of University Pedagogy, University of Toronto
Mississauga, Mississauga, ON, Canada
`chris.eaton@utoronto.ca`
[4] Department of Mathematical and Computational Sciences, University of Toronto
Mississauga, Mississauga, ON, Canada
`bogdan@cs.toronto.edu, michael.liut@utoronto.ca`

Abstract. To address the scalability of feedback in computer science while mitigating the privacy and cost limitations of commercial Large Language Models (LLMs), this study evaluates a locally hosted Small Language Model (SLM). We deployed a quantized Llama-3.1, GPT-4, and human instructors across introductory programming ($N = 176$), operating systems ($N = 80$), and a writing seminar ($N = 7$). Mixed-methods analysis of student perceptions reveals that while the local SLM matched commercial LLMs and was rated higher by students for readability and actionability in technical courses, human feedback remained more favoured for highly specialized writing tasks. We demonstrate that local SLMs offer a privacy-preserving, zero-marginal-cost alternative for foundational feedback, supporting a tiered pedagogical framework where AI handles structural guidance while instructors focus on high-level conceptual scaffolding.

Keywords: Technical Writing · Small Language Models · Large Language Models · Intelligent Tutoring System · Computer Science Education

---

S. Liu, R. Ye—These authors contributed equally.

E. G. Blanchard et al. (Eds.): AIED 2026, LNAI 16583, pp. 577–592, 2027.
https://doi.org/10.1007/978-3-032-29760-0_57

1   Introduction

Feedback enables students to understand their progress and identify areas that require improvement [8,13]. In education, both in the computing and writing/communication domains, where complex concepts and technical proficiency must be acquired, timely and constructive feedback is integral to student development [2,16]. Traditionally, formative feedback in such contexts is often provided by Teaching Assistants, who guide learners through assignments, projects, and exercises. Although the quality and consistency of TA-generated feedback can vary [6], students perceive it as a valuable and supportive resource [18].

As artificial intelligence (AI) technologies continue to evolve, recent work has proposed leveraging LLMs such as GPT [1] or Llama [10] as scalable, automated feedback generation tools [17,24,25,36]. These AI-driven approaches hold the promise of delivering timely and consistent feedback at scale. Other work shows the impact of SLMs, lightweight models optimized for efficiency and accessibility, that have been used in place of LLMs [35] as a time-efficient and cost-effective alternative.

This research aims to address a gap in understanding how AI-generated feedback compares to human-provided alternatives by examining student perceptions of feedback quality and contextual suitability. Specifically, it evaluates the potential for LLMs and SLMs to deliver clarity, specificity, and actionable insights and to meet the nuanced requirements within computing education. Our key research questions (RQs) are:

> **RQ1**: How does students' perception of feedback quality differ between humans and language models? Furthermore, can students discern if the feedback is human[1] or machine-generated?
>
> **RQ2**: How do local SLMs, commercial LLMs, and human instructors compare in terms of operational efficiency and scalability when providing technical feedback?

2   Related Work

2.1   Pedagogical Foundations of Effective Feedback

Hattie and Timperley [13] found that students place a premium on feedback that is personalized and actionable, enabling targeted improvements and fostering engagement. In computer science education, Fisk et al. [9] observed that automated personalized feedback on code significantly improved persistence, while Liu et al. [22] found that timely, individualized feedback enhanced conceptual understanding during writing-to-learn activities. Similarly, Suraworachet et al. [28] showed that combining human and analytics-based feedback improved student engagement in reflective writing tasks. This evidence aligns with Watling's [32] emphasis on constructive, actionable, and iterative guidance. Such approaches ensure that students not only receive critiques, but can also integrate changes that lead to learning gains.

---

[1] We define a *human* as either a Teaching Assistant or Course Instructor.

2.2 Cognitive Load and Scaffolding

The efficacy of such personalized guidance can be understood through the dual theoretical lenses of Cognitive Load Theory (CLT) [29] and instructional scaffolding [34]. CLT posits that working memory is limited; therefore, effective educational interventions must minimize extraneous cognitive load, such as poorly formatted or unstructured text, so learners can allocate mental resources to germane, schema-building tasks [30]. For novice learners, rigid instructional scaffolding is essential to manage this cognitive load by breaking complex logic into manageable, step-by-step components. However, as learner expertise increases, the "expertise reversal effect" dictates that highly structured scaffolding becomes redundant, and learners instead require nuanced, high-level conceptual guidance [15]. This theoretical dichotomy directly informs our investigation into whether the structured formatting of AI feedback acts as an effective cognitive scaffold, and how students' perceptions of machine versus human quality shift alongside their developing expertise.

2.3 AI-Driven Feedback Systems and SLMs

The use of LLMs as virtual teaching assistants has been explored, demonstrating their effectiveness in providing clear, engaging feedback in programming courses, though human supervision remains crucial [7,20]. Automated Feedback Systems (AFSs), driven by advancements in NLP and machine learning, offer scalable solutions for generating personalized feedback on writing [26]. Son et al. [27] highlight the growing adoption of AI-driven feedback for grammar, structure, and coherence in language learning, effectively reducing instructor workload through the integration of automated grading and feedback systems (reducing instructor grading hours from 15 to 9.75 per week). Similarly, in computer science education, studies by Wei [33] demonstrates how AI systems can provide error-specific feedback. Beyond individual courses, AFSs have been linked to improved engagement and retention in online education [31]. Students receiving AI-generated feedback were more likely to complete assignments and show deeper engagement, suggesting that real-time, automated guidance can be a powerful motivator.

While prior research highlights the benefits of AI-generated feedback, comparisons against human feedback from the student perspective remain sparse. For instance, although Guo and Wang [11] found complementary affordances between ChatGPT and teacher feedback in an EFL context, their evaluation centered entirely on teacher perceptions (N = 5). How computing students perceive this dynamic, particularly when utilizing locally deployable SLMs for data privacy and scalability [35], has not been thoroughly explored. We address these gaps by conducting a comprehensive, mixed-methods comparison of the perceived feedback quality generated by LLMs, SLMs, and humans across diverse instructional contexts.

3 Methodology

This study was conducted at a large, publicly funded, research-focused university in North America. We selected three distinct undergraduate courses to evaluate students' reception of feedback efficacy across varying levels of domain complexity and technical depth. All data collection was approved by the Institutional Review Board (IRB), and students provided informed consent for their data to be used for analysis.

3.1 Course Context and Participants

Introduction to Computer Science (CS2, $n = 176$): This large first-year course (694 students enrolled) focuses on software design fundamentals in Python, including object-oriented programming, recursion, and complexity analysis. For this study, students submitted a class hierarchy implementation accompanied by a technical design document. The document was assessed on structure, writing mechanics, and audience awareness. There were 190 unique survey submissions from this class, 176 of which passed the survey's attention check.

Operating Systems (OS, $n = 80$): This specialized third-year course (143 students enrolled) covers system-level concepts such as concurrency, memory management, and file systems. The study focused on a synchronization assignment where students were required to submit two technical artifacts: a bug report detailing a race condition and a README discussing starvation risks in their design. These tasks emphasized precise technical reasoning and concise communication. There were 83 unique survey submissions from this class, 80 of which passed the survey's attention check.

Writing on AI Topics ($n = 7$): This third-year seminar course (13 students enrolled) explores the intersection of artificial intelligence and communication design. Students produced an eight-page professional proposal aimed at industry decision-makers. The assignment required the integration of peer-reviewed research and multimodal elements to argue for AI-driven workflow improvements. There were seven unique survey submissions from this class, all of which passed the survey's attention check.

3.2 Feedback Generation System

Our RAG pipeline builds on insights from our prior work [21,35]. In particular, we adopt and adapt the recommendations around vector database design, retrieval accuracy, and hallucination mitigation, tailoring the approach to support rubric-aligned feedback rather than open-ended student assistance.

Two distinct model architectures were employed:

1. **Large Language Model (LLM):** GPT-4o, selected to represent state-of-the-art cloud-based reasoning.

2. **Small Language Model (SLM):** Meta's `Llama-3.1-8B`[2], deployed locally using 4-bit quantization and `torch.compile()` optimization. This model served as a privacy-preserving, low-latency alternative. See Appendix for complete technical specifications of local SLM deployment.

Both models used identical system prompts (see Appendix) designed to generate constructive, criterion-based feedback without assigning numeric grades.

3.3 Data Collection and Survey Design

We employed a blinded, within-subjects experimental design. Students accessed a web interface displaying three anonymized feedback responses for their submission: one from the LLM, one from the SLM, and one from a human evaluator (TA or Course Instructor). The display order was randomized.

The survey consisted of three components:

1. Preference & Rationale: Participants selected their single most preferred feedback source and provided a qualitative justification (Q_{Reason}).

2. Quantitative Ratings: Students evaluated each feedback source on a 7-point Likert scale (1=Lowest, 7=Highest) across six dimensions derived from feedback literature [13,23]: *Readability, Detail, Specificity, Actionability, Helpfulness,* and *Overall Quality.* An attention check item was embedded to validate response quality.

3. Source Discernment & Reflection: Students attempted to identify the origin of each feedback item (AI vs. Human) ($Q_{AIHuman}$). Finally, two open-ended questions invited suggestions for system improvement ($Q_{Improve}$) and broader reflections on the role of AI in assessment ($Q_{Discern}$).

3.4 Evaluation

Quantitative Analysis. As the Likert data violated normality assumptions (Shapiro-Wilk, $p < .05$), we utilized non-parametric methods. Differences between feedback sources were assessed using the Friedman test for repeated measures. Significant omnibus results were followed by post-hoc Wilcoxon signed-rank tests, with p-values adjusted using the Holm-Bonferroni correction to control for family-wise error rates.

Qualitative Analysis. Responses to open-ended items (Q_{Reason}, $Q_{Improve}$, $Q_{Discern}$) were analyzed using a consensus-based thematic analysis [3]. Rather than relying on a rigid, deductive codebook, two researchers independently reviewed a subset of responses to generate an initial thematic framework, which was iteratively refined through collaborative discussion. This organic process focused on identifying the specific textual features, such as tone, structural specificity, and perceived correctness, that drove student preferences.

---

[2] Specifically, we used `unsloth/Meta-Llama-3.1-8B-Instruct-bnb-4bit`, available on Hugging Face.

Following the methodological arguments of Hammer and Berland [12], we prioritized negotiated agreement over statistical inter-rater reliability. In this paradigm, coding is not the independent categorization of isolated statements, but rather a reflexive process of developing a shared understanding of complex, subjective student data. Therefore, rigour was established through the dialogic resolution of discrepancies, the maintenance of a transparent audit trail, and the deliberate discussion of negative or disconfirming cases across varying levels of student expertise.

4   Results

We present our quantitative results in Fig. 1. The x-axis represents mean student ratings, where 7 indicates the best score and 1 the worst. The y-axis captures feedback dimensions, ranging from readability and detail to overall quality.

Below, we report on the student ratings on the various dimensions of feedback quality from LLMs, SLMs, and human.

4.1   Quantitative Findings

Statistical Power and Pilot Designation. Before evaluating specific feedback dimensions, we conducted a post-hoc power analysis to determine the statistical adequacy of our sample sizes for the Wilcoxon signed-rank tests. Assuming a medium effect size ($r = 0.3$) and $\alpha = .05$, the analysis confirmed that our largest cohort, the introductory CS2 course ($n = 176$), was highly powered at 97.8%. The advanced Operating Systems course ($n = 80$) achieved 76.5% power, which is marginally below the 80% standard but sufficient for detecting moderate-to-large effects [5]. Expectedly, the Writing on AI Topics cohort ($n = 7$) achieved only 12.5% power. Consequently, we excluded the writing cohort from any cross-course inferential generalizations and treated it as exploratory pilot data.

General Trends in Technical Courses. Across the two adequately powered technical courses (CS2 and OS), a distinct hierarchy in student preference emerged. The Small Language Model (SLM) consistently achieved the highest mean ratings for *Overall Quality* and *Detail*, considerably outperforming the Human baseline. While the commercial LLM was generally rated higher than Human feedback overall, it did not consistently match the *Specificity* and *Actionability* of the locally hosted SLM. However, the dynamics between the models shifted based on learner expertise, as detailed below.

Course-Specific Quality Analysis: CS2. In the introductory CS2 course ($n = 176$), students consistently rated Human feedback lower than both AI sources. The mean Overall Quality for Human feedback was 3.62, significantly lower than that of the LLM ($M = 5.48, p < .001, r = 0.82$) and SLM ($M = 5.73, p < .001, r = 0.83$). Notably, while the SLM received the highest ratings for content-related metrics such as Detail ($M = 6.20$) and Helpfulness ($M = 5.86$), the

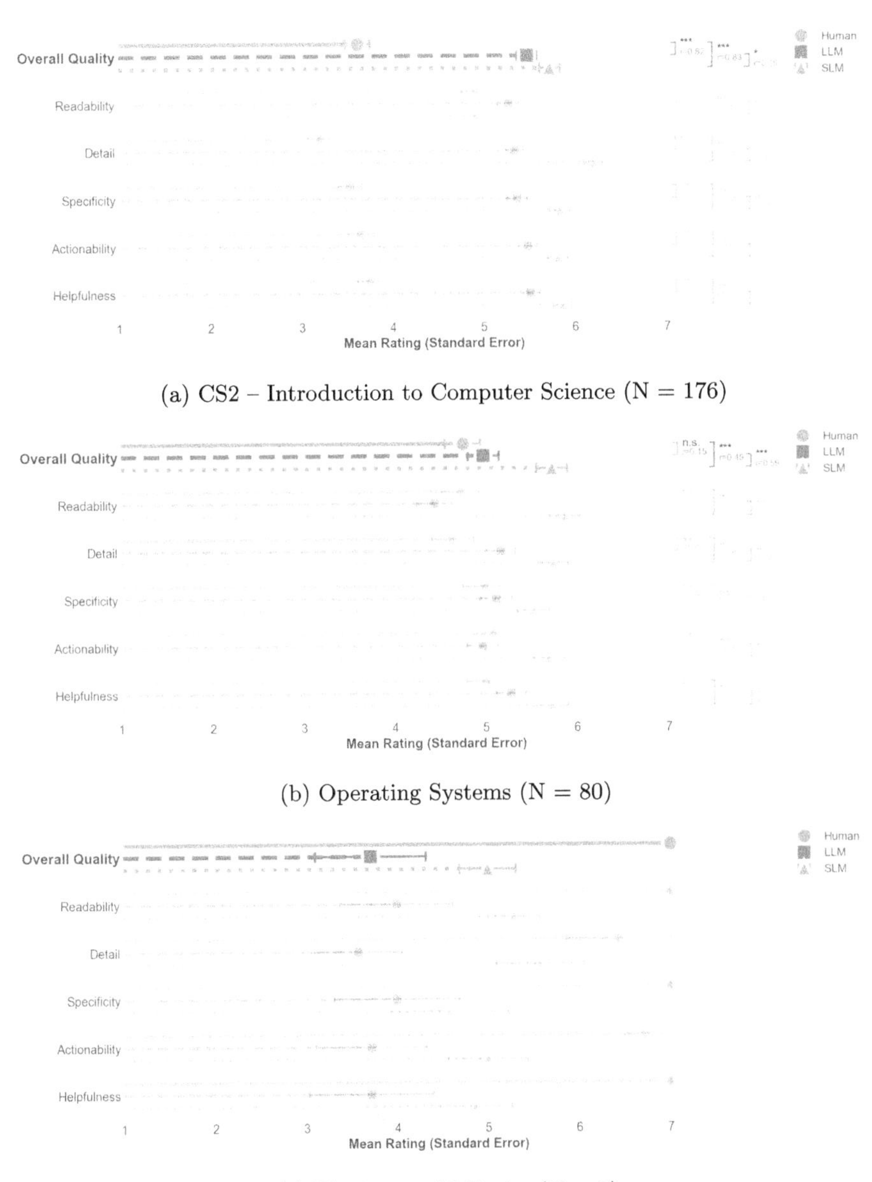

(a) CS2 – Introduction to Computer Science (N = 176)

(b) Operating Systems (N = 80)

(c) Writing on AI Topics (N = 7)

Fig. 1. Student feedback ratings across three courses. Ratings are measured on a 1–7 Likert scale (x-axis: higher is better). **n.s.**: $p \geq .05$; *****: $p < .05$; ******: $p < .01$; *******: $p < .001$ (Holm corrected). Effect sizes are reported as rank-biserial r. Inferential statistics are omitted from (c) due to the pilot's small sample size.

generic LLM was rated highest for Readability ($M = 5.27$), significantly outperforming the SLM ($M = 4.91, p = .024, r = 0.26$) and Human feedback ($M = 4.91, p = .021, r = 0.23$).

Course-Specific Quality Analysis: Operating Systems. In the advanced Operating Systems course ($n = 80$), the advantage of the generic LLM disappeared. There was no significant difference in Overall Quality ratings between the LLM ($M = 4.97$) and Human feedback ($M = 4.75, p = .28, r = 0.15$). However, the specialized SLM maintained its lead, achieving the highest ratings in the cohort for Overall Quality ($M = 5.72$), significantly outperforming both the Human ($p < .001, r = 0.49$) and LLM baselines ($p < .001, r = 0.59$). A key divergence occurred in Readability: unlike in the introductory course, OS students rated the SLM as the most readable source ($M = 5.86$), significantly higher than the LLM ($M = 4.44, p < .001, r = 0.82$) and Human feedback ($M = 4.72, p < .001, r = 0.54$).

Exploratory Pilot Data: Writing on AI Topics Quality Analysis. Descriptive statistics for the Writing on AI Topics pilot ($n = 7$) show a trend reversal compared to the technical courses. Human feedback received a high rating for Overall Quality ($M = 7.00$), Descriptive Specificity ($M = 7.00$), and Helpfulness ($M = 7.00$). In contrast, the AI models were rated substantially lower, with the SLM ($M = 5.00$) and LLM ($M = 3.71$) failing to match human performance. While the underpowered sample size prevents inferential generalization, the descriptive data suggest a strong domain-specific preference for human feedback in high-context rhetorical scenarios.

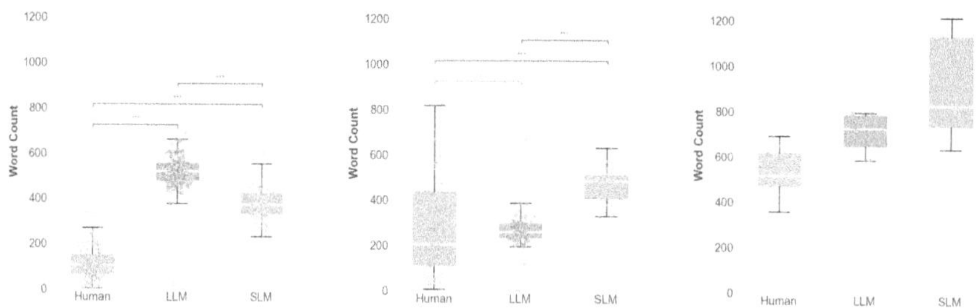

(a) Response word count: CS2

(b) Response word count: OS

(c) Response word count: Writing on AI Topics

Fig. 2. Word count distributions of feedback generated by Human, LLM, and SLM across (a) CS2, (b) Operating Systems, and (c) Writing on AI Topics. Statistical significance is derived from post-hoc Wilcoxon signed-rank tests (**n.s.**: $p \geq .05$; *: $p < .05$; **: $p < .01$; ***: $p < .001$, Holm-corrected). Inferential statistics are omitted from (c) due to the pilot's small sample size.

Feedback Length Analysis. To objectively compare the structural differences between the feedback sources, we analyzed the word count distributions across all three courses (Fig. 2).

In the introductory CS2 course ($n = 176$), a Friedman test revealed significant differences in feedback length ($\chi^2 = 313.99, p < .001$). Post-hoc Wilcoxon signed-rank tests (Holm-corrected) indicated that both the LLM and SLM generated significantly more text than human instructors ($p < .001$, with large effect sizes of $r > 0.99$ for both). Furthermore, the LLM's feedback was significantly longer than the SLM's ($p < .001, r = 0.92$).

In the advanced Operating Systems course ($n = 80$), the length dynamics shifted ($\chi^2 = 65.75, p < .001$). Here, the SLM produced significantly longer feedback than both human instructors ($p < .001, r = 0.73$) and the LLM ($p < .001, r = 0.98$). Notably, there was no significant difference in word count between the human and LLM feedback ($p = .79$). Finally, descriptive data from the Writing pilot ($n = 7$) indicated a similar trend where the SLM generated the highest volume of text, though inferential testing was omitted due to the underpowered sample size.

Table 1. Confusion matrix of feedback source attribution: actual source vs. student identification.

	Introductory CS2			Operating Systems			Writing on AI Topics		
Actual Source	AI	Human	Acc.	AI	Human	Acc.	AI	Human	Acc.
LLM	61	115	34.66%	41	39	51.25%	7	0	100%
SLM	93	83	52.84%	61	19	76.25%	7	0	100%
Human	51	125	71.02%	15	65	81.25%	0	7	100%

Distinguishing AI from Human Feedback. Discernment accuracy varied significantly by student experience and model sophistication (see Table 1). Advanced Operating Systems students (69.58% overall accuracy) reliably distinguished Human (81.25%) and SLM (76.25%) authors, but found the commercial LLM nearly indistinguishable from human feedback (51.25%). Novice CS2 students were even more susceptible to the AI's "human-like" quality, correctly identifying the LLM and SLM sources only 34.66% and 52.84% of the time, respectively.

OS students distinguished AI from human feedback more reliably, whereas CS2 students were near chance overall and frequently misidentified the commercial LLM as human-generated. The writing seminar result should be treated as descriptive only due to the small number of students.

4.2   Qualitative Findings

Formatting as Function: Students Prefer the SLM's Rigid, Step-by-Step Structure for Technical Tasks. Contrary to the expectation that quantized models might degrade coherence, students in technical courses specifically favored the SLM for its rigid adherence to formatting. The local `Llama-3.1` model consistently generated feedback with explicit headers, bullet points, and distinct "Reasoning" sections (a byproduct of the system prompt). For CS2 and OS students, this structural rigidity mirrored technical documentation standards, making the feedback appear more rigorous than the conversational style of the human instructors. One student noted, *"The layout [of the SLM] makes it easier to debug my logic step-by-step,"* indicating that for technical writing, formatting is a functional component of feedback quality.

Mistaking Length for Quality: Novices View Longer AI Responses as More Thorough. A clear divergence emerged based on learner expertise regarding how students perceived the SLM's lengthy outputs. Novice (CS2) students frequently equated the SLM's high token output with high effort and quality, interpreting "wall-of-text" responses as thoroughness (*"It looked very detailed... I felt the AI read every line"*). However, this effect diminished in the advanced Operating Systems course, where students were more critical of generic volume. This suggests that SLMs, which often generate highly repetitive text, inadvertently create an illusion of thoroughness for novices seeking reassurance, even if the semantic density, the ratio of actionable critique to total word count, is lower than that of a human expert.

Low-Stakes AI Feedback Reduces Social Anxiety and Encourages Iterative Drafting. Students explicitly recognized the trade-off between the "warmth" of human feedback and the immediate utility of the local model. The perception of the SLM as a *"helpful and cheap service"* highlights a shift in student expectations: they view the local model not as a teacher replacement, but as a high-availability tool for logic confirmation. By removing the social anxiety of submitting to a human, the SLM encouraged iterative drafting. One participant noted, *"AI is friendlier than a human because I don't feel judged for bad drafts,"* suggesting that the "cold" tone of the local model acts as a privacy-preserving feature that encourages experimentation.

The Limits of Local AI: Quantized Models Fail to Grasp Rhetorical Nuance in Writing Tasks. While the SLM excelled at syntax and structure, qualitative responses revealed the semantic limitation of 4-bit quantization. In high-context scenarios (i.e., the Writing seminar), the SLM struggled to interpret editorial intent, often correcting stylistic choices as if they were objective errors (*"The AI missed the point of what I was trying to argue"*). This limitation validates the quantitative drop in performance for the writing course; while the SLM can parse technical specifications in a prompt (RAG), it lacks the sufficient context window and reasoning resolution to critique rhetorical nuance, delineating a clear boundary for where human-in-the-loop intervention remains mandatory.

5   Discussion

5.1   RQ1: Novices Prefer AI Structure, Advanced Learners Demand Human Semantic Nuance

Our findings suggest a tiered utility for AI in technical education, where the efficacy of the model depends on the pedagogical goal rather than model parameter size. Viewed through the lens of Cognitive Load Theory [29], the local SLM matched or outperformed human instructors in introductory contexts because its rigid adherence to structural constraints acted as effective instructional scaffolding. Novice learners, who benefit from guided, step-by-step support [19], associated the explicit headings and bullet points of the SLM with high perceived feedback quality because this formatting actively reduced the extraneous cognitive load required to parse the critique. This structural advantage inadvertently triggered a verbosity heuristic: because the SLM's lengthy, structured outputs were easy to read, novices conflated high word count with high effort and actionability. Furthermore, the automated system successfully provided a low-stakes environment that reduced the social anxiety of human judgment, encouraging iterative drafting.

However, as predicted by the expertise reversal effect [15], this structural advantage diminished in high-context tasks. In the advanced operating systems and writing seminar contexts, students were more critical of generic volume. Here, the SLM's semantic limitations were exposed. While it produced lengthy text, its semantic density (the ratio of actionable, nuanced critique to total word count) was perceived as lower than that of a human expert. The 4-bit quantized model lacked the reasoning capabilities to critique rhetorical intent or complex architectural trade-offs, delineating a clear semantic ceiling for local models in advanced coursework.

Perception and Detection. Our findings reveal a clear dissociation between AI detection and perceived utility. Because students who reliably identified the AI still rated its feedback highly, it is evident that successful deception is not a prerequisite for user acceptance. Students embraced the SLM as a distinct, pragmatic tool rather than a simulated teacher, proving that "human-like" text generation does not inherently guarantee superior educational value. This also echoes recent studies [4, 14], in which learners are developing assessment literacy in which the actionable content of a critique supersedes the attributed identity of its author.

5.2   RQ2: Efficiency, Sustainability, and Data Sovereignty

The deployment of automated feedback pipelines highlights a stark contrast in resource utilization between human and AI workflows. Human graders in the operating-systems course invested approximately 40 h (grading plus training) to generate feedback, while the instructor in the writing seminar spent 4.5 h ($\sim$ \$500 equivalent). In contrast, our automated pipeline processed the entire operating-systems cohort in 1.8 h and the writing seminar in under 10 min. This 95%

reduction in routine workload suggests that AI can effectively shift instructor effort from summative assessment to high-value pedagogical interventions.

However, the divergence between the two AI approaches offers the most critical insight for institutional adoption. The commercial LLM (GPT-4), while offering high inference throughput ($\sim$26 tokens/s), accumulated approximately \$500 in API usage fees across two rounds of feedback. This variable cost structure presents a scalability barrier for large-enrolment courses.

Conversely, the locally hosted SLM demonstrated that data sovereignty is achievable on consumer-grade hardware. By applying 4-bit quantization to the Llama-3.1-8B model, we reduced the memory footprint to fit comfortably within the VRAM limits of a standard GPU ($\geq$12 GB). Although the local inference speed was lower ($\sim$15 tokens/s), this latency is negligible in an asynchronous batch-processing context. Crucially, the local SLM incurred near-zero marginal cost per student once deployed. This decoupling of enrolment size from operational cost, combined with the assurance that student data never leaves institutional infrastructure, positions local SLMs as the only sustainable architecture for privacy-compliant, large-scale educational feedback [35].

6 Limitations and Future Work

Our results are constrained by the context window limitations of local models, which occasionally resulted in generic feedback when the error required deep knowledge of assignment constraints. Additionally, our sample skewed toward upper-year students, and generalizability to non-technical domains remains untested. Methodologically, as indicated by our post-hoc power analysis, the advanced and writing-intensive cohorts possessed limited statistical power. Consequently, findings from the writing seminar must be treated as exploratory pilot data rather than inferential generalizations.

Crucially, our evaluation is bounded by student self-reports and ratings. While these metrics provide valuable insights into user acceptance, readability, and perceived utility, they do not substantiate claims of objective educational effectiveness. As noted in prior literature, students may prefer feedback that reduces cognitive load rather than feedback that maximizes learning. Future work must incorporate pre- and post-learning assessments, learning analytics (e.g., LMS logs), and student revision tracking to determine whether highly-rated SLM feedback translates into measurable pedagogical outcomes.

On the technical side, our evaluation focused on a single commercial LLM and a locally hosted SLM. Refining the system prompt for AI models to strictly enforce a rigid structural template or evaluating state-of-the-art frontier models could alter the preference gap. Furthermore, our pipeline utilized a fixed 4-bit quantization; future technical evaluations should include a sensitivity analysis across various depths (e.g., 2-bit, 8-bit, 16-bit) to map the precise trade-off between memory footprint and feedback quality. To efficiently scale these comparative studies, future work could leverage unified API routing tools, such as OpenRouter, to query and benchmark feedback quality across a wide range of open-source and proprietary models without increasing infrastructure overhead.

7   Conclusion

To address the privacy, cost, and scalability bottlenecks of commercial language models in computing education, this study evaluated the perceived feedback quality of a locally hosted, quantized Small Language Model (SLM) compared to GPT-4 and human instructors. Through a mixed-methods, within-subjects evaluation across introductory programming (CS2), operating systems (OS), and an exploratory writing pilot, we demonstrated that parameter size does not strictly dictate pedagogical utility. For foundational tasks, novice learners rated the local SLM highest in readability and actionability, as its rigid formatting provided effective structural scaffolding that reduced cognitive load. Conversely, human expertise remained critically necessary for the nuanced, high-context reasoning required in advanced writing scenarios. Regarding efficiency and sustainability (RQ2), the local SLM processed entire course cohorts at near-zero marginal cost while guaranteeing institutional data sovereignty, directly overcoming the recurring financial barriers of cloud-based APIs. In the end, these findings suggest a tiered, privacy-preserving framework for the future of AI in education. By deploying local SLMs to handle routine, syntax-level structural critique, institutions can sustainably improve assessment scalability crises while alleviating the workload of human educators, allowing them to focus their limited bandwidth on high-level conceptual scaffolding and pedagogical motivation.

Acknowledgments. We would like to thank the Learning & Education Advancement Fund (LEAF) from the Office of the Vice-Provost, Innovations in Undergraduate Education, University of Toronto, and the Natural Sciences and Engineering Research Council of Canada (NSERC) Discovery Grant (#RGPIN-2024-04348). We would also like to thank Dr. Antoine Deza for his continued support, guidance, and mentorship.

Appendix

SLM Technical Specifications

The SLM was locally hosted on a high-end Ubuntu workstation with an AMD Ryzen Threadripper PRO 7965WX 24-core/48-thread CPU, paired with 192GB of 6400MHz DDR5 memory, a 4TB Samsung 990 Pro NVMe SSD, and a GIGABYTE AORUS GeForce RTX 5090 GPU.

LLM/SLM System Prompt

You are an experienced writing professor teaching a course on [COURSE TOPIC]. Students were required to complete the following assignment: [ASSIGNMENT INSTRUCTIONS].
Your student submitted the following work for your feedback: [SUBMISSION]. You are required to provide constructive feedback and meaningful steps for improvement based on the "criteria" and "description" outlined in the rubric. Your feedback must address each of the criteria from the rubric and must not assign a numerical grade.
For each criterion, provide the following information:
 1. The criteria name
 2. Feedback on the student's performance
 3. Reasoning behind the feedback
 4. Specific suggestions for improvement
Grading rubric: [Grading rubric of given course]
Structure your feedback using the following format:
 Criteria: [Name of criteria]
 Feedback: [Detailed feedback]
 Reasoning: [Why this feedback was provided]
 Suggestions for Improvement: [Steps to improve on this criterion]

References

1. Achiam, J., et al.: GPT-4 technical report. arXiv preprint arXiv:2303.08774 (2023)
2. Bonsu, E.: The influence of written feedback on the writing skill performance of high school students. Int. J. Appl. Res. Soc. Sci. **3**(3), 33–43 (2021)
3. Braun, V., Clarke, V.: Using thematic analysis in psychology. Qual. Res. Psychol. **3**(2), 77–101 (2006)
4. Chan, C.K.Y., Hu, W.: Students' voices on generative ai: perceptions, benefits, and challenges in higher education. Int. J. Educ. Technol. High. Educ. **20**(1), 43 (2023)
5. Cohen, J.: Statistical Power Analysis for the Behavioral Sciences. Routledge (2013)
6. Cook, A., Phan, V., Windsor, A.: Improving ta feedback on in-class coding assignments for introductory computer science. In: Proceedings of the 27th ACM Conference on on Innovation and Technology in Computer Science Education, vol. 1, pp. 421–427 (2022)
7. Denny, P., MacNeil, S., Savelka, J., Porter, L., Luxton-Reilly, A.: Desirable characteristics for AI teaching assistants in programming education. In: Proceedings of the 2024 on Innovation and Technology in Computer Science Education V. 1, pp. 408–414 (2024)
8. Evans, C.: Making sense of assessment feedback in higher education. Rev. Educ. Res. **83**(1), 70–120 (2013)
9. Fisk, S., et al.: Automating personalized feedback to improve students' persistence in computing. In: Proceedings of the 53rd ACM Technical Symposium on Computer Science Education V. 2, p. 1197 (2022)
10. Grattafiori, A., et al.: The llama 3 herd of models. arXiv preprint arXiv:2407.21783 (2024)

11. Guo, K., Wang, D.: To resist it or to embrace it? Examining ChatGPT's potential to support teacher feedback in EFL writing. Educ. Inf. Technol. **29**(7), 8435–8463 (2024)
12. Hammer, D., Berland, L.K.: Confusing claims for data: a critique of common practices for presenting qualitative research on learning. J. Learn. Sci. **23**(1), 37–46 (2014)
13. Hattie, J., Timperley, H.: The power of feedback. Rev. Educ. Res. **77**(1), 81–112 (2007)
14. Henderson, M., et al.: Comparing generative ai and teacher feedback: student perceptions of usefulness and trustworthiness. Assess. Eval. High. Educ., 1–16 (2025)
15. Kalyuga, S.: The expertise reversal effect. In: Managing Cognitive Load in Adaptive Multimedia Learning, pp. 58–80. IGI Global Scientific Publishing (2009)
16. Karnalim, O.: Automated, personalised, and timely feedback for awareness of programming plagiarism and collusion. In: Proceedings of the 17th ACM Conference on International Computing Education Research, pp. 393–394 (2021)
17. Kazemitabaar, M., et al.: CodeAID: evaluating a classroom deployment of an LLM-based programming assistant that balances student and educator needs. In: Proceedings of the 2024 CHI Conference on Human Factors in Computing Systems, pp. 1–20 (2024)
18. Kristiansen, N.G., Nicolajsen, S.M., Brabrand, C.: Feedback on student programming assignments: teaching assistants vs automated assessment tool. In: Proceedings of the 23rd Koli Calling International Conference on Computing Education Research, pp. 1–10 (2023)
19. Kumar, H., et al.: Guiding students in using LLMS in supported learning environments: effects on interaction dynamics, learner performance, confidence, and trust. Proc. ACM Hum. Comput. Interact. **8**(CSCW2), 1–30 (2024)
20. Liu, M., M'hiri, F.: Beyond traditional teaching: large language models as simulated teaching assistants in computer science. In: Proceedings of the 55th ACM Technical Symposium on Computer Science Education V. 1, pp. 743–749 (2024)
21. Liu, S., Yu, Z., Huang, F., Bulbulia, Y., Bergen, A., Liut, M.: Can small language models with retrieval-augmented generation replace large language models when learning computer science? In: Proceedings of the 2024 on Innovation and Technology in Computer Science Education V. 1, pp. 388–393 (2024)
22. Liu, Y., Xiong, W., Xiong, Y., Wu, Y.: Generating timely individualized feedback to support student learning of conceptual knowledge in writing-to-learn activities. J. Comput. Educ. **11**(2), 367–399 (2024)
23. Nicol, D.J., Macfarlane-Dick, D.: Formative assessment and self-regulated learning: a model and seven principles of good feedback practice. Stud. High. Educ. **31**(2), 199–218 (2006)
24. Pădurean, V.A., et al.: Humanizing automated programming feedback: fine-tuning generative models with student-written feedback. arXiv preprint arXiv:2509.10647 (2025)
25. Prather, J., et al.: The robots are here: navigating the generative ai revolution in computing education. In: Proceedings of the 2023 Working Group Reports on Innovation and Technology in Computer Science Education, pp. 108–159 (2023)
26. Shi, H., Aryadoust, V.: A systematic review of ai-based automated written feedback research. ReCALL **36**(2), 187–209 (2024)
27. Son, J.B., Ružić, N.K., Philpott, A.: Artificial intelligence technologies and applications for language learning and teaching. J. China Comput. Assist. Lang. Learn. **5**(1), 94–112 (2025)

28. Suraworachet, W., Zhou, Q., Cukurova, M.: Impact of combining human and analytics feedback on students' engagement with, and performance in, reflective writing tasks. Int. J. Educ. Technol. High. Educ. **20**(1), 1–24 (2023)
29. Sweller, J.: Cognitive load during problem solving: effects on learning. Cogn. Sci. **12**(2), 257–285 (1988)
30. Sweller, J., Van Merrienboer, J.J., Paas, F.G.: Cognitive architecture and instructional design. Educ. Psychol. Rev. **10**(3), 251–296 (1998)
31. Villegas-Ch, W., García-Ortiz, J., Sánchez-Viteri, S.: Application of artificial intelligence in online education: influence of student participation on academic retention in virtual courses. IEEE Access (2024)
32. Watling, C., Lingard, L.: Giving feedback on others' writing. Perspect. Med. Educ. **8**, 25–27 (2019)
33. Wei, L.: Artificial intelligence in language instruction: impact on English learning achievement, L2 motivation, and self-regulated learning. Front. Psychol. **14**, 1261955 (2023)
34. Wood, D., Bruner, J.S., Ross, G.: The role of tutoring in problem solving. J. Child Psychol. Psychiatry **17**(2), 89–100 (1976)
35. Yu, Z., Liu, S., Denny, P., Bergen, A., Liut, M.: Integrating small language models with retrieval-augmented generation in computing education: Key takeaways, setup, and practical insights. In: Proceedings of the 56th ACM Technical Symposium on Computer Science Education V. 1, pp. 1302–1308 (2025)
36. Zhang, J., Li, D., Kolesar, J.C., Shi, H., Piskac, R.: Automated feedback generation for competition-level code. In: Proceedings of the 37th IEEE/ACM International Conference on Automated Software Engineering, pp. 1–13 (2022)

Teachers' Perspectives on Decision-Making in AI-Supported Classrooms: A Cross-Cultural Study of Germany and Japan

Tomohiro Nagashima[1]([✉]) [iD], Shintaro Sato[1] [iD], Mirella Hladký[1] [iD], Niklas Scholz[2] [iD], and Lisa Siegrist[3] [iD]

[1] Saarland Informatics Campus, Saarland University, Saarbrücken, Germany
{nagashima,sato}@cs.uni-saarland.de, mirella.hladky@uni-saarland.de
[2] RWTH Aachen University, Aachen, Germany
niklas.scholz@rwth-aachen.de
[3] University of St. Gallen, St. Gallen, Switzerland
lisa.siegrist@unisgh.ch

Abstract. As AI technologies become increasingly integrated into classrooms, the field of AI in Education (AIED) emphasizes the need to understand stakeholder perspectives to ensure AI is designed and implemented in ways that support both teachers and students. However, previous research has not fully examined how these perspectives may vary across cultural contexts. Given the complexity of classroom dynamics and the role of cultural and social values in shaping learning experiences, it is crucial to explore how contextual factors might influence stakeholder views. This study presents a qualitative investigation involving 15 German and 10 Japanese teachers, using a storyboard-based speed-dating approach to examine their perspectives on student-led versus AI-led decision-making in the classroom. Our findings reveal commonalities between the two groups, such as the shared belief in the importance of teacher involvement in both students' and AI's decision-making processes and concern about excessive AI monitoring. However, we also identified notable differences: Japanese teachers expressed a stronger preference for greater access to student data, while German counterparts preferred student autonomy in decision making. We discuss these findings in relation to their cultural contexts, including classroom norms such as the "silence" in Japanese classrooms. This study contributes to the field by demonstrating how stakeholder perspectives on AI in education can vary across cultural contexts and highlighting the need to account for cultural and social factors when designing and integrating AI systems in classrooms.

Keywords: AI-Supported Classroom · Student Agency · Intelligent Tutoring Systems · Classroom Orchestration

E. G. Blanchard et al. (Eds.): AIED 2026, LNAI 16583, pp. 593–607, 2027.
https://doi.org/10.1007/978-3-032-29760-0_58

1   Introduction

1.1   AI Use in the Classroom: Towards Hybrid Intelligence

Across the world, an increasing number of classrooms are adopting or considering the integration of Artificial Intelligence (AI)-powered technologies to enhance the efficiency and effectiveness of learning [16]. Notable examples are seen in North America, where a number of schools have incorporated advanced intelligent tutoring systems, such as Cognitive Tutors, to support student learning in subjects such as mathematics and reading [8,14]

The integration of AI-powered learning tools in classrooms results in complex dynamics among the AI systems (such as Intelligent Tutoring Systems, ITSs), students, and teachers [18]. For example, when students independently use tutoring software on their own devices during class, challenges may emerge if the provided content does not align with the curriculum or the teacher's planned instruction. Additionally, teachers may interrupt students' progress to address widespread misconceptions identified through the system [6]. In these scenarios, students or teachers might request that the AI adjust tasks to offer further practice, teachers may pause progress to enable classroom discussions, or they may pair higher-performing students with those who need additional support, leveraging AI-based tutoring to reduce instructional workload while enhancing student learning outcomes [3].

Recognizing the critical role of human actors in AI-assisted classrooms, recent research highlights the necessity of teacher involvement in these complex interactions [9,11]. Aligning with the concept of "hybrid intelligence," which refers to synergetic collaborations between AI tutors and human educators [6,9], studies have examined teachers' preferences regarding AI-assisted group formation in classrooms [3]. Additionally, researchers have co-designed AI-based tools together with teachers to ensure their needs and preferences are embedded in the design process [9]. Findings consistently show that teachers do not favor fully letting AI systems take their responsibilities [3,9].

1.2   Cross-Cultural Stakeholder Views on AI Use in the Classroom

Despite progress in AI in Education (AIED), much of the research on human-AI hybrid intelligence in school classrooms remains focused on North America, especially the United States [3,7,9]. In contrast, there is a lack of studies capturing perspectives from stakeholders in other cultural settings. While some research does examine stakeholder viewpoints in other countries, these studies target contexts other than K-12 classrooms [5].

Given that an increasing number of school classrooms across the world have been equipped with advanced technologies, with a focus on AI [16], it is vital to explore how stakeholder views might or might not be similar across cultural contexts. The field requires context-specific interpretations of design studies with stakeholders; otherwise, we risk that findings from existing studies (from a single cultural context) might be advocated for greater generalizability. Indeed, studies have documented that schools and classrooms in different cultures adopt instructional technology in various ways [13]. Further, cultural and social norms also play an important role in influencing peoples' views towards AI technologies [4,15]. For example, Brauner et al. [2] compared Chinese and German citizens' perception towards benefits and risks of AI in the society, finding that Germans are more cautious attitudes towards AI than Chinese people, who are more optimistic about the use of AI in the society. In a complex multi-stakeholder environment such as in a classroom, it is possible that certain social practices and norms affect how stakeholders see the technology.

To explore stakeholder views on AI use in the classroom across cultures, we conducted a qualitative speed-dating study with a total of 25 teachers in Germany and Japan. We chose these two countries because both countries are starting to integrate adaptive learning software in school environments (examples include *bettermarks*[1] in Germany, *Qubena*[2] in Japan), supported by governmental policies (in both countries, all students from secondary schools are provided with a laptop or tablet device). Compared to countries with advanced implementation of AI-based systems in everyday instruction (e.g., Cognitive Tutor-based tools, such as a full curriculum implementation using MATHia[3] in the US [14]), classrooms in Japan and Germany have not yet used adaptive learning software to its full potential, instead only to the limited extent (e.g., homework practice). While we made this characterization first based on our own experience in working with schools in Germany, Japan, and US, international surveys also support the claim; PISA2022 shows that US schools have much more availability of computers for students (mean: 1.74 devices per student), while Germany (mean: 0.55) and Japan (mean: 0.76) did not yet have many computers available in 2022, below OECD average (mean: 0.81) [13].

This setup offers study contexts that are similar to each other in terms of AI integration in the classroom. As well, the authors of this paper include two Japanese and three German citizens, and have worked with schools in Japan and Germany in the last few years. Therefore, we chose the countries in which we could provide a detailed account of the observed phenomena and relevant social and cultural contexts in these countries.

Despite such commonalities that make a comparison useful, it is noteworthy that Germany and Japan have several distinctive differences that might or might not influence how stakeholders view AI use in the classroom. PISA2022 [13] has revealed some differences in how teachers support student learning (perceived by students). For instance, Japanese students consistently report that their teachers are dedicated in helping students understand mathematics with interest, while German students do not feel that level of teacher support in the classroom. Regarding technology use, German students are more open to teacher monitoring during laptop use in the class compared to Japanese students [13].

---

[1] https://de.bettermarks.com/.
[2] https://qubena.com/.
[3] https://www.carnegielearning.com/solutions/math/mathia.

These differences in how classroom climate is maintained and managed might mediate/moderate how they would interact with AI systems.

1.3 The Current Study

In this paper, we ask the following research question: *How do teachers in Germany and Japan differ in their preferences regarding student-AI decision-making control in school classrooms?* We conducted a speed-dating study with 25 teachers from both countries to obtain deep insights into how they envision the future of AI-supported classrooms.

The study contributes cross-cultural insights into teacher preferences for human-AI hybrid intelligence in the classroom, addressing the current North American bias in AIED research. In particular, our study identifies key cultural differences (along with similarities), where German teachers emphasized student autonomy in decision making while Japanese teachers preferred stronger control over students' data sharing. We also find differing views on AI-supported help-seeking, with German teachers favoring help-seeking within AI systems and Japanese teachers preferring direct teacher-student interaction, which implies broader cultural differences in classroom communication.

2   Method

2.1   Participants

We recruited 15 school teachers in Germany and 10 school teachers in Japan through previous contacts and direct emails/visits to nearby schools (Table 1). Teachers participated in a study session individually, which was conducted in German with the German teachers and in Japanese with the Japanese teachers. They attended the session online or in-person in a university lab or at the teacher's school. We did not have any concrete knowledge of how much AI tools have been used (if any) in the participants' specific classes prior to data collection. Participants received a consent form prior to the study, and only after signing the form, participated in the study. German teachers received 40 Euros and Japanese teachers received 2,500 Japanese Yen after participation (which are within a standard level of compensation given in respective countries). Participation in the study was fully voluntary, and the study had been approved by the university ethical review board before data collection.

2.2   Materials

To facilitate our sessions, we developed eight storyboards that show hypothetical situations of AI use in the classroom. Storyboards are a typical design material for speed-dating studies [19]. Each storyboard has five scenes, in which the first three scenes set the context of the story and behaviors of stakeholders in the classroom (Fig. 1). The last two scenes show the outcome of the action, where one (4A) shows a positive consequence, while the other (4B) shows a negative

Table 1. Participants' years of teaching experiences, grade levels taught, and whether they have participated in the study online or in-person. Participant ID with "G" and "J" represent German and Japanese teachers, respectively.

Participant	Years of teaching	Grade levels taught	Participation mode
G1	10	5th–12th	Online
G2	3.5	1st–4th	In-person
G3	4	5th–12th	Online
G4	15	5th–12th	Online
G5	15	5th–12th	Online
G6	7	8–10th, 12th	Online
G7	1.5	7–8th, 10th, 12th	In-person
G8	2	5th, 7th, 10–11th	Online
G9	2.5	3rd	Online
G10	2	5th, 7–9th	In-person
G11	1	6th–12th	Online
G12	0.5	6–7th	Online
G13	21	5th–9th	Online
G14	10	11th–13th	Online
G15	28	5th–10th	In-person
J1	23	3rd–6th	In-person
J2	3	7–9th	In-person
J3	7	7–9th	In-person
J4	10	7–9th	In-person
J5	4	7–9th	In-person
J6	2	7,9th	In-person
J7	7	7–9th	In-person
J8	7	2–7th	Online
J9	8	2–6th	Online
J10	7	10–12th	Online

ending. For instance, in Fig. 1, 4A illustrates a positive consequence of giving students a greater decision-making control over data sharing where students feel comfortable as they were able to choose what (not) to choose with the teacher. On the other hand, 4B shows a negative consequence that the teacher cannot offer help as they cannot view student data. We included both positive and negative consequences intentionally to avoid receiving biased responses. In this study, we use Intelligent Tutoring Systems (ITSs) as an example of common classroom AI technology [8,14].

Japanese and German versions were created; these two versions of the eight storyboards did not differ, except for the language used for captions and for

Scenario #3

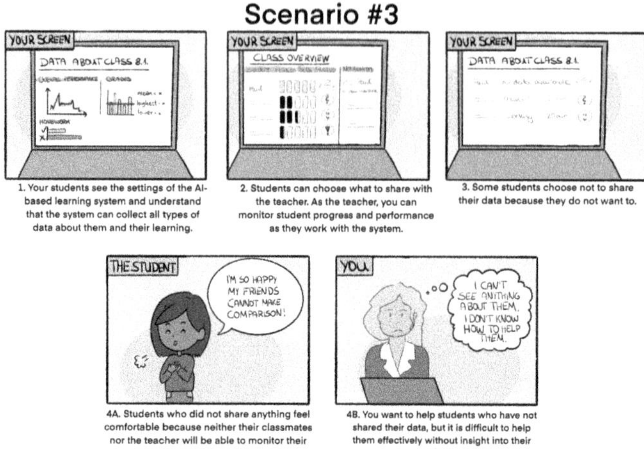

1. Your students see the settings of the AI-based learning system and understand that the system can collect all types of data about them and their learning.

2. Students can choose what to share with the teacher. As the teacher, you can monitor student progress and performance as they work with the system.

3. Some students choose not to share their data because they do not want to.

4A. Students who did not share anything feel comfortable because neither their classmates nor the teacher will be able to monitor their performance.

4B. You want to help students who have not shared their data, but it is difficult to help them effectively without insight into their data.

Fig. 1. A scenario illustrating students' high degree of control over data sharing with teachers through an AI system.

names of the students who appeared in the scenarios (common names in the respective country were used).

We chose eight different scenarios that cover across multiple dimensions of student-AI decision making control so that the insights would not be specific about one aspect of decision making. Namely, we followed Vincoli et al. [17]'s multi-dimensional model of student-AI agency in the classroom. In their agency framework, they define four types of student-AI decision-making control: *Content Control* (student deciding what content to learn next vs. being assigned by AI), *Help-Seeking Control* (student autonomously asking for help vs. AI prescriptively gives hints when identifying struggles), *Data Control* (student deciding what learning data to share vs. AI automatically sharing data with teachers) and *Co-Orchestration Control* (student deciding with whom to work with in a group work vs. AI assigns groups based on students' performances).

We generated the scenarios such that they represent student-led decision making and AI-led decision making in a systematic way; specifically, each scenario shows a situation that corresponds to each *end* of the decision-making spectrum presented above (four spectrums * two ends, resulting in a total of eight scenarios) [17]. In other words, these eight scenarios depict situations of AI use where one with students having greater decision-making control whereas the other with AI possessing greater power over decision-making control power across the four spectrums of AI use in the classroom. All eight scenarios are available online.[4]

---

[4] https://tinyurl.com/teacherstoryboards.

2.3   Procedure

One or two researchers (who are native speakers of the language) conducted each session. After several warm-up questions on participants' years of teaching, how they normally use technology in the classroom (e.g., AI technologies), we introduced the eight scenarios, following the speed-dating technique [19]. We presented scenarios in a random order to avoid any potential influence of what participants see earlier in the session on their sharing for later scenarios. The participants were asked how they would feel in the depicted situations for both positive and negative outcomes. All sessions (which took about 40–60 minutes) were video recorded for analysis.

2.4   Analysis

We collected video recordings of approximately 17.4 h from 15 German teachers and 8.6 h from 10 Japanese teachers. Two German native speakers and two Japanese native speakers transcribed and then coded the data based on our research question. We did not include data on the warm-up questions as they were meant to create a friendly study environment. During the initial coding process, each researcher looked for teachers' quotes that show their preferences and opinions on the presented scenarios. This coding process resulted in 648 individual quotes for German data and 386 quotes for Japanese data.

Then, within each data group (German and Japanese data), the four researchers conducted Affinity Diagramming (AD) analysis separately to find common themes within each country group without being biased by the other group. AD is a qualitative data analysis technique that involves organizing quotes and codes into clusters based on shared ideas and themes. This process creates hierarchical structures that help identify overarching patterns across multiple levels of themes [10]. We conducted AD using a virtual whiteboard, which allowed for iterative refinement. Researchers who transcribed the data performed AD (two researchers for each), which was then reviewed and revised by researchers who transcribed the other country's data. Applying AD, we generated 70 and 29 low-level themes/groups for German and Japanese data, respectively. We chose not to form a higher-level structure for each dataset as we realized that it would make comparison ambiguous; we decided to stay in low-level categories for a more fine-grained comparison between data groups.

Next, to identify the differences between German and Japanese teachers' views, we combined the two resulting AD structures. Specifically, all the researchers examined each low-level theme ($n = 70$) from the German data (as there are more themes in German data) by reviewing a represented them and individual quotes included, as well as the number of quotes and participants represented for each low-level theme. Then, we compared each of the low-level themes from German teachers against all 29 low-level themes from the Japanese data. During this process, we annotated Japanese low-level themes with either "similar" or "opposing," depending on the *direction* of the theme. For example, a German theme of "students should be notified of how AI is used in the classroom" was annotated as "opposing" against a Japanese theme of "I don't think students care about their data being shared" as they show opposing views towards AI monitoring. After reviewing all German data, we also reviewed individual Japanese themes to apply the same procedure. As a result, we generated 32 "similar" matching pairs and 15 "opposing" pairs between German and Japanese data. We also recorded non-matching themes as distinct themes unique in each data group.

Finally, we synthesized the resulting low-level matches and distinct themes (n = 95) into five high-level theme categories. Four individual low-level themes were disregarded as irrelevant later in the analysis process. During the entire analysis process, all researchers met regularly to share the coding/analysis process and discuss to resolve any disagreements.

2.5   Positionality Statement

The team includes five researchers (including three native German citizens and two Japanese citizens, born and raised in the respective country till in their 20 s). The team has prior experience working with school teachers in Germany, Japan, and the United States. They also have research expertise with ITSs, which serve as the primary platform examined in the scenarios. It is of note that their background and past experiences may have influenced the design of the study, study materials, analytical approach, and interpretation.

3   Results

In this section, we report the main high-level themes, categorized into whether the teachers' views are similar or different (combination of opposing and distinct themes from the analysis) between German and Japanese teachers.

3.1   Shared Views on AI Use in the Classroom

First, we identified several overarching themes that were common across teacher groups in all countries. These include teachers' recognition that AI cannot fully capture the complex social dynamics of the classroom, their concern for maintaining safety in AI use, and their preference to retain control over key decisions as the "gatekeepers" of teaching and learning. Each of these findings is discussed in detail below.

"AI Cannot Consider Social Aspects of Teaching and Learning."
Teachers in both countries share the concern that AI is not capable of detecting social dynamics in the classroom. This is most often mentioned while participants were discussing scenarios on pairing students up into groups (i.e., Co-Orchestration Control). For example, J1 (23 years of teaching) said:

"It's quite difficult, you know [...]. For example, when making group in the class, it should include information such as 'this child and this child should not be close to each other' or 'this child and this child will have a fight'."

Teachers in both countries are also concerned that reliance on AI that overlooks social relationships may undermine teacher-student relationships:

"If this were to be used everywhere and all the time in every subject, it would mean that a little bit of the social interaction would be lost. And also the teacher-student relationship is a completely different one" (G3: 4 years of teaching).

In these situations, a majority of teachers in both data groups reported that they would discontinue using AI, as they do not find it meaningful to rely on AI systems that make decisions without considering classroom social dynamics. For teachers, building strong, sustainable relationships with students is critical, and AI systems that disregard these relationships are viewed as unacceptable.

"I'm trying to build a good relationship with my kids on a daily basis. I think that is a very important aspect of classroom activities, regardless of whether it is AI or not. In all teaching situations, I think building a good relationship with kids is important regardless of whether it is AI activity or not" (J9: 8 years of teaching).

"We Need to Ensure the Safe Implementation of AI Systems in the Classroom." Another area of agreement concerns the safe use of AI systems in the school environment. For example, teachers in both groups emphasized the importance of obtaining *buy-in* from all relevant stakeholders. Most importantly, while recognizing the benefits of AI use (e.g., for better personalization), teachers thought that creating a safe environment might be difficult with increased AI monitoring:

"Yes, not nice, [...] the children would come to school with stomach aches and that would not be nice. Because then you can't remember anything and you can't learn anything if you go to school with these fears" (G2: 3.5 years of teaching).

"From the student's point of view, if the student is being monitored by the teacher, and if the student does not want to be monitored in this way, he or she will not be able to study with peace of mind" (J7: 7 years of teaching).

This concern also extends to how AI technology may be accepted by stakeholders outside the classroom, such as parents:

"[When discussing scenarios for Data Control] This is incredible. A real monitoring system. It's scary if it goes this far, though. The school is becoming scary for kids. I think the teachers are going to notice that we are not studying. There's going to be complaints from parents" (J5: 4 years of teaching).

Importantly, many teachers emphasized the need to maintain the classroom as a safe and relaxed environment where students can make mistakes, openly acknowledge them, and engage in transparent discussions with their teachers. Although AI may enable faster and more efficient communication between students and teachers, teachers did not find it meaningful to use AI for all classroom activities, as this could result in constant monitoring and further offloading of teacher-student communication.

"As a Teacher, I Should Be Able to Intervene Student-AI Interactions." Both groups of teachers have a strong desire to proactively intervene in situations where AI tries to make decisions for students. Teachers shared that there should be a way for them to over-ride AI's decision making [6] when their perception of what is best for students differs from that of AI (across all scenarios and aspects of control). This tendency of teachers' proactive intervention desires replicates prior findings in the US [3]:

"It would be difficult if we couldn't change the assignments when what the AI thinks and what we believe about the children differ, especially in terms of the points/areas where we really want students to educate. It would be a problem if the AI's perception and our perception don't match." (J3, 7 years of teaching).

This desire for intervention often comes from their belief that AI can never be perfect (as shown above regarding social dynamics). However, teachers' sharing also implies that they are worried about AI disrupting the hierarchical structure of authority in the classroom, thinking that AI's "dictatorship" (G10: 2 years of teaching) gives students a wrong impression (that teachers would not like):

"[When seeing a scenario that shows a situation where teachers cannot change AI's content assignment] This would weaken my role in the class. And it could also give students a false sense of hierarchy in the classroom. So suddenly the technology is above the pedagogically trained force" (G14: 10 years of teaching).

3.2   Differing Views on AI Use in the Classroom

While teachers from both countries shared their views on the aforementioned aspects, there were several notable themes on which German and Japanese teachers expressed different thoughts. These distinct differences include teachers' perception on how AI could help students become metacognitive and students' data sharing with teachers.

"Use of AI Would Not Help Promote Students' Metacognitive Skills (Japanese)." First, there is a differing view regarding the benefits of a help-seeking feature embedded in a typical AI tutor (depicted in our scenario (Scenario 1). This help-seeking function illustrates a common problem-solving hints [1] that are adapted based on students' problem-solving state. While German teachers generally liked that students can ask for such adaptive hints (thinking that it would be useful for their learning), many Japanese teachers rejected it:

> "Not only Kazuya [student illustrated in the scenario who is struggling with their task], I will tell all students that 'if you don't understand something, just ask me.' It is important to proceed on your own, but if you don't ask and end up not understanding, it won't be for your own good, so if you don't understand, just ask me! This is not to hurt Kazuya's dignity – I will tell all students in classroom, 'Please ask me question if you have any issues'" (J9: 8 years of teaching).

We speculate that this difference might be attributed to the reported characteristic among Japanese "silent" students (i.e., Japanese students tend to keep silence in the classroom, begin reluctant to initiate interactions with teachers [12]); it might be that Japanese teachers prefer inter-personal, transparent communications more than what German – or *Western* – teachers would prefer [12].

"Students' Data Should Always Be Shared with Me (Japanese)." Another notable difference between the teachers was on the topic of data sharing. Japanese teachers were more optimistic regarding getting access to students' data (i.e. students having less control over data sharing through AI) while German teachers are more restrictive and conservative. Specifically, many German teachers emphasize students' right regarding data ownership and sharing, and that students should be given at least a formal consent (in accordance with legal requirements e.g., GDPR) and also an opportunity to make decisions about what data to share with teachers:

> "So somehow it would be quite fair for the children to have a say. And that's also what we promote at school: the right of co-decisions, that children are allowed to have a say at a very early age in what concerns them or, in this case, what data they want to disclose, is a good thing" (G2: 3.5 years of teaching).

Although German teachers, too, recognize the importance of having access to basic learning data from students to conduct their teaching, Japanese teachers insisted on students' data sharing more strongly, indicating that students would not care much about their data being collected and shared:

> "I'm thinking that there probably aren't that many kids who feel fear from the system, because they would rather use it as something like that. They probably don't know that data is being collected, but they don't care that much" (J7: 7 years of teaching).

"I think only some students would choose 'not to share.' In my case, I would tell the students, 'Show it to me.' If everyone in the class were to use this system, I would want to know about the students' situations too" (J4: 10 years of teaching).

In both countries, there are several teachers who stated that students would be fine with data sharing as long as teachers clearly explain its purpose, but we observe the pattern that Japanese teachers are more open to students' data. This tendency is notable, as Japan also has a GDPR-equivalent law ("Act on the Protection of Personal Information," while GDPR requires more strict data protection practices).

4   Discussion

It is increasingly important to fully understand stakeholder views to promote effective, ethical, and safe use of AI in a complex, multi-stakeholder environment such as in a school classroom. Past work has yet to reveal how stakeholder views might (or might not) differ across cultures. We conducted a speed-dating study with 15 German teachers and 10 Japanese teachers to gain insights into how teachers perceive decision-making control owned by AI or student, what preferences they have towards the use of AI, and how their views differ between the two cultures (which share a similar pace of technology adoption in schools).

Our study shows that while both German and Japanese teachers deeply value the *human touch* in teaching, they differ significantly in how they view data privacy and the way students and teachers should talk to one another.

4.1   Preserving the Human-in-the-Loop Student-AI Interactions

A primary finding of this study is the agreement that AI cannot (and should not) replace the social identity of a teacher. Across both groups, teachers expressed skepticism about AI's ability to navigate the complex social dynamics of the classroom, such as interpersonal conflicts or student friendships, which they think they can better handle (therefore prefer to be able to intervene). This finding aligns with prior work conceptualizing how teachers and AI could work together [7,11], with the unique implication that AI is viewed as a tool that must be subordinate to human judgment.

A central tension in our findings is the perceived threat AI poses to the pedagogical hierarchy. Teachers in both countries did not view AI merely as a neutral assistant but as a potential "dictator" (G10) that, if misused, could undermine their professional authority.

Although it was expected that these feelings might have been influenced by the design of our storyboards that illustrated *extreme* cases, teachers' reflections also pose important implications regarding how they consider the hierarchical structure in the classroom. When German teachers expressed concern that technology might rank "above the pedagogically trained force," they were defending a specific professional identity: the teacher as a critical decision-maker who possesses context that an AI algorithm lacks. This finding suggests that hybrid intelligence might not look as simple as a 50/50 split of power. Instead, they desire a model where AI provides data, while the teacher retains the power to make critical decisions.

4.2 Individual Rights Vs. Pedagogical Responsibility

Our study also revealed a few critical differences between the two groups, especially around how they perceive student data and privacy. For German teachers, the classroom is an environment where student autonomy is protected by formal rules. Their focus on the "right of co-decision" indicates that German teachers view students as an individual with distinct rights that exist independently of the teacher. In this context, AI monitoring is seen as a potential violation of the student's private space.

Japanese teachers in general, however, prioritize the teacher's ability to support the student over the student's individual privacy. Their claim that students would not care much about data collection implies that their relationship building and how much teachers perceive student autonomy is based on their trust (rather than social norms or legal boundaries). For them, access to data is a prerequisite for fulfilling their professional duty. If the teacher does not have full visibility into the student's progress, they cannot intervene effectively. This aligns with the PISA2022 findings [13] that Japanese teachers are perceived as highly dedicated to individual support; they see data not as a surveillance tool, but as a necessary resource for high-quality instruction.

Further, another clear difference around help-seeking reveals an unique pedagogical strategy and social dynamics in the classroom. Although a deep cultural comparison between Germany and Japan is out of scope for this paper, prior work conducted in Japanese classrooms [12] suggests the special "silent" culture present in Japanese classrooms (which also resonates with authors' impression as someone who have experienced and seen both Japanese and German classrooms). This distinct difference may form teachers' preferences and strategies differently; for example, it may be that Japanese teachers need to actively ask students to share their thoughts (because otherwise students would not ask questions). On the other hand, German teachers may have a tendency that they would let students freely interact with help-seeking features as teachers are not concerned about the "silence" that Japanese classrooms have.

4.3 Limitations

We acknowledge a few limitations of the study. First, our sample included only 15 and 10 German and Japanese teachers, respectively. Insights from this sample might therefore not generalize across the population. Further, the design of storyboards might have biased teachers' conception of AI.

5 Conclusion

It is essential to gain a comprehensive understanding of stakeholder perspectives on classroom AI to promote its effective, ethical, and safe use in classrooms and to identify how they differ between cultures. We conducted a speed-dating interview study with a total of 25 German and Japanese teachers, examining how their preferences align or diverge across these contexts. Our findings show that while Japanese and German teachers share similar views regarding the limitations of AI, concerns about safety, and their desired level of control over classroom decision-making. At the same time, we also found notable differences in their attitudes toward student data sharing and the role of AI in supporting students when seeking help.

Acknowledgements. This work was supported by JST, PRESTO Grant Number JPMJPR2318, Japan. We thank all the participants in the study.

References

1. Aleven, V., Roll, I., McLaren, B.M., Koedinger, K.R.: Help helps, but only so much: research on help seeking with intelligent tutoring systems. Int. J. Artif. Intell. Educ. **26**(1), 205–223 (2016)
2. Brauner, P., Glawe, F., Liehner, G.L., Vervier, L., Ziefle, M.: Ai perceptions across cultures: similarities and differences in expectations, risks, benefits, tradeoffs, and value in Germany and China arXiv preprint. arXiv:2412.13841 (2024)
3. Echeverria, V., Yang, K., Lawrence, L., Rummel, N., Aleven, V.: Designing hybrid human-AI orchestration tools for individual and collaborative activities: a technology probe study. IEEE Trans. Learn. Technol. **16**(2), 191–205 (2023)
4. Ge, X., Xu, C., Misaki, D., Markus, H.R., Tsai, J.L.: How culture shapes what people want from AI. In: Proceedings of the 2024 CHI Conference on Human Factors in Computing Systems, pp. 1–15 (2024)
5. Han, B., Coghlan, S., Buchanan, G., McKay, D.: Who is helping whom? Student concerns about ai-teacher collaboration in higher education classrooms. Proc. ACM Hum. Comput. Interact. **9**(2), 1–32 (2025)
6. Holstein, K., Aleven, V., Rummel, N.: A conceptual framework for human-AI hybrid adaptivity in education. In: International Conference on Artificial Intelligence in Education, pp. 240–254. Springer (2020). https://doi.org/10.1007/978-3-030-52237-7_20
7. Holstein, K., McLaren, B.M., Aleven, V.: Co-designing a real-time classroom orchestration tool to support teacher-ai complementarity. Grantee Submission (2019)
8. Kulik, J.A., Fletcher, J.D.: Effectiveness of intelligent tutoring systems: a meta-analytic review. Rev. Educ. Res. **86**(1), 42–78 (2016)
9. Lawrence, L., Echeverria, V., Yang, K., Aleven, V., Rummel, N.: How teachers conceptualise shared control with an ai co-orchestration tool: a multiyear teacher-centred design process. Br. J. Edu. Technol. **55**(3), 823–844 (2024)
10. Lucero, A.: Using affinity diagrams to evaluate interactive prototypes. In: IFIP Conference on Human-Computer Interaction, pp. 231–248. Springer (2015). https://doi.org/10.1007/978-3-319-22668-2_19

11. Molenaar, I.: Towards hybrid human-ai learning technologies. Eur. J. Educ. **57**(4), 632–645 (2022)
12. Nakane, I.: Silence in intercultural communication (2007)
13. OECD: PISA 2022 Results (Volume I): The state of learning and equity in education. OECD (2023). https://doi.org/10.1787/53f23881-en
14. Ritter, S., Yudelson, M., Fancsali, S.E., Berman, S.R.: How mastery learning works at scale. In: Proceedings of the Third (2016) ACM Conference on Learning@ Scale, pp. 71–79 (2016)
15. Sindermann, C., et al.: Acceptance and fear of artificial intelligence: associations with personality in a German and a Chinese sample. Discov. Psychol. **2**(1), 8 (2022)
16. Topali, P., Haelermans, C., Molenaar, I., Segers, E.: Pedagogical considerations in the automation era: a systematic literature review of AIED in k-12 authentic settings. Br. Edu. Res. J. **51**(6), 2777–2809 (2025)
17. Vincoli, M., Scholz, N., Nagashima, T.: Multidimensional student agency in learning with ai: a conceptual framework and design implications. In: International Conference on Artificial Intelligence in Education, pp. 218–232. Springer (2025). https://doi.org/10.1007/978-3-031-98459-4_16
18. Xu, W., Ouyang, F.: A systematic review of ai role in the educational system based on a proposed conceptual framework. Educ. Inf. Technol. **27**(3), 4195–4223 (2022)
19. Zimmerman, J., Forlizzi, J.: Speed dating: providing a menu of possible futures. She Ji: J. Des. Econ. Innov. **3**(1), 30–50 (2017)

AI Partners that Support Productive Uncertainty Within "Jigsaw" Activities During Small Group Collaborative Learning in Classrooms

Mon-Lin Monica Ko[(⊠)] ⓘ, Chelsea Chandler ⓘ, Sierra Rose, Brooklyn Cline, Emily Watts, Jason Reitman ⓘ, Peter W. Foltz ⓘ, and Sidney K. D'Mello ⓘ

University of Colorado, Boulder, Boulder, CO 80309, USA
`monlin.ko@colorado.edu`

Abstract. We report on the design and formative evaluation of an AI tool, JIA (Jigsaw Interactive Agent), that supports productive uncertainty during a collaborative "jigsaw" activity where students first build individual expertise and then work collaboratively to solve complex problems that require pooled expertise. We developed and contrasted a rule-based, LLM-based, and hybrid (rule + LLM) AI Partner that analyzed students' open-ended spoken discussions during the jigsaw activity and responded with one of four productive uncertainty intervention types (support, connect, problematize, stabilize). We formatively evaluated JIA in a user study with 16 small groups ($n = 64$) of middle school students in 11 classrooms. We found that the three approaches differed in the types of interventions provided, and that the LLM and hybrid approaches were deemed to be more appropriate and elicited more affective responses from students. We discuss insights for developing AI-based supports for collaboration in classrooms.

Keywords: Pedagogical agents · human-AI collaboration · learning sciences · productive uncertainty · LLMs · Jigsaw tasks

1 Introduction

The application of AI in education has seen great growth over the last decade, sparking new ideas and conversations about how AI systems can deepen student engagement in classrooms. Much of the recent work that leverages large language models (LLMs) within education focuses on creating personalized and adaptive learning experiences that cater to the needs of individual learners [1]. While this approach holds much promise, learning is not only personal, but also a social activity situated within a cultural system [2], which underscores the importance of collaborative, social, and open-ended learning environments for fostering learning [3], as supported by meta-analyses [4]. Accordingly, this study explores new possibilities for AI in supporting collaborative learning in real-world classrooms.

Collaborative learning often occurs through small group interactions; here, students talk about their ideas, make connections, and explore and experiment to develop a

E. G. Blanchard et al. (Eds.): AIED 2026, LNAI 16583, pp. 608–622, 2027.
https://doi.org/10.1007/978-3-032-29760-0_59

shared understanding. One way to foster effective collaborative learning is by designing and enacting instructional tasks that require students to meaningfully engage with one another's ideas [5]. These tasks often involve a combination of taskwork – individual or group activities in service of the task goals – and teamwork – the interpersonal communication and coordination needed to effectively collaborate. Jigsaws are one type of activity where students engage with different aspects of a topic to develop initial expertise (individual taskwork) and then work together with peers to build joint understanding and solve complex problems that require everyone's expertise (collaborative task- and team-work) [6]. Recent studies found that students engage in higher levels of collaboration, motivation, metacognitive, cognitive, and social skills after engaging in jigsaws [7]. However, the effectiveness of jigsaws is determined by how they are enacted within classroom contexts—how the activity is structured, how teachers support groups, and how students engage with the activity [8]. This also highlighted challenges for teachers who have facilitated multiple student groups at the same time. Concomitantly, this also poses challenges for technological solutions in that they require capturing and analyzing the rich multiparty, multimodal data that flows from these collaborations and turning it into actionable insights to support learning.

The present study examines the role of an AI tool, the *Jigsaw Interactive Agent* (JIA), which functions as an AI Partner to support jigsaw activities by providing timely support to students in ways that teachers are unable to do in large classrooms. We designed JIA to support collaborative dialogue through *productive uncertainty,* where students notice gaps, ambiguities and contradictions amongst multiple ideas and engage with one another to address these uncertainties [9]. We developed and contrasted three implementations of the AI Partner (rule-based, LLM, and a hybrid of the two) and formatively evaluated their potential for fostering collaboration in real-world classrooms.

2   Background and Related Work

Small Group Discourse Promotes Collaborative Knowledge Building. In real-world classrooms, collaborative knowledge building occurs in messy, socially negotiated spaces. Here, a confluence of factors shapes how collaborative interactions unfold: classroom culture, curriculum and disciplinary norms for talking, speaking, and interacting shape how students engage with one another, their teacher and disciplinary content. Grounded in sociocultural view of learning [10], we view learning as constituted within these interactions, with classroom discourse mediating knowledge building processes. Instructional tasks that are cognitively demanding and open-ended provide a strong foundation of student disciplinary discourse during collaboration. Jigsaws are one such task because they invite multiple points of view, provide opportunities for students to do evidence-based reasoning about the topic [11], and encourage students to navigate productive uncertainty.

Supporting Productive Uncertainty during Small Group Collaboration. As AI technologies become more prevalent in K-12 classrooms, there is an increasing interest in understanding if, when, and how these technologies can support learning. In the context of learning environments that are designed to promote collaborative knowledge building, AI tools must be designed in ways that preserve and enhance the conditions for rich disciplinary learning, rather than reducing the cognitive load of complex tasks. In this study, we anchored the development of our AI partner in the idea of *productive uncertainty*. Productive uncertainty is a pedagogical approach that seeks to center the non-obvious and contingent aspects of knowledge-building, rather than reducing them [12]. In classrooms that foster productive uncertainty, teachers might make aspects of students' ideas uncertain, "de-settle" aspects of agreed-upon knowledge that may seem obvious. Teachers might also help make uncertain aspects of their activity visible and assist in students resolving or learning from uncertainty [13]. Problematizing aspects of students' collective sensemaking invites students to work collectively to figure out solutions to complex, open-ended problems. However, fostering productive uncertainty is metacognitively demanding; teachers struggle to monitor classroom discussions in ways to foster productive uncertainty [14], suggesting the potential for AI support.

AI Agents that Support Small Group Collaboration. Recent work points to the potential of AI-based methods for analyzing, assessing, and providing feedback to support collaboration. Much of the work has focused on assessing collaboration skills and processes from student discourse [15] with fewer studies providing real-time feedback and support. One class of tools has focused on promoting after-action reflection on student small group collaborative discourse, such as Discussion Tracker [16], IneqDetect [17], CPS Coach [18], and the Community Builder (CoBi) [19]. Fewer studies have provided real-time feedback to support ongoing collaborations. One early example is [20] who developed an agent that monitored student discussions (via chat) and encouraged students to explain their own reasoning.

The closest study to our work is that of [21], who developed an AI agent to support triads as they engaged in jigsaw tasks involving sensors in a lab environment. The agent sensed the state of the triadic collaboration (via speech recognition and discourse classifiers) and responded with a set of hand-crafted rules and LLM-generated intervention prompts that were fed to a human wizard, who adjudicated communication with the students. A quasi-experimental analysis of 145 students in three lab-based conditions (no agent, human Wizard of Oz [WoZ] only, and LLM-WoZ) revealed that both WoZ and LLM-WoZ supported groups showed stronger collaborative behaviors, compared to the control groups.

3 Contributions, Novelty, and Research Questions

The central **contribution** of this study is **in the** development and formative evaluation of a new generation of fully-automated AI Partners that provide real-time facilitation of productive uncertainty during small group jigsaw activities in middle-school classrooms. Our work is **novel** in multiple ways. First, to the best of our knowledge, our work represents the first attempt at near real-time AI-driven small group support during open-ended spoken collaborations in authentic classroom environments. The real-world context poses several technical challenges involving child speech diarization and noisy automatic speech recognition (ASR), analyzing collaborative discourse in light of imperfect ASR [22], and User Experience (UX) interaction design that facilitates but does not detract from student-student interactions.

Second, there is limited work that explores how *fully-automated* AI pedagogical interventions might support students in jigsaw collaborations. Our study builds on and significantly extends prior work that used a semi-automated approach in the lab [21].

Third, our work represents the first attempt at developing AI that can support the socio-cognitive pedagogical practice of *productive uncertainty* in small groups. We contrast our three approaches (rule-based, LLM-based, and a hybrid), resulting in two related **research questions**:

RQ1: How do the three JIA approaches differ in providing real-time support for productive uncertainty to small groups of students engaged in a jigsaw task?
RQ2: How did students respond to the varied support from the three JIA approaches?

To address these questions, we conducted a formative user study to investigate how to instantiate complex pedagogies from the learning sciences into actionable AI tools for real-world classrooms. As such, our focus was on assessing how the three JIA approaches behaved in this complex environment and how students responded to them. This is a critical step prior to evaluations that study their effectiveness in promoting learning.

4   AI Partner Design

We situate our AI tools as part of a larger curricular activity system [23], comprising: (1) an AI literacy unit; (2) AI partners to support collaboration within the unit and (3) teacher professional development (PD) to support implementation of the unit and AI.

4.1   Lesson and Curricular Context

Our AI partner, the Jigsaw Interactive Agent (JIA), was embedded in a co-designed AI literacy curriculum unit that invites students to experience, critique, build and test how moderation systems can foster equitable and welcoming online gaming communities. The AI partner was embedded in Lesson 4 (jigsaw activity) of this 7-lesson three-week unit. In this lesson, students work together in small groups to generate a set of criteria that could be used to evaluate moderation systems. Then, students independently become an expert on one of 5 different moderation approaches (that utilize human, AI, and humans-and-AI-based moderation). After independent work, students return to their groups to share their new expertise and then work together to rank them from *most* to *least* effective, using criteria they generated earlier in the lesson. Successful completion of the task requires collaboration because each student only has partial information that needs to be shared/exchanged, and the group needs to come to consensus on the efficacy of these approaches.

We designed JIA to be integrated within a web interface where students input their written responses to questions during the jigsaw (Fig. 1A). A scribe from the group typed out their responses to each question. As students worked collaboratively on the questions (Fig. 1B), JIA listened to their conversation and would respond with interventions that supported the collaborative dialogue on the right side of the screen. Interventions were provided at one-minute intervals to avoid overwhelming students and allow them to engage in discussion before receiving additional guidance. This approach ensured that

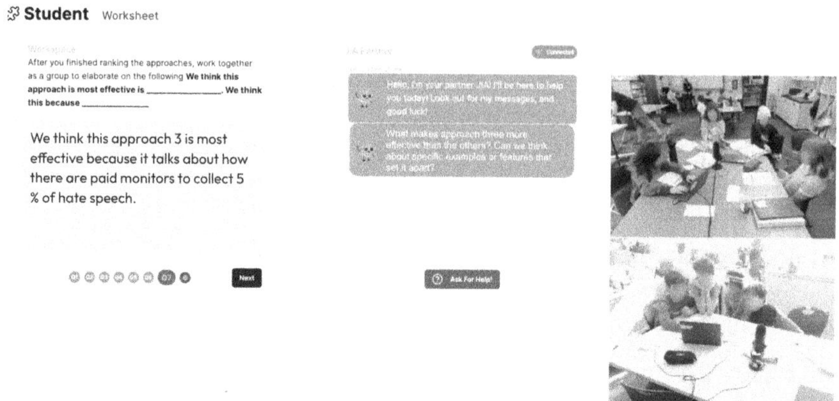

Fig. 1. (A) Screenshot of interface with prompt, student response on left and JIA support on the right; (B) Student groups engaging with interface in classroom

feedback was not overly disruptive to the students' conversations, and students could decide whether and how to respond to JIA feedback.

4.2 AI Partner Dialog Policies to Support Productive Uncertainty

We designed dialog policies that provides four interventions derived from research on how teachers support productive uncertainty in classrooms [13]: (1) *Social support* encourages students to join the ongoing conversation in the group and contribute their thinking; (2) *Connection* interventions invite students to make connections between one another's ideas; (3) *Problematizing* interventions juxtapose, compare, and contrast aspects of students' ideas; (4) *Stabilize* interventions supports taking stock of conversational flow, marking areas of convergence/divergence in thinking within the group talk.

We implemented and tested three different approaches for the dialog policy. They all operate on one-minute intervals, analyzing the immediately preceding segment of group conversation to determine which of the four interventions would best support the groups. We used a near-real-time student discourse analysis pipeline comprising a Whisper-Large-v2 ASR model and a customized speech diarization module to assign utterances to the relevant speakers. The word error rate (WER) in benchmark datasets in similar classroom contexts is about 58% highlighting the challenges of obtaining accurate transcripts pf child speech in noisy classroom environments.

Rule-Based Approach. This approach selected the intervention based on the group "state" derived from indicators capturing *participation structure, task engagement,* and *collaboration quality.* Participation structure included conversational statistics such as the number of utterances produced in the last minute and whether participation is uneven (e.g., one student dominates while others are silent). Task engagement was estimated with a RoBERTa model developed to detect whether student conversation has drifted off topic. Finally, collaboration quality was measured using validated RoBERTa utterance-level classifiers. These included Constructing Shared Knowledge, which captured whether students were sharing knowledge and building on each other's ideas, and Moving Thinking Forward, which reflected whether the group's dialogue advanced understanding by asking questions and proposing ideas. Accuracy of these classifiers significantly outperformed chance (Area Under the Receiver Operating Characteristic Curve [AUROC] from 0.60 to 0.77) and was deemed sufficient for the present purposes.

The rule-based approach triggered the four interventions based on these indicators Because the goal of the *Connect* intervention was to invite others into conversations and make connections, it was triggered when there was uneven discussion, the conversation went off topic, or students were having difficulty sharing knowledge and moving the group's thinking forward. A sample message for this intervention was *"I wonder how these criteria would be implemented in an online community your teammates are a part of. Can you all discuss that a bit?"*. In contrast, the *Problematize* intervention occurred when students were speaking but not meaningfully sharing knowledge or advancing thinking, or when the group had stalled entirely (e.g., no speech) because it was intended to juxtapose or question existing ideas. For example, the feedback might have been *"Do you think any of these approaches are similar or different from one another?"*. Similarly, *Support* interventions focused on re-engaging students when participation was off topic, minimal or uneven (e.g., *"Keep going and be sure to invite others into the conversation!"*), while *Stabilize* interventions were used when students have generated ideas but may have benefitted from consolidating, reviewing, or aligning their thinking before proceeding (e.g., *"Can you take a minute to review it with your team and see if there are more to add?"*).

LLM-Based Approach. This approach operated solely on student speech (i.e., without the aforementioned indicators) as input and used an LLM (Llama 70b) to interpret dialogue and generate feedback, allowing for more context-sensitive and adaptive responses. The prompt consisted of definitions of the four intervention types, examples of candidate interventions, the agent's role, and descriptions of the jigsaw task. The prompt also included what the AI agent should pay attention to within the discourse, emphasizing that the interventions should support the students in co-constructing their solutions. For example, the LLM was prompted to: *"Pay attention to make sure that all students are contributing ideas and support them in generating new ideas of criteria."*

The LLM was also prompted to generate a summary of the students' discussion the minute prior to the intervention, select an intervention type, and provide a justification for its decision. To illustrate, when JIA summarized that *"The group started brainstorming criteria for evaluating a moderation system's effectiveness, but the conversation seems to be struggling to take off, with some students not contributing and others dominating the conversation."*, it determined that the *Support* intervention would be most appropriate because *"The group needs encouragement to keep generating ideas and build on each other's thoughts to establish common knowledge and negotiate/coordinating"*. In this scenario, the feedback was *"Great start! Let's hear from everyone - what else do you think makes a moderation system effective?"*.

An example of a transcript of student discussion and JIA feedback using the LLM model is shown in Table 1. In the discussion, the LLM has first prompted the students to consider how moderation affects people with different backgrounds and experiences. The students pick up on this feedback and start elaborating by discussing how the meaning of words may be interpreted differently in different languages. The LLM then summarizes the conversation up to that point as *"The group is brainstorming criteria for evaluating effective moderation systems, considering perspectives and equity, and sharing everyday experiences"* and suggests a "connect" intervention to encourage them to relate their ideas to a prior part of their discussion around understanding the context of language usage, saying *"That's a great point about different backgrounds. Can someone connect that to our idea about context being important?"*.

Table 1. Example transcript of ASR-derived student discourse and the LLM-JIA feedback.

Student ID/Agent	ASR transcript or Agent Feedback
LLM Agent	*Let's consider how our ideas about moderation might affect people from different backgrounds or with different experiences.*
Student 1	Like… We don't want any offensive comedy.
Student 2	And if you do, you will be banned from the game for 3–7-2.
Student 3	I'm just gonna do this.
Student 4	might affect people from different backgrounds or different identities.
Student 4	might affect people from different backgrounds or different identities.
Student 3	If people from like different countries and stuff play on the same game and like words mean different things in different languages
Student 4	What was your layout?
Student 1	Like if they're trying to translate, like If they say they're trying to have-They're trying to say that they have a female dog And then they go on like Google Translate
Student 4	then like
LLM Agent	*That's a great point about different backgrounds. Can someone connect that to our idea about context being important?*
Student 2	Maybe there's like an auto-translate, so instead of like showing it in English for everybody…
Student 3	That's a great point about…
Student 4	Someone connect that to our idea about context being important.

Hybrid Approach. Combining the strengths of the other two approaches, the hybrid approach used the same LLM to integrate indicators of collaboration (i.e., the states detailed in the rule-based policy section) and utterance-level indicators (e.g., predictions from the RoBERTa models) with the conversation transcript, which were analyzed through a curated prompt very similar to that provided in the LLM-based approach.

5   Method

5.1   Participants, Design, & Procedures

Participants. A total of 64 groups of 8th grade students aged 13–14 from two school districts in the United States participated in the study. All students were enrolled in English Language Arts (ELA) or Math classes. Both student and parent consents were required for a student to participate. Those who opted out engaged in the same activities without JIA support as part of normal instruction, and no data was collected. Students were grouped by their consent status to form groups of 3–6 students. All study procedures were approved by the authors' IRB and school districts' Research Review Board.

Design and Procedures. The study adopted a quasi-experimental design where each classroom group interacted with only one of the three AI partners throughout their activity. Through the process of iterative design, the rule-based and LLM models were first deployed in two classes and groups were randomly assigned an AI partner. Based on feedback from students and a review of the data, the hybrid model was then deployed in place of the other two models for the final classroom.

Researchers were present in the classroom daily during the unit enactment to help troubleshoot technical challenges. Each group of students used a single Chromebook laptop equipped with a Yeti microphone and customized software was used to stream the audio to the JIA Web app, which provided the interventions in 1-min intervals (Fig. 1). Cameras were also placed in the classroom to capture the interactions of the students for human annotation of data.

5.2   Data Treatment

Data Selection. Of the 64 groups of students, 23 groups had poor audio or video quality, while 41 groups had usable audio. Four members of the research team reviewed the ASR-generated transcripts and videos from these 41 groups and categorized the videos based on students' level of engagement with JIA: (1) no engagement (n = 10), (2) low (1–2) interaction (n = 15), (3) moderate (3–4) interaction (n = 11), and (4) high (sustained throughout) interaction (n = 5). The low interaction and poor-quality audio were primarily due to misconfigurations of hardware/software in the classroom and/or limited instructions on how to work with JIA. These issues are critical in the design and deployment of AI technology in classrooms because they pertain to issues of usability, which is not the present focus. Instead, we focused on the moderate and high interaction groups (N = 16) as they are germane to our research questions focused on analyzing the quality of the interventions and students' responses to them.

Automated and Human Annotation. The data comprise two categories. The first was automatically generated data including timestamped responses from JIA, intervention type, and a summary and justification (for LLM approaches). The second category of data was human annotations performed to characterize the quality of each piece of JIA feedback as well as the impact of the feedback on the direction of student conversations (see Table 2 below). Four researchers annotated the data by reviewing videos around the time of each intervention (typically the minute before through the minute after the intervention). Annotators also had access to the ASR transcripts and the text of the interventions. There were 341 total interventions across the 16 student groups; a subset of 137 interventions wherein students explicitly reacted to the feedback were further analyzed for *level of uptake* and *emotional valence* of reaction. Student reactions could be both verbal and/or non-verbal. Level of uptake included Acknowledgement (e.g., reading responses aloud), Basic Response (e.g., short answers to questions posed), Integrated (e.g., discussing or implementing a suggestion in the conversation), Ah-ha moment (e.g., expressing a new understanding or resolving confusion) or None (e.g., no response). Since we were interested in understanding not just the content of student reactions but also their affective experience, each reaction was additionally coded for emotional valence. Example of emotional valence include neutral, confused, curious, frustrated, etc.

Table 2. Human-annotated data.

Annotation Dimension	Example
Rating of the appropriateness of the partner feedback	Yes, Maybe, No
Did the students react to the feedback (and reaction modality)	Verbal, Non-verbal, Both, None
Level of uptake of the information from the intervention	Acknowledgement, Basic Response, Integrated, Ah-ha moment, None
Emotional valence of the student reaction	e.g. Neutral, Confused, Curious, Excited, Frustrated, Stressed

Analytical Approach. The data were analyzed at the level of individual JIA intervention responses via mixed-effects linear regression models to account for repeated measurement and nesting of responses within student groups (random intercept). The main fixed effect in all models was the the JIA approach (LLM, Rule-based, Hybrid) as a three-level categorical effect. We included the intervention number within each question to ascertain if effects varied as the activity progressed. Question number was included as a categorical covariate to account for any question-related effects. We used pairwise comparisons with false-discovery rate (fdr) corrections to probe significant main effects. A two-tailed $p < 0.05$ criteria was used for statistical significance. Since all outcome variables were binary, we used logistic regression models in R (see Table 3).

Table 3. Mean proportion (SD in parentheses) by AI Partner type; n.s. = not significant.

Intervention Type	Rule-based [R]	LLM-based [L]	Hybrid [H]	Pattern of Sig.
Intervention				
Connect	0.21 (0.41)	0.59 (0.49)	0.62 (0.49)	[L = H] > R
Problematize	0.17 (0.38)	0.07 (0.26)	0.06 (0.24)	n.s.
Stabilize	0.20 (0.40)	0.12 (0.32)	0.13 (0.34)	n.s.
Support	0.41 (0.50)	0.21 (0.41)	0.19 (0.40)	R > [L = H]
Appropriateness	0.63 (0.49)	0.82 (0.38)	0.87 (0.34)	[L = H] > R
Student Reaction				
Students Reacted	0.24 (0.43)	0.49 (0.50)	0.29 (0.46)	L > R
Neutral Valence	0.78 (0.43)	0.40 (0.49)	0.67 (0.49)	[R = H] > L
Negative Valence	0.11 (0.32)	0.34 (0.48)	0.33 (0.49)	n.s.
Positive Valence	0.06 (0.24)	0.26 (0.44)	0.00 (0.00)	n.s.
Elaborated Uptake	0.28 (0.46)	0.29 (0.46)	0.21 (0.43)	n.s.

6 Results

6.1 How Do the Three JIA Approaches Differ in Providing Real-Time Support for Productive Uncertainty During Jigsaw Activities? (RQ1)

First, we examined whether the implementation of the four intervention types (overall occurrence: connect [51%], problematize [9%], stabilize [14%], and support [26%]) varied by approaches via four separate mixed-effects logistic regression models contrasting the presence (coded as 1) vs. absence (coded as 0) of each intervention type (n = 341). The results indicated that the LLM and hybrid approaches were significantly (*pfdr's* < .001) more likely to apply the *Connect* intervention (e.g. *"How does this moderation approach relate to our own experiences with online gaming?"*), compared to the rule-based approach, which was more likely (*pfdr's* < .01) to apply *Support* intervention (e.g. *"Great job listening to each other and asking questions!"*). There were no significant differences for the *Problematize* (e.g. *"How do you think the approaches compare in terms of effectiveness?"* and *Stabilize* interventions (e.g. *"I notice we're not really discussing...how can we work together to make sure everyone's ideas are heard and respected?"*).

Next, we examined the extent to which the interventions were deemed appropriate - those that built upon students' conversations, deepened their thinking, or re-oriented them to the question at hand - by human coders and if the students' reactions to the interventions varied by AI type. Of the n = 341 interventions, human coders deemed 79% appropriate overall and 40% received some type of student reaction. These (and all subsequent) models also examined if effects varied by type of intervention by including it as a categorical covariate. Compared to the Rule-based agent interventions (63%), human coders were significantly (*pfdr's* < .05) more likely to judge the LLM- (82%)

and Hybrid- (87%) agents' interventions as being more appropriate. Human coders judged appropriateness based on the substance and flow of the students' conversation the minute prior to the AI Partners' intervention. Most often, inappropriate responses misunderstood students' contribution or misjudged where students were relative to the jigsaw task goals, moving students away from the task at hand when they were not yet ready to move on.

6.2 How Did Students Respond to Varied Support from the Three JIA Approaches? (RQ2)

We examined variations in patterns of whether students responded to the three approaches at all, as well as the nature of their responses. We found that overall, students were more likely ($pfdr < .05$) to respond to the LLM approach (49%) compared to the Rule-based (24%) and Hybrid approaches (29%), although this latter difference was not significant.

Next, we examined whether the approach type predicted students' emotional valence (overall occurrence: neutral [48%], negative [31%], and positive [20%]) and level of uptake (defined below). The analyses were conducted on the subset of 137 interventions where students reacted to JIA. Results for emotional valence indicated that students were significantly (p_{fdr}'s $< .05$) more emotionally neutral in response to Rule-based (78%) and Hybrid (67%) approaches compared to the LLM (40%) approach. The LLM approach, in turn, evoked a combination of positive (26%) and negative responses (34%) compared to the two other implementations, but the differences were not statistically significant. Qualitatively, the LLM approach tended to generate more varied and contextually-sensitive interventions, more closely tied to the specifics of students ideas, compared to the Hybrid and Rule-based approaches. The Rule-based approach generated the most repetitive interventions, overall. In terms of type of intervention, the *Stabilize* intervention evoked more (p_{fdr}'s $< .05$) negative responses (57%) than the *Connect* (26%) and *Problematize* (8%) interventions, but not the *Support* intervention (32%). The *Stabilize* interventions tended to make judgements on the state of students' collaboration, using prompts such as "I notice….Let's shift…", or invite students to determine if they were in agreement or disagreement. The other three interventions made less overt judgements on the state of students' knowledge building and collaboration.

Finally, the level of students' uptake was coded as elaborated (28% overall) when aspects of the intervention were taken up in subsequent discussion. Reactions were coded as 'elaborated uptake' when students up aspects of JIA's input by "borrowing" language from the AI Partner, acknowledging the insight of the intervention, or shifting the direction of the conversation based on the intervention. For example, in one group, the JIA intervention sparked their first in-depth conversation about the jigsaw activity, as the minute prior students were discussing off-topic ideas. When the scribe read, "*recognizing hateful words is a great point. How does that relate to our criteria for effective moderation systems?*" [*Connect* intervention], students began calling on their group members to elaborate on their criteria for evaluating moderation approaches. Students then added aspects of their conversation as answers to the online worksheet. An elaborated response contrasted responses that merely acknowledged the prompt (e.g., reading it aloud). The regression model revealed that there were no statistical differences in level of uptake among the three approaches. However, there was a main effect of intervention, where students had significantly (p_{fdr}'s $< .03$) more elaborated uptake with the *Connect* (35%) and *Problematize* (58%) interventions compared to the *Support* (9%) intervention, while there were no significant differences with the *Stabilize* (18%) intervention.

7 Discussion

We reported on the novel approach of developing and implementing the Jigsaw Interactive Agent (JIA), a fully-automated AI Partner that promoted productive uncertainty for small groups of middle school students as they engaged in a jigsaw task within an AI literacy curriculum. Designing three types of AI dialog approaches to provide four possible intervention types allowed us to enact pedagogical theory in an AI Partner implementation and test the impacts of the different approaches and interventions during jigsaw tasks in middle school classrooms. We discuss our main findings followed by limitations and future direction.

7.1 Main Findings

Overall, our study found that it was feasible for JIA to support small group collaborations during a complex jigsaw activity in authentic classroom environments despite the challenges inherent in this context. From our larger sample of participants with usable audio ($n = 41$ groups), we found 16 groups of students with moderate to high engagement with the AI Partners. There were, however, key differences in patterns of engagement among the three approaches, potentially due to their selections of intervention types and quality of their responses.

Specifically, the LLM- and Hybrid approaches were more likely to utilize the *Connect* intervention compared to the Rule-based partner, which was more likely to provide *Support* interventions. The LLM and Hybrid approaches also provided more appropriate interventions, and the LLM approach elicited more responses from students compared to the other two approaches. We suspect that the low performance of the Rule-based interventions was due to the repetitive nature of its feedback. While it was able to assess the collaborative state of the students, it was not as effective at providing varied and context-aware interventions to students. For example, in one group, the Rule-based approach stated, *"This list is looking great. Can you take a minute to review it with your team and see if there are more to add?"* when students had not generated much of a list at that point in the activity. This misunderstanding of the students' progress likely influenced the relevance and potential impact of the student-AI interaction. Conversely, the LLM approach was successful in incorporating pieces of the conversational history in its responses, thereby providing a greater sense of relevance. At the same time, this approach also triggered more of a range of emotional reactions from students including being dismissive, amused, confused, excited, and annoyed. For example, one student dismissed the partner, *"We can ignore the partner. It doesn't matter,"* whereas another was amused by the Partner's response saying *"Thank you, JIA!"*.

In terms of level of uptake, there was no significant difference among the three approaches, but the *Connect* and *Problematize* interventions generated more elaborated uptake compared to the *Support* intervention. Elaborated responses showcased the potential for JIA to deepen students' collaborative sensemaking. For example, when JIA said: *"What makes you think the paid moderators approach is the most effective? Are there any potential downsides to this approach?"* [*Problematizing* intervention], students elaborated on the pros and cons of choosing AI + paid moderators as the best approach. In another example, JIA intervened with the question, *"How does that idea about humans deciding consequences relate to the idea about tone and context? Can we connect those?"* [*Connection* intervention]. One student responded by sharing that AI can't interpret the tone of conversations, so humans should help determine the criteria for evaluating the feedback. These examples illustrate how JIA's *Connect* and *Problematize* interventions could effectively prompt students to articulate and integrate ideas, fostering deeper collaborative reasoning.

In summary, our results support the potential for developing an AI Partner that can support the socio-cognitive pedagogical practice of *productive uncertainty* in small groups, thereby demonstrating how to instantiate complex pedagogies from the learning sciences into actionable AI tools for real-world classrooms.

7.2 Limitations and Future Work

First, this study focused on groups with high quality interactions with JIA; these interactions are not fully representative of our larger sample. The lack of engagement by the other groups can be attributed to technical issues as well as problems with UX interaction design where JIA was unable to direct and maintain student attention. That said, the more suggestive and background (rather than directive and central) role for JIA was a design decision to foreground student-student interactions rather than student-AI interactions. Future work is needed to strike a more appropriate balance among the two depending on goals and values.

Second, this study reflects an iterative design study without random assignment, so causal claims cannot be made about the JIA's influence on student collaboration. For this reason, we also did not examine the impact of JIA on student learning, because we deemed such formative studies as being an essential step to refine the designs prior to larger-scale evaluation studies.

To this point, the study provided several themes to pursue. Specifically, our findings point to the promise of LLM- and Hybrid- approaches to AI Partner design. A future direction involves developing dialog policies that better approximate the relevance of student dialogue in connection to the overall goals of the jigsaw task, lesson, and the larger curriculum unit. This will sharpen our theory of action around when and what types of interventions are most appropriate, given students' collaborative dynamics and curricular context.

These findings also point us to new directions in thinking about AI-human interactions. JIA was developed to be student-facing, providing just-in-time support for small group collaboration. Investigating the ways that AI Partner designs and interventions can scaffold and improve student dialogue (as opposed to an increasing reliance on the Partner) is one productive direction. Analyzing the ways that JIA interventions influenced students' perceptions of the tool and participation in group work can also more clearly illuminate the promise of AI Partners in supporting collaborative learning.

Concluding Remarks. While assessing and supporting real-time multimodal collaboration in classrooms is inherently complex, this study reveals much promise in AI-based approaches to supporting collaborative learning. This work underscores that understanding how AI supports learning in the classroom requires that researchers go beyond just measuring the accuracy of an AI assessment model. Researchers must consider a wider context of how students interact with AI Partners, when they notice or don't notice feedback, how and when that feedback is communicated to other students, whether the feedback is taken up into student's collaborative discussions, and the emotional tenor of their reactions which may indicate how much they trust or value the contributions of the AI Partner. These are all vital precursors towards leveraging the benefits of complex theories of pedagogy into AI tools for real-world classrooms.

Acknowledgments. This research was supported by the NSF National AI Institute for Student-AI Teaming (iSAT) under grants DRL 2019805 and DRL 2454151. The opinions expressed are those of the authors and do not represent views of the NSF.

Disclosure of Interests. The authors have no competing interests.

References

1. Penuel, W.R., Philip, T.M., Chang, M., Sumner, T., D'Mello, S.K.: Responsible innovation in designing AI for education: shifting from personalization to collaborative problem-solving. Educ. Res.
2. Bransford, J.D., Brown, A.L., Cocking, R.R., et al.: How People Learn. National Academy Press, Washington, DC (2000). http://csun.edu/~SB4310/How%20People%20Learn.pdf
3. Roschelle, J., Teasley, S.D.: The construction of shared knowledge in collaborative problem solving. In: O'Malley, C. (eds.) Computer Supported Collaborative Learning. NATO ASI Series, vol. 128, pp. 69–97. Springer, Heidelberg (1995). https://doi.org/10.1007/978-3-642-85098-1_5
4. Jeong, H., Hmelo-Silver, C.E., Jo, K.: Ten years of computer-supported collaborative learning: a meta-analysis of CSCL in STEM education during 2005–2014. Educ. Res. Rev. **28**, 100284 (2019). https://doi.org/10.1016/j.edurev.2019.100284
5. Fransen, J., Kirschner, P.A., Erkens, G.: Mediating team effectiveness in the context of collaborative learning: the importance of team and task awareness. Comput. Hum. Behav. **27**(3), 1103–1113 (2011). https://doi.org/10.1016/j.chb.2010.05.017
6. Aronson, E.: The Jigsaw Classroom. Sage, Thousand Oaks (1978)
7. Hind, N.S., Astuti, P.: How jigsaw worked in a middle school classroom for enhancing students' reading comprehension. Eur. J. Engl. Lang. Stud. **4**(2), 81–87 (2024). https://doi.org/10.12973/ejels.4.2.81
8. Cochon Drouet, O., Lentillon-Kaestner, V., Margas, N.: Effects of the Jigsaw method on student educational outcomes: systematic review and meta-analyses. Front. Psychol. **14**, 1216437 (2023). https://doi.org/10.3389/fpsyg.2023.1216437
9. Manz, E.: Designing for and analyzing productive uncertainty in science investigations. In: Kay, J., Luckin, R. (eds.) Rethinking Learning in the Digital Age: Making the Learning Sciences Count, 13th International Conference of the Learning Sciences (ICLS) 2018, vol. 1, pp. 288–295. International Society of the Learning Sciences, London, UK (2018)
10. Greeno, J.G.: The situativity of knowing, learning, and research. Am. Psychol. **53**(1), 5–26 (1998)

11. Martin, D.S., Manzano, C., de Camargo, V.V.: Do students learn better together? Teaching design patterns and the OSI model with the aronson method (No. arXiv:2508.16770). arXiv (2025). https://doi.org/10.48550/arXiv.2508.16770

12. Manz, E., Suárez, E.: Supporting teachers to negotiate uncertainty for science, students, and teaching. Sci. Educ. **102**(4), 771–795 (2018). https://doi.org/10.1002/sce.21343

13. Watkins, J., Manz, E.: Characterizing pedagogical decision points in sense-making conversations motivated by scientific uncertainty. Sci. Educ. **106**(6), 1408–1441 (2022). https://doi.org/10.1002/sce.21747

14. Chen, Y.-C.: Dialogic pathways to manage uncertainty for productive engagement in scientific argumentation: a longitudinal case study grounded in an ethnographic perspective. Sci. Educ. (2020). https://doi.org/10.1007/s11191-020-00111-z

15. OECD: PISA 2015 Collaborative Problem Solving Framework (2015)

16. Lugini, L., Olshefski, C., Singh, R., Litman, D., Godley, A.: Discussion tracker: supporting teacher learning about students' collaborative argumentation in high school classrooms. In: Proceedings of the 28th International Conference on Computational Linguistics: System Demonstrations, pp. 53–58 (2020). https://doi.org/10.18653/v1/2020.coling-demos.10

17. MacNeil, S., Kiefer, K., Thompson, B., Takle, D., Latulipe, C.: IneqDetect: a visual analytics system to detect conversational inequality and support reflection during active learning. In: Proceedings of the ACM Conference on Global Computing Education, pp. 85–91 (2019). https://doi.org/10.1145/3300115.3309528

18. D'Mello, S.K., Duran, N.D., Michaels, A., Stewart, A.E.: Improving collaborative problem solving skills via automated feedback & scaffolding: a quasi-experimental study with CPSCoach 2.0. User Modeling & User-Adapted Interaction (2024)

19. Breideband, T., et al.: A feasibility and implementation integrity study of the community builder (CoBi): an AI-based collaboration support system in K-12 classrooms. Int. J. Artif. Intell. Educ. **35**, 3579–3613 (2025)

20. Dyke, G., Adamson, D., Howley, I., Rosé, C.P.: Enhancing scientific reasoning and discussion with conversational agents. IEEE Trans. Learn. Technol. **6**(3), 240–247 (2013). https://doi.org/10.1109/TLT.2013.25

21. Doherty, E., et al.: Piecing together teamwork: a responsible approach to an LLM-based educational jigsaw agent. In: Proceedings of the 2025 CHI Conference on Human Factors in Computing Systems, pp. 1–17 (2025). https://doi.org/10.1145/3706598.3713349

22. Cao, J., et al.: A comparative analysis of automatic speech recognition errors in small group classroom discourse. In: Proceedings of the ACM International Conference on User Modeling, Adaptation and Personalization (UMAP 2023), pp. 250–262. ACM (2023)

23. Roschelle, J., Knudsen, J., Hegedus, S.: From new technological infrastructures to curricular activity systems: advanced designs for teaching and learning. In: Jacobson, M., Reimann, P. (eds.) Designs for Learning Environments of the Future, pp. 233–262. Springer, Boston (2010). https://doi.org/10.1007/978-0-387-88279-6_9

Impact of Multimodal and Conversational AI on Learning Outcomes and Experience

Karan Taneja[1]([✉])[iD], Anjali Singh[2][iD], and Ashok K. Goel[1][iD]

[1] Georgia Institute of Technology, Atlanta, GA 30332, USA
{karan.taneja,ashok.goel}@cc.gatech.edu
[2] University of Texas at Austin, Austin, TX 78712, USA
anjali.singh@ischool.utexas.edu

Abstract. Multimodal Large Language Models (MLLMs) offer an opportunity to support multimedia learning through conversational systems grounded in educational content. However, while conversational AI is known to boost engagement, its impact on learning in visually-rich STEM domains remains under-explored. Moreover, there is limited understanding of how multimodality and conversationality jointly influence learning in generative AI systems. This work reports findings from a randomized controlled online study ($N = 124$) comparing three approaches to learning biology from textbook content: (1) a document-grounded conversational AI with interleaved *text-and-image* responses (MuDoC), (2) a document-grounded conversational AI with *text-only* responses (TexDoC), and (3) a textbook interface with semantic search and highlighting (DocSearch). Learners using MuDoC achieved the highest post-test scores and reported the most positive learning experience. Notably, while TexDoC was rated as significantly more engaging and easier to use than DocSearch, it led to the lowest post-test scores, revealing a disconnect between student perceptions and learning outcomes. Interpreted through the lens of the Cognitive Load Theory, these findings suggest that conversationality reduces extraneous load, while visual-verbal integration induced by multimodality increases germane load, leading to better learning outcomes. When conversationality is not complemented by multimodality, reduced cognitive effort may instead inflate perceived understanding without improving learning outcomes.

Keywords: Multimodal AI · Conversational Multimedia Learning · RCT

1   Introduction

Multimedia learning integrates verbal and visual representations and has been shown to improve knowledge retention and transfer compared to learning from text alone [15]. This is particularly important in visually rich STEM disciplines, where visual representations such as diagrams and graphs are central to learning.

E. G. Blanchard et al. (Eds.): AIED 2026, LNAI 16583, pp. 623–638, 2027.
https://doi.org/10.1007/978-3-032-29760-0_60

Recent advances in Multimodal Large Language Models (MLLMs) create new opportunities to support learning by enabling conversational systems grounded in educational content that can generate personalized multimedia explanations in response to learner inquiries [23]. This potential is especially salient given the adoption of AI tools in classrooms [8], and recent large-scale deployments of generative AI tools in higher education [10]. However, empirical evidence regarding the educational impact of AI chatbots remains mixed. While some studies report improvements in learning outcomes and student engagement [24], others raise concerns such as overreliance and reduced metacognitive effort [26]. Additionally, the impact of AI-generated multimedia content on learning outcomes is still not well understood. Finally, there is limited work examining how conversational interaction and multimodality jointly influence the learning process.

To investigate how multimodality and conversational AI—both independently and jointly—influence students' learning outcomes and experience, we conducted a randomized controlled trial (RCT) on Prolific with $N = 124$ participants learning meiosis cell division, a fundamental topic in cell biology. We compared three systems: (i) **MuDoC 2.0** (henceforth referred to as MuDoC), an AI system for *conversational multimedia learning* that uses text and visuals from learning material to construct interleaved text-and-image responses, extending our previous system **MuDoC 1.0** [21], (ii) **TexDoC**, a system that is identical to MuDoC, except that it generates text-only responses without images, and (iii) **DocSearch** (DOcument SEARCH), a semantic search tool that supports multimedia learning by highlighting relevant content in the textbook in response to students' search queries. Participants first completed a pre-test, then learned the assigned topic using one of the three systems, and finally completed a post-test and a survey probing their learning experience.

Results show that MuDoC led to significantly higher post-test scores compared to TexDoC, whereas no significant differences were observed between the remaining pairs of systems. For learning experience, MuDoC and TexDoC were rated similarly, while DocSearch received significantly lower ratings. Interpreting these findings from the lens of the Cognitive Load Theory (CLT) [20] suggests that conversational multimedia learning supports learning by reducing extraneous load through conversationality while increasing pedagogically-effective germane load through visual-verbal integration. On the other hand, conversational interaction without accompanying visuals enhances perceived learning experience despite resulting in poorer learning outcomes. These findings provide evidence in support of using MLLMs for conversational multimedia learning to enhance both students' learning outcomes and experience. Further, by examining learner behaviors and the disconnect between subjective satisfaction and objective performance of the TexDoC group, this work offers a new perspective on the effects of conversational AI on learning and over-reliance.

2 Related Work

Cognitive Theory of Multimedia Learning (CTML) [15] posits that learners process verbal and visual information through separate, capacity-limited channels.

Learning is enhanced when these representations are meaningfully integrated with one another and with prior knowledge in long-term memory [15]. This integration supports deeper cognitive processing and leads to improved learning outcomes compared to verbal information alone.

Multimodal AI systems have also been explored for multimedia learning in several domains [2–4,23], but the impact of AI-generated multimedia content on learning outcomes remains unclear. Chen et al. [4] generated visualizations as learning aids for poetry but did not compare against a non-visual baseline. Bland et al. [2] used AI to generate cinematic clinical narratives for pharmacology but focused only on student experience. In mathematics, the *Interactive Sketchpad* [3] tool uses an MLLM to generate and manipulate diagrams within a conversational tutoring setting. While learners reported a better learning experience and problem-solving efficacy using this tool compared to using ChatGPT, this study did not examine the impacts on their learning outcomes. *MuDoC 1.0* [23] enhanced learner engagement and trust but did not significantly improve learning outcomes compared to a baseline system with text-only responses. To the best of our knowledge, prior work does provide evidence for the effectiveness of MLLMs in generating multimedia content for improving learning outcomes.

Regarding the effects of conversational AI, recent studies with educational chatbots, such as ChatGPT-style systems, report gains in academic performance, engagement, and perceived personalization, though effects vary across domains and contexts [5,24]. At the same time, researchers have also raised concerns about overreliance and shallow processing due to undermined cognitive and metacognitive processes that are essential for durable learning [6]. Further, it is unclear how conversational interfaces for interacting with textbooks compare to more classical document or semantic search baselines, which we address in this work.

3   MuDoC, TexDoC, and DocSearch

In this section, we first describe MuDoC, an AI system that answers queries with interleaved text-and-image responses, extending MuDoC 1.0 [21], using the 'Reason-and-Act' (ReAct) framework [25] (see Fig. 1). We then discuss TexDoC and DocSearch made with minimal modifications to the MuDoC pipeline to isolate the effects of visuals and conversational AI on learning. Additional details about these AI systems are provided in the supplementary material[1].

3.1   Preprocessing and Response Generation in MuDoC

Document Preprocessing: The document processing pipeline involves parsing the document layout to extract content from each page, which is subsequently processed and stored in a vector database to facilitate the retrieval process. We utilize the HURIDOCS document layout analysis parser [1] to extract text, figures,

[1] Supplementary material (including demo videos): https://tinyurl.com/IMCAILOE.

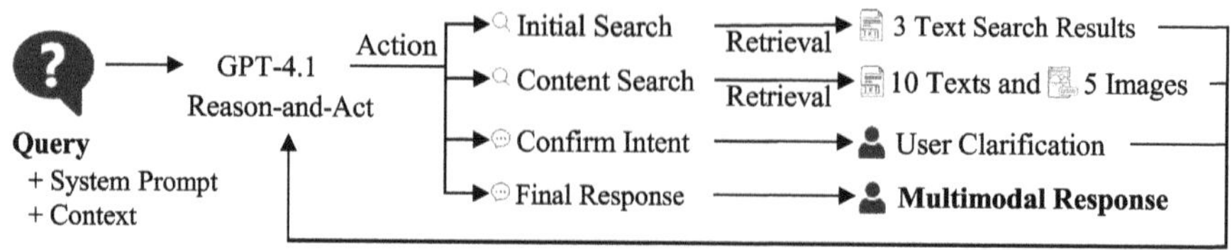

Fig. 1. MUDOC uses GPT-4.1 for Reason-and-Act (ReAct) loop with 4 possible actions viz. Initial Search, Content Search, Confirm Intent, and Final Response.

and other structural elements from the document. These *blocks* extracted during the layout analysis are combined into partly overlapping *chunks* of at least 8,000 characters. For each text chunk, we generate and store a succinct summary using the OpenAI `gpt-4o-mini-2024-07-18` model (see Footnote 1). Similarly, for every extracted image, we store a caption and a detailed image description generated using the same model. We employ the OpenAI `text-embedding-3-large` model for text embeddings and the `google/siglip-so400m-patch14-384` model for image embeddings [27]. The resulting chunks and their embeddings are stored in a vector database for retrieval (described later). Compared to MuDoC 1.0, among other differences, we now use a more recent and performant layout parser and text and image embedding models along with larger context windows.

Response Generation: MUDOC uses OpenAI `gpt-4.1-2025-04-14`, which supports multimodal inputs and function calling capabilities, for response generation. It now uses reasoning, unlike MuDoC 1.0, by structuring response generation as a ReAct [25] loop to improve search functions usage and generation quality. In each iteration of the ReAct loop, the model first Reasons its current state within the conversation, and then decides to take an Action to search for additional context or to generate a response (see Fig. 1).

Reasoning: Prior to executing an action, the LLM is instructed to perform the following three reflection steps (see Footnote 1). (i) **Query Reflection:** The model evaluates the user's intent, identifying any unknown terminology, acronyms, typos, or misconceptions within the query, and determines whether a search is necessitated by the request. (ii) **Search Content Reflection:** If content has been retrieved during the current or past conversation turns, the model assesses content relevance and identifies any missing information that requires further retrieval. The model also reasons about the most pertinent textual and visual content and determines how to structure a self-contained response, including definitions for terms that may be unfamiliar to the student. (iii) **Action Reasoning:** In this final step, the model synthesizes the previous reflections to select the most appropriate course of action. The possible actions are detailed next.

Actions: The model can execute four distinct actions, categorized into search and generation functions. If the model requires foundational information to interpret the query, such as definitions for unfamiliar terms or acronyms, it utilizes the **Initial Search** action. This retrieves the top three text results, ensuring a low-overhead clarification of the problem space. Conversely, if the model understands the query sufficiently but requires a search, it can trigger the **Content Search** action and subsequently generate specific search queries for text and image retrieval function calls, which can return up to ten text chunks and five images respectively. The remaining two actions are generative. If the model determines that the user's intent is ambiguous, it utilizes the **Confirm Intent** action to request a clarification, ensuring a precise final output. Finally, once the model possesses a clear understanding of the query and the necessary retrieved context, it executes the **Final Response** action to synthesize a comprehensive response for the user. In the event of a search action, the retrieved results are appended to the conversation history, serving as updated context for the subsequent ReAct loop. Conversely, when a generation action is performed, the model delivers the response and awaits the user's input to proceed.

Text and Image Retrieval: As opposed to purely embedding-based retrieval in MuDoC 1.0, MuDoC now employs a hybrid search strategy [11] combining dense vector embeddings with sparse keyword-based retrieval for both texts and images. For text retrieval, we utilize both the original content and the generated summaries (from preprocessing) for embeddings and keyword-based scoring. We found that prioritizing vector embedding similarity (75% weight) over keyword-based BM25 [18] score (25% weight) led to the highest retrieval accuracy in hybrid ranking. After text retrieval, we sort retrieved results in the natural order of the textbook and remove redundancy caused by overlapping chunks, leading to a leaner and organized context for the LLM. In image retrieval, the raw text index includes the image captions and descriptions while the image vector is the mean of the image and caption embedding. For ranking images, we found that prioritizing BM25 score (75% weight) led to better retrieval, potentially because image descriptions focus on key terminology, where keyword matching works well, rather than semantically-rich explanations. We plan to release a thorough evaluation of text and image retrieval methods used in MuDoC in future work.

Interleaved Grounded Generation: MuDoC synthesizes an interleaved, grounded response based on retrieved texts and images while providing explicit references to the source material. To incorporate visuals, the model is instructed to generate HTML `figure`, `figcaption` and `img` tags, based on source links and corresponding raw retrieved images. Textual claims are supported by in-text citations, similar to WebGPT [16], referring to the original document name and block IDs to ensure that the generated response is grounded and verifiable. We found that block-based in-text citations (using LLMs directly) had higher reliability than embedding-based source attribution used in MuDoC 1.0.

Pedagogically-aligned Prompt: The model's generation is guided by the principles of CTML [15]. Specifically, the model is prompted to prioritize functional visuals over decorative ones to minimize cognitive load. Information provided via images should be complementary rather than redundant to the text, and visual elements should be spatially integrated near the relevant text. The model is instructed to utilize concrete examples and analogies rather than abstract definitions in accordance with CTML's worked example effect. Further, explanations should follow a 'simple-to-formal' progression, grounding new concepts in the context of prior conversation turns. At the conclusion of a response, MuDoC can pose reflective questions to encourage active learning, invite the user to explain concepts in their own words or make follow-up inquiries. The system prompt (see Footnote 1) also includes instructions to ensure that all responses remain safe, polite, and constructive.

Response Post-processing and Rendering: Following response generation, we employ regular expressions (regex) to identify in-text citations and image placeholders within the model's output. These identifiers are dynamically replaced during token streaming with interactive link icons that connect directly to the source document. When a user clicks a citation link, the system retrieves the precise coordinates of the target block from the backend, triggering the frontend to switch to the 'Document' tab, navigate to the corresponding page, and highlight the relevant passage for several seconds to facilitate verification. For HTML figure references, the specific image—extracted from the source document during document preprocessing—is embedded directly into the chat message. Similar to text citations, each image is also accompanied by a link icon that allows the user to locate the figure within the original document. To ensure transparency, the model's reasoning process is accessible via a dedicated icon adjacent to the agent's avatar. Furthermore, the token stream is monitored in real-time to detect ReAct loops, allowing the interface to display agent status indicators when the system is performing reasoning and retrieval.

3.2 TEXDOCand DOCSEARCH

TEXDOC, a TEXt-only version of MuDoC, lacks the image retrieval pipeline of MuDoC, image-related prompt instructions, the image search function call, and raw input images. As a result, it provides text-only responses similar to Jill Watson [7,8,22], but with interactive citations, indirectly allowing users to find visuals in the textbook. Aside from the omissions, TEXDOC is identical to MuDoC and helps us isolate the impact of multimodality in our experiments.

DOCSEARCH is a stateless semantic search tool integrated within the document viewer. It employs the same retrieval pipeline as TEXDOC and uses the same LLM to select the most relevant text and image blocks from the retrieved content to provide up to ten search results. Users can navigate these results using arrow keys or by clicking corresponding buttons. As a user navigates to a search result, a block of text or image is highlighted for a few seconds, similar to MuDoC and TEXDOC citations. Overall, DOCSEARCH is a convenient way to navigate a document with very specific search queries, but it does not synthesize responses or use past context for follow-up questions, helping us study the impact of conversational AI compared to non-conversational multimedia.

4   Experimental Methods

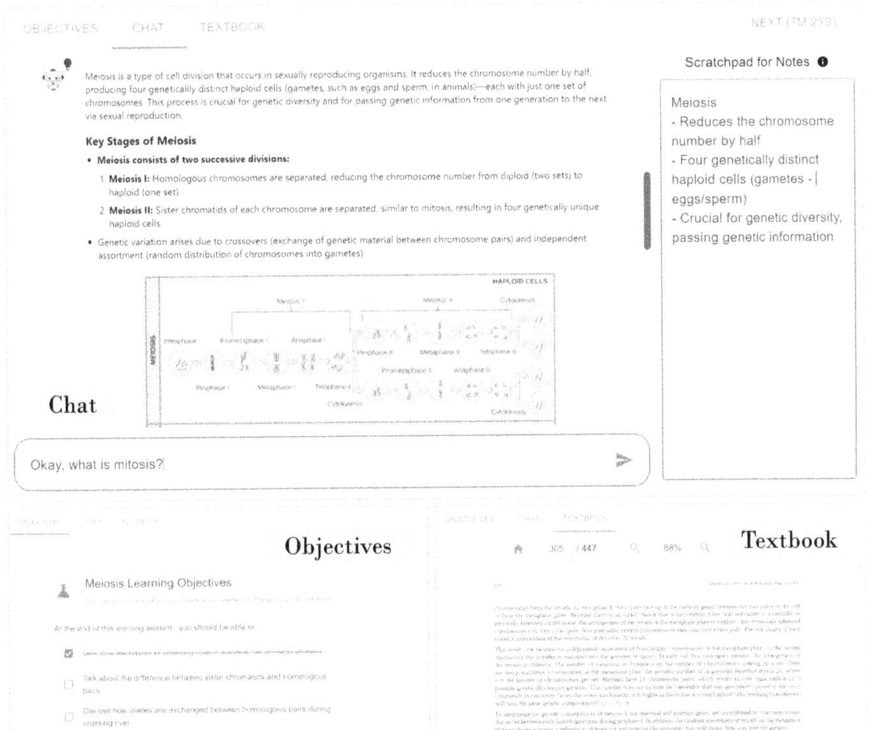

Fig. 2. Snapshots from self-learning session: 'Chat' tab shows the conversational AI interface (MuDoC and TexDoC). 'Objectives' tab contains the learning objectives with checkboxes to track progress. 'Document' tab shows the source document for all AI systems. A 'Notepad' box is present on the right for note-taking.

Participant Recruitment: We conducted the study using the online platform Prolific, recruiting participants aged 18+, residing in the US, who had a major in biology and had completed at least a high school diploma. The compensation was US$20 for completing the study with an estimated duration of 75 min.

A total of 162 participants completed the study, of which 17 were excluded for not passing attention checks, 18 were excluded for insufficient activity during the learning session, and 3 were excluded due to technical issues, resulting in a final sample size of $N = 124$. Out of 124, 117 (94%) of participants were 18–35 years old, and 112 (90%) had basic familiarity with AI as end users.

Study Protocol: The participants first signed the consent form for our study, approved by the Institutional Review Board (IRB) at Georgia Tech. Following

Table 1. M, SD values for **Pre-**, **Post-test** scores (out of 10), **Time** (mins) spent interacting with AI, number of **Queries** and edits to **Notes** (highest in bold).

System	N	Pre-test	Post-test	Time	Queries	Notes
MuDoC	42	6.92 (1.25)	**7.24** (1.15)	17.6 (2.9)	7.26 (3.32)	7.1 (7.3)
TexDoC	41	6.91 (1.32)	6.55 (1.11)	**18.0 (3.7)**	**8.29 (5.02)**	7.5 (8.2)
DocSearch	41	**6.98** (1.29)	6.77 (0.93)	17.6 (3.5)	5.27 (2.74)	**11.4 (8.4)**

consent, they were randomly assigned to one of the three experimental conditions, viz. MuDoC, TexDoC and DocSearch. In each condition, participants first completed a pre-test with 10 multiple-choice questions (MCQs) covering basics of cell division. Participants who scored fewer than 4 correct answers were screened out. Those who scored 4 or higher proceeded to watch a 15-minute instructional video on the meiosis cell division process and a two-minute video on the AI system they would subsequently utilize for learning.

In the next step, called "self-learning with AI", participants were instructed to learn about meiosis cell division using only the assigned system, guided by three predefined learning objectives, and informed that they could use the provided notepad (described below) for note-taking to support their learning. The system interface displayed two tabs for the DocSearch condition and three tabs for TexDoC and MuDoC. The first 'Objectives' tab, in all conditions, presented the learning objectives. For the TexDoC and MuDoC conditions, the middle 'Chat' tab contained the chat interface. The final 'Document' tab, in all conditions, displayed the source document, the OpenStax Biology textbook [9] (Chapter 4–14, 447 pages (see Footnote 1)), and a search bar in the case of DocSearch. In all conditions, the notepad was displayed on the right side, occupying one-fourth of the interface width. The interface required participants to spend at least 15 min (by disabling the 'Next' button) and at most 25 min (by automatically advancing the session) on self-learning. Snapshots from the self-learning session are shown in Fig. 2.

Next, participants completed a post-test with 10 MCQs related to the three learning objectives. Unlike the pre-test which focused on broader knowledge of cell division with 3 visual-based questions, the post-test focused on three specified learning objectives related to meiosis cell division with 7 visual-based questions. Finally, they answered survey questions with Likert-scale responses (see Fig. 3), provided subjective feedback and answered demographic questions. The survey, learning objectives, pre- and post-tests, and other materials are provided in the supplementary material (see Footnote 1).

Data Collection: In addition to test scores and surveys, we measured the time spent using the assigned system, the number of queries, and the frequency of adding or editing notes in the provided notepad across all three conditions (Table 1). For MuDoC and TexDoC, we also measured the average response length from participants' conversations, usage of interactive citations, and the proportion of time spent on the textbook tab (Sect. 5.2).

5   Results

5.1   Pre-test and Post-test Scores

Descriptive statistics for performance across the three experimental conditions are presented in Table 1. To test analysis of variance (ANOVA) assumptions, normality was assessed using Shapiro-Wilk tests for each group (all $p > 0.05$) and homogeneity of variance was confirmed using Levene's test, $F(2, 121) = 0.117, p = .89 > .05$ for pre-test scores and $F(2, 121) = 1.711, p = .18 > .05$ for post-test scores. A one-way ANOVA on pre-test scores indicated no difference across the three groups, $F(2, 121) = 0.27, p = .97, \eta^2 < .001$, confirming that participants had comparable prior knowledge across the three groups.

A one-way ANOVA on post-test scores revealed a statistically significant effect of the AI system type with a moderate effect size, $F(2, 121) = 4.60, p = .012, \eta^2 = 0.071$. Post-hoc comparisons using Tukey's honestly significant difference (HSD) test showed that MuDoC participants achieved significantly higher scores than TexDoC ($p = .010, diff = 0.69$). While MuDoC also outperformed DocSearch ($diff = 0.47$), this difference did not reach the threshold for adjusted significance in the Tukey HSD test ($p = .11$).

We also examined the influence of prior knowledge (pre-test scores) on learning outcomes (post-test scores) using an Ordinary Least Squares (OLS) regression model while controlling for the experimental condition. As expected, pre-test scores were significantly positively associated with post-test scores ($\beta = 0.21, p = .005$), providing evidence that the tests are sensitive to differences in prior knowledge and learning gains.

5.2   Why MuDoC is Better than TexDoC?

To confirm that MuDoC leads to better performance than TexDoC due to its high-quality multimedia content, we performed in-depth analysis of user interactions and system behavior. While none of the behaviors we captured showed a statistically significant difference, MuDoC group consistently had lower mean values. They jumped to the textbook using interactive citations less frequently ($p = .08, d = -0.38$ using t-test), asked fewer questions ($p = .27, d = -0.36$), spent less time with the AI system ($p = .31, d = -0.11$), spent a lower proportion of time on the textbook tab ($p = .60, d = -0.12$), and made fewer updates to their notes ($p = .80, d = -0.06$). In terms of system behavior, the average response length of MuDoC (excluding figures) was lower than that of TexDoC , but not significantly ($p = 0.10, d = -0.36$). Besides text, an average conversation with MuDoC had $M = 3.1, SD = 1.2$ unique images and a total of $M = 6.2, SD = 2.3$ images.

These results show that there was no significant differences in learning behaviors and system behavior, except for the visuals included in MuDoC responses, which likely drove the improvements in learning outcomes. Further, if we examine the weak trends discussed above, their consistency suggests that MuDoC group may have allocated more time to examining the visuals rather than relying on the textbook or asking follow-up questions. TEXDOC users likely had to read complex text, ask follow-up questions, and seek visuals in the source textbook, all of which are time-consuming and cognitively demanding.

How does DOCSEARCH *compare?* Compared to the systems with conversational AI, the DOCSEARCH group made significantly fewer queries ($p < .001, d = -0.63$), but made significantly more updates to their notes ($p = .008, d = 0.50$). This group made $M = 5.27$, $SD = 2.74$ queries and examined $M = 18.8$, $SD = 10.1$ search results. In summary, DOCSEARCH interactions show a more traditional approach to reading with fewer queries and more note-taking.

	Completely Disagree	Disagree	Neutral	Agree	Completely Agree
(1) Is easy to navigate					
MuDoC	3	19		20	
TEXDOC	1 2	16		22	
DOCSEARCH	1	8	24		8
(2) Is engaging to use					
MuDoC	2 1	8	23		8
TEXDOC		10	15	16	
DOCSEARCH	3	8	12	14	4
(3) Gives results/responses that have adequate level of detail					
MuDoC	1	5	20	16	
TEXDOC	1	6	22	12	
DOCSEARCH		5	12	20	4
(4) Gives results/responses that help me learn					
MuDoC		5	22	15	
TEXDOC		5	20	16	
DOCSEARCH	5	6	23	7	
(5) Gives easy to understand results/responses					
MuDoC	1	9	20	12	
TEXDOC		6	22	13	
DOCSEARCH	6	14	16	5	
(6) Helps me think of new questions					
MuDoC	1 2	14	15	10	
TEXDOC	3	10	18	10	
DOCSEARCH	2	11	15	9	4
(7) Makes me think					
MuDoC	2	9	17	14	
TEXDOC	2	13	17	9	
DOCSEARCH	4 3	13	17	4	

Fig. 3. Perceived Learning Experience with MuDoC, TEXDOC and DOCSEARCH.

5.3   Quantitative Data on Learning Experience

The results from seven Likert-scale survey questions are summarized in Fig. 3. Since normality and homogeneity of variance are not satisfied by Likert-scale data, we used the non-parametric Kruskal-Wallis test. The results revealed significant between-group differences across all seven questions ($p < .05$), with effect sizes (η^2) ranging from moderate (.051) to large (.123). Post-hoc analyses were performed using Dunn's test with Holm correction for multiple comparisons.

Usability (1, 2 in Fig. 3): The analysis indicates that conversational interfaces (MuDoC and TEXDOC) provided a superior user experience compared to DOCSEARCH. Participants found the two systems significantly easier to navigate

$(p = .002, \eta^2 = .09)$ and more engaging to use $(p < .001, \eta^2 = .12)$. No significant differences between MuDoC and TexDoC suggest that conversationality was the primary driver of better usability ratings.

Response Quality (3, 4, 5 in Fig. 3): In terms of perceived quality, both conversational AI systems outperformed DocSearch in providing detailed $(p = .001, \eta^2 = .10)$, helpful $(p = .017, \eta^2 = .05)$, and clear responses $(p = .001, \eta^2 = 0.10)$. Again, we did not see a difference between MuDoC and TexDoC, suggesting that conversationality in AI systems leads to better perceived quality for information needs as compared to stateless semantic search in DocSearch.

Cognitive Engagement (6, 7 in Fig. 3): Both conversational systems significantly outperformed the baseline in helping users formulate follow-up questions $(p = .001, \eta^2 = .10)$, indicating a shift from passive reading to active cognitive engagement. However, for the question 'makes me think' $(p = .012, \eta^2 = .06)$, MuDoC was the only system to maintain a statistically significant advantage over the DocSearch baseline $(p = .010$ in Dunn's test). TexDoC showed a positive trend but did not reach statistical significance $(p = .163$ in Dunn's test). This suggests that the integration of visuals, unique to MuDoC, helps learners integrate information from two modalities, therefore making them think more.

5.4   Qualitative Data on Learning Experience

Participants answered two survey questions about the strengths and limitations of the AI systems they were assigned. We split their responses into distinct assertions and thematically organized similar assertions, of which the most common ones are elaborated below.

What was the best part of using 'System X' during the self-learning session? DocSearch was primarily lauded by 18 participants for its *efficiency*, specifically its ability to act as a 'smart' search tool; one participant noted that it "likely saved 20–30 minutes of reading" by streamlining the identification of relevant material in the textbook. In contrast, TexDoC's main strength was in its *transparency* (14 participants), with users appreciating the "links back to where in the textbook [it] was referencing," which served as a vital tool for information verification, corroborating findings from MuDoC 1.0 [23]. While MuDoC had identical source attribution, these strengths were overshadowed by participants' appreciation for its *multimodal grounding* and *simplified responses* (9+9 participants). Users highlighted that the system "integrated visual aids to help explain the concepts" while "summariz[ing] text that is typically long and tiring."

What are some frustrations you experienced when using 'System X'? DocSearch users reported significant frustration with its perceived lack of 'intelligence', with 10 participants noting it felt like a 'glorified search tool' rather than a helpful AI. In the TexDoC condition, the most prominent frustration was the *lack of visual aids* (9 participants), which forced users to "switch back and forth between tabs" to view necessary diagrams. While MuDoC success-fully addressed the visual needs, a few participants mentioned limitations such as *cognitive overload* (7 participants) and *system latency* (6 participants) that were also brought up by 5 and 3 TexDoC participants respectively, while only 4 DocSearch participants indicated the former as their biggest frustration. Very few participants in each group (1–2) reported difficulties with the document or chat interface, which alleviates concern about the interface design negatively impacting the learning experience.

Summary: For DocSearch, across the two responses, 13 participants expressed a desire for content summarization, reflecting the prevalent expectation of syn-thesized summaries from AI systems. For TexDoC, the feedback centered on the limitations of a text-only conversational AI, particularly for the complex STEM topic they were learning. MuDoC received the most enthusiastic feed-back overall, particularly for learning "without needing to look at paragraphs of text" and "the fact [that] it pulled [visuals] from the textbook".

6 Discussion and Future Work

The results of our study suggest a complex interplay between multimodality, conversationality, learning experience, and learning outcomes.

MuDoC enabled conversational multimedia learning that led to significantly better *learning outcomes* with a moderate effect size compared to TexDoC. It also led to better learning outcomes compared to DocSearch , although this result was not statistically significant. In terms of *learning experience*, includ-ing ease of use, engagement, and perceived helpfulness, MuDoC is at par with TexDoC and outperforms DocSearch. Loosely speaking, trends show that MuDoC > DocSearch ≥ TexDoC for learning outcomes (Table 1), while MuDoC = TexDoC > DocSearch for learning experience (Fig. 3). We inter-pret these results through the lens of Cognitive Load Theory (CLT) [20].

According to CLT, effective learning occurs when instructional design reduces extraneous cognitive load and promotes germane load within the limits of work-ing memory [20]. *Extraneous load* is the mental effort caused by poorly designed learning materials or distracting environmental factors, while *germane load* is the beneficial mental effort used to process new information, build mental models, and integrate knowledge into long-term memory.

Multimedia learning leads to higher germane load through careful content design [15]. In the case of DocSearch, while the presence of multimedia content would have led to high germane load, lack of conversationality likely increased extraneous load—by requiring learners to repeatedly search and integrate frag-mented content—potentially exceeding cognitive capacity. This imbalance may explain the poorer learning experience observed with DocSearch. In the case of TexDoC, low extraneous load due to conversationality likely led to better learning experience, but lower germane load due to lack of multimodality could have resulted in poorer learning outcomes. Compared to TexDoC, in Doc-Search, in addition to the multimodal content, the more frequent note-taking

(Table 1) would have also contributed to higher germane load. This may explain why, despite higher extraneous load and a poorer learning experience, the DOC-SEARCH group's learning outcomes were comparable to TEXDOC. Finally, in the case of MUDOC, conversationality reduced extraneous load, thereby enhancing the learning experience. This preserved cognitive capacity could have enabled learners to capitalize on the heightened germane load due to multimodality, leading to better learning outcomes. In summary, these findings suggest that *conversationality reduces extraneous load by maintaining contextual continuity, eliminating the need for repeated search and simplifying the integration of information. Further, conversational multimedia learning exhibits an improved cognitive load balance by lowering extraneous load and increasing germane load, leading to both improved learning outcomes and experience.*

It is also worth noting that there is a striking disconnect between participants' perceptions of TEXDOC and its actual impact on learning outcomes—participants rated TEXDOC as highly engaging and easy to use, yet it yielded the lowest post-test scores. While many in the TEXDOC group realized that visuals would support learning, they did not spend significantly more time exploring visuals in the textbook compared to the MUDOC group, likely as that would have led to increased extraneous load [13]. In contrast, by reducing the effort required to access and interpret visuals, MUDOC facilitated integration between text and graphical visuals, therefore replacing extraneous load with germane load. This suggests that *when reduced extraneous load from conversationality is not complemented by higher germane load, it can lead to a fluency effect where ease of digesting information is mistaken as a sign of learning* [17].

Finally, MUDOC establishes the efficacy of recent MLLMs to adaptively generate high-quality multimedia content for educational contexts. Further improvements in image retrieval, image understanding in MLLMs, and generative AI for diagram creation and editing will also enhance context-specificity of visuals. Our results also highlight opportunities for future research on how conversational AI can be effectively designed to enhance learning. While conversational interaction appears beneficial for improving subjective learning experience, text-only conversational systems may be insufficient for improving learning outcomes. In visually rich STEM domains, the inclusion of relevant textbook-based visuals alongside textual explanations is both necessary and beneficial for learning, as evidenced by our findings. In domains where visuals are less critical, future work should explore alternative design strategies for introducing desirable germane load—such as metacognitive prompting [19] or introducing "friction" in human-AI interactions [12]—within conversational AI systems to support learning outcomes.

Limitations: First, the study was conducted within a single domain and for a single biology topic. Second, the time constraints (15–25 minutes) may have affected learning outcomes, but this effect should be minimal as 88% of participants completed the learning session before the time limit, suggesting that the time allotted for the task was sufficient. Third, we assessed learning immediately after the intervention; future work should also consider measuring impact on long-term learning outcomes such as retention. Additionally, we grounded our interpretation in CLT, but did not directly measure cognitive load during learning. Future work should include explicit cognitive load measures [14] to better understand the influence of conversational multimedia learning. Fourth, the study recruited participants via Prolific. Future research should examine these findings in more authentic educational settings. Finally, MuDoC's performance may be dependent on the quality of the source textbook and visuals which impacts the accuracy of the document preprocessing pipeline, a subject of system evaluation that is outside the scope of this work.

7   Conclusion

In this paper, we described MuDoC, a conversational multimedia learning system that generates grounded, interleaved text-and-image responses based on textbook content, and compared it to two baselines—TexDoC (TExt-only MuDoC) and DocSearch (DOCument with semantic SEARCH)—through an RCT with $N = 124$ participants. MuDoC led to the highest post-test scores and a better learning experience based on qualitative and quantitative feedback, showing that multimodal LLMs can be effectively leveraged for learning by introducing interleaved responses containing grounded visuals. Examining the results through the lens of Cognitive Load Theory (CLT), we argued that *conversational multimedia learning* improves cognitive load balance by reducing extraneous load as a result of conversationality while increasing germane load as a result of multimodality. Our findings also suggest that conversational AI systems can lead to an illusion of learning, unless complemented by strategies to cultivate higher germane load, such as visually-enriched explanations. Future work should explore the application of conversational multimedia learning across diverse domains and develop improved methods for image retrieval, understanding, and context-specific visual generation to further enhance instruction.

Acknowledgments. We are grateful for the support provided by National Science Foundation under Grant No. 2247790 and Grant No. 2112532. We also wish to thank Dr. Emily G. Weigel and Joon Kum for support in creation of assessments.

References

1. huridocs/pdf-document-layout-analysis (2025). https://github.com/huridocs/pdf-document-layout-analysis. Accessed 06 May 2024
2. Bland, T.: Enhancing medical student engagement through cinematic clinical narratives: multimodal generative AI-based mixed methods study. JMIR Med. Educ. **11**, e63865 (2025)
3. Chen, S.S., Lee, J., Liang, P.P.: Interactive Sketchpad: A Multimodal Tutoring System for Collaborative, Visual Problem-Solving. CHI Extended Abstracts 2025 (2025)

4. Chen, X., Wu, D.: Automatic generation of multimedia teaching materials based on generative AI: taking tang poetry as an example. IEEE Trans. Learn. Technol. **17**, 1327–1340 (2024)
5. Deng, R., Jiang, M., Yu, X., Lu, Y., Liu, S.: Does ChatGPT enhance student learning? A systematic review and meta-analysis of experimental studies. Comput. Educ. **227**, 105224 (2025)
6. Fan, Y., Tang, L., et al.: Beware of metacognitive laziness: effects of generative AI on learning motivation, processes, and performance. Brit. J. Educ. Technol. (2024)
7. Goel, A., Nandan, V., Gregori, E., An, S., Rugaber, S.: Explanation as question answering based on user guides. In: Explainable Agency in Artificial Intelligence, 16p. CRC Press (2024)
8. Goel, A.K., Polepeddi, L.: Jill Watson: a virtual teaching assistant for online education. In: Education at Scale: Engineering Online Teaching and Learning. Routledge, New York (2018)
9. Zedalis, J., Eggebrecht, J.: Biology for AP Courses. OpenStax, Houston, Texas (2018). https://openstax.org/details/books/biology-ap-courses
10. Kakar, S., et al.: Jill Watson: scaling and deploying an AI conversational agent in online classrooms. In: Intelligent Tutoring Systems, pp. 78–90 (2024)
11. Karpukhin, V., et al.: Dense passage retrieval for open-domain question answering. In: EMNLP 2020, pp. 6769–6781 (2020)
12. Kazemitabaar, M., Huang, O., Suh, S., Henley, A.Z., Grossman, T.: Exploring the design space of cognitive engagement techniques with AI-generated code for enhanced learning. In: Intelligent User Interfaces, pp. 695–714 (2025)
13. Kool, W., McGuire, J.T., Rosen, Z.B., Botvinick, M.M.: Decision making and the avoidance of cognitive demand. J. Exp. Psychol. Gen. **139**(4), 665–682 (2010)
14. Korbach, A., Brünken, R., Park, B.: Measurement of cognitive load in multimedia learning: a comparison of different objective measures. Instr. Sci. **45**(4), 515–536 (2017)
15. Mayer, R.E.: Multimedia learning. Psychol. Learn. Motiv. **41**, 85–139. Academic Press (2002)
16. Nakano, R., Hilton, J.: WebGPT: browser-assisted question-answering with human feedback (2022). arXiv:2112.09332
17. Oppenheimer, D.M.: The secret life of fluency. Trends Cogn. Sci. **12**(6), 237–241 (2008)
18. Robertson, S., Walker, S., Jones, S., Hancock-Beaulieu, M., Gatford, M.: Okapi at TREC-3. In: Text Retrieval Conference (1994)
19. Singh, A., Guan, Z., Rieh, S.Y.: Enhancing critical thinking in generative AI search with metacognitive prompts. Assoc. Inf. Sci. Technol. **62**(1), 672–684 (2025)
20. Sweller, J.: Cognitive load theory. Psychol. Learn. Motiv. **55**, 37–76. Academic Press (2011)
21. Taneja, K., Goel, A.K.: MuDoC: an interactive multimodal document-grounded conversational AI system. In: AAAI Machine Learning and Knowledge Engineering (MAKE) for Trustworthy Multimodal and Generative AI (2025)
22. Taneja, K., Maiti, P., Kakar, S., Guruprasad, P., Rao, S., Goel, A.K.: Jill Watson: a virtual teaching assistant powered by ChatGPT. In: AIED 2024, pp. 324–337 (2024)
23. Taneja, K., Singh, A., Goel, A.K.: Towards a multimodal document-grounded conversational AI system for education. In: AIED 2025, pp. 92–99 (2025)
24. Wu, R., Yu, Z.: Do AI chatbots improve students learning outcomes? Evidence from a meta-analysis. Br. J. Edu. Technol. **55**(1), 10–33 (2024)

25. Yao, S., et al.: ReAct: synergizing reasoning and acting in language models. ICLR 2023 (2022)
26. Zhai, C., Wibowo, S., Li, L.D.: The effects of over-reliance on AI dialogue systems on students' cognitive abilities: a systematic review. Smart Learn. Environ. **11**(1), 28 (2024)
27. Zhai, X., Mustafa, B., Kolesnikov, A., Beyer, L.: Sigmoid loss for language image pre-training. In: ICCV 2023, pp. 11941–11952. IEEE (2023)

From Examples to Rules? Exploring Inductive Reverse Engineering and Deductive Few-Shot Coding via LLMs for Qualitative Data Analysis

Zifeng Liu[1]([envelope]) [iD], Anupom Mondol[2] [iD], Xinyue Jiao[3] [iD], Jie Chao[4] [iD], Linlin Li[5] [iD], and Wanli Xing[6] [iD]

[1] University of Florida, Gainesville, FL, USA
liuzifeng@ufl.edu
[2] Texas Tech University, Lubbock, TX, USA
a.mondol@ttu.edu
[3] New York University, New York, NY, USA
xinyue.jiao@nyu.edu
[4] Concord Consortium, Boston, MA, USA
jchao@concord.org
[5] WestEd, San Francisco, CA, USA
lli@wested.org
[6] University of Miami, Coral Gables, FL, USA
wanli.xing@miami.edu

Abstract. This study examines how two LLM prompting paradigms support qualitative coding of students' open-ended responses in an AI-integrated learning module on sentiment analysis. The dataset includes approximately 110 students' responses to three model-revision tasks of increasing abstraction: (Q1) handling negative sentiment words, (Q2) handling multiple sentiment words, and (Q3) weighting mixed sentiment. A human-coded baseline was established through iterative codebook development and three rounds of double coding across two dimensions, Interpretation and Proficiency, achieving high reliability (round-level Cohen's k ranging from .80 to 1.00). We explored (1) an inductive reverse-engineering pipeline, where the LLM inferred an executable codebook from labeled input-output pairs and was evaluated on held-out test sets, and (2) a deductive few-shot pipeline, where the LLM applied the finalized codebook with 1-, 3-, or 5-shot demonstrations under three context levels (simple, some, full), yielding 27 experimental conditions. Results show that task complexity is the dominant constraint: performance is high for Q1 and Q2 but degrades sharply for the more abstract Q3, especially for Proficiency. Increasing shots generally improves accuracy, yet gains are non-linear and depend on context; "Some" context often matches or exceeds full context. Error analysis reveals systematic failure modes, including proficiency overestimation driven by surface completeness, forced interpretation under ambiguity, keyword-triggered misclassification, weak differentiation among low-information labels, inconsistency blindness, and task-goal misalignment. Findings suggest LLMs can

© The Author(s), under exclusive license to Springer Nature Switzerland AG 2027
E. G. Blanchard et al. (Eds.): AIED 2026, LNAI 16583, pp. 639–653, 2027.
https://doi.org/10.1007/978-3-032-29760-0_61

assist with lower-abstraction coding and triage, but complex interpretive judgments require human oversight and error-aware workflow design.

Keywords: Qualitative Data Analysis · Large Language Model · Reverse Engineering · Few-shot Learning

1 Introduction

Qualitative data analysis (QAD) plays a central role in educational research, enabling researchers to interpret open-ended student responses and examine learning processes [15,18]. While traditional qualitative analysis supports in-depth, context-sensitive interpretation of data, it is labor-intensive and often limited by the availability of trained human coders [15]. These approaches are also not intended to prioritize scale, but rather to provide rich, interpretive understanding based on relatively small datasets. At the same time, contemporary learning environments generate large volumes of open-ended student data through online platforms and AI-supported tools. In these settings, applying traditional coding approaches can become practically challenging. This has led to growing interest in AI-assisted methods that can help organize and interpret large collections of qualitative data.

Recent advances in large language models (LLMs) have renewed interest in automating qualitative coding [4]. Prior work has demonstrated that LLMs can approximate human judgments in tasks such as sentiment analysis [12], topic classification [11], and rubric-based scoring [9]. Existing approaches to LLM-based qualitative coding largely fall into two paradigms. The first is a *deductive* approach, in which researchers directly prompt an LLM with a predefined coding scheme and a small number of labeled examples (e.g., [14,22]), commonly operationalized as few-shot prompting [21]. This approach is attractive due to its simplicity and low setup cost. However, it implicitly assumes that the coding rules are transparent, unambiguous and readily internalized by the model. In practice, many educational coding schemes involve abstract constructs and tacit human judgment, raising potential concerns about overgeneralization and forced classification in certain contexts. The second paradigm is an *inductive* approach, in which coding rules are inferred from data rather than explicitly provided (e.g., [7,20]). Recently, researchers have begun to explore prompting LLMs to infer operational rules from example input-output pairs and create codebook (e.g., [3]). While inductive approach holds promise for capturing latent coding logic, its reliability and alignment with human reasoning remain underexplored in educational qualitative coding contexts [6].

This study explores how two distinct LLM-based prompting paradigms (i.e., inductive reverse engineering and deductive few-shot coding) can be applied to qualitative coding tasks in AI education. Reverse engineering refers to the process of inferring underlying rules, structures, or mechanisms of a system by analyzing its observable inputs and outputs, rather than relying on explicit specifications provided a priori [5]. This approach differs from prior studies that treat zero-shot prompting as an inductive approach [20], or that rely on purely data-driven label emergence [17], which raise important challenges for uncovering deeper meanings and emergent interpretations [6]. Instead, this study uses reverse engineering to learn underlying coding logic from human-labeled data.

Rather than positioning the two paradigms in competition, we discuss their workflows, affordances and limitations across tasks of varying abstraction. Our goal is not to identify a universally superior approach, but to characterize how different prompting strategies interact with task demands, contextual information and coding dimensions, as well as the types of systematic errors that emerge. By foregrounding both performance patterns and error behaviors, this work contributes to a deeper understanding of when and how LLMs can meaningfully support qualitative analysis in education. Our findings aim to inform both methodological practice and the design of future AI-assisted analytic tools that respect the interpretive nature of educational data.

2   Recent Work: Qualitative Data Analysis Using LLMs

QAD using LLMs has recently emerged as a promising research approach for analyzing large-scale textual data in education research [7,22,23]. A wide range of applications, including both inductive and deductive LLM-based coding pipelines, reflects a growing interest in leveraging LLMs to accelerate qualitative analysis and enrich the interpretive process in education research [1,14].

Existing work has predominantly focused on *deductive* LLM coding pipelines. For example, [9] analyze transcripts from 262 one-on-one tutoring sessions using GPT-3.5 with few-shot prompting to detect tutoring strategies. Their results show that GPT-3.5 can moderately identify ineffective tutoring strategies, achieving true negative rates ranging from 0.655 to 0.738. However, the model struggles to correctly identify effective strategies, with recall values ranging from 0.327 to 0.432. In a related line of research, [13] introduce a collaborative AI tool based on GPT-4o to support thematic analysis of student group discussion transcripts. They demonstrate that the tool produces themes comparable to those generated by human coders with substantially greater efficiency; however, unlike human analysts, the model does not iteratively refine or reshape the research questions during analysis. Similarly, Sankaranarayanan et al. [19] propose a multi-agent LLM-based system using Claude Sonnet 3.5 for thematic analysis of 200 open-ended survey responses. While human analysis remains more detailed and conceptually deep, their system achieves over 75% alignment with human coding.

In contrast, research on *inductive* LLM-based qualitative analysis remains relatively limited but is gaining increasing attention. For instance, Barany et al. [3] examine the use of GPT-4 for inductive codebook development, evaluating its potential to address common challenges in manual qualitative coding, such as time constraints, inconsistencies, and human error. Shah et al. [20] further investigate the use of LLMs for qualitative data annotation in requirements engineering by explicitly comparing inductive and deductive coding strategies. In their study, inductive annotation is treated as zero-shot learning, whereas deductive annotation is implemented using one-shot or few-shot prompting. Evaluating three LLMs on two real-world datasets, they find that deductive (few-shot) annotation consistently shows higher agreement with human experts, with GPT-4 achieving Cohen's kappa values up to 0.738. In contrast, zero-shot inductive performance remains limited across all evaluated models. Their findings also highlight the importance of prompt design, demonstrating that context-rich and longer prompts significantly improve accuracy, consistency, and reliability in LLM-supported qualitative analysis.

LLMs are also increasingly being adopted in education research to support inductive qualitative coding. Parfenova et al. [17] present a systematic comparison between human experts and LLMs for inductive open coding. Evaluating six open-source LLMs across zero-shot, few-shot, and fine-tuned settings, they find that human coders outperform LLMs on semantically complex and ambiguous excerpts. In contrast, LLMs show stronger alignment with gold-standard labels on simpler and more explicit text segments.

Beyond task- and domain-specific applications, recent work has examined the methodological and collaborative roles of LLMs in QAD, with particular attention to how LLM outputs compare with human coding and how they can be integrated into collaborative qualitative workflows. For example, [2] propose a human-in-the-loop workflow using GPT-4 and Claude Sonnet 3.2 to analyze student perspectives on generative AI in higher education, drawing on twenty focus groups conducted across four universities. Their findings suggest that LLMs can effectively assist in generating and organizing qualitative themes while keeping researchers actively involved in validating and interpreting model outputs. Similarly, Jiang et al. [10] investigate how GPT-4o can support collaborative qualitative coding using 104 interview transcripts with artists. They examine whether LLMs can help resolve coding disagreements, clarify ambiguous codes, and improve alignment during collaborative coding and peer debriefing. Their results show that integrating LLM support improves alignment with human coders (average F1 score = 0.83) and helps surface ambiguities in code definitions.

In summary, despite growing interest, the use of LLMs for QAD remains in an early stage of development. As noted by [13], the field is still at the early stage. Most existing applications of LLMs for qualitative coding and content analysis emphasize deductive approaches, in which human analysts first establish a gold-standard codebook and test reliability across multiple raters before applying LLMs [2]. In contrast, inductive LLM-supported qualitative analysis requires further exploration. As [6] caution, LLMs primarily rely on surface patterns present in the input data, which raises important challenges for uncovering deeper meanings, contextual nuances, and emergent interpretations that are central to inductive qualitative inquiry.

3   Method

Dataset and Context. The dataset consists of approximately 110 students' open-ended responses to three AI model revision tasks collected from an online AI learning module (see examples in Table 1). The module was designed to support students' understanding of sentiment analysis and AI-based classification through multiple instructional components and consisted of five sequential activities, each building on the previous one, for a total of approximately 250 min of online learning. The module included three open-ended model revision questions that encouraged reflection and allowed students to articulate their understanding in their own words. These three AI model revision tasks required students to revise an existing sentiment analysis model to address its limitations. Specifically, the first task (Q1) asked students to modify the model so that it could correctly identify reviews containing negative sentiment words (see Fig. 1). The second task required students to revise the model to handle reviews containing multiple positive and/or negative sentiment words. The third task asked students to assign different weights to positive and negative words so that the model could determine the final sentiment label for reviews with mixed sentiment. Students' responses to these tasks capture their reasoning processes and conceptual understanding of AI model behavior and were structured into three parts: assumptions, verbal expressions, and algebraic expressions.

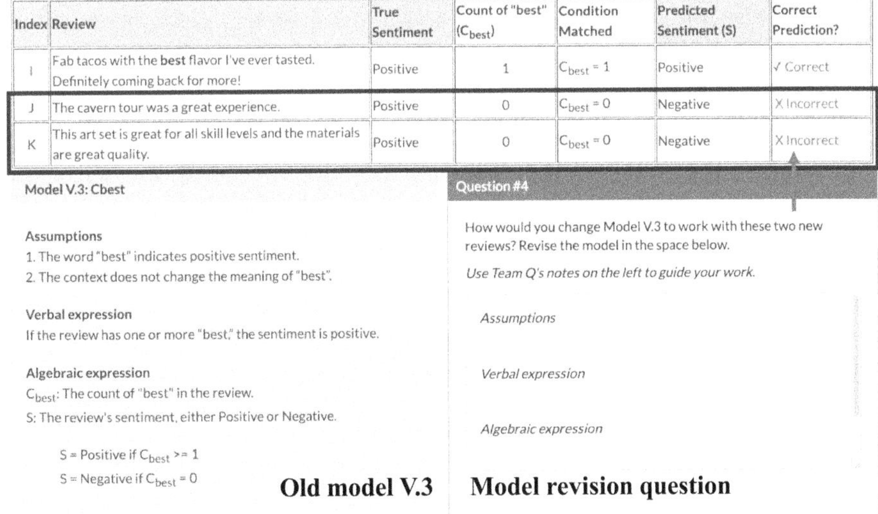

Fig. 1. An example of the model revision question (Q1)

Human Coding Process. Three researchers collaboratively developed and applied the codebook. First, the three researchers met to discuss and refine a

Table 1. Example Student Responses for Q1 and Q2 Model Revision Tasks

Component	Q1 Student Response	Q2 Student Response
Assumptions	The word "best" indicates positive sentiment.	− Multiple words can indicate positive or negative sentiment. − The context does not change the meaning of these words. − Define arrays of positive words (P_i) and negative words (N_i).
Verbal Expression	If a review contains one or more instances of "great" or "best," the sentiment is positive.	If the number of positive words exceeds the number of negative words, predict the sentiment as positive; otherwise, predict it as negative.
Algebraic Expression	− C_{best} = count of "best" − C_{great} = count of "great" − S = review sentiment (Positive or Negative)	− $P_{list} = P_1 + P_2 + \cdots + P_n$ − $N_{list} = N_1 + N_2 + \cdots + N_n$ − If $(P_{list} - N_{list}) \geq 1$, then S = Positive − If $(P_{list} - N_{list}) \leq 0$, then S = Negative

draft version of the codebook. Two dimensions were determined for analysis: interpretation and proficiency. Interpretation captures whether a student correctly understood the goal of the question and the task being asked, whereas proficiency reflects the extent to which the student's response successfully addressed and solved the problem. Following the initial discussion, a preliminary version of the codebook was established, including definitions and examples for each coding level.

Next, two of the three researchers independently applied the preliminary codebook to responses from 26 students across the three model revision questions. Percent agreement for each question and each dimension was calculated and recorded (see Table 2). After this first round of coding, the two researchers met to discuss cases with discrepant labels. Based on these discussions, ambiguous descriptions in the codebook were clarified, and additional coding levels (e.g., *Can't tell* for interpretation coding) were introduced. The two researchers then conducted a second round of independent coding on responses from an additional set ($n = 32$). The resulting percent agreement is reported in Table 2. Cohen's kappa was calculated separately for interpretation and proficiency. For each round, question-level kappa values were aggregated using a sample-size-weighted average to obtain round-level reliability estimates. For Q1 and Q3, agreement exceeded 90%, and no further coding rounds were conducted for these two questions. The researchers again discussed all remaining disagreements and reached consensus. The codebook was further refined by adding and revising coding examples specific to the second model revision question. A third round of coding was conducted for Q2, as the agreement did not exceed the 90% threshold in the second round. The third round met the required threshold, and the two researchers discussed the conflicted labels and finalized the codebook. The finalized codebook has three levels for interpretation (*intended, not intended,* and *can't tell*) and five levels for proficiency (*advanced, proficient, developing, lack of effort*, and *blank*). The final labeled datasets for Q1, Q2, and Q3 consisted of 58, 88, and 58 responses.

Table 2. Interrater Agreement and Reliability Across Coding Rounds and Dimensions

Round	Dimension	Q1	Q2	Q3	Cohen's k
1 (N = 26)	Interpretation	76%	88.6%	96.2%	**0.82**
	Proficiency	96.2%	100%	88.5%	**0.93**
2 (N = 32)	Interpretation	96.9%	87.5%	93.75%	**0.88**
	Proficiency	90.6%	75%	93.75%	**0.80**
3 (N = 30)	Interpretation	/	100%	/	**1.00**
	Proficiency	/	90.6%	/	**0.90**

Inductive Reverse Engineering Pipeline. For the inductive condition, the LLM (ChatGPT-5.2) was prompted to infer emergent coding categories without access to a researcher-predefined (human) codebook. The LLM was asked to reverse engineer the underlying coding logic directly from labeled examples. Post-hoc category alignment was conducted to enable evaluation against researcher-defined codes. This approach is particularly meaningful in contexts where labeled data are available (e.g., from experienced teachers or expert raters), but no formative codebook exists. In our case, inductive reverse engineering supports the construction of an initial, operational codebook for QAD in educational research when some human-labeled data are available. Figure 2 shows the overview of the approach.

In this study, we designed a structured prompt to guide the LLM in generating an executable codebook. Specifically, the LLM was instructed to infer coding rules from a set of input–output pairs and to produce a codebook that included: (a) operational, decision-ready definitions for each category and level in the *interpretation* and *proficiency* dimensions; and (b) at least three diagnostic cues (e.g., linguistic indicators, mathematical structure, reasoning steps, completeness, correctness, or clarity) for each category or level. The LLM was asked to regenerate the output if any required component was missing. Beyond this verification step, the researcher made no additional interventions in the final version of the codebook. The chatbot version of ChatGPT-5.2 was used as in prior work, in anticipation that future researchers may prefer the web-based interface for more straightforward interaction when developing and refining a codebook [3]. The dialogue sessions for all three tasks are available at this link.

After generating the codebook using the LLM, we evaluated the effectiveness of the reverse engineering approach by assessing classification accuracy on held-out test data. For each question, the dataset was randomly split into training and testing subsets. Specifically, for Q1 ($n = 58$), 40 responses were used for training (for generating the codebook) and 18 for testing; for Q2 ($n = 88$), 60 responses were used for training and 28 for testing; and for Q3 ($n = 58$), 40 responses were used for training and 18 for testing. Researcher-labeled data served as the ground truth for evaluation. Both ChatGPT and an additional researcher who was not involved in the original coding process were asked to code the test dataset using the AI-generated codebook.

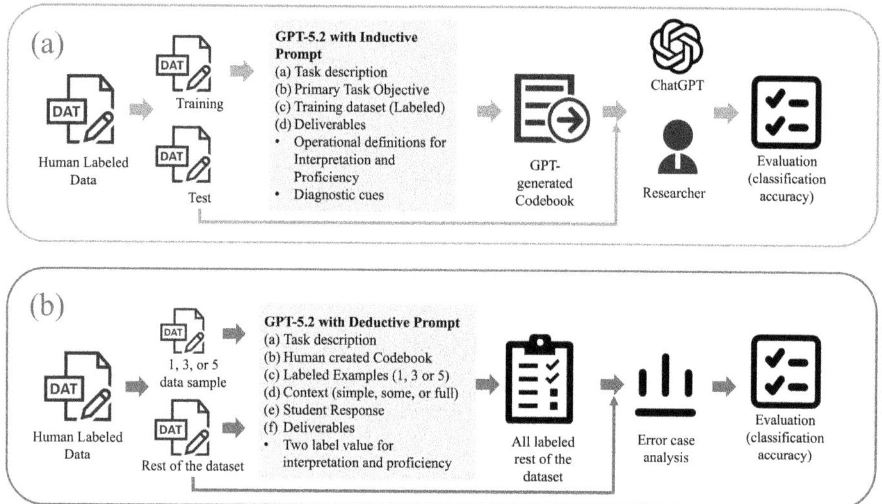

Fig. 2. Overview of the (a) Inductive Reverse Engineering and (b) Deductive Few-Shot Coding Pipelines. *Notes:* (a) illustrates the inductive reverse engineering pipeline, in which the LLM is not provided with a predefined human codebook. Instead, it infers operational coding rules directly from labeled training examples and generates an executable codebook, which is then applied to held-out test data and evaluated against researcher labels. (b) shows the deductive few-shot pipeline, where the LLM is given an explicit human-developed codebook along with a small number of labeled examples and varying levels of contextual information. In both pipelines, researcher-labeled data serve as the ground truth for evaluation, but the role of human knowledge differs fundamentally: inductive prompting emphasizes rule inference from data, whereas deductive prompting emphasizes rule application under predefined constraints.

Deductive Few-Shot Coding Pipeline. For the deductive condition, the LLM was provided with the finalized codebook along with a small number of labeled examples ($n = 1, 3$, or 5). One-shot, three-shot, and five-shot configurations were examined. In addition, the prompt context was manipulated at three levels: *simple, some,* and *full.* In the simple context condition, only the student's open-ended response was provided. In the some context condition, the prompt included the original question, the previous model description, and the student response. In the full context condition, the entire instructional page content was provided along with the student response. As shown in Table 3, in total, 27 experimental conditions were tested, reflecting all combinations of shot number and context level. All experiments employed the same state-of-the-art LLM (GPT-5.2) with fixed decoding parameters (temperature = 0.0, maximum output tokens = 500) to ensure comparability across conditions. In Fig. 2(b), the blue block illustrates the composition of the prompt used. To evaluate model performance, accuracy was calculated using the remaining unlabeled portion of the dataset after the few-shot examples were selected. For example, for Q1, when three labeled examples were used as in-context demonstrations, the remaining 55 responses were used to compute classification accuracy. Researcher-assigned codes were treated as the ground truth for evaluation.

Table 3. Experimental Design: Shot and Context Conditions

Dimension	Description
Shot Setting	One-shot, Three-shot, and Five-shot prompting configurations
Context Level	**Simple**: Student response only
	Some: Original question, prior model description, and student response
	Full: Entire instructional page content and student response
Task	Three model revision questions (Q1, Q2, Q3)

4 Results

Overall Coding Performance. For the reverse-engineering approach, Table 4 reports accuracy results for the AI-generated executable codebook, evaluated by both human coders and ChatGPT on the test dataset. ChatGPT achieves high accuracy on less abstract tasks (Q1 and Q2), approaching human coding performance. However, substantial performance gaps remain for the more abstract task Q3, particularly for Proficiency judgments. A similar performance pattern is observed for human coders.

Table 4. Test Accuracy of Human and ChatGPT Coding using AI-generated Codebook

Coder	Metric	Q1 (N = 18)	Q2 (N = 28)	Q3 (N = 18)
ChatGPT	Interpretation	88.89%	96.43%	55.56%
	Proficiency	94.44%	96.43%	44.44%
Human	Interpretation	83.30%	58.60%	30.00%
	Proficiency	94.40%	82.80%	60.00%

Table 5 summarizes the accuracy of few-shot LLM-based coding across tasks, shot settings, and context conditions. Three consistent patterns emerge. First, task complexity shows a dominant correlation with LLM coding performance. Across all context conditions and shot settings, performance on Q1 is consistently higher than on the other two tasks for both Interpretation and Proficiency, whereas more abstract tasks remain challenging for the LLM to code (e.g., Q3). Second, increasing the number of few-shot examples generally improves coding accuracy, with particularly pronounced gains for Proficiency judgments. For example, Proficiency accuracy for Q1 and Q2 tends to increase from one-shot to three- and five-shot settings (with the exception of Q2 under full context), although these improvements are non-linear and vary by task and context. Third, moderate contextual input ("Some") combined with three-shot prompting often yields performance comparable to, or even exceeding, that of full context, suggesting diminishing returns from additional contextual information. Interestingly, for more difficult tasks such as Q3, increasing the number of shots becomes more beneficial when richer context is provided: under full context, Q3 accuracy increases from 63.79% in the one-shot setting to 67.42% with three shots and further to 79.31% with five shots.

Table 5. Performance of Few-Shot LLM Coding Across Different Conditions. Best performance within each context is shown in bold.

Context	Metric	One-shot			Three-shot			Five-shot		
		Q1	Q2	Q3	Q1	Q2	Q3	Q1	Q2	Q3
Simple	Interpretation	89.66%	69.32%	43.10%	**98.28%**	73.86%	67.24%	96.55%	77.27%	72.41%
	Proficiency	**87.93%**	61.36%	41.30%	**87.93%**	68.18%	77.59%	**87.93%**	76.14%	84.48%
Some	Interpretation	96.55%	76.14%	62.07%	**96.66%**	76.14%	67.24%	94.83%	82.95%	70.69%
	Proficiency	86.21%	53.41%	55.17%	86.21%	62.50%	77.59%	**87.93%**	70.45%	79.31%
Full	Interpretation	93.10%	76.14%	63.79%	**98.28%**	72.73%	67.42%	93.10%	81.82%	79.31%
	Proficiency	75.86%	55.68%	60.34%	86.21%	54.55%	68.97%	**89.66%**	70.45%	75.86%

Error Case Analysis. Accuracy answers how often a model is wrong, whereas error analysis addresses how and why the model is wrong. We conducted a focused error case analysis for each task by examining the experimental settings with the lowest accuracy under fixed shot conditions. Specifically, we analyzed error cases across nine experimental combinations, corresponding to the three tasks and three shot settings, under the full-context condition.

Across these analyses, we identified six main recurring error types. (**T1**) Systematic overestimation of proficiency. GPT frequently treats formal completeness and keyword density as primary indicators of proficiency. In contrast, human proficiency judgments emphasize whether the response genuinely addresses the core challenge of the task, particularly for Q3, and whether it provides an executable, internally consistent revision that adequately covers critical cases. (**T2**)

Over-commitment in interpretation. The human label *Can't tell* is applied conservatively and indicates insufficient evidence or unclear intent. However, under one-shot prompting, GPT exhibits a strong tendency toward forced classification, often assigning definitive interpretation labels in cases where ambiguity remains. (**T3**) Keyword-triggered misclassification. This error type is relatively limited in Q1 due to the lower task complexity, becomes more noticeable in Q2, and is particularly pronounced in Q3, where it represents a critical failure mode. Under one-shot conditions, GPT lacks a clear completion threshold and tends to interpret isolated ideas or keywords as a complete solution rather than as an incomplete proposal. (**T4**) Boundary confusion among low-information categories. GPT often struggles to distinguish between low-information labels such as *Blank*, *Lack of Effort*, and *Can't Tell*, resulting in inconsistent classification of responses with minimal or insufficient content. (**T5**) Consistency blindness. GPT frequently fails to penalize internal logical inconsistencies, such as contradictions between algebraic and verbal expressions or reversed decision rules. While human coders typically classify such responses as *Not as Intended*, GPT often assigns *Developing* or *Proficient* labels. (**T6**) Task-goal misalignment. In some cases, student responses merely restate the original sentiment model rather than revising it. Human coders consistently label these responses as *Not as Intended*, whereas GPT frequently classifies them as *As Intended*, indicating a misalignment in task-goal interpretation.

5   Discussion

Across both prompting paradigms, task complexity emerged as the most consistent determinant of coding performance. For less abstract tasks (Q1 and Q2), the LLM achieved accuracy levels approaching those of human coders (see Tables 4 and 5), regardless of whether coding rules were induced through reverse engineering or provided via few-shot examples. In contrast, performance degraded substantially for the more abstract revision task (Q3), particularly for Proficiency judgments. Importantly, a similar pattern was observed among human coders when applying the AI-generated codebook, suggesting that these difficulties cannot be attributed solely to model limitations, but instead reflect the inherent ambiguity and interpretive demands of the task itself. Tasks that involve identifying surface-level features or applying relatively explicit criteria are more amenable to automation, whereas tasks requiring judgments of conceptual adequacy, internal coherence, or alignment with task goals remain challenging even under favorable prompting conditions. This pattern is consistent with prior work showing that LLM-human agreement varies systematically with the clarity and objectivity of the coding construct, with constructs that are difficult to define or difficult to reach consensus on posing greater challenges for automated coding [8,14]. Unlike prior inductive coding work that focuses on label emergence [17], we explicitly require the LLM to surface the underlying decision logic as an executable codebook. Moreover, our approach extends prior work on LLM-assisted codebook development [3] by explicitly treating codebook generation as a reverse-engineering task and evaluating the induced rules on held-out data.

Results from the few-shot experiments further indicate that increasing the number of examples generally improves coding performance, particularly for Proficiency judgments. However, these improvements are neither linear nor uniform across tasks. For simpler tasks, performance often plateaus after three shots, whereas for more complex tasks such as Q3, additional shots are most effective when combined with richer contextual information [14,16]. In this study, moderate contextual input ("Some") frequently yielded performance comparable to, or even exceeding, that of full context, suggesting that more information does not necessarily translate into better alignment and may, in some cases, dilute task-relevant signals.

The error case analysis provides deeper insight into how and why LLMs fail in qualitative coding tasks. Several systematic error types were observed under full-context conditions. First, GPT consistently overestimates proficiency by treating formal completeness and keyword density as proxies for conceptual adequacy. Human coders, by contrast, emphasize whether a response genuinely addresses the core challenge of the task and whether proposed revisions are executable, internally consistent, and comprehensive. This discrepancy is particularly salient in Q3, where superficial plausibility often masks substantive inadequacy. Second, GPT exhibits over-commitment in interpretation, especially under one-shot conditions. Whereas human coders reserve the *Can't tell* label for cases with insufficient evidence or unclear intent, GPT tends to force definitive classifications, thereby reducing its sensitivity to ambiguity. Third, keyword-triggered misclassification becomes increasingly pronounced as task abstraction increases. In Q3, isolated ideas or familiar terms are frequently interpreted as complete solutions, reflecting the absence of an internal "completion threshold" for complex revision tasks. Additional error types, including boundary confusion among low-information categories, failure to penalize internal logical inconsistencies, and task-goal misalignment, further illustrate that GPT often prioritizes surface coherence over deeper task understanding.

These findings suggest that LLMs can support qualitative coding in educational contexts, although their role is best understood within certain limits. For tasks with lower abstraction and more clearly defined criteria, both inductive and deductive prompting approaches can approximate human coding with relatively high accuracy. In these cases, LLMs may be useful for initial coding or screening, helping to reduce the time and effort required when working with larger qualitative datasets, while offering a consistent starting point for further analysis. For more complex, open-ended tasks that involve judging conceptual soundness, goal alignment, or internal consistency, LLMs show systematic limitations that are not fully resolved by adding more examples or context. Rather than replacing human coders, they are more appropriately used to support early-stage coding, assist in refining codebooks, or flag ambiguous cases that require closer human interpretation. The results suggest a workflow in which LLMs and human coders serve different but complementary functions. LLMs can help organize larger volumes of data and apply coding criteria consistently, whereas human analysts remain essential for handling ambiguity, interpreting meaning, and maintaining analytic rigor. From this perspective, LLMs do not replace qualitative analysis, but can extend its use in settings where data volume or practical constraints make fully manual coding difficult.

6   Conclusion

This study investigated how two LLM-based prompting paradigms (i.e., inductive reverse engineering and deductive few-shot coding) support qualitative coding of students' open-ended responses in an online AI learning context. Grounded in a carefully constructed human coding baseline, our results show that task complexity is the dominant constraint shaping LLM coding behavior. For less abstract tasks with relatively explicit criteria, both prompting strategies achieved accuracy approaching human performance. In contrast, for highly abstract tasks requiring judgments of conceptual adequacy, internal consistency, and task-goal alignment, LLM performance degraded substantially and exhibited systematic error patterns. These limitations persisted across prompting paradigms, suggesting that they stem from the epistemic demands of the task rather than from prompt design alone. Taken together, the findings indicate that LLMs can meaningfully assist with routine or surface-level qualitative coding, but remain limited in supporting deeply interpretive judgments central to educational research.

Several limitations should be noted in this study. First, the study draws on data from a single AI-integrated learning module focused on sentiment analysis, and the coding tasks all involve model revision within this domain. Although the tasks varied in abstraction, the findings may not fully generalize to other disciplines, data types, or qualitative traditions. In addition, the dataset is relatively small (approximately 110 student responses), which may limit the robustness and generalizability of the findings. Second, researcher-assigned codes were treated as ground truth for both inducing coding logic and evaluating model performance, meaning that the induced codebooks necessarily reflect the assumptions and interpretive stance of the human coders. This study therefore does not address contexts in which coding frameworks are contested or where multiple interpretations are equally plausible. Finally, all experiments were conducted using a single LLM with fixed decoding parameters, and other models or configurations may exhibit different behaviors.

Future research should extend this comparative framework to a wider range of qualitative data sources (e.g., interviews, classroom discourse and collaborative learning interactions) to assess the generalizability of the observed patterns. Hybrid workflows that combine inductive reverse engineering with human refinement warrant particular attention, as LLM-generated codebooks may function more effectively as provisional analytic artifacts than as finalized instruments. In addition, evaluation frameworks should move beyond accuracy to incorporate uncertainty estimation and error sensitivity, which are more closely aligned with qualitative research norms.

References

1. Preface. In: From data to discovery: LLMs for qualitative analysis in education (LLM-QUAL). ACM (2025). workshop preface, LAK 2025
2. Bakharia, A., Shibani, A., Lim, L.A., McCluskey, T., Shum, S.B.: From transcripts to themes: a trustworthy workflow for qualitative analysis using large language models. In: Proceedings of the 15th International Conference on Learning Analytics and Knowledge (LAK 2025). ACM, New York, NY, USA (2025)
3. Barany, A., et al.: ChatGPT for education research: exploring the potential of large language models for qualitative codebook development. In: Artificial Intelligence in Education, vol. 14830, pp. 99–107. Springer (2024). https://doi.org/10.1007/978-3-031-64299-9_10
4. Barros, C.F., et al.: Large language model for qualitative research: a systematic mapping study. In: IEEE/ACM International Workshop on Methodological Issues with Empirical Studies in Software Engineering (WSESE), pp. 48–55. IEEE (2025)
5. Chikofsky, E.J., Cross, J.H.: Reverse engineering and design recovery: a taxonomy. IEEE Softw. **7**(1), 13–17 (1990). https://doi.org/10.1109/52.43044
6. Davison, R.M., et al.: The ethics of using generative AI for qualitative data analysis. Inf. Syst. J. **34**, 1433–1439 (2024). https://doi.org/10.1111/isj.12504
7. De Paoli, S.: Performing an inductive thematic analysis of semi-structured interviews with a large language model: an exploration and provocation on the limits of the approach. Soc. Sci. Comput. Rev. **42**(4), 997–1019 (2024). https://doi.org/10.1177/08944393231220483
8. Dunivin, Z.O.: Scaling hermeneutics: a guide to qualitative coding with LLMS for reflexive content analysis. EPJ Data Sci. **14**, 28 (2025). https://doi.org/10.1140/epjds/s13688-025-00548-8
9. Gu, M., et al.: Toward automated qualitative analysis: leveraging large language models for tutoring dialogue evaluation. arXiv preprint arXiv:2504.13882 (2025)
10. Jiang, H., Corrigan, S., Peppler, K., Erana, T.I.: Bridging human and machine perspectives: integrating large language models into collaborative coding and peer debriefing for qualitative inquiry. In: Joint Proceedings of LAK 2025 Workshops (2025)
11. Kapoor, S., Gil, A., Bhaduri, S., Mittal, A., Mulkar, R.: Qualitative insights tool (qualit): LLM enhanced topic modeling. arXiv preprint arXiv:2409.15626 (2024)
12. Lacy, J.W., Nnoka, C., Jock, Z., Morreale, C.: LLM sentiment quantification reveals selective alignment with human course-evaluation raters. Comput. Educ. Artif. Intell., 100545 (2026)
13. Lin, G.C., et al.: Collaborative AI for qualitative analysis: bridging AI and human expertise for scalable analysis. In: Proceedings of the 15th International Conference on Learning Analytics and Knowledge, ACM, LAK (2025)
14. Liu, X., et al.: Qualitative coding with GPT-4: where it works better. J. Learn. Anal. **12**(1), 169–185 (2025). https://doi.org/10.18608/jla.2025.8575
15. Miles, M.B., Huberman, A.M., Saldaña, J.: Qualitative Data Analysis: A Methods Sourcebook, 3rd edn. SAGE Publications, Thousand Oaks, CA (2014)
16. Min, S., Shi, W., Yao, M., Zhou, Y., Zettlemoyer, L., Hajishirzi, H.: Rethinking the role of demonstrations: what makes in-context learning work? In: Proceedings of the 2022 Conference on Empirical Methods in Natural Language Processing (EMNLP), pp. 11048–11064 (2022)

17. Parfenova, A., Marfurt, A., Pfeffer, J., Denzler, J.: Text annotation via inductive coding: comparing human experts to LLMs in qualitative data analysis. In: Findings of the Association for Computational Linguistics: NAACL 2025, pp. 6456–6469. Association for Computational Linguistics (2025)
18. Rogers, R.: Coding and writing analytic memos on qualitative data: a review of johnny saldaña's the coding manual for qualitative researchers. Qual. Rep. **23**(4), 889–892 (2018)
19. Sankaranarayanan, S., et al.: Automating thematic analysis with multi-agent LLM systems. In: Joint Proceedings of LAK 2025 Workshops (2025)
20. Shah, S.T.U., Hussein, M., Barcomb, A., Moshirpour, M.: From inductive to deductive: LLMs-based qualitative data analysis in requirements engineering. arXiv preprint arXiv:2504.19384 (2025)
21. Song, Y., Wang, T., Cai, P., Mondal, S.K., Sahoo, J.P.: A comprehensive survey of few-shot learning: evolution, applications, challenges, and opportunities. ACM Comput. Surv. **55**(13s), 1–40 (2023)
22. Tai, R.H., et al.: An examination of the use of large language models to aid analysis of textual data. Int. J. Qual. Methods **23**, 1–16 (2024). https://doi.org/10.1177/16094069241231168
23. Yan, L., et al.: Human-AI collaboration in thematic analysis using ChatGPT: a user study and design recommendations. In: Extended Abstracts of the CHI Conference on Human Factors in Computing Systems, ACM (2024). https://doi.org/10.1145/3613905.3650732

Author Index

GPSR Compliance
The European Union's (EU) General Product Safety Regulation (GPSR) is a set
of rules that requires consumer products to be safe and our obligations to
ensure this.

If you have any concerns about our products, you can contact us on

ProductSafety@springernature.com

In case Publisher is established outside the EU, the EU authorized
representative is:

Springer Nature Customer Service Center GmbH
Europaplatz 3
69115 Heidelberg, Germany